A DIPLOMATIC
DOCTOR

A DIPLOMATIC DOCTOR

David Holbrook M.D.

To Joanne
All the best
with thanks for
making my
... meet ...
David

iUniverse, Inc.

New York Lincoln Shanghai

A DIPLOMATIC DOCTOR

iUniverse books may be ordered through booksellers or by contacting:

iUniverse
2021 Pine Lake Road, Suite 100
Lincoln, NE 68512
www.iuniverse.com
1-800-Authors (1-800-288-4677)

ISBN-13: 978-0-595-36493-0 (pbk)
ISBN-13: 978-0-595-80926-4 (ebk)
ISBN-10: 0-595-36493-4 (pbk)
ISBN-10: 0-595-80926-X (ebk)

Printed in the United States of America

THE SAGA OF A MEDICAL DOCTOR
AND HIS FAMILY ABROAD

Contents

INTRODUCTION

Turning forty was a signal to me that it was time to move on to the next chapter in my life.

After fifteen years as a family practicioner, I had reached a point where the practice, although very stimulating and fun was getting the better of me. Even after an excellent physican joined me, the hours seemed to get longer and my time with my family shorter.

I missed the moments when I didn't have to worry about patients committing suicide, or having to deal with a complicated obstetrical problem. I missed not being able to get home before the children were in bed and not having dinner with Lauretta.

When the opportunity arose to take an overseas posting with the government, how could I turn it down?

This memoir recounts a number of years in my life as a physician and foreign service officer for the Canadian government in the Caribbean, Asia, Latin America and Europe.

It also recounts the joys and the difficulties in raising a family overseas. After some years of being childless, Lauretta and I had adopted three children with the help of obstetrician colleagues. Chris and Sue arrived at ten days of age, two weeks apart. Thirteen months later, Matthew joined our crew. We did not think a great deal at the time about how we were all going to fit into our Porsche.

As the early childhood years passed, Matthew began to have difficulties in school. Teachers complained bitterly about his behaviour. A psychological assessment resulted in a diagnosis of Attention Deficit Hyperactivity Disorder.

A child with ADHD presents difficulties ranging from parental guilt at not being able to find a logical approach to managing the child to embarrassment at appearing to be a poor parent. The effect on other family members takes a toll but perhaps the saddest element is the inability of the ADHD child to under-stand the reason for the turmoil.

The irony is, as a physician, I could deal with a myriad of problems, but not our own son.

I hope that this memoir will give readers a glimpse of how one family dealt with it for better or worse.

1

CARIB COUNTRY

1

The name of the pub was obliterated. The dingy interior of the establishment was lit by daylight streaming in through the bank of open doors that stretched across the entire front of the one storey concrete block building. The place stank of stale beer. Two white-haired regulars were leaning back against the side wall in the shade, on the hind legs of their metal chairs. An old sign on the wall above the oldsters, peeling from years of no care, stated clearly

'*A BEER's A CARIB!*'

Taking a moment for my eyes to adjust from the bright sun, I approached the stocky barman, who was decked out in a red-checked shirt and denim Oshkosh overalls, his curly black hair turning gray. "We don't see many white faces in here, maan. You new here?" He spoke with a lyrical Trinidadian accent.

"Yes, I work next door."

"Thought so. You're *Canajian* ."

"Yes. Is this a good place for lunch?"

"Depen on what ya want."

"O.K. a Carib and an egg sandwich."

With his thick fingers, he dug into a fat jar of hard boiled pickled eggs and plopped one on a plate with two pieces of white bread. "Did you say sandwich?" I nodded and he held the red-labelled beer bottle by the neck, put the egg between the two slices of bread and slammed the bottle down on the bulge of the egg. I looked on in amazement at this culinary display as he pushed the plate toward me. "Der yar, maan."

I chose a black steel table with a wobbly chair and ate as I looked out into the harbour, watching as the small fishing trawlers and tramp freighters from Domenica and St. Lucia unloaded their cargo of fish, vegetables and lumber onto the crammed docks. Shirtless labourers in colourful wool tams and trousers, tightly belted to keep them up, clambered over piles of crates. Skillfully manoeuvring my crumbling Wonderbread sandwich into my mouth and downing the end of my 'Carib', I leant back against a pillar and thought back on how I had landed in Carib publand.

Our introduction to Trinidad at Port of Spain's Piarco Airport was a blast of heat after leaving Toronto on a cool autumn day. It was dark and steamy in the early evening. Palm trees swayed in the hot breeze engulfing us in a sweet fragrance that neither of us recognized. I could feel my face dripping with perspiration and my clothes, suddenly drenched in sweat, sticking to my body.

People were everywhere, pushing, shoving and shouting, hauling masses of luggage. As we stood surveying the situation with rambunctious six year old Matthew whining and Sue and Chris, both seven, sleepy and dazed hanging on to Lauretta, a voice from the maze was calling our name and waving frantically with both arms.

"Doctor Holbrook! Doctor Holbrook! Hello! I'm Nathan. Welcome to Trinidad." A short white-uniformed man with a red maple leaf pin in his lapel rushed toward us. "What a relief! I didn't know if I could find you."

Beaming from ear to ear his mouth slightly askew after a bad hare-lip repair, Nathan shook hands with each of us. Matthew squirmed away from the handshake and tried to pull away from my grasp. I was tempted to let him go, but knowing it would take ages to find him again, I tightened my grip.

"Dad, you're hurting my wrist."

"Well, stop pulling then. You're staying with me." Matthew groaned, put his head down and snarled but stopped yanking my arm.

In a blur of frantic activity, Nathan and I collected the luggage. I had to let go of Matthew who scooted off ahead of us and was soon out of sight. When we did catch up to him, he had collected shells, coins from a fountain and who knows what else in a cast-off plastic bag, which he refused to give up without a fight which I was not about to get into.

Nathan collected our passports and pushed his way through the dank, dingy, stifling immigration and customs hall, urging his new charges to follow closely, bypassing the long lines, chatting amiably with the officers who were obviously buddies, expediting our entry. We were suddenly outside, no questions asked, in the steaming night air.

After bundling us into the Canadian High Commission van, we were soon rocketing towards Port of Spain, Nathan driving like a speed demon on the crowded narrow road with deep ditches on either side, weaving in and out as he passed everything on the highway. Driving with caution obviously did not cross anybody's mind in Carib country.

"I feel sick, Dad."

"No you don't, Matthew." I reassured him but dumped out the plastic bag, in case. The coins, stones and a dead fish fell on the floor of the van.

"Ooh! Dad. That stinks. Now we're all going to be sick." Sue sat with a scrunched up expression on her face and covered her nose with her sleeve.

I opened the window for some air and Matthew promptly put his head out and lost his dinner. I couldn't look at the car travelling closely behind us.

"I'm taking you to the Hilton, the nicest hotel in town," chirped Nathan. "You will have a rest until your house is ready."

I was jolted back to the activity on the docks as my wobbly chair legs slipped, jerking me forward against the grimy steel table. I slowly stood, paid for my lunch, waved to the barman and stepped out into the scorching sun.

Taking a chance, I crossed the boulevarded highway separating the pub from the harbour, dodging beat-up Datsuns with so much glitter stuck on the dash and hanging from the mirror that I knew the drivers couldn't possibly see me.

As I walked along the crumbling sidewalk, I listened to the water lapping against the side of the wharf. Chains attached to cranes on the piers clanged as the cargo was hoisted from the decks and holds of the vessels moored in the harbour. Men dressed in scruffy jackets carrying clipboards with sheaths of lading bills, were milling about negotiating the sale of the goods. The stink of day-old fish was ruining the fresh smell of recently cut lumber and that combined with the noise of the traffic made walking intolerable. I beat a quick retreat back across the road.

Returning to the Gaines and Webber Insurance Company building housing the High Commission, I stumbled over the worn patches of humidity-rotted carpet and climbed the stairs rather than wait for the cramped elevator. My breath and clothes stank of stale beer. I was sure to give the wrong impression and vowed to bring my lunch from then on. Besides, I preferred a different variety of egg sandwich. The beer-induced drowsiness did not help me stay awake reviewing medical forms and chest x-rays for migrant farm workers going to Canada which Aliza, my secretary, dressed in her pleated red georgette skirt, had plunked on my desk. All the forms and x-rays had to be reviewed and given medical clearance before their visas could be issued.

2

Our hotel stay, a happy two week vacation initially, had begun to lengthen as no decision was forthcoming on a suitable house. The extra time enabled us to register the children in school which was a relief as they were becoming more and more fractious and bored with hotel living. It also gave us time to deal with the red tape of living in a new country: residents' permits and drivers' licences.

Meanwhile Lauretta struck a deal with the maids to save recent foreign newspapers for her. The local *Trinidad Guardian* was the only newspaper in the hotel shop and was fine for news of Port of Spain and Boisey's column, an hilarious sketch of local lore which poked gentle fun at the inhabitants of Port of Spain, but was devoid of news from outside the Caribbean.

"Maybe we could sell the papers you get." Matthew's entrepreneurial skills had started early.

The '*Welcome to the Hilton*' parties were the highlight of the week for hotel guests, generally tourists who stayed from Thursday to Sunday. Not the Holbrooks. We had lost count of how many we'd attended.

Rum and fruit punches were served along with shrimp on coloured swizzle sticks. The game for the children was to see who could collect the most swizzle sticks and umbrellas. It started off innocently enough with the kids begging the waiters for umbrellas before they were put in the glasses. Matthew supplemented his take by collecting umbrellas already in the punch. I should've watched more closely but it was hard to carry on a lucid conversation and watch the children all at the same time. If Matthew had been draining the glass before taking the prize, the rum certainly didn't slow him down.

There was always a fancy 'international' buffet dinner after the cocktails, supposedly representing the cuisine of countries around the globe. The dining room was festooned with the flags of the country of the week, but the food was always the same: deep fried plantain and shark steaks with a hot chili sauce. After sixteen weeks, even the children noticed the similarity in the food.

"Mom, do they have plantain and sharks in Lebanon?"

"Good question, Sue."

"Of course they don't, Sue." Chris, as well as being a constant reader, had become fascinated by geography.

"Why don't they call plantain, bananas, Dad? They look like big bananas to me."

"I don't know, Matthew." Matthew always wanted facts not speculation. It was easier to deny any knowledge. Our three collectors always took a healthy number of decorative flags from the 'International 'display which they used to barter among themselves and to plaster their rooms.

With Christmas approaching, Sue had come up with the brilliant idea of using the cocktail umbrellas as tree decorations, but the children were horrified at the thought of not having a real pine tree to decorate.

"Dad. We can't have this one. It's only a felt tree outline. It's flat. How will we decorate it?" With difficulty, I thought to myself, as Matthew stamped his feet and pouted.

"The manager has given you six scarlet ibis decorations. It's the national bird of Trinidad. You saw them in the bird sanctuary. Look. There are even feathers on the wings. You've got all the umbrellas, as well. It'll look wonderful."

"No it won't!" Chris was not convinced. "It'll look stupid, Dad."

He turned to Lauretta when sympathy was not forthcoming from me. In fact, it didn't look bad hanging on the wall.

"It's not traditional, Dad." Chris was right.

Lauretta and I sat by the pool each night before dinner with a rum punch. It was a time for us to chat while watching the children play, Chris and Sue in the pool, Matthew looking for something different to do. Always independent, he took great pleasure in picking fights with Chris when bored or simply disappearing which was a constant worry.

As we sat and watched the sunset, we commiserated about the events of the day.

The transition from being self-employed to being low man on the totem pole was harder than I had anticipated.

"I have all this time to read forms and look at chest x-rays. It's almost sinful. "Doctor Castillon, the doctor in charge, had not yet appeared. His substitute had a meeting at five every day to give endless instruction to the new recruit. It didn't occur to him that I could figure out a lot of the requirements on my own.

"Is there any word about a house? Maybe they'll leave us here for the entire posting. The kids are really good but somebody has to watch them every moment by the pool. 'Don't throw paper in the pool!' 'Stay away from Chi-Chi's cage. He's a nasty chimpanzee. You'll get bitten.' 'Don't go in the long grass. There might be snakes or insects that bite.' Yes, you have to wear uniforms to school and, no, there is no alternative.' I'm getting to be such a nag."

"You're not a nag, Darling, far from it. You've got three kids and only two eyes and two hands. However, I'm sure it won't be long. It's costing them a fortune to keep us here."

In the hotel lobby arriving from work earlier than usual one evening, I was stopped by the desk clerk.

"Doctor Holbrook. I was just about to call your wife. Would you please go to the manager's office?" I smiled, walked to the office and knocked thinking that perhaps we were going to receive a medal or at least a bottle of scotch for lasting so long at the Trinidad Hilton.

"Please come in." Standing by the desk was a tall well dressed blond young woman looking tense as she clutched Matthew's grimy hand. Dirt was smeared on his face and his clothes were dishevelled.

"Hi, Dad." Matthew's cheery retort was meant to cover any wrongdoing. I stood bewildered, looking first at my wiry son and then the manager, then the soot smudges on her tailored beige suit.

"Doctor Holbrook, your son has just climbed onto my balcony from the floor below. I was panic-stricken for fear he might fall before he was safely on the balcony. He says he has climbed the eight floors from the ground."

Matthew butted in with an explanation in his own defence.

"Dad, a man at the pool said the hotel is called the upside-down Hilton. The lobby is on the top level and that's why we always have to take the elevator down to our room. So I went to the ground and climbed up. It was easy and makes more sense than taking the elevator."

"I apologize for my son's behaviour. It won't happen again."

"I was very concerned for your son's safety, Doctor Holbrook. We don't want this type of thing happening at our hotel. Please keep a closer eye on him if you can."

I grasped Matthew's wrist, thanked the manager again and quickly left the office, dragging Matthew along with me.

"Dad, you're hurting my wrist. I can walk by myself."

"Do you not realize how dangerous and stupid that was?"

I continued to drag him at a fast trot to our room as he whined and wept.

"Don't you ever do anything that idiotic again."

I unlocked our room door and found Lauretta, looking frantic, with the phone in her hand. Sue and Chris were sitting calmly at the table playing Monopoly.

"Thank God you're here! David, I was at my wits end. I just called the High Commission and they couldn't find you. Matthew! Where on earth have you been? We've looked everywhere for you! Look at you! What have you been doing?" Matthew stood with the corners of his mouth turned down so far that his chin puckered.

"He was rummaging about outside. I was called to the manager's office as I was walking through the lobby. She was worried that he might hurt himself and took him to her office." I thought that explanation would suffice, though it was a wonder nobody saw him climb by the window.

"Dad hurt my wrist," Matthew moaned. Chris sniggered, knowing Matthew probably deserved it.

I took Matthew aside, "A lot more than your wrist is going to hurt if you ever pull a stunt like that again."

3

'Diego Martin', an area of new 'fancy homes' was the site of our long-awaited piece of Caribbean paradise. Ten San Diego Park, a large L-shaped house, had many unique features. The east wall of the living room was a series of floor to ceiling dark-stained wood-framed windows that folded back to the wall leaving the room open to a patio. The spacious backyard had an easily climbed Julie mango tree which would no doubt see the children in the top branches picking the best large dark green mangos. A tall coconut tree curved over the corrugated steel flat-roof of the family room which projected into the yard. Ferns filled what would normally have been flower beds.

The front of the house facing west was made up of brick lattice work open to the elements. The kitchen, also on the west side, was spacious with two large barred and glassless windows making access difficult for everything except Matthew and the neighbourhood stray cats.

"What about the rain?" Chris, always thinking ahead, looked at Lauretta and me and raised his eyebrows in a worried expression.

"Chris you've got a point. We'll have to wait and see." The roof of the house had a wide overhang that probably would reduce the flood in the kitchen. A waist-high brick fence surrounded the property with a deep culvert on the road side.

The three bedrooms were in a separate 'secure' area off the living room, which could be sealed off from the rest of the house by an alarm system placed in a cupboard outside the master bedroom. When the alarm was on, and an outside door opened, it had to be turned off in thirty seconds with a key or sirens screeched in the backyard.

"Now tell me, David, how will the kids manage alarms and locks? They can't even reach the alarm box to put the key in it!"

"Don't worry. It only has to be used at night."

"Is it really necessary?"

"Apparently, just at night."

"What difference will it make? We don't have a phone."

"It will alert the neighbours. We're supposed to get a phone soon." I said all this knowing it made little sense.

Lauretta grimaced. I put my arms around her and hugged her.

The house backed onto a drab, brown hill dotted with a few trees, low scrub and dozens of shacks, connected by a zig-zagging dirt path which led to a stand-pipe, the only source of water. There were throngs of people on the hill which Lauretta thought might be a good thing in case of an emergency. God knows they'll all hear the alarm!

The neighbours on either side appeared prosperous with large homes and fancy cars for Trinidad and most importantly, youngsters our children's age. The kids were excited about the prospect of once again living in a house and having other young people to play with.

Moving from the hotel with our luggage was nothing. Arriving at our new home with a mammoth steel container blocking the road was another story. Seventy-one boxes were piled in our living room. The three movers waved good-by and vowed to be back soon.

"David, remember this is Carib country. What day do you suppose 'soon' means?" Lauretta had a sly expression on her face. We laughed. I threw up my arms and muttered, "Why don't we start?"

The movers surprisingly reappeared at dusk to set up the beds and cart in the mattresses.

"Don't we have any sheets?" Matthew wanted everything to be done properly and to his specifications.

"Matthew don't be stupid." Chris had to get into a scrap with the little 'brat' as he called him. Intervention was the only way to prevent a punch-up.

"Enough you two. Go lie on your beds. When we find sheets we'll tell you. Sue, look for cartons with your names on them and drag them to your rooms." Lauretta looked at me as if I'd lost my mind, rightly visualizing chaos.

4

Because our car hadn't arrived yet, Lauretta was isolated during the day. According to the neighbours, the nearest taxi stand was two miles away. It was a relief when Nathan found us a used car we could rent, even if it was for an exorbitant sum which apparently went to his church. The adjustment to driving on the left-hand side of the road was only one part of the 'Trini' driving experience. Not only did you have to concentrate on changing lanes, but you also had to avoid the local drivers who careened like maniacs down the middle of the potholed roads.

I had made the mistake of saying that the container with our car would arrive quickly from Toronto, without consulting a map which would have pointed out that Trinidad was the furthest south of the Caribbean islands, only twelve miles from the coast of Venezuela.

With our furniture unpacked and pictures on the wall, our new abode began to feel like home. We spent our late afternoons on the patio with our new frangipani tree, watching the children playing in the yard with their new friends.

"Is it my imagination or are the children really making strides at school?"

"David, they're actually becoming numerate and literate. It's none of the 'would you like to do this' attitude so prevalent in Canada. It's back to the basics and the kids love it."

"No wonder Matthew wasn't getting anywhere. His answer was always, 'No, I don't want to do it'. And he wouldn't."

"I still laugh when I think of you walking him to school on your way to the office every day only to discover that he was going in one door of the school and out the other to play in the park." Lauretta smiled at me as I shook my head.

"The incredible thing was that he was so naughty that none of the teachers ever asked us why he wasn't at school. It was such a relief."

Matthew was pleased with the decision to have him attend a Benedictine monastery school in Grade 2 as a boarder during most of the week. He would be away from the prying eyes of his brother and sister to say nothing of his parents. The brave fathers were happy to have such a free spirit. The school, in Tunapuna, in the country in Matthew's mind, was on a hill overlooking Port of Spain.

At St. Martins, a day school in Port of Spain, the principal had told us that Sue and Chris were a pleasure to have in their Grade 3 program. The teachers, all trained in England, were dedicated and keen. There were extra-curricular activities at both schools which included rugby and ballet, and for Matthew, science programs which were amazing to us as they were not available in Toronto.

Lauretta and I had had many discussions about our three adopted children and particularly Matthew who had always had an uncontrollable independent streak. He would participate in family activities that interested him but not to please anyone but himself. On the other hand Chris and Sue wanted love and affection, something Matthew spurned. We assumed it was one of the difficulties of adopting children so close together in age.

We could be talking to Matthew one minute and then once our backs were turned, he would disappear for hours without any explanation.

Sue, had activities closer to home and had become quite interested in ballet, as had Debbie, our neighbour the judge's chunky daughter, who started the ballet craze. Chris was fascinated by geography and spent hours reading and drawing maps for various school projects.

The children's friendships gave us an opportunity to meet Debbie's parents next door. The heavy-set bespectacled judge with the reputation in the community of being a 'hanging judge', and his diminutive wife stood at their door and waved politely. They appeared uncertain as to whether they wanted to accept our invitation to venture onto our patio.

Chris and Loulou, the tomboy who lived at the corner of our street, along with her younger brother Rocky, had become great bug collectors. They were constantly asking Lauretta for empty jars and boxes they could punch holes in for their live catches. It was dangerous to walk into Chris's room especially if dropped towels and clothes concealed boxes and jars of live inhabitants.

"Chris, what's that?" Lauretta pointed to a container on Chris's desk.

"It's a tarantula, mom. Loulou says it won't bite." Crammed into a large 'Mason' jar was a black tarantula the size of a very large fist.

"You cannot have that in the house!"

"Ah, Mom. Loulou says you don't have to worry about it."

"Take it outside!"

With a disgruntled look on his face, he picked up the jar and went off to find Loulou and her brother Rocky. They dutifully took the jar to a corner of the garden and sat cross-legged opposite each other, Rocky kneeling, leaning on Chris's shoulder.

They carefully opened the bottle and the giant hairy creature slowly eased itself out of the jar, stretched its multiple joints and walked away on its stilt-like legs. The three observers leaned back quickly giving their latest creepy-crawly the right of way.

They watched in disbelief as it climbed up the long elephant grass that separated the lawn from the property behind. The grass bent under the weight of the giant spider but it soon disappeared over the boundary. We would have reservations about going in that corner of the garden ever after.

It was a joy for us to see how easily our 'whitey' kids were adopted by their new friends. Loulou and Sue, when they could coerce their brothers to turn rope, rattled off universal double-dutch rhymes:

Mable, Mable, dressed in sable,
if you're able, set the table,
don't forget the salt and pepper,
pitch, patch, PEPPER!

Sue's and Loulou's braids bobbed in unison, their legs a blur as the boys turned faster and faster. Matthew often appeared from nowhere and skilfully flew into the middle of the rope, not missing a beat to the chagrin of Chris and Rocky.

5

"Good morning. I'm Mrs. Henry, da Taxi Lady. I'm goin ta be drivin your children to da school." Standing at the gate was a plumpish, stern-looking East-Indian woman trying to smile, though it didn't come naturally to her. She had taken over the contract to drive the Canadian children to and from school for the High Commission. She was the voice of doom and gloom for the kids who came home and reported the latest outrageous story about what was going to happen next in our neighbourhood.

"Mrs. Henry says our house is going to flood."

"Mrs. Henry says the shacks are going to burn."

Mrs. Henry says…

When the children arrived home with the latest story of pending disaster, Lauretta calmly reassured them.

"Mom, she did say we have in our garden the best mangoes in all of Port of Spain ." Chris was pleased that she had had something positive to say.

If Lauretta wanted to go anywhere during the day, Mrs. Henry came back after the school run and picked her up. But downtown Port of Spain had few charms. Scores between families in the predominitably Black and East Indian communities were settled with arson, leaving gutted ruins along many streets. The smell of charred wood irritated the nose and throat and made walking on many streets disagreeable.

Rastas celebrating their anti-establishment, Ganja-based religion, lounged about in the main square. They sat around their wooden shacks, their long dreadlocks stuffed into colourful knitted wool berets or slightly askew leather caps, watching all of each woman go by. The homemade leather goods they had for sale hung from hooks on the shacks and trees. Their marijuana was sold in tins like pipe tobacco. Lauretta was slightly uneasy but amused as she crossed the square walking through clouds of sweet-smelling smoke. It wasn't a trip she'd make alone at night. Lauretta bypassed the sugar cane vendor with his cane press but often bought a coconut, served to her by a seller who gripped the coconut in one hand, lopped off the top with his machete and offered it to her with a straw to drink the clear sweet liquid from the shell. She smiled and paid a Trini dollar for his effort.

She often walked down to HiLo (high prices, low quality, according to the locals), to see if there were road runner chickens larger than a kilo or even a piece of cheese. It would bring such joy to the children, tired of fish dinners.

She did enjoy making regular trips to Anderson's Bookstore, with its selection of Penquin paperbacks on the worn, musty shelves, to buy yet another V. S. Naipaul novel. His stories of Trinidad painted a vivid picture for her, one that she could relate to now that she was in the middle of it. She could even see 'Mr Biswas' house' quite clearly, perched on stilts, prayer flags fluttering above the door on the hill behind our home. Reading was the mainstay of her day.

Afterwords she would go to the Anglican Cathedral Church of the Holy Trinity, a calming oasis from the noise and clatter of Port of Spain. It was our meeting place on the days that Lauretta ventured into town. The slowly rotating ceiling fans squeaked a musical accompaniment to the chirping sparrows and created a breeze which was a relief from the sticky heat.

We sat on the benches in the park adjacent to the cathedral, and had our lunch, brought from home. It beat crowding into the din of McDonald's or eating roti, an Indian flat bread wrapped around various fillings most commonly gamey goat with its splintered bones. It was definitely more relaxing than taking Lauretta to the pub next door to the High Commission for an egg sandwich and a *Carib*. It was doubtful a woman had ever ventured into the place.

Our lunch in town was the calm before the storm for Lauretta. The children arrived home from school in the mid-afternoon, tired and irritable, with the inevitable question, "What'll we do now, Mom? Not homework yet! We want to do something different."

6

The weekends were a respite.

"Dad, can we go to Maracas today?" Maracas was a beautiful beach twenty kilometres from Diego Martin. The route took us through Maraval, the 'upper class' area of Port of Spain where the large houses were surrounded by iron fences and 'Beware of the Dog' signs. It eventually went by the Osborne's pasture. Doctor Osborne was a Scottish-born local physician who, in his paranoia, had arranged an evacuation plan for his family in case of an island uprising against foreigners.

"We'll be first off the island. I've made all the arrangements with the Prime Minister."

His wife was a middle-aged hippy who smoked and drank incessantly.

"Dad. She runs the local chapter of the Mustard Seed Trackers and Racers club."

"What on earth is that?"

"Maybe we should join and then we would know what it's all about."

"Chris, I don't think so."

"I think it's a game the Boy Scouts play." Matthew always came up with his two-cents worth.

"How would you know, Matthew?" Chris didn't get a reply.

"See their horse, mom? His name's Bert. You know he swallowed a mango pit. Jenny told me." The old bay gelding stood by the Osborne's empty swimming pool, skin and bones, head down, back hollowed, looking like the horse in Dali's Don Quixote.

"The pit's probably still there. That's why he looks like that." stated Sue.

"Bert can go in the kitchen. That's where he swallowed the pit. Jenny said he took it out of the garbage." Matthew continued the story.

"Jenny's not even in your school, Matthew. She's in Chris's class, isn't she, Chris?" Chris nodded and poked Matthew.

"Can they ride him when he's so thin? He might break."

"Don't be ridiculous, Matthew."

"Can we have a pony, Mom?" The banter went on for the entire trip.

The road wound through long stretches of rain forest teeming with lush vegetation, before opening up into a stunning blue lagoon.

"We should have brought our tarantula here, Mom. Maybe I can find another one. Look! There's one squished on the road. Yuk!"

"Let's stop, Dad. I want to get out and see it. Maybe another will come out of the rain forest to see that dead one and I can catch it."

"Matthew. Stop grabbing my shoulder! You can't get out and I'm not stopping. We're going to Maracas."

We always tried to arrive early, to stake out our area between the red and green flags denoting the safe zone for swimming, before what seemed like the arrival of the rest of Port of Spain. To satisfy Matthew, our spot had to be close to the shark-burger stand. The agitation for his first burger began thirty seconds after our arrival.

"Dad. Can I have a Trini dollar? I'm hungry. I'm going to have a sharkburger with hot sauce."

"Matthew, you wouldn't eat your breakfast. You can just wait. You can't swim right after eating."

"I don't want to swim."

"The answer is still no." Matthew trooped off kicking sand in clouds. It was hard to ignore the harassment.

The undertow at Maracas was treacherous and the kids were not allowed to go in the ocean beyond their knees without one of us holding on to their hand firmly.

Our first trip to Maracas was almost our last. Chris and I were no more than four feet from shore when we were hit by a wave and swept out thirty feet, twirling underwater. I couldn't stop spinning and couldn't get my head to the surface. I remember thinking that my lungs couldn't hold more water. I knew I was still alive because my heart was pounding, a deafening thumping in my ears. Was Chris alive? I clutched his arm like a vice. When finally we were propelled to the surface, sweeping back toward shore on another wave, I dug my feet in the sand and pushed Chris's head out of the water still holding on to him for dear life. Gasping for breath, we were swept onto the beach.

The lifeguard, who had been at the sharkburger stand with Matthew, rushed to help Chris as Lauretta ran to me. The acid vomitus and salt paralysed the back of my throat. I was unable to speak.

Seeing that I was breathing, she held my head in her lap until I could move and sit on my own.

When finally Chris could talk, all he was able to say was, "That was too scary, Mom. I don't want to do that again."

I sat on the beach, weeks later wondering how we survived. There will be no need to warn the children about an undertow again, except for Matthew, forever fearless, who would probably want to try it for himself.

"Look, Dad. I found it." Matthew stood with a stinking four foot Morey eel, draped over his arms, its needle teeth grotesque and threatening even in death.

"Get rid of it, Matthew."

"OH NO! Dad, I want to take it home for my room!"

"Forget it Matthew. Get rid of it now!" He sulked and stomped away once again, no doubt intending to hide it for future investigation.

San Diego Park Port of Spain Trinidad

Boredom with a smile   Trinidad

Chris and friends San Diego Park Port of Spain Trinidad

Sue, Chris and Matthew Maracas Trinidad

Chris and friends Port of Spain Trinidad

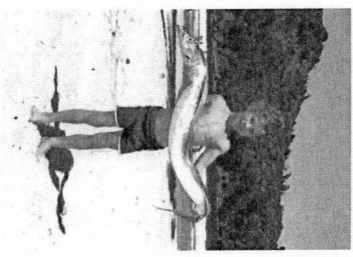

Matthew and eel on Maracas Beach Trinidad

7

Lauretta filled the monotonous weekday mornings with household tasks and reading. Twice a week she came to town for our lunch dates. The afternoons in Diego Martin were endless. She sat on the stoop at the kitchen door in the shade on hot humid afternoons, chin in her hands, alone with her thoughts, waiting for the children to come home from school at three-thirty and for me to arrive at six. The heat made any activity uncomfortable. The women in the neighbourhood either worked in Port of Spain or played bridge. If only the government allowed foreign wives to work. She watched the inevitable brush fires on the surrounding hills. Fire crews and shack dwellers used garden hoses with what little water they could muster, using brooms and long branches to beat out the flames.

It was on just such an afternoon that a tall local woman, perhaps from the shacks on the hill, slowly ambled to the gate in her multi-coloured calico skirt, flowered apron and white blouse, her gnarled feet bare, her face wrinkled from age and sun. Tight cornrows covered her head like a shiny helmet.

"Missus, you have any work? I'm Myrtle, missus. I wash and sew."

Lauretta had been told that you must get references for local servants, but Myrtle was different. Her calm, peaceful face imparted a feeling of confidence. Lauretta looked at Myrtle, a woman the age her mother would have been were she alive, and a warmth came over her.

Lauretta slowly nodded, "Yes, Myrtle, I do need help. Do you enjoy caring for children and doing housework?"

"Ah surely do, missus. Ah hav a boy but he go to school in the day."

"When can you start, Myrtle?"

"Now, missus."

Myrtle, a woman of an indeterminate age perhaps even in her seventies, was quickly a very special part of our family. She was our bridge to the local culture and customs. She always surveyed the neighbourhood prior to her arrival at eight in the morning, and announced whether there were too many 'ordinary mistahs' lurking in the area for women to venture beyond the gate.

"Myrtle, what are 'ordinary mistahs'?"

"Some people, they jus miscreants. They jus lookin fer trouble."

"David, what are we supposed to do if there are 'too many ordinary mistahs' out there?" Lauretta and I chatted as we lay in bed that night.

"You should take Myrtle with you as a bodyguard." We laughed.

"Maybe she knows all the local miscreants."

Weeks passed. Finally our last shipment of personal belongings arrived.

"Where are the sheets and other things that were in the car? Where is the car?"

"There's some bad news." I hesitated, trying unsuccessfully to soften the blow. "As they were unloading the ship, the Renault fell into the harbour."

"What!? No! How? I don't believe it! What are we supposed to do now?" I put my arms around Lauretta as any cheer at the thought of having our car packed with our remaining possessions, quickly vanished. "David, what next? It's a catastrophe."

"The winch on shore gave way. It can happen. They're going to compensate us for the car, after they decide whose fault it is."

"What about the stuffed animals and sheets and stuff?"

"They'll have to be replaced, too."

"How can you be so relaxed about this? Dammit, it's sickening. What do you suppose the children are going to do when they find out that their teddys are floating in the harbour?"

"They'll want to fish them out. They'll simply see them floating on their backs looking up at the sky, at peace with their new surroundings. "Lauretta looked up and her tears changed to giggles.

"Be serious, David, this is hideous. Those beautiful bears their grandparents gave them. The kids will be heartbroken."

"I know, but it was an accident. It's just one more thing we'll have to get through. It won't bring the teddys back to life but we'll survive."

"Now we have to try and remember what else we put in the poor old Renault?" Lauretta bit her thumb nail thinking back on the packing.

"At the last moment we just shoved in all the left overs.

The only way we'll know is when we can't find things. Bloody hell. What a pain!"

8

"Missus, dis maan at de gate, he come fix da sick tree."

Lauretta looked through the bars of the glassless kitchen windows and saw an emaciated floppy-eared donkey harnessed to a wooden, two-wheel cart. A wiry, grey-haired Indian dressed in tattered shorts, was standing outside the gate in the hot late afternoon sun.

"What sick tree, Myrtle?"

"Da coconut, Missus."

"What's he going to do to it?"

"Salt it, Missus."

"Salt it?"

"Yes Missus".

"What's that supposed to do to it?"

"It makes da fruit healthy missus."

"Okay, Myrtle. Tell him to fix the tree."

Lauretta and the kids watched in disbelief as he took a twenty-five pound sack of salt from the heap on the cart and padded into the yard in bare feet. They expected him to put the salt around the base of the tree but no. He tossed the sack over his shoulder as if it weighed nothing, looked at the tree from bottom to top and shinnied up the twenty-five foot trunk holding it with hands and soles of his bare feet, the bag of salt balanced on his neck and shoulders.

"Mom, he climbs like a monkey." Sue can't believe her eyes.

"It's amazing." Lauretta, too, was incredulous.

"What's he going to do with the salt, Mom?" Matthew was intrigued. "Look, Mom, he's pouring it in the top of the tree. Is it hollow?"

"No, chile, he jus puttin da salt around da cocanut and da leaves." Myrtle helped Lauretta with the explanation.

"Oh no, he's covering up the coconuts. I wanted them, Mom."

"Da'll be fine, chile. Don' worry."

"How's he going to get down?"

"Don't be stupid, Sue. The same way he got up."

"Don't call me stupid."

"Okay, you two. Just wait and watch." Lauretta worried that the next thing we knew, Matthew would be checking out the top of the tree.

"You see, he comes down the same as he went up, Sue. It was a stupid question." Sue poked him. He was so engrossed, he didn't respond to her prodding.

"I still don't understand what the salt is supposed to do?"

"Chris, I haven't the foggiest idea either." He shrugged and watched the tree-salter take the empty bag back to his wobbly cart.

"Myrtle what shall I pay him?"

"Four trini dollar, missus."

We were wakened in the middle of the night by what sounded like a bomb exploding in the living room.

"My God, David! What was that!"

The kids rushed into our room.

"I don't know. Everybody stay here. I'll find out."

Looking out the bedroom window, I could see nothing amiss in the yard and so I turned off the alarm and went into the living room. I didn't smell smoke or anything other than the new frangipani tree on the patio. As I looked again into the yard, a coconut slowly rolled off the corrugated metal roof of the family room onto the patio.

"It's okay, kids. It's just the coconuts falling." I turned and tripped over Matthew in the dark.

"Come on Matthew, I told you to wait inside."

"But, Dad, I want the coconut."

"Not tonight you don't. Back to bed, kids. It's a false alarm."

"The salt in the tree is really working. The coconuts are falling." Lauretta and I laughed as we crawled back into bed.

"Do you suppose the salt really causes them to fall?"

"Who knows? Let's try to get some sleep before the next one falls."

"I'm going to change the garden. Some colour will add some cheer. What do you think, David?"

"I think it's a great idea."

"I'll get rid of the ferns and put in some flowering tropical plants, maybe some red, bottle-brush trees, oleander or a hibiscus hedge."

Uprooting the ferns sparked a rebellion. An army of geckoes, small green ugly creatures, wriggled into the open living room and hid behind every picture, chair and table. Now, they had taken over the house instead of the garden.

Lauretta, overcoming her initial fear of the little horrors, launched a counter-attack, wacking them with a broom. Every gecko she swatted dropped off its tail, leaving it twitching on the floor as it squirmed away and hid behind another picture.

Lauretta muttered to herself as she swept the wriggling tails into the yard.

The next morning as I was about to sit down on the patio with a cup of coffee, I suddenly noticed a slight movement in the grass by my feet. A three-foot long chameleon with a multi-coloured spiked tail blinked a heavily-lidded eye at me as its tongue lunged out at who knows what?

"Oh damn, I whispered under my breath as I pulled my feet under the chair." Slowly the large lizard slithered away. Lauretta nonchalantly walked towards me with her cup of coffee. I watched the lizard out of the corner of my eye to be sure it was out of her sight before she reached the patio.

9

"Lauretta, I'm taking you out for dinner. Just the two of us." Evenings out alone had all but disappeared. It was a shock to Lauretta when I arrived home with my great announcement.

"You must be joking. Where do you propose to get a baby-sitter?"

"I've got it all organized. Beulah's going to come. She's a secretary at the office and is delighted to babysit. All I have to do is pick her up. We'll go to either Luciano's or the Chaconia Inn. Which would you prefer?"

Luciano's, at the end of a long winding lane, was the childrens' favourite restaurant not because of the food but because of the tree toads which produced cacophonous croaking in the pitch black hill top surroundings in the evening. Matthew, determined as he was, never managed to get close enough to catch one as the noise stopped the instant he tried to sneak up on them.

"You *are* joking. It's not fair to tease me."

"Come on. I'm serious. It'll be fun without the kids. I'm going to pick up Beulah at seven."

"Let's go to Lucianos. I can't imagine what it's like without children."

At seven it was already dark. I was sitting in the car on a normally quiet street lined with one and a half storey wooden cottages, most with verandahs and low picket fences surrounding their front gardens. A few street lamps arced over the road and the lights from the houses filtered through coloured curtains projecting various hues onto each verandah. I waited in front of the People's Fellowship Church, a vertical clapboard rectangular, unchurch-like building where I had arranged to meet Beulah. I was hoping the raucous clapping and singing would soon be over; at the same time remembering that Trinidadians were not time-bound, I got out of the car and leaned on the front fender thinking I might catch a cooling breeze.

"Mistah, I wan ya money." I froze, then turned calmly, slowly, and saw a hulk emerging from the darkness at the back of the car, outlined by the street light in the distance. I could hear Myrtle saying: 'He's so black, he's navy blue'. It was her favourite term for what she perceived as undesirables or miscreants.

"Sorry, man, I don't have any."

"Wha ya mean, no money?" I shrugged and put my hands out so he could see them. Then he pulled a knife from his belt. The blade glistened, reflecting light from the church windows. A very long couple of moments went by. He stood and looked at me in disbelief. I could hardly believe my reaction either.

"Ummh." A long pause followed with only the 'praisin da Lord' drowning out the sound of my heart thumping in my ears. "Den take me ta San Fernando."

I shook my head. "Sorry, not enough gas." He looked down at his knife, but didn't edge any closer. Minutes passed. I could feel my face flush, my heart pounding faster. I didn't move.

"What ya doin here?"

"I'm waiting for Beulah. She's at church." I hoped Beulah would appear and he'd feel outnumbered. Perhaps she could deal with miscreants.

"Wher ya come from?"

"Canada."

"I bin dere. Mm'a sailor. I bin ta Montreal."

"Where else have you been?"

"I bin ta Shanghai."

"I've been there too." He scratched his head, shuffled his feet and contemplated his next move. I waited.

"Nice meetin ya." The knife went back in the belt and he disappeared into the dark. I slowly got back in the car, clutched the steering wheel with both hands and took a deep breath. That had been too close for comfort. He was one of Myrtle's ordinary mistahs.

The stranger, the knife and I had conversed for twenty minutes. Forget Beulah. I headed home still shaking. Luciano's would have to wait for another day.

10

Seated in my office in front of my radiology screens with another pile of chest x-rays and completed medical forms, I was paid a rare visit by Doctor Castillon.

Paul Castillon, shock of white hair, beard and rotund body, was the senior physician in the office. He rarely appeared choosing to spend his days on his yacht.

"I'm on the way out, David. Why would I spend my time sitting in this crappy place? At sixty-two, I've got better things to do."

His wife, a native Carib, had a fighting spirit that was enough to prevent pirates from attacking their boat as they cruised the Caribbean. When posted to Trinidad, the two of them sailed their boat from Athens to Port of Spain.

That same spirit was enough to get her to King Farouk's court where she had been a famed belly dancer. She still wore the gold, jewel encrusted, engraved bracelet to prove it. I learned early in our posting to pay attention to her Spanish conversation. She refused to speak English. My attention lagged only once. The resultant punch to the shoulder knocked me off my bar stool at their favourite watering hole at the time of our first meeting. Her father had been a heavyweight boxing champion.

"David, I know you've been paying a huge amount to rent that car from Nathan and I heard the news about your Renault at the bottom of the harbour. I'm going to do you a favour." I smiled, anticipating what was coming, knowing Doctor Castillon's reputation as a practical joker. "You're aware that I'm leaving shortly. I'm going to sell you my car for one Trinidad dollar. It's old, but it runs. There's only one proviso. You must sell the car for only one dollar when you leave." Doctor Castillon looked at me to make sure I was listening carefully. "Now, the car is parked in the bushes near our boat mooring at Chaquaramas. I'll draw you a map."

I thanked him profusely to be polite but was still uncertain as to whether this was a joke.

Finding it without a map would have been impossible. The car, an antique 1949 model Triumph coupe resembled a shoe box with four wheels and looked not unlike a child's depiction of what a car should be. We gaped in wonder at our new car camouflaged in a bush as he had described.

"This reminds me of the '59 Porsche we had with the seat that kept sliding away from the steering wheel, leaving me hanging on for dear life!"

"Lauretta, at least the Porsche had style. It was round. This is a rectangle. The seat in this doesn't even move. You'll love it. There are only four gears, three forward and one back. Try it." The long gear shift handle with a black bulb on top was too high and far for Lauretta to reach comfortably. "We're going to have to get a thick telephone book for you to sit on."

Once we got our little black box with wheels onto the road, Lauretta struggled initially with the odd clutch and shift position.

"Don't say a word, David! Give me a chance. The lurching will stop."

Arriving at the High Commission the next day, I found Paul Castillon sitting in my office with his feet on my desk.

"Well? How is it? Did your bride figure out how to drive it?"

"Yes she did. The car's great. Thank you, Paul. We really appreciate it."

11

With the departure of the Castillons, my job changed. In addition to reviewing file after file, I was now required to travel to various sites in Latin America to choose and supervise the physicians who complete medical forms and do x-rays for the Canadian immigration programme.

Doctor Steiner, who was now my supervisor, planned the trips.

"First, I would like you to go to Paramaribo in Surinam and then Sao Paulo, Rio and Brasilia. There are five physicians to see. We haven't visited these doctors for a number of years. It's your job to bring them up to date on changes in the requirements."

"May I take my wife with me?"

"Of course, as long as she pays her own way. When you get your schedule confirmed, I would like to see it before you finalize it."

Returning to my office and looking at the map, I understood why there hadn't been frequent visits. It was a vast area to cover in one trip.

Lying in bed at night, was always our chance to chat without including the children in our conversation.

"Lauretta, would you like to go to South America with me?"

Lauretta sat up in bed and laughed, her arms around her knees.

"You're serious?"

"Yes, of course I am. I'd love you to come with me on my immigration trip."

"O.K. And the children? Are you going to take them too?"

"No. You've forgotten. In three weeks, my parents are coming to Tobago for a few days on their way home from the Galapagos. It would be easy for them to come to Trinidad to see their grand-children. They'll be able to babysit. We'll have time with my parents when we come back. Myrtle will be here to help. The kids will be at school for a good part of the day and Matthew for most of the week.

"Do you think they would want to babysit for that long? What about Matthew? Would he be too much for them on the weekends?" Lauretta raised her eyebrows and looked at me.

"They brought up three children. It'll be easy for them."

Lauretta lay back on the pillow, arms behind her head, and smiled at me.

"Yes. That would be great. I'd love to go."

After approving my plans, Doctor Steiner announced that he was going to drive us to the airport. He picked us up late and then drove like a fiend, despite poor eyesight, his nose inches from the windshield.

"I have reserved a suite for us at a lovely hotel. There will be one bedroom for you and Lauretta. I'll take the other. The sitting room we can use if you have any trip plans to discuss." Lauretta and I looked at each other in disbelief.

"Us? Do you mean to tell me that we're going to share our hotel room?" whispered Lauretta.

"I didn't realize he was coming too."

"What's that?" Doctor Steiner's hearing was surprisingly good.

"I didn't realize you were joining us, Jeff."

"I'm only going to Caracas for a few days."

I smiled at Lauretta who rolled her eyes still uncertain with the arrangement.

The trip from the Caracas airport to the city centre was up a gorge, dotted with long tunnels cut through the rock, from the sea at La Guaira. It was a long drive for a short stopover before our flight to Surinam. The hotel was beautiful, the face shrouded in greenery drooping from balcony to balcony. The suites were part of a high-rise building that included a shopping plaza and church complete with spire on the sixteenth floor.

"Holbrooks, it's getting late. Let's go for dinner." Close to midnight, Jeff hit the deserted streets. We tagged along, our hunger having passed hours ago. "I'm going to take you to a traditional Venezuelan restaurant. You must order a char-broiled steak with chimi-churri and the special bread which is a cross between pita bread and Indian naan."

The restaurant was crowded despite the few people in the street. Only crazy gringos took a chance and walked at night. We were seated next to a roaring fire with sparks periodically flying out into the room.

"David, can we move away from the fireplace? It's so hot. Lauretta spoke to the waiter in Spanish and he led us to another table.

"What's wrong with the table by the fire?" Doctor Steiner was accustomed to making all the decisions even if I was paying the bill.

"I hope you don't mind but we'd prefer to sit where its a bit cooler."

The dinner was very good, particularly the steak with chimi-churi, an Argentine sauce made with a combination of green onions, garlic, parsley, oregano, cayenne pepper, oil and vinegar slathered on an enormous rare steak, the surface charred in the open fire next to which we were supposed to be sitting.

Awakening the next morning with difficulty after spending much of the night awake as our suite-mate had left his radio on all night, we found the bathroom occupied. After a half-hour wait we were both becoming desperate, not only for obvious reasons but for the fact that our flight departure time was fast approaching.

When finally he opened the door, a blast of steam poured into the room. Every available towel lay wet on the floor. The sink and tub were full of hair.

"Lauretta, I think I'll go first."

"No you won't. We're in this together. You see if you can find a dry towel and I'll have a shower." Our trip was not off to a good start.

When we arrived in Surinam, the former Dutch portion of the Guyanas, south of Venezuela, there was a seventy-five kilometre drive from the airport to Paramaribo, the capital. At night, it was a surreal world.

We drove past clusters of lean-tos made of boughs, nestled in palm groves in the rain forest, tribesmen in sheep-skins clustered around bonfires. The road then passed through great expanses of rural Surinam populated by descendents of escaped slaves. They had chosen, over the generations, to maintain their African village life rather than adopt the urban style of the Surinamese Dutch settlers in Paramaibo. Some huts did have kerosene lamps shedding an eery light on the brush around the open doors.

Our hotel in Paramaribo, a minor Ritz in that it had running water, was primitive but had a comfortable bed. The heat in the room made nightwear and the blankets on the bed unnecessary.

We woke in the morning to a roaring noise that turned out to be pelting rain on the corrugated steel roof of the building next to our window. I got up to close the window.

"Lauretta, look at this." She wrapped the sheet around herself and came to the window dragging the sheets behind her. Much to our amazement, a marching band in full dress red regalia complete with gold epaulettes was marching down the middle of the main street below, in the pouring rain, rivulets of water streaming down their faces from their scarlet kepis.

"Oh no! That can mean only one thing. It's National Day. Look at the banners on the poles. I didn't notice them when we arrived."

"David. It's going to be hard to find any doctor on a national holiday in Surinam."

"There's a solution for that." I deftly picked up Lauretta and we headed back to bed.

By midday, the sun appeared. We emerged and walked with the crowds, not knowing where we were going. Hawkers with huge bunches of green, white and red balloons and ice cream vendors with boxes hanging around their necks, crammed with tubs of multi-flavoured ice cream surrounded by dripping ice, shouted out their wares in Dutch or a patois neither of us understood.

We were able to move in one direction, finally reaching the 'White House', the Surinamese President's residence, bedecked with green, red and white flags, a yellow star in the middle. The large white clapboard mansion looked like some-thing transplanted from the southern United States.

We stood in the background, watching the milling crowd, the marching band having passed. Children dripped ice cream down their clothes, as it melted faster than they could get their tongues around the cones.

"I'm going to go back to the 'Ritz' to call the doctor. Do you want to come?"

"I'm not going to stand here on my own looking like a hooker." We laughed and walked hand-in-hand in the direction of our hotel. The shops were closed with their metal grills pulled down leaving us no chance to even window shop.

I sat on the bed and waited for a dial tone while Lauretta opened the window for some air before she lay on the bed and undid her shirt. I knew it wouldn't take long for the shirt to come off as the air filling the room was hot.

"It's Doctor Holbrook calling. I would like to speak to Doctor Van Heuys, please." There was a long pause.

"I'm sorry Doctor Holbrook. We were unable to locate you to cancel your appointment. Doctor Van Heuys is out of the country. I do apologize." As I hung up, I looked at Lauretta smiling and thought I didn't need any doctor's appointment. I had more recreational activity to occupy my time.

We headed for the airport late in the afternoon hoping for better luck with our visits in Brazil.

It was to be a seven o'clock flight. Twenty of us congregated in the departure lounge. Eight o'clock came and went, as did nine. At nine-thirty, we were asked to go through security.

At ten, the runway lights were turned on. We clapped, and hoped for the best.

With a tremendous roar, we heard an approaching aircraft. The 747 with BWIA emblazoned on the side, flew past literally thirty feet above the runway without touching down. We looked at each other in disbelief. I remembered Matthew's 'joke' about the acronym for BWIA—But Will I Arrive.

"Perhaps the pilot was testing the length of the runway," a young sales-person with the tell-tale square black bag of samples commented.

After a few minutes, we could hear the aircraft returning for a second attempt at landing. It was not as close to the runway as the first approach. The runway lights were then extinguished. That was a bad sign.

"Lauretta, it's time for cribbage." We returned to our seats. Two couples from France pulled up their chairs to watch. Eleven o'clock passed, then twelve. At two-thirty, we were asked to go through security again.

"Pack up all belongings and come this way please." There was a good deal of consternation among our fellow would-be passengers, particularly as there had not been one announcement about when the departure time would be. We followed orders.

After going through everything in our hand luggage again, we returned to our game and our chats in French, Spanish and English. I did struggle with the two Japanese bankers' English.

Still no runway lights came on.

Three o'clock passed then four. Most of us were now stretched out on benches. At four-thirty, the lights came on to a cheer.

A mere eight and a half hours late, we left for Brazil.

"Varig would like to apologize for the delay. We would like you to accept a glass of champagne with our compliments. Please enjoy your flight to Belem."

"They should be giving us the whole bottle," Lauretta muttered loud enough to be heard.

"Excuse me. My wife and I are going to Sao Paulo."

"Oh, I'm sorry sir, this flight will terminate in Belem. We'll arrange for an ongoing flight for you the next day. We'll pay all your expenses in Belem."

"Whoopee," murmured Lauretta. "I'm going to spend the time in Belem in bed."

"I'm going to join you."

12

Arriving in Sao Paulo a day late, left me only one day to cram in all my appointments and little time for Lauretta to have the joy of shopping in a large city with great department stores. The manager of the Hilton Hotel had assigned us the bridal suite perhaps recognizing our lengthy stay at the Trinidad Hilton. Now it was to be one night rather than the originally planned two. The suite with its enormous white canopied king-sized bed was a lovers' dream. We could easily have stayed another day. However, the pollution in the streets left us gasping for clearer air.

Rio was not a vast improvement for different reasons.

The Copacabana Hotel, reserved for us by the Canadian consul, was a beautiful historic hotel. It overlooked the famous beach, jam-packed with string-bikinied women of all ages with countless 'lifts' of everything, from face to buttocks and G-stringed men probably 'lifted' as well. Our room did overlook the beach and had many original features including an enormous bathtub and an ancient porcelain basin. The problem was the water supply. After many blasts of pent up gas, a trickle of brown liquid dribbled from the tap.

"David the only advantage of the tub is that if we have a bath we will have an all-over tan without a moment in the sun. The rust stain will last for weeks."

"I agree, Babe, but I can't postpone the appointments. Let's sort it out when I get back."

"Okay." There's a smile and a tone of voice that I know means 'I'll do it for us'.

Returning from my local immigration doctor visits, I was not totally surprised to find Lauretta reading in the lobby, bags beside her.

"We're moving to Ipanema." I laughed and asked about the bill. "There isn't one. They apologized and made the reservation for us."

The hotel in Ipanema was pristine with clear running water but without the beautiful antique fixtures. There were also safety concerns on the deserted beaches.

"Do you mean I'm going to the beach at Ipanema and I can take nothing but the bathing suit I'm wearing?" Lauretta wrinkled her forehead in a quizzical expression.

"Wear a serape and shoes in the lobby and take a towel, but from what is said, they frequently disappear when we're in the water."

"Maybe I'll just sit. There's no one on the beach."

"Okay. You sit, 'My girl from Ipanema'. I'll look at you from the water." When we did sit in the middle of the vast beach by ourselves it didn't last long. From nowhere, two hawkers descended on us, trying to strike up a conversation in a combination of Portugese and English.

"You would like to buy a hat and perhaps some sunglasses too and a key chain with the statue of Jesus? You see the statue, Señor? It is above the bay." Who could miss it?

Lauretta and I shook our heads, got up and started to walk, hawkers in tow. We went into the water up to mid-thigh level, the hawkers followed. We gave up and headed for the hotel.

We were happy to be alive after the ride from Ipanema to downtown Rio. We careened around curves at incredible speeds too close to the brink of the cliff separating the road from the sea. We did arrive at the airport in one piece but not rested enough for the adjustment to Brasilia, a strange city planned by the Brasilian architect Lucio Costa, who used the original design ideas of the French architect Le Corbusier in cleared jungle in the middle of nowhere.

The city was designed in the shape of an airplane. The commercial area was in the nose; the government, entertainment and diplomatic area in the centre; the residential areas in the wings and the industrial zones in the tail section. Vast expressways, so wide it was impossible to walk across them safely, connected each zone. Tunnels went under the roadways and the small shops lining the tunnels were gathering spots for local teens with nothing to do but get into trouble. Because the plans did not provide sufficient housing, huge shanty towns had grown around the city.

In addition to my roster doctor visits, I had an opportunity to return to general practice. The recreation area of the embassy had been set up as an office for 'consultations', which turned out to be chats with the staff about the problems of living in Brazil, the worries about anti-malarial pills and the cobras.

The cobras were discovered in a Canadian family's living room in rugs rolled up while the floor was being repaired. The teenage daughter, in a panic, called the US Marines at the suggestion of her best friend who was brought up to expect the US Marine Corps. to solve all problems large or small. The cobras were diposed of by the Marines within minutes of the call.

"Lauretta, this evening we're going to the ambassador's for dinner."

"Oh great. I'll unroll the dress I brought."

Lauretta, looking wonderful in her unrolled chartreuse dress, shook hands with the Ambassador and his wife, who were happy to see a new face.

"Have you ever been in a living room with three television sets?" Lauretta whispered.

"Oh sweetheart, I forgot to tell you. Tonight is the World Cup final."

"Oh no. I don't know a thing about football."

"Don't worry. I'll explain as we go. I don't even know who's playing."

We were separated for dinner at tables of ten. Lauretta sat with a Thai woman and the Japanese Ambassador. She looked comfortable and I tried to concentrate on my dinner partner's Spanish conversation. Being the Argentine Ambassador's wife, she berated me on my poor Spanish and attempted to explain to me that I was very stupid not to be going to Argentina, the heart and soul of Latin America. I decided that smiling and saying nothing was my only option.

As the brandy was passed, the television sets were turned on. I was nowhere near Lauretta to give her a play by play description. I watched with amusement as the Japanese Ambassador struggled to explain to his female dinner partners, the subtleties of European football.

"I still know nothing about football, David." Lauretta laughed as we departed smiling sweetly to our hosts who suggested that we'll all do it again in four years, the next Cup final.

At long last, the holiday portion of the trip took us to Salvador in Bahia, the province of Brazil on the east coast north of Rio. The white beaches stretched for miles from the beautifully designed new hotel where we were staying.

Salvador is the centre of black culture in Brazil. The original settlers, African slaves, arrived in the early sixteenth century, bringing with them the deities of the Yoruba religion from south-western Nigeria and Benin. It's now combined with Roman Catholicism. Having two religions and many gods is considered better than one by the black natives of the area. The Cathedral Church of Our Lord of Bonfim, sitting on a cliff, towered over us as we sat under multi-coloured umbrellas in the lower town, and lingered over our strong black coffee. Small children tried to sell us a variety of voodoo charms. One pretty, black-haired, green-eyed teenager gently tied a pink 'fita' around Lauretta's wrist and told her the ribbon was for Lemanja, the goddess of the sea.

This was relaxation we had missed for the past few years. It was b.c. (before children), back to a time when we were free to dine when the urge prompted us. It was the freedom to go out, walk, or sit in a café without having to arrange for a babysitter.

Our room, furnished with modern red wooden furniture, gave us a panoramic view of the long stretches of white beach below our window and the ocean beyond.

Walking in the warm sand was a joy particularly for me watching Lauretta, not a true beach lover in her new red Rio bikini, her parrâo in her hand.

"Wow! What a body." Lauretta looked over her shoulder and grinned slyly. I walked behind her for a few yards just watching.

We walked a great distance down the deserted white sand beach.

"Look at this, David." The tide was going out, leaving lagoons of warm water. We sat up to our shoulders and lounged in the water without the fear of being pulled away by the undertow, like our, not to be repeated, Maracas experience. We returned to our room, dropped our bathing suits at the door and jumped into bed for a rest before dinner.

Three days of walking on the beach, and of intimacy without the inevitable interruptions of children, passed far too quickly.

We did feel rested and relaxed as we returned to the stress of airports and delayed flights.

Our next overnight stop was Manaus where the Rio Negro and the Solimões join and flow into the Amazon basin as it heads for the sea at Belem. It was also where Caruso came to inaugurate their opera house built with vast amounts of money from the rubber plantations in the area. We laughed trying to imagine Caruso's expression and comments when he reached the city, a thousand kilometres from the next town of any size.

The opera house was memorable by its sheer existence. It was difficult to imagine luring Caruso and a host of opera afficionados to this place in the middle of Amazonia.

"I'd love to stay longer, David. Just look at that." As we wakened in our isolated cabin in a lodge on the edge of the jungle a magnificent electric-blue, swallow-tailed butterfly, the largest we had ever seen, was immobilized on our window by the overwhelming humidity.

"If we miss our flight, we'll be here for an another four days." As great as it would have been for us, it wouldn't have been a popular move back home in Trinidad.

13

As Nathan, the driver, greeted us at the airport, he quickly added,

"Doctor Holbrook, I think your parents are eager to get off to Tobago."

Arriving home at 10 San Diego Park, the grandparents were indeed sitting by the front door waiting for us. Father, his cold blue eyes staring at us as Nathan carried our bags to the door, chomped on his pipe, barely concealing his anger and pointed to the bags.

"We're packed and ready to leave for Tobago."

My parents' enthusiasm for caring for their grandchildren had waned to put it mildly. The litany of devilry began.

Mother, I now realized in retrospect, would never have had the patience to deal with their youngest grandchild.

"Matthew lost the key to the living room doors. We couldn't put the alarm on and the little devil spent most of the time sleeping in the garden. The kids are tired of eating fish and Myrtle wasn't able to buy anything else. We've run out of scotch. We're sorry to leave in such a hurry, without staying to hear about your trip. Write us a letter."

"We understand." Lauretta and I looked at each other and shrugged realizing there wasn't anything we could say or do to lighten the tension.

"Thank you so much for offering to come and stay with the children." Lauretta, the true diplomat, tried to defuse the situation.

"I'll drive you to the airport first thing in the morning."

"No, no, David. Nathan is taking us now."

It was clear that the days of looking after grandchildren had come and gone. Lauretta and I waved and breathed a sigh of relief as Nathan's car drove away.

"Ah, David. That was a great holiday. I feel years younger."

"I agree, now let's find the damn key." We shook our heads and smiled at Matthew's knack of creating havoc.

"I never thought I'd say it but it's fun to be home."

Lauretta pulled me down to her five foot two level by the front of my shirt and planted a kiss on my lips.

14

While Chris and Sue were excelling in school and becoming avid readers, Matthew was adopting his own curriculum with the Holy Fathers in Tunapuna. Rather than be bored in school, he skipped the classes he had no interest in. That included everything except science and animal care. His favourite hideouts were the chicken pens and the kennels. It had not taken him long to realize that the Benedictines were having no more success than anyone else in the teaching profession dealing with his individuality and transgressions.

He was always enthusiastic about his time at school. Our discussions on the weekends never touched on the academic topics that Chris and Sue brought up. Matthew's idea of academe was decidedly different.

"Mom, you should come to see the beautiful Alsatians at my school. They are my friends. There are six and I know their names."

"Should you be playing with the dogs, Matthew?"

"The're looking after the special science rooms behind the school where the snakes are. They have beautiful snakes at the school too, you know."

"Are you supposed to be there?"

"Oh yes. The teachers don't mind. They're happy that I'm interested in science."

"Matthew. Always ask permission first."

"Okay Mom," blasé as always.

Matthew went off to rummage in the culvert around the house looking for living organisms.

Lauretta and I sat and listened to his conversation with himself as he poked along with a stick.

"Maybe we should get him a microscope to give him ideas for his science projects." Lauretta spoke as she continued to observe his lone pursuits. He rarely joined activities with his brother and sister.

"It's probably also time to pay the Benedictines a visit and see if they have any suggestions.

Aliza staggered into my office with another heavy stack of farm worker's medicals and x-rays as I finished my take-out goat roti lunch. I couldn't help but ask myself how it was possible that so many farm workers were needed in Canada. I wondered how many would actually return to their homes in the Caribbean.

"I know what you're thinking, David." Ben Crosby from the immigration department stepped into my office. "You want to know how come there are so many. A lot of these guys don't come back. So we've started asking for the same requirements which regular immigrants need, the medical and police check rather than just handing out visitors' visas. Then if they do stay, at least we have a partial file."

"I thought so. I suppose you're looking for somebody in this pile who has to be on the next flight or the apples will rot?"

"Doctor Holbrook! Doctor Holbrook! You must come with me to the hospital!" Nathan charged into my office, interrupting the conversation.

"What's the trouble?"

"It's Matthew, Doctor! He's been bitten! He's dying!" I charged out of the office with Nathan.

I ran into the emergency to find him in shock, a doctor at his left side with the paddles of the defibrillator in his hands attempting to jolt his heart back to regular activity.

"Oh God! He's not dead!?"

"No. We've got his heart going again. His pulse is back. His breathing is more regular." He had an intravenous in both arms. A nurse stood at his head holding an oxygen mask over his nose and mouth. "We're just going to start the anti-venom. We only have two vials at the moment. We might need more. We've requested three more. He has multiple bites on his hands and arms." I stood at the foot of the bed feeling useless, watching as our son's life ebbed and flowed. I was totally overwhelmed. I felt guilty about every scolding, every recrimination given in exasperation.

I sat down on the only chair in the emergency cubicle and stared blankly at the ceiling and tried not to panic. I did my best not to listen to the orders being barked back and forth. I prayed for a miracle to pull him through this.

It was typical of Matthew. He'd been told regularly at home and school never to go near the colony of small striped coral snakes raised at the monastery to be milked for their venom to produce an anti-venom. His love of animals and moving creatures of all kinds, coupled with his enjoyment of breaking free of any strictures, had led to this. He'd charmed the Alsatians guarding the snake pits but was unable to charm the snakes. His inquisitive spirit could not squelched by anyone or anything.

I could imagine Matthew saying, "I thought I could, Dad. I thought I could."

I heard his whisper over and over in my head. It haunted me. Lauretta arrived and we held each other and watched as the frantic activity calmed as his condition stabilized. We sat by his bed, and waited for him to awaken.

"Why didn't we call the school to tell them that Matthew had befriended the dogs and knew about the snakes?"

"David, we can't redo anything now. He's going to get better. Matthew can't die."

At that moment, Father Doughlin, the school principal, knocked softly on the door. I stood and we shook hands in silence.

He shook hands with Lauretta. "We did everything we could with Matthew short of having somebody watching him every minute."

"We understand, Father." We bowed our heads as he said a prayer. We sat in silence for a few moments. He then shook our hands again and departed.

We'd been at his bedside for twenty-four hours waiting for the lethargy and muscle weakness to dissipate when finally he was able to keep his eyes open long enough to say: "Hi, Mom. Hi, Dad. I didn't know you were here." His lids lagged and he went back to sleep. We smiled. Tears that couldn't be held back any longer, followed.

Two days later, when we came into the room after a night at home, he was sitting up in bed ready to go, no I.V., looking as if nothing had happened. A nurse peered in. "Is this Matthew's idea or can he go home?"

"I think it's his idea but I'll check his chart."

"Dad, the doctor said I could because you're a doctor and will know what to do." Oh great, I thought to myself. I hated the pressure of having to be medically responsible for my own family.

Sue and Chris welcomed him home as a returning hero.

That night, Sue knocked on our bedroom door. We raised ourselves on our elbows.

"What's the matter?" She came into the room.

"Matthew's not in his room." I jumped out of bed to look for myself. No Matthew. The alarm had been turned off and the living room door was open.

"Matthew. What are you doing out here?"

"I felt like a mango." He was sitting under the mango tree with a smirk on his face.

"Get in the house, Matthew. It's not funny."

I got back in bed and looked at Lauretta.

"What are we going to do with this child of ours? He's irrepressible."

"David, I'm stumped. I don't understand how his mind works or how he can can be so impervious to everything except his own rules."

We made the trek to Tunapuna the next day at the request of the Benedictines. We were ushered into the principal's office to wait, side by side, hands folded in our laps, knowing what we were going to hear.

Father Doughlin arrived after a short wait and sat down behind his desk.

"Doctor and Mrs. Holbrook, I'm sorry but we do not have the staff at the school to give your son the individual attention that he needs."

Realizing that there was nothing to be gained by prolonging the conversation we slowly stood, shook Father Doughlin's hand and left. As we coasted down the hill from the school, we decided on an alternate course of action.

"The school year has only a few weeks to go. We have already registered all three in summer camp in Haliburton. It starts in four weeks. I think we'll just have to keep Matthew home until Chris and Sue are finished. Myrtle is one of the few who has Matthew's number."

I was late arriving at the office the next day. (So late that Jeff Steiner was already in his office as I passed.)

"David. I would like to speak to you." He motioned to a chair in his tatty office. "I've been on the phone to Ottawa. They feel, as I do, that you have done a very good job here for the past year and they would like to move you to Singapore. There is a serious refugee crisis in South-east Asia that needs someone who isn't afraid of hard work. This post has had its ups and downs for you and your wife. A change will be beneficial for all of you."

"Thank you very much. Would you mind if I went home to tell Lauretta?"

"Go." I jumped up and shook his hand.

"I don't believe it." Lauretta threw her arms around my neck.

"Not only that. It's a promotion and a pay increase."

"I'm ecstatic. We'll be moving half way around the world. It'll be a fresh start, David."

2

REFUGEES IN SOUTH-EAST ASIA

1

I walked home along the footpath beside the Singapore River and was overcome by the stench of excrement from the newly fertilized gardens. When I reached Killaney Road, I passed oldsters who stopped in mid-conversation to look at the 'round eye' appearing out of the darkness. After I passed, they blew snot into the gutter, already wet with spit from their tuberculous lungs. Continuing past the fruit stand which had no regular hours, I was bowled over by the smell of the huge ripe durians, a foulness not unlike that of a full diaper. It was an odour that masked the delicious fruit within, a stink I couldn't bring into my hot and humid apartment with the air-conditioning still not repaired.

Once I reached River Valley Road and passed the vacant lot the Chinese triads had been known to use as a place to dump the bodies of those who stepped out of line, I finally arrived at the iron grill that protected my empty apartment. I took time only to light mosquito coils before I fell into bed exhausted after a day of arguing with local authorities about refugees. I thought of Lauretta and the children but before I could finish the thought, I was asleep.

Morning. The sun was streaming into my curtainless room. I could hear the sweet chirping of song birds. Was I imagining things? I dragged myself out of bed to the window. In a corner of the adjacent lot, free from pile drivers, squatted half a dozen cronies in their singlets and pajama bottoms, sitting on their heels in clouds of smoke from their filterless '555' cigarettes, eyeing each other's caged song birds with a combination of scorn and nonchalance.

The infernal construction was about to begin for the day, pitching more buildings toward the sky. Before long, this place would be sunless, as this once sleepy town, with its quaint low rise shops and colourfully shuttered houses, strove to become a metropolis.

The *Straits Times* was inched under my door. As I picked it up, a yellowed sheet of paper fell out.

'Come quick, Mister Kok is dead!'

I read the note thinking that it had to be a joke. I had not met my neighbours and didn't recall mentioning to anyone that I was a doctor. I climbed the stairs to 601 and Alice, Mr. Kok's girlfriend, frantically waved me in. Stretched out on what served as a couch was a wasted old man. Kok, pale and breathing slowly and deeply, was out cold from another night of opium. I propped open his eyelids revealing dilated brown pupils. I listened to his heart beating regularly, and took his blood pressure. The stench of rancid cooking oil constricted my nostrils.

"Oh doctor, he never smokes opium," piped up Alice, before I had uttered a word.

Was she reading my mind? No doubt their regular doctor refused to come, knowing old Kok's history of opium stupors. "He'll wake up," I reassured her, "just like the last time."

She looked uncertain as I let myself out knowing there was nothing more that I could do.

I locked my apartment and headed for Orchard Road and the bus that would take me to the pile of hastily thrown together lean-tos on an abandoned wharf on the other side of the island.

2

Sitting on the packed bus, dripping with sweat and hoping for a hint of a breeze, I wondered what Lauretta and the children were doing in Canada at that moment. I daydreamed between stops as the bus lurched down Orchard Road passing fancy shopping plazas that Lauretta was going to find infinitely more enjoyable than the town centre of Port of Spain. No wonder refugees want to come to this place.

In Canada, in early 1978, the Liberal government of Pierre Trudeau had agreed that Canada had to do something to alleviate the refugee crisis in South-East Asia. My posting from Trinidad to Singapore was to oversee the medical program for the refugees Canada was willing to accept. I mulled over how I was going to do the medicals for the Canadian immigration department. Many of the hundred or more refugees I was on my way to see, were going to be accepted by Canada. How would they manage the winter?

When I arrived at the pier, I was stunned by the size of the force of the Singapore constabulary milling around the chain-link fence keeping this motley crew of temporary migrants penned in like convicts. It was amazing that so many had been able to get here through the net of patrol boats trying to push them away from Singaporean territory. I presented my credentials and was allowed into the enclosure.

Tan Dinh, paper thin and tense, sat opposite me at a wobbly picnic table set up by the camp leaders for me to interview the new arrivals. His wife and children huddled behind him, terrified, clutching each other, looking sallow and gaunt after weeks at sea. The two children, who were about four and six, were softly weeping, unsure of what was going to happen to them next. I realized they had all been so traumatized by the events of the past weeks that questions were going to be difficult.

"Do you take any medicines, Tan?"

"Yes, I was taking medicine in my country."

"What were the pills for?"

"I do not know." I looked at the translator for some help. He gave none.

"What did they look like?"

A stupid question. I likely wouldn't have recognized them anyway. It would have been equally stupid to ask where they were now. No doubt they were on the bottom of the South China Sea with everything else that had fallen out of their packed flimsy boat. I wondered how many relatives went the way of the pills.

"Have you been ill?" I asked. He shrugged.

"Tan, stand up please. How long have you had the rash on your legs?"

"A long time. The doctor in Saigon gave me the pills for it."

"Ah. Is it getting better?"

"It was."

I ran my hand over the odd-shaped, brown patches of toughened skin on the inside of his right knee and thigh. I checked his hands for telltale deformities. Was this leprosy? If it was, it was my first case in this endemic area. I examined the family and found nothing...not surprising as the disease spreads so slowly.

"O.K. Tan. We'll give you more pills."

I decided it was best to keep my suspicians to myself. If the Singaporean authorities discovered they had a possible case of leprosy brought in by a refugee, God knows what would happen. They have tried to convince the world that they have eradicated the disease.

The UN director motioned me over. I thought he, too, had noticed.

"Doctor, this group is being moved tomorrow to Galang in Indonesia to join the rest of their group. Transport will be arranged from there for any that are accepted by Canada." Twenty-four hours would get Tan out of here. I gave him a prescription to be filled by the nurse in their new compound in Galang where I would see him and his family next.

At the picnic table that served as my office, I saw family after family, physically in relatively good health but all in shock from their harrowing experiences. Recovery was going to be slow. The United Nations High Commission for Refugees (UNHCR) representative now asked me to see a young woman sitting at the back of the group alone with her knees drawn up to her chest, staring at her feet. She stood out from the rest because her hair was crinkly and a reddish hue rather than black. Could this be a nutritional deficiency or some illness that I was totally unfamiliar with and peculiar to Vietnam? Had she been poisoned by chemicals from the war?

"Do you feel ill?" I looked to the interpreter for assistance. He repeated the question.

I squatted to try to see her face. She had lovely features with green eyes. Tears overflowed and dripped onto her dirty white cotton blouse. I waited to see whether she was going to speak. Silence.

"Do you have any family here? Where is your mother?" At this point, a woman who had been squatting nearby, spoke up.

"She and her mother were separated when their boat left Vietnam. It was dark and they didn't get on the same boat."

I was silent for a moment thinking how frightened the poor teenager was and wondered what I could do. The group director motioned to me to come with him.

"We don't know whether her mother made it or if she was on one of the boats that capsized and sank. Her father was an American soldier. Because of this, she's a fifteen year old outcast."

"She should be going to the US not Canada." I said, thinking I had come up with a solution to the problem.

"They don't want her because they say they can't trace the father. Could there be a family in Canada who would adopt her?"

I leaned forward, put my hands on my knees and wondered what to say. I walked around for a moment and glanced in the woman's direction as she continued to crouch and stare at her feet.

"I'm sure a family could be found to sponsor her. I'll put her on the list for the immigration officers when the group gets to Galang. I can only recommend her on her medical admissibility. She would have to pass their criteria. It's worth a try."

"David, thanks. You've seen all the refugees on the Canadian list." We chatted briefly and I was about to leave when I felt a tugging at my sleeve.

"Would you please see my granny?" I turned and faced a teenager, a boy of fifteen or sixteen who grabbed my arm and pulled me back into the group. The director tried unsuccessfully to shoo the boy away.

Granny was a forlorn tiny woman who appeared truly ancient, with translucent skin, a wrinkled face and arms and a miniscule body dressed in black. She was squatting, surrounded by a cluster of elderly women. The woman sat motionless and seemed completely oblivious to the activity around her. Traditionally, she was every person's granny as she was likely the oldest of the group.

"We have not found any relatives as yet," explained the UNHCR representative. "She's not on the Canadian list at this point."

"I'm sorry."

"But…please, Sir." The teen pointed to the 'Canadian group' to make sure I understood what he wanted. When I shook my head, he looked at the ground dejectedly. I felt awful, knowing that teenagers take everything so personally but what on earth would a single elderly woman, steeped in an Asian culture, unable to speak English or French, do in Canada? How long would she survive in the winter? Perhaps she would simply die pining away for her native Vietnam and her ancestors' graves.

At the end of the day, after examining forty-seven prospective Canadians, I was tired and numb. I decided to walk home from the dockside confinement area. What was there about Singapore that resulted in a deluge of rain every evening? Thoroughly drenched, I reached the footpath by the Singapore River, the shortcut to Killaney Road.

3

Lauretta and I embraced as she stepped into the arrival area of Changi airport. Chris and Sue wrapped themselves around us.

"Hi Dad." An accolade from Matthew as he wandered off. I watched him as he checked out his new environs. I prayed that he would have an easier road than in Trinidad. "This is okay, Dad."

"Wait until you see the apartment."

Lauretta's first comment was, "I hope it's air-conditioned. I'm drenched. The heat and humidity are incredible."

"Yes it is." I didn't mention the fact that the repairs had just been completed. "Suite 401 needs lots of your decorating skill and imagination and we'll need some furniture, but, it'll be super and you kids have your own rooms."

"What about school, Dad?"

"You're all going to go to Tanglin School. It's the same type of school as St. Martins in Trinidad. You'll love it."

"Can we wear what we want?"

"No, there are uniforms just like St. Martins." They groaned in unison. I did't have the heart to tell Chris and Matthew they'd still be wearing short pants even though they were almost ten and eleven and 'grown up'.

"We don't miss Trinidad." Chris put into words what we had been thinking. Lauretta and I glanced at each other and I put my arm around her waist as we moved through the immigration line.

Arriving at the apartment on River Valley Road, the kids bounced out of the car to survey their new home before Lauretta and I could lead the way.

"Dad. Dad. There's a swimming pool." Matthew was ecstatic, as he and Chris skirted the pool and Sue checked the bounce on the diving board.

"Come on you kids. I want you to see the apartment."

"David, it's huge." Lauretta was amazed.

"What will we do with this furniture?" I looked at Lauretta hoping that she would have some suggestions.

"It's awful!" Lauretta laughed. "I've never seen such peculiar stuff. Look at that sofa. The headrest slopes forward. And that fuzzy blue green and mustard material! Look at the chair. It's mauve and gold." I grinned and put my hands on my hips, waiting for ideas to flow from the assembled crew.

"We have permission from the High Commissioner to change whatever we want."

"Hey, Mom, the floor's marble. We can play floor hockey."

"I don't think so, Matthew."

"Let's get some of that grass matting. It's a huge space and it would look really nice." Lauretta surveyed the room with her hands in her pockets. It was such a relief to have her home. "We could get wicker furniture. It's inexpensive and would look wonderful with the matting. Let's take down that partition that separates the dining area from the rest of the living room. It's only attached with bolts to the floor. We'll have one huge space."

"Mom, look at the balcony. It's enormous." Chris was on his own tour. "We need some furniture out here too."

"Look down there, Mom. It's a village." Matthew had discovered the Malay kampong tucked up against the other side of the apartment wall.

"Slow down, Matthew. Give us a chance to catch up. We want to look at the balcony first."

"It already has some plants, Mom," Sue added, knowing Lauretta's love of gardening. "What's that tree?" Lauretta walked over to smell the small white flowers.

"It's jasmine. Isn't it beautiful? Perhaps We'll grow orchids, too."

"This is going to be fun, David. Incidentally, is there a phone that works?" We laughed. "Yes. It's one of the first things I checked."

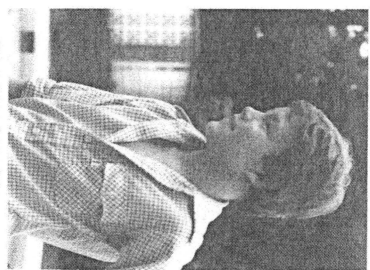

Chris at River Valley Road Singapore

· Sue and Lautetta by pool River Valley Road Singapore

Matthew and friend Singapore

Chris in Malaysian refugee camp

4

At sunrise a week later, having revamped the apartment and registered the children at school, Lauretta waved as I left the apartment for Kalang, the port for Kuala Lumpur. It was hard to leave so soon after Lauretta and the children had arrived but travelling was a crucial part of the job.

I was the only passenger in a Malaysian police launch, on my way to international waters, the sun hot on my back even at this early hour. A burly Malay policeman stepped back from the front of the launch and shoved a red arm-band in my face.

"Put this on! Wear it at all times! This is your pass. We will be in a security zone." As a diplomat, I was being offered no favours.

The launch blasted off from the jetty, the wake flooding the numerous dugouts and their occupants, fishing in the shallows of the Kalang harbour.

I watched as the Malay fishermen struggled to right their boats and bale them out with their rusty tin cans. There were no angry gestures. Flocks of screeching sea gulls circled and zoomed in on fish the locals couldn't retrieve. Navigating past collossal container ships, we finally came into the Straits of Malacca, leaving behind the stench of rotting fish and garbage.

The salt sea smell in the Straits was a relief but the noticeable swell was not. The rising sun on the waves in front of the launch painted the water with green and gold highlights as we cut through it. Anchored in the distance was a rusted, sickly-looking freighter, my destination.

The *Hai Hong*, ('Sea Breeze' in Chinese) was a floating piece of scrap, which had secretly left Singapore and anchored in the estuary of the Saigon River near the town of Vung Tau, south of Saigon, in October 1978. There, it took on a load of 2510 desperate people willing to pay $3200 US or 16 pieces of gold to leave Vietnam. Children were supposedly half-price.

The cost was worth it to many in South Vietnam's middle class. They were facing re-education camps and hard labour, separation from their families and, at worst, long prison terms for supporting the losing side in the war. The final blow was that these families were then obliged to move out of Saigon to 'new economic zones', a euphemism for a plot of jungle where new communities were to be established. They comprised the part of Vietnamese society that could not and would not support a unified Vietnam under a 'socialist' regime governing from Hanoi in the north, the traditional rival of Saigon in the south. There were no longer positions for teachers, doctors and lawyers in Saigon, which were now all taken by northern newcomers.

The syndicate responsible for the Hai Hong was made up of Vietnamese officials, Singaporean promoters and the Hong Kong owners of the salvaged freighter. They made a profit of $4 to $5 million on this voyage alone. Trafficking in human lives had become an easy way to make money, if you didn't give a damn about what happened to them.

As the *Hai Hong* left Vietnam and moved into the South China Sea, neighbouring countries were alerted to its presence. All had refugee camps overflowing from earlier arrivals. A year earlier, another supposedly scrapped freighter, the *Southern Cross*, had floated into Indonesian waters and dumped 1200 refugees for the government of Indonesia to house. The *Hai Hong* was going to be forbidden to land anywhere in South-East Asia. After weeks of drifting back and forth at sea, refused entry over and over again and battered by a typhoon, the diesel engines failed, leaving the 1600 ton freighter drifting off the Malaysian coast.

The United Nations High Commission for Refugees appealed to Canada, and others, to share the responsibility for the *Hai Hong*'s cargo as a humanitarian gesture. When finally an agreement was reached to launch a relief mission, Malaysia would still not allow the *Hai Hong* to enter its waters. The processing had to be done at sea. As part of that team I was responsible for the health of the refugees bound for Canada.

As the launch approached, I could see the rusted orange hull looming over me. A squiggly white strip painted without care, white paint dripping into the rusty black, stretched from bow to stern, with the new name, '*Hai Hong*' printed on both sides of the bow, in white. Streams of dirty bilge water poured out holes in the hull and splashed into the sea beside me. Was this from the engine room? Was this the toilets draining? Toilets? There probably weren't any. Three decks teemed with bodies pushing against the rail, men, women and children of all ages, shouting and waving banners:

'FEED US.' 'TAKE US TO YOUR COUNTRY!'
'WE WANT TO GO TO AMERICA!'
'NO FOOD!' 'NO WATER!'

I felt sick.with horror and disgust at what was happening in front of my eyes. Could these people have expected this when they paid their money? Would they still think it worthwhile? The sight of this mass of desperate humanity shouting and screaming was overwhelming.

The police launch was now circling the Malaysian Navy frigate already at the scene. It kept the *Hai Hong* from going anywhere. The launch finally came alongside and I was waved to the front to transfer to the larger Navy vessel. Five Canadian immigration officers stationed in Malaysia were already on board.

"Welcome aboard, David. We sure need a doctor," quipped a smiling Dick Williams.

I tried to stand still on the deck of the frigate to get my balance back. Over the side of the *Hai Hong* dangled a rotting wooden ladder with rungs missing, pieces of frayed rope filling the gaps.

"O.K. Holbrook, you're the doctor. You go first.

The ladder thudded back and forth against the hull. It stretched from just below the first deck railing to three feet above my head. By standing on the steel railing of the frigate, I could just reach the first rung, with a boost from my compatriots. I didn't have much choice and so rather than think about it, I grabbed the end of the ladder. Careful not to fall through the holes where rungs once were, I hauled myself up the side to the first deck. I was met by a cheering mob of people who grabbed my arms and pulled me over the rusty uneven railing onto the deck. The stench of sweat, stale urine and feces was nauseating. I was now jammed into the mass of people, moving as one, as the ship swayed. I was tugged away from the rail by an unseen arm and found myself closer to the centre of the deck. There was a noticeable listing, sending pots and various containers sliding past me. I watched a giant tub of thick brown slop slip by without tipping.

I suddenly realized that there were jagged holes in the deck above, allowing excrement and garbage to drop from deck to deck. No wonder the spot I was trying to stand on was so slimy. I pushed through the crowd to the port side thinking there might be more air.

Four people were laid out on the deck with filthy sheets over them. There was no movement and only the tops of their heads were visible. I asked the nearest person, motioning at the four bodies.

"Are they sick?"

"Oh yes, sir!" said a woman hauling me by the elbow to their side.

She gingerly pulled back each sheet. Was the odour the horrid sweet smell of rotting flesh or the filthy sheets? I crouched beside the first of the four.

Under the sheet was a teenager with third degree burns, grey patches roughly six inches wide on her shoulders and chest oozing and peeling around the edges. The sheet, her only covering from the waist up, stuck as I tried to peel it off to expose the entire burn. She wouldn't look at me or the burn.

I didn't have any instruments to remove the dead skin or any dressings to cover it properly.

"Is there anyone here who speaks English?"

The woman beside me nodded.

"Please tell her that we'll get bandages for her burns and clean sheets."

"Can I still go to Canada?" moaned the burned teenager.

I smiled, looking back, surprised to hear her talk.

"Yes, I'm sure we'll find a way."

Next was an elderly man with a crinkly face, papery skin and a toothless grin or was it a grimace? What looked like a jagged puncture wound was surrounded by burned, grey, dead skin in the centre of his abdomen. Surprisingly, there seemed to be little blood loss around the wound. I held his arm and took a closer look. It was hard to tell if it was only superficial but surely he'd have been be dead if his bowel had been punctured. He tried to lift his head to see what I was looking at. I didn't want to touch the wound as my hands were filthy, although I don't suppose I would have introduced any bacteria he didn't already have.

"Boiler blew, Doctor." I held his arm as I explained to the woman by my side how to clean the wounds.

The middle-aged woman next to him had red blotchy burns on her neck. She could not move her head without grimacing in pain. There wasn't the dead greyish hue of third degree burns, but weepy red patches. It would be a nasty scar but it would heal better than the other two. Finally, the teenager next to her had red streaked burns across the tops of both feet. They stretched up his legs. He seemed blasé about it all but obviously could not stand up or move his feet. An antibiotic ointment was needed.

Propped up nearby was a young woman with a right ankle protruding at an odd angle. "Not much doubt about that fracture," I said to myself thinking finally I had something relatively simple to deal with. All that could be done was to find a piece of wood for a splint until we could get it x-rayed and set properly.

"Is there a nurse in this group?" I asked the woman helping with the sheets.

"I'm a nurse, Doctor."

I did know that there was a provision for taking a small number of ill or injured refugees. These four would qualify.

"I'm going to send you bandages and a splint. Please do the best you can to dress the wounds and we'll try and move these people to shore soon."

The old man tried again to raise his head and held up his arm to shake my hand. I was swarmed by people on all sides trying to grab me to get assurances that they could get off this floating hell hole and go to Canada. Neatly printed, pleading letters in Vietnamese, French or English were stuffed in all my pockets. I smiled without agreeing to anything and made my way to the ladder.

Going back down the side was worse than going up. The ladder slammed back and forth with the swell, out, then in, crunching against the side of the freighter. I didn't want to get my hand caught between the side of the ladder and the hull, so I moved down slowly, trying to time each step with the motion of the ship. I breathed a sigh of relief as I jumped from the last step onto the deck of the frigate.

I jotted down a list of necessities I needed for the nurse. I wondered where I'd collect it all. The captain of the frigate joined us as we set up a table for the interviews on the deck under the canopy shielding the Bofors anti-aircraft gun.

"Captain. Would it be possible to have some sheets and burn dressings for four patients on the freighter?"

I looked him the eye, bit my lip and hoped for a positive reply.

"Yes, we can help with that." The problem was solved easily.

"We'll interview refugees claiming to have relatives in Canada first," announced Dick Williams, the immigration officers' leader. "Then, David, you do your medical examination on the other side of the gun and send them to Bill who'll try and do a police report. Sorry Bill, you're going to be in the sun."

I smiled to myself wondering what good a 'police report' was going to be. Would anybody with a police record be honest under these circumstances?

"How on earth are we going to get them off the *Hai Hong* and then back on it after the interview?" I asked.

"We interviewed a spokesperson for the refugees while you were on board and he has chosen an individual on each of the three decks who can speak English. That person will get two people from each deck at the top and bottom of the ladder to help move the people off and on the ship. The spokesman will be the overall organiser," explained Dick. "It's his task to coordinate the interview process, deciding who is to be interviewed on the frigate."

"We're going to have to stop if the sea gets any rougher. We can't afford any catastrophes."

Dick continued, "Lists are being prepared and submitted to the captain who in turn will tell us how many he will allow on the deck of the frigate each hour, from dawn to dusk."

"I am Dat Luu Phuoc." He put out his hand and smiled. Tall and gaunt, the *Hai Hong* appointed leader was the first person down the ladder with the initial list of interviewees in his hand. I watched in amazement as he navigated the ladder with ease. He spoke fluent English and agreed to translate for us on the Navy vessel. We went over the procedures with him. Phuoc's wife and five daughters had disappeared at sea or were in another refugee camp. The details were neatly written on a folded piece of paper and stuffed in my pocket. He wanted me to look in the camps for them.

Day one was over at sunset. We fell exhausted into the launch for the trip back to Port Kalang before total darkness. Looking back at the *Hai Hong*, I could only see the vague outline of the black hulk in the water with a few candles flickering on each deck.

Dawn to dusk. Dawn to dusk. For a week, it was the same seafood dinner, the same grimy roach infested room in the Port View Hotel with the flashing red neon sign outside my window that made it seem even hotter. In my narrow bed, I twisted around, flipped my pillow and kicked off the sheet. I was unable to put the thoughts of the previous day out of my mind.

The interviews had to be makeshift at best. Applicants ranged in age from 2 weeks, born during the voyage, to 82 years. To get so many down the decrepit ladder and back up was a major logistical feat. I examined each person with my hands and a stethoscope, attempting to rule out tuberculosis, leprosy and as many other communicable illnesses as I could detect on a swaying ship on a choppy sea. This was good old-fashioned medicine, the way my grandfather said it should be. But then, my grandfather could never have envisioned this scenario. A chest x-ray would certainly have helped confirm tuberculosis-free lungs. The refugees should have received extra health credits for having the agility to manage the ladder as it swayed precariously back and forth against the hull.

The youngest of the refugees was virtually a newborn.

"When was your baby born? Is he your first child?"

"Yes. He was born twenty days ago." I could barely hear her over the screaming of the thin but clear-eyed infant. The baby didn't look sick. The umbilical cord however, was a soggy mess, still attached and with no sign of drying up. I couldn't pull it for fear of making it worse.

Tetanus? There didn't seem to be any muscle tightness other than that caused by the yelling. There was no question about being able to open his mouth and swing his arms around. The only case of tetanus I had ever seen was two weeks ago in one of the camps…a baby with an infected umbilical cord. Could this be another? I dressed it as well as I could, cleaning away as much of the grunge around the cord as possible, and used the antibiotic ointment the captain had given me.

I made a mental note to get some anti-tetanus toxin from the US Embassy doctors, who were always lifesavers when all else failed.

Being the only one with a camera and extra film, I took the 700 passport pictures. It was soon working like clockwork.

"Please come here and lie on the couch while I examine you and go there and smile because I'm going to take your picture. No arguments allowed." There were none. There was apprehension. I doubted that any of the oldsters had ever had their photograph taken. In Asia, it was thought that a photo could take away part of your soul that could never be retrieved. In this case, was it a fair price to pay for freedom and a new life? The background, an anti-aircraft turret and flapping khaki canvas, no doubt added a nice touch to the travel permits.

The transfer to the airport in Kuala Lumpur from the *Hai Hong* began with the burn victims. They were lowered over the side on borrowed stretchers, each of us manning a rope and praying that the rusted railing would not give way. As the sun set on the final day of the *Hai Hong* for me, I looked at all those still waiting, standing by the rail at the top of the flimsy ladder, softly weeping, wringing their hands, and waiting and waiting as the launch sped away.

Hai Hong in the South China Sea

Hai Hong

Hai Hong

On our way to the mainland, dry land for the first time in weeks for these poor souls, no conversation could be heard over the roar of the launch's engines. The Red Cross completed the journey to the airport where I bade farewell to those on stretchers and the young woman, with her baby still screaming, with handshakes, bows and tears. They were all to go to military bases across Canada for their chest X-rays and any other necessary documentation. We knew that in a week we'd accepted 700 people to fill the two Air Canada charter flights waiting at the airport.

I found a bench to sit on in silence for a few minutes, exhausted, physically and emotionally, tears running down my cheeks, staring at nothing in particular, thinking of Lauretta and the children. Could we do what these people had done? Would we ever have to? I found it difficult to imagine even though I'd just observed first hand what it would be like.

5

"Dad, great. You're home. You've got to come to the tombola. I think I've figured out how to win." Chris greeted me, opening the door before I could get my key out. He was counting on hauling all of us to the Tanglin School fête.

We walked around the grounds of the school, a complex of two storey buildings with external staircases, while mobs of kids streamed in and out, leading their parents to their classrooms to see the accomplishments of the first months of school. Sue, eager to show us her prize winning art, disappeared with Lauretta, leaving me to try to find Matthew who had distanced himself from us. Chris watched with interest the activities at the tombola and to my amazement managed to win three bottles of Johnny Walker Black Label before he had finished.

My week at home was a chance for me to have fun with the children and Lauretta. Chris's and Sue's school marks had improved dramatically. We credited much of the change to a far better education foundation built up in Trinidad, something lacking when we moved from Canada. Their grades were now in the upper half of their class which gave them more confidence. Matthew received praise from his science teacher but the other teachers complained of a lack of interest. We had heard it before.

The time in the office was spent trying to define the duties of the two additional doctors sent to help process the thousands of medical reports the eight secretaries had prepared. Personality clashes were inevitable but I was surprised by their reactions. Two professionals, grown men behind their closed office doors, refused to speak to each other. I decided to ignore the nonsense and simply have the secretaries divide evenly the cases to be reviewed. The fact that they refused to travel to the camps for fear of contracting some disease, I chose to ignore. In retrospect, I should have requested their recall and replacements sent.

6

It was another Monday at sunrise. Another day, another camp, another box lunch, more sunburn, and hurried goodbyes to Lauretta and the children. This time it was an hour on the ferry from Singapore to Tanjungpinang in the Indonesian archipelago. On arrival most people were elbowing their way onto the ferry as I struggled to get off.

"Sir, you the doctor?" I was surprised to be picked out in the mob.

I nodded to the short, wrinkled Indonesian boatman who had singled me out. He presented me with his laminated UNHCR ID badge with his picture in the corner.

"Follow me, Sir." I dutifully walked along the shore away from the ferry terminal, leaving the din behind.

"Here, please, Sir."

I looked at him, at the skiff with the tiny motor on the back, at the long stretch of sea beyond us, and said, "No, you must be mistaken." He didn't speak enough English to have the faintest idea what I was saying and continued to point at the rowboat, a flat bottomed wooden skiff with three planks as seats. I shook my head in disbelief and got into the rowboat.

"Sir, for the sun." He handed me an umbrella.

"A long way, Sir." The aged Evinrude was cranked up and off we went. Conversation, even if I did speak the language, was impossible because of the engine racket. Half an hour later, we chugged into open water. There was absolutely nothing appearing on the horizon to even suggest an island, Galang or otherwise. Time for the umbrella. We slowed down as he stood up to help me unfurl it. Heaven help us if he fell overboard. I didn't know enough about operating the motor to even turn it off. Ah, the umbrella's spokes were there but little or no black nylon between. My hat would have to do. The sun blazed down from a cloudless sky.

Half an hour later still with nothing in sight but sea, the motor sputtered and quit.

The boatman hooked up the extra petrol supply.

"No problem, Sir." He cranked the motor. Nothing happened.

I continued to look at the horizon as if I expected the vague image of an island to pop up. The motor was well on the way to being dismantled.

"We get help, Sir." I didn't ask how. Which was better, to sit here and fry, or get into the water against the side of the boat in partial shade?

"Are there sharks in these waters?" He shrugged as I put my feet over the side. I eased myself into the water being careful not to dump him in as he probably couldn't swim. Ahhh! The feel of the sea was like cold water on a hot skillet. I sizzled and sputtered.

Sharks? I hadn't seen any, yet. Just stay still I told myself. My waterproof watch proved not to be. As I tried to keep myself in the shade of the bow, the skiff drifted powerless on the calm sea, and I slowly splashed the pools of purple oil slick away from me. The sun was directly overhead when I finally heard more positive noises from the motor. I hoped the boatman remembered that I was still here. Could he give me a hand to get back in or would I just hang on to the painter? I filled my hat with water and plopped it on my head to make enough noise to remind him. Once I carefully tumbled back in, the wet clothes reduced the heat somewhat.

"Sorry Sir. Motor old. Fine now. Galang close."

Before my clothes had a chance to dry, I could see a gray outline on the horizon.

Previously uninhabited Galang island was now packed with 8500 refugees. The place had become a dusty town stuffed with Coke stands and fast food stalls serving a variety of steamed dumplings and fried rice. The rancid smell of old cooking oil filled the air. There was a stall stacked with piles of red and blue flip-flops. People rummaged through the heap looking for a match to the one already on one foot. White tee-shirts with pictures of Bob Marley, the Rolling Stones and Elvis hung from a rope across the front of the stall. God knows what the supply route was for all this stuff.

There were official white canvas tents emblazoned with the UN emblem for the United Nations rep and other occasional visitors. The camp director and his staff were housed in yet another. They were responsible for producing a list of applicants for the immigration and medical interviews.

The camp was a labyrinth of heavy blue plastic sheeting, rows and rows of it, flapping and undulating in the hot air. Yards of plastic served as dividers for the living quarters such as they were. Two boards roughly the size of a large door maybe five feet by four feet separated the bottom berth occupied by one family from the upper occupied by another family. It was a duplex, refugee camp-style.

The roof and the sides were the ubiquitous blue plastic sheeting. It was no won-der that they needed a camp police force to keep peace among so many piled on top of each other with frayed tempers and squalling babies.

I was greeted by Jim Weston, the UNHCR representative on the island. We had met previously in Thailand in similar camp conditions on the Thai coast.

"How have things been going?"

"Well with the exception of trying to control the teenage rowdies scrapping with each other and harrassing the young women, I'm fine. The oldsters who complain about their living conditions and their neighbours are also a pain. I can understand the teenage boredom but the bickering among their parents about their social class or how hard they fought during the war is ridiculous, given our circumstances here."

"How do you handle them?"

"It's easy. I just move the complainers to the other side of the island and threaten the bad actors with removing their names from the interview list. The belief is that the closer you are to the gate, the sooner you will be interviewed. It isn't true but try and tell them that."

A young Vietnamese, wearing a once white singlet and blue striped pajama bottoms, slipped into the tent and then apologized for interrupting our conversa-tion.

"David, this is Liam Fuk, our camp leader. He is going to take you to the clinic." He bowed and we shook hands. A giggling bunch of little children peered around the tent flaps. "Oh David, wait a minute. I have another bag of letters for you."

"That reminds me, Jim. You wouldn't have a single woman with five children on the camp lists, would you? Her husband's name is Phuoc Dat Luu. He's in Malaysia and thinks his wife and children either drowned or are here."

"I'll check the list and get a message to you."

I followed the tall and, as always, reed thin Vietnamese camp leader down the path past rows of shelters, kids in-tow. It was like walking down a street in a scruffy town anywhere in Asia, no trees or grass, just dust, dirt and humidity. The dust stuck to my face and was irritating.

"This is our clinic." A large well-lit blue plastic tent appeared to be clean and well equipped for a camp setting. There were two cots, a few boxes of supplies and a refrigerator hooked up to a small generator whirring in the corner. The nurse, young, wearing a white blouse and bulky black trousers, was also from the camp community.

"How do you do, Doctor. My name is Thieu Ba. She bowed. I have a list of people who would like to see you, please. They have been diagnosed as having tuberculosis when they had a chest x-ray on arrival here."

"Thank you, Ba. I'll be happy to see them." She already had them lined up outside the clinic tent. I chatted with each patient with the help of the nurse who spoke impeccable English. I made sure they understood why they had to take three medicaments and that they could not leave for Canada until they had taken the medication for six months. Each had to come to the clinic three times a day for medicine and have their names recorded. She assured me that the patients with tuberculosis lived in a separate area of the camp.

"Let's go and see it."

"Follow me, please." We set off down more pathways followed by the little kids who had been watching my every move. They peeked through the tent flaps, chattered and poked each other, happy for the change in their routine.

As I stumbled over tree trunks, I realized this island was practically denuded of trees, perhaps mahogany trees like the few that remained. They had been hauled off to the mainland. Every remaining scrap of wood was used as fuel for cooking in the camp.

The island was also much larger than I had thought, but there was no peace, no silence anywhere. The racket was almost unbearable: babies screaming, children arguing and fighting, adults yelling at each other.

After a ten minute walk through the blue nylon labyrinth, we came to a four strand wire fence separating the 'isolation' portion from the rest of the camp. I peered over the fence and saw no difference, a sea of blue. I turned and looked behind me. By now, a flock of kids was swarming around us. I felt like the Pied Piper of Galang. Isolation? I looked back at the nurse who anticipated my question.

"We try our best, Doctor."

We walked through the 'gate' cut in the fence and along the narrow pathways separating the living quarters.

"Is the isolation going to work with all these families crammed together?"

The nurse didn't hear me as the children, now in the isolation area with us, were making so much noise. It was highly unlikely but I couldn't come up with a better solution.

Explaining the care that must be taken, I chatted with a few families, thanks to Nurse Thieu's translation. Some understood the reasons for not hacking up sputum and spitting in the corners of their blue plastic-draped abode. Others, perhaps because they didn't understand her dialect, looked blankly into space. After completing my grand tour, we started our long walk back to the clinic. We were intercepted by the camp leader with a message from Jim Weston.

"Sir, there is a woman that fits the name and description except that one of the children was washed overboard soon after leaving Viet Nam."

"Nurse Thieu. Could you take me to where this woman is?"

I passed the details to her. The kids were pushing and shoving to get closer to hear what we were talking about. I guess it was their English lesson for the day. The nurse told them who we were looking for.

"Oh, I know Sir," piped up a squirt of a kid with a brush cut, faded red shorts and bare feet. Off he ran at break-neck speed, expecting the nurse and me to follow closely behind. Fortunately, this band of helpers kept him in view. "Over here!" he shouted through the maze of blue lean-tos.

"There he is," shouted the boy next to me pointing through a crack in the blue plastic sheets. There was so much shouting around me, I wasn't sure who to listen to. I had lost track of where I was.

In the last row of dwellings, close to the shore of the South China Sea, a small, tired-looking woman crouched, her elbows resting on her thighs, her hands cupped around her chin. She watched a group of children swimming in the sea outside the curls of barbed wire, the perimeter fence which surrounded the island. My loyal band of helpers now crowded around and the woman stood alarmed at what was happening. I shooed them away as best I could.

"*Chao Bà.* (Hello Madam) Are you Dat Lai?"

"Yes." Frightened, she turned to look at me. Her face was gaunt. Dark circles drooped under her penetrating black eyes. Her mouth was partially open and her brow furrowed. Not taking her eyes off me, she quickly moved away.

"I'm the Canadian immigration doctor, Dat Lai. Is your husband's name Dat Luu Phuoc? Did you live on Tu Do Street in Saigon?" She nodded hesitantly. "Do you have five daughters?

Madam Dat, I met Dat Luu Phuoc in Malaysia. He asked me to look for you."

"Oh, Oh!" Her cheeks flushed and a smile slowly broke across her face. She uttered a nervous cry and covered her face with her hands.

"He was terrified that he would never see you and his girls again."

She lunged forward and grasped my hand with both of hers and looked at me with her watering dark eyes. Moments of disbelief passed as we stood silently, hands joined, then tears began trickling down her face.

"Are you sure?" she whispered.

"I am positive. You and your daughters will be joining him in Canada." She shook and shook my hand. Then she turned to the sea waving her arms trying to call her daughters but they couldn't hear her shouts because of the squealing and laughing of the kids playing in the water.

She bowed again, her shoulders straighter than before. Still thanking me, she backed toward the bank not wanting to be impolite by turning her back to me but desperate to slide down, under the barbed wire, into the water with her daughters.

I watched as they jumped up and down screaming and splashing water over each other.

Forlorn Gentleman Galang

Child in Galang Camp Indonesia

Swimming on shores of Galang Indonesia

Camp Life in Mersing Malaysia

7

Back in Singapore, I was met by silence as I opened the apartment door.

Chris came to greet me. "Guess what, Dad? Matthew has been expelled from school." I was stunned.

"Chris! I told you I was going to deal with it." Lauretta rushed across the room to greet me. Chris marched off grinning, pleased with himself that he was getting back at his brother for yet undescribed crimes.

"I'm sorry, David. I had no idea that was going to happen." We embraced and she took my briefcase of files and more packages of letters from the refugees pleading with me to find their lost relatives. "Put those clothes in the garbage. Have a shower. Put on some clean things and come and sit." I returned to the living room after a shower and change of clothes.

"Where's Matthew?"

"He and Sue are at Annalisa Chou's home swimming. Chris didn't want to go. He has an architectural project he's having fun with."

"I'll be back in a minute. I'll get us a Campari and soda."

I sank into a chair and waited for Lauretta to reappear. "What happened?"

"The teacher was just fed up with having Matthew disrupt the class. She claimed that he talked out all the time, didn't pay attention and got up when he pleased and traipsed around the room. Instead of telling him to stand in the hall as she usually did, she sent him to the office. He was furious and went out muttering and slammed the door. He didn't have the same luck at the office. The principal phoned and told me to pick him up. He was tired of being told how to run his school. He would like us to find another school for him. He had no suggestions."

I took a deep breath and let it out slowly. I looked at Lauretta.

"Damnation. I thought he had adjusted well to school."

"Now what do we do?"

"What baffles me is that his behaviour is never great at home but it's normal for his age, don't you think? What are we missing, David?"

"He's always into something but there's nothing I can put my finger on. It is odd I guess that he doesn't crave attention. He never seems to want love or cuddling and yet he always expects us to be there for him."

I slumped back in my chair.

"I wonder whether his behaviour would be the same if we were living in Canada? Frankly, I think it would be, but are we kidding ourselves? Let's try boarding school again. But where?"

"I think we'll have to send him back to Canada. I'll take him to Toronto if you can make some appointments for me."

"There's not much choice. Oh Matthew, Matthew. It's never-ending."

Four days later, with appointments at five schools, I tearfully hugged and kissed Lauretta and Matthew at Changi Airport.

In Lauretta's absence, Mimi, a gentle young Malay whose allergies caused constant sniffing and the need for multiple boxes of Kleenex, stayed in the apartment during the day.

"Now listen you two. I have to go to work and Mimi is going to be here. Behave yourselves."

"We're not babies you know, Dad. We're eleven years old. We can be on our own."

"Not a chance."

"Oh Dad. You don't have to worry about us." Chris and Sue have felt the family tension and stress surrounding their ten year old brother.

"We can't blame everything on Matthew. It's just that he doesn't see the need to follow others' rules. You don't have that excuse."

After a week of abortive interviews, Matthew was accepted by a boarding school in Peterborough, a long drive from Toronto. The school was pleased with Matthew's 'individualistic' streak as they so aptly called it. There was a catch.

"If your son repeatedly breaks the school rules, Mrs. Holbrook, we will request that you remove him immediately."

Lauretta returned to Singapore feeling anxious and depressed.

"I feel as though I have let Matthew down, David. It was awful leaving him and yet he simply said, 'See ya Mom.' and went off with a group of kids. He isn't connected with us somehow."

"Darling, you have not let him down. It's not you. It's all of us if anything. Honestly I can't figure him out either. I think we're doing the best we can." I put my arms around her and we held each other in silence.

My 'home' time with the children had given me an opportunity to get through the mountains of medical forms and x-rays for the hundreds of refugees leaving every week for Canada. Because of the high incidence of tuberculosis, requests had to be made for TB cultures and treatment records and then follow-up, much to the chagrin of the immigration officers trying to fill the planes, chartered by the Canadian government, on time.

8

It was a relief to get back to the camp visits leaving the secretaries and bickering doctors, to deal with the paperwork.

Before leaving for Indonesia, I received a call from Ted Hasan, a cheery Malaysian veterinarian that I had met earlier in Kuala Lumpur.

"David, I know you're going to be on Galang and thought you might like to come to my clinic and give me a hand for a day. I have an immunization program to do and I could really use the help. I know you don't want even more time away from Singapore, but..."

After so many weeks in refugee camps, a change was welcome.

"Where is your clinic?"

"It's in the jungle about ten miles out of Sandakan."

Sandakan is at the eastern end of Sabah, one of two provinces of Malaysia which share the island of Borneo with Indonesia.

Ted, a burly, bearded, jolly looking man, picked me up at the small airport in his old Land Rover and took the gravel road out of town. We chatted about the refugee camps and their negative effect on the region and its economy during the thirty minute trip from town.

The gravel gradually gave way to a dirt path which began to have more and more grass growing down the middle leaving room for only tire tracks. As the road narrowed, the jungle thickened, the low hanging branches of the eucalyptus trees scraped along the top and sides of the vehicle. We stopped in front of a chain-link fence. Ted unlocked the sturdy gate and I drove the Land Rover into the yard. The low-rise cement block building in the compound looked newly built. We strolled through the yard and Ted again got out his heavy key ring.

"Why all the locks and fences?"

"You'll see." He undid the double locked door of the clinic and Ted gestured with his arms. "It's great, isn't it? This serves as the examining/operating room."

The examining room was spotlessly clean, lined with sheets of stainless steel. Two shiny stainless steel examining tables were in the centre of the room. The pungent smell of disinfectant reminded me of the myriad of other examining rooms I had been in in my life.

"Ted, how did you get this assignment?"

"It's a funny story. The Malaysian government has passed a law forbidding private citizens from keeping wild animals as pets. Consequently the animals were all confiscated and the orang-utangs were brought here.

"We immunize them in case they have been exposed to any illness they could introduce into the wild, then we set them free. This reserve is surrounded by water, and because orang-utangs hate water, they are contained in this area of the jungle which enables us to keep track of them."

I followed him into a large room next door to meet my first patient. There was the pleasant smell of fresh jungle grass in the cages along one wall.

"Just put your hand out." I did what I was told and Tigus, a young orang-utang put his rough and hairy paw in my hand and we walked into the examining room for my introduction to veterinary medicine.

"Are all orang-utangs well behaved?"

"I don't usually have trouble but I'm always happy when I have help."

The syringes with the polio vaccine already drawn up from the 10cc.vial were lined up on a tray on the counter.

"O.K. buddy, this is not going to hurt a bit." I took his furry right arm, swabbed a patch with alcohol on the inside above the elbow where there was the least fur, and quickly slid the needle under the skin. Aside from scrunching up his nose, the orang-utang showed no reaction as I eased the needle out of his arm. Next, Romulus. The same reaction. Tigus bounced up and down in his cage mocking his friend.

"Where on earth did the incredible names come from?"

"Somebody's vivid imagination." Ted laughed.

After completing the four injections, Ted with his charges, and I with Tigus in one hand and Romulus in the other, went out the clinic door and walked to the edge of the jungle behind the clinic.

"O.K., just stand still," whispered Ted. For a moment all was quiet.

Suddenly, there was a great rustling above us. An enormous male orang-utang swooped down swinging from branch to branch and moved towards us, just like a scene from the Tarzan movies of my youth. My two charges panicked and grabbed my legs with all their considerable strength. He stopped ten feet in front of us and mumbled to himself glaring at my two young ones and then at me with yellow streaked sorrowful eyes.

"Don't move," whisperd Ted.

In front of me ten feet off the ground was a wooden platform built between two tall bamboo trees. Sitting on the platform were two wild females calmly eating bananas, seemingly oblivious to the goings on in front of them.

"Now, let go of your friends," Ted murmured.

"I'm not holding them, they're holding me." My legs were sweating from being wrapped in furry, shaking orang-utangs. One of the females suddenly swung down from the platform and meandered towards us. She slowly walked around me showing gums and teeth and chewing as if about to spit. Or was she smiling? I couldn't tell whether she fancied my two charges or me. I sure as hell was not going to move. She took a swat at Tigus and then jumped away as if it was a private little joke. Tigus buried his head in my pant-leg. The female abruptly stopped teasing, sauntered back, and gently took hold of Tigus' forearm. I didn't move. Was this only part of the act? Suddenly I felt the grip on my leg slacken. Slowly but surely, Tigus let go and was dragged away by the female, like a young child being hurried along. Romulus seeing his friend leave, looked up at me and then at Tigus, let go of my other hand and loped after his buddy, squealing.

Ted was more adventurous. He walked closer to the platform with his charges. Three females stepped from the shadows, pawing at the dirt around him, baring their gums in what looked like a laugh but was more likely a snarl. It was as if they were warning him he was trespassing, and also guilty of kidnapping. His two young ones let go in order to follow Tigus and Romulus. Was it the call of the wild or a craving for a banana?

Ted turned to me, "O.K. let's..." at that instant, he was swatted by one of the females. His wallet dropped out of his shirt pocket. The nearest orang-utang quickly grabbed it, swung onto the platform and up a nearby tree where she gleefully dropped every bill and bit of paper piece by piece to the jungle floor. Then she dropped the empty wallet at his feet and bared her teeth in a toothy grin.

"Now what?"

"I'm going to move very slowly and try and pick up as much money as I can. You stay where you are. Don't move."

I could see the clinic door out of the corner of my eye, but it was too far to run without the pack swarming us. Ted slowly managed to pick up his credit cards, driver's licence and wallet and left the rest.

We cautiously backed up the path to the clinic but kept our eyes on the scene in front of us, our footsteps silent on the moist jungle soil. The male orang-utang stood on all fours humming to himself while staring at us with his deep set dark eyes. Any quick move and I was sure he would have jumped us. By breathing slowly and moving backwards a cautious half step at a time, we reached the clinic door.

"Phew! That was close. I usually don't have that many wild ones to contend with in this area. My mistake was putting that whole branch of bananas on the platform."

"Thanks for helping because as you can see, you never know what's going to happen. With so many milling about, we could have been hauled off into the jungle."

Orangutangs Sandakan Sabah Malaysia

Sandakan Sabah Orangutan Reserve

9

After every camp visit, I was met with an outpouring of questions and a fascination with the hundreds of letters I received. Sue and Chris separated them into Vietnamese, French and English.

"Dad, I'd really like to come with you sometime. Just once. May I? Please? Just once?" Chris was insistent. I finally gave in and requested permission from the Malaysian authorities to take a member of my family with me.

"Chris, crowds of people will have lots of questions to ask you."

"It'll be fun, Dad."

"There is one problem. You'll have to have a shot of gamma globulin to protect you against hepatitis."

"Oh no!" Chris winced as he hated needles.

"You'll survive it kiddo, I have to give mine, myself. At least you'll have me to do it for you. You'll have to restart your antimalarial pills tonight and you'll have to carry your own bag. So, don't pack too much. Don't forget your mosquito lotion." Chris nodded, excited by the prospect of actually seeing what he had been hearing so much about.

Chris and I waved to Lauretta and Sue as we left for our pre-dawn flight to Khota Bharu on the north-east coast of Malaysia near the Thai border.

"Dad. Did you know that Khota Bharu is where the Japanese landed in south-east Asia in World War II?" I looked at Chris, surprised by his comment.

"How did you know that?"

"I read it in the library at school. You told me where we were going, remember?"

I smiled. "No. I'd forgotten."

"Will there be kids my age in the camp?"

"Yes. I'm sure. They'll ask you what school is like in Canada. Can you remember?"

"Oh course. School is school. Will they speak English?"

"Some do. You'll have to use your imagination to explain some things. But you'll find some who can speak English who can help you with those that don't."

Chris could not believe that after a ninety minute flight, we still had a one hundred mile three hour taxi ride to get to our destination, Kuala Trengganu. It was long enough to give me a chance to realize how mature Chris and his sister were now that they were eleven. The conversation, about everything from tuberculosis, which was the reason for the trip, to why some classmates do so poorly and behave so badly at school, shocked me into accepting the fact that we now had a young man in our midst. Lauretta had been telling me for ages but I had not experienced it until now.

"You know Dad, more kids should do things like this. It would really help kids to understand people better. I bet they have the same problems most kids have. Like, kids hate to have parents that fight or drink too much. Kids like rules that are fair."

I sat back and let him talk as I took in all he said. The comments from our eleven year old were so wise. Our taxi to Kuala Trengganu also gave Chris a chance to point out the similarities and differences in the jungle we were driving through to that of southern Malayasia. The Tanglin School had taken ten kids on a four day trip earlier in the year. They had stayed in a jungle campsight and, from Chris's recounting of the adventure, learned a great deal more than I'll ever know.

Sue had chosen mountain climbing in Sarawak on the north-west shore of Borneo instead and regaled us for days afterwards with tales of the two gin-toting crochet-bikinied chaperones.

I told Chris some of the stories I had heard, stories of the refugees being shot at from the shore in an attempt to keep them from landing, or being robbed of what few possessions they had managed to get ashore. Chris would want to know the truth before he got there.

The taxi finally turned off the road and stopped at a tall chain-link gate manned by Malaysian security forces.

Gerry Sorensen was one of a group of Scandanavians who had been running the Malaysian camps for the UNHCR. A number of physicians from Scandanavia had been responsible for doing the immigration medical examinations for Canada.

"Gerry, I would like you to meet my son." They shook hands.

"Hi, Chris. I have lots of people who are very eager to talk to you. David, there are twenty-two people with TB waiting to see you. Chris, you can come with me." Chris put up his hand in a self-conscious half wave as he went to meet the camp group of children and teenagers who were going to Canada. I headed for the nursing area to answer questions about TB medicines and when they leave for Canada.

The camp was not allowed to spread beyond the beach area. With more than two thousand people crammed into this miniscule space, it was a sea of blue plastic from the high tide mark to the trees. The nurse had an area just off the beach and from where I stood, I could see Chris's blond hair poking up in a crowd of hundreds of young people.

"There are a lot of objections." The nurse looked tense as she explained her difficulties with some of the oldsters who wouldn't take their medication unless she stood and watched them.

"I do have one patient I would like you to see. He has swollen glands in his neck." The nurse walked to a group of refugees standing nearby and pulled a man out of the crowd.

"This is Nguyen Nhin and his wife Venh Anh." A young shirtless man and his pretty wife in the ubiquitous black trousers with a white blouse approached me.

"Hello, I'm Doctor Holbrook. I would like to examine you." The nurse translated. She gave me their latest chest x-rays. I held them up to the light and compared them with earlier ones. The fluffy looking shadows in the upper right lobe of Anh's x-ray were now clearing leaving stringy fibrous lines in their place. That was a good sign which meant that the pulmonary tuberculosis was gradually becoming inactive.

"Nhin, how long have you had the swollen glands in your neck?"

"Many months, sir."

"Are you taking the medicines that the nurse has been giving you?"

"Yes, Doctor."

"Do you have any pains in your stomach?" I put the screen around the wobbly stretcher and checked his abdomen and did not find an enlarged liver or spleen. He did not have swollen glands in his groin.

"The swollen glands are likely caused by the tuberculosis. The medicines that you're taking will help them to clear. The glands will get harder and less sore as the medication continues to clear up the infection." I explained as much as I could so that the nurse would know what to expect over the next few months.

"Dad, that was really fun. They wanted to know about snow. I said that snow was like sugar only cold, also what our houses are like and whether it is hot like here. I told them what the schools were like and what time school starts and finishes. They wanted to know if teachers were strict. The man who translated said there were too many questions. He asked me if I could come again. I said I would ask you. Could I, when you come again?"

"Chris, have you forgotten about school?"

"This is educational, Dad. I could go here and then I could help."

"You have to complete your school year. The answer's no. Furthermore we still have another stop, Chris. You're still going to have many more people to see. Are you ready?" Chris nodded less enthusiastically, disappointed at my not agreeing to his plan.

We continued our taxi trip to Mersing and another round of questions for Chris and from the camp nurse for me before returning by car to Singapore.

10

Sue arrived home from an afternoon at her friend Brenda's and came onto the balcony where Lauretta was pruning her jasmine trees.

"Mom, a weird thing happened at Brenda's house. We were playing in the 'rec' room and we heard someone knocking at the window. We looked and there was a huge snake knocking with its hood. Her dad says it is a king cobra that lives in the ravine."

"It can eat chickens you know, Sue," piped up Chris.

"Now, remember Sue, you're never to play outside at Brenda's! We've heard all we ever want to hear about snakes in our lifetime."

"We don't play outside because she knows about the cobra. Don't worry, Mom. I hate snakes. You know that."

"Relax, Mom, we're old enough now. We're not going to do anything foolish." Chris and Sue, now in their twelfth year, were becoming the voices of reason and maturity. Sue was going to need a new beige striped uniform as she was getting so tall that her uniform was fast becoming a micro-mini. Chris went through a shirt a week thanks to the rigours of rugby. He was hoping that school rules would soon allow him to wear long pants.

"Let's change the subject, everybody. The good news is that this year we're going to have a real Christmas tree."

"Great, Dad. Where are we going to get it?"

"Jason's supermarket is importing some trees from the Black Forest in Germany. They arrive today. We must go and choose one we like before they're all sold."

"We can use the decorations we made in Trinidad."

"If you can find them, Chris. You'll have to make some extras."

"I can make some origami decorations like the ones Matthew and I made at the Hilton for that horrible flat felt tree."

"First, let's get the tree and then we'll know how many decorations you will have to make."

We set off for Jason's parking lot prepared for the extortionate cost of our real German Christmas tree.

"I want this tree, Dad." Lauretta and I looked at the monster tree Chris had chosen. "It's a fir tree. Look. It's blue." It's also the largest of the dozen remaining.

"It won't stand up in the apartment. It's huge."

"Mom, all we have to do is cut a bit off the bottom."

"It makes up for not having a tree for the past few years." Lauretta smiled raising her eyebrows as we glanced at each other trying to figure out how we were going to get it home.

The children were right. It looked spectacular even if it did take up half the living room.

"I hope Matthew likes it too. We've saved all these things for him to put on the tree when he arrives from Canada." Both Chris and Sue were very conciliatory to Matthew and missed him despite the frequent skirmishes.

He wasn't due to arrive until two days before Christmas. His flight by way of Hong Kong would normally be enough to knock over a dozen people for days. Not Matthew.

As he pushed through the frosted doors of the customs area, he rushed headlong into Lauretta and me.

"Matthew, you've grown so much. Your hair is turning brown."

"Dad, I'm five foot four." Wiry Matthew is now taller than Lauretta.

"Mom. You should see all the food sellers in Hong Kong riding bicycles with live chickens all over their bikes."

"Matthew. How did you get to see that?"

"The flight had a long delay. A stewardess from the airline took me to Kowloon because I didn't want to stay in the airport that long."

"I don't believe you, Matthew." Chris said what the rest of us were thinking.

"I don't care. I had fun." He continued with stories of his escapade, describing in detail the new tall buildings for our benefit and how he managed to buy Christmas gifts, a bangle each for Sue and Lauretta and postcards for Chris and me.

As we reached home Matthew ran ahead and was first through the door.

"Wow. I like the tree. Who chose it?"

"I did." Chris stood proudly with his hands in his pockets.

"We saved a lot of decorations for you to put on it."

"How did you get the angel on top."

"I had to use a ladder." Sue's angel, minus a halo but with a silver hem on the skirt, had to be perfect and so had to be put on the tree by Sue.

"I would like the ladder. Show me where it is, Sue?"

Lauretta and I decided to sit on the balcony and watch the scene rather than argue about who was going to do what. Hours passed before our Matthew began to show signs of tiring. Chris and Sue could barely hold their heads up.

"Okay kiddies it's time for bed." There were no complaints.

The mood over Christmas gradually changed as Matthew got bored and wandered further afield in his explorations. He left silently and unnoticed despite being told to tell us if he was going out. After the first few times this happened, he came home smelling of cigarette smoke.

Sue noticed it initially. "Matthew, you've been smoking."

He put his finger to his mouth, "Shhh".

Lauretta happened to come in from the balcony in the middle of the discussion.

"What's going on, you two?"

"I was over looking at the old men with the birds in the lot across the street." Matthew was quick with a reply. Sue didn't bring up the subject of smoking.

"Mom, when am I going back to school. There's nothing to do." Despite trips to the zoo, the botanical gardens, swimming with Sue and Chris's friends, Matthew felt like an outsider. Sadly, it was a relief as we stood and waved as Matthew boarded the plane to return to school.

11

With some apprehension and uncertainty, my next project was a two week visit to Ho Chi Minh Ville, formerly Saigon with Georges Fenier, an experienced immigration officer stationed in Bangkok. We had been asked by the United Nations to go to Vietnam to try and arrange a program for the orderly departure of migrants directly to Canada, rather than taking the sea route to Vietnam's neighbours, across the South China Sea to the south, west and east.

As the Air France 737 landed on the worn runway of the Tan Sun Nhut airport in a western suburb of Saigon and approached the rundown terminal building, I knew we were not going to be welcomed with open arms. As we passed through the arrival room the customs officers were not disagreeable. I did wonder how they could sit in the heat and humidity in the large dingy room with one antique ceiling fan whining above them, pushing down the hot air. There were no smiles but no delays either.

The UN representative, Yves Dumont, was happy to see us, new faces in what had to be a difficult job.

The pot-holed road to downtown Ho Chi Minh Ville was enough to shake my fillings loose. We rode in the only automobile on the road—an ancient Peugeot—in a land of bicycle riders, one, two, three, whole families on one bike; mother and the baby on the back fender, one child on the cross-bar and one on the handlebars. Father got the seat and the responsibility for balance, steering and pedal power. The feeble Peugeot horn was drowned out by the ringing of bicycle bells. The trip to the Caravelle Hotel on Lam Son square was a slow one. It was difficult to ignore the sinister glares of the riders who pulled alongside the car as we eased our way through the bike congestion. Yves looked at us, his face lined with fatigue.

"All the people in charge from the hotel clerks, to the teenage soldiers are from the North. They are furious with all southerners who did not wholeheartedly support them through the civil war. They have fired all South Vietnamese officials from government posts and even school teachers. They are being forced out of the city." Yves continued. "To make matters worse, the Americans, who were supposed to act as advisors to build up the South Vietnamese army, got caught in a role reversal. The southerners became dependent on them to fight their war. It's still a mess. You're going to get antagonism everywhere."

Georges and I looked at each other.

"We'll manage." I smiled at Yves. Georges nodded. In truth we didn't know what we were getting into.

As we entered our hotel, a somber clerk eyed us from behind his desk.

"Leave your passports on the counter."

I pushed my passport across the desk with some trepidation. The hotel clerk then tossed two keys on the counter with a clatter.

"Take the stairs to the second floor. The elevator isn't working."

We struggled with our suitcases and boxes of immigration forms up the two flights realizing that the rez-de-chausée did not qualify as the first floor. The hallway, for inexplicable reasons, was lined with plush maroon armchairs. We trudged down the hall and tried to see our room numbers in the gloom.

I was happy that Georges Fenier was with me for a number of reasons. He was oblivious to people's negative reactions and didn't notice the sullen hotel clerk. He was also brilliant when it came to the minor pleasures in life. Take Scrabble for example.

We had no board or letters. No problem. Georges could make them all. No chess board or pieces. George made them. I knew I would eventually use my shirt cardboards for something essential. His night time reading was Homer and Ovid. I forgot to bring a book.

I returned to the front desk to request an extra room in which to conduct our interviews. The clerk slowly stood, scowling and stated, "That will have to be discussed with the management."

"But there is no one else on our floor."

"We have our rules."

"It's not for another person. It's to interview people who hope to rejoin their relatives in Canada."

"*Nguys*! Those who left are traitors."

We decided that my room, being the largest, would be the interview room. Two French doors opened onto a small balcony and the ceiling fan kept the temperature bearable. This hotel did reveal its French heritage: floor to ceiling doors, wrought iron decoration on the balconies, little things that reminded me of Paris. Paris with geckos zipping up and down the walls.

Tonight I decided to read my borrowed book. Turning on the light, I soon forgot that idea. The twenty-five watt bulb gave off barely enough light to see my hand in front of my face. Sleep was the only option.

Soft knocking on the door wakened me. I got up and stumbled to answer it in my T-shirt and gym shorts. Standing in front of me, head bowed, was a beautiful young woman with waist-length satin-black hair. Her spotless high-collared white cotton *ao dais* was buttoned to the neck skintight to the waist and then slit from the waist to the ankles with black trousers underneath.

"Sir, are you the Canadian doctor?"

"Yes, I am. May I help you?" We had been warned about women appearing at our door in our briefings. I reminded myself of what was said:

'Beware of locals who are too friendly.'

'Do not invite locals into your hotel room. You may compromise them as well as yourself.'

'Do not accept sexual favours or money.'

If I had paid more attention, I might have remembered more. She didn't look like a prostitute but what did a prostitute look like in Vietnam?

"My name is Liam Hoa. I have been sent by Monsieur Dumont to be your interpreter."

I looked back into the room: clothes, files and scrabble everywhere.

"We are not quite ready to start. Would you please have a seat."

I motioned to one of the plush chairs against the wall outside my room. I banged on Georges's door. No response. I grabbed the scrabble tiles, stuffed the clothes into my suitcase and piled the boxes of files on the bed.

I splashed water on my face from the basin in the corner of the room and put on a clean shirt to go with my beige trousers. I found socks and remembered to bang out any lurking scorpions from my shoes.

"Would you please come in, Miss Liam?"

"There are many people waiting." She motioned to the window. They were lined up the length of the block in twos and threes. The banana-leaf conical hats, *non las,* on the women were over their shoulders and tied with ribbon under the chin. It looked like an abstract painting from where I stood. This crowd was going to get us deported for promoting a demonstration. There was, no doubt, a strict regulation that no more than three people could meet without a permit. There were hundreds.

"Please leave the door open." With the door to the hall shut, the heat of the room was overwhelming as the humidity increased. The geckos flitted up and down the walls after the bugs that were trying to escape the ceiling fan which was otherwise useless.

Bleary eyed, Georges appeared at the door.

"Thank God you're awake," I realized I should not use profanities in front of our guest interpreter.

"How do you do? I'm Georges Fenier." He put out his hand and she shook it. I watched his eyes look her up and down.

In Asia, as in most countries, the woman was expected to put her hand out first, if she intended to shake hands at all. I thought to myself 'Bow, Georges. Put your hands in your pockets.'

"Miss Liam, let me explain what we are going to do. Many of these people outside have relatives in Canada and would like to join them either for a visit or to help the family. We hope to reunite as many people as possible. We have a list of families in Canada who are willing to sponsor their relatives, by paying for their airfare and permits. We can only interview those who are being sponsored by relatives in Canada."

I knew that many were here trying to escape the harsh reality of their calamitous change in life style. The sad fact was that they had no connection with Canada which would permit us to issue a visa.

The smell of cooking wafted through the open balcony windows. We had not eaten and our stomachs rumbled. Hoa excused herself. She returned a few minutes later with take-out food, Saigon-style, from the vendor, who sat in the shade of her *non la* below our window.

"I hope you like petit pain with fried tomato, onions and garlic?"

"Hoa, thank you very much. This is very kind of you." I reached for the roll of dong notes stuffed in my pocket.

"I'm sorry. I cannot accept payment."

Georges and I looked at each other and decided it was one more thing that we could do nothing about. It was time to get to work.

"Sir, my name is Tran Dinh and this is my wife Li and my three children. The Americans called me Charles, sir," he whispered, embarrassed.

Georges and I both sat at our makeshift table, head resting on our elbows as we looked at the scene playing out in front of us for the umpteenth time today. So many were obviously poor souls who had worked for the Americans and were unable to get into the American compound or the nearby building with the helicopter landing pad because of the chaos during the final hours of the evacuation on that Wednesday, the 30th of April 1975.

"Do you have relatives in Canada, Mr. Tran?"

"I think so."Everybody thought so and in order to satisfy the Vietnamese authorities, we had to have something more substantial to get an exit permit.

"What are their names?"

He gave us a list of names impossible to trace. He then told us they were in Montreal. Finally. Something concrete.

"My uncle sent me this letter."

Georges and I sat back in our chairs and breathed a sigh of relief. It might be adequate to get this family to Canada. It even had an address we could trace. To try and validate the claim we asked as many pertinent details as we could.

"Mr. Tran, where is Montreal? How many children does your uncle have? How long have they lived in Canada?" When Georges was satisfied with all the answers, he nodded. It was such a joy to see the family so elated at our acceptance.

Sadly, more than half of the families that had lined up for hours had no connection with Canada, not even a faint hope that we could stretch into an exit permit especially with our interpreter no doubt reporting to the Vietnamese authorities, even though she worked for the United Nations High Commission for Refugees. After fifty-six interviews, we sat in our 'interview' room with our feet on the bed. Numerous applicants were left for another day.

Now that we had accepted all these people, I was faced with the problem of how to get their medical examinations and x-rays completed. My only hope was the Health Ministry.

Doctor Thieu Duk Dinh, the Assistant Minister of Health for the southern portion of the united Vietnam, politely asked me to sit down. He wore a white lab-coat over khaki trousers and an open-necked shirt. Tea appeared quickly.

"I hope that you are having a pleasant stay in Vietnam."

I assured him that I was. I didn't go into the details of the chaos at our hotel. He got to the point quickly.

"What can I do to help you with your work?"

"My colleague and I would like to be able to arrange for relatives of Canadian citizens to leave Vietnam by air instead of by sea as many do at the present time."

He twirled a pencil on his desk and said nothing for a moment as if trying to predict what it was that we required from him. "What is it that you need?"

I explained the requirements and offered to get him the x-ray film and developer from Bangkok. He agreed that if I supplied the x-ray materials, he would get the medical examination completed.

We stood, shook hands and he walked me to the door.

As I walked through the drab hospital, I mulled over how I would get the x-ray film and developing materials to Ho Chi Minh Ville from Bangkok the only direct air route to Vietnam.

By the end of the day our room looked like a tip. Applications were strewn on the chairs, bed and floor. As we attempted to bring some order to the place, there was a knock on the door.

"How would you like to go out for dinner?" Yves Dumont joined us as we tried to cram the files into the appropriate boxes.

"Well, we could pry ourselves out of this room for dinner," sighed Georges.

Yves smiled and continued, "There is only one problem. We have to find the food."

"Find the food? Do you mean scavenging? Is this a party game?"

I had visions of scurrying between the garbage cans in the dank back alleys surrounding the hotel.

"Almost. We'll go to the black market. Bring your greenbacks but don't flash them."

The three of us were hardly inconspicuous, the only 'Americans' to be seen. Georges, with his dirty blond hair slicked back, and both of us with our 'yankee' style chinos, traipsed off toward the large downtown central market.

On the way, we were swarmed by a group of women likely left destitute when their husbands were forced to report to the re-education centres to have their European-style bourgeois thinking changed to that of their northern brethren. Their wives, left with only the funds that they had managed to hide from the new rulers, were forced to panhandle. We pushed through the mob as best we could without knocking anybody over while hanging on to our cash.

Yves went staight to the back corner of the market to a nameless stall. The child behind the counter disappeared as we approached. Yves motioned to us to stop and wait. Eyes stared at us, curious and not friendly. Yves spoke to a young man who came out from behind the plastic multi-colour strips that acted as a door. Yves then motioned to us to follow him to the market exit.

"Have a ten dollar bill ready," he whispered.

The child who was originally behind the stall appeared from nowhere with a large bundle wrapped in newspaper. We quickly passed him our US dollars.

"We're going to have roast beef. Now let me explain how this soirée works. I'll take the meat to the home where we're going to have dinner so the cooking can begin and meet you at the hotel at seven. Don't get arrested in the meantime!"

Yves was only half joking as he walked off, the newspaper bundle under his arm leaving Georges and me to spend time wandering around Ho Chi Minh Ville.

"This looks interesting." Georges strode off down an alley lined on both sides with plastic sheets laid on the ground. The sheets were covered with trinkets and treasures of every kind from cooking pots to a service for twelve of Christoffle silver. "Do these people own this or is it loot from abandoned homes?" I wondered out loud.

"How much is this?" I motioned to a large lacquer box with inlaid ivory sides and doors locked by a Chinese square lock. The only response was a slow motion move to unlock the doors with a key pulled from an inside vest pocket. At this point, I didn't know whether the vendor was male, female, or a police agent. The doors when opened, revealed six small silk-lined drawers with red satin handles. One drawer had a double string of large cultured pearls. That would be a great gift for Lauretta. I wondered if there was a penalty for buying these treasures?

"Dollar not dong." Finally, some action from the sinister character in the shadows.

"How many?"

"Dollars twenty-five."

"And the silver?"

At eighty dollars, it was an unbelievable bargain, but I would have had to return to the hotel and then find this place again. I looked up and down the alley and saw no one looking like an official. I took the chance.

I picked up the box for a closer examination. It was signed on the bottom by Than Le, the foremost Vietnamese lacquer maker at the turn of the century. He had left for Paris in the 1920's.

"I will take the box and the pearls." The vendor slowly budged from the squatting position, picked up the box and tied it in an ingenious way knotting binder twine through the handles and then finally making a carrying loop. I put it nonchalantly under my arm. I wished that it was less conspicuous.

I was not much further down the lane when I spotted a magnificent blue and white Ming bowl, fifteen inches in diameter, and a small pale green Sung bowl wrapped in paper inside it. Chances were they were fake but they were beautiful.

After much bargaining, a price of thirty-five dollars was agreed upon. I now had serious qualms about how I was going to get this loot first to the hotel and then out of the country. Georges doubled up with laughter when he saw me.

"I couldn't stop myself." He had bought nothing.

The alley opened onto a large square with a waterless fountain filled with dried leaves and litter. Sturdy benches with curls of cast iron at each end, once again reminiscent of Paris, circled the fountain. We sat and looked out on the Saigon River, wide enough at this point to serve as the port of Ho Chi Minh Ville. Three dirty tramp freighters all with Russian names on their bows were being unloaded at the sea wall. Sheds lined the far bank of the river.

"What do you suppose is hidden over there, Georges?"

"Just munitions," he quipped.

"Taxi, Mister, Taxi, Taxi." We smiled politely as we started our walk back to the hotel. Were we going in the right direction? We were amused by the three taxi drivers and their 1961 Chevrolets. The Vietnamese may hate the Americans but they love American automobiles.

"No. We don't want a ride." We smiled at the drivers who leaned on the hood of a particularly garish orange Chevy. We kept walking. Along the way, we were pestered by an avalanche of bicycle rickshaws.

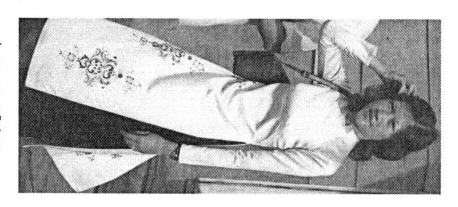

Interpreter Saigon

Tanh Le lacquer box

Our walk in the evening from the hotel to the 'bibliothèque', the venue for our dinner, was beautiful. The avenue of tamarind trees with their gnarled boles and plane trees with their scaly bark and tall trunks created an umbrella over the street which opened onto the cathedral square. The red brick Dứ'c BÄ Cathedral in the centre of the square, had a magnificent rose window over the door. Twin spires flanked the window.

"It was built in 1888, styled after Notre Dame in Paris," added Georges, the font of knowledge. "A high percentage of the population is Roman Catholic but most have a buddha in their parlour as well."

"Does that mean two religions are better than one?" We smiled at the pragmatism of the Asian psyche.

Mass was still celebrated at noon daily, a surprise as I wrongly associated a revolution with the withdrawal of religious freedom. It was obviously not necessarily so. It had been said that Viet Cong infiltrators met with conspirators from the south during services in the cathedral. A cooling breeze swept across the square, a relief after a stifling day.

Turning west at the cathedral, we walked half way down a block of once stately homes, Plane trees still flanked the street. The grand white stucco mansions were now dirty and yellowed. Balustrades masked the flat roofs. Most homes had crumbling walls surrounding the property, walls that were now showing the yellow bricks under the grimy stucco coating, some with jasmine bushes pushing through the gaps.

We entered the hardened clay courtyard in front of the Thieu's home and approached the large white double door between grand white Corinthian columns now urine coloured around the base with white paint chipping at the top. Madame Thieu, our hostess, grey hair pinned back with bobby pins, dressed in a white *ao dai* with gray trousers, welcomed us and ushered us into the wide hallway, a room in itself with twelve foot ceilings and a checkered black and white tiled floor. Directly in front of us was a large official portrait of Ho Chi Minh.

Madame Thieu had noticed the surprised expression on my face.

"We must hang the portrait in the hall to please the authorities."

A large mirror hung on the wall to my left with a three legged marble topped walnut table under it, the type of antique gold-trimmed table one sees in French chateaux. I was still gawking when she urged us to follow her to the library, a room leading off the hall to the right and the same size as the hall. Floor to ceiling books lined three walls. A large family portrait of an ancestor, I would guess, was on the other wall. The dining table in the middle of the room sat on a worn oriental carpet over the tiled floor. The table was set for five, with what my grand-mother would call, the good silver, on a white damask tablecloth.

The three of us were joined by Doctor and Madame Thieu. She had been a Supreme Court Judge in the previous regime. Her husband had been Dean of the Medical School and Vice-Chancellor of the University of Saigon.

"We did not agree with or support the regime that was propped up by the United States. The war that began as an uprising against colonialism and esca-lated into a civil war was misinterpreted by America as a communist takeover fuelled by the Chinese. Vietnam had been battling the Chinese for years and China would not have been allowed to take an inch of Vietnamese territory. If we had known what grief was to follow the fall of Saigon, we might have thought differently about leaving." We were surprised by her frankness. "Our daughter did think differently and went to Canada in 1973."

"How interesting. Is she enjoying Canada?"

"She enjoys Canada very much, Doctor Thieu continued. She's a doctor and lives near Ottawa. We hope to visit her when the situation is calmer."

The smell of the black market beef was tantalizing. Beans with almonds and garlic and sweet local rice from the Mekong delta were also being prepared. Fresh picked rice tasted so different from the stale packaged rice that we were used to.

"The aromas are wonderful, Madam."

"Thank you. We do not have much meat and to have buffalo is a special treat."

Georges and I looked at each other and then at Yves who was smiling politely. Buffalo was going to require a good set of teeth and a sharp knife.

Doctor Thieu uncorked a bottle of red wine.

"Would you like some wine while we wait?"

I was stunned by the wine. The Thieus' wine cellar had not been confiscated. Two bottles of 1961 Charmes-Chambertin, the best of Burgundy, were placed on the table.

"Yes, I will have some wine, thank you." I savoured the smoky, leathery bou-quet of this grand wine amazed that it could be kept properly in this tropical cli-mate.

12

A few days later, our office/bedroom was still a mess. We answered a knock on the door frame. The door was propped open with boxes to allow a through breeze.

"Doctor, I would like you and your colleague to come to Vung Tau with me." Lysiane Goulet, an officer at the French Consulate was going to visit the former resort town, thirty kilometres south of Ho Chi Minh Ville. Lysiane was an anomaly for a number of reasons. She refused to transfer to Hanoi when the French Embassy was forced to move from Saigon. After long negotiations, the French government was allowed to have a small Consulate in the former Saigon recognizing the long association the French and the Vietnamese had had since 1859 when the French first captured Saigon. Lysiane stayed in Saigon in 1975 as a consular officer. She brought French chic to a society with its own style, the elegant *ao dais*. Tall with greying blond hair, she stood out in any crowd. Today, with a khaki shirt and trousers, brown sandals and a gold chain around her neck, she looked soigné, even when we were wilting from the heat and humidity.

"I should explain that Vung Tau, on the estuary of the Saigon River is the starting off point for the majority of small boats trying to leave Vietnam," Lysiane added, "I have permits for today only. It'll get us past the road blocks I know about. They're always changing them. The regime doesn't like foreign visitors in Vung Tau and doesn't want 'collaborators' escaping to the countryside to avoid the hard labour prescribed for the 'bourgeoisie' whom they still consider enemies of the regime in Hanoi."

Highway One had not been repaired since the worst bombing of the south in 1975. The craters were large enough to swallow the car. It made it impossible to drive more than forty kilometres an hour.

Vung Tau, once the Las Vegas of south Vietnam, was now a delapidated bombed out shell. The crumbling former nightclubs stood hollowed by fire which left only crumbling walls. Metal awnings fronting on the narrow streets tilted and dangled at odd angles, a surreal picture of what must have been a swinging scene two decades ago.

The one redeeming feature of the place was the seashore which was separated from the nightclubs by Highway One. A boardwalk lined the beach which extended for almost two kilometres. Rocky promontories jutted into the water at either end of the littoral, creating a wonderful calm expanse of water before opening into the broad estuary which emptied into the South China Sea. Two small children, unaware of our presence, walked along the shore collecting firewood for their family.

"This is the site which the government claims is the starting off point for the boats of escapees, as the officials call them," Lysiane explained. "It's rumoured that the *Hai Hong*, which you are familiar with, actually anchored just off-shore, with the collusion of the authorities. Many taels of gold changed hands. They say they are now confiscating fishing boats and shooting anyone on the beach after dark. They also say there are patrol boats on the other side of the promontories preventing people from leaving."

"And still people get through," I said to myself.

"No wonder the line up of applicants at our hotel stretches around the block." Georges commented. "This is bloody risky."

As I turned to take photos of the children, a young girl came up to me out of the blue. I recognized the distinctive features of an Amerasian child, probably waiting to get on a refugee boat out of this place. Without money or gold bars, she didn't have a hope.

"Sir, will you take me with you?" I stared at her pleading face as she stood, waiting and hoping I would agree.

"I'm sorry. It would not be possible. I'm so sorry," I said softly as I watched her face drop. She quickly moved away. My heart ached for her. I stood and watched her go away repeating I'm so sorry to myself as she faded out of view in the distance. I turned and saw an armed soldier running toward me. I froze.

"STOP! STOP! No camera!" He pointed his rifle at me. I put my camera under my shirt.

We quickly left the seashore, returned to the rubble-filled streets of the town, and climbed the hill to the heights above the night-club strip. A sprawling hotel stretched along the crest of the hill.

The approach to Vung Tau

Amerasian Child hoping for Adoption

Refugee child on the beach in Vung Tau

Refugee Family in Trengannu Malaysia

Collecting Wood Vung Tau Vietnam

Beach in Vung Tau Vietnam

"Bienvenue a L'Auberge, Madame." Lysiane, after receiving kisses on both cheeks, introduced us to the proprietor, a short, stocky, balding Frenchman, an anachronism in this strange town. To have survived the fall of the French regime at Dien Bien Phu in 1954, and then the Americans in 1975, and still be in business, was a remarkable feat.

L'Auberge des Roches Noires, the Inn on the Black Rocks, had a blue tiled lobby with a fish sculpture in the middle of it that squirted water in all directions. We were ushered into the open air dining room where one table in a room of fifty was set with a blue cloth, blue cotton napkins and polished cutlery. The blue matched that of the proprietor's apron.

"Aujourd'hui, nous avons poisson. C'est le bar." (sea bass).

Translated, it meant, if you don't like fish, you're out of luck in this place.

"For you, madam, one of my best bottles of wine." Le patron brought a bottle of rosé, sadly well past its prime. The brownish colour told the story and the acrid taste made it undrinkable. We raised our glasses in a toast to the proprietor. The grilled sea bass however was marvellous with home-grown potatoes and rolled fried spinach with garlic.

Despite urging from all of us, the owner was unwilling to discuss how and why he had stayed in Vung Tau all these years. All questions were met with a Gallic shrug.

13

Sunday. There was a shorter line in front of the Caravelle Hotel. I wondered whether the authorities were curtailing the permit seekers. Two men with cameras had been sitting in Lam Son Square obviously photographing every person in the line for days. God help those we didn't accept. They risked everything to come to the Caravelle. If only we could have taken everybody.

Once again, a knock on the doorframe. There stood Yves Dumont in a spotless white safari suit.

"Are you on your way to a wedding?"

"No, to see the daughter of the last Emperor. Would you like to come?"

Georges and I looked at each other and laughed. "We don't have a comparable outfit but, yes, why not."

Leaving the Caravelle, was a trial. There was always a crowd milling about. They tugged at my sleeve as we made our way to the old Peugeot. I half expected to see the same young girl from Vung Tau. Would I sponsor her without talking to Lauretta first? Probably. We do think alike and agree on courses of action. As I stepped out a young man blocked my way.

"Sir, sir, You American, Why you here? Why you come back?"

There was no sense trying to explain. I smiled and moved as quickly as possible without crashing into anybody.

"*Xuo Gua!*" Big liar, he shouted after me.

The journey to our country destination required two permits. As we moved out of Cholon, a downtrodden suburb of Ho Chi Minh Ville, and crossed an ageing bascule bridge, left over from the speedy repairs at the end of the war, we came to an unexpected sentry post, a scowling uniformed soldier in the road blocking our way. He motioned to the driver with his rifle barrel to pull over. He then ordered the driver to get out.

"No!" Yves grabbed the driver's arm. "Tell him we have permits and diplomatic privileges."

The poor teenage North Vietnamese army conscript had no idea what we were talking about. He put the barrel of the gun in the window and motioned to us in the backseat. We slowly pulled the red diplomatic passports from our pockets.

"Don't give them to him," said Yves, "Just hold them up."

He pulled his gun out of the car and slowly walked around it as if it was some kind of trapped beast. Minutes went by and we couldn't imagine what he was going to do next. By the time he reached the front, he banged the fender with the butt of his rifle and motioned us on.

"How many times do we have to go through that?" I muttered from the back seat.

"I didn't know about that one." Yves admitted. "Maybe twice more."

The highway sliced through bright green rice paddies. Ditches and levees created neat rectangles with six inches of water covering the plants. Women bent to pick the tender shoots. Their conical banana leaf hats shaded their faces. We passed the two sentry points uneventfully and turned off the main road after an hour's slow drive. The narrow strip of macadam was not wide enough for two cars. I chose not to think about the possibility of a car coming in the opposite direction.

We soon turned into a narrow tree-lined dirt laneway with an unobtrusive diamond-shaped red sign hanging from a tree: 'La Biche Aux Abois' (The Doe at Bay). A six-foot vertical bamboo fence funneled into an iron gate manned by a lone guard. He saluted our driver and waved us past.

Princess Phùòng Liên and her seven year old daughter, Gnuyet, came to meet us. The very thin, thirty-something daughter of the last Emperor was wearing black jeans with a red, belted jacket and red sandals, a western style outfit for a cosmopolitan member of a family with strong European connections.

Bao Dai succeeded his father as Emperor in 1925 at the age of twelve. He was then sent to France to study. In 1932, he formally took the throne of Indochina and was strongly influenced by the French until 1939 when he declared Vietnam independent with the concurrence of the Japanese, the subjugators of South East Asia during the Second World War. He abdicated in 1945 and went into self-imposed exile in Hong Kong. There he had a reputation as a philanderer and playboy. He kept three wives the second of whom, was the mother of our hostess.

He returned to his homeland in 1949 and ruled under French auspices until 1955 when he was ousted in a rigged referendum. He was appointed supreme counsellor to the provisional government in Hanoi. It was rumoured that he spent his days sitting by the Perfume River in Hué writing poetry and fishing, with time out to drink his green tea made with dew. This Hanoi connection accounted for the luxury that Princess Phùòng enjoyed today.

We introduced ourselves and were ushered into the main house to meet her husband, Tui Ba, and their three year old daughter. The stone house was cool compared to the steamy exterior. Though not lavish, the main room was lined with books, and deep comfortable chairs. In one corner of the room wasan elaborate shrine with a photograph of her grandfather, circa 1880, with a white flowing beard. He was dressed in ceremonial robes—his young Empress at his side. Flanking the picture were two metal candles with large Christmas tree-like bulbs on top. In front of the picture sat a brass pot with a dozen joss sticks. A bronze portrait of Bao Dai sat on a table in the centre of the room. Wisps of sweet-smelling incense drifted around us.

We looked at each other unsure how to break the awkward silence. Were we to sit down in the plush chairs or ask about grandfather?

"You must be hungry. We shall have lunch." Princess Phùòng motioned toward the door.

"If this is to be a picnic," I whispered to Georges, "I'll be able to watch the giant red ants I've been stepping around march off with my food."

"Let us go to the dining area." Princess Phùòng led us outside to a large vertical bamboo building with horizontal open windows on two sides. A huge wooden table was set simply with a blue table cloth and napkins to match. A servant brought salt, pepper and sugar shakers reminiscent of a 40's diner. A bottle of warm Beaujolais and a cold Tavel Rosé also appeared. The main course of rice with chunks of chicken, hot peppers and some type of squash was surpassed by the crepes with fruit and a liqueur sauce. We each were given a small battered tin café filtre dripping strong Ban Me Thuot coffee into the tin base. Next, the Martell cognac. Conversation seemed to be easier.

"Madame, how long have you lived here?"

"We moved south in 1975. The home was built for us a year later."

I wished I could keep her talking but she stood and offered to show us the grounds. I would love to have known more about her parents. The focus appeared to be on her grandparents. Did she dislike her parents? I wondered.

We walked through a mango orchard, mother and daughter walking ahead of us. Nobody said anything as we strolled casually down the path until finally the daughter, Gnuyet, turned to me and said, "Would you like to play pétanque?" Finally some action. Trust a child to break the ice. She came and stood in front of me.

"Yes. Great. Can you show me how to play?"

"We have two teams. Each team has four people. Mommy will be one captain and I will be the other." She took my wrist and pulled me out onto the path. "I pick first. I pick you, Dad, and the driver."

We each took one palm size, polished silver steel ball. The other team had four bronze coloured balls. We flipped a coin to see who threw the small wooden ball we were supposed to be aiming for. The team with the most balls close to the small wooden one won. The course, instead of being flat which was usual, was bumpy and around trees, a true obstacle course. Gnuyet had done this before as she told us exactly where to throw the boule.

"No, no. Not that way!" she admonished and showed me how to toss the ball with my palm down. She took great pleasure in challenging her mother and made sure we were going to play the game her way. We had a great team. Despite heated arguments and with the help of precise measurements with a tape measure, we were victorious.

The prize: "Can you come again?"

"I assured her that I would enjoy that very much. We thanked our hostess and family for an enjoyable visit and departed before dark in order to avoid the highway with bomb craters difficult to see at night.

I sat in the front seat for the return trip to Saigon. I was in another world, a world which will always include the expression on the teenager's face on the beach in Vung Tau, the exuberance of Gnuyet, a child shielded from all the strife around her. Her parents who by their silence revealed an anxiety that I, too, would have had, had I been Vietnamese, from the North, the Highlands or the South.

Emperors Ancester's Home

Saigon Cathedral

Last Emperor's great granddaughter

Shrine to Emoeror and one of his wives

Author with family of the last Emperor

Breakfast at the Caravelle

12

It was a shock to return to Singapore and its pristine but stilted life style after the tension of Vietnam. Just stepping off the plane in the brightly lit, spotless airport was a blast to a system numbed by even a few weeks of repression. It was a joy to be with Lauretta and the children.

"Did you bring more letters to sort? I'll write to the some of the kids and they can become pen pals. They must be so bored."

A dinner out in Singapore was met with some trepidation by Chris and Sue. Neither was too keen on food not immediately identifiable.

"Now kids, you must be polite and eat a little bit of everything. It's very kind of Doctor Hong to invite us all to his party."

"You know Dad we don't like fish." I nodded.

"You don't have to eat fish. There will be lots of other things."

Doctor Hong, a radiologist had been a great help in interpreting suspicious chest x-rays for me. He had also been very helpful in getting x-ray film for the refugee camps.

"Now Holbrooks, we have an array of Chinese delicacies especially for you and the children to choose from. There is shark fin soup in that bowl in the centre. Next to that are almond shrimp and then crispy duck with a hot chili sauce or hoisin. There's beef and chicken and then bird's nest soup. We put a fork and spoon for you children in case you don't like chopsticks. Now please start." We obliged and took plates and chopsticks.

Lauretta and I watched the children cringe but they dutifully followed as we tried a myriad of unknowns on the buffet. Chris and Sue were taken downstairs by an amah to eat with the other young people at the party.

We mingled in the huge chandeliered dining room and on the terrace. The main interest was food rather than conversation. Most people we attempted to talk to had a mouthful. We sipped the small glasses of Chinese wine that was more like port. This group was not interested in small talk.

When the children reappeared, to see when we were leaving, we sought out our host.

"This has been a sumptuous feast, Doctor Hong. I can't tell you how much we've enjoyed ourselves."

"Well, I'm very happy you could all come."

After thanking our host profusely, we set off for home.

"Dad, do you know that Doctor Hong loves horses?"

"How do you know that, Chris?"

"Well, he has computers in the basement and he has all the horses running at the race track down the street, listed with their pedigrees and past racing record. He chooses a horse he likes and sends an amah to the track with money to bet on that horse."

Lauretta and I looked at each other in amazement wondering how a child, our child, could figure out that scheme.

"Chris, I guess he does like horses a lot."

"He makes pots of money too, I bet." Chris had a good mind for money matters. We smiled at each other thinking back to the fact that the main part of any conversation we had at the party was related to money and the profits to be made on the Singapore Stock Exchange.

"Did you enjoy the dinner, Sue?" Lauretta changed the subject from the grand gambling system.

"Yes and I didn't have to eat any fish."

"I had a lot of trouble picking up those button mushrooms with chopsticks," Lauretta added.

"No wonder. They were fish eyes.

"They were what!?" All three exclaimed in unison.

"How do you know?" Lauretta asked.

"Mrs. Ho thought we would enjoy them. They're a delicacy."

"Stop the car, Dad. We're going to be sick.

14

Helping the children pack for their Canadian summer at camp in Ontario's Haliburton Highlands was always a nightmare.

"No, Sue, you don't need all that stuff. Remember the two of you are going on your own and you have to keep track of all your luggage."

"Oh Mom, you worry too much. We've done this before."

"We get great treatment when we're UM's," Chris added.

"Okay but remember unaccompanied minors have to take some responsibility for their belongings. Grandmother and grandfather are going to have to help you cart this load all the way to camp."

"We'll be fine. Honestly." Lauretta and I shrugged and gave up. "Will Matthew be there to meet us too?"

"Yes. He's going to camp the same day."

Despite our protestations, we took them to the Changi airport with two enormous canvas dunnage bags, nylon sleeping bags and an extra suitcase each. Our goodbyes were always tearful. Lauretta and I inevitably went home worrying about air disasters and everything else that could possibly go wrong.

15

"Being on our own together had been a rare occurence in Singapore. To take advantage of it, I had planned a trip to parts of the area Lauretta hadn't visited. In order to leave the High Commission, given the refugee crisis, permission had to be sought from the Head of Post.

"David. By all means take the time. You deserve it." The High Commissioner, a fit man without a grey hair, only slightly older than I was, had helped me through the refugee programme throughout my two year posting in South East Asia. It had been a situation not experienced by the government since the mass migration after the Second World War.

"David, the twenty-year old twins of our closest friends in Ottawa are coming to Singapore and need a place to stay. Would you mind if they stayed in your apartment while you're away?"

"Of course not." I hoped Lauretta's reaction would be the same.

On the day of our departure, we greeted our two charming apartment sitters.

"Doctor and Mrs. Holbrook, I'm Kate Cruikshank and this is my brother, William." They stood surrounded by backpacks as Lauretta opened the door "This is so kind of you. We promise the apartment will be just as you left it when you return."

"Thank you, Kate, I'm sure it will."

"We understand that you are going to Burma. We were just there. The women really love to get cosmetics, especially Estée Lauder lipsticks if you have any you no longer use. They can't buy lipstick. Also, take '555' cigarettes. They are a status symbol. You can trade these things for crafts. I traded some lipstick for this great silver bracelet." Kate removed the bracelet for Lauretta to try on.

"It's beautiful." Lauretta held her arm up to show me.

"That's great advice. Thank you."

The trip from Bangkok's Don Muang airport to the city core was always a nightmare. I assured Lauretta that this was the worst part of the trip.

Our ninth floor corner room in the Oriental Hotel overlooked the Chao Phraya River a beehive of activity with every conceivable type of watercraft, some going upriver, some down toward the Gulf of Siam. Narrow rocket-like 'cigarette' boats roared up the river. An enormous fish-tail of water shot into the air. They carried passengers from wharf to wharf. Tugs chugged, lugging strings of huge barges of grain and other commodities. Dual tugs towed eight to ten barges at once. Ferries crammed with commuters sat in the middle of the river waiting for the barges to pass. Skiffs loaded with vegetables and a single rower, drifted in and out of the river traffic floating markets for the wooden houses built on the water's edge of the narrow klongs, canals substituting for streets, emptying into the river.

"Look at that." Lauretta pointed to a lone swimmer doing the crawl from the ferry dock below our window to the dock on the other side.

"He's got a tube on his back." We watched mesmerized as he reached the other side, undid the tube, took out his clothes, dressed and resumed his journey.

"That was amazing. It's better than sitting in traffic. He must be nice and slick from the oil in the river."

"It's a wonder he doesn't get run over in the water."

"Let's just order room service for dinner and sit in front of the window and watch the river. It's fascinating."

"That's a great idea. I'm tired and the room is so beautiful. Look at the deep red silk wall covering and the vases of orchids. We don't need to go anywhere."

"This dinner is stunning in more ways than one. Is it the lemon grass in the hot and sour soup or is it my imagination?" I looked at Lauretta with my mouth open trying to cool my mucous membranes.

"It's hot but delicious. Don't drink water. It'll only make it worse. Maybe you swallowed a hot chili." Lauretta giggled looking at the small bowl of tiny green sliced chilis accompanying the dinner.

"Why did I order spicy calamari?"

"It'll be wonderful with the Thai rice. You'll be accustomed to the heat after the soup." Lauretta laughed but was not totally reassuring.

We sat and lingered over our wine and watched the lights on the river now that darkness had descended. It was hard to make out the outline of the tugs but the thumping noise of their engines churning was as distinctive as is the high-pitched whine of the cigarette boats with their single lights at the stern. They looked like fireflies scooting along the water. Faint lights on the tugs and barges outlined families cooking their rice and fish as clothes flapped on lines strung from any attachment which made the lights appear to flicker.

The red roofs of the royal palace trimmed with gold were partially visable along the river's edge. The ends of the roofs twisted up like steers' horns and the gold trim shimmered in the distance lit by floodlights.

Thailand for many years had been known as the source of fine silk.

The industry was virtually destroyed during World War II. An American, a former OSS operative, (the precursor of the CIA), restarted the Thai silk industry in the late 1940's. In 1967, he disappeared without a trace, while on a holiday near Penang in Malaysia. Nobody has any idea what happened to him. During the time he lived in Bangkok, he was instrumental in preserving Thai architecture and his home is an excellent example.

"I'd really like you to see the house. He bought all or parts of six beautiful old traditional houses and put them together as one large house on a tree-lined klong somewhere near here."

"Let's take a taxi rather than get lost." Lauretta sensed some doubt in my voice as to where the house actually was located.

Sitting in the smog waiting for a break in the traffic so that our smoke-spewing beat-up taxi could crawl between the buses and trucks, was exasperating. I looked at Lauretta chagrined, "We could probably have walked faster than this."

"Why have you got the money out already, David?" I smiled.

"You have to learn the idiosyncratic rules of life in Bangkok. If there's an accident involving this taxi, we're going to jump out, leaving these baht on the seat. If there's a crash, the driver runs away leaving the passengers to face the music. It's not going to be us."

"Thanks for telling me." Lauretta rolled her eyes.

It was hard to imagine that the Thompson home was made up of pieces of many old houses. The teak walls and the carvings around the top of the dormers all matched perfectly. The wide floorboards were worn from centuries of use. The door frames were raised so that if the klong flooded, the water wouldn't pour in. Lauretta was intrigued as she moved slowly from room to room.

"Look. His cockatoo is still here in its cage." Lauretta emphasized the cage, hating birds on the loose, especially indoors. "The bird must be ancient."

After lingering in the house and surroundings for over an hour, we decided to try walking back to the hotel along Sukumvit Road. We were trailed by young boys.

"You big boss, sir?"

"No. No."

One lad took the edge of my tropical suit jacket and pulled it open.

"Ah. Nice suit, sir."

"Now they've looked and know I don't have a wallet in my pocket, maybe they'll leave us alone."

Lauretta put her hand to her neck, reassuring herself that her gold chain was still there. "Let's take a taxi after all. I don't want to be mugged."

Our trip back to the airport after our brief stopover in Bangkok was fortunately faster than the incoming one. Lauretta was feeling unwell after lunch with a American friend in a touristy restaurant.

"I don't know whether I can get myself on a plane, David."

"Darling, just relax. I'll look after you. We'll never be able to get another Burmese visa. If we're ever going to do this, it'll have to be now."

It was not long before our flight was called. As we got into the bus taking us across the tarmac to the Thai Airlines flight to Rangoon, a fellow passenger said politely to me, "Your friend should really see a doctor."

"Thank you but I think she's feeling better." The woman turned away not believing a word I'd said.

I held Lauretta tightly and said, "You're going to be okay, Darling."

Lauretta nodded afraid to say anything for fear of being sick on the spot. The worried passenger looked at me in disgust.

"I hope there's a sick bag in the seat pocket."

"I'll make sure there is." I tried to be reassuring, praying at the same time that the nausea would pass quickly.

The trip from the airport to the Strand Hotel in Rangoon was relaxed and slow. Lauretta didn't need one of the usual careening taxi rides to which we were accustomed.

The traffic, light by Bangkok standards, meandered along at a creeping pace, partly because of the many school 'buses' which consisted of a bicycle pulling a wooden crate on dual wheels. They were crammed with young primary school pupils in white shirts and navy skirts or pants who peeked out between the slats. The local 'buses', pick-up trucks with benches in the back, were jammed with office workers on their way to work dressed in beige or brown ankle-length longyis.

"Is this the Strand Hotel?" I asked the taxi driver, as we stopped at a dirty cream-coloured building. The taxi driver didn't understand and looked at us, waiting for his payment. Ten kyat, roughly two U.S. dollars for the fare was all he managed in English.

The pillars on either side of what was a grand entrance were peeling. The steps leading up to double doors opening into the lobby still had brass clips sticking up where carpet was once attached. I took Lauretta's arm and we climbed to the foyer. The doors were opened for us and we entered the middle of a hubbub which turned out to be a wedding party.

Incredulous, finding ourselves in the middle of a celebration, we sat in two shabby once-elegant armchairs on the perimeter of the festivities and waited for a chance to register. For the first time in many hours a smile came over Lauretta's face.

The bride was dressed in a long white organza wedding dress with a scalloped neck line and intricate embroidery down the front, rather than a more traditional red gown as was the custom in Asia. The groom did follow local tradition and was wearing a long gray longyi, a wrap-around ankle-length skirt, with horizontal stripes of gold thread. Dozens of gold thread stars were woven between the stripes. He wore a puffy white linen shirt buttoned to the neck.

The guests chatted and laughed among themselves, and smiled at the two unexpected foreign guests. The wedding pictures were taken in the hotel lobby, for some unknown reason, when there were a number of lovely parks and pagodas in the area.

"It must be some sort of status symbol. Look at the other wedding pictures hanging on the walls. They're all taken in this lobby." Lauretta had always been more observant than I was. It was also an indication that she was feeling better.

We were finally ushered to our room down a long dark corridor on the second floor covered with shabby mud coloured carpet. The room smelled musty and dusty, likely uninhabited for a long time. A yellowed blind covered the window reflecting a sepia colour on the walls. The double bedstead was dark stained wood.

"Look at the bathroom." Marble floors and antique fixtures were left-overs from another era. Lauretta was happy when the blast of air in the pipes was followed by running water—a luxury in this part of the world.

"I bet there'll be a cloud of dust when we lie down on the bed."

"We'll both have an asthma attack." We chuckled as we stretched out carefully.

Leaving Lauretta to rest, I returned to the lobby. Stepping out into the heat of the street, I was amused by the trees growing out of the foundations of the hotel, as I walked along the uneven sidewalk towards the British Embassy, the Union Jack flapping in the breeze.

"We don't get too many visitors here." The consul commented as I introduced myself. "We don't have a doctor on our staff list but have you met Joe Fricker, the American Embassy doctor? He's usually out in the Gulf of Martaban sailing. I doubt that he could be reached in an emergency. Perhaps you would like to move to Rangoon." He smiled as I shook my head.

"Thank you for the offer but no thanks. My wife and I are going to Maymyo. On our way back to Bangkok, I'll try and contact Doctor Fricker." I smiled at the thought of spending my time on a boat off Rangoon rather than sitting in an office in the heat of this run-down city.

The taxi driver on our trip to the airport the next morning wanted to make sure we didn't miss anything as we meandered along in his decrepit taxi.

"Oh sir. You must see the Shwe Dagon Pagoda. It's two thousand years old. The largest stupa as you can see, sir, has eight sides and is covered with many tons of gold leaf. Precious stones are embedded in the top."

"Can you tell us the difference between a pagoda and a stupa, please?"

"Yes, sir. A pagoda is a temple for us Buddhists. The stupa is like a gravestone for a saint or buddha. I'm sorry, sir. My English is not very good."

"It's very good. Thank you for explaining it."

"Would you like to stop?" As I said no, I felt sorry that we were discouraging him after he had taken such care in explaining everything.

"No thank you. We'll be back in a few days then we'll have more time."

After checking in at the Burma Airways counter, we were given an orange boarding card. The card said nothing. Flights were called in Burmese leaving us no choice but to join any line where others appeared to have the same colour boarding card.

"Do you suppose we're really on the flight to Mandalay?"

"It's too late now." The aircraft was taxiing down the runway.

"It'll be a mystery until we land."

"And how will we know then?" We looked at each other and laughed.

"Is this Mandalay?" I asked an official-looking airline attendant. She nodded, amused. "Where can we get a taxi?"

"Over there under the tree." We looked under the tree and then at each other.

"That's a stagecoach with one horse. It's skin and bones at that."

We carried our two bags over to the tree.

"We're going to Maymyo." He opened the door to the stage and put our bags on the seat. We sat opposite. The stage jerked into motion.

The stage coach was obviously becoming obsolete in Mandalay. We were in the only one visible. We clip clopped down the street fighting for road space with bashed-up taxis, three-wheeled Lambretta trucks and pedestrians spilling out of the open front concrete block shops. We turned into a side street and stopped.

"Now what?" asked Lauretta.

"I have no idea."

We had stopped at a street corner where six other people were waiting. For a stage?

The door opened and the driver took out our bags and put them on the dirt sidewalk in front of a line of market stalls of fruit and vegetables.

"I guess this is where we get out."

"Maymyo?" I asked, looking quizzically at the people standing on the corner. They nodded. Lauretta and I looked at each other and smiled.

In due course, a US army surplus Second World War jeep appeared, the windshield folded down on the hood. A short wiry middle-aged driver hopped out.

"Maymyo," he shouted and motioned towards the jeep. Five locals jammed into the back. Lauretta, I, and a heavy-set woman with a bushel of cabbages and the driver crowded into the front. The low-cut doors helped as the person on the edge could have his foot on the running board. Our bags were tied to the spare tire on the back. The remaining parcels and baskets went on the laps of the back-seat travellers. As we lurched away from the corner, our driver pulled out a stogy and lit up. We traveled only two blocks before pulling into a gasoline station.

The driver jumped out and asked me to move over, virtually onto Lauretta's lap. He took out the driver's seat and opened the gas tank as he puffed on his thick acrid smelling stogy.

On our way at last. He kept dropping his glowing ashes on the floor in front of the gas tank, so I had visions of exploding in an orange ball of flame.

Maymyo, a hill station in the Shan Highlands, had for many years been a summer residence, first for the British and most recently for the army generals who rule Burma. The wooden shops with a raised wooden sidewalk in front, were open to the street . This town did look like the Wild West and public transit was by stage coach.

Candacraig, our destination, was a Tudor-style government guest lodge that had seen better times. The jeep navigated the once well-groomed circular driveway with rose-coloured wisteria bushes in full bloom and pulled up to the front door. Our driver untied our two suitcases from the spare tire and saluted. He drove off leaving us on the doorstep of our vacation hotel.

"Oh I'm sorry sir. We don't have any room."

"But we've come all the way from Singapore." Lauretta and I looked at each other in shock. We always tried to anticipate potential difficulties. This was totally unexpected. We stood and stared at each other not knowing what to do or say.

"Well, we do have a small room for two. The boy here will take you."

I looked at Lauretta as if to say I knew it would work out.

"What a relief. I had visions of sleeping under the stars."

We smiled as 'the boy', actually an elderly servant, took our bags up the polished oak staircase, the fanciest part of the building so far.

"Oh David. This is no good. The room is separated from the others by a sheet. We might just as well be dressing and undressing in the lobby."

We tried to explain our concern to 'the boy' who had no idea what we were talking about. We returned to the main desk and the manager.

"We don't want that room. What else is there?"

"We'll take it." The couple behind us in the line jumped at the chance.

The manager muttered something to 'the boy' who picked up our bags and motioned to us to follow him.

We went back up the stairs and to the rear of the building. By now, the heavy cloud of marijuana hanging over the lobby was intoxicating. He opened the door without a key and we were ushered into a large room with ten beds. A large fire place covered the wall at one end of the room.

"This looks like a hospital ward." We giggled, now slap-happy and exhausted from our travel, Lauretta particularly so after her bout of food poisoning.

"Look at the roaches in the fireplace, some only half-smoked. David this place is for left-over hippies."

"That's us. However, unless we want to share with eight others, I'm going back to rent the other eight beds."

I returned after my successful foray to the front desk and found Lauretta sitting on a bed laughing so hard tears were streaming down her face.

"What happened?"

"Go into the bathroom."

I walked into the room attached to the bedroom and found that it was part of a verandah that spanned the back of the lodge. A huge galvanised metal tub filled with dirty water from the previous tenant's baths sat in the middle of the room.

There was a free standing white porcelain sink in one corner. I turned on the tap to make sure there was running water.

"Ahhh!" I exclaimed. That only made Lauretta laugh harder as my legs were soaked from the knees down. There was no pipe from the drain in the sink.

"Great, an open air bathroom. Where's the toilet?"

"Right here." Lauretta shoved a potty out from the edge of the bed with her foot. "I guess you're supposed to throw the contents to the landscape. *You* have to head for the bushes in the middle of the night."

I chose another bed, sat and laughed, wondering how on earth we got ourselves into this.

"It's time for a change. Let's try the dining room."

"That should be fun. Shall I pull on my dinner dress?"

"Tonight, we are serving vegetable curry and meat curry." The efficient maitre d' who was a one man dining room service, ushered us to a table spread with a white linen table cloth and with white linen napkins. Coffee and curry stains marred the once clean cloth.

"Do you have soup?"

"No, Sir. The curry is a full meal. We do have beer."

"We'll have vegetable curry and two beers." Lauretta did the ordering relieving me of the stress of choosing. The waiter headed for the kitchen.

"We can't try any more mystery meat. Being sick once is enough." I was relieved that Lauretta was well enough to eat at all.

"Before we go back to our 'palatial room', let's go for a walk." As we strolled down the driveway and along the road to the west, the sun, by now a red-orange ball, was setting. The vermilion sky was streaked with slits of clouds. The sky behind us was turning a magnificent blue-black.

"This is like walking in the country at home." Open fields were in front of us as we walked past a long one storey windowless warehouse with a metal peak roof. Suddenly, a dozen white China geese ran at us, wings flapping madly, making a tremendous squawking commotion. Lauretta jumped back and we crossed the road to get away from the racket.

"Thank heaven there's a chain link fence between us."

"I'll bet that's an opium processing plant. The crop from the fields in front is probably opium poppies. It's the Shan tribe's main cash crop."

"David, it's getting dark. Let's go back."

As we came into the lobby, we were offered a candle, an ominous sign.

"Which bed will we choose?" We tried them all, bouncing to test the thin mattresses and putting down the mosquito netting to find the one with the fewest holes.

"This one is closest to the open window. I might get a breath of air. You take that one opposite. Incidentally, don't forget your trip to the bushes. Don't step on any snakes." Lauretta laughed.

"I can hardly wait."

In the middle of the night we were awakened by streaks of lightning and crashes of thunder. With each flash the thunder was almost simultaneous.

"My God the storm must be right over this place! This isn't even the rainy season."

"Well sweetheart, you're not dreaming. Listen to the rain pounding on the roof and dripping into the fireplace."

"What roof. It's pouring in on my bed." Lauretta laughed as I jumped out of bed and tried to find the candle and a dry match. "The power's off."

"Oh hell. Now it's pouring in on my bed."

"Let's change. We've got eight more to choose from."

With only one dry bed left in the room of ten, we prepared for a hot night together, not a bad idea. I struggled to tuck in the mosquito netting and get back to sleep, difficult with the persistent dripping all around us.

"Lauretta, do you want the tub first?" Lauretta gave me a 'you've-got-to-be-kidding' look. "I'll dump it out for you." Together we dragged the tub as close to the verandah as possible and tipped it over.

"That should wash out the kitchen below." We waited to hear any protestations before dragging it over to the drain hole under the sink.

"This is going to be a fast, cold sponge bath."

"The water looks clean. Wait. I'll do your back."

We were exhausted from the hilarity of our night from hell as we waited for our jeep ride back to Mandalay.

The same jeep and driver arrived on schedule, this time with the windshield up meaning we wouldn't have to be swallowing bugs as we cruised down the road. The back is already packed with sacks of who knows what. It could be processed heroin from the warehouses of Maymyo for all we know. The driver deftly tied our bags on the rear tire for the return trip.

We stopped for passengers in front of what looked like the general store in Maymyo, brooms and mops hung from the ceiling. Bolts of cloth, most a drab brown or green, were piled on a counter. The two customers, one a very young woman with a baby in a sling tied around her middle, the other, perhaps her mother joined the shopkeeper staring at the two 'Yankees' in the jeep. The jeep was quickly full to capacity, passengers sitting on sacks and on each other. An elderly stout woman sat on the handbrake lever next to the driver. Lauretta got a bit of the torn vinyl seat and I got the other portion, with my leg out the side on the step.

Street Scene Maymyo Burma

Public Transportation

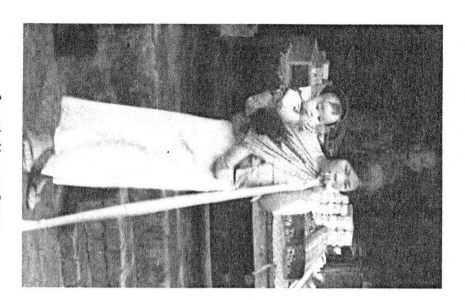

Street in Maymyo, Burma

Candacraig Maymyo Burma

The ninety minute twisting downhill route to Mandalay, went through scrub forest, all that was left after the mature teak trees had been cut down. The trip was marred by a sudden downpour. The driver struggled to get the canvas roof over the sacks, baskets and bodies in the back. An elderly man wrinkled with age and sun stopped to survey this curious scene, as he clutched his thick bamboo cane, a cheroot dangling on his lower lip. A cloud of foul smelling smoke encircled him.

Finally, with a mighty yank, the driver freed the canvas roof from behind the sacks and attached it along the top the windshield. There were no side panels. I resigned myself to a good soaking. The driver took time out to chat with the old gentleman and smoked his long vertigal bamboo pipe.

We arrived at the market in Mandalay and retrieved our soaked luggage and scraped off the mud. We did not see any stagecoaches and so took a motorised tricycle to a restaurant we had passed.

It was restful sitting outside on the banks of the Irrawaddy River, eating our vegetable curry and drinking cold beer, now staples in our diet. The view across the river of the stupas and pagodas poking up through the trees was beautiful, with the sun now shining from the west on the golden tips.

The river was busy in a lazy sort of way. Long narrow wooden fishing boats, their small motors put-putting slowly up the river were dragging fishing nets, or simply trolling. They were interspersed with skiffs rowed by a lone oarsman standing on the back working two oars, transporting everything from bicycles to a load of soccer balls. Two bullocks pulled a barrel of water on a two-wheeled cart out of the river.

A procession of saffron-robed Buddhist monks of all ages walked by us with their alms bowls and then stopped, as a young woman offered them sliced mango from a brass tray on her head. There was a gentleness in the Burmese that was sadly lacking in the neighbouring countries.

"Lauretta, Let's save the rolls. It'll be the only food we'll have on the seventeen hour train trip back to Rangoon."

"Let's try to get some bottles of soda too."

"Remember—the less input, the less output."

The station was a chaotic muddle, with families camped everywhere, kids screaming and people arguing. One train was sitting on a track at one of the three platforms.

"Do you suppose that really is our train?" Lauretta anticipated confusion comparable to the airport on our trip up-country from Rangoon.

"Well, Babe, it looks like the only one. Let's try it." We walked the length of the train before we came to an open door.

"Excuse me sir. You must have a ticket." I waved my tickets in the air as the conductor tried to get us to stop.

After checking and punching our tickets the conductor obligingly led us to seats at the front of an empty car.

"Is this train supposed to be air-conditioned?" Lauretta was already melting in the sweltering coach.

"I guess that means you can open the windows."

"I'm glad we have two seats to ourselves. I hope they turn the lights off so we can sleep."

"We'll have to wait and see."

The window had a metal blind which I pushed up to let in more air. After a half hour wait, the train began to move. The conductor came through the car and pulled down the blind. After he passed, I pushed it up again.

"Sir. Do not touch the window. It is too dangerous. Rebels shoot at open windows and throw stones. When the train stops, miscreants climb in. You must keep the blind down."

"Can some of the lights be turned off?"

"No sir. It is for your own safety. We do not want thieves to take your belongings."

We looked around and counted only seven other people in the car, mainly Burmese businessmen in beige suits and open-necked white shirts.

"David. This is a bit excessive." Lauretta was exasperated and tired.

Seventeen hours on a boiling hot train stopping every fifteen minutes with hucksters banging on the metal window blind, was enough to finish us both. We dozed but didn't sleep. I watched the flies crawl up the wall in front of us, buzz around and then start the climb again.

"Let's be daring and eat our roll and drink our soda. We only have seven hours to go."

"That's a great idea. To hell with everything." We feasted on our precious buns and soda, accompanied by the snoring of our neighbours.

"Rangoon!" shouted the conductor from the other end of our coach.

We stumbled to the door only just having gotten to sleep. As I turned to pick up the bags on the platform, a middle-aged man approached Lauretta.

"Madam. Would you like to come to my house for a bath? Oh by the way, you are Mrs. Holbrook aren't you?"

"You know, that's the best offer I've had all day."

"Perhaps I should introduce myself. I'm Dennis Cartwright and I work for the Canadian Wheat Board. I heard from the British Embassy that you and your husband were in Burma. You are of course both welcome to use my bath and shower." We laughed and took him up on his offer.

"By the way, we're all invited to the US Embassy canteen for a breakfast of eggs and bacon. Joe Fricker, the doctor at the Embassy, says he knows you, David, from somewhere. He'll be there too."

The breakfast on the deck outside the American Recreation Centre was complete with orange juice and freshly brewed coffee as well as the promised eggs and Canadian bacon as the Americans choose to call it. The baseball game between the Embassy and the Japanese Embassy 'Kamikazis', was for fourteen year olds and under. It was all enough to make us forget where in the world we were. We were revived in time to board our return flight to Bangkok and on to Singapore.

The telex from Ottawa didn't come as a complete surprise. I knew it was time for me to change postings. My request for a posting in Latin America or Hong Kong was not granted. Instead, we were asked to move to London. They must really think I should slow down. Lauretta continued to read the posting confirmation letter.

"David, you'd better keep reading. It states that your duties will be in Eastern Europe: Moscow, Prague, Budapest and Warsaw. That's not exactly an easy posting and you have to visit each one every three months. You're still not going to be home much."

3

COLONIALS IN SUBURBIA

1

Our move to England immediately brought back memories of our meanderings in London in the sixties. Despite jet lag, we set off from our hotel near the High Commission on Grosvenor Square for Sloane Street and Kings Road to refresh those memories.

"Penny for the Guy. Penny for the Guy." Young lads were on corners with their rag doll-like mannequins propped against buildings collecting their alms for Guy Fawkes Day.

The subtle pleasures that were lacking in Asia temporarily overwhelmed us. We could barely imagine a metropolis with activities other than shopping. Singapore did have a symphony orchestra but only if it made a profit each year. Here we could go to recitals at Wigmore Hall and drink vintage wine at sixties' prices at the Tate Gallery. Fortunately few knew about it which made it a treat whenever we had the opportunity.

I was still able to rent a studio by the hour to resume my lapsed piano efforts on a Bösendorfer grand.

But there were disappointments. The home assigned to us was an hour's train ride from the High Commission in Mayfair. As Londoners would say, 'Oh my dear, do you *really* live all the way out there?'

The house, in a cul-de-sac of identical homes, circa 1975, looked brand new, but we soon learned it wasn't the case. It was pseudo Georgian with deficiencies. Neither the doors nor windows fitted well enough to stop the rain or cold from seeping into the house. In fact, I was almost able to put my hand under the front door. Double patio doors opened from the living room onto a small sitting area under a large pine tree in the backyard. With the space under the patio doors, there was a brisk through breeze, front to back. On a positive note, we hoped the tree would absorb some of the noise from the trains at the foot of the garden, four British Rail lines and the Metropolitan Line, our ticket to town.

There were four miniscule bedrooms on the second floor. The dampness was enough to make the sheets clammy. It was not Chelsea, but it was to be our home for the next few years.

The jaunty roly-poly neighbours to our right came to the door within fifteen minutes of our arrival.

"Welcome to Woodbridge Way. I'm Edith and this is my husband, Russell." Edith, dressed in a fully-filled flowered house dress and comfortable shoes and Russell, a few steps behind, in a blue button-down shirt and gray flannels were quick to make us feel at home. "We are very happy to see you here. The previous tenants were colonials. They didn't know a thing about looking after the garden or even mowing the lawn."

"You mean they were colonials like us." Lauretta couldn't contain herself."I assure you I love to garden and yes, I do cut the grass."

"Oh, beg your pardon. You don't sound like colonials."

"Think nothing of it" Lauretta continued without skipping a beat.

"Perhaps I could take you to the high street and show you the shops. There's a lovely green grocer, a chemist and a fine butcher. Oh, and a fine fashion shop with lovely frocks. You know, the shops are much smaller than in America." She seemed unembarrassed by her 'colonial gaffe'.

"That would be lovely, Edith. Perhaps tomorrow."

Husband Russell didn't get a word in. He stood with his hands stuffed in his pockets.

Our move was like all moves. On a positive note our belongings arrived speedily for a change. However, something was always lost. In this case sadly, the carton, carefully packed with our Tanh Le lacquer box carried from Vietnam with such care, never arrived. With it was my collection of Japanese netsuke and inro, small accessories worn on kimono sashes, collected in Singapore. I imagined that someone, thinking that it was full of precious stones, would take an axe to the box with its Chinese square lock on the outside. I had foolishly left the lock on the box and so made it irresistible to a petty thief.

I realized how much I enjoyed those connections to the past.

"David, they're only possessions."

"I know, Darling but…I admit it's stupid of me to get attached to these things but I do."

The children, after bouncing from school to school, were quite excited about going to boarding school in England, or so we thought. The decision, made in Singapore, meant that their new school in Suffolk, would be close enough for them to come home on some weekends.

"Dad, could Matthew come to our school?"

"Chris, it's a nice idea but he's doing well where he is. He wanted to go to the school in Canada because many of his camp friends go there too."

"You know we try to get along. It's just that he bugs me so much."

"We're still a family, even though Matthew's in Canada. You're all going to boarding school so it's fair for everybody." Chris, no doubt mulling over what I'd said, sat down to read.

"Mom, the problem is we're still going to have to wear uniforms." The idea of uniforms was becoming more and more difficult to promote as they considered being twelve practically adult.

"It's part of the school rules, sweet. You will have lots of time to wear clothes you like after school and on weekends."

"Can we choose a school where we don't have to wear uniforms? I don't think this boarding school is a good idea after all." Chris now tried to reinforce Sue's argument.

"No kids. We've made the decision and paid the fees. You'll get used to it." I tried not to let this get out of hand by adding, "Now stop the whining."

Lauretta and I looked at each other as they stomped off to Chris's room and slammed the door. I put my arm around her shoulder.

"Did you see the list of required clothes? Three pairs of black Oxfords. One pair of plimsolls (sneakers). Three pairs of socks. Three sets of undergarments; they say it's one on, one in the laundry and one in the drawer. What are they supposed to do with more shoes than socks and underwear? I guess kids' socks and underwear never get dirty in Britain." We laughed at the thought.

"Let's try it for six months and see how we all adapt."

"I hope your parents managed to get Matthew back to school on time."

"I'm sure they did. He was keen and they offered to do it. We'd have heard by now if he hadn't arrived."

The children reluctantly helped pack the car with their trunks, bags, and tuck box for our trip to Suffolk and boarding school.

"Now remember. On the weekends just bring a small bag and your homework. We're going to meet you on Friday evening at the Liverpool Street Station. Stay together and don't wander off."

We waved and tried to leave quickly not wanting to make it any more agonizing than it already was. We looked at each other both with tears in our eyes as we waved to Chris standing alone with his hands in the pockets of his dreaded short pants as he watched us leave.

"I don't know why I'm so upset!" Lauretta was shaking her head.

"I think we're so accustomed to having them at home. We'll miss that. I do think it'll be great for them. It'll be a more stable environment than moving every few years."

"Sue is so gregarious and outgoing. It's Chris I worry about."

Two weeks after the beginning of school, Lauretta answered the telephone.

Matthew, who refused to write letters, was brief in his monthly phone calls. "Hi, Mom. School's fine. I saw a bear at camp. I'm on the swim team. I love you." Click.

"I wonder who moved first, Matthew or the bear?" I laughed.

Lauretta added, "I wonder whether there was a counsellor with him?"

Meanwhile, Woodbridge Way was turning out to be a gold mine for any amateur psychologist. Sam, our other next door neighbour, was a case in point. Candy, his latest long-legged blonde bombshell, had taken to sunbathing, making sure to get an all-over tan much to the relish of Chris, whose hormones were beginning to bubble.

"Chris, are you doing your weekend homework?"

"Yes." There were no books in sight.

"By the way, give the woman some privacy."

She looked as though much of the tan was from the high street (the English equivalent to the main street) tanning parlour, or the south of France, particularly since our pine tree kept a good deal of the sun from their backyard.

The blondes changed often, usually every few months, much to the disgust of the other neighbours. It was rumoured that Sam was one of the great train robbers, which accounted for his expensive red sports cars and his ability to change ladies so often; to say nothing of the fact that he did not work outside the home. We were told that his house had been burgled three times and he never called the police. No wonder rumours were so prevalent. It didn't take us long to understand why any blondes living in the neighbourhood were interested in Lauretta's garden. It was adjacent to Sam's.

"Dad, Betsy has two mothers."

"Well, Sue, perhaps one or both women are divorced."

"No. She says they're lesbians. What does that mean?"

"Well, Sue, it simply means that they prefer other women to men."

"Oh." Sue walked off mulling that over.

"I'm glad you're home for some of these questions." Lauretta smiled as she came into the room. "Betsy's mothers have the most beautiful lavender bush at the end of their driveway. It's enormous. Run your hand up a stem next time you pass and then smell your fingers."

Two boys with a sudden keen interest in turning skipping ropes for Sue and her friend Betsy lived further up the street. Julia, their pretty fair-haired mother had become a frequent visitor, offering help with our adjustment to the street. It turned out that she, too, had a great interest in our neighbour, Sam.

"Lauretta, it's going to take me a while to get accustomed to the intrigue in this neighbourhood."

The weekends passed quickly. Sunday evening it was back to the Liverpool Street Station for Sue and Chris's return to Bury St. Edmunds and school.

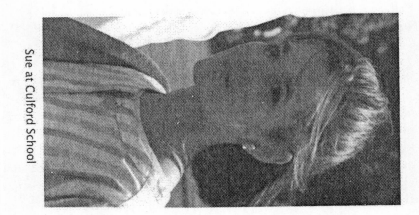

Sue at Culford School

The dreaded uniforms in London

Sue's Prom

Matthew at Millfeld

2

My quarterly trips to Eastern Europe began in the autumn of 1980 with an early morning flight to Moscow. My arrival at Sheremetyevo Airport was nerve-racking. Moscow was buried in an early November snowfall as my flight landed.

"Stand there." A gruff immigration official pointed to the line on the concrete where I was supposed to put my two feet. It wasn't until I'd done it a few times that I realized I was standing with my back to a mirror with calibrations measuring height. It had to match what was stated in the passport. "Why aren't you in a group?" I explained my job with the Canadian Embassy. The fact that I was alone, meant one person had to be assigned to watch me, a wasteful use of manpower.

The airport bus to Red Square seemed easy enough until I realized it was filling with smoke and not moving. I barged off, pushed by the other passengers with their luggage smashing into me, as I tried to hold on to my own bags.

"Oh, there you are, sir. You're supposed to wait inside for me until I get the Embassy car."

I smiled and shrugged. How I'd missed the driver with his huge fur hat with a red Canadian insignia on the front, I don't know. Even in the crush of people, he towered over the mob the hat adding an extra six inches on top of his six foot frame.

"The buses are not safe, Sir. It is so cold, they try to make sure the motor will start by heating the radiator with a wood fire. It often gets out of control."

"I can see that. I'll remember in the future."

"My name's Alexander, Sir. Welcome to Moscow. The Counsellor has given me this letter to give to you."

It was a schedule of Canadian and British Embassy diplomats and their families who had made appointments to see me during my three day stay. I was suddenly back in general practice. The British resident doctor was on vacation and so I was left with the British and Commonwealth Embassy staff to see as well as the Canadians.

The clinic, a tiny room in the embassy basement next to the furnace room, had been fitted with a couch and drapes. There was even a nurse to help. The Embassy, an historic home in central Moscow not far from Red Square, housed a large staff and living quarters on the upper floors for the Ambassador and his wife. The appointment schedule was posted at the top of the basement stairs.

Office hours began the moment I stepped in the door.

The first patients were waiting and we descended to the basement for their appointment. "Doctor, Paul and I are expecting a baby. Could you do my prenatal care?"

"Yes, of course, but I will only be here every three months. I'll arrange for you to see the British or American doctor in between my visits." I wondered what I'd do if she went into labour prematurely. "Where are you intending to have your baby?"

"We thought I should return to Norway. My mother's there and if my baby is born in Norway, the child allowances I'm entitled to are very generous. I'm Norwegian as well as Canadian." I must have looked stunned. "Is that not possible, Doctor?"

"Of course." I always assumed people would want to return to Canada but then what is Canada but a melange of the world? "You choose what's best for you and your family." I prescribed the necessary prenatal supplements and arranged for her initial examination at the better-equipped British clinic.

No sooner had she left than a guard from the Embassy entrance was brought down to the clinic with his right palm full of blood. He spoke no English as he held out his hand. Once I got it cleaned up with the few disinfectant pads I had in my bag, all I could find was a laceration on the side of his middle finger. Not having any sutures, I decided that the only way to repair this was to make some tape closures and a good finger bandage. I rummaged through my meagre supplies and found enough tape and bandage to produce my rendition of the Stelco bandage. It was one of the only things I learned while working as a First Aid attendant at the Steel Company of Canada during my student days. There was nothing I could do if anyone fell in a vat of molten steel but I could bandage hand lacerations, the most common minor injury.

At the end of a long first day, Jim Reynolds and his wife were determined to show me how to eat and drink in Moscow. Jim, a commercial counsellor at the Embassy, had invited me out for dinner. He was specific about where I was to meet them.

"Remember, go to the *soft* currency restaurant at the Hotel Nacional." I was relieved because I was not looking forward to spending any longer than absolutely necessary in my hotel, a monstrous thirty-three storey wedding cake-like creation which ranked with the worst architectural designs I had ever seen. Stalin favoured the architect and had him design two identical buildings one as a hotel and the other to house government departments. It generally took twenty minutes to get an elevator after having dealt with the babushka, a stout sour crone who kept the keys on my floor as well as observing all activity. In these days of Andropov, she probably went through my luggage twice a day.

I managed to get a taxi from my hotel. The driver spoke no English and let me off miles from my destination. I had no idea where I was.

A huge Russian policeman came up to me, no doubt wondering what I was doing, a foreigner standing alone.

"Hotel Nacional?" I asked quizzically.

He stepped into the road and stopped the traffic. Next, he pulled out his baton and cracked it down on the roof behind the driver's door of a taxi which had stopped. He ordered him to take me to Red Square. It wasn't a happy trip. The driver cursed the entire fifteen or more blocks.

As we pulled into the vast square, I was stunned by the beauty of St. Basil's Cathedral, resplendent with spotlights highlighting the seven cupolas I could see, all topped with gold. Snow coated some of the façade. The spirals of colour below the gold cupolas were breathtaking.

"Hotel?" I'd not been watching where we're going. He swung the taxi around and screeched to a halt at the front doors of the Nacional.

Jim Reynolds and his wife were already seated when I arrived."Now David, in Moscow, we go to the soft currency restaurants so that we can pay in rubles rather than U.S. dollars. They have excellent Russian vodka and caviar. It makes a meal. You don't have to eat greasy day-old chicken Kiev." The restaurant had been elegant at the beginning of the century. Three enormous chandeliers hung from the high-ceilinged room. The tables were covered with yellowed linen cloths. The furniture, antique in North America, was merely old in Russia. We were seated for a few minutes when a large silver ice bucket arrived at the table with an ice cold bottle of Stolichnaya vodka, a bottle of Russian champagne and a bottle of mineral water.

Next three large bowls of caviar, one a golden colour, one silver and one black, were placed in a tripod in the middle of the table, a colossal quantity compared to the usual dollop of Danish lumpfish one sees on fancy sandwiches. Despite my increasing vodka haze, I did relish the sensation of the smooth caviar melting in my mouth.

As the caviar bowls were taken away, Jim announced the next part of the evening. "David, we would like you to come back to our place and have some of the Russian champagne we have on ice." I groaned. Would I make it? My legs were numb from the knees down.

Entering the Reynolds' apartment building was akin to walking into a seedy tenement building in Manhattan. The stink of the garbage piled up in ugly open black dumpsters practically made me sick on the spot. There was one dim light bulb illuminating the door from the parking lot and none in the stairwell as we climbed to the first floor and the elevator. Their apartment on the eighth floor of the building was beautiful, a startling difference from the first impression in the parking lot. The dry, toasty champagne was delicious but almost finished me.

The stern, disapproving look of the key lady on my return to the hotel was all I remembered of the rest of the evening. Perhaps she had to unlock the door for me. I fully expected a horrendous hangover from my vodka dinner but awakened quite lucid for reasons I still don't understand.

The Embassy driver picked me up at the hotel early for my trip to the British clinic for the day. I was in the clinic no more than ten minutes, when a middle-aged Australian diplomat, doubled up with pain was helped in. With the help of the young woman I assumed was his wife, I got him onto the examining table.

"I'm going to be sick to my stomach." We helped him to sit up again and I grabbed a waste basket.

"George has had this pain twice before but not this bad. It started in the middle of the night. He wouldn't go to the local hospital and I don't blame him. It's so dirty." Rosalie, his young wife, was helpful with the history.

"Okay, George, do you feel well enough to lie down again?" I get him supine with difficulty.

"When did the pain start?"

"A couple of weeks ago, Doctor, but it wasn't like this" Examining his abdomen, the tenderness extended from the base of his sternum to his groin.

"Now George, on a measure of 1 to 10, I want you to tell me where the pain is worst." I gently palpated each quadrant. The right upper quadrant and the right loin were the worst and were extremely tender.

"Does the pain go anywhere else, George?"

"Yes, I seem to have pain in my right shoulder blade."

"George, you likely have a blockage of your bile duct leading from your gallbladder to the duct that flows into your stomach, which means that not only does your gall bladder swell, but the duct from the liver and pancreas can back up too. You may have to have your gall bladder removed and the duct cleared. First, I'm going to give you something for pain, start an intravenous and get your stomach settled. Then we'll decide what to do next."

I excused myself and quickly phoned the United States Embassy doctor to ask what he did about surgical emergencies.

"Well, David, if he's an ambassador, the Kremlin will sometimes allow a patient to be admitted to the fancy hospital used by government officials. However it's a security problem, so you'll have to make sure somebody from the Australian Embassy is with him all the time, especially if he has to have an anaesthetic. He cannot be allowed to give away commercial or military secrets while anaesthetized. If you can't get him into the top hospital here, you'll have to send him to Helsinki. Standard care here is not reliable and can be medically dangerous. Finnair and Lufthansa are great for evacuations."

"Thanks, Ben." I went back and explained the plan to George.

"As soon as the pain eases, I'm going to arrange for you to be flown to hospital in Helsinki." Turning to Rosalie I asked, "Perhaps you could accompany him? The flight's about three hours. The Helsinki General Hospital has more up to date methods of dealing with gall bladder surgery than are available here. Their surgeons will make the decision as to whether you keep or lose your gall bladder. I'll contact the hospital for you."

"Thank you, Doctor." Rosalie watched as I tore off pieces of tape to secure the needle once I got it in a good vein in his left forearm. I didn't expect to be starting I.V.'s on these trips and I was relieved when I saw the drip running smoothly.

"I'm sorry we don't have a nurse to stay with him. The injection of Demerol should make him more comfortable. I'll be back every chance I get." I left them behind the curtain and moved on to the throng of other patients including a screaming three year old.

By the end of the day, the Australian was much improved. I decided to take the easiest course of action. I disconnected the I.V. and sent him home on fluids. The travel arrangements would be made by his Embassy.

The British Embassy was directly across the Moskva River from the Kremlin walls. As I left the British compound, I couldn't resist walking to the entrance in Red Square. As I walked over the bridge spanning the river, I thought of the notorious torture chambers in the prison supposedly under the bridge. My step quickened.

Bypassing Lenin's tomb, I slipped through the gates expecting to be stopped by the usually vigilant guards. I was not. The Kremlin was magnificent with its beautiful fifteenth century buildings floodlit in the early evening. Every city in Russia has a Kremlin. It houses the officialdom of that city or area. Though some Kremlins are older, I'm sure that in sheer size, this was the most stunning.

As darkness fell, I decided to walk to the Canadian Embassy to get a lift to the hotel rather than try the taxi system again. I couldn't resist walking around St.

Basil's Cathedral. It was built in the mid-sixteenth century by Ivan the Terrible, to replace a wooden church that was torn down because it was a fire risk for the wooden walls of the Kremlin. The walls were later rebuilt in stone. The twists of colour on the domes lead up to a golden onion shape on the top of each spiral. Rumour has it that Stalin had decided to tear down the Cathedral so that his soldiers would not have to break ranks to go around it as they marched into Red Square. Luckily he was thwarted.

I moved on to the second half of my trip. Poland.

Warsaw, devastated on the first days of the Second World War, had been rebuilt mainly in Eastern European schlock, concrete blocks being the main ingredient. The exception was the downtown core which had been lovingly restored. The Canadian Embassy sat on a hill in a park overlooking the Wistula River just outside the core of the city.

Once again, I was given an office to use as a clinic during my visit. I hoped not to be practising my bandaging skills and I.V.starting procedures here. I enjoyed my chats with the Canadian staff and their families. Their problems focused on the stress of impending martial law and the secret police watching one's every move.

The British Embassy, my second family practice clinic for the next two days, was in a pre-war building, adjacent to 'my club'. It was, in fact, a literary club, dimly lit and smoky, with dark wood panelling, reminiscent of Paris in the twenties. The consul at the Canadian Embassy, was a club member and she had kindly chosen to take me there for lunch. I thought of myself as a two silver brush, English toff when I mentioned 'my club'. I envisioned myself, brush in each hand smoothing my silver hair behind my ears. I laughed as the years of having enough hair to brush had passed.

I was flattered by the hospitality both in Moscow and Warsaw. I was a new face and connection with life outside the Iron Curtain.

Ambassador Findlay was a professorial gentleman, complete with tweed jacket and leather elbow patches. Quiet and studious, I could imagine him in a university setting rather than as the Canadian Ambassador to Poland. His wife was in many ways the opposite, a human dynamo who never stopped.

"My wife and I would like you to join us for dinner, David."

As I was welcomed at the residence, Mrs. Findlay announced that 'Liminal the Criminal' had just delivered fresh produce, which he smuggles from Scandinavia and then sells at extortionate prices from the back of his truck to the expatriate population. It was fortunate that the dinner of over-done pork chops did include a salad of lettuce and tomatoes, courtesy of Liminal.

"Doctor Holbrook, tomorrow I would like you to accompany me to the Sue Ryder Home which the Embassy and I support." I agreed, not about to say no to the Ambassador's wife. Sue Ryder was an English Baroness, who twice a year, drove her three-ton truck with donated supplies for the needy from London to Warsaw and other destinations in Eastern Europe. She had established a number of homes in her name to treat the homeless and infirm. The situation in Poland had been very hard on the Sue Ryder Home on the outskirts of the city.

The building, a long brown horizontal one storey clapboard structure in a pine grove, was in a distant suburb of Warsaw. Ramps led to the main entrance.

"David, I should explain that all of the twenty-six residents are young women between the ages of sixteen and thirty-eight, all with crippling juvenile rheumatoid arthritis."

Five ancient wheelchairs with wicker seats and tall backs were the first thing I saw as I stepped in the door. The backs were so tall it was hard to see anybody sitting in them as I waited for my eyes to adjust from the bright sunlight. The wheelchairs were shared by the entire group.

I was greeted in the large dining hall as I entered to introduce myself. The charm and positive attitudes of these women astounded me. Their beautiful faces and grotesquely distorted bodies were a stark reminder for me of what others were forced to tolerate. The crippled limbs were, undoubtedly, extremely painful.

"Doctor, it's so kind of you to come." Elisabet Walenski, a woman in her late thirties, dressed in an indigo blue dress with a lace collar was the spokesperson. I bowed and smiled rather than shake hands knowing how excruciating it would be for her with her red swollen knuckles. She walked slowly around the room, showing me the dolls, dressed in Polish folk costumes, made for sale in Sue Ryder charity shops in Britain. I tried to chat but did not know who spoke English. There were no blank expressions. One young woman showed me how she painted the faces on the wooden dolls by clutching a fine brush with her right fist before she passed them on to be dressed in wonderful long-sleeved blouses and full skirts with aprons, made from scraps of material salvaged from many sources.

"Elisabet and I would like you to come to our room for coffee. We would like to make a gift for your wife." Angelica spoke the words haltingly, struggling with her English. I felt as though I should apologize for not speaking Polish.

I pushed Angelica, a perky twentyish woman, down the long hallway in one of the rickety wicker wheelchairs to her shared room. The coffee was already brewing on a hot-plate. Three mugs and a plate of oatmeal cookies were produced from a sideboard jammed in the corner. Elisabet's excellent English and Angelica's lack of it made our conversation awkward but amusing as translations had to be made.

"We enjoy making paper decorations by cutting out designs. It's such good therapy." I looked at the gnarled, twisted hands and watched in disbelief as she cut an intricate pattern from a small piece of folded paper. Just holding the scissors was a miraculous feat. Angelica carefully put them in an envelope for me.

I was ushered back to the dining area where the dolls were being packed with the help of Mrs. Findlay.

"Mrs. Ryder takes them back to England to be sold to help us buy more materials." I smiled and once again expressed my appreciation for their hospitality. After I assured the women I would bring my wife with me on my next visit, Mrs. Findlay and I departed.

In the car enroute to Warsaw, the driver tried to avoid the wretched looking draught horses pulling their decrepit carts of everything from people to manure.

"David, I would like you to get some more manoeuvrable wheelchairs for the home?"

"I'm sure I could try. I'll ask the Canadian Womens' Club in London to help. They're always looking for worthy projects."

It was startling to find such a large group of young women wracked by such a debilitating disease all under one roof. How interesting it would be to know if there was an environmental reason for such a high prevalence of rheumatoid arthritis.

3

My return to London was a joy after trips to Eastern Europe and the uneasy feeling one has of living even briefly in authoritarian regimes. There was also the joy of catching up on family happenings. On one occasion, I was met by Lauretta standing on the lawn with a gorgeous smile on her face.

"You won't believe this, David. Voilà! Our new lawnmower."

"Wow, that's going to keep you busy and the neighbours happy."

Our shiny red electric 'Flymo' looked as though it could cut a swath through anything. Lauretta had gone to the High Street and bought enough extension cord to cut most of the lawn on the street. As she plugged it in for the first time the next morning and started to cut our grass, Edith appeared.

"Oh. Are *you* going to mow the lawn? Shouldn't your husband be handling that machine?"

"Oh, no. He's having a bit of a lie-in this morning," coining an English phrase that was perfect for the situation. In fact, when Edith returned to her place behind the curtains, she would likely spot me sitting under the pine tree writing trip reports. Cutting our small patch wasn't nearly enough for Lauretta. She moved on to the large patch across the street.

"Oh my dear." Out came Edith once again. "That grass is the responsibility of the town council."

"But Edith. If I cut it rather than wait for the council, it makes the view of that beautiful Lutyens house on the next street more agreeable from our living room." The hip-roofed wood-shingled white stucco house designed in the twenties, was a feast for our eyes, tired of the sameness of our street.

"No. The Lutyens don't live there. The Thompsons do." There was no sense trying to explain who the English architect Lutyens was.

"Edith. I enjoy mowing grass. Would you like me to do yours?"

"Oh no, thank you very much. It's Russell's job."

Lauretta's love of gardening and her new 'Flymo' convinced her to take her first overseas paying job, a gardener's position for the High Commission. It involved caring for the gardens of their unoccupied properties in our suburb, eight in total. Her physical strength soon surpassed mine as she heaved the 'Flymo' in and out of our ten year old Toyota Estate Wagon. Lauretta, now adept at right hand drive after Trinidad and Singapore, was in her element.

Having Chris and Sue home for Easter was a great help with my entertaining plans.

"Sue, we're going to have a party for mom's birthday. I need you and Chris to help me. First of all, we have to make the house easier to find. What should we do?"

"I can draw a really good map, Dad."

"Okay, Chris. That's your project."

"Dad, we need a bigger number on the house. Nobody will ever find it."

"That's a great idea, Sue. What's the first thing you see when you look at this house?"

"The garage."

"Let's paint the number on the garage door."

"I can make a stencil. How big do you think?"

"The bigger the better. A five foot '6'. Can you make a stencil that big?"

"Sure. Then let's paint it silver like the old Porsche."

Our garage door was to become the focus of the street. I'm sure many of the comments were not complimentary but Edith was the only one to challenge our silver '6' directly to our faces.

"Do you not think that door is too ostentatious?" Edith came out with both barrels blasting. "And by the way, can't you afford a better car? We pride ourselves on our motors. Yours is very dated."

Lauretta, tired after a day's mowing, couldn't let that go by.

"No, we can't. We choose to pay to send the children to great schools instead. Furthermore, we think the garage door looks vastly better. Would you like Sue to paint yours?"

Edith returned to her house in silence.

"It's so hard to be patient with that woman, David. Should I go and apologize?"

"No. She was rude and the comments uncalled for. But then we're only colonials remember." I put my arm around Lauretta's waist and we retreated to the house smiling at the thought of our old banger and the new Saab in our neighbour's driveway.

Lauretta's birthday party, originally meant to be a small affair, had mushroomed.

The High Commissioner's butler had insisted on organizing the event as a means of thanking me for looking after his sick children. He'd convinced the chef at the High Commissioner's Residence to prepare the food, supposedly finger food, meaning no cutlery. Or so I thought. Cake? Of course, but that meant something to put it on and eat it with. In the end, there were so many guests that every plate in the house, including those under the plants, was brought into service. When anybody put down a fork, someone snatched it, washed it and put it on the next saucer.

The High Commissioner was in his element in a corner of the living room, holding forth with a bottle of cognac at his elbow.

"Doc. You've got to do this more often. I'm meeting the damndest people. I just met a chap who works for Planned Parenthood. I was telling him about my daughter's illegitimate child. The poor man was so surprised to have such a frank conversation with a High Commissioner, that he went off to get a drink. I even got an invitation for a weekend at a country inn courtesy of that lady over there with the flowers on her hat."

He raised his glass as she looked his way. Her husband, a crotchety, considerably older man, sat oblivious to the goings on. He seemed to be staring at the young, mini-skirted women through his cataract-clouded eyes.

It was the first and probably last time Woodbridge Way ever required a police presence to control traffic.

4

My second trip to Eastern Europe began in Czechoslovakia in late spring.

Prague was one of the most beautiful European cities I had seen. Unfortunately, it was also one of the grimiest because of the pollution from coal burning furnaces, the polluting Travant two-cylinder plastic automobiles and the clouds of black smoke from the large, Second World War vintage Russian trucks.

The Czechs seemed resentful of foreigners like me, Americans in their minds.

Walking over the Charles Bridge, past blackened statues every few yards, was dauntingly beautiful, despite the soot and the sour attitude of the locals. I could not walk on the cobblestones without wondering who had been doing the same, six hundred years before.

The U Tri Pstrôsu, nestled at the end of the bridge, was a perfect hotel for me. The garret, my room for all of my stays, overlooked the bridge. I couldn't stand upright without banging my head but I could put the one chair next to the window and watch the strollers, lovers, hippies and those striding purposefully to and from work as they crossed the bridge just below me.

"I would like room service at seven in the morning, please."

"Oh, I'm sorry. We don't do that here." I shrugged and went to my room.

At seven in the morning, there was a knock on the door. I got up from my chair at the window where I'd been watching the mist rise from the Vltava River (known as the Moldau in Germany) and my fellow early risers walking on the bridge with their dogs.

"It's room service, sir." I didn't believe it. A tray with fresh-baked bread, cheese and ham with a pot of strong coffee was brought in and put on my rustic pine table by the window.

Once again, I was back in practice. The British and American Embassy doctors rotated with me so that we shared the duties from month to month. The stress of living with the harrassment in the Soviet bloc countries was overwhelming for many families. There was little joy for the citizenry and the dour, sullen expressions on many passersby in the street were depressing for the staff of the Embassies, few of whom spoke the local language. As a result, most of the patients I saw, came for psychotherapy. Part of my day was spent in the Canadian Embassy where the commercial counsellor had kindly vacated his office to give me a consultation room and a private place to chat. The feeling of being able to talk to a doctor from 'back home' was comforting to many.

The rest of my day was spent in the US Embassy Health Unit, a fully equipped out-patient clinic. The American Embassy personnel had a remarkable support system overseas. It reduced the isolation felt in other diplomatic missions. Consequently, the morale was better.

The US Embassy, a small converted seventeenth century palace, was on Nerudova Street named after the nineteenth century Czech poet. The Chilean poet, Neruda, adopted the name. The cobblestoned street rose steeply from the US Embassy. A walk up Nerudova Street was a joy. Houses were tucked into the hill on the right, to the top of the hill where a gate house protected the upper limits of the Seminar Gardens with its neat rows of cherry and pear trees. The American Embassy staff could stroll through the gardens now overflowing with late daffodils and beautiful pink cherry blossoms. I continued my walk to the observation platform atop Petrín Hill with its panoramic view of the Old Town.

The house where Mozart lived with his mother during his Prague years was nestled into the hill half way up Nerudova Street. After entering Mozart's house, you had to climb to the second floor which opened into a large living room with one of his fortepianos, the precursor of the modern piano, in the corner. The room looked out on a large garden cut into the hill. Enormous tulips and white lilacs were in bloom. I felt as though I were living in another century. My visit corresponded with the opening of an art exhibition of drawings by Kramule, a Czech master with pen and ink, in the garden.

My two days in the Health Unit at the US Embassy passed uneventfully, if you consider caring for Marines with colds and others with sore knees from running on cobblestones, not too taxing.

I was under some stress when asked to take a visitor to Prague, a doctor attending a medical conference, out for dinner and then to a concert. The latter I looked forward to but the former posed a problem. It was hard to find anyone who knew a great deal about fine dining in a city known for its beerhalls. The commercial counsellor at the Embassy finally helped me out.

"It's easy, David. You go to Wenceslaus Square, you know the square with the fantastic clock that chimes every fifteen minutes." I thought he meant the thirteenth century 'clock of the seasons'. "Turn left. Halfway down the block is a restaurant with a metal sign hanging out in front. The sign has a cutout of a bunch of grapes. You can't miss it. It's great."

I took his word for it and went to the Intercontinental Hotel to meet the visitor. I was surprised to see a lovely, bejeweled, elegantly dressed silver haired woman standing in the lobby waiting for somebody. Could it be me? I looked around and didn't see anybody else who looked as though they were going out for dinner and so decided to ask.

"Hello. Are you Doctor Shurlin?"

"Yes. Are you David Holbrook?"

"Yes, I am." We shook hands. I went to the front door and asked for a taxi.

"Where are you going?" asked the driver. I explained as best I could.

"Sorry, I can't take you there." After three attempts, I decided that it was only five blocks or so, we would walk. I then looked at her three inch heels and wondered how I was going to manage this. Should I carry her?

I had not counted on it being so dark, black as pitch with the occasional twenty-five watt light bulb twinkling as we slowly walked down the street. Her arm was firmly grasping mine. It was silent. There were no people, no cars, just stillness.

Half way down the street, there was the outline of a bunch of grapes mounted on a dimly lit wall. There was no actual sign hanging into the street. Still silence.

I pushed open the door and the place exploded with noise from within. Stairs led down to the beamed basement. We carefully navigated the stairs without my guest tipping on her heels. I found an empty table and we sat. The din was almost too great to allow conversation. Out of nowhere, two waitresses appeared with table settings, white linen napkins, wine glasses and a carafe of red wine. I laughed out loud wondering what my guest was thinking at this moment.

"Sir, day's special?" The waitress looked at me quizzically.

"Yes, please." She never asked my guest. Within minutes, soup arrived, a beef broth with small dumplings floating on the top.

"This is delicious," I was relieved to hear her say it.

All of a sudden the din stopped. Silence again.

"What's happening?" My guest whispered looking anxiously around.

"I have no idea." At that moment, three uniformed policemen appeared on the staircase.

"Just keep quiet and hope we blend in." The three walked around the outside of the room peered at each table and then left. The din erupted again.

"What was that about?"

"I'm not sure, but perhaps they're looking for student agitators. I guess neither of us fits the description."

The main course, identified by my dinner companion, an experienced food and restaurant connoisseur as it turned out, was noisettes of venison, with a dollop of creamy mashed potatoes and yellow squash topped with a delicious red wine sauce.

"This dinner is outstanding, David. Do you come here often?"

"Well no. But I did think you would find it interesting." I should have bitten my tongue uttering that line. "I wasn't counting on subjecting you to a visit by the police."

The concert was also a success, the Borodin String Quartet playing Smetana and Dvorak quartets, true Czech fare to leave a lasting impression of Prague. I chuckled to myself wondering if she had any idea that I, too, was a neophyte in Prague.

5

On returning to London, I decided it would be wise to arrive at work early a few mornings a week to get my immigration medical cases reviewed in peace before the staff appeared and the phone started ringing. The second day of my new policy, I was paid an early visit by the High Commissioner.

"David. I have a job for you. I would like you to be at Canada House for the Royal Wedding tomorrow. We are expecting a contingent of Monarchists from Canada most of whom are elderly. It's an excellent vantage point so you will see it all if you are not busy with the sick and suffering. Bring your black bag." The High Commissioner smiled. "Oh and by the way, Mr. Trudeau, the Prime Minister, would like to see you today. He's staying at Claridges and needs some immunization for his trip to Africa."

"Thank you, I'll do that this morning." Africa? Where in Africa? What would I take to the hotel, vaccines? antimalarials?

Claridges was not a hotel I frequented. It's an exclusive base for Kings, Queens and Prime Ministers. I went to the second floor as instructed and a security officer told me to stop. After an adequate explanation, I was ushered down the hall to a door flanked by two uniformed Royal Canadian Mounted Policemen. One knocked on the door for me.

The door was answered by a young Margaret Trudeau in a short skirt and green turtleneck. I was surprised to see her given their turbulent marriage and separation details I had read in the media including her supposed fling with the Rolling Stones. Her marriage to the Prime Minister had produced three children who bounced to the door to greet me.

"Please come in." She introduced herself. We shook hands.

"Are you the doctor? Are you the doctor?" The boys rushed up to me and asked to carry my bag. I obliged.

"How do you do." I shook the Prime Minister's outstretched hand. "I would like to introduce my sons." They each shook hands."It's good of you to come. I just need a gamma globulin shot unless you find something else we should have when you check our vaccination books."

I breathed a sigh of relief as I didn't have an array of vaccines with me.

"What about the boys?" the Prime Minister's former wife asked.

"Where are you going?" I asked.

"Mainly to Tanzania."

"Do you have a supply of antimalarials as well?"

"No. Will you please organize that for me and work out the paediatric dose?" I agreed that I would.

"The antimalarials have to be started a week in advance of your arrival in Africa. You must continue them for a month after your return." I left it to him to figure out the timing. "The gamma globulin has to be given in your hip. Do you want to lie down in the bedroom?" He agreed and we walked down the long hall to one of the bedrooms.

"We want to come too, Dad." There was no objection.

I drew the 5cc. into a syringe with a large enough needle to ease the flow, swabbed an area on his hip and injected the gamma globulin.

"Does it hurt, Dad?" Justin grimaced as he watched the procedure.

"No."

"Then why is your face red?"

We all laughed.

"Tomorrow, could you bring the boy's gamma globulin and the antimalarials to Canada House? What you don't know is that they're going to be there to help you with your elderly patients in exchange for being brave when they have their injection."

"Mom is going to come with us too."

"Oh great. I'll see you tomorrow."

The Prime Minister accompanied me to the door. We shook hands and a uniformed mountie with the familiar red tunic walked me down the hall.

The next day, Canada House was abuzz even at eight in the morning.

"Hello Doctor, can I carry your bag?" The Prime Minister's sons, Sasha, Justin and Michel had already arrived. I'm not sure whose turn it was to carry my black bag, but I gave it up anyway. Their mother was smiling in the background.

The Monarchists and retired armed forces officers had already staked out their places at the windows. The boys and I retired to the office designated as the medical suite.

"Can I put some bandaids on the desk in case we need them?"

"Sure. What a good idea. By the way, who wants to have their gamma globulin first?" That created a sudden silence.

"Don't forget the deal." Margaret appeared at the door. They looked at her and then at each other and couldn't decide.

"Okay, let's flip a coin to see who goes first." It was a complicated coin flipping making the rules to cover three.

"This isn't fair, mine was heads." It mattered little as he quickly received his injection.

"That didn't hurt at all." Tears trickled down his cheeks as he twisted to try to see where the needle had left a mark.

His brothers' tears had already begun before their injections. The anticipation was worse than the reality. They were the speediest injections I'd ever given.

"Aren't you glad you had those bandaids ready?"

That prompted a giggle and all was forgotten. I explained the antimalarials to their mother and gave her an instruction sheet.

The pomp and circumstance of the Royal Wedding Procession on the street had almost lost out to the activities inside. From my vantage point, I managed to catch only a glimpse of the horse-drawn bridal carriage bearing the young Princess and her older Prince, the future British monarch. We listened to the cheering, as the monarchists clapped politely.

After the procession passed, I was amused at the guests who sidled up to me and said, "Is that her?"

I agreed and offered to introduce them to the Prime Minister's separated wife.

"Oh, no thank you."

One retired general, dripping in decorations and braid, relented and said: "Yes, I would like to meet her after all," after which many in the group changed their minds too. Margaret was gracious, almost regal, as she stood smiling, offering her hand.

The only casualty of the day was a temporarily lost diamond earring found by the boys in the women's washroom.

Our Yuletide preparations started earlier than expected.

"Hi, Mom. You said I was going to come to England at Christmas."

"Yes, Matthew. Of course you are. But it isn't December yet."

"When is my ticket coming?"

"Well, soon. What's the rush?"

"I've decided not to go to school here anymore. I'm going to go to school in England."

"Now wait a minute, Matthew. What's going on?"

"I'm changing schools. It'll be fine, Mom."

Matthew, unbeknownst to us had been reprimanded for the umpteenth time and had managed to call us before the headmaster of his school reached us to say that he was no longer welcome at the school.

"Now what are we going to do?" Lauretta asked, looking at me with a tense, worried expression. I sighed and said nothing, trying to get my thoughts straight.

"Let's try and find a school here. Maybe a fresh start is the answer. There has to be some place suitable."

With the help of a number of English friends, a school in Somerset appeared to fit the bill. The school was near Glastonbury, with its abbey, and reputation as a centre of learning dating back to the Middle Ages, as well as its Arthurian legends.

"It says in this brochure that Millfield caters to strong-minded independent, intellectual individuals with musical talent." Lauretta put down the booklet and smiled slightly.

"Do you think that sounds like Matthew?"

"Let's take him for an interview. We've nothing to lose."

Matthew, never slowed down by things like jet-lag, bounced off the plane and gave each of us a hug at Heathrow Airport. "Good to be home, Mom and Dad. Where are Chris and Sue?"

"They're at school Matthew and you should be, too." He shrugged off my nasty remark.

"This time it's going to work well, Peach. You're going to go to a wonderful school but first we have to take you for an interview. The headmaster wants to meet you."

Matthew looked upon it as a social occasion rather than as assessment of character and intelligence.

"They're going to take me, Mom." Matthew bounded out of the principal's office after his fifteen minute 'discussion' with a broad smile on his face. We put our arms around him and waited for the headmaster to appear.

"I must tell you Doctor Holbrook, we have rules at this school. Any pupil who breaks the rules three times is dismissed without recourse. Matthew and I discussed that and he assured me he understands."

We shook hands and departed with a list of uniform requirements, once again enough to break the bank.

"Matthew, we're going to stay overnight in Bath to celebrate."

The Royal Crescent Hotel was part of the Georgian Royal Crescent, designed by the architect John Wood and his son, as part of Nash's restoration of Bath in the eighteenth century. Its sumptuous rooms and fine dining room were suited to Matthew's extravagant tastes.

Dressed in his blazer, now with the Millfield crest hurriedly sewn on before dinner, grey flannels, white shirt and Millfield tie purchased in the school tuck shop before leaving for Bath, Matthew now thirteen, looked like a young toff expecting a glass of champagne with his dinner. We obliged with a sip and proposed a toast to a new school and a fresh start.

6

Taking Lauretta to snow-bound Moscow in the middle of a record-setting January deep freeze did not bother her in the least. Mind you, neither of us was able to take off our fur coats for any length of time.

Our host, Jim Collinson, the British doctor and his wife, Vi, had invited us to stay in their flat in the British Embassy annex, with its fine view of the Kremlin.

The British Embassy, housed in a mansion built by a sugar baron in the eighteenth century, was magnifcent with its palatial rooms, now serving as offices for the staff as well as a residence for the Ambassador. Jim and his wife lived above the medical clinic with their cat, Pectopah, named after the first sign the Collinsons saw when they arrived in Moscow. 'Pectopah', in Russian means restaurant. The cat was named before they managed to translate the word.

"David, I'm so glad that you've arrived for dinner. We're celebrating Robbie Burns day tomorrow and we're going to warm up by taking you and Lauretta to the Hotel Nacional for vodka, caviar and champagne." I didn't have the heart to tell him that I knew all about the Nacional. At least we won't have to get a taxi as I did the last time.

"Lauretta, you must have more vodka." Jim topped up Lauretta's glass from the bottle in the ice bucket with the two bottles of champagne.

"We can't wait for the caviar. Let's dance." Before I knew it, Jim and Lauretta were flying around the dance floor. I sat, hesitating to ask Vi to dance as I was always clumsy with partners other than Lauretta. I looked up just in time to see my bride, separated from her partner, body-checked by a pair of large buxom Russian women, dancing together, the bleach barely dry on their blonder than blond hair. Lauretta was sent reeling across the floor into the potted palms. I jumped up but Jim had come to her rescue and after much laughing and apologies from the culprits, they continued to dance.

"Phew, I have to sit down." Lauretta, accustomed to my sedate fox-trot, was in a lather. Before I could ask my hostess to dance, the caviar arrived.

By the end of the evening both Lauretta and I were wobbly from a vodka and champagne overload.

The Collinsons were smokers, two packs of Dunhills a day, each. Knowing that we were not, they had eased the windows in our room open a crack, enough to clear the air but also enough to reduce the temperature to near freezing.

"It's not possible to undress in this room, David."

"Let's go to the bathroom. I want a bath anyway. Come on, we'll both go. Once the hot bath is running, we can take off our fur coats."

Pectopah was occupying the only seat in the room. As Lauretta descended to her neck in the bath, I leaned over to remove the cat from his perch. With the speed of lightning, he cuffed me across the face.

"Oh! You miserable cuss!" I swatted him back. He took a flying leap out a previously unseen 'cat door' fitted to the second floor window. Lauretta and I look at each other in disbelief.

"Look at your face." Blood was oozing from a gash on my nose. I washed the cut with soap and water.

"I wonder when I had my last tetanus shot?"

"It was two years ago in Singapore before one of your camp trips. I remember your arm being sore."

"Thank God you've got a good memory. Maybe I'll only get cat scratch fever."

"Lord, I wonder where he jumped to? Cats aren't stupid. He must do it all the time."

"Hurry up and get in the bath while it's still hot." I sank down in the tub facing Lauretta, being careful not to flood the bathroom.

"Now quickly get dry and put your fur coat back on. It's the only sensible bedtime outfit for Moscow at thirty-five below." I heartily agreed. "Shall we share one coat?" We laughed and speedily headed for our room.

Opening the door, there was Pectopah on our bed.

"Well, you nervy beast. You're not going to win, buddy. Out you go." Not the window this time, but into the hall with our bedroom door firmly shut.

Lauretta, more than fortified with vodka and champagne, couldn't sleep for inexplicable reasons.

In the morning, she could not believe that I had slept through the racket she'd heard.

"Didn't you hear that bumping in the middle of the night?"

"You were dreaming, Darling." I had no trouble remembering the hallucinations after my first vodka, caviar and champagne dinner.

"I'm serious. Could it have been bodies? It sounded like heads bumping on every step as they were dragged down."

"Oh Lauretta, I don't think so."

There was a sharp knocking on our door.

"Rise and shine. It's Robbie Burns day." We pulled the duvet and fur up to our neck as Jim carried a tea tray into the room. We hadn't had a chance to get out of bed and put on some clothes.

As Jim and I left for our respective clinics, Lauretta and Vi, cosseted in fur, set off for the Pushkin and Tretyakov Galleries.

It wasn't until Lauretta and I had a chance to put our feet up before dinner that we had a chance to chat about our experiences during the day.

"Well let me tell you about our day." Lauretta began. "The Tretyakov Gallery was closed for 'remontre'. Apparently that means refurbishing. They don't know when it's going to open. That's where the great twelfth century icons are. I asked about contemporary art and an old man told me that somebody at the Canadian Embassy has it all, because it's banned. What's he talking about?"

"The old man at the gallery is right. Mr. Coustaki was in charge of the cars and drivers at the Embassy. He and his wife were fascinated by contemporary Russian art. He used much of his salary to buy more and more paintings until their apartment was chock-a-block covering the walls floor to ceiling. He had a Greek passport and the authorities couldn't stop him. The Embassy paid Mr. Coustaki in dollars so the artists were always eager to sell their paintings to him for hard currency. Sadly he's retired and moved to Greece. To get the art out of the country, he had to give a portion of his collection to the government. It's supposed to go to the Tretyakov Gallery. If it's always closed for renovations, we'll never see it."

"We did have a lot of fun. We took the trolley bus to Gorky Park and watched the skaters and cross-country skiers. It cost all of five cents each way on the bus. We went into a restaurant for a cup of coffee where there must have been a hundred tables. Our KGB shadow didn't sit on the other side of the room as you told us he would. He sat right next to us pretending to read a book."

"Tomorrow, the Embassy has offered us a car and driver for the afternoon. I'm going to take you to Peredelkino. It's in the country slightly beyond the twenty mile limit that we're allowed to travel outside of Moscow. The Embassy doesn't think we'll have any trouble."

"What trouble could we have, David?"

"Just passport checks. Don't even think about it."

Peredelkino is a small nineteenth century town, a retreat for the aristocracy. It's known for its magnificent dachas, the country homes of the rich. Generally located behind high wooden fences, the dachas are built of vertical clapboard unpainted to blend into the natural setting. The snow, unshovelled, drifts in wonderful dune shaped curves up to the fences, swirls around the trees and drifts up the doors of the dachas.

"Doctor, this is where the novelist Nabokov's family lives. I'll stop so that you can walk up to the gate."

"I don't think we should, David." Lauretta thought I was reckless.

"Come on, Babe".

We walked up to the gate in the deep fresh snow, following the lone track made since the recent snowfall. The gate was off its hinges and tipped open when I touched it. I couldn't resist going a few more steps leaving Lauretta standing at the gate. The snow was above our knees. I ploughed ahead to the side of the dacha listening to a wonderful jazz pianist sounding very much like Oscar Peterson.

I couldn't help but wonder whether the basis for his novel Lolita, had anything to do with this place. Knowing I could be arrested for trespassing and the inhabitants could be charged with harbouring a foreigner, I shuffled back through the snow to the car. The driver produced a whisk to brush off our clothes and Lauretta looked daggers at me for taking such risks. We began our return trip to Moscow and our preparations for departure.

"Lauretta, those 'bodies' you thought you heard being dragged in the night, were bodies! They were sides of beef that the Embassy has imported. They were being unloaded during the night." Jim smiled.

Lauretta raised an eyebrow toward me in an 'I told you so' gesture.

We all laughed as we left the Collinsons for the airport.

"I'm sorry we can't go on to Budapest together, David. I'll save it until one of your next visits. I have to get back now that I have an 'indoor job' at the High Commission." We were both delighted that Lauretta would be working as a clerk in the Immigration Department. She had moved up a rung or two from her gardening position. "Have a safe trip and get home soon."

We embraced and I watched her walk down the ramp looking happy. She turned and waved before boarding her flight to London.

Budapest no longer had the charm it once held for me. Perhaps it had to do with the embarrassment of dropping and smashing a bottle of red wine in the supermarket as I packed my few items bought for a hotel room home-made dinner on a previous visit. It was upsetting to splash a dozen people with red wine and not be able to apologize in Hungarian, an impossible language to learn. I was lucky to get out of the place without being lynched.

I was met at the airport by the Embassy office manager.

"Doctor Holbrook, one of the office staff became ill in the night. We took him to the General Hospital. They wouldn't allow us to see him after he was admitted. We're going to take you there now. Would you please decide what we should do next?"

Walking into a huge hospital ward crammed with rusting metal frame beds was like stepping back fifty years. Ferencz Tibor, the physician who completed the immigration medical forms for the Canadian government, joined me at the door.

"David, he's supposed to be along this wall of beds." I had no idea what the man looked like. "It must be this bed." Drying socks hung over the end of the bed. "George, there you are." Fortunately, Tibor recognized him.

"Hello, I'm David Holbrook the Canadian doctor from the Embassy."

"Doc, I'm ready to leave this place. I've passed a piece of gravel. I heard it splash in the toilet bowl. My pain has disappeared. I want out o' here. Somebody even stole my baked apple from dinner."

We all laughed and Tibor went to find the physician in charge to thank her and tell her George was leaving.

"Your socks are still wet."

"I'll wear them anyway."

The clinic at the Embassy was quiet now that the hospital admission had been dealt with. I was about to go to my hotel to read and write reports when the Ambassador asked to see me.

"I need an escort tonight, David. I would appreciate it if you would do me the honour." How could I refuse an Ambassador's request? The Canadian Ambassador to Hungary was a glamorous woman of a certain age.

"I would be delighted, but I don't know whether I have the proper attire."

"I have a dinner jacket for you. I'll have it delivered to your hotel." I thanked her and tried to look as though it was a common occurrence for me. It wasn't. "The driver will pick you up at 6:45."

At 6:45, I was in the lobby, wearing my borrowed formal wear, the waist cinched in a few inches with the cummerbund and the shirt sleeves hiked with elastic bands still enabling me to reveal someone's gold cufflinks below the jacket sleeve.

"The Ambassador would like you to wait in the lounge for her."

I smiled to myself thinking if only Lauretta could see me now. She would hoot with laughter.

After a half-hour wait, the Ambassador, in a long flowing red dress, dark hair newly coiffed, floated down the stairs.

"I don't like to arrive at these dinners precisely on time. By the way, the dinner is at the American Ambassador's residence and it's for Billy Graham, the evangelist." I swallowed hard wondering what on earth I was going to talk about and to whom.

As we swept up the grand staircase of the American residence, there, at the top of the stairs waiting for us, was the Ambassador and Mr. Graham. This was like the movies.

After exchanging greetings and being introduced, we were ushered into the formal living room. I thought this would be a large affair, but soon realized it was a dinner for eight which meant I was going to have to converse a lot more than I expected.

"Well, Doctor, what do you do?" I sipped my wine and gave the brief version.

"I wish you'd been around when I had my plane crash."

"When was that, Mr. Graham?"

"Why don't you call me Billy." I was stumped at that. He didn't look like a Billy. Could I do it with a straight face?

"The Cessna I was piloting went down in a storm in Montana a number of years ago. I got banged up pretty badly. I had broken bones and a bang on the head. The power of prayer certainly guided me through that horrible time. Do you believe in the power of prayer, Doctor?"

"I do." I quickly tried to think of a way of describing what prayer meant to me or how to change the subject, keeping my religious feelings to myself. It would be an impossible task for a shy individual like me to express my religious beliefs. "I'm concerned with the inequities I see particularly in refugee camps and poverty stricken areas of the world."

"That can be a focus for your prayer. You know, Doctor, you have a knowledge that gives you a clearer insight into people's physical and emotional health. I envy you that. I think you can use that talent to guide folks to good health both physically and spiritually."

"I do try. I find that you can only help those who are receptive to what you say."

"Now, you, Doctor, can tell when you're getting through to people."

I agreed that I usually could. Our conversation ended abruptly when our host proposed a toast to the honoured guest which gave me an opportunity to contemplate the extraordinary conversation I had just had and to think of the remarkable charisma that this man had. It also gave me a chance to begin a chat with the guest to my right.

At the usual diplomatic leaving hour of half past ten, the guests, having ajourned to the sitting room for coffee and cognac, stood, gave their salutations and departed, with the exception of the Canadian Ambassador. I silently hoped that her intense conversation with Billy didn't last too long as I had an early morning flight back to London.

An hour later after too much cognac, we left with a flourish, Madam Ambassador having mesmerized our host and his guest.

7

Prior to my return from Hungary, Edith had caught Lauretta as she left the house to head for the Metropolitan Line train and work.

"Lauretta, my church is having a jumble sale and I wondered if you have any old clothes to donate."

"Oh yes, that would give me an opportunity to get rid of a lot of my husband's clothes that he really doesn't need to cart around the world."

"Anything would be appreciated."

"I'll send over a bag or two in the next few days."

Thus began a full scale clean out of many of the clothes I was sure I was going to need someday. In fact I didn't realize they had gone.

The next week returning home to the burbs, I happened to be on the same train as our neighbor. "I met Russell on the train, Darling." She opened the door as I tried to shake my dripping umbrella. "He was wearing a really nice tie. I hope it wasn't wrecked in the rain." Lauretta waved at Russell as he made his way up his driveway.

"Come in and get dry. We received some of Russell's mail by mistake. I'll use your umbrella and take it over."

Lauretta returned laughing. "Russell does look a little flushed. He was holding their scrawny little dog in front of him."

"What's so funny?"

"Well, sweet, I can't keep the secret any longer. The tie you really liked was one of yours. I donated a load of the ties you never wear to Edith's church rummage sale. She must have kept all of yours and given his away. The poor man will be so embarrassed every time he sees you."

"How many ties do I have left?"

"More than enough. You'd never have noticed any missing if it hadn't been for Edith getting rid of Russell's."

"The poor guy. Shall I offer to take them back?"

"Absolutely not."

8

In the early 1980s, Poland was in the grips of a crisis that resulted in a flow of refugees into Austria. Students and workers in Lodz, the textile capital of the country with the poorest workers, rebelled against the government. The demonstrations spread to the Gdansk ship-building yards on the Baltic Sea. Lech Walesa, a dynamic speaker and union organiser, became the leader of the new movement now called Solidarity.

The Prime Minister and Defence Minister General Jaruzelski, faced with a worsening financial crisis as the country teetered on the brink of bankruptcy, massive increases in the price of food, and a Russian invasion to stop the anti-communist demonstrations, declared martial law in December 1980.

Thousands were jailed without charge. Public meetings were banned and the Solidarity uprising broken or so the government believed. There was a huge influx of refugees crossing the border into Austria. Once again, Canadian assistance was requested.

I was asked first to go to Vienna to help process refugees who had already crossed the Austrian border and then to go on to Warsaw.

Lauretta joined me in Vienna for a night at the Staatsoper. This was followed by a rough flight to Warsaw. The Canadian Women's Club had gone to a lot of trouble to get the wheelchairs for the Sue Ryder Home. Lauretta was determined to meet the women in the home and make sure the chairs had arrived.

Warsaw was an armed camp. Police, soldiers and tanks were everywhere. The local population surprisingly ignored the army but they couldn't help but be demoralised by the conditions, the cost and paucity of food. They couldn't get together in groups larger than three.

"David, there's nothing in the shops. I can't even stand in front of a store window without a line of people forming behind me. They must think I know something they don't. Worse still, they think I might buy something which would deprive them further. I'm sure this is one of the reasons the Embassy families are having such a miserable time."

"What I really want to do is take you to meet Zofia Demkowska, an artist whom I met briefly on my last visit." Lauretta and I, map in hand, wound our way on foot into the depths of what was the historic core of the city rebuilt in the style of the old city. With difficulty, we found the bell to the garrett at the address on my map. We climbed the steep steps to the top floor and knocked on the only door. A short elderly gray-haired woman answered the door.

"Good afternoon, I'm Zofia. You must be Lauretta. Your husband has told me all about you." She shook hands with Lauretta and invited us into her high-ceilinged single room, the walls lined with full bookcases.

Three chairs were placed around an old oak table with three places set with lace placemats. Beautiful antique ruby-red porcelain cups with gold trim sat on over-sized saucers at each place, a silver dessert fork alongside the saucer. A cake with white icing sat in the middle of the table, silver cake cutter at the ready.

"Please. Come and sit down."

"A friend in Canada has told us about your superb medals." Lauretta was wonderful at initiating conversation.

"Oh. How kind. I must show you my latest." She got up from the table and climbed the stairs to her loft. "Please help yourself to tea. It is ready."

"This is my bedroom up here." A deck protruded out into the room with a low railing to prevent her from rolling out of bed and falling the twelve feet to the floor. "I have my kiln up here too. Sadly there is not enough power to heat it to high temperatures but it has to do."

Lauretta and I were amazed at the resourcefulness. She quickly returned to the table rubbing a thick oblong talisman in her hands. She passed it to Lauretta.

"It's magnificent." Lauretta put the bronze medal in the palm of her hand. "Are you a pianist as well as an artist?" Looking over Lauretta's shoulder, I could see an image of a grand piano with a woman playing.

"I used to play but I don't have a piano any more. Just my memories. I must do many things to keep myself from becoming old. It is very difficult in Poland now."

"When we met earlier, you mentioned that you were taking photographs when you had film."

"Yes, that's part of my art. It gives me images that I can use for my sculpture."

"Lauretta and I have brought you some black and white film, some developing liquids and some print paper. I hope you can use it."

"Oh how kind! Oh, how wonderful!" She jumped up, clapped her hands together and kissed us on both cheeks. She rushed to find photographs.

The conversation moved from topic to topic for another hour until we realized that it was starting to get dark. We thanked her so much for the tea and stood to go.

"I want you to have something that will remind you both of me." She returned to the table, picked up the medal of the pianist and pressed it into Lauretta's palm.

We never did cut the cake. How could she have known that it was my birthday? We retraced our steps to the taxi stand near the Polish Pope's parish church and returned to our hotel.

We had one more stop on our agenda, the Sue Ryder Home.

"I'm so happy you'll have a chance to meet Angelica and Elisabet."

As we walked up the ramp to the front door, I tried unsuccessfully to remember the names of more than two of the residents. All twenty-six were clapping as we came in the door. The new wheelchairs were lined up as if for inspection. It was so moving, it was hard to keep our composure.

After chatting briefly, Lauretta was given a tour of the dining room and doll construction area. We were then ushered down the hall by Angelica to her room with Elisabet where the tea and biscuits were waiting.

"Elisabet, that is wonderful." Elisabet had deftly cut another paper figure multiplied by eight as it was unfolded for Lauretta. The small scissors were squeezed onto two fingers, the least swollen by her arthritis.

As we walked back down the hall to the door, I couldn't think of a happier conclusion to a tense visit to Warsaw.

It would be a wonderful picture to describe to the Canadian Women's Club members who raised the money for the wheelchairs.

9

On my return to London, I was asked to go to the High Commissioner's office.

"David, I'm unable to attend this function for the Anniversary of the Discovery of Insulin. It's in conjunction with a World Congress on Diabetes being held in London. I would like you to go in my stead." The High Commissioner presented me with an invitation embossed in gold.

"Have you read this invitation?" Lauretta realized I likely hadn't. "It's for tomorrow afternoon, and it's for you alone." So much for the fact that I had already asked Lauretta to go with me. "You're going by yourself, Sweet. By the way, it's a white shirt, dark suit event."

I arrived at Westminster Abbey by Underground and after a long walk from the Charing Cross Station, I presented myself to an usher in morning suit and white gloves. I followed him until he pointed to a seat high above the choir stalls, obviously a seat of honour for a Bishop or Prince. I looked across at the comparable seat opposite me to which the Lord Mayor of London was being ushered. Perhaps I should have pointed out that I wasn't the High Commissioner. It was a little late for that. Throngs filled the body of the Abbey as the organ played Bach and Pergolesi.

The service was beautiful, the singing of the choir magnificent. Homage was paid to Banting and Best and the work of diabetes specialists around the globe. I was almost relaxed until I realized it was approaching the end and time for me to make an inconspicuous exit. It was not possible.

Two ushers walked up the aisle toward me. One motioned to the Lord Mayor, the other to me. I stood, stumbled over the feet of the choir boy in the aisle, descended the stairs and joined the Lord Mayor. We casually walked down the aisle chatting while a great organ voluntary was playing in the background. I suppose I should have been talking about Banting, Best and diabetes but the time was too short. We shook hands at the door. She got into her Rolls Royce limousine. She didn't offer me a ride assuming, no doubt, that I had my own Rolls. So much for pomp and circumstance. Nobody had mentioned a reception so I neatly skirted the limousine behind hers and headed for the Mall and a contemporary art exhibition at the ICA before heading back to the underground.

As Lauretta and I sat and chatted about the day's happenings, the phone interrupted our conversation.

"Hi, Mom. I'm fine. I'm coming home this weekend. See ya." Click.

"That's strange, David. Matthew's supposed to be at school for games this weekend. He says he's coming home." We looked at each other both thinking the same thing.

"Oh no. Not again." Before we could call the school, the phone rang.

"We're sorry, Doctor Holbrook. Your son is completely unwilling to take instruction. He's leading a number of his classmates astray and flatly denying any wrong-doing. He disappears in the middle of class while the instructor is occupied with other things. He has damaged his trumpet in a fit of anger. He is simply incompatible with our school aims. We will expect you to collect him as soon as possible."

"Does Matthew know of your decision?"

"I have an appointment with him this afternoon." Little did he know that Matthew was planning his exit as he spoke.

"Now what do we do?"

"Lauretta, I don't know what to say. This is the school that had expelled only two students. Can he be that bad?"

Our trip to Somerset to pick up our wayward son was silent as we contemplated his future.

"Hi, Mom and Dad. I've got my stuff ready."

"That isn't all of your 'stuff'?"

"I gave some things away so that we wouldn't have so much to carry. Can we go to Bath?"

"No. This isn't a celebration, Matthew. You've got to get it through your head that school is to prepare you for what you want to do as an adult."

"But Dad, I know what I want to do. I don't need school. If I have to go to school, I'll go in Canada. There are no rules and I can learn what interests me. It won't be like the last time. I'm fourteen now. Soon I'll be sixteen and I won't have to go to school at all."

"But Matthew, let's be realistic. Life has rules. You've got to learn that others might have a better understanding of things than you.

"Dad, they didn't understand me." Lauretta and I looked at each other and shook our heads.

Our trip back to London brought us no closer to a solution. Lauretta and I were overcome with sadness at the reality of having failed again.

"We have to face the facts, Darling. We can all go back to Canada and get family counselling in the hope that we can guide Matthew into being a more conventional kid."

"Yes, but that is punishing all of us. You would have to start up a practice again and we would have to uproot Chris and Sue who are doing so well. I don't think that's the answer."

"Frankly, I think we're going to have to admit failure in dealing with Matthew. He has a 'King' complex. The world revolves around him. I don't know what the answer is and we're never going to know. We could blame ourselves, his natural parents, the schools, but the bottom line is we have to handle it as best we can.

After umpteen phone calls, Matthew was accepted in his previous school near Peterborough, albeit with a number of provisos.

"Matthew, you understand that there are a number of conditions. You must follow the rules. I want you to pay attention in class. You must realize that if you do well in high school, it will help you get into university. You've always said you want to be a veterinarian. It's not going to happen without a high school diploma no matter how smart you are."

"I know all that stuff, Mom. Don't worry. I'm serious now."

On a warm spring day, I embraced Lauretta and hugged Matthew as they boarded their flight to Toronto.

"I'm sorry to do this to you, Darling."

"Stop fretting, David. I did it before. I'll do it again."

A week later, Lauretta returned looking drawn and tense. It was a combination of jet-lag and having been put through the wringer by the school.

"They think we should move back to Canada to keep an eye on him. The school had a social worker sit in on the interview. The implication was that if we cannot or are unwilling to take proper care of Matthew, as they put it, he should be made a ward of the Children's Aid Society. It was so awful, David. I'm supposed to be a mother to each of our children in the same way. There was no recognition of the fact that Matthew is totally different from other children. He doesn't even have anything in common with Chris and Sue. He won't take part in their activities. Are we awful parents? Are we too selfish? I'm lost David."

I put my arm around Lauretta and hugged her.

"Darling, we're doing the best we can. We've discussed it over and over. We can't enable Matthew to derail Chris, Sue and you and me. If the Children's Aid becomes involved, so be it. They're not going to have any better luck dealing with his psychological problems whatever they are, than we're having. We love Matthew and he loves us. That bond can't be broken. He's a loner, he's not psychotic, he isn't schizophrenic. He's not suicidal. It all defies a sound diagnosis. They can say we're terrible parents, selfish and uncaring but in our hearts we know that isn't true."

"The school asked whether he is on ritalin. I told them that he had been and the only difference was that he was wild twenty-four hours a day."

"I've decided that we need a week to get over this. I'm taking you to a Club Med. I've made all the arrangements. Chris and Sue have a school trip to Amsterdam. It's perfect timing. I've even arranged for your leave from work to be extended."

"Oh David. I'm so tired and depressed. Let's wait."

"No, Babe. We're going this week. We're going to be in Paris overnight, just long enough for a couple of pichés of Beaujolais Nouveau."

Arriving in Port St. Louis, in Senegal after a hair-raising flight from Dakar, we were exhausted after spending thirty minutes careening up, down, and sideways through air pockets. Was this really what we needed? I asked myself. Once settled in our adobe-style apartment, I decided it was. The ambience, the food, wine and the private beaches were idyllic. Watching Lauretta frollicking topless in the surf as I lay on the beach resting on my elbows wiped out everything else on my mind. I was convinced that I was in heaven.

Our four years as colonials in London was slowly coming to an end.

"Lauretta we're going to have to think seriously about our next posting. We'll probably have a choice of Ottawa, New Delhi or Mexico City."

"There's no doubt in my mind. I'd hate to go to New Delhi or Ottawa."

"I'll send a fax asking for Mexico City."

The posting ritual, a trial for us every two to four years, always caused major turmoil in our lives. It was starting over with a new home in a different country with local customs to learn.

"Lauretta, I think it would be better for the children if they stayed in school here in England. That would reduce the stress of another move for them. We hope that Matthew will manage in Canada."

"At least they'll be together at camp in the summer."

Two weeks passed before we heard any word from headquarters in Ottawa. The news when it finally did arrive was not good.

"Lauretta, they say we must go to New Delhi or return to Ottawa."

"That sounds like an ultimatum."

"It is."

"Why is it that we can't go to Mexico City?"

"They claim that they need a francophone doctor."

"That's ridiculous. You speak French."

"Yes but I'm not a native speaker." We looked at each other, smiled and said in unison, "Mon Dieu! Let's fight it!"

The next day after mulling over responses together for hours, my petition included my right to be able to use the official language of my choice, a suggestion from one of my Francophone superiors at the High Commission.

"You've got to stress that we both speak Spanish as well as French." Lauretta was enjoying this fight more than I was, knowing the intransigence of the hierarchy when it comes to changing decisions.

Two weeks more passed without a reply.

Finally a missive: 'We have decided to change your posting instructions. You are to be posted to Mexico City. Report for duty August 1.'

Lauretta and I hugged each other and cheered. "We won!"

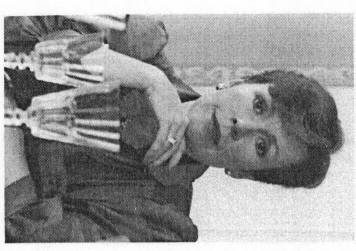

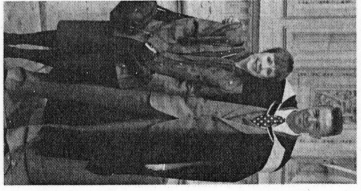

Lauretta's entertainment commitments London   Chris's Graduation from the London School of Economics

4

GRINGOS IN LATIN AMERICA

1

Mexico City, 7:19 a.m. on the 19th of September 1985, the radio died, the lights went out and the bowels of the house erupted.

"My God, it must be an earthquake!" We looked at each other for an instant then jumped up from our breakfast and rushed out the front door into the court-yard. The shaking, like a major epileptic seizure, was worse. The ground was rumbling and shaking under our feet. There was a peculiar roaring sound like a train approaching. The air felt humid and suffocating. The wind blew the trees as if a hurricane was about to strike. They were horizontal, or was the earth vertical? Charley, our Alsatian guard dog, howled and tried to jump over the ten foot out-side wall one instant and then crashed into the plate glass window at the side of the house the next. I tried to grab her but couldn't hold on.

"We're not supposed to be outside!" screamed Lauretta! I could barely hear her. "Quick! Stand in the doorway!" she shouted.

We could see the paintings on the walls flip out from their bases and smash back against the wall. We waited for the windows to buckle and smash. We could hear the dishes rattling and see our breakfast plates slowly sliding to the edge of the table.

Three *minutes* later, an eternity, the tremor slowly stopped. We breathed a sigh of relief and gingerly moved away from the door to survey the damage. We got to the dining room and the rumbling began again. We ran back to the door-frame.

"They must be after-shocks, Lauretta." She wasn't sure whether to believe me. They lasted another minute. Hesitantly, we stepped back to the dining room. The after-shocks continued less violently every few minutes. We tried to collect our wits and assess the state of the house.

The walls had not cracked. There were no broken pipes visable. I couldn't hear water gushing. I didn't smell gas. No power, no phone and a mad dog, but otherwise, 83 Ahuehuetes Norte, our home for the past year, in Bosques de Las Lomas, a suburb of Mexico City, was miraculously unscathed.

"We'd better go to the Embassy, Lauretta. They'll wonder if we're still alive."

We slowly drove down Avenida Reforma, the boulevarded main thoroughfare to central Mexico City. Normally it was crowded with all forms of vehicular traffic and Ruta 100 buses with their vertical exhaust pipes belching black pollutants into the already thickly contaminated air.

"Do you feel an earthquake in the same way if you are in a moving car?"

"I don't know, Darling. I hope we don't find out." We watched the few cars in front of us closely, hoping they would give us adequate warning of any collapse of the road. Fortunately, there were no bridges to cross. There was an eerie silence but no hint of damage around us aside from broken tree limbs and a few bricks in the road. Most houses were surrounded by high walls making it impossible to know what state they were in. We drove past the civic auditorium which appeared undamaged, through Chapultepec Park, and into the Colonia Polanco.

Walking into the Embassy, we were met by George Davids, the communications officer. We lived furthest from the office and at the rate we had driven were the last to arrive.

"In my forty years doing this bloody job, I've never seen this happen. We only have one communication link. That's to Paris, of all places. Paris will have to relay all of our messages to Ottawa. It'll take forever. An avalanche of messages has already arrived. From Ottawa via Paris! The quake was only an hour and a half ago. How does news travel so fast? Where do we start?"

"Slow down! Slow down, George!" The shock had him talking even faster than his usual staccato rate. He was more concerned with his communication links than with what was going on around him.

"Let's divide everything up. Do you want some help in the communication centre?"

"You know nobody is allowed in the centre, David, except the Ambassador and me. The union doesn't permit it. Furthermore, you couldn't run the machines."

"Forget the union. One of us can help you. We can learn, George." There was no answer. He shook his head and walked away.

"Give up, David." Lauretta had a better idea.

"Let's divide this list of Canadians who have signed the visitors' book and take the addresses of those Canadians we know live here. We'll try to make sure all are accounted for. You and I can take the downtown area. Somebody else San Angel and somebody Hipodromo. We'll go door to door."

Lauretta and I got back into the car and divided our list into streets.

"David. What if there's another earthquake?"

"Let's pray that there isn't."

We turned off Reforma into the Zona Rosa to start our search.

At 9 Rio Escondido, Hector Rodriquez was sweeping the walkway in front of his home. He likely always did it at this time. It was shortly after nine on what had turned out to be a lovely sunny morning. He swept, oblivious to the mass destruction surrounding him. He thought nothing of the weird creaking of timbers in the buildings on either side. According to our records, Anita Brown, his grand-niece and her friend Carla Andreolis from Toronto had been staying with Hector for the past two weeks. They'd come to the Embassy and signed the book. In fact, it was a late Friday afternoon and they sat with the group of us enjoying 'Happy Hour'.

"Good morning, Señor Rodriquez. I'm David Holbrook from the Canadian Embassy. Are your niece and her friend staying with you?"

"*¿Disculpe, Señor?* Hector cupped his hand to his ear. He hadn't heard a word. I loudly repeated my query.

"*Oh no Señor*. They left for Oaxaca two days ago."

Hector's neighbours' homes were reduced to rubble as was most of the street. Inexplicably, Hector's home was spared. Hector, now in his eighties, his blue eyes foggy from cataracts, was unaware of what was going on around him. Surely he must have wondered why there was so little activity on the street? The roadway beyond his house was virtually blocked by chunks of bricks and concrete.

The house of Maria and Jorge Ojeda, Hector's neighbours at number 11, was flattened like a pancake. It was difficult even to know where the door and windows were. We stood on the sidewalk and shouted their names as Hector Rodriguez stood on his swept sidewalk. We listened and heard nothing but the grinding of timber and metal. There was no reply.

"There's nothing we can do Darling, without more help."

Driving further was impossible because of the rubble on the road.

"God, David, you're going to have to back up a long way. Do you want me to clear a path?"

"No, No. Let's turn around and try another street."

For reasons known only to nature, this pattern was repeated all morning. Some streets were virtually unscathed while others were impassable.

There appeared to be a total absence of rescue crews or help of any kind. We felt so useless. It was a sickening feeling as we knocked on doors not knowing what to expect. Those that answered were fine, all busily sweeping up broken crockery and shattered windows. We found no Canadians. We hoped those on our list were safe somewhere.

We drove down Avenida Reforma toward the Zocalo and suddenly realized the damage in the centre of the city was even more horrendous. The structure, adjacent to the *Excelsior* building, home of the largest daily newspaper, was literally hanging out into the street on a weird angle. The building next door had whole floors accordioned into each other. The floors of the building had gone from twelve feet apart to twelve inches apart. We were both dumbfounded. People were milling about in an aimless fashion in shock.

"Do you think that building was evacuated in time?"

"Oh Lauretta, I don't know how. I think it would be impossible. Just look at it. The building must have been packed with people who had just arrived for work."

There was a weird silence broken every few moments by a crunch and puff of dust as buildings subsided a little further into the earth.

"Perhaps rescue crews are around the back on Constituyentes. You know when you think about it, the slightest noise or movement might cause the building to collapse on top of us."

"Look at Avenida Juarez. That pile of rubble was a High School." Smoke and flames were billowing into the sky as we stared in disbelief. Students wandered around, arms around each other.

"David, we can't go further. Let's get out of here quietly, so we don't disturb any structure that's about to fall down."

"Why don't we try to get to Tlaltelolco?"

It took us half an hour to travel half a dozen blocks. Buildings on both sides of the road were jarred off their foundations, if not in heaps on the roadway. People sat on the curb some with bandaged cuts and most coated in grey plaster dust.

"I can't see the Televisa tower. Could it have collapsed?"

"I don't know but this is hopeless. Let's go back to the Embassy, David. It's hours past lunch. I'm starving and you must be too."

As we entered the building, we were met by the harried communicator, "Lauretta, your children's school in England called Ottawa because the television news in Britain had reported that Mexico City had been largely destroyed. We didn't know when you would be back, so, we sent word to Paris to call the school in England to assure them that you and David are safe. Do you want to send a personal telex?"

By this time we were both in a daze, partly from exhaustion and partly shock, as the size of the catastrophe slowly sank in.

"Yes please, George." Lauretta and George set off for the telecommunications room, the inner sanctum.

"Darling, tell them even the dog is okay." I sat for a moment in the foyer thinking of what to do next.

The Ambassador's secretary, Judy Bell, came out of her office and called my name.

"Will you please come to a meeting in the Ambassador's office, David?" Ambassador Gould had had a number of ambassadorial postings prior to Mexico, and his calm demeanor leant an air of control to this chaotic situation.

"Come in, David, and sit down." Gilles Lefevre, the political officer and Andy Stinson, the commercial officer, and the rest of the post management team, were already there.

"We would like you to get some information for us, David. The official word is that many have been injured and the damage is heavy, but the government says they are handling the situation well. We need to know what the Red Cross assessment of the situation is and what they think would be the most needed supplies that Canada could send. While you are there, ask them for an ID badge. You're going to need it." I left for the Red Cross office, three blocks from the Embassy, on foot.

Jaime Diaz, the Red Cross Society Area director, sat at his desk resting his chin on his hands looking down blankly at his desk. He outlined the scene for me.

"Despite the fact that Mexico City has had numerous earthquakes, nobody was prepared for this. The quake has been recorded at 8.3 on the Richter scale. The entire Nuevo León housing project, buildings of ten stories, have simply tipped over on each other. Five thousand people are unaccounted for!" If five thousand people were presumed dead, I couldn't imagine how many injured there must be. Jaime continued, "People are digging in the rubble with their bare hands trying to find relatives. Placido Domingo's aunts lived in the building. He has been to every government agency trying to borrow a crane to lift the slabs of concrete. He apparently got one from Pemex, the state oil company. Buildings with the slightest aftershock are still collapsing all around them. The National Health Hospital and the Juarez Hospital the two largest hospitals in the city have collapsed, crushing patients and staff and the entire fleet of ambulances." He gave his impression of how this had happened.

"The contractors have simply stolen materials by altering plans and using a fraction of the steel and cement required. This has resulted in the buildings collapsing with the slightest quake. Not even the hospitals are built to the government standard. It's criminal! Everybody knows it's happening but nothing is done about it. Now ten, maybe twenty thousand people have died." Jaime was becoming more and more flushed as his anger boiled over. "Skyscrapers in the Zocalo banged together. Segments of floors have been knocked off."

"What can Canada send that would be most helpful?" He sighed and leaned forward on his desk, palms of his hands flat against his forehead.

"You can send blankets and tents to the Red Cross depot at the airport. We'll distribute them for you."

"Great. We've already requested them. I was thinking of additional things that would make a difference."

"If there are any ambulances that we could borrow, I'll try and make sure they're returned. The Americans will send medical teams and the Mexicans will think it's an invasion. The Russians will send a million aspirin tablets. The Germans will send dogs and their trainers to dig in the rubble and they'll have a battle to get visas. David, it'll be a political fight to see who will get their name in the newspaper first to show how generous they are in another's hour of need. Forget the glory, David. It'll be old news soon. Plan some good long term aid: equipped clinics, for example. We have no idea how extensive the damage is outside the city. The Mexicans are going to need clinics, not just in the next few days, but for weeks and years to come."

Returning to the Embassy in the early evening with my information, I was stopped in the hall by Judy Bell. "The Ambassador would like you to go to the airport, David, to meet a Canadian military cargo plane with a load of blankets and tents. Try to expedite their clearance. Also, a team of firemen and their dogs are on their way from Edmonton. We told them not to come unless they got permission from the Mexican Embassy in Ottawa. They didn't wait. By the way, Lauretta has gone back out with two other spouses and another list of addresses."

I was worried about Lauretta being on her own in case there was another quake and depressed about Jaime Diaz's claims about the political overtones affecting aid in a catastrophe. I had had no idea that this went on. I realized how naive I was.

The airport was chaotic. Tourists were milling about. Airline personnel tried to help, but with little to do as there were no commercial aircraft coming or going. With difficulty, I found the gate leading to the cargo depot on the other side of the airport. A guard opened the gate for a US Embassy van in front of me. I pulled up as close to it as I could, intending to follow it onto the runway leading to the cargo area.

"*¿Dondé esta su permiso?*" I stopped and tried to think of a way to con the guard and get myself through the gate.

"I'm with him," I said as I pointed at the van in front of me while I fingered my laminated official-looking Red Cross card.

"*Okay Señor. Pasale.*"

The cargo area was crammed with aid workers and various embassy officials waiting for aircraft. There were no customs people in sight.

"David, isn't that the Hercules from Canada?" a US Embassy colleague said as he came up beside me.

"It beats me, I don't know much about aircraft."

"It's got a maple leaf illuminated on the tail."

I walked out to the area where the Canadian forces Hercules had parked for unloading. Just as promised, they were piling up the palettes of tents and blankets, as well as two portable field hospitals complete with stretchers and bags of intravenous fluids. They even had their own forklift truck to move everything. I was proud of being a Canuck at that moment.

"Where do we put this stuff, Doc?"

I looked over my shoulder expecting to see some diligent customs official heading my way. There was none in sight.

"Let's put it in the Red Cross warehouse. They'll know what to do with it." I pointed to the well-marked building behind me. "Can I get you a place to stay the night?"

"No thanks, it's just a turnaround." I smiled at the jargon as I made my way back to the car thinking who in their right mind would stay in case there was another quake.

Lauretta was waiting for me in the foyer as I stepped into the embassy. We hugged each other so happy to be in one piece.

"We found an injured old woman sitting on the sidewalk in the rubble on Constituyentes. We took her to the hospital that the people on the street told us was the closest. They wouldn't take her because they said she wasn't sick enough! Furthermore, she wouldn't be able to pay. They sent us to the Escuardo Hospital in another district. They're putting patients on blankets on the floor. One teen-age girl, obviously in shock, hasn't spoken. I sat with her and kept telling her everything would be okay. A single tear finally trickled down her cheek. David, she had lost a leg. They have a coat hanger on a nail on the wall to hold her IV drip." Lauretta's eyes filled with tears.

"There were people of all ages with broken bones, head injuries, and their x-ray machine was broken. It was incredible to see these people working so hard with so little. As I was leaving, an old couple who looked like campesiños stopped me to ask if I could help them find their daughter. I didn't know what to do. I wrote down all the hospitals I could think of and then made sure they talked to a nursing sister. I should have taken them from hospital to hospital but they disap-peared. We have to help that hospital, David. Can we get them some cots and IV fluids?"

"Sweetheart, let's both go to the Ambassador and ask him to request supplies on the next Canadian forces flight. Tell him what you just told me. We might even get a portable X-ray machine for them."

It was almost four in the morning and we'd forgotten about Charley. We didn't even know if our power was back on. "Let's go home."

As we drove carefully back up Reforma, we couldn't help but think back on the trials of our first year in Mexico: the living room window being shot out, the razor blades in our mailbox, our tires slashed. The torment stopped only after we painted a huge red maple leaf on our gate establishing the fact that we were Cana-dians and not Yankees. The neighbours soon rallied around us and the local police, who cruised the neighbourhood in their Volkswagen beetles, were now our protectors, no doubt helped by our healthy Christmas cash 'mordida'. It was an improvement on the single guard sitting by the front door with his pearl han-dled revolver at the ready. We had been afraid that he might mistakenly shoot one of the children on their visits from school.

Earlier in the year, a tremendous explosion at the Pemex plant had cut off the gas supply for our appliances. Lauretta resorted to the 'helpless, hopeless female' role to persuade the few suppliers still in existence to bring gas to our roof-top tanks. Macho Mexican men couldn't handle Lauretta's pleading and invariably relented, filling the tanks under the watchful eyes of Charley. The problem was that Charley went mad when she saw them. She barked so hard, they were petri-fied. Lauretta held on to her with difficulty until they were finished."

"Senora. El perro morde?"

"No se, Senor." Lauretta had never seen Charley bite but she was her sole protection against the hombres in charge of the gas supply. But now we had to contend with this catastrophe.

After a second twenty hour day, my third started on a different note. The Ambassador met me in the hall.

"We have a visitor from the Prime Minister's Office. I would like you to take him to the Zocalo so he can take some pictures of the earthquake damage to take back to Ottawa. It will reinforce our requests for additional aid."

Expecting the usual pin-stripe-suited lawyer, I was surprised when the Ambassador introduced me to an ageing, paunchy, sloppily dressed man with bare feet and sandals. He was carrying an inexpensive instamatic camera.

The visitor, a Doctor Patel, piped up immediately.

"Please, I would like to go right away. This is an important mission."

"Of course, Doctor. I'm David Holbrook. I'm the doctor here at the Embassy." He reluctantly shook my hand with a weak, clammy handshake. Not a good start.

"What field of medicine are you in, Doctor Patel?"

"I'm a specialist working in the Prime Minister's office."

As no more information was forthcoming, I gave up. It was useless to try querying someone from the Prime Minister's Office.

For a change, I had gone back to wearing a suit and tie. It's the normal business garb in Mexico City. As I ushered Doctor Patel to the car, he stated that he would sit in the backseat. What a twit, I mumbled to myself. I can play chauffeur but I don't have the proper headgear. That will be a black mark beside my name in the PM's Office.

"I'm going to take you down Reforma, the main boulevard, to the *Excelsior* newspaper building. The building next to it, directly in front of us on the right, has been virtually untouched since the quake as rescuers are still hoping there will be survivors."

"No, I want to go further." Doctor Patel ordered from the backseat.

I weaved around piles of rubble finally reaching the turn to Alameda Park and the Zocalo, the main square of the city. An army officer orderd me to stop.

"Park the car over there if you are planning to stop. Otherwise turn around and get out of the area."

"I'm from the Prime Minister of Canada's Office," piped up Doctor Patel.

"I'm sorry, sir, those are my orders."

"How rude. He can't tell me what to do." He talked to himself loud enough for me to hear.

"Doctor Patel, he's not rude. He *can* tell you what to do. He's in charge here. This is where we're stopping." I got out of the car and began to walk to the corner of Constituyentes and the junction with Reforma. From the corner of my eye, I could see Patel still sitting in the car waiting for me to open his door I suppose. I left him to figure it out.

Standing on the corner, I found it strange that the military officers next to me were dressed in full regalia, even white gloves. I was surprised when a Cadillac limousine turned the corner and stopped in front of me. The backdoor was opened and a woman in a beautiful yellow Chanel-like suit stepped out and came directly to me. She put out her hand.

"Good morning, I'm Nancy Reagan."

"How do you do. I'm David Holbrook."

I was quickly surrounded by embarrassed secret service officers and the press as I stood stunned. My new friend, Nancy, was quickly ushered away to be greeted by the actual United States Ambassador, a former movie star, and his wife, an opera diva (as in soap opera).

I casually walked around the corner and back to the car where Doctor Patel was waiting for me. He had missed a great photo opportunity.

"I would like to return to the Embassy now," Patel stated in a pompous voice.

No sooner had we entered the Embassy than I was paged.

"David we've just had a urgent call from the Canadian firemen. They're digging with their dogs in a building downtown and think they have found three Canadian students. Please take a driver and see if you can find out what's happened. They were last heard from on Escandido."

I grimaced, remembering the rubble Lauretta and I tried to get through a couple of days ago. I grabbed my stethoscope and blood pressure cuff and ran to the car only to hear Doctor Patel shouting at me to wait. He chugged to the car and got into the back seat. Kevin Saunders, one of the consuls in the office, joined us.

"Doctor, I can't go any further. The road is totally blocked." Guillermo, our driver, had managed to get further than Lauretta and I had, but we were still a long seven blocks from where the Canadians were digging. Kevin and I ran the remaining distance. I was not a runner and had trouble keeping up with Kevin. Glass and bricks littered the road. Doctor Patel was nowhere to be seen.

"The rescue team went in there." The volunteers on the street pointed at what had been the entrance. Kevin and I looked at the hole in the side of the hotel building, the floors squashed into each other. I couldn't even tell how tall the building had been. It was like a cake that had collapsed in the middle.

"Is the building stable?" I asked stupidly.

"As long as there isn't another earthquake. Don't shout because the building next door is not safe. The less noise the better."

"How many people are in there?" Kevin sensibly tried to confirm what we knew.

"There are two Canadians and a paramedic. They have two dogs." The volunteers were very helpful.

"Do you think one of us should go in and try to help?

"It's too risky. Sit here, and wait. I'm sure they're okay and will be out soon. It's likely they just don't want to make any extra noise. The dogs can detect voices if there is no extraneous noise."

There was still no sign of Doctor Patel. We sat in silence, hard for me because I talk too much when under stress.

"There's someone coming out now." An Alsatian crawled from the hole coated with white dust, a rope attached to his harness. Next, one of the fireman coated like the dog. Together, they looked like a Segal sculpture.

"We've found the bodies of two young women. Where is the temporary morgue?" The first man out asked in a raspy voice spitting muck out of his mouth. "The lad's still alive but he's pinned and we're going to have to amputate his arm."

"I'll find out where to take the body bags." I stumbled over the rubble to the corner, two blocks down the street, feeling sick at the thought of the young people in the bags and, my God, the amputation. Do they have a saw? Oh God, how awful. I was in a cold sweat thinking about it.

The two policemen at the corner of Avenida Juarez were directing the rescue teams in the area.

"¿Donde esta....el morgue?" They didn't know what the hell I was talking about. I didn't have my dictionary. I pointed down the street and convinced a policeman to follow me until I could see a body bag that had been pulled out of the hole.

"Ah. Señor. El depósito de cadáveres. Ahi." He pointed at a large building opposite the police booth. By now, the remaining Canadian, their dogs and the paramedic had emerged, the two body bags had been pulled out. The young student was on a litter with an IV drip, bandaged leaving only his head visible. I managed to get my blood pressure cuff on his remaining arm. The paramedic had a tourniquet on the stump and the vessels clamped to reduce the bleeding.

"Kevin, I think I'll stay here and then go to the hospital with him so we don't lose track of where he is. We've done what we can, here. Why don't you go back to the Embassy and tell them what's happened. See if you can find Doctor Patel. Please call Lauretta if the phone is working and tell her that everything is okay and I'll be back as soon as I can."

The trip to the Humana Hospital was nerve-wracking. The young man whose name I didn't know, stared straight ahead in shock, eyes wide open. I'd swear he was dead but I could still get a pulse. What was I going to say to his parents? Worse still, what would I say to the parents of the two young women who are dead? I gently massaged his head as I thought of the dreaded conversations.

After collecting my stethoscope and blood pressure cuff, I went to the doctors' lounge in the hospital and found a working phone. The only thing I could do was phone the emergency Embassy number and dictate a telex to George to send to Ottawa. I felt sick as I hitched a ride back to the Embassy. Sick with anguish for the young man and the parents. Sick with fatigue and desperately needing to be home with Lauretta.

On my arrival at the Embassy, I heard my name called. Gilles Lefevre looked tense. Doctor Patel was in my office, sweating profusely, mopping his brow. His handkerchief looked like it had been dropped in the dirt.

"That was the most irresponsible performance by a physician that I have ever seen," began Doctor Patel, "I am going to report you to the Medical Council and to the Prime Minister's Office."

I was flabbergasted by the outburst. If it hadn't been for the fatigue, I would have laughed. I felt myself flushing with anger.

"What are you talking about?"

"You didn't carry your black medical bag! You were totally unprepared! I have not seen you do one thing that merits your position here. Sit down! I am waiting for the Ambassador! I will have you sent back to Canada and expelled from the service!"

My head was reeling.

"Listen!" I shouted, "You sit down and shut up! I'm not going to put up with this nonsense from the likes of you, you arrogant jerk."

Surprisingly, he did sit down, sputtering as he lowered his flabby body into the chair. Gilles, surprised at my atypical outburst broke into the discussion.

"David, we'll get this settled. Why don't you go home? I'm sure Lauretta is eager to see you."

"I'll take you home, sir," piped up Guillermo, who was standing in the hall. "Your wife has taken the car."

A few hours later, Lauretta answered a knock at our door. "David, the Ambassador's driver has just delivered a note."

Dear David,

I have spoken to Doctor Patel and explained that conditions overseas are very different for doctors in the service. He was not happy with the explanation but, as far as I am concerned, there is no need for any action on my part. We appreciate what you are doing and stand by you 100%.

You will be interested to know that the Prime Minister's Office has never heard of a Doctor Patel. How he got here at government expense, nobody knows. He has been told to leave the country.

You don't have to worry about anything.

Gould

"Now, David, just calm down. You've been vindicated." Lauretta put her arm around me.

"I hope he didn't forget his Kodak Instamatic, the pompous ass!"

Three months later, as our lives slowly returned to normal and we awaited the children on their Christmas break from school in Britain and Canada, we sat in our den with a glass of wine and looked back on the aftermath of the earthquake. I thought of the fruitless meetings, the times that I accompanied the Ambassador to pointless high level government discussions with ministers, the demands for aid that seemed to me unrelated to any relief operation, the political manoeuvring and photo-op sessions that served no purpose.

We did have happy memories despite the terrible circumstances. The fact that we were able to get medical equipment and supplies for two hospitals that previously had only makeshift facilities was a joy. The neighbourhoods in some of the poorest areas of Mexico City celebrated the opening of their clinics, supplied by Canada, with unforgettable street parties. The resilience of the populace would be one of the indelible memories of Mexico. The suffering, with estimates of thirty thousand casualties, left few unscathed.

2

Chris and Sue were always the first to arrive at Christmas. Now both seventeen, Chris appeared to have grown another six inches and had to bend over to give his mother a kiss. Sue was also taller, slim and gorgeous. They were happy to be home where they had many friends who invited them to dance clubs for teens in Techamachalco, a neighbouring suburb. Their friends' parents sent a driver and bodyguard with them to ensure their safety.

Matthew, at sixteen, was more interested in exploring but unfortunately we didn't have a household staff to accompany him. We did make sure he had mugger money in case he was accosted on the street.

Gumercinda had worked in our home since our arrival in Mexico City. She returned to her village after the earthquake and had now reappeared two months later, telling us that her family would like us to come to their Posada at Advent. She wanted us to bring our children. We were honoured to be invited.

On the appointed day the car crammed, with Lauretta, Chris, Sue and Matthew, gifts and Gumercinda squeezed into the seat next to me, we sailed down the Puebla highway.

"*Aquí, Señor!*" As she had not said anything until then, it was a surprise. Somehow, we avoided the ditch as we swung into a gravel road that took us miles into the interior.

"*Aquí, Señor.*" Another swift manoeuvre took us onto a grass path that did not see many cars. By now we were in a forest. At the top of a hill we came into a clearing surrounded on all sides by pine trees. In the middle of the clearing was a rectangular red mud-brick building with a flat roof. One orphaned deciduous tree with bare spindly branches stood adjacent to the mud hut. A grove of large yucca plants with tall sharp green leaves was thriving in the sandy soil. The air was chilly but smelled fresh. We enjoyed the aroma of pine and grasses after the oily pollution of the city. We bundled ourselves up from the cold wind.

"*Disculpe Señor y Señora.*" Gumercinda backed away from the car. She told us that she would return with her family and disappeared into the pine forest. An hour went by and dusk brought a bitterly cold wind. The hut with its dirt floor was empty. Without climbing the tree or marching off into the woods, there was little else to investigate. Chris and Sue, got the huge star-shaped piñata out of the back of the car and held it up while Matthew climbed the lone tree and attached it to a branch making sure the multi-coloured streamers were straight.

"Dad look!" From unseen paths, emerging from the forest were adults and children coming from all directions. Some pregnant women on horseback, old men with home-fashioned canes and crumpled straw hats, women carrying babies in slings around their shoulders, wrapped in multicoloured serapes, the children and adults in brown raw wool ponchos. Most had bare feet. The children all had runny noses, a yellow crust around their nostrils.

We watched, intrigued by the size of the 'family' of thirty of all ages. We bowed, as they did in a mass greeting.

"Now what?" whispered Lauretta. The car was packed with Christmas gifts carefully wrapped by Chris, Sue and Matthew.

"Do we have enough?" whispered Sue. "Where should we put them?"

While we tried to make up our minds, teens in the group had collected firewood and started a bonfire which added a shimmering light to the very dark evening. Each person was given a burning piece of wood to act as a torch. A procession was started. It wound into the building which we now realized was a chapel. Gumercinda, who had been in the background until now, asked us to join in and follow the group into the chapel. Torch in hand, we walked around the interior twice singing what I guessed was a hymn, then around the outside of the chapel and back inside repeating the course. This time, everyone knelt in pew-less rows. The clay floor was cold and damp on our knees. More songs were sung and then silence. We filed out of the chapel. The sky was a mass of stars.

Next, the *piñata*. The smaller children were blindfolded and with the help of their taller siblings, attacked the swaying sparkling bloated star with flailing sticks. It lasted only a matter of minutes, breaking open after being blasted by a mighty blow from one of the smallest girls. It was mass hysteria, with kids and young adults scrambling for the candies flying in all directions from the smashed piñata. Two children brought candies to Sue, Matthew and Chris, a great lesson in sharing with the few gringos they had ever seen. Finally, it was time for our young to distribute the gifts that they had wrapped so carefully. We watched them as they tried to keep tabs on the number of children left in line. They hoped they had enough gifts for all.

A horse pulling a primitive cart came out of the woods. It was loaded with clay pots full of frijoles refritos, refried beans being a staple in the rural diet. There was some kind of mole or salsa. Chris and Sue looked anxious. Not Matthew. He had few qualms about eating anything.

"How are we supposed to eat this?" asked Chris.

"Just watch what they do," said Matthew with a shrug.

With plastic spoons from the car, we shovelled some of each cauldron onto tortillas, rolled them up and ate enough to be polite.

"Remember, drink only what's in a can that you have opened yourself. The water and juice are loaded with bacteria that our systems will not be accustomed to."

As the evening went on, it became frigid. The children not only had bare feet but thin cotton tops. Gumercinda announced that they must now go home.

"Señora, I will return to the city in two weeks." She got into the horse drawn cart, waved and disappeared into the darkness.

"It's fortunate I have a good sense of direction," I muttered to Lauretta. "Otherwise we might be wandering around the countryside for days trying to find our way home."

"You should put one of the Canadian-supplied clinics in their village, David. Did you see the state of those children, and the young pregnant teens, and the adults with the hacking cough? I hope they don't all have tuberculosis."

"I'll have to come back and see where they get their water. I hope they don't have to carry it for miles. The clinic will need a water supply."

The next day, at home after our Advent posada, the children were eager to get out their Christmas decorations.

Posada near Puebla Mexico

Opening of Canadian donated clinic in Guerrero State

Posada near Puebla Mexico

Xochimilcho, the flower market in the south of the city, was the only place to get a tree. We went through the groves of living tall pines at the back of the market looking at hundreds of cut spruce and scotch pine, until finally one was chosen that everybody was happy with. Chris and Matthew were left to load it into the borrowed van.

"We have to get some noche buenas as well." Lauretta commented.

"What colour poinsettias do you want? Look at the huge red ones."

"Señora, You must take these noche buenas."

"There are far too many."

"It's the same price, Señora." Rather than bicker, Lauretta agreed. Sue took the huge flat to the van.

"Oh, look at these azaleas. Let's get some of them too."

"How are we going to get all this stuff in the van?" I asked.

By the time it was all loaded, I could barely see out the windows.

"Dad, we want to set up the tree and do the decorating."

"Okay. Okay. You won't get an argument from me."

"Don't forget you have to go to the San Juan Market to get the turkey,"

Accompanied by Matthew, I arrived at the market assuming it was going to be an easy transaction.

"*Oh no, Señor.* You didn't tell me you wanted a turkey."

"*Si Señor.* I did ask you last week. You wrote it in that book. It's in the order book sitting on the chopping block right there."

"*Oh no Señor.* You didn't come early enough. The turkeys are all gone." I put my hands on my hips in anger, and stared at him in disbelief. He turned and shouted at a butcher friend.

"*Amigo*, do you have a turkey?"

"*Si, mi amigo. Uno.*"

"*Señor*, it's for you." They laughed. I didn't. It was cheaper than the original was to be but looked as though it had been run over by a truck. There didn't seem to be a breast bone. Ah, a turkey was a turkey.

"Dad. Dad. I found one. It might be better." I took the one I had and followed Matthew to his find.

"That's a goose, Sweet. I think we'll stick with what we've got."

"I'm going to get some extras. What's this?"

"It's jicama. You peel it and eat it raw. Get one if you want."

"Ugh. Let's get away from the fish. I have refused to eat fish since Trinidad."

"Matthew, I thought you liked fish. You said you eat everything."

"Oh yeah, Dad. You eat it. I bet Chris and Sue don't eat it either."

I shrugged and didn't admit that he was correct. When I got my poor excuse for a turkey home, Lauretta was amused.

"David, this is going to be hellish to cook. Between the altitude altering the cooking time and the size and shape of the thing, I give you the job of cooking it. Pull out *Julia Child*. She'll have some ideas." I laughed and looked at my mutilated bird.

"Maybe I can surgically repair it."

Sue offered to help by assisting with the trussing and the preparation of the stuffing.

Chris stormed into the kitchen swearing at Matthew who had locked the door of Chris's room. I could see Matthew from the kitchen window hitting a croquet ball around the garden.

"Matthew isn't in your room. Maybe the wind blew it shut."

"We'll get a ladder and you can climb in the window. But you'll have to wait until we're finished here."

When I finally got to walk around to the modern orange trapezoidal house behind ours, the servant gladly lent us an extension ladder. The problem was quickly resolved.

The Christmas dinner met with the approval of the family which put me in the unenviable position of likely having to do it again next year.

Matthew home at Ahuehuetes Mexico

Sue, Lauretta and Chris at home in Mexico

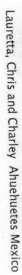

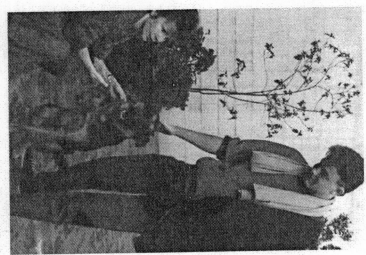

Lauretta, Chris and Charley Ahuehuetes Mexico

Chris and Charley

3

My first day back at work started with a request for an urgent visit to Peru.

I left Lauretta with the job of marshalling the children and their belongings back to the airport for their return to school.

I was met at the airport in Lima by the Canadian consul.

"We have a medical problem with a Canadian who happens to be residing, at the moment, in jail. I will take you to the jail but they will only let one Embassy official in. They requested an Embassy doctor. You'll be on your own."

"Thanks, Jean." The thirty-something consular officer, Jean Clermont always appeared tense and twitchy. I knew he was hoping that I wouldn't refuse which would leave him no alternative but to go himself.

My frequent immigration medical trips to Latin America from Mexico always involved some bizarre twist which added credence to the strange writings of Gabriel Garcia Marquez or the paintings of Orosco. Peru was no exception.

The prison in a dirt poor suburb, was surrounded by flimsy shacks put together with pieces of wood, the occasional concrete block or brick and corrugated metal sheeting. Dust rose everywhere. Stand-pipes were the only source of water and the ditch running down the side of the road served as a communal latrine. The stench was nauseating. Children with few clothes, oblivious to the stink, ran around chasing rolling rubber tires, their hair gray with dust.

The prison was a daunting site pushed into the side of a hill, a medieval 'castle' with turrets at the corners and high concrete walls. We drove up to solid steel gates which blocked any view of the inside from the dirt bowl below. Four white-helmeted army security guards armed with sub-machine guns checked our credentials and waved us inside. There, an armed guard asked us to wait while our credentials were confirmed again.

"We would like you to leave your passport and wallet with the security guard at the desk in the guard house over there." I felt as though I was being checked in as an inmate. I was given a large brass disk in order to claim back my valuables.

"Sir, I apologize but we will have to frisk you. It's policy. Hands up, legs apart." This was a first.

"You may now pass through the gate to your right. They're expecting you."

There was a small door cut into the solid twelve foot steel doors with razor wire curled along the top. A guard slid the bolt across the door. I went in alone and the door banged shut behind me. I heard the bolt sliding into its socket.

Once I was inside the solid door, an electronically controlled link fence slid open. I stepped over the second threshold. That gate clanged shut behind me.

"Welcome, Doctor. I'm Jorge Cruz. I'm president of the prisoners' executive," I smiled and shook hands. "Come with me." I followed this tall, brown-haired man dressed in a brown tweed jacket, blue open-neck shirt and grey flannels. I quickly realized that there were no guards inside the gates I had just entered. I could be here forever and no one could do anything about it. We walked through a barren patch of packed clay which lead to one of the two large concrete buildings.

"This way, please." We went into the main cell-block and climbed stairs to the second level. The damp stale smell of tobacco gave me an instant sore throat. Half-way down the block of cells, all with doors open, we entered a cell with a picnic table in the middle and a bare light bulb hanging from the ceiling. It cast eerie shadows as it swayed back and forth. Seated around the table were the other five members of the executive, all dressed in their Sunday best—or was this the uniform? As I stepped into the cell it was reassuring to see the bars behind me remain open.

"Doctor, you're from the Canadian Embassy. Is that correct?"

"Yes."

"We have one of your fellow Canadians here who is too sick to be in this prison. We want him moved to a hospital as soon as possible." That was blunt. I obviously was not being given any choice.

"What's the matter with him?"

"He has a God-awful cough and he is spitting up a lotta stuff. We don't want him here." I looked to my left at the balding heavy-set man speaking, his striped shirt stretched over his corpulence and bare ham-like tattooed arms. The others nodded their approval.

"May I see him?"

"Follow me, Doctor."

We went back down the stairs to the last cell on the lower level. "This is George Mayler." Seated on a bench at the back of the dank cell was a gaunt man with a scruffy beard whose age might have been forty, maybe fifty. It was impossible to guess. He did look ill. His skin was gray and face drawn.

"Hello, I'm David Holbrook from the Canadian Embassy. I'm a doctor and I understand that you're sick." We shook hands. His was weak and sweaty. He looked at me and then at Jorge, who made no move to leave us alone.

"When did you get sick?"

"I guess it started about a year ago but it has been worse in the past month or two."

"How long have you been here?"

"Three years now."

"I understand you have a bad cough."

"Yes and I've been losing a lot of weight."

"How long have you had the dark patch on your forehead?"

"A couple of months."

"May I look at your legs?" His legs were like matchsticks with balloons at the ankles.

"Oh yes, they've been swelling too." I pushed on his ankle. It left a noticeable dint. I ran my hand over the nubbly purple patch on his calf.

"We're going to get you to a hospital as soon as we can, so take it easy. We'll try to make the arrangements quickly."

"Doc., I do nothing else but take it easy." He looked down dejectedly. Jorge and I left him in his misery and went back to the 'conference' cell.

"Thank you Doctor. You'll see that he's moved quickly?" I nodded.

Jorge and I returned to the main gate and shook hands. I stepped through the first gate. A grill opened on the small door as the gate snapped shut behind me. I held up my brass ID disc and stepped over the threshold. I breathed a sigh of relief. I had just been behind bars with murderers, muggers and misfits of every kind and had survived. I retrieved my belongings and gave up the large brass disc. It would have been a good souvenir.

I didn't have the nerve to tell them that George had AIDS with Kaposi's sarcoma and to complicate matters likely tuberculosis. Be damned if I was going to go back with the news, when it's confirmed. Maybe that's the real reason they wanted him out of the prison. I wondered how many of his fellow prisoners were HIV positive. I was surprised that he was still alive if they did suspect him of spreading HIV.

I was relieved to get an appointment with the director of the University Hospital.

"Doctor Guzman. It's kind of you to see me on such short notice." Doctor Guzman's stocky frame was stuffed into a buttoned white lab coat, many pens protruding from his upper coat pocket, ballpoint marks on the coat. When he stood up in his platform shoes, he was still short.

"Doctor Holbrook, how can I help you?"

"The Canadian Embassy has asked me to see a sick Canadian presently living in Lima. I would like to send him home to Canada but he will need hospitalization until I can make the necessary arrangements."

"What's his diagnosis?"

"He probably has tuberculosis."

"Ummm. Well, we could take him for a few days, but no longer."

"We'd be very grateful."

"Send him to the Admitting Department this afternoon."

"Many thanks. The Embassy is making flight arrangements for him. It should only be a short time before we can reach his relatives."

"Oh…and the Embassy will pay the hospital bill?"

"Yes, of course. The consul will make the arrangements." You put me through the jail scene, Jean. You sort out the hospital bill.

Lima was always grey when I appeared. A fog rolled in off the Pacific, coating Miraflores, the affluent area of the city where the Canadian Embassy was located, with a cool damp pall. My small hotel, away from the posh tourist establishments, was thought to be less likely a target for the Shining Path guerrillas, eager to disrupt the tourist trade and the Peruvian economy in general. I still crossed the road when I saw a bank with a cash stop, another favourite target.

I was usually on my way home to Mexico from La Paz in Bolivia when I stopped in Peru. I always felt as though I had the bends, moving from 15,000 feet to sea level in one swoop. At least this time I was not short of breath.

After completing my medical clinic at the Embassy and sorting out the medical emergency at the prison, and with the rest of the day to spare before my early morning flight, I decided that I should see more of Lima before moving on to Bogotá and finally home to Mexico City.

"Is the Gold Museum very far?"

"No sir. Just follow this map and you will come to it quite soon."

I looked at the small map the hotel clerk had given me and the problems of scale and distance didn't occur to me. I decided not to take my camera or much of value. I'd heard horror stories of Lima and didn't want to be a statistic. I made sure I had enough money to satisfy at least one mugger and set out as the day brightened. Leaving Miraflores, I crossed the Panamerican highway and noticed a distinct change in the neighbourhood from rich to poor, to poorer still. The sidewalk served as part of each home. Children poured out of the houses, and took over the block with rusty bikes, old rubber tires, skipping ropes and hop-scotch drawn on the sidewalk with chips of brick. The parents sat on the doorsteps or leaned back against the walls on teetering chrome chairs with torn vinyl seats, stuffing oozing out, watching the goings-on. Some had chrome-legged tables on the pavement for outdoor eating and maybe schoolwork.

I was so engrossed in the street scene that I suddenly realized that the sidewalk was gradually narrowing. What I thought would be a twenty minute walk had turned into more than an hour. It was too late to turn and retrace my steps. I went into the local smoke shop, the last building before the sidewalk dwindled to a dirt path.

"Donde està el Museo d'Oro?"

"No se, Señor Americano."

I pulled out my map and showed it to the two others in the shop. They shrugged.

I kept walking past treeless vacant lots with long grass and the odd pile of concrete blocks. I had to be going in the right direction as I had not strayed off the main road. I came to a complex of four shops, all with a 'cerrado' sign hanging from a suction cup on the doors. I cupped my eyes with my hands and squinted in the window of the first shop. There were beautifully tooled saddles with silver tipped pommels, cantles and tapadors with bridles and decorated martingales to match hanging from hooks on the wall. Closer to the window was a pile of magnificent panama hats. Next door was a shop with Amazonian crafts. A floor length 'cuchma' hung in the window. A cuchma was a long woven garment which was supposed to keep out the heat. It no doubt kept in the mosquitos. There was no sign to say when the shops were open. I had to come back. I chuckled at the thought of another endless walk.

The neighbourhood began to improve as I continued walking. The sidewalk reappeared again and the houses suddenly had front lawns. A father and his teenage daughter were on their hands and knees looking for something in the grass.

I repeated the question in my best Spanish.

"Oh, Señor, you're a long way from the museum. We'll take you in a few minutes if you care to wait. We must find a diamond earring. It has to be here on the lawn. Perhaps you could help us. It's about this big." He held up his thumb and forefinger indicating the size. The balding elegantly dressed man resumed his search, kneeling in his expensive suit on the lawn, talking as he ruffled the grass with his hands.

"Señor, do you live here or are you staying at a hotel?"

"I'm staying in the Hotel Florida, a small hotel in Miraflores. Do you know it?"

"Yes. It's comfortable, is it not?" They tried to make small talk as they sifted through the grass. I tried to explain why I was in Lima in unintelligible Spanish. My misuse of the language at least brought some humour to the situation for them.

Finally, success. Patricia jumped up, her green eyes sparkling, waving a gold and diamond earing. Her GUESS jeans and white T-shirt identified her as one of the well-to-do teens in Lima, those that the poor kids I had just passed on my route only see in magazines and vice-versa.

"You have walked many miles. Would you like something to drink?"

I couldn't refuse. We sat on the grass and drank coke from plastic cups.

They drove me the final three or four miles to the museum. I thanked them profusely and waved as they drove away.

"*Desculpe Señor. Hoy, el Museo es cerrado.*"

I wasn't sure whether to laugh or cry or kill the hotel clerk.

I turned around and began the long walk back to the hotel. I hoped to stop a taxi along the way.

Prior to departing, I decided to check on Mr. Mayler in the hospital.

"Nurse, where is Señor Mayler?" She said nothing, only pointed to the end of the ward. The ward was a thirty foot wide corridor that seemed a mile long. Huge shiny redwood pillars held up the thirty foot ceilings. I walked down the middle of the black and white tiled corridor towards what looked like a white tent covering the last bed on the left. Fans droned every ten feet above me as they slowly oscillated and drew a warm breeze from the large open window at the end of the corridor.

"Mr. Mayler?" I pulled back a corner of the white netting and found a smiling shaven patient. He looked considerably happier than the last time we met in prison. Even his handshake was stronger and less clammy. I sat on the edge of his bed.

"Doctor, I've got to thank you. This is like a grand hotel compared to my cell."

"We're trying to reach your sister in Toronto. Does she know what's been happening to you?"

"I wrote and told her I was sick. I left out the prison bit."

"Did you tell her much about your illness?"

"You mean AIDS? I did tell her I suspected it."

I breathed a sigh of relief knowing that I didn't have to tell him or his sister.

"We're trying to make the flight reservations for you as soon as possible. Someone from the Embassy will be here as soon as they have the tickets confirmed."

"Thanks, Doctor, for everything." We shook hands again. I folded the 'tent' flap down and retraced my steps down the ward, with its white sheeted beds pushing out from the walls on both sides. I felt relieved that I didn't have to explain AIDS and its complications to him. I was happy to be getting him home to Canada. I was curious to know how Jean Clermont was doing with the legal extradition arrangements. No. On second thought, I didn't want to know. It was Jean's problem.

When I returned to the Embassy to collect my belongings, the receptionist asked me to accept a telephone call. It was from the airline reservation desk. "I'm sorry, Doctor, we cannot transport anyone who has AIDS."

"I don't believe it. How many people do you suppose you have transported already with AIDS?"

"That's not the point, Doctor. We have our regulations."

"I would like to speak to your supervisor."

"I am the supervisor. The medical director is on vacation in the United States."

She had anticipated my next question. The lack of understanding of the disease astonished me. No amount of explanation was going to achieve anything. I gave up and tried another airline to get him to Miami and then Toronto. My next problem was going to be getting him a medical escort.

The phone by my bed woke me from a sound sleep. It took a moment to realize where I was. I assumed it was the driver who would take me to the airport for my flight.

"*Digame,*" I mumbled into the phone.

"Doctor, Señor Mayler has disappeared!"

"*¡Cómo!* What do you mean disappeared?"

"You must come immediately!" Click. The phone disconnected.

At one o'clock in the morning, as I walked down the now familiar corridor, strange shadows patterned the walls of the ward as the trees blew outside the windows. The fans still whined but the breeze was cooler. George's 'isolation tent' was deserted.

"This is very serious, Doctor. The hospital doctors are responsible for any patient transferred from prison. They could go to jail."

"Have you searched the grounds?" I peered out the window and of course saw nothing but shadows. "He'll be back." I said, having no idea what to do next. I knew that he couldn't go far in his state. "He knows I will be in to see him later today with his tickets to Toronto. He'll be here for that." I walked out of the hospital and around the grounds. It was a chance to enjoy the cool air and the quiet, something rare in a Latin American city. I saw a shadow beneath plumes of cigarette smoke.

"George, how long have you been sitting here? The nurses are having a conniption! You've got to go back in. For heaven's sake, ask permission next time." I knew full well there wouldn't be a next time. They would have a guard sitting outside his 'tent'.

"Okay. Okay. I just needed some air. They won't let me smoke in there."

"Come on, George." I took his arm and we slowly made our way back in the front door.

The nurses stared angrily as we shuffled past and didn't say a word as we made our way down the long corridor to the 'tent'.

"George, this ordeal is almost over for you. You have to stay in this place for only a few more hours. Please do what they ask. Someone from the Embassy will bring your ticket and arrange for your trip to the airport soon."

I returned to the hotel to snatch a couple more hours' sleep.

"I'm sorry to call you so early, Doctor Holbrook, but the doctors at the hospital cannot travel with the patient. We have arranged a ticket for you on the same flight as Mr. Mayler. The Embassy driver will pick you up at seven in the morning for your flight to Toronto." I slumped back on the bed and cursed. I was now faced with cancelling the Bogotà portion of the trip.

I was met in the Departure lounge by the consul, Jean Clermont and Georges, my companion for the trip to Toronto.

"Welcome aboard, Doctor Holbrook, and you, Mr. Mayler. We have reserved a special section for you both."

We were ushered to bulkhead seats on the left side of the 747. The seats behind were taped off and marked reserved.

"The washroom just on the other side of the bulkhead is for your use."

George thanked the steward for his care.

"Okay George, this is going to be a long day. I hope you have a book."

"Do you think I can smoke?" I assured him he couldn't.

"Doctor, it's good of you to accompany me. I'm sure I could do it alone but it's nice to have somebody to talk to. You know my illness. Do you think I should tell my relatives?" I suspected that that was the end of my plan to finish my Vargos Ilosa book.

"It has to be your decision, George. Do they know you're gay?"

"My sister does."

"It's your sister who's going to meet us, correct?" He nodded. "Then you don't need to worry about anyone else right now. You said she knows you are ill."

"I'm going to miss Peru. I didn't have to worry about relatives' reactions. Living with homophobia is so trying. My parents never accepted it. I knew I was gay from my early teens. I tried to avoid telling my family but finally couldn't live a lie any longer. Only my sister was sympathetic. I moved to Latin America to start fresh with my life as I was living it. I had good friends until I went to prison. It was a trumped up charge for an assault that was fabricated. It was one lousy mistake. I hit a guy because he said rotten things about my friend and me. It was a bad rap. Until I got AIDS, I thought I would stay in Peru forever. I never thought it would happen to me. Most of my friends dropped me when I went to prison. I don't know whether I got AIDS in prison or before."

"You can't redo the past. Let's just get you home to Toronto."

The stewardess pushing her trolley of meals down the aisle stopped at our row.

"Would you like chicken or steak, sir?" George's chicken came on a plastic plate with plastic utensils and cup. My steak came with a china plate and stainless steel utensils and a regular wine glass.

"Oh I wish I had ordered steak." George looked truly disappointed.

"Well, we'll trade. Here. You take this one."

I realized that they intended to throw away everything that poor George touched. Now they were going to have to destroy their 'finest china', such as it was. Even though they didn't have anything to worry about, regulations must be followed.

After a long choppy flight, I was happy to land in Miami, an airport I usually tried to avoid.

"Sir, you must clear immigration and customs before going to your connecting flight. Turn left at the top of the ramp. The attendant will direct you."

I thanked the stewards for their attention. George and I walked up the ramp and turned left as instructed. The door in front of us led to stairs and another door. We passed through the second door and found ourselves on the street.

"My God! This is wrong!" We tried to get back in the door but it was locked.

"Excuse me, Officer, we're lost. We made a wrong turn and came out to the street. We must go back in to collect our luggage."

"You've been through immigration?"

"No. Not yet."

The policeman was speechless. He called for some help and we were escorted, an officer at each elbow, back into the airport. We soon had an audience of police, airport security staff and airline officials listening to how we'd pulled off our caper and become illegals in the US. I was now worried about catching our next flight to Toronto.

"How long will you be in the United States?"

"We are just connecting to a flight to Canada."

"Are you leaving anything in the United States?"

George and I looked at each other and tried not to laugh. We realized we had almost left our luggage. I was hoping George would keep his mouth shut. If he mentioned AIDS, we were finished. Goodbye flight to Toronto.

Thinking I was home-free, we got to the customs to retrieve our luggage, only to find a perky beagle with a United States agriculture sweater on, standing over my bags. As I reached for the handle, the dog growled.

"Open your bags sir." I watched George pick up his bags and move on.

"It's the smell of coffee beans." I invariably packed the suitcase with bags of beans from Colombia. As I had had to cancel my visit to Colombia, only the smell lingered from previous bags of beans but it was enough to alert the perky beagle.

When we finally reached our destination and made our way through the immigration and customs inspections in Toronto, we passed through the sliding doors into the throngs waiting for relatives and friends.

"Thanks, Doctor," George tossed a wave in my direction and rushed toward his waiting sister. I stood a few minutes thinking he might introduce me but he put his arm around her, turned and disappeared in the crowd. I shrugged, disappointed, and moved on to get my flight to Dallas and finally Mexico City and home. I was alone at last with time to read my book, if I could keep my eyes open.

4

I was happy to see Lauretta's smiling face as I climbed the ramp from the aircraft at the Mexico City Airport. We hugged and kissed and got through the formalities speedily thanks to Lauretta's airport pass. I put my hands on her shoulders and held her at arm's length so that I could see the freckles and auburn hair that I loved. I spun her around to see the navy pants that fit perfectly over her hips and a new white blouse.

"I'm eager to get back to my Mexican routine."

"I'm eager for you to be home to walk the cursed dog. She's impossible. I get dragged after every stray dog she sees." We laughed. Lauretta worked her way into the heavy traffic on the Periferico, the jammed expressway which took us to Bosques de las Lomas and home. Driving with Lauretta was great fun. She drove like a Mexican modifying many of the rules that governed the roads in other parts of the world.

One of her rules was to completely ignore the police, assuming that they were only trying to shake you down. In fact, they generally didn't stop a woman unless she was blond.

Lauretta was now a volunteer teacher at the Embassy.

"It's fun and so much better than sitting at home while you are travelling. All the students are teens or adult refugees from Guatemala or Nicaragua. They are so eager to learn English. I just wish I had my textbooks from Canada. I didn't realize how much I miss teaching."

My few weeks at home passed far too quickly. Most of my time was consumed with the heaps of medicals and chest Xrays to review. However I did take time to enjoy our dog. We walked through our area of Bosques de Los Lomas with its twisting streets and extraordinary homes all designed seemingly to outdo each other. Contemporary Mexican architects were all influenced by the great Mexican architect, Barragán who used concrete and colour in such interesting ways.

Though obliged to do our share of official entertaining, I did get myself in hot water with my bride over entertainment that I didn't have a chance to mention to her before the fact. One particular event was on a day when the last thing we needed to do was entertain.

"Thanks for picking me up, Babe. Could we stop at Gigante or Superama on our way home?"

"No. I think we have everthing we need for a couple of days. I've just been shopping."

"Well I thought I would pick up some extra wine. I forgot to mention that I asked the Ambassador for dinner."

"You what!?"Lauretta almost ran into the rear of a Ruta 100 bus.

"He's on his own. His wife is in Canada and I thought it would be a nice gesture. I asked the commercial counsellor to make it an even number. The problem is his wife is coming too."

"David! David! How could you do this to me? You can make the bloody dinner yourself!"

"I could but I've already told them it's a family dinner with lasagne. It'll be great."

"Don't you ever do this to me again."

"Oh Babe, it'll be wonderful. I just needed some extra wine." I apologized profusely but Lauretta remained silent for the remainder of the trip home.

It was only when the time of arrival was imminent that Lauretta began to mellow. After drinks and conversation we moved to the table decorated with splashes of colour in the Mexican style, purple, yellow and orange placemats and napkins of various colours, colour coordination only Lauretta could do.

"This is very generous of you to ask us for dinner, Lauretta." My Darling grinned and practically choked as the Ambassador smiled and savoured his wine. "The wine is lovely as well."

5

No sooner was I relaxed and reacclimatized to the altitude, than I was obliged to leave Lauretta and Mexico for a trip to Honduras. I was met at the airport in San Pedro Sula by Doctor César Romero. This city on the north-east coast of Honduras, near the border with Guatemala, was a prosperous town, known mainly for its bananas rather than the Nicaraguan refugees I was there to examine, change camped around the town. I was surprised by how neat and clean the streets were, reminiscent of any 'modern' suburban development.

The residential area I was being driven through had likely been built by the United Banana Company, the main employer in the region. There were no pedestrians or people wandering about, as was the case in most of the Latin America I knew. It was almost sterile.

"Call me David, Doctor Romero." He didn't suggest I use his given name. He was one of a family of physicians at whose clinic the chest X-rays and medical examinations were completed for me to review. A tall dapper man of forty, his dark hair was slicked back and his goatee neatly trimmed. He pointed out the highlights of the town as we drove to his house.

"This is our cinema." 'Pronto Adios, Señor Chips', with Peter O'Toole in the lead role, the current feature, was a little dated. He pointed out a huge equestrian stature of somebody whose name I missed. Surely not another one of Bolivar.

"It is kind of you to invite me for comida, Doctor Romero." Having a large meal at two in the afternoon would spare me from having to worry about anything more than a snack later. The 'town' horn of his Mercedes summoned the children to open the grill at the front of the property. The ranch-style one storey house had incongruous Corinthian columns on either side of the front door and a porte cochère, a fancy covered drive-through for the big Mercedes to float up to the front door.

After being introduced to his wife, a svelte thirty-something woman with long curly black hair, green eyes, perfect makeup and manicure and the latest New York couture—Ralph Lauren or is it DKNY? I had to shake hands with the four children ranging in age from Pedro who was six, to Alesia at twelve, in their Sunday best—frilly blouses, starched shirts and shiny shoes—all in a rush to sit down for lunch. Given the setting I could have been having a meal in New York, Madrid or Paris.

I was ushered into a beamed, elegant dining room where I was asked to sit at an elaborately carved mahogany table, an antique Spanish colonial masterpiece. It could easily seat twenty-four with its high backed chairs. A sparkling crystal chandelier flooded the dark room with light. The household staff descended upon the table once we were seated and a formal Latin grace had been said. The children were remarkably quiet until the grace ended. At that point, they jumped up to reach for what they wanted. Mama looked daggers at them and peace was quickly restored. The steaming hot tortillas came first accompanied by at least three types of chili. Not knowing one from the other, I scalded my tongue. So much for tasting the rest of the meal.

The soup was a lobster bisque. Next came shrimp with lemon, garlic and more chilis. I had more than my share of tortillas to soothe my burnt mouth, much to the chagrin of the children. The maid finally brought them their own plate of steaming tortillas in a red checked napkin. Remarkably, they offered me some of theirs which I accepted. I expected bananas flambé for dessert since it was banana country. Instead, I got an array of tropical fruit. Star fruit and rambutans, I recognized, but had no idea what the rest were.

"I apologize for not having a Honduran wine. It's not very good yet." I assured my host and hostess that I had enjoyed the food and the Argentine wine enormously.

"Now you must meet father." I smiled and agreed.

Propped up against a pillar behind my chair, was what at first glance could have been a mummy from a museum, fully dressed in a navy suit, white shirt, silk tie, and highly polished black shoes. He stared straight ahead, eyes open. His waxen skin was stretched over facial bones, hollowing his cheeks and sinking his eyes, his mouth slightly open, a ghoulish image I guessed everyone in the family was accustomed to. I wasn't. He stood strapped to what looked like the two wheeled dolly that the Coca Cola man used to wheel crates of pop.

"Father had a stroke a few years ago and he doesn't communicate, but we get him up every day. We don't know whether he hears us but we talk to him anyway and bring him to comida. We feed him by tube."

I couldn't help but think of the rest of the tubes required to service this living cadaver.

I was speechless. I hoped that he didn't notice my shock. I quickly closed my mouth. I didn't know what the proper comment should be. It would be a good scene in a Buñuel movie.

"I understand that you are going to Tegucigalpa for your flight to Mexico City," Doctor Romero said when we met again later in the week.

"There is a problem at our airport, David. Your flight to Tegucigalpa has been cancelled. You are welcome to stay at our home instead of the hotel." I hesitated not wanting to spend more time with 'dad'. "Or you could always take the bus?"

"Thank you so much for the offer and your hospitality. I think I'll take the bus and get the work completed."

I bought the six dollar bus ticket and boarded the Blue Bird Coach Lines bus, a yellow school bus painted blue. I sat at the back. This enabled me to see the circus going on in front of me rather than having my head on a pivot. Each of the forty-four seats was taken. Though it was an 'express', we did make frequent stops. The driver did allow goats and chickens inside the bus, but the bushels of fruit and vegetables went on the roof. The livestock produced a pongy smell which took me back to my youth on the farm. The scrawny men all had their hand-rolled, pinched, yellowy cigarettes dangling from their mouths and spoke to me through a cloud of bitter smelling smoke. The alcohol breath was probably from yesterday's hooch. The women held the chickens upside down by the legs in the aisle. The chickens pecked at the lone goat as it wandered up and down the passageway, and were bunted in return clouding the air with downy feathers.

"Señor, donde va usted?" I hesitated to try my poor Spanish in reply. When I did, it produced gales of laughter. I wondered what I'd said. I mixed a combination of gestures, English words and Spanish grammar and ended up with acceptable but bizarre communication. When the talk turned to the Americanos, I made sure that they realized I was Canadiense. I had realized that we were passing a large American armed forces base in the centre of Honduras complete with its high link fence with barbed wire curled along the top.

"Señor, ahora, el reposo." I guessed this meant it was time for a break. The bus stopped at a Coke stand at the side of the road. We were now in the middle of a magnificent pine forest. I had been so engrossed in my conversation, that I had not noticed that the bus had been going uphill for the past few hours. The temperature was cooler. I walked about scuffing the pine needles, breathing in the fresh aroma.

To sit on a bench after three hours on a board in the bus was not appealing, so I remained standing. I picked up a few pine cones to save for the children for Christmas wreaths, another Christmas in the tropics.

"Señor, qué bueno." My companions, with a sweeping gesture, motioned to the panoramic view in front of the bus. Forested hills, a dark emerald green in the distance, separated us from the Honduran capital at the bottom of the gulley which sliced down between the highlands. I guessed they thought I was going to enjoy the downward plunge of the bus back to the plains as much as they did. I was offered a hand-made cigarette by a short, smiling local devoid of front teeth. Not having the heart to tell him I didn't smoke I accepted. When he also offered me a light, I too, contributed to the cloud of acrid smoke wafting through the bus.

Fortunately I was not sitting at the window as we came perilously close to tumbling into the valley hundreds of feet below. The Honduran hombres loved this roller-coaster ride as the bus picked up speed and rocketed around corners with screeching tires. Some of the fruit and vegetables on the roof did not fare well. They tumbled onto the road as we careened from one side to the other. The chickens cackled and even the goat struggled to keep its balance. There was a communal sigh as the bus slowed, and we could see the twinkling lights of Tegucigalpa in the distance.

At the bus terminus I shook hands with many of my companions and collected my bag still wedged in an overhead compartment behind baskets of root vegetables I didn't recognize. A taxi got me to the hotel on a hill overlooking the bustling low-rise town where the hotel clerk greeted me with a smile.

"Doctor Holbrook, we were expecting you earlier. We have saved a room for you. Perhaps you would like to speak to Doctor Estaban first." Before I could say no, a young man, doused in aftershave was at my elbow.

"I know you are leaving early tomorrow, Doctor Holbrook, but I would like you to see my clinic first. We need some help from Canada for our aid projects. Would you be so kind as to request some things from your country for us?"

I was taken aback by the boldness of this guy. I explained that my purpose was to visit doctors on my immigration list. His name was not on it. "Canada is more interested in clinics for campesiños and their families outside the main centres."

"Yes but in Honduras the transportation is good. They could come to my clinic from all over." I tried to be polite but I was tired and my patience was running out.

"I will pick you up here tomorrow, give you a short visit to my clinic and then take you to the airport." I gave up and agreed to accept the ride to the airport with the side trip to his hospital. The drive to his clinic was in silence.

"Now you see, Doctor Holbrook, this is where I'm going to put my ultrasound equipment. I am going to devote a good percentage of its use to the poor."

I smiled knowing 'the poor' were going to need basic care before they needed an ultrasound. Maybe he was going to give ultrasounds to everybody. I smiled and apologized saying that Canada didn't have funding for private ultrasounds.

"Good luck and thanks for the ride to the airport."

I hoped my stopovers in Costa Rica and Guatemala on my way home would be quiet. I needed time to write my reports and sleep.

6

While Lauretta and I had our breakfast on a day early in October 1986, ominous vibrations shook the breakfast table.

"Oh God. Not this again."

"Lauretta, let's stay calm and wait a minute." The vibration, faint but noticeable, stopped.

"I am still panic-stricken at the thought of going through another earthquake," murmured Lauretta as we sat prepared to jump for a few more minutes before relaxing.

Arriving late at the Embassy, I was surprised to be greeted by the Ambassador as I stepped into my office. "I know that you haven't had much time at home of late. I do, however, have an urgent request for help from El Salvador. I would like you to deal with it. As you know, they had an earthquake earlier today. Because of your experience assisting with aid projects here, I felt you would be an enormous help."

I went home to break the news to Lauretta.

The airport in El Salvador was an hour's drive from the city of San Salvador in normal conditions.

"Doctor, today it's going to take us a long time to reach the city." Juan, the Red Cross driver who had picked me up, was not exaggerating. "The main bridge two miles down the road has fallen into the valley below. We will have to take another route. It will add an hour to the trip. I will have to drive slowly in case some of the other bridges are unsafe."

"Take your time Juan. I'm in no rush."

"There is no power in the city. Your hotel has a generator and I hope they have enough fuel to keep it going."

"What about your family, Juan? Are they safe?"

"Oh yes, sir. We live outside the city. Our walls are cracked but I can fix them. Many dishes are broken but my wife and our six children are fine."

The small talk continued until we reached the outskirts of San Salvador, a spooky sight, with darkness descending and none of the usual glittering lights. Juan slowed to a crawl to avoid fallen trees and live wires still sparking with the slightest breeze.

My last visit to San Salvador was nerve-racking. I was edgy just thinking about it. Some US Marines were shot and killed as they sat in a café close to the Camino Réal Hotel where I usually stayed. Ever since, I'd been wary of the black pick-up trucks with darkened windows the rebels used to cruise the streets. I made a point of finding the closest building to deek into at the slightest glimpse of any suspect vehicles heading in my direction. Maybe the rebels would be busy putting their own houses and families back together.

The hotel was an eerie sight. The lobby, usually bright and sparkling, was lit by dim lights in a perpetual brown out. Candles shed an odd wavy shadow on the counter as I signed in.

My first challenge was to find my friend, Doctor Alejandro Castillo and his wife, Bridget, an elderly couple who had always gone out of their way to make my stay in San Salvador a happy one.

"Oh, Señor, it's not possible to get you there at this hour. It's past midnight and there are many wires down." The only taxi driver available thought I must be out of my mind.

"Look, it's just up the hill overlooking the city. I'll direct you."

"*Si Señor, pero…*"

"Just try. Turn here. Okay now it's just a bit further on the left."

"No, Señor. There is no house there."

"Stop by that gate and let me out. Please wait." I knew he thought I was crazy as I walked up the grass path to the wooden slatted gate with the large sign ¡Cuidado! Perros de Guardia! It was so dark that I could barely see my hand in front of my face. I climbed over the fence and started up the grass path. I'd taken two or three steps when I heard two barking dogs running down the path toward me. Did I rush for the gate or keep going? It was too late. I could normally calm dogs and babies. I hoped they would remember me from my previous visits. I began my banter as the two Dobermanns skidded to a stop in front of me. I slowly reached for my flashlight. I tried not to alarm them.

"Where are your masters, guys? Let's go and find them." I continued walking as I got the once-over from the dogs, one on each side of me. I kept up the chatting and moved toward the darkened house. Not even the flickering of a candle could be seen. I skirted the swimming pool, now covered with fallen branches and moved slowly, hoping not to trip over any live wires. I was surprised to find the front door of the large ranch-style home, ajar.

"Alejandro! Bridget! Are you here?" The dogs in their smooth loping gait breezed from room to room without any indication of where their masters might be. I slowly moved from the front to the back of the house checking each room as I went, finally reaching the kitchen and breakfast room. There, sitting at the table were the Castillos, both in a state of shock. The dogs poked each on the leg and got no response. I wondered if they were dead. I called their names again and got no reply. Bridget sat at the table, her greying blond hair unbrushed, looking down at the broken Scandinavian china in front of her, china she had shown me on a previous visit. It had been hand-painted by her grandmother in her native Sweden. She appeared in a trance, the broken china being the blow that tipped her into this catatonic state. Neither had any physical injuries I could see.

I put my hand on Alejandro's shoulder. He slowly moved his head toward me. He didn't look up. I couldn't imagine how long they had been sitting there. The earthquake was almost twenty hours ago. There were no food remnants but the dogs would likely have cleaned up anything edible. I dragged a chair over the pile of broken china to the table.

"The china was my wife's prized possession." Alejandro finally said something. "It was the last of her family heirlooms. I am heart-broken for her."

"Alejandro, have you or Bridget eaten anything?" He shook his head. "It's dark. I'll get you and Bridget to bed. Which way is the bedroom?" He slowly rose from his chair. I took his arm as he stumbled. He pointed in the direction I had to go. I had him sit again while I went around the table to take Bridget by the arm. I thought she was going to collapse. I put her arm around my neck, my arm around her waist and started to half drag, half lift her toward the bedroom. I hoped that I didn't fall through a hole in the floor or have the ceiling fall on us. I unceremoniously dropped her on the bed and returned to the kitchen to do the same for her husband.

After making them as comfortable as I could, I found some biscuits and bottled water in the kitchen and tried without great success to get them both at least to drink. Finally I left the water at their bedside. There was nothing in the refrigerator that would be safe to give them since the power had been off too long. Perhaps daylight would revive them by which time I could get some help. The dogs, despite the food that I'd left for them, returned to the road with me and growled only when I climbed back over the gate. Either they didn't want me to leave or they didn't like me the climbing on their gate. Incredibly, the taxi driver had waited for me.

I was awakened at daybreak by the telephone.

"Would you please come to the paediatric hospital with me, David? It has been severely damaged. They would appreciate your help." Ian Lawrence was the director of the Latin American office of the International Red Cross.

"First I have to get some help for some friends in Monte Esidro. It's a Doctor Castillo and his wife. They are in shock and have no food."

"I know Doctor Castillo. We'll send some workers as soon as possible."

"Be careful of the dogs."

The San Salvador Childrens' Hospital had been a striking modern building on a tree-lined boulevard in the city centre. It was now tilting on a forty-five degree angle. It had sunk two stories as the earth opened up around it.

"Doctor, I'm Julio Gomez, the hospital director." He came right to the point. "There was a nuclear medicine department in the basement of the hospital. The entire staff of the department are missing and presumed dead. I don't know whether there is any danger from the isotopes that were stored, and I don't know whether any were in use at the time of the earthquake. What should we do? I know this might not be your field but do you have any ideas that could help us? We could get some protective clothing for you to wear if you would go in with some of the rescue force to check the nuclear medicine department for us."

"You're right. It's not my field. Do you remember who supplied the nuclear material?" I tried to ignore the idea of going into the ruins.

"Yes. The original equipment was from the Atomic Energy of Canada in Chalk River Ontario. The isotopes are from a nuclear medicine supply company in Toronto. All the manuals were in the basement."

"I'll contact Ottawa from the Red Cross office and we should find out what to do later today."

I hesitated to ask whether anyone got out of the hospital alive.

Doctor Gomez continued, "Two hundred and twenty bodies have been found and ninety-two are still unaccounted for among the staff and patients." I wiped my wet cheeks with my sleeve. After the Mexico City earthquake, with an estimated thirty thousand people dying and now this, I felt emotionally drained.

I returned to the office with Ian to sort out the radioactivity problem and then prepared to go back to check on Alejandro and Bridget.

"We moved Doctor Castillo and his wife to a shelter temporarily." We contacted the Castillos' son in Miami. He's going to take his parents back to the States until they've recovered and their home can be repaired."

"I'm relieved. I didn't know what more I could do."

"Also, we've just received a reply from the pharmaceutical firm. They say the isotopes obviously must be handled with care. The only sales slip they have is for radioactive iodine. All the instructions are in the manuals. They'll send duplicates."

I kneaded my forehead trying to ease my headache and wondered what more I could do.

"Surely there must be someone experienced in this field, Ian. I have no training at all in handling radio-active material. I do know the type of isotopes they would be using for children would have a short half-life which means that after about three days, there would be little or no danger. But, if they had a reactor to create the isotopes in the first place, the danger would be far greater. I suspect they have a reactor if they were dealing with Chalk River."

"Let's request that a specialist be sent from Chalk River to help them. That will prompt Atomic Energy of Canada to check their invoices to confirm what they did sell the Salvadorans."

"That's a great idea. I wish I could be more help, Ian. I'll go back to the hospital and explain what we're going to do."

I walked back to the hospital from the Red Cross office through the streets which had become virtual campsites teaming with people already made homeless as well as with those afraid to return to their homes in case of another quake or powerful after-shock. It was early evening and I walked the mile or so, slowly. I worried that there was little more I could do before heading back to Mexico. When I finally did make it home, I was depressed and tired.

7

"I'm so glad you're here, David. We've been invited to a soirée in your honour by Conchita Sanchez who is a director of the Humana Hospital."

My shoulders sagged as I wondered how I was going to muster the strength to go. "I guess I'll know who she is when I see her." I racked my brain. "Are you all right, Babe? You look awfully pale."

"I feel terrible. It must be something I've eaten."

"Why don't we go for just for a few minutes and then we'll know who she is, thank her and quietly leave? From the map they've sent, it looks quite close to here."

The first indication that this was not going to be an ordinary party was the valet parking. Our hope for an early retreat was soon dashed by the white-gloved servants with trays of *Pol Roger* champagne.

"My stomach feels more settled already." Lauretta had sprung to life.

The next surprise was the opera singer on the grand spiral staircase. She was a Mexican version of Maureen Forrester, without the humour.

We were gradually sucked into the house and away from our exit by the multitude of people still arriving late in the Latin tradition.

"I feel remarkably restored, David."

"I'm pleased, Darling. It's the champagne. M. Pol Roger always says if you drink 'quality bubbles', you'll be cured of whatever ails you. Let's move further away from the singer before I'm deaf."

In the crush of people, it was impossible to chat because the noise level was so great. We did say a few words to Conchita, enough to realize who she was and pleased that I had written a note to thank the hospital staff for their help during the earthquake and the handling of the cases I had sent over the past few years.

"Oh, Doctor. You cannot leave yet. I have some words to say." She moved to the grand staircase and silenced the throng.

"I have been asked to present to you the Mexican Legion of Honour, on behalf of the people of Mexico, for your contributions during the Mexico City earthquake. I would like you also to accept this silver plaque." Lauretta and I looked at each other dumbfounded. I was speechless unable to say more than a simple thank you.

Having had our fill of honours, hors d'oevres and *Pol Roger*, we departed.

"You realize Lauretta this award is as much for you as me.

8

After a couple of weeks of catching up in the office, I prepared for another trip to Havana to assist the Canadian Embassy staff with health and immigration problems. I did not look forward to my Cuba trips. The state of the island was depressing and the citizens suspicious of foreigners and in many cases of each other. The zealous block chair-person kept the cadres under strict control.

The José Martí airport in Havana was a hot hellhole. The line-up for immigration and customs clearance usually extended onto the tarmac. I could feel my shoes sinking in the hot tarvia. I was generally unlucky enough to be behind a contingent of the Russian army when I was in line for my passport check. Because of my red diplomatic passport, I was not allowed in the regular line. All the Russian soldiers carried red passports too. I kept telling myself that patience was a virtue.

"It's kind of you to wait for me." I was happy to see Charles, the Consul at the Canadian Embassy. The thought of taking an ancient decrepit taxi was almost too much to handle. "I was hoping it might be cooler in the middle of the night, but no such luck."

"I'm surprised you came because we're expecting a tropical storm in the next few days. I hope you don't mind staying awhile." I smiled trying not to betray the fact that there were many places I would rather be.

"We've put you in a newly renovated hotel near the Malecón.

It is closer to the United States Interest Section. The Americans are eager to see you too. The Marines are planning a chili-dog supper for you at Marine House." I smiled at the thought of it.

The Hotel Esmeralda was a majestic nineteenth century mansion on the Calzada del Cerro, the main boulevard of the once prosperous El Cerro district of Havana. Decorated with antiques confiscated from the pre-revolutionary rich, the Esmeralda was normally reserved for visiting dignitaries from Eastern Europe. Things must be slow if there was room for me.

The antique cage elevator took me to my elegant third floor bedroom. The large walnut bed was so high that I practically needed a stool to get onto it. I could see the sea while lying in bed. The tiled bathroom had an enormous tub with sculpted legs, taps in the middle, and was large enough for two. If only Lauretta had been here. It was too bad that only a cold trickle came from the taps. A makeup table, with what had once been a beautiful gold framed mirror above it, was by the bed. The glass in the mirror was now pock-marked with black patches.

It was an easy walk to the Malecón, the sea-wall and roadway to the heart of old Havana. I set off on a Sunday morning walk realizing that the same walk any later in the day was down prostitutes' alley. As I reached the decaying eighteenth and nineteenth century core of Havana, I was stunned by the magnificence of the buildings. Some dated from as early as 1775 when they were rebuilt after yet another sack of the city.

"Señor, Señor. Es muy peligroso." A passerby pointed up to the cracked cornices which hung precariously over the street. The buildings eaten away by the passage of time, salt air and neglect were in deplorable condition. I decided to walk in the middle of the road and take my chances as I shared the thoroughfare with the circa 1950s autos which would barely start let alone roar down the street.

En route to my hotel, I passed the American Interest Section, as the US Embassy was euphemistically called. Huge sign boards facing the Embassy cartooned 'Uncle Sam' and screamed in huge letters:

YANKEES GO HOME.

WE DON'T WANT YOU HERE.

WE KNOW WHAT YOU ARE DOING IN THERE.

Loudspeakers mounted on either side of each sign blared out antagonistic messages at regular intervals. Ignoring it all, Marines in full dress uniform greeted visitors at the door

I walked through a park, bought an ice cream cone and Granma, the Havana newspaper to read the latest propaganda as I sat at the base of the statue of José Martí, the nineteenth century socialist hero. I knew the name from listening to *Güantanamera*, a Pete Seeger folk song known in my youth. Exploring in Havana could include everything from watching a good baseball game, to a ballet class in the once magnificent, now tumble-down theatre serving as the ballet school.

Near the hotel, I passed the basement shops in old apartment buildings which reeked of rotting potatoes. Women of all ages and a few old men stood around chatting. They no doubt listened to the latest reports from the block committee, with news about foreigners like me. It was not that I was a threat but rather that I might have some US dollars to give up.

The US Head of Mission, or Ambassador anywhere else but Cuba, welcomed me to the well-equipped clinic in the American Interest Section. My days in Cuba were always busy. There were many patients to see, both American and Canadian. The frantic pace continued into the evenings with chili-dogs and beer at the United States Marines' residence one night, and then dinner at the Canadian Ambassador's the next.

Marine House was a typical fraternity house transplanted from a college campus in the States to Miramar, a wealthy section of Havana.

I was ushered into the living room, handed a bottle of beer, (Budweiser was the favoured brand) and given a comfortable seat to watch last week's National Football League game between the Green Bay Packers and the Detroit Lions. I could be almost anywhere but Havana.

I never did learn the final score as I was whisked off to help myself from the huge pot of chili. Being a jock for a few hours added a new dimension to my character.

The Canadian Residence was also in Miramar. I always hoped that their neighbour, Fidel, would drop in unannounced as he had been known to do. He had so many residences supposedly for security reasons, it was hard to know when he was a neighbour. Fidel's personal firing range was behind the Canadian Residence which was unnerving for the Ambassador and his wife, especially as they had young children.

The Canadian Ambassador's dinners were, in addition to being a warm and happy occasion, an enormous help in keeping me up to date on Cuban health care.

"You know, David, health care here in Cuba is excellent." This served as part of the introduction to Doctor Jorge Léal, the Minister of Health, who was a guest at one of the dinners arranged for me by the Ambassador.

"Yes, we have excellent facilities but we are very short of medication. We would be most grateful for any assistance." I was relieved that the request was directed at the Ambassador as I smiled and listened.

"Doctor Léal, as you know, we are having serious concerns about the best treatment for the virus causing AIDS. How is it handled in Cuba?"

"We don't have many cases in Cuba, but those that are confirmed are sent to a sanatorium on the other side of the island."

I thought of asking how there could be so few cases when Haiti, the supposed source of many of the North American cases, was Cuba's neighbour.

After dinner, I was driven back down Fifth Avenue, a boulevard with swaying palm trees, deserted at ten o'clock at night, to my hotel.

My trip to the airport, courtesy of the Marines with their airport passes, was always entertaining and often resulted in an invitation to the V.I.P. lounge for a brandy snifter of incredible rum, and another Montecristo cigar. My wooden box of Montecristo Joyitas packed in my case would have to last until my next visit to Havana, who knows when.

I felt fortunate to have missed the expected hurricane. Maybe my luck was changing.

9

Arriving home, I was met at the door by a smiling Lauretta.

"Come and see what I've bought."

"What beautiful pottery. Where did you get it?"

Lauretta began to laugh. "Four of us decided to go to Puebla. The wife of the RCMP. officer at the Embassy, the wife of the FBI officer at the US Embassy and two friends of hers. They claimed that they had been before and that none of the shops would accept credit cards. We each took a lot of cash. We hid the cash in our bras or pantyhose.

"All went well until men kept pointing at us as they drove by. We thought it was a ploy to get us to stop. That could only mean rape and robbery. But soon I began to have trouble steering the car. Finally, we pulled into a truck stop. A number of men surrounded the car and we thought we were in dire straits. I decided that we had to pull the helpless female routine.

"Oh Señor, can you help us? There is something wrong with the car."

"*Si Senōra.*" He laughed and pointed at the tire. I got out, threw my arms in the air and waited. He waved at his friends to come and help. They asked for the trunk key. My three friends promptly got out of the car and went to find the washroom which turned out to be an outhouse in an adjacent field. I hesitated to join them in case the car disappeared. Twenty minutes passed.

"*Senōra.*" He gallantly swept his right hand toward the car and handed me back the key.

"David, he refused to let us pay him. Finding this great pottery was an anticlimax after that. Incidentally all of the shops took Visa."

"Every time we use the pottery, we'll think of the trip rather than the purchase." I laughed and hugged Lauretta.

Dr. Holbrook, you have now completed your four year posting in Mexico City. You are requested to submit your preferences for your next posting. Keep in mind that all officers are expected to spend every third or fourth posting in Ottawa.

"Lauretta, the dreaded telex has arrived telling us we have to move. What are we going to say this time?"

"What choices do we have?"

"Hong Kong, Nairobi or Abijan. And also New Delhi and Ottawa."

"Let's choose Hong Kong. I don't want to go to New Delhi."

"I think maybe Africa would be interesting from a work point of view, but I agree Hong Kong sounds great."

After weeks of waiting, we were given a choice. New Delhi or Ottawa.

"What'll we do?"

"I think we should stay overseas at least until the children finish school. It would be unsettling to move them when they have such good friends and are so close to finishing. David, I guess it will have to be India."

5

THE JEWEL WITHOUT ITS CROWN

1

Our move to India with its heat and dirt, slums and hordes, was something neither Lauretta nor I wanted.

We arrived in the middle of the night to face an endless immigration line of shoving, irritable people which did little to allay our feelings about the place. The only positive note was that Indira Gandhi Airport was air-conditioned.

As we dragged our many suitcases out of the customs hall past sleepy inspectors and through the doors, a blast of hot humid air hit us as the doors opened. Even at four in the morning, the 'cool' time of the day, it was hotter than we had ever experienced. A brownish yellow haze enveloped the airport and a heavy barnyard smell overwhelmed us. We were set upon by a myriad of eager helpers, grasping for the handles of our suitcases in hope of a tip. The stench of stale urine irritated my nostrils.

We suddenly noticed a large white placard bobbing up and down in the mass of people. Our name was written on it in bold black letters.

"Please, Doctor Holbrook, over this way. Please! I'm Lakshmi, Doctor. I'm the driver for the High Commission." This middle-aged man in a white safari suit with a red maple leaf over the right chest pocket, herded us and the suitcase haulers toward the High Commission van. Dozens of small calloused hands were pushed in Lakshmi's face as he shoved the cases into the car. He paid them, which was a relief, since we had no rupees.

"Now that July has arrived for us, Sir, the thermometer has fallen." Lakshmi was amused as we mopped our brows. "It is very hot and dry from April until June, Madam, and then if we're blessed with a good south-west monsoon and if she's not delayed over the Andaman Sea, the rains arrive and it becomes cooler with more humidity." Cooler meant 36° degrees instead of 45°. We smiled as the monsoon is talked about like a goddess.

"Lakshmi, what's the smell?"

"Sir, it's burning cow dung patties. They're used as fuel for heating and cooking."

It was certainly a different pollution smell from what we had grown accustomed to in Mexico. Now it was dung as well as auto fumes.

"I'm going to take you to your temporary quarters. Your permanent housing is not ready yet, Sir." At this point we couldn't have cared less where we were as long as we could get some sleep after our sixteen hour flight.

We sped down the airport road as the driver weaved in and out to avoid the three-wheeled brown and yellow Bajaj taxi-scooters jammed with three or four people and their luggage. Clouds of black smoke billowed from their three-stroke engines as they swerved to get out of our road. As we pulled onto the main road our car slowed behind garishly decorated Tata trucks portraying every conceivable goddess in the wet sari look, all overloaded with cargo hanging out over two lanes of traffic. Lone people, oblivious to the passing vehicles, wandered aimlessly on the road. They were barely visible in the shadows. We were told human life was cheap in India. I knew pedestrians couldn't last long. The cows grazing along the median were held in higher esteem.

When we pulled into the driveway of our temporary abode, we had no idea where we were. Lakshmi took the suitcases to the house. He insisted on our not helping.

"What's the noise on the other side of the fence?" asked Lauretta anxiously as the lights were turned on.

"It's just a neighbourhood pig going through the garbage, Madam. It's quite safe."

Lauretta glanced at me. I wasn't sure whether she was thinking of the garbage or the pig.

"I'll turn on the 'AC' for you, sir. These are the keys. Be sure to keep the gate shut." Lakshmi excused himself and left us in our temporary abode. When we found the light switches in the kitchen, we discovered a welcome note from the High Commission and a cache of food, a huge box of cornflakes, a loaf of bread and milk.

"Let's start this with a blast." Lauretta had her sense of humour back. We sat down to a bowl of cornflakes with hot UHT milk which tasted like infant formula.

We were awakened at eight in the morning by the ear-splitting ring of the doorbell. When I got myself to the door, I gasped at the hot, humid blast of air that hit me in the face. I had already grown accustomed to the air-conditioning. There was no one at the door.

"Here Sir. Here Sir." I looked out and saw a group of people standing at the white wrought iron gate. I soon realized the bell was on the gate.

"Buy some baskets today, Sir?"

"You need a maid? I can start now, Sir."

"You buy best oranges from me, Sahib." No wonder the driver said to keep the gate shut. I walked towards it in my pajamas, not the proper garb for a sahib. I was supposed to be dressed in an ironed shirt and pressed trousers or a dhoti which I would have to learn to tie it properly or face embarrassment.

"No, no, no. We are only staying here for a few days." A moan of disappointment went up from the throng who thought they had come across a gold-mine. I returned to the house in a lather. I was not yet accustomed to the drenching humidity and wondered why I had ventured out at all.

No sooner had I stepped in the door than the bell rang again.

"This time, I'll go." Lauretta, dressed at this point in her coolest Mexican market dress, felt confident she could handle the mob at the gate with greater success than I managed.

"Okay, Sweet, give it a try." No sooner had I said that than I knew she would have more success than I did. She was more rational.

I soon heard Lauretta chatting in the driveway, talking about our flight from Mexico. I opened the door to find out what was going on.

"David, I'd like you to meet Percy and Beverly Baker. Percy works in the commercial department at the High Commission and lives across the street. They were waiting at the gate hoping we would answer the bell. They knew about the frustration of the string of bell ringers."

"Welcome to India, David. We hope you and Lauretta have everything you need here until your assigned house is ready for you." We must have look bewildered as the Bakers, both jolly and roly-poly, went on to explain how to start the generator, how to run the washing machine and where the extra towels and sheets were.

"Later in the morning we'll drop by and take you on a tour of the neighbourhood."

We headed for the kitchen and the giant box of *Kelloggs* corn flakes.

The Bakers soon returned. "It'll probably take another week or so for your house in Shanti Niketan to be ready. We'll take you past it so that you can get your bearings. This part of New Delhi will be confusing for a while." Percy Baker was trying to prepare us for the inevitable delays with the house repairs and painting.

"Is there a market near here where we can buy fruit and vegetables?"

"Yes, but, we should tell you that we buy most of our staples at the United States Embassy Commissary. They have lettuce you can eat without having to treat it to remove the bacteria. They sell bottled water which has not been opened and refilled locally. You'll get used to all this. If you buy food at the local markets you will invariably be sick the next day. If your servants know nothing about hygiene, you'll be sick all the time. Incidentally, you have the best servants in the area. None of us could get them to move. They wanted to stay with the house in Shanti Niketan. It's called the Doctor's house." The Bakers chatted as we began our drive.

We drove slowly past our future home, a red brick and concrete block, two storied, flat roofed house with the entrance on the side.

"It looks very interesting. I can hardly wait to move in, unpack and make it our next home," Lauretta said in a positive tone. A hedge separated the front garden from the street. It was a beehive of activity as workmen, went in and out. We decided not to stop.

"It's a double house unfortunately." Beverly now filled in the negatives. "The landlord lives in the rear with a huge garden. Ambassador (ret'd) V.J.R. Kapoor is how he refers to himself. I think he's quite old and so it's not likely you'll be wakened in the night by rock and roll."

The streets of Shanti Niketan were festooned with signs:

'DR. RADHU, M.B.CAMBRIDGE (failed), PILE DOCTOR.'

'DR. MEHTA, M.B. U.of MADRAS, BONE SETTER.'

'DR. RAJMAR, M.B. U.of PUNE, MRI. NO WAITING.'

"Are doctors proud enough of failing to put it on a sign?"

"Well, David, half the battle here is getting to Cambridge. If you fail you can at least advertise that you got there and gave it a try."

"Here is the 'mall' in your neighbourhood. That's PIG PO. I couldn't recommend their meat. It all smells slightly off. This is MEHTAS CATERING. They mix up their dal, lentils and various other ingredients under that tree. They cater for many fancy parties which is why we're often sick after dining out. This shop over here will be one of the most important for you. It's a good video shop. If he doesn't have the movie you want, try next door. They try to outdo each other. If they have to, they will send somebody to make a video of the movie you want in a theatre in the US. The colour is a little weird, but the movies are current." Beverly paused. "You've probably guessed that we're a little negative about this place. We're eager to move on to our next posting."

"Incidentally, while you're waiting to move to your house, would you be interested in a trip to Kashmir next weekend? We have two tickets we can't use. We'd be happy to sell them."

"Don't the air tickets have your name on them?"

"Yes, but Indian Airways never looks." Percy was not entirely convincing.

Lauretta and I looked at each other and smiled.

"Sure. It would be fun."

2

We were apprehensive as we presented ourselves at the ticket counter on the domestic side of the Indira Gandhi airport on our second weekend in New Delhi. The harried counter clerk looked briefly at our tickets and our passports.

"Go over there. The flight for Srinagar will be called soon." We seemed to be the only people waiting.

"Perhaps they've noticed the tickets weren't ours and will wait until the flight has left before they tell us."

"Excuse me, sir. If you are going to Srinagar, you must go to the aircraft and claim your luggage."

"I knew this wouldn't work," Lauretta muttered as we went out of the building into the mid-day sun to collect our two bags lined up with everyone else's on the tarmac.

"Is this all of your luggage, sir?" We nodded. "Open it please." We glanced at each other and did as we were told. An armed soldier virtually dumped everything out and fingered it all for odd bulges.

"What do you think they're looking for?" Lauretta looked at me.

"Maybe hand guns or grenades." We laughed as he told us to put it back in and return to the waiting room. We watched as each passenger went through the same routine.

"We seem to be still on the flight, David." Having been warned that the flights never left on time, we sat down and pulled out our scrabble.

When we arrived in Srinagar three hours later, we were faced with the same baggage search on the tarmac. This time, Lauretta and I were separated. She realized too late that I had her bag and she, mine. By the time the army sergeant got to the personal items, creams, tampons and womens' knickers, I was getting peculiar looks. He was unsure what to do about this odd man. He said nothing as he jammed everything back into the bag. I saw Lauretta trying to keep a straight face at the end of the line as they looked at 'her' razor and masculine clothing. We left the small terminal and took one of the two ramshackle taxis. I gave the driver, a sinister grey-robed man with a matching hat not unlike a soufflé, the name and address of our houseboat.

As we approached Nageen Lake along the rutted gravel road from the airport, the beauty of the snow-capped Himalayas across the lake was breathtaking. A dozen large houseboats were moored along the shore, their verandahs facing the lake.

Our once fine teak houseboat, 'THE KASHMIRI QUEEN', moored to the shore with two thick hausers, was a little the worse for wear. The verandah with its steps down to the water looked out on the white-capped Himalayas and the Mughal gardens designed in the sixteenth century across the lake which was rumoured to be bottomless.

"I'm Mr. Abdul. You're renting my houseboat. It's made of teak you know. You must keep the curtains pulled in the sitting room."

We were speechless, at such a strange welcome from this short, middle-aged, well-dressed Kashmiri, in his white gown and Haj cap, indicating that he had been to Mecca. "Oh, thank you for the house rules, Mr. Abdul. We're going to enjoy sitting on the verandah and also in the sitting room. We may need the curtains open for the view."

Mr. Abdul grumbled and left.

"We are paying for this."

"David, don't let the man irritate you. It's a weekend holiday. His teak won't be ruined in three days." Lauretta spoke calmly as we sat down in the plush horse-hair stuffed arm chairs in the living room. A metal based floor lamp reminiscent of my grandmother's was capped with an ancient cream shade, allowing light to focus on a mounted elk's head with huge multi-pointed antlers hanging above it, a peculiar highlight for this room.

"Concentrate on the lake and mountains. In fact the hand-carved teak on the verandah and the doors is amazing." It was intricately carved in geometric patterns. It smelled like cedar, or was it furniture polish?

"Hello, Sahib. I'm Aziz, your bearer. I will do the cooking and cleaning. Come. I will show you the bedroom and bathroom. This ladder goes to the roof where you will get a better view."

The bedroom, a large square room with Constable-like tranquil scenes of the English countryside hanging on the wood-panelled walls had a low double bed in the middle of the room.

Aziz, dressed in a stained white jacket with a few brass buttons remaining, gave the boat an air of faded charm. We went out to try the cushioned benches on the verandah.

As we sat, relaxed at last, we were surprised to see a skiff filled with flowers, being paddled by an elderly, white capped bearded man silently gliding towards us.

"Hello. Hello. I'm Mr. Wonderful. You need flowers? Very fresh, memsahib, very fresh."

We smiled and waited to see what was on offer.

"Okay, Mr. Wonderful. We will have some of the tall white flowers."

"Oh yes, Memsahib, a good choice. Very fresh."

"What is the name of the flower?"

"It is rhojangandha. Here, Memsahib. See how fresh it is."

"It has a lovely aroma, David. Smell it. It smells like jasmine."

"In India, it's the flower for the bridal night, memsahib."

Lauretta and I looked at each other and said "Why not?"

How many you want? Try twelve." Mr. Wonderful was no doubt figuring that he could charge as much as he wished, taking into consideration the cost of the houseboat, the fact we were foreigners and maybe it *was* our bridal night. "That will be five US dollars."

"Let's say one dollar." Lauretta took on the bargaining, a concept I was still uncomfortable with. I smiled and sat back contentedly.

"Oh Memsahib, too little. Three dollars."

"Oh no. Two dollars."

"You are getting them for nothing. Okay, this time." Mr. Wonderful took his money. He put the heart-shaped blade of his paddle back in the water and moved on. We sat back and relaxed for a few minutes.

"Hello. Hello. You need a haircut, Sahib or a new suit? Very good price."

"No thank you."

"Then, antiques. Antique jewellery for memsahib?"

"No. No. No." Now Lauretta was the irritated one. "How are we going to handle this? Let's go inside for a while. I could do with a rest. What about you?"

"Sounds great to me."

The thin-mattressed double bed was very lumpy and uncomfortable. We looked at each other and rolled off opposite sides to look underneath. Someone else's luggage was stuffed under the bed.

"Do you suppose the owner of these bags is sharing the bed, David?"

We looked at each other and shrugged. We pulled the bags out and lined them up along the wall.

"Now let's try the mattress again."

"Ah. This is great," as we rolled together in the middle of the bed with the mattress now almost touching the floor.

"I guess that's why the luggage was under the bed."

No sooner had we stretched out and stopped laughing, then there was a loud persistent knock on the verandah window.

"Let's let Aziz deal with this." The knocking was now a pounding. I got up and went to the door.

"We don't want anything. Get off the verandah!" The three vendors stared at me. I banged the door leaving them standing there and returned to bed.

Soon, we heard the backdoor open and assumed that finally Aziz has reappeared and would deal with the tormentors on the verandah.

"Hello. It's Mr Abdul. Are you here? Would you like some apples from my orchard? Perhaps you would like to see my fine Kashmiri carpets. It's a special price for you." Lauretta and I looked at each other and groaned in exasperation.

"This is going to be hopeless. Let's go up on the roof." Lauretta had probably chosen the only escape. "We'll wait until we hear him leave."

We furtively climbed to the roof.

"There you are." Mr. Abdul, standing on the planks leading from the boat to the moorings on the shore, spotted us with ease. "I will arrange a trip to the Mughal Gardens for you. You can also go through the canals of Srinagar."

"Thank you Mr. Abdul. Perhaps tomorrow."

"Sahib, what will you have for breakfast? I will serve porridge, fried eggs and sausages, 'toasts' and drinks." Lauretta felt sick at the thought of fried eggs swimming in grease. We chose porridge.

Next morning, awakened at five by the wailing call to worship from the mosque across the lake, we arrived in the dining room, and found the table set and a large platter of fried eggs in the middle with 'toasts' in the platter to soak up the grease. Lauretta couldn't look at it. Yet another giant box of *Kelloggs* corn flakes sat on the table and there was no porridge in sight. Aziz appeared from the galley kitchen, wearing the same jacket but now with a towel over his arm. He was carrying two bowls of porridge.

"Perhaps he trained at the Ritz," muttered Lauretta.

The back door opened and Mr. Abdul appeared and sat down at the table.

"I should tell you that your Prime Minister stayed in my houseboat. Yes, Mr. Trudeau, I believe his name was. Do you know him?"

"Well no, but I do know who you mean."

"I'm here to tell you that this morning Mr. Butt is coming to take you to the Mughal gardens across the lake. It will take forty minutes. You must be ready." It didn't sound as if we had any choice. It was better than fending off the vendors.

We were still drinking our strong Kashmiri coffee when we were summoned to the verandah. Mr. Butt, a wizened elderly man wearing a long cream-coloured kurta sherwani, (a pajama coat), his clean white embroidered skull cap pulled down tightly on his head was standing on the back of his colourfully cushioned shikarra, a Kashmiri gondola with a canopied section and enough room for two small people. Still standing with his oar on the platform behind where we were to sit, he said nothing. We crawled under the covered portion without dumping him into the lake and lounged on the once multi-coloured cushions.

The only sounds we heard as we floated through clumps of lotus blossoms with large peony-like flowers were the drips from Mr Butt's heart-shaped paddle. Trimmed down shikarras piled high with loads of straw, perhaps reeds from the lotus plants, all powered by locals with a paddle, drifted silently by.

We were startled when a skiff came up beside us and a young girl with dancing huge chestnut-coloured eyes, handed Lauretta a lotus blossom.

"Thank you." Lauretta smiled and admired the gorgeous pink flower.

"Temoney. Temoney." The girl's smile was gone. With one hand holding on to our shikarra, she thrust her other hand at us. Mr. Butt stopped paddling and waited to see what we would do.

"David, she means tip money, I think. Or, maybe it's to bribe her to let go of the shikarra."

"I have a rupee." We smiled and obliged.

She didn't seem too pleased but at least she let go and moved on.

Shikarra in Lotus Blossoms

Shikarra near houseboats on Nageen Lake

Canals of Srinigar Kashmir

Shalimar Gardens Kashmir

As we neared the shore, we could no longer see the houseboats across the lake. We floated through a narrow crumbling tunnel which once served as the gate to the Chasma Shai (the Imperial Spring), a small Mughal garden designed by Shah Jehan in the seventeenth century for his wife. We docked at a pier at the foot of the garden.

"Temoney." Mr. Butt now had his hand out.

"Not again." Lauretta grimaced. We looked at each other.

"Later. At the houseboat." I pointed across the lake realizing that if we paid him now, he might disappear.

Rows of lilac bushes, mauve, purple, light and dark blues, were divided in four sections on the first terrace. Other white aromatic flowering bushes, perhaps orange blossoms, were interspersed. The perfume was glorious.

Throngs of Kashmiris and other Indian families walked the paths around the fountain in the centre. These walkways meandered to patchy lawns where families had laid out picnics. Two rows of fruit trees led to the top of the hill and the ruins of a pavillion. To get away from the crowds and to get the best view across the lake in front of us, and the Himalayas behind us, we walked up the hill along the stream that fed the fountain. We sat on an ornate iron bench with a slatted wooden seat and watched the passing parade, all in party clothes: Indian men in black suits and white shirts open at the collar and Kashmiri men in long flowing grey robes, 'haj' hats pushed on their heads. Some women wore saris, others, shoulder-covering dresses. Most wore a scarf over their heads. The girls wore fancy dresses and white knee socks, the boys long pants and white shirts, as they ran and shouted together seemingly unaware of the Hindu-Muslim-Kashmiri friction.

"I'm glad I didn't wear a sun dress. It's probably worse than a mini-skirt. Nobody is wearing slacks or jeans either. I don't have a shawl to wear over my head." Lauretta looked down at her mid-calf length flowered skirt.

"I don't have a jacket or a white shirt, so let's not worry about it."

"What do you suppose is the occasion?"

"It must be a holy day of some sort. Heaven knows."

We slowly made our way back down the hill to the water's edge. We could see Mr. Butt waiting impatiently, shifting from foot to foot, his oar in the water ready to push the shikarra away from the pier.

"David we're not going to rush. I'm on my holiday." We took our time reaching the pier. I helped Lauretta into the shikarra as he glowered.

As the KASHMIRI QUEEN came into view, we saw the vendors drifting around our verandah likes sharks around bait. We were surprised to see another couple sitting on the verandah with Mr. Abdul.

Mr. Abdul jumped up and jauntily announced, "My next clients are here."

"But we don't leave until tomorrow."

"Perhaps you would like to take an overnight trek in the Himalayas? Very nice. My son will take you."

"No thank you. We'll leave tomorrow as planned." Lauretta was not budging from our plan.

"Hello. I'm Jim Spence. This is my wife Carol. I'm sorry about this. We had no idea. He turned to Mr. Abdul. "We'd be happy to take a trek."

"Just put your luggage under the bed then, Mr. Spence."

Mr. Abdul quickly suggested.

"Pay in dollar! Pay in dollar!" We had forgotten about Mr. Butt still standing on his shikarra.

"No. Rupees. You said two hundred rupees." Fortunately, I had the money ready. As I put the money in his hand he looked at me with his jaw set and eyes now slits. He was ready to kill me on the spot.

"Sahib, for dinner we have lamb chops and rice." Aziz smiled with his brown-toothed grin as he came to save me from Mr. Butt's temper.

We sat at our dining room table and awaited our dinner. A single candle flickered, creating shimmering shadows on the shiny, flowered oil cloth table covering. Aziz finally appeared with what looked like two *Swanson*'s TV dinners except that they were served on a plain iron stone dinner plate rather than an aluminum tray. They tasted bland without a hint of spices.

Once again Mr Abdul appeared and sat at the table. Not a mention of the poor Spences who had disappeared after leaving their luggage under the bed.

"Tomorrow, I have arranged another shikarra trip for you to the canal in Srinagar." We said nothing realizing there was no way we would be able to sleep past eight on this vacation with Mr Abdul organizing our every moment.

Mr. Khan, the antithesis of Mr. Butt, greeted us in the morning. Smiling and helpful, he assisted Lauretta into his fancy shikarra gold tassels hanging from the cabin portion. We set off for the Jhelum canal in Srinigar.

We silently floated into the canal and passed large squat houseboats with curved sides and horizontal, open, glassless windows, moored to the bank. Each housed many families. We were happy to be at least partially covered. Kitchen slop was pitched out the windows into the water.

"They look like duplicates of Noah's ark." Lauretta smiled.

Children bathed in the dirty brown water in the shallow areas, laughing and splashing each other. Some swung toward us on rubber tires on ropes tethered to sturdy willow trees along the bank. The ancient stone houses of Srinigar leaned precariously over the waterway as we glided by. We wended our way up the canal until it became too overgrown with weeds to go further.

Reversing our direction, we stopped at a landing jutting out from a large stone house.

"Here you buy honey from Kashmir to take home to Canada." We were not sure if it was an order or merely a suggestion. We did accept the offer. How we would get it home to Delhi without smashing the jar was a mystery. After our purchase we floated back into the channel and headed across Dhal Lake to Nageen Lake and the houseboat.

"I hope you have enjoyed the tour I arranged for you with Mr. Khan and that you like our city." Mr. Abdul welcomed us back from our excursion as we stepped onto the verandah of his KASHMIRI QUEEN. "Now you must come to see my carpets."

"Lauretta, we're not going to get out of this," I mumbled.

"That would be lovely, Mr. Abdul." Lauretta smiled.

We walked up the path behind the boat to a large multi-family house on a hill in the middle of an apple orchard. It was home to his many wives and children. We were ushered into a large display room on the top floor. Mr. Abdul clapped his hands and sent acolytes scurrying to get us coffee. We sat on leather three-legged stools and the show began.

"I would like you to see one of my prize carpets." The two men standing in a corner hauled a large rolled carpet to the edge of the room and started to unroll it on the polished wooden floor.

The wool carpet was magnificent, shades of red, crimson to red-orange, a tessellated design in the middle and four different patterns in the four quadrants. A geometric motif surrounded the outer edge. At twenty-four by thirty feet, the carpet would require a colossal room to house it. It was luxurious to stand on, almost sensuous. We smiled at the thought of having a suitable abode for such luxury.

"I think this is a bit too large for us, Mr. Abdul."

"Ah. Well we do have something smaller."

Carpet after carpet was unrolled as we sat and sipped our coffee.

"This has been a wonderful display of fine carpets, Mr. Abdul. I think we will have to wait until we have moved into our house and then decide what is best for us. We'll have to come back or perhaps you will bring some of your carpets to New Delhi."

"As you wish." Mr. Abdul looked glum as his helpers started rerolling the carpets and we excused ourselves to walk slowly back to the houseboat. We enjoyed the clear air prior to returning to the pollution of Delhi.

At the crack of dawn, we were picked up for the trip to the airport.

"It's kind of you to drive us to the airport, Ahmed."

"My father would have driven you, but he is busy with the new occupants of the houseboat." Lauretta and I smiled knowing the harrassment the new occupants would be subjected to.

"Srinigar is very quiet and tense, Ahmed." Lauretta had struck a nerve. Well-armed Indian troops crouched in the shade of buildings or behind walls of sandbags. With the exception of a few crotchety old men, no locals were on the streets as we drove past. Ahmed must have been known to the military since he was not stopped.

"We don't want to be part of India. We're an independent state. The Indians have put all those soldiers you see here. Look. Soldiers at every intersection. They think the Pakistanis are going to take us away from Mother India. It's ridiculous." We passed the Shakara Hazratbal mosque with minarets at each corner. Loudspeakers at the top of each minaret were the source of the five a.m. call to prayer which had been waking us.

At the airport we laughed and made sure we had our own bags for the security inspection. The Indian Airways 737 was sitting by the terminal, but it didn't mean we were going anywhere for a while.

3

Our return to New Delhi from Kashmir happily corresponded with our move to our refurbished quarters in Shanti Niketan.

As we stepped through the door of our Delhi home, we were greeted by a thin tense man with a pleasant smile who was sweating profusely, likely more from nervousness than the heat.

"I'm Simon, your bearer, Sahib. This is my sister, Sheela." Traditionally, the bearer was the most important of the servants in the household. We could not have survived without Simon's help. He knew the markets, what to buy, what was horrible and which vendors were cheats. He knew that the beautiful watermelons sold by the pound were deadly because they were injected with contaminated water to make them weigh more. He knew where to buy good fish and vegetables without having to depend on the US Commissary. His knowledge was invaluable.

As we introduced ourselves, Simon blurted out some of his culinary expertise.

"Madam, I can make chocolate cake with spangles, Tandoori chicken and I bake naan."

"Simon, that's wonderful. We probably won't need the cake unless our children are home but the chicken sounds wonderful with your naan. I'll help you with some new recipes as well."

Lauretta's offer was accepted graciously. Thus began Simon's training which in two years, would give him the reputation of being the best cook and bearer in the servant hierarchy among the staff at the High Commission, as well as the posh Shanti Niketan area.

Sheela was the sous-chef and cleaner and lacked the intellectual capacity of her brother. She sang as she dusted, and carried pails and various other things on her head for reasons unknown. Her hair was pulled back tightly into a bun on the back of her head, and she wore bottle-bottom glasses. She could read and write. Both were Christian which meant that someone of a lower caste did not have to be hired to clean up spills.

The caste system is horrid in the inequities that it perpetrates, all in the name of the Hindu religion. The four designated castes, starting with the so-called Brahmins at the top, do not recognize the untouchables who barely reach the bottom rung and are responsible for cleaning up the filth of those above them in the system. Moving out of your social position is not permitted. It was the most disturbing of the many features of India that we had to contend with.

The dhobi, another member of our inherited staff, was a wizened silent man who floated from the kitchen to his work area on the roof.

"Actually, it wasn't my fault but the iron was being too hot and the back came out of Sahib's shirt. What to do? What to do?" The dhobi combined this statement soon after our arrival with the requisite head swaying from side to side in a smooth swivel. Not a good beginning to our two years in New Delhi. The laundryman's ironing woes were not frequent after that unless I was missing other shirts that I was not aware of. To avoid having him boil socks, stockings and Lauretta's underwear, as was his normal practice, on Sundays we did the 'smalls' ourselves to spare the elastic. He probably now thought I never washed my socks and Lauretta never wore underwear.

The washing machine, dryer and a huge horizontal freezer were on the top floor which opened onto the roof with clotheslines stretching every which way. We discouraged hanging things out to dry. They were dirtier when the dhobi brought them in than when they went out. The freezer rarely had anything in it but occasionally word went out that the Commissary had hams or a roast of some sort. They went into the freezer and we hoped the power didn't go off for long stretches before they could be consumed.

The mali had been the gardener for years. His main claim to fame were the enormous prize-winning chrysanthemums that he nurtured every year and entered in the February Delhi Flower Show. He was not happy with the vegetable seeds that Lauretta had brought from Canada and asked him to plant.

The sweeper, whose main task was sweeping up the curved brown pods from the caesalpinia trees shading the driveway, had been waiting in the wings for the mali to drop dead so that he could show the memsahib what great things he could grow. In fact, nothing grew in the garden except the chrysanthemums which had adapted to the pollution and dirt from the main road in front of the house.

The two guards in their cast-off military uniforms, dutifully saluted when I arrived home in our miniscule Peugeot, swung the gates open with a flourish, saluted again, shut the gates and went back to sleep. In this male-oriented society, Lauretta did not get the same treatment. She often had to put her hand on the horn or open them herself to get action.

"Simon, what's that huge contraption in the driveway?"

"Sahib, that's the generator. We often have power outages in New Delhi. When it's off, the guards are supposed to turn on the generator."

"How often does the power go out?"

"Once or twice a day, Sahib."

"Does the phone work, Simon?"

"Usually, Sahib."

Three weeks after our arrival, I realized having a phone was not always a benefit.

"Hello, Hello. Doctor Holbrook? This is Siva Rama here. Remember me. You came to my restaurant in Toronto. I'm coming to India to buy spices. I would like you to do me a favour."

"Mrs. Rama, it's three o'clock in the morning."

She carried on, without listening to my objection. "I would like you to get a visa for my uncle. He lives in Chandigarh in the Punjab. I will come to see you, introduce you to him and pick up the visa. I don't have very much time so I hope you will see me promptly."

"I'm sorry, Mrs. Rama. It's not my department. You'll have to call the Immigration Department at the High Commission in the morning." I hung up.

From that point, I quickly discovered what this posting was going to be about. 'Hello. Remember me? I would like a visa for my auntie or my uncle or both.' I felt constantly on the defensive. Indians seemed proud of their country on the one hand, but in a great hurry to get out of it on the other.

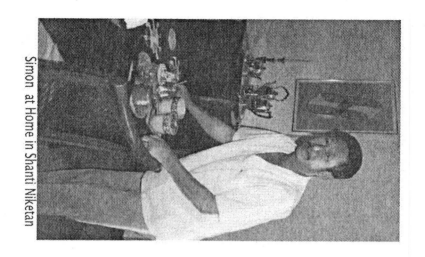

Simon at Home in Shanti Niketan

Lauretta and friend

4

In India, it was the custom for most to drive in the middle of the road unless the driver behind blasted his horn. Trucks all drove in the middle and had a 'HORN PLEASE' sign on the back. In order to pass, one had to blare the horn continuously. It took a long time to figure out that driving down the middle of the road probably gave the sacred cows more room on either side of the road. They stood with their hind quarters in the passing lane cropping the grass in the median. Heaven help you if you hit one. Though they appeared to be strays, they were all owned by a herder camped nearby who would demand an extortionate payment if his cow was maimed.

Our garden was separated from the main highway by a deep ditch and an access lane to the houses in our area. The racket prevented us from using the front garden for everything except the mali's handiwork. It also meant we couldn't sleep with a window open and had to leave the air-conditioner fan on to create a steady background noise.

Returning home from work only weeks after our arrival, the access road was blocked by two enormous trucks.

"Lauretta, our shipment has arrived!" I rushed to the house to get her.

"Actually, it wasn't my fault, Doctor Holbrook, but there was a problem with your possessions." Something always went wrong. We were used to it. I waited for the bad news. The shipping supervisor prepared us.

"The crates were unloaded from the container on the runway at the airport ten days ago and were covered in plastic sheeting for protection. Because the monsoon was so bad this year, Sir, people living in the shacks by the runway needed the plastic to cover their shacks and scooters. The wooden shipping boxes have filled with water."

This time I was speechless, as was Lauretta. We watched as the wooden crates were broken open and waited while the torrents of water poured out. The cardboard packing boxes inside had disintegrated.

"What shall we do with the clothes, sir?" They were saturated. A greenish mould coated everything.

"Hang them on the fence." With sixty degree centigrade heat in the crate, it was a wonder they didn't boil away to nothing.

"What's that?" asked Lauretta. We looked at what had been wonderful photographs from Mexico now shrivelled blobs. Then we stared at some of our most loved prints and paintings, stained and likely damaged beyond repair.

"Look at my desk!" Lauretta was aghast. Her pine desk was now a lime green.

"You are not to worry, Memsahib, not to worry. We have the finest craftsmen here in India who will put it right, Memsahib." We went into the house, leaving Simon and Sheela to fret about the mess.

Two weeks later, Simon announced excitedly, "The clothes are back, Sahib, from the cleaners."

Despite double doses of carbon tetrachloride, the clothes looked the same. I was sure we would have exploded if a match had been lit anywhere near us.

The insurance adjuster from McCormicks and Greaves looked at the clothes and promptly said that they looked quite fine to him.

"I could wear them." He took out his stubby pencil and laboriously wrote something on the forms he carried on a clipboard. These were in quadruplicate, but without carbon paper so that four entries were required for each item.

"This broken bowl is just old. It might have broken anyway."

"No! It is an antique and I want it mended." He looked at me in disbelief. Four more entries were made.

"The desk is quite fine."

"No. It's green from mould. It's pine wood. It should look like wood not green paint." Lauretta could barely contain herself.

"It's not our fault you know. It's caused by the airline." The adjuster put the tip of the pencil on his tongue and began another comment on his form in quadruplicate.

After losing our car in Trinidad, we knew what happened next.

"But Sahib, it wasn't our fault.

5

A few months after starting work at the High Commission, as I reviewed the medical examination results and chest Xrays for prospective immigrants to Canada, I was more and more aware of discrepancies in the documents I received from the examining doctors outside of New Delhi.

The Director of the Immigration section, Bill Rowland, stepped into my office as I flipped chest x-rays onto my radiology screens.

"David, we're having a great deal of trouble organizing visas for applicants from the Punjab. Local doctors supposedly perform the medicals for visa applicants and send them to you for processing. We have been informed that most people or their relatives simply buy a completed form and x-ray from the doctor without undergoing an examination. I think you should come and meet a man who has appeared to pick up his visa. His brother came earlier and we told him that we would only give it to the applicant in person. The applicant has arrived with his daughter."

An elderly wrinkled man with an orange turban and tan kurtah sat in a wheelchair in Bill Rowland's office. "Hello, Mr Singh. I'm Doctor Holbrook." There was no acknowledgement. I tried louder. Still nothing.

"My father is a little deaf." His daughter took the end of the pallu draped over her left shoulder and gently wiped the drool from the edges of her father's mouth. Her white and red flowered salwar kameez was a pleasant contrast to her father's drab outfit.

"Does he have to be in the wheelchair or can he stand and walk?

"Oh no, sir. He had a stroke many years ago."

"Tell me, why does he want to go to Canada."

"He doesn't wish to, but your medical care is much better. His brother in Canada will look after him and be able to get him better medical care than here."

I patted Mr Singh on the shoulder and asked his daughter to wait a few minutes. I returned to my office and looked up the medical file which I had passed as healthy. The forms from the doctor in Jallandur stated that he was in perfect health. I wondered how many others supposedly in perfect health were already in Canada. I returned to Mr. Singh.

"I'm sorry but Mr Singh is going to require more medical tests before he will be able to travel. We will keep his visa until the tests are completed."

"But sir. We've already purchased the plane ticket for two days hence." She swiveled her head as if it was my tough luck.

"Perhaps you should speak to Doctor Benhri in Jallandur. If Mr. Singh is not able to pass the tests, he will not be able to travel to Canada."

Two days later I answered the phone.

"Benhri here. You are quite right. I must have inadvertently sent the wrong form. Quite right, Doctor Holbrook, quite right. Mr. Singh is not a well man. I tried to tell them so, but they insisted that he go. You see actually it wasn't my fault."

A week later, I had another call from Bill Rowland in the immigration department.

"Remember that chap in the wheel chair, David? Somebody looking surprisingly similar to the woman who was pushing the chair has applied for a visitor's permit for her father. If we give it and it's the same man, he will apply for refugee status for sure when the permit runs out."

"They certainly know every angle. Why don't you suggest they come here for a medical examination? I'd be happy to see them and do the examination personally. In his condition, he would be medically inadmissable."

They did not show up for the appointment. By now, they would have skirted the sytem and be in Canada.

Bill Rowland appeared at my door a few days later looking exasperated.

"David, I don't like to ask but, if we can get permission from the High Commissioner, will you visit the doctors in the Punjab? Then you could make a decision about how we could change the system." I thought it would be a waste of time but I reluctantly agreed.

The Punjab was in the midst of civil strife in support of demands for an independent Sikh state. Sikh separatists were carrying on a terror campaign against the central government in New Delhi. I would be disappearing into this morass leaving poor Lauretta to deal with the shipment of our belongings and the work it involved.

I was promptly called into the High Commissioner's office once he had read our memo about the proposed visit.

"The Punjab is a restricted area as you know, David. You will have to take the bullet-proof car and Rajinder, my driver, will drive you. He has been specially trained to deal with terrorist situations." This all sounded a bit like James Bond but at least I wouldn't have to worry about driving.

"We will be going to Chandigarh first, Doctor. Tomorrow, we will go to Ludhiana, Jallandhar and finally Amritsar."

Chandigarh, another city designed by Le Corbusier, unlike Brasilia, was never quite finished.

As we drove around trying to find the physician's house, I tried to envision what the city would have looked like if it hadn't been overgrown before it was completed. It was to have had a lake with the Corbusier designed state government buildings reflected in the water giving the citizens of Chandigarh an escape from the humdrum of the city and a chance to enjoy the beauty of nature and silence. No lights were to be allowed at night to enable only the stars to be reflected in the lake. Alas there wasn't enough water to fill the lake.

After an hour's search, success at last. I was greeted warmly by Doctor K. L. Singh, the first physician on my list of medical practioners who examined the applicants for immigration to Canada. Over tea and biscuits he explained how the immigration medical system operated in the Punjab.

"Doctor Holbrook, you don't realize how things work here."

"You're right, Doctor Singh. Please tell me."

"Tourist agencies and real estate agencies are often combined. As a result, when a relative or 'close friend' asks a person to come to Canada, first, the agency sells them a ticket. In order to pay for it, the agency sells the person's property and their livestock. Because the person leaving now has no place to return to, the agent must ensure that the medical requirements are met. So, the doctor is paid a bribe to make sure the medical examination and x-ray are normal."

No doubt the doctor got a healthy stipend for his assistance not his medical expertise. I soon realized the only solution would be to bypass the tourist/real estate agent and have each applicant examined in Delhi before the air ticket was purchased. I would, no doubt, have a price on my head in the Punjab.

"Now I understand." I thanked Doctor Singh. We shook hands and I returned to the car. It was disgusting to think that the medical requirements have probably never been met in this area. The drain on the Canadian health care system and taxpayers was undoubtedly huge. It was obvious that the immigration programme had to be altered to take into account local conditions such as these.

For the rest of the four day trip, I did not find another of the appointed immigration doctors willing to see me. Word spread quickly in the community.

"We will stay in Amritsar, Doctor Holbrook. I would like to take you to the Golden Temple." I agreed but was apprehensive. I didn't know any of the religious customs and didn't want to make a fool of myself, or of Rajinder.

After a sleepless night in a room thick with clouds of mosquitos and not enough geckos to keep them under control, I was met at the hotel by Rajinder. As we walked to the main entrance of the Temple, Rajinder started his instruction.

"Please leave your socks and shoes here." I put them in a slot in the shelves along the outside wall and took a number card. "Let me help you tie this white head cover securely. Now please follow me." As we walked up the steps and through the large main arch of the entranceway built originally in the sixteenth century, the beauty of the temple was stunning, with the reflection of the gold temple and the arcade around the pool shimmering in the water. We walked down steps inside to the marble pathway that surrounded the lake or Pool of Nectar as it is known. The marble was cold, a welcome change from the blistering heat of the steps. "Please keep up, Doctor." I followed Rajinder clockwise along the sisal matting covering the marble.

In the middle of the pool sat a small gold-domed pagoda-like structure, the Harmandir Sahib, which created a shimmering golden reflection in the water.

This jewel of a small temple, the most holy shrine of the Sikh religion, was connected to the walk-way by a narrow causeway. I was the only non-Sikh in view and had strong reservations about crossing the bridge for fear of insulting the three priests robed in gowns of white with gold trim, their heads covered with the equivalent of a bishop's mitre.

They sat at the back of the marble and gold inlaid room which was much smaller than I expected. A soft ragh, an Indian melody, was played as background music. One priest read from the Siri Guru Granth Sahib, the Sikh bible.

The priests blessed the supplicants as we slowly moved past. I was pushed from behind and realized there was no turning back. I slowly bowed in front of the priests and was blessed. I was happy that Rajinder was in front of me. We then recrossed the causeway.

I was very moved by the whole experience. I now understood the outrage of Sikhs around the world when Mrs. Gandhi sent troops into the Temple searching for supposed Sikh terrorists. Hundreds of unarmed men, women and children were killed both in the Temple and the environs.

Having completed what I set out to do in the Punjab, my trip back to New Delhi was at breakneck speed. I guessed that was part of the avoidance plan. It certainly would prevent any terrorist from taking pot-shots at the car. We did have to stop at many railway crossings to allow trains to pass. The Indian railway system in this area was dependent on cast-off Canadian Pacific Railway Hudson steam locomotives, the huge ones I loved as a child. Every rail crossing had fruit peddlars who waited for the next train. They knew that every automobile would have passengers willing to buy some of their oranges or papadoms, a spicy, crisp flat bread. I couldn't resist.

"We have to be careful, doctor. You must stay in the car. I'll get what you wish." I reluctantly agreed. I knew that Rajinder would be blamed if anything went wrong.

The Punjab was the agricultural heartland of India. Driving at high speed through it was hair-raising. Enormous wheat racks pulled by slow moving tractors did not respond to the 'HORN PLEASE' signs. The car just slipped under the wheat sheaves piled horizontally on the rack, the sheaves jutting out over the road. They brushed the roof of the car as we passed on the shoulder. Heaven help us if we knocked any off the rack. Rajinder didn't slow down. I breathed a sigh of relief as we entered the outskirts of Delhi.

Bill Rowland came to my office the day of my return.

"Bill, the only way we can do this is to have all immigration medicals for applicants from the Punjab completed at one of the two High Commission medical clinics. Perhaps at some later date I'll be able to find another set of doctors who will not be coerced into faking the examinations."

6

It was a relief to be home with Lauretta for at least a few weeks. We waited until evening when the heat dissipated somewhat and walked to the video store to see what great flicks had arrived from Hollywood and Bollywood. The latter were wasted on us though they generally were of comedic value for locals and foreigners alike. With every walk, we were astounded by the number of new ultrasound clinics opening to satisfy the demands of families wanting to know the sex of their child. The girls were aborted early. No thought seemed to be given to what would happen when there was a shortage of potential child-bearing women in the country.

Our neighbourhood was becoming more and more expensive and rental properties were rare. The home owners had come up with a new strategy, build up, add a storey or two. The construction mess made walking less enjoyable and the clouds of dust added to the pall of smog which had started to descend over our home.

7

Calcutta and Bangladesh took me away from our peaceful evenings.

Arrival at Dum Dum Airport on the outskirts of Calcutta and the taxi ride to the city were always a miserable experience. Driving through the early morning haze, passing fields of odiferous decaying cauliflowers, I was soon overcome by the stench of rotting flesh from the tannery on the outskirts of the city. The traffic chaos began inside the city limits. The traffic lights didn't work. The police, who tried to bring order to the scene, were ignored. Gaping holes cut down the middle of the road were evidence of the ongoing subway construction, a subway which regularly filled with water from the Hooghli River. Clouds of dust blanketed everything and black fumes belched from the lumbering trucks which clogged the traffic.

The sidewalks were taken over by hordes of unfortunates who had lived on their patch for years.

Reaching Chowringhee and the The Oberoi Grand, my Calcutta hotel, was, in contrast, luxury out of the Raj. As the taxi turned into Jawaharlal Nehru Street, bystanders and the destitute stood and peered into the private laneway separating the privileged class from the have-nots. It was embarrassing to be divorced from the population in general.

Doormen in plumed hats took my bags and ushered me into a grand salon where I was invited to sit at a desk to register. What opulence compared to the street scenes only meters away.

Calcutta was a city of contrasts. The capital of Bengal was home to many of India's finest writers, artists and musicians. Numerous coffee houses had poetry readings every evening. On the other hand, the grinding poverty and decay were appalling. One Mother Theresa was not going to make a dint here.

Next morning I looked out my window and thought I was dreaming. The ground was blanketed with snow. I rubbed my eyes, put on my glasses and took a closer look. The chicken market was below my window. The ground was covered by a sea of white-feathered chickens tied together by their legs in bunches. All upside down, feathers to the sky, they blanketed the pavement. Bunches were chosen by buyers, picked out of the pile and tied to bicycles, rickshaws or flung over the shoulder. The 'snow' melted over the time it took me to eat my room service breakfast. When next I glanced out the window all that was left of the snowy down was being swept away.

As I stepped out onto Chowringhee Road from the sterility of Nehru Street, I quickly realized that walking was not possible. To step over families and around armless, legless lepers and beggars, was too much to tackle.

I crossed the road to what at first looked like a clearer area. That was equally hopeless. Hulks rolled in steely grey blankets were either sleeping or dead. The smell of urine and excrement was overwhelming. On taking a closer look around me, I soon realized that the subway entrance next to me was used by all on the street as an open public toilet.

I took a trishaw pedalled by a wiry grey-haired man. He stood on the pedals of his heavy double cross-barred Enfield and strained to propel me to Ho Chi Minh Street, the site of the clinic where the majority of the medical examinations for Canadian visas from West Bengal took place.

The elderly Bengali physician was nattily dressed in a three piece suit, odd with the temperature hovering in the nineties. I got the impression that this was his regular outfit.

"Doctor Ghosh, I have had to send to you requests for additional information on the forms. Do you fill them out or does your secretary? Do you take the x-rays here in your office? Who interprets them for you?"

He nodded between each question. It could have been a yes or a no. The nod was the same. "Oh, I do all those things. I am sorry for any mistake. I will be taking greater care." His head swiveled as if to shake off any criticism. I was embarrassed to have had to bring up the subject. He wasn't at all.

"Now you must join me for lunch at my club."

"Thank you. That would be very nice." The thought crossed my mind to refuse, to emphasize the problems with the medical forms, but what was the use.

"It's the Calcutta Club. Shall I meet you there?" We agreed on a time and I moved on with my morning calls.

The home of the British Council counselor and vice-consul for the British Embassy was beautifully restored. I felt as though I had stepped back into the thirties in the heyday of the Raj. From the thin bamboo awnings lining the balcony verandah, to the white wicker lawn furnishings, to the carpets and decor of the interior, it was like a magazine layout. A striped canvas shamiana (a fancy open-sided tent-like structure) was being erected on the spacious lawn for an afternoon British Council event.

Allister Somers, the British Consul, seemed adjusted to Calcutta. In addition to his work for the British Embassy, he assisted Canadians in distress in West Bengal.

"The problem is the longer one lives here, the less you notice the enormous disparities. People get on with their lives. The caste system makes it easy. You don't have to worry about somebody in a lower caste and they don't worry about you."

I thought of the lovely teenage girl I had passed on my way here. She was carrying baskets of feces on her head to some unknown destination. Would she ever progress to something better?

Not in the caste system. Not with arranged marriages. Not in India.

The Calcutta Club, formerly elegant, now tacky, was also a throwback to another era. The waiters' white jackets looked as though they hadn't been white for years.

Going out for a meal in India was a problem. One had to become a picky eater to avoid being sick afterwards. When the waiters' uniforms were dirty, one could usually assume that the kitchen was filthy too.

"The curry is very good at lunch." Dr. Ghosh helped me out. I ate my naan and little else and drank coke rather than the Indian wine from Italian grape varietals, imported by Rajiv Gandhi's Italian wife. "We make good champagne I understand. Would it be that you would prefer it?"

"No, thank you, Doctor Ghosh. I'll wait until dinner."

"You must have some mangoes." He called for the waiter.

"Tell me what mangoes you have on the trolley."

"Sir, we have some fine Safedas, and a few Langras left. Would you be wanting some of each?"

"Yes, well prepared and not stringy." He turned my way, "You have to be quite specific with these servants."

The mangoes arrived in perfect wedges arranged artistically on a platter. I felt like asking how they did it. Eating a mango was usually something I did in the garden. I was incapable of eating or cutting up a mango without dribbling it all over myself and the surrounding area.

"Now, I think you will savour a hint of rose petals in the Safedas."

Not knowing one from the other, I nodded.

I thanked my host for lunch and returned to the hotel to prepare for the next part of the trip.

8

My wait at Dum Dum Airport for my Biman Airways flight to Bangladesh was always a chaotic experience. Checking in was total mayhem. There was no line. You took out your ticket and started waving it as you pushed to the front of the mob.

"I'm sorry sir, the flight is full."

"Oh no it isn't. My name is right there." I pointed to a name which I couldn't read upside down. "Here is my ticket."

The exasperated attendant took my ticket without looking at it and gave me a purple boarding card. I stuck out my elbows and squeezed my way out of the crowd. Being taller than the Bengali passengers was a help. I found a stained metal chair in the lounge, its walls, originally cream, now a dirty brown. The stale urine stench came from the grubby washrooms and from the corners of the waiting room where males, young and old relieved themselves, not bothering with the formalities of a washroom. It was nauseating. I tried to ignore it and concentrate on my book.

The next push was to get a seat on the aircraft. Boarding cards meant little. More were issued than there were seats.

When the boarding was announced, I jumped up, stuck my elbows out again and charged for the gangway to the aircraft. At the top I looked behind to ensure that I was not near the last to board. A seat was now a certainty. I stopped for a spoonful of fennel seeds in a bowl held by a welcoming sari-clad stewardess. I rudely took two spoonfuls to treat myself with the refreshing licorice taste for the whole trip. I politely declined the cardboard box of food offered—a curried ball of rice and a samosa filled with curried vegetables and E coli to which my system was not yet accustomed.

The chaos of Dhaka began in the partially constructed airport. I was always surprised when the Embassy driver found me as I wandered around the crumbling pillars trying to find what looked like an exit. A string of gypsy children tagged along beside me each with a hand on some part of me or my bag. I didn't have a free hand to keep them out of my pockets which were always empty. I smiled at them as more joined in, all eager for a tip to take back to the elderly minder who was squatting against a pole and watching my reaction.

The drive into the city was an obstacle course. It meant avoiding pedestrians, bicycle rickshaws and enormous potholes. The main road past the presidential palace was suddenly smooth. It was either an attempt to show the power of the President or to prevent back damage as he drove to the magnificent National Assembly buildings designed by the American architect Louis Kahn. They were built over a number of years beginning in 1962.

Bangladesh, despite the opulence of the National Assembly, was dirt poor, almost totally dependent on aid from the rest of the world. To make matters worse, it had one of the largest populations on earth all living at or close to sea level. On average, five thousand people were crammed into every acre of land. How or why the British thought that at partition, the place could be run as East Pakistan from Islamabad, a thousand miles away, I didn't know. The 1947 partition of India into Muslim Pakistan and Hindu India was cavalier at best, pure stupidity at worst. Not only was the Punjab sliced in two. Pakistan was divided into East and West separated by a tiny isthmus high in the Himalayas. In 1971, the eastern section declared independence and became Bangladesh.

As we slowly bumped down the road to downtown Dhaka, the only noise seemed to be the car horn. The bicycle rickshaws moved silently with only the occasional grating of a bicycle chain or hacking of phlegm from one of the emaciated, white lungi-garbed peddlers wrapped in scarves to protect them from the early morning mist. The tricycles with a high back over the passenger seat and a canvas convertible-style roof were decorated elaborately with drawings and pictures of goddesses living and dead, gold streamers and multi-coloured flags. It was cheery after the drabness of Calcutta. Large billboards advertised the merits of Suntory whiskey and Sony stereos.

The hotel like the rest of Dhaka was in the midst of a brown-out. The lobby was dimly lit and my room was without power. The phone rang as I stepped into the room.

"I know you've just arrived, Doctor Holbrook, but I would like to take you to the diarrhoea hospital."

"Well, that sounds exciting." I shuddered. Doctor Peter Reed was a visiting physician from the United States posted in Dhaka for six months on a project sponsored by the Carnegie Foundation.

"Your High Commissioner thought you might be interested in the work I'm doing. I'll pick you up in half an hour."

Peter Reed was as good as his word. Half an hour later, there was a knock at the door. Dressed in a well-ironed safari suit, he introduced himself. He explained his project as we drove.

"David, I've been sent to Bangladesh as part of an aid project to train technicians in identifying diarrhoea-causing organisms. The knowledge will help health care workers treat the enormous number of water-related illnesses and reduce the mortality rate."

Walking in the front door of the hospital, I was practically overcome by the fetid fecal stench, mixed with a hint of carbolic acid. We walked first through the paediatric ward. Some squalling but mostly silent children, some too weak to peep, lay flat on their backs, arms and legs spread, unmoving in cribs. Their mothers sat with them giving them fluids constantly. We walked into the adult ward where only soft moaning could be heard. The beds were all designed with a hole in the middle, a bucket under the hole, making bed soiling less troublesome and sample collection easier.

"I'm never going to get the smell out of my sinuses," I muttered as we continued the tour. He laughed. He was obviously accustomed to it.

"Most have cholera. The fluid loss is so great that it's a real battle to keep up. Oral and intravenous fluids, when you can find a vein, are the only hope. Most die before they get here. Trying to get people to boil water seems to be hopeless." I must have looked about to pass out from the stench.

"Come and see the lab I've set up. The nursing staff are incredibly dedicated to be measuring the volume of feces and then pumping in the correct replacement fluid volume, morning, noon and night."

I followed Peter into a well-lit lab in the centre of the ward. "We had to have a generator." He laughed as I took a deep breath of air once inside the air-conditioned fresh smelling laboratory. Three technicians were doing stool cultures.

"David, I think you get so used to this, it's easy. We have nine hundred beds packed into two buildings and they're usually full."

The visit completed and not being keen to linger longer, I thanked the nurses and Peter who walked with me to the door.

I hailed an auto-rickshaw to the High Commission Recreation centre in Gulshan for a hamburger. I smiled at the thought of eating after a morning of wall-to-wall diarrhoea.

My next stop was the United States Embassy, a modern square brick fortress which would have been helped by some of Louie Kahn's brilliant flowing design ideas. George Bower, the physician-in-charge was awaiting my arrival.

"Well, David, how did you like the diarrhoea hospital? It's a real tourist highlight. The other day, I talked to Peter Reed, that lad from New Jersey and he mentioned he was going to give you a tour."

"It was certainly a different start to the day."

"Meet Susie Gordon. She's our nurse from stateside." The three of us sat and drank coffee and discussed the problems of being posted in Bangladesh: boredom, illness and the pluses: R & R in Calcutta.

"Calcutta for R & R? Wow! I must have missed something."

"By the way, we'd be happy to see any of your sick compatriots. Just tell them to call first so that the Marines will let them in."

I thanked them for their hospitality.

9

Returning home for me was usually a respite, a time of less stress. In India, it never worked that way.

"Sahib! Sahib! Come! Please come without delay!"

"Simon, what's the matter?"

"It's the bus, Sahib."

Buses in New Delhi were all in disrepair, windows broken, no springs and exhaust pipes belching clouds of pollutants into the already dense pall of poisonous air above the city. Opposite our house was a government housing estate of numerous five-storey apartments buildings, home to thousands of poorly paid civil servants. It was also the terminus for one of the many bus routes in Delhi.

Despite the fact that this was the beginning of the route, the buses were always packed to capacity. An extra dozen people clung to any appendage at the front or rear doors.

This particular bus had roared out of the estate and crossed the main highway, somehow thinking that the Goddess of Rules had given special dispensation to protect it from oncoming traffic. The bus didn't make it, but rolled into the gulley in front of our home, pitching people through the hedge and into our garden.

"Sahib, there are people lying all over the garden. They are dead."

Sheela was standing at the door looking bewildered.

"Sheela, take some sheets and tear them up for bandages."

People were lying on the grass moaning, but definitely not dead. The bus must have veered wildly as it turned out of the housing estate, and careened into the ditch which tipped it on its side in front of our house, tossing passengers in all directions.

"Simon, we'll first see if there is anybody pinned in the bus."

Simon climbed on the upturned side of the bus to peer in the windows while I tried to see whether there was anybody underneath within reach. Seeing no one, I returned to the garden.

Now strangely silent, people sat, a few writhed on the ground in pain while others milled about. Sheela, the bandage lady, appeared and the repairs began. I was amazed that nobody was dead, unless there was some poor unseen soul under the bus.

Once bandaged or simply reassured, people got up and left as if it was the end of a party. There were no broken bones, no lacerations requiring stitches and no apparent deaths. Soon the garden was emptied of people which left only the shell of the bus in the ditch.

"The driver has run away." Simon offered this information and I wondered whether this meant the wreck would be a permanent fixture in the Holbrook ditch.

When I returned from work at the end of the day, I was flabbergasted but happy to see that the bus had been removed, probably back in service without any repair.

President's Estate Polo Club

Ditched Bus in front of our Shanti Niketan home

10

We looked forward with great joy and pride to Sue, Chris and Matthew's annual visits to Delhi. Now twenty and a glamorous trio, Sue, slim and tanned with long dark brown hair and a smile to add to the beauty and Chris, tall with smiling hazel eyes and light brown short hair, arrived during their university break. Sue was now attending St. Martin's School of Art in London and Chris, the London School of Economics. Matthew, always scrawny was in his punk phase and 'not interested in education'. It was fascinating to watch the children's reactions to the parts of the world that we have called home.

Sue's initiation to India a year ago was a blast of reality for her. She rolled up the chicks (Indian blinds) in her room on her first morning in Delhi to face a funeral procession passing by her window on its way to the ghats on the Jumna. It was bearing the body of a young woman covered with orange marigolds her flowing black hair dotted with orange petals, her feet protruding from the end of the litter. She immediately equated what she saw to an article she had read on dowry deaths, the misfortune that faces those women and their families who are unable to supply the increased dowry demands of some in-laws after a year of marriage. The experience had left a pall over her impression of South Asia. It was not helped by the local youth who shoved his hand between her legs while she was looking in a craft shop in Connaught circus. She wheeled around and decked him with a right hook.

Chris, on the other hand, had been fascinated by the Indian experience. He was adventurous and wanted to see as much of India as he could. He had just returned from a camel safari through Rajasthan, an early twenty-first birthday present, which he wouldn't forget in a hurry.

"There were ten camels and a horse. The eight American girls each had a camel handler. One sat behind each girl supposedly to hold them on but in reality to cup their breasts." We all laughed knowing he was right. "I had my own camel, a nasty piece of work she was, but I didn't fall off. We stopped to take photos and some women in the desert thought we were taking pictures of them and started throwing stones at us.

Everthing was a tan colour, the clothes, the landscape, the camels, the buildings, everthing. There were some beautiful maharajah's palaces near Faridabad where we started but it was six hours from New Delhi on the bus before we even arrived there."

"Where did you stay?"

"Not at the places we were supposed to. There were no fancy hotels like the brochure described. The hotels were ghastly. There was no wallpaper over the concrete walls just postcards stuck up. I can hardly wait to have a bath. What's for dinner, Simon?" At the kitchen door, Chris noticed Simon and Sheela smiling and listening to the stories.

Matthew had decided to quit school after grade ten, figuring that parents, schools, social workers and the Children's Aid Society had no idea what course he had mapped out for himself. We certainly didn't. Despite formally being a ward of the state he still considered us his family and we assumed the same. We sent him the funds to come to New Delhi for Christmas and he arrived in punk attire, not a good blend with the local scene. On his own he recognized that a change in garb was required.

Matthew had us in a quandary. At nineteen, he was still incapable of taking advice from anybody. He chose instead to antagonize anyone in authority which resulted in his expulsion from every school we had tried. We now found ourselves chastised by the Children's Aid Society in Toronto for adopting him in the first place.

"Do you feel that Matthew is distancing himself from Chris and Sue as well as us?" Lauretta and I, as we lay in bed, thought over the first week of our family holiday in New Delhi. "Do you think it's the differences in schools and friends or just personality clashes?"

"I don't know, Babe. It's a mystery. He certainly has changed."

"He seems happy on the surface when he arrives for school breaks and when we see him in Canada."

"But there's definitely been a change in his psyche in the past six months. I can't put my finger on it. He doesn't seem interested in any of us."

"Could it be drugs? How could we tell?

"We've had chats with each of them about drugs and birth control. Obviously they're not going to come out and say 'Dad, I'm an addict', but at least they know we're not going to banish them if there's a problem. They know we'll help them deal with it."

"Maybe it's just the earlier separations from his brother and sister."

"Do you suppose he's in some kind of trouble?"

"I'll ask him but there is not much hope of getting a straight answer."

"I'm so depressed when I think back on the funny high-spirited kid he used to be. Now when I look at him, he looks back as if he doesn't know us or care. Is it our fault?"

"Lauretta, no, it's not. We are doing and have done the best we can. Chris and Sue have thrived. Matthew will still make it in his own time and way. I don't think he's any different from the very beginning, self motivated, self contained with an impenetratable psyche."

We put our arms around each other, fell back on the bed, and stared at the ceiling in silence.

Chandi Chowk, the main street of Delhi since the seventeenth century, was still the heart of the old city. Driving was virtually impossible with motorized rickshaws chugging out fumes and noise, and pushcarts weaving all over the road laden with everything from grain to spices to lumber. A fence down the centre of the boulevard did not keep people from crossing or the cattle off the road. Trucks, oblivious of the pedestrians and the sweating labourers pushing and pulling the over-loaded two-wheeled carts, bounced down the thoroughfare horns blaring.

Sauntering through this maze was a weekend family experience when we were together on their break from university or in Matthew's case from the unemployment rolls.

"Will you tell me what spices you have for sale?" Sue couldn't resist asking partly for the interest in colour and partly to be able to perfect the lilt of the language.

"Memsahib, we have every spice." The head rotated in the typical swivel. The pyramids of yellow turmeric, red cinnamon, the rich colour of allspice and nutmeg, numerous masalas of undetermined ingredients were piled high in perfect peaks on counters. The aroma was wonderful. An awning covered the seller.

"That's a first. It's fun to be a bride briefly. Nobody calls me memsahib." We laughed realizing that at twenty, she was well past marrying age for most Indian women with arranged marriages.

"Dad, let's have a glass of milk." Chris smiled slyly knowing that a communal cup of warm fresh unpasteurized milk from a large bowl sitting on the counter of a stall would give us a good chance of getting sick. "If we lived here permanently I would probably adjust to the bacterial changes in my system."

"You're right, Chris. Are you planning on staying?"

He smiled. "No thanks, Dad. I like London too much for that. I'll stick with the visits."

Lauretta, Sue and Matthew had disappeared down a narrow alley to the shops which specialized in ribbon and lace and, in Matthew's case, incense. Invariably, Lauretta emerged with a skein of silk ribbon or gold thread in a small paper bag while Matthew came out of another shop with a wooden box of incense of many types. I couldn't imagine what his room in Toronto must smell like.

The narrow lanes housed small, crowded shops selling everything imaginable. One of our favourites was Rajiv's. He had a bullock turning a wheel to grind millet all day in his living room. He sold bags of ground seed while his wife sat on her haunches with a switch to keep the bullock moving in circles. After a twelve hour day the bullock was ushered out of the living room to a stall in the kitchen no doubt suffering from vertigo. The couch was moved back into the living room for guests.

"What's this, Dad?" Matthew picked up a sliver of black wood from a vendor's stall.

"It's bark for cleaning your teeth."

"The man leaning against the tree over there watching you is the tooth-puller and bone-setter. He'll show you how to use it. He's Mister Fix-it. He is the handy dentist and surgeon."

Matthew wandered over to chat. Chris, serious all of a sudden, said, "Dad, I'd like to go to a fortune teller."

"Are you sure, Chris?"

"Why not? It'll be fun. I don't have to believe what he says."

"I'll ask one of the secretaries at work where to go."

On a Saturday morning, we climbed the worn rickety staircase to Mr. Dipanji's small room above one of the tiny shops in an alley off Chandi Chok. Sitting cross-legged in a shaded corner half-asleep, the soothsayer mumbled a greeting.

"I'm fine Dad, you don't have to stay." I looked at the ancient, turbaned, white-bearded soothsayer and decided Chris was right. I descended the uneven circular stairs.

Twenty minutes later, Chris appeared looking pale and shaken.

"What's the matter? What did he say?"

"He said that I am going to become very ill unless I carry a five-carat ruby next to my heart. Of course I don't believe him. He also said that Sue is going to be much wealthier than me." Chris paused and looked off into the distance. "This wasn't a very good idea, was it?" I reached up and put my arm around his shoulder and we walked back to Chandi Chowk.

"Chris, he can tell you any story and apply it to you. Relax." It was difficult to think of anything reassuring to say.

"I'll take you to Sundar Nagar before you go back to London." Precious and semi-precious stones had always been a part of life in India. Well-to-do families had drawers of stones carefully wrapped in tissue paper for their own enjoyment. I guess it was the same as having a stamp collection. The Sundar Nagar market had a shop that specialized in gems.

"My son would like a five-carat ruby." Without a moment's hesitation, the owner turned and pulled out a drawer of rubies and a scale. He weighed five stones that were five carats.

"Which one do you like?" I asked as Chris looked at me bewildered.

"What is the price range?" Chris asked in a very business-like manner.

"This star ruby you can have for three thousand rupees. This one will be eighty thousand rupees. It is of very high quality." Chris glanced my way again.

"How much is three thousand rupees?" Chris asked me.

"About one hundred dollars." Chris turned to the clerk.

"I would like the star ruby please." Chris pulled out his wad of ragged rupees, his travel allowance accumulated over the past weeks.

The ruby was carefully wrapped in tissue paper and put in a navy blue pouch with a gold chord to pull it shut.

"I think I need a chain to hang it around my neck." Another drawer was pulled out and an array of chains displayed. "I'd like this one please." The thin chain of tiny gold balls was wrapped.

"I'll put a loop on the ruby so that it will fit on the chain."

"You know, Dad, I should never have had my fortune told. I feel awful. I didn't want to spend my money on that, but what if the fortune teller is right?"

"Hey, cheer up. This is India. You don't have to believe everything." I put my arm around his shoulder again and we headed back to the car hoping that now having filled the soothsayer's prescription he felt reassured.

Having the children home for Christmas was a joy but trying to keep them occupied was another thing. Sue was content to read and stay home to paint and draw. She was beginning to make a mark for herself in graphic design at St. Martins. She was into her Camden market-used-clothing-phase wearing a collection of cottons that were cool but eccentric.

We did not encourage Matthew to go Rajasthan with Chris. We were afraid that he might have turned the seven day safari into a two month trek in the desert. On the other hand, that might have been better than having him sneaking around the alleys of Shanti Niketan in his worn jeans, studded belt and snake tattoo on his arm, smoking my Montecristo cigars.

Simon, with Lauretta's urging, was embarking on a new culinary endeavour, making the finest Christmas cake in India. He had been to the market with a detailed list and now had everything spread out in the kitchen waiting for Lauretta to give him the signal to start. The day long process was to be capped by an entire twenty-six once bottle of rum being poured into the mix.

Chris, having recovered from his Rajasthani journey, came up with another activity proposal.

"Dad, will you and Mom take us to Fatepur Sîkrî? We missed it when we went to the Taj Mahal." I shuddered to think of the God-awful traffic.

"Sure. Let's. I'll book a car and driver." I tried to be cheery not wanting to dampen any enthusiasm they might have had for India.

The Grand Trunk Road from Delhi to Agra was a traveller's nightmare. Indian lorries were simply truck frames with four wheels and a motor. The purchaser had to build his own cab and cargo space, using wood and tin and then decorate it in the most garish style possible. Multi-coloured goddesses, bodies painted in the draped wet sari look, nipples prominent with streamers attached strategically, incense burning on the wooden dashboard and prayer flags fluttering on the roof did not protect these vehicles from the most catastrophic accidents.

The trucks, always travelling at break-neck speed, ploughed into cars on the two lane Grand Trunk Road with wild abandon and then careened into the deep ditches. This left bodies strewn on the pavement, hanging limbless or decapitated from the tin remains of the cabs of the trucks. The death toll every week was appalling.

"Ugh. Look at that!" Chris couldn't believe his eyes as our pale blue Ambassador with its tiny powerless engine rolled to a halt immediately behind an accident scene. A truck laden with bricks had overturned in the ditch. A brown body hung out of the cab motionless. Bricks littered the road.

"Don't look." Sue and Chris scrunched down in the back seat with Lauretta in the middle looking sick. Matthew's morbid curiosity got the best of him.

"It's best if we pull out of the traffic, Doctor. I'll drive into this dhaba." The tea station, which smelled of curry and spilled motor oil, didn't help the three back seat passengers to revive quickly. Old tires cut in half, painted white and stuck in the ground, lined the driveway.

"I'll go and see if I can help any of those people."

"I'll come with you, Dad," Matthew volunteered.

"Oh no you won't," exclaimed Lauretta. "Neither one of you. Even I can see they're dead or beyond help." Lauretta grabbed my arm and was not about to let go.

"Doctor, don't go. Petrol is pouring out of the lorry and people are standing over there smoking." I stood with my hands on my hips in disgust unable to believe such carnage. I resigned myself to staying out of it and turned away.

"There's a washroom over there beside the tea shack if anybody needs it." I offered the information knowing from our last stop here that the toilet was simply a hole in the ground.

"Sahib, where have you been missing?" The proprietor of the outdoor tea stand with a tin awning over the counter remembered seeing Lauretta and me before. His slatternly wife was pulling teacups from a tub of dirty water.

"Memsahib, you would like tea?"

"No thank you." Lauretta walked toward the only bench in the shade. The cars in the traffic jam shimmered in a wavy blur as the heat rose from the hot pavement.

"Let's turn the bench around." Chris and I struggled to push the old iron seat. It had probably never been moved. Matthew, for reasons known only to him, was now walking into the field of grain behind the dhaba, towards a group of women bent ninety degrees at the waist, hoeing between the plants. He probably wanted to know what they were growing.

"I wonder how he proposes to carry on a conversation?" Sue laughed.

"He'll think of some way. I hope their husbands are not watching," Chris added.

I cupped my hands around my mouth and shouted at him. "We're leaving, Matthew." He heard and came back.

"Women do the manual jobs. Men run the machines and rest on their charpoys during the heat of the day. No rest for their wives." Lauretta was observing first-hand what the women in the crèche, where she tried to volunteer, had been telling her. Her efforts were thwarted because she didn't speak Hindi. She also felt that being a farangi, the locals thought a foreigner might give Mother India a bad reputation.

"I bet most of those women are younger than me," Sue muttered.

"Yes, and probably married, Sue, You're slow." Chris smirked.

"If they get rid of so many female babies, who's going to grow up to do the work? Men will soon far outnumber the women." Sue had been reading the Hindustan Times' reports about infanticide.

"You're right, Sue, but this attitude is centuries old and it takes a long time for old habits to die." Lauretta found it difficult to answer Sue's query logically.

We sat in the heat waiting for the driver to reappear from the back of the dhaba. It was better than sitting in the stifling Ambassador.

"Sahib, the police have finally arrived and will let us pass." We unenthusiastically returned to the car.

"Let's hope that this will be the last time we have to tackle this road. I did think the kids should see Fatehpur Sîkrî. It's such a marvellous example of sixteenth century Moghul architecture."

Fatehpur Sîkrî was a long deserted royal city built by the Moghul Emperor Akbar in the mid sixteenth century. It soon ran out of water and was abandoned.

After walking through the huge main gate flanked by enormous stone elephant statues, we were soon approached by umpteen potential guides.

"I do not charge very much money, Sahib, I am a brahmin."

A greasy, short middle-aged man came up to Lauretta and tried to take her arm.

"Thank you but we don't want your help." Lauretta recoiled as he pushed closer. "Brahmins do not act as tour guides." I stepped between Lauretta and the weaselly character. Realizing we saw through his upper class pretentions he stopped. The five of us entered the vast plaza within the walls, alone. The dry furnace-like heat pounded down on us and Lauretta was ready to leave.

"Let's go over there in the shade before I faint." We climbed to an alcove and looked out over the empty plaza. Our three, still referred to by us as kids despite being young adults, climbed the stairs behind us and looked down on us from the arcade above.

"Come up here, Mom. It's cooler." Chris's shouting echoed around the empty plaza sending clouds of pigeons out of their roosts under the ramparts.

"Oh Chris. You know I hate birds flying at me."

We appeared to be the only visitors. Perhaps this accounted for the guides circling like vultures around us outside the gate.

Out of the blue, a short, aged, white-bearded and mustachioed man sporting an unkempt grayish white turban, and loose fitting gray ankle length kurta, appeared from a passageway behind us.

"I will show you the palace." He spoke in a slow quiet voice.

"Are you a guide?"

"No, Sahib, I'm a caretaker." He spoke slowly and sadly as if he was tired of his lot in life. We got to our feet without falling off the edge of the alcove. "Are those young people with you?"

"Yes they are. It would be kind of you to show us the palace." We slowly walked down a narrow passageway after climbing a flight of stairs to an upper level. Sue and Chris joined us. Matthew was nowhere to be seen.

"If you look down at the plaza from here, you can see that it's divided into squares," explained our new found guide.

"Look, Mom. It's a chess board." Matthew shouted from an alcove above us.

"It was like a board game that the Emperor played with his servants acting as board pieces."

"Come over here, Dad." Matthew pointed to the arched windows looking out over the western plain outside the wall.

"That is where elephant polo was played" explained our guide. "The mahouts carrying long mallets and the elephants using trunks and feet had long battles on that field." He talked as though he had been there four hundred years ago.

"This is the harem." A maze of rooms with a double wall of miraculously filigreed red sandstone allowed some light in but very little chance of seeing out.

"I can't imagine being part of a harem" Sue mused to no one in particular.

"It would be a good place for you," Chris suggested. Sue stuck her tongue out at him unable to ignore the jibe.

We slowly walked in and out of the harem, descended to the plaza and caught up with Matthew now below us. We thanked our guide who nodded and started to walk away without expecting to be paid.

"Chris, take these rupees and give them to the gentleman and thank him." The caretaker bowed to Chris and carried on into the shadows and disappeared.

11

As we turned into the driveway on our return home, we were greeted by a torrent of water pouring out under the front door.

"Sahib there has been an accident." Simon shouted as he ran out to greet us. "It's the geyser."

"The what?"

"The geyser which heats the water in the young memsahib's bathroom. It exploded. The water was hot and difficult to turn off."

After making my way up the sodden carpeted staircase and into the bathroom, I could not believe my eyes. Shards of metal from the hot water heater were lodged in the door and ceiling. It looked like a nail bomb had been detonated.

"Thank God none of the children was in the bathroom."

"Thank heavens for Fatehpur Sîkrî." Sue added. "It saved me."

"I will call maintenance, Sahib. They will get a new geyser quickly."

"Thank you, Simon." We looked at the sodden mess and knew that it wasn't going to dry quickly.

"We'll have to get this place fixed before the cocktail party we're supposed to be giving for the delegation of government ministers from Canada. Simon has been working for days preparing hors d'oeuvre."

The party of big eaters and drinkers were in India to converse briefly with local officials and have photo-ops on elephants or camels for their office walls. They would not likely venture up the sodden staircase. The reception was larger than expected. Lauretta became desperate as she watched the food disappear.

"Simon. Where are the shrimp?" Lauretta always the observant hostess, knew there were pounds of shrimp.

"Oh Mehmsahib, the Big Boss in the dark suit ate them all." Lauretta looked skyward and said nothing.

Once the throng realized that the food and drink were drying up, they left. They now felt that they had received their tax dollars' worth from their civil servants. We could now move to the living-room with our invited extras and finish what was left over.

"David. Pull out your champagne." Bubbly, as the woman in the crimson and gold sari was fondly known, shouted at me from the middle of the living room where she sat crosslegged, sari spread out around her, crimson scarf wrapped around her neck. She was hoping for a reprieve rather than a tipsy journey home with her sullen husband. Simon and Sheela in their serving finery watched the scene from the kitchen in disbelief. Simon looked at me for instructions and soon appeared with my one bottle of champagne made in India from Sonia Gandhi's varietals and imported expertise.

Chris, Sue and Matthew, much to their chagrin, had to return to college and in Matthew's case a job search. The departure was always sad for us all. Matthew, having arrived from Canada in jeans, insisted on travelling back in the middle of winter in a grey suit that he had lifted from Chris's closet. Needless to say, Chris had outgrown it. He refused a coat and boarded the aircraft wearing a white shirt and tie with the suit.

Chris and Lauretta and their camel

Chris and Lauretta and their elephant party

12

Getting to Islamabad was an exhausting adventure. The first leg of the trip from Delhi to Lahore in Pakistan, usually involved a delay resulting in a mad scramble to get on the connecting flight to Rawalpindi and Islamabad.

To make matters worse the change of aircraft was often to a smaller plane and thus a fight for a seat. There were always losers.

The one time Lauretta accompanied me, we were among the losers. Lauretta had agreed to come to Pakistan to become familiar with as much of South Asia as possible.

"Lauretta, we're going to spend your first night in Pakistan in Lahore." Lahore was the capital of the Punjab for centuries prior to the Partition of India into Hindu and Muslim states which was orchestrated by the British in 1947. The Punjab was slashed in two leaving Lahore, just north of the border with India, as the capital of the Pakistani half of the Punjab. We sat and watched the sun set over the dome of the Golden mosque in the brief time we had before our return to the airport early the next morning.

Islamabad, like most newly-built capitals in the world, was an uninteresting city built in the early 1960s. Our arrival on a Friday, the Islamic holy day, gave us an opportunity to reconnoitre.

Lauretta did not conform to the stereotypical Muslim woman. We enjoyed walking down the street holding hands rather than having the dutiful wife walking a few paces behind her husband. In fact we were the only people walking with the exception of a few young Muslim men walking hand in hand. I suspected no sexual innuendo but merely friendship. It was interesting that it wouldn't be seen that way in America. We were gawked at by the men washing their souped-up Japanese sedans in the stream adjacent to our hotel.

The immigration problems I was asked to deal with at the Embassy, centred around the Afghan refugees in the north of the country.

Peshawar in the North-West Frontier Province was a remarkable city of a million smugglers, arms dealers and refugees from the Afghan war. The British tried on many occasions to bring some order to the area without any success and finally gave up thus splitting the area from the rest of the Indian subcontinent into a province of unruly warlords. At partition it was stuck on to the newly formed Pakistan.

Our driver had remained quiet throughout our trip on the Grand Trunk Road from Islamabad. We crossed bridges over deep gulleys, passed ancient Moghul forts with crenellated walls, and over riverbeds far below.

"Is walking safe, David?" I shrugged and asked.

"Sir. Peshawar is always dangerous. I will accompany you to the bazaar. Madam, keep your head covered." The Chawadi bazaar was a maze of alleys with two storey wooden structures on each side, each with a verandah hanging over the narrow lane allowing a view of the action below. We were drawn into a shop by a beautiful crimson and blue patterned carpet in the window. Our driver waited outside the door.

"Welcome. From where is it that you are coming?" The short wizened shop-keeper clutched his hands as if in prayer, hoping for a monumental sale no doubt.

"From Islamabad." We couldn't pass for locals or Pakistanis if our lives depended on it.

"You are not interested in munitions?"

"What do you have?" Lauretta looked at me as if I'd lost my mind.

"We have some AK47 rifles if you are wishing some. Imported. Also grenades. We can get whatever you are requiring, from ammunition to shoulder missiles." Having satisfied my curiosity, I smiled.

"No, I think today we'll just look at your carpets."

"As you wish."

"We would like to see the carpet in the window as well as the silk coat." Our host pulled out two small leather stools for us to sit on and two small glasses of black espresso were brought by a minion from the arms area behind a vertical multi-coloured plastic strip curtain.

"This is a clan elder's formal coat. Please try it." Horizontal bands of maroon, gold and green silk stretch to my ankles, and the sleeves were practically as long. He handed me a silk sash to tie the buttonless coat.

"It's magnificent, David." Lauretta turned to our host. "What is your best price for this coat?" He muttered an amount that neither of us heard. "The carpet is what price?"

"Well madam, perhaps I should show you other carpets first." He went off to get a helper to bring half a dozen more rolled up carpets.

"This place gives me the creeps." Lauretta whispered. "What if his ammunition dump blows up. Let's get out of here." As the shopkeeper re-entered the room, the helper began to unroll other carpets.

"I don't think we'll see any more today, thank you."

"But sir. I can give you a special price on any carpet."

"What is your price for this carpet?" We pointed to our original choice. He was silent for a moment as he sized up his potential customers.

"Five hundred dollars for the carpet and coat." Lauretta and I conferred. "and I'll give you this antique silk sash for the coat."

"We'll give you two hundred dollars." Lauretta stated.

"Madam, that is an insult. It will cost me money if I sell them to you for three hundred dollars." Dealing with a woman would be enough of an insult.

"We will offer you two hundred dollars." Lauretta repeated.

He was silent pondering whether we would walk out. As we rose from our stools and slowly headed for the door, he called after us.

"I will only accept cash." Lauretta and I looked at each other and pooled our resources, bills stuffed in every pocket to avoid losing it all if mugged. "Do not tell anybody what you paid for these items."

The carpet, four feet by six, was rolled and tied securely. "That was a weird experience, 'Will it be arms or carpets'. The coat is a masterpiece." Lauretta breathed a sigh of relief as the door shut behind us and we were ushered to the car by the driver concerned for our safety.

The purpose of our visit to Peshawar was to see a large refugee shelter on the outskirts of the city.

"This refugee camp is primarily for women, children and wounded men," Doctor Abdul Shayeed explained as we walked into the courtyard of an enclosure of three two storey wooden buildings in a field surrounded by barbed wire. "Madam Holbrook, there are two young nursing students who would like to take you on a tour." Lauretta, her scarf over her hair, was ushered into the paediatric and women's ward. "Doctor Holbrook, I would like to discuss with you the possibility of getting some assistance from Canada to purchase medication for this hospital. We have prepared a list of things we need desperately."

"May I have a copy of the list? I will discuss it with the Embassy in Islamabad and I'm sure we will be able to assist you with some things you need." It was hard to know what the official policy was. I hoped to convince the Embassy to help now that I had got myself into this. However, it was awkward because of not knowing which factions were being supported and which were not. On humanitarian grounds, I could see no difference but the politics of the situation was beyond me.

"May I walk through the wards with you?"

"It would be a pleasure." Doctor Shayeed chatted with patients as I smiled, unable to communicate in any other way.

"This is a good example, Doctor. This woman has uncontrolled diabetes because we do not have any insulin."

"I am amazed, Doctor, at the high incidence of diabetes in women in South Asia. Is it because of eating habits or malnutrition?" I would have liked to ask if it was because the females in the family get what was left over when the men were sated.

"It is a perplexing question. Studies have not been done."

"In Islamabad I do have some insulin which I'll send to you."

After many handshakes and pleasantries, we returned to our car for our return to Islamabad.

Peshawar Munition and Carpet Shop

Afghan Refugee Camp in Peshawar

"Lauretta, I think we'll save our trip to the Khyber Pass until our next visit."

"One visit to Pakistan might be enough for me." Lauretta laughed. "There is something eerie about this place. I don't quite know what it is. Is it the sneers I get on the street from both sexes? I'm not flaunting my body, I'm not knowingly tempting Muslim men to anger their women. I'm covered from head to toe albeit with slacks rather than a burqa but this is too much for me."

"Lauretta. There is one more stop."

Karachi, Pakistan's main port and the capital prior to the building of Islamabad, was a city in dire straits. Armed private armies frequently fought in the streets, battling over corruption in the local government and conditions in the ghettos. Mohajirs, Muslim refugees from India, also raised the ire of many resulting in more outbreaks of violence. Dacoits, often disaffected students turned terrorists, murdered and kidnapped with impunity the wealthy and foreigners.

Much of the city was a shambles. The oranji neighbourhood, a slum area near the city core, tired of open sewage drains running down the streets and angered by the authorities who simply pocketed the allocated funds, finally raised the money themselves and paid for their own neighbourhood sewage system.

The only way to understand a city and feel a part of it is by walking through the markets and observing the locals. In this case though bodyguards were offered, I didn't want to put Lauretta in any danger from random acts of sectarian violence and so we cancelled our usual meandering. To avoid spending time on the streets or in markets it was simpler to stay either at the hotel or the hospital.

The Agha Khan Hospital and Medical School, one of the finest in Asia, met the standards of the best in North America. The wards in this hospital put many Canadian hospitals to shame. The physicians, most with some British or North American training, were excellent. Doctor Imran Khan, the director, came out of his office, hand extended.

"We are so pleased that you, Doctor and Mrs. Holbrook, have come.

"Doctor Khan, the reason for my visit is to ask whether your hospital could offer Canadians specialized care if required. It's always a concern for my department if individuals are too ill to be evacuated to Canada."

"It would be my pleasure to offer any care required while in Pakistan. We even have our own helicopter and rescue service. I would like to take you on a tour of the hospital. The director as you probably know is the chief of the Mayo Clinic. He is here for a six month term." I didn't know, but I was impressed. "The director of our Emergency Department is a nurse from McMaster University in Hamilton, Canada."

After visits to almost every department, admiring everything from the state of the art equipment to the indigo blue wall tiles with beautifully written Arabic script of passages from the Koran, we excused ourselves, thanked our host and headed for the airport through the chaos of Karachi. Garishly decorated trucks, one, a tanker of gasoline with 'HIGHLY INFALLIBLE' in enormous letters on the back, buses and the ubiquitous rickshaws pushed by their lawn mower motors, puffed black smoke into the already sulfurous atmosphere. Clouds of dirt and soot hung over the streets and the noise of blaring horns and shouting people was deafening, the fumes and stench of rotting food, nauseating.

13

On our doorstep we were met by Simon in a greater than usual state of agitation.

"Sahib, my daughter is very sick. Would you please see her for me?"

"Simon, I'm not on the staff of a hospital here but I can make sure she gets proper care. Is she here now?"

"Oh no, Sahib. She is in Darjeeling with my mother."

"Where is her mother?"

"My wife, she has died, Sahib."

"Oh, I'm sorry." I grimaced. "Can you bring your daughter to Delhi?"

"Oh yes, Sahib. May I go now to fetch her? My sister will be here in my place until I return. It will take me one week."

One week later, Simon walked toward the house from the servants' quarters above the garage. Clutching his hand was a short, scrawny child, pale and short of breath. She appeared to be seven or eight years old.

"Thank you Sahib for helping us." I put out my hand and Seama raised hers to grasp mine.

"Please come in." She stepped gingerly into the hall accompanied by her father, grandmother and Sheela, Simon's sister.

"How long have you been short of breath?" I mimicked a deep breath and pointed to Seama as I pulled out my stethoscope.

"Oh, she doesn't understand." offered Sheela.

"Two months." answered Seama.

"How old are you, Seama?"

"Fifteen, sir." I was taken aback, astounded by the difference between her actual and apparent age.

"I'm just going to listen to your lungs, Seama." Simon undid her clean white cotton shirt. I could hear only faint breath sounds on either side of her upper chest, none in the lower lobes. "We're going to go to the hospital and get an x-ray of your chest." I left it to Simon to explain what an X-ray was.

Cramming Seama, Simon, granny, an ample wrinkled elderly lady, and Sheela into our little Peugeot and still have space to drive was a feat.

"We're going to the Hospital for Chest Diseases. It's somewhere near Connaught Circus (the commercial centre of New Delhi). Simon, you hold the map for me." We found the hospital with difficulty.

After a lengthy wait during which time many chest x-rays were taken, the radiologist finally appeared.

"Doctor Holbrook, please come with me." I followed Doctor Khosla into his x-ray viewing room. "This child has fulminating pulmonary tuberculosis. Look at this."

"There's only minimal air entry into her upper lobes."

"The two lower lobes and the right mid lobe are obliterated. We'll have to get her into the Tuberculosis Hospital."

"Where is it?"

"It's on Mehrali Road in the north of the city, past the All India Medical Centre. You'll find it. I'll call my friend Doctor Chopra. He'll make the arrangements and will be expecting you."

"May I take the chest x-rays with me? It'll save time and the need to have them repeated." They were stuffed in an envelope and I put them under my arm.

The Tuberculosis Hospital was out of the Middle Ages. To drive through the broken down gates and up the pot-holed road to the entrance was bad enough but once inside, the dark, dingy hallways, hot as an inferno, airless, and smelling of disinfectant, were horrible. The admissions room was packed. Every iron chair was taken. Holding on to his daughter Simon leaned against the wall.

I knocked on the admitting doctor's door. Getting no answer, I opened it and stepped into the room. It was dark and cramped with its cluttered desk, a single wicker chair piled high with files and a black vinyl surfaced examining table without a sheet. The thought of lying on the black sticky vinyl was horrible. Two dirty french doors opened onto a verandah where two lab-coated doctors stood and chatted. I walked to the verandah door as they obviously didn't hear me or if they did, paid no attention.

"Excuse me for interrupting." I introduced myself.

"Oh yes. We heard from Doctor Khosla about the teenager with tuberculosis you have working for you. Is she here now?"

"Yes she is." I didn't get into the details of how Seama got to our house.

"Please bring her in." As I went to get Simon, I thought of all these other poor souls who had been standing for hours.

After a cursory examination, they agreed that she should be admitted. He gave me directions to the nursing station on the women's ward.

The ward which would house Seama for at least three months if she didn't get worse and die, was horrid. The vast women's section on the second floor of the sprawling two storey nineteenth century brick building was divided into areas of eight iron beds separated by curtains which were drawn open to let in whatever breeze drifted by.

The bed I assumed was Seama's was the only empty one I saw on the entire ward. It had a rolled up, dirty, paper-thin mattress on ancient springs. A rusted bedside table had a white enamel cup sitting on it.

I waited while Simon tried to comfort his tearful daughter.

"Seama, we will be back in a few hours with some covers for the bed."

Granny volunteered to stay until our return.

On our return to Shanti Niketan, Lauretta met me at the door.

"You won't believe the hospital."

"I'll come back with you. Let's take the children's Snoopy sheets and a pillow. They're a little young for a teenager but she won't mind."

We walked into the dingy building from the sweltering sun looking for the stairs to Seama's ward. Lauretta suddenly jumped and grabbed my arm.

"My God, look at that! They're chewing on the bandages soaked with pus." Rats the size of small cats were milling around the room adjacent to the staircase to the second floor. "That's appalling." Lauretta looked sick.

"Wait until you see the ward." With both hands on the edge of the bed, Seama leaned forward to make her breathing easier. She had a hint of a smile as she recognized us.

"Seama, we're going to put these sheets on the bed. Why don't you go outside on the balcony with Simon?" Simon, confused and helpless, took Seama by the hand and walked out into the heat, dust and sun on the balcony.

"Let's put this towel over the mattress and the sheets on top of that."

Together we got the bed made and covered the bedside table with a towel.

"Do you suppose there's a shower?"

"Probably in the room with the rats."

"Let's leave these extra towels anyway."

After reassuring Seama that we would be back soon, we went down a different staircase to avoid the rat-room. Instead we walked past a 'treatment room' where the only nurse visible was probing a tuberculous boil with a clamp and sponges. She tossed the yellowy, putrid gauze into a beat up garbage can, more fodder for the rats.

"This is unbelievably ghastly. Let's get outside so I can breathe without getting sick to my stomach." I agreed as we moved out into the heat and waited for Simon. "David, would she be better at home?"

I sighed and shrugged my shoulders. "Darling, I don't know. The only advantage to this hell-hole is that they have the required medication. I doubt that they would have supplies in Darjeeling." Simon finally appeared.

"Simon, every day, after you serve lunch, prepare a meal for Seama and take a taxi to the hospital. Bring the sheets and towels home to be washed as often as you wish. There is an extra set of sheets and towels when you need them."

"Thank you, memsahib. How long will she be there?"

"The doctor thinks at least two months, Simon." Simon walked away downcast and alarmed for good reason

14

The heat, dirt and workload in New Delhi severely reduced the urge to get any exercise.

The President's Estate Polo Club (PEPC) became not only a source of good execise for me but a stress reducer. My efforts to talk Lauretta into joining me failed.

"David, you can leave me out of that. Furthermore, they're not going to want a woman playing polo."

"I'm sure you don't have to play polo. You can come riding with me in the early morning when the sun is rising or as the sun is setting in the evening. It'll be beautiful."

The formalities involved in trying to join a sacrosanct semi-official group such as The President's Estate Polo Club were daunting. Getting past the sentries at the military base that houses the office of the PEPC was only the first hurdle. Finding the windowless hut which safeguarded the club records and the harried looking membership clerk with nothing to do but keep records in quadruplicate with a stubby pencil, was the next.

The crumbling building was reminiscent of the doctor's office at the tuberculosis hospital. Stacks of files were piled on every flat surface or dumped on the floor.

"Yes, Sir. We would welcome you as a member and would you be stabling your ponies with us?" I smiled at the thought of travelling around the world with a stable of polo ponies at my disposal.

"No, unfortunately not." He went on to give me a copy of the club rules and a map of the estate.

The polo grounds on the President's thousand acre estate in the middle of New Delhi, not only had a polo field but a large wooded area which rose over a rocky knoll high above the city. The President's guard stabled their horses on the estate. The cavalry officer in charge decided which horses could be ridden by club members.

Riding up the rocky slope at seven in the morning, watching the sun rise over the dome of the Lutyen's designed viceroy's house and the orangy mist rising over the city, was an exhilarating experience. Ever mindful of the chattering monkeys and the yakking swooping peacocks, flying like the Concorde, nose down tail feathers trailing, I stuck to the horse like glue. I did not want to be dumped in the middle of nowhere, the horse heading back to the stable alone.

I quickly learned to give the horse plenty of loose rein, as we slipped down precipitous rock trails from my sunrise vantage point high over the city. I leaned back against the cantle of the saddle, feet straight out in front of me in the stirrups to keep the horse balanced as we went down hill at a sixty degree angle.

The monkeys, cute from a distance, gibbering and screaming to each other, could be a menace. They bit like fury. I didn't relish the thought of having one jump on me as I rode past rocky outcroppings.

They'd been known to jump in open car windows at nearby traffic lights. They could also be unwanted guests at outdoor dinner parties as they landed in the middle of the table. The host was obliged to keep a golf club handy to convince the intruders to leave.

Though Lauretta's riding forays were infrequent, a confrontation with a monkey would finish her riding forever.

After one of my early morning rides, I was surprised to see Jean Lemoine, a young Canadian officer working at the High Commission, and his wife, Claudette sitting in our living room chatting with Lauretta.

"David, my husband and I are hoping to adopt a baby. We have investigated orphanages in New Delhi and I think we have found a baby."

"I'd be happy to help but what would you like me to do?"

"Do you know about the 'blue basket'?" I admitted that I didn't.

"There's a blue wicker basket in an alcove outside the entrance of the Our Lady of Mercy orphanage in New Delhi. Every week two or three infants are left in the basket." The infants are nearly all girls, unwanted in families wanting only male heirs. "The baby we have chosen is a 'blue basket baby'. They say she's healthy but we'd like you to examine her for us."

Usually unwanted female fetuses were aborted long before their due date. Almost every street had a sign, large or small, advertising clinics that performed amniocenteses to determine the sex of the fetus. Abortions of unwanted females were readily available.

If a female was born, many families, particularly the mothers-in-law, implored the new mother to get rid of it, drown it or give it up for adoption. Refusals only added to the very difficult time many brides had as they tried to live with their mothers-in-law who ran the household and supervised the care of their sons after marriage.

Once past early childhood, schooling, particularly in lower caste families, was reserved for the sons. Next, the dowry started to loom large. Marrying age, once again depending on caste, began at thirteen. The families of potential husbands decided what dowry demands had to be met. The dowry was turned over to the mother-in-law thus leaving the bride possessionless and penniless.

After the first year of marriage, extra dowry demands were often made. If they were not agreed to, the bride was sacrificed, often by being burnt alive, often in a 'kitchen fire'. The son was now free to marry and accept another dowry. The practice was against the law but that was not a deterrent. The newspapers had frequent stories of young women committing suicide by shooting themselves with numerous shots to the head. If it wasn't so ghastly, it would be ludicrous to think anyone could be gullible enough to believe the stories.

Accompanying the Lemoines to the orphanage, we were met by a sour woman who, with her beady black eyes, looked me up and down.

"Who are you?"

After explaining my role to the rude nursing sister, I was given permission to examine the infant under her watchful eyes.

I smiled and checked the baby's joints and spine. She followed my finger and moved her head as I flicked my fingers near her ears.

"Have you had any problems with her feeding, Sister?"

"We only have donated formula here. The kind varies. As a consequence, she doesn't feed well. As a result, she must stay a few weeks longer."

I looked at the Lemoines as they slowly shook their heads behind the nursing sister's back.

"My friends will be able to handle the baby well at home, I can assure you. There will be continuity with the formula."

"You must realize you will be taking the infant against my judgement."

"I realize that, Sister, but you can be assured that all will be well."

"You will have to complete all the documentation before I will release the baby."

"Of course, Sister. I will ensure that that is done." The Lemoines nodded and we went into the office to complete the file of forms.

The Lemoines were ecstatic as we walked to the car with their pink bundle.

"Thank you, Doctor. We do have formula from the American Commissary and my mother is here from Quebec City. She's going to help me. We're quite confident that everything will be fine."

"If you have any questions just call me at any time."

15

Bombay from the air revealed little of the true nature of the city. The pattern of the shore line outlining the harbour on the Arabian Sea was known as the The Queen's Necklace, India Gate being the pendant. On the ground it no longer suited a queen. Queen Victoria for whom it was named would not have been pleased.

Dharavi, the shanty town that consisted of miles of slums, known as jhuggie settlements, lined both sides of the highway for miles from the airport to the city core. At every stoplight on the route swarms of people poured out of the hodge-podge of shacks. Some of the huts were fashioned from mismatched pieces of wood, some of concrete blocks. The mobs at the stoplights and bus stops were dressed for work in the city or for school or simply for getting out to make money in whatever way they could.

Some women in saris with fresh black or red bindis on their foreheads waited for the battered maroon buses which would take them to offices in town. These people were moving up in the world. They were descendents of the original squatters who had taken over this area years ago. Perhaps they had grown out of the harijan label denoting untouchables. Perhaps they simply couldn't afford the exorbitant rent in one of the world's most expensive cities.

Garish billboards of smiling white-toothed Indian beauties advertising shampoo covered parts of the slum with images to dream about.

There was no way to hide the stench of sewage in the ditches or to mask the young and old squatting to defecate by the side of the road.

The traffic was horrendous, stop and go for miles. The dirt blowing into my black and yellow Maruti taxi stuck to my face. I should've worn dirt coloured clothes. When I finally arrived at the Oberoi Hotel, my first wish was to have a shower.

Before I could make it to my room, a voice behind me called my name.

"Doctor Holbrook, I presume? Would like you to join me for lunch? Are you free now? Oh by the way, I am Doctor Rylie. I am one of the roster doctors for your immigration medical program."

"I'm pleased to meet you, but I won't be able to join you for an hour. May I call you?"

"No. I'll wait."

"As you wish." So much for a relaxed adjustment to the whirl of Bombay.

"Before we go to lunch I would like to take you to the Candy Hospital. I have been on the staff for fifty years." Doctor Rylie was obviously older than he appeared to be. When I finally got myself pulled together, I smiled at my host as he ushered me to his white Ambassador parked in front of the door.

The Candy Hospital was meticulously clean. We walked down the ward to the remarkable laboratory which was obviously his pride and joy. Dated equipment sat next to the latest in computer driven machines to measure every cell in every body fluid.

I listened politely as he recounted his life history, as the elderly are wont to do.

"I was a pioneer in working out a mechanism for administering blood transfusions at the beginning of the World War II. I thought perhaps mercury would reduce reactions between donors and recipients. The first couple of recipients died so I gave up on that idea. It was probably the mercury. I then just hooked up a tube from the donor to recipient and that seemed to work nicely, until we started analysing the blood more carefully. It was a time for innovators like me."

"This laboratory certainly reflects your interest, Doctor Rylie. When did testing for blood types begin? Did you start that as well?"

"I wish I could take credit but no. I'm sure my innovations led to that discovery." I was amused at how much modern medicine seemed to owe to this man. I was learning that Indian physicians are not noted for their modesty. Perhaps he was the originator of the blood transfusion though I somehow doubt it.

"I don't see as many people going to Canada any more from Bombay. I think it's because your predecessor appointed another doctor in a zone outside the centre of the city. He probably thought I was too old. I'm not, you realize. I might be in my eighties but I continue to study."

"No, Doctor. It's Canadian policy to have at least two doctors for the visa medicals in a city the size of Bombay." That excuse was probably not good enough for him but it was the best I could come up with on the spur of the moment. He had no doubt noticed a reduction in income.

"Now that we have toured the hospital, I would like to take you to lunch at the Willingdon Gymkhana Club." It turned out to be a golf club in the centre of Bombay.

"We'll sit here on the verandah." I sank into a cushioned wicker chair and looked out over a row of pink flowering shrubs which divided the fairways.

"May I order you a drink?"

"I would like a glass of wine, please."

"You could have imported scotch whiskey, you know, Johnny Walker Black Label." I smiled and declined remembering Simon telling me that the chowkidar collected and sold any empty scotch bottles he found. They were then refilled with a caramel coloured liquid, sealed and sold as the real thing.

"I'll take you for a stroll before lunch." Doctor Rylie stood and picked up his scotch. I followed with my wine glass filled to the brim. We walked as far as the flowering shrubs which disappointingly had no scent. As we turned to walk back to the verandah, I felt something drop on my shoulder. Bird dirt on the shoulder of my navy jacket. No mark. I look down and jumped back slopping my wine down my tie and trousers which made me look incontinent. A gray, bloodless thumb, lay at my feet.

"Oh, I do apologize. Sometimes vultures drop body parts as they fly over. Malabar Hill is close by. The Parsi Towers of Silence are situated there. The Parsis believe that their bodies should not contaminate the earth, water or fire. As a result the body is left for the vultures to dispose of."

I took a slug of wine and changed the subject. I didn't remember much of the vegetable curry. I wasn't able to forget the pitiful digit on the lawn. I wondered if the vulture returned for it or if guests would simply step on it.

The only time to walk in India is early in the morning or in the evening. Walking to Victoria Station in Bombay was something farangi or foreigners like me didn't usually do. Those that did were thought to be out of their minds. Why would you walk when you could afford to have a car and driver at your disposal? In fact I had a better understanding and feeling of where I was, if I walked.

The sidewalk was just beginning to come alive with naked children running around, babies wailing, mothers trying to scrape scraps of food together and men sleeping. I crossed the street to get out of the way of the family activities. Arbours of greenery covered some stretches of sidewalk adjacent to a small park filled with beds of flowering rose bushes. At the entrance to the station, I left the oasis of green and rejoined the multitudes of people. Diesel locomotive horns echoed in the high iron girders of the station as commuter trains poured in and out disgorging mobs from who knows where. Those without space inside the coaches hung onto the sides, pulling themselves in an extra inch as a train passed on the next track or piled onto the roofs of the carriages.

Enough bedlam for one day. I returned to the hotel to prepare for my medical visits. As I entered the lobby and requested my key, I was approached by a young woman.

"Are you Doctor Holbrook?"

"Yes"

"I'm Jenny Newsome. This is my husband Bill. We're from Toronto and we hope to adopt a baby here in Bombay. We have been waiting with the baby for three weeks. We still don't have a visa for her. Can you help us? We don't know what the problem is."

"Have you had the baby medically examined for the Canadian immigration?"

"No. Nobody mentioned that."

"That's probably part of the problem. There are two doctors here in Bombay who are appointed to do the medicals. You could make an appointment. I'm sure they'll expedite everything for you."

I left them to reread the requirements and headed for my room to prepare my notes for my afternoon visits.

In the lobby I was met once again by the Newsomes.

"Doctor, the immigration doctors can't see us until next week. Should we go to New Delhi and try there?" I looked at them and knew how frustrating the system was. I thought of our own adopted children and the rigamarole we had to go through twenty years ago.

"No. I think the best thing to do is to bring the baby to my room and I'll do the medical for you. Do you have the form with you?"

"Oh yes, Doctor. We would be very grateful." The baby with shocks of black hair and large chestnut eyes looked at me and smiled.

"Please come with me. I'd be happy to complete the forms for you."

The infant gurgled through the entire examination. "I hope this will speed up the process for you." The Newsomes left relieved and happy. It was such a joy to have people appreciate the little things you do for them especially here where the obstacles can seem insurmountable.

Next day, my return to the airport in the early morning was eerie. Mist rose from the jumble of shacks in the jhuggie settlement. Outlines of people emerged from the haze as they headed for the bus stops.

The taxi driver was silent. His hand was constantly on the horn which made a croaking racket inside the cab and probably gave little warning to the images appearing out of the mist.

"We *are* going to the *International* Airport?" I asked, uncertain of the route he was taking. He nodded and swivelled his head.

We pulled up to the doors of the terminal. I paid and got out with all my belongings. He left quickly.

Inside, I checked my flight on the departure board. There were no flights to Colombo. I pushed my way to the check-in counter.

"Oh sir, you are at the wrong airport. You must go to the International Airport."

I cursed the taxi driver and cursed myself for not being sure of my route.

"How do I get there?"

"By taxi, sir." I dragged my baggage back outside only to be met by the same gypsy children who once again were all over me like a swarm of bees.

"I want to go to the International Airport."

The taxi driver said nothing, just shook his head in refusal. I tried the next. The same response. Finally, one quoted an exorbitant fee, equivalent to the charge from the centre of Bombay. I checked my watch and realized I had twenty minutes to catch my flight so I accepted.

I left a handful of coins for my gypsy helpers, got in and started the ten minute drive down a lane in the slum settlement to the International Airport.

16

Sri Lanka once a calm peaceful Buddhist nation was now wracked by civil war. The Tamils in the north fighting for an independent territory for themselves managed to disrupt most of the country with their terrorist activities.

I no longer felt free to walk on the beach near my hotel on the sea. I was told to take a different route to the High Commission each day.

"Don't worry, Doctor, you'll be safe." My driver informed me as he told me to sit on the passenger side of the car in the rear seat. "If we are shot at, they won't kill us both. I'll still be able to drive you to the hospital quickly."

"I'm not worried, Raja." The High Commission driver who had picked me up at the airport must have noticed me grimacing in his rear-view mirror as we left the heavily fortified airport and drove towards Colombo, on what used to be a picturesque drive along the banks of the Kelani River. I was horrified by the bloated, blackened human bodies floating naked, half submerged down the river beside the road.

"That is just to frighten us Doctor."

"It's certainly a brutal way to do it."

The neat bungalows along the river seemed to look away, the wash now hung in the front yard, the prayer flags flapping at the front door as usual. Groves of trees along the river bank masked parts of the yellowy green water flowing to the sea. I wondered what happened if a body got stuck in a grove at the foot of your garden. Do you bury it or just shove it back out into the current?

My hotel room was on a secure floor. The elevator would not open without a special key. Access to the stairs was blocked by armed guards.

A commuter train crammed with passengers on a single track below my window indicated to me that the city, contrary to terrorist wishes, was still functioning.

The High Commission, a two-storey formerly elegant home on a quiet tree-lined street, was a hive of activity. A crowd of locals lined up for visa applications on the verandah that extended from one end of the house to the other. Inside one Canadian immigration officer and four locally engaged officers ploughed through mountains of forms.

Bernie Whitman, wearing what looked like the same worn guayabara he wore when we worked together on the *Hai Hong* off the coast of Malaysia ten years ago, looked tired and tense.

"David, we would like you to appoint two more local doctors to do the immigration medical exams. The two on our list are swamped. We've had a flood of applicants because of the Tamil uprising in Jaffna. I hate the interviews these days. There seem to be flocks of teenage males all telling me the the most improbable stories. They think it's going to be enough to give them a visa to Canada. If they don't get the visa, they just get on the next plane to Canada and immediately claim refugee status. It's a good deal, David. They get welfare, housing, schooling and send money back to the Tamil cause to buy arms. The poor doctors here get blamed if they're found to be ill." Bernie finally smiled and put his hand on my shoulder. "The High Commissioner would like to see you."

I climbed the wide staircase to the second floor and knocked on the heavy mahogany door.

"Ah. Doctor Holbrook. I'm Mary Lalonde." A vivacious woman of about forty-five got up from her large rectangular desk buried in paper and files and came around to shake my hand. She smiled warmly. "Welcome to Colombo." She motioned to the two plush wingback chairs in front of her desk. She pulled at her tight skirt and sat down. High Commissioner Lalonde had actually asked for this posting. I can't imagine why. Maybe it was the challenge of a potential war.

"I'd like you to do a few things for us while you're here. I would like to have an evacuation plan for our staff, in place. That should include emergency hospital care, a list of doctors, and some medical supplies deemed essential. I have made arrangements for you to visit the military hospital. It would probably be the safest place for us. I'm sure that Bernie Whitman has brought you up to speed with our immigration concerns. I hope you will have enough time to help him out."

"I'm sure I will." I couldn't imagine telling her anything was impossible.

"Oh by the way. I'm having a dinner party tonight and I would like you to attend." I smiled. I thought that I wasn't going to have a moment to myself. Maybe just as well as there was no place to walk safely. I thanked her and left the office where the driver was waiting for me outside the door. He already knew where I was going.

By the time Raja got through the third set of gates at the military hospital on the outskirts of Colombo, every inch of the car had been inspected. It was well past lunchtime.

I introduced myself to the white-coated, middle-aged physician who met me at the door.

"I'm Doctor Rajaringum. Welcome. I would like you to join my colleagues and me for tea." He motioned to me to join him as we walked down the hall with its polished gray linoleum floor. The modern, clean, well-equipped hospital was a surprise in a country suffering such hardship. But then, of course, the military were looked after first. I was ushered into a conference room where Earl Grey tea and Peak Frean biscuits were served.

"Would you like to join us on rounds?" I was given a white coat. We started the tour on the medical and surgical wards, moving on to the paediatric and maternity unit.

"I'm surprised, Doctor Rajaringum. I thought I would see only wounded soldiers."

He smiled and looked back down the paediatric ward.

"This medical facility is for the military and their families. As you can see, we offer all services."

"It's very impressive and much like our general hospitals in Canada." The government had obviously spared no expense.

In the conference room after rounds over more tea and biscuits, it was finally agreed that the hospital would treat Canadian diplomats with life-threatening illnesses or injuries until evacuation from Sri Lanka could be arranged. I was relieved because I knew that it was better than taking a chance at the other local hospitals.

Back at the hotel I unpacked my suit for the dinner party.

At the High Commissioner's residence I was ushered into a small pale yellow sitting room jammed with guests, none of whom I knew. By the time dinner was served, I had figured out who my dinner partners were though their names had escaped me. The woman to my right was approaching fifty, I would guess. Wrapped in a long red flowered dress with little to cover her ample breasts, she smiled too affectionately at me much to the chagrin of her husband who sat opposite straining to hear what she was saying to me. I felt that she was eager to antagonize him for some private reason. He had a sour look on his face. Was she going to give away family secrets?

"We have decided to sell our tea plantation in Kandy and return to England. We've been here for many generations and I'm sure my grandfather would be horrified at the thought." I nodded in agreement as if I had known who Grandfather was.

"It is not the unrest, you realize." The husband interrupted, to clarify his wife's conversation. "We would have to replace many of our tea bushes if we were to stay. You Americans insist on using tea bags rather than leaf tea. 'Real' tea drinkers drink tea brewed from leaves rather than the broken bits of leaves and dirt enveloped in a tea bag for convenience with very little flavour or aroma. It's a matter of appreciating quality." He stroked his moustache, a self-satisfied look on his face.

I smiled and tried to continue my conversation with his wife.

"My husband is referring to the fact that tea bags are filled with the dregs left over when the leaves are packed." He smiled now in agreement with the course of his wife's discussion.

At this point, I decided the tea conversation had gone far enough and tried to change the topic. "Did you go to school in England?"

"Oh yes, boarding school. As a child, I fell down a chute in the tea drying house where the leaves are packed." I was having trouble getting out of the volatile tea conversation. "I had to have medical treatment in England and stayed on for my schooling. You're a medical doctor. Is that correct?" Oh no, not a free medical consultation at dinner!

The High Commissioner seated to my left must have noticed my feigned smile and pulled me into the conversation she was having with a Sri Lankan legislator. Since I had missed the beginning of the discussion, I smiled and listened. I hoped not to be accused of not pulling my weight when I next met with Madam Lalonde.

The job of finding prospective doctors for the immigration programme was not easy. Many refused once they realized that they would be deluged with so many applicants it would be difficult to accomodate their regular patients. They were correct and in the end I had to settle for two physicians on a part time basis.

At the end of the day I returned to my secure room with the view of the train track and the commuters once again clinging to the sides of the coaches. Some were heaped on the roof as the train left the city for the nearby villages.

17

Republic Day parade in New Delhi on the 26th of January was a glorious display of pomp and circumstance, a reflection of what had been the Raj and the Imperial Throne. The parade of camel battalions, their riders in scarlet tunics and plumed turbans, battalions of Sikh and Gurkha militia in stunning dark green uniforms with plumed helmets and turbans of many colours and a brass band mounted on elephants, all marched down the hill on Rajpath, the wide ceremonial avenue with the dome of the Ratrapati Bhavan designed by Edward Lutyens for the Viceroy, behind them on their way to India Gate, the Lutyen's War Memorial Arch at the end of the processional route more than a mile away. There could be nothing like this, even in England whence had come the pageantry.

"I'm sorry that the kids are not here to see this."

"I think they would be objecting to the heat by now." Lauretta was right. Having managed to pass through the security net and find our seats, we soon realized that the sun blazing down on the bleachers was only for mad dogs and

Englishmen. After two hours we retreated to Shanti Niketan to watch the remainder of the spectacle on television.

The most moving part of the day was beating retreat, the flag lowering ceremony, as the sun, now a huge orange ball, slowly receded behind the dome of the Viceroy's lodge. Camels and their riders slowly and silently moved one by one from the ramparts of the legislative buildings at the top of the Rajpath hill, as a single bugle sounded the retreat. The crowds of people were suddenly silent. Even the mounted battalions stopped shuffling. The elephants, their howdahs resplendent with crimson banners and tassles, stopped swaying and only the occasional ear flapped as the mahouts with their long thin bamboo switches sat like tiny statues behind the elephant's ears.

"That was one of the most beautiful and moving sights I have ever seen."

"Lauretta, it's overwhelming," I whispered as my eyes filled with tears.

Two weeks later on a sunny day that was not yet stifling, I followed my customary route to the High Commission. I stopped at the traffic light at the end of our lane to chat with the gypsy kids and buy the Times of India newspaper. They insisted on selling me garlands of jasmine wrapped in banana leaves for my 'pretty lady'. Rather than take them home, I decided to leave them to perfume the little Peugeot as it sat in the forty degree heat at work.

Hoping that the headache I had awakened with would soon ease, I drove up to the gates of the High Commission in Chanakyapuri as usual and said good morning to the guards. As they checked under the car for bombs, I suddenly realized that I couldn't speak. I couldn't reply to their greetings. I couldn't move. I could see them calling to me and I could see the dashboard of the car. I realized the door was being opened, but as they undid my seatbelt and slowly lifted me from the car, the world went blank.

Two nights later, I awoke briefly in the British Embassy 'cottage' hospital, flickering candles in the periphery of my vision. I thought I could hear Lauretta talking but then, perhaps I was dead. This was the next life. I lapsed into unconsciousness before I could continue the thought.

My swift horizontal departure from India was a discouraging end to another chapter in my life. The flight to Frankfurt on a stretcher at the back of a 747 and on to the Neurological Institute in Montreal was lost somewhere in my memory. I did later remember it as the Valentine's Day I didn't want to repeat.

6

REBIRTH IN CANADA

1

I knew I would miss being comatose. Even now the beautiful calming gemini blue of the inside of my eyelids was fading and the flashes of orange streaking across my retina were less frequent. I had reached the time to make the effort to keep my lids open.

Valentine's Day, 1990, the Montreal Neurological Institute. I could smell antiseptic as the cleaner with the yellow wheeled bucket squished the excess from his mop and swept the long tendrils under my bed.

I was finally conscious enough to be aware of my surroundings, a busy ward of umpteen beds, my clothes in a green plastic garbage bag on a pole at the end of the bed. My left arm was taped to the side frame of the bed, tubing tracking from the frame to a bag on a hook above my head. The bag dripped liquid slowly into the tubing. I wasn't sure what I was doing here.

In the next bed, a teenager was wearing a football helmet.

"He's a head banger," the obese young person opposite shouted over the din of his radio, so loud my ears rang as they did after the last Rolling Stones concert I had attended. He'll be stone deaf in the near future I thought to myself.

"Yeah. Well, wait 'til ya hear him snore," shouted the teen with the helmet making sure the snorer could hear him. "They're doing tests to see if he's the loudest snorer on the planet. He wants to be in the Guinness Book of Records."

The cleaner shook his head muttering about the insane mass of humanity cluttering up his floor.

Before I could attempt a relationship with this odd crew, I was moved to a room in the surgical wing of the hospital.

Surgery. How could I prepare myself for that? Before I thought of an answer, I could hear the soft lilting Trinidadian accent of the head nurse on my new ward. I was in a single room next to the nursing station. "You have the best neurosurgeon in the world, Doctor Holbrook. All you have to do is relax and let him work his magic. There is some investigation that has to be completed." It was obvious that surgery was a foregone conclusion.

"First, an electroencephalogram. Now I'm sure, as a physician, you know all about that." I agreed that I did. Within minutes, I was being whisked down endless corridors to be wired. "You'll be living better electrically" the smiling attendant informed me. Wires were pinned around my skull and graphs made measuring blips in my brain activity supposedly to pinpoint where my brain was short-circuiting.

Once shuttled back to my room, I tried to relax enough to sleep. It wasn't to be.

"I'm sorry to waken you, Doctor Holbrook but there is another test we must do now." The ward appeard dark. The clock on the wall in the nursing station indicated five minutes to midnight.

"What now?" I asked sleepily.

"It's just an MRI. It's a magnetic imaging device, Doctor. It's a new machine for taking images of slices through your brain that assists the surgeon in deciding how to approach the surgery. It's more precise than a CAT scan."

I was half asleep and didn't know what she was talking about. I was wheeled into a dimly lit room with an adjacent control room with a series of screens which reminded me of an air-traffic controller's panel.

"I would like you to slide onto this table." I looked at the slab the technician was motioning to. In the middle of the night, it looked like a dug-out canoe. "I'm just going to do up these straps and put these pillows against your head so that it doesn't move. Now, you must stay perfectly still during the tests. They will take about forty-five minutes. I'm just going to roll you into the machine." I was suddenly in the pitch black. Was I dreaming that I was being buried or was I buried? I heard a door shut in the background and a clicking somewhere in my dug-out.

Suddenly, a racket like a pneumatic drill on concrete crashed into my head. It was now a repetitive pattern, click, click, click then 'wham' the drill. Stay still! I said to myself. God. I'm going to panic. Maybe my tomb is being sealed. I had never had claustrophobia but I sure as hell had it now. My heart was racing and my face flushing. I tried counting the minutes, thinking of Lauretta, thinking of Chris, Sue and Matthew. All to no avail.

Nothing worked. I was spastic by the time I heard people talking and the lid of my coffin sliding open. Unable to talk, I was wheeled back to my room.

My date with the surgeon began early the next day. Soap and a razor made fast work of my remaining head of hair.

"David, you won't remember any of this. We're simply going to cut a flap from your skull so that we will have a good visual field." I swear I could hear the saw cutting the top off my head like slicing off the top of a coconut. The surgeon pulled a mask over his nose and mouth as I drifted away for a day lost in a fog without the benefit of the memories of my coma.

Eight hours later, I was aware of being in a bed with intravenous tubes now taped to both arms. All I could see was a haze in front me. I tried to move only to be stopped immediately by a tugging on my penis. Oh my God. Me with a catheter. There had to be a mistake. The shock awakened me and I realized I was in a room full of every conceivable apparatus to keep people alive and monitored. I was next to a woman with even more machines attached than I had.

A blond nurse stood over me adjusting the bag of intravenous liquid. I seemed to be lying on a brick. "Doctor Holbrook, there's a drain in the back of your skull." I wondered whether that attachment was permanent. "The urinary catheter will only stay until your bladder works on its own." I then realized that Lauretta with her auburn hair, freckles and hazel eyes with flecks of gold in the iris was clutching my right hand in both of hers. It was such a relief to see her. Finally there was something I could connect to emotionally in this technological jungle.

My two day stay in the intensive care unit was more than enough for me. The last act was the removal of my tubes and encumbrances.

"Today we're going to remove the drain." Oh Lord. Will half my brain come with it? A resident, two interns and two nurses crowded around as I was turned, somebody holding the drain and somebody holding me. I felt nothing as the stitches were removed and the metal brick was cut loose. "Now, next we'll remove your catheter and you can return to your room." The blond grasped my penis with one hand and pulled the catheter with the other. Wow. I took a deep breath. Free at last.

Now, back in my room, I was paid a visit by Doctor Villefranche.

"David. You are going to be fine." He rested his hand on my arm as he smiled down at me. Unfortunately, we weren't able to remove the tumour as it was too large and diffuse but we're going to shrink it." He sounded so positive that it seemed pointless to worry.

"Someone has told me that the brain is never the same after it has been exposed to the air. Is that true?"

He smiled. It was a warm comforting smile. "I don't know, David. You're going to have to tell me. There'll certainly be changes. There'll be gaps because of the surgery and radiation. Your brain will be a bit like Swiss cheese. All those gaps will have to be filled again."

"That sounds like a great project for me. When can I go back to work?"

"You must give yourself time. You have a lot of relearning to do." He paused. "We have to look at the pathology and plan a rehabilitation programme and your course of radiation." Reality was setting in as the surgeon left the room. I was tearful as Lauretta came in trying to look cheery.

"It's going to be fine, David."

"I know. I'm depressed because of the cortisone medication to keep my brain from swelling." She knew that wasn't the whole reason. It was partly the 'why me?' syndrome. As I lay in bed I could only think of the horrors I had experienced overseas and now I too had succumbed to illness and thoughts of death.

Within days, I was finally moved from the hospital to a suite in a nearby hotel where Lauretta and I could at least share the same bed. I had graduated to a cane but accepted the company of Lauretta, Sue, Chris or Matthew for the trip to the hospital for my daily radiation treatments.

The voice of the technician I could hear ringing incessantly in my ears as I lay on the table with the huge radiation cone looming menacingly above me.

"Now don't move your head," a command that automatically caused me to panic again leaving me in a frantic state at the end of each segment. I convinced myself that six weeks of this was going to put me over the edge.

Recuperation was slow as I began to fill in the patches in my brain chewed up by the tumour and fried by the radiation. Sitting in the hotel garden, I thought back on my early days in family practice. The never ending pressure that was relieved by a change in direction and our move overseas. Now I began to plot what changes I would have to make to get back on track after this rough patch.

2

Eight months after leaving India on a stretcher, after I had completed my radiation treatments and allowed time for my brain swelling to recede and the surgery to heal, I decided I had to return to India to help Lauretta supervise the packing of our belongings. We had left hurriedly leaving everything in limbo.

I had taken the time to fill in as many of the gaps as possible at that time and felt I couldn't sit and brood over my illness any longer.

"David, it's ridiculous for you to come to India with me. I can manage perfectly well on my own."

"I'm not denying that, Darling, but I want to do this. I know all the government regulations and the hassles with packers. I'm coming with you. Furthermore, I'm looking forward to it. It'll help me get my confidence back. I feel well.

"Now you know that's not true. You're still having seizures."

"They're much better and they're now only on my left side. I know how to control them. I just have to stop for a few minutes. I'll use a wheelchair if I need to."

"David, you're impossible. You've got to realize that everything has changed. You can't drive. You can't work. You've got to relax and let your body heal. You were so depressed after the surgery. Have you forgotten?"

"That was related to all the medication, I'm sure. I feel great. Lauretta I can't sit and wait. I'm going to get on with my life, our life together. Stop worrying so much, Babe. I'll be fine. I can deal with a few bumps along the way."

Our house in Shanti Niketan appeared strangely quiet. There was no chowkidar in sight as we let ourselves in the front door.

"Simon. Sheela." No answer. Everything looked unchanged. We climbed the stairs to our room, and heard a rustling on the third floor and smelled a putrid odour. We continued up to the laundry room on the top floor and found Sheela taking hideous smelling meat and produce that had been in the freezer, outside onto the roof.

"What on earth are you doing, Sheela?"

"Oh Memsahib. It wasn't my fault." The dhobi had accidentally pulled out the plug to the freezer when he was ironing. The food had thawed. "I'll put it out on the roof to dry. Then put it back in the freezer."

"Oh no. No, Sheela. You must throw it out. It will make us all sick." Lauretta couldn't believe she would even think of it. The stench of rotting food was nauseating.

"Where is Simon, Sheela?"

"Oh Memsahib, he's dead." We gasped and looked at her in disbelief, our mouths gaping. "Memsahib, doctor say Simon's liver exploded and he died." She uttered the news nonchalantly, without any great emotion.

"His liver exploded?!" Lauretta and I cried out in unison.

"When did this happen?"

"In June, Sahib. We took him home to Darjeeling."

"We're very sorry, Sheela."

"He was very sad that Sahib got sick."

Simon was so distraught at the thought of losing his status, Sahib and Memsahib in one swoop, that he had drunk our entire stock of liquor and wine in a matter of weeks, gone into liver failure and died.

"Sheela, what has happened to Seama, Simon's daughter?"

"Oh, she died too, Sahib. She was not getting better in the hospital. Simon took her home to Darjeeling. She died two weeks after Simon. Seama was very frightened in the hospital here in New Delhi. Simon thought she would be better with granny. But she got pneumonia and died, Memsahib." Sheela's blasé attitude was baffling.

"Oh, poor Seama, We're very sorry." We both stood staring at each other, our eyes filling with tears. India had been a cruel and crushing experience for us. It was a surreal world where emotions were distorted and humans counted for so little. I was not going to miss the despair or the society crippled by the caste system. Lauretta and I could put it behind us but a billion others could not.

We sat through the two days of packing, said our goodbyes at the High Commission and left India.

3

We knew that it was going to be difficult moving back to Canada. We had become temporary citizens of so many countries in so many parts of the world. We had come to enjoy the diverse city life in Singapore, London and Mexico City.

We felt at home in cities from Tokyo and Jakarta to Paris, Bogata and Lima.

Now Torontonians again, we were living in a multicultural society, a microcosm of the world we had come to know. Little things were major events for us. It was awesome to be able to turn on a tap and have potable water flow, to say nothing of not having to keep your mouth shut in the shower.

The bureaucracy continued to plague us. The storage shipment, the contents of our three storey former home, had to be delivered before our shipment from overseas could be released from customs. The former filled our entire apartment from floor to ceiling. Furniture we could accommodate we set aside. The remainder went to an auction house.

Our goods from India posed a new problem. Giant ants were found by the movers who refused to unload anything from the containers. The entire shipment had to be moved to a remote lot and left in the freezing weather until it was deemed safe with all the unwanted insects frozen solid.

4

Being put on leave indefinitely, left me with more than enough time on my hands. Though I missed the daily challenges and the camaraderie of life overseas, I decided to tackle as many diverse projects as possible.

The seizures, a result of the tumour,surgery and radiation were now controlled and my position with the government was kept open in the hope that I might return, albeit to Ottawa rather than abroad.

I turned to other pursuits. The drawing course at the Royal Ontario Museum was a disaster. The instructor rolled her eyes every time she peered at my work. The art history courses were more satisfying.The required research introduced me to many periods of art previously unknown to me.

My piano studies were hampered by a residual hand weakness although my reconditioned piano provided an enjoyable form of physiotherapy.

I realized that while living abroad the computer age had descended. I felt left out. Consequently, I started to bring myself into the high tech nineties with computer software courses to supplement my love of graphic art.

I volunteered at a local high school assisting teachers with large classes of unruly teens. Lauretta then convinced me to start writing. I took courses at Ryerson University and finally at the Humber College School for Creative Writing. It was the stimulus that I needed.

All went well until my health once again fell apart. I developed Stevens-Johnson Syndrome, a combination of skin and renal failure which required stopping medications and so my seizures recurred in earnest. The hope of returning to work seemed more distant. The seizures became worse and it was discovered that my tumour had recurred in a more malignant form necessitating more brain surgery.

The craniotomy was booked as a 'day' procedure which caused a great deal of apprehension for both Lauretta and me. At the appointed hour, I arrived and was told the surgery would be done under local anaesthetic. The experience of having another flap sawed out of my skull while awake to hear the goings-on, did not thrill me. A nurse, with squiggles of blond hair and dangly orange earings peeking out from under her surgical operating room cap, tried to reassure me. She produced the opposite effect. When I heard the host of neuro-surgeons shouting at her to bring pitchers of cold water to pour on my exposed brain in order to stop the generalized seizure that enveloped me, I was wondering how I could ever have agreed to this.

The recovery was slow and arduous but there was an incentive.

Sue was to be married a month after my surgery. I had no intention of being wheeled down the aisle or using a sroller. A cane was barely tolerable. I was still faced with a year of chemotherapy. So much for my government position. I formally retired.

I decided there was no sense in waiting a year to finish the chemotherapy. So I prepared to return to employment. Over the years I continued my medical education. It was now time to start over in medicine. I found working in a walk-in clinic challenging and fun as well as a focus other than my illness.

The clinic, in a feisty area of downtown Toronto, services a huge and diverse community ranging from the shelter and homeless population to the affluent of nearby Rosedale. I feel I am doing something with a cross-section of the world that I can assist. I have quickly become attuned to the needs of addicts, troubled teens, new mothers without a clue as to how to care for four day old infants, plus the intricasies of treating AIDS.

Many of my patients from the Caribbean, South Asia, Africa and Latin America feel comfortable knowing that I know their countries and customs. I can't help but wonder whether I knew some of the families. Had I examined them for immigration on the Hai Hong in the South China Sea or perhaps in the refugee camps in Pakistan?

Many refugees bypass the system leaving me with many basic concerns. I am very aware of the high incidence of tuberculosis in their countries of origin and find myself treating active cases. Culture shock, so common among diplomats serving abroad, is now a worry for many of these new Canadians unsure, or, in some cases, unwilling to give up customs incompatible with their new environment. This is particularly evident in the teenagers who are so eager to fit in with their peers, yet who face intolerable restrictions at home. I reassure them that they can be proud Canadians like me and still not lose sight of their heritage. Convincing their parents is often impossible. Because I see thirty to forty patients in a six hour period, I must focus on the most pressing issues.

Meanwhile, Lauretta returned to teaching French and English as a Second Language. Her knowledge of many cultures, like mine, has been a great bonus in helping teens striving to adjust to life in Canada, a dream many thought was unattainable. In addition, she returned to college and took a course in Colour Theory preparing her for another career, this time in design.

Our 'children', now adults, have moved on with their lives.

Chris graduated with an Honours degree from the London School of Economics. He chose to return to Canada but found the job market in the early nineties very trying. His British degree did not hold the same caché as a Canadian university diploma.

He returned to the University of Toronto to study Modern Languages. The fact that he now spoke French, German and Spanish still left him with only an entry level position in the insurance industry.

He went back to economics, earned his securities licence and upgraded his insurance credentials. He's now looking at a much brighter future. Listening to his discussions about investing in Japan, China and Vietnam is enlightening for us.

Sue decided to stay in England after studying art and design and graduating from St. Martins Central School of Art in London. She began to work for 'Elle' magazine and then for a British film company as a graphic designer. She soon moved into public relations and marketing. She has now begun an independent career in children's television film promotion and joined forces in business and in marriage with an Englishman who is involved in music promotion and marketing.

Matthew, despite our efforts and those of umpteen others, continues to refuse to comply with any rules. He still sees himself as the sole ruler of his universe and indeed he is. One could say he has been consistent from a very early age. Sadly, he had disappeared from our lives into a blur of addictions and petty crime. After four years with no communication, he suddenly resurfaced in typical style.

"Hi, Mum. How's Dad? I'm fine. Guess what? I've been married for two years. I have a beautiful Japanese wife, Noriko, and we have a rottweiler." It was a relief as we had serious concerns about having a grandchild beginning life as an addict.

His methamphetamine addiction has been impossible to beat. He has tried on many occasions.He has even signed himself into rehabilitation programs only to be defeated soon after release.

Not surprisingly, his marriage has ended. The occasional request for money is refused because we know that it would be fuelling the very thing, deep down, he would like someday to stop. We hope for a miracle.

ABOUT THE AUTHOR

David Holbrook is a physician living in Toronto Canada.

He graduated in Medicine from the University of Toronto and practiced Family Medicine prior to joining the Canadian government and serving overseas as a Foreign Service Officer.

He recently returned to medical practice in Toronto.

ACKNOWLEDGEMENTS

I would like to thank the Ryerson University writing program and in particular Ann Ireland and Sarah Sheard for getting me started on this project. The input from the writing group under Sarah's guidance was an enormous help.

I am also deeply indebted to the Creative Writing Program at Humber College especially the editing of Antanas Sileika without which this book would not have been completed. I would also like to thank Bruce J. Friedman, Charles Tisdall, John Parry, Bill Belfontaine and Helen McLean for their valuable assistance and encouragement. I am indebted to Mark Patterson and Karen Beutler for their technical expertise.

Finally, to my wife Lauretta for her constant love and support through thick and thin. The idea of writing about this chapter in our lives was hers and it is to her this book is dedicated.

978-0-595-36493-0
0-595-36493-4

Printed in the United States
38756LVS00011B/47

9 780595 364930

HISTORICAL DICTIONARY

The historical dictionaries present essential information on a broad range of subjects, including American and world history, art, business, cities, countries, cultures, customs, film, global conflicts, international relations, literature, music, philosophy, religion, sports, and theater. Written by experts, all contain highly informative introductory essays of the topic and detailed chronologies that, in some cases, cover vast historical time periods but still manage to heavily feature more recent events.

Brief A–Z entries describe the main people, events, politics, social issues, institutions, and policies that make the topic unique, and entries are cross-referenced for ease of browsing. Extensive bibliographies are divided into several general subject areas, providing excellent access points for students, researchers, and anyone wanting to know more. Additionally, maps, photographs, and appendixes of supplemental information aid high school and college students doing term papers or introductory research projects. In short, the historical dictionaries are the perfect starting point for anyone looking to research in these fields.

HISTORICAL DICTIONARIES OF AFRICA

Jon Woronoff, Series Editor

Namibia, by John J. Grotpeter. 1994.

Senegal, Second Edition, by Andrew F. Clark and Lucie Colvin Phillips. 1994.

Comoro Islands, by Martin Ottenheimer and Harriet Ottenheimer. 1994.

Benin, Third Edition, by Samuel Decalo. 1995.

Uganda, by M. Louise Pirouet. 1995.

Côte d'Ivoire (The Ivory Coast), Second Edition, by Robert J. Mundt. 1995.

Togo, Third Edition, by Samuel Decalo. 1996.

Congo, Third Edition, by Samuel Decalo, Virginia Thompson, and Richard Adloff. 1996.

Tanzania, Second Edition, by Thomas P. Ofcansky and Rodger Yeager. 1997.

Chad, Third Edition, by Samuel Decalo. 1997.

Guinea-Bissau, Third Edition, by Richard Lobban and Peter Mendy. 1997.

Tunisia, Second Edition, by Kenneth J. Perkins. 1997.

Burkina Faso, Second Edition, by Daniel Miles McFarland and Lawrence Rupley. 1998.

Equatorial Guinea, Third Edition, by Max Liniger-Goumaz. 2000.

Kenya, Second Edition, by Robert M. Maxon and Thomas P. Ofcansky. 2000.

South Africa, Second Edition, by Christopher Saunders and Nicholas Southey. 2000.

Swaziland, Second Edition, by Alan R. Booth. 2000.

Djibouti, by Daoud A. Alwan and Yohanis Mibrathu. 2000.

Liberia, Second Edition, by D. Elwood Dunn, Amos J. Beyan, and Carl Patrick Burrowes. 2001.

Zimbabwe, Third Edition, by Steven C. Rubert and R. Kent Rasmussen. 2001.

Sudan, Third Edition, by Richard A. Lobban Jr., Robert S. Kramer, and Carolyn Fluehr-Lobban. 2002.

Somalia, Second Edition, by Mohamed Haji Mukhtar. 2002.

Mozambique, Second Edition, by Mario Azevedo, Emmanuel Nnadozie, and Tomé Mbuia João. 2003.

Egypt, Third Edition, by Arthur Goldschmidt Jr. and Robert Johnston. 2003.

Lesotho, by Scott Rosenberg, Richard Weisfelder, and Michelle Frisbie-Fulton. 2004.

Ethiopia, New Edition, by David H. Shinn and Thomas P. Ofcansky. 2004.

Central African Republic, Third Edition, by Pierre Kalck, translated by Xavier-Samuel Kalck. 2005.

Guinea, Fourth Edition, by Thomas O'Toole with Janice E. Baker. 2005.
Western Sahara, Third Edition, by Anthony G. Pazzanita. 2005.
Ghana, Third Edition, by David Owusu-Ansah. 2005.
Madagascar, Second Edition, by Philip M. Allen and Maureen Covell. 2005.
Sierra Leone, New Edition, by C. Magbaily Fyle. 2005.
Morocco, Second Edition, by Thomas K. Park and Aomar Boum. 2006.
Libya, Fourth Edition, by Ronald Bruce St. John. 2006.
Gabon, Third Edition, by David E. Gardinier and Douglas A. Yates. 2006.
Algeria, Third Edition, by Phillip Naylor. 2006.
Burundi, Third Edition, by Ellen K. Eggers. 2007.
Republic of Cape Verde, Fourth Edition, by Richard A. Lobban Jr. and Paul Khalil Saucier. 2007.
Rwanda, New Edition, by Aimable Twagilamana. 2007.
Zambia, Third Edition, by David J. Simon, James R. Pletcher, and Brian V. Siegel. 2008.
Mali, Fourth Edition, by Pascal James Imperato, Gavin H. Imperato, and Austin C. Imperato. 2008.
Botswana, Fourth Edition, by Fred Morton, Jeff Ramsay, and Part Themba Mgadla. 2008.
The Gambia, Fourth Edition, by Arnold Hughes and David Perfect. 2008.
Mauritania, Third Edition, by Anthony G. Pazzanita. 2009.
Nigeria, by Toyin Falola and Ann Genova. 2009.
Democratic Republic of Congo (Zaire), Third Edition, by Emizet Francois Kisangani and F. Scott Bobb. 2010.
Republic of Cameroon, Fourth Edition, by Mark Dike DeLancey, Rebecca Mbuh, and Mark W. DeLancey. 2010.
Eritrea, Second Edition, by Dan Connell and Tom Killion. 2011.
Angola, Second Edition, by W. Martin James. 2011.
Malawi, Fourth Edition, by Owen J. M. Kalinga. 2012.
Niger, Fourth Edition, by Abdourahmane Idrissa and Samuel Decalo. 2012.

Historical Dictionary
of Niger

Fourth Edition

Abdourahmane Idrissa
Samuel Decalo

The Scarecrow Press, Inc.
Lanham • Toronto • Plymouth, UK
2012

Published by Scarecrow Press, Inc.
A wholly owned subsidiary of The Rowman & Littlefield Publishing Group, Inc.
4501 Forbes Boulevard, Suite 200, Lanham, Maryland 20706
www.rowman.com

10 Thornbury Road, Plymouth PL6 7PP, United Kingdom

Copyright © 2012 by Abdourahmane Idrissa and Samuel Decalo

All rights reserved. No part of this book may be reproduced in any form or by any
electronic or mechanical means, including information storage and retrieval systems,
without written permission from the publisher, except by a reviewer who may quote
passages in a review.

British Library Cataloguing in Publication Information Available

Library of Congress Cataloging-in-Publication Data

Idrissa, Abdourahmane, 1971–
  Historical dictionary of Niger / Abdourahmane Idrissa, Samuel Decalo. — 4th ed.
    p. cm. — (Historical dictionaries of Africa)
  Decalo's name appears first on the earlier edition.
  Includes bibliographical references.
  ISBN 978-0-8108-6094-0 (cloth : alk. paper) — ISBN 978-0-8108-7090-1 (ebook)
  1. Niger—History—Dictionaries. I. Decalo, Samuel. II. Title. III. Series: Historical
dictionaries of Africa.
  DT547.5.D4 2012
  966.26'003--dc23

                                                                    2012001590

∞™ The paper used in this publication meets the minimum requirements of
American National Standard for Information Sciences—Permanence of Paper
for Printed Library Materials, ANSI/NISO Z39.48-1992.

Printed in the United States of America

To Idéal

Contents

Editor's Foreword

When the third edition of this volume was published in 1997, the editor—like many others—was relatively pessimistic, citing the great promise of independence and the high expectations of the people offset by poor economic performance once uranium prices fell and, even worse, a series of military coups d'état. So it is nice to be at least cautiously optimistic that the situation is improving. Perhaps most important, democratization does seem to have taken root; in many fields, more constructive policies are being followed. Niger is again a major uranium producer, to which other ores have been added, and its agriculture and industry are holding up. What now looks like perhaps the most serious problem, although not really verbalized as such, is the constant growth of the population—not terribly big in numerical terms but certainly more than can be sustained by a vast but largely arid land without creating tensions within and a push toward emigration abroad.

This rather bumpy trajectory since independence, although quite calm and peaceful when compared to even earlier periods, is told in this historical dictionary several times over. It is perhaps clearest and crassest in the chronology, which is a blow-by-blow description of very "interesting" if often depressing times. The introduction puts things in context and provides the basis for a better understanding of the present situation and prospects for the future. But the most important section remains the dictionary, with an amazingly large number of impressively detailed entries on the leading figures in every facet of national life, both present and past. These are embedded in broader entries on politics, economics, and social and artistic life, to say nothing of religion and the military. For those who want to know more, the extensive bibliography is a very good place to look for other works on this still under-researched country that deserves to be known better.

The first three editions of the *Historical Dictionary of Niger* were written by Samuel Decalo, who is a specialist both on Francophone West Africa and the military—the ideal combination in this case. He has taught at various universities, including the University of Natal in South Africa and University of Florida at Gainesville. Over the years, he has written more than a dozen books and dozens of articles on Africa. Among his works are five historical dictionaries. This fourth edition was written by Abdourahmane Idrissa, who is a Nigerien political scientist. Born and brought up in Niger, he studied political science at the University of Dakar in Senegal and then moved to the United States, where he obtained a doctorate from the University of Florida and did postdoctoral work at Oxford and Princeton. Among his main focuses are African democratization and political Islam, which also turns out to be a good combination. Building on the previous editions but adding an impressive amount of new material, he gives our readers a new look at a hopefully new Niger.

Jon Woronoff
Series Editor

Acronyms and Abbreviations

ABN	Autorité du Bassin du Niger
ACCT	Agence de Coopération Culturelle et Technique des Pays Francophones
ACP	African, Caribbean and Pacific
ACTN	Association des Chefs Traditionnels du Niger
ADINI ISLAM	Association pour la Diffusion de l'Islam au Niger
AFC	Alliance des Forces du Changement
AFD	Agence Française de Développement
AFD	Alliance des Forces Démocratiques
AFDS	Alliance des Forces Démocratiques et Sociales
AFJN	Association des Femmes Juristes du Niger
AFMN	Association des Femmes Musulmanes du Niger
AFN	Association des Femmes du Niger
AGIR	Amélioration Gestion Intégrée des Ressources
AIN	Association Islamique du Niger
ALG	Autorité du Liptako-Gourma
AMACA	Association Mutuelle pour la Culture et les Arts
AMM	Affaires Militaires Musulmanes
ANASI	Association Nigérienne pour l'Appel et le Salut Islamique
ANDDH	Association Nigérienne pour la Défense des Droits de l'Homme
ANDP	Alliance Nigérienne pour la Démocratie et le Progrès
ANPI	Association Nigérienne de la Presse Indépendante
AOF	Afrique Occidentale Française
AQIM	Al-Qaeda in the Islamic Maghrib
ARCI	Association pour le Rayonnement de la Culture Islamique
ARCN	Association des Radio-Clubs du Niger
ARD	Alliance pour le Renouveau Démocratique
ARLA	Armée Révolutionnaire de Libération de l'Azawad
ARLN	Armée Révolutionnaire de Libération du Nord Niger
ARM	Autorité de Régulation Multisectorielle
ARMP	Autorité de Régulation des Marchés Publics

ASECNA	Agence pour la Sécurité de la Navigation Aérienne en Afrique et à Madagascar
ASFAN	Association Sportive des Forces Armées Nigériennes
AU	African Union
AUF	Agence Universitaire de la Francophonie
BAGRI	Banque Agricole du Niger
BALINEX	Banque Arabe Libyenne Nigérienne pour le Commerce Extérieur et le Développement
BCC	Banque du Crédit et du Commerce
BCEAO	Banque Centrale des États d'Afrique de l'Ouest
BCL	Bureau de Coordination et de Liaison
BCN	Banque Commerciale du Niger
BDRN	Banque de Développement de la République du Niger
BEPC	Brevet d'Études du Premier Cycle
BIA	Banque Internationale pour l'Afrique
BIAO	Banque Internationale pour l'Afrique Occidentale
BICIN	Banque Internationale pour le Commerce et l'Industrie du Niger
BNA	Bloc Nigérien d'Action
BOA	Bank of Africa
BRANIGER	Sociétés des Brasseries et Boissons Gazeuses du Niger
BRIMA	Briquèterie de Maradi
BRS	Banque Régionale de Solidarité
BSIC	Banque Sahélo-Saharienne pour l'Investissement et le Commerce
BUNIFOM	Bureau Minier de la France d'Outre-Mer
BUREMI	Bureau des Mines
CAMAD	Club des Amis de Moumouni Adamou Djermakoye
CBLT	Commission du Bassin du Lac Tchad
CCAIAN	Chambre de Commerce, d'Agriculture, d'Industrie et d'Artisanat du Niger
CCFN	Centre Culturel Franco-Nigérien
CCN	Conseil Consultatif National
CCOG	Centre Culturel Oumarou Ganda
CDS	Convention Démocratique et Sociale
CDTN	Confédération Démocratique des Travailleurs du Niger
CEA	Commissariat à l'Energie Atomique
CEAO	Communauté Economique de l'Afrique de l'Ouest
CEDAW	Convention for the Elimination of all Discriminations against Women
CELTHO	Centre d'Étude Linguistique et Historique par la Tradition Orale

CENI	Commission Electorale Nationale Indépendante
CENSAD	Communauté des États Sahélo-Sahariens
CESOC	Conseil Economique Social et Culturel
CFA	Centre de Formation Administrative
CFA	Communauté Financière Africaine
CFAO	Compagnie Française d'Afrique de l'Ouest
CFD	Coordination des Forces Démocratiques
CFDR	Coordination des Forces Démocratiques pour la République
CFDT	Compagnie Française pour le Développement des Fibres Textiles
CFEPD	Certificat de Fin d'Études du Premier Degré
CFN	Commission du Fleuve Niger
CFPM	Centre de Formation et de Promotion Musicale
CILSS	Comité Inter-États de Lutte contre la Sécheresse au Sahel
CMS	Conseil Militaire Suprême
CNCA	Caisse Nationale de Crédit Agricole
CND	Conseil National de Développement
CNDP	Conseil National de Dialogue Politique
CNE	Caisse Nationale d'Epargne
CNES	Centre National d'Energie Solaire
CNNC	China National Nuclear Corporation
CNPC	China National Petroleum Corporation
CNRS	Centre National de la Recherche Scientifique
CNRSH	Centre National de Recherches en Sciences Humaines
CODDAE	Collectif de l'Organisation pour le Droit à l'Energie
COMINAK	Compagnie Minière d'Akouta
CONGAFEN	Coordination des ONG et Associations Féminines
CONOCO	Continental Oil Company
COPRO-NIGER	Société Nationale de Commerce et de Production du Niger
COSIMBA	Comité de Soutien des Amis de Maïnassara Baré
CPCT	Caisse de Prêts aux Collectivités Territoriales
CRA	Coordination de la Résistance Armée
CRD	Conseils Regionaux de Développement
CRDTO	Centre Régional de Documentation pour la Tradition Orale
CRN	Conseil de Réconciliation Nationale
CROISADE	Comité de Réflexion et d'Orientation Indépendant pour la Sauvegarde des Acquis Démocratiques
CSLTN	Confédération des Syndicats Libres des Travailleurs du Niger

CSN	Conseil de Salut National
CSON	Conseil Supérieur d'Orientation Nationale
CSPPN	Caisse de Stabilisation des Prix des Produits du Niger
CSRD	Conseil Suprême pour la Restauration de la Démocratie
CUN	Communauté Urbaine de Niamey
CVD	Conseils Villageois de Développement
ECOWAS	Economic Community of West African States
EEC	European Economic Community
EITI	Extractive Industries Transparency Initiative
EMAIR	Ecole Minière de l'Aïr
ENA	Ecole Nationale d'Administration
ENAM	Ecole Nationale d'Administration et de Magistrature
ENIPROM	Entreprise Nigérienne de Production de Mousses
ENITEX	Entreprise Nigérienne des Textiles
ENITRAP	Entreprise Nigérienne de Transformation du Papier
EU	European Union
FAC	Fonds d'Aide et de Coopération
FAN	Forces Armées Nigériennes
FDD	Front pour la Défense de la Démocratie
FDN	Forces Démocratiques Nigériennes
FDN	Front Démocratique Nigérien
FDR	Front pour la Démocratie et la République
FDU	Front Démocratique Uni
FEANF	Fédération des Étudiants d'Afrique Noire en France
FED	Fonds Européen de Développement
FESPACO	Festival Panafricain du Cinéma de Ouagadougou
FIAA	Front Islamique Arabe de l'Azawad
FIDES	Fonds d'Investissement pour le Développement Economique et Social des Territoires d'Outre-Mer
FIMA	Festival International de la Mode Africaine
FFR	Front des Forces de Redressement
FLAA	Front de Libération de l'Aïr et de l'Azawak
FLT	Front de Libération Temust
FNIS	Force Nationale d'Intervention et de Sécurité
FOI	Front de la Oumma Islamique
FPLA	Front Populaire de Libération de l'Azawad
FPLN	Front Populaire pour la Libération du Niger
FPLS	Front Patriotique pour la Libération du Sahara
FRDD	Front pour la Restauration et la Défense de la Démocratie
FUSAD	Forum Uni pour la Sauvegarde des Acquis Démocratiques
GAP	Groupe d'Action Politique

GRGN 21	Groupe de Réflexion sur le Genre au Niger au Vingt-et-unième Siècle
HCCT	Haut Conseil des Collectivités Territoriales
HCI	Haut Conseil Islamique
HCR	Haut Conseil de la République
HCRP	Haut Commissariat pour la Restauration de la Paix
HIPC	Heavily Indebted Poor Countries
IDB	Islamic Development Bank
IFAN	Institut Fondamental d'Afrique Noire
IFAN	Institut Français d'Afrique Noire
IFTIC	Institut de Formation aux Techniques de l'Information et de la Communication
IHEOM	Institut des Hautes Études d'Outre-Mer
IMF	International Monetary Fund
INDRAP	Institut National de Documentation, de Recherche et d'Animation Pédagogiques
INRAN	Institut National de la Recherche Agronomique du Niger
IOM	Indépendants d'Outre-Mer
IPDR	Institut Pratique de Développement Rural
IRD	Institut de la Recherche pour le Développement
IRSH	Institut de Recherches en Sciences Humaines
ITIE	Initiative pour la Transparence dans les Industries Extractives
JAD	Journées d'Action Démocratique
JID	Journées d'Initative Démocratique
LOSEN	Loi d'Orientation du Système Educatif Nigérien
MDD	Mouvement pour la Défense de la Démocratie
MDDR	Mouvement pour la Défense de la Démocratie et de la République
MDG	Millennium Development Goals
MDP Alkawali	Mouvement pour la Démocratie et le Progrès
MEBA	Ministère de l'Education de Base et de l'Alphabétisation
MECREF	Mutuelle d'Epargne et de Crédit des Femmes
MFUA	Mouvement des Fronts Unifiés de l'Azawad
MNJ	Mouvement des Nigériens pour la Justice
MNSD	Mouvement National pour la Société de Développement
MODEN/FA	Mouvement Démocratique Nigérien pour une Fédération Africaine
MOUNCORE	Mouvement Nigérien des Comités Révolutionnaires
MPA	Mouvement Populaire de l'Azawad
MPLA	Mouvement Populaire pour la Libération de l'Azawad

MRLN	Mouvement Révolutionnaire pour la Libération Nationale
MSA	Mouvement Socialiste Africain
NEPAD	New Economic Partnership for African Development
NIGELEC	Société Nigérienne d'Electricité
NIGERTOUR	Société Nigérienne pour le Développement du Tourisme et de l'Hôtellerie
NITEX	Société Nigérienne des Textiles
NITRA	Niger Transit
NNJCC	Nigeria-Niger Joint Commission for Cooperation
OAU	Organization of African Unity
OCAM	Organisation Commune Africaine et Malgache
OCBN	Organisation Commune Bénin-Niger
OCDN	Organisation Commune Dahomey-Niger
OCRS	Organisation Commune des Régions Sahariennes
OECD	Organisation for Economic Co-operation and Development
OFEDES	Office des Eaux du Sous-Sol
OIC	Organization of the Islamic Conference
OIF	Organisation Internationale de la Francophonie
OLANI	Office du Lait du Niger
ONAHA	Office National des Aménagements Hydro-Agricoles
ONAREM	Office National des Ressources Minières
ONERSOL	Office de l'Energie Solaire du Niger
ONPE	Office National des Postes et de l'Epargne
ONPF	Observatoire National de la Promotion de la Femme
ONPPC	Office National des Produits Pharmaceutiques et Chimiques
OPA	Organisations Paysannes Agricoles
OPT	Office des Postes et Télécommunications
OPVN	Office des Produits Vivriers du Niger
ORA	Organisation de la Résistance Armée
ORCONI	Organisation des Consommateurs du Niger
ORTN	Office de Radio-Télévision du Niger
PAIPCE	Programme d'Appui à l'Initiative Privée et à la Création d'Emploi
PCF	Parti Communiste Français
PDDE	Programme Décennal de Développement de l'Education
PDP Daraja	Parti pour la Dignité du Peuple
PFPN	Plateforme Paysanne du Niger
PII	Parti Islamique Intégriste
PINE	Parti Indépendant du Niger-Est

PMT Albarka	Parti du Mouvement des Travailleurs
PNA Al' Ouma	Parti Nigérien pour l'Auto-gestion
PNDS	Parti National pour la Démocratie et le Socialisme
PPN	Parti Progressiste Nigérien
PRA	Parti du Regroupement Africain
PRDS	Poverty Reduction and Development Strategy
PRLPN	Parti Républicain pour les Libertés et le Progrès du Niger
PSDN Alheri	Parti Social-Démocrate Nigérien Démocratique
PSR	Parti Socialiste Révolutionnaire
PUND	Parti pour l'Unité Nationale et la Démocratie
RDA	Rassemblement Démocratique Africain
RDFN	Rassemblement Démocratique des Femmes Nigériennes
RDP	Rassemblement pour la Démocratie et le Progrès
RECAN	Rencontres du Cinéma Africain de Niamey
RINI	Riz du Niger
ROPPA	Réseau des Organisations des Paysans Producteurs d'Afrique de l'Ouest
ROTAB	Réseau des Organisations pour la Transparence et l'Analyse Budgétaire
RPN Alkalami	Rassemblement des Patriotes Nigériens
RSD Gaskiya	Rassemblement Social-Démocrate
RTD	Radio-Télévision Dounia
RTT	Radio Télévision Ténéré
SAFELEC	Société Africaine d'Electricité
SAMAN	Syndicat Autonome des Magistrats du Niger
SAP	Structural Adjustment Program
SCIMPEXNI	Syndicats des Commerçants, Importateurs et Exporteurs du Niger
SCN	Société Cotonnière du Niger
SEEN	Société d'Exploitation des Eaux du Niger
SEPANI	Société d'Exploitation des Produits d'Arachide du Niger
SHN	Société des Huileries du Niger
SIAM	Société Industrielle et Alimentaire de Magaria
SICONIGER	Société Industrielle et Commerciale du Niger
SIP	Sociétés Indigènes de Prévoyance, de Secours et de Prêts mutuels
SIP	Société Industrielle Pharmaceutique
SMDN	Société Minière du Dahomey-Niger
SMDR	Société Mutuelle de Développement Rural
SMN	Société Minière du Niger
SNC	Société Nigérienne de Cimenterie
SNE	Société Nigérienne des Eaux

SNEN	Syndicat National des Enseignants du Niger
SNTN	Société Nationale des Transports Nigériens
SNTV	Société Nigérienne de Transport des Voyageurs
SOCOGEM	Société de Construction et de Gestion des Marchés
SOLANI	Société de Lait du Niger
SOMAIR	Société des Mines de l'Aïr
SOMINA	Société des Mines d'Azelik
SONAL	Société Nigéro-Arabe-Libyenne
SONARA	Société Nigérienne de commercialisation de l'Arachide
SONERAN	Société Nigérienne d'Exploitation des Ressources Animales
SONIA	Société Nigérienne d'Alimentation
SONIBANK	Société Nigérienne de Banque
SONICA	Société Nigérienne de Crédit Automobile
SONICERAM	Société Nigérienne de Produits Céramiques
SONICHAR	Société Nigérienne du Charbon d'Anou Araren
SONIDEP	Société Nigérienne des Pétroles
SONIFAME	Société Nigérienne de Fabrications Métalliques
SONIPHAR	Société Nigérienne des Industries Pharmaceutiques
SONIPRIM	Société Nigérienne des Primeurs
SONITAN	Société Nigérienne de Tannerie
SONITEL	Société Nigérienne des Télécommunications
SONITEXTIL	Société Nigérienne des Textiles
SOPAMIN	Société du Patrimoine Minier
SORAZ	Société de Raffinerie de Zinder
SOTRAMIL	Société de Transformation du Mil
SPCN	Société des Produits Chimiques du Niger
SPEIN	Syndicat Patronal des Entreprises et Industries du Niger
SPEN	Société du Patrimoine des Eaux du Niger
ST	Syndicat des Transporteurs
STIN	Société des Télécommunications Internationales
SYMPHAMED	Syndicat des Pharmaciens, Médecins et Chirurgiens Dentistes
SYNTRACOM	Syndicat National des Transporteurs et Commerçants
SYNTRAMIN	Syndicat des Travailleurs des Mines du Niger
TOM	Territoire d'Outre-Mer
UAM	Université Abdou Moumouni de Niamey
UCFA	Union pour la Communauté Franco-Africaine
UDFP Sawaba	Union Démocratique des Forces Populaires
Sawaba UDFR	Union Démocratique de Forces Révolutionnaires
UDN	Union Démocratique Nigérienne
UDP Amintchi	Union pour la Démocratie et le Progrès

UDPS	Union pour la Démocratie et le Progrès Social
UDPS Amana	Union pour la Démocratie et le Progrès Social
UDR Tabbat	Union pour la Démocratie et la République
UEMOA	Union Economique et Monétaire Ouest Africaine
UFCN	Union des Femmes Catholiques du Niger
UFDP	Union des Forces pour la Démocratie et le Progrès
UFN	Union des Femmes du Niger
UMOA	Union Monétaire Ouest Africaine
UN	United Nations
UNCC	Union Nigérienne de Crédit et de Coopérative
UNDP	United Nations Development Program
UNE	Union des Nigériens de l'Est
UNESCO	United Nations Educational, Scientific and Cultural Organization
UNI	Union Nationale des Indépendants
UNIRD	Union National des Indépendants pour le Renouveau Démocratique
UNIS	Union Nigérienne des Indépendants et Sympathisants
UNTN	Union Nationale des Travailleurs du Niger
UPDP Chamoua	Union des Patriotes Démocrates et Progressistes
UPN	Union Progressiste Nigérienne
URANIGER	Office National de Recherches, d'Exploitation et de Commercialisation de l'Uranium au Niger
USAID	United States Agency for International Development
USCN	Union des Syndicats Confédérés du Niger
USN	Union des Scolaires du Niger
USTN	Union des Syndicats des Travailleurs du Niger
WAEMU	West African Economic and Monetary Union

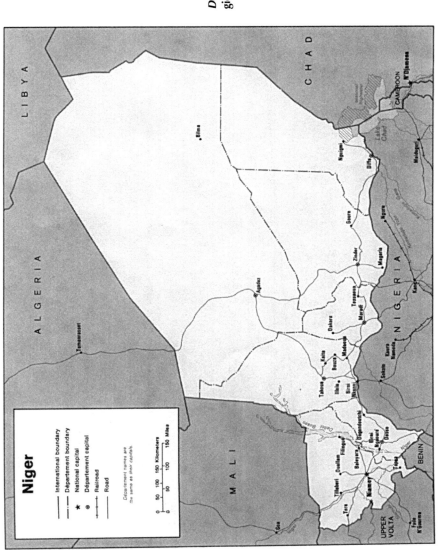

Départements became re-
gions after 1999

Chronology

3000–2000 BCE   Desertification of the Sahara. Populations of agriculturalists and ceramists trek south, leaving behind pastoralists, who draw large herds of cattle on rocks. Elephants, hippos, and a great variety of savannah fauna are also represented.

7th century BCE   A Songhay state is founded around Koukya or Gounguia, a site in Mali, near the border with Niger.

1010   The monarchs of Koukya move to Gao and embrace Islam. Trade routes to the Middle East develop.

11th century   Tuareg move south from areas now in Algeria and Libya. They displace populations that will settle south to form the Gobir branch of the Hausa people. Agadez founded as a trading junction.

14th century   The Songhay kingdom put under vassalage by the powerful Mali Empire. This will last about a century.

15th century   The Songhay king Sonni Ali Ber throws the yoke of Mali, which he proceeds to conquer, founding the Songhay Empire. His warfare will extend its territory over much of what today are Mali, Niger, and northern Nigeria.

1497   Askia Mohammed makes the pilgrimage to Mecca, where he receives the title of "Lieutenant of the Caliph for the Land of the Blacks." Back to that land, he decides to build an Islamic empire on the basis of the Songhay state.

1515   Agadez is captured by the Songhay, who turn it into a trading outpost on a par with Timbuktu.

1591   Battle of Tondibi, a Moroccan expedition armed with firearms, opposes the Songhay army. The defeat of the Songhay leads to the rapid collapse of their state.

17th century   Rise of the Katsina kingdom in the Hausaland. Its capital, Birnin Katsina, overtakes Kano as the commercial heartland of the Hausaland. Its northern fringe (Maradi) is threatened, however, by the growing power of the Gobir.

18th century Katsina suffers major setbacks from the Gobir, but the latter eventually concentrates on Zamfara. Successive Gobir monarchs annex chunks of Zamfara territory and found their capital, Alkalawa, on conquered land.

1740 The small state of Damagaram is founded by Mallam Yunus as a tributary chiefdom of the Bornu Empire.

1750 Boukar, a descendant of a great Zarma warrior Tagour, establishes the settlement of Dosso.

1774 Usman Dan Fodio, a radical Fulani Qadiriyya cleric, settles at Degel, in Gobir territory, and secures the autonomy of its community from King Bawa Jan Gwarzo.

1795 Death of Jan Gwarzo. The ideological bases of the Hausa monarchic system are threatened by the mounting Islam-based criticism flowing from Degel.

1804 Dan Fodio issues his *Letter to the People of the Land of the Blacks*, which declares his jihad. At Alkalawa, Gobir king Yunfa proposes a reform of the monarchy on the basis of both Islam and the customary rites and beliefs of the Hausa. A showdown develops between the Fulani jihadist and the Gobir king, which rapidly escalates into war.

1807 The Fulani strike at Katsina, which they seize, expelling the ruling dynasty.

1808 Jihadists storm Alkalawa and King Yunfa dies defending his capital, which is completely destroyed. Both the Gobir and the Katsina overthrown ruling families move north into what is now Niger.

1825 Alfa Mamane Diobbo, a pious Fulani Qadiriyya cleric, founds the community of Say. Although the settlement resembles the process through which Usman dan Fodio established Degel, Diobbo has neither radical politics nor is intent on waging a jihad war. Instead he becomes popular through his meekness and liberality.

1841 In Damagaram, Sultan Tanimoun starts his first reign. Deposed two years later, he comes back to power in 1851 and continues to rule over the state of Damagaram during its height until his death in 1884, turning it into the last major Hausa power.

1854 In Dosso, the *Zarmakoy* Kossom pushes back the encroachments of the emirate of Gwandu—the Western branch of the Sokoto Empire—and defeats the Tuareg to the extent that he captures their tribal drum, the Toubal.

1898 **5 May:** Captain Gabriel Marius Cazemajou, leader of the French exploratory expedition "Mission du Haut-Soudan," is murdered in Zinder on orders from the sultan of Damagaram, Amadou Kouran Daga. **June**: An Anglo-French agreement establishes the boundary between French and British zones of intervention in the Central Sudan. **11 August:** A decree dated that day and issued from Porto-Novo makes the village of Doulsou (about 100 km north of Niamey) the administrative center of the French "middle Niger circle." **November:** The infamous Voulet-Chanoine mission sets out from Dakar.

1899 **8 January:** Voulet and Chanoine, a 2,000-men strong expedition, sacks the village of Sansanné-Haoussa, south of Tillabéri. **16 April:** They battle against the forces of the *Sarraounia* Mangou, queen of Lougou, in the Arewa. **8 May:** Massacre of Birni-N'Konni; thousands are slaughtered by Voulet and Chanoine men. **16 July:** Voulet and Chanoine are murdered by their African troops at Dankori. **30 July:** Lieutenant Pallier, who took over the Voulet and Chanoine mission, defeats Sultan Amadou Kouran Daga at Tirmini. **15 September:** Sultan Amadou Kouran Daga is killed in Roumji to avenge the death of Cazemajou.

1900 **11 October:** Cercle du Djerma is established and seated in the village of Sorbon Haoussa, about 60 km north of Niamey. **20 December:** Creation of the French Third Military territory for the Central Sudan, provisionally headquartered at Sorbon Haoussa.

1901 **1 January:** Creation of a Tirailleurs (French African colonial troops) battalion in Zinder. **20 April:** Lieutenant-Colonel Peroz arrives in Zinder, where he installs the headquarters of the Territoire Militaire de Zinder.

1902 **April:** The first French school in the Cercle du Djerma opens in the village of Filingué. Three more schools open their doors that year in the villages of Dosso, Niamey, and Sandiré. **15 May:** The village of Niamey is chosen by Captain Salaman, *commandant de cercle* (circle commander), to become the administrative center of the Cercle du Djerma.

1903 Niamey replaces Zinder as the administrative center of the military territory until 1911. A famine in western Niger that started the previous year begins to abate.

1905 **December:** Two *garde-cercles* (colonial gendarmes) come to Kobkitanda to levy taxes and are murdered by the villagers.

1906 **4 January:** Colonial forces rout Kobkitanda forces, led by the blind cleric Alfa Saibou. Oumarou Karma attacks Goudel that same day. **March:** Oumarou Karma killed in a battle in the Zarmaganda. Alfa Saibou is executed at Sokoto by the British. The sultan of Damagaram, Amadou dan Bassa, accused of plotting a massacre of the European population of Zinder, is arrested and exiled to Côte d'Ivoire. He will return in 1922.

1910   22 June: The Territoire Militaire du Niger is established.

1911   2 January: Zinder is reinstated as the administrative center of the territory and will remain so until 1926. **September**: The regional school of Zinder opens its doors.

1912   1 January: The Territoire Militaire is put under the jurisdiction of the General Government of the Afrique Occidentale Française (AOF, French West Africa).

1913   The territory is hit by a famine that kills thousands and decimates cattle, abating only in the following year.

1914   The First World War begins. France recruits most of its so-called Tirailleurs Sénégalais in the colonies of French Sudan (Mali) and Niger: 31,000 men out of a total of 164,000 for the entire AOF. AOF will lose over 30,000 men in the conflict, which is more than any other colonial ensemble. The bulk of Nigerien conscripts are drawn from the Zarma-Songhay western part of the territory, triggering a 10-month period of unrest along the Niger River valley.

1916   17 December: Kaocen, a Tuareg warlord, besieges the French fort near the town of Agadez, in the Aïr. Kaocen attacks the fort unsuccessfully on 18 and 20 December but ambushes and massacres the French military escort to the Azalai caravan on 28 December.

1917   3 March: Siege of Agadez lifted by French reinforcements sent from Zinder; Aïr subsequently pacified.

1919   September: The *Foyer des Métis* (the "Home of the Half-Caste") is created in Zinder.

1920   Second great famine hits Niger, devastating the regions bordering Nigeria.

1921   1 January: A decree written the previous month changes the Territoire Militaire du Niger into the Territoire du Niger.

1922   1 July: The Territoire du Niger becomes the Colonie du Niger, ruled by a lieutenant-governor and endowed with administrative and financial autonomy; Niger must pay for its government by France through taxes and requisitions. **27 December:** Constitution of the first Conseil des Notables (Notables Council) of the colony, in the circle of Tessaoua.

1926   28 September: The administrative center of the colony definitively transferred from Zinder to Niamey.

1927   25 June: The French military cantonment of Tessaoua is attacked by a band of Hausa men from Nigeria, fired up by the clerical leader Malam Moussa. Suspecting him of complicity, the French exile Barmou, the chief of Tessaoua, to the French Sudan (Mali), where he dies.

1929   24 December: On Christmas Eve, a Songhay man by the name of Douraman becomes the first Niger convert to Roman Catholicism.

1930   The apostolic vicar of Dahomey, Monsignor François Steinmetz, arrives in Niger with a priest, Father François Faroud, and establishes the Roman Catholic mission of the colony.

1931   A third great famine started the previous year and hits especially the Zarma regions where entire villages disappear. **31 May:** The Jules Brévié Hospital is founded in Niamey; this is the nucleus of the current Hôpital National de Niamey.

1932   Father François Faroud builds the first Catholic church of Niamey. **5 September:** The colony of Haute-Volta (now Burkina Faso) is dismembered and its eastern divisions (Dori and Fada N'Gourma) allocated to the colony of Niger. Haute-Volta will be reconstituted in 1947.

1937   March: Slight opening up of the colonial regime, with the right of unionization extended to colonial subjects with a primary school certificate (a tiny number, especially in Niger).

1939   World War II begins. Some 30,000 of the 75,000 African conscripts for France's war effort are recruited in AOF. France's early defeat halts conscriptions.

1942   20 April: Monsignor Hyppolite Berlier is appointed first bishop of Niger by Pope John XXIII.

1944   16 September: Rights of unionization are extended to all AOF populations, with no conditions of literacy or formal French education. **24 December:** Abolition of political censorship.

1945   22 August: The Colonie du Niger becomes a Territoire d'Outre-Mer in the framework of the Union Française imperial ensemble. **21 October:** Maurice Kaouza and Fily Dabo Sissoko are elected deputies for French Sudan and Niger at the French constituent assembly. That same day, Djibo Bakary creates in Agadez the Groupe d'Action Politique (GAP), a civil rights organization directed against forced labor, cattle and property requisitions, and native courts. The GAP joins a similar group founded in Niamey by Hamani Diori and Boubou Hama, leading to the establishment of the Parti Progressiste Nigérien (PPN) the following year.

1946   13 March: Freedom of association is extended to overseas territories. **11 April**: Freedom of congregation extended to overseas territories; forced labor abolished. **30 April:** Native courts are abolished; establishment of the Fonds d'Investissement pour le Développement Economique et Social des Territoires d'Outre-Mer (FIDES) and of the Caisse Centrale de la France d'Outre-Mer (CCFOM). France pledges to fund development in the colonies and to lend state funds to private businesses and public collectivities there. **7 May:** Extension of French citizenship to all populations in the Union Française. **12 May:** Creation of the PPN, chaired by the chief of Dosso, Issoufou Saidou Djermakoye. **10 November:** Hamani Diori is elected at the French national assembly.

1952   28 April: Publication of the first Nigerien newspaper, the union broadsheet *Talaka* (The Commoner).

1953   13 April: Publication of the weekly *Le Niger*, the newspaper of PPN and predecessor of the future government dailies *Le Temps du Niger* (1960) and *Le Sahel* (1974).

1956   19–22 September: Boubou Hama attends the first congress of black writers and artists in Paris. **19 November:** Creation of the Sawaba party, following the merger of two parties and under leadership of Issoufou Saidou Djermakoye and Djibo Bakary.

1957   Traces of uranium are detected at Azelik by the Bureau Minier de la France d'Outre-Mer. **11–13 January:** Djibo Bakary attends the constitutive congress of the radical inter-African Mouvement Socialiste Africain (MSA) in Conakry (Guinea). Sawaba affiliates with the MSA. **31 March:** The MSA wins the first legislative election on universal and direct suffrage. Bakary heads the first government council from the colony.

1958   26 April–1 May: Series of violent confrontations between MSA and PPN militants: two dead and 111 hurt. **1 June:** In France, Charles de Gaulle returns to power and comes up with the idea of a referendum to bind the colonies to France in a Franco-African community. **28 August:** Djibo Bakary declares himself against the Franco-African community. The French decide to back the PPN against the MSA. **28 September:** The Nigeriens allegedly vote for the Franco-African community at 78 percent, but with an abstention rate of 62 percent. **19 October:** The Bakary government resigns. The territorial assembly is dissolved the following month. **14 December:** Early legislative elections, heavily rigged in favor of the PPN, are held. **18 December:** The new assembly is a constituent assembly, which proclaims the Republic of Niger, a member-state of the Franco-African community. Hamani Diori heads the new government council.

1959 Uranium is found at Azelik and Abokorum by the French Commissariat à l'Energie Atomique (CEA). **23 January:** The municipality of Niamey, a Sawaba bastion, is dissolved. **22 February:** Political meetings are forbidden in Niamey. **17 March:** Creation of the Union des Femmes du Niger (UFN), Niger's first women's association. **15 July:** Boubou Hama is elected vice-president of the Senate of the Franco-African community. **12 October:** The Sawaba party is decreed out of existence; Djibo Bakary and other Sawaba leaders leave Niger. **23 November:** Niger adopts its current motto (*"Fraternité, Travail, Progrès"*) and flag. **18 December:** The first pavilion of the Musée National is inaugurated.

1960 4 June: The French constitution is revised to allow for independence in the framework of the Franco-African community. **28 July:** The Union des Scolaires Nigériens (USN) is created but will not be recognized until 1990. **29 July:** The National Assembly is created to replace the legislative assembly in preparation for formal independence. **1 August:** The state of Niger becomes an independent and sovereign republic; the Forces Armées Nigériennes (FAN) are established. **3 August:** Niger's formal independence is proclaimed. **9 November:** Hamani Diori is elected president by the National Assembly. **15–19 December:** Niger becomes a founding member of the Union Africaine et Malgache (UAM, later Organisation Commune Africaine et Malgache (OCAM)), a pro-French group of Francophone states.

1961 13–17 January: Meeting of anti-imperialist states and groups in Casablanca (Morocco), attended by the heads of state of Ghana, Guinea, Mali, Morocco, Egypt, a delegation of Algeria's liberation fronts, and members of Niger's Sawaba. **24 April:** Signature in Paris of the Accords de Coopération (Cooperation Agreements) between France and pro-French states, formalizing the multifarious bonds that survived decolonization. Moreover, France signs a military cooperation agreement (Accord de Défense Commune) with Côte d'Ivoire, Dahomey (Benin), and Niger. The agreement allows for the posting of French troops in Niamey and will be terminated in 1974. **25 May:** Creation of the Banque de Développement de la République du Niger (BDRN), a development bank owned 55 percent by the state of Niger and 45 percent by Nigerien nationals; it will operate until 1990. **12 July:** Adoption of the national anthem "La Nigérienne."

1963 Uranium is found at Madaouela by the CEA. **24 April:** Niger is admitted into the International Monetary Fund (IMF), the World Bank, and the International Development Association (IDA). **25 May:** Niger becomes a founding member of the Organization of African Unity (OAU) in Addis-Ababa (Ethiopia). **3 December:** Zodi Ikhia and Captain Amadou Hassane Diallo are arrested for plotting a coup d'état scheduled to happen during the 18 December celebrations of the proclamation of the Republic. **4 December:** In neighboring Dahomey, three Nigeriens are killed following events that developed after the coup d'état of Captain Christophe Soglo there on 11 November; tensions grow between Niger and Dahomey. **23 December:** The Nigerien government asks the 16,000 Dahomey residents of Niger to either opt for Nigerien citizenship or leave Niger; thousands leave. Niger concentrates forces along the Niger River border with Dahomey and claims islands on the river. Beginning of the Benin-Niger border dispute.

1964 **27 May:** Twenty-one men suspected of Sawaba membership are arrested in Girataoua and transferred to Maradi's prison, where they die of suffocation. **17 July:** Administrative reorganization of the territory: *départements, arrondissements*, and communes replace the older, colonial subdivisions of *cercles* and *secteurs*. **27–28 September:** Sawaba commandos infiltrate Western Niger. **3–4 October:** Sawabist insurrections break out in various parts of the country and are quashed.

1965 More uranium findings in various locales in northern Niger. **19 January:** An agreement is brokered in Abidjan to settle the border dispute between Niger and Dahomey; this will prove to be temporary. **13 April:** Grenade attack against President Diori by Sawabist Amadou Diop, during the Id-al-Kabir prayer, in Niamey. Diori survives. **25 May:** Trials of Sawabists in Tillabéri; five death sentences are pronounced and 875 political prisoners enter Niger's jails. **30 September:** Diori is re-elected president with allegedly 99.98 percent of valid voting. **21 October:** The PPN single list for 50 deputies is elected at the national assembly with allegedly 100 percent of valid voting.

1966 Uranium is found at Imouraren.

1967 Uranium is found at Akouta.

1968 Beginning of a dry cycle in the Sahel, which will culminate in the major droughts of 1972–1973 and will end only in 1975. Six crop years out of eight will be in severe deficit in Niger during this period, and 80 percent of the cattle will be wiped out. **1 February**: The Société Minière de l'Aïr (SOMAIR) is set up to begin uranium mining.

1969   December: The new, post-Nkrumah Ghanaian government expels non-Ghanaian residents from the country; thousands of Nigeriens return to Niger.

1970   20 March: The Agence de Coopération Culturelle et Technique (ACCT), later Agence de la Francophonie, is created in Niamey. **1 October:** Diori is re-elected president, with allegedly 98.98 percent of valid suffrage. **22 October:** The PPN single list of 50 deputies re-elected to the National Assembly with allegedly 100 percent of valid suffrage. **18 December:** Inauguration of the Pont Kennedy (Kennedy Bridge) in Niamey; it is 740 m long and was funded by the United States. This will lead to the right bank expansion of Niamey and the establishment of the University of Niamey there.

1971   4 February: Marketing of uranium begins. **12 April:** Boubou Hama is awarded the Grand Prix littéraire d'Afrique Noire for his 1968 book *Kotia Nima*. **6 September:** The Centre d'Enseignement Supérieur (CES) of Niamey is established.

1972   18 February: The airport of Niamey is inaugurated. **12 March:** Oumarou Ganda's film *Le Wazzou polygame* wins the Etalon de Yennega at Ouagadougou (Haute Volta)'s third pan-African film festival (FESPACO). **11 September:** The boxer Issaka Daboré wins the bronze medal at the Olympic Games in Munich (Germany); this is as yet the only medal won by a Nigerien sportsman at the Olympic Games.

1973   4 January: Niger breaks off diplomatic relations with Israel, in solidarity with the Arab states. **20 September:** The CES of Niamey becomes the University of Niamey. **November**: The *Arbre du Ténéré* (the Tenere desert's only tree) is discovered dead by participants in the Raid Afrique rally. In December, the tree is carried in a military truck by Lieutenant Ali Saibou (Niger's future president of the late 1980s) to the Musée National at Niamey, where it will be put in a mausoleum in 1977. **13 November:** First Franco-African summit at Paris, in which only nine African countries (including Niger) took part.

1974   9 March: Treaty of defense and security with Libya. **14 April:** Lieutenant-Colonel Seyni Kountché topples Hamani Diori. The constitution is suspended, the National Assembly is dissolved, and all political organizations are suppressed. **22 April:** The Conseil Militaire Suprême (CMS) and a provisional government are established. **26 April:** A commission is created to investigate misappropriations and prevarications under the overthrown government; it is headed by Lieutenant Gabriel Cyrille. **16 May:** The CMS breaks off the military cooperation agreement with France and evicts French troops. **26 July:** The first version of the Conseil National de Développement (CND) is established; it is presided by battalion chief Sani Souna Siddo. **2 August:** Kountché announces the project of turning Niger into a *société de développement* (development society). **7 September:** Kountché announces the reestablishment upon new bases of the youth organizations of the Samariya. **13 September:** The Association Islamique du Niger is created.

1975 28 May: The Economic Community of West African States (ECOWAS) is founded in Lagos, Nigeria; Niger is a founding member.

1976 15 March: A coup attempt involving Commander Bayéré Moussa, Captain Sidi Mohamed, and the secretary-general of the union federation Union Nationale des Travailleurs du Niger (UNTN), Ahmed Mouddour, is thwarted. **15 September:** Niger signs a contract with seven mining companies for the building and operation of a 700-km road between Arlit and Tahoua. The so-called Route de l'Uranium (Uranium Road) will be inaugurated in 1981 and will cost 8.1 billion CFA francs. **21 September:** The Route de l'Unité (Unity Road), started under Diori, is inaugurated at Gouré, in Niger's far east. **22–27 September:** The UNTN becomes the Union Syndicale des Travailleurs du Niger (USTN), a reframed federation somewhat closer to the government. **17 December:** The power line between the Kandji Dam (Nigeria) and Niamey is inaugurated. It is 600 km long and had cost 9 billion CFA francs; construction had started in May 1974.

1977 23–26 May: First congress of the Association des Femmes du Niger (AFN), a new women's organization created two years earlier, is held; Fatoumata Diallo is elected its first national president.

1978 19 December: The writer Idé Oumarou wins the Grand Prix littéraire d'Afrique noire for his novel *Gros Plan*.

1979 7 April: Niger's national television starts broadcasting. **29 October:** Creation of the commission in charge of establishing the société de développement. It is headed by Moumouni Adamou Djermakoye.

1982 29 January: Boubou Hama dies in Niamey. **30 March:** Niamey's central market is destroyed by a fire.

1983 17 January: The Nigerian government decides to expel 3 million non-Nigerian nationals, among whom tens of thousands are Nigeriens. **24 January:** The office of prime minister is created for the first time in Niger, and Mahaman Oumarou is appointed to the position. The new government is largely a civilian one. **3 August:** The second version of the Conseil National de Développement is established, with Mahaman Oumarou as its president.

6 October: A coup is thwarted; it was masterminded by Kountché's close advisor, Amadou Oumarou aka Bonkano.

1984 **11 January:** A national commission is set up to prepare a constitutional charter. **4 April:** Both Hamani Diori and Djibo Bakary are released from house arrest. **16 November:** Under pressure from the IMF, the financially restricted state of Niger announces the future privatization of 54 parastatals (companies or agencies owned or controlled wholly or partly by the government) but faces unionist opposition as well as difficulties in securing the best conditions for selling enterprises to private interests.

1985 **February:** The Union Nationale de Crédit et de Coopératives is privatized, signaling that Niger is starting to give up the policy of agricultural development. **24 April:** The second Nigerian expulsion of "illegal immigrants" is in violation of ECOWAS treaty; this concerns about 100,000 Nigeriens at a time when drought has hit hard regions bordering Nigeria, causing a famine there. **29–30 May:** An armed group of 14 Tuareg men attacks the small town of Tchintabaraden, killing two republican guards and wounding a gendarme; one of the assailants is killed and 10 other are arrested. This is labeled the Affaire de Tchintabaraden. **20 July:** Idé Oumarou is elected secretary-general of OAU at Addis-Ababa.

1987 **25 January:** Inauguration of Niamey's new central market. With a graceful neo-Sahelian architecture and a rational plan, it cost 5 billion CFA francs and its management was contracted out to the Société de Construction et de Gestion des Marchés (SOCOGEM). **21 March:** The CND adopts the draft of the national charter. The government follows suit on 11 May. **14 June:** The national charter is adopted by referendum, with 99.58 percent of voters approving it. **22 October:** A plan of civil service early retirement intended to reduce the state's wage bill is adopted, the Programme d'Appui à l'Intiative Privée et à la Création d'Emploi (PAIPCE). **10 November:** President Seyni Kountché dies of a brain tumor in a Paris hospital. **14 November:** The CMS designates Colonel Ali Saibou as Kountché's successor.

1988 **6 January:** A Second Republic is decreed. Two days later, a commission is set up to prepare its constitution. **1 December:** The CND adopts the draft constitution for the Second Republic. The government follows suit in February 1989.

1989 **23 April:** Hamani Diori dies in a hospital in Rabat (Morocco). He had been rearrested following the Affaire de Tchintabaraden, in which his son was involved, but Saibou had released him again upon coming to power. **15–18 May:** The Mouvement National pour la Société de Développement (MNSD) is established as a single party for the Second Republic. Ali Saibou is nominated sole candidate for the presidential election. **24 September:** The constitution of the Second Republic is adopted, with 99.28 percent of voters approving it. **10 December:** Ali Saibou is elected president with 99.60 percent of valid suffrage; the MNSD single party list of 93 candidates is elected to the National Assembly with 99.52 percent of valid suffrage. **20 December:** The new government is formed and conspicuously does not have a prime minister. It announces a policy of drastic austerity, including especially in the financing of education—this through a plan pushed by the World Bank and known as Project Education III. Student unrest immediately starts.

1990   9 February: Students march against the government's new education policy and clash with security forces on the Pont Kennedy. Three and perhaps more students die; dozens more are injured. Saibou hurries back from Benin, where he was making a state visit. **2 March:** A prime minister is appointed, presumably to give a less authoritarian air to the government. **6–8 March:** At a high level meeting of the MNSD, a number of officials are held accountable for the deaths on the Pont Kennedy and are removed from the party. **1 May:** The USTN demands a constitutional revision and multipartism as a guarantee for citizens' rights and democratic freedoms. Publication of Niger's first independent newspaper, *Haské*. **6–7 May:** Armed Tuareg men attack Tchintabaraden, killing five persons. This is the beginning of a period of insecurity, during which 63 persons will be killed in the *départements* of Agadez, Tahoua, and Tillabéri, mostly among the assailants themselves. Though 44 men are arrested by the end of the year, they will all be released in April 1991 for insufficient evidence. The military operations involved the death of an unknown number of Tuareg civilians in various locales: 70 according to the government, several hundred people according to international organizations, and several thousand according to future Tuareg rebel leaders. The deaths are called "the massacre of Tchintabaraden" by the international press and Tuareg rebel fronts, though they occurred in various places and at various points in time, in May–June 1990. **16 June:** The government announces that the constitution will be revised. **15 November:** Ali Saibou announces that the constitution has been revised and includes multipartism. **1–4 December:** The MNSD high-level organ, the Conseil Supérieur d'Orientation Nationale (CSON), holds a series of meetings at the end of which it announces that the government will organize a National Conference.

1991   10 January: The USTN ends all participation in MNSD's organizations and activities. **8 March:** The army breaks off ties with the MNSD. **12–18 March:** The MNSD holds an extraordinary congress during which it becomes a normal political party as MNSD Nassara. **24 April:** The constitution is revised and Niger becomes a multiparty democracy. **4 May:** A national commission is set up to prepare the National Conference. **13 May:** Nationwide demonstrations of women erupt against the fact that the national commission does not include a single female; women in Niamey storm into the commission's building and five seats are granted to them. **2 June:** Six Tuareg men attack the border control station of Yassan, at the Niger-Mali border, north of Tillabéri, and kill two policemen. **27 June:** First issue of *Le Républicain*, Niger's flagship independent newspaper. **12 July:** Ali Saibou resigns as president of the MNSD, for the sake of political neutrality during the imminent National Conference. **29 July:** The National Conference starts at Niamey's Palais des Sports. The following day, it proclaims itself sovereign. In August, it will dissolve the government (which will become a caretaker government) and establish a commission in charge of investigating all state crimes and offenses covering "the past thirty years." **26 October:** Cheiffou Amadou is elected prime minister of the transition government, with the task of adopting a series of fundamental texts, including a controversial Family Code. **2 November:** André Salifou is elected president of the Haut Conseil de la République, a provisional parliament. **3 November:** The National Conference ends. Initially scheduled for 40 days, it had lasted three months.

1992   28 February: Mutiny of soldiers over two-month nonpayment of salary; unions strike for the same reason. **27 March:** Cheiffou Amadou reshuffles his cabinet to better cope with the budget crisis; he also seeks a truce with Tuareg rebels in the north. **15 May:** The government reaches a truce with Tuareg fronts, but the latter will not respect it, owing to their own internal divisions. **31 July:** Niger sells official recognition to Taiwan, receiving $50 million in aid from the island, a welcome respite in the budget crisis. The People's Republic of China breaks off diplomatic relations. **26 December:** The constitution of the Third Republic is approved with 89.79 percent of the suffrage.

1993   12 February: Creation of the Alliance des Forces du Changement (AFC), a gathering of the new parties opposed to a return of the MNSD to power through elections. **14 February:** Legislative elections give AFC parties 50 of the 83 seats of the National Assembly. **27 February:** First round of presidential elections; Tandja leads with 34.22 percent of the vote, with Mahaman Ousmane of the Convention Démocratique et Sociale (CDS) a challenger with 26.59 percent of the vote. **27 March:** Second round of presidential election: Ousmane, with the backing of other AFC parties, wins with 54.42 percent of the vote. **18 April:** Mahamadou Issoufou of the Parti Nigérien pour la Démocratie et le Socialisme (PNDS) is appointed prime minister. **23 April:** The first government of the Third Republic is formed and includes 5 women out of 28 ministers and state secretaries.

1994 **12 May:** A Toubou group starts a new Saharan rebel front; it will operate mostly in far eastern Niger, clashing there with Fulani herdsmen and Niger's military. **28 September:** Mahamadou Issoufou leaves the government coalition over disputes with President Ousmane on the control of market contracts allocation and public service appointments. The minister of commerce, Souley Abdoulaye, replaces him. **16 October:** The PNDS joins the MNSD in a no-confidence vote that brings down Souley Abdoulaye's cabinet. **17 October:** Ousmane dissolves the National Assembly and confirms Souley Abdoulaye as interim prime minister.

1995 **12 January:** Legislative elections at which the MNSD, the PNDS, and some smaller parties win a plurality of the seats—43 out of 83. **7 February:** In a ploy to split the MNSD, President Ousmane appoints an MNSD official, Amadou Boubacar Cissé, prime minister. This backfires, as Cissé is evicted from the MNSD and his government quickly ousted by a no-confidence vote on 20 February. **21 February:** Ousmane is forced to appoint the MNSD's secretary-general Hama Amadou as prime minister. **24 April:** The Amadou government signs a peace agreement with the Tuareg Organisation de la Résistance Armée (ORA), a federation of rebel fronts. This chiefly commits the state of Niger to find military and paramilitary jobs for disbanded fighters. However, dissident Tuareg fronts continue to sporadically attack travelers in the north. **10 December:** Niger reluctantly signs an IMF prepared structural adjustment package.

1996 **27 January:** Colonel Ibrahim Baré Maïnassara, chief of defense staff, overthrows the government, which had been paralyzed for months, as President Ousmane refused to attend cabinet meetings and to thus allow the government to operate. Baré Maïnassara establishes a 12-member Conseil de Salut National (CSN) and suspends all political parties. France supports the coup and becomes the new regime's international patron; the United States condemns it. **30 January:** Boukary Adji is appointed prime minister by the CSN. **1–7 April:** The CSN convenes a 700-member Forum pour le Renouveau Démocratique to write a new constitution. **12 May:** The constitution of the Fourth Republic is adopted through a referendum by allegedly 90 percent of voters, with a turnout of 35 percent. **20 May:** The suspension of political parties is lifted in preparation for presidential and legislative elections. **12 June:** The CSN commits the state of Niger to an IMF Enhanced Structural Adjustment Facility (ESAF), leading to a large-scale privatization scheme. **7–8 July:** Ibrahim Baré Maïnassara is elected president in the first round with 52.22 percent of the suffrage. The voting, however, is heavily manipulated, and is immediately called into question by the major political parties. **14 September:** The MNSD, PNDS, CDS, and a number of other minor parties form the Front pour la Restauration et la Défense de la Démocratie (FRDD), which claims Baré Maïnassara's rule is illegitimate. **23 November:** Legislative elections are held but are boycotted by the FRDD. The new National Assembly is entirely made up of a coalition of pro-Baré Maïnassara parties, earning the nickname "Assemblée Balsa" (*balsa* being Hausa/Zarma slang for "profiteering"). **12 December:** The CSN is dissolved. **21 December:** Amadou Boubacar Cissé is appointed prime minister. His main mission is to end the unions' unrest, which paralyzes the civil service and creates an atmosphere of political crisis supportive of FRDD goals. He is not successful.

1997 **20 March:** Agreement with the World Bank to trim the public sector, which leads to further union unrest. **21 June:** The Cissé government dismissed for "incompetence." Ibrahim Hassane Mayaki is appointed prime minister.

1998 **23 March:** The National Assembly votes a general amnesty for disbanded Tuareg and Toubou rebels. Rhissa ag-Boula, the key leader of the Tuareg rebel fronts, is appointed minister delegate to tourism. **31 July:** Agreements are reached with the FRDD on the first local elections of Niger, to be held in early 1999. The FRDD agrees to participate since the electoral commission is reconstituted on its original bases (1992). The agreement was brokered behind closed doors by the French. **August:** Several former Tuareg rebel fronts morph into a Niamey-based liaison committee in charge of overseeing the Tuareg-side recruitment of former fighters into Niger's military and paramilitary forces; this becomes a source of patronage for former rebel leaders. **September:** An IMF delegation congratulates the government for its financial management under the ESAF and World Bank agreements. Donors and development banks shower Niger with funds to further push through the policies. Union strikes completely paralyze the civil service; the government freezes salaries in retaliation.

1999 **7 February:** Local elections are largely won by the opposition, despite heavy-handed attempts at manipulating the voting. Thus, for example, in Madarounfa, masked security forces opened fire on electoral commission officials who were protecting the ballot boxes from them. **7 April:** The constitutional chamber of the Supreme Court validates the opposition's victory and then voids it of its meaning by deciding that 80 percent of the voting was flawed and should be done again. The opposition immediately demands Baré Maïnassara's resignation and calls Nigeriens to arms. **9 April:** Baré Maïnassara is killed at the military airport of Niamey by coup leader Major Malam Daouda Wanké. **12 April:** Wanké becomes head of state and installs a Conseil National de Réconciliation (CNR). The Mayaki government remains in office as a caretaker government. Wanké promises a speedy return to democratic governance. **18 July:** Constitutional referendum is declared; the results, proclaimed on 9 August, adopt the Fifth Republic constitution with 89.57 percent of the suffrage. Voting-weary Nigeriens go to the ballot at only 31.2 percent turnout. The new constitution in particular creates a constitutional court, unattached to the Supreme Court and constituted in ways that extensively protect its independence—this in light of the negative role played by the constitutional chamber of the Supreme Court in the final crisis of the Fourth Republic. **3 October:** First round of the presidential election, with MNSD's Mamadou Tandja (32.22 percent) ahead of PNDS's Mahamadou Issoufou (22.79 percent) by about 10 percentage points. **24 November:** Tandja wins the runoff with 59.89 percent of the suffrage, largely thanks to CDS support. Legislative elections held that day give the MNSD 38 percent of the 83 National Assembly seats against 17 percent for the CDS and 16 percent for the PNDS. **31 December:** Hama Amadou is appointed prime minister; his 23-member cabinet includes only two women.

2000   3 January: Prime Minister Amadou asks deputies to forgo their first salary, in view of the budgetary situation: "The coffers of the state are absolutely empty." **7 January:** The National Assembly votes an amnesty law for the perpetrators of the coups d'état of 1996 and 1999. Only Baré Maïnassara's party, the Rassemblement pour la Démocratie et le Progrès (RDP), opposes this. **March:** Twelve opposition parties are led by the PNDS and the Alliance Nigérienne pour la Démocratie et le Progrès (ANDP) into a National Assembly coalition, the Coordination des Forces Démocratiques (CFD). The CFD's main plank is to denounce the allocation of senior parliamentary commission positions to the majority. The majority responds with a 17-party group, the Alliance des Forces Démocratiques (AFD). **June:** Ten soldiers are arrested for the temporary kidnapping of Major Djibrilla Hima, former CRN permanent secretary. A government speech read by acting prime minister Wassalké Boukary (Amadou being in France), calls for a republican army. **1 November:** Creation of a High Court of Justice, empowered among other things to indict high state officials for treason or process impeachment cases—a fallout from Baré Maïnassara's actions. **8 November:** Islamist demonstrators destroy betting kiosks and attack bars and other so-called "perdition places" in Niamey and Maradi, in protest against the second edition of the African fashion festival FIMA, which opens in Niamey on the following day. Several Islamic associations are subsequently dissolved and 25 Islamists arrested.

2001   16 January: The CFD fails to have a no-confidence vote passed at the National Assembly; it will try and fail again in March. **21 February:** Students demonstrate against their deteriorating living and working conditions;

prevented from crossing the Pont Kennedy, the students turn violent. A group of students beats up a gendarme, Adamou Bizo, who will die on 14 March from the injuries and 16 students are arrested. **15 May:** The soldiers involved in the kidnapping of Major Hima are released by decision of the court of appeal. **10 June:** The sultan of Damagaram, Aboubacar Sanda, is sued by the government; a month later, the Ministry of the Interior dethrones him, even though there was no judicial decision yet. **8 September:** The leader of the Toubou rebel front Forces Armées Révolutionnaires du Sahara (FARS), Chahai Barka, is killed by the Nigerien army in an attack 300 km north of Dirkou.

2002 31 July: Troops in the far eastern garrisons of Diffa, N'Guigmi, and N'Gourti organize a mutiny against their deteriorating living and working conditions and take hostage all state authorities in the area, including traditional chiefs and a religious dignitary, the imam of Diffa. **4 August:** In Niamey, a band of military men tries to seize an arms depot and is thwarted. The government arrests several military personnel—mostly junior officers—accused of plotting a coup in connection with those events. **9 August:** Talks are organized between the mutineers in Diffa and the government, through the released hostages, including the imam of Diffa. **31 August:** The government decrees an *état de mise en garde* of the region of Diffa, a form of state of emergency that essentially restricts the press from investigating the target district. The constitutional court judges the procedure of the decree anticonstitutional, but the government ignores its decision. Its president and vice-president (Sani Koutoubi and Lawan Ari Gremah) resign, creating an impending political crisis. **11 September:** The Benin–Niger border dispute is brought to the International Court of Justice. **17 September:** The government lifts the *état de mise en garde* on Diffa. **2 December:** The government fails to pass a law reforming the judicial system to introduce a military tribunal integral to it. This is an outcome of the decree mini-crisis, as a reform would have needed an agreement with the opposition group CFD, which questioned the motivations of the government given the September blunder with the constitutional court. The government instead adopts a military justice code with its own court.

2003 3 January: Three Italian tourists are killed in the Orida sector by a landmine left by Tuareg rebels in the 1990s. The year will be dotted with incidents of Tuareg men attacking isolated individuals, remote state posts, and faraway dwellings, though not as part of any organized rebellion as in the 1990s. The government considers the incidents acts of armed banditry. **25 May:** A political truce is reached by CFD and AFD in the framework of a Conseil National de Dialogue Politique (CNDP), supposed to design consensual solutions to certain types of political issues. Though the truce will be very short-lived, the CNDP will be maintained. **4 August:** Mamane Abou and Oumarou Keita, the director and editor of *Le Républicain*, are arrested for defamation after the publication of an article that claims Niger was shifting allegiance from the West to Iran. In reality, *Le Républicain* had published, at several points since 2000, confidential state papers unearthing shady financial deals by government officials. Under cover of judicial slowness, Abou and Keita spend a few months in jail.

2004   27 January: Tourism minister and ex-rebel leader Rhissa ag-Boula is arrested for the murder of Adam Amagué, president of the MNSD branch of Tchirozerine. Ag-Boula will shortly thereafter be released on bail, after his brother, Mohammed ag-Boula, kidnaps two gendarmes near Arlit and threatens to kill them. **15 March:** The CNDP convenes for the first time to discuss the voting systems and electoral circumscriptions; a consensus is reached. **24 July:** Regional elections are held. **12 August:** Moussa Kaka, director of the private radio Sarraounia and correspondent for Radio France Internationale (RFI), is arrested after an interview with Mohammed ag-Boula for RFI. **October:** The government and donors estimate that 3.5 million people will face a severe food shortage in the coming months owing to drought and also the rise in food prices. The government announces a plan for selling grain at subsidized prices. **16 November:** First round of the presidential election: the MNSD's Tandja (40.67 percent) ahead of the PNDS's Mahamadou Issoufou (24.49 percent). **4 December:** Runoff to presidential election: Tandja wins with 65.53 percent of the suffrage, thanks to the widest coalition supporting a presidential candidate until then. At legislative elections, 14 women enter the 113-member National Assembly, dominated by the MNSD (47 seats against 25 for the PNDS and its allies). Amadou is reappointed prime minister.

2005   The food crisis rages: President Tandja denies a famine, sacking government workers who publicize it and intimidating foreign workers and reporters; Prime Minister Amadou takes the opposite stance and ends up calling for international assistance on 28 May. **4 January:** Under pressure from the IMF, the National Assembly adopts a law that extends value added tax (VAT) to milk, sugar, corn flour (essential for the French-inherited baguette bread), and other foodstuff. Food prices soar in urban areas too. **5 March:** A large-scale protest coalition of unions and civil society organizations mobilizes hundreds of thousands throughout the country's towns. The showdown with the government lasts a full month and involves a complete stop of all economic activity, including in the huge informal sector, through "ghost city" operations. **20 April:** The government revises the tax bill: VAT on most foodstuffs and some usage of water and electricity are lifted, but not the 19 percent VAT on sugar. The burden is shifted to other sectors of economic activity. The government and deputies commit to reduce their own so-called operational spending. Foodstuffs in rural areas (millet, sorghum, etc.), though not taxed, remain dear due to market speculation on the food crisis. **12 July:** The ruling of the International Court of Justice adjudicating the Benin–Niger border dispute is largely in favor of Niger. **7 December:** The fifth games of the Francophonie start in Niamey and last for 10 days. **22 December:** The IMF cancels $111 million of Niger's debt.

2006 February: Creation of a Haut Conseil Islamique, the government's response to the proliferation of Islamic associations. **27 June**: The previous and current national education ministers are sacked. The government had come under attack at the National Assembly for financial improprieties related to the funding by the European Union of Niger's primary education system. An audit earlier in the year disclosed a muddle amounting to 4 billion CFA francs. This has come to be known as the "Affaire MEBA" (from Ministère de l'Enseignement de Base). **September**: Twenty persons (including the two ministers) are arrested in relation to Affaire MEBA. The government thus responds to threats from the European Union to suspend indefinitely disbursements on its education aid program if some punishment was not meted out somewhere.

2007 February: The cyclical 10-yearly Tuareg rebellion resumes in the north with a new generation of fighters who found the Mouvement des Nigériens pour la Justice (MNJ) with much the same planks as fighters in the mid-1990s. The government's official line is that they are armed bandits, though a rift exists between President Tandja (hard line) and Prime Minister Amadou (favorable to dialogue). **1 June:** A no-confidence motion successfully brings down the Amadou government through the combined efforts of the opposition and the Tandja faction of the MNSD (62 deputies out of 113 voted the motion, though MNSD rode a coalition of 88 seats). Seyni Oumarou (MNSD) is appointed prime minister two days later. **24 August:** Tandja decrees an *état de mise en garde* over the region of Agadez. This gives the army full repressive powers in the region.

2008 Sporadic rallies are organized throughout the year to call for a third—anticonstitutional—term of office for Tandja; these are most intense and frequent in Zinder. **14 June:** The National Assembly strips former prime minister Amadou of his parliamentary immunity and sends him to trial at the High Court of Justice for allegedly embezzling 100 million CFA francs. **26 June:** Amadou is arrested and sent to a high-security prison outside of Niamey. **19 October:** A rally of thousands in Niamey protest Amadou's imprisonment; another rally scheduled a week later is forbidden. **15 December:** A Canadian United Nations representative, Robert Fowler, ventures in an insecure district of the northern part of the Tillabéri region and is kidnapped by a group of armed men. This draws the attention of Western officialdom to Niger's new Tuareg rebellion.

2009   8 January: The French uranium corporation AREVA signs a contract to exploit the giant mine of Imouraren starting in 2012. This means a €1.2 billion investment in Niger, a country that provides over a third of the fuel used by French nuclear plants. **22 January:** Four European tourists are kidnapped in Nigerien territory while traveling to a music festival in northern Mali. A month later, the Islamist terrorist group Al-Qaeda in the Islamic Maghrib (AQIM) will claim their abduction, as well as that of the UN envoy Fowler. **27 March:** French president Nicolas Sarkozy travels to Niamey "to defend the interests of France" with regard to uranium. At an event with Sarkozy later that day, Tandja declares his intention to stay in power in order "to finish up the job underway." **23 April:** A court orders the release of Hama Amadou for health reasons; Amadou leaves for France. **3 May:** Tandja in Agadez meets with leaders of MNJ and another rebel front, the Front des Forces de Redressement (FFR), an offshoot of the former. However, he extends the *état de mise en garde* on Agadez, which leads the MNJ and FFR to keep on fighting. **8 May:** Consulted by opposition deputies, the constitutional court delivers a nonbinding decision against a referendum. The following day, Tandja dissolves the National Assembly. Opposition parties then join forces with unions and civic associations to create the Front pour la Défense de la Démocratie (FDD). **29 May:** Tandja announces in a rambling and paternalistic televised speech that he intends to continue serving the Nigerien people and will organize a referendum to request a term extension. **12 June**: The constitutional court issues a binding decision against the referendum. **23 June:** Propaganda speech by finance minister Lamine Zeine, who grotesquely inflates Niger's economic performance to give credence to Tandja's claims of being indispensable. The following day, Tandja writes an official letter to the constitutional court requesting it to rescind its decision on the basis that it had "exceeded its competencies." The court refuses. **26 June:** Tandja announces that he invests himself with "exceptional powers" in view of the constitutional court's refusal to authorize a referendum. The adoption of a new constitution will furthermore entail a three-year transition period during which he intends to bring everyone to heel. The FDD calls the move a "constitutional coup d'état" and publicly asks the army to intervene. **29 June:** Tandja scraps the constitutional court. **9 July:** The European Union suspends its €9 million aid program. **4 August:** The referendum is organized, with a few clashes in Tahoua and Illela (PNDS's Issoufou's fiefs) and Dosso (ANDP's Djemakoye's fief). The turnout is a trickle, except for the regions of Zinder and Maradi where there is some enthusiasm for Tandja's project.

The constitution will be promulgated on 18 August. **31 August:** The Tuareg rebellion peters out as its leader, Aghali Alambo, settles in Libya with blandishments from that country's president, Colonel Muamar Kaddafi. The MNJ vows to reorganize itself for further struggle but seems to grow irrelevant, especially given the emergence in the area of the AQIM (constituted chiefly of Algerian and Tunisian Islamist militants). **20 October:** Legislative elections, boycotted by the opposition and leading to Niger's automatic suspension from ECOWAS. The new National Assembly is comprised of Tandja's faction at the MNSD and a smattering of small parties and nonentities. It gains the nickname "Assemblée Balsa," earlier given to the Fourth Republic's Parliament.

2010   18 February: Tandja is toppled by a coup d'état led by squadron chief Djibo Salou. Thousands celebrate on the streets in Niamey and other towns. Tandja is put under house arrest in a posh villa next to the presidential mansion. A largely civilian caretaker government is appointed, under Mahamadou Danda, while the ruling organ is a military Conseil Supérieur pour la Restauration de la Démocratie (CSRD). **10 March:** All new regional governors, with the exception of the one in Dosso, are military officers. **29 March:** Greenpeace accuses AREVA of poisoning the area around Arlit and Akokan with radioactive pollution in land, water, and air. **1 April:** Journalists and government officials gathered in an "estates-general of the media" push through a legal text replacing prison terms with fines for press offenses (defamation, insult, and propagation of false news, all indictments previously used to jail journalists). **2 April:** A new food crisis breaks out throughout rural Niger and especially in the region of Zinder. It will be more serious than the one in 2004 but will be stemmed more easily, thanks to full government cooperation with food aid specialists. **10 May:** The Comité des Textes Fondamentaux, in charge of writing a new constitution, passes on its final draft to the provisional parliament, the Conseil Consultatif National, for amendments. **17 September:** Seven expatriate workers (five French and two Africans) are kidnapped by AQIM in Arlit. **15 October:** Colonel Abdoulaye Badié, CSRD's second in line, and Colonel Abdou Sidikou, are arrested. They are accused of plotting a coup. Two other high-ranking officers are arrested the following day. **31 October:** The constitution of the Seventh Republic goes through a referendum. Turnout is high at 54.16 percent, reaching rates unheard of since the early 1990s, and 93.48 percent of voters approve the constitution.

2011   8 January: AQIM kidnaps two young Frenchmen in a restaurant in Niamey, but a high-powered intervention of French security forces leads to the death of the abductors and their victims. **11 January:** Regional elections are held. **31 January:** Legislative elections, at which the PNDS wins 39 seats against 26 for the MNSD (led by Tandja's former prime minister Seyni Oumarou) and 23 for an offshoot of the MNSD led by Tandja's former antagonistic prime minister Hama Amadou, the Mouvement Démocratique Nigérien pour une Fédération Africaine (MODEN/FA). Of the traditional major parties, the ANDP wins fourth place (8 seats) while the CDS falls back with only 3 seats, after its ill-constituted lists are invalidated by the constitutional council in its stronghold of Zinder. The first rounds of the presidential election are also held that day: Mahamadou Issoufou (PNDS) comes ahead with 36.06 percent of the suffrage, followed by Seyni Oumarou (23.24 percent) and Hama Amadou (19.82 percent). **12 March:** Runoff to the presidential election: With the support of Amadou, Issoufou beats Oumarou with 57.95 percent of the suffrage against 42.05 percent. **22 April:** First government of the Seventh Republic is appointed and headed by Brigi Raffini, a seasoned Tuareg state official. The 24-person government includes 6 women and 5 ministries for the PNDS's ally, the MODEN/FA Loumana. **12 July:** A coup d'état attempt is averted. Ten days later, on 22 July, 10 persons are arrested after police investigations, while others flee the country. The would-be coup-makers are mostly people fearful of the new government's anticorruption probes. **28 November:** First oil barrels come out of the refinery at Zinder. The government lowers gas prices to 579 CFA francs per liter, down from 670 CFA francs. This is met with public anger as Nigeriens had been expecting a sharper price reduction. The government stresses that the new price is temporary and likely to decrease. In Zinder, a supporter of former President Tandja's constitutional coup uses the malaise to call for an uprising. He is arrested a few days later. **5 December:** Violent demonstrations erupt in Zinder, as the trial of the Tandja supporter starts there. Police repression leads to three deaths, including a high school student accidentally hit by a tear gas grenade in his school's yard. Zinder's police chief is sacked. In the following days, primary and secondary students demonstrate throughout the country, while security forces are put on hold.

Introduction

Sitting on the cusp between Mediterranean and sub-Saharan Africa, Niger is in many ways a remarkable place, blending in the harsh Sahelian environment a great diversity of cultures and lifestyles to make up a poor but resilient nation. The country was established in the early 20th century in what used to be the busy crossroad of exchanges between the kingdoms and empires of West Africa and the Arab-Islamic world. The resulting melting pot is a blend of Western Sudanic cultures, manifest in particular in food, music, and dance as well as in the enduring rituals and practices of animist religions, with a good deal of Arab culture imported through the Islamic religion and a dash of French culture notable in formal schooling and the state.

The Sahara desert, which played such a vital role in the evolution of Niger's peoples, lost its role as a commercial and cultural crossroad when European occupation of West Africa shifted the bulk of the region's exchanges toward the southern coast and the Atlantic. Niger is arguably the most typical manifestation of this historic division. The country now stitches together two regions polarized by southern centers of gravity: the Zarma-Songhay West, orientated toward the Gulf of Guinea (Benin, Togo, Ghana, and Côte d'Ivoire) and the Hausa Center-East turned toward Northern Nigeria (where the majority of the Hausa reside), leaving only the sparsely populated Tuareg-Toubou North to remain linked to the Arab world through Libya and Algeria. These varied outside pulls do not compromise Niger's national makeup (with the exception of the peculiar case of the Tuareg), as they are powerfully counterbalanced by the traditions of interdependence that tie together Niger's ethnicities, often specialized in their economic activities and maintaining vibrant customs of hospitality and goodwill that were greatly shaped by the severe constraints of the Sahelian environment.

Niger generally suffers from extreme marginalization in the world economy and has inherited very little in terms of infrastructure and modern education from French rule, which developed here the shortest-lived (1922–1960) and flimsiest colonial regime in West Africa. It has therefore tended to hedge its bets on volatile primary commodities (groundnuts in the 1960s–1970s, uranium since the late 1970s, and oil coming in the picture in recent years). Foreign aid, though important in the state's budgets and the shaping of its

1

economic policy, has tenuous impacts on the country's great poverty. Austerity programs and privatizations have installed a small market economy in the country in the 1990s, but economic development remains elusive as structural factors, such as high demography or environmental degradation, are still mostly uncontrolled. Despite these adverse circumstances and also a military accustomed to plotting and making coups, Niger is remarkably successful in establishing, restoring, and maintaining democratic governance. Tuareg uprisings and more recent Islamist attacks organized by Saharan-based Algerian armed groups are contained chiefly in the northern deserts, in good deal owing to the country's social cohesion and religious moderation. Niger's dominant options today are to deepen democratic governance, to better organize the country's integration in the West African economy, and to make the most of its territory's primary commodities, among which oil is scheduled to become an important element in the years to come. These are certainly wise choices, and ones that allow Nigeriens, if they have the will, to be true agents of their destiny.

LAND AND PEOPLE

Except for its northern regions, Niger is a relatively flat country with monotonous topographical features, numerous depressions, and a harsh climate. It has three distinct climatic regions: (1) The intensely cultivated south, and especially the fertile Niger River region, with a mean altitude of 300–350 meters above sea level, and with a Sahelian climate with one rainy season between June and October (preceded in May by powerful dust tornadoes). (2) The arid transitional center of the country, suitable for nomadic pastoralists raising cattle, and with a sharply lower rainfall. This region is usually divided into the South Sahel belt (including Niamey), which receives between 350 and 750 mm of rainfall, permitting three to four months of agriculture, and the North Sahel belt (which includes Agadez), with a maximum of 350 mm of rainfall, in which true agriculture is impossible except in oases. Finally, (3) the desert expanses in the middle of the Ténéré where there is little rainfall, and which includes Bilma.

It is essentially only in the first area, comprising roughly 120,000 sq km—or some 10 percent of Niger's total territory—that intensive and/or regular agricultural activity is possible. The Sahel belts, marginally self-sufficient in good years, suffer tremendously in periods of drought. The overall population density of Niger, estimated at 12.52 people per sq km for 2010, reflects both the higher density in the south, and the relative absence of population in the desert areas of the north.

Niger is one of the hottest countries in the world, although it also presents some extremes of cold owing to the continental nature of its climate. Niamey's temperature range is 8°C–45°C (47°F–114°F); Tillabéri's annual average maximum is 41°C (106°F); and in the Aïr, the range is from 5°C to 50°C (23°F to 122°F) in the shade. The country's wildlife, much decimated, includes small numbers of elephants; hippos in the Niger River; in the W National Park lions, buffalo, and antelopes; and, in the area of Kouré, the last population of giraffes in West Africa, saved by a protection program set up in the late 1990s.

In terms of relief, the ruggedly beautiful Aïr mountains in the north are extensions of the Algerian Ahaggar Mountains, and include the core north–south 80,000 sq km Aïr massif (with an altitude of 700–800 meters), bisected by numerous ravines (koris) and punctuated by a north–south line of volcanic crests, as well as other isolated outcroppings. The northernmost of these includes Niger's highest elevation, the 2,022-meter-high Mont Baguezane (until 2001, measurement flaws had attributed this position to the 1944-meter-high Mont Gréboun, farther north). In the northeast, a series of high plateaus form a ridge between Chad's Tibesti (until 1929 governed by Niger) and Algeria's Ahaggar massifs. These include the plateaus of Djado, Tchigai, and Manguéni. On each side of Aïr extends the Sahara sand lowlands. In the west is found the Talak desert, which includes in its northern segment the Tamesna region, where fossilized river valleys filled with shifting sand dunes flow south, and in the south the Azaoua region. In the east stretches the huge (400,000 sq km) Ténéré desert, with its large ergs interrupted only by the remote Kaouar oases to which caravans from Agadez (in Aïr) still trek for their salt output. Fossilized river valleys (dallol) "flow" from Aïr southward into the Niger River. Once filled with water some 5,000 to 6,000 years ago, these tributaries of the Niger (and the drainage system of Aïr) enabled the desert north to support large populations of fishermen, hunters, and pastoralists, as was stunningly revealed in ancient cave drawings of rivers and wildlife.

In the east, Niger includes 2,560 sq km of Lake Chad, which, in times of intense drought (as in the early 1970s and again in the early 1980s), greatly contracts (being essentially very shallow), allowing a dry crossing to Nigeria and Chad. Part of the frontier in this area—for 150 km—is formed by the Komadougou Yobé river system (dry 1974–1984), which flows from the west into the lake. In the southwest, the Niger River—the ninth longest in the world, and Africa's third longest—flows for about 500 km through Niger, from the rapids of Labezanga on the Malian border to Gaya on the Nigerian border. It receives several tributaries on its right side, notably the Gorouol, Sirba, Tapoa, and Makrou, all intermittent trickles now. Its left bank is joined by the dry fossilized valleys that once drained the northern regions.

The landlocked country is bordered on the south by the long frontier with Nigeria and by Benin, on the west by Burkina Faso and Mali, on the north by Algeria and Libya, and on the east by Chad. Though caravans do travel in the east–west direction, communications are mostly along the north–south axis and along the southern road system connecting the towns of Zinder, Maradi, Dosso, and Niamey to Nigeria, Benin, Burkina Faso, and Mali. The southward route that starts at Arlit—far north—is utilized for the evacuation of all of Niger's exports and for the importation of the country's needs, via Cotonou in Benin, Lomé in Togo, Tema in Ghana, Abidjan in Côte d'Ivoire, as well as some of the Nigerian ports. Niamey itself is, as the crow flies, 2,591 km from Algiers (Algeria), 2,432 km from Tripoli (Libya), 1,413 from N'Djamena (Chad), 1,100 km from Bamako (Mali), 797 km from Cotonou (Benin, and the nearest port), 767 km from Abuja (Nigeria), and 415 km from Ouagadougou (Burkina Faso).

Most of Niger's population of 10.8 million people (2001 census) resides in the southern regions, with those in Maradi (2.2 million), Zinder (2 million), Tahoua (1.9 million), Tillabéri (1.8 million), and Dosso (1.4 million) being the most populous. By contrast, in the huge region of Agadez, only 203,000 people are to be found.

Most of the people are from one of eight basic ethnic groups. Just over half the population is Hausa (6,069,740), to be found in a broad arc north of the Nigerian border and in the key regions of Maradi and Zinder. Slightly less than one quarter of the population is of Zarma-Songhay ethnicity (2,300,880), usually residing west of the Hausa in a belt stretching into Mali. According to the 2001 census, the Fulani of Niger number 935,600 and are scattered in small concentrations in the south center of the country. In the extreme east are found the Kanuri and Manga (513,200), while the Tuareg (and their former slaves), comprising 10 percent (1,017,000) of the population, are nomadic or settle the vast expanse of the region of Agadez, north of the Hausa, the Fulani, and the Zarma-Songhay belt, but at times in their close proximity. Tinier ethnic groups exist in the far north and far east—such as the Arabs (40,085) and Toubou (42,200)—and in the far west, the Gourmantchés (40,000).

Most of Niger's peoples are settled agriculturalists, with only about 20 percent of nomads, whose populations are dwindling, and 16 percent of urbanites, whose population is growing. Niamey was virtually nonexistent prior to the 20th century but has today over 750,000 people, while Zinder and Maradi, both important economic centers in relation with northern Nigeria, are closely tied for second place, with a population of 170,000 for the former and 150,000 for the latter. The highest population densities are also found in these two regions, with especially 116.5 people per sq km in the *département* of Madarounfa (in the vicinity of Maradi) as against 0.1 people per sq km in the *département* of Bilma. The population of Niger has been growing at a fast rate of over 3 percent per year and is estimated at over 16 million in 2011. Though still massively rural, Niger's urbanization is on the increase, as is shown especially in the case of Niamey, which has grown from independence, and swelling from 31,000 people in 1960 to nearly 800,000 today.

THE PRECOLONIAL ERA

Prior to the imposition of French influence and control in the area, Niger was the meeting ground of Songhay and Bornu power, exerted from the west and east respectively, and later Tuareg and Fulani power from the north and south.

Until the collapse of the Songhay Empire in Gao (Mali) at the end of the 16th century, parts of Niger, including Aïr, were under Songhay control. With the defeat of Gao to musket-bearing troops from Morocco, Aïr fell temporarily under the control of Bornu. The eastern provinces of Songhay—most currently in Niger—retained their independence but soon disintegrated into a series of small chiefdoms, easy prey to assaults from both north and south.

In the east, Bornu's weakening hegemony over the territory was first challenged by the coalescing sultanate of Damagaram, based in Zinder, which emerged as a powerful factor in what is now eastern Niger, and later by nascent Fulani power in the south. The latter displaced certain Hausa dynasties northward, and much of the history of southern Niger in the 19th century is the story of a tug-of-war between these two ethnic groups along a frontier coinciding with the current Niger–Nigeria border.

The Tuareg, arriving in the 11th century in Aïr and strengthened by further waves from the north (many coming from Algeria's Ahaggar), created a population pressure in the north resulting in the migration of various clans (*kel*) southward, to clash with established sedentary groups. From this were born the persistent sedentary-versus-nomadic clashes of central and southern Niger that affected many Zarma, Songhay, Maouri, and Hausa settlements, and remain as bitter memories to many to this day.

FRENCH OCCUPATION

With the entry of French exploratory missions and then military force in the region in the last few years of the 19th century, the various ethnic groups reacted in accordance with their varying situations, but with a greater or lesser degree of initial hostility. To the Tuareg—many of whom had been converted to the Sanusiya Sufi order—the French were infidel conquerors threatening their culture, way of life, and control over sedentary groups in the area, and thus had to be expelled. The concomitant Franco–Tuareg conflicts, fiercely fought, greatly decimated the superior castes of most Tuareg confederations and partly laid the ground for future Tuareg unrest in more recent decades. The Toubou in the Kaouar region similarly suffered devastation, and this points to the fact that colonial government was more favorable to settled populations than to the nomadic ones, including for obvious administrative reasons.

This is shown by reactions in the Zarma-Songhay area, where the French were sought after by many chieftains as allies who could assist them in stemming the dual pressure from the Fulani in the south and the Tuareg in the north, while also playing in the complex politics of consolidation of executive power positions in their rather anarchistic polities. The crucial case in point was the city state of Dosso, where the chief, Aouta, ingratiated himself with the French through much-needed assistance for their "pacification" operations, to be rewarded by a strengthening of his grip over Dosso and the extension of Dosso's dominance over adjacent regions. The Hausa élites, on the other hand, were alienated to some extent by France's inability to assist them in regaining their territories lost to the Fulani—and subsequently to the British—in the south (in what became northern Nigeria) and by the heavy-handed abolition of the sultanate of Damagaram in 1906. In both the Zarma-Songhay and the Hausa area, sporadic revolts broke out until the end of the first decade of the 20th century, but the sedentary organization of life in these regions was ultimately amenable to a colonial government of agricultural labor, taxation, and commerce. Southern Niger, especially in the Zarma-Songhay areas, also provided large contingents of soldiers for France's war effort in World War I.

It was only in 1922 that a civilian-headed Colonie du Niger was set up. Some areas of the vast territory were not secure until the 1940s, with one (desert) region being under military administration until after World War II, and in general the flavor of military rule never quite faded out in colonial Niger.

The Colonie du Niger was a poor relative of France's West African empire. At first France sought to preserve the trans-Saharan trade that imparted its economic value to the territory, especially since it also controlled most of the northern termini of the trade, in Algeria and Tunisia (though not Libya, which was occupied by Italy). This proved nonviable, owing to the insecurity created by Tuareg attacks and, in 1911, the arrival of the railway to the northern Nigerian city of Kano. France then started to develop a groundnut basin in the Zinder and Maradi areas, similar to the one that became successful in Senegal, around Kaolack. However, this really took off only in the 1930s after the system of colonial trade (with French companies and banks and African middlemen) was finally established. Given the principle that a colony must pay for its improvement and considering the poverty of this colony, Niger lagged far behind in terms of investments in education and infrastructures. The colonial regime, just like subsequent independent governments, was also unable to stem the devastating hunger that regularly broke out in the colony, at a time when the population was much smaller (during the colonial period, it progressed from 1 to 2 million approximately).

After 1945, the Colonie du Niger became a Territoire d'Outre-Mer (TOM, overseas territory), with different rights and obligations. In particular, the notion that it must pay for its development was replaced by the concept of development assistance financed by a fund created in 1946 and fed by annual French state subventions and contributions from the territories. This had a modest impact on urban infrastructures and education, but mostly allowed the French to reorganize the colony's import/export network by deviating it away from northern Nigeria and through the French colony of Dahomey (now Benin). When Niger became independent in 1960, it had a 2 percent school attendance rate, a few hundred kilometers of paved roads, some mining of cheap minerals (cassiterite), and no industries. The challenge thus looked immense for the newly independent state.

It must be noted that the colonial regime, which was a form of administrative dictatorship until 1945, started to organize representative democracy throughout France's empire after that year. Multiparty politics quickly developed in the colony, although chiefly in its Western, Zarma-Songhay parts, where French education had grown more rapidly than elsewhere. By the late 1950s, when it became clear that the colony would inevitably evolve into an independent nation-state, the main stake of Nigerien politics became the nature of the future polity—meaning, would it be a pro-French, pro-capitalist entity, or a pan-African socialist polity?

INDEPENDENCE

The politics leading to independence explains most of Niger's crucial early years as an independent country. As elsewhere in Francophone Africa, the post–World War II emergence of local parties in Niger was a complex process full of splits and mergers that finally resulted in the ascendance of the Parti Progressiste Nigérien (PPN), which was affiliated with the Rassemblement Démocratique Africain (RDA), an inter-African umbrella led by Côte d'Ivoire's Félix Houphouët-Boigny. Just prior to independence, however, the dominant power was the neo-Marxist Mouvement Socialiste Africain (MSA, later Sawaba), which was itself a section of the Parti du Regroupement Africain (PRA), another inter-African umbrella party led by Senegal's Léopold Sédar Senghor. Both RDA and PRA cultivated some form of African nationalism and were staunchly opposed to French rule. However, the RDA's strategy was more elitist and also rejected cooperation with traditional authorities, with the result that in Niger the PPN was unable to secure the support of that group, a very important one in the colony's context. The PPN was therefore essentially a party of educated men from the more schooled western Niger. The PPN and the Nigerien branch of the MSA were led by two cousins, respectively Diori Hamani and Djibo Bakary. But given the MSA's more open-ended strategy, Bakary had made of Niger's MSA the more important party by forging a coalition of Hausa chiefs, militant unionists, nationalist petty traders and laborers, and some conservative Zarma nobility.

Given this broad power base, Bakary felt confident he could challenge the French when they tried to shape Niger's independence through a referendum in 1958. However, the very size and heterogeneity of the coalition made it vulnerable to pressures, and when the French found a champion in Diori, they were soon able to detach from Bakary's party the more conservative elements, especially the chiefs. This weakened the MSA—which radicalized into the Sawaba party—and a few additional manipulations and fraud led to its defeat in 1958. That event led to bitter and at times violent confrontations between the two parties, until the now-prevailing PPN decided to ban Sawaba altogether, causing its leadership to opt for militant exile. As a result, Niger became independent as an authoritarian single-party, French-controlled post-colony, an outcome that considerably shaped its subsequent evolution. What follows is a description of that process, divided in the three eras of contemporary Nigerien history—the First Republic, the Regime of Exception and Second Republic, and the Democratic Era, the latter being itself subdivided into the four regimes that it spawned.

First Republic

The regime of the First Republic organized a civilian authoritarianism led by a duumvirate comprising President Hamani Diori and the National Assembly speaker, Boubou Hama, a famous writer. Its 14-year rule was divided in two periods, one that was generally positive in its results and that lasted to the end of the 1960s, and the following one that saw it speedily deteriorate and collapse. Through the 1960s, the First Republic was sustained by the export of groundnuts and a modicum of foreign aid. The state was able to fund a rapid growth of education to create a modern elite, establishing in a little more than a decade a full educational system to the level of university in a territory with only a small number of primary schools at independence. It also developed an economic policy based on the setting up of parastatals that organized and marketed agricultural production and ran factories, processing some of the produce into consumer goods. Like many African states in the 1960s, First Republic Niger pursued its aims of national development and food self-sufficiency through corporatist control of society—with the establishment of women and youth associations and rural cooperatives—as well as development plans. Trade unions were cowed into cooperation with the rulers, though their subservience was always limited, and students were turbulently opposed to the regime.

Much of the students' criticism targeted the regime's subservience to France, and indeed, until the late 1960s, the First Republic was closely aligned with France's international policy. This was a legacy of the manner in which Diori came to power, as well as an imperative, given the intent of the excluded Sawaba party to fight its way back to power by planning attacks, insurgency, and coups. Thus, since Sawaba supported Algeria's struggle for independence and was in turn supported by the newly established Algerian state of 1962, Diori followed the lead of France in that period, incurring the hostility of independent Algeria. As a result, the First Republic was particularly generous with the Tuareg, fearing that Algeria might use that volatile community to destabilize Niger. In general, Diori maintained Niger in all the French-inspired intergovernmental organizations that replaced to an extent the colonial empire, and he was instrumental in the creation of the Francophone organization in February 1969, at Niamey. The previous year, Diori had signed a treaty granting to France the exploitation of Niger's uranium with little returns for the Nigerien state. However, there were limits to subordination, and Diori refused Nigerien support of France's policy of assistance to the Biafran rebels during Nigeria's civil war of the late 1960s.

The 1970s decade started with a severe drought throughout the Sahelian region, causing large-scale starvation from Senegal to Niger through Mali. Like the colonial regime, and for very similar reasons—lack of preparation and of adequate transport infrastructures—the First Republic's rulers were unable to stem the disaster in short order. As a result, they suffered a crisis of legitimacy, as internal criticism focused on corrupt management and distribution of food aid. The hunger in the countryside was compounded by the effects of the oil shocks of the mid-1970s on the townspeople. Moreover, at about the same period, Niger's main export commodity, groundnuts, started to rapidly lose its market value. Foreign aid was very limited and inadequate. In disarray, the Diori regime pressured the French, in 1974, to renegotiate the uranium mining agreement of 1968 in order to increase Niger's income. Diori was toppled in April that year by a team of military plotters led by

Lieutenant-Colonel Seyni Kountché. The First Republic's constitution was scrapped and party politics suspended.

Regime of Exception and Second Republic

Niger inherited from French colonialism the notion that a "normal" regime is a republic with democratic institutions. Although the First Republic effectively suppressed the pluralist substance of democracy, it always retained a pretense of constitutional, republican governance with elections and a national assembly. Blaming the failures of the First Republic—and especially its corruption—on party politics, the new military rulers installed a "regime of exception," which disallowed republican institutions and resolved to pragmatically focus on the technical problems of development. They were initially helped in this by a boom of demand for uranium on the world market that started in 1974–1975 and that led to a huge increase of Niger's income. The military regime's policy was, however, not substantially different from that of the First Republic. To be sure, reacting ruthlessly to early plots in the army, Kountché purged the ruling organ of the Conseil Militaire Suprême (CMS) and essentially neutered it by the end of the 1970s, emerging as the sole strongman of the country. But he sought to achieve control over society through the same corporatist organization of social groups, subordination of trade unions, and persecution of student militants and other malcontents as the rulers of the First Republic—only with vastly increased means. He also retained an economic policy based on parastatals and development plans, all stepped up through the uranium income and easy borrowing.

But the prosperous years of the Regime of Exception were even shorter than those of the First Republic. By 1980 a uranium glut was already becoming evident on the international market and the commodity very abruptly lost its value. The regime had put all its eggs in the ore's basket and neglected rent crops to boost food crops. Peasant cooperatives had been turned into acclamatory groups that were told to organize food production, and a very positive outcome was obtained in the Niger River valley with the tremendous growth of rice production. With the drying up of uranium revenue, however, the option was no longer sustainable, and when the 10-yearly Sahelian drought-cum-hunger hit again Niger in 1984–1985, the whole edifice of the rural economy collapsed.

In the early 1980s, the regime had started a "normalization" process—that is, a "return" to republican governance. Military officers were gradually replaced in government by civilian officials, a civilian prime minister was appointed, and the technical development council set up in the late 1970s became a consultative body, akin to a national assembly (though not elected) that was tasked with the preparation and adoption of a national charter. The project was to create a republican system based on a "movement" rather than a party, and the movement was to be developed through "consultation, *concertation,* participation" (consultation, dialogue, participation) instead of competitive elections. A movement, Kountché's ideologues pondered, was more suitable to the creation of a "development society" than a party, as again the collapse of the First Republic seemed to indicate.

Nonetheless, in the process leading to the adoption of the charter, the regime granted limited freedoms of expression and association, and thus opened up the public space for groups (unions and associations) that became vocal in clamoring for multiparty democracy, which they saw as the true substance of a republic. The regime reacted feebly, given the austerity program that undermined the rulers' legitimacy and the illness of strongman Kountché. When the latter died in 1987 of a brain tumor, things quickly moved forward, and away from his project of a movement-based republic.

Kountché was replaced by his close friend Colonel Ali Saibou, an easygoing man with little taste for power who was propelled there to defuse the rivalries between more ambitious high-ranking military officers—especially Mamadou Tandja and Moumouni Adamou Djermakoye. Saibou proclaimed that his rule would be that of "*décrispation*" (easing of tension), as a token of which he freed political prisoners and abolished the secret police. He also attempted to blend Kountché's vision of a movement-based republic with the party-based republic demanded by a budding civil society. The outcome was the curiously imbalanced Second Republic. It was outwardly a single party regime, though its party, the Mouvement National pour la Société de Développement (MNSD), sought to retain the movement organization planned by Kountché's ideologues by keeping for its internal organization the principles of cooptation devised by the national charter. Elections were held, but they were, like those of the First Republic, noncompetitive. At the same time— and unlike with the First Republic—the regime permitted a large extent of freedom of expression and association, thus setting off the train of organized contestation that would ultimately put an end to its rule.

Democratic Transition

A number of factors contributed to tilt Niger toward democratic governance in the early 1990s. First among those was the fact that, as the Cold War was coming to a close at an international level, the claims of opposition groups started to be much more about liberal democracy than about a communist system. Then there was the humbling of the state by economic and financial crises, which scuttled its coercion capacities and general authority, as it proved unable to maintain and expand its services and salaried positions. To these elements that were found at the time in most African countries must be added the peculiar nature of the Second Republic in Niger, a hesitant dictatorship manned by a halfhearted autocrat. When a small number of students were killed in the course of a demonstration—an unprecedented event in the country—the regime came under heavy internal pressure from the democracy militants, and Saibou quickly organized its transformation into a multiparty regime. When this momentous concession was not considered enough by his opponents, he accepted the holding of a National Conference that would in effect terminate the Second Republic and organize a transition to democracy.

The conference started on 29 July 1991 to end only three months later on 3 November. It tried to indict people—especially military officers—who were accused of corruption and use of excessive force during the previous regimes, but the arrested people were all released within a year, chiefly through rulings of the Supreme Court. The genuine and enduring legacy of the National Conference was instead the establishment of a constitutional tradition—that of the semi-presidential system imported from France—and of an institutional practice that would survive recurring setbacks in the development of democratic governance through the 1990s and 2000s.

The Third Republic

An acrimonious and unstable affair, the Third Republic started and ended in an atmosphere of crisis. The state was financially bankrupt, and its increasing inability to pay salaried personnel—including soldiers—led to permanent unrest in the workforce and a number of mutinies in the military. Government was largely inoperative, owing to bitter squabbles between the leaders of the parties who came to power through a pragmatic alliance designed only to keep the MNSD out of power. When the first government of the Third Republic fell in 1995 and was replaced by a cohabitation government between an MNSD prime minister (Hama Amadou) and President Mahaman Ousmane of the Convention Démocratique et Sociale (CDS), the quarrels worsened and completely paralyzed the state. Meanwhile, Tuareg insurgents took up arms in the north, with the ambiguous backing of Libya, hoping to wrest the northern regions from Nigerien sovereignty. Trade unions maintained the pressure on Niger's rulers to prevent them from signing any meaningful agreement with the International Monetary Fund (IMF), which conditioned assistance to a trimming of the civil service and a boosting of the market economy through privatizations and austerity measures. Nevertheless, many parastatals were either restructured or scrapped in that period.

The crisis at the top of the state led the military to come back to power. In January 1996, Chief of Defense Staff Colonel Ibrahim Baré Maïnassara toppled President Ousmane and forced both the president and the prime minister to sign a resignation letter. The constitution of the Third Republic was at first simply suspended and then repealed.

The Fourth Republic

The organizers of the Fourth Republic blamed all Niger's troubles on the semi-presidential system of the previous regime and crafted a presidential system with a clear-cut separation between executive and legislative powers. However, the new constitution was also intended for a strong presidency occupied by coup-maker Baré Maïnassara. When elections were organized in this framework, Baré Maïnassara realized that his presidential projects would be thwarted by the electoral return of the leaders of the Third Republic. He therefore resorted to a brazen electoral coup, reshuffling the independent electoral commission and immediately afterward coming off first at the polls. The event returned Niger to political crisis, as the main parties refused to recognize Baré Maïnassara's fabricated victory and strived to induce indocility throughout the country. Baré Maïnassara further antagonized powerful political players by signing agreements with the IMF and the World Bank and selling off most of the state's medium-sized parastatals to his cronies. The larger parastatals, on the other hand, did not immediately attract serious bidders.

To resist the pressures of the big parties and trade unions, Baré Maïnassara courted cash-strapped or greedy civil society leaders as well as traditional chiefs (the palaces of the main chiefs were fully redecorated by the state) and Muslim clerics (graciously sent to the pilgrimage at Mecca by the state), among other perks. But the state of tension remained very high, and Baré Maïnassara was in the end advised by the French government—the only Western government to have maintained its support to Niger after the coup—to mend fences with his opponents. In view of the regional elections scheduled for February 1999, Baré Maïnassara restored the independent electoral commission to its older state—a major demand of the opposition. This brought about a massive victory of the big parties at the regional elections, leading a furious Baré Maïnassara to browbeat the Supreme Court into nullifying most of the results in April 1999. Two days after this action, he was assassinated at Niamey's military airport by men from his presidential guard.

The Fifth Republic

The constitution of the Fifth Republic returned Niger to the semi-presidential system, with some modifications designed to guarantee stability. Key among these was the establishment of an autonomous constitutional court to avoid a repeat of Baré Maïnassara's cowing of the Supreme Court. The

10-year existence of the Fifth Republic proved indeed to be Niger's longest period of stability since the end of the Regime of Exception. Elections were peacefully held in 1999 and 2004, all of them won by the MNSD and its allies against the rising Parti Nigérien pour la Démocratie et le Socialisme (PNDS). The MNSD governments were run chiefly—under President Mamadou Tandja—by Prime Minister Hama Amadou, a committed liberal who maintained the entente with the IMF and stepped up Niger's maintenance of the convergence criteria of the regional grouping, the Union Economique et Monétaire Ouest-Africaine (UEMOA).

This stability period also revealed the limitations of the reformed Nigerien state: aid dependent, negligent of most of its sovereign duties, and receiving no transformative vision from a political class patently governed by self-interest and factionalism. In 2004–2005, a food crisis and urban revolts against regressive taxation underlined the aloofness of the political class, which made damaging decisions on all these scores right after the elections of 2004 that had brought them back into the halls of power. When a new Tuareg revolt broke out in 2007, led by a group called Mouvement des Nigériens pour la Justice (MNJ), it became very popular in urban areas, where it was at first thought to be genuinely borne out of general frustration with the government. The MNJ lost its popularity, however, when public opinion judged that it was simply another Tuareg irredentist undertaking.

Meanwhile a crisis was brewing at the top of the state, when President Mamadou Tandja started to push forward his plan of seeking a third term in office, despite the two-term limit locked into the Fifth Republic's constitution. Tandja first got rid of Prime Minister Amadou through a no-confidence vote at the National Assembly in June 2007, where the MNSD faction close to the president voted with the PNDS-led coalition to oust the government. He then floated the idea of a third term and of a constitutional revision that would "re-found" the republic. The street tersely and accurately dubbed the ploy "Tazartché" (Hausa for "overstaying") and Nigeriens were soon divided between "Tazartchistes" and "Anti-Tazartchistes."

Tandja managed to ram his way to a constitutional coup, dissolving the National Assembly, illegally abolishing the constitutional court, and finally organizing a referendum to install a Sixth Republic. Niger seemed to be returning to the political crisis and instability that had marred the 1990s.

The Sixth Republic

An attempt by Mamadou Tandja to establish a dictatorship disguised in democratic garb, the Sixth Republic was Niger's shortest regime to date, lasting only about seven months (August 2009–February 2010). It was a solidly presidential regime with the pronounced conservative character (including a senate of traditional chiefs) distinctive of Tandja's entourage. Though the Sixth Republic antagonized most of Niger's modern elite—the big parties, the trade unions, the civil society, the private media—it also revealed surprising levels of opportunism and a lack of commitment to democratic governance among historically militant groups, such as the students' union, the university professors' union, and others. The disconnect between politicized urbanites and apathetic rural dwellers was also evident through the period, as well as the divergence of views between the central Hausa regions of Zinder and Maradi, supportive of Tandja, and the rest of the country, which was clearly hostile to his project. In the end, however, it was the hostility of the army that counted, and Tandja was forcibly removed from a usurped presidency (his legal term had expired in December 2009) on 18 February 2010 by a military squad.

The Seventh Republic

The military organized a civilian transition to the Seventh Republic that lasted exactly 12 months. The transition was chiefly run by civil society leaders, owing to their strong and risky participation in the struggle against Tandja's dictatorial project. The Seventh Republic basically reinstated the Fifth Republic, with some minor adjustments. Innovations mulled over by the modern elite—degree requirements for elective positions—were defeated in the debates preceding the constitutional referendum, although the subsequent victory of the PNDS—the so-called "intellectuals' party"—may seem a victory of the modernists over the traditionalists who had appeared to triumph under Tandja. Just how much this is the case, and just what it means, will become clear in the years to come.

ECONOMIC, SOCIAL, AND POLITICAL DEVELOPMENT

Niger is, in many regards, an odd product of modern history. It is essentially a narrow band of relatively fertile lands in its southern stretch—running thin over 1,500 km from west to east—that hugs an immense northern expanse of 700,000 sq km, made up of a dry geography of arid valleys; craggy plateaus; dusty, windswept plains; and in the far north, a glorious but deadly desert of sand dunes, the Ténéré, a section of the world's largest desert, the Sahara.

This territory—the second largest in West Africa and landlocked with the capital farthest from a port in the region—was acquired somewhat by accident in the early 1900s by France. The colonial plans of France involved a drive east from Dakar on the Atlantic Ocean to Djibouti on the Red Sea, crossing through the promising regions of Lake Chad and the Nile (eastern Sudan). On the way there, there was a sandy corridor that had only one politically developed area, the kingdom or sultanate of Damagaram, an important southern terminus for Saharan trade routes to North Africa. But the French move east clashed in 1898 at Fashoda, on the Nile, with the British move south, which aimed at linking Cairo to the Cape. Given the superior force of the British, eastern Sudan had to be left to the British, leading the French to look for what compensations could be had elsewhere. At that juncture, the British consented to cede to France the slim far northwestern corner of the colony of Nigeria, so that the sandy corridor it used as a way east might become a bit more viable. This added the current region of Maradi as well as the prosperous kingdom of Konni to Damagaram, all of which were sewn to the corresponding section of the Niger River valley—called Cercle du Djerma—to form the southern band of Niger. The territory was completed when France took full control of the desert north (Aïr and Ténéré) toward the end of World War I.

The new territory thus formed belong to the Sahel-Sahara zone of West Africa which, historically, had been the cradle of the greatest imperial states created in the region and indeed in the whole of Africa. However, by coincidence, Niger's territory is made up only of the fringes of these empires, whose centers now lay in Mali (Mali and Songhay Empires), Nigeria (Sokoto and Bornu Empires), and Chad (Kanem-Bornu Empire). Most of the peoples in what is now Niger were thus never organized by large states and their land chiefly served as a crossroad of exchanges among the various great centers in West Africa and out toward North Africa and the Middle East through the Sahara desert. This role provided important economic returns to the elite groups in the small kingdoms and marginal imperial provinces that existed in the area, and it also fed the development of an economic base resting on the production of sturdy local cereals—millet and sorghum—and the nomadic or semi-nomadic farming of cattle, sheep, and dromedaries whose meat, hide, milk, and cheese are today constitutive of Nigerien identity. Certain preparations of meat—the pemmican-like *kilishi* (meat), the flimsy but tasty *chuku* (cheese)—are indeed unique to Niger and are in great demand in other West African countries.

Arguably, the economic fortunes of the colony of Niger, and subsequently those of the republic of Niger (independent in 1960), are of a very different nature than what used to be true historically. The new country emerged in a changed world, in which the Sahara desert had lost its ancient role in international trade, and the peoples of Niger had at the outset little on which to hedge their bets aside from the groundnut trade that was developed by the

French colonial government in the 1930s in the regions of Maradi and Zinder. The earnings from groundnuts were used to fund a developmental state that planned the growth of education, agriculture, and industries, all sectors left pretty much fallow under French rule. The new independent government set up parastatals to spur agricultural production and market agricultural produce, and opened factories in all the main towns of the country to transform agricultural raw materials into flour, milk, leather, textiles, tableware, and so forth. While the state received a modicum of bilateral cooperation aid, especially from France, its efforts were completely dependent on national income, and the regime that ruled it—called "the First Republic" in Niger's officialdom—was rent with internal contradictions. For one thing, it was dominated by men from the Zarma-Songhay minority, which fueled resentment from the Hausa majority. During much of its existence, the regime was opposed, sometimes violently, by a banned political party (the Sawaba), which blended political and social grievances with this ethnic resentment motif to unsettle the regime. Moreover, the regime created a single-party rule that covered the entire social space through state-sponsored civic associations and peasant cooperatives, thereby stifling private initiative and concentrating power—and attendant animosity—in the party's leadership.

The ramshackle edifice of the First Republic did not resist the first serious crisis of independent Niger: the combination, in the period 1969–1974, of a protracted drought and the oil shock of 1973. Although internal criticism stridently pointed at the regime's corruption, the main problem was that a cash-strapped state—groundnuts had started to flounder as a rent crop—received in fact minimal help from the outside world and was not up to the task of distributing food in an immense territory sorely lacking in good transport infrastructures. The regime's head, President Hamani Diori, sought to replace groundnuts by newly exploited uranium as Niger's key foreign exchange earner, but France, which controlled most of the ore production through an exclusivity contract, was displeased with this and quietly created the conditions for the overthrow of Diori in April 1974.

There was a short uranium boom in the second half of the 1970s, leading the new Nigerien rulers—a military junta—to step up the functions of the developmental state, to set up additional parastatals, and to borrow extensively with private financial institutions then awash with funds and actively seeking borrowers. The situation swiftly changed at the beginning of the 1980s: A uranium glut rendered the ore virtually worthless while groundnuts had already lost their international market value by the mid-1970s; the United States needed to repatriate capital, leading the Federal Reserve to raise interest rates and the U.S. dollar to appreciate considerably. As a result, the debt of Niger, which was expressed in U.S. dollars, swelled in real terms. American deficit-financing also led to stringent borrowing restrictions on the international financial market and pushed the price of debt (i.e., debt interests) to stratospheric heights. To these international deteriorating circumstances must be added an ill peculiar to the former French colonies of Africa that, like Niger, were members of the Franc Zone single-currency organizations—that is, the mid-1980s appreciation of the French franc, anchor currency for those countries. The real exchange rate of the CFA franc, the currency that Niger shared with other West African countries formerly ruled by France, rose in relation notably to the currencies of Nigeria and Ghana, with a profound negative impact on the country's trade balance and competitiveness.

By 1985, the Nigerien state was virtually bankrupt, and the effect on its development plans was devastating. Niger's rulers had first tried to win time through heterodox financing tricks, using one parastatal's gains to offset the loss of another, thereby generating a state of disorder upon which administrative corruption quickly festered. Moreover, they started to listen to the instructions of the only easy lenders left, the International Monetary Fund and the World Bank, despite the fact that those institutions tied their assistance to a rapid dismantling of the developmental state, now portrayed as the main culprit in the country's economic collapse. Parastatals were restructured, the civil service underwent a first trimming, and the government actively sought to promote the private sector, notably prodding the wealthy traders of Maradi (known as the "Alhazai of Maradi") to invest in the manufacturing sector from which the state was retreating.

In the midst of this evolution, Niger's authoritarian regime collapsed (1991) and the new democratic dispensation that replaced it was pushed through by those forces—trade unions especially—most opposed to the end of the developmental state. Until Niger's next authoritarian phase (1996–1999), therefore, collaboration with the IMF and the World Bank was unsteady and sporadic. Meanwhile, the CFA franc currency was devalued (1994), the burden of the debt service asphyxiated the state, inflation skyrocketed, and the recession deepened. Civil service and armed forces salaries were left unpaid sometimes several months on end, Tuareg armed bands waged war on the state in the desert north, and austere forms of the prevailing Islamic religion gained ground, in good deal to cope with despair. In 1996, the chief of defense staff colonel Baré Maïnassara overthrew the inept President Mahaman Ousmane and appointed a former World Bank official prime minister of his would-be authoritarian regime. Fences were mended with the two international financial institutions, and Niger committed to their preferred economic policy of liberalization and privatization.

The commitment survived the fall of Baré Maïnassara's regime in April 1999, and defined the evolution of the Fifth Republic democracy that succeeded him and lasted through the decade of the 2000s. Niger embraced a minimal state policy, tempered with a poverty reduction strategy strongly shaped by Western aid agendas and the United Nations Millennium Development Goals. Most of the parastatals created in the 1960–1970s were scrapped, and the state tried to sell those that were left, with moderate success. Foreign investors' interest in Niger is indeed very limited and a vibrant class of local modern businesspeople failed to materialize as rapidly as was expected or wished by reform programs. By 2010, the economic landscape has certainly changed to the advantage of the private sector, and Nigeriens enjoy much more economic and political freedoms than used to be the case. However, the country has grown poorer, in great deal owing to the fact that the brisk dismantling of the public sector had left most of the structural factors of Niger's evolution unattended. This includes importantly agricultural policy or the areas of state social legitimacy that would sustain typically invasive policies—i.e., birth control or taxation.

The new uranium boom that started in 2007, the exploitation of oil in the far eastern regions of the country, and the emergence of new, non-Western global partners lead some among the contemporary Nigerien ruling elite to dream of a reinvention of the public sector and of a stronger role of the state in the economy. This is stimulated by the continuous growth of the state budget in the 2000s. Of around 400 billion CFA francs (less than $1 billion) at the beginning of the decade, it grew to 900 billion CFA francs in 2009 following investments in mining from the French and the Chinese, and jumped to nearly 1 billion CFA francs in 2011. Moreover the new state budget is balanced, with internal revenue providing 616 billion, significantly overtaking for the first time in decades external resources (aid and borrowing). Clearly, a new page of Nigerien history is in the works, one that has a fair chance of success, as the state is gaining much-needed financial leverage while the population has learned—generally the hard way but with no bloodshed—the lessons of democracy and liberal economy.

It is not sure, however, how these improvements could help the people of Niger to withstand the worsening of their traditional challenge—the bleakly arid environment. A Malthusian school of thought views in the growing population of the country a portent of doom in the medium term, especially since the very fertile Nigeriens have barely begun their so-called demographic transition (itself a condition as well as an outcome of more prosperity), and global warming will likely take further toll on the already gasping Sahel. Others, however, point out that solutions found in other arid lands—irrigation in particular—are grossly underused by Nigeriens and other Sahelian populations, and stress that the problem is one of policy and agency, more so than one of nature and fate. Whatever the case, the coming decades will present Nigeriens with hardships that will continue to put them to the test, especially if the population continues to grow at the current rate.

A

ABACHÉ, CHAIBOU (1937–). A mathematician, Abaché was educated in Dahomey (now Benin) first at the high school Lycée Victor Ballot (1956–1957), then at the University of Dakar (1957–1962) for a bachelor's degree in mathematics, before heading to **France** where he completed a Certificat d'Aptitude Pédagogique pour l'Enseignement Secondaire (CAPES) at the University of Paris in 1962–1964. Abaché pursued a distinguished career in Niger's national **education** system both as a teacher and an administrator. This was crowned by his appointment as minister for higher education, research, and technology from June 1988 to May 1989. He was a member of the Comité des Textes Fondamentaux (the constitutional texts drafting committee) of the **Second Republic** in 1989 and became deputy for **Tessaoua** in December 1989 on a national list presented by the **Mouvement National pour la Société de Développement** (MNSD), then the only existing party in the country. As a member of the Second Republic's **National Assembly**, he was National Assembly representative at the **Conférence Nationale** in August–November 1991—despite the fact that the institutions of the Second Republic were then extinct. He retired from the **civil service** in early 1993 to run the private high school Lycée Kouara as vice-principal and then headmaster.

ABALAK. Small town of some 13,000 people, 590 km northeast of **Niamey**, in the region of **Tahoua**. It is 150 km from the city of Tahoua, on the road to **Agadez**, in the historic region of **Azawagh**. It possesses scenic charm, lying in a seasonal wash (*kori*, in **Hausa**), which retains underground water even during the long dry season. Known for this reason as Abalak Mai Ruwa (Hausa for "Abalak-that-has-water") in Niger's lore, the town has developed, quite unusually for the Azawagh, a fishing industry around an artificial lake dammed out of the *kori*. The main population is made up of half-settled **Tuareg** and **Fulani** (especially the **Woodabe**), with a fraction of **Ader** Hausa.

Since the administrative reforms of the late 1990s, Abalak has become the headquarters of the *département* of Abalak.

ABALAMMA. *See* DALLOL MAOURI.

ABANI, ABDOULKARIM (1934–). Abani is, in a rare combination, both a businessman and a civil servant. After primary **education** in **Zinder** (1941–1948) and **Niamey** (1948–1949), he took up an internship in **banking** at the **Colonie du Niger**'s treasury office, and started a professional career in finance and commerce. Among other positions he was the commercial manager of the now defunct **groundnut** trading company **Société Nigérienne de commercialisation de l'Arachide** (SONARA) in 1976–1977 and has been the president of the Zinder Chamber of Commerce since 1964. In December 1989, he became deputy for the **commune** of Zinder on the **Mouvement National pour la Société de Développement** (MNSD)'s single-party national list and was selected as the secretary of the bureau of the **Second Republic**'s **National Assembly**. After the dissolution of the Second Republic in 1991, he became one of the key MNSD leaders for the region of Zinder.

ABARA, DJIKA (1945–). Abara is a public administrator who completed higher **education** at Niamey's École Nationale d'Administration (1966–1968)—now the **École Nationale d'Administration et de Magistrature** (ÉNAM)—and at the Cairo's Planning Institute (1970), topped off by an internship at the French national assembly. In the 20 years between 1969 and 1989, Abara's career was essentially administrative, as he filled positions ranging from head manager for the rural development division at the presidency's General Commission for Development to Niger's consul in Kano or *sous-préfet* in several *arrondissements*. In 1989, he became deputy for **Guidan Roumdji** on the **Mouvement National pour la Société de Développement** (MNSD)'s single-party national list and held several terms at the **Second Republic**'s **National Assembly** (*questeur* and member of the commission for finances and planning). He took part in the **Conférence Nationale**'s preparatory commission as a representative from the government and was subsequently elected deputy for **Maradi** on the list presented by the MNSD (which by then had become a normal party within a multiparty political system). After President **Mahaman Ousmane** dissolved the first **Third Republic**'s National Assembly in 1994, Abara reverted to his administrative career and was appointed *sous-préfet* of several *arrondissements*, including **Tchintabaraden** in 1996–1997. Abara is the author of two monographs of an administrative nature: *Monographie de l'arrondissement de Say* (1987) and *Étude sur le développement intégré de l'Ader Doutchi Maggia*.

ABARCHI, DANDI (Lieutenant Colonel). Former member of the **Conseil Militaire Suprême**, the military organ that presided over the *régime d'exception* of General **Seyni Kountché**, with whom he was very close. When Kountché died in 1987, his successor, General **Ali Saibou**, dispatched some of Kountché's allies on diplomatic postings. Abarchi was appointed ambassador to Senegal, and in January 1991 was sent to Benin in the same position. After the onset of civilian rule, Abarchi returned to Niger and retired from military service. *See also* ARMED FORCES.

ABASS, SERKIN ABZINE (1949–). Abass is one among the many businesspeople who entered electoral politics when Niger adopted liberal democratic institutions in 1991. In 1993, he was elected **Convention Démocratique et Sociale** (CDS Rahama) deputy for **Tahoua** and was reelected in 1995 for the same circumscription. This term in office was shortened by the **coup d'état of 1996**. He afterward focused his efforts on onion exports, founding the company NIGER-OIGNON, and thus illustrating how many enterprising businesspeople moved out of politics as a way to ensure better business into the private sector once **liberalization** legislation was consistently adopted by the state of Niger in the late 1990s and early 2000s.

ABDON, DOURAMANE (1946–). Abdon acquired professional training as a teacher at the elementary teachers' school Cours Normal of **Zinder** in 1961–1965 and started out his career as director of Wanzarbé's primary school from 1966 to 1968. In the next three decades, he held similar offices in four other primary schools in the area of **Téra**. This was interrupted when he moved to **Niamey** as deputy for the *arrondissement* of Téra on the **Mouvement National pour la Société de Développement** (MNSD)'s single-party national list in 1989. He left politics, however, when the **Second Republic** was dissolved in 1991, typifying the second generation of Niger's political elite, which thrived mainly as the backbone of the authoritarian *régime d'exception* and **Second Republic**.

ABDOU, ALI TAZARD (1928–). Abdou went on from the elementary school of **Tessaoua** to pursue primary **education** in **Niamey**, entering the French Sudan (now Mali)'s renowned teachers' school, the École Normale Frédéric Assomption of Katibougou, in 1945. After a few years heading the primary school of **Tahoua** (1948–1950), he was temporarily removed from the **civil service** (*mise en disponibilité d'office*) for political reasons but was soon appointed to the Niamey inspectorate as head of the examinations bureau in 1953. He spent the following two decades as primary education inspector in most of the country's regions before a final position as legislation professor at the teaching school (*école normale*) of **Maradi** in 1981–1983. Upon retirement in 1984, he became the director of the private high school Bosso in **Zinder** (1984–1990). In 1993, he was elected deputy for the Union Démocratique des Forces Populaires (UDFP Sawaba) for Maradi and filled various positions at the **Third Republic**'s first **National Assembly** until its dissolution in October 1994. He was a member of the Conseil des Sages (Council of the Wisemen) instituted in 1996 to broker an agreement with the parties that opposed President **Ibrahim Baré Maïnassara**'s regime.

ABDOU, IDRISSA (1949–). Abdou is a medical doctor who earned his degrees at the universities of Abidjan (Côte d'Ivoire), Montpellier, and Creteil (**France**). He combined an administrative career (at the Hôpital National in Niamey) and a teaching career. He represented the order of physicians, pharmacists, and dentists of Niger at the **Conférence Nationale**, in 1991, and he was elected member of the transitional parliament, the Haut Conseil de la République (HCR). Abdou returned to his professional work afterward.

ABDOULAYE, HOUDOU (1944–). Radio broadcaster and poet. Born in 1944 in **Tillabéri**, Houdou was director of programming at **Radio Niger**, the secretary of state of the Ministry of Information, and after August 1985, director of Niger's radio and television services. He is the author of two volumes of poetry, one of which (30 poems constituting *Sahéliennes*) received a prize for poetry. He is now retired. *See also* MEDIA.

ABDOULAYE, KHAMED. A journalist (he was director of **Radio Niger** in the early 1980s) and administrator, he had, by the early 1990s, reached the inner circles of power in the authoritarian dispensation established after the **coup d'état of 1974**, when the **Conférence Nationale** dissolved the **Second Republic** and established a multiparty system in the summer of 1991. Abdoulaye, a **Tuareg** dignitary of **Tchintabaraden**, joined the largely Tuareg party Parti pour l'Unité Nationale et la Démocratie (PUND). He was subsequently involved, directly or indirectly, with unrest in his region, and on 2 September 1992 was arrested in the military sweep of Tuareg leaders that the army decided as a rebuff of what they perceived as the government's slipshod handling of the Tuareg unrest. Released shortly thereafter, Abdoulaye resumed his political and administrative career, winding up as director-general of the country's journalism school, the Institut de Formation aux Techniques de l'Information et de la Communication (IFTIC) in December 2010.

ABDOULAYE, SOULEY (1965–). A member of the **Convention Démocratique et Sociale** (CDS Rahama) in 1991, Souley was appointed minister of trade, transport, and **tourism** in the **Alliance des Forces du Changement** (AFC) coalition government of 1993–1994. As such he skillfully dealt with the Nigerian hijacking crisis of October 1993, securing the release of passengers of a Nigerian plane diverted to **Niamey** and subsequently organizing the storming of the aircraft and the arrest of the hijackers. After the **Parti National pour la Démocratie et le Socialisme** (PNDS Tarayya) withdrew from the AFC coalition, Abdoulaye was appointed prime minister by President **Mahaman Ousmane** on 5 October 1994. The minority government that he formed was 10 days later overthrown by a no-confidence vote. After the **coup** that ousted Ousmane in January 1996, Abdoulaye left CDS, moved into the camp of the coup-maker, Colonel **Ibrahim Baré Maïnassara**, and was appointed minister of transport (1996), and following a reshuffle, minister of the interior in 1997–1999. In that capacity, Abdoulaye vigorously organized the repression through which Baré Maïnassara intended to suppress opposition to his authoritarian designs. When Baré Maïnassara was assassinated in April 1999, Abdoulaye, who had been tainted by the ruthlessness with which he had organized repression, saw his political career ended, though he eventually escaped judicial sanctions.

ABDOULMOUMINE, KHAMED-ATTAHER (1964–). After his primary and secondary **education** in **Abalak**, **Agadez**, and **Tahoua**, Abdoulmoumine was due to enter the public high school in Tahoua when he left Niger for a period of exile in connection with **Libya**'s efforts to create a **Tuareg** "Islamic legion." He underwent military training in Libya in 1981–1984 and operated in several West African countries, including Mali, Burkina Faso, and **Nigeria** as a fighter for Libya's leader, Muammar Kadhafi. He was arrested in Niger following his involvement in the **Tchintabaraden** attack of May 1990 but was detained for only three months. Abdoulmoumine then settled in Niamey where he started campaigning to persuade the newly formed political parties that there was a Tuareg predicament in Niger. His efforts led to the foundation of the Comité pour la Défense des Victimes de Tchintabaraden (Committee for the Defense of the Victims of Tchintabaraden), over which he presided and which secured the liberation of 44 Tuareg men arrested in the northern sections of the *département* of Tahoua by the **armed forces**. Abdoulmoumine was afterward a founding member of the **Association Nigérienne pour la Défense des Droits de l'Homme** (ANDDH) and took part to the **Conférence Nationale** as a journalist and a victim of the Tchintabaraden repression. In November 1991, he was appointed head of the administrative post of Takiéta, in the region of **Zinder**. However, shortly thereafter, the army began rounding up certain Tuareg individuals whom they deemed suspicious and, fearing for his security, Abdoulmoumine left for the northern regions of Niger and reentered armed struggle as a member of the **Front de Libération de l'Aïr et de l'Azawak** (FLAA). He soon afterward left that organization to set up his own **Armée Révolutionnaire de Libération du Nord Niger** (ARLN). In 1995, after signing the peace agreement between the government and rebel organizations, Abdoulmoumine was appointed vice-president of the Comité Spéciale de Paix (Special Peace Committee), established to implement the provisions of the agreement. He was then elected deputy for Abalak on an independent list in 1996 and became second vice-president of the **Fourth Republic**'s **National Assembly** in December that year. After the Fourth Republic was terminated by the **coup of April 1999**, Abdoulmoumine was unable to restart a successful political career and returned to private life.

ABDOUSSALE, TANKARI (1914–1994). Longtime deputy to the **National Assembly** under the **First Republic**. Born in 1914 in Bouza, and a local notable, Abdoussalé was a civil servant by profession. In March 1957 he was elected deputy to the **Territorial Assembly** from **Madaoua** on the **Mouvement Socialiste Africain** ticket (later the **Sawaba**). He subsequently left Sawaba to form a small parliamentary group, the Groupe Indépendant Populaire, and in December 1958 joined the pro-French coalition of the Union pour la Communauté Franco-Africaine (UCFA). Under leadership from **Hamani Diori** of the **Parti Progressiste Nigérien** (PPN-RDA), UCFA campaigned for the "yes" in the referendum organized by the French with respect to adherence to the French Community, a late colonial federal ensemble of **France**'s African possessions. UCFA predictably won—the poll was organized by the colonial administration with some rigging here and there— and was later merged into PPN altogether. As a result, Abdoussalé retained his deputy seat for Madaoua as a PPN member and was active until 1974 in various National Assembly commissions. After the coup d'état in 1974 that ended PPN's rule, Abdoussalé retired from political life but became *chef de canton* of Bouza in 1983. *See also CHEFFERIE TRADITIONNELLE*; COUP OF 15 APRIL 1974.

ABODAN, SAADOU (1958–2008). Better known as Saadou Bori from the **Bori** animist rite of possession central to traditional **Hausa** religion, Abodan's music dominated the stage in **Niamey** in the early 1990s, together with the work of **Moussa Poussi Natama**. Saadou Bori blended Hausa traditional music with the characteristic beat of Niamey's nightlife, and his powerful voice allowed him to develop a late-career focus on praise-singing in Niger and northern **Nigeria**. He died in a car crash while traveling between **Maradi** (his hometown) and Nigeria.

ABOU, MAMANE (1948–). Born in a **Tuareg** community of Belbeji, in the region of **Zinder**, Abou entered Niger's public scene as head of the Commission Crimes et Abus (Crimes and Abuse Commission) investigating instances of abuse of power during earlier regimes at the **Conférence Nationale** in

1991. By then he had also founded the weekly *Le Républicain*, which grew over the years into Niger's flagship independent paper with serious journalism and a knack for investigative work. A close friend of **Mahamadou Issoufou** and other leaders of the longtime opposition party **Parti Nigérien pour la Démocratie et le Socialisme** (PNDS Tarayya), Abou and his editor Omar Lalo Keita frequently published reports and articles that uncovered details of government malfeasance, often leading to their arrest. Abou was thus jailed in a remote prison at Ikarfane, in the desert of **Abalak**, together with PNDS official **Hassoumi Massaoudou** and others, under President **Baré Maïnassara**. In 2006, he was arrested and momentarily detained at the prison of **Say**, near **Niamey**, after having penned editorial articles on the financial mismanagements of the government (though the arrest was cunningly made for an entirely different editorial article that claimed that Niger was switching its international allegiance from the West to Iran, prompting an accusation of "propagation of false news").

When President **Mamadou Tandja** dismantled the **Fifth Republic** during the **Tazartché** constitutional coup, *Le Républicain* published essays from Nigerien intellectuals calling for resistance and continued its damaging reporting on the regime's mismanagement and corruption. After Tandja was toppled by the military in February 2010, Omar Keita was appointed special advisor for the press to transition prime minister **Mahamadou Danda**. At the **elections** that followed the military restoration of democracy, Abou's friends at the PNDS won both at the legislative and the presidential polls, an event that will perhaps influence the editorial line of his paper and check its vaunted independence. *See also* COUP OF 18 FEBRUARY 2010; MEDIA.

ABOUBA, ALBADÉ. A **Fulani** man from the **Ader** (historical region of **Tahoua**), Abouba served in minor administrative positions before emerging as a protégé of President **Mamadou Tandja** at the onset of the **Fifth Republic** in 1999, becoming in 2002 minister of the interior and decentralization. After a second victory of the MNSD-led coalition at the 2004 **elections**, he kept the rank of a minister but was appointed advisor to the presidency. In 2007, he was returned to the position of minister of the interior, when President Tandja's bid to overstay his last term began to take shape. As a result, through summer and fall 2009, Abouba was in charge of controlling the situation on the streets as Tandja was busy overthrowing the Fifth Republic. He, however, failed to nab exiled Tandja's rival **Hama Amadou** when the latter returned to Niger in July 2009 to attend the funerals of **Moumouni Adamou Djermakoye**, and more importantly, he failed to prevent Amadou from creating a new party on that occasion.

In August–November 2009, Abouba ruthlessly organized the repression of anti-Tandja demonstrations in **Niamey** and other places. After the ousting of Tandja in February 2010, Abouba was arrested together with a number of other ministers. The latter were promptly released but not Abouba, who remained the only Tandja associate to be kept in custody with no charge. After over a year spent in a barracks in Niamey, he was finally freed in March 2011 and returned to his position as secretary general of the **Mouvement National pour la Société de Développement** (MNSD Nassara). *See also* TAZARTCHÉ.

ABOUSSA, SANI (1968–2004). Aboussa was perhaps the most celebrated of a crop of young pop singers who emerged from **Zinder**'s musical scene and took over the floor in **Niamey** in the late 1990s and early 2000s. His airy and dynamic style of music combined the traditional Nigerien light percussion and flute instruments to modern beats shaped by the sound of the *maquis* (Ivorian-style bars which became popular youth hangouts in the 1990s and broadcast the latest musical trends from Côte d'Ivoire, Togo, Benin, and Burkina Faso). His lyrics were openly or cunningly dirty, highlighting a lifestyle of sex and booze, which goes a long way toward explaining his premature death in 2004. The most popular of his 37 known numbers is "Aya baya." His band, the Super Haské, survived thanks to new talents such as Tambalio and Ali Atchibili.

ABZINE. Hausa name of **Aïr**.

ADA DA RABIOU. Hausa for "Ada and Rabiou." Ada Maikano and Rabiou Adamou, both born in the early 1950s in the region of **Maradi**, met at the bus station of the town, where Ada Maikano was a freelance entertainer. For his day job, he was an officer in the Waters and Forestry Department. Rabiou Adamou was a petty tradesman and, unbeknown to most, an Islamic scholar. The two men teamed up as stand-up comedians for the *samariya* (youth organization) of their neighborhood and triumphed at the national youth festival of **Zinder** in 1986. They were then offered the opportunity to create a show on national television which parodied the weekly advising show of the **Association Islamique du Niger** (AIN), purporting to speak in the name of Adinin Buslunci (the Buslim Religion) and satirizing Nigerien society. Their show ended with the onset of the **democratization** era, which also saw the rise of rigorous Sunni orthodoxy. Ada Maikano remained a somewhat successful stand-up comedian, but Rabiou Adamou turned into an austere Muslim cleric.

ADAMUSAWA. **Hausa** name for the resident merchants from Ghadames, a Libyan town at the border with Tunisia and, historically, a trans-Saharan trading emporium. The term is now chiefly used to refer to any person originating from north of **Aïr**. *Adamusawa* merchants were especially important in the trade that the **sultanate of Damagaram** maintained with Tripoli (then part of the Ottoman Empire) in the 19th century. *See also* GHADAMSI.

ADARAWA. **Hausa** for the Hausa-speaking natives of the **Ader**. The singular form is *Ba'adare*. They are known as *Adarance* in **Zarma**. Current president **Mahamadou Issoufou** is a *Ba'adare*.

ADER. A mostly arid, windswept region with permanently eroded soil occupying much of the region of **Tahoua**. In prehistoric days, heavily wooded, fertile, and full of big game, Ader (pronounced locally *Adar*) has remnants of some very ancient settlements. Closer to the desert than other Nigerien regions, it has a longer dry season during which sandy tornadoes sweep the bleak, inhospitable area, while the *harmattan* fog covers all with dust.

The region's history has been intertwined with that of **Aïr** and **Azawagh**, and its name derives from a **Tamashaq** (**Tuareg** language) word, *ader*, meaning "foot." The Tuareg leader of the late 17th century, Aggaba, established a capital in **Birnin Ader**, south of Tamaské, using the place as a base for trade and *razzia* (plunder expeditions, especially for making slaves) in the **Gobir**. In the 18th century, however, the political center shifted to **Illela**.

Ader's population is mostly **Hausa**, with strong minorities of **Fulani** and Tuareg (in the north especially). The region lends itself better to stockbreeding than to **agriculture**, and its Hausa population, which lacks the nomadic traditions of the Fulani and the Tuareg, has developed a famed seasonal trade and emigration pattern, which resulted in a big *zongo* (Muslim foreigners' neighborhood in coastal countries) in Cotonou (Benin) and the control of the huge retail market of Katako in **Niamey**. The Ader is the political fief of **Mahamadou Issoufou**, the leader of the **Parti Nigérien pour la Démocratie et le Socialisme** (PNDS Tarayya) and current president of Niger.

ADMINISTRATIVE ORGANIZATION. Among the last territories conquered by **France** in Africa (1900), much of the area now making up the Republic of Niger began as a tentative military frontier area consisting of the Territoire Militaire de Zinder (July 1900) and the Cercle du Djerma (*Djerma* being French pronunciation for **Zarma**). These two floating entities were at first attached to the Colonie du Haut-Sénégal-Niger, which stretched from today's Mali through Burkina Faso into Chad. On 22 June 1910, the territory was renamed the Territoire Militaire du Niger, into which was included the Cercle de Gao, which was later (21 June 1911) returned to the Timbuktu (French Sudan, now Mali) region and the *territoire* was directly attached to the **Afrique Occidentale Française** (AOF) federation. On 13 October 1922, the area was finally designated a colony (i.e., came under civil administration) as the **Colonie du Niger**. During this period the capital shifted a number of times, from Sorbon-Haoussa (until 1903) to **Niamey** (1903–1911), to **Zinder** (1911–1926), and back to Niamey (in 1926).

A French colony was subdivided into *cercles* and *secteurs*, run by European administrators, under which came a hierarchy of customary chiefs under control of the colonial administration: *chef de canton*, *chef de village*, and *chef de tribu*. The administration was in fact essentially military, even under a colony, as it was performed by military *commandants de cercle* (circle commanders). The *cercle* commander was, however, assisted by a Comité des Notables, i.e., a committee of local persons of influence and authority (including the local customary chief and often noted clerics) useful in legitimizing foreign overrule.

The July 1922 administrative organization of Niger included nine *cercles*—**Agadez**, **Dosso**, **Gouré**, **Maradi**, **N'Guigmi**, Niamey, **Tahoua**, **Tillabéri**, and Zinder—each with a Comité de Notables. The *cercles* were in turn composed of 27 subdivisions. This administrative organization lasted until independence; the internal breakdown was as follows:

Cercles	Subdivisions
Agadez	**Bilma**, Agadez
Dosso	Dosso, **Dogondoutchi**
Gouré	Gouré, **Mainé-Soroa**
Maradi	Maradi, **Dakoro**, **Tessaoua**
N'Guigmi	N'Guigmi
Niamey	Niamey, Niamey-Centrale, **Boboye**, **Filinqué**, **Say**
Tahoua	Tahoua, Tahoua-Nomade, **Birni-N'Konni**, **Madaoua**
Tillabéri	Tillabéri, **Djermaganda**, **Téra**
Zinder	Zinder, Zinder-Centrale, **Magaria**, **Tanout**

The N'Guigmi and Agadez *cercles* were exclusively administered by a military bureaucracy until 31 December 1946, with the Bilma subdivision remaining under military rule for another decade.

At various times, parts of other colonies have been administratively lumped into the territory of the Niger colony. Apart from the previously noted Gao *cercle*, between 1932 and 1947 two regions of Haute-Volta (which disappeared as a separate colony)—Dori and Fada N'Gourma—were attached to Niger, as was a border region of Dahomey, while all of Tibesti (now in Chad) was also part of the Niger colony until 1930.

The *cercles*, whose number increased to 16, were replaced on 1 January 1961 by 31 *circonscriptions*—several with internal subdivisions. Following the *Réforme Administrative* of 1964 (effective 1 October 1965), these were regrouped into seven **départements** and 32 **arrondissements**, the number of which inched upward to 36 by 1998 with the creation of new units, and specifically the 1969 creation of the **uranium** center of **Arlit**, the 1972 split of the Maradi, and the 1973 split of the Tessaoua *arrondissements* each into two separate units. With the explosive urban growth of the city of Niamey, the headquarters of the *département* of Niamey was transferred to Tillabéri in 1989, with Niamey itself removed from the new *department* and erected into a *communauté urbaine*. The new entity, the Communauté Urbaine de Niamey (CUN), was given the status of a *département* in its own right.

In September 1998, a decentralization law erected the *départements* into regions, conferring also to Niamey the status of a region as a *communauté urbaine*. Moreover, all Nigerien cities of over 100,000 inhabitants became also *communautés urbaines*, but without the status of a region; such is the case of Maradi, Zinder, and Tahoua (even though the latter has fewer than 100,000 people). Lastly, while the 36 *arrondissements* in the former scheme have been erected into *départements*, communalization has been extended to the entire territory of the country, reaching the smallest districts through the cantons of the settled communities and the *groupements* (groupings) of the nomadic communities. Since the local **elections** of 1999, citizens elect local council representatives in each **commune**, chosen by subdivision of the commune (*quartiers* in town, villages in the rural areas, and *groupements* in nomadic zones). There are currently 36 *départements*, divided into 265 communes, 122 cantons, and 81 *groupements*. The regions and their first level (*départements*) internal divisions are as follows:

Regions	Départements
Agadez	Agadez, Arlit, Bilma, Tchirozérine
Diffa	Diffa, Maïné-Soroa, Nguigmi
Dosso	Boboye, Dogondoutchi, Dosso, **Gaya**, **Loga**
Maradi	**Aguié**, Dakoro, **Guidan Roumdji**, Madarounfa, **Mayahi**, Tessaoua, Communauté Urbaine de Maradi
Tahoua	**Abalak**, Birni-N'Konni, Bouza, **Illéla**, Keita, Madaoua, **Tchintabaraden**, and Communauté Urbaine de Tahoua
Tillabéri	Filingué, Kollo, **Ouallam**, Say, Téra, Tillabéri
Zinder	Gouré, Magaria, Matameye, **Mirriah**, Tanout, and Communauté Urbaine de Zinder
Communauté Urbaine de Niamey	

Decentralization has shifted important financial rights and decision-making responsibilities to elected local officials. It is thus an expression of Niger's overall democratic experiments of the 1990–2000s. The country also has, at local levels, the older administrative map of the *chefferie traditionnelle* (traditional chieftaincy) put in place by the colonial regime to create a sense of political legitimacy where democratic accountability was impracticable. Elected local authorities and the *chefferie* often collide.

AFFAIRES MILITAIRES MUSULMANES (AMM). Elite, Muslim-affairs intelligence-gathering military unit (in which many scholars worked) set up by the French government in June 1938, on the basis of the corps of military interpreters operating in North Africa, and harking back to Napoléon Bonaparte's invasion of Egypt in the late 18th century. The officer corps was deployed not only in Niger but also in other predominantly Muslim French colonies in North and West Africa. In Niger, its actions were geared to curtailing the expansion of militant, nonaccommodating **Islam** in the colony, which the AMM thought would come down from the Middle East. The corps was disbanded in 1962, though it has left a tradition of Islamophobia in the French army to date.

AFRIQUE OCCIDENTALE FRANÇAISE (AOF). French West Africa; one of two colonial federations set up by the French in Africa. AOF was the earliest and was created in 1895, only a year after **France** defined its colonial policy and established a minister of colonies and a training school for colonial administrators (1894). AOF grew from Senegal, where its governor was seated, and at first included only the coastal colonies and the French Sudan (Mali). Niger was the last territory to be attached to the ensemble (1 January 1912). AOF started out as a fairly centralized organization, run by a general-governor residing in Dakar (Senegal) with direct administrative authority over the lieutenant-governors who headed the different colonies. Over time, it became a more federal entity, as lieutenant-governors became full governors and the general-governor evolved into a representative of the minister of colonies. AOF ceased to exist in 1958, when a referendum organized the transformation of the colonies into autonomous republics federated within the Franco-African Union, itself dismantled two years later.

Structures grounded in AOF survived to a large extent the independence of France's colonies, and France has successfully retained a great deal of control over its former possessions through the successor organization of the **Union Economique et Monétaire Ouest Africaine** (UEMOA), which gathers all of AOF's former members.

AOF was 4,689,000 sq km large. It had 10 million people at creation in 1895, and 25 million at dissolution in 1958.

AG BOULA, RHISSA. A **Tuareg** politician and former leader of rebel factions in the Tuareg-based insurgencies of 1990–1995 and 2007–2009. Ag Boula had headed the **Front de Libération de l'Aïr et de l'Azawad** (FLAA), one of the main rebel armed groups, before signing a peace agreement with the Nigerien government (April 1995) and securing a position as minister of **tourism** under President **Ibrahim Baré Maïnassara**, in 1997. Following the **coup of April 1999** and the return to democracy, he was appointed minister of tourism again, until 2004, when he was arrested for the murder of an activist of the **Mouvement National pour la Société de Développement** (MNSD Nassara), Adam Amangué, in Tchirozérine. In July 2005, Ag Boula's brother, Mohammed Ag Boula, formed an armed group and kidnapped three gendarmes, demanding in exchange for their release the freeing of Rhissa Ag Boula. The exchange was eventually organized by **Libya**, and Ag Boula, now provisionally released, fled to **France**.

In 2007, when another Tuareg insurgency broke out in Niger's desert north, Ag Boula attempted to pose as a mediator, was refused by the government of Niger, and announced that he was setting up his own rebel group, the Front des Forces de Redressement (FFR), splintered off the **Mouvement des Nigériens pour la Justice** (MNJ), which was then the main rebel group. In 2008, a court in **Niamey** tried him in absentia and condemned him to death. His smallish and rather irrelevant group was, however, included in the peace agreement brokered by Libya in 2009. Ag Boula did not return to Niger though, since the amnesty included in the agreement covered only crimes committed in the course of the insurgency.

Following the **coup of February 2010**, Ag Boula returned to Niamey in order to pressure the new authorities on the integration of his followers into Niger's armed forces and thus restore a position to himself in the Tuareg game. He was arrested, together with Kindo Zada, an army major who had deserted to the rebels in 2007. However, Ag Boula was released a few months later under pressure from Libya's Colonel Muammar Kadhafi, who conditioned Ag Boula's liberation with the freeing of Nigerien immigrants arrested in Tripoli on trumped-up charges. Ag Boula then fled to Libya, soon joining Kadhafi's struggle against his own rebellion and the attack of Western powers in March 2011. After the fall of Kadhafi in September of the same year, he was invited back to Niger by President **Mahamadou Issoufou**, who appointed him special advisor to the president, a sinecure also bestowed on Aghali Alambo, his colleague of the MNJ, clearly as a conciliatory ploy to end the cycle of **Tuareg rebellions**.

AGADA, NAGOGO (1919–1997). Born in **Tibiri Maradi** in the main chiefly lineage of the **Gobir**, Agada was trained as an agricultural technician in Tarna, serving in that capacity in various Nigerien regions between 1940 and 1958. That year, he started a political career as the Union pour la Communauté Franco-Africaine (UCFA) deputy for Maradi at the colony's **Territorial Assembly**. After acceding to the Tibiri chieftaincy in 1963, he was elected to the **National Assembly** on the **Parti Progressiste Nigérien** (PPN-RDA) single-party list in 1965 and reelected in 1970. After the **Seyni Kountché coup d'état of 1974**, Agada returned to his chieftaincy seat in Tibiri and became a prominent member of the Association des Chefs Traditionnels du Niger (ACTN). In 1989, he was appointed member of the **Conseil Supérieur d'Orientation Nationale** (CSON), the highest body of the ruling single party, the **Mouvement National pour la Société de Développement** (MNSD), and likewise in 1996, he was a member of the mediatory organ, the Conseil des Sages (Council of the Wisemen) created by the **Ibrahim Baré Maïnassara** after the coup which he made in January that year. He died in December 1997.

AGADEZ. A historically important town, capital of **Aïr**, major center of Niger's **tourism** until the 1990s **Tuareg** rebellion, and also the name of Niger's northern region. Its name possibly derives from the Tuareg name for "to visit," *egdez*, from the fact that the Tuareg, who are not settled town dwellers, considered the town as a place of congregation of visitors. Its main population has probably been always **Hausa**, as with the very similar town of Timbuktu (Mali), which is essentially a **Songhay** town with Tuareg visitors. It was also likely founded in the 11th century and grew into a sultanate in 1449, reaching perhaps as much as 30,000 inhabitants at the time. It owed much of this development to the organization of the western Sudan by the **Songhay Empire**, and was subsequently captured by the Songhay in 1515. Agadez then became a trade port toward the Middle East, through Ghat, Ghadames, and Tripoli, just as Timbuktu was a trade port toward the Maghrib. After the fall of the Songhay Empire, Agadez slowly went downhill, and when the German traveler **Heinrich Barth** visited it in 1850, he found it a shadow of its former self, with many houses in ruins, even though the famed obelisk-shaped mud minaret still stood at 88-feet the tallest monument in the Sahara (it dates back to the 16th century after having been rebuilt in the mid-11th century).

In the 18th century, Agadez came under the influence of the Ottoman Empire, but it remained politically an autonomous city-state ruled by a **Hausa** dynasty with nominal authority on the surrounding Tuareg clans. Its trade had sunk to the level of a trickle, dealing essentially in **millet** from Central Sudan (Hausaland) as opposed to gold from the western Sudan (Songhay) in its heyday. It was, however, a reputable center of Islamic learning, where the future Sokoto empire-builder **Usman dan Fodio** underwent his early schooling. In the early 1900s, the French erected a fort near the small town or large village that it had become, to support their policy of gradual control of the southern Sahara. They also protected Agadez's trade by organizing and providing an escort to the *azalay* caravan that commercially linked North Africa to Central Sudan, with Agadez as its axis. That fort was besieged over four months in 1916–1917 by the Tuareg warlord **Kaocen ag-Mohammed**, in his objective of uniting the Aïr Tuareg against the intruders. Eventually defeated by the French, Kaocen retreated north into what is now Libyan territory, where he was executed by an **Arab** empire-builder at Mourzouk.

From its flourishing in the 16th century and its commercial prosperity in the 17th century, Agadez has evolved a typical clay and warm brown mud-brick architecture of terraced houses with openwork balustrades and various embossed motifs quite similar to that found in Timbuktu and, to some extent, **Gao**. The city is monochromatically brown to date, with modern buildings made to adopt the hue, and the cityscape seems to merge into the sandy brown of the desert at the horizon. Its famed gold and silver filigree "cross of Agadez" circulates throughout large parts of Africa from this region, though artisans now reproduce the item in much of West Africa.

Throughout most of the 20th century, Agadez was a small, drowsy town. But it knew wild demographic swings starting in the 1970s, first under pressure from the **droughts** of the early 1970s, which saw thousands seeking refuge within its walls, and then following the **uranium** boom of the late 1970s. It has grown to be Niger's third- or fourth-largest city, in competition with **Tahoua**.

Agadez is the headquarters of the region of Agadez, which covers an area of 667,000 sq km (about 52 percent of Nigerien territory) but has a regular population of 310,300, with 78,000 (2001 **census**) in the town itself. The main populations throughout the region are the Tuareg, the **Toubou**, and the Arabs, with a **Kanuri** minority and Hausa as the main population in the town itself. The region is divided into the *départements* of Agadez, **Arlit**, **Bilma**, and Tchirozérine, and borders Algeria and **Libya**, the latter claiming a large slice of its northeastern quarter on the basis of a never ratified Franco-Italian agreement of the 1930s (**Mussolini-Laval Boundary Agreement**). This claim served at times as a rationale for Libya's support for **Tuareg rebellions** in Niger.

The lucrative center of Niger's uranium and **cassiterite** mines, and a magnetic attraction for tourists from afar, Agadez was given an international airport connecting it directly to Marseilles in **France**, but the Tuareg rebellions of the 1990s rapidly put an end to an anticipated major tourist boom. Following the peace agreement of 1995, Agadez saw a revival of its fortunes, and the area's many other opportunities (abundant aquifers, the nearby lake of **Abalak**) were discovered by other Nigeriens, while the decentralization law passed in 1998 started to have favorable effects on its pastoral **economy**. In fact, in the early 2000s, the region of Agadez became the second internal migration destination in Niger, after **Niamey**. However, this revival was ruined again by the Tuareg insurgency of 2007–2009, which incurred a heavy-handed reaction from President **Mamadou Tandja**. Tandja accused the insurgents of being mere armed bandits, a finger-pointing founded on the fact that the region, like neighboring northern Mali, had effectively become a zone of much illicit trafficking, including drugs and cigarettes, to Europe through Algeria. In 2008–2009, Agadez was put under an *état de mise en garde* (a newfangled sort of state of emergency) that gave extensive powers of control and repression to the military while severely restricting access to most areas of the region, especially since many roads and tracks had been mined by the insurgents. Another peace agreement was brokered by Libya in May 2009, but Agadez has not yet fully recovered.

AGENCE FRANÇAISE DE DÉVELOPPEMENT (AFD). In December 1941, the Free French Forces created the Caisse Centrale de la France Libre to serve as a central bank for the French territories (chiefly those in the African colonial empire) not occupied by the forces of the Axis during World War II. The Caisse issued **CFA francs** in the African colonies as well as other **currencies** in the overseas *départements*. At the end of the war, it became the Caisse Centrale de la France d'Outre-Mer (1944), and its currency issue responsibilities were gradually phased out and replaced with development missions. These were paired with efforts at tying African economies to French capital and industrial interests, since development funding was tied to deals with French contractors and manufacturers. The institution was renamed Caisse Centrale de Coopération Economique (CCCE) in 1958. In Niger, it worked with the **Banque de Développement de la République du Niger** (BDRN) and funded mostly projects in which French interests and Nigerien development needs appeared to converge. Thus the Caisse often assisted the **mining** companies in charge of mining the **uranium** ore vital to **France**'s industry. In 1992, the CCCE was renamed Caisse Française de Développement, and then Agence Française de Développement in 1998, with a much broadened development agenda, including almost the entire African continent into a "zone of priority solidarity." This is consonant with the European Union's new focus on Africa as the primary recipient of their development aid. Thus, in Niger, AFD now concentrates, in addition to the traditional areas of interest of its sponsor, on projects relevant to poverty alleviation and the United Nations Millennium Development Goals, using appropriations from the French state's Fonds de Solidarité prioritaire. *See also* ECONOMY.

AGGABA (r. 1687–1721). Son of the reigning sultan in **Agadez**, Aggaba imposed, with Lisawan (a **Tuareg** clan of the **Ader**) help, a Tuareg chiefdom in the Ader, which he conquered what is referred to by the **Adarawa**, in **Hausa**, as *yakin Aggaba* ("the war of Aggaba"). The Magorawa community was the only group in that region to withstand his invasion. In 1687 he succeeded his father as sultan in Agadez and further expanded **Aïr**'s dominions. Deposed by his brother in 1721, Aggaba took refuge in Ader, which he had set out to conquer 37 years previously, and died discomfited.

AGRAM. Another name for Fachi.

AGRICULTURE. Agriculture—farming and herding—is the primary activity of the majority of Nigeriens, although it is practiced in a particularly arduous environment. Much of Niger's 1,267,000-sq-km territory lies in the arid Saharan zone of West Africa, which receives on average less than 200 mm of rain per year, and is thus considered a desert for all practical purposes. This includes the entire region of **Agadez** (667,799 sq km or 52 percent of the landmass), the northern fringes of the regions of **Tillabéri** (**Filingué**), **Tahoua** (**Tchintabaraden** and **Abalak**), **Maradi** (**Dakoro**), and **Zinder** (**Damergou**), as well as most of the territory of the region of **Diffa**, making up around 70 to 74 percent of the country's territory. The remaining 26 percent of the landmass is divided between the Sahelian zone (on average 200 to 600 mm of rain per year) and a tiny bit of Sudanic zone occupying Niger's southernmost *département*, that of **Gaya** (above 600 mm of rain per year). Northern soils are sandy and shifty (dunes system), and those in the west (the region of Tillabéri) are dominated by arid plateaus cut by fossil valleys (the *dallols*), while the east offers more agriculturally propitious plains. This rather bleak environment presents, however, some favorable ecological enclaves, including oases in the **Aïr** growing on fat aquifers, large ponds emerging in the **Ader** (including the lake of Abalak) and in the Gorouol and the dry but alluvial valley of the Tarka in the **Gobir**, washed over by seasonal streams. The country has in total 2.7 million hectares of arable lands, which are only partially cultivated, and which would yield much more than they now do with adequate irrigation; only about 40,000 hectares were irrigated as of the mid-2000s.

Niger's agriculture has four main sectors: stockbreeding, subsistence farming, commercial farming, and fishing. The latter occurs mostly in the **Niger River** valley and on the **Lake Chad**, and the fish is consumed locally and in **Niamey**, owing to the lack of a countrywide distribution infrastructure and investment. This disorganization also characterizes the very large stockbreeding sector, which numbered, in 2009, 9.2 million **cattle**, 10.5 million sheep,

13.1 million goats, 1.6 million camels, 1.5 million donkeys, and 240,000 horses. Figures on cattle, sheep, and goats diminish significantly in case of **droughts**, and stockbreeders tend to maintain large herds precisely in consideration of such a contingency. Modern herding systems are incipient in ranches especially in the western regions of the country, which can rely on supplying the substantial market of Niamey, while animals in the eastern regions are largely bought from the so-called nomadic zone (the slim belt of transition between the Sahara and the **Sahel**) and sold into **Nigeria**.

All Nigerien farmers practice subsistence farming, producing essentially **millet** and sorghum, and in some areas (essentially the Niger River valley), rice. In the past, the dominant production system was that of large patriarchal farms (called *gandu* in **Hausa**) apportioned from communal lands and leaving only small plots to married **women** and unmarried young men for producing special rent crops (cowpeas, chufa). Labor was to a large extent collective, especially at harvest time, and nonmonetary. The development of large towns and a cash **economy**, as well as desertification and demographic pressure, have radically transformed this model throughout most of the country, and the typical farm today is a small, individually held plot on which farmers combine to the extent possible the cultivation of subsistence crops, commercial crops, and small stockbreeding. Successful commercial crops— **groundnut, cotton, onion**—tend to be cultivated chiefly in the southeastern plains, ranging from southern Zinder (the region of the "Trois M," i.e., **Mirriah, Matameye, Magaria**) through Maradi to the area of **Birni-N'Konni**. Other commercial crops—including cowpeas, chufa, and sugar cane—are more widely cultivated, though the bulk of chufa is produced in the region of Maradi and exported into Nigeria.

Niger's subsistence production of cereals presents a chronic deficit and has never known a year of genuine surplus. In the years of the developmental state (1960–1980), **development plans** were chiefly geared toward ensuring food self-sufficiency, against quite daunting odds. The great hungers of the early 1970s and of 1983–1984 paid to the endeavor, and the country struggled—and still struggles—to establish a policy of food security, combining more intensive production and larger imports. The dismantling of the food self-sufficiency policy in the late 1980s and early 1990s considerably disorganized the agricultural sector, especially as it did away with marketing boards and the associated public agricultural credit associations. In the 1990s, the vagaries of the **democratization** process and the difficult **economic liberalization** turn prevented the development of a new agricultural strategy, leaving the entire sector essentially to its own devices. Commercial agriculture did benefit in that period from the devaluation of the **CFA franc** against the naira, the **currency** of the main importer of Niger's agricultural produce, Nigeria. However, intensification inputs, such as artificial fertilizers and machines, also became extremely expensive at a time when the credit systems made viable by the state had disappeared (the **Caisse Nationale de Crédit Agricole**, in particular).

Recent trends point toward the establishment of larger landholdings for commercial purposes as well as the development of a private credit system, rendered difficult, however, by the country's long distances and poor road systems, and which produces very high interest on credit. Moreover, while the state-supervised cooperatives of the early periods have either disappeared or become inactive, peasant organizations emerged in the 1990s, on the basis of management autonomy, freedom of association, and the ability to negoti-ate directly with national and foreign partners of interest (for further details on this evolution, see the **Union Nigérienne de Credit et de Cooperative**). Niger's Organisations Paysannes Agricoles (OPA) consolidated in the Plate-forme Paysanne du Niger (PFPN, 1998) and have linked up regionally (West Africa) with the Réseau des Organisations des Paysans Producteurs d'Afrique de l'Ouest (ROPPA), headquartered in Ouagadougou (Burkina Faso), to develop an agenda of agricultural development that focuses on subregional networks and lobbying, via the **Economic Community of West African States** (ECOWAS) and (to a lesser extent) the **Union Economique et Moné-taire Ouest-Africaine** (UEMOA). These evolutions have resulted in the establishment, in July 2010, of a Banque Agricole du Niger (BAGRI, a public institution working with the Ministry of Agriculture), the **Institut National de la Recherche Agronomique du Niger** (INRAN), the **Office National des Aménagements Hydro-Agricoles** (ONAHA), and the OPAs to organize strategic funding for the sector. In April 2011, the bank raised 2 billion CFA francs to fund a fertilizer and seed selection program, in line with the chal-lenge of agricultural intensification. The operation also aims at providing easier credit to peasant producers and sustaining the "Trois N" (*Nigériens Nourrissant les Nigériens*, "Nigeriens feeding Nigeriens") electoral promise of President **Mahamadou Issoufou**. It remains to be seen whether the bank could survive the pitfalls—including especially the difficult collection of past due debt—that bankrupted earlier public agricultural credit institutions.

As of the 2001 **census**, 79 percent of Nigeriens live in the rural areas, with a projection of 70 percent in 2020. The main crop productions in terms of economic profitability are millet (38 percent), onion (27 percent), and cowpea (10 percent). Sustainability in the stockbreeding sector is highest with cattle (21 percent), followed by poultry (16 percent), cattle dairy (15 percent), and goats (13 percent). Niger's economy is strongly dependent on performance in the agricultural sector, which is in turn too disorganized to reduce dependence on the climate. Thus, in 2008, Niger's economy grew at the rate of 9.3 percent of GDP but brutally contracted to 1.2 percent in 2009 following weak rainfall. Greater organization, more flexible credit systems, and better infrastructure could render the Nigerien agricultural sector much more profitable than it now is, especially considering some of the untapped potentials, including even in terms of arable lands. However, agriculture is here, as in many African countries, one of the most neglected fields of international funding, on which the state of Niger is dependent for large-scale investments. The international agricultural market is at the same time unregulated (in Africa) and unfree; Organisation for Economic Co-operation and Development (OECD) countries create major market distortions by allocating around $360 billion annually to their farmers in generally protectionist and unproductive ways. As a result, Niger's agriculture languishes in the hands of small-scale farmers and uneducated traders. This is one of the paradoxes that explain the country's great poverty. (See Table 1, a statistical history of agricultural sectors.)

AGUIE. A *département* in the region of **Maradi**, with a total population of 435,200 and headquarters in the small town of the same name, population, 11,475. It produces large amounts of chufa for export into **Nigeria**. In recent years, its industrious peasant population—a mix of **Katsina** and **Gobir Hausa**—has managed to recover much land from the desert through a technique of tree regeneration.

AÏR. Mountainous massif in northern Niger in the **Agadez** region of which the administrative capital is also Agadez. It was widely known until the 20th century under its Hausa name of **Abzine**. Geologically the upper basin of the fossilized valley of **Azawagh**, Aïr is largely a Precambrian granite massif with previous volcanic activity. Some 400 km from north to south, 100 to 200 km from east to west, and peppered with fertile valleys and hidden oases of great beauty, Aïr encompasses some 61,000 sq km between the desert plains of Azawagh and **Ténéré** and provides pasturage for animals as well as adequate water in its subterranean water table to form oases. Aïr receives an average rainfall of 169 mm per year (1940–1970), with the highest ever recorded being 288 mm, and the lowest ever recorded (in 1970) being 40 mm. During the **Sahel drought** of the 1970s, which hit Aïr very hard, rainfall averaged (between 1969 and 1974) only 73 mm, and only in 1974 did it rise somewhat to 136 mm.

The region has salt pans of considerable regional importance in In Gall and Teguidda-n'Tesemt, cassiterite at El Mecki and elsewhere, **uranium** in several localities (with the earliest to be exploited at **Arlit**), coal in the south, and several other minerals in what is Niger's **mining** center and from the mid-1970s to the mid-1980s its prime source of foreign revenue. Occupied by

Table 1. Statistical History of Agricultural Sectors

Food Crop	1960	1970	1980	1990	2000	2009
Millet	718,000 tons	870,900 tons	1,362,800 tons	1,110,600 tons	1,679,200 tons	2,677,900 tons
Sorghum	222,000 tons	230,200 tons	368,000 tons	281,300 tons	370,700 tons	738,700 tons
Rice	7,400 tons	37.1 tons	29.9 tons	9.8 tons	62.9 tons	20.1 tons
Cowpea	46 tons	84,300 tons	268,700 tons	223,600 tons	262,700 tons	787,500 tons
Rent Crop						
Groundnut	150,500 tons	204,600 tons	226,100 tons	17,600 tons	113,200 tons	305,000 tons (**2008**)
Cotton	—	—	—	4,900 tons	2,400 tons	—
Onion	—	—	—	220,000 tons	178,700 tons	373,600 tons (**2008**)
Livestock						
Cattle	3.5 million	4 million	3.3 million	5.4 million	6.6 million	9.2 million
Sheep	1.8 million	2.7 million	3 million	5.9 million	8 million	10.5 million
Goat	5 million	6 million	7 million	7.7 million	10 million	13.1 million
Camel	349,000	345,000	391,000	1.2 million	1.4 million	1.6 million

France in 1904, and center of a major **Tuareg** uprising during World War I, Aïr has been settled since prehistoric times, when its ecology was much more hospitable. Relics from this early period are continually discovered.

Aïr's earliest known inhabitants were probably **Hausa**. These were chased out to the south (to become the Azna, Gobirawa, etc.) starting in the 11th century by successive waves of Tuareg confederations coming out of what are today **Libya** and Algeria. The bulk of the **Bella** and **Buzu** in Aïr and elsewhere may be descendants of early Hausa captives of the Tuareg. Among the first clans to arrive in Aïr were the Sandal and the Kel Gress, later the Kel Owey. In internecine fighting among these three, the Sandal were nearly annihilated as a separate clan (some remnants, the Lisawan, remain). Most of the Kel Gress were chased out of Aïr by the Kel Owey in the middle of the 18th century to settle north of **Gobir** in the **Madaoua** area where they are still to be found. The Kel Owey remained more or less in control of Aïr. Other clans arrived later, some continuing on south. Thus, from the Ahaggar Mountains (Algeria) came the Kel Ferouane, Kel Fadey, and the Ouilliminden. The Sandal (also Issandalan) who came to Aïr in the 12th century, and among whom the Itesen were the most important component, founded **Assodé** as their capital, the latter becoming the oldest city in Aïr. It was also the Sandal who sparked the foundation of the Sultanate of Agadez prior to their clashes with the Kel Gress and Kel Owey. Aïr was visited by Ibn Batuta in the middle of the 14th century.

With the collapse of Assodé, the principal center in Aïr became **Tadeliza**, then Tin Chaman, and finally Agadez. The fact that a number of important trans-Saharan routes criss-crossed Aïr gave the area much of its importance from the 16th through the 18th centuries. These were the Gao–Tibesti–Kufra and Tripoli–Kano routes in particular. With the Aïr towns at the edge of the Sahara desert, they acquired prominence as important caravan stops just before or at the conclusion of the difficult desert crossing.

Aïr repelled an assault from the **Bornu Empire** around 1450 but was conquered by the **Songhay Empire** in the early 16th century. After the fall of the Songhay Empire, Bornu gained dominance over the area, loosely controlling it between 1600 and 1750.

Prior to the 1970s swell in the population of Aïr with the influx of refugees from the Sahel drought from farther north and west (Mali and Algeria), the Tuareg population of Aïr was composed of the Kel Owey, around 6,000, residing in the most mountainous regions and in the east; and the Kel Tamat—including the Ikazkazan—found west of the former group with a population of around 4,800. These groups are under the direct authority of the ***anastafidet***, the leader of the Kel Owey, the true power wielder in Aïr though only second most important traditional Tuareg leader, after the sultan of Agadez, also called "Sultan of the Aïr" in Niger's traditional peerage. The other groups in the region include the Kel Ferouane (6,000) found west of the massif, south toward **Damergou**, and also in the vicinity of Agadez.

Drought-triggered population dislocations during the 1970s altered these figures—at times quite dramatically—and increased Aïr's sedentary population. Most of the Tuareg in Aïr who are pastoralists are not under the rule of the *anastafidet* and are collectively known as the Kel Amenokal.

Until the Tuareg rebellion in the 1990s, Aïr was one of Niger's major tourist attractions with its stunning desert scenery, Tuareg oases, and historic relics. The Agadez–**Iférouane**–Igoulaf–Timia–El Mecki–Agadez route is an unforgettable basic staple for the venturesome, with the difficult track passing through some of the wildest and most spectacular Saharan scenery. *See also* ARCHAEOLOGY; *CHEFFERIE TRADITIONNELLE.*

AIR NIGER. Niger's defunct domestic airline. Formed on 10 February 1966 with capital from the state of Niger, two French airlines (Air France and the now defunct UTA), and the now defunct Air Afrique. It had taken over Air France domestic service in Niger and to Haute-Volta, **Nigeria**, and Chad, although by the late 1980s it was operating mainly domestic flights connecting **Niamey** to **Maradi**, **Zinder**, and **Agadez**. It folded in 1993, a victim of the state's financial collapse and Niger's catastrophic economic crisis of the 1990s. Since then, and apart from a brief inroad of the Nigerian airline company Arik, no airline company has served the interior of Niger, despite the enormous distances and potential demand. See also CHEIFFOU AMADOU; TRANSPORTATION.

AKOKAN. Niger's second "**uranium** town," over 800 km north of **Niamey**, 265 km from **Agadez**, near **Arlit**, and home base of the labor force working the Akouta mines of the **Compagnie Minière d'Akouta** (COMINAK). Akokan now forms with Arlit an urban area of 80,000, with upper-scale quarters for the French uranium giant **AREVA** workers (complete with hotels, sports centers, and a cultural hall) and large surrounding shanty towns that have attracted chiefly people from the region, the **Tuareg** and **Toubou**. In 2009, Greenpeace reported alarming levels of radioactivity in and around Akokan (and Arlit as well), and AREVA, which exploits the mine in both Arlit and Akouta, eventually confirmed the reports the following year and committed to cleaning the spots.

AKOUTA. Second major site of **uranium** ore to be exploited in Aïr. At first exploited by a small outfit uniting **France**'s COGEMA to Japan's Overseas Uranium Resources Development Company (OURD) and the Nigerien state, it was enlarged into the **Compagnie Minière d'Akouta** (COMINAK) under the new military regime, in 1974. The first ore from the mine was processed in 1978. After a depressed period in the late 1980s and through the 1990s, COMINAK has been more recently revived as the biggest underground uranium **mining** company in the world, as a branch of **AREVA**, the French uranium behemoth that succeeded GOGEMA. Thirty-four percent of the company's capital is owned by AREVA, 31 percent by Niger's Société du Patrimoine Minier (SOPAMIN), 25 percent by Japan's OURD, and 10 percent by Spain's Empresa Nacional del Uranio SA (ENUSA). Approximately 98 percent of its 1,200 employees are Nigerien. Workers are lodged in the new town of **Akokan**.

ALASSANE, MOUSTAPHA (1940–). Born in Djougou (northern Benin) of Nigerien parents, Alassane was educated locally and in **Niamey**. He was a worker at the **Musée National** in Niamey when he met and befriended the French anthropologist and cinematographer **Jean Rouch**. Under Rouch's influence, his ambitions shifted to cinematography, and between 1962 and 1982, he made dozens of full-length, short-length, and animated movies. Two of his full-length features have become important references in Nigerien culture: *FVVA: Femme, Villa, Voiture, Argent* (1972), which satirizes the greed of the new modern elite, and *Toula ou le génie des eaux* (1974), recounting an old **Songhay** legend. His *La Mort de Gandji* (1962) is the very first African animated movie, an art he learned with the celebrated Canadian animated movie maker Norman McLaren. He was also an actor in Jean Rouch's *Petit à Petit* and in **Djingareye Maïga**'s *L'Etoile noire* as well as in his own *Toula*.

Alassane was the driver in the car crash that killed Jean Rouch in February 2004, after the latter had gone to visit him in the hotel he now runs in **Tahoua**.

ALFA SAIBOU (1865?–1906). An Islamic cleric from Kouré, a village between **Niamey** and **Dosso**, Alfa Saibou (Alfa is a shorthand for the **Zarma** word *Alfaga*, which means "cleric") moved to the newly created village of **Kobkitanda** in or around 1902. Kobkitanda, like Sambera farther south, was a refuge village of people discontented by the emerging regime which saw a collusion of French colonials bent on extracting poll taxes and forced labor from locals, and ambitious chieftains ready to assist them in return for new privileges. At Kobkitanda, Alfa Saibou, though blind and frail, engaged in fiery preaching calling for revolts in the name of justice and **Islam**, and even toured the region to attract adherents. His charismatic personality worked wonders but also alerted a staunch ally of the French, the **Zarmakoy Aouta** of **Dosso**, to the danger he represented. In December 1905, the French sent tax collectors to Kobkitanda, but they were set upon and killed, triggering a combined attack of the French and forces from Dosso. Defeated in a scuffle in February 2006, Alfa Saibou fled to Sambera which was in turn attacked. He ended up reaching the village of Satiru, some 70 km north of Sokoto, in British **Nigeria**, where he soon took the lead of another revolt. While there, he was contacted by the sultan of **Damagaram, Amadou dan Bassa**, who was plotting against the French overlords. That plot unravelled, however, in March 1906, a month in which the British managed to capture Alfa Saibou and to have him beheaded on the marketplace of Sokoto.

ALFARI, KAMPAIZE (1944–). Kampaizé is a businessman who was co-opted into politics by the late President **Baré Maïnassara**, who appointed him a member of the Conseil des Sages (Council of the Wisemen) in 1996. He is famous for being one of the most vocal cheerleaders of Baré's short-lived regime at the **Fourth Republic**'s **National Assembly**, and the **coup d'état of 1999** terminated his political career.

ALGABID, HAMID (1941–). Born to a noble **Tuareg** family of Belbedji, near **Tanout**, in the region of **Zinder**, Algabid is a lawyer and a technocrat who first worked in the financial departments of the Nigerien state in the early 1970s, before occupying the posts of country representative for the **Banque Centrale des États d'Afrique de l'Ouest** (BCEAO), and then country representative of the Islamic Development Bank, while being concurrently secretary general of finance (1973–1979) in Niger's government. After a couple of senior government positions, he was finally appointed prime minister in 1983 under President **Seyni Kountché**. President **Ali Saibou**, Kountché's successor, cut out the office of prime minister but provided the backing of the state of Niger for Algabid's successful application to the highly prestigious executive position of secretary-general of the Organization of the Islamic Conference (OIC). In 1996, he was nominated as a candidate to become secretary-general of the United Nations, a post eventually won by Koffi Annan.

After this, Algabid reverted to Nigerien politics, bringing his support to President **Ibrahim Baré Maïnassara**, who put him at the helm of his party, the **Rassemblement pour la Démocratie et le Progrès** (RDP Jama'a). He also headed the Convergence pour la République, a conglomerate of pro-Baré Maïnassara parties established in response to opposition coalitions. After the assassination of Baré Maïnassara and the installation of the **Fifth Republic**, Algabid fought for the control of RDP with his vice-president, **Amadou Boubacar Cissé**, and won in the courts. He then came fourth out of seven candidates in the first round of the presidential election and supported

Mahamadou Issoufou of the **Parti Nigérien pour la Démocratie et le Socialisme** (PNDS Tarayya) at runoff. Issoufou was defeated by **Mamadou Tandja** of the **Mouvement National pour la Société de Développement** (MNSD Nassara), but Algabid had secured a seat at the **National Assembly**. In January 2001, he was reelected president of the RDP and stressed on this occasion that the party must "secure the opening of an international commission of inquiry into the assassination of President Maïnassara." In 2004, Algabid moved to Sudan where he had been appointed the African Union's special envoy for the Darfur. He was therefore largely absent from Niger during the **elections** that year and came last out of six candidates at the presidential election. RDP supported MNSD and the candidacy of Tandja. Reelected at the National Assembly, Algabid was also rewarded for his support with the position of president to the decentralization supervisory body, the Haut Conseil des Collectivités Territoriales (HCCT).

During the crisis caused by Tandja's decision to illegally stay in power through a **constitutional referendum** in 2009, Algabid's RDP supported Tandja, first under condition of eliminating from the Fifth Republic's constitution the clause of amnesty preventing investigations in the conditions of the death of Baré Maïnassara, and then unreservedly. The RDP was subsequently given two posts in government and the HCCT was extended by six months. In November 2009, Algabid was sent, together with other pro-Tandja dignitaries, to Abuja (**Nigeria**'s capital) to plead the cause of their patron at the **Economic Community of West African States**, which had suspended Niger from its ranks. After the fall of Tandja in February 2010, the financial inspectorate set up by the military to retrieve some of the monies spent by Tandja to fund his project investigated Algabid. In January 2011, Algabid announced that RDP will not have a candidate at the presidential election, and he subsequently brought his support to PNDS's Issoufou, a wise bet given Issoufou's final victory at the presidential runoff election of March 2011.

Apart from **Akoli Daouel**, with whom he has some traits in common, Algabid is Niger's eldest politician, having been in activity since the **First Republic**. Algabid is also one of the best and longest-serving high officials in Niger. *See also* FOURTH REPUBLIC.

ALHAJI. One who has performed the *hajj*, the main annual Islamic pilgrimage to Mecca. In contemporary Niger, the term has tended to become chiefly honorific, and can be given to notable persons even if they are known not to have carried out the requisite pilgrimage. It also has a connotation tied to wealth and social prestige. Feminine: *Hajia. See also* ISLAM.

ALHAZAI **OF MARADI.** The phrase designates **Maradi**'s merchant class, whose activities provide the state of Niger with one fifth of its customs revenue. *Alhazai* is **Hausa** plural for *Alhaji*. The fortune of the *Alhazai* of Maradi originates in the needs of the great Kano (northern **Nigeria**) market for hide and skin. Kano had been for centuries a leading exporter of fine leather goods to North Africa, and much of the raw material came from the **cattle**-rearing northern fringes of the Hausaland, situated in today's Niger. The wealth of the Garki family is testimony to that fact. They had specialized, in the early 20th century, in the selling of hide and skin on the Kano marketplace, thanks to stocks of cattle and networks of buyers set up throughout the **Katsina** and the **Gobir**. The main architect of the current Garki wealth, Gonda Garki, did not invest in colonial trade (**groundnuts** and the seasonal trading known as *traite*) and instead relied on the Nigerian market, using capital earned through the hide and skin trade to become a wholesaler for current consumption goods.

After Niger's independence, Gonda Garki become one of the key suppliers of the Nigerien state trading store, **COPRO-NIGER**. With support from the **banking** system, Gonda Garki then moved into the tobacco market and diversified his import and export schemes. But like other businessmen of his generation, he resisted pressure from the state to invest in industrial production. The current head of the family, Sani Gonda Garki, has taken control of a big chunk of Maradi's real estate market, but with his sons as managers, he is also expanding the family's interests into industrial production (Niger Plastique).

The wealth of the Koudizé family has similar origins, since it started when Djibo Mossi (whose nickname means, in a blend of **Hausa** and **Zarma**, "Child of Money," which became the name of the family), a man from Nikki, near **Dosso** (in the Zarmaland), sold his father's cattle and sheep on the market of Abeokuta, in Nigeria and later on the Gold Coast (Ghana). In that period, Koudizé understood the strategic position of Maradi as a gateway to the Nigerian market, as well as the strong commercial culture brewed in the town, and he settled there, building a fortune in the re-exportation of American and British cigarettes into Nigeria. He also built a reputation as the rich man who cared for the handicapped, not only in charitable actions but also in employment.

Even the chief of province of Maradi, the late *sarki* (king) **Bouzou Dan Zambadi**, was a member of the merchant class, owning important import/export and transport businesses, and being during his lifetime the honorary president of the Bureau Départemental des Commerçants de Maradi (Maradi's district office for traders) and the Bureau Départemental des Transporteurs de Maradi (Maradi's district office for carriers). He also held very large agricultural estates in the area of Dan Issa, a market town hugging the border with Nigeria.

By the late 1980s, the generation of self-made men gave way to that of the heirs, many of whom proved to be skillful businessmen. This is certainly the case of Sani Gonda Garki, heir to Gonda Garki, although the classic story in that regard is that of the Guizo succession. Alhaj Issoufou Guizo died in 1988, childless, but leaving an enormous wealth in real estate, trucking, and shares in the capital of various state businesses and banks. He also left a will sharing his money between nine heirs, two of whom—Alhaj Souley Miko dan Rani and Alhaj Sani Souley Nassaley—united their resources to carry on the business. Nassaley, a nephew of Guizo, had studied economics at the University of Dakar and he invested heavily and successfully in the stock markets. The noted effect has been to raise the interest of Maradi's merchant class for modern **education** and technology, as is now seen with many of the younger, emerging businessmen.

Maradi's position rests on the two facts that it sits on the border with Nigeria and has developed (unlike **Zinder**, also close to Nigeria) a dynamic money-making culture. This is assisted by the state of Niger, which has made of Maradi a dry harbor for northern Nigeria through the mechanism of the so-called special transit. Through this organization, which builds on the **Organisation Commune Bénin-Niger** infrastructure, the great northern Nigerian traders of Kano and Katsina bypass the problem-fraught ports of southern Nigeria by using Niger's quays at the ports of Cotonou (Benin) and Lomé (Togo). The goods are ferried across Benin and southern Niger and de-livered through Maradi to northern Nigeria, with the state of Niger charging handsome re-exportation duties. A percentage of the goods stay in Maradi, in the hands of local merchants, for sale throughout Niger.

Maradi's merchant class is cosmopolitan in the Nigerien context, welcom-ing Zarma businessmen in this thoroughly Hausa city, but it counts very few **women**, and none of much note.

ALI DIALLO, BOULI (1948–). Ali Diallo is one of the most distinguished **women** scholars of Niger. In the early period of her **education**, she attended several teaching institutions, including the teachers' school Cours Normal of **Tillabéri**, then a women-only institution. She afterward studied chemistry and biology at the University of Dakar and at the Science and Technology Uni-versity of Languedoc (Montpellier, **France**), earning a doctorate in applied microbiology in 1978. This was followed up, in 1991, by a *doctorat d'État* (the highest degree then awarded by universities in France, now replaced by the habilitation to supervise research award) in applied entomology.

Ali Diallo combined a brilliant career in Niger's educational system with activism in the cause of women's advancement in Niger and Africa. On the first score, she has been teaching biology at the **University of Niamey** since 1978 while also serving in many administrative capacities: director of the university's external relations services (1987–1993), vice rector of the University of Niamey (1993–1995), minister of national education (1995–1996), rector of the University of Niamey (1999–2005), vice president of the African Virtual University (2002–2004), and member of the administrative board of the French Institut de la Recherche pour le Développement (IRD). As a **civil society** activist, Ali Diallo presided over the Forum for African Women Educationalists (FAWE) from 1999 to 2005, of which she founded the Nigerien chapter, and she works on the administrative board of the international nongovernmental organization Aide et Action. She was awarded several decorations in France, including the Officier des Palmes Académiques de la République Française medal for distinguished academic accomplishments.

As rector, Ali Diallo had to tackle the crisis in early 2001 that saw the university campus rocked by a particularly violent series of student demonstrations. She was appointed to the position by Prime Minister **Hama Amadou** in part to oversee the implementation of measures that enabled the government to post security forces in an around campus, at the expense of the conventional *franchises universitaires* that used to make of the campus an off-limit territory for the state.

ALI DJIBO, AMADOU. Better known in Niger as Max, Ali Djibo started his political career as treasurer for the **Mouvement National pour la Société de Développement** (MNSD Nassara), which he left in the early 1990s over a dispute with the party's leadership. He attempted to launch an independent political career while also working as an accountant, before finding an unexpected opportunity in the coup d'état of January 1996, when Colonel **Ibrahim Baré Maïnassara** overthrew the **Third Republic**. Ali Djibo soon tied himself to Baré Maïnassara's chariot, organizing first a support committee (the Comité de Soutien des Amis de Maïnassara Baré, COSIMBA) to position him as a valid candidate to the post-coup presidential election, and then managing Baré Maïnassara's electoral campaign. When Baré Maïnassara quite fraudulently won the **elections**, Ali Djibo was rewarded with the lucrative position of director-general of the **Société Nigérienne des Pétroles** (SONIDEP), the company that manages Niger's petroleum importation and distribution systems. In February 1999, Ali Djibo founded the Union Nationale des Indépendants (UNI) in view of the local elections, and, under the regime's open manipulations of the ballot, the new party had a good performance.

The regime was ended however by a **coup d'état in April 1999**, and Ali Djibo quickly moved to realign UNI by campaigning as its presidential candidate and then by using his paltry score (1.7 percent of the vote) as a means to piggyback his party onto the **Parti Nigérien pour la Démocratie et le Socialisme** (PNDS). In the ensuing years, Ali Djibo concentrated on local elections as a way to bolster his party's political significance, and succeeded into getting elected municipal councilor in Kirtachi in 2004. He subsequently was elected mayor of Kirtachi, while also earning a deputy seat at the **National Assembly**. Secure in those positions, Ali Djibo maintained the UNI into PNDS allegiance. However, he changed sides again in August 2009, when it appeared that President **Mamadou Tandja**'s attempt at ending democratic governance might be successful, a move for which he was rewarded with a seat at the fabricated National Assembly formed in October 2009. After the fall of Tandja, Ali Djibo was able to make the most of a bad situation, and won back his party's only seat at the National Assembly at the January 2011 elections. *See also* COUP OF 27 JANUARY 1996.

ALIDOU, BARKIRE (1925–). Former minister of justice and one of the more important leaders of the ruling **Parti Progressiste Nigérien** (PPN-RDA) prior to the **coup d'état of 1974**. Alidou was born in 1925 in **Niamey**, where he was also educated (1933–1947). He continued his studies at the teachers' training college at Katibougou (French Sudan, now Mali), and after military service in the colonial army (1947–1948) he taught in the French Sudan for several years (1948–1958). In 1959 he returned to Niger and was appointed *chef de cabinet* of the minister of interior. In 1962 he was further promoted to become secretary-general for national defense and director of national defense. In 1965 he dropped his security responsibilities when he attained full ministerial rank as minister of **economy**, trade, and industry. He then moved to head the Ministry of Justice in 1970, a post he held until the April 1974 coup d'état.

During the years 1952 to 1974, his career was strongly advanced by his being the first vice-president of the Veterans Association (Office des Anciens Combattants et Victimes de Guerre)—a powerful pressure group—and president of the Association Amicale de Niamey. His early affiliation with the PPN brought him membership on the latter's political bureau in 1956, as well as the post of PPN treasurer (the same year), both positions he retained through the 1974 upheaval; as such, more than for his ministerial duties, Alidou was one of a small group of politicians who were the ultimate source of power in Niger in the **First Republic**.

ALKALAWA. Longtime capital of the **Gobir** Kingdom. After repeatedly besieging it, the **Fulani** armies of Shehu **Usman dan Fodio** took Alkalawa and destroyed it in 1808, killing Gobir King **Yunfa** in the process. Alkalawa was in the part of Gobir that is now in **Nigeria**. In 1815 the site was abandoned in favor of **Kadaye**. *See also* GOBIRAWA.

ALKASSOUM, AL BAYHAKI. Secretary-general of the **Association Islamique du Niger** (AIN) since its foundation in 1974. Alkassoum had previously been the director of the *medersa* in **Say**, and just prior to his appointment as head of the first **Franco-Arabe** high school in Niger. In 1979 he was also appointed director of Arabic **education** in the Ministry of Education. After 1991, Al Bayhaki and other AIN officials worked to define AIN's stance in Niger's liberalized religious landscape, bestowing on it a mild but very characteristic Sunni orthodox coloration, opposed to both Sufi orders and possible Shi'a inroads. *See also* ISLAM.

ALLAKAYE, JOSEPH SEYDOU. Longtime editor of the governmental daily *Le Sahel*. He moved to the private independent weekly *Le Républicain* in 1991, where he is one of the more prominent journalists and editorialists. *See also* ABOU, MAMANE; MEDIA.

ALLÉLÉ, EL HADJ HABIBOU (1938–). A teacher by training, Allélé was a school director in this first decade of his working life (1957–1969) before entering an official career in 1969 as cabinet director for the minister of public **health**. He afterward took up a string of ambassadorships in Côte d'Ivoire (1971–1974), Ghana (1974–1980), and Senegal (1980–1982). After spending a year as mayor of **Niamey**, Allélé was appointed minister, first of justice (1983–1985), then for **agriculture** and environment (1985–1987), mines and energy (1987–1988), and foreign affairs and cooperation (1988–1989). In 1989, Allélé became deputy of Tchirozérine on the list of the ruling single-party **Mouvement National pour la Société de Développement** (MNSD), a term in office interrupted by the dissolution of the **Second Republic** in 1991. Two years later, however, he was elected deputy for **Agadez** on the MNSD (now in a multiparty context) list and further reelected in 1995. In more recent years, Allélé has been in turn CEO of the **Compagnie Minière d'Akouta** (COMINAK) and advisor to the president. Allélé's signature as minister for mines and energy was famously used on a document dated October 2000 and produced in the United States and Great Britain as evidence of Niger's attempts at selling **uranium** to Iraq. As Allélé's appointment in that position dated back more than a decade ago, the document was easily proved a forgery, apparently perpetrated by the Italian military intelligence service.

ALLIANCE DES FORCES DU CHANGEMENT (AFC). After the adoption of multiparty democracy with the constitution of 1992, the newly created **political parties** feared that the **Mouvement National pour la Société de Développement** (MNSD Nassara), the successor party to the **Second**

Republic's single party, would poll its way back to power. The apprehension was justified by the fact that, unlike the new parties, the MNSD, owing to its history, had a true national base with strongholds in all the regions of the country, especially in the *départements* (now regions) of **Tillabéri**, **Maradi**, and **Diffa**, and also in bits of the *département* of **Zinder**; it had lost the *département* of **Dosso** to **Moumouni Adamou Djermakoye**'s **Alliance Nigérienne pour la Démocratie et le Progrès** (ANDP Zaman Lahiya) created after Djermakoye left MNSD. All the new parties were preponderant only in the region of origin of their main leader—thus, the **Convention Démocratique et Sociale** (CDS Rahama) in Zinder and the **Parti Nigérien pour la Démocratie et le Socialisme** (PNDS Tarayya) in **Tahoua**. Nine of the new parties united therefore in the AFC, pledging to support the candidate who, in a runoff, would challenge the MNSD candidate (already expected to reach the second round). AFC won over MNSD by close margins, even at the legislative **elections** where all nine parties secured 50 seats against 33 to MNSD, and as the history of the **Third Republic** will soon show, the alliance was not viable. Of all AFC parties, only the CDS, the PNDS, and to some extent the ANDP were to become key political parties in the future.

ALLIANCE NIGÉRIENNE POUR LA DÉMOCRATIE ET LE PROGRÈS (ANDP ZAMAN LAHIYA). *See* DJERMAKOYE, MOUMOUNI ADAMOU; POLITICAL PARTIES.

ALMOU, ALKA. Political leader of the Parti Républicain pour les Libertés et le Progrès du Niger (PRLPN-Nakowa), a small post-1991 party, part of the AFC alliance, though it failed to secure representation in the 1993 parliamentary **elections** and dwindled out of existence in the late 1990s.

ALPHADI. *See* SIDHAMED, SEIDNALY.

AL-QAEDA IN THE ISLAMIC MAGHREB (AQIM). An Algerian-Tunisian Islamist terrorist group that arose from the struggle, in the late 1980s, of Algeria's military and secular regime and several Islamist groups aiming at creating an Islamic state in that country. The Algerian military forcibly suppressed the project even though the Islamist party Front Islamique du Salut had won at the polls in 1990; the Islamist movement therefore went underground and turned violent. In the course of the 1990s, it engaged in guerrilla warfare and terrorism against the Algerian state and society, until it was finally driven out from the centers of the polity in the 2000s. Radical Islamism then organized itself within the Groupe Salafiste pour la Prédication et le Combat (GSPC), which operated mostly in the Sahara desert, from

Mauritania to Chad through Mali, Algeria, and Niger, targeting Western tourists and interests—as in Niger with **AREVA**'s desert **uranium** mines. GSPC later became AQIM, claiming collusion with the international Al-Qaeda terrorist network.

Niger became one of its choice targets, given the importance of French interests there, the existence of illicit trade networks throughout the Sahara, and the insecurity created by **Tuareg rebellions** and volatility in many parts of the country. The main hits of AQIM in Niger include the kidnapping of elderly French aid worker Michel Germaneau in 2009 (leading to the latter's death a year later); the kidnapping of five French people, one Togolese, and one Malagasy in **Arlit** in October 2010; and the ill-fated kidnapping of two Frenchmen at a **Niamey** restaurant in January 2011, which led to the heavy-handed intervention of French military units and the death of the abductors and of their victims as well as of three Nigerien gendarmes.

AQIM does not represent a serious security risk for Niger or for French interests there, but its threatening and unpredictable presence has led to a considerable dampening of **tourism** and foreign cooperation work in the country. It must be noted that it is based in northern Mali, and that interventions in Niger are carefully prepared remote operations benefiting from paid local complicities. Recently, however, governments in the region fear that AQIM is stepping up efforts to recruit and train young Nigeriens as militants and to link up with the Nigerian Islamist terrorist group Boko Haram. *See also* FRANCE.

AMADOU DAN BASSA (1878–1950). Last independent sultan of **Damagaram**. Born in 1878, and the younger brother of **Amadou Kouran Daga**, who was killed by the French in 1899, dan Bassa ascended the throne upon his brother's death. The French upheld his government and paid him a salary, chiefly in order to consolidate their grip on the region, while also contemplating a weakening or abolition of the sultanate in line with their "direct rule" political doctrine. To buttress the administrative post they opened at **Gouré** in 1903, they recreated the Mounio kingdom (a state absorbed by the sultanate in the 1870s) and appointed at its head Mai Moussa, the old king who had been living under house arrest in **Zinder** since 1877. Moreover, the Franco-British convention of 1903 quashed dan Bassa's ambitions to include into Damagaram territory regions south of **Magaria**, which were left to the British. A disgruntled dan Bassa resolved, in 1906, to shed the white man's yoke and put his court (clerics, traders, and even the *cercle* interpreter, a man in the employment of the French who brought him from Senegal) to work to organize an uprising. **Malam Yaro**, an old ally of the French, was very active among the conspirators. Dan Bassa strove to unite several anti-European forces, sending missions into British **Nigeria** at Kano, Sokoto, Hadeja, and Satirou (where contact was made with the **Kobkitanda** leader **Alfa Saibou**, who had fled there to become the leader of the revolt against the British). The French discovered the conspiracy before it developed and arrested dan Bassa in March 1906. The sultanate was abolished and the sultan exiled to Dabou, in Côte d'Ivoire. He was eventually released in 1919, returning to Niger where, after a few years spent in **Niamey**, he resettled in the Damagaram, residing there with his family until his death in 1950. *See also* DAMAGARAM, SULTANATE OF.

AMADOU, HAMA (1948–). Born at Youri near **Niamey** in the **Kurtey** community (a mixed **Songhay/Fulani** ethnicity), Amadou was educated locally and trained as customs inspector. He entered the customs service and served as regional inspector of **Zinder** and **Maradi** (1971–1974). He then undertook further studies at Niger's École Nationale d'Administration (ENA, now **École Nationale d'Administration et de Magistrature**), following which he was appointed assistant *préfet* of **Agadez** (1980–1982) and secretary-general of the prefecture of Zinder (1980–1982). After further studies at the Institut d'Administration Internationale in Paris, he returned to a posting as *sous-préfet* of **Tahoua**. In 1984 he was appointed director of Niger's national radio and television services, and in 1985 he joined President **Seyni Kountché**'s staff as his cabinet director. After Kountché's death, he continued in this capacity under President **Ali Saibou**.

In 1988, Saibou appointed him minister of information, ignoring a ploy by Amadou to head the national electricity company **Société Nigérienne d'Electricité** (NIGELEC). He resigned from the cabinet about a year later to concentrate on his work as the secretary-general of the newly institutionalized single-party **Mouvement National pour la Société de Développement** (MNSD). When the **democratization** process was launched in 1991, the emerging political class strove to dismantle the MNSD, and the party was saved chiefly by Amadou's strategizing and political acumen. Amadou has also been credited for MNSD's strong showing at the 1993 **elections** and was as a result the party's choice for the prime-ministership when the **Alliance des Forces du Changement** (AFC) coalition government collapsed in 1994. At that point, however, President **Mahaman Ousmane** declared new legislative elections, in which an MNSD-led coalition emerged victorious, forcing Ousmane to finally appoint Amadou as prime minister.

The cohabitation situation (in which the president and the prime minister belong to opposing parties) quickly resulted in an institutional gridlock, as Ousmane refused to attend cabinet meetings, effectively preventing the government from operating. Amadou governed as best he could under the circumstances, knowing full well that Ousmane would dissolve the **National Assembly** and call for new legislative elections in January 1996. However, a coup organized by Colonel **Baré Maïnassara**, the chief of defense staff, ousted Ousmane a day before he could declare legislative elections, and soon thereafter, Amadou, Ousmane, and all major politicians agreed to approve the putsch and call the military to restore civilian rule.

Baré Maïnassara intended, however, to stay in power and went in for a showdown with the political class now united against him. Over the next three years, Amadou was instrumental in fanning civil disobedience (in the form of strikes and demonstrations) against Baré Maïnassara in Niamey, a city in which he had grown immensely popular. He is also rumored to have incited army officers uneasy with the situation and angry at the arrogant behavior of Baré Maïnassara's entourage to rebel against the new regime. Baré Maïnassara was finally overthrown and killed by his enemies in the **armed forces** in April 1999, and a short transition process reinstated civilian rule by the end of the year. An MNSD-led coalition won the presidential election, which resulted in the activation of a power-sharing pact Amadou had made with the new president, **Mamadou Tandja**, in the early 1990s. In exchange for his support against **Moumouni Adamou Djermakoye**, who was also seeking control over the party for presidential ambitions, Amadou had then promised Tandja to engineer his accession to the presidency, if Tandja would agree to groom him as his successor. In this perspective, Amadou actively shaped key aspects of the new constitution that was written in 1999, in particular locking with unbreakable provisions the two-term limit in presidential tenure to ensure that Tandja would respect the agreement.

Amadou was appointed prime minister, a post in which he remained throughout Tandja's first term, and in which he returned after the MNSD coalition emerged victorious again in the 2004 **elections**. By then, however, serious rifts had started to develop between Tandja and Amadou, which showed in the divergent stances taken by the two men regarding the key issues of Niger's 2004 food crisis and the **Tuareg** insurgency in early 2007. While Tandja insisted in denying that there was a famine in the country, Amadou vocally acknowledged the situation and called for international aid. And while Tandja chose a hard-line position of considering Tuareg insurgents as armed bandits and drug dealers, Amadou publicly supported negotiation and compromise. These divergences, reflecting deeper divisions which were renting the MNSD into Tandjiste and Hamiste factions, could not be solved by a simple dismissal of the prime minister; although it appeared that the president had the constitutional power to remove the prime minister, Amadou made clear his intention of fighting a dismissal in the courts. Such was the case because Amadou had realized that Tandja would not respect their gentleman's agreement and would in all probability want to establish a new regime to perpetuate his rule.

Tandja then orchestrated the fall of Amadou through a cunning ploy. He faked a rapprochement with the opposition's leader Mahamadou Issoufou and organized a tactical alliance between the opposition and the MNSD's *Tandjistes* in order to pass a successful no-confidence vote against the government in June 2007. Defeated in the National Assembly, Amadou resigned and soon became vulnerable to Tandja's plans to terminate his political career through judicial penalties. A first lawsuit for battery against the leader of the youth section of the MNSD unraveled, and after a few months of judicial harassment, a prosecution file for corruption was finally mounted against Amadou. Using his alliances at the National Assembly, Tandja managed to strip Amadou of his deputy immunity, and he was jailed in the top security Koutoukalé prison after a hearing at the **Haute Cour de Justice** (June 2008). In a regular trial, which was postponed month after month, Amadou would face a jail term and the loss of the right to hold political office in Niger. It was, however, proving hard to destroy his position, due to his immense popularity in Niamey and **Tillabéri** (the two most important bases of the MNSD), his influence with the military, and the hold that he maintained on the MNSD. Moving with caution, Tandja worked to undermine his position in the MNSD, finally succeeding in stripping him of the presidency of the party (which he had kept even in jail) in early 2009. A special congress of the party, held in **Zinder** in February 2009, elected his erstwhile close friend and new prime minister **Seyni Oumarou** as president of the party.

Meanwhile, Amadou was briefly brought back to Niamey for **health** reasons, and while physicians disagreed on the seriousness of his illness, this provided his legal team with further reasons to press for a trial at the Haute Cour de Justice. The court, headed by his friend Djermakoye, ordered his release, and Amadou left Niger for Paris (**France**), officially for health reasons although he later told the press from his French retreat that, in Niger, he feared for his life. Amadou did return briefly to Niger to attend Djermakoye's funeral in June 2009, and on this occasion managed to arrange the creation of a new party, the Mouvement Démocratique Nigérien pour une Fédération Africaine (MODEN/FA Lumana Africa), which quickly began to bleed MNSD dry of supporters. Amadou then fled back to France, escaping arrest by a hair's breadth. He stayed there until the ousting of Tandja in February 2010, at which point he returned to Niger to launch his presidential campaign for the 2011 elections. He first tried wresting MNSD from the surviving Tandjiste faction (now called *Tazartchiste*, from the Hausa name given to Tandja's constitutional coup) and then led MODEN/FA to substantial victories at the legislative (third party at National Assembly with 23 seats) and presidential elections. Coming third in the first round, Amadou emerged as the kingmaker at runoff and brought his support to **Mahamadou Issoufou**, allowing him to crush the MNSD candidate, Seyni Oumarou.

AMADOU, IDRISSA (Lieutenant). Key conspirator in the **1983 attempted coup** against **Seyni Kountché**. Amadou's role was central to the conspiracy since he was at the time commander of the presidential guard. After the collapse of the conspiracy, Amadou fled to Europe.

AMADOU, ISSAKA (1924–2004). Born into the main chiefly lineage of Kantché, near **Magaria**, he became the chief of that canton in 1954. After a string of elected positions under the colonial regime, aided by his rather opportunistic affiliations to the **Mouvement Socialiste Africain** (MSA) and then to the Union pour la Communauté Franco-Africaine (UCFA), Amadou filled highly distinguished parliamentary positions as a grand councilor for French West Africa (1958–1959), senator of the Communauté Française for Niger's legislative assembly, and finally vice-president of the Legislative Assembly and then of the **National Assembly** right after independence. In the decade leading up to the **coup d'état in 1974**, the Kantché absentee lord took up several ministerial positions (public service, labor, **economy**, commerce, and industry). **Seyni Kountché**'s coup d'état destroyed his political career as he was deposed from his chieftaincy and detained in a military camp in **Agadez** for over a year. However, he was released in August 1975 and reinstated as chief of Kantché. He was called up to be a member of the **Fourth Republic**'s Conseil des Sages (Council of the Wisemen) in 1996 and died at Kantché in November 2004.

AMADOU KOURAN DAGA (r. 1893–1899). Known also as Amadou dan Tanimoun and Amadou mai Roumji. Sultan of **Damagaram** in 1893–1899, he was the son of Sultan **Tanimoun**, the greatest Damagaram monarch. At the time of his rule, the kingdom was a major power in Central Sudan, prospering on trade with the North African territories of the Ottoman Empire. In early April 1898, when the French colonial expedition led by Captain **Marius-Gabriel Cazemajou** approached the Damagaram territory, Kouran Daga sent emissaries to let them know that the sultanate recognized only Ottoman sovereignty. Then the sultan invited Cazemajou to his capital city, **Zinder**, and treated him magnificently. But this proved to be only a trap, as members of the Damagaram court fearful of French intentions arranged for Cazemajou and his second-in-command Olive to be treacherously murdered: readying to make a good-bye visit to the sultan on their way out toward the **Lake Chad**, Cazemajou and Olive were knocked out, their throats were slit, and their bodies dumped in a well.

The main motivation of the Damagaram court appears to have been fear of a French alliance with the Darfourian empire-builder **Rabah Zubayr**, who had already conquered the **Bornu Empire** (southern neighbor of Damagaram) and was openly preparing to strike the kingdom. Kouran Danga was also influenced by zealous Islamic clerics hostile to what they perceived as a Christian crusade. After these dramatic events (for which Kouran Daga is mostly remembered and celebrated in Niger as an opponent of colonial takeover), Kouran Daga resumed the old wars of Damagaram against the emirate of Kano. In July 1899, however, a new French colonial expedition (the **Mission Afrique Centrale-Tchad**), led by Lieutenant Pallier, defeated Damagaram forces at Tirmini. A desperate Kouran Daga ordered the evacuation of Zinder and fled into the countryside. He was pursued by the French and killed in the village of Roumji on 16 September 1899.

These events have inspired the Nigerien television movie *Si les cavaliers* (1981) by **Mahamane Bakabé**.

AMADOU, MAROU (1972–). Amadou hails from Kotaki, in the **Boboye**, a region of the Zarmaland not far from **Dosso**, where he earned his *baccalauréat* in 1992. He studied business law at the University of Cotonou (Benin) and private law at the **University of Niamey**, receiving a master's degree in 2001. The **civil service** froze staffing and the private sector was undeveloped and unorganized; Amadou found himself among a throng of ambitious young graduates who sought an outlet in the foreign-funded **civil society** of the country. He was first an active militant of the civic association, the Comité de Réflexion et d'Orientation Indépendant pour la Sauvegarde des Acquis Démocratiques (CROISADE, an acronym corresponding to the French word for crusade), which had been founded in 2000. It was as member of CROISADE that he led, together with **Moustapha Kadi** and **Nouhou Arzika**, the 2005 social movement of the Coalition Equité Qualité contre la Vie Chère au Niger (Fairness and Quality Coalition against the High Costs of Living in Niger), which was successful in checkmating an International Monetary Fund–backed valued added tax on goods and services in Nigerien cities. Amadou, Kadi, and Arzika became instantaneously famous both in Niger (where the government ended up hiring them as consultants in the charting of a new tax scheme) and abroad (an IMF official flew from Washington to meet them).

After these heady days, the trio fell apart, as Amadou had to retreat in the Boboye to cure an illness. He re-emerged in 2008 to become the staunchest and most outspoken civil society opponent to President **Mamadou Tandja**'s subversion of the **Fifth Republic**, as leader of a new association, the Forum Uni pour la Sauvegarde des Acquis Démocratiques (FUSAD). Amadou resisted all attempts made by Tandja to intimidate him, including two trials, several stays at Niamey's detention center, and an illegal internment in the top-security prison of Koutoukalé orchestrated by the military corps of the Force Nationale d'Intervention et de Sécurité (FNIS). This made him a cause célèbre in Niamey where "Libérez Marou" (Free Marou) posters sprouted in all corners of the city. Eventually freed and unrepentant, he became one of the major actors in the crisis triggered by Tandja's project. After the coup d'état that overthrew Mamadou Tandja on 18 February 2010, Amadou was appointed president of the **Conseil Consultatif National**, the transitory parliament set up by the military to oversee the return to civilian rule. Amadou's objective in that office was to further strengthen Nigerien democratic gains (*acquis démocratiques*). After organizing the adoption of a new constitution in December 2010, he coordinated work on two texts that form his mission legacy at the Conseil Consultatif National: a charter for civil society organizations providing them with a constitutional legal framework that strengthens their position as the bulwark of democracy, and the quite solemn adoption of a *Pacte Républicain* (Republican Compact), an unprecedented legal text (published in the country's official journal) through which Nigeriens have been essentially called to sign a formal social contract defining their obligations and commitment toward each other and toward the state.

After the **elections** of 2011, he was appointed minister of justice and created a telephone green line at the ministry to allow citizens to act as whistleblowers for administrative corruption. *See also* FORCES ARMÉES NIGÉRIENNES; SALOU, DJIBO.

AMADOU, OUSMANE (1948–). A journalist and author, Ousmane has become known in Niger when he published, in 1977, the political novel *Quinze ans ça suffit!*, an attack on the corruption of the **First Republic** which also played well as propaganda for the newly established regime of **Seyni Kountché**. He later developed an interest for the judicial system, authoring a kind of judicial novel, *Le Nouveau juge* (1985), and a lively, semifictionalized collection of court stories, *Chronique judiciaire* (1987), and was very productive in the 1990s. That decade saw the publication of an essay comparing Seyni Kountché (who had long fascinated him) and the 1996 coup-maker **Ibrahim Baré Maïnassara** (a man who, at some levels, was consciously trying to reenact Kountché's rule), *L'Itinéraire* (1996); it was very much a propaganda work like his first novel and Baré Maïnassara tapped him as a Kountché aficionado. He had earlier put out two political novels building loosely on Niger's **democratization** processes, *L'Honneur perdu* (1993) and *Le Temoin gênant* (1994). *See also* LITERATURE.

AMARYAL BORI. "The newly wed wife of **Bori**"—that is, the woman possessed by the spirits in the Bori ritual.

AMBARKA, HASSANE (1946–). A cultural worker by training (he attended two cultural monitoring schools in **France** in 1965–1966 and in 1980–1982), Ambarka served as director of several Culture and Youth Halls in 1966–1974. After a number of positions in public administration, he wound up as assistant director of the Centre Culturel Franco-Nigérien (CCFN) in **Niamey** (1995–1996) before being appointed judge at the **Haute Cour de Justice** (1996–1999). Ambarka is notable for his role in the training of the **Parti Progressiste Nigérien** (PPN-RDA)'s (then the de facto single party) armed militia in 1966–1974. During that period, he was also involved in the management of the youth organizations orchestrated by the party (Camp de Jeunesse of 1964–1965, Semaines de la Jeunesse Nigérienne of 1966–1974), which logically led him to be co-opted by the new regime after 1974 as one of the key organizers of the celebrated national youth festivals (1976–1989) and national traditional wrestling championships (1978–1995) organized annually through the *régime d'exception* and a few years afterward.

AMENOKAL. **Tuareg** title of suzerains of both large Tuareg political units and territories. It is usually applied to the chiefs of the large Tuareg confederations.

ANAFI, SOULEYMANE (1967–). Anafi is a French professor and the youngest deputy of the **Third Republic** (for **Tillabéri** on a Parti pour l'Unité National et le Développement (PUND Salama) list in 1995–1996). Under the **Ibrahim Baré Maïnassara** regime, which came about after the **coup of January 1996**, Anafi was appointed director of university provisions, a notoriously difficult but financially rewarding position.

ANAGOMBA. Name by which the **Wodaabe** are called by outsiders. *See also* BORORO; WODAABE.

ANAKO, MOHAMMED. Tuareg rebel leader of the 1990s, founder of the insurgent group Front Patriotique pour la Libération du Sahara (FPLS). During the **Fifth Republic**, he became head of the Haut Commissariat pour la Restauration de la Paix (HCRP), an institution tasked with the mission to oversee the implementation of the 1995 peace agreements. The HCRP essentially redistributed benefits and employments (mostly in the **armed forces**) to former rebels but also to clients of Anako and other prominent Tuareg leaders. *See also* TUAREG REBELLIONS.

ANASTAFIDET. Head of the Kel Owey **Tuareg**, once resident in **Assodé** but since the 1920s in **Agadez**. Historically, this was the most powerful position in Aïr, though its holder cedes primacy of status to the sultan of Agadez. Of noble birth, the *anastafidet* is elected for three years and is subject to annual recall by the Kel Tafidet and Kel Azanieres Tuareg groups. The Ikazkazan—junior clan of the confederation—have little voice in his selection. The *anastafidet*'s symbol of office is the confederation's drum.

Since the dislocation effects of the **droughts** of the 1970s, most Tuareg pastoralists who became refugees as a result do not fall under the authority of the *anastafidet*. *See also* AGADEZ, SULTANATE OF.

ANEY. Small oasis 89 km from **Bilma** and traditional residence of the sultan of **Kaouar**, who is always of **Toubou** origin.

ANGLO-FRENCH TREATIES (1890–1906). Of the various Anglo-French treaties that demarcated the borders of the colony of Niger, the following are the most important:

Treaty of 1890, which delineated the Say–Baroua Line (a straight line between the two localities) as the boundary separating the British and French spheres of influence. The haste with which the line was accepted by **France** was indicative of the latter's gross overestimation of the extent to which British influence was to be found south of it. This cost France the populated centers of **Nigeria**, including the former **Bornu Empire** itself, while pushing its own dominions to the edge of the **Sahel** belt. More intensive and careful exploration of the region revealed the weakness of Great Britain's presence in the area, and the nonviability of the agreed-to boundaries, leading to demands for border revisions. (Great Britain's vast claims over the area were based on **Heinrich Barth**'s explorations and included claims over **Ader, Aïr, Gobir, Maradi,** and **Tessaoua**.)

Treaty of 1892, in which Great Britain renounced its claims to Aïr, Gobir, and stipulated a 100-mile zone around Sokoto as an integral part of the future colony of Nigeria. The French agreed to these provisions in order to have their claim to Aïr and **Agadez** validated, losing in essence all the **Hausa** border towns except for **Zinder**. In light of the fact that without the existing wells in these border towns little east–west traffic was possible, another border revision treaty was signed.

Treaty of 1904 and 1906, a "package deal" treaty that involved contested areas outside Niger-Nigeria, indeed, some non-African ones. The treaty shifted south the British boundaries, to within 60 miles of Sokoto (or just south of British boundaries, to within 60 miles of Sokoto (or just south of **Birni-N'Konni** and Maradi), conforming somewhat more to traditional boundaries in the area and placing under French jurisdiction the border towns and their wells. Still, the French complained that though the centers of the kingdoms in the area (**Maouri**, **Konni**, **Damagaram**, Gobir) had been allocated to France, their peripheral dominions ended up in Nigeria. These complaints were in sync with the Hausa subjects of these European transactions, who referred to the divisions as *yanken kasa* (Hausa for "the partition of the land").

ANGO, YAKUBA (1948–2001). A **Maradi** African or traditional wrestling champion under the name of **Kantou**, Ango was one of the stars of the national wrestling championship set up by the **Seyni Kountché** government in 1975, and which made African wrestling Niger's most popular sport. Kantou won the top champion saber (and the attendent substantial financial rewards from the government and wealthy private persons) four times, more than any other Nigerien wrestler. These were at the very first championship in **Tahoua** in 1975, then in **Dosso** in 1977, in **Zinder** in 1978, and in **Agadez** in 1980. In 1983, President Kountché offered Ango gifts and a large cash award to help him retire from wrestling. Ango then moved into business and farming, where he was active until his premature death in August 2001. The traditional wrestling stadium of Maradi has been named after him.

ANNOU, FATOUMATA DJIBO (1949–). Annou was a civil servant whose career chiefly evolved as the personal assistant of a number of high officials, including President **Hamani Diori** in 1971–1973. Elected deputy for **Tillabéri** on a **Mouvement National pour la Société de Développement** (MNSD Nassara) list in February 1993, she resigned her office in July of the same year for reasons of "personal convenience" that had much to do with fending for herself as a woman in Niger's male-biased legislatures.

ANOU ARAREN. Site of extensive coal deposits 50 km northwest of **Agadez**. Reserves are estimated at over 10 million tons and were discovered in 1964 during prospecting for **uranium**. In 1976 the **Société Nigérienne du Charbon d'Anou Araren** (SONICHAR) was set up to exploit the coal deposits and convert them into electric energy to serve the uranium mines. A thermal complex on the site was inaugurated on 14 April 1981; at the time it had an electricity output of 16,000 kw, with a second plant scheduled to enter into production. Other coal deposits were discovered by Canadian and Chinese companies in the 1990s and in 2004. The most promising are those at Salkadamna in the region of **Tahoua**, which harbors, within a 28-sq-km perimeter, an estimated 30 million tons of coal. The Chinese company Géo-Ingénierie de Chine is currently studying the feasibility of coal **mining** in the area.

AOUTA, ZARMAKOY (1846?–1912). Ruler of the **kingdom of Dosso** in the early 1900s, with the colonial title of *chef de canton* (canton chief). Aouta is the nickname of Idrissa Kossom, and he was one of the sons of the famed Dosso ruler **Zarmakoy** Kossom, born in the Sirimbeye nobility. In the late 19th century, Kossom had defeated **Tuareg** warlords in a battle called Ta-angam Takio (The Four Glorious Fights, in **Zarma**), capturing the Tuareg's war drum, the *Toubal*, which became one of the symbols of executive power in Dosso. Dosso's political system rotated the office of *zarmakoy* through the neighborhoods of the town. The French colonial government put an end to the system when, upon the death of *Zarmakoy* Attikou in 1902, it imposed its favorite Aouta in the office, even though the latter's turn was not up yet.

Aouta, having early understood the power of the French from what he had heard of them even before they arrived in the Dosso area, ingratiated himself with them as soon as they came in in 1898. He assisted them—through levies in men and the supply of horses, food, and fodder for their expeditions—in their conquest of the area surrounding Dosso, including the Goubé village of Sargadji which defeated one French attack in 1899. He also was very instrumental in quashing the large-scale revolt of **Kobkitanda** in 1905–1906, as well as in the repression of more localized uprisings in the **Dallol Maouri** valley. In this way, the French came to consider Aouta as their best ally in western Niger, while Aouta drew from his association with them rights and powers that had thus far eluded the rulers of Dosso. He also had cleverly understood the French concept of "canton," i.e., a coherent territorial unit formed for administrative purposes, and he creatively made such concept to apply to a Dosso country (*laabu*) that had never existed before but that included all the lands that Aouta and earlier rulers of Dosso had ambitioned to conquer. In October 1901, when creating the cantons of the Cercle du Djerma, the French apportioned to Dosso all the conquests made with the assistance of Aouta, although, faced with the bitter complaints of other local leaders, they belatedly understood his actions and removed the most hostile quarters (**Kiota**, **Loga**, Kobkitanda, and the **Maouri** country) from his canton in 1903 and 1908.

However, the colonial government continued to buttress Aouta's authority, ensuring that the office of *Zarmakoy* of Dosso remained in his family. In 1926, the government declared the canton of Dosso a province, bestowing on *Zarmakoy* Saidou (Aouta's nephew and one of his successors) indirect power over the areas that had previously been removed from the canton's purview as well as a status equal to that of the historical kings of **Gobir**, **Katsina** (**Maradi**), **Damagaram**, and **Aïr**. The very title of *zarmakoy* became the family name of Aouta's descendants and relatives, under its Frenchified form, Djermakoye.

When he was simply a prince in the court of the *zarmakoy*, Aouta helped and befriended the exiled **Fulani** king of the Wolof (Senegal) Alboury N'Diaye, who was retreating before the colonial advance and waging war on his way to Central Sudan. Alboury was eventually killed in a scuffle at the border between Dosso and Sokoto territory. On orders from Aouta, his indefatigable right arm was cut, brought back to Dosso, and buried in the courtyard of the palace of the *zarmakoy*, to be honored. *See also* FRENCH OCCUPATION; SARGADJI REVOLT.

AOUTA, ZARMAKOY ABDOU (1909–1998). Son of the *chef de canton* of **Dosso** and faithful French ally **Zarmakoy Aouta**. Abdou Aouta was educated in Dosso and **Niamey**, where he went to a vocational school in mechanics and electricity. He afterward served in several somewhat menial capacities in the administration until 1962, when he was designated *chef de province* and *zarmakoy* of Dosso. He then became president of the association of Niger's customary chiefs, a position he retained until his death 36 years later. During the **Second Republic**, he was a member of the **Conseil Supérieur d'Orientation Nationale**, the consultative organ of the single-party **Mouvement National pour la Société de Développement**. He died in Paris on 31 July 1998, having been flown there for treatment of his last illness. His body was repatriated and buried—like that of other *zarmakoys* of Dosso—in the grounds of the palace of the *zarmakoys*.

ARABS. The Arabs in Niger are a very small minority found in the northern and far eastern parts of the country. Arab groups include the Kounta, most likely originating in the Touat (now in Algeria) and living in the regions of **Tahoua** and **Agadez**; the Shoa in the region of **Zinder**; and the Ouled Slimane, who came down into the **Lake Chad** area from the Fezzan (now in Chad and **Libya**) in the 19th century. There, the Chadian conflicts had pushed thousands of Mohamid Arabs into Niger in the early 1980s, and their arrival caused some disturbance, which eventually prompted a threat, from the Nigerien government, to deport them in 2006. The Arabs are mostly business folks, respected by the state as good taxpayers in their districts. Despite their tiny number, some of Niger's more prominent politicians are Arab, such as **Bazoum Mohamed (Parti National pour la Démocratie et le Socialisme)** and Mohamed ben Omar (Rassemblement pour la Démocratie et le Progrès). Arabic is one of the nine national **languages** of Niger.

ARAWA. A **Hausa**-speaking ethnicity living in the **Arewa** and thought to be an offshoot of the **Kanuri**. Singular form is *Ba'aré* (masculine) and *Ba'ara* (feminine). There are also **Zarma**-speaking Arawa, who are called **Maouri**.

ARBRE DU TÉNÉRÉ. The **Ténéré** desert's best known landmark until 1973. A lone, straggly tree—the only one on a vast area the size of **France**—in the middle of sandy dunes, it was found 270 km east of **Agadez**. The tree was uprooted accidentally by a truck in 1973, and then carried over to **Niamey** where its fossilized remains are exhibited in the **Musée National** since 1977.

ARCHAEOLOGY. Possibly not as profuse with prehistoric relics and sites as neighboring Chad, Niger nevertheless is extremely rich in prehistoric remains, including cave engravings and fossil remnants. They are found mostly in **Aïr**—which in prehistoric days had a much wetter climate and was home to large populations—though the region did not yield its treasure until 1938, and the major sites were not discovered until after 1946. Indeed, a large number of sites peppered with cave drawings were not discovered until 1960 by the Mission Berliet-**Ténéré** in the Ténéré desert. The latter was also climatologically much more hospitable in prehistoric days, having had profuse vegetation and being criss-crossed by rivers. Many remains of former human habitation have been found, including pottery and fishhooks. In Aïr at least 5,000 cave engravings are known to exist, with scores also in the **Kaouar** district. In the southern regions there is practically no cave art but instead numerous invaluable ancient village sites have been located. One of these is close to **Niamey,** and another some 15 km north-northwest of the city. Many archaeological sites have also been found along the **Niger River**, especially of *donborey kwaray* (in **Zarma**) or *tombo* (in **Hausa**), both terms denoting "place of inhabitants of the past." In the **Filingué** region, for example, many such sites of ancient villages have yielded much pottery and jewelry of historic interest. In the **Dosso** and W area of the Niger River, ancient **Gourmantché** villages have been excavated; at Rosi—15 km southwest of Birni N'Gaouré—scientists have investigated a 15th-century village.

AREVA. A world leader in nuclear energy, AREVA was created in 2001 from the merger of several French nuclear agencies and corporations, namely the Commissariat à l'Energie Atomique (CEA), Framatome ANP, COGEMA, and FCI. Until the creation of AREVA, Niger's **uranium** was exploited by COGEMA through the two companies jointly set up with the state of Niger, the **Société des Mines de l'Aïr** (SOMAIR) and the **Compagnie Minière d'Akouta** (COMINAK). AREVA succeeded COGEMA in Niger in 2006, creating the subsidiary firm AREVA NC Niger as its representative in the country. It then moved to sign new agreements with the Nigerien government in 2007, in view of the upturn in the market for the commodity and the immense prospects offered by the new site of **Imouraren**. In January 2008,

AREVA announced it would invest over €1 billion in the Nigerien mines. The mines in Niger are AREVA's most important asset. Even before the opening of the giant mine of Imouraren, the company drew one third of its ore from Niger—about 3,000 tons of uranium annually. Imouraren will yield 5,000 tons annually, which will propel AREVA to the rank of the world's first producer of uranium. Niger will be allowed to sell 300 tons of the ore on the market for its own profit, besides revenues accruing from its shares in the **mining** companies. This explains why AREVA cannot leave Niger despite the great risks caused by the activities of insurgent **Tuareg** and the Islamist terrorist group **Al-Qaeda in the Islamic Maghreb.** AREVA is accused of dangerously polluting the areas of Nigerien territory where it extracts uranium.

AREWA. The Arewa is a region where the Hausaland transitions into the Zarmaland, which presents a number of important anthropological features. The region covers the districts of Tibiri Doutchi, **Dogondoutchi**, Guéchémé (prefecture of Dogondoutchi), Sokorbé (prefecture of **Dosso**), and Kara-Kara and Zabori (prefecture of **Gaya**), all of which are part of the administrative region of Dosso. Historically it is a melting pot of a variety of **ethnic groups** usually practicing, in sections (i.e., not in a bilingual mode), the **Hausa** and the **Zarma languages**: the Gubawa, who came from the **Gobir** and the **Ader** in the 16th and 17th centuries (called Goubé when they speak Zarma); the Basuwa, from farther east; the Darayawa from Darai, in the Ader; and who settled along the **Dallol Maouri** valley; the lion hunters Yarawa, who came from the area of **Birni-N'Konni**; and finally the Magorawa, from Magori in the Ader in the early 19th century. The origins and date of arrival of the dominant group, the **Arawa** (called **Maouri** when they speak Zarma), is uncertain, but most stories point to the **Kanuri**-speaking **Bornu Empire**, and the name itself would on this account derive from the name of a Bornuan prince, Ari (and not from the Hausa word for "North," *arewa*).

The Arawa rose to prominence in the region (to which they ended up giving their name) because they brought with them traditions of centralized power and organized **religion** (an animistic pantheon centered around the **Doguwa** family of spirits) and were able to establish a state around the Dallol Maouri. In a pattern that is widespread in West Africa, the Arawa, as conquerors, unified political power, setting up state capitals in **Matankari** (under a male Ari dynastic lineage) and in **Lougou** (under a matriarchal queenship with great spiritual sway), while power over the land remained entrusted to the older settled groups. The main animistic priesthood, headed by the *Baura*, was for its part established in the town of Bagaji. Moreover, the western Arawa (Sokorbé, Kara-Kara, and Zabori) are minority groups settled among the Zarma, whose language they eventually took, thus losing usage of the Hausa language and being renamed (by the Zarma) Maouri.

To all these particularities, the Arawa add the fact of having kept their ritual identity and autonomy despite being tucked in between major expansionist poles: the Gobir kingdom to the east, the **Tuareg** to the north, the colonizing peasantry of the Zarma to the west, and the Sokoto Empire to the south. The sturdiness of their political system was symbolized by the way in which succession was tied into their religious rituals through the *tarkama* in the spiritual centers of Lougou and Bagaji (the corpse of the deceased priestess or priest, borne by porters, designates the successor).

Arawa chronicles tend to disparage mere temporal power, as is betokened by the dark legend of the arbitrary King Kabarin Kabara, famous for having ordered a massacre of the elders and the building of a palace suspended in the air, between earth and sky. The story says that his subjects got rid of him by tying him up on a wild stallion offered as a gift, and by then letting the horse run into the wilderness with its burden, never to be seen again. A darker, and certainly truer story, pitched the Arawa, led by the priestess queen of Lougou, **Sarraounia Mangou**, against a renegade French colonial expedition which had left a trail of blood in the area in the late 1890s, the Voulet and Chanoine column. After having lost troops to the Arawa guerrilla, the Voulet and Chanoine column succeeded into storming Lougou but were not able to seize the queen. The column's leaders were eventually killed in Matankari by their own troops.

The Arewa has remained a stronghold of animism in Niger. While **Islam** has made some inroads, especially in Dogondoutchi, it is here balanced by **Christianity**, and both religions have been unable to displace the older rituals of the region. It is therefore in an **Arna** enclave, not far from the Arewa, in the town of Massalata, that Niger holds its only annual animist festival. *See also* MISSION AFRIQUE CENTRALE-TCHAD.

ARFAI BOGERMI (1885?–1960). Chief of Séguédine, and in his day the prime entrepreneur in the entire canton. Arfai Bogermi left his home village of Emi Tchouma in 1940 and settled in Séguédine (then badly devastated by bandits), some 100 km to the north. Through his efforts the village revived and commerce recommenced. By 1943 the *azalay* caravans once again began to call upon Séguédine, and in return for his initiative the French administration recognized Arfai Bogermi as chief of Séguédine. The village saltpans are widely recognized as producing the best-quality natron in the entire **Kaouar**.

ARLIT. Located 200 km from the border with Algeria and 1,237 km north of **Niamey**, Arlit is a boom town created in 1969 after the discovery of huge

uranium deposits in the area by the French Commissariat à l'Energie Atomique. There are two mines: Arlit, which is open air, and Akouta, which is underground. These have been dwarfed by the recently opened mines at **Imouraren**. The mines at Akouta are exploited from the smaller town of **Akokan**, very close to Arlit. Both Arlit and Akokan grew in accordance with the fortunes of uranium mining. Large and flush with first-rate modern amenities in the period of uranium boom of the late 1970s to early 1980s, they shrank considerably when uranium's prices collapsed in the late 1980s, and they have recovered to some extent with the commodity's upturn of the 2000s.

By the last **census** (2001), Arlit has about 67,400 inhabitants, mostly from other parts of Niger, with a small community of French and other expatriates. Although cordoned off as a high-security zone owing to the activities of **Tuareg** insurgents, sometimes with ties with the **Al-Qaeda in the Islamic Maghreb** (AQIM) armed group, marauding armed men at times attack it.

Arlit is the capital of the *département* of Arlit, in the region of **Agadez.**

ARMA. Name of the much-intermarried descendants of the Moroccan conquerors (1591) of the **Songhay Empire**. Most are found in Mali, though descendants have made their way down the **Niger River** to Niger.

ARMED FORCES. *See* FORCES ARMÉES NIGÉRIENNES.

ARMÉE RÉVOLUTIONNAIRE DE LIBÉRATION DE L'AZAWAD (ARLA). One of several **Tuareg** armed groups which fought in the 1990s Tuareg irredentist rebellion. The ARLA was originally part of the Mouvement Populaire pour la Libération de l'Azawad (MPLA) but seceded in June 1993, together with three other movements, after the MPLA signed peace accords in Mali. In 1992 it joined with two other movements to form the Mouvement des Fronts Unifiés de l'Azawad (MFUA), and in 1993 it joined in the more all-encompassing **Coordination de la Résistance Armée** (CRA). It was dismantled after the Ouagadougou accords which ended the rebellion in 1995. *See also* TUAREG REBELLIONS.

ARMÉE RÉVOLUTIONNAIRE DE LIBÉRATION DU NORD NIGER (ARLN). One of several **Tuareg** armed groups which fought in the irredentist Tuareg rebellion of the early 1990s. Its geographical sphere of operations was contested by a second group, the Front Patriotique de Libération du Sahara (FPLS). Led by **Khamed-Attaher Abdoulmoumine**, in 1993 the ARLN joined the more all-encompassing group, the **Coordination de la Résistance Armée** (CRA). It was dismantled after the peace agreements signed with the Niger government in April 1995. *See also* TUAREG REBELLIONS.

ARNA (also *Anné, Azna***).** A term used by post-Sokoto jihad **Fulani** to designate animists in Hausaland and now especially restricted to animist groups from areas ranging from the southern districts of **Maradi** to the **Dallol Maouri** through **Madaoua** and **Birni-N'Konni**. Their origins are uncertain: They may be **Songhay** who had colonized the **Aïr** region in the 15th century and subsequently moved south after the collapse of the **Songhay Empire** and under pressure from the **Tuareg** and desertification. The "Azna" version of their name may thus derive from the way in which the **Hausa** designate the Aïr, **Abzine**. The Arnas, in any case, though they are Hausa speaking, claim that they are not Hausa but had lost usage of their own language over time. Their identity is enshrined in their religion, the **Bori**, which presents strong affinities with the Songhay **Holley** religion.

The political system of the Arnas is more spiritual than temporal: two priestly officers, the Dagel and the Matsafi, lead them. The Dagel resides in Massalata, now the capital of the Arnas, after they left Birni-N'Konni to **Islam** in the era of the Sokoto jihad (early 19th century). In the view of the Arnas, Massalata, a town 5 km away from Birni-N'Konni, is the spiritual center of the world and the place in which the ceremony of the **Aroua** uncovers the future of people and things. This ceremony has been consecrated as an annual animist festival in Niger. *See also* AREWA.

AROUA. Common divination method whereby marks on the sand are read and interpreted by a qualified diviner. This procedure takes on a particular importance in the great meetings of geomancers organized annually at Massalata, capital of the **Arnas**, usually in the cooler part of the dry season (December to February). The ceremonial meeting, at which geomancers "turn the soil" and reveal events that will mark the year, is preceded by ritual sacrifices and *trance danse* made in Massalata and nearby Dagarka. The *aroua* is an ancient festival, predating the foundation of the historical state of **Konni**, on the territory of which Massalata is located. Given the recent upsurge of Islamic orthodoxy, it has lost a significant fraction of its following, but it still retains its importance for the Arnas; as such, it has a place in the calendar of Nigerien festivals. The *aroua* day, which is chosen by Massalata's elders, is celebrated only in that village, but it is usually attended by local state officials and covered by the national media.

ARRONDISSEMENT. Older administrative division. In 1998, the 36 *arrondissements* then extant were erected into *départements*, the upper level administrative division, while the *départements* became regions. *Arrondissements* became thin administrative units, rather irrelevant as decision-making centers within the decentralization scheme, and headed by a state-appointed official, the *sous-préfet*. *See also* ADMINISTRATIVE ORGANIZATION.

ARZIKA, NOUHOU (1968–). Born in the **Arewa**, Arzika studied economics at the **University of Niamey** (1988–1995) where he became famous as one of the most vocal and aggressive among the leaders of the turbulent students union, the **Union des Scolaires du Niger** (USN). During that period he also worked for the radical weekly *Alternative* (1994–1998) owned by the leftist militants of the Groupe Alternative but was mostly busy as a **civil society** activist in the ranks of the more mainstream **Association Nigérienne de Défense des Droits de l'Homme** (ANDDH). While plying his trade as a management consultant, he founded a consumer's defense organization (Organisation des Consommateurs du Niger, ORCONI) and joined **Marou Amadou** and **Moustapha Kadi** to spearhead a resistance movement to the passing, in Niger's parliament, of a value added tax on goods and services which affected the price of running water, power, bread, and other primary commodities, the Coalition Equité Qualité contre la vie chère au Niger (Fairness and Quality Coalition against High Costs of Living in Niger).

The success of the movement, which organized "ghost city" operations in Niger's cities and towns for several days and an impressive mass demonstration in Niamey, rendered Arzika and his friends famous overnight. The trio was subsequently co-opted by the government in consultations to chart a new tax scheme. In 2006, Arzika and Kadi fell out (while Amadou returned to his rural home to cure an illness); the former drifted out of human rights and consumer defense and into vocal and rambling Nigerien patriotism. Arzika's new stance soon proved to be a close political rapprochement with President **Mamadou Tandja**, as the civil society activist turned into a firebrand propagandist for the president's hardline approach to a **Tuareg** insurgency that started in 2007. In that year, Arzika set up a new organization, the Mouvement Citoyen pour la Paix, la Démocratie et la République (Citizen's Movement for Peace, Democracy and the Republic) and became one of the key orators in the Réfondation de la République (Refounding of the Republic) debate pushed through the national media by the president's advisors to start undermining the **Fifth Republic**. Despite his efforts, Arzika failed to disseminate the concept of a Tandja third term and regime change within Niger's civil society and instead appeared increasingly isolated as Tandja's project of overthrowing the Fifth Republic took shape. He then became a fixture in Tandja's entourage and a strident and often incoherent orator in the promotion of the regime change project, delivering brutal announcements laced with slurs against other politicians and his own former friends in the civil society.

After Tandja was toppled in February 2010, Arzika vociferously called for his release while condemning the coup d'état, but public threats issued by the new authorities and the irrelevance of his new position eventually silenced him. *See also* TAZARTCHÉ; TCHANGARI, MOUSSA; TUAREG REBELLIONS.

ASKIA. Songhay dynasty established in **Gao** in 1493 when one of **Sonni Ali Ber**'s lieutenants, a Sarakholle general named Mohammed Touré, overthrew Sonni Barou, the legitimate successor. Barou's sisters reportedly protested against the coup by yelling *"A si kia"* (Songhay for "it will not happen"), a phrase which Touré defiantly affixed to his name, or which was in any case affixed to it by commentators at the time. Hence, he ruled under the name **Askia Mohammed**, and the phrase evolved into the dynastic title of his lineage. There were eight subsequent Askias before the dynasty collapsed. The new dynasty expanded the power of the empire into **Aïr** and other Saharan regions to the west and ruled between 1493 and 1591, when the Moroccan invasion from the north destroyed it. The southern part of the empire (now in Niger territory) continued on as an independent unit under a legitimate Askia lineage but slowly disintegrated into a series of small states. *See also* DENDI; TONDIBI, BATTLE OF.

ASKIA MOHAMMED I (1440–1538). One of the most successful generals of **Sonni Ali Ber**, the king of **Gao** whose warfare transformed the kingdom into the **Songhay Empire**, Mamar Touré (as he was known in **Songhay**) seized power in 1492, overthrowing Ali Ber's son and successor, Sonni Barou, in the name of **Islam**, and ruling until his deposition by his son, Askia Moussa, in 1529. His family—originally from the Sarakholle rather than the Songhay ethnicity—ruled the empire until its collapse at the end of the 16th century. Askia Mohammed was a lesser war leader than Sonni Ali but a greater organizer, who consolidated Songhay rule over far-flung possessions and dominions, including the **Hausa** states in the east, **Aïr** and Teghazza in the north, and much of what used to be the Mali Empire in the west. Though centered along the **Niger River** valley—original home of the Songhay—the empire thus became, under his leadership, the largest state ever built in Africa. Askia Mohammed is important also for having stimulated the expansion of Islam in the area through war and policy, basing Islamic identity on both the **Zarma-Songhay** and the Hausa populations of Niger.

ASSAO (1850?–1910). *Kaura* (war chief) of **Maradi** in a troubled period of its history and a strong figure comparable to **Dan Kassawa** and **Dan Baskoré**, at the end of the 19th century. Son of a **Fulani** father from Mobiraya (near Sokoto), and a simple trader at the outset, Assao profited from the period of upheaval during which King Mijinyawa fled to **Tessaoua**, to become named *kaura* of Maradi. Widely detested by many, he became a maker and breaker of kings. Appointed by Nabo (1892–1894), Assao died in 1910 after being poisoned by one of his wives. *See also* NORTHERN KATSINA.

ASSEMBLÉE CONSTITUANTE. Constituent assembly created in December 1958 out of the **Territorial Assembly**, after the elimination of the **Sawaba** party from the public stage (subsequently banned in October 1959), to adopt the constitution of 25 February 1959, which it did (by 44 votes to 8). The body was then dissolved on 12 March 1959, becoming the Legislative Assembly, and later, on 29 July 1960, the first **National Assembly** of the **First Republic**.

ASSIMILATION POLICY. Theoretical underlying tenet of French colonial policy in Africa, which assumed the gradual assimilation of colonial populations to the essentialized view of French culture held by the elite of the French Third Republic (1871–1940). The status of the *assimilé* (assimilated) or *évolué* (evolved) was acknowledged to colonial subjects who acquired the accoutrements of French civilization—including **language**, dress, customs, **education**, and **religion**—or who had served with distinction in the French colonial armies or **civil service**. This was monitored through inspections, including in the running of household life, by specially appointed French examiners. The status conferred the right to petition for French citizenship, a process so cumbersome that in the entire **Afrique Occidentale Française** (AOF) barely 2,000 Africans acquired it. The advantages of being classified an *évolué* and attaining citizenship included voting rights, falling under French republican civil and penal codes (instead of the *Indigénat* code), and freedom from *corvée* labor. The basic assumption of the assimilation policy was the unquestioned superiority of French culture and its suitability for all populations. However, its mode of operation was so cumbersome and indeed costly (it required educational efforts similar to those deployed in metropolitan **France** itself) that it could touch only a tiny fraction of the colonial population. After the fall of the **Third Republic**, colonial philosophy shifted to the concept of association, a watered-down version of assimilation that was never as clearly worked out.

The French concepts of *assimilé* and *évolué* were translated into Niger's social context by different concepts and meanings. *Assimilé* itself never became current in Niger's common speech, while *évolué* was and is still used by the French-educated minority to designate someone who has acquired modern education and outlook. While the word is used even in France with that meaning, in Niger it might have negative connotations of designating someone who traded his or her roots for modern delusions. After independence, it was largely replaced, in public discourse, with the word *intellectuel*, which designates anyone who has attended modern French-based schools at least up to the high school *baccalauréat* level. *Intellectuel* functions as the code name for the sociocultural minority of the Francophones, and is a distant but direct outcome of the assimilation policy. In local languages, a variety of **Hausa** and **Zarma** terms designate this group of people. Hausa refers to them as *yan boko* (the secular-educated), *masu ilimi* (the enlightened), and *mushanu* (plural for the Hausa rendition of the French word for sir, *monsieur* [*mushe* in Hausa singular form] that was applied at first to French teachers). Zarma calls them *ilimi koyey* (the enlightened) and *komiyey* (plural of *komi*, the Zarma rendition of the French word *commis*, office clerk, the menial job to which most *évolués* were consigned during the colonial regime, and which was, despite its modesty, a sign of social elevation in the emerging modern Nigerien society). *See also* FRENCH OCCUPATION.

ASSOCIATION DAHO-TOGO. Mutual-aid and cultural association grouping all those in **Niamey** (mostly merchants and civil servants) from the coastal areas of Dahomey and Togo, except for the Yoruba who had their own organization (the Ajo Omo Sahki Kparapo). The association collapsed with the expulsion of the Dahomeans in 1964–1965 from Niger. It had been mostly involved in sponsoring cultural activities and helping members with loans and other assistance. The organization was actively supported during the colonial era by the French administration, which regarded it as a grouping of successful *évolués*, a fact that rankled with the local population, given that they were foreigners, Christian, and tended to be condescending in outlook. All of these facts explain the peculiarity of the grudges harbored against Dahomeans in Niger in the early 1960s. *See also* ASSIMILATION POLICY; BENIN-NIGER BOUNDARY DISPUTE.

ASSOCIATION DES FEMMES. A 1956 alliance of **Niamey**'s **women**, organized by the town's four *magajiyas*. The association was superseded at the end of 1958 by the wider **Union des Femmes du Niger**, which the *magajiyas* also helped set up, under leadership from **Diori Hamani**'s wife, **Aissa Diori**.

ASSOCIATION DES FEMMES DU NIGER (AFN). The AFN was established in September 1975 by the military regime which had come to power over a year earlier and on the occasion of the first International Year of **Women**. AFN replaced the Diori-era **Union des Femmes du Niger** (UFN) and was staffed with highly educated women in **Niamey** and **Zinder**, tasked with the mission to mobilize women, especially in the rural areas, for participation in the regime's "development society" agenda. In this context, specific women's problems were sidelined, as is shown by the fact that AFN never succeeded in pushing through the adoption of a Family Code organizing Niger's civil legislation in ways more favorable to women, and the association was generally better funded yet less militant than the UFN. In the early 1990s, political liberalization led to the emergence of more combative women's associations, though none of these has the reach, resources, and level of coordination attained by AFN when it was a state organization. *See also* WOMEN.

ASSOCIATION DES FEMMES JURISTES DU NIGER (AFJN). The Nigerien **women** lawyers association is a civic association established in 1991 under the leadership of attorney **Bibata Niandou Barry**. Its main initial aim was to lobby the emerging democratic institutions of Niger for the adoption of pro-women legislation, especially a Family Code. Since that period, its goal has shifted to providing legal assistance to poorer women, though its rather lackluster organization is not adequate to the challenge. AFJN is part of the umbrella feminine organization **Coordination des ONG et Association Féminines du Niger** (CONGAFEN), whose strategy is to shape Nigerien legislation through ratification and implementation of international conventions, scaling down domestic mobilization and confrontation.

ASSOCIATION ISLAMIQUE DU NIGER (AIN). The AIN was established in September 1974 as a state-sponsored guardian of Nigerien **Islam**, on the basis chiefly of prominent religious groups and leaderships across the country. In this way, AIN emerged as a religious equivalent to the *chefferie traditionnelle* and was given some of the latter's functions as a semiformal arm of the state, especially when it comes to the governance of marriage problems and inheritance issues. AIN was able to fulfill that role in particular through the development of a system of Islamic courts which, though they are not officially part of the Nigerien judicial system, are nonetheless backed by the state when they adjudicate divorce and inheritance issues. The preferred arbitration method, based on Sunni Maliki law, does not require state-sanctioned procedures, and the courts never venture into the domain of penal and business law.

The first meeting of the AIN took place in 1974 under its still-current president, Alfa Oumarou Ismael, son of a venerated cleric of **Say**, and its vice-president, Malam Moussa, son of a prominent cleric from **Abzine (Aïr)**. Unlike the Islamic association put together under the **First Republic**, AIN had a degree of autonomy, owing to the facts that it was not a party organ and was run by people who had social authority and prestige through family and learning. On that latter score, the **Seyni Kountché** regime benefited from the policy set up under **Hamani Diori** to create literate and learned Islamic scholars through the **Franco-Arabe** educational system and an active policy of scholarships to and from Middle Eastern countries.

In the 1980s, the authority of AIN was slightly disturbed by the emergence, within Niger's religious landscape, of a Wahhabi-inspired trend from northern **Nigeria (Izala)**. A more serious disturbance came about with **democratization** and the falling apart of the corporatist system put in place by Kountché. After an initial loosening up of ties, the state of Niger ultimately did not sever its connection with AIN. The association did lose its budgetary appropriation but it continued to receive state subsidies. By then, freedom of association had led to the creation of dozens of independent Islamic associations, all more or less patterned on the model of AIN. The ensuing changes in the public space led the Nigerien state, by the 2000s, to start accommodating the Islamic **civil society**, even while still upholding the hallowed French-inherited principle of *laïcité* or public secularism. The government thus created an Islamic consultative body, the Haut Conseil Islamique, in 2005, constituting all the associations the rulers of the day intended to favor. The state also included Islamic associations in the subsidy that it allocates to formally recognized associations, but it channeled these monies through the hierarchy of AIN, thus intentionally reinforcing that association.

In the world of Niger's Islamic associations, AIN represents a force of moderation which has steadily cooled down some of the most radical associations of the early 1990s. This was also a result of the model it offers: To become a truly national association like AIN, moderation appeared inescapable. But AIN was also transformed, in turn, by the new religious landscape, defining Nigerien Islam in ways that are closer to Wahhabi strictness than was the case in the 1980s. *See also RÉGIME D'EXCEPTION.*

ASSOCIATION NIGÉRIENNE POUR L'APPEL ET LE SALUT ISLAMIQUE (ANASI). Islamist association with a modernist outlook founded in 1991 by a group of Islamist intellectuals. Its main plank in the early phase of its existence was the wholesale adoption of an Islamic state by Niger, though it later retreated (faced with the impossibility of that proposition) to defending the Islamic identity of the Nigerien nation through fighting—somewhat successfully—the characterization of the state as *laïc* (secular) or the adoption of a Family Code which rearranges husband-and-wife relationships as well as inheritance rules in ways deemed un-Islamic. In fact, Niger's state secularism has been largely upheld, including in constitutional texts, but ANASI was generally more effective in its **National Assembly** lobbying against the feminist cause, especially when the Additional Protocol of the African Union on **Women**'s Rights, which the state had signed, was rejected at parliamentary ratification level in 2006. ANASI's modernism shows however in its stance in other domains, opposing, for instance, the popular Islamist rejection of the poliomyelitis vaccine which had spread into Niger from northern **Nigeria** in the late 1990s. In 2009, ANASI also condemned President **Mamadou Tandja**'s bid to overstay his last term, refusing to join in the chorus of popular preachers who claimed that he could do so despite having sworn on the Quran that he would respect and maintain the constitution. ANASI's membership is small and elite, but unlike many independent Islamic associations of Niger, the association has branches throughout the country's territory and a good deal of influence through its partnership with Islamist media in Niamey (the biweekly *As-Salam*, the Radio Television Bonferey). *See also* ISLAM.

ASSOCIATION NIGÉRIENNE POUR LA DÉFENSE DES DROITS DE L'HOMME (ANDDH). ANDDH was founded by a group of lawyers in April 1991, as Niger was formally adopting a liberal democratic regime. The initiative was motivated by the notion that democracy is a package that comprises, besides **elections** and representation, the defense and promotion of individual human rights. Many such associations cropped up in Niger at the time, greatly thanks to funding from Western organizations intent at promoting human rights in the country, but ANDDH is the only one to have survived and expanded beyond that early period, becoming a national organization and a fixture of Niger's **civil society**. Owing to the rise of an Islamist agenda, ANDDH *cause célèbre* battles in the 1990s included efforts to promote **women**'s civil rights in a liberal framework through a Family Code (1993), the Convention for the Elimination of Discrimination against Women (1999), and the Additional Protocol to the African Union Charter on Women's Rights (2007). In most of these struggles, ANDDH was checkmated by Islamist associations backed by conservative politicians, but its most valued work is of a more unobtrusive kind and is performed by regional committees and judicial clinics that propagate information on Niger's laws and the rights and obligations of citizens, relay campaigns on issues such as discrimination or living conditions in prison inter alia, and assistance to individuals in solving disputes, dealing with the state, or setting up voluntary groupings.

ANDDH has two broad components: a political section which leads the association at national and regional levels, making decisions, maintaining relations with the state and other organizations, and recruited through elections by the membership; and a technical staff of lawyers and voluntary workers who perform the day-to-day activities of the association. ANDDH publishes regular reports and memoranda on Niger's human rights records as well as a monthly bulletin (*Le Bulletin de l'ANDDH*), makes frequent public interventions on national affairs, hosts frequent seminars and conferences, organizes regular human rights courses for Niger's military and police, and maintains a reference center with a library in **Niamey**, as well as headquarters in Niamey and all seven regional capitals of the country. It was a vocal opponent of President **Mamadou Tandja**'s attempt at establishing a dictatorship in 2009.

ASSOCIATION POUR LA DIFFUSION DE L'ISLAM AU NIGER (ADINI ISLAM). One of the new independent Islamic associations with national scope and relevance, founded in 1993, with a stronghold in **Maradi** where it benefited from the patronage of wealthy Islamist businessman Alhaj Rabé dan Tchadoua. ADINI Islam's doctrinal position was shaped by the popular Wahhabi-slanted Islamism of the **Izala** movement. In the 1990s, it promoted its agenda of making Nigeriens lead more religious lives through preaching and high-profile issues such as the fight against condom use, the Family Code, and the Festival International de la Mode Africaine (FIMA) fashion show. On the latter occasion, ADINI Islam was involved in the organization of a demonstration-cum-riot in Niamey in November 2000, and the ensuing violence led the government to ban the association. It survived, however, though mostly in the guise of local associations with an Arabic name stressing their Sunni orthodoxy orientation: *Kitab wa Sunna* and *Ikhya wa Sunna* (Maradi), *Alkitabbal Sunna* (Filingué), etc. *See also* ALPHADI; ISLAM; WOMEN.

ASSODÉ. Older capital of **Aïr** and one of the most ancient known towns of the area. Established around 880 CE by the head of the Isandalen **Tuareg** clan. The site—completely deserted since 1917—still has the ruins of some 200 houses and a mosque originally built over several centuries previously. Assodé's decline is linked with the creation of the sultanate of **Agadez** by 1405 and its rise to prominence. It used to be the headquarters of the *anasta-fidet*—supreme chief of the Kel Owey—whose relocation to Agadez in 1917 sounded the death knell of the city. Destroyed during internecine fighting between the Kel Gress and Kel Owey, the ruins lie 216 km from Agadez on one of the routes to Algeria.

ATAKORA. Mountain range mostly in northwestern Benin and northeastern Togo. The Atakora ends in Niger between **Say** and **Gaya**, where it is traversed by the **Niger River** (between Kirtachi and Boumba), which traces a sinuous W outline, giving the name to the **Parc National du W**.

AUTORITÉ DE RÉGULATION MULTISECTORIELLE (ARM). The multisectoral regulation authority was created on 26 October 1999 to supervise the lawfulness of private sector activities in the domains of water, energy (electricity and hydrocarbons), transport, and telecommunications, and more generally to ensure that Niger's **economic liberalization** policy develops in an orderly fashion. Its mission includes the surveillance of legislation implementation and the protection of consumers' interests under conditions of free and fair competition. ARM was effectively set up only in 2003 and started to recruit its staff in 2004. This means that the great water and telecommunication services privatizations of the early 2000s occurred with little regulatory surveillance.

By 2010, ARM was fully established, as the Conseil National de Régulation and its four sectoral divisions (Transport, Telecommunications, Water, and Energy) had become operational. It issues decisions on private companies' conduct, which are enforceable through the justice system, with a right of appeal at the administrative chamber of the **Cour Suprême**.

AUTORITÉ DU BASSIN DU NIGER (ABN). Interstate organization of which Niger is a member, charged with coordinating the development of the **Niger River** basin. The Niger Basin Authority includes countries directly crossed by the river valley (Guinea, Mali, Niger, **Nigeria**) as well as countries touched by it and by its tributaries (Benin, Burkina Faso, Cameroon, Chad, and Côte d'Ivoire). It originates in a colonial (French) agency, the Mission d'Étude et d'Aménagement du Niger (MEAN), and was established in **Niamey** (where it is still headquartered) in 1964, at first under the name Commission du Fleuve Niger. After a period of some activity in the 1970s, ABN had become largely a dormant organization in the following two decades but was recently revived when its member-states adopted a "shared vision" agenda at the summit of Abuja (Nigeria), in 2002. The main result of this evolution is that ABN has become an active coordinator of programs and projects focused on the Niger River valley and funded by a variety of European donors, including the **Agence Française de Développement**. The development and preservation challenges faced by the agency are impressive: The river is 4,184 km long (the third longest in Africa) and traverses all the ecosystems typical of West Africa—the tropical forest, the grassland savannah, the **Sahel**, and the Sahara desert. It contributes to the livelihood of 110 million riverines in nine countries, including a densely populated, **oil**-rich delta in southern Nigeria.

AUTORITÉ DU LIPTAKO-GOURMA (ALG). Interstate authority created on 3 December 1970 and headquartered in Ouagadougou (Burkina Faso). The organization covers the frontier areas of Niger, Burkina Faso, and Mali, with a territory of 370,000 sq km, landlocked and semiarid. ALG contributes to reducing the isolation of Burkina Faso's and Mali's poorest regions (the far northeastern **Sahel** region of Burkina and the far eastern region of **Gao** in Mali), while serving, in Niger (where it covers the region of **Tillabéri**), to establish transborder connections with communities in a common neighborhood of economic and societal activities. Initial ambitious projects aiming at building connecting roads and setting up electric energy producing plants inter alia have been shelved over the years, given their impracticability, and ALG was long dormant in the 1980s and 1990s. It was revived in the early 2000s, and now endeavors to define its vision in relation chiefly to the important stockbreeding resources of the area.

AYOROU. Small but important **Songhay** town of around 5,000 people on the **Niger River**, near the border of Mali, 30 km northwest of **Tillabéri** and 210 km north of **Niamey**. This *commune urbaine* has a picturesque Sunday market, which draws islanders from the river and **Fulani** and **Tuareg** nomads as well as *pirogue* boats from Mali. The market, the town's setting on the Niger River, its tourist facilities, and the wildlife (especially hippos) along the scenic drive from Niamey have made Ayorou a regular staple of Niger's tourist industry. This has been jeopardized somewhat in recent years by the inroads of Tuareg rebels, including from nearby Mali, and the area is now heavily patrolled by Nigerien military.

Ayorou is important historically, since this is where Sonni Barou retreated after he was overthrown by **Askia Mohammed** in 1493. He reigned over a small kingdom there.

Ayorou is administratively in the Tillabéri *département* of the region of Tillabéri and is slated to be moved a few kilometers away from its current location as the **Kandadji Dam**'s work progresses. *See also* DENDI; SONGHAY EMPIRE.

AZALAY. Historically important semiannual salt caravans plying the **Ténéré** desert between the oases of **Bilma** and Fachi, and **Agadez**. They are also known as *taglem* or *tagalem* in **Hausa**. The *azalay* usually travel in October and November and in March and April, bringing food and other commodities to the desert oases, as well as for their entire round trip, returning with the salt cakes produced in **Kaouar**. In the colonial period, a strong French military escort accompanied them, but it was nonetheless often prey to **Tuareg** raiders. Thus, in1904, the *azalay* was plundered in front of Bilma's walls by 200 Ouled Sliman from Borkou (Chad), while the 1906 *azalay* was destroyed at Fachi. The latter caravan numbered 20,000 camels. No caravans plied the route between 1916 and 1924 due to generally unsettled conditions. Afterward, the caravan dwindled in importance, and in 1948, the *azalay* numbered only 8,000 camels, while the average caravan in the precolonial era was composed of 10,000 camels stretching in a file 25 km in length. Traditionally, a representative of the *amenokal* of **Aïr** heads the caravan, followed by the camels of each Tuareg drum group.

The round trip across the Ténéré takes about three weeks. Previously all *azalay* were exclusively Tuareg (and specifically Kel Gress), but since the onset of the colonial era the Hausa have also become deeply involved. In more recent decades, the profitability of the *azalay* has declined as trucks have begun to link the Agadez–Kaouar routes. On the other hand, post-1973 increases in gasoline prices have somewhat reversed this trend, since salt is a heavy and cheap commodity, sensitive to fluctuations in transport costs. With the onset of the Tuareg rebellion in the north in 1990, however, they have virtually ceased plying their ancient routes.

AZAWAD. *See* AZAWAGH.

AZAWAGH (Also Azawak and Azawad). Vast area between the **Ader** plateau and the valleys of **Aïr**, or more specifically the dry sandy plateau north of **Tahoua**, between Ader, the Tiguidit fault, Talak in the north, and Ménaka to the west. Composed of sand dunes at its center, the **Ténéré** in Tamesna in the north, and the sandstone plateau of Tegama in the northeast, Azawagh in prehistoric times was part of a drainage system for the Ahaggar mountains (now in Algeria) and Aïr, and extended to the south via the **Dallol Bosso**, which joined the **Niger River** at Boumba just before the current **Parc National du W**.

Modern Azawagh extends into Mali (where the term *Azawad* is more common), is 80,000 sq km large, and very sparsely populated. In Niger, its main human settlements are **Tchintabaraden** and **Abalak**, small centers of congregation for largely nomadic peoples: the **Tuareg** Ouilliminden Kel Dinnik, the **Woodabe Fulani**, and an **Arab** minority. Azawagh was one of the areas which Tuareg insurgents in the 1990s wanted to detach from Nigerien and Malian territory.

AZELIK. Political center of **Aïr** before the foundation of **Agadez** and also site of the ancient town of Takedda (Teguidda), visited by the **Arab** traveler Ibn Battuta in the 14th century, and an important copper-smelting center at the time. About 20 km northeast of Teguidda-n'Tesemt and 30 km southwest of Agadez, it is referred to by oral tradition as the oldest settlement in the area, ruling over a mixed population of **Hausa**, **Songhay**, and **Tuareg**. Indeed, the names of the archaeological sites associate the Berber sounding name of Azelik to Hausa (Azelik wan Birni) and Songhay (Azelik Bangu Beri) descriptions. The rise of the sultanate of Agadez brought about clashes with Azelik in which a stalemate developed. One surprise attack, however, finally succeeded, and all residents of Azelik were killed except (according to tradition) one boy and one girl. They settled at Teguidda-n'Tesemt where some Azelik workers were established at the salt pans, perpetuating the clan though now under Agadez suzerainty. According to some traditions, the ancestors of Azelik come from Fès.

Azelik was the site at which **uranium** ore deposits were first found by the Bureau Minier de la France d'Outre-Mer, in 1957. However, the site was left unexploited until the late 2000s, when the China National Nuclear Corporation (CNNC) purchased **mining** concession, in the framework of Niger's policy of partners' diversification initiated by former president **Mamadou Tandja**. CNNC created, together with the state of Niger (33 percent of shares), the Chinese investment fund ZXJOY Invest, and the Korea Resources Corporation the Société des Mines d'Azelik (SOMINA), which produced its first yellow cake barrel in 2011. SOMINA is scheduled to produce 700 tons of uranium annually, compared to the yearly output of 3,000 tons in the mines of **Arlit** and **Akouta** exploited by the French uranium giant **AREVA**.

AZU. Title of one of the important chiefs of **Maradi**. The first holder of the post, from Kano (capital of one of the seven **Hausa** states) was given command over the Maradi market by the king of **Katsina**; later a Katsinawa dignitary was appointed sovereign of the region, and the two split up the area between them. A descendant of the original *azu* still lives in the town of Maradi today.

B

BA, ABDOUSSALAM (1939–). Physicist specializing in solar energy and an international administrator. Ba was trained in physics at the **University of Niamey** except for a year (1973–1974) at the University of Pennsylvania's Solar Energy Utilization and Energy Conversion unit. He has served as an electronics technician and researcher with the **Office National de l'Energie Solaire** (ONERSOL) (1968–1981) before becoming its deputy director in 1981. In 1986 he became project director of the West African Economic Community and director general of the region's solar energy center. He is currently the director of the **Centre National d'Energie Solaire**, formerly ONERSOL.

BA, BOUBAKAR (1935–). Educator and former rector of the **University of Niamey**. Born in Diapaga, now in Burkina Faso (formerly Haute-Volta), at a time when the eastern regions of the colony of Haute-Volta were merged in the colony of Niger, Ba completed a rather privileged educational career, moving from the upscale colonial high school Lycée Van Vollenhoven (Dakar, Senegal) to the Institut des Hautes Études (Dakar), and the Lycée Hoche (Versailles, **France**) before entering the elitist French Lycée Louis le Grand (Paris, 1955–1956) and the École Normale Supérieure (Paris, 1956–1959), obtaining a mathematics degree. He continued his studies in mathematics at several French institutions (the Fondation Thiers and the Centre National de la Recherche Scientifique, CNRS, 1959–1961) and at Princeton University (1961–1962), and again at the CNRS (1962–1964), obtaining a doctor of science degree in 1965. Between 1965 and 1968, he was a lecturer at Dakar's Faculty of Science and afterward served as professor of mathematics at the University of Madagascar (1969–1971) and in 1971 returned to Niger to assume the post of director of what was to become the University of Niamey. In September 1973 he was appointed rector of the university, serving for two terms of office before joining the university's **health** sciences faculty. Ba has published several scholarly papers.

BA, OUMAR (1906–1964). Ba was born in Bandiagara (French Sudan, now Mali). A *médecin africain* (African physician), he served in several districts of **France**'s Sahelian colonies before settling in Niger where he worked in **Niamey** (1941), **Tessaoua** (1942–1943), **Tillabéri** (1944–1947), and **Birni-N'Konni** (1947–1948). He started a political career in 1946 and was elected as the **Parti Progressiste Nigérien** (PPN-RDA) general councilor for Tillabéri (1946), French West Africa grand councilor for the Overseas Territory of Niger (1947), and president of the financial commission of French West Africa's grand council. Ba filled a few other distinguished political offices before returning to his medical career in 1952. He was instrumental in the founding of the Union des Syndicats du Niger (1947), a forerunner of the **Union des Syndicats des Travailleurs du Niger** (USTN), the biggest union federation in Niger. He died in Niamey in 1964.

BABARI DAN UBAN ICHE (r. 1742–1770). King of **Gobir**. His rule consolidated the Gobir monarchy and set it on track for its apogee, through a policy of successful warfare against neighboring **Hausa** states (**Katsina**, Kano, Zamfara) as well as the **Bornu Empire**. His most signaled success was when he captured the Zamfara capital by resorting to a fifth column of Gobir settlers, in 1762. Having thus checked the rise of Zamfara, Babari built his capital at **Alkalawa**, in annexed Zamfara territory, and died soon thereafter.

BAKABE, MAHAMANE (1947–). Born in Gazaoua (region of **Maradi**), Bakabé, a teacher by profession, also developed a career as a television moviemaker in the 1970–1980s. He mostly made documentary movies on issues of national interest but is famous in Niger principally for having authored the historical film *Si les cavaliers*, on the event surrounding the deaths of French colonial leader Captain Marius-Gabriel **Cazemajou** and the sultan of **Damagaram**, **Amadou Kouran Daga**. *See also* CINEMA; MISSION DU HAUT-SOUDAN.

BAKARY, DJIBO (1922–1998). Former secretary general of the **Parti Progressiste Nigérien** (PPN-RDA) and head of the banned **Sawaba** party, first mayor of **Niamey** (1956), first vice-president of the colonial Executive Council of Niger, and, in later life, political leader of the small Union Démocratique des Forces Progressistes (UDFP Sawaba) party. Born in 1922, Bakary, who is a cousin of his great rival, **Hamani Diori**, was educated locally and at Dakar's **École William Ponty** (until 1942). A teacher by training, Bakary entered political life at the end of World War II, becoming secretary-general of the then-new PPN party, and a leading figure in the interterritorial **Rassemblement Démocratique Africain** (RDA) party. Extremely active as a politician, journalist, and trade unionist, Bakary was one of the top militants in the RDA's struggle with the administration in Côte d'Ivoire (1949–1950) but devoted his attention fully to Niger after 1950. His active support for **groundnut** farmers in eastern Niger gradually assisted his electoral aspirations.

When the RDA broke with the French communist party (following Côte d'Ivoire's Houphouët-Boigny's lead), Bakary refused to follow suit and was expelled from the party. The local PPN then promptly split into two factions, with Bakary's renamed the Union Démocratique Nigérienne (UDN) and based mostly on his unionist support in western Niger.

In the 1956 **elections** for the French **National Assembly**, Bakary ran against Hamani Diori; despite active French manipulations in the latter's favor, Bakary nearly beat him. In that year's municipal elections, the UDN won 10 seats to the PPN's 13 and the Bloc Nigérien d'Action (BNA)'s 4, and an alliance of the UDN and the BNA made Bakary Niamey's first mayor. The two parties later merged to become the Niger branch of the interterritorial **Mouvement Socialiste Africain**, which was founded in 1957 by Senegal's Lamine Gueye and backed by **France**'s SFIO (socialist party). In the 1957 **Territorial Assembly** elections, the MSA scored a dramatic success, gaining 41 seats to the PPN's 19, and Bakary was appointed vice-president of the Executive Council (a post normally becoming the premiership with the grant of full internal autonomy). The next year, the MSA joined the new interterritorial Parti du Regroupement Africain (PRA) party of Senegal's Leopold Sédar Senghor and changed its name to Sawaba (Freedom). In the September 1958 referendum regarding the future status of French Africa, the party campaigned strongly for a "no" vote (and for immediate independence) but was deserted by many of the country's customary chiefs, who swung the electorate against the party. Moreover, France had commissioned its last colonial governor in Niger, Dom Jean Colombani, to rig and otherwise bend the voting in favor of the supporters of the "yes" vote.

The party was thus badly trounced, while the former BNA faction (led by the *zarmakoy* of **Dosso**, **Seydou Issoufou**) deserted Bakary to join the PPN party. In the December 1958 elections, the PPN led a coalition of parties to unseat Sawaba, gaining 54 seats to the latter's 4. These were also heavily rigged, leading the Sawaba to take to the streets and attempt to rouse the city of Niamey against the PPN. Faced with the PPN's repression, Bakary left Niamey for Conakry (Guinea) in September 1959, officially to attend the congress of that country's Parti Démocratique party, but in fact starting his long, 15-year exile. The following month, Sawaba was banned and many of its leaders arrested. Establishing himself in Bamako (Mali), Bakary made several efforts to topple the Diori regime. In 1963–1964, an attempted coup d'état followed by a guerrilla attack on Nigerien border posts caused considerable unrest in Niamey, though the attack was clumsily organized. Bakary was allowed to return to Niger only after the 1974 coup d'état. Then ailing, he had to pledge to the military regime to refrain from political activities. This pledge was perhaps not kept, for soon afterward Bakary and several other members of his old Sawaba party were implicated in the attempted coup of Major **Sani Souna Sido**. Bakary was arrested in August 1975 and imprisoned until April 1984. He was held in the isolated garrison of **N'Guigmi** near **Lake Chad**, in far eastern Niger.

After his release, Bakary remained out of politics until the **Conférence Nationale** in 1991. Though by now 73, he founded a new **political party**, the Union Démocratique des Forces Progressistes (UDFP Sawaba) but with only a segment of his lieutenants, the others forming "another" Sawaba party, the Union Démocratique de Forces Révolutionnaires (UDFR Sawaba). Bakary contested the presidential and legislative elections of 1993. His personal candidacy garnered only 1.71 percent of the vote and the party likewise. Largely shunned by the **Alliance des Forces du Changement** (AFC), he threw his lot behind the **Mouvement National pour la Société de Développement** (MNSD Nassara), in the coalition of which his party became a member. The other Sawaba party aligned with the AFC.

In 1992, Bakary published an autobiography which revisited the most dramatic and, for Niger, crucial epoch of his life, the late 1950s: *Silence, on décolonise! Itinéraire politique et syndical d'un militant africain*. He died in Niamey in 1998.

BAKO, MAHAMANE SANI (1951–1997). Twice foreign affairs minister under the *régime d'exception* and the **Second Republic**. Born on 25 April 1951, at **Tessaoua**, and educated at the University of Benin in Lomé, Togo (1971–1974), Bako then proceeded to the University of Abidjan (1974–1975), where he studied law and international relations, and to the University of Yaoundé, Cameroon. He joined Niger's Ministry of Foreign Affairs' United Nations' desk in 1976 and the next year was promoted to director of the Division of International Organizations in the same ministry. In January 1979 he again moved up, to assume the post of assistant secretary-general of the ministry and in October became the secretary-general. In September 1981 he was brought into General **Seyni Kountché**'s staff as his cabinet director, and on 23 September 1985, moved into the cabinet as foreign affairs minister after the incumbent, **Idé Oumarou**, was elected secretary-general of the Organization of African Unity. After General **Ali Saibou**'s accession to the presidency, Bako was retained in his old post for a year, but in September 1988 he was dispatched as ambassador to Belgium. He returned to head the Ministry of Foreign Affairs in May 1989 and stayed in that office until the **Conférence Nationale** government was set up in September 1991, when he was attached to the foreign office in **Niamey**. He also became an influential power broker in the **Mouvement National pour la Société de Développement** (MNSD Nassara) party until the coup d'état of Colonel **Baré Maïnassara** in January 1996. The new ruler, who was Bako's brother-in-law, appointed him his cabinet director, a position he kept until his untimely death the following year.

BALABILI. One of **Bilma**'s oldest quarters, some 200 meters south of the center of the settlement. Balabili is a venerated graveyard today, marking the site of the massacre in the 18th century of over 200 townspeople during an attack by **Arab** marauders from Ouadai (Chad). Remnants of the old mosque, ruined in the attack, are still visible.

BALLA ARABÉ, CHAWEYE (1925–1991). Colonel Balla Arabé was a high-ranking officer in the Nigerien army, trained in Saint-Louis (Senegal) and Saint-Maixent (**France**) in 1956. A private of the French army since 1944, he was stationed in Madagascar, the Sahara, Algeria, and Cotonou between 1946 and 1958. After Niger's independence, he was appointed assistant chief of the defense staff of the **Forces Armées Nigériennes** (1961–1962) and then general chief of the defense staff (1962–1973) and special chief of the defense staff for President **Hamani Diori** in 1973–1974. After **Seyni Kountché**'s **coup in 1974**, Balla Arabé paid for this closeness to the president by being removed from the Nigerien army (September 1975) and detained in the military camp of **N'Guigmi** (in the far eastern desert) from 1974 to 1978. Afterward, he was more or less under house arrest in his hometown of **Maradi**. After the death of Kountché in 1987, Bala Arabé was rehabilitated and became a deputy of the **Mouvement National pour la Société de Développement** (MNSD) for the **commune** of Maradi in 1989 and second vice-president of the **National Assembly** until its dissolution in 1991. He was the representative of war veterans at the **Conférence Nationale**, at the end of which he died.

BALLA DAN SANI. See DAN GARA, SOULEY.

BANK OF AFRICA–NIGER (BOA). Established in April 1994 to acquire the assets of the **Nigeria** International Bank–Niamey. Capitalized at 1,000 million **CFA francs**, it is owned by the Groupe Bank of Africa, founded in 1982 in Bamako (Mali) and operating in 12 mostly West African countries. *See also* BANKING.

BANKING. The banking sector of Niger followed the economic evolution of the country. Established in the 1960s through mostly a development bank (the **Banque de Développement de la République du Niger**, BDRN) and a number of agricultural and consumer credit institutions, it expanded in the late 1970s with the short-lived **uranium** boom, then contracted in the 1980s with the onset of the fiscal crisis, consolidated in the 1990s with the policy of **economic liberalization**, and expanded again in the 2000s.

In the 1980s—at which time the sector had matured—Niger had the following banks: Banque Internationale pour le Niger (BIPN); Banque Arabe Libyenne Nigérienne pour le Commerce Extérieur et le Développement (BALINEX); Citibank Niger; Banque du Commerce et du Crédit (BCC); Banque Internationale pour le Commerce et l'Industrie du Niger (BICIN); Banque Massraf Faycal al-Islami-Niger; Banque de Développement de la République du Niger (BDRN); **Caisse Nationale de Crédit Agricole** (CNCA); **Crédit du Niger**; and **Union Nigérienne de Crédit et de Coopérative** (UNCC). Other financial establishments at the time included Société Nigérienne de Crédit Automobile (SONICA); Caisse de Prêts aux Collectivités Territoriales (CPCT); Caisse Nationale d'Epargne (CNE); Fonds de Garantie des Petites et Moyennes Entreprises Nigériennes (FIPMEN); and Société Islamique d'Investissement du Niger. Of note is that banking facilities were very limited, with at most only 27 branches of all institutions in the entire country, one third of these in the capital.

With the onset of a major fiscal squeeze in the mid-1980s, several of these banks collapsed; in the case of the state organs, the government was unable to sustain the deficits any longer. The ones that closed their doors included BICIN, BDRN, BCC, FIPMEN, SONICA, and BIN. BALINEX was also on the verge of closure but was rescued in March 1992 by the infusion of 746 million CFA francs from **Libya**. Several other private banks closed their doors, finding banking operations in Niger at the time not profitable. As a result of this weeding out, the following banks existed in 1992 in the country: BALINEX; Banque Meridien BIAO Niger, rescued by the Belgian group Belgolaise and a European investment fund (Cofipa) to become the Nigerien branch of the Banque Internationale pour l'Afrique (BIA Niger); Crédit du Niger; Nigeria International Bank; and **Société Nigérienne de Banque** (SONIBANK).

From 1993 through 1995, several major consolidations and changes took place on Niger's banking scene. Among these could be noted the 1994 establishment of the **Bank of Africa–Niger**, taking over the assets of the Nigeria International Bank–**Niamey**. Also in 1994 the former BALINEX became a private bank, coequally owned by Libyan and Nigerien interests and now trading under the name Banque Commerciale du Niger (BCN). The

Banque Massraf Faycal al-Islami entered a period of restructuring in 1994, to reemerge as the Banque Islamique du Niger. And the Nigerian Trust Bank opened its doors, taking over the assets and liabilities of the defunct BCC.

These consolidations led to a profound transformation of the banking scene in the country, with in particular the large-scale expansion of operations into the rest of the country, both in the regional capitals and in smaller, commercially important towns, such as in **Gaya** at the border with Benin.

Moreover, the end of the decade was marked by the arrival of ECOBANK, a banking institution tied to the financial institutions of the **Economic Community of West African States** (ECOWAS) and now, with branches in 30 African and European countries, the biggest African bank, and arguably the one most present across Nigerien territory (1999). This was followed in 2004 by the installation of the Libyan-originated Banque Sahélo-Saharienne pour l'Investissement et le Commerce (BSIC), tied to the Sahelo-Saharan community of states promoted by the Libyan government under Colonel Muammar Kadhafi. The same year, the Banque Régionale de Solidarité (BRS), a credit-boosting institution set up by the **Banque Centrale des États de l'Afrique de l'Ouest** (BCEAO) throughout the countries of the **Union Economique et Monétaire Ouest Africaine** (UEMOA) regional organization opened doors. The Banque Atlantique Côte d'Ivoire, a smallish Francophone version of ECOBANK, founded in Côte d'Ivoire but seated in Togo (like ECOBANK), followed suit two years later in 2006. The last addition to Niger's banking system is the Banque Agricole du Niger (BAGRI), created in July 2010 and geared to improving credit access for the peasantry.

In recent times, the aggregate **currency** and demand deposits, savings deposits, small time deposits, and money market mutual funds of Niger averages $190 million. The same aggregate for the biggest regional **economy** in West Africa, Nigeria, averages $12 billion. Moreover financial intermediation is very limited, with credit to the economy representing on average 6 percent of GDP. Niger's banking sector is therefore a very small one, with much room left for development. *See also* UNION ECONOMIQUE ET MONETAIRE OUEST-AFRICAINE.

BANQUE CENTRALE DES ÉTATS DE L'AFRIQUE DE L'OUEST (BCEAO). The BCEAO originated in the Banque d'Afrique Occidentale (BAO), also known as Banque de l'AOF (AOF being the French acronym for French West Africa), which itself was an expansion, in 1901, of the colonial Banque du Sénégal, created in 1853. Although a private investment bank, it was authorized to print the colonial **currency** which **France** promoted in its African colonies, including those in Equatorial Africa. In the late 1930s, France gradually worked out the Franc Zone system, and ended up spinning off the BAO a currency issue institute, the Institut d'Emission de l'Afrique Occidentale Française et du Togo, to administer the Franc des Colonies Françaises d'Afrique (**franc CFA**), in 1945. This institute was transformed into a central bank, the BCEAO, in 1959, in preparation for the independence of France's West African colonies, and the currency was renamed Franc de la Communauté Financière Africaine (franc CFA).

Tightly tied to France through a fixed parity between the franc CFA and the French franc as well as operational accounts at the French treasury to guarantee its currency's convertibility, BCEAO was for a while headquartered in Paris, under close control from the French. In fact, when BCEAO took its current form in 1962, its director general was a French administrator, Robert Julienne. After several reforms and the independent evolution of West African economies, the BCEAO was eventually transferred to Dakar in 1978. However, its essential ties to French finances were maintained, and the bank functions to a large extent as a glorified currency board, with its monetary policy decided at the French Treasury (by direct administration) and the European Central Bank (by derivation).

BCEAO regulates all **banking** activities in the states of the **Union Economique et Monétaire Ouest-Africaine** (UEMOA), the regional organization that gathers the countries that use the West African variant of the franc CFA. By an unwritten rule, its governor is always from Côte d'Ivoire (currently Koné Tiémoko), while the vice-governor is often either a Burkinabe or a Nigerien. In Niger, BCEAO has its principal office in **Niamey** and auxiliary branches in **Maradi** and **Zinder**. The current national director for Niger is Mahamadou Gado, a financier who worked at Niger's finance ministry before entering the BCEAO in 1993. He took office in February 2009.

BANQUE DE DÉVELOPPEMENT DE LA RÉPUBLIQUE DU NIGER (BDRN). National development bank created on 29 May 1961 and inaugurated on 8 November 1961, with technical assistance from the Société Tunisienne de Banque, and with **Crédit du Niger** as a major shareholder. **Boubou Hama** served until 1974 as its director general. In 1984 the BDRN had a capitalization of 2.5 billion **CFA francs** (compared to 450 million in 1961). With **parastatal** and state bodies in the majority, the BDRN was until 1978 the only public bank in the country. Controlled by the state, it was as much an economic as a political instrument, and it was notably used by the government to spur business activities in the regions of Niger which lacked a substantial business environment in the precolonial and colonial periods—chiefly the **Zarma-Songhay** west and the **Tuareg-Arab** north. Suffering from the illiquidity of the **parastatal sector** to which most of its loans had been made, in 1989 the bank was rescued from bankruptcy with new state and external funds. At the time it had 44 billion CFA francs of unpaid debts. Its liabilities proved too important, however, and the fiscal crisis of the state too unremitting for further rescue packages. In August 1990, its more viable assets were stripped off to establish the private **Société Nigérienne de Banque** (SONIBANK) bank, again with participation from the Société Tunisienne de Banque, but with much less ambitious objectives and much stricter rules of operation. The collapsing BDRN was written off the following month.

BAOUA, SOULEY (1922–). Trained as a nurse, Baoua served in several Nigerien localities in 1940–1950 and was elected **Mouvement Socialiste Africain** (MSA) territorial councilor for **Maradi** in 1957. After the assembly was dissolved through maneuvers from the **Parti Progressiste Nigérien** (PPN-RDA) and Sawaba was outlawed, Baoua attempted reinstating the party, was fined and then pardoned in 1960. He left Niger in 1963 in a self-imposed exile following Sawaba's proscription, briefly lived in East Germany, and returned to his home area of **Gaya** where he led several subversive armed actions against the Nigerien government. In 1965, he was sentenced to death in absentia and fled to Lagos, in **Nigeria**, where he was eventually arrested and repatriated to Niger. The death sentence against him was not executed, however, and was instead converted to 20 years' imprisonment. Baoua was released from jail upon **Seyni Kountché**'s coup d'état and returned to his professional occupation as a nurse. He retired in 1989.

BARÉ MAÏNASSARA, IBRAHIM (1949–1999). Born in **Dogondoutchi** in the **Hausa Arewa** region, Baré Maïnassara led a successful career in Niger's military and was appointed Army chief of staff by President **Mahaman Ousmane** in 1995. The next year, he toppled Ousmane (27 January 1996) as the country was caught up in a political crisis that resulted from Ousmane's refusal to cooperate with the government headed by a rival party and prime minister, **Hama Amadou**. Niger's politicians expected Baré Maïnassara to then restore civilian rule after a brief transition; instead, Baré Maïnassara created a political support group, the Comité de Soutien à Ibrahim Maïnassara Baré (COSIMBA), and proceeded to install several institutions that worked to change Niger's political regime. A presidentialist constitution replaced the French-style semipresidential constitution of the **Third Republic** in May 1996, and Baré Maïnassara emphasized its authoritarian streak when he stated in a televised speech that "*la recréation est terminée*" (the playtime is over). The COSIMBA became a **political party**, the Union National des Indépendants pour le Renouveau Démocratique (UNIRD), and campaigned for Baré Maïnassara's election as president.

At the **elections** held in July, Baré Maïnassara reshuffled the **Commission Electorale Nationale Indépendante** (CENI) as early announcements were pointing to his defeat at the polls, coming last of all candidates. Thereafter, he came in first and "won" in the first round (first-round victory being a very unlikely event in Niger's normal electoral process) with 52 percent of the vote. The UNIRD was subsequently replaced by a new party, the Rassemblement pour la Démocratie et le Progrès, which captured most of the seats at the **National Assembly**, as the major parties decided to boycott the legislative elections. United in umbrella movements, the major parties organized mass demonstrations against the new regime, and their leaders were twice put under house arrest. Baré Maïnassara's actions were condemned by the United States but supported by **France** and West Africa's then leading dictators, **Nigeria**'s Sani Abacha and Burkina Faso's Blaise Compaoré, as well as by **Libya**. More importantly, he struck several agreements with the International Monetary Fund and the World Bank for the **privatization** of nearly all of Niger's **parastatals** and a trimming of the **civil service**. As a reward, the World Bank led a funding boon by international development banks for a variety of Niger's reform policies.

By starting in earnest the implementation of structural adjustment, however, Baré Maïnassara further antagonized the trade unions, which were already opposed to his government on political grounds, and he trenchantly dismissed their incessant strikes by stating that they will help the government to spare money on their salary (not paid during strike periods). The nasty political and labor atmosphere nonetheless took a heavy toll on the country's stability, creating a situation of permanent political crisis, until the French were able to persuade Baré Maïnassara to reach for a compromise with the political parties on the occasion of the local elections of February 1999. A gentleman's agreement was brokered in 1998 to the effect of reconstituting the CENI on its former bases in view of the elections. Predictably—though it seemed to have taken the presidential camp by surprise—the outcome was a crushing electoral defeat for RDP, despite a few crude maneuvers (including attempts to seize ballot boxes by force in certain localities) from Baré Maïnassara's coterie.

The political tension, which had abated somewhat after the victory of the opposition parties, rose again very quickly when Baré Maïnassara pressured the **Cour Suprême**'s constitutional chamber into declaring flawed 80 percent of the voting. Incensed, the political class fell back on radical demands, clamoring for the president's immediate resignation and even calling the people to arms. When Baré Maïnassara was toppled on 9 April 1999, just two days after the Supreme Court's ruling, the relief was general, though tainted by the fact that the coup had led to the brutal killing of the overthrown ruler at

Niamey's military airport. Baré Maïnassara was the only target of the coup, and his government remained in office as an interim government, with Prime Minister **Ibrahim Hassane Mayaki** famously announcing Baré Maïnassara's death by the understatement that he had been a victim of an *"accident malheureux"* (unfortunate accident). Under the aegis of the leading coup-maker, Major **Daouda Mallam Wanké**, a new constitution was drafted during a short transition. It included a provision granting general amnesty for all collateral damage in the coups of 1996 and 1999, though the intention was obviously to protect Baré Maïnassara's killers. The provision thus became one of the main fighting points of the RDP but was never removed.

BARKA ALAFOU (?–1876). Important **Toubou** chief of the Kecherda clan who, allied with the **Tuareg** of the Koutous, soundly defeated the Ouled Sliman **Arab** group in 1845. The latter, who had displaced the Toubou in Tibesti (now in Chad), had continually harassed neighboring regions and disrupted the *azalay* trade by attacks on the **Kaouar** oases. Barka Alafou died in a round of fighting that erupted in 1876.

BARKA, MALAM MAMANE (1958–). Born in Tesker in the desert of **Gouré** among the **Boudouma** community (nomadic fishers), though himself a **Toubou**, Barka paired a teacher's career with his vocation of musician. He was celebrated as a singer in the 1980s but is also well versed in the history and arts of Niger's traditional music. This led to his appointment first as director of the musical cultural center Centre de Formation et de Promotion Musicale (CFPM Taya) of **Niamey** (1997–2009), then as director of the Centre Culturel Oumarou Ganda in the same city (since 2009). He is adept at the typical Nigerien instruments of light percussion, air and cord, and is especially known as the last master of the *biram*, a harpsichord-like instrument anciently played by the Boudouma, who believed it to be protected by their spiritual ancestor, Kargila. *See also* DANCE AND MUSIC.

BARMOU. Small village north of **Tahoua** in **Ader**, and a rural **commune**, Barmou has Niger's biggest cattle market. The second biggest market is **Zinder**.

BARTH, HEINRICH (1821–1861). Famous German traveler into West Africa. Born in February 1821 and educated in the classics and linguistics, Barth toured North Africa from Tangier to Egypt between 1845 and 1847 and went up the Nile as far as Wadi Halfa, publishing accounts of his explorations. Following his return to Germany, he was invited by the British government (at the suggestion of expedition leader James Richardson) to join the forthcoming expedition of European exploration into West Central Africa, also called Central Sudan. The expedition started from Tripoli in 1850. After Richardson's death in 1851, Barth assumed leadership, reaching the capital of the **Bornu Empire** in April 1851. He later mounted expeditions to neighboring areas, including **Aïr** and **Zinder**, returning to England in 1855. In 1857–1858, he published a five-volume account of his travels on the regions he visited. The wealth of data provided by Barth, including detailed linguistic studies, made him the greatest of the 19th-century explorers of Central Sudan. In April 1990 the German government announced that it would further honor Barth by donating 18.89 million **CFA francs** to construct a German pavilion in the Zinder museum as homage to Barth. The museum specializes in the colonial history of Niger.

BATTLE OF TONDIBI. See TONDIBI, BATTLE OF.

BAWA JAN GWARZO DAN BABARI (r. 1777–1795). King of **Gobir**, son of King **Babari dan Uban Iche** (r. 1742–1770). He succeeded his brother, King Dan Gude dan Babari, who died fighting **Tuareg** invaders. Bawa vigorously strengthened Gobir's defenses and presided over the kingdom's apogee, as it emerged as the most powerful of the **Hausa** states of the late 18th century. His nickname, Jan Gwarzo (also spelled Jangorzo in Niger), literally means (in Hausa) "the Red Dauntless," a testament to his energetic leadership. Bawa Jan Gwarzo had welcomed the establishment of the **Fulani** preacher **Usman dan Fodio** in the village of Degel, on Gobir territory, but soon found reasons to regret it, as dan Fodio started to attack his tax policy and even more radically, the principles of his government, on the basis of **Islam**. While under his rule, dan Fodio and his companions never appeared quite as threatening as they really were, but Bawa's successors had to face the mounting peril until a full blown jihad dislocated the kingdom and killed his nephew King **Yunfa** within only 13 years of his own death, in 1808.

BAYARD, MARIAMA GAMATIE (1958–). Born in **Maradi**, Mariama Gamatié, better known as Madame Bayard, earned her high school degree in 1976 at **Niamey**'s high school Lycée Kassaï (named after an iconic **Songhay** woman leader, Kassaï, sister of 15th-century emperor **Sonni Ali Ber**) and went on to study political and social **economics** at the University of Montpellier (**France**). After obtaining a degree in that discipline in 1979, she studied sociology at the University Paul Valéry of Montpellier for a master's (1980) and eventually worked on a doctorate in international relations at Cameroon's Institute for International Relations.

Bayard returned to Niger in time to become a leading force in the Nigerien **women**'s movement. As **democratization** picked up pace in the early 1990s, she founded, with a group of women jurists, the **Rassemblement Démocratique des Femmes Nigériennes** (RDFN), a feminist association that was instrumental in the organization of the 13 May 1991 demonstration which forced the organizing commission of the **Conférence Nationale** to guarantee women's participation in the assembly. She was subsequently appointed president of the Rural Development Commission of the Conférence Nationale.

In 1997, and despite her militant commitment to democracy, she became part of a government set up by **Ibrahim Baré Maïnassara**, who had toppled President **Mahaman Ousmane** in 1996 and had grossly manipulated the ensuing presidential election to ensure that he remained in power. Bayard was given the Ministry for Culture and Communication, and her tenure was marked by the organization of a national festival of Nigerien traditional **dance and music** held in **Zinder**, and for which thankful Nigerien artists bestowed on her the title *Marraine des Arts du Niger* (Godmother of the Arts of Niger). She also presided over the introduction of mobile telephones in the country and continued her feminist activities through the establishment of the nongovernmental organization Femme et Famille pour l'Auto-Promotion des Femmes.

In 2003, after a stint in conflict resolution organizations in Niger, she undertook a career as an international official in the United Nations and was posted to conflict resolution secretariats in Guinea Bissau (2003–2005), Côte d'Ivoire (2005–2007), Burundi (2007–2008), and Dakar in Senegal (2008), before returning to the cultural activities fold at UNESCO in Paris.

In 2009, Bayard left her position in Paris and returned to Niger to fight against President **Mamadou Tandja**'s overthrowing of the **Fifth Republic**. She was famously beaten during a demonstration in October 2009, which led to a hospitalization. She emerged from the adventure unrepentant, and after the eventual toppling of Tandja, she launched, in her hometown of Maradi, a campaign to become president of Niger as an independent candidate. Bayard never stood a chance of winning the position, but her score as the last of 10 candidates, with only 0.38 percent of the vote—even below previously unknown male newcomers on Niger's political stage—shows that women still have a long way to go to change Nigerien perceptions of female leadership. *See also* WOMEN.

BAYERÉ, MOUSSA (Major) (1936–1976). Key conspirator in the **15 March 1976 attempted coup d'état**. Born in **Filingué** on 7 February 1936, Bayeré was, during the **Hamani Diori** era, director of materials and housing on secondment from the army. Following the 1974 coup, Bayeré, a captain, was integrated into the cabinet as minister of public works, transport, and urban affairs. On 30 November 1974, he was reshuffled to head the Ministry of Rural **Economy**. He was dropped from the cabinet on 21 February 1976, shortly before the attempted putsch in which he was the driving force. When arrested, he had on his body three kilograms of amulets and charms to help him in his assault. Blinded by utter hatred of President **Seyni Kountché**, Bayeré's motives in the conspiracy were purely personal. The other conspirators wished power; he desired solely Kountché's death. In his trial he reiterated his belief that Kountché was the devil incarnate. Sentenced to death for his role in the attempted coup, Bayeré was executed on 21 April 1976.

BAZEYE, FATIMATA SALIFOU (1954–). A jurist, born in **Zinder** and trained in **France** at the École Nationale de la Magistrature, better known as Madame Bazeye. Upon returning to Niger, she rapidly rose in the ranks of the judgeship to a prominent position at the **Cour Suprême**. There, in 2005, she became famous for resisting pressures from the government of Prime Minister **Hama Amadou** to transfer magistrates who were on strike. She was subsequently nominated by the judgeship to one of the seats of the **Cour Constitutionnelle** reserved for jurists and was accepted by the government in 2007, despite her earlier obstructions. The court immediately elected her its president, which placed Bazeye in the fateful position of confronting President **Mamadou Tandja**'s maneuvers against the **Fifth Republic**'s constitution in 2009. Firmly opposed to the project, Madame Bazeye led the court in two unanimous decisions against Tandja's move. The first decision, on 8 May 2009, was nonbinding and responded to a **National Assembly** application made in the process of forming a parliamentary high treason motion against the president, which prompted the latter to dismiss the National Assembly. The second one, on 12 June 2009, was a binding decision, for which the president vainly pressured the court to recant. When eventually Tandja extraconstitutionally dismissed the court, the notion that he had thus made a constitutional coup d'état crucially eroded the legal legitimacy of his power.

After the toppling of Tandja in February 2010, the military **Conseil Suprême pour la Restauration de la Démocratie** (CSRD) appointed Bazeye head of the Constitutional Council, a consultative constitutional court in charge of providing a legal framework to the transition back to democratic governance.

BAZOUM, MOHAMED (1960–). Bazoum is a philosophy teacher hailing from the **Arab** community of Tesker, not very far from **Zinder** and **Diffa**. After primary and secondary **education** in Tesker, **Maïné-Soroa**, **Gouré**, and Zinder, he studied philosophy up to the predoctoral DEA degree (Advanced

Studies Diploma) at the University Cheikh Anta Diop of Dakar (1982–1984). He then taught philosophy in high schools in **Tahoua** and **Maradi** while rising to prominence in the teacher's union Syndicat National des Enseignants du Niger (SNEN) and in the **Union des Syndicats des Travailleurs du Niger** (USTN), in which he became the coordinator for Maradi (1989–1991). He took part in the **Conférence Nationale** as a representative of the USTN, and after a stint as state secretary at the Ministry of Foreign Affairs in the transition government (1991–1993), he was elected **Parti Nigérien pour la Démocratie et le Socialisme** (PNDS Tarayya) deputy for Tesker in 1993. As vice-president of a major party (PNDS Tarayya), Bazoum became a well-known politician in Niger and was appointed foreign affairs minister when his party came to power in 1995. This was ended by the **coup d'état of January 1996** and its aftermath of repression and struggle against **Ibrahim Baré Maïnassara**'s attempt at restoring authoritarian government in the country.

Maïnassara's was eventually toppled and killed in 1999, and at the **elections** organized shortly thereafter, Bazoum secured a seat at the **National Assembly**. There, he worked in the ranks of the opposition to undermine the government of the **Mouvement National pour la Société de Développement**'s (MNSD Nassara) prime minister **Hama Amadou**. During the **Tazartché** political crisis triggered by President Mamadou Tandja's overthrowing of Niger's **Fifth Republic** constitution, Bazoum was very active in a coalition of parties aiming at restoring constitutional order in the country, the **Coordination des Forces Démocratiques pour la République** (CFDR). After the toppling of Tandja in February 2010, Bazoum went on the campaign trail for PNDS, and his party emerged victorious in both the legislative and presidential elections held January–March 2011. Bazoum was subsequently appointed minister of foreign affairs.

BEIDARI, MAMADOU (Lieutenant Colonel). Former minister of labor and the **civil service**, President **Ali Saibou**'s right-hand man, and for a long time pillar of the military regime. His reputation of strict technocratic efficiency, acquired as quartermaster general of the **armed forces**, impelled President **Seyni Kountché** to bring him into the cabinet to streamline the **parastatal sector**, when Niger endeavored to implement its first structural adjustment program. He was appointed, in August 1984, minister in charge of the supervision of public enterprises, parastatal and mixed-economy companies. From that position, Beïdari was moved to the Ministry for the Civil Service and Labor with the mission to implement the government-sponsored early retirement program that led to a first trimming of the civil service in the late 1980s. In November 1987, crowning a career of managerial reforms, he was finally appointed finance minister, where his measures considerably irritated Niger's business class. He was removed a year later, in November 1988, lingered in the cabinet as a minister without portfolio, before being dropped into the diplomatic service in May 1989, with a posting as ambassador in Cameroon. He returned to Niger in 1992 to live in retirement.

BEIDOU, BAGNA (Colonel). A key member of the ruling centers of the *régime d'exception* and of the **Second Republic**. At the **Conférence Nationale**, in 1991, he was indicted for his responsibility in the execution of Major **Sani Souna Siddo**, leader of an attempted coup in 1976, as well as for his role in the repression of the **Tuareg** civilian population in the area of **Tchintabaraden** in 1989. Beidou was arrested owing to the climate of virtuous indignations in which the Conférence Nationale basked, but a ruling of the **Cour Suprême** ordered his release in April 1992.

BELLA. Name, in **Zarma** (or **Songhay**) of the lowest caste of the **Tuareg**, the slaves called *Ikelan* in **Tamashaq**. The Bella are perceived, by the **Zarma-Songhay**, as Black Tuareg plying the trade of wood and garden produce sellers. The Bella originate in captured or enslaved black minorities—who had stayed in the **Aïr** after the arrival of the Berber Tuareg in the 13th century—and were historically given the task of tending their overlords' gardens when the latter left the oases in their nomadic treks. Most Bella are no longer actual slaves, but slavery—always of dark-skinned Tuareg—is still illegally practiced in the Tuareg society, triggering the recent emergence of the identity of Black Tuareg, to which the Bella belong. The Zarma-Songhay call the Berber, or Red Tuareg, *Surgu*.

BENIN–NIGER BOUNDARY DISPUTE. A boundary dispute which erupted in December 1963 and was put to rest only in the early 2000s. Involving the question of ownership of the **Niger River** island of Lété (between **Gaya** and Malanville) as well as 24 other smaller islands, the crisis resulted in the dispatch of troops by Niger and Dahomey (older name of Benin) to the area and the sealing of the international border. Other by-products of the clash were the disruption of the **Opération Hirondelle** import/export scheme and the expulsion of Dahomeans working in Niger. The conflict, dormant for quite some years, had other causes: the takeover by the military in Dahomey and the ensuing toppling of President **Hamani Diori**'s good friend, President Hubert Maga. There was a tentative resolution of the dispute in 1965, under the aegis of Côte d'Ivoire's president, Felix Houphouët-Boigny, to the relative dissatisfaction of both parties. The case was eventually revived in the 1990s as Benin claimed ownership of all 25 islands, with the symbolic prize being the island of Lété. This time, the two states finally posted the case to the International Court of Justice (ICJ) of The Hague in July 2005, agreeing to abide by its decisions with no further appeal. The ICJ found that 16 islands (including Lété) were Nigerien and 9 islands were Benin territory. The decision has ended the dispute.

BERI BERI. Name by which the **Kanuri** of East Niger are popularly known in Niger.

BILMA. *Département* encompassing 260,000 sq km and a total population of 14,000 people, mostly **Toubou**, the headquarters of which is the village of the same name, which has a population of 2,300. The most important settlement in the **Ténéré** desert, Bilma is also the smallest *départément* headquarters of the country. The village has extensive natron salt pans (called *balma* by the **Hausa**) and is important because of the 500 to 800 tons it exports annually. Bilma is actually the principal and biggest oasis of 10 such salt-pan sites in the **Kaouar** and also has large date plantations and plentiful water. Found on the main historic Fezzan–Tibesti–Bornu route, Bilma (as also Fachi) has for a long time been a **Kanuri**-populated island in the desert. Natron extraction plummeted in the modern era, though until the **Tuareg** rebellion of the 1990s it was still the principal economic activity of the population. In 1907, 15,000 camels came to Bilma to transport some 1,600 tons of salt, bringing into the community meat and cereals. By 1929 only 9,094 camels were involved in the *azalay* that evacuated 727 tons of salt. The natron itself is of very poor quality, especially compared to that of Amadror in the north, but is still widely used for human and animal consumption. Trade in natron declined in profitability in the 1970s due to cheap imports from **Nigeria** and the cost of the long and hazardous Ténéré crossing.

Half a kilometer from Bilma is **Balabili**, an old quarter and now a venerated graveyard marking the spot where Bilma's population was massacred in the 18th century by **Arab** marauders from Ouadai, Chad. Separated from **Agadez** and the **Aïr** massif by the Ténéré, Bilma is one of the most remote spots in the world. Surrounded by sand dunes, it has been used as a natural prison. In the 19th century, Bilma was very much a slave town, with the masters living in Kalala near the salt pits themselves, which was raided so frequently that the residents finally moved in within Bilma's walls. The salt pans are 2 km northwest of the town and are the scene of hectic activity when the *azalay* season arrives. The pans are divided into concessions held by various **ethnic groups**. Until the arrival of the Tuareg in the area, the Kanuri (the original inhabitants of Kaouar) held most of the plots. With the Tuareg domination of the trade established, other groups have been given concessions and until today most have a plot, though a few powerful families own the biggest and best.

BIRNI. In **Hausa**, "city." The plural is *birane*. The term signifies a walled city, and more specifically designates the moat-like ditch which surrounds the wall. Historically, most *birane* were capital of the Hausa city-states of the 14th–19th centuries, and hence the contemporary meaning of big city.

BIRNIN ADER. Former capital of **Ader** after its 18th-century conquest by **Aggaba**, who set up his administration in there but was later (around 1738) forced to relocate due to the incessant assaults against it by various groups in the area. At the time (after Aggaba's death), **Illela** was founded as the new capital.

BIRNIN LALLE. For two centuries the capital of the Gobirawa before the relocation to **Alkalawa**. The name, in **Hausa**, means Welcome City. *See also* GOBIR.

BIRNI N'GAOURÉ. Small town of 10,530 people, midway between **Niamey** and **Dosso**, on the **Route de l'Unité**. Situated in the **Dallol Bosso**, its population is mostly **Zarma** and **Songhay**. It is the seat of the *département* of the **Boboye**, which has a population of 265,000 people.

BIRNI-N'KONNI. Important border town (with **Nigeria**) of 57,000, and *département* with a population of 364,000 in the region of **Tahoua**. Birni-N'Konni is 422 km east of **Niamey** and 95 km north of Sokoto in Nigeria. Its big Wednesday market, sitting close to the Nigerian border, is a major commercial magnet for the entire area. The surrounding region is a bastion of **Hausa** animism in Niger, with the principal center being Massalata in the vicinity of Birni-N'Konni. A reunion of traditional fetishists can bring thousands of participants into Birni-N'Konni, as it indeed does from time to time.

The town was crushed in battles during the **Fulani** Sokoto jihad in the early 19th century and was later brutally sacked by the Voulet-Chanoine mission. It is now a major market town, connecting Nigerien and Nigerian trades through its Nigerian border equivalent, Illela, just 18 km to the south. *See also* AOURA; ARNA; MISSION AFRIQUE CENTRALE-TCHAD.

BOBOYE. Zarma name for the **Dallol Bosso** in the **Dosso** region. It is also a *département*, headquartered in **Birni-n-Gaouré**.

BOGU. Working songs aimed at giving rhythm to cultivators in the fields, from the **Zarma** term for the collective labor obligation a farmer could invoke by declaring a *bogu* on his plot of land.

BOKAYE. **Hausa** plural for *boka*. *Bokaye* are traditional healers, referred to by diviners (*madiba*), who also sell traditional medicines, treatments, amulets, aphrodisiacs, and sundry other items.

BONKANO. *See* OUMAROU, AMADOU.

BORI. Type of spirit ritual that is prevalent in native **religions** in many parts of Africa, including throughout Niger, where another one, very close to the Bori, is the **Holley** ritual of the **Zarma-Songhay**. Bori ritual is integral to the **Hausa Arna** pantheons, which is now actively practiced especially in the areas of **Maradi, Dogondoutchi, Birni-N'Konni**, and among the Maguzawa in northern **Nigeria**. It is an appropriation ritual of the powers of spirits in the pre-Islamic Hausa pantheon, the *iskoki* (plural of *iska*, which means, literally, *wind*) and the **Hauka** (spirits of a form of ritual which merged into the Bori and Holley rituals only after the 1940s). There are several kinds of *iskoki*, male and female; red, white, and black; with characteristics derived from known human individuals from the remote past as well as from more contemporary periods. Thus, some Bori spirits derive their character from a truck driver, a **Zarma** blacksmith, a French colonial military officer, even a Muslim cleric. The ritual, which is under certain circumstances part of an initiation ceremony and under other circumstances part of a healing ceremony, consists in the spirit taking possession, "mounting" the medium, who thus becomes his or her "horse," and performs an exhausting and sometime, hazardous *trance danse*.

Historically, Bori mediums have developed into an organization of priests, most of whom are in fact priestesses, headed in the Maradi area by the *Iya* (for the Katsinawa of Maradi proper) and the *Inna* (for the Gobirawa of the surrounding region) and recruited among categories of **women** who are morally but not socially marginalized in the Islamized Hausa context: runaway girls, multiple times divorced, or prostitutes, chiefly of the popular classes. Many women used to join, however, to cure an illness or infertility.

In an older context, Bori women were an important center of social influence, as *magajiya*, and they indeed formed the backbone of the Hausa chapters of the **Union des Femmes du Niger**, the earliest national women's association of Niger. In the area of Dogondoutchi, men tend to lead the priesthood.

With the advance of **Islam**, Bori has become far less central to Hausa culture in Niger than it used to be. It is now more present in the countryside, though it has not been quite blotted out from the urban centers. In contemporary common Hausa, the words associated to it often describe a state of dementia. Thus, the modern Hausa word for madness is *hauka*, from a category of Bori spirits which appeared in the early 20th century.

Aspects of Bori ritual and of the Hausa pantheon are very similar to old animist and communal religions the world over, but they are most closely related to the Holley of the Zarma-Songhay from which many of their traits derive, and they have spread into North Africa as a result of the trans-Saharan slave trading of past centuries.

BORNU EMPIRE. One of the most powerful and longest lasting Sudanic states in Africa. Originally one of several small trading principalities in the ninth century in Kanem (Chad), in the 12th century the kingdom began to expand and to control major east–west and north–south trade routes, prospering in the process. A major split among the federated clans in the middle of the 13th century resulted in the expulsion of the ruling Sefuwa dynasty to Bornu, west of **Lake Chad**. There it rapidly expanded and became one of the most powerful states in the entire region. The empire's capital was at Birni Ngazargama (founded in 1484) and later (in 1815) in Kukawa. Bornu conquered Kanem at the beginning of the 16th century and exacted tribute over a wide-ranging number of states, including **Aïr**, **Damagaram**, Kano, **Katsina**, and **Kaouar**. In the 17th and 18th centuries, the empire's control began to crumble in the peripheral areas, and in the 19th century the **Fulani** of the Sokoto Empire detached from it most of its Hausa dominions. The empire fell in 1893 to **Rabah,** who had just started to organize his rule there when he was overran by the combined assaults of the British and the French (the latter defeating and killing him at Kousseri in 1900). The richer, southern parts of the empire were incorporated in the British colony of **Nigeria**, while Chad and Niger inherited its desert north, including (for Niger), much of the region of **Diffa** and the *département* of Bilma.

BORORO. *See* WOODABE.

BORREY, FRANCIS (1904–1976). Colonial administrator, surgeon, and early political leader in Niger. Born in Besançon, **France**, on 8 April 1904, and a physician and surgeon by profession, Borrey was director-general of the Centre d'Études et d'Information des Problèmes Urbains dans les Zones Arides (PROHUZA). In 1946 he entered the political sphere when he competed in the French National Assembly **elections** from Niger and placed second after **Hamani Diori**. Originally a cofounder of the **Parti Progressiste Nigérien** (PPN-RDA), Borrey later became a prominent leader of the Union Nigérienne des Indépendants et Sympathisants (UNIS) party and dominated its activities until 1955, when the party split over his insistence that it affiliate with the Indépendants d'Outre-Mer (IOM) parliamentary group. Since the bulk of the membership followed the dissidents led by Amadou Mayaki and **Zarmakoy Issoufou Seydou**, his faction fared poorly in the subsequent elections and eventually changed its name to the Forces Démocratiques Nigériennes (FDN). Borrey served as IOM councilor from Niger at the French National Assembly and president of its Social Affairs Committee (1947–1953). In 1952 he was the IOM assembly faction vice-president and also served as future Côte d'Ivoire's president Houphouët-Boigny's technical councilor, as well as minister of **health** in the French government of 1959. A former technical councilor also in Hamani Diori's 1959 cabinet (and just prior to that, district officer in **Zinder**), Borrey was appointed Niger's representative to **France**'s Social and Economic Council and Niger's deputy delegate to United Nations Educational, Scientific and Cultural Organization (UNESCO). After Niger's independence, Borrey returned to France and served as representative of French Polynesia at the Social and Economic Council (1964–1966), playing a role in the administration of the New Hebrides, and he was later integrated into the French cabinet first as minister of agriculture, then of national education.

BOUBACAR, TOUMBA (Colonel). Former chief of staff of the Niger **armed forces**. Boubacar, a career soldier, undertook prompt and loyal action in October 1983, defusing the attempted coup of Lieutenant **Amadou Oumarou**, and rescuing then-colonel **Ali Saibou**, who had been captured by the plotters. In September 1985, Boubacar was brought into **Seyni Kountché**'s cabinet as minister of youth and sports. Boubacar, also vice-president of the **Conseil National de Développement** (CND), was brought into this key ministry (which controlled the *samariya*) after administrative inquiries into general mismanagement under its previous minister. He was promoted within the armed forces by Kountché to deputy chief of staff in 1984, and by General Saibou to succeed him as chief of staff when he assumed the presidency in 1987. In August 1991, Boubacar showed bitter irritation at what he took to be the **Conférence Nationale**'s attempt at humiliating the armed forces, chiefly over the handling of the growing **Tuareg** unrest in the north. He was replaced the following month as army chief of staff by Major Mazou Issa.

BOUBE, IDRISSA (1938–1976). Former director of the Sûreté Nationale, which in March 1976 joined in the attempted coup of Major **Moussa Bayeré**. Prior to the attempt, Boubé had been the Sûreté's deputy head (1967–1973) and its head until shortly before the **Kountché** takeover. His support for the

Bayeré conspiracy cost Boubé his life; sentenced to death in court martial, he was executed in April 1976.

BOUBON. Small fishing village on the **Niger River** some 23 km from **Niamey** on the road to **Tillabéri**. It is a very popular weekend congregation point for the capital's Western expatriate community.

BOUBOU, HAMA. *See* HAMA, BOUBOU.

BOUDOUMA. A population of fishermen, living on the islands of the **Lake Chad**, and known by this Kanembou word which means "those who live near the *douma*" (the *douma* being a tall water grass). The names with which they designate themselves are Yetena, Yedina, and Worwei. They live in close connection with the **Kanuri**, and most of them reside in Chad. There are smaller populations of Boudouma in the Nigerian and Cameroonian parts of the lake.

BOUKARY, SANI MALAM CHAIBOU (1958–). Best known as Zilly, he is a teacher turned businessman who held the position of personal assistant to Prime Minister **Hamid Algabit** in 1983–1987. He took part in the **Conférence Nationale** as representative for the Chamsiya party before moving into the **Convention Démocratique et Sociale** (CDS Rahama), where he was appointed head of propaganda in the political bureau of the party. He was elected CDS deputy for **Zinder** in 1993 and 1995. After the **coup in 1996**, he opportunistically moved closer to **Baré Maïnassara**, the man who removed his party leader, **Mahaman Ousmane**, from the presidency, and was appointed public relations secretary of Baré's party, the **Rassemblement pour la Démocratie et le Progrès** (RDP Jama'a). After the assassination of Baré Maïnassara in April 1999, Zilly remained one of the heavyweights of the RDP thanks to his influence on electors in Zinder, and he polled his way back into the **National Assembly** at the first legislative **elections** of the **Fifth Republic**, in November 1999. He eventually left the party in 2010, after the latter again unsuccessfully bet on yet another authoritarian restoration attempt (the **Mamadou Tandja** constitutional coup of late 2009).

BOUKARY, WASSALKE. Senior civil administrator and former minister of finance. A former treasurer-general of Niger, Boukary was brought in 1988 into Prime Minister **Hamid Algabid**'s staff as director of the prime minister's office and secretary of state in charge of the budget. A few months later, in November 1989, he was appointed minister of finance. He left the cabinet in January 1991, rejoining the treasurer general's office. During the 1990s he became one of the grandees of the **Mouvement National pour la Société de Développement** (MNSD Nassara), maintaining a hold on his fief of Bankill-aré in the Gorouol (**Songhay** country). He was appointed minister for rural development in 2002, eventually becoming a staunch supporter of President **Mamadou Tandja** in the rift that divided MNSD as Tandja's projects to eliminate Prime Minister **Hama Amadou** matured. In 2009, Tandja rewarded his support with an appointment as the executive secretary of the busy and important market regulation agency, the Autorité de Régulation des Marchés Publics (ARMP). After Tandja was toppled in February 2010, Boukary was duly removed from his post in June of the same year, and in response, he attacked the state of Niger for abusive dismissal. However, the state inspectors appointed by the **Conseil Suprême pour la Restauration de la Démocratie** (CSRD) investigated him and determined that he had diverted some of his agency's resources to fund Tandja's project, and the judicial wrangle took a new twist.

BOUREIMA, DOULAYE (1973–). The dominant voice on **Niamey**'s music stage in the 2000s, this **Songhay** language singer born in Sirfi Koyre, near **Tera**, is better known as Mali Yaro in Niger. After leaving school in 1987 for *la débrouille* (getting by) in Niamey, he soon became a minor celebrity entertainer in the city's nightlife in the late 1990s, using the characteristic Songhay *goumbé* instruments and rhythms. He founded his band, the Goumbé Star, in 1995. In the 2000s, Mali Yaro became the most prolific musician in the country, issuing five albums between 2000 and 2010. He mixes the modernization of traditional Songhay and **Zarma** language songs to the updating of national hits from the 1970s and 1980s and more original creations conveying popular messages on social problems or the "culture of peace" (a theme Mali Yaro shares with the couturier **Seidnaly Sidahmed**). This approach proved very successful, as Mali Yaro quickly grew into the best name in musical entertainment for all kinds of events (marriages and baptisms, advertisement, political functions, concerts), touring also the Nigerien diaspora within West Africa and in such faraway places as the United States and Belgium. Along with the slightly older but very similar (in terms of career arc) singer **Yacouba Moumouni**, Mali Yaro belongs to the small coterie of Nigerien musicians savvy in career building. *See also* DANCE AND MUSIC.

BOUREIMA, MALIKI (Captain). Commander of the unit involved in the reprisals against **Tuareg** insurgents after the 1990 **Tchintabaraden** assault. Boureima was arrested in October 1991 for his role in the use of force on civilian Tuareg populations, which the **armed forces** at the time suspected of assisting attackers. Army mutineers in February 1992 called for him to be released (which he ultimately was), pointing out that he was simply obeying orders. His release was also supported by the new chief of staff in order to boost the morale of Nigerien forces in the north, though it led to the resignation of the minister of trade, Mohamed Moussa, then negotiating with the Tuareg rebel leaders, and himself a Tuareg.

BOUREIMA, MOUMOUNI (General) (1952–). Better known as Tchanga in Niger, from the **Zarma-Songhay** subethnicity of the **Tyenga** of the area of **Gaya**, where he was born. After studying up to the high school degree, he received military training at Cherchell (Algeria, 1976) and Angers (**France**, 1978–1979), as well as in Germany (1989–1991). He had started his military career in 1974, notably heading the **armed forces** instruction center at **Tondibia** and being posted in various military stations throughout the country. In 1992, he took up the important position of commander of defense for zone one—that is to say, of all military commands in **Niamey**. After the **coup d'état of 1996**, he was appointed to the **Conseil de Salut National**, the military executive organ created to rule over the transition to the restoration of civilian government. He moved from there to the office of *préfet-président* of the Communauté Urbaine of Niamey.

In April 1999, Boureima supported the coup d'état that removed **Ibrahim Baré Maïnassara** from power and became a member of the transitional military executive organ, the **Conseil de Réconciliation Nationale**. He was also made army chief of staff (July 1999) and minister of the interior of the interim government set up for the duration of the nine-month period of restoration of civilian government.

Extremely popular and influential with the armed forces, Tchanga kept his chief of staff position throughout the **Fifth Republic**, right up to the coup d'état of February 2010. When discontent with **Mamadou Tandja**'s attempt to install an authoritarian regime in 2009 led to a political crisis, Tchanga was widely believed to be part of a caste of enriched military who lent their support to the ploy. However, after the fall of Tandja, whom he did nothing to defend, he unreservedly participated in the army consensus that defined the provisional rule of the **Conseil Suprême pour la Restauration de la Démocratie** (CSRD). Thus, Tchanga's career offers a shortcut vision of the institutional operation of the Nigerien armed forces, and notably of their repeated interventions in the political arena, showing great adaptability, cohesion, and will to relinquish power.

BOUZA. *Département* in the region of **Tahoua** with a population of 280,000 and headquarters in the small town of the same name. The latter is some 50 km north of **Madaoua** on the Madaoua–Tahoua road. Its population is 8,400.

The **economy** of the region is chiefly pastoral (**Fulani** and **Tuareg**), though the bulk of the population is made up of **Hausa** agriculturalists.

BOUZOU. *See* BUZU.

BOUZOU DAN ZAMBADI (1911–2004). Elhadj Mahaman Sani Bouzou dan Zambadi has been the longest reigning *sarki* (monarch) of Katsina in **Maradi**. He succeeded his brother **Dan Baskoré dan Kouré** in 1947 and remained on the throne until his death in 2004, with a brief crisis period when he was temporarily revoked by the president of the council **Djibo Bakary** in 1958, when customary chiefs incurred the latter's hostility for their support for **France**'s neocolonial agenda. Bouzou dan Zambadi became a faithful servant of Niger's successive regimes, presiding over the rise of Maradi to the position of "economic capital" and getting himself involved in business and commercial **agriculture**. Along the years, he grew to become representative of the "old chiefs" class, inherited from the **Colonie du Niger**: generally illiterate, authoritarian, and traditionalist. He died childless and was succeeded by another member of the house of Korau, **Maremawa Ali Zaki**. *See also* NORTHERN KATSINA.

BRAH, MAHAMANE. Brah joined the **Seyni Kountché** cabinet in September 1979 as minister of rural development. He was shifted in February 1981 to head the Ministry of Planning, and in July 1983 again, this time to head the Ministry of Posts and Communications. He was dropped from the cabinet in November 1983 to be, a few months later, appointed the executive secretary-general of the regional grouping the Comité Inter-États de Lutte contre la Sécheresse au **Sahel** (CILSS, the Inter-State Committee for the Combat of **Drought** in the Sahel). Brah, together with **Idé Oumarou** (secretary-general of the Organization of African Unity) and **Hamid Algabit** (secretary-general of the Organization of the Islamic Conference), was thus one of the diplomatic successes of the *régime d'exception*, and the most lasting one, since Brah still heads the CILSS today.

BRANIGER. *See* SOCIÉTÉ DES BRASSERIES ET BOISSONS GAZEUSES DU NIGER.

BRÉVIÉ, JULES (1880–1964). A colonial administrator, Brévié made most of his career in West Africa, starting as circle commander of Bamako in the French Sudan (now Mali) and becoming the first lieutenant-governor of Niger in 1922–1929. As such, he is often presented in Niger's official stories as the country's first ruler. He moved from **Niamey** to Dakar in 1930, where he was appointed general-governor of **Afrique Occidentale Française** (AOF), which gave him the opportunity of promoting his vision of a methodically scientific colonization. He notably founded the Institut Français d'Afrique Noire (Black Africa French Institute), now Institut Fondamental d'Afrique Noire (IFAN) in 1936. After a short tenure as governor of Indochina, Brévié accepted in 1942 the position of minister of the colonies and the overseas territory under the government of Pierre Laval, which was running France in collaboration with Nazi Germany. There, he tried to develop to the full his vision of scientific colonization, setting up an Office de la Recherche Scientifique Coloniale (Colonial Scientific Research Office). Upon the defeat of Germany in 1945, he was indicted as a member of France's collaborationist regime, losing his rank and retirement pension as a result. In Niger however, a street in Niamey's administrative quarter still bears his name.

BUDE N'DAJI. Major ritual celebrations in **Birni-N'Konni** and Massalata—*arna* centers of importance—which attract large delegations from various **Hausa** communities, including Kano, Zaria, and **Katsina**, as priests unite to offer ritual sacrifices to the **Doguwa** spirit and others.

BUREAU DE COORDINATION ET DE LIAISON (BCL). Secret police created by President **Seyni Kountché**, put on hold by President **Ali Saibou**, and dissolved in 1991. Its sinister reputation is borne out by the practice of torture and insidious surveillance, though it was certainly not as active as those that existed in many other African countries at the time.

BUZU. Equivalent, in **Hausa**, to the **Songhay Bella**. For further details, see entry for *Bella*. Hausa plural for Buzu is Bugaje.

C

CAISSE CENTRALE DE COOPÉRATION ECONOMIQUE. *See* AGENCE FRANÇAISE DE DÉVELOPPEMENT.

CAISSE DE PRETS AUX COLLECTIVITES TERRITORIALES (CPCT). Banking agency, 100 percent owned by public bodies, with 94 percent of the capital belonging to territorial collectivities. It was founded in 1970 with 1.4 billion **CFA francs** in capitalization. The CPCT is the leading banking agency for credit to regions, *départements*, and **communes**.

CAISSE DE STABILISATION DES PRIX DES PRODUITS DU NIGER (CSPPN). Price stabilization office for Niger's agricultural crops, the CSPPN guaranteed prices to farmers and ensured that no major variations develop from year to year. It was founded in 1960 and was liquidated in 2003, in the context of trade liberalization.

CAISSE NATIONALE DE CREDIT AGRICOLE (CNCA). Agricultural development was considered the mainstay of national economic development in Niger as in most of the newly independent African countries in the 1960s. Thus, in 1962, a first agricultural public financing scheme was set up with the Sociétés Rurales de Crédit et de Coopération (SRCC), state-funded units working in tandem with the **Union Nigérienne de Crédit et de Coopérative** (UNCC), the farmer's cooperative system established the same year. SRCC being deemed insufficiently ambitious, they were replaced with a more insti-tutionalized outfit in 1967, the CNCA. The mission of the CNCA—a credit institution endowed with financial autonomy with original capitalization of 67 million **CFA francs** (later raised to 650 million)—was to provide afford-able loans in the rural areas with the view of assisting the improvement of ag-ricultural, pastoral, and artisanal production. UNCC's member cooperatives prepared borrowing applications and, together with CNCA agents, organized funding for the purchase of approved inputs and collected the debt. CNCA focused its funding on the supply of fertilizers, the purchase of low-cost, low-technology agricultural machinery, and the marketing of agricultural produce. However, it gradually ran into financial jams, owing at first to high operational costs and poor repayment rates and then, as Niger's financial crisis grew in the 1980s, excessive financing of parastatal deficit. The final blow came when the international prices for rent crops fell drastically in the 1980s, with **groundnut** in particular becoming unprofitable, rendering peasants financially insolvent. By 1986, CNCA was plagued with payment arrears in the amount of 5 billion CFA francs and could no longer perform. It was scrapped the following year, and its disappearance deprived Niger's farmers of a lifeline access to credit which has started to be remedied only in 2011, with the creation of the Banque Agricole du Niger (BAGRI).

CAMARA, MAURICE (1922–). Born in Kissidougou, Guinea, of French and African parents, Camara was a *vétérinaire africain* (African veterinarian) posted to Niger by the colonial government. He was elected **Mouvement Socialiste Africain** (MSA) territorial councilor for **Birni-N'Konni** in 1957, and then French West Africa grand councilor the same year. He was expelled from Niger upon the dissolution of **Sawaba** in 1959.

CARAVAN ROUTES. Several major caravan routes cross Niger, both east to west and north to south. Of the former, the *azalay* route linking **Agadez** with **Kaouar** (including **Bilma** and Fachi) is still important and allows for the evacuation of Kaouar's natron, though competition from trucks has recently reduced the profitability for caravans, and the **Tuareg** rebellion in the 1990s has curtailed them severely. The classical western route linking In Gall and Teguidda-n'Tesemt with **Gao** is no longer of any importance, though in former centuries it was a major trade artery. The north–south routes have similarly ossified, though there are still caravans plying the routes from **Tahoua** through the **Aïr** massif to Algeria and **Libya**.

Prior to the colonial era, important caravan routes from the north, most passing via Agadez, terminated at **Zinder**, the capital of **Damagaram**, which benefited greatly from this fact. These routes, traversing both Damagaram and **Damergou**, gave rise to many caravan stops that flourished in the 17th through 19th centuries. The ancient Garamantian route (Tripoli–Fezzan–Bornu), which was the mainstay of Kanem and Bornu until the 19th century, also benefited towns now in Niger territory, since caravans needed to stop in Kaouar, and at times branched off westward. The collapse of the route in the 19th century (due to mounting insecurity caused by Tuareg raiders) led to a major shift in caravan routes to the east, resulting in a decline in many of the Niger centers along its southern end.

Historically, most of the caravan routes that crossed Nigerien territory had the purpose of linking Hausaland to the central sections of North Africa. The routes started therefore from the southern side in **Katsina**, Kano, and

Zinder and ended in Algiers, Tunis, Tripoli, and Benghasi. In the south, they interlinked to the central markets and several satellite markets, most of which are now in Niger territory: **Maradi, Tessaoua**, and **Gouré**, in particular. The routes from Hausaland would then unify prior to reaching Agadez, which functioned, in connection with Iferouane, as a hub from where the route would branch off westward to Algiers (through Tarrhou Haout and In Salah, now in Algeria) and eastward to Tunis, Tripoli, and Benghasi (through Ghat, Ghadames, and Mourzouk, now in Libya). Other routes used to link Agadez to the hub of Timbuktu (now in Mali) via In Gall, and major stopovers in the Algiers route included Tamanrasset and Touat. These routes tended to shift in accordance with the highly fractious politics of the Tuareg confederations, which occupied the crucial desert area between Agadez and Ghadames. When Tuareg—and at times **Toubou** and **Arab**—warfare and raiding made a segment of the route exceedingly insecure, it would shift to such an extent that prosperous stopovers would go downhill overnight or the nature of trade would change.

Thus, in the mid-19th century, when **Heinrich Barth** visited the Aïr, the basis of Agadez trade was millet, which clearly signified a major downturn tied to higher security risks. In good times, trade from the Hausaland included slaves, cloth, hide and skin, ostrich feathers (in great demand in Europe), ivory, and gold, though the latter in far lesser amounts than what used to be traded in the centers of the western Sudanic empires (Mali and **Songhay**). The Tripoli trade brought south mostly guns, horses, textiles, **Maria Theresa dollars**, and Ottoman **currency** as well as a variety of manufactured goods. The Zinder–Tripoli route was so profitable that important communities of merchants from Ghadames (an oasis south of Tripoli) established themselves all along it until the onset of the colonial era. Commercially, the Tripoli–Ghadames–Aïr–Zinder–Kano route (taking from 70 to 90 days to traverse) was the most important one in the 19th century. Even at the turn of the 20th century, large caravans used it. In August 1904, for example, 8,000 camels passed along this route. By the second decade of the 20th century, however, caravanning became increasingly unprofitable due to competitive prices of the same commodities arriving across the Atlantic and shipped north by rail, the decline of North Africa as a commercial powerhouse and more generally the large-scale reorganization of West African trade by colonial policy. Today only limited local trade and the *azalays* ply the desert routes.

CARTATÉGUY, MICHEL CHRISTIAN (1951–). Born in Hasparen (**France**) and a Roman Catholic priest in the African Missions Society since 1968, he was appointed auxiliary bishop of **Niamey** in 1999 and then bishop of Niamey (after the retirement of Bishop Guy Romano) in 2003. In 2007,

Niamey became an archbishopric. Under Archbishop Cartatéguy, the Catholic Church maintains its profile in Niger as a moderating Christian religious force (as opposed to Protestant denominations whose conversion missions often clash with orthodox Muslim groups), devoted chiefly to catering to its congregations and work in formal schooling (*Écoles mission*, prized, private, Catholic-run schools with a secular curriculum) and charity (notably through the organization Caritas Niger).

CASSITERITE. Tin dioxide, one of the principal minerals for the production of tin, found mostly in El Mecki mountains and in Tarroundji and Timia south of **Aïr**. The El Mecki deposits and sites produce fully 60 percent of Niger's output. Total production in 1960 was 76.8 tons; in 1971, 125.9 tons; and 38 tons in 1990. Production could be increased if a more automated system were adopted, at the cost of some 300 million **CFA francs**. The first explorations commenced right after World War II, and the ore was first discovered at Tarroundji. The Société Minière du Dahomey-Niger (SMDN), formed to exploit the concessions, encountered major difficulties, including water shortages and the problem of evacuating the ore to the coast. Nevertheless regular production commenced in 1950 with the entire output sold to a smelting firm in Northern **Nigeria**. In 1964 the Niger government took over 75 percent of the shares of the SMDN (renamed the Société Minière du Niger). In 1966 two other sites were discovered in the vicinity of **Zinder** with excellent conditions for **mining**.

CATTLE. Niger is an important stockbreeding country, with a favorable pastoral zone covering around 240,000 sq km and a total livestock (cattle, sheep, goats, camels, horses, donkeys, and a small population of pigs in the far western Gurma region) population of 38.2 million. Eighty percent of Niger's population practices some herding, although the large-scale, productive cattle rearing remains the purview of the 20 percent (mostly **Fulani** and **Tuareg**) who practice it in the pastoral zones. Niger's cattle population periodically suffers from **droughts** (it was reduced by 15 percent in the early 1970's catastrophe) but remains on average on the ascendant. Stockbreeding is chiefly destined for export markets, the most important of which are in **Nigeria**, where the animals used to be driven on hoof, with truck **transportation** becoming more economical in recent times. Long underestimated by official records, livestock export is calculated today to be second only to **uranium** in the country's export charts, and cattle markets within Niger itself have become treasure troves for decentralized taxation. Cattle export revenue and subsequent regulations were boosted by the devaluation of Niger's **currency** in 1994 and by the decentralization law of 1998.

Meat production in Niger satisfies internal demand and is steadily growing (25 percent growth rate between 1995 and 2003) and Nigerien grilled meat and *brochettes* seasoned with traditional **Hausa** spice mixes (*yaji*) is a very common snack in the country's towns. Consumption is, however, indeed much higher in town than in the rural areas, and is highest in **Niamey** where it reaches, at 28 kg per person per year, double the national average. Niger could thus export more meat but is hampered by its inadequate infrastructures (only 3,760 km of paved roads, which is 27.1 percent of the country's network of roads and highways). *See also* AGRICULTURE.

CAZEMAJOU, MARIUS GABRIEL (Captain) (1864–1898). French colonial officer. Born in Marseilles on 10 December 1864 and commissioned in the army in 1886 (becoming a captain in 1889), Cazemajou first served in Indochina and Tunisia before being dispatched to West Africa in 1896. There, he headed the **Mission du Haut-Soudan** sent to contact the Sudanese slave raider **Rabah Zubayr**, in order to negotiate some form of agreement allowing contiguity of the French possessions in West and Equatorial Africa (threatened by Rabah's conquests). On his way to Rabah's court, Cazemajou stayed three weeks in **Damagaram** and was murdered in **Zinder**, the sultanate's capital, by a faction fearing that a Franco-Rabah link would free the latter to attack Zinder. Subsequently the **Mission Afrique Centrale-Tchad** was mounted to punish Zinder and carry on Cazemajou's mission, which led to the occupation of Damagaram in 1899. Cazemajou was honored when the main garrison camp in Zinder was named after him. Following independence, however, the camp was renamed after Zinder's greatest sultan, **Tanimoun**.

CENSUSES. Niger's first census, conducted in 1977, revealed that the country's population stood at 5,121,000 people, with projections of 6,265,000 in 1985; 8,370,000 in 1995; and 9,796,000 in the year 2000. Niger's urban population, it was estimated, would grow to 982,000 in 1985, and more dramatically to 2,182,000 in 2000. These projections assumed the 1977 demographic growth rate of 2.33 percent would rise to 3.19 in 1995.

The second census took place in 1988 (results were published at the end of January 1992). It revealed that the country's population had grown at a faster pace than projected (at a rate of 3.3 percent) to 7.25 million people, of whom 49.5 percent were below the age of 15. Life expectancy in 1988 was now up to 47 years, and infant mortality rates had dropped to the still-high 140 per 1,000 births.

The third census was organized in 2001, and counted 10,790,352 people. Reports (first published in 2003) showed an average national density of 8.5 people per sq km, with the highest density in the regions of **Maradi** (52.7) and **Dosso** (43.7) and the lowest in the regions of **Agadez** (0.5) and **Diffa** (2.1). There were 5,410,065 **women** and 5,380,287 men. The total urban population (distributed in 40 urban centers) was of 1,749,095, making up just 16.2 percent of the country's total population. Fully half of the country's urban population resided in the country's three main cities, **Niamey** (674,950), **Zinder** (170,574), and Maradi (147,038). Thirty-eight percent of the urban population lived in medium-size towns (of 10,000 to 99,999 people according to Nigerien categorizations) and 5 percent lived in small towns (2,000 to 9999 people).

Niger's fertility rate, though one of the highest in the world, seems to have stabilized at around 3.3 percent. The projection of 2,182,000 urban population by 2000 has indeed proven excessive and the notion entertained in 1988 that the country would reach 22 million in 2018 now looks off the mark. Currently (2010), Niger's population is estimated at 14 million, and a fourth census is in the works for 2011 (census is ten-yearly in Niger). Results consistently show a very young population, with a majority of **Hausa** (52 percent), followed (in this order) by the **Zarma-Songhay**, the **Tuareg**, the **Fulani**, the **Kanuri**, the **Toubous**, the **Gourmantchés**, and the **Arabs**.

CENTRE D'ENSEIGNEMENT SUPERIEUR. Precursor to the **University of Niamey**. It originally opened with only a sciences section, in October 1971. The center was transformed into a university on 7 June 1973. In 1976 it had a budget of 420 million **CFA francs**, a 75 percent increase over the 1975 budget. By 1988 this figure had doubled again. *See also* EDUCATION; UNIVERSITE ABDOU MOUMOUNI DE NIAMEY.

CENTRE D'ÉTUDE LINGUISTIQUE ET HISTORIQUE PAR LA TRADITION ORALE (CELHTO). Originally the Centre Régional de Documentation pour la Tradition Orale (CRDTO), founded in July 1968 through an agreement between the state of Niger and United Nations Educational, Scientific, and Cultural Organization (UNESCO), and as the result of intensive diplomacy on the part of **Boubou Hama** to have this West African outfit based in **Niamey**. CRDTO's scope was later broadened to the rest of the African continent, and became, as CELHTO, an organ of the Organization of African Unity (now the African Union). Underfunded and understaffed, it now mostly hosts conferences and seminars.

CENTRE NATIONAL DE RECHERCHES EN SCIENCES HUMAINES. *See* INSTITUT DE RECHERCHE EN SCIENCES HUMAINES.

CENTRE NATIONAL D'ENERGIE SOLAIRE (CNES). This is a successor organ to the **Office National de l'Energie Solaire (ONERSOL)**. **Abdou**

Moumouni Dioffo, Niger's greatest scientific figure, whose interest in solar energy had led to several practical inventions that ONERSOL was meant to disseminate, created the agency in 1965. In 1975, a commercialization company, the Société Nigérienne d'Energie Nouvelle (SONIEN), opened a plant in Niamey's industrial area in order to build and sell ONERSOL-patented devices. Though backed by several foreign donors, it did not thrive, failing to attract the interest of local investors willing to run the plant and sell the products while paying royalties to ONERSOL. These products included cooking devices, devices powering community television, and food preservation in nonelectrified regions, brick-making ovens, and the ONERSOL-spilling solar engine. Foreign partnerships proved also unpromising, especially after ONERSOL's industrial plans were compromised by the bankruptcy of the French company SOFRETES with which it had associated to produce solar panels for thermodynamic solar pumps in villages. Moreover, ONERSOL never succeeded in developing a strong and growing team of researchers. A two-person agency at creation, it seriously took off in 1974, growing then to include four researchers. This figure did not change until 10 years later, when it swelled to eight, before declining to six currently.

While ONERSOL was chiefly a scientific center tied to the **University of Niamey** and the Ministry of Higher **Education** and research, CNES is defined less ambitiously as an agency tasked with the mission of promoting renewable energy use in the country, and it has been put under the supervision of the Mines and Energy Ministry. As such, CNES offers a suitable ground for international scientists—many from Western countries—interested in developing solar energy solutions for developing countries. Its current director, **Abdoussalam Ba,** strives to orient the center toward the marketing of solar energy producing devices, a not unreasonable endeavor in view of the continued fall of the price per watt in developed countries and the growing size of the market for this commodity.

CFA FRANC. *See* COMMUNAUTÉ FINANCIÈRE AFRICAINE (CFA) FRANC.

CHAAFI, LIMAN. A Libyan adventurer who operated, chiefly with instructions from **Libya**'s president, Colonel Muammar Kadhafi, in various West African countries, including Niger twice. Chaafi was involved in the coup d'état attempted against the newly established regime of Lieutenant-Colonel **Seyni Kountché** by Commandant **Moussa Bayéré** in 1976, in cahoots with two **Tuareg** officials who felt they had lost more than they gained by the overthrowing of **Hamani Diori** two years earlier. Captain **Sidi Mohamed** was *chef de cabinet* of the defense minister under Diori, and **Ahmed Mouddour,** then director of the **COPRO-NIGER,** was the son of Diori's finance minister, **Mouddour Zakara**. At the time, Colonel Kadhafi was endeavoring to create puppet regimes in the sub-Saharan countries to the south, with a view to establishing a pan-Islamic United States of the **Sahel**. He also claimed a large chunk of Niger's northeastern territory. He had attacked Chad directly and sought to use the ever-turbulent Tuareg of Niger to destabilize that country and remove its government. Chaafi fanned revolt among the Tuareg in the north and supplied weapons to conspirators in **Niamey** to overthrow Kountché, famously using sheep carcasses to do so. The plan unraveled, and Chaafi fled to Libya. In 1985, he was involved in the attack of **Tchintabaraden** organized from Tripoli by Tuareg insurgents led by former president Diori's son, **Abdoulaye Hamani Diori**. Chaafi's own son, Mustapha Ould Liman Chaafi, has continued serving Kadhafi's designs in West Africa, in cahoots with President Blaise Compaoré of Burkina Faso, brokering many underhanded deals in troubled spots that recently included Guinea after President Lansana Conté's death and Mauritania in the course of a string of coups d'état and fractious **elections**.

CHAMBRE DE COMMERCE, D'AGRICULTURE, D'INDUSTRIE ET D'ARTISANAT DU NIGER (CCAIAN). Set up by parliamentary statute in June 1964 as the Chambre de Commerce, d'Agriculture et d'Industrie du Niger, the chamber initially had 40 members and 20 associates elected by a college of heads of industrial and commercial firms. For a long time under direction by COPRO-NIGER general manager, Jacques Nignon, it was reorganized in 1998 shortly after the election at its presidency of Ibrahim Idi Ango (1997). Expenditures of the chamber are financed by a tax of 0.25 percent of the market value of all goods entering Nigerien territory. A directorate called the Compagnie Consulaire, assisted by the Bureau National, and a general secretariat in charge of technical services, run the chamber. The president of the Bureau National and of the Compagnie Consulaire is the effective president of the chamber, and is elected every four years by the members of the Assemblée Consulaire Nationale. The chamber has representations and assemblies in each headquarters of the eight regions of the country, though the most important are those in **Niamey**, **Maradi**, and **Zinder**. This is reflected in the current composition of the Bureau National, whose members hail from these three regions (with the president being from Zinder). The chamber strives to promote business acumen and professionalization among Niger's business classes, while also providing a channel of communication with the state and defending the country's commercial interests in certain capacities—for instance, as regards the relations of Nigerien tradesmen with port authorities in Benin, Togo, Ghana, and Côte d'Ivoire.

CHAOULANI, TANKARI (1909–1977). Parti Progressiste Nigérien (PPN-RDA) councilor for **Tahoua** in 1946–1952, Chaoulani was the canton chief of **Bouza** from 1944 to his death in 1977.

CHEFFERIE TRADITIONNELLE. Niger, like many postcolonial sub-Saharan countries, especially in West Africa, has a dual administrative structure: one constituted by the modern state and comprising the hierarchical echelons from the president of the republic to the subprefect and the canton judge and gendarmerie, and the other formed out of the country's historical authorities into a complex traditional peerage with recognized powers and compensations, which came to be called *chefferie traditionnelle* (traditional chieftaincy). This traditional peerage emerged from the colonial government's need for local intermediaries, especially for collecting taxes and recruiting men for the *corvée* (forced labor) and the army in times of war. The colonial government also needed local first-degree courts capable of dealing with small claims and petty community litigations. Most importantly, it needed a cheap administrative structure that could be supported without funding from the metropolis. In the territory of Niger, there were not many opportunities for finding such intermediaries on a grand scale. The only state of some size and substance was the **sultanate of Damagaram**, centered around **Zinder**. Then there were the small but well-organized kingdoms of the **Katsina** in **Maradi** and of the **Gobir** in **Tibiri**; the ambitious lord of **Dosso Zarmakoy Aouta**; the patchy desert sultanate of the **Aïr**; and the dominant **Tuareg** *amenokals* in the transition zones from the **Sahel** to the Sahara (**Ténéré**) desert. These lords and kings represented patches of organized authority submerged in a land dominated by the little patriarchal (and in some areas matriarchal) democracies and anarchies of villages, hamlets, and communal fields.

Colonial policy extended and assisted organized authority where it existed, scoring its greatest success with the *zarmakoy* of Dosso, whose power was consolidated by the French in a polity otherwise characterized by a civic constitution that rotated the executive office among the leading families of the town. Where organized authority did not exist, or existed less, the French installed cantons and *groupements nomades* (the equivalent of cantons for nomadic people), erecting to the chieftaincy of the cantons the head of the family that was most prominent when they arrived in the area, or sometimes, as in the Gobir democratic constellation of villages and hamlets of the area of Shadakori, importing princes from more hierarchical places (here Prince Jika, from the Gobir court in Tibiri). In this way, the Nigerien territory was transformed, at the level below the *cercle* (now *département*), into a maze of cantons and *groupements nomades* assisting the commander of the *cercle* (almost always a European), while the greater customary chiefs (the sultans of Damagaram and Aïr, the kings of Maradi and Tibiri, the *zarmakoy* of Dosso) enjoyed more direct contacts with the colony's lieutenant-governor.

Niger's traditional peerage as it stands today is thus a creation of the colonial government, useful for governing on the cheap and masking the unaccountability of colonial power with the legitimacy of traditional signs, symbols, and gestures. This policy was perpetuated by the independent state of Niger, which further shaped the *chefferie* as auxiliaries of the administration by formally intervening in their elevation (chiefs are usually elected from within the ruling family by an electoral college, then appointed by the state after a gendarmerie inquest, and finally enthroned in pomp and ceremony) and by putting them on its payroll in accordance with their rank in the peerage. The long evolution that led to the present status of the *chefferie* was formalized in 1993 by the adoption of an ordinance which regulates that status. As a result, the state also takes pain to buttress the authority of the *chefferie* through formal deference and the upholding of the fact that they are judges of first resort in villages for small claim cases. But it can remove a chief, as it did with the sultan of Damagaram, **Sanda Aboubacar**, in 2001, and it can change their status at will. Thus, until 2010, there were only two sultans in Niger (Damagaram and Aïr), followed by chiefs of province, and chiefs of canton and *groupement nomade*, with chiefs of village and neighborhood at the tail end. In September 2010, the **Conseil Suprême pour la Restauration de la Démocratie** (CSRD) promoted all the chiefs of province to the rank of sultan.

The chiefs' legitimacy had suffered from their association with President **Mamadou Tandja**'s attempt at ending democratic rule in 2009. Their attitude was partly explained by the fact that the decentralization program launched in the late 1990s had considerably eroded their authority and resources in many areas and at many levels, since elected officials were given powers in local councils that conflicted with those which they had customarily held. To incur their support, Tandja promised to curtail decentralization and set up a senate in which they would get a strong showing. In the regions most opposed to Tandja's plans, however, chiefs were either reluctant to obey (**Songhay** northwestern corner) or when they complied, they were attacked by the population (parts of the famed palace of the *zarmakoy* of Dosso were burned down in July 2009). The *chefferie* has, however, survived this trial, as it did many others in the past.

CHEIFFOU, AMADOU (1942–). Former interim prime minister of Niger and longtime director-general of **Air Niger**. Born in Kornaka and educated locally, at the University of Dakar (1961–1966), and the University of Toulouse (1966–1967) as an engineer, he afterward went to Toulouse's school of civil aviation, graduating in 1969 as a civil aviation engineer. Cheiffou then served in a variety of capacities with the Agence pour la Sécurité de la Navigation Aérienne en Afrique et à Madagascar (ASECNA, the African civil aviation authority), as commander of **Niamey**'s airport (1970–1975), deputy director-general of ASECNA in Dakar (1975–1985), and West Africa's representative to the International Civil Aviation Organization (ICAO) in Dakar (1985–1991). A militant socialist in his student days, he became a champion of competitive **elections** and gained entry to the **Conférence Nationale** in 1991 as a delegate for the Association des Nigériens de l'Etranger (Association of Nigeriens Living Abroad).

Chiefly because of his political inexperience and lack of association with the ancient regime, he was selected by the National Conference over six other competing candidates to be Niger's interim prime minister during the 15-month transitional period (1 November 1991 to 31 January 1993) leading to elections and a new government. The office came with prohibition to stand as a candidate for the 1993 presidential office, and Cheiffou resumed his professional career after Niger's transition period, climbing, in 2002 to the position of the regional director for ICAO's Western and Central African Office. Meanwhile, he had become involved with the **Convention Démocratique et Sociale** (CDS Rahama), the party of **Mahaman Ousmane** (president of Niger in 1993–1996). In 2004, he split with the party and created the Rassemblement Social-Démocratique (RSD Gaskiya) in order to run for president that year. He came off fourth of six candidates with 6.35 percent of the vote and won a **Maradi** seat at the **National Assembly** in the following legislative elections.

In 2006, President **Mamadou Tandja** attracted him into his camp by appointing him president of the Conseil Economique Social et Culturel (CESOC), and in 2009, Cheiffou duly supported his patron in his attempt at changing Niger's political regime and to stay in power beyond the term limit. The RSD participated to the October 2009 legislative elections which the major opposition parties had boycotted, and still serving as president of CESOC, Cheiffou also ran for the local office of municipal councilor in Kornaka, where he won a seat. These various terms of office were annulled upon the termination of Tandja's **Sixth Republic** in February 2010. However, and to the shock of many who remember his role in Tandja's constitutional coup, President **Mahamadou Issoufou** chose him for the office of mediator of the republic in August 2011, a lofty and lucrative sinecure.

CHEIK ABOUBACAR HASSOUMI (1914–2004). Also called Sékou **Kiota** (Sékou being a **Zarma** pronunciation of *Shaikh*). Spiritual leader and founder of the Nigerien branch of the Niassite **Tijaniyya** brotherhood, which has its roots in Senegal. Cheik Aboubacar Hassoumi embraced the Tijaniyya liturgy at first through meetings with a Nigerien Tijaniyya cleric, **Cheik Hanafi Moustapha** (known also as Sékou Bali Bali), before becoming a disciple of the great Senegalese Tijaniyya master Cheikh Ibrahima Niass, whom he met in Kano (**Nigeria**) where he was a religious student. He reputedly accomplished the pilgrimage to Mecca twice on foot, the first time over 30 months, in 1931–1932. He launched the annual celebration of the Prophet Muhammad's birthday, the Mawlid, in Kiota, in 1954, an event that gathers thousands from Niger, **Nigeria**, and other neighboring countries. His most celebrated wife is a daughter of the Cheikh Niass, **Saïda Oumoul Khairy Niass**, known in the community as Maman Senegal. Maman Senegal, who had become a driving force in organizing Tijaniyya **women** throughout western Niger, now pretty much runs the show in Kiota, while an elder son of the late *cheik* has been installed as the new spiritual leader of the community. Like Senegalese **Niassism**, Nigerien Niassism as promoted by the Kiota family is politically quiescent but socially and culturally active, functioning therefore as a moderating force in Niger's often heated religious climate. At the death of Sékou Kiota in 2004, the head of the country's Roman Catholic Church, Bishop **Michel Cartatéguy**, was invited to pray over his remains before even the ceremonies performed by Muslim faithfuls, an indication of the broad irenicism of Sufi liturgies. He was succeeded by his son Cheik Moussa Aboubacar Hassoumi. *See also* ISLAM.

CHEIK HANAFI MOUSTAPHA (1874–1945). The earliest introducer of the **Tijaniyya** liturgy in western Niger (then chiefly adhering to the **Qadiriyya** liturgy brought in by **Mamane Diobo** when he settled in **Say** in the early 19th century), Cheik Hanafi Moustapha received the Sufi teachings of the Sudanese master Cheikh Al-Qadarify, whom he met in Sudan during his pilgrimage to Mecca in the late 19th century. In 1909, he settled in Fandou Bali Bali, in the **Boboye** (**Zarma** country), soon became a major spiritual leader, and earned the appellation Sékou Bali Bali (Zarma for "the *shaikh* of Bali Bali"). He was the first to initiate **Cheik Aboubacar Hassoumi** into the Tijaniyya liturgy, though the adoption by the latter of Niassite organization eventually made of his own congregation of **Kiota** bigger and better known. *See also* ISLAM.

CHIEFS OF STAFF. Since their creation, the Niger **armed forces** have had 14 chiefs of staff, 8 of these during the current civilian era: 1961–1968, Colonel Demba Maïnassara; 1968–1973, Colonel **Balla Arabé**; 1973–1976, Lieutenant-Colonel **Seyni Kountché**; 1976–1987, Colonel **Ali Saibou**; 1987–1991, Colonel **Toumba Boubacar**; 1991–1993, Lieutenant-Colonel

Mazou Issa; 1993–1995, Colonel Mahamane Koraou; 1995–1996, Colonel **Ibrahim Baré Maïnassara**; 1996–1997, Colonel **Moussa Gros**; 1997–1999, Colonel Moussa Moumouni Djermakoye; 1999, Colonel Soumana Zanguina; 1999–2010, General Boureima Moumouni; 2010–2011, General Souleymane Salou; 2011– , General Seyni Garba.

CHRISTIANITY. Christianity is a minority **religion** in Niger. Before 2001, religion was not recorded in Niger's **censuses**, but the numbers in 2001 indicate that only about 1 percent of Nigeriens are Christians. Christianity often thrives in Niger in regions where animism holds out against **Islam**; thus, in Western Niger among the **Songhay** and the **Gourmantché** and in the Hausaland among the **Arawa** and the **Arna**. Migration from coastal **Nigeria**, Benin, and Togo introduces a great influx of Christians in Nigerien towns and, in later days, these carry with them missionary Protestant denominations (that of the evangelicals in particular) that tend to antagonize the now-dominant Sunni orthodox Muslims.

CHRONIQUES D'AGADEZ. Historical records of the dynasty of the sultans of **Aïr**, resident in **Agadez**. They contain some ancient manuscripts, chronologies, and king lists, and a brief history of the sultanate, all written and rewritten over the ages. The material comprises around 70 pages of texts and is much cited in the scholarly literature.

CINEMA. Niger has one of the earliest cinemas in sub-Saharan Africa, as it emerged in the late 1950s and knew its golden age from the late 1960s to the early 1980s. Nigerien cinema afterward declined for much of the 1980–1990s before experiencing a timid revival in the 2000s.

Nigerien cinema grew out of the work of French anthropologist Jean Rouch, who moved from ethnographic filmmaking to producing narrative movies set in Niger or within the Nigerien diaspora in the Gold Coast (Ghana) and Côte d'Ivoire, thereby training a number of young Nigeriens in acting and directing. Actors **Damouré Zika** and **Zalika Souley** as well as future movie directors **Oumarou Ganda** and **Moustapha Alassane** all worked with Rouch in this period. Some of Rouch's later work (*Petit-à-petit*, 1971; *Cocorico Monsieur Poulet*, 1974) may be considered to fully belong to Nigerien cinema, as they were in particular written in collaboration with Rouch's Nigerien cast and crew. However, while Rouch's inspiration is mostly humoristic and poetic, Nigerien cinema generally devoted itself to the criticism of Niger's social ills and prejudices and the adaptation of fictional stories set in historical or legendary times.

The first among Rouch's friends to direct and produce movies was Mousta-pha Alassane, who developed a rich and varied filmography in the 1960s and 1970s, including animated movies, fiction, and documentaries. He is mostly known in Niger for his social satire tale *FVVA, Femmes, Villa, Voiture, Ar-gent* (1972), which upbraided the new modern elite of the country, and for his crisp take on an old **Songhay** legend narrated in one of **Boubou Hama**'s collections of tales, *Toula ou le génie des eaux* (1973). His animated short, *La Mort du Gandji*, was the first Nigerien movie to win an award, at the Festival Mondial des Arts Nègres of Dakar (Senegal), in 1966.

In 1969, it was the turn of Oumarou Ganda's **Zarma** language *Cabascabo* to be rewarded first by being shown at the Cannes Film Festival in **France**, and then by winning the Grand Jury prize at the Moscow Film Festival the same year. *Cabascabo* tells the poignant story of a veteran of the French wars in Indochina (where Ganda himself fought as a *tirailleur sénégalais*, i.e., a West African colonial foot soldier) who returns home with some money only to get fleeced out of it by his so-called friends and turn half-mad after so much betrayal. The movie is at the same time a response to Rouch's *Moi, un noir* (a documentary movie in which the same story is glossed over with an unwitting ethnographic distance) and a bitter criticism of Nigerien or African mentality. Ganda afterward proved to be the most serious and purposeful of Nigerien moviemakers, winning several awards in the 1970s at the African Film Festival FESPACO of Ouagadougou (Haute-Volta, now Burkina Faso) and concluding his career with the haunting tragedy of *L'Exilé* (1980), argu-ably his greatest film, both in terms of narrative cogency and poignancy and of coherence between content and form. A story of integrity and sacrifice which takes as much inspiration from Greek tragedy (in particular *Oedipus*, with the motive of the riddle that leads to both victory and death) as from **Zarma-Songhay** lore, *L'Exilé* was also clearly a political message addressed to the new African elites, who are seen in contrast as dishonest and as all too ready to sacrifice others to their privileges rather than sacrificing themselves for others, as did the king in the movie. Ganda sadly died shortly thereafter, at the age of 46.

Other moviemakers who deserve mention in that period are Abdouraha-mane Gatta (his *Gossi* of 1979 also won a FESPACO prize), **Djingaraye Maïga**, **Mamane Bakabé**, Inoussa Ousseini, and **Moustapha Diop**. Niger-ien cinema used chiefly French and local Nigerien **languages** (with French subtitles) and found its main market in Francophone Africa. It never became an industry, however, and could not live on without subsidies, which mostly came from the state of Niger and French cultural cooperation—although *Cabascabo*, for instance, was largely financed by German sponsors. The fiscal crisis of the state of Niger in the 1980s dried up state-sector financing and also curtailed national television sponsorships, which had supported in particular the work of Djingaraye Maïga and Mamane Bakabé. Most movie directors turned to other activities to earn their living and thus were unable to train a new generation of moviemakers. In 1994, a cinema aficionado, Ousmane Ilbo Mahamane, tried to revive Nigerien cinema by founding a prize-less biennial festival, the Rencontres du Cinéma Africain de Niamey (RECAN), which brought back filmmaking to the attentions of the Nigerien public. RECAN presented mainly original movies from other parts of the world, until 2005 when it was able to show a **Hausa**-language Nigerien film, *Tuwo yayi magani*, from a film team known as *Tarbiyya* of **Niamey**.

Since then, a number of young filmmakers have emerged on the Nigerien stage. They all, however, have specialized in the documentary form. The most talented are Malam Saguirou and Sani Elhadji Magori. For Nigerien cinema to rebound, all recognize that there is need for a policy of investment in the training of technicians and actors and in support for movie theaters, which have steadily shut down throughout the country in the 1990s, asphyxiated by the development of television and home video, and the lack of coping and reorientation measures. The younger generation of Nigerien moviemakers struggles to draw the attention of the state and potential donors to these tasks.

CIROMA. In the **sultanate of Damagaram** state hierarchy, the commander of the armies, chosen from the brothers and nephews of the reigning sultan. With a personal tribute from a number of outlying villages, the *ciroma* was normally a very important official in the court.

CISSÉ, AMADOU BOUBACAR (1948–). Engineer and twice prime minister of Niger. Born in **Niamey** in a **Fulani** family from **Say**, Cissé graduated in 1975 from the Paris École Nationale des Ponts et Chaussées as an engineer. He then worked as advisor for infrastructure to the president of the republic (1975–1979) and chairman of the department of public works (1979–1982). In 1982, he was sent to the World Bank to represent Niger, and the following year (1984) assumed in that agency a post responsible for transport projects in Benin, Côte d'Ivoire, Chad, and Guinea-Bissau. With the onset of competitive party politics in Niger, Cissé joined the **Mouvement National pour la Société de Développement** (MNSD Nassara), thus rather as an outsider than as an early member. After the legislative **elections** that followed the fall of the **Alliance des Forces du Changement** (AFC) government in 1994, the MNSD emerged as the largest party in the legislature and expected to have its secretary-general, **Hama Amadou**, appointed prime minister. President Ousmane instead chose Cissé in February 1995, in an attempt to divide MNSD.

Cissé was, however, promptly faced with a no-confidence vote in parliament and was duly ousted.

After **Ibrahim Baré Maïnassara** overthrew the **Third Republic** in January 1996, Cissé turned his coat again, ingratiated himself with the new ruler, and was appointed prime minister in December. As a former World Bank functionary, he saw to it that Niger's government signed an agreement with that institution in March 1997, committing the state to an extensive trimming of the public sector. This backlashed into immediate and continuous union strikes which finally overwhelmed his government by preventing it from operating. President Baré Maïnassara sacked him in June 1998 for incompetence. He then returned to the World Bank as a councilor attached to the executive vice-president of the bank (1999) before moving to the Islamic Development Bank as vice-president (2002–2008).

After retiring, Cissé returned to Niger where he reactivated the party he had founded in 1999, the Union pour la Démocratie et la République (UDR Tabbat), eagerly joining the opposition parties which were fighting President **Mamadou Tandja**'s bid to overturn Niger's constitution and stay in power with no limitation. Cissé linked up his party to the umbrella **Coordination des Forces pour la Démocratie et la République** (CFDR) and, following the toppling of Tandja and the launching of an electoral process in 2010, he positioned himself as candidate for the presidency. He came off eighth with 1.61 percent of the vote at first round. He then brought his support to **Mahamadou Issoufou** of the **Parti Nigérien pour la Démocratie et le Socialisme** (PNDS Tarayya) at runoff. After his victory of March 2011, President Issoufou appointed Cissé minister of state, minister for planning, territory management, and community development.

CISSÉ, AMADOU ISSA. Current *alfaize* (a title which means, in **Zarma**, "the cleric's son") of **Say**, the town founded as a shrine of **Qadiriyya** Sufism by the **Fulani** cleric *Alfa* **Mamane Diobo** in the early 19th century. A direct descendant of Diobo, Alfaize Amadou Issa Cissé is the 12th *alfaize* (not counting Diobo, who was *Alfa*, "the cleric," the founder of the lineage) and came to office in 2002.

CISSÉ, BOUBACAR (1909–1989). Politician and senior civil administrator. Born in **Say** in 1909, and an administrator by training, Cissé was elected to **Niamey**'s municipal council in December 1956, serving on it until January 1959. In March 1957 he was also elected **Parti Progressiste Nigérien** (PPN) deputy to the **Territorial Assembly** and was reelected in both 1958 and 1965 in that regime's acclamatory polling. Prior to his retirement in the mid-1980s he also served as the administrator of the **Société Nigérienne de Produits**

Céramiques (SONICERAM) and of the Société Mutuelle de Développement Rural (SMDR), as well as director-general (since 1964) of the Société Nationale des Grands Travaux du Niger (SNGTN) and president (since 1971) of the Syndicat Patronal des Entreprises et Industries du Niger (SPEIN), the employers' union of Niger. He was the father of **Amadou Boubacar Cissé**.

CISSÉ, SEKOU OUMAROU (1944–). Maître Cissé, as he is best known in Niger (*maître*, i.e., master, is an honorific title for lawyers in the French system), initially worked in the state justice system as judge and deputy public prosecutor in various localities before establishing himself in **Niamey** in 1978 in his capacity as a bailiff and an auctioneer. In 1995, he represented the **Tillabéri** electoral district for the **Mouvement National pour la Société de Développement** (MNSD Nassara) at the National Assembly and was a key member of the transition parliament of 1999, the **Conseil Consultatif National**.

CIVIL SERVICE. Niger barely had a civil service under the colonial regime. Until 1960, the country had only 13,824 salaried personnel for a population of 2,600,000. Most of this workforce was made up of unskilled laborers and blue-collar workers, many of them recruited seasonally and on construction sites. In August 1959, a year before independence, Niger had only 5,970 permanent salaried workers, among whom only 3,021 were Nigerien nationals (the others came from Dahomey, Senegal, Mali, and Haute Volta). The spirit of Niger's colonial administration remained chiefly militaristic, even though the era of military government had ended in 1922, and this partly accounts for the role that the Nigerien **armed forces** will continue to play under Niger's independent governments.

At independence, Niger strove to create a civil service that would be in the hands of nationals, greatly in reaction to the negative prejudices which foreign personnel had developed against the local populations (often termed "incapables" by their foreign-born administrators). This led to xenophobic policies directed especially against the Dahomeans. Around 850 to 1,300 Dahomeans were thus forcibly repatriated in 1964, under pretense of a border dispute that took a bad turn that year between the two countries. Regarding officials from the Sahelian countries (Haute Volta, Mali, Senegal), Nigeriennization did not entail eviction but rather the adoption of Nigerien nationality by civil servants; this is the origin of some very prominent Nigeriens, including the scholar and writer **Abdourahamane Mariko Keletigui** (family from Mali), the founder of Niger's first independent newspaper **Ibrahim Cheick Diop** (family from Senegal), and former president **Mamadou Tandja** (family from Mauritania/Senegal).

The civil service grew after independence. By 1974, following the establishment of an independent state and the project of state-led development which most postcolonial states pursued at the time, the civil service comprised around 19,000 workers out of a total pool of salaried workers of 36,000. With the boom in state revenues consequent to the coming on-stream of **uranium** exports, numerous new state enterprises were set up in Niger, with the regular civil service also expanding for a decade. Those in one way or another on the public payroll (civil service and **parastatal** workers) were estimated in 1984 at 51,000—with 31,000 directly in the civil service. But at about that time, Niger's major economic slump and dire fiscal straits led the government to launch a first trimming of the civil service, through an early retirement plan, the Programme d'Appui à l'Initiative Privée et à la Création d'Emploi (PAIPCE). Under President **Ali Saibou** (1987–1991), there was a selective pruning of the state payroll and freeze of new recruitment, as well as a first series of closure or **privatization** of parastatals. As the number of state employees declined, however, unrest grew in the country, especially after Saibou agreed to a Structural Adjustment Program that would have entailed even harsher budgetary (and hence employment) cuts. All these measures had been strenuously resisted by the country's trade unions, and later—when the government announced that it would no longer automatically hire graduates from the **University of Niamey**—by students as well.

In 1990s, the civil service paradoxically continued to grow, even as state capacities and services steadily continued to decline. The situation was particularly dire in the early parts of the decade, when pay backlogs of up to six months combined with the political vagaries of the **Third Republic** to reduce operation of the civil service to shambles. Western donors continued to press for employment cuts as precondition of bailing out the country's parlous finances while also pushing for advances in **democratization**, which in turn imparted more resistance power to malcontents.

A reform agenda to trim down the civil service and revise its statute was adopted by the authoritarian government of **Ibrahim Baré Maïnassara** in 1998, in agreement with the World Bank and the International Monetary Fund (IMF). In particular, the reform introduced mandatory retirement after 30 years of service or at age 55, and based promotion on merit only, while 12 enterprises (including the three major public utilities and the national petroleum companies) were slated for privatization, with the attendant layoffs. Under Baré Maïnassara, the regime's bad relations with trade unions stalled the reform, but it was gradually implemented in the early 2000s (all candidates at the 1999 **elections**, which followed the toppling of Baré Maïnassara, had pledged to implement the reforms designed by the IMF and the World Bank). It was eventually the educational system which, here as in many other African

Table 2. Civil Service Workforce since Independence

Year	1961	1976	1985	1995	2005	2009
State workers	3,755	19,902	32,297	40,857	34,288	34,682

countries, bore the brunt of the efforts to stem the salary bill, as professional teachers were mostly replaced by voluntary and contractual workers. The ensuing recruitment drive partly accounts for the swelling in the state's payroll. On the other hand, the freeze in recruitment in other services gradually led to the de-staffing of state services, especially in remote regions and rural areas, where traditional recruitment cycles had tended to send beginners in the service. In many Nigerien regions, by the early 2000s, the civil service all but disappeared, and the presence of the state was typically signaled by a lone administrator and a squad of security forces (gendarmes or the military). The Nigerien civil service took on the characteristic tadpole-like structure of a big head—in the capital and main towns—and a thinning body. Moreover, administrative corruption, which was minimal in the previous era, became endemic by the late 1990s, triggered at first by pay backlogs and pay freezes, and subsequently by the disorganization of administrative services under pressure from party politics and the country's successive political crises and gridlocks. While Niger's civil service started to recover from the stormy 1990 decade in the 2000s, it is now faced with the daunting task of rebuilding the traditions and conscience of an administration (see Table 2). *See also* BENIN–NIGER BORDER DISPUTE; COLONIE DU NIGER.

CIVIL SOCIETY. Prior to the **Second Republic** (1989–1991) and the **Conférence Nationale** (1991), Niger knew two traditions of organized social groupings in relation to state power. One was hostile and expressed itself virulently in the illegal but very active **Union des Scolaires Nigériens** (USN) and more moderately through trade unions, while the other was accommodating and was essentially a set of organizations coopted and subsidized by the state (**Union des Femmes du Niger, Association Islamique du Niger, Association des Femmes du Niger,** Association des Chefs Traditionnels du Niger, *samariya*). A dozen or so independent associations of minor relevance existed by the mid-1980s, when the *régime d'exception* granted freedom of association. Many of these where the nuclei of future **political parties**. Under the favorable regime of the Second Republic and even more so, of the **democratization** era (1990–1993), this number grew to around 60, with new orientations germinating—thus, human rights defense associations and associations for the promotion of **Islam**. By the mid-2000s, Niger counted about 1,200 nongovernmental organizations (NGOs) and civic associations of more or less national scope, as well as four union federations, not counting over 5,000 local associations which make up the localized civil society. This boom, of course, covers heterogeneous situations, with a great number of organizations existing only on paper or in response to funding offers from donors pursuing their own agenda. In general, Niger's civil society was profoundly shaped by donors' imperatives, as its units acted as foot soldiers for **foreign aid** and adopted the required perspectives on most socioeconomic issues relevant to the country. A key effect of this was to render Niger's civil society accountable and much more responsive to foreign donors than to their alleged constituencies—a feature especially stark in the case of **women**'s issues.

Yet in many instances, Niger's civil society has also proven fiercely united and combative in relation to attempts at undermining democratic rule. Thus, while many civil society organizations were initially supportive of the January 1996 coup which ended the **Third Republic**, a majority sided with the opposition political parties when it became clear that coup-maker **Ibrahim Baré Maïnassara** wanted to use the coup to restore authoritarian government. Similarly, in 2009, the civil society was arguably even more active than the political parties in opposing **Mamadou Tandja**'s **Tazartché** constitutional coup. These political battles have defined the identity of the civil society, which largely ran the transition period of 2010–2011 under the aegis of the **Conseil Suprême pour la Restauration de la Démocratie** (CSRD) and adopted an organizing charter in January 2011. The charter in particular stresses the need for Nigerien NGOs and civic associations to distinguish their agenda from that of political parties, as well as for striving toward independence from foreign money—a difficult proposition in a country where the bulk of the funding of Niger's main donor (the European Union) goes to the civil society. Another defining moment of Niger's civil society was the March–April 2005 actions against value added taxes which saw the largest civil society coalition ever formed mobilize tens of thousands in **Niamey**, **Zinder**, and **Maradi** to defeat the government and the International Monetary Fund, which together had devised the policy. That victory was short-lived, however, and as high costs of living have spiraled out of control, civil society organizations have gradually lost their legitimating aura as the defenders of the Nigerien citizen's purse. *See also* COUP OF 27 JANUARY 1996.

COLONIE DU NIGER. On 20 December 1900, the Territoire Militaire de Zinder (dating back to 23 July of the same year) and the Cercle du Djerma (created on 11 October of that year) were merged into the larger West African set of French colonies then called the Troisième Territoire Militaire du Haut-

Sénégal-Niger. Thus, the nucleus of the colony was the Territoire Militaire de Zinder, which was given more substance by the addition of the Cercle du Djerma. The date 20 December must therefore be noted as the founding date of Niger by the political union, effected under French aegis, of its two key populations, the **Hausa** of the east-central region and the **Zarma-Songhay** of the west. On 7 September 1911, the region was renamed Territoire Militaire du Niger, and on 4 December 1920, it was rendered autonomous from the Haut-Senegal-Niger block (centered on the French Sudan, i.e., today's Mali), dissolved at that point. Finally, on 3 October 1922, the military territory was deemed in sound enough possession of **France** (after the **rebellions** of the period 1898–1918) to become the Colonie du Niger, with its own budget, administration, and security forces. It had by then grown to include the northern desert, with its **Tuareg** population, the third-largest ethnic group of Niger.

The colony's territory initially included the nine *cercles* of **Agadez**, **Dosso**, **Gouré**, **Maradi**, **N'Guigmi**, **Niamey**, **Tahoua**, **Tillabéri**, and **Zinder**, and 27 subdivisions. The original capital of the colony was Zinder (1911–1926); previously it had been Sorbon-Haoussa (until 1903) and Niamey (1903) before shifting back, in 1926, to Niamey. It was first put under the executive jurisdiction of the larger ensemble of the **Afrique Occidentale Française** (AOF), meaning that its governor was the governor of AOF (headquartered in Dakar), with lieutenant-governors as his executive assistants in the colony. (At the earlier time of the Territoire Militaire, Niger was ruled by commissioners.) In 1937, though remaining formally a member of the AOF, Niger gained further autonomy when its executive ruler became a governor with all the prerogatives and powers attached to the position. It was, however, only an autonomy of administration, not a political autonomy.

After World War II, Niger was endowed with an increasing amount of political autonomy and right of representation at the French parliament, first as a Territoire d'Outre-Mer (TOM) in the Union Française (as per the new French constitution of 27 October 1946), then as a member state of the federative Communauté Française (as per the French constitution of 1958). In this latter guise, the TOM of Niger became the République du Niger (18 December 1958), even though it did not have full political independence. The executive ruler was for the first time an elected Nigerien politician, the president of the government council, while the head of state was the French president, represented by a high commissioner (the governor of yore, with diminished formal powers). Hardly was this new status formalized by the adoption of a constitution as a member state of the Communauté Française (12 March 1959) when it was discarded owing to Niger's accession to independence on 3 August 1960. Thus did the country's colonial history end, just 60 years after it had started. *See also* FRENCH OCCUPATION.

COMMISSION DU BASSIN DU LAC TCHAD (CBLT). Interstate agency for the joint development and protection of the **Lake Chad** basin, covering 200,000 sq km. The commission was founded on 22 May 1964, when a convention was signed following five meetings between March 1962 and April 1964. The participating states are Chad, Cameroon, Niger, and **Nigeria**, which pledged that they would act to prevent policies or action likely to pollute the lake or drain its waters, and would act to promote cooperation on projects affecting the basin. The commission is composed of eight delegates, two from each state, with a secretariat in Ndjamena, Chad, and it meets at least once a year.

COMMISSION ELECTORALE NATIONALE INDÉPENDANTE (CENI). The first Nigerien independent electoral commission was set up in 1992 to organize the first **elections** of the **Third Republic**. It proved to be a competent outfit, capable of organizing credible polls. Indeed, none of the countless vagaries of the Nigerien democratization process is attributable to the CENI, and the only time when the fairness of elections was contested by losing parties was when, in July 1996, coup-maker **Ibrahim Baré Maïnassara** illegally reshuffled the commission to ensure his victory at the elections that year. Thenceforth, opposition politicians made reconciliation with Baré Maïnassara contingent on a restoration of the CENI in its original composition and rules of operation. In August 2009, President **Mamadou Tandja**, planning a constitutional coup, killed off the independent commission and replaced it—under the same name—with a fraud-mongering outfit which organized the **Sixth Republic**'s elections in a most slapdash and financially lax fashion.

The CENI's makeup is based on the idea of representativeness, and the small alterations that have been made to it since 1992 tend to reinforce that feature. Thus the CENI that organized the elections of 2011 has as one of its statutory vice-president a representative of the organizations promoting **women**'s rights. Owing to its marked success in Niger's democratization story, the CENI is the recipient of much Western aid.

The current CENI was instituted on 27 May 2010 by the **Conseil Supérieur pour la Restauration de la Démocratie** (CSRD). It has one president (currently Ghousmane Abdourahamane), two vice-presidents (an attorney and a representative of women's organizations), a reporting official representing the state, and a reporting official representing human rights defense organizations. It has 100 members drawn from the political parties and the **civil society** and runs eight regional electoral commissions, 36 departmental electoral commissions, 266 municipal electoral commissions, 310 local electoral commissions, and 20,900 voting stations. Over time, and in reaction to previous problems and issues, the CENI has grown into an impressive bureaucracy complete with a permanent secretariat and five subcommissions: defense and security, communication and registration, administration and law, finances, and logistics.

COMMUNAUTÉ FINANCIÈRE AFRICAINE (CFA) FRANC. Established between 1939 and 1945 as the Franc des Colonies Françaises d'Afrique (French Colonies of Africa's franc), the CFA franc restored **France**'s monetary authority in its African empire after World War II and was afterward included in the monetary zone organized by France in the interest of colonial mercantilism. One of the missions of the CFA franc was to ensure that the trade of France's African colonies was made primarily with France, and although the **currency** has evolved considerably in some aspects since that period, it still carries many effects of its origins, which contribute to explaining the economic conditions in countries such as Niger.

The CFA franc was at first an autonomous currency sharing a common pool with the metropolitan currency, conditions of parity established at the newly created International Monetary Fund (IMF), and exchange control mechanisms. After the French franc was redenominated into the stronger *nouveau franc* (new franc) in 1958, the CFA franc (by then renamed to its current designation) was pegged to it at a fixed rate (1 FF = 50 CFA franc) to gain from its convertibility. The currency zone subsequently underwent several minor reforms in the 1960s–1970s to register the move into independence of the colonies, including the relocation of the central bank in Dakar (for the West African section of the Franc Zone). Indeed, the more radical former colonies, Guinea and Mali, moved out of it altogether, but Mali returned in 1973 (not Guinea so far).

The monetary authority for the CFA franc was, and is still largely, detained by the French treasury which, through the mechanism of the operations account, is able to offer France's convertibility guarantee. The Franc Zone countries are required to deposit at least 50 percent of their foreign exchange at the French treasury (down from 100 percent until 1973, and 65 percent until the mid-2000s), and have in this way immobilized about €5 billion in that institution. It is also the French treasury which regulates the issue of the currency—so much so that the central bank (**Banque Centrale des États d'Afrique de l'Ouest**, BCEAO) is a specie of currency board. This has both positive and negative effects. The CFA countries cannot issue money by fiat and are thus able to maintain very low inflation rates and a stable currency over time. They are also ruled by strict budgetary control, since the bulk of their foreign exchange reserves is deposited at the French treasury and resort to it is capped at 20 percent of any country's international trade revenues.

So states in trouble cannot be bailed out by the zone (as happens in the Euro Zone) and must control public expenditures or pay for "their excesses" (such as Niger's salary backlogs in the early 1990s).

But the CFA countries imported the inflation from the French franc and were also repeatedly victims of the French franc's frequent devaluations of the 1970s–1980s, which meant that their dollar-denominated debt soared while, as producers of raw material and agricultural commodities, they were not able to recoup their losses on the export side. Moreover, for much of the 1960–1980s, the interest rate in the Franc Zone was lower than the one in France, officially to make credit cheaper in the impoverished countries. However, owing to the rule of free transferability of capital between the African Franc Zone and France administered by the Bank of France, the period was marked throughout by massive capital flight from Africa into France, where capital was on the lookout for high and easy returns on that country's interest rates market. The system, in this way, chiefly benefited France, which was moreover able to export manufactured products at (automatically) preferential rates into what came to be known as its *pré carré* (preserve). The history of Niger's late 1970s–1980s is partly explained by these facts: The state, flush with **uranium** money, was able to take advantage of the credit boom of the late 1970s and got heavily in debt. When the boom ended, uranium revenues plummeted and the French franc devalued, all in the early 1980s, and Niger's financial status crashed. The story did not end there, since the French franc revalued considerably in the mid-1980s, making of the CFA franc such a strong currency that the competitiveness of the zone's production was eroded—a development that, in the case of landlocked Niger, was counterbalanced by the possibility of cheaper imports.

Lastly, it should be noted that the rigorous budget control mechanisms also mean that CFA states cannot allocate credit for development through the **banking** system according to their changing circumstances, and are in essence frozen in the roles that they had under the colonial empire: thus, the 20 percent cap of international trade revenue as a bailout mechanism means that Côte d'Ivoire, which has a vastly superior international trade, will always have access to more monetary resources than Niger, ensuring that the winners and losers of the colonial system remain the same into independence.

In 1993, France ended the free convertibility between its currency and the CFA franc, in preparation for its bowing to the pressures of the IMF to devalue the CFA franc. France was in effect reluctant to radically reform the mechanisms of the zone, and thought it was unable to cope alone with the recession which hit CFA countries more seriously than any other African region in the late 1980s. The currency was devalued in 1994 (1 FF = 100 CFA franc), with some positive effects on exports (including, for Niger, exports of agricultural produce into **Nigeria**) and more negative effects on the costs of living. In January 1999, the CFA franc was pegged to the euro under sponsorship from the French treasury (1 euro = 654 CFA franc). The new anchor currency is stronger than the French franc, which means that the CFA Franc suffers again from the overvaluation which was deemed a crucial factor in the recession of the late 1980s, and also that the French preserve has been expanded to other members of the Euro Zone.

Although (or because) it can be defined as the poor man's hard currency, the CFA franc is attractive to many states outside of the zone, and took in Equatorial Guinea (1983) and more recently Guinea Bissau (1997). Strong and diversified economies may have less need for its onerous protections. *See also* ECONOMY; FRENCH OCCUPATION.

COMMUNE. Since the decentralization law of 1998, the commune, which was restrictively defined in the past as a unit of urban government headed by a mayor (and for a long time there had been only 11 such units in the country), is now the prevalent form of local government in Niger. There are *communes urbaines*, which are small towns of over 10,000 people (including the subdivisions of the large towns of over 100,000 inhabitants which have the status of *communauté urbaine*) and *communes rurales*, grouping sets of villages and *tribus* (nomadic) in a predefined district (*terroir*), often corresponding to the cantons and having at least 5,000 inhabitants. The commune has an elected mayor and a local assembly of elected municipal councilors.

COMMUNICATIONS. *See* SOCIÉTÉ NIGÉRIENNE DES TELECOMMUNICATIONS.

COMPAGNIE MINIÈRE D'AKOUTA (COMINAK). Founded on 12 June 1974 by the Niger government, the French Atomic Energy Commission (CEA), a Japanese consortium (Overseas Uranium Resources Development Ltd.), and a Spanish company to operate **uranium** concessions in the **Akouta** region. The mines, 10 km west of **Arlit**, were scheduled to yield 2,000 tons of processed ore by 1980. Capitalized with 35 billion **CFA francs** to exploit the ore field discovered in 1966–1967 by the CEA (and more precisely pinpointed 1970–1973), COMINAK is the second such uranium company (after the **Société des Mines de l'Aïr**) to be established in Niger. Its plant opened in 1978, with further buildings completed in the 1980s. As of 2009, estimated reserves should suffice for 17 years of production at current pace. They should suffice for the production of 25,000 tons of processed ore. Of the COMINAK shares, the French nuclear behemoth **AREVA** owns 34 percent, Niger's Société du Patrimoine des Mines du Niger (SOPAMIN) 31 percent,

OURD 25 percent, and the Spanish Empresa Nacional del Uranio S.A. 10 percent. The company works from a new city, **Akokan**, smaller than and very close to Arlit. In 1986, as a result of a global uranium glut, production was cut. The rebound of the commodity in the 2000s led to a new **mining** convention between AREVA (successor to the earlier managers of **France**'s uranium interests, CEA and COGEMA) and the state of Niger, reviving COMINAK's production in 2001. In recent years, AREVA and COMINAK have come under heavy fire from environmentalists, owing to the high rates of radioactivity detected far around the exploitation sites. They have adopted corporate accountability strategies, sponsoring social services in the region, and seeking clean energy certifications.

CONDAT, GEORGES MAHAMANE (1924–). The son of a French father and a Nigerien mother, Condat attended the **Foyer des Métis** of **Zinder** (1933–1936) and graduated from the **École William Ponty** of Sébikhotane (Senegal) in 1944. He afterward worked at the Institut Français d'Afrique Noire (IFAN) in Dakar and at Niger's national archives before being elected Niger's deputy at the French National Assembly in 1948. Condat shifted between a number of **political parties**: Union Nigérienne des Indépendants et Sympathisants (UNIS), of which he was the assistant general secretary, Union Progressiste Nigérienne (UPN), of which he was the president, and finally the Bloc Nigérien d'Action (BNA), created in 1956 and of which he became the secretary-general, the BNA emerging from a coalition of disgruntled UPN and UNIS members.

He allied himself to the policies and objectives of **Djibo Bakary** and the BNA and Bakary's party Union Démocratique Nigérienne (UDN) merged to become the Nigerien branch of the **Mouvement Socialiste Africain** (MSA), later **Sawaba**. When Sawaba came to power in 1957, Condat assumed the office of president of the **Territorial Assembly**, becoming thus the first president of a representative assembly in Niger's history. After the dissolution of the assembly in 1958, he was reelected deputy for **Tessaoua**, but the election was voided in April 1959 and Sawaba itself was banned. Condat did not afterward join the resulting Sawaba **rebellion** but instead chose to work with the **Parti Progressiste Nigérien** (PPN-RDA) regime and was appointed ambassador in Germany, the Benelux, and the European Economic Community (1962–1964). After a second ambassadorship in the United States (1970–1972), he was sent to the African **Groundnut** Council in Lagos (1972–1975) but was forced to retire in 1976. He lives in Niamey.

CONFÉDÉRATION DES SYNDICATS LIBRES DES TRAVAILLEURS DU NIGER (CSLTN). Breakaway confederation of trade union affiliates formerly grouped within the **Union des Syndicats des Travailleurs du Niger** (USTN). The CSLTN was formed in 1993 with 4 of the USTN's 35 affiliates.

CONFÉRENCE NATIONALE. The National Conference of 1991 presided over the redistribution of power that saw the emergence of multiparty democratic rule in Niger. The immediate cause of a movement that started in Benin and spread throughout Francophone Africa is the state of acute economic crisis that plagued all African countries at the time, but even more so the countries in the Franc Zone. During the 1980s, the International Monetary Fund (IMF) and the World Bank had pressured those countries for economic and political liberalization, which drastically called into question their preferred development strategies and the security of key state constituencies (civil servants and **students**). **France**, at the time, provided enough support to regimes such as the one in Niger to counterbalance somewhat the pressures of the IMF. By the late 1980s, however, that support was not much forthcoming, and Niger's rulers, under President **Ali Saibou**, installed a semi-authoritarian **Second Republic** which attempted to combine political liberalization with the implementation of unpopular measures. The explosive mix could not be handled; the implementation of the World Bank's sponsored educational reform policy Project Education III led to student unrest and the clash on **Niamey**'s Kennedy Bridge in February 1990, which eventually led to the collapse of the Second Republic. Students, labor unions, and politically based associations clamored for full democracy and the government ended up offering a multiparty constitution tailored on France's Fifth Republic. In the meantime, however, the example of neighboring Benin's National Conference led protesters to demand one in Niger, and France announced at a summit with African states in the town of La Baule that it intended to support **democratization** on the continent.

The National Conference opened on 29 July 1991, with the participation of 1,204 delegates from all walks of life, including 24 **political parties** (newly emerging), 69 mass organizations, students, religious leaders, the government (100 delegates), the **armed forces**, and others. Though the government did succeed in packing the conference in its favor, this had little effect on the outcome.

The conference elected **André Salifou**, a noted history professor and writer, as conference president, and on 31 July declared itself sovereign; on 9 August it suspended the recently revised constitution. It decided, however, to retain Saibou as interim head of state, though it dismissed key officers (including the chief of staff and his deputy) with whom relations had grown tense over criticism of the army's handling of the budding **Tuareg** insurgency. It also had arrested the retired colonel responsible for the liquidation of Major **Sani Souna Sido** after the latter's abortive coup in 1975, and bound the security forces to Salifou directly. These decisions set the stage for one of the missions that the conference assigned itself: trying the crimes of the *régime d'exception* and of the Second Republic (and even to the extent possible the **First Republic**, though not those of the colonial government).

On 14 August, a 30-man commission on crimes and political abuses was elected under the chairmanship of **Mamane Abou**, leader of a human rights organization and founder of the liberal weekly *Le Républicain*. It was charged inter alia with investigating 185 instances of embezzlement during the 1959–1991 period. It was before this commission that **Amadou Oumarou**, better known as **Bonkano**, famously revealed stunning but somewhat contrived and certainly braggadocio details about misrule under the *régime d'exception*.

Originally scheduled to last for 40 days, the conference continued deliberations for 3 months, setting up a 15-month interim government and legislature from its membership, to resign after the holding of legislative and presidential **elections**. It is noteworthy that despite a few pay-related mutinies by armed units, continued social unrest linked to the state of the **economy**, and the political instability of the successor civilian regime, the armed forces accepted their subordination to civilian leadership without demur, and indeed, even before the convening of the conference, distanced themselves politically from the erstwhile single party, the **Mouvement National pour la Société de Développement** (MNSD). *See also* EDUCATION.

CONSEIL CONSULTATIF NATIONAL (CCN). Name of consultative organs in operation during Niger transitions to democratic governance. One was established by Major **Daouda Malam Wanké** after his **coup d'état of 9 April 1999** and another one was decreed on 22 February 2010, just four days after Squadron Chief **Djibo Salou** ended **Mamadou Tandja**'s short-lived personal rule period. The consultative councils were given the power to adopt a new constitution after it has been prepared by a writing committee and before it underwent popular ratification through a referendum. The 1999 consultative council was strongly supervised by the executive military organ headed by Wanké, the **Conseil de Réconcilation Nationale** (CRN). The process under the 2010 **Conseil Suprême pour la Restauration de la Démocratie** (CSRD) was more open, with very little interference from the CSRD. At that time, the 131-member organ was composed of representatives of various sectors of national activity and responsibility, without participation from the politicians. But the latter strongly lobbied it to secure changes in the proposed constitution of the **Seventh Republic**, and a number of controversial innovations were eventually dropped prior to the referendum. These included the higher **education** criteria for candidates to the presidency, and a maximum age of 70 for the same position.

CONSEIL DE L'ENTENTE. A regional club of pro-French West African states, led by Côte d'Ivoire's Félix Houphouët-Boigny as a countermove to the Mali Federation which Senegal and the former French Sudan sought to establish as a pan-African nationalist initiative. Created in May 1959, it included, besides Côte d'Ivoire and Niger, Dahomey (now Benin), Haute-Volta (now Burkina Faso), and Togo. It theoretically provided for freedom of movement across state boundaries, coordination of policies in the judicial, **communications**, fiscal, economic, and developmental matters, and had a solidarity fields aimed at fiscal redistribution of accumulated funds in favor of the weaker members. President **Hamani Diori** signed Niger up to it in relation to his pro-French **foreign policy** of the 1960s as well as to his belief that by tying Niger strongly to other Francophone countries in West Africa, he would reduce its dependence on **Nigeria** and what he feared was an eastern (**Hausa**) Niger tendency to increase that dependence. After the unraveling of the Mali Federation (1962) and the later development of other regional groupings, the Conseil de l'Entente became largely inactive.

CONSEIL DE RECONCILIATION NATIONALE (CRN). Executive military body installed on 11 April 1999 by Major **Daouda Malam Wanké**, two days after he had organized the overthrowing and assassination of President **Ibrahim Baré Maïnassara**. It was headed by Wanké, who received from it the powers of head of state and of government. It also expressed the **armed forces'** consensus on a speedy restoration of democratic and civilian governance, and scheduled its own dissolution to occur within nine months of its creation. The council was disbanded following the first **Fifth Republic**'s **elections** in November 1999, after only eight months in existence. The council had 14 members, including Captain **Djibrilla Hamidou Hima** and Lieutenant-Colonel **Moumouni Boureima** who would, throughout the ensuing Fifth Republic, become the most influential military officers in the country.

CONSEIL DE SALUT NATIONAL (CSN). A military executive directorate made up of 12 high officers, and set up after the **coup d'état of 27 January 1996**, when army chief of staff Colonel **Ibrahim Baré Maïnassara** toppled President **Mahaman Ousmane** following the political gridlock then stalling the **Third Republic**. It was headed by Baré Maïnassara and the gendarmerie high commander, Colonel **Youssoufa Maïga**. Other key members were Lieutenant-Colonels **Moussa Moumouni Djermakoye** and **Moussa Gros**, Battalion Chief **Moumouni Boureima**, and Captain **Daouda Malam Wanké**. All of the latter will be involved, directly or indirectly, in the coup d'état that will remove Baré Maïnassara in 1999 and they will come to constitute the mainstay of the hierarchical military consensus behind army interventions in politics, including after the **coup d'état of 18 February**

2010. Unlike the executive military organs set up after 1999 and 2010, the CSN ushered in a period in which, under the trappings of a civilian democratic regime—the **Fourth Republic**—President Baré Maïnassara essentially endeavored to restore authoritarian government. The eventual failure of this attempt seems to have shaped future military consensuses strongly in favor of democratic governance.

CONSEIL GENERAL (General Council). Niger's first colonial **territorial assembly**, when the colony became a French Territoire d'Outre-Mer—a more liberal status. It was set up by decree on 25 October 1946, in Niger as well as in the other colonies of **France**, and its first local **elections** (in two stages) took place on 15 December 1946 and 5 January 1947. The double electoral college elected 10 councilors from the first college (European) and 20 from the second (African). The first president of the council was the *zarmakoy* of **Dosso**, Moumouni Aouta. On 6 February 1952, the General Council was transformed into the Assemblée Territoriale.

CONSEIL MILITAIRE SUPRÊME (CMS). The Supreme Military Council was a formalization of the military clique which plotted and implemented the **coup d'état of 15 April 1974** against President **Hamani Diori**. After the coup, Lieutenant-Colonel **Seyni Kountché** emerged as the leader of the council but the consensus was only apparent, and two attempted coups d'état from within the council were averted in 1975 and 1976, including one from the council's vice-president, Major **Sani Souna Siddo**. Afterward, Kountché relied on the military and on close friends, including future presidents **Ali Saibou** and **Mamadou Tandja**, and the future political rival of the latter, **Adamou Moumouni Djermakoy**. The council remained in place to signal the military nature of the regime but did not play any politically significant role. It was disbanded in 1989, when Ali Saibou decided to push Kountché's normalization process into the restoration of republican order in 1989. *See also RÉGIME D'EXCEPTION.*

CONSEIL MUNICIPAL. The municipal council is the first-level deliberative institution of Niger's decentralized regions, running the **communes**. Councilors are elected through direct universal suffrage, and they then form the electoral college that chooses the mayor of the commune. Their term of office runs for four years and each councilor can be reelected only once. The council itself comprises the councilors, the mayor, and his assistants, and it must be made up of at least 10 percent of the least-represented gender (generally female). Traditional chiefs and deputies from the area who were not elected councils can still sit in it but have only a consultative voice. In many rural communes, councilors are educated men and **women**, often civil servants, who do not actually reside in their villages and *tribus* but in a nearby town or in **Niamey**.

CONSEIL NATIONAL DE DÉVELOPPEMENT (CND). The highest bureau of the military regime's "development society" vision, an epistemological, ideological, and structural innovation of the 1980s, lauded (and derided) as Niger's noncapitalist, nonsocialist approach to development. A first CND had been put in place in 1975, but the infighting in the **Conseil Militaire Suprême** put a hold on its development. Finally, in 1978–1979 President **Kountché** mobilized all the top Nigerien technocrats that he could to ponder a structured purpose and ideology for his administration on the basis of the prevailing ideals of national development of the day. Following in the footpath of such luminaries as Mamadou Dia of Senegal and Julius Nyerere of Tanzania, though with less ideological fanfare, Niger's developmentalists designed the system they thought was suitable to the economic conditions and general characters of the country.

Ultimately a system of hierarchically organized development agencies was ratified in which primacy was granted, at the base level, to the local *samariya* (youth organization) and the agricultural cooperatives. At the top of the hierarchy stood the national-level Conseil National de Développement, which became also the first deliberative assembly since the 1974 **coup d'état of 1974**. The CND was composed of 150 delegates elected from the seven *départements* of Niger, and included the entire CSM and other military representatives via the *préfets*, who were all officers. The function of the CND—whose first meeting took place in November 1983—was to propose to the cabinet fundamental development options. It was regarded as an agency of greater importance than the cabinet, with the leadership of the CND entrusted to the hands of the former prime minister, **Mamane Oumarou**.

Elections for the CND took place by "consensus voting" in July 1983, with the ballot box being bypassed owing to a conception of Niger's traditional culture that favored consultation over competition. The basic unit of the hierarchy was the village CND, followed by the local (canton), subregional, regional, and ultimately the national CND.

This system of organization was meant to spur the development of a movement that would transform Niger's national society for development without going through a state revolution, as had happened in Burkina Faso in the early 1980s. But the initiatives taken in this regard were doomed by Niger's acute economic crisis of the late 1980s, which eroded the legitimacy of the regime. After the death of Kountché and the rise to power of **Ali Saibou**, the **Mouvement National pour la Société de Développement** (MNSD) of which the CND was an integral part, was institutionalized as a **political party** in a further attempt to legitimate the regime through national elections. The entire structural hierarchy disappeared as MNSD turned into a normal party with the onset of competitive multiparty politics in 1991.

CONSEIL SUPERIEUR D'ORIENTATION NATIONALE (CSON). State/party organ formally set up by President **Ali Saibou** in May 1989 as the top level of the newly institutionalized single **political party** of Niger (hitherto a "movement")—the **Mouvement National pour la Société de Développement** (MNSD)—replacing to an extent the **Conseil Militaire Suprême**. Saibou was both the president of the CSON and, after the **elections** of 1989 in which he ran as the sole candidate of the sole new political party, of Niger. The CSON, composed of 77 civilian and military members, was elected by a 750-man constituent congress of the MNSD on 17 May 1989. It had a 14-man executive organ—the Bureau Exécutif National—which included six cabinet members and eight without specific portfolios. The council was in place until 1991.

CONSEIL SUPRÊME POUR LA RESTAURATION DE LA DÉMOCRATIE (CSRD). Executive military organ established on 19 February 2010 by Squadron Chief **Djibo Salou**, the day after he had removed **Mamadou Tandja** from the presidency. Tandja had committed a constitutional coup d'état against the **Fifth Republic** in July–August 2009, and had stayed on beyond the expiration of his term of office (December 2009). The council expressed the **armed forces'** consensus for a speedy return to democratic and civilian rule, which was processed in stages and completed in March 2011. Throughout, Djibo Salou—later appointed general to end hierarchical tensions in the military—presided over the state and the government. The council was dissolved following the **election** of a legislature and a president in March 2011. The CSRD had wanted to distinguish its tenure from that of the **Conseil de Réconciliation Nationale** (CRN), which fulfilled a similar mission in 1999, by also attempting to clean up Niger's finances. It was not clear that the CSRD was successful in this effort however.

CONSTITUTIONAL REFERENDUMS. Referendums in Niger have so far been used exclusively to adopt new constitutions. Eight such consultations have been organized so far, all leading to a positive response.

Constitutional Referendum of 18 September 1958: Approval of the constitution meant internal autonomy within the Communauté Française federation, while rejection meant immediate independence. Voting was manipulated by the administration. With a somewhat low turnout of 36.7 percent, 78.43 percent of voters approved the constitution against 21.57 percent who rejected it.

National Charter Referendum of 16 June 1987: Approval of a national charter issued by decree and establishing nonelective, consultative institutions at national and local levels, while also granting freedom of association and limited freedom of expression. The heavily controlled voting yielded the unanimous approval of 99.58 percent of voters, said to have turned out at 96.8 percent.

Constitutional Referendum of 24 September 1989: Approval of a single-party presidential system, at 99.28 percent of valid suffrage.

Constitutional Referendum of 26 December 1992: Approval of a multiparty semipresidential system, with a president and legislature serving for five years with no term limits. Turnout was high at 56.6 percent and 89.79 percent of this free ballot approved the constitution against 10.21 percent who rejected it.

Constitutional Referendum of 12 May 1996: Approval of a multiparty presidential system. Turnout in this somewhat free ballot was low at 35 percent and the proposed constitution was approved by 92.34 percent of voters.

Constitutional Referendum of 18 July 1999: Approval of a multiparty semipresidential system, with two-term limits on the presidency and a judiciary with enhanced review powers. Turnout very low at 31.2 percent, but 89.61 percent of voters nodded the constitution into existence.

Constitutional Referendum of 4 August 2009: Approval of a multiparty system removing presidential term limits, granting absolute executive powers to the president, and creating an upper house of the legislature (the Senate). The opposition boycotted the voting. Turnout was alleged to have enthusiastically climbed to 68.3 percent while unofficial observations estimated it at less than 10 percent; 92.5 percent of alleged voters approved the new constitution.

Constitutional Referendum of 31 October 2010: Return to a semipresidential system with two five-year terms for president. Turnout was comparatively high in this free ballot, at 52 percent, and the constitution was approved by 90.19 percent of voters.

See also ELECTIONS.

CONSTITUTIONS. Niger has had eight constitutions, one national charter, and two major constitutional revisions—though it should be said that three of its constitutions are in fact the same one interrupted and revised by political transition committees (see below, points 7, 9, and 11):

1. *The constitution of 25 February 1959*, ratified by the Constituent Assembly. The constitution set up a quasi-parliamentary system with a president

of the council with executive powers invested by an assembly to whom he was responsible. The assembly, elected for five years, was composed of 60 deputies.

2. *The constitution of 8 October1960*, ratified by the **National Assembly**, set up a presidential system in which the executive president was to be elected by universal franchise simultaneously with deputies for the assembly who, as before, were elected for five years. The constitution also transferred to the Nigerien government powers hitherto lodged in the French Community, including defense, **foreign policy**, and **currency** matters. The constitution further provided that cabinet members could not also be members of Parliament. This was the constitution of what came to be known as the **First Republic**. It was suspended on 15 April 1974 and subsequently abrogated that year.

3. *The constitutional reform of 7 September 1965*, disassociated the election of the president of the republic from the **elections** of the National Assembly, and specified that deputies would be elected on the basis of national lists.

4. *The Charte Nationale* was adopted by the **Conseil National de Développement** on 21 March 1987 and from there went into several other procedural adoptions until its ratification by referendum on 14 June 1987 and its enactment the following September. The charter was only a step in the future adoption of a constitution. It defined the development society, the concept of the state, and the organization of the executive councils tasked with the mission of pushing the country forward using rules for (the motto went) "consultation, dialogue and participation." It also made room for "freedom of association of a political nature," leading to the emergence of the nuclei of the future **political parties**.

5. *The constitution of 24 September 1989*, ratified in these unanimous times by 99.28 percent of those who voted, and 95.08 percent of the total electorate. The constitution saw the reemergence of party politics via a single governmental party headed by President **Ali Saibou**—the recently institutionalized **Mouvement National pour la Société de Développement** (MNSD)—and a national assembly elected for the first time since the onset of military rule in 1974. It should be noted that the first draft of the constitution included provisions for multipartyism, which were removed however before the referendum. The constitution was short-lived since the demonstrations that ushered in multiparty democratic rule came shortly after. It was specifically abrogated by the **Conférence Nationale** in 1991 (with the National Assembly dissolved and replaced with an interim Haut Conseil de la République, elected from the conference's membership), which in due course codified a new constitution. This was the constitution of the **Second Republic**.

6. *The constitutional revision of 24 April 1991* brought some radical modifications to the constitution of 1989 by putting in place a semipresidential,

multiparty regime and by completely doing away with the last remnants of the **armed forces'** influence on executive power. It also moved a step further toward the rule of law at the political level by bestowing on the **Cour Suprême** the power of constitutional review. The revision was meant to salvage the Second Republic, which it failed to do.

7. *The constitution of 26 December 1992*, enacted on 22 January 1993. The constitution was ratified by 89.79 percent of those who voted vs 10.21 percent who rejected it. Of Niger's total population at the time, 3.9 million were entitled to vote, 2.7 million registered to vote, and 2.2 million actually voted. The constitution set up a dual executive with a head of state (elected for five years in two electoral rounds, and reelectable only once) who named a head of government responsible to an 83-man National Assembly elected by proportional representation. This was the constitution of the **Third Republic.**

8. *The constitution of 12 May 1996*, allegedly voted in by 92.26 percent of those who voted, with an alleged participation rate of 34.94 percent. The constitution established a presidentialist system, rather than a purely presidential one: While the head of state, elected for five years in two electoral rounds, was the actual head of the government, and while the government was not accountable to Parliament (which in turn could not be dissolved by the president), Article 48 gave as much legislative powers to the president as to Parliament and Article 86 enabled the president to request from Parliament the right to change the law in order to implement his programs. The balance of power inherent in a pure presidential system is therefore absent from this constitution. This was the constitution of the **Fourth Republic.**

9. *The constitution of 9 August 1999.* Voted after a sluggish referendum campaign with a participation rate of 18 percent, but under excellent conditions of freedom and fairness, this constitution is a restoration of the constitution of 1992, with a few modifications destined to dampen the risks of institutional instability that had bedeviled its Third Republic antecedent. Thus, it erected the constitutional chamber of the Supreme Court into a true judicial power, organized under the name of **Cour Constitutionnelle** in a way that would make political manipulation of the judicial review authority of the constitution extremely difficult (as President **Mamadou Tandja** was to discover in 2009). It also extended the time after which the president would be able to dissolve Parliament after an earlier dissolution, changing it from one year to two. This was the constitution of the **Fifth Republic.**

10. *The constitution of 4 August 2009*, adopted through a referendum organized by President Mamadou Tandja in extremely coercive conditions, and with a national rate of participation estimated to be below 10 percent by most independent observers. It established a presidentialist system giving extensive executive and legislative powers to the president and weakening

oversight mechanisms; enacting that before it came into full effect, President Mamadou Tandja would have been allowed to govern for three years as he saw fit. This is to date the shortest-lived of Niger's constitutions, since it ruled the country—or tried to—for only about six months. This was the constitution of the **Sixth Republic**.

11. *The constitution of 2 November 2010*, adopted through a referendum organized by the **Conseil Suprême pour la Restauration de la Démocratie** (CSRD), restores Niger to the semipresidential system of the Third and Fifth Republic's constitutions. Coming after the divisive and oppressive Sixth Republic regime, this constitution was adopted by 90 percent of voters with a voting turnout of about 53 percent, not seen in the country since 1992. The day of the constitution's enactment (26 November 2010) was declared a festival. In the draft constitution, candidates to the presidency were required to have a university degree (and deputies a secondary school degree) while the age at which one could bid for the presidency was capped at 70 (deposed President Tandja was 71 when he tried to suppress democracy). These innovations were removed from the final text. This is the constitution of the **Seventh Republic**. *See also* CONSTITUTIONAL REFERENDUMS.

CONVENTION DÉMOCRATIQUE ET SOCIALE (CDS Rahama). The **Hausa** word appended to the acronym of the party derives from the Arabic *rahama*, meaning divine mercy. The CDS was founded in January 1991 under the leadership of **Mahaman Ousmane**, evolving from an ethno-regional organization established by cadres from **Zinder** and **Maradi** during the liberalization period that preceded Niger's adoption of multiparty democracy, the Association Mutuelle pour la Culture et les Arts (AMACA). While keeping Zinder as its stronghold, the CDS has managed over the years to become one of the four major **political parties** of the recent period, with some national reach.

During the run-up to Niger's first free **elections** in 1992–1993, the CDS joined a coalition of parties, the **Alliance des Forces du Changement** (AFC), cobbled together by the opponents of the ancient regime party, the **Mouvement National pour la Société de Développement** (MNSD), in order to prevent that party from winning its way back to power through elections. Upon AFC's victory, Ousmane became the first president of Niger's **Third Republic**. The CDS was ousted from power by the coup d'état of **Ibrahim Baré Maïnassara** in January 1996. It then associated with its former rivals, the MNSD and the **Parti Nigérien pour le Socialisme et la Démocratie** (PNDS Tarayya), to form a dissenting coalition, the Front pour la Restauration et la Défense de la Démocratie (FRDD), which contested the legitimacy of Baré Maïnassara and his regime.

After the **coup d'état of 1999**, which put an end to Maïnassara's rule, the CDS allied itself with the MNSD and its chairman, Ousmane, became the president of the **National Assembly** upon the electoral victory of the MNSD-led coalition. When President **Mamadou Tandja** started to subvert the **Fifth Republic** in June 2009, the CDS drifted away from the MNSD alliance, removing its members from the Nigerien government (although not all of them complied), and finally creating a pro-democracy coalition with five smaller parties, the Mouvement pour la Défense de la Démocratie (MDD). But Tandja had managed to carve out a base in Zinder, chiefly through weakening CDS's hold on that region. As a result, when the **armed forces** eventually restored democratic governance in February 2010, CDS struggled to regain its full power and influence. Moreover, it failed to present at the legislative **elections** of 2011, lists that conformed to the new electoral rules on quotas of **women** and the illiterate, leading to an invalidation of its list in its stronghold in Zinder. This explains its terribly dismal showing at those, where it secured only two seats at the National Assembly. At the presidential election, however, Ousmane came off fourth of 10 candidates, with 8.42 percent of the vote. In the Nigerien context, the CDS may be defined as a centrist party.

COORDINATION DE LA RESISTANCE ARMÉE (CRA). Early co-ordinating group of several of Niger's **Tuareg** irredentist movements. The CRA was formed on 11 September 1993 by **Mano Dayak** and grouped the Front de Libération Temust (FLT), the Front Patriotique de la Libération du Sahara (FPLS), the **Armée Révolutionnaire de Libération du Nord Niger** (ARLN), and the **Front de Libération de l'Aïr et l'Azawad** (FLAA), the last having been the first to form. The president of the FLAA, **Rhissa ag Boula**, was the vice-president of the CRA. The CRA gave way, in 1995, to the Organisation de la Résistance Armée (also headed by Rhissa Ag Boula), which in April 1995 signed a peace agreement with the government of Niger. *See also* TUAREG REBELLIONS.

COORDINATION DES FORCES DÉMOCRATIQUES POUR LA RÉPUBLIQUE (CFDR). Initially a large coalition of **political parties** and trade **unions** created on 16 July 2009 to oppose President Mamadou Tandja's plans of establishing personal rule in the country. The CFDR united a coalition of political parties, civic associations, and trade unions set up under the leadership of future president **Mahamadou Issoufou**, the Front de Défense de la Démocratie (FDD), a smaller coalition of political parties led by former president **Mahaman Ousmane**, the Mouvement pour la Défense de la Démocratie et de la République (MDDR), a **civil society** coalition, the Front pour la Démocratie et la République (FDR), and the seven trade union federations of the country. The CFDR organized the boycott of the August 2009 referendum through which Tandja instituted the short-lived **Sixth Republic**, as well as the subsequent legislative **elections** of October 2009. It also organized several demonstrations which were violently repressed by security forces and installed its own "authentic" Parliament after the Sixth Republic's legislative elections of October 2009. However, thanks to the support of the **Economic Community of West African States** (ECOWAS), it became the protagonist to which Tandja was required, by the organization, to talk in order to solve the political crisis into which his actions had plunged Niger. In the end, Tandja rejected ECOWAS's demands and was eventually removed by Niger's **armed forces** on 18 February 2010.

A few months later, in July, the original CFDR disappeared and was replaced by a group of political parties that signed an agreement in view of the elections of 2011. The agreement, called a *pacte politique* (political compact), had the quixotic aim of suppressing all conflicts and tensions between Nigerien politicians, under the impression that it was such divisions that had paved the way to Tandja's constitutional coup. As the date of elections neared, however, the compact unraveled, and CFDR lost some of its key members—especially the Convention Démocratique et Sociale of former president Ousmane—to become an electoral machine for Mahamadou Issoufou and former Prime Minister **Hama Amadou**. Many parties, sensing the chances of Issoufou, knocked at the door of CFDR, but not all were admitted. The updated coalition eventually triumphed at all the elections of 2011. *See also* TAZARTCHÉ.

COORDINATION DES ONG ET ASSOCIATIONS FEMININES (CONGAFEN). A collective of feminine nongovernmental organizations (NGO) and civic associations, founded in 1995 and now gathering together 51 organizations. CONGAFEN is chiefly a lobbying group which coordinates the forces of its member associations for pressure on the government on key **women**'s issues. Its membership includes historic associations such as the **Association des Femmes du Niger** (AFN) and the **Association des Femmes Juristes du Niger** (AFJN) as well as NGOs focused on very specific issues (SRMSR Dimol, for instance, a reproduction **health** task force) or credit and development institutions, thus the women's savings and credit outfit Mutuelle d'Epargne et de Crédit des Femmes (MECREF). CONGAFEN also counts in its membership the Union des Femmes Catholiques du Niger (UFCN), the only religious group admitted in the federation, chiefly on account of the minority position of **Christianity** and the fact that Islamic associations are the ideological antagonists of Nigerien feminism. *See also* CIVIL SOCIETY.

COPRO-NIGER. *See* SOCIÉTÉ NATIONALE DE COMMERCE ET DE PRODUCTION DU NIGER.

COTTON. There were only a few spots of traditional cotton cultivation in Niger, until 1956 when modern and intensive modes of cultivation were introduced by the state-owned French company Compagnie Française pour le Développement des Fibres Textiles (CFDT). CFDT had been created by the French government to get cotton going in the Franc Zone countries of Africa (CFDT worked also in Benin, Burkina Faso, Cameroon, the Central African Republic, Chad, Côte d'Ivoire, Guinea, Madagascar, Mali, Senegal, and Togo). The CFDT ventures were generally a success, thanks to a commercial model that guaranteed the price of purchase to peasant producers and integrated community benefits to credit systems and individual profit. The most palpable evidence of CFDT's success is the fact that West Africa's Francophone countries produce vastly more cotton—and of the highest grade—than the much more populated Anglophone **Nigeria** and Ghana. In Niger, CFDT's cotton zones included the *gulbi* areas of the **Gobir**, the valleys of Ader–Doutchi–Maggia, and the lower **Dallol Maouri**.

Commencing from 112 tons in 1956, cotton harvests went up to 10,000 tons before plummeting with the onset of the **Sahel drought** in the 1970s, to revive in the 1980s. The purchase of the cotton harvest was then allowed only to the CFDT and the state cooperative umbrella **Union Nigérienne de Crédit et de Coopérative** (UNCC), with the price (for the highest purity) set at 37 **CFA francs** per kilo in the mid-1970s. In 1988, CFDT retreated out of Niger's cotton sector and was briefly replaced by a state company, the Société Cotonnière du Niger (SCN), to which was added, the following year, a private Nigerien-Chinese company operating in the region of **Gaya**. By 1998, production had been pushed up again from the lows of the early 1980s (1,000 tons on average) to around 11,000 tons. In recent years, the average production has tended to peak at 8,000 tons, although the government is mulling over plans to drastically develop the sector, with a 100,000 ton peak output as its target.

COUP OF 3 DECEMBER 1963 (Attempted). Little-publicized mutiny and attempt at sedition that was a prelude to a coup attempt. The key figures were Captain **Hassan A. Diallo**, who was arrested on 3 December 1963, then released and arrested again on 13 December, and **Ikhia Zodi**, at the time the minister of African affairs, who lost his post over the affair and was imprisoned. There was in this event an element of ethnic and social resentment. Both Diallo and Zodi were **Fulani**, and Diallo in particular was impatient because he had received orders from a government dominated by **Boubou Hama**, a man of servile status in the **Songhay** society to which he belonged. There were also contacts between Diallo, Zodi, and **Sawaba** elements. However, the entire affair was quite muddled, and its key casualty was the Ministry of African Affairs, which the government had created to define Niger's **foreign policy** in terms of openness on the African continent.

COUP OF 15 APRIL 1974. Led by the chief of staff of two years, Lieutenant-Colonel **Seyni Kountché**, the 1:00 a.m. coup had the almost total support of the **armed forces**. The only unit to resist, spurred on by President **Hamani Diori**'s wife, **Aissa Diori**, was the **Tuareg** Presidential Guard. Aissa Diori was one of the few victims of the coup.

The army had developed throughout the years a variety of grudges against the regime. Used to enforce highly unpopular tax collection, the army was also vividly aware of the effects of the **drought** in the countryside and the discrimination against certain groups in the government and the countryside. In like manner, the mutual-defense treaty signed with **Libya** shortly before the actual coup was deeply resented (according to many observers, this was the prime cause of the coup), as were Diori's efforts to harness the army for political tasks. Paradoxically, President Diori had been forewarned, as early as 1973, that Kountché was unreliable but had nevertheless promoted him to chief of staff. The officially stated reasons for the coup were slightly different: wide-scale corruption, the absence of democracy in Niger, and the government's overinvolvement in foreign affairs to the detriment of domestic concerns. Many observers believed that **France** played a role in the coup, angry at Diori's attempts to draw non-French commercial interests into Niger's **uranium** industry. On the other hand, the resident French military mission was expelled immediately after the coup.

Following the coup most government agencies were abolished, and most high government officials were placed under house arrest subject to charges being levied against them. The military regime also immediately opened up grain-distribution centers in **Zinder**, **Maradi**, **Birni-N'Konni**, and **N'Guigmi**, and began expeditiously to move goods destined for drought relief but bottlenecked all the way to the Atlantic ports. Large amounts of **groundnut** seeds were also distributed, even though it was known that farmers would consume them rather than plant them. Support for the coup was immediate from most circles, including Niger's exiled opposition groups who were reinvited back to **Niamey** on condition that they would avoid political activity.

At first mostly military, the regime slowly introduced more civilians until on 21 February 1976, a government shuffle resulted in a majority of civilian appointments, most unconnected to the former regime. During the first year the government's stress was on drought relief and on preventing speculation, which, then as now, was being practiced on a large scale. Internal competition within the armed forces resulted in at least five major challenges to Kountché's leadership.

COUP OF AUGUST 1975 (Attempted). Conspiracy aimed at overthrowing the newly established military regime of President **Seyni Kountché**. The vice-president of the **Conseil Militaire Suprême**, Major **Sani Souna Sido**, headed the conspiracy, allegedly in coordination with the recently returned **Sawaba** leader, **Djibo Bakary**, and with the involvement of a variety of individuals. The coup was nipped at the bud, and some of the key conspirators died in prison, while others were not freed until 1983. Sani Souna Sido was officially executed for his role, but at the 1991 **Conférence Nationale**, it was revealed that the deed was closer to being a murder. *See also* ARMED FORCES.

COUP OF 15 MARCH 1976 (Attempted). An attempted coup against the government of President **Seyni Kountché** that lasted only a few hours. In the uprising—which resulted in the capture by rebels of the radio station, the army headquarters, and a few other installations—the regime stated that eight government soldiers were killed. Outside observers put the total killed in very fierce fighting at over 50. An attack on the presidential palace was repulsed. Captain Mohamed Sidi and Major **Moussa Bayeré** led the uprising. Arms were brought into Niger from **Libya** via the latter's diplomatic pouch (allegedly without the knowledge of Libyan authorities) and transported by trucks of the **COPRO-NIGER** company at the orders of former director **Ahmed Mouddour**, through the ministrations of Libyan adventurer **Liman Chaafi**. Most of the plotters were **Hausa**, and there were a variety of personal motives behind the assault, including a ploy by Libya's Colonel Kadhafi to unsettle Niger and annex its northeastern section. Courts-martial after the attempted putsch issued a number of harsh sentences, including 28 life imprisonment and nine death sentences. The key leaders were executed on 21 April 1976. They included Mouddour, Bayeré, Sidi, former chief of general intelligence **Idrissa Boubé**, and Issaka dan Koussou. *See also* ARMED FORCES.

COUP OF 5 OCTOBER 1983 (Attempted). Carefully organized coup attempt during President **Seyni Kountché**'s absence abroad, masterminded by his friend and security advisor, *chef de cabinet* of the prime minister, Lieutenant **Amadou Oumarou**, nicknamed Bonkano, who was also in charge of security in the presidency. Among those involved, apparently solely for reasons of self-advancement, were Lieutenant **Idrissa Amadou** (commander of the Presidential Guard) and Major Amadou Seydou (commander of the **Niamey** garrison). The coup attempt collapsed when officers loyal to Kountché questioned the orders aimed at their entrapment. Most of those involved escaped the country, including Bonkano, immensely rich from his control of the portals of the presidential office. In 1991, granted personal immunity for his misdeeds, he returned to Niger to testify before a committee of the **Conférence Nationale** investigating corrupt practices during previous regimes. *See also* ARMED FORCES.

COUP OF 27 JANUARY 1996. Organized by army chief of staff Colonel **Ibrahim Baré Maïnassara**. The coup was motivated by the institutional gridlock which had been paralyzing the state since the legislative **elections** of January 1995. The elections had been won by a coalition led by the **Mouvement National pour la Société de Développement** (MNSD Nassara), forcing President **Ousmane (Convention Démocratique et Sociale)** to appoint a prime minister from the MNSD. This led to a government headed by the MNSD's secretary-general, **Hama Amadou**, with whom Ousmane stubbornly refused to collaborate to run the country. Resorting to several obstructions—including refusing to show up at cabinet meetings and sign decrees—Ousmane stalled government operation, waiting for the date of 28 January 1996, when he would be able, as per the constitution, to again dissolve the **National Assembly** and seek a more compliant legislative majority. When this was happening, Niger's financial crisis had reached extremely serious levels, and it was not clear that new and costly legislative elections would lead to an outcome acceptable to Ousmane. In these circumstances, the coup of 27 January 1996—on the eve of the day at which Ousmane would have been able to dissolve the National Assembly—was welcomed with a sigh of relief in Niger. The coup-makers organized a so-called *action militaire de rectification* (corrective military action), attacking the presidential palace and arresting the president and all members of the government. Ousmane and Amadou were then made to both sign their resignation, while Baré Maïnassara promised that regular democratic governance would be restored in four months' time. While Western countries (with the exception of **France**) condemned the coup, the entire Nigerien class called for support for Baré Maïnassara, partly because they recognized their responsibility in causing the coup, and greatly because they were expecting Baré Maïnassara to keep his promise of quickly restoring democratic governance. In this, however, they were deceived. *See also* BARÉ MAÏNASSARA, IBRAHIM; FOURTH REPUBLIC.

COUP OF 9 APRIL 1999. The coup of April 1999 was the outcome of the political crisis escalation caused by President **Baré Maïnassara** when he pressured the constitutional chamber of the **Cour Suprême** to declare flawed 80 percent of the regional **elections** voting of February 1999, in which opposition parties had routed his party despite heavy-handed attempts at manipulation. The elections themselves had been organized after lengthy negotiations the previous year between the regime and the opposition, and they were considered a step in the reconciliation between the two camps, which would end the ambiance of political crisis in which Niger had been living since Baré Maïnassara had stolen the presidential election in 1996. The court issued its ruling on 7 April 1999 and two days later the president was killed with a machine gun by his personal guard at the military airport of **Niamey**, as he was preparing to board a plane, at 10 in the morning. The coup had been masterminded by Major **Daouda Malam Wanké**, chief of the armored squad and a partner of Baré Maïnassara in his own coup of 1996. It was a quiet coup with few casualties, the principal one being the president himself, whose death was later announced by Prime Minister **Ibrahim Hassane Mayaki** as the result of an "*accident malheureux*" (an unfortunate accident). The government appointed by Baré Maïnassara remained in place during the nine-month period that returned Niger to democratic governance. *See also* ARMED FORCES; COUP OF 27 JANUARY 1996.

COUP OF 18 FEBRUARY 2010. Niger's most popular coup to date, it was the outcome of the protracted and divisive political crisis caused by President **Mamadou Tandja**'s will to stay indefinitely in power beyond his final term under Niger's **Fifth Republic**'s constitution. The coup leader was a junior officer, squadron chief **Djibo Salou**, who led the attack of the presidential palace at noontime, as Tandja was presiding over a cabinet meeting. There were no civilian casualties, despite the violence of the attack. The coup was followed by a curfew which was lifted a day later, allowing Niameyans to come out and celebrate on the streets by the thousands. The following week, transition institutions were put in place together with a new government, and the restoration of democratic governance was organized to be concluded in a 12-month process.

In the arc of Niger's military coups, this one signals a deeply changed context. The coups and coup attempts in the 1960–1980s sought to take over the state and conquer power at all costs. The **Baré Maïnassara** coup was a transitional putsch, with the coup-maker retaining power even as he attempted to put a democratic makeup on his actions. By 1999, it had become impossible to keep power after a coup. A coup now simply removes the cause of political crisis and stops there. The Djibo Salou coup of 2010 not only recognized this but drew the consequence of therefore achieving removal with the minimum casualties and a show of decency. Tandja, the victim of his coup, benefited from this evolution by being put under house arrest in a luxurious state villa, instead of being murdered as was Baré Maïnassara. *See also* ARMED FORCES; COUP OF 27 JANUARY 1996; TAZARTCHÉ.

COUR CONSTITUTIONNELLE. At independence in 1960, constitutional review powers were given, in Niger, to the constitutional chamber of the **Cour Suprême**. The military regime that took power in 1974 changed the Supreme Court into a Cour d'État (State Court) which did not have a constitutional chamber, owing to the fact that Niger was in a *régime d'exception* (regime of exception)—that is to say, a regime without a constitution. Although a constitutional text (the National Charter) was eventually adopted in 1986, it is only on 13 June 1990 that a Supreme Court was reinstalled, complete with a constitutional chamber. The Supreme Court survived the **Conférence Nationale** and to the **coup d'état of 1996**. Following the **coup d'état of 1999**, and during the transition period when there was no constitution, it was transformed into a Cour d'État but still retained a constitutional chamber, in view of the speedy process of democratic restoration then put underway. The new **constitution** adopted that year eliminated the constitutional chamber, however, owing to the negative role it played in the crisis that led to the assassination of President **Baré Maïnassara**. It was deemed that the chamber was not independent enough, and it was replaced by a new judicial body, completely separated from the Supreme Court, and composed in such a way that its independence seemed guaranteed: the constitutional court.

The court has seven members, each aged 40 or above. Of these, the president of the republic and the **National Assembly** nominate one member each, the judge's body elects two members, the attorneys elect one member, a law scholar with a doctorate in public law is elected as a member by the Law School, and human rights associations elect a member from the **civil society** known to master public law (generally therefore a jurist). Members are elected for a six-year nonrenewable term, must desist from absolutely any other office and occupation, and while they can resign, they cannot be dismissed. However, the great originality of the Niger constitutional court is that the court's president and vice-president are both elected by its members, instead of being appointed by the president of the republic as happens elsewhere. The court's rulings are binding and suffer no appeal.

Since its creation, the court has tackled two major crises. In August 2002 it issued a binding decision about the government's policy in the region of **Diffa**, following a military mutiny there. The government had put the region under state of emergency through a decree, which was an unconstitutional procedure. Although the government creatively called its policy "*état de mise en garde*" and not "*état d'urgence*" in order to avoid an attack by the court, the latter did strike its policy down. The government refused to comply, however, and in protest the president and vice-president of the court resigned. The following month, the government lifted the emergency state to quell an impending political crisis. More famously, the court, under its president, **Fatimata Salifou Bazeye**, twice denied—in May and June 2009—then-president **Mamadou Tandja** the right to hold a referendum on a new constitution, thereby effectively ruining his ploy to legally terminate the **Fifth Republic**. Tandja had to dissolve the court on 30 June, an action which, being out of the scope of his powers as president of Niger, formally signaled his move into a coup d'état mode. Indeed, it is then that the phrase "constitutional coup d'état" started to characterize his actions in Niger. Tandja promptly recreated a constitutional court, but it was an illegal one since he handpicked its membership. In February 2010, after the toppling of Tandja, a consultative constitutional review body was constituted under the name Conseil Constitutionnel (constitutional council), headed by Bazeye, and it remained in place throughout the yearlong transition to the **Seventh Republic**. Restoration of democracy in January 2011 also restored the constitutional court in the form and shape it had under the Fifth Republic. *See also* FOURTH REPUBLIC.

COUR DE SÛRÉTÉ D'ÉTAT. Formed in April 1964 as a court for crimes against the state and, specifically, plots and attempted coups. The impetus for its creation was the revelation of the Diallo plot. In June 1964 the court became a *cour martiale* empowered to judge, in accord with specific procedures, flagrant antistate activities. The president of the Cour de Sûrété was **Boubacar Ali Diallo**, who had been aware of the Diallo plot. Among cases heard by the court was that of Amadou Diop—of the grenade attack on President **Hamani Diori**—in which the death sentence was meted out (but not executed), and of some 80 political prisoners from **Tahoua** and **Agadez**, sentenced to life imprisonment in connection with the **Sawaba** uprising. *See also* DIALLO, HASSAN A.

COUR SUPRÊME. Court of last resort, not to be confused with the **Haute Cour de Justice**, which was a section of the Cour Suprême, or with the **Cour Constitutionnelle**, erected in 1999 on the ashes of its constitutional chamber. As Supreme Courts elsewhere, it fulfills the role of highest judicial review institution, and must promote jurisprudential unity over the country's territory. It was first created in 1960 with four specific chambers: civil affairs, constitutional affairs, audit matters, and the Haute Cour de Justice. Under the **First Republic**, it was headed by Ousmane Bassarou Diallo. The military regime that came to power in April 1974 replaced it with a Cour d'État which had only three chambers: judicial, administrative, and audit matters. The Cour Suprême reemerged with the constitutionalization of the **Ali**

Saibou regime in 1990, under Mamadou Malam Awami, with a fourth chamber, the constitutional chamber. It was reconstituted and kept by the **Conférence Nationale** in 1991 and the subsequent **constitution** of 1992. In April 1999, its constitutional chamber was used by President **Baré Maïnassara** to cheat the opposition parties of their electoral triumph of February that year, and after the removal of Baré Maïnassara in a coup, the 1999 constitution abolished the chamber and erected in its stead an independent institution, the **Cour Constitutionnelle**.

COURMO, BARCOURGNÉ (1916–1993). Former cabinet minister and early secretary-general of the **Parti Progressiste Nigérien** (PPN-RDA), ruling party of the **First Republic**. Born in 1916 in **Say**, Courmo has been one of the inner circle of PPN politicians and cabinet ministers. Educated in **Niamey** and at the **École William Ponty** in Dakar, Senegal (1933–1936), he continued his studies in Paris before returning to Niamey to become an administrator in the local treasury, where he was to work for the next 17 years. Between 1946 and 1955 Courmo was the secretary-general of the PPN, and by 1953 he had become head of the Equipment Department of the treasury. In 1956 he transferred to become personnel manager of the Ministry of Public Works. In 1958, also briefly deputy prefect of the **Madaoua** district, he became minister of finance after the fall of the **Djibo Bakary** government the same year. In 1963 his ministry was enlarged to include economic affairs, but returned to its former size in 1965. Cuormo remained in that position until 1970, when he was appointed minister of foreign affairs for a few months, before being shifted to head the Conseil Economique et Social, serving as its president until 1974, and as political secretary of the PPN politburo. He has served also on a number of other administrative boards, including that of the **Banque de Développement de la République du Niger** (BDRN), and between 1959 and 1963 was president of the Organisation Commune Dahomey-Niger (OCDN, later **Organisation Commune Bénin-Niger**). After the **coup d'état of April 1974**, he was arrested and interned at a military camp in **Agadez**, like most high-level officials of the toppled regime. He was subsequently put under house arrest until President **Ali Saibou** released him (together with other dignitaries of the **First Republic**) upon his accession in 1987. He died at Say, where he had retired as a gentleman farmer, and was interred in his hometown of Dalway, not far from Say.

CREDIT DU NIGER. Opening in 1958 and by 1970 Niger's sixth-largest enterprise, Crédit du Niger is headquartered in **Niamey** and has a capitalization of 220 million **CFA francs**, of which the government holds 53.5 percent of the shares, the national security fund 20 percent, the **Caisse des Prêts aux**

Collectivités Territoriales (CPCT) 11.6 percent, the **Banque Centrale des États d'Afrique de l'Ouest** (BCEAO) 9.10 percent, the **Agence Française de Développement** 3.5 percent, and the SONIBANK 2.3 percent. This capital composition followed a **privatization** process that occurred in 2005. *See also* BANKING.

CURE SALÉE. Annual trek of **Tuareg** and **Fulani** herders, whereby flocks of **cattle**, sheep, goats, and dromedaries are led through bands of pastures over 300 to 400 km and two or three months, toward the area of In Gall. The flocks converge in the salt-rich pastures of the Irhazer by mid-September and herders celebrate in a three-day festival—the *cure salée* proper. On this occasion, Tuareg dromedary riders engage in spectacular dromedary races while the **Woodabe** organize a *gerewol* dance.

CURRENCY. A variety of currencies circulated in the part of West Africa in which Niger was to later emerge, including iron bars, pieces of cloth, and cowry shells, as well as foreign currency from the Middle East, especially Ottoman money and **Maria Theresa dollars** (*thalers* in German) in the 19th century, in the **sultanate of Damagaram**. French currency was introduced with some difficulty in Niger, becoming successful only in the late 1920s, and prevalent after World War II. Before that development, caravans from North Africa commonly imported shells in cases of 30,000, and the *thaler*—not used in Austria since 1854, though over 2 million were minted between 1891 and 1896—was much sought after. The rate of exchange fluctuated around 5,000 cowrie shells per thaler in 1890. The introduction of French currency did not immediately displace the thaler and cowries. Thus, the 5-franc piece was exchangeable in 1902 in **Zinder** at the rate of 4,000 cowries. Coins were always more valued than paper money, and a 5-franc bill was commonly exchanged for a 2-franc coin. Only in the 1920s did the French colonial franc become more prevalent in Niger, though right up to 1945 other currencies circulated alongside it. Its spread was greatly assisted by the shift of colonial taxation from goods to currency, as French overrule gradually settled. The colonial franc was afterward replaced by the **CFA franc**, the current currency of Niger. In Niger's **languages**, money is called *dala*, which is a local pronunciation of the *thaler* (or dollar).

CYRILLE, GABRIEL (Captain). Promoted from lieutenant shortly after the 1974 coup d'état, Cyrille was brought into the cabinet of President **Seyni Kountché** as minister of public works. Shifted to head the Ministry of Posts, Telecommunications, and Information, he was also appointed chairman of the special committee of inquiry into the financial abuses of the **First**

Republic. The committee issued a large number of stiff penalties against many individuals who occupied office under President **Hamani Diori**. Some time after the committee ended its investigations, Cyrille was purged from all offices (3 March 1975) for "being a threat to the state," in a period when Kountché was fearful of plots against his newly established regime. President Kountché justified jailing Cyrille by claiming that he had used his position as chairman of the committee to wreak vengeance, resulting in abuses of justice. He remained in prison until released in 1987 by President **Ali Saibou** after the death of Kountché, when he was appointed head of **NIGELEC**, Niger's electricity company, in part compensation for his lengthy incarceration.

Anecdotally, Cyrille was a friend of **Abdoulaye Hamani Diori**, and famously led the search in the presidential palace's private apartments during the **coup of 15 April 1974**, using his acquaintance with the premises gained during previous friendly visits.

D

D'ARBOUSSIER, GABRIEL (1908–1976). Born in Djenné (French Sudan, now Mali), d'Arboussier was the son of a colonial governor hailing from a wealthy planter family from the French Caribbean and a Sudanese mother descended from the famous Muslim empire-builder El Hajj Umar Tall. After graduating from the École Coloniale (1935), he was posted to the cabinet of the general governor of French West Africa and started a career as colonial administrator which led him successively to Haute-Volta (now Burkina Faso), Congo, Côte-d'Ivoire, and eventually the French National Assembly, where he represented the Middle Congo and Gabon electoral district. He was a founding member of the **Rassemblement Démocratique Africain** (RDA) in 1946, and his subsequent electoral career is emblematic of the federal and quite amalgamated nature of French West African politics before independence. He represented at various French Union legislatures Côte d'Ivoire and Niger while being an active member of the executive committee of the Union Démocratique Sénégalaise, the Senegalese section of the RDA. D'Arboussier, who was not very popular among African politicians at the time, had been assisted by Félix Houphouet-Boigny in securing the support of Niger's RDA leader **Hamani Diori**, in order to be elected to the French West Africa grand council in 1957. Using Niger as a launching pad, he landed in the highest office of the grand council, its presidency, in 1958, the year in which Niger's **Territorial Assembly** was dissolved. D'Arboussier worked behind the scenes to ensure that Niger responded "yes" in the 1958 French Union referendum, although his efforts were not crucial to the final outcome. He ended his career in the Senegalese diplomatic service and died in Geneva in 1976.

DABGUE, HAMA. Born in Loga, in the vicinity of **Dosso**, Dabgué is the most famous lyrical **Zarma** singer in the so-called traditional manner, flourishing chiefly in the 1980s, with songs that (with very few exceptions) focus humorously on incidents in his personal life. This makes Dabgué's art a close cousin to that of the **Songhay** song-makers of Mali (such as Ibrahim Hama Dicko and the late Ali Farka Touré), who are neither social satirists nor praising griots, but primarily take their own life and feelings as the matter of their art. However, his music is less somber. Starting in the 1990s, Dabgué suffered from both his unhinged lifestyle, marked by alcoholism and profligacy, and by the decline of state and social sponsorship of his form of art that set in during that decade. He now lives in near misery, despite the great popularity of most of his songs—a victim of the underdevelopment of copyright law in Niger. *See also* DANCE AND MUSIC.

DAGRA, MAMADOU (1953–). Dagra started a public career in the early 1980s when, as a successful law scholar, he was appointed president of the board of directors of Niger's École Nationale d'Administration (1984–1989), which is now the **École Nationale d'Administration et de Magistrature** (ÉNAM). In 1988 he moved closer to the circles of state power as cabinet director to the prime minister, before becoming minister for national **education** (1989–1990) and minister for **civil service** and labor (1990–1991). That was in the framework of the **Second Republic**'s single-party rule of the **Mouvement National pour la Société de Développement** (MNSD). The defeat of the MNSD at the first multiparty **elections** of the country in 1993 put an extended hold on his political career, and he concentrated on teaching and administrative duties at the **University of Niamey**. Apart from a brief stint as a special councilor at the cabinet of the prime minister in 1996, Dagra chose to remain active as a university professor and a legal expert above all, notably working to revive Niger's law journals with the assistance of the Danish Institute for Human Rights and other Western donors and providing consultant services to various organizations.

In 2009, Dagra accepted an appointment as justice minister and then as professional and technical training minister in the government of the faithful formed by President **Mamadou Tandja** as he was undertaking to overthrow the **Fifth Republic**. This stunning move was accounted for by the ethnic and family relations between Dagra (a man from the **Kanuri** far east) and Tandja, and was perhaps calculated to enable Tandja to win over university professors. After the fall of Tandja in February 2010, Dagra returned to the university fold.

As perhaps the most prominent law scholar in Niger after **Abdourahamane Soly**, Dagra is highly regarded as a teacher and a university worker. He has published extensively on Nigerien and diplomatic affairs.

DAHOMEY-NIGER BOUNDARY DISPUTE. *See* BENIN-NIGER BOUNDARY DISPUTE.

DAKAOU, BIBATA ADAMOU (1941–). Dakaou attended primary and secondary school in Fada N'Gourma and Ouagadougou (both places now in

Burkina Faso) and then studied teaching and pedagogy in Paris (**France**) and **Niamey**. After a distinguished career as a teacher and a school headmaster and primary **education** inspector (1960–1986), she became one of the main leaders of the state feminine organization **Association des Femmes du Niger** (AFN) and was appointed national director for **women** empowerment in 1986–1989. In this new career, she also worked as technical director for population and family life in 1992–1996, and retired in 1996. In 1989, she had become deputy for Kollo on the single-party list of the **Mouvement National pour la Société de Développement** (MNSD) and survived the dissolution of the **Second Republic** to be elected a member of the Haut Conseil de la République (HCR), the first transitional parliament of 1991, as a women's representative. She afterward adhered to the **Convention Démocratique et Sociale** (CDS Rahama) but put more efforts into union (Syndicat National des Enseignants du Niger, SNEN) and feminist nongovernmental (Fahamay) work.

DAKORO. *Département* in the region of **Maradi** in the transition zone between the Sahelian band and the Sahara desert, a nomadic zone par excellence. It is centered on the town of Dakoro, about 500 km east of Niamey and 128 km north of Maradi. The main populations are **Gobir Hausa**, **Fulani**, and **Tuareg**. The small town of Dakoro (5,000 people) is known in Niger for its juvenile detention center, the only one in the country.

DALLOL. **Fulani** term equivalent to the **Hausa** *goulbi*, i.e., valley. It now designates the fossilized valleys, usually very fertile, of which the two principal are **Dallol Bosso** and **Dallol Maouri**. In wetter prehistoric times, these were major affluents of the **Niger River**, which drained the entire northern regions of Niger up to and including **Aïr** (especially the Bosso) and into Ahaggar (Algeria).

DALLOL BOSSO. Called Boboye by the **Zarma** (its main population), the Dallol Bosso is a large fossilized valley in the *département* of **Birni N'Gaouré**—one of two major ones in Niger—which in prehistoric times drained from **Aïr**. Called a variety of names along its various segments (including **Azawagh** in the plains of the same name), the Dallol Bosso is a dry valley, 300 km in length and between 5 and 15 km wide, whose western "bank" is a major geological fault. *See also* DALLOL.

DALLOL FOGA. *See* DALLOL MAOURI.

DALLOL MAOURI. One of Niger's two major fossilized valleys, which in wetter prehistoric times drained the entire region to the north. The Dallol

Maouri runs from **Matankari** to south of **Gaya**. In theory a basin that extends up to the Tidjeddi fault (50 km south of **Agadez**), it is in reality a series of different affluent basins (Abalemma, **Keita**, Badaguichiri) joined by the **Dallol Foga** around 20 km north of Gaya, and joining the **Niger River** around Dole. The **Dallol** has some water in its lower course. *See also* AREWA.

DAMAGARAM, SULTANATE OF. Malam Yunus, a man from the Bornu (**Lake Chad** area), founded a small state in the village of Damagaram around 1740. Damagaram was surrounded by a number of other villages, including that of Zindir (now **Zinder**), which gradually came under its authority. The new state was very unstable, owing to squabbles among potential successors to the throne, and the sultan of Bornu often intervened in its internal affairs. In fact, the state was very much a satellite of the **Bornu Empire**. The capital moved from Damagaram to Zindir or Zinder in the early 19th century, though the title Sarkin Damagaram (**Hausa** for king of Damagaram) prevailed over that of Sarkin Zinder. At that point, the Bornu Empire's power declined, partly owing to the rise of the Sokoto Empire, and the state of Damagaram was able to develop a policy of independence from both powers as they weakened each other. The policy was also enhanced by the geographic situation of the state, at the edge of the desert, far beyond the centers of Sokoto power, as well as by the mastery of cannon-building technology, unique in the region.

Soon, the little kingdom graduated into a sultanate and knew its apogee under the two reigns of Sultan **Tanimoun dan Sulayman** (1841–1843 and then 1851–1884). Damagaram policy was then defined as first and foremost remaining independent from the **Fulani** Sokoto Empire—the only Hausa state to be entirely successful in this—and second, strengthening its position as a trading center between the Central Sudan and North Africa. In view of the first tenet of its policy, Damagaram helped the former ruler of **Katsina** to settle in **Maradi** which then became a buffer state between Damagaram territory and the Sokoto Empire. After the Sokoto Empire became a loose federation of emirates, Damagaram put all its efforts into undermining the position of the nearby emirate of Kano, which its rulers saw as their main rival in both trade and political ambition. In view of the second tenet, Tanimoun conquered the northern region of the Mounio and adjacent areas, erstwhile dominated by the **Sossebaki**s, thus reinforcing the security of the commercial route to Tripoli, vital to Damagaram prosperity.

As the 19th century wore on, Damagaram shifted its allegiance from Bornu to the faraway Ottoman Empire—a testimony not so much of Ottoman power as of Bornu's decline. In this regard, however, a crisis arose when, toward the end of the century, the Darfourian empire-builder **Rabah** the Black successfully attacked a weakened Bornu and suddenly became a major threat to the sultanate. When a French expedition appeared in its territory in 1898, the Damagaram court was mostly worried that it might have been sent to strike an alliance with Rabah, and Sultan **Amadou Kouran Daga** ordered the murder of its leader, Captain **Marius-Gabriel Cazemajou**. Kouran Daga then seized the weapons of the French column in order to use them against Kano and increase his power and prestige. The following year, however, a new French expedition showed up to avenge the death of Cazemajou. Kouran Daga was defeated and killed at the battle of Tirmini (1899). Damagaram thus came under French rule and formed the nucleus of the Territoire Militaire de Zinder. It was at the time over 70,000 sq km large, with a population of around 400,000 people. The slim southern portion of its territory was incorporated into the British colony of **Nigeria** while the vaster northern portion makes up today much of the region of Zinder.

The sultanate of Damagaram was initially maintained by the French, who abolished it in 1906 after having discovered a conspiracy against them masterminded by Sultan **Amadou dan Bassa**. At that point, the sultanate was divided into three districts, which soon fell under the leadership of Ballama Ousman, a eunuch court slave of the deposed sultan acquired from the Bagirmi (Chad), who gained the trust of the French through clever intrigues and strategic denunciations. In 1915, Ballama managed to drive away his principal challenger, Barma Moustapha, a descendant (through his mother) of Sultan Tanimoun, by falsely accusing him of a plot against the French regime in Damagaram. The French eventually realized the ploy, removed Ballama (who returned to the Bagirmi where he died in 1953) in 1922, and reinstated the sultanate under Barma Moustapha the following year. Damagaram's official records consider the period 1906–1923 a regency. A list of Damagaram rulers follows: Malam Yunus Dan Ibram, 1731–1746; Baba dan Malam, 1746–1757; Tanimoun Babami, 1757–1775; Assafa Dan Tanimoun, 1775–1782; Abaza Dan Tanimoun, 1782–1787; Mahaman Dan Tanimoun Babou Tsaba, 1787–1790; Daouda Dan Tanimoun, 1790–1799; Ahmadou Dan Tanimoun Na Chanza, 1799–1812; Suleyman Dan Tintouma, 1812–1822; Ibrahim Dan Suleyman, 1822–1841; Tanimoun Dan Sulayman, 1841–1843; Ibrahim Dan Sulayman, 1843–1851; Mahaman Kace, 1851; Tanimoun Dan Suleyman, 1851–1884; Abba Gato, 1884; Suleyman dan Aisa, 1884–1893; Ahmadou Dan Tanimoun Mai Roumji Kouran Daga, 1893–1899; Amadou Dan Tanimoun Dan Bassa, 1899–1906; Ballama's regency, 1906–1923; Barma Moustapha, 1923–1950; Sanda Oumarou Dan Amadou, 1950–1978; **Aboubacar Sanda Oumarou**, 1978–2000; Mamadou Moustafa, 2000–2011; Aboubacar Sanda Oumarou (restored), 2011– . *See also* COLONIE DU NIGER; FRENCH OCCUPATION.

DAMERGOU. Region immediately northwest of **Damagaram**. With the onset of the colonial era, the area was administered from Djadjidouna, at the time a major caravan stop on the Tripoli–**Zinder**–Kano route. A vast, monotonous pastureland plateau, Damergou was dominated by the Imouzourag **Tuareg**, who protected sedentary groups in return for payment in kind against predatory attacks by the Kel Owey, who traditionally led all caravans through the region. These two Tuareg groups continually clashed in the area in the 19th century, leading to the intervention of the French. Solicited by each for military help against the other, **France** promised assistance to the group that would provide the most mounts for the expedition then being prepared against **Rabah** in Chad. The Kel Owey, the only ones with camels (due to their role in the caravan trade), donated 200 mounts, and the subsequent battle of Tanami saw the defeat and dispersal of the Imouzourag. The ***anastafidet*** of the Kel Owey was then appointed head of Damergou. In due time, the abolition of slavery in the area brought about the collapse of the **economy**.

The name *Damergou* comes from "the country of meat," because of the **Hausa** hunters who were its original inhabitants. Damergou is a geographical entity; no protostate ever developed in the region, which remained one of scattered millet-growing villages. In recent times, its name has become almost synonymous with famine in Niger, as most hunger cycles appear early in that area.

DAN BASKORE. Sarkin **Maradi**, 1858–1879; successor to **Dan Kassawa**, and with him one of the two greatest kings of precolonial Maradi. Son of Maroua (r. 1825–1835), Dan Baskoré ruled at the time of Maradi's apogee, after Dan Kassawa had organized it. He was also the last of the Dan Kassawa successors to mount truly serious expeditions at **Katsina** aimed at reconquering the area from the **Fulani**. Of his 80 battles in that direction, one reached within 6 km of Katsina in a campaign that included a force of 10,000 from Maradi, **Gobir**, **Damagaram**, and the **Tuareg** Kel Owey. Under him Maradi prospered greatly and built walls, becoming a ***birni***.

DAN BASKORE DAN KOURE, MAHAMAN (1897–1947). Born in **Maradi**, Dan Baskoré dan Kouré was chief of the province of **Katsina** for only three years (1944–1947), much less than his famous namesake of the 19th century or his famous successor **Bouzou Dan Zambadi**. Prior to acceding to the Nigerien Katsina throne, he was a teacher in **Zinder**. He was elected **Parti Progressiste Nigérien** (PPN-RDA) general councilor for Maradi in 1946 but died the following year.

DAN BOUZOUA, MAHAMANE (1933–1997). Dan Bouzoua's political career presents the interest of spanning colonial and independent Niger in the rank and file of ordinary elected representatives. His father, Abari Dan Bouzoua, was a colonial interpreter who was elected a **Parti Progressiste Nigérien** (PPN-RDA) deputy for **Zinder** in 1946, while the son was finishing primary school in **Tanout**. Dan Bouzoua was afterward trained as a nurse and an administrator in Paris (**France**) and Geneva (Switzerland). After working for the French colonial commercial giant Compagnie Française d'Afrique de l'Ouest (CFAO), Dan Bouzoua started a political career as a member of the **Mouvement Socialiste Africain** (MSA), later **Sawaba**, the rival party to the PPN, and was elected Sawaba general councilor for Zinder. It is to be noted that the PPN was the radical anticolonial party when Dan Bouzoua senior adhered to it, and that Sawaba had replaced it in that role by the time Dan Bouzoua junior took to political militancy.

After the dissolution of the party, dan Bouzoua pursued an administrative career as labor inspector in Zinder and **Maradi** and was appointed mayor of Maradi (1974–1975). Forced to retire from the public service in 1979, he was recruited by the French postcolonial public works giant SOGEA SATOM 13 years later in 1992 and was elected in 1993 Union Démocratique des Forces Populaires (UDFP Sawaba) deputy for Zinder. In a twist evoking his one-year mayorship of Maradi, he was appointed *préfet* of **Tillabéri** (1995–1996) upon the dissolution of the **National Assembly** in 1995. He died in **Niamey** in 1997.

DAN DOBI, MAHAMANE (1923–1981). Dan Dobi studied in **Birni-N'Konni**, **Niamey**, and at the **École William Ponty** (1938–1942) in Dakar, Senegal, from which he graduated as an administrator. A founding member of the **Parti Progressiste Nigérien** (PPN-RDA), he was moved to Guinea after having signed a petition demanding the removal of Niger's governor, Jean Toby, but was soon posted back to his home colony in 1954. In 1957, he became PPN territorial councilor for **Dogondoutchi** and then a senator of the French Community in 1959. After independence, he started a distinguished government career as justice minister (1965–1970), public works minister (1970–1972), and rural **economy** minister (1972–1974). He had moreover been enthroned as *chef de canton* of Guéchémé, his family seat in 1960.

All this came to an abrupt end with **Seyni Kountché's coup of 1974**, when he was arrested and removed from his chieftaincy. Jailed first in a military cantonment in **Agadez**, he was afterward moved to the Bagagi barracks in Niamey, temporarily released in 1978, and arrested again in 1980, in **Dosso**. He died the following year, at the hospital of Niamey. Dan Dobi is the author of several published and unpublished literary works, among which might be mentioned the early piece *La Chèvre* (1947), one of the very first productions of Nigerien **literature** in French. He also penned *Les Invités du Bar Welcome*, *Kabrin Kabra* (1958) and *Moumouna*.

DAN FODIO, USMAN (1754–1817). **Fulani** Islamic **Qadiriyya** preacher, scholar, and empire builder. Dan Fodio was born in the kingdom of **Gobir**, in Marata (now included in the Republic of Niger) and is popularly known as *Shehu* (a **Hausa** rendition of *Shaykh*). His name means, in a mix of Hausa and Fulani, the son of the cleric. Dan Fodio was a member of the settled Fulani urban elite, who, living among the Hausa as a minority group, tended to lose the nomadic ritual culture of the Fulani but also to intensely cultivate the Islamic religion. Having studied theology in **Agadez** under a celebrated clerical teacher, Jibril ibn Umar, dan Fodio sought to create an ideal Muslim society in the town of Degel (Gobir) in the 1780s. The Degel experiment gradually unsettled the ruling *sarauta* (royalty) system of the Gobir, especially as it incited Islamized slaves to rebel against their condition and generally criticized the non-Islamic political principles upon which most states in the Hausaland were based.

In 1802, the Gobir king **Yunfa**, a former student of dan Fodio, canceled the autonomy granted to Degel and tried to have dan Fodio executed or murdered. Dan Fodio fled into the wilderness where he secured the alliance of the warlike Fulani nomads and had himself proclaimed *Amirul Muminin*, Guide of the Believers. He also secured the backing of much of the Hausa peasantry, who were resentful of the heavy taxation that supported the *sarauta* regime. Starting in 1804, he was able to launch a jihad, issuing his famous *Letter to the People of the Sudan*, a list of personal rights and obligations sanctioned by Islamic legality, to announce the dawn of a new era. Coming after years of preaching and Sufi organization, the jihad was as much a war of conquest as it was a social revolution, and within 10 years, it had engulfed all the Hausa kingdoms with the exception of the **sultanate of Damagaram** and minor rulers in today's Niger. A number of Hausa dynasties relocated to the fringes of Hausaland, such as **Northern Katsina**. After the conquests, the new empire was divided into a western wing with its capital in Gwandu, and an eastern wing centered at Sokoto. The *shehu* himself returned to his religious studies and died in 1817 a private person, having two years earlier transmitted his sultan title to his son, Muhammad Bello.

A key effect of the Sokoto Empire has been to entrench **Islam** as the dominant cultural and religious formation in this area of West Africa. This is so much the case that future Nigerien territory, which was not subjected to the Fulani Islamic government of Sokoto, remained an area of thriving animism far into the 20th century.

DAN GALADIMA, OUSMANE (1927–). A post office official, Dan Galadima joined **Djibo Bakary**'s Union Démocratique Nigérienne (UDN) in 1956 and was elected territorial councilor to the **Mouvement Socialiste**

Africain (MSA), later **Sawaba**, in **Madaoua** in 1957. After the interdiction of Sawaba, he joined in the armed struggle decided by the party's exiled leadership and was designated chief of staff of the Liberation Army. He was captured in 1967, tried, and sentenced to death, but a decree of 1971 commuted this into life imprisonment. He was released after the **coup d'état in 1974**.

DAN GARA, SOULEY (1932–1997). Souley Dan Gara, better known as **Bala Dan Sani** (and even better known as BDS when he was alive), was born in 1932 in Dan Gara, a village not very far from the **Gobir** capital, **Tibiri**. He first grew up to be a village weaver with a small plot of land, until the early 1960s. Then, starting with a 60,000 **CFA franc** loan as his capital (this was a good amount of money in the 1960s Niger), the weaver soon turned into a cunning businessman, capitalizing on profit made on moving goods from cheap places to places of relative scarcity and high demand—in one event buying truck tires in **Niamey** and selling them for more than three times the price in **Birni-N'Konni**, a town just about 300 km east of Niamey. His business model was chiefly based on speculation on agricultural produce, something typical of many of **Maradi**'s *Alhazai*. By the late 1980s, Bala dan Sani (he took the surname dan Sani, which means in **Hausa** "son of Sani," as a tribute to his father-in-law, whose first name was Sani) had become a major farmer and speculator in the region's agricultural markets, often at the expense of petty peasants, and in a way that portended the economic causes of the Maradi famines of the late 2000s.

DAN GURMU (Late 19th century–1985). Dan Gurmu is the artistic name of **Hausa** singer Mahamadou Bohari, author of a celebrated lyrical ballad on alcoholism and its social consequences, *Muugun Maagani* (Hausa: "Bad Medicine"). As with most Hausa singers, Dan Gurmu's work moderates deepseated conservatism with a streak of satirical drollery. The rhythm and accent of his melodies make them close cousins of American blues. His name was given to the Nigerien annual music awards. *See also* DANCE AND MUSIC.

DAN KASSAWA (?–1831). True founder of the **Katsina** successor **Hausa** state of **Maradi**. After the Hausa expulsion from Katsina by the **Fulani** and the suicide of the exiled Sarki Magajin Halidou in 1807, dan Kassawa was selected as his successor. After two years in **Zinder** dan Kassawa and his followers settled at Gafai on the **Damagaram** border. After 10 years there, during which dan Kassawa's strength was augmented by new refugees from the Fulani, an assault was mounted against Maradi—a former Katsina province—after the **Arna** to the South of the town (from Gawon Barki and Soumarana) revolted against the Fulani, beheading the ruling emir, Mani, very likely at Soumarana, and sending over his head to dan Kassawa. Maradi then became the center of Hausa resistance against the Fulani in Katsina. By the time dan Kassawa died, the town was totally entrenched.

The main legacy of dan Kassawa was the reconstruction of a Katsina state in Maradi, even though it was certainly one adjusted to the customs and traditions he found there. The system was rather typical of what a Hausa *sarauta* regime looks like, even today. At the top of the state (*daula*), is the *Sarki'n Katsina*, born in the ruling dynasty but elected by an electoral college (*rukuni*) constituted by the four highest state officials. The *rukuni* is divided in two groups of officials, the left hand of the king (*hannu na auni*), which used to comprise the war chief (**kaura**) and the police intendent (*durbi*); and the right hand of the king (*hannu na daama*), which includes the state intendent and master of the palace (*galadima*), in times of yore a eunuch, and his assistant (*yan daka*). These four officers had a great many aides and retainers, 130 under the great reign of **dan Baskoré**, including a few **women**.

DAN KOULODO, DAN DICKO (1934–1998). Scientist and one-time secretary-general of the Agence de Coopération Culturelle et Technique in Brussels. Born in 1934 in **Maradi** and the son of the then-reigning *Sarki'n Katsina* (king of Maradi), Dan Koulodo was educated in Maradi, **Niamey**, and at the prestigious colonial high school Lycée Vollenhoven, in Dakar, Senegal. After attending the academies of Dakar (1953–1954), Montpellier (1954–1958), and the Collège d'Agde (1959), at which he studied science, he graduated with a doctoral degree in organic structural chemistry. He then joined the faculty of the University of Montpellier (1959–1961) and the center for higher studies, Abidjan (1961–1968). While in Côte d'Ivoire, he also taught at the École Nationale Supérieure des Travaux Publics (1963–1968). He remained in Abidjan, at the newly created University of Abidjan, through 1971 before returning to Niamey to teach at the new **University of Niamey** and to assume the post of vice-president of the Conseil Economique et Social. In August 1972 he was brought into the cabinet as minister of **education** and after the **coup d'état of 1974** he was sent abroad to head the Agence de Coopération Culturelle et Technique des Pays Francophones (ACCT). Dan Koulodo was the author of several scientific research papers. *See also* ORGANISATION INTERNATIONALE DE LA FRANCOPHONIE.

DANCE AND MUSIC. Like most African societies, Niger is extremely rich in dance and music traditions, although, as a country sitting on the cusp between sub-Saharan Africa and North Africa, it has the added peculiarity of mixing traditions stemming from very different worlds of culture and civilization. These traditions were greatly shaped by French colonialism, which introduced the modern band and orchestra and also connected Niger to music and dance produced in other Francophone African countries, which influenced its more recent evolutions, especially Dahomey (Benin) in the 1960s–1970s, Zaïre (Democratic Republic of Congo) in the 1980s–1990s, and Côte d'Ivoire in the 2000s. What follows is a review of the four dominant Nigerien dance and music traditions—**Hausa**, **Tuareg**, **Zarma-Songhay**, and **Fulani**—and of current trends.

Hausa: Dance and music traditions are somewhat distinct among Nigerien Hausa. Hausa masculine dance is chiefly a form of acrobatic dance which likely derives from **Bori** trance dance, but stylized to follow the rhythm of drums, in celebrations called *kidi* (literally, "drumming"). Feminine dance follows specific social occasions, especially marriage and baptism (*aure* and *buki*). Here, as in many African societies, dance is a youthful occupation performed by *samariya* (youth) clubs, whose members are generally individuals aged less than 30. On the other hand, music is ageless and often performed by older men and **women** (the women are called *zabiya*). It is both business and entertainment. Singers form companies with a lead singer, a chorus, and a smallish orchestra—generally of light percussion—to praise the wealthy and mighty and enliven social occasions, while also very often developing a repertoire of satirical songs, as did **Dan Gurmu**, **Idi Nadadaw**, Ali Konko, Dan Koyro, and others. Indeed, Hausa singing is most potent in this vein, especially when satirizing destructive vices (alcohol with Dan Gurmu's poignant, blues-sounding *Mugun Maagani*, narcotics with Ali Makaho's funnier *Mandoula*, which is apparently self-deprecating), or commenting on social change in constructing often ambiguous stories.

Tuareg: Tuareg masculine dance is acrobatic and warlike, involving energetic jumps, sword playing, and vigorous yells. It is often performed against the backdrop of music—of flute, the single-cord violin called *goge*, and light percussion—and singing made by seated women. Women very rarely dance, and usually do so in the hieratic manner best exemplified by the **Songhay** *takamba*.

Zarma-Songhay: The dance traditions of the Zarma-Songhay generally mix men and women, and are shaped by the fact that each village develops its own air or hymn, sometimes called *bitti* from the **Holley** ritual of seasonal appropriation. In village life, dance is generally a trepident affair, rythmed by drum and calabash percussion and the very expressive small guitar-like *kountigui*. Among especially the Songhay of **Gao**, the dominant dance, both for men and women, is the *takamba*, a slow and seemingly easy dance which plays exactly on the flexibility of the torso, the legs, and even the arms, and is attended by a suitably slow-playing music. *Takamba* probably developed in the **Songhay Empire** as a court dance, strongly influenced by

Tuareg or more generally Saharan music, but the disappearance of that state may explain why Zarma-Songhay male singers are chiefly lyrical poets, not much interested in praising the great, but rather dwelling on personal feelings and adventures, often with the accompaniment of a *moolo* (three-cord guitar) player and a listener. Female singers, for their part, specialize as wordsmiths and proverb makers, often drawing, in past times, the generous admiration of wealthy patrons.

Fulani: Fulani music is shaped by herding and thus dominated by the flute and very light percussion (calabash and gourd) serving as background for airy songs, often celebrating **cattle**.

Niger is also home to more marginal music traditions which produced musical instruments not found outside the area: thus, the harpsichord-like *biram* of the **Boudouma** and the better known *algaita* of the **Kanuri**, a kind of trumpet which produces an extremely plastic and fluid stream of music.

These various traditions were very localized and distinct in the past. But in the late 20th century, with the development of an urban Niger, they gradually mixed with each other to produce modern Nigerien music, often through the organization of social ceremonies and festivals. Though the dominant **languages** of star singers are Hausa, Zarma and, to a lesser extent, French, the music itself characteristically fuses instruments and rhythms from Tuareg and Fulani traditions as well. The main genres that came to the fore are Nigerien pop (often described as Afro-pop in international charts), *maquis* music, and more recently, *dandali*. Nigerien pop—dominated in the 1980s by **Elhadj Mahamane Taya** and the Orchestre Guez Band, in the 1990s by **Moussa Poussi Natama** and **Saadou Bori**, and in the 2000s by **Denké-Denké** and **Mali Yaro**—represents the kind of modern music which is popular through all classes and ages in Nigerien society, while wilder and generally more outrageous scores (**Dargné**, **Sani Aboussa**) dominate the *maquis*, a boisterous kind of music bar that was imported from Côte d'Ivoire in the 1990s to spread especially in **Niamey** and **Dosso**. *Dandali* music emerged from the fashion of Indian-style romantic musicals that became all the rage in northern **Nigeria** in the late 1990s and crossed over in the 2000s into Niger, where the suave Hausa-language songs delivering niceties and bubbly feelings are backed up by synthesizers and computerized gimmicks. *Dandali* songs, in Niger more so than in Nigeria, are performed with a modernized form of Hausa acrobatic dance, though now with no ethnic connotation, since companies of performers are multiethnic, a condition of success in Niamey. Most representative of this multiethnic Nigerien hodgepodge is the currently predominant music group, **Tal National**, whose success is tied to the *gabdi* lifestyle characteristic of Niamey.

DANDA, MAHAMADOU (1951–). An administrator and political scientist with degrees from universities in Burkina Faso and Canada, Danda was briefly a cabinet minister in the late 1980s under **Ali Saibou**'s presidency and later in **Daouda Malam Wanké**'s transitional regime in 1999. He was then appointed embassy advisor in Canada and cultivated a profile of technocratic neutrality by avoiding party affiliations while maintaining ties with all the major Nigerien political leaders. This, and the fact that General **Djibo Salou** explicitly wanted to avoid an ethnic characterization of his coup d'état against President **Mamadou Tandja** (a **Hausa** for all practical purposes, like Danda, but unlike Salou), are reasons he was chosen as prime minister of the transitional government that followed the toppling of Tandja in February 2010.

DANDOUNA, ABOUBACAR (?–1964). Militant **Sawaba** activist, born in **Maradi** and a joiner and carpenter by trade. Dauntless, committed, and a formidable speaker, Dandouna was a typical representative of the "little folks" core of the Sawaba movement. He learned to read and write through his contacts with French communists and traveled extensively in Eastern Europe in the 1950s, developing staunch pro-labor ideals and attending in 1958, in New York, a training course under sponsorship from the International Labor Organization. As a pillar of the Marxist-oriented Sawaba in the populous region of Maradi, he was harassed by the regime that emerged from the referendum of 1959 and ended up escaping **Niamey** in August 1961 as a wave of repression was brewing. He spent the following years in military training in China, North Vietnam, and Ghana, which enabled him to become a Sawaba commando leader as the exiled party was preparing a guerrilla invasion in 1964. Dandouna led a unit that crossed the border in the **Konni** sector and was arrested at Dibissou. Having killed a local schoolmaster who betrayed him, he was lynched (October 1964) and his body was brought to Niamey, where it was laid to rot in desecration.

DANGI. Basic clan unit among the **Hausa**.

DAOUEL, AKOLI (1937–). Akoli was educated as a nurse, an administrator, and a teacher but became well known in Niger as a journalist. His early career was spent as director of the national **tourism** office, a position often held by **Tuareg** or more generally Saharan officials. In 1970, he became deputy on a list presented by the single-party **Parti Progressiste Nigérien** (PPN-RDA) and was a member of the Radio Niger programs committee as a **National Assembly** representative. Although his legislative term was interrupted by the **coup in 1974**, his professional career received a boost as he was appointed program director at the state radio **Voix du Sahel**. Among several other state technical appointments, Daouel also became the general manager of the then freshly established Nigerien national television corporation in

1981. This was followed by a very different appointment, at the general directorship of the Société Minière du Niger in 1985.

After the advent of multiparty democracy, Daouel created the largely Tuareg-based Union pour la Démocratie et le Progrès Social (UDPS Amana) in January 1991 and took part in the **Conférence Nationale** as leader of that party. But he left it in May 1992 to found another party, the Parti pour l'Unité Nationale et le Développement (PUND Salama), another chiefly Tuareg outfit, over which he still presides. In the 1990s, Daouel was in turn an assistant official to the transition prime minister **Cheiffou Amadou**, CEO of the **Société Nigérienne de Charbon d'Anou Araren** (SONICHAR), and minister for **agriculture** and livestock farming until 1997. He was a member of the Conseil des Sages (Council of the Wisemen) in 1996 and of its 1999 equivalent, the **Conseil Consultatif** (Consultative Council). In that latter body, he presided over the commission for rural development and the environment, a position from which he predictably moved to the post of minister for water resources in the first **Fifth Republic** government in 2000. Initially opposed to President **Tandja Mamadou**'s constitutional coup of July–August 2009, Akoli ended up joining his camp when it looked as if it was winning. After Tandja was toppled, he attempted linking up PUND to the new winners of Niger's political stage, the **Coordination des Forces Démocratiques pour la République** (CFDR), but was refused entry.

Akoli is admittedly the veteran of Nigerien politics, having served and survived all of the country's regimes since independence, although he might be at the end of his run with the new ruling coalition that emerged from the 2011 **elections**. *See also* FOURTH REPUBLIC; TAZARTCHÉ.

DARGNE. See MAMIDOU, SEYDOU.

DARGOL. Small **Songhay** kingdom that became a major center of anti-Moroccan resistance after the 1591 **battle of Tondibi**. It corresponds to the southern area of the **Soney**, extending between **Téra** and **Tillabéri**. Later, in the 18th and 19th centuries, Dargol had a series of violent confrontations with both **Fulani** and **Tuareg** invaders. The kingdom was centered on the town of the same name, which today has a population of around 5,000 and is located in the Téra *département*. *See also* DENDI.

DAYAK, MANO (1949–1995). Born in the Tidene Valley, north of **Agadez**, and a successful businessman (owner and manager of Temet Voyages, the most important tourist agency in the region of Agadez in the early 1990s), he took up arms as a rebel leader in the **Aïr** during the spate of mid-1990s **Tuareg rebellions**. Specifically, he was a leader for the Front de Libération de

Temust (FLT). He had written a book delineating **Tuareg** grievances against **Niamey** (leading to a rebuttal in a book by historian **André Salifou**), became a spokesman of the Tuareg in Paris, and became a vice-president of the **Coordination de la Résistance Armée** (CRA), formed in 1993. Two years later, he agreed to take part to peace negotiations but died in the crash of the plane (supplied by the French government) which was carrying him to Niamey. He had famously lamented that Niger and Mali's Tuareg are the only "white people" to be under the domination of "black people" in the entire world. The international airport of Agadez has been named after him.

DAZA. A branch of the **Toubou** found both in northern Chad and in northeastern Niger. They call themselves Dazagada ("those who speak Dazaga"). The other Toubou branch, the **Teda** (or Tedagada), speak a very similar **language**. The Daza are found in Chad in Ennedi and Borkou, and in Niger in **Manga** and **Kaouar**. They are divided into numerous small clans, the total population of which is hard to estimate but is placed at around 50,000. Some non-Nigerien elements filtered in from Chad after the ouster there of former president Hissene Habré.

DELANNE, RENE (1910–1985). Born in Doulsou, in the vicinity of **Tillabéri**, and educated in **Niamey** and at **École William Ponty**, he worked in various capacities in the colonial government's financial departments in Niger (1937–1944), Guinea (1945–1953), and Senegal (1953–1956). Delanne was the secretary-general of the **First Republic**'s **National Assembly**, of the Union Nationale des Travailleurs du Niger (UNTN), and of several other agencies until the **coup of 1974**, and a key and loyal second-echelon personal aide of President **Hamani Diori**. Between 1956 and 1971, Delanne was the social affairs secretary of the political bureau of the **Parti Progressiste Nigérien** (PPN-RDA), deriving his power from this appointment. Though he was to be a key personality in the Diori regime, Delanne sided with his UNTN lieutenants in demanding major pay raises—rejected by the government—and was consequently purged from his PPN posts, becoming one of only two politburo members the PPN ever dropped, losing his post in 1971. Since Delanne—who is of mixed parentage—was very visible in all the posts he occupied, he was one of the most detested members of the Diori regime and was immediately arrested after the 1974 coup d'état, to be released only about a decade later.

DEMBÉLÉ, HIMA (1928–1968). A key **Sawaba** figure, Dembélé was a **Niamey**-based cinema operator by trade and a fervent unionist. He helped **Djibo Bakary** found his party, Entente Nigérienne, after he had left the **Parti**

Progressiste Nigérien (PPN-RDA) in 1952, and before the establishment of the Union Démocratique Nigérienne (UDN). Dembélé was especially famous for editing the union broadsheet *Talaka*, the organ of the umbrella **union**, Union des Syndicats Confédérés du Niger (USCN). He later headed Sawaba's press organ, *Unité*. A municipal councilor for Sawaba in Niamey in 1956, Dembélé was afterward elected deputy for **Tessaoua**, a Sawaba stronghold. He worked for Tessaoua to vote "no" in the 1958 referendum and thereafter developed active contacts in Eastern Europe as part of his radical anti-imperialist politics. Upon the banning of Sawaba, Dembélé helped develop clandestine cells for the party in West African countries, especially Mali. Arrested and quickly released in 1960, he was eventually sent to the penal colony of **Bilma**, in the far northeastern desert, following a bout of repression by the PPN regime in the fall of 1961. He was set free in 1965 after a prolonged ordeal and died three years later in Niamey in a car accident.

DEMOCRATIZATION. Most African countries started a democratization process in or after 1990, although few successfully transformed their political regime to operate a functional democratic system, one which actually ends entrenched authoritarianism instead of merely holding cosmetic **elections** and façade representation. Niger is one of the successful cases, but its democratization process was not smooth. The process started on 9 February 1990, when a **student** demonstration ended for the first time in Niger's history in fatalities, with three students dead on the Kennedy Bridge in **Niamey**. The deaths happened when the government was already under pressure from trade **unions** and newly created civic associations—following the freedoms granted under the constitution of the **Second Republic** adopted the previous year—to further open up and adopt multipartyism. A week after the students' demonstration, a general demonstration of all unions and associations was held to commemorate the event, and the government decided to dismantle single-party rule.

The trade union federation and the **armed forces** formally broke their ties with the single-party **Mouvement National pour la Société de Développement** (MNSD) and on 24 April 1991, the government revised the **constitution** to include multipartyism. At that point, however, the coalition of pro-democracy movement clamored for a national conference, on the model of that which was held in Benin in 1990, and the government bowed to the pressure the following month (4 May) by setting up a commission to prepare a national conference. Incidentally, on 13 May, **women**'s associations organized demonstrations throughout the country, with the one in Niamey ending at the conference preparation commission building, where women's leaders forced their way into the meeting and secured five seats for themselves. The

Conférence Nationale started on 29 July and the following day proclaimed itself sovereign, thereby ending the Second Republic and officially starting the democratization process.

The conference lasted much longer than initially planned—three months instead of 40 days. The dominant forces—the trade unions and the **Union des Scolaires Nigériens** (USN) as well as budding civic associations—turned it into a cathartic event, revisiting the "crimes and abuses" of all Nigerien regimes since independence, and occasionally putting military personalities under arrest. (They were eventually all released in 1992–1993.) Despite dire financial straits (which led to sporadic mutinies from the unpaid military), the process moved to a transition government, a **constitutional referendum** (26 December 1992), and the first fair and competitive **elections** in the country (February 1993).

Since then, Niger's democratization has come under attack twice. In 1996, the first democratic regime (**Third Republic**) unraveled under the acrimonious struggles of inexperienced politicians, leading to a **coup d'état on 27 January 1996**. The coup resulted in an attempt to restore authoritarian entrenchment over three years of a **Fourth Republic**, often seen as a second "regime of exception" or dictatorship in Niger. In July–August 2009, after 10 years of stable democratic governance, the then-president again attempted to restore despotic rule, establishing a ludicrously authoritarian **Sixth Republic** in an ambiance of political crisis. The attempt was much shorter than the earlier one, as it was terminated in February 2010 when the army moved in to remove the president. It therefore appears that Niger's option for democratic governance resists challenges and may only deepen in the predictable future. *See also* ARMED FORCES; CIVIL SOCIETY; TAZARTCHÉ.

DENDI. Both a geographical term referring to the country around **Gaya** and a **Songhay** province centered on the section of the **River Niger** which now forms the border between Niger and Benin. Dendi means, in the Songhay **language**, "water flow," especially downstream, and so by implication, it is also the south. At the time of the **Askia** dynasty, the area included the **Niger River** valley downstream from Goungia; it slowly began to refer more narrowly to the southernmost segment and especially to the sinuous W region of the river at later dates. Also, the term was used to refer to the almost totally Songhay population of this region, which has retained a dialect much more similar to the Songhay of **Gao** than to **Zarma**. Currently there are large minorities of those Songhay in the region of **Dosso**, with a smaller minority farther south, in neighboring Benin's Nikki region.

Dendi became the last remnant of independent Songhay after the Moroccan invasion and conquest of Gao, and the **battle of Tondibi**. Based in **Loulami** (since disappeared), they accepted the authority of **Askia Nouhou** (ruled 1592–1599). A total break with Gao occurred in the 17th century, and several attempts were mounted to liberate the ancient empire's core. The frontiers with the Moroccans eventually stabilized in the vicinity of the contemporary Niger–Mali borders (between **Tillabéri** and Ansongo). The new dynasty in Dendi continued its Askia titles and traditions for some time. Eventually Dendi disintegrated into five or six smaller kingdoms, each with a genuine Askia descendant at its head. Among these states are **Téra**, Gorouol, and **Dargol**, in the Soney.

DENKE-DENKE. *See* MOUMOUNI, YACOUBA.

DÉPARTEMENTS. Administrative regions into which Niger is divided, as subdivisions of the regions. Initially, the *département* was the highest territorial subdivision of Niger, the colonial *cercle* until October 1965. The original seven *départements* were headed by a *préfet* appointed by the minister of interior. Since the decentralization law of September 1998, the older *départements* have been changed into regions, while their own subdivisions, the *arrondissements*, were erected into *départements*. The new *départements* are run by a deliberative *conseil départemental* and an executive president of the *conseil départemental*, in collaboration with a *préfet* appointed by the minister of the interior. *See also* ADMINISTRATIVE ORGANIZATION.

DEVELOPMENT PLANS. In the 30 years between 1961 and 1991, Niger has had 12 development plans and programs. Planning was the preferred method of action of the developmental state (1960 into the early 1980s), while programs characterize the agendas developed by the international financial institutions (the International Monetary Fund and the World Bank) starting in the early 1980s. The developmental state corresponded, in poorer countries such as Niger, to the welfare state that existed in the developed countries at roughly the same period, the 1960s through the mid-1970s. This means in particular that the state was made to assume extremely ambitious roles in economic policy, providing all kinds of services, organizing all key sectoral activities, and doing so through administrative planning sometimes directly inspired by the Soviet model but also by the modernization theory produced in American universities. Development plans required that the new states train a great number of specialists and operate a large administrative service to run all kinds of activities, all at the same time. In fact, they relied a great deal on foreign cooperation and investments, and the means were vastly inferior to the goals. Thus, all Nigerien plans had to be downscaled at midpoint or failed to attain their targets, generally for lack of sufficient funding.

Development plans disappeared with the passing of the developmental state in the mid-1980s. The new wisdom that emerged at the time pushed for the drastic reduction of state ambitions and the opening up of space for private economic activity. The **civil service** was deemed unreasonably large, and the competence and motivations of its staff were called into question. Yet, after over 20 years of **privatization** policy, there is a timid return to the notion of state planning in the late 2000s, owing to the realization that many of the functions erstwhile devolved to the state cannot be adequately performed by private actors, especially in contexts of great poverty and persistent dearth of solid investors.

During the developmental state's period, Niger's most important plan was the fourth full-fledged plan, the Plan Quinquennal de Développement Economique et Social for 1979–1983. It was the most ambitious, being predicated on the continuation of substantial **uranium** exports and revenues, and the end of the **Sahel drought** of the 1970s that put to shambles the previous development plan which had stayed in draft form. The 1979–1983 plan had to be revised, however, due to the onset of another drought in the Sahel, and to grossly declining uranium receipts. Total anticipated expenditures had been targeted at 730,223 million **CFA francs** with a 53 percent (384,493 million) contribution from the public sector and the remainder from private sources. The major emphasis was, as in previous plans, on attaining self-sufficiency in food production. Public-sector contributions were targeted in the following sectors: rural development (116,450 million CFA francs); mines and industry (70,206 million); human resource development (84,847 million); **communications** (67,762 million); administrative infrastructure (26,266 million); and commerce and **tourism** (19,962 million). Subsequent to the failure of the Fourth Plan, a cadre meeting in **Zinder** in 1983 oriented Niger toward austerity policies shaped by the advice of the International Monetary Fund (IMF) and included into two structural adjustment programs. One of these, the Programme d'Ajustement du Secteur des Entreprises Publiques, did away with much of the **parastatal sector** put in place in the period 1960–1980, thus profoundly redefining Niger's entire economic policy. In essence, these programs phased out the era of state-led national development in Niger, even though there was a last plan in 1987–1991, and the IMF and donors complained of the fact that the state of Niger was dragging its feet in implementing the instructed policy packages (see Table 3).

DEVELOPMENT SOCIETY. *See* CONSEIL NATIONAL DU DÉVELOPPEMENT.

Table 3. Development Plans between 1961 and 1991

Plan	Duration	Story
Plan intérimaire (Interim Plan)	1961–1964	First three-year plan submitted on 15 June 1961 as an intermediate research plan to permit the enactment of a comprehensive economic plan in 1964. Anticipated expenditures in 1961–1964 were 30 billion CFA francs, of which 63 percent was to come from public sources. Only 84 percent of the anticipated expenditures was in the end available.
Perspectives décennales (Decennial Outlook)	1965–1975	Overview for the decade ahead. Included the first Four-Year Plan (1965–68).
Plan quadriennal (Four-Year Plan)	1965–1968	The first Four-Year Plan anticipated financing in the amount of 43.2 billion CFA francs for infrastructures (in decreasing order for the productive sector, social issues, economic issues, administration) and research. Though the expenditures amounted to a 71 percent increase over the previous plan, the plan was subsequently revised downward to a grand total of 30 billion CFA francs, or a 31 percent cut. The revised goals of the plan were only partially achieved.
Plan quadriennal (Four-Year Plan)	1969–1973	Second Four-Year Plan. Less ambitiously envisaged 37.1 billion CFA francs of public expenditures and 10.7 billion CFA francs of private funds, with much expectation about foreign funding. This was not forthcoming and the Sahel drought quashed the better parts of the expectations and goals.
Projet de plan (Draft Plan)	1971–1973	Revised previous plan based on drought and oil shock.
Projet de perspectives décennales (Draft Decennial Outlook)	1973–1982	Attempted new decade-long overview based on grimmer parameters.

Plan	Years	Description
Programme triennal (Three-Year Program)	1976–1978	Adopted on 30 April 1976 by the newly established military regime to free the country from "outside geographical factors" and install a "dynamic development society." The plan included an administrative reorganization of state agencies, especially limiting the Société Nigérienne de Commercialisation d'Arachide's activities to the marketing of groundnuts and derivatives (oil), while COPRO-NIGER was given a monopoly over the import of consumer goods and their sale through retail outlets. The government also took over all outstanding shares in Crédit du Niger. Total investment envisaged during the life of the plan was 1,024 million CFA francs in industry (11 projects) out of a grand total of 135.2 billion CFA francs. The plan was described as an intermediate one with the primary aims being (1) feeding the population and attaining self-sufficiency, especially in cereals; it stressed accelerated growth in food crops and the opening up of virgin lands along the fertile Niger River valley to reduce peasant dependence on volatile cash crops such as cotton and groundnuts; (2) compensating as fast as possible for the decimation of the country's livestock herds by the Sahel drought and bringing them up to 1972 level; and (3) research on the Kandadji dam leading (once constructed) to a major growth in electricity production and also of solar power. The plan had a reasonable chance of attaining most of its goals, especially at the outset, but like other plans, it fell short in the long run.
Plan quinquennal de développement économique et social (Five-Year Social and Economic Development Plan)	1979–1983	An amplification of the objectives of the previous plan, which saw the establishment of dedicated technical parastatals, such as the Office National des Aménagements Hydro-Agricoles, and the design of agricultural development projects.
Programme Intérimaire de Consolidation (PIC) (Interim Consolidation Program)	1984–1985	Adjudicated the failure of the great ambitions of the previous two plans.
Programme d'Ajustement Structurel (PAS) (Structural Adjustment Program)	1986–1987	First attempt at economic liberalization.
Programme d'Ajustement du Secteur des Entreprises Publiques (PASEP) (Parastatal Sector Adjustment Program)	1988–1989	Restructuring of the parastatal sector in view of economic liberalization.
Plan de développement économique et social (PDES) (Economic and Social Development Plan)	1987–1991	Last gasp of the developmental state in Niger.

DIALLO, BOUBACAR ALI (1906–1965). Born on 6 February 1906, in **Niamey**, and a *chef de canton* and secretary-general of the Association des Chefs Coutumiers du Niger (Association of the Customary Chiefs of Niger), Diallo was elected to the **Territorial Assembly** in March 1952 on the Union Nigérienne des Indépendants et Sympathisants list. Serving concurrently as councilor to the **Afrique Occidentale Française** (AOF) Grand Council in Dakar (1952–1957) he was reelected to the assembly in December 1958 as **Parti Progressiste Nigérien** deputy from Niamey and was appointed minister of **health** (18 December 1958 to 31 December 1960). He was subsequently appointed minister of justice (1961–1962) and minister of labor and social affairs. At the time also president of the **Cour de Sûrété de l'État**, he was dropped from all his positions in September 1964 for involvement in the military plot of that year by withholding information he possessed about it. He died of fever in prison on 11 May 1965. *See also* ZODI, IKHIA.

DIALLO, HASSAN A. (Captain). Former military officer. One of the two key instigators of the 1963 attempted coup d'état. Arrested on 3 December 1963, Diallo was released after strong protests of his colleagues in the army. He was rearrested on 13 December, following a cabinet shuffle that saw the eclipse of one of his protectors, Minister of Defense **Ikhia Zodi**. In 1964 came a series of **Sawaba** guerrilla attacks on border posts; in 1965, cashiered from the army, Diallo was condemned to death for his earlier plot, seen to be connected to the attacks, though the two events were very likely separate actions. Eventually granted clemency in 1969, he was released from prison in 1971. *See also* COUP OF 3 DECEMBER 1963.

DIAWARA, IRENE MEON (1946–). Diawara is an administrator and a sociologist trained at the Universities of Caen (**France**) and **Niamey**. She had a very active administrative career in various ministries between 1968 and 1991, and was a dynamic union leader. As such, she took part in the **Conférence Nationale** as a **Union des Syndicats des Travailleurs du Niger** (USTN) representative and was elected member of the transition parliament, the Haut Conseil de la République. She afterward preferred municipal to national politics (serving in two **communes** of Niamey as general secretary) and became one of the key figures of the feminist **civil society** as president of the **Rassemblement Démocratique des Femmes du Niger** (RDFN) and of the Fédération Kassaï. (Kassaï is the name of the celebrated sister of the 15th-century **Songhay** emperor **Sonni Ali** and a symbol of feminine heroism in Niger on par only with the **Arewa** queen **Saraounia Mangou**.) *See also* WOMEN.

DIFFA. Far eastern region bordering Chad, **Nigeria**, and (through **Lake Chad**) Cameroon, while within Niger it borders the regions of **Agadez** and **Zinder**. It encompasses a vast territory of 156,906 sq km with a sparse (density of 2.1 percent per sq km) population of 216,245 inhabitants, mostly **Kanuri** (the majority population in the region), **Hausa**, **Toubou**, **Tuareg**, **Arab**, and **Fulani**. The town of Diffa, headquarters of the region and over 1,000 km away from **Niamey**, is the smallest regional capital (25,000 inhabitants). Located on the **Komadougou Yobé** River, it has a big Sunday market of regional importance in which the main commodities are **cattle** and the famed Diffa pepper.

The region includes the *départements* of Diffa, **Maïné-Soroa**, and **N'Guigmi**, three urban **communes** (the three *département* headquarters), nine rural communes, and 20 Fulani, Toubou, and Arab *groupements*. Internal routes in the *département* are very sandy and poor, passable (between Diffa and N'Guigmi, for example) only during the dry season. In the mid-1990s, the region was troubled by the emergence of a "liberation front," mostly of Toubou insurgents, who carried out several assaults. In recent years, it has benefited from more attentions from the central government, owing to the fact that President **Mamadou Tandja** hailed from Maïné Soroa—a welcome change for a region which has been perhaps the key victim of Niger's administrative recession of the 1990s.

DIOBO, ALFA MAMANE (1768–1834). Fulani cleric and founder of **Say**. Born around 1768 in the Macina (Mali) and trained as an Islamic cleric, Diobo first settled in **Gao**, then in **Zinder** and **Dargol**. He was there widely acclaimed as a great saint by the **Kado**, **Kurtey**, and **Wogo**. He moved then to the immediate vicinity of contemporary **Niamey**, where he lived for seven years, and finally settled at Say and established it as a holy city in the Sufi **Qadiriyya** persuasion. As a Fulani island in **Zarma** country, Say also attracted many new Fulani immigrants who bolstered its position in the region, as well as the protection of the Sokoto Empire. One of Diobo's followers, Boubakar Louloudji, settled in the **Dallol Bosso** and helped the Fulani conquest of the area, further consolidating the position of Say, which grew to become a major market town linking the northern **Songhay** areas to Sokoto and beyond. As it was founded and settled essentially by voluntary converts to the faith, Say acquired a reputation as a saintly town, though it had grown into an ordinary small Nigerien town by the late 20th century. Thanks to its old reputation, though, it hosted the first Islamic school in Niger, a *madrasa* founded in 1957, and then the **Islamic University** established there in 1986 by the Organization of the Islamic Conference. After Diobo's death in 1834, his sons succeeded him as rulers of Say; the current chief of Say, *Alfaize* **Amadou Issa Cissé**, is a direct descendant of Diobo.

DIOFFO, ABDOU MOUMOUNI (1929–1991). Born on 26 June 1929 at **Tessaoua**, but in a **Fulani** family from Kirtachi, not far from **Niamey**, Dioffo went to primary and secondary school in **Zinder** and Niamey and studied mathematics at the **École William Ponty** (1944–1948). He moved from there into a brilliant student career in physics in French universities, culminating with an *agrégation* (a very prestigious and highly competitive higher education rank in the French system) in 1956 and a *doctorat d'état* (then the highest university degree in the French system) in 1967. Dioffo had also been teaching at high schools in West Africa, moving from Dakar (Senegal) to Conakry (Guinea) and finally Niamey in 1956–1959. His early interest in solar energy led him to take up a specialization in that field at a Moscow (USSR) university in 1961–1964, creating, upon his return to West Africa, the **Office National de l'Energie Solaire** (ONERSOL) in Niamey and then a solar energy laboratory in Mali, which he ran until 1969. In that period, he also taught at the Bamako (Mali) teaching school and was Mali's general inspector for physics. This stint in Mali was tied to Dioffo's radical politics and the connection he had built in that regard with Mali's ruler, Modibo Keita, a leading anti-imperialist.

After the fall of Keita in 1968, Dioffo returned to Niger (1969) where he revived ONERSOL. At ONERSOL, he invented several devices for harnessing solar energy in cooking, conservation, and general energy use, although the team he created there failed to draw in enough investors to commercialize the inventions in Niger. He directed the outfit until 1985. Dioffo was also very active in the creation of the **University of Niamey** and was appointed its rector in 1979–1983, teaching there until 1989. After his death on 7 April 1991, the university took his name. His remains were buried at Kirtachi. He had published in 1964 *L'Education en Afrique*, arguably the most thoroughgoing reflection on **education** in Africa in the French **language**. *See also* CENTRE NATIONAL D'ENERGIE SOLAIRE.

DIOP, MOUSTAPHA (1945–). Born in Cotonou (Benin), Diop studied modern **literature** in Abidjan and Ouagadougou before turning to **cinema** studies in Paris (**France**) at the Conservatoire Libre du Cinéma Français (1975–1978), graduating as director and film editor. By then, he had already made a movie, *Synapse*, in 1974. Upon returning to Niger, he was hired by the national television corporation, the **Office de Radio-Télévision du Niger** (ORTN), as movie director and shot for them the short movie *La Tomate* with Isabelle Calin (1981) and, in 1982, a full-length movie, *Le Médecin de*

Gafiré, for which he received several awards, including the Prix de la Critique Internationale at the festival of Locarno (Switzerland) and the Grand Prix of the festivals of Mannheim (Germany) and Perugia (Italy). He shot another full-length film in 1990, *Mamy Wata*, but this one was a flop. He then turned to journalism, founding *Le Paon Africain* in 1992, *Alfazar* in 1994, and *Sportissimo* in 1994. He is the secretary-general of Niger's filmmakers' association, the Association des Cinéastes du Niger.

DIORI, ABDOULAYE HAMANI (1945–2011). The son of former president **Hamani Diori**, Abdoulaye Diori was an international businessman who, in the 1980s, was involved in several attempts to destabilize the regime of **Seyni Kountché**, in connection with **Libya**. In one of these attempts, Diori partnered with the **Tuareg** commandos who raided **Tchintabaraden** in 1985, following which his father, who had been freed the previous year, was rearrested. After Niger's adoption of democratic institutions in 1991, Diori was elected a **Parti Progressiste Nigérien** (PPN-RDA) deputy for **Dosso** in 1995 and became the second vice-president of the **National Assembly**. In 1999, he was a member of the **Conseil Consultatif National**, the transitory parliament put in place by the military after the coup that year. Diori was afterward elected deputy in the **Fifth Republic**'s National Assembly in 2000 and reelected in 2004. During the **Tazartché** crisis, he sided with **Mahamadou Issoufou** and in opposition to President **Mamadou Tandja**'s attempt at ending democratic governance in Niger. After Issoufou's victory at the **election** of April 2011, he was appointed councilor to the president with the rank of a minister, but died shortly thereafter, on 25 April 2011, at Niamey's national hospital.

DIORI, AISSA (1928–1974). Wife of President **Hamani Diori**, born in **Dogondoutchi**. During her husband's administration, she personally amassed a large fortune, including quality buildings in **Niamey**, and was greatly detested especially in the more militant student circles where she was referred to as "l'Autrichienne" ("the Austrian," after French Queen Marie Antoinette who was thus dubbed in the period leading to the French Revolution). She was also a patron of the **Union des Femmes du Niger** as well as of several praise-singing artists, such as **Bouli Kakassi** or the Nigerian Maman Shata. Of Fulani origin, she was the mother of six. She was killed brutally in the **coup d'état of 15 April 1974**.

It must be noted that wives of president, especially when they remain in power for an extended period of time, often earn a reputation for greedy acquisitiveness in Niger, for good or exaggerated reasons; such has been the case of Mintou Kountché, wife of President **Kountché**, who ruled from 1974 to 1987, and of Laraba Tandja, one of the two wives of President **Tandja**, in power in 1999–2009.

DIORI, HAMANI (1916–1989). Diori was born in Soudouré, a village near **Niamey**, in June 1916, and was registered in a French school by his grandmother, Waybora Koundoum, seven years later, in 1923. In 1929, he obtained the native primary **education** certificate which led him to further studies at the French West Africa's teachers' schools of Porto-Novo and Gorée (**École William Ponty**). He subsequently served as a teacher in 1935–1938 in Niamey and **Maradi**, before being dispatched to **France**'s national school for overseas territories in Paris, also known as the École Coloniale. There, he tutored prospective colonial officials in the **Zarma** and **Hausa languages**. After the Second World War broke out, he was repatriated to Niger, where he returned to teaching and dabbled in linguistics and ethnology with his friends **Boubou Hama** and **Léopold Kaziendé**.

Diori entered politics in 1945 as leader of the **Parti Progressiste Nigérien** (PPN-RDA), which became a local affiliate of the then radical anticolonial West African party, the **Rassemblement Démocratique Africain** (RDA). He lost an early electoral bid to represent western Sudan and Niger to French Sudan's Fily Dabo Cissoko before being elected deputy for Niger, with the notable support of Boubou Hama and **Djibo Bakary**. At first perceived as an extremist party by the colonial government, in part owing to its association with the French Communist Party, the RDA was everywhere opposed by the administration, and Diori lost the 1951 **elections** to the French-backed **Georges Condat**. But by the end of the decade, the PPN evolved into an accommodating outfit while Bakary's parties (the last of which was **Sawaba**) grew more radical, especially in relation to the way the French intended to shape African independence. The PPN came to represent the kind of party that the colonial administration had tried to cobble together at various points in the 1950s, one that would ensure that strategic French interests would be safeguarded after independence, on the basis of conservative stability, allying modern leaders to traditional authorities (chiefs and clerics).

While liberal critics of Diori's regime emphasize its ethnocentricity (in particular the political bureau of the party was entirely constituted of **Zarma-Songhay** and **Maouri** officials), contemporary critics, including the radical insurgents of the Sawaba movement (also led by a Zarma leader and cousin of Diori, Djibo Bakary) chiefly insisted on its subservience to France and privileged groups. Indeed, the dominant character of Diori's regime was conservatism (the **National Assembly** was packed with traditional chiefs, mostly from the Hausaland) and accommodation of French interests (Diori, a founding father of the **Francophonie** organization which saw the light of day in Niamey, also granted special monopoly rights to France on the exploitation of Niger's **uranium**, in 1968). It was a French intervention which saved his regime from a military coup in 1963, and it is owing to his ties with France, which helped him organize repressive measures, that Diori faced an assassination attempt by a Sawaba militant in 1965.

Diori made creditable efforts to better Niger's situation in the 1960s, having inherited easily the most backward colony of the **Afrique Occidentale Française** (AOF). He established a number of **parastatals** and light manufacturing plants, mainly aimed at processing agricultural produce, and he extended the road system of the country by hundreds of kilometers with the building of the **Route de l'Unité** connecting Niamey to the far eastern regions of the country. The school attendance rate also soared under his regime to provide staff for the new state, moving from a paltry 2 percent to 17 percent by the early 1970s. But the **groundnut** economic rent flowing from the fields of Maradi and used by the state of Niger to finance these efforts dried up by the 1970s, as a **drought** cycle was settling in the **Sahel** region and the political crisis in the Middle East was leading to the 1970s **oil** shocks.

Famine in the countryside and various shortages and price hikes in town combined to bring the Diori regime to its knees, especially since the inefficiency to adequately respond to the cataclysm was widely ascribed to corruption in the establishment. A harried Diori looked for solutions up and down, allegedly contemplating the sale of northeastern Niger to **Libya**, but mostly putting pressure on the French to revise the uranium agreements and return to the Nigerien government a greater share of the profits, especially since the oil shocks were boosting the price of that commodity. It was two days before a high-level meeting with French officials on the uranium issue that Diori was overthrown by the **coup d'état of 15 April 1974** led by army chief of staff Lieutenant-Colonel **Seyni Kountché**, and which the French did nothing to stop as they had done some 10 years earlier. The coup was in particular tainted by the brutal assassination of Diori's wife, **Aissa Diori**.

Diori spent the remainder of his life mostly in house arrest. Released in 1984, 10 years after the coup that removed him from power, he was rearrested the following year, after his son **Abdoulaye Hamani Diori**, attempted to engineer a **Tuareg**-based, Libya-supported coup against Kountché's regime in 1985. After Kountché's death in 1987, he was freed by President **Ali Saibou** and died in Rabat (Morocco), where he was flown on a medical emergency, in 1989. *See also* OPERATION CHEVAL NOIR.

DIRKOU. Oasis at the foot of the **Kaouar** cliffs. With a population of 4,000, it is a rural **commune** in the *département* of **Bilma** (region of **Agadez**). At 1,600 km northeast of **Niamey**, Dirkou is the remotest Nigerien administrative subdivision. Historically an important oasis on one of the Central Sudan-to-North Africa **caravan routes**, it is now chiefly a military outpost guarding entry into and exit from Algeria and **Libya**. West African migrants to Libya use the village as a transit point, both for going into that country or when they are expelled from it. Several rock engravings from prehistoric times are to be found in the cliffs behind the oasis. *See also* ARCHAEOLOGY.

DJERMAKOYE, ADAMOU MOUMOUNI (1939–2009). Djermakoye was born in **Dosso**, in a family which the colonial government had promoted to an elevated position in the normally egalitarian structure of **Zarma** political organization. They acquired and retained the title of Djermakoye (or more properly, *zarmakoy*, i.e., lord of the Zarma) of Dosso, the greatest Zarma town. After secondary **education**, Djermakoye joined the military and became one of the closest friends of another officer, **Seyni Kountché**, who masterminded the **coup d'état of 15 April 1974** against the **Hamani Diori** regime. A key member of the **Conseil Militaire Suprême**, which was the highest government body under the new regime, Djermakoye was also appointed minister of foreign affairs and cooperation in 1974–1979, and then minister of youth, sports, and culture (1979–1981) and minister of public health and social affairs (1981–1983). He afterward served as ambassador to the United States and as Niger's permanent representative to the United Nations (1988–1991).

After Niger adopted a multiparty political system in 1991, and as the former single party, the **Mouvement National pour la Société de Développement** (MNSD) had become a normal **political party**, Djermakoye developed presidential ambitions which he hoped MNSD would harness. However, he was defeated by an alliance between another party bigwig, **Mamadou Tandja**, and the house strategist **Hama Amadou**. Djermakoye's defeat was ultimately good for MNSD: given that both Amadou and he were from the **Zarma-Songhay** regions of Niger, a Djermakoye-Amadou tandem would have made of the MNSD an ethno-regional party just like **Mahaman Ousmane**'s **Convention Démocratique et Sociale** (CDS Rahama) or indeed Djermakoye's own **Alliance Nigérienne pour la Démocratie et le Progrès** (ANDP Zaman Lahiya). By siding with a man from the **Hausa-Kanuri** East, Amadou ensured that MNSD would remain a party of national scope and relevance.

A disgruntled Djermakoye did not see it that way, though, and went on to establish a Club des Amis de Moumouni Adamou Djermakoye (CAMAD), a faction of the MNSD which evolved into ANDP. The new party thrived on its stranglehold over Dosso and its region, aligning itself with CDS in the anti-MNSD coalition of the **Alliance des Forces du Changement** (1993), and was rewarded for its support with the speakership of the **National Assembly**, which Djermakoye kept until the **Baré Maïnassara coup d'état of 1996**. After initially approving Maïnassara's actions and being rewarded with the presidency of the **Haute Cour de Justice**, Djermakoye ended up joining his opponents, peeved at what he saw as the arrogance of Maïnassara's entourage. After the 1999 coup d'état that did away with both Maïnassara and his regime, Djermakoye was appointed head of the **Conseil Consultatif National**, the organ tasked with overseeing the restoration of democratic governance.

By then, the position of his party had been firmly established as that of a support party, unable to win the highest prize (the presidency) but a necessary element of credible coalitions. In the 1999 presidential election, he came fifth at the first round and sided, for the runoff, with the main opponent to the MNSD, the **Parti Nigérien pour la Démocratie et le Socialisme** (PNSD Tarayya). The coalition lost the presidency, but ANDP gained four seats at the National Assembly, allowing Djermakoye to be an opposition deputy. However, he was persuaded in 2002 to switch to the ruling coalition and was rewarded with the position of minister of state for African integration and New Economic Partnership for African Development (NEPAD) programs. He resigned in view of the 2004 **elections**, in which he came fifth again and in which he backed the MNSD-led coalition at runoff.

In May 2005, Djermakoye was elected president of the **Fifth Republic**'s Haute Cour de Justice, a special judicial body composed of National Assembly deputies and endowed with the authority to indict high state personalities. The next year he lost a bid to become the speaker of the **Economic Community of West African States**' Parliament to Mahaman Ousmane, an event he bitterly resented and publicly ascribed to the support of **Nigeria**'s Hausa to their brethren from Niger.

In 2009, Djermakoye became the most dangerous (to Tandja) opponent to the president's bid to change the country's political regime in order to stay in power. His military past ensured that he remained very influential within the **armed forces** and could not be physically intimidated as were all the other major political leaders. Moreover, his grip on Dosso made of him an ethnic leader who saw behind Tandja's actions the project of establishing a Hausa-Kanuri political hegemony and a threat to national unity. After the **Cour Constitutionnelle** ruled against Tandja's project, the National Assembly began drafting a treason indictment against the president, which, if it had come into effect, would have landed Tandja at the Djermakoye-presided Haute Cour de Justice. To avoid this outcome, Tandja dissolved the National Assembly before it completed the indictment. Djermakoye then joined a coalition of Tandja's opponents from the political class and the **civil society**, becoming the most outspoken and fearless orator of the movement to resist regime change. He died from heart arrack at a rally in **Niamey**, on 14 June 2009. Both Tandja and the self-exiled Amadou attended his funeral, in an eerie respite in the political crisis—a tribute to his commanding presence in Nigerien politics.

His party survived under the leadership of one of his younger brothers, Colonel Moussa Moumouni Djermakoye, and it has kept its stranglehold over Dosso.

DJERMAKOYE, ISSOUFOU SAIDOU (1920–2000). Politician, diplomat, international administrator, and *zarmakoy* of **Dosso**. Born on 10 July 1920 in Dosso, he was the grandnephew of *Zarmakoy* **Aouta** (founder of Dosso's ruling dynasty) and the son of one of Aouta's successors, *Zarmakoy* Saidou (r. 1924–1938). He first studied at Dosso's elementary school and at **Niamey**'s regional school before attending secondary school at Algiers (Algeria) and Paris (**France**). When he was there, World War II broke out and he interrupted his studies to fight in the operations of the campaign of France. After France's defeat, Djermakoye remained in Paris to complete his studies at the Lycée Saint-Louis, becoming in 1943 the first Nigerien to earn a *baccalauréat* degree.

He returned to Niger in 1946, where he started working at the economic bureau of the colony's government, before taking up politics and presiding over the first central committee of the **Parti Progressiste Nigérien** (PPN-RDA). He later left PPN for the Union Nigérienne des Indépendants et Sympathisants (UNIS) in 1948—a party normally more friendly to the colonial government than PPN—before becoming a founding member of the Union Progressiste Nigérienne (UPN) and of the Bloc Nigérien d'Action (BNA), which merged with **Djibo Bakary**'s Union Démocratique Nigérienne (UDN) to engender the Nigerien branch of the **Mouvement Socialiste Africain** (MSA), later **Sawaba**. Djermakoye was the president of the party and became Sawaba municipal councilor for Niamey in 1956, keeping that position until the dissolution of the municipal council in 1959. Meanwhile, he had also served as a councilor of the French Union (1947), a member of the Grand Council of **Afrique Occidentale Française** in Dakar, Senegal (1952–1957), a member of the French Senate in Paris (1957), a vice-president of the Council of Ministers of Niger (1957–1958), and a minister of justice (1959–1960).

In the critical referendum period which saw a clash between the pro-French PPN and the anti-French Sawaba, Djermakoye eventually moved in the PPN's camp. After the latter's victory and Niger's independence (August 1960), he was briefly attached to **Hamani Diori**'s presidential office and then was sent for a year to represent Niger at the United Nations. On his return in

1963, he again put in two years as minister of justice (1963–1965) and then joined the United Nations until his retirement as undersecretary for trusteeship matters (1967–1972), undersecretary-general for economic and social affairs (1973–1978), secretary-general for technical cooperation (1978–1979), and secretary-general for political affairs and decolonization (1979–1982). He retired in 1982 and returned to Niger, where he was appointed *chef de province* of Dosso upon the death of his uncle, *Zarmakoy* **Abdou Aouta**, in 1998. He, however, died two years later.

***DJINN* (Also *Zinni*).** Among the **Songh**, the *djinn* are local spirits, protectors of villages or small localities, to whom offerings are made. According to mythology, the *djinn* were the first inhabitants of Earth but became invisible when people were created. They continue, however, to inhabit inanimate objects such as trees, rocks, rivers, and mountains.

***DOGARI*.** Mounted guards in Niger's principal kingdoms, usually wearing resplendent and colorful tunics, nowadays often in the colors of the Republic of Niger (orange, white, and green). The most famous are those in **Zinder** and **Dosso**. The word is **Hausa** in origin (but adopted into the **Zarma language**), with plural *dogaray*.

DOGBE, ALFRED (1962–2012). Playwright, writer, journalist, and dramatist, born in **Niamey** on 9 September 1962. He taught **literature** in several high schools in Niamey and other parts of the country in 1981–1997 before being appointed lecturer for literary criticism at the **University of Niamey**'s Letters Department. He then created several cultural organizations, including the center for cultural training CLEF of Niamey and the theater company Arène, which tours Niger and West Africa to present his productions as well as adaptations of European stage classics. He has published a great number of collections of short stories and plays, demonstrating easily the greatest stylistic abilities and creative spirit among Niger's contemporary writers. These works include *Bon voyage, Don Quichotte et autres textes* (1997), *L'homme-braise* (1997), *La Vie au brouillon* (1997), *La Geste de Zalbarou* (2000), and *Richard III/Africa* (2004). Dogbe died of cancer at Lome (Togo) in 2012. *See also* LITERATURE.

DOGO, YAZI (1942–). Born in **Dogondoutchi** where he received his primary **education**, Dogo went afterward to a Roman Catholic secondary school in the neighboring colony of Haute-Volta (now Burkina Faso) in 1953–1956 and worked for a while in the Catholic school system of Niger, first as a teacher at **Niamey**'s École Canada (1960–1967), then at **Zinder**'s École Mission Garçons (1967–1970). In 1970, he joined the national education system by taking up a teaching position at Zinder's École Birni Garçons. His next position as a teacher in the newly established **Hausa**-language school École Expérimentale Haoussa of Zinder highlighted his interest in local arts and culture. While pursuing a steady career in the national education system (he lectured on teaching at the **University of Niamey** in 1982–1984 and was in turn primary education inspector and general supervisor of Niamey's Centre de Formation Professionnelle until his retirement in 1997), he developed a vigorous vocation in theatrical arts, founding the most famous comedy group of the 1970s–1980s in Niger, the Troupe Théâtrale de Zinder (1972–1982). The Hausa-**language** classics of the *Troupe* offer vivid, sometimes moving, and always humorous portraits of traditional Hausa society and blends situation comedy lightness with the clever exposition of complex and at times intriguing characters and types.

In 1983, Dogo settled in Niamey and founded the Troupe Théâtrale du CCOG (CCOG being a cultural center in Niamey, the Centre Culturel **Oumarou Ganda**), which afterward became the Troupe Théâtrale Yaji Dogo.

Dogo's cultural career reached its high point in the 1980s, when the Nigerien government was interested in sponsoring cultural activities, notably through the annual youth and culture festivals started in 1976; at the time, he was a very public person and a national celebrity. In subsequent decades, however, with the retreat of the state and the advent of the Nigerian Hausa movie industry, Dogo had to reinvent himself as a private entertainer, working on contracts, including for public television. He remains an icon of Nigerien culture.

DOGONDOUTCHI. A town of 30,000 people some 140 km northeast of **Dosso** (237 km from **Niamey**) in the **Arewa**, of which it is the major center. The area is a center of the **Bori** cult, whose possession dances traditionally take place between April and June. Following the **French occupation**, Dogondoutchi became the regional French district headquarters, prompting the *sarkin* Arewa to relocate there from his previous capital at Matankari. Dogondoutchi has an important regional market and is also the name of the *département* of which the town is the headquarters. The short Dogondoutchi–Matankari stretch of road is very picturesque.

DOGUWA. "The Long One" (feminine) in **Hausa**. A family of potent female spirits native of the **Arewa**. Spirits—in Hausa, *iskoki*—in the ancient Hausa **Bori** pantheon dwell in the bush (*daaji*) and usually existed before the birth of human races, who are weaker kinds of beings needing to appropriate or tame spirits or in any case find ways in which to protect themselves from their often nefarious powers. Arewa chiefdoms often became entwined with in particular the Doguwa spirits, propitiating them for their role in warfare, their ties to the land, and their capacity to ensure communal prosperity. They were honored in Bori rituals and would receive the sacrifice of a bull on certain occasions. But many Doguwa remained untamed and nameless, keeping their wild will and propensity for wreaking havoc in human's lives, which is why the Arewa is reputed to house the most dangerous spirits of Niger. And although the progress of **Islam** has greatly reduced the scale of the collective cult of the Doguwa and the hold of Bori rituals, the spirits remain feared and often venerated forces in the Arewa.

DOSSO. Region encompassing 33,844 sq km and a population of 1,505,864, the second most densely populated subdivision of Niger, after the region of **Maradi**. The administrative capital is in the important town of the same name, which has around 44,000 people. Most of the people in the region are **Zarma** with minorities of **Maouri**, **Arewa Hausa**, **Fulani**, **Tuareg**, and **Dendi Songhay**.

Dosso was founded in the 18th century after a period of population dislocations consequent to a tug-of-war with the Tuareg, and it has been dominated by its white princely palace since 1904. It is 139 km east of **Niamey**. Its name derives from *do-so*, a spirit. It is the headquarters of the sultan (formerly *chef de province*) or *zarmakoy* of Dosso, the most important Zarma leader.

A stronghold of **Adamou Moumouni Djermakoye**'s **Alliance Nigérienne pour la Démocratie et le Progrès** (ANDP Zaman Lahiya), Dosso was fiercely opposed to President **Mamadou Tandja**'s objective of staying in power after his term, in 2009. The *Zarmakoy* Maidanda had, however, been enlisted by Tandja as a clapping hand, to the anger of his population. When in June 2009 he decided to bestow on Tandja the customary honor of *mazayaki* (war strategist, an office traditionally held in Dosso's old constitution by the Sirimbeye quarter), riots erupted and parts of the *zarmakoy*'s palace were burned down while a party of Tandja supporters was molested.

The region has five *départements* (Dosso, **Boboye**, **Dogondoutchi**, **Gaya**, and **Loga**), one sultanate, and 15 cantons. *See also* DOSSO, KINGDOM OF.

DOSSO, KINGDOM OF. The kingdom of Dosso was until the 20th century a small but plucky **Zarma** state which emerged in the mid-18th century under *Zarmakoy* Boukar or Aboubacar. The encroaching Zarma displaced **Sabiri** rule in the area, but struck a pact with them to maintain the high Sabiri office of *sandi* as almost on par with the kingly office of *zarmakoy*. In particular, the *sandi* enthrones and inters the *zarmakoy*. The office of *zarmakoy* was established as a supreme executive office that rotated among the various small villages which were grouped in the area that would later extend and coalesce into the town of Dosso. Various assistant offices were allocated to each village: thus the *sandi* (who presides over enthronement) must come from the Sabiri quarter of Dosso Beye, the *wonkoy* (war lord, as in commander in chief) from Oudoungkoukou, the *mazayaki* (war strategist) from Sirimbeye, and so on. In fact, the names of Dosso's offices are often borrowed from the **Hausa** states to which it was adjacent: thus the court of the *zarmakoy* was a *fada*, like in the Hausaland, and the dignitaries were titled *yerima* (the successor of the *zarmakoy*) and *galadima* (the official who organized slave labor), words derived from the **Bornu Empire** through the **sultanate of Damagaram**; *marafa* (chief of the government) and *waziri* (chief intendant), words derived from the Hausa states. When he took over the office of *zarmakoy*, **Aouta** created the office of *maizindadi* (from Hausa *maijindadi*, "the merrymaker") for his court treasurer.

The kingdom was essentially a warrior state, thriving through victories over rival kingdoms and the attendant capture of people reduced into slavery. Its higher ambition was to unify the Zarma in the southern quarters of the **Zarmaganda**, but throughout its existence, and until the 20th century, it only ruled over a small hinterland cultivated by communities of peasants who paid to the ruler a seasonal land tax (*laabu albarka*) and an inheritance tax (*usiri*). The booty of war, including the acquisition of slave labor, was a much greater source of wealth than these revenues.

Thanks to its organization, the state of Dosso was able to ward off the first attacks from the Sokoto Empire (early 19th century). When it finally fell into the power of the emir of Gwandu (a Sokoto-anointed ruler) toward the mid-19th century, it still retained its organization and was quickly able to reassert its independence. This happened under the leadership of *Zarmakoy* Kossom (1854–1865), who also inflicted a crushing defeat to the **Tuareg**, capturing their war drum and considerably increasing the prestige of Dosso in the Zarmaland. It is at that point, as the authority of the *zarmakoy* of Dosso started to reach beyond the four gates (Kofadeye, Deye Gorou, Tombokireye, Takamargou) of the town, that it is possible to talk of a kingdom of Dosso.

In 1902, the French changed the civic constitution of Dosso into a dynastic monarchy, fixing the office of the *zarmakoy* in the family of their favorite interlocutor in the town, Idrissa Kossom Aouta. *Zarmakoy* Aouta subsequently persuaded the colonial government to erect Dosso into a canton, ruling over a much larger section of the Zarmaland than it used to, before the arrival of the French. The revolution introduced by the colonial government entailed the suppression of slavery and its replacement, as source of revenue, with a steady land tax. Thus the *laabu albarka*, which was levied in accordance with the season (some years not at all, when the harvest was bad or the crop eaten by locusts), became a permanent annual impost with a fixed amount, to be paid to the *zarmakoy* who acted as a tax collector for the colonial government. The **bogu**, which used to be an invitation issued by the *zarmakoy* to come and work on his fields, and was thus a voluntary labor rewarded by festivities and the distribution of kola nuts, **millet**, and meat, became a *corvée* (forced labor) due to the *zarmakoy*. In this way, the transformation of the kingdom by the colonial regime largely benefited the *zarmakoy*, at the expense of the warlike aristocracy which was the backbone of the kingdom, and which disappeared as a class. Moreover, starting in 1903, the *zarmakoy* started to receive a salary which, by 1944, was equal to that paid to the sultan of **Aïr**, though slightly inferior to that paid to the sultan of **Damagaram**.

In 1946, the land tax and the *bogu* were abolished after a campaign against them engineered by the **Parti Progressiste Nigérien** (PPN-RDA), which correctly denounced them as colonial innovations and earned them great popularity among the rural populations in western Niger. Afterward, the *zarmakoy* of Dosso became, like all other so-called customary chiefs in Niger, a full salaried member of the **civil service**, even though this was masked by the maintenance of old etiquette and court mannerisms. The kingdom's administrative names were in turn: canton of Dosso (1903–1926); province of Dosso (1926–2010); and sultanate of Dosso, since September 2010. For a list of rulers, *see also* DOSSO, *ZARMAKOYS* OF.

DOSSO, *ZARMAKOYS* OF. The title of *zarmakoy* designates an executive office in the government of **Zarma** villages. It knew its greatest development in **Dosso**, where the descendants of the warrior Tagour founded a state in the mid-18th century, through efforts at protecting and unifying Zarmas in that area against the **Tuareg** and the **Fulani**. In the constitution of Dosso, the political egalitarianism of the Zarmas was maintained by rotating the office through the various small villages composing the polity. The office was retained by Dosso even when it was conquered by the emir of Gwandu, the western province of the Sokoto Empire, toward the mid-19th century. In 1854–1865, it was held by *Zarmakoy* Kossom, who consolidated independence from Gwandu and defeated the Tuareg at a battle known as Taangami Takio (the Four Glorious Battles) in which he captured the Tuareg commandment drum, the *Toubal* (now kept in the palace of the *zarmakoy* and beaten at important occasions).

In 1902, the French colonial authorities ended the rotating system by conferring the office to a son of Kossom, Idrissa, nicknamed **Aouta**, while it was not yet his turn. Ever since, the office of *zarmakoy* of Dosso has remained in the family of *Zarmakoy* Aouta Kossom, to the extent that the name of the office has become (in its Frenchified form, Djermakoye) the name of that family. *Zarmakoy* Aouta built the current palace of the *zarmakoy* (1904), thus marking the passage from the ancient, civic constitution to the monarchical constitution, under French protection. The *zarmakoy* of Dosso is, since September 2010, a sultan in Niger's traditional peerage. Between 1938 and 2000, the sons of *Zarmakoy* Aouta and of his brother *Zarmakoy* Saidou alternated on the throne. The prominent Dosso politician **Adamou Moumouni Djermakoye** was a grandson of *Zarmakoy* Aouta. The list of the *zarmakoys* is as follows: dates unknown: *Zarmakoy* Aboubacar (mid-18th century), *Zarmakoy* Laouzo, *Zarmakoy* Gounabi, *Zarmakoy* Amirou. Dates known: *Zarmakoy* Kossom, 1854–1865; *Zarmakoy* Abdou Kiantou Baba, 1865–1890; *Zarmakoy* Alfa Atta, 1890–1897; *Zarmakoy* Attikou, 1897–1902; *Zarmakoy* Aouta Kossom, 1902–1913; *Zarmakoy* Moussa Kossom, 1913–1924; *Zarmakoy* Saidou Kossom, 1924–1938; *Zarmakoy* Moumouni Aouta, 1938–1953; *Zarmakoy* Hamani Saidou, 1953–1962; *Zarmakoy* Abdou Aouta, 1962–1998; *Zarmakoy* **Issoufou Saidou**, 1998–2000; *Zarmakoy* Maidanda Hamadou Saidou, 2000–. *See also* DOSSO, KINGDOM OF.

DOUTCHI. *See* DOGONDOUTCHI.

DROUGHTS. As a chiefly Sahelian and Saharan country, Niger has been periodically ravaged by devastating droughts and famines affecting diverse regions of the country but usually **Damergou**, **Damagaram**, and **Aïr**. Until the major **Sahel** drought in 1968–1974, the 1913–1914 famine had been the most vicious in living memory. The droughts of the 1970s, however, surpassed the earlier ones, especially given their length, since they actually began in 1968.

Droughts and famines in the 20th century have included one in 1902—coinciding with the **French occupation** of the country—that saw many **Hausa** relocate to the Sokoto region in **Nigeria** and played a part in the **Zarma-Songhay** revolts of 1905–1906; the 1913–1914 famine that raged throughout the country; the 1919 drought that hit **Zarmaganda**; the 1920–1921 drought that affected all of southern Niger along the Nigeria border; and the 1930–1931 drought in the west–central part of the country—with the last two triggering major migrations from **Ader** (the hardest hit) to Nigeria.

The recent series of Sahel droughts commenced in 1968, with progressively less rainfall each succeeding year. In 1972 there was a major migration south of **ethnic groups** and **cattle** normally resident in the areas affected as the Sahara gradually expanded southward into the Sahel. Rainfall in **Agadez** in 1970 was 40 mm; in 1972, 74 mm, contrasted with the 33-year average for the city of 164 mm per year. Forty-four food and seed distribution centers were established in Aïr to assist the local population to survive the worst drought to hit Niger. Each center was headed by a committee of government officials and local notables entrusted with the equitable distribution of ration cards. Much of the grain intended for the stricken populations was not delivered, however, due to mismanagement and the country's poor infrastructures. The **Tuareg** of Aïr were forced to give up their nomadic patterns and congregate around boreholes southeast of Agadez, where aid was also given, and they lost around 95 percent of their cattle. The town and region of Agadez greatly swelled consequent to this southward migration of refugees, and the population of Agadez itself (normally 20,000) jumped to 105,000 in 1972.

Complaints of corruption, hoarding, and speculation with grain intended for the starving were heard and were one motivation invoked for the **coup d'état in April 1974**. In its efforts to delegitimize the **First Republic**, the new military regime extensively documented malfeasance, including government speculation on donated grains. Some of the accusations were very likely exaggerated or unfounded, but they brought to light for the first time the fact that the famines in Niger do not have purely natural causes. However, the country's poor road networks and generally bad infrastructures are a more daunting problem than mismanagement and speculation. The drought was Sahelian and not purely Nigerien, and at its height nearly 500,000 refugees from Mali (mostly Tuareg) entered Niger seeking relief. At the same time, however, some 500,000 Nigeriens had moved into Nigeria for the same reason.

In the mid-1980s another drought afflicted Niger. In 1985—as during the mid-1970s—**Lake Chad** shrank so much in size that it no longer extended into Niger territory, and the **Niger River** itself was nearly dry at **Niamey**—reaching its lowest levels since 1922.

Though the **Kountché** regime's main post-1974 economic emphasis was on making Niger self-sufficient in food in case of future droughts, by 1984 the country was again on its knees. In 1985 over 500,000 people were displaced by the drought. The economic effects of the drought were worsened by the decision taken by Nigeria's president, Muhammad Bohari, to shut down his country's border with Niger, thus cutting a major lifeline for Niger's eastern regions. The famine was known in those parts as *El Bohari* (Hausa for "The Bohari One"). The onset of good rains later that year allowed the country to become self-sufficient once again.

While Niger's food problems did not result in a famine in the two decades following the 1985 crisis, they grew more acute and complex, owing to the increased pressure of demographic growth, the 1990s dismantling of government monitoring systems (in relation to the freeze in **civil service** recruitment), and the adoption of premature liberalization strategies for the purpose of food security. The demographic issue combined with the advance of desertification and the lack of a rural development agenda left Niger's vast agricultural and pastoral areas in precarious condition. In 2004, the early end of rains combined with an infestation of desert locust (that damaged some pasture lands) and high food prices to trigger severe food crises in the northern fringes of the regions of **Maradi** and **Zinder**, as well as in the large areas of the regions of **Tillabéri** and **Tahoua** which had been taken over by desertification since the 1980s. The international consensus was that the crisis was not a famine, but while the Sahelian region recorded overall a grain surplus of about 85,000 tons, Niger suffered a deficit of around 224,000 tons. The situation in Niger was in particular worsened by exports of grains to Nigeria, a bigger market with constant large demand, which also contributed to driving the price of food up in the regions of Maradi and Zinder. The crisis hit Niger in 2005 and was the fodder for a summer media frenzy in Western countries, while in Niger itself, it marked an episode in the rift between President **Mamadou Tandja** (who maintained that it was not a famine) and Prime Minister **Hama Amadou** (who argued that it was one). The United Nations and international organizations defined the situation as a food crisis (rather than a famine) and assessed that 800,000 people faced acute food insecurity in the affected regions. Despite the media coverage, donors gave less than half the $81 million appealed for by the United Nations.

Another drought hit the Sahelian region, including Niger, in 2010, causing spikes of food shortage and hunger in the regions of Maradi and Zinder. New theories about the natural causes of the problem point to global warming as an additional, serious trigger of the droughts in this part of Africa. *See also* AGRICULTURE; ECONOMY.

DUMI. Among the **Songhay**, the extended family unit. It encompasses all descendants from a common founder. Members are the *hamay*, as in *Si hamay*, "descendants of Si." (*Hamay* is the plural of *hama*, which also means grandchild.)

DYA (also *Za*). **Songhay** dynasty established around the year 690, and ruling for some 600 years, with the foundation of **Koukya** (also **Goungia**), the pre-Islamic capital of the Songhay. The 21st *dya* of the dynasty, in the mid-15th century, revolted against the suzerainty of the Mali Empire and took office as Sonni, or Si. (The Songhay had become Muslim with the conversion of the 15th *dya*, Kosoy, at which time the center of the kingdom shifted to **Gao**.) Though the lineage of the kingdom remained intact, future kings were known under the new prefix, Si, or Sonni. In 1493 one of the lieutenants of **Sonni Ali**—one of the kingdom's greatest rulers and true founder of the **Songhay Empire**—seized power and set up the **Askia** dynasty, which itself was to be shattered with the invasion from the north of Moroccan armies in the waning years of the 16th century.

E

ÉCOLE DES MINES DE L'AÏR (ÉMAÏR). "Hands-on" **mining** school set up in 1975 in **Aïr** by the **Société Minière de l'Aïr** (SOMAÏR) and the **Compagnie Minière d'Akouta** (COMINAK) in order to assist in the training of local engineers and technical staff, and as part of the mining companies' pledge to bring about a localization of staff—to the 50 percent level by 1983. The goal was not attained; indeed, by 1983 only 52 Nigeriens had graduated from the school, even as the number of mining expatriates in the country went up. Following the global **uranium** glut, ÉMAÏR was downsized in the 1990s, and shut down many of its training programs. In recent years, the new uranium boom has led to its revitalization by **AREVA**, the French uranium giant which exploits Niger's huge deposits. Some 150 young Nigeriens were enrolled in 2009 to be trained as drivers and technicians for the mines at **Arlit, Akokan**, and **Imouraren**. Students flock from all over the country, though the majority of them are from the region of **Agadez**.

ÉCOLE NATIONALE D'ADMINISTRATION ET DE MAGISTRATURE (ÉNAM). About two months away from formal independence (June 1960), Niger set up a training center for administrators, the Centre de Formation Administrative (CFA). Three years later, the CFA was developed into an undergraduate higher **education** outfit for training in administration, the École Nationale d'Administration (ÉNA). Gradually the school added graduate echelons, first in 1972, the Level II (master's) and then in 2002, the Level III (post-master's) with the creation of a section for training judges. In June 2005, 25 years after the creation of the CFA, ÉNA became the École Nationale d'Administration et de Magistrature, the highest development of this kind of school in the system inherited from **France**. In the period 1987–1992, ÉNA had undergone thorough restructuring owing chiefly to Niger's dire financial straits. This included, among other things, the adoption of more demanding selection criteria for admission in the school for high cadre training and a greater reliance on foreign financing (rather than the state of Niger). Thus, the judges' training section opened thanks to French money, while the public management program was partly funded by Quebec's École Nationale d'Administration Publique. After a period of crisis in the late 1990s, ÉNAM has harnessed with some success a strategy used by many African higher education institutes to cruise a globalizing context: higher learning networking. It has thus linked up, through conventions and agreements, with administration schools in the wealthy Francophone world (France, Belgium, Switzerland, Quebec) as well as with projects aiming at a regional, West African development of public management studies. In 2006-2008, a Canadian-trained scholar, Mamoudou Djibo brought to this very French type of school some of the zest of the North American academe. The school is currently headed by Boucar Abba Kaka.

ÉCOLE WILLIAM PONTY. Prestigious high school initially on Gorée Island off Dakar, Senegal, which trained many among the African elite of **Afrique Occidentale Française**. Later, at Sebikhotane and then Dakar, much of Niger's early elite attended the *lycée*: Abdou Sidikou, **Djibo Bakary**, Harouna Bembello, **Georges Mahaman Condat**, **Barcougné Courmo**, **Mahamane Dan Dobi**, **Hamani Diori**, Yacouba Djibo, **Pierre Foulani**, Amadou Gaoh, **Boubou Hama**, Ibra Kabo, **Noma Kaka**, Garba Katambe, **Leopold Kaziendé**, Abderahmane Keita, **Harou Kouka**, Mai Maigana, and Amadou Mossi.

ECONOMIC COMMUNITY OF WEST AFRICAN STATES (ECOWAS). A regional economic and political integration organization founded in 1975, mostly under the leadership of the Federal Republic of **Nigeria**. ECOWAS's membership extends to all West African countries, with the exception of Mauritania, and it also includes the Cape Verde islands, comprising in all 15 member states. The organization was long dormant in the 1980s but knew a revival in the 1990s, as it transformed itself with the view of becoming the African Union's agenda bearer, or "pillar," for West Africa. Important developments include the creation of a security force, the Economic Community of West African States Monitoring Group (ECOMOG), a community Court of Justice (1991), a Protocol on Democracy and Good Governance (2000), a common market agreement (2002), and pacts on a common agricultural policy (ECOWAP, 2005) and on a common industrial policy (WACIP, 2010). ECOWAS has become increasingly important in the West African political landscape in the 2000s, notably through its normative defense of democratic governance and rule of law. It thus suspended Niger on 20 October 2009, after **Mamadou Tandja** ignored its request not to hold controversial, antidemocratic **elections** that month and year, and reintegrated the country only after Tandja had been removed (18 February 2010) and democracy had been fully restored, on 23 March 2011.

ECONOMIC LIBERALIZATION. The philosophy of economic policy under the colonial regime—a philosophy largely inherited by Niger's early governments—was in theory liberal, since colonial territories were acquired in view of expanding metropolitan trade and productive investments, which were private enterprises. The state intervened to ensure that colonial subjects provided a suitable labor force and consumer population for French capitalists. At independence, the new project of national development led to a combination of economic liberalism and direct intervention of the state in the productive sector. This was partly due to the fact that domestic private capital was too meager to take up productive activities, while foreign capital often did not find Niger profitable and safe enough for investments. The state also adopted a regulatory framework which created a system of public monopolies, especially in so-called strategic sectors, such as water, telecommunications, and electricity. Moreover, the ideal of national development was vetted at the international level, and public bilateral **foreign aid** was generally geared to help the state develop the productive sector, especially in the 1960s. Private enterprise was confined to services, particularly trade in the so-called informal sector.

After the **uranium** boom of the mid-1970s, the state stepped up investment in the **parastatal sector** in the framework of the ambitious three-year program and five-year economic and social development plan of 1976–1983. These developments were financed by both uranium income and foreign borrowing which rewarded Niger's apparent solvability, boosted by the ore. The collapse of the uranium market put paid to these ambitions and processes in the early 1980s; by 1985, Niger was saddled with an external debt which represented 51 percent of its fiscal revenue, and the situation was particularly dire in the parastatal sector. In 1983, it was calculated that total indebtedness of that sector had reached the grand total of 87 billion **CFA francs**, or 31 percent of the country's total external debt. In 1986, the government committed to an International Monetary Fund's (IMF) restructuration prescription which sought to jumpstart economic liberalization through privatization and closure of parastatals—a first step toward the removal of the state from the productive sector. Most parastatals were evaluated as noncompetitive, wasteful, and overstaffed, and government control also meant large-scale public payment arrears as well as diversion of funds and profit away from the economic objectives of the enterprise, owing to the fiscal crisis and to corruption.

However, public opposition to the dismantling of the developmental state implied by the IMF reforms ran high among trade **unions** and much of the emerging **civil society**, and economic liberalization got underway by fits and starts. A series of restructuring plans was adopted starting in 1986, regarding a variety of service sectors, including **banking** and **transportation** (1994), and these reforms helped in opening up professions and business segments hitherto heavily controlled by vested interests. The monopolist outfits were either scaled-down to make room for competition (**Office National des Produits Pharmaceutiques et Chimiques, Société Nationale des Transports Nigériens**) or written off (**COPRO-NIGER**). However, democratically elected Nigerien governments tended to shy away from the more radical prescriptions of the IMF for fear of antagonizing organized labor.

It took the authoritarian leadership of President **Ibrahim Baré Maïnassara** (1996–1999) to develop a full-fledged privatization process and attendant reforms. Thus, in 1996, the government set up the Cellule de Coordination du Programme de Privatisation and a Department of Privatization was added to the Ministry of Finances to pilot the process. By 1998, Niger had reached an agreement with the IMF on the implementation of a large-scale privatization program which meant a full removal of the state from the productive sector. This included sectors such as water, electricity, telecommunication, and fuel importation and distribution, which the state of Niger had thus far considered too strategic to be handled by private hands.

The various reforms undertaken between 1994 and 1998 led to the development of formal private domestic activities in the service sector and in some aspects of the productive sector, but in fact the liberalization movement encountered the same obstacle as the state, when it used institutional measures to try and stimulate private activity in the 1980s; Niger sorely lacked a competent private business class with the level of **education** which would lead to innovations and calculated risk taking. Indeed, it was in all cases modern-educated businessmen, members of a tiny minority in Niger's business environment, who spurred the modest development that occurred in **agriculture** and small manufacturing. Moreover the privatization process of the erstwhile strategic sectors—which required foreign capital—eventually yielded mixed results. The water sector was taken over by the French company Vivendi Waters (now Veolia), solving the myriad financial problems of the erstwhile state-run Société Nigérienne des Eaux (SNE) but also leading to the collapse of modern water supply in the unprofitable countryside; the telecommunication privatization scheme ended in relative failure, leading the state of Niger to renationalize the **Société Nigérienne des Télécommunications** (SONITEL) in 2009; the electricity company **Société Nigérienne d'Electricité** (NIGELEC) did not attract serious bidders, and in 2007, the government agreed with the World Bank to give up its privatization. Likewise, the government eventually kept in its portfolio the oil company **Société Nigérienne des Produits Pétroliers** (SONIDEP). The **Société Nigérienne de Cimenterie** (SNC) performs less well than when it was state run and notably fails to meet increasing demand for cement in the country. While a number of state societies thrived after privatization (**Société de Lait du Niger, Entreprise Nigérienne des Textiles**), other privatized companies ended in bankruptcy shortly after having been sold out.

It has thus appeared that while state management in the productive sector has its many dilemmas, full-out privatization might not be the panacea that it was believed to be in the late 1990s, especially given conditions in Niger. Privatization, however, is only one component of economic liberalization, the other one being reforms undertaken to promote private activities and attract foreign direct investment. Niger was relatively more successful in these latter fields. While foreign investors do not flock to the country (which has tiny markets, poor infrastructure, considerable bureaucratic delays, a shortage of local capital, lack of skilled labor, and exorbitant transportation costs), negative rates of investment—which were frequent in the 1990s—have disappeared in the 2000s and the positive rates tend to be higher than what they were in the past, even though much of this remains tied to the **mining** sector. And local capital has become more active with the opening up of the agricultural productive and trading sector. The impending trend, however, is clearly to bring the state back into the productive sector, though through modalities different from those in the 1960s and as yet to be defined. *See also* AUTORITÉ DE RÉGULATION MULTISECTORIELLE; DEVELOPMENT PLANS; ECONOMY; SOCIÉTÉ D'EXPLOITATION DES EAUX DU NIGER.

ECONOMY. Niger's tiny and vulnerable economy yields a GDP of $359 per inhabitant, leaving over 60 percent of Nigeriens under the poverty line and the country at the bottom of the United Nations Development Program's human development index. The economy is dominated by the trade and service sectors (43.7 percent) and the agricultural sector (41.2 percent), with the secondary sector (15.1 percent) being itself shaped much more by **mining** activities than by industries (figures of 2009). Crucially, much of the primary and tertiary sector activities develop in the so-called informal economy, estimated at about 75 percent of GDP (compared to 65 percent of GDP for Côte d'Ivoire, the leading economy of Francophone West Africa). This means low productivity, low levels of skills, low and irregular generated incomes, a lower level of organizations that limits business expansion, and lower acumen for competitive technological innovations. Moreover, lacking proper accounting and recording systems, the informal economy is not easily taxable, and indeed prospers on its ability to evade or compromise the state's fiscal attempts. While it certainly provides some employment for millions of Nigeriens, its disproportionate importance in the country's economy is a negative factor for wealth and job creation.

Niger's economy is shaped by a number of regional agreements and by the state's relationship with the international financial institutions (see Table 4). The country is a member of the **Union Economique et Monétaire Ouest-Africaine** (UEMOA), the regional economic organization which gathers all the users of the **CFA franc currency** in West Africa. Through its convergence criteria, UEMOA determines Niger's macroeconomic policy, notably the level of inflation to be kept (must hover around 3 percent), the level of tax burden to be reached (17 percent), the wage bill (must be of 35 percent of fiscal revenues), or the level of investment funding using internal resources (20 percent). In recent years, Niger has been successful in meeting some of these criteria, especially as regards the reduction of the wage bill (26.9 percent), but not the important one on tax burden (hovering around 14 percent). Moreover, the state's indebtedness is generally within UEMOA's norms, as it is incurred with development banks for infrastructural development purposes (recently, the **Kandadji Dam**). UEMOA is also a customs union which determines Niger's rates of external tariffs, which are quite low (the highest rate being of only 20 percent) and criticized for being inadequate if the country is to develop an industrial policy, as is inscribed in its latest constitution. The **Economic Community of West African States** (ECOWAS), which includes all UEMOA member-states and the other (English-speaking) West African countries, has less impact on Niger's economic policy, though it is scheduled to supersede UEMOA in the near future. Niger's relations with the International Monetary Fund (IMF) and the World Bank have been stable since the late 1990s, with the IMF regularly renewing its budgetary support, even during political crises. On 12 February 2010, six days before the toppling of the illegal president **Mamadou Tandja**, the IMF had disbursed a 3.3 million SDR loan in favor of Niger's government. The World Bank runs, as

Table 4. Niger's Economic Indicators

Indicator	Rate & Ranking (Est. March 2010)
Nominal GDP	2,764 billion CFA francs ($5.6 billion)
Growth rate per GDP percent	8 percent
Investment rate per GDP percent	41.5 percent
Inflation rate	2.9 percent
Tax burden per GDP percent	13.7 percent
Fiscal revenue	14.3 percent
Aid rate per GDP percent	7.2 percent
Net external debt outstanding per GDP percent	24 percent
World Bank Doing Business ranking	173 out of 183

of July 2010, 16 projects in the country, representing a total commitment of $292.8 million. This is to reward the country's relative abidance by the institutions' strict criteria of macroeconomic stability, which supplement those of UEMOA, with the World Bank intervening in the improvement of public finance management.

Niger's growth rates are heavily dependent on the primary sector and are subject to wild swings: Very high at 9 percent in 2008, the rate abruptly fell to 1.2 percent in 2009, owing to the **agricultural** sector's negative growth that year. With the recovery of the primary sector in 2010, the growth rate rebounded to 5.8 percent, but still below the 7 percent steady growth rate which, according to UEMOA, would trigger economic change over time. It was recently boosted by a brighter outlook in the mining sector.

The rebound was also tied to the growing dynamism in the mining sector: In 2009, Niger's **uranium** production showed a 2.6 percent increase, yielding 5 percent of GDP and 5 percent of fiscal revenue—and this is prior to the opening of the **Imouraren** mine, which is likely to propel Niger to the rank of second or even first world producer of the ore. The Fukushima nuclear catastrophe in Japan (March 2011) will have an impact on Niger's uranium sales, insofar as Japan was the second buyer of the country's ore after **France**, and the catastrophe is likely to have a negative impact on French investments and those of an emerging economic partner, China. In 2007, Sino Uranium, a subsidiary of China National Nuclear Corporation (CNNC), invested $300 million USD in the exploitation of mines at Tegguida and **Azelik**. Niger has some other untapped mineral riches, in phosphate (**Ader**) and **oil** and natural gas (Agadem). In 2007, the country applied to the Extractive Industries Transparency Initiative (EITI), an international monitoring system aimed at shielding mining revenues from corruption and misappropriation, and it was admitted in 2011, after delays caused by the **Tazartché** political crisis in 2009–2010.

Niger's industrial sector is puny and remains concentrated on a few low-end activities: agribusiness, textiles, building trade, and public works. It contributes very little to the country's GDP growth (0.7 points in 2010 as opposed to 2.8 points for the primary sector and 2.3 points for the tertiary sector). The tertiary sector has been here (as in other sub-Saharan African countries) boosted by the development of telecommunications, chiefly the mobile phone subsector. Inflation in Niger is vulnerable especially to food prices and energy costs (oil). In 2008, high global food prices sent inflation in the country to the heights of 11.3 percent, and the relative decrease in 2009 (4.3 percent) was still too high (relative to UEMOA criteria), owing chiefly to domestic food prices after the poor performance of the agricultural sector that year. Inflation fell however to below 1 percent in 2010.

Imports and exports grow minimally but regularly. In 2010, imports (chiefly of cereals and consumer goods) grew by 8.3 percent while exports (chiefly of uranium and gold) grew by 7 percent. Niger's trade balance is therefore negative, a situation also reflected in the country's public finances, where the budget deficit is only very incrementally reduced, for instance from 3.3 percent in 2009 to 2.9 percent in 2010.

Niger's external debt has considerably lowered since the cancellation, in 2006, of the 784.3 billion CFA francs debt in the framework of the Multilateral Debt Relief Initiative engineered by the IMF, the World Bank, and the African Development Fund. Since then, it has remained constant at around $965 million, meaning a servicing of 4.1 percent of fiscal revenue in 2007 and 2.7 percent in 2008, down from double-digit rates in the 1990s. The expected production of refined oil (on stream in 2012) and of Imouraren uranium (2013) has led the World Bank to assess Niger's external debt as a sustainable one.

Niger's **banking** system—in 2010, consisting of 11 banks—has recently strengthened in terms of profitability, with a net aggregate result of 12.6 billion of CFA francs in 2009 as opposed to 3 billion in 2008, chiefly because the banking system has been stepping up ways to tap into the vast unincorporated pool of potential customers in the country. Microfinance—which comprises 10 decentralized financial institutions—is also on the increase, concerning about 350,000 customers in 2009 (20 percent higher than 2008) and 7.4 billion CFA francs in deposits, that is, 3.4 percent of total deposits in the banking system.

Economic indicators for Niger are moderately optimistic for the future, chiefly owing to observed improvements in tax collection, **foreign aid** (notably tied to the restoration of democratic governance), as well as on a prudent management of external debt and of inflation, and the expected improvement of the trade balance with the coming on-stream of Imouraren's uranium and the refined oil from Agadem. However, Niger's economy is heavily shaped by an agricultural sector exceedingly dependent on climatic vagaries and on the quite erratic mineral commodities markets.

Niger's main trading partners are France and **Nigeria** (with a generally negative trade balance with the former and a positive one with the latter), followed by Japan (uranium exportations essentially), Côte d'Ivoire, China, the United States, Switzerland, and the Netherlands. Imports progressed in the 2000s from $949 million in 2006 to $2.2 billion in 2009 and exports from $508 million in 2006 to $900 million in 2009. Niger is also a member of the World Trade Organization. *See also* ECONOMIC LIBERALIZATION.

EDUCATION. The Nigerien educational system is currently constituted of one primary education cycle (*Cycle de Base 1*), two secondary education cycles (*Cycle de Base 2* and *Enseignement Moyen*), and higher education programs offering bachelor's (*licence*), master's, and doctorate degrees at the Universities of **Niamey** and **Say** (the latter being an Islamic university). In 2011, three new (secular) universities were opened in **Maradi, Tahoua,** and **Zinder**. The Ministry of National Education runs the *Cycle de Base 1*, while the secondary education cycles and higher education are under tutelage of the Ministry of Higher Education. The system has a predominant secular school system and the semi-Islamic system of the Franco-Arabic schools. Most schools are public, though most religious schools (Islamic and Roman Catholic) are private and there is a fast-growing private schools system in urban areas.

Cycles of general (nonvocational) formal education in Niger include:

Preschool (kindergarten and **Koranic schools**).
Cycle de Base 1: accessed at age six minimum, lasts six years, ends with a degree called Certificat de Fin d'Études du Premier Degré (CFEPD).
Cycle de Base 2: lasts four years, ends with a degree called Brevet d'Études du Premier Cycle (BEPC).
Enseignement Moyen: lasts three years (high school), ends with a degree called *Baccalauréat* (Bac).
Enseignement Supérieur: university.

Historically, Niger's educational system was extremely narrow prior to independence. In 1927 the barely established educational network counted only 700 pupils in all the country, and this figure was modestly increased to 1,629 by 1942. These were all students at the primary education level, and those who wished to or could pursue further formal education would leave the colony, generally for Dakar (Senegal) and Cotonou (Dahomey, now Benin), though some went to **France**. Even in 1958, shortly before independence, the rate of school attendance had not risen above 2.5 percent. Then it jumped dramatically to 7.7 percent under the independent government of **Hamani Diori**, which wedded the growth of national education to the prevailing concept of national development. The first legislation on national education was decreed under the Diori government in 1965–1966 and aimed at a steady development of the secular education sector in order to ensure a modicum of educational self-sufficiency. At the time, in the absence of a local university, students had to pursue higher education abroad, especially in France, at very high costs. The Franco-Arabic semireligious system was legislated into existence in 1966. The Diori government also established local **language** schools, chiefly in **Hausa** and **Zarma**, but did not allocate sufficient resources for these schools to develop beyond the experimentation stage (they are still called *écoles expérimentales*). The greater proportion of resources was allocated to the secular, French-language schools that are called *écoles traditionnelles* in Niger's officialdom.

As a result, by 1968, the total of children enrolled in primary school amounted then to 77,300 (boys, 68 percent; girls, 32 percent), a staggering increase of 556 percent over the past decade. Secondary education, lagging even more in the country, reached barely 4,100 in 1968, but this was practically a doubling of registrants from the figures of only four years previously (1964: 2,015 students). In 1968 there were also 167 students studying abroad in colleges or universities, but as early as 1973, a national university was opened in Niamey. By 1980 the rate of school attendance had gone up dramatically to 23 percent (vs 13 percent in 1976, itself nearly double the 1968 rate). In that year there were 230,000 primary school pupils (vs 139,000 in 1976), 29,607 were in secondary schools, 2,452 at the **University of Niamey**, and 3,691 in various professional schools.

One educational experiment for which Niger became widely known and cited was the use of educational television. Begun in 1965 with only 80 students, by 1967 the program eventually encompassed 800 students tied into a closed-circuit television. Though only 167 finished their courses of study, when the project was terminated in 1971 it was considered a technical success. The next phase, for some time seriously considered, would have involved an expansion of the program to include some 80 to 85 percent of all pupils in the country. The immense cost of the program prevented its implementation, but this eventually led to the establishment of the country's national television agency in the late 1970s.

School attendance rates increased dramatically in the 1970s but began decreasing in the 1980s. Government spending on education had become stagnant at 17 percent of budget allocations. A reaction in the late 1970s increased it to 22 percent, and schooling rates increased in real numbers but not in proportion of a booming education-age population. Moreover, the financial recession of the state had led to a collapse of government employment, in which over half of salaried employees found positions (in the absence of a developed private sector), and this further discouraged formal education. The response urged by the World Bank and Western donors, consisted in shifting some of the costs of education to parents while also reallocating most of the state educational budget (partly financed by aid and bilateral cooperation) to primary schooling at the expense of higher education. This policy, at first resisted by the Nigerien government, then accepted under President **Ali Saibou**, led to the conflicts between the government and university students, which culminated in the deaths on the Kennedy Bridge (February 1990) and the eventual fall of the **Second Republic** (1991). The following Nigerien governments initially committed to satisfy the students' demands, especially given the fact that they had been a numerous and vocal section of the **Conférence Nationale**, the national gathering that presided over the establishment of a democratic regime in the country. However, they eventually implemented the reforms dictated by the International Monetary Fund and urged by the World Bank, reducing dramatically the state scholarship tab and cutting funds for the university and higher learning more generally.

Programs for boosting primary education were at the same time designed and funded by donors, including the Islamic Development Bank for the Franco-Arabic sector. In 1998, a framework bill, the Loi d'Orientation du Système Educatif Nigérien (LOSEN), was adopted to give some coherence to these varied efforts and to prepare the ground for the European Union–funded Programme Décennal de Développement de l'Education (PDDE) in Niger, which started to run in 2001. The objective of these reforms and efforts is to work toward reaching the United Nations' Millennium Development Goals of full scholarization by 2015, and there was a remarkable surge in primary education enrollment rates in Niger in the period, reaching 78 percent by 2010. However, this was achieved at the expense of quality teaching (career teachers, deemed expensive, were replaced by voluntary and contract teachers with no training and even less dedication) and sustainability (dropout rates are also very high). The multiplication of schools throughout the country's territory accounts for the rise in enrollment rates, but the shift of financing to parents and local communities in a context of deep poverty seriously impairs the sustainability of this development.

In the early 2000s, university students, still on the losing end of Niger's World Bank–inspired educational policies (steep increase in registration fees and further funding cuts) wrangled with the government of Prime Minister **Hama Amadou**, which incurred considerable unpopularity from the episodes. This was compounded by a mismanagement of PDDE credit lines uncovered by an independent audit and very successfully exploited by opposition parties under the headline name of *Affaire MEBA* (from Ministère de l'Education de Base et de l'Alphabétisation, then the name of the primary education ministry). The crisis was defused by the arrest of two successive national education ministers; the Nigerien governments has since been trained in a more principled use of PDDE funds. However, the issue of a sustainable national education policy still remains daunting.

Thus, although in the period 1998–2004 records show that enrollment rates have steadily progressed, moving overall from 30 to 50 percent, the gender and geographic imbalances persist. In 1998, the rate for boys was of 37 percent against 23 percent for girls, and the gap remains at 59 percent for boys against 41 percent for girls in 2004. Similarly, in 1998, urban school attendance rate was at 51 against only 22 percent in rural areas. In 2004, there was

Table 5. Growth of Niger's Formal Educational System

	1955	1965	1975	1985	1995	2005	2009
Preschool			686	3,259	—	19,597	48,119
Primary	7899	49,921	110,437	254,000	427,000	1 million	1.5 million
Secondary	277	2,327	10,500	—	87,000	177,000	250,000
University of Niamey	—	—	—	—	5,000	8,000	9,882
Islamic University of Say	—	—	—	—	—	616	1,100

a dramatic increase in these latter quarters (48 percent), but urban centers still lead with a 54 percent schooling rate. The key issue remains, however, the quality of the teaching, which has collapsed to the point where Nigerien students may not reach normal levels of literacy and numeracy before entering higher education—which is still, under World Bank aegis, the poor relative of Niger's educational system (see Table 5). *See also* FRANCO-ARABE.

ELECTIONS. Since the first national (noncolonial) elections in Niger in 1958, parliamentary and presidential elections have been regularly organized, except for the period of the *régime d'exception* (1974–1987). It is, however, only after 1993 that Niger started to organize free and competitive elections. It must be noted in this regard that elections under the **Fourth Republic** (1996–1999) were heavily manipulated, as well as the legislative elections of October 2009. With these exceptions, Nigerien elections have all been free and fair, with results calmly accepted by all contestants. Starting in 1999, Niger also organized regional elections, in the framework of its decentralization process. The following is a list of presidential and parliamentary elections in Niger in the period 1958–2011, followed up by a list of referendum voting.

Parliamentary Elections of 14 December 1958: The elections led to the installation of a constituent assembly which established the Republic of Niger four days later, on 18 December. The main stakes were whether Niger would be a pro-French or a pan-African republic, and the elections were preceded by a referendum voting on this very issue, which saw the heavily engineered defeat of the anti-French party, the **Sawaba**. The forces in presence were the pro-French coalition of the Union pour la Communauté Franco-Africaine (UCFA), led by the **Parti Progressiste Nigérien** (PPN-RDA), and the Sawaba. Total voters turnout was officially at 36.7 percent, and UCFA won with 49 seats against 11 seats to Sawaba. The elections were competitive but not fair.

Presidential Election of 30 September 1965: Noncompetitive election to reelect President **Hamani Diori**. The acclamatory result was 100 percent of a unanimous turnout of 98.4 percent.

Parliamentary Elections of 21 October 1965: Noncompetitive elections to elect a PPN-RDA legislature. Results were 100 percent for the list, voted by 98.2 percent of registrants.

Presidential Election of 1 October 1970: President Diori was reelected unopposed at 100 percent by 98.3 percent of voters.

Parliamentary Elections of 22 October 1970: Noncompetitive ballot returning a PPN-RDA list at the **National Assembly**, with 100 percent of votes and a turnout of 97.1 percent.

Presidential and Parliamentary Elections of 12 December 1989: Noncompetitive ballot; President **Ali Saibou** elected unopposed and a **Mouvement National pour la Société de Développement** (MNSD) rubber-stamp National Assembly voted in. Saibou had garnered 99.6 percent of the votes and the 93 deputies had the same score.

Parliamentary Elections of 14 February 1993: Competitive, free, and fair elections, opposing the coalition of the **Alliance des Forces du Changement** (AFC, six parties) and an alliance of three parties led by the MNSD. The AFC parties were united to prevent MNSD to poll its way back into power. Of the 83 seats of the National Assembly, AFC won 50 against 29 for MNSD and 4 (two each) for its allies. The turnout was 32.7 percent. Below is a breakdown of results, with number of seats:

AFC Parties

Convention Démocratique et Sociale (CDS Rahama)	22
Parti Nigérien pour la Démocratie et le Socialisme (PNDS Tarayya)	13
Alliance Nigérienne pour la Démocratie et le Progrès (ANDP Zaman Lahiya)	11
Parti Progressiste Nigérien (PPN-RDA)	2
Union pour la Démocratie et le Progrès Social (UDPS Amana)	1
Parti Social-Démocrate Nigérien (PSDN Alheri)	1

MNSD and Allies

Mouvement National pour la Société de Développement (MNSD Nassara)	29
Union des Patriotes Démocrates et Progressistes (UPDP Chamoua)	2
Union Démocratique des Forces Populaires (UDFP Sawaba)	2

Presidential Election of February/March 1993: Competitive, free, fair two-round ballot. The first round, on 27 February 1993, had a voter turnout of 32.5 percent. MNSD's candidate, **Mamadou Tandja**, came first with

34.22 percent of votes, followed by **Mahaman Ousmane** (CDS) with 26.59 percent of votes, **Mahamadou Issoufou** (PNDS) with 15.92 percent of votes, and **Moumouni Adamou Djermajoye** (ANDP) with 15.24 percent of votes. Issoufou and Djermakoye sided with Ousmane at runoff (27 March, with 35.2 percent voter turnout), allowing him to beat Tandja with 54.42 percent of votes against 45.58 percent.

Parliamentary Elections of 12 January 1995: Elections called by President Ousmane after falling out with his principal ally, Issoufou, and thereby losing the control of the National Assembly, PNDS having moved into the MNSD camp. Ousmane dissolved the National Assembly, and the new legislature confirmed his defeat. MNSD and PNDS won 43 seats against 24 to CDS. Below is the breakdown:

MNSD	29
CDS	24
PNDS	12
ANDP	9
UDFP	3
UDPS	2
PSDN	2
PPN	1
UPDP	1

Presidential Election of 7–8 July 1996: The election was heavily manipulated by **Ibrahim Baré Maïnassara**, the military officer who overthrew President Ousmane on 27 January 1996. When he realized that his party was coming off last in the ballot, Baré Maïnassara reshuffled the electoral commission—against the law—and suddenly came first. The official results allege a 66.4 percent voter turnout (inconsistent with numbers in previous elections) and are shown below:

Ibrahim Baré Maïnassara	52.22 percent
Mahaman Ousmane (CDS)	19.75 percent
Mamadou Tandja (MNSD)	15.65 percent
Mahamadou Issoufou (PNDS)	7.6 percent
Moumouni Adamou Djermakoye (ANDP)	4.77 percent

Parliamentary Elections of 23 November 1996: The elections were boycotted by CDS, MNSD, and PNDS, Niger's three greatest parties, which opposed Baré Maïnassara's intention to create a subservient and an authoritarian system. The provisional party put together by Baré Maïnassara, the Union Nationale des Indépendants pour le Renouveau Démocratique (UNIRD), won 59 seats out of 83 during a heavily controlled voting, and all participant parties were allied to UNIRD. The resultant legislature was therefore lifeless. Below is a breakdown of results:

UNIRD	59
ANDP	8
UPDP	4
UDPS	3
Parti pour la Dignité du Peuple (PDP Daraja)	3
Parti du Mouvement des Travailleurs (PMT Albarka)	2
Mouvement pour la Démocratie et le Progrès (MDP Alkawali)	1
Independents	3

Presidential Election of October/November 1999: Free, fair, and competitive election. Voter turnout was 43.6 percent at first round and 39.4 percent at runoff. The election was won by MNSD candidate Mamadou Tandja against PNDS's Mahamadou Issoufou. Among the kingmakers, Tandja was supported by Ousmane (CDS) and Issoufou by Djermakoye (ANDP). Tandja came first during the first round with 32.33 percent and won with 59.89 percent of votes at runoff. Issoufou earned 22.79 percent of votes during the first round and 40.11 percent at runoff. Ousmane was third (22.51 percent), **Hamid Algabid** (Rassemblement Démocratique Populaire, RDP Jama'a) was fourth (10.83 percent), and Djermakoye fifth (7.73 percent).

Parliamentary Elections of 24 November 1999: The elections gave control of the 83-seat National Assembly to an MNSD/CDS coalition, to which RDP was also tied. ANDP sided with PNDS, but left its camp in 2002. Breakdown follows:

MNSD	38
CDS	17
PNDS	16
RDP	8
ANDP	4

Presidential Election of November–December 2004: President Tandja was reelected during the runoff with 65.53 of votes, against Issoufou (34.47 percent). At first round, Tandja had led with 40.67 percent of votes vs 24.6 percent for Issoufou. All kingmakers sided with Tandja, including CDS's Ousmane (17.43 percent), **Cheiffou Amadou** of the Rassemblement Social-Démocrate (RSD Gaskiya, 6.35 percent), and ANDP's Djermakoye (6.07 percent). Algabid came last with 4.89 percent.

Parliamentary Elections of 4 December 2004: The elections created a 10-party legislature, with seat numbers increased to 113. MNSD and its allies dominated the legislature, while PNDS broke its isolation by heading a small but very active coalition. Turnout was comparatively high at 44.7 percent (2,358,213 voted out of 5,278,598 registered voters). Breakdown follows:

MNSD and Allies	
MNSD	47
CDS	22
RSD	7
RDP	6
ANDP	5
PSDN	1
PNDS and Allies	
PNDS	17
PNDS/PPN/ Parti Nigérien pour l'Auto-gestion (PNA Al Ouma)	4
PNDS/Union des Nigériens Indépendants (UNI)/Union pour la Démocratie et la République (UDR Tabbat)	2
PNDS/PPN	2

Parliamentary Elections of 20 October 2009: Organized in the framework of the **Sixth Republic**'s constitution controversially adopted by President Tandja in August 2009. The largest parties—PNDS, CDS, and a faction of the MNSD which created the Mouvement Démocratique Nigérien pour une Fédération Africaine (MODEN/FA Lumana Africa)—boycotted the ballot. MNSD won the elections and was surrounded by allies, producing a lifeless, rubber-stamp legislature. Voter turnout was allegedly at 51.3 percent. The legislature was the shortest of Niger's history, as it was dissolved five months later, in February 2010.

MNSD	76
RSD	15
RDP	7
PMT	1
PNA	1
Rassemblement des Patriotes Nigériens (RPN Alkalami)	1
UNI	1
Independents	11

Parliamentary Elections of 31 January 2011: Free and competitive elections, though with some fairness issues. It established the first legislature of the **Seventh Republic**, dominated by PNDS and its allies, including ANDP and a breakaway of the MNSD, MODEN. Turnout was high at 49.2 percent (3,317,935 of 6.740.493 registered voters went to the ballot). Breakdown follows:

PNDS	34
MNSD	25

MODEN	23
ANDP	8
RDP	7
UDR	6
CDS	3
UNI	1
Invalidated (by-election held afterward)	6 (Agadez)

Presidential Election of January–March 2011: The first round held on 31 January (voter turnout of 51.6 percent) ranked Mahamadou Issoufou (PNDS) first with 36.16 percent of votes, followed by **Seyni Oumarou** (MNSD) with 23.23 percent of votes, **Hama Amadou** (MODEN) with 19.82 percent of votes, and Mahaman Ousmane (8.33 percent of votes). Anecdotally, the first female candidate in a Nigerien presidential election, **Mariama Gamatié Bayard** (independent) came last with 0.38 percent of votes. New kingmaker Amadou sided with Issoufou at runoff, and the latter beat Oumarou with 58.04 percent of votes against 41.96 percent. The runoff was held on 12 March 2011 and registered a voter turnout of 49 percent. *See also* CONSTITUTIONAL REFERENDUMS.

ENTREPRISE NIGÉRIENNE DE TEXTILES (ENITEX). Joint company founded in 1968 as the Société Nigérienne des Textiles (NITEX) with the participation of the Agache Willot group (70 percent) and the Niger government (15 percent). In 1978, when faced by major financial problems, the Nigerien government assumed 49 percent of the shares of NITEX, and the company was renamed SONITEXTIL. Capitalized at 725 million **CFA francs** (later increased to 1 billion) and employing 830 workers (up from the original complement of 609), NITEX was Niger's third-largest company. Production in 1975 was 6 million meters of textiles, and by that date plant expansion had raised the number of workers to 950. The plant was involved in all aspects of textile and fiber production and printing using local **cotton** and had an annual capacity of 7.5 million meters of yarn and printed cloth. The highly automated factory covers 15,000 square meters in the industrial zone of **Niamey** and used to satisfy 80 percent of Niger's textile needs.

In 1996, Niger was pressured by the International Monetary Fund (IMF) to sell the company, which was suffering from high productions costs and had been somewhat scuttled by the rising competition of cheap imports from Asian countries. Two years later, SONITEXTIL was bought by China's World Best with 80 percent of capital, it was renamed ENITEX, and its plant was renovated. Initial relations between the new Chinese management and Nigerien workers were tempestuous, with the latter complaining about the harshness of Chinese labor practices and engaging in strikes. When the situation later calmed down, it appeared that ENITEX was also suffering from the Asian competition that plagued SONITEXTIL, leading the government to hike antidumping duties in 2005. The measures had no immediate impact, and the following year, the company laid off two thirds of its 715 workers. ENITEX remains somewhat in difficulty but seems to have carved out a niche for itself in Niger's market. *See also* ECONOMIC LIBERALIZATION; PARASTATAL SECTOR.

ETHNIC GROUPS. Niger has eight main ethnic groups, themselves subdivided into groups claiming separate or mixed origins. The main groups are, in order of demographic size: the **Hausa**, the **Zarma-Songhay**, the **Tuareg**, the **Fulani**, the **Kanuri**, the **Toubous**, the **Gourmantchés**, and the **Arabs**. Most Hausa live east of **Dogondoutchi**, and most Zarma-Songhay west of that town. The Tuareg are found in the desert north and also in small groups in the northern fringes of the eastern and western regions. There are Fulani in most parts of the country, either settled or nomadic. When settled, the Fulani tend to use the **language** of the main neighboring ethnic group and to gradually lose their own language. The Kanuri reside in the far eastern **Lake Chad** area, together with a number of tiny ethnicities such as the **Boudouma**, usually lumped together with them. The Toubou are a smallish population occupying the northeastern desert, along the border with Chad, while the Gourmantchés live in the southwestern savanna, at the border with Burkina Faso. Arab communities are found especially in the northern parts of the region of **Zinder** and the southern parts of the region of **Agadez**.

These eight broader groups denote especially common language and shared customs, even when differences of origins among the subgroups are stressed. However, in the transition areas between Hausaland and Zarmaland occurs the rather peculiar phenomenon of subgroups claiming common origin but using the Hausa language in Hausaland and the **Zarma** language in Zarmaland: the **Arawa/Maouri** around Dogondoutchi, the Tyengawa/**Tyenga** around **Gaya**, and the **Kurfeyawa/Soudiés** around **Filingué**. From the Nigerien point of view, these subgroups therefore belong each to two different ethnic groups.

Ethnicity has some relevance in Nigerien politics but only when combined with the geopolitical regions of the country—i.e., the east, the west, and the north. These geographic terms are proxies for the Hausa, the Zarma-Songhay, and the Tuareg respectively, but include also the various minority ethnic groups who dwell in each of the regions and are consequently pulled to the dominant regional ethnicity—the Zarma-speaking Fulani of **Say**, for instance, or the Hausa-speaking Fulani of **Dakoro**. During the colonial period and Niger's first three decades of independence, the geopolitics of east, west, and north was the source of an important underlying political fissure, with notably the west being deemed by the east as far too powerful for its smaller population and paltrier contribution to national wealth. However, this never led to physical confrontations as happened in some other African countries.

After **democratization**, the establishment of **political parties** modified this early context by creating subregional fiefs for the major leaders: thus, for instance, **Mahaman Ousmane** of the **Convention Démocratique et Sociale** (CDS Rahama) in Zinder, **Moumouni Adamou Djermakoye** of the **Alliance Nationale pour la Démocratie et le Développement** (ANDP Zaman Lahiya) in **Dosso**, and **Mahamadou Issoufou** of the **Parti Nigérien pour la Démocratie et le Socialisme** (PNDS Tarayya) in **Tahoua**. In the case of the **Mouvement National pour la Société de Développement** (MNSD Nassara), the fiefs cut through ethnic and regional lines, as the party has a stronghold in both east (in Zinder and **Maradi**) and west (in **Tillabéri**). This feature greatly explains its electoral successes and has inspired the PNDS in particular to develop a strategy of expansion beyond its leader's regional base. This was successful, as the party's gradual progress at the **elections** of 2004 and 2011 demonstrated. The MNSD's and the PNDS's successes also means that while it is easier for party leaders to rely on ethnic or regional voting, an ideological message that transcends these categories is key to national political victory in Niger. *See also* KADO; KANEMBU; KURTEY; SABIRI; SOSSEBAKI; WOGO.

F

FIFTH REPUBLIC. The **constitution** of the Fifth Republic was adopted in August 1999, returning Niger to a semipresidential system with a few constitutional fixes, and the locking of the number of presidential terms to two. The Fifth Republic was the most stable of the Nigerien regimes, one which led many commentators to believe that the Nigerien political class had learned to work peacefully with liberal democratic institutions. The Fifth Republic was notably marked by the holding of the **elections** of 2004, which threatened the position of the incumbent **Mouvement National pour la Société de Développement** (MNSD Nassara) and ended with the defeated **Parti Nigérien pour la Démocratie et le Socialisme** (PNDS Tarayya) gracefully accepting the results.

However, in 2009, the third election year of the regime, President **Mamadou Tandja**, who had been in office since 1999, sought to change the constitution of the Fifth Republic in order to stay in power and, faced with the resistance of the political class, he did away with the regime altogether, replacing it in August 2009 with a **Sixth Republic** after a heavily controlled referendum voting. Tandja's starkly authoritarian Sixth Republic lasted for about seven months, before being terminated by the military through a **coup d'état on 18 February 2010**. In November 2010, Niger adopted by referendum a new semipresidential constitution not very different from that of the Fifth Republic, and introduced a **Seventh Republic**.

The Fifth Republic chiefly presided over the liberalization of Niger's **economy**, accelerating the **privatization** process and creating the institutional and fiscal framework congenial to the policy, almost exclusively under instructions from the International Monetary Fund. One result of this orientation was the budget bill of January 2005 which extended value added taxes (VATs) to foodstuff and raised them for water and electricity consumption, prompting the development of a major urban-based social movement in March–April 2005. The VATs were finally repealed for the most part, and the government raised instead corporate taxes, a breach of the liberalization policy. The general orientation of the regime was not reversed, however, and the Fifth Republic has considerably expanded Niger's private sector. Its achievements in rural development, **education**, and **health** are much grimmer. *See also* TAZARTCHÉ.

FILINGUÉ. Important and historic **Hausa** town, 187 km northeast of **Niamey** and 256 km southwest of **Tahoua**, with a population of nearly 12,000, up from 7,051 in 1970. Also a *départment* within the region of **Tillabéri**, with a population of 250,000. On the right side of the **Dallol Bosso**, at the foot of the fault, Filingué is the site of a major convergence of several **ethnic groups**. A very picturesque town (though with few tourist amenities), its huge Sunday market brings into town large camel and **cattle** herds and **Tuareg**, Hausa, **Fulani**, and **Zarma-Songhay** traders. The first French-**language** school in Niger was opened here in 1902.

FIRST REPUBLIC. The regime of the First Republic was proclaimed on 18 December 1958 by a constituent assembly succeeding the **Territorial Assembly** that represented Niger in the framework of the French Community. But it was only on 1 August 1960 that the republic's sovereignty was legally instituted in agreement with **France**. The independence proclamation was read out by **Hamani Diori** two days later, on 3 August 1960, marking that day as the formal date of Niger's independence. The constitution of the First Republic was adopted on 8 November 1960 by the **National Assembly**, which elected the president of Cabinet Council, Diori, president of the republic the next day.

The new **constitution** was presidentialist and concentrated executive powers in the hands of the president, who headed the government and could serve as a minister (as happened in the cases of strategic ministries led by Diori: foreign affairs and defense). It led to the dominance of a single-party system known as "parti-État" in Nigerien parlance, in which the structures of the ruling party, the **Parti Progressiste Nigérien** (PPN-RDA) effectively trumped state administrative organization over which was superimposed its own organization. Under the First Republic regime, Niger was thus ruled by the leadership of the PPN, which included President Diori and the president of the National Assembly, **Boubou Hama**.

The First Republic was an ideologically moderate political system with an authoritarian mode of operation. While it severely repressed the insurgent **Sawaba** movement that offered a radical alternative to its rule, it carefully toed the line between the competing interests of the day, associating power with both traditional society and modern educated groups, and attempting to reconcile French and Nigerien interests in the formal **economy** and the **mining** sector—in effect often subordinating the latter to the former. Its records include a rapid development of the formal **education** system, a concerted

Nigerienization of national administration still largely performed by French and natives of neighboring former French colonies in the first years of independence, the building of Niger's main national highway known as the **Route de l'Unité**, and the establishment of **parastatals** and factories aimed at transforming **agricultural** produce into processed food and domestic commodities.

The First Republic was, however, destabilized by grave crises in the early 1970s: a **drought**-related famine in most of the countryside in 1971–1973 compounded the next year by the effects of the Arab **oil** embargo on urban populations and local trade. Furthermore, President Diori antagonized the French government by demanding a renegotiation of **uranium** contracts to increase state revenue, while local critics denounced his failure to suppress elite corruption. On 15 April 1974, the **armed forces** carried out a coup d'état which ended the First Republic.

Many commentators relate the First Republic to the dominance of the ethnoregional group of both Diori and Hama, the **Zarma-Songhay**, though PPN policies do not seem to bear this out and the notion is unrelated to its fall. *See also* COLONIE DU NIGER; ELECTIONS.

FLAG. Niger's flag was adopted, together with the country's motto "Fraternité, Travail, Progrès" (Brotherhood, Labor, Progress), on 23 November 1959. The flag has three horizontal strips of equal width, with the top one being orange, the middle one white, and the bottom one green. The white strip carries an orange circle in its middle. The flag represents Niger's geography, with the orange symbolizing the Saharan and Sahelian regions and the green the **Niger River** valley and the Sudanic far south. The white strip represents the clear skies of the Sahel which would incite Nigeriens to strive for purity and innocence, while the orange circle is the radiant and fiery sun which, as an image of the state of Niger, shines over the citizens.

FONDS D'AIDE ET DE COOPÉRATION (FAC). French financial and technical-assistance development fund, the successor, in 1959, of the **Fonds d'Investissement pour le Développement Economique et Social des Territoires d'Outre-Mer (FIDES)**. Similarly, FAC was lodged in the Ministry of Cooperation which, for all practical purposes, had succeeded the Ministry of the Colonies. The Ministry of Cooperation worked only with former sub-Saharan colonies of **France** until 1995, when its geographic purview was extended to other developing countries. The idea behind FAC was to assist the newly independent countries, which, by 1960 (independence year for the vast majority of France's colonies), still had fledgling **economies** and administrations. FAC therefore granted subsidies for projects and loans at generous interest rates and long-term repayment periods. During the period 1980–1987, Niger received from FAC annually between 20 and 60 million French francs, for a grand total of 269,296,000 French francs. In later period, amounts tended to sink to below 10 million French francs annually. This included grants and scholarships for **students**, technical assistance, and investment aid which was a form of tied aid, functioning also as a market subsidy to French industries. In 1999, FAC was transformed into a Fonds de Solidarité Prioritaire. *See also* AGENCE FRANÇAISE DE DÉVELOPPEMENT.

FONDS D'INVESTISSEMENT POUR LE DÉVELOPPEMENT ECONOMIQUE ET SOCIAL DES TERRITOIRES D'OUTRE-MER (FIDES). Established on 30 April 1946 and the precursor of the postcolonial **Fonds d'Aide et de Coopération**, FIDES was the development fund that dispensed development capital to the French colonial territories following their transformation into *territoires d'outre-mer* with limited autonomy. FIDES was an expression of the rise of the concept of "development" in the world after World War II.

In Niger, FIDES lines of credit were chiefly useful in building urban public infrastructures (65 percent of funds), with some monies going to the productive sector (19 percent) and social equipment (16 percent). FIDES's development vision—as later that of FAC—was essentially technical and gradualist, and although disbursed funds were substantial in Niger's context, they were never close to amounts required to transform the colony's **economy**.

FORCES ARMÉES NIGÉRIENNES (FAN). The Nigerien Armed Forces originate from the three companies of the French Colonial Forces recruited in Niger, which were united with national police and gendarmerie forces by a decree in July 1960 to form an organization that has played important roles in Nigerien politics on many levels. At first there were only 10 African (Nigerien) officers, all of low rank, and though President **Hamani Diori** legislated the end of the employment of expatriate military officers in 1965, some continued to serve until the **coup d'état of 1974**. At that point the practice was ended and also the 1,000 French troops of **France**'s Quatrième Régiment Interarmes d'Outre-Mer based in **Niamey** were evacuated.

In purely military roles, the FAN have been fighting almost continuously since the early 1980s **Tuareg** and, less often, **Toubou** insurgents in the desert northern and northeastern regions of Niger, and have served in several peacekeeping missions under the banner of the Economic Community of West African States Monitoring Group (Liberia, Guinea Bissau), the African Union (Burundi, Comoros), and the United Nations (Saudi Arabia in the first Gulf War, Rwanda, Côte d'Ivoire, Democratic Republic of Congo).

But the army also developed a tradition of intervening in state politics through coups d'état, four of which have been successful, and all of which appeared to solve problems which threatened to rend the state. The first in this series toppled the **First Republic** in April 1974, leading to the extended tenure of the **Conseil Militaire Suprême** headed by General **Seyni Kountché**, until his death in 1987. Although the most controversial of all Nigerien military coups—it has been criticized for serving French interests in the exploitation of Nigerien **uranium**, which were jeopardized by the maneuvers of the ousted president, Hamani Diori, and upended the civilian movement toward the opening of Niger's political system—it led to a government which Nigeriens now generally praise, in retrospect, for its integrity and purposefulness. In 1991, Niger returned to full civilian government and adopted liberal democratic institutions, but this did not prevent the army to conduct another **coup d'état in January 1996** under the leadership of Chief of Defense Staff Colonel **Ibrahim Baré Maïnassara**, ending an institutional gridlock caused by the refusal of President **Mahaman Ousmane** and Prime Minister **Hama Amadou** to collaborate in the framework of a cohabitation. While the coup d'état was welcomed as a way out of political paralysis, Maïnassara's intention to remain in power by changing the **constitution**—moving from the Third to the **Fourth Republic**—and heavy-handedly controlling voting rendered him widely unpopular. His rule was beset by incessant **union** strikes and the confrontational attitude of the main **political parties**, leading to another political crisis and another **coup d'état in April 1999**, in which Maïnassara was shot dead. This time, the army organized a nine-month transition to a **Fifth Republic** and quickly left the stage. Under the new constitution, Niger's institutions of liberal democracy appeared to mature and Niger's constitution was in particular viewed as a model in the circle of the French-speaking countries of West Africa. However, at the end of his last, nonrenewable term, **Mamadou Tandja**, who had presided over the Fifth Republic since its foundation, and himself a retired military officer, decided to dissolve it in order to remain in power, initiating a new political crisis which was predictably ended by another **coup d'état on 18 February 2010**. The 2010 coup d'état, conducted by a junior officer, Squadron Head **Djibo Salou**, was even more popular than the two previous ones, triggering spontaneous mass demonstrations of support that never before followed such an event, and the army organized a 12-month transition toward a **Seventh Republic** (the deposed president Tandja having given the name "**Sixth Republic**" to his six-month regime). Despite their repeated coups d'état, or perhaps because of them, the FAN insists on its attachment to *républicain* (Jacobin and constitutional) norms and values.

In 1974, when the army took power under Seyni Kountché, it numbered some 2,500 troops, 500 of whom were National Police. Today, there are 600 policemen in the city of Niamey alone, and the army is currently made up of around 9,000 troops, which include draftees, around 4,000 members of the Garde Nationale (FNIS, formerly the Garde Républicaine), and career soldiers. Units include logistics, motorized infantry, airborne infantry, artillery units, and armored companies. Of the 10 pure motorized infantry battalions, three are Saharan. Furthermore, there are mixed or interarms battalions in Niamey, **Zinder**, **Tahoua**, and Madaouela. Each battalion comprises a logistics and engineering company, an infantry company (airborne and land), an armored squadron, and an artillery company. Nigerien officers are trained locally at a national officers' training school in **Tondibia**, near Niamey, on the road to **Tillabéri**. There is also a paramedical personnel training school in Niamey.

In December 2003, the Groupement Aérien National became the Forces Aériennes du Niger, with operation and technical units and a company of infantry. It is a smallish outfit, with around 300 people, 25 of which are pilot officers. Some units of the gendarmerie are also trained in military fashion, although the gendarmerie's main role is law enforcement outside urban **communes** (while the National Police force patrols the towns).

Niger allocates only 1.6 percent of government expenditures to the defense budget. While France has been in the past the dominant partner in terms of providing military assistance to Niger (in the form of military advisors), China has come to the fore in recent times, especially in terms of equipments. The United States assisted the Nigerien military in the 2000s, in the framework of the Department of State Pan-**Sahel** Intiative to monitor and oppose armed Islamist groups in the Sahelian band of West Africa. *See also RÉGIME D'EXCEPTION*; THIRD REPUBLIC.

FOREIGN AID. Niger is heavily dependent on foreign aid, a volatile and cumbersome source of income which, over the five decades of the country's independence, has had little effect on its continuous sinking into poverty. As for most other African countries, there have been three periods of foreign aid provision in Niger: the developmental period (1960–1985), the transition period (1985–1996), and the poverty reduction period (1996 to date). In none of these periods did foreign aid have a noticeable improving effect on Nigerien lives, but in each, it has had a significant impact on the determination of Niger's economic policy, with increasing force in more recent years.

The Developmental Period. In the 1960s, the dominant economic policy for then-called underdeveloped countries was the implementation of modernization plans under the aegis of the state, and aid was therefore channeled into the public sector, mostly in the framework of bilateral agreements between governments. In this period, aid was greatly determined by recipient states, which were understood to be building national infrastructures and capacities. It therefore took the form of scholarships to train national experts, as well as the building of strategic infrastructures such as, in Niger, the **Route de l'Unité**, a segment of which was funded by Canada; the **Niamey** Kennedy Bridge, funded by the United States; and a number of industrial installations to process **agricultural** produce throughout the country funded through foreign investments, chiefly French and from the European Economic Community (EEC). The EEC also developed the ambition to help the newly independent African nation-states to take off—in particular, the former colonies of **France** and Belgium—at a time when Great Britain was not part of the EEC. This was organized by the European Development Fund (EDF), created in 1957 and renewed every five years. The EDF is an instrument that helps spur investments in countries like Niger which are members of the African, Caribbean, and Pacific (ACP) group that signed a series of economic partnership conventions with the EEC. The first of these in 1963 was the conventions of Yaoundé (1963 and 1969), followed by those of Lomé (1975, 1984, 1989, 1995) and of Cotonou (2000). These economic partnership conventions have, in theory, a central aid and development orientation. The Yaoundé and early Lomé conventions (1963–1984) negotiated trade arrangements normally favorable to the ACP countries by giving them privileged access to the European market for the selling of tropical crops. In particular, the conventions granted public aid to assist underdeveloped countries in setting up schemes that would enhance the cultivation and commercialization of rent crops. Such aid targeted in Niger the state-run cooperative system of the **Union Nigérienne de Crédit et de Coopérative** (UNCC) which organized the exploitation of **groundnut**, and the **Société Nigérienne de Commercialisation de l'Arachide** (SONARA) which organized its marketing. This form of aid was strengthened with the Convention of Yaoundé II, when development projects became its key mode of operation. Niger benefited when the decline of groundnut production was temporarily stemmed in the late 1970s with Project Revival of Groundnut Cultivation (1972–1987).

The conventions signed in the 1970s (Lomé I, 1975–1980, and Lomé II, 1980–1985) were in particular aimed at compensating the drop in the price of the raw materials (crops and minerals) which constituted the principal source of independent revenue of countries such as Niger. Groundnut indeed lost its market value by the end of the 1970s, and **uranium**, Niger's prime mineral, knew only a very short-lived boom in the late 1970s before losing much of its worth in the 1980s. The two Lomé conventions put in place funding systems—the Income Stabilization Fund for Agricultural Produce, or STABEX, and the Income Stabilization Fund for Mineral Production, or SYSMIN—that sought to cushion states from these losses, although by the mid-1980s, the conventional wisdom had shifted and negative perceptions on the shortcomings of states (corruption, administrative inefficiencies, and political interference) eventually put paid to bilateral agreements and public sector aid.

The results of aid in this period are mixed. Some improvements in **health** and **education** are clearly attributable to foreign cooperation in Niger, especially from **France**. However, aid had little to show in terms of agricultural and infrastructural development, certainly the two most important sectors in an **economy** such as that of Niger. The failure was ascribed to Niger's governments and state that donors, in subsequent periods, sought to control, curtail, and discipline.

The Transition Period. In the 1980s, Niger's main bilateral cooperation partnership—that established with France—declined, as the World Bank and the International Monetary Fund (IMF) were gaining ground in the promotion of the new vision of aid tied to the expansion of the private sector and the maintenance of macroeconomic stability on the basis of sound and austere financial management. In this new vision, investment in infrastructures, industrial policy, and agricultural development became less important than rigorous ethics and frugal management. The main actions to be undertaken under the aegis of the IMF were not positive but rather negative: reducing the state's wage bill, reducing deficits, selling or closing down unproductive units owned by the state, and stemming corruption. In this way, factors of production would become efficient, and the economy would grow. Indeed, in this new vision, development was seen as a natural outcome of economic growth and would be freely organized by economic agents rather than by state intervention and coordination. These new imperatives were turned into a variety of conditionalities tied to the bailing out of Niger's finances, but they came with considerable political costs for Nigerien leaderships. This was especially true for the reduction of the state's wage bill and, to an extent, the selling and closing down of **parastatals**, which often involved laying off hundreds of salaried personnel. The military regime appeared to have sufficient control over society to start implementing a Structural Adjustment Program in 1986 as well as an early retirement plan the following year. In this new configuration, the mission of the World Bank seemed more positive, as the bank started to coordinate a number of aid projects—in particular, in education and health—funded by Western state donors. However, the World Bank's aid also came with reform conditionalities, notably in the domain of public education, and one of these reforms—Project Education III, which shifted resources from higher education to primary and secondary education—was the trigger that started the chains of events concluded by the fall of the **Second Republic** in 1990–1991.

After Niger democratized in 1991, a new form of aid emerged, one which targeted society directly and bypassed the state and the public sector. It was based on the idea that democratic rights and governance would also lead to economic change through the rapid institution of the Western-style rule of law, stable property rights, and modern modes of behavior in society. This extremely ambitious vision led international programs, Western state initiatives, and nongovernmental organizations (NGOs) to flood the country with funds destined to induce the emergence of a vibrant public sphere and **civil society**. As a result, countless local NGOs sprouted and specialized in democracy promotion, human rights defense, and **women**'s emancipation. The majority of these local NGOs later appeared to be enterprising outfits more interested in grabbing foreign money than in achieving their stated goals, even though others failed chiefly for lack of the required skills and vision. A few among the early local NGOs, such as the **Association Nigérienne de Défense des Droits de l'Homme**, survived to become competent fixtures of Nigerien civil society in the late 1990s and 2000s and are supported essentially by foreign money. Aid targeting the state was also shaped by democracy promotion, and in particular one of the main successes of French cooperation in this period was the training of several cohorts of Nigerien judges in a program that had been launched in the early 1980s. By 1988, the French-trained judges had secured from the state an organization of their legal status, and in May 1991, they founded a union, the Syndicat Autonome des Magistrats du Niger (SAMAN) which was very active in the drafting of Niger's democratic texts in 1992 (codes and constitution).

Economic aid, on the other hand, declined sharply, chiefly because it had become the purview of the World Bank and the IMF, whose conditionalities Nigerien rulers in the early 1990s were extremely reluctant to accept. Thus, in 1992, the bankrupt Nigerien state replenished its coffers only through the (temporary) recognition of Taiwan as the only Republic of China, receiving in return a loan of $50 million from the Taiwanese (Niger later shamelessly returned to the fold of the People's Republic of China, in 1996). During the **Third Republic**, Niger's resistance to reform and conditionalities led to very limited foreign aid and a deterioration of budgetary conditions famously marked by months of pay backlogs for all state sectors (including the army) and state grants (including scholarships). Successive Nigerien governments attempted difficult political maneuvering to start negotiations with the international financial institutions without antagonized the unions, and secured debt relief in March 1994 from the Club of Paris lenders group; the servicing of the debt represented 47 percent of the value of all Nigerien exports. Much of the benefit that came from this was lost, however, when the **CFA franc** was devalued the same year, propelling Niger's economy into heights of hyperinflation (around 44 percent).

In 1998, the authoritarian government of **Ibrahim Baré Maïnassara** finally signed agreements with the IMF and the World Bank which made Western economic aid possible, despite the suspensions caused by the **coup d'état of January 1996**, which notably led to United States Agency for International Development (USAID) leaving the country. Much of the aid came from France, which supported the new regime in view of its own interests (propping up stability in Niger), and from Japan, a key contributor of the IMF and of the World Bank with less commitment to the expansion of liberal democracy than the United States or Germany, both of which pointedly shunned the regime. Incidentally, the motive of political instability became at that point an important one in Western aid processes in Niger. Thus, substantial loans and subsidies from the European Union (EU) were withheld after the **coup of 1999**, President **Mamadou Tandja**'s illegalities in 2009, and the **coup of 2010**. In 2008, foreign aid represented 8.6 percent of the country's GDP but fell to 4.5 percent under Tandja's **Tazartché**, before rebounding to 7.2 percent in 2010.

The Poverty Reduction Period. After the restoration of democratic governance (1999), Western aid in Niger was organized in relation to the United Nations Millennium Development Goals (MDG), signed in New York in September 2000. The MDG aim at (1) reducing poverty and hunger, (2) ensuring primary education for all, (3) promoting gender equality, (4) reducing child mortality, (5) improving maternal health, (6) fighting HIV/AIDS and malaria, (7) protecting the environment, and (8) establishing a global partnership for development. Thirteen other targets were added in 2005 to this list, and countries are supposed to reach specific measures of development in relation to 60 indicators by 2015, with 1990 as starting year. All Western aid to Niger in the 2000s was determined by this new framework and was buttressed by budgetary support received from the IMF through yearly Poverty Reduction and Growth Facilities. To absorb aid and satisfy IMF criteria, Niger adopted as its key economic policy document a Poverty Reduction and Development Strategy (PRDS) paper which highlights the promotion of the private sector and the maintenance of macroeconomic stability, chiefly through frugal government spending. In the period since the new policy came into force, poverty has been slightly reduced in the country, with 59.5 percent of the population living below the poverty line in 2008, as opposed to 63.6 percent in 2002, and much of this may be attributed to aid. However, given the high demographic growth, there were in fact more people living under the poverty line in 2008 (8 million) than in 2005 (7.8 million). It is projected that between 55 and 60 percent of Nigeriens will still be living under poverty line in 2015, much more than the goal of 40 percent targeted by the MDGs. In general, the MDGs will not be reached by Niger by 2015, a failure that draws attention now also to some of aid's inefficiencies.

The politics of conditionalities and liberalization in the 1990s had brewed an aid culture which sidelined the state, urging it to reform its services in order to adjust to the requisites of a great variety of donors and often censuring it for its failure to do so. This led to the logics of policy transfer, where aid organizations devise strategies independently from local actors, and implement them in the country by striving to prompt "ownership" by the civil society and politicians. Both of these two groups tend, in their differing ways, to view aid principally as a source of rent which can be appropriated for very different purposes, leading at times to corruption scandals, the most famous of which was the so-called *Affaire MEBA* of 2006. In 2002, the European Union granted budgetary aid to the Ministry of Basic Education (MEBA) to fund the Programme Décennale de Développement de l'Education (PDDE), and over 1 billion CFA francs were misallocated over several years, chiefly through fraudulent contracting and lack of congruence between the ministry's accounting services and the funding criteria of the EU. The political opposition, the media, and civic associations uncovered the issue and made of it a major public scandal, prompting donors to demand judicial redress and a refund of the dissipated funds in 2006. The state restored 1.3 billion CFA francs in the PDDE funds. However, the permanent issue in this instance is not government malfeasance but the mismatch between funding strategies and the capacities of the state, at times described from donors' side as an inability of Niger to "absorb" aid. The disparity is all the more significant because different donors have different agendas and timings, and they all still favor funding through projects over more coordinated and pluralist programs.

In recent times, non-Western donors have emerged on the Nigerien development stage, working outside the MDGs framework and with no programmatic conditionalities imposed on the state or society. Thus, in the late 1990s, the Islamic Development Bank (IDB) came to the fore, providing loans and subsidies in 1998 to considerably boost the **Franco-Arabe** educational sector some four years before the EU started the PDDE financing. The IDB and the African Development Bank also focus on infrastructure building, and it is at Jeddah (Saudi Arabia) that the government of Niger signed in December 2007 the financial convention in the amount of 110 billion CFA francs that funds the building of the **Kandadji Dam**, a structure that could considerably impact the country's economy by stepping up electrification. Niger is also the French-speaking West African country most favored by China, which has become a prime source of foreign direct investments as well as of infrastructural development aid. By 2010, the country had benefited from $184 million in Chinese foreign direct investments—beating Benin (54 million) and Côte d'Ivoire (37 million). China also built a second bridge in Niamey in 2009 as well as an **oil** refinery in **Zinder**. But most of these Chinese actions are economically motivated rather than aid related.

It must be noted that while Niger is arguably the poorest country in West Africa, it is also the one which receives the least aid in the subregion—and perhaps in Africa as a whole—with only $4 per capita in 2010, twice or three times lower than in other West African countries. This may be explained by the fact that aid is motivated by many more things than acuteness of need or vulnerability, and is in particular greatly driven by the geopolitical calculations of rich countries, for which Niger has no strategic importance in that regard. Thus, it is especially France which maintains permanent aid relationships with the country, owing not only to postcolonial ties, but also to the importance of Niger's uranium to French industry. *See also* ECONOMIC LIBERALIZATION; FOREIGN POLICY; STUDENTS.

FOREIGN POLICY. Niger does not have an expansive and ambitious diplomacy. Through much of its existence, the state of Niger has chiefly endeavored to defend narrowly defined national interests, shaped by the maintenance of territorial integrity, reliable access to ports, and the construction of the country, an economic process heavily dependent on **foreign aid** and cooperation. Aside from short bursts of diplomatic activism, especially under the **First Republic** (1960–1974) and the *régime d'exception* (1974–1987), Niger's foreign relations have therefore been mostly consequent to decisions taken by more vigorous and stronger external powers, the most remarkable of which have been **France**, **Nigeria**, Algeria, **Libya**, and more recently China. Niger was or is also a member of a number of international organizations, some of which have, at times, played a defining role in its foreign relations: the **Conseil de l'Entente**, the **Union Economique et Monétaire Ouest Africaine** (UEMOA), and the **Economic Community of West African States** (ECOWAS). The evolution of Niger's foreign relations can however be parsed in three moments: the postindependence moment, dominated by Cold War dynamics as they played out in the era of African nationalism; the *régime d'exception*; and the contemporary period.

Postindependence. The First Republic's international positions were initially determined by the internal conditions through which it came into being. It was established by the camp led by the **Parti Progressiste Nigérien** (PPN-RDA), which sided with France in the **elections** and referendum of 1957–1958 about the nature of political independence—whether it meant complete rupture with the colonial overlord or some form of continuity. Those conditions also prevailed in the early Francophone West African landscape, dominated by radical, anti-French leaderships in Conakry (Guinea), Dakar (Senegal), and Bamako (Mali), opposing the accommodating, pro-French Côte d'Ivoire. The victory of PPN over the radical **Sawaba** party in **Niamey** meant that Niger followed the lead of Côte d'Ivoire, with which it formed—together with Dahomey (Benin), Haute-Volta (Burkina Faso), and Togo—the Conseil de l'Entente. Both radicals and accommodating camps adhered however to the then-inescapable force of African nationalism which led to the foundation of the Organization of African Unity (OAU) in 1963. In fact, however, the continent of Africa itself was divided in radical, anti-imperialist forces (the Group of Casablanca, based in Morocco, in which the exiled Sawaba insurrectionary party represented Niger) and accommodating pro-Western ones (the Group of Monrovia, established in Liberia, and supported by the majority of French-speaking countries which had already promoted its orientations in an earlier, purely Francophone "Group of Brazzaville").

The radical camp basically lost out at the foundation of OAU, as its ideals of rapid continental integration were sidelined by the vision of the Group of Monrovia, which privileged above all the sanctity of the boundaries inherited from colonialism. That vision led Niger to define its foreign policy first and foremost on the defense of its borders, leading to at least two protracted—though rather bloodless—border conflicts with Dahomey (the **Benin–Niger border dispute**) and Libya (the **Mussolini-Laval boundary agreement**). Niger's membership in the Conseil de l'Entente and the general tenor of its pro-French foreign policy also defined its position with regards to its two biggest neighbors, Algeria to the north and Nigeria to the south. Regarding Algeria, Niger was bribed by France into supporting the creation of the Organisation Commune des Régions Sahariennes (OCRS), a French attempt at excluding the Sahara desert—rich with **oil** and gas and offering the space needed for France's early nuclear bomb tests—from independence processes. Thus, in 1962, out of a total French aid of 1.9 billion French francs, Niger received 750 million in the framework of cooperation (scholarships, subsidies, investments, and loans), 400 million in the form of budgetary support, and 750 million as a member of OCRS. This incurred considerable hostility from Algeria, which hosted Sawaba exiles and sought to prompt **Tuareg** irredentism in Niger's north. To counter possible destabilization from the northern regions, President **Hamani Diori** created a Tuareg-cajoling Ministry of Saharan Affairs, partly supported by OCRS funds.

With respect to Nigeria, Diori's policy was determined by fears that eastern Niger, where the majority of the country's population (**Hausa**) resided, would become an economic appendage of that country, with the result of neutering Nigerien sovereignty. In response, Diori developed ties with Dahomey—a smaller French-speaking country with no significant economic or ethnic impact on Niger—through the Organisation Commune Dahomey-Niger, despite the border tensions with Cotonou. This effectively diverted Niger's import-export trade away from Nigeria at enormous cost, although "informal" trade remained in place. Diori nevertheless declined to assist French efforts at breaking up the Nigerian federation during the Biafran War (1967–1970). He also endeavored to practice a more activist diplomacy to improve Niger's very marginal situation on the world stage, securing help from the United States (which built Niamey's sole bridge until 2011, the Kennedy Bridge), Canada (which helped complete the **Route de l'Unité**), and other Western countries. He also promoted the creation of a French equivalent to the Commonwealth organization, with the organization of the Francophonie (the **Organisation Internationale de la Francophonie**) which saw the light of day in Niamey in March 1970.

In the early 1970s, the **Sahel drought** and **oil** shocks put the First Republic's foreign policy in disarray, as its traditional support, France, proved unable to help Niger cope with the crisis. Diori sought help in all corners of the world, including especially the **Arab** world and Libya, and gradually antagonized France. A beleaguered Diori tried to force the latter to revise **uranium** contracts so as to increase Nigerien revenue from the ore, but was toppled in the **coup of April 1974**, a few days before a high-level meeting on the issue, and with no intervention from the French troops stationed in Niamey to protect the regime.

Régime d'exception. The military regime that succeeded the First Republic maintained its newly found orientation toward the Arab world—based on Niger's majority religion, **Islam**—but soon became hostile to Libya, whose erratic leader, Colonel Muammar Kadhafi, wanted to enlist Niger as a pawn in his pan-Islamic vision of the world. Niger initially accepted Libya's largesse (including the Grand Mosque of Niamey) and activities (including a Libyan cultural center in Niamey), but the two states soon fell out as Libya claimed large sections of Niger's northeast. Thenceforth, Libya tried to engineer the fall of President **Seyni Kountché** through a series of coup attempts and Tuareg-led attacks on Niger's military installations—a rather low-key version of the full frontal attack Kadhafi launched against neighboring Chad, from which it also claimed a northern territorial strip, the Aouzou Band. At these junctures, Kountché received the support of other African and Arab countries, especially as he engaged in his own bit of activist diplomacy, successfully placing a Nigerien at the head of OAU (**Idé Oumarou**) and of the Organization of the Islamic Conference (**Hamid Algabid**). Kountché also maintained good relations with Western countries, notably restoring France in its central role in Niger's foreign policy, while also developing special relationships with the People's Republic of China, which established an extensive medical cooperation program with the country and, in a pattern found throughout Africa, offered Niamey a stadium (named after General Seyni Kountché after his death) and a housing project.

Contemporary Period. In the more recent period, the earlier tense relationships with Algeria and with Libya abated, while Niger's foreign policy was marked by three new elements. One was rather negative, since the crisis of the state in the 1990s meant that any kind of activist diplomacy became inconceivable, and the country fell back on pure interest opportunism. Thus, in 1992, it broke its diplomatic relations with China to recognize Taiwan and thus secure a much-needed $50 million loan in view of the state's fiscal crisis and reluctance to cave in to the International Monetary Fund's instructions. But Niger also started to develop a more independent foreign policy with respect to France, chiefly in reaction to the fact that France itself was scaling down in considerable measures its African policy. And lastly, West African, close-to-home regional integration bodies (UEMOA and ECOWAS) gradually became important factors in the country's foreign policy, pushing it to develop international regulatory norms and legal frameworks shaped by these organizations' agendas and orientations. The now traditional relationship with the Arab world led Niger to break up diplomatic relations with Israel over the violence of the Second Intifada (2000–2005), in 2002. In 1996, Niger had returned to the fold of the People's Republic of China (the Taiwan recognition had been deeply unpopular in the country), and the latter soon grew to be one of the key international partners of the country in the 2000s, notably becoming its leading foreign investor after France. In 2005, the border dispute with Benin was finally put to rest by a ruling of the International Court of Justice, and Niger's regional environment became generally a peaceable one, marked much more by all manner of technical cooperation than by conflict and tension. No grand vision has, however, emerged from this new context to redefine the country's international position, and its foreign policy has not found new ambitions comparable to those which characterized the short-lived periods of diplomatic activism in the two previous eras. *See also* OPERATION CHEVAL NOIR; ORGANISATION COMMUNE BENIN-NIGER.

FOULANI, PIERRE (1939–). Professor at the **University of Niamey**. Born in Zaziatou, near **Dogondoutchi**, in 1939, and educated in **Zinder**, **Tahoua**, and at **École William Ponty** in Senegal (1957–1960), Foulani continued his higher **education** at Abidjan's Centre d'Enseignement Supérieur, obtaining a number of certificates in physics and chemistry. He then taught for one year (1963–1964) at the École Normale teaching school of Zinder before going to the University of Bordeaux (1964–1970) in **France**, where he obtained his doctorates in chemistry (1967) and in physics (1970). Between 1967 and 1970 he also served as an engineer with the French Centre National de la Recherche Scientifique in Bordeaux and between 1970 and 1971 as principal engineer at Grenoble's center for nuclear studies (France). Since 1971 he has served as professor of physics and in 1972 also assumed the directorship of the School of Science at the University of Niamey. In the 1980s he was promoted and served as dean of the Faculty of Sciences and vice-rector of the university. He has published a number of scholarly papers and also served on the Franco-Nigerien commission on **uranium** and on the interministerial technical committee on uranium.

FOUMAKOYE, GADO (1950–). Academic and minister of mines. Born in 1950 and holding a degree in chemistry from a French university, Foumakoye taught at the pedagogical school of the **University of Niamey**. In April 1993 he was appointed minister of mines and served until the government fell after the October 1994 parliamentary crisis. He is the first assistant secretary-general (i.e., the second highest office) of the **Parti Nigérien pour la Démocratie et le Socialisme** (PNDS Tarayya). He was appointed minister of mines and energy after that party came to power at the 2011 **elections**, and a later technical shuffle of the government landed him in the newly created Ministry of **Oil** in September of the same year.

FOURTH REPUBLIC. The Fourth Republic was proclaimed on 12 May 1996, after a controversial **constitutional referendum** organized by Colonel **Ibrahim Baré Maïnassara**, former President **Mahaman Ousmane**'s chief of defense staff, and the man who overthrew him in January of that year. The referendum, organized under heavy state control, drew record low participation levels; regional administrations were ordered to inflate numbers, incurring vocal criticisms from the judge's union, the Syndicat Autonome des Magistrats du Niger (SAMAN), which withdrew from the **Commission Electorale Nationale Indépendante** (CENI). The new **constitution** ostensibly strove to solve the ills that undermined the **Third Republic** by arranging a presidential system with a strong executive separated from the legislative body. But the text was also visibly tailored to suit the ambitions of Baré Maïnassara who, after repeatedly claiming that he did not intend to bid for the presidency, finally announced his independent candidacy after the adoption of the constitution.

The history of the Fourth Republic ended up being every bit as troubled as that of the Third Republic. It was tainted by the original sin committed by Ibrahim Baré Maïnassara when he stole the presidential **election** of July 1996: after early results showed that he was ranked last among the candidates, he replaced a recalcitrant electoral commission with a pliable committee staffed with handpicked members. The new, rubber-stamped results announced his victory but were not accepted by the major political parties.

The **Mouvement National pour la Société de Développement** (MNSD Nassara), the **Parti Nigérien pour la Démocratie et le Socialisme** (PNDS Tarayya), and the **Convention Démocratique et Sociale** (CDS Rahama) created an umbrella organization, the Front pour la Restauration et la Défense de la Démocratie (FRDD), boycotted the legislative elections, and took many measures to undermine Baré Maïnassara's grip on power: diplomatic campaigns (when Baré Maïnassara was sworn in, only one of his peers, Burkina Faso's dictator Blaise Compaoré, showed up) and internal agitation in the form of strikes and demonstration. Civil disobedience events, called Journées d'Initative Démocratique (JID) and Journées d'Action Démocratique (JAD), were mounted in **Niamey** and other towns, harassing the government and perpetuating an atmosphere of crisis and gridlock. Moreover, in 1998, the only parties of some note, the **Alliance Nationale pour la Démocratie et le Progrès** (ANDP-Zaman Lahiya), the Parti Nigérien pour l'Autogestion (PNA Al'Ouma), and the Parti pour l'Unité Nationale et la Démocratie (PUND Salama), which had initially supported Baré Maïnassara, left his camp and created another opposition umbrella, the Alliance des Forces Démocratiques et Sociales (AFDS). FRDD and AFDS then united their forces, and in July 1998, the regime was forced to sign an agreement with the opposition whereby it promised not to steal the incoming regional elections. The stakes in these elections were high, as they were following the first decentralization reform of the country, through which extensive management and tax collection powers were being devolved by the state to regions and their subdistricts. The agreement notably insisted on the reconstitution of the CENI as it had been set up since the establishment of the institution in 1992.

As a result, the regime was routed at the regional elections in February 1999, despite bizarre attempts at seizing ballot boxes by armed and turbaned men, who quickly faced the physical resistance of house vigilantes at the commission's headquarters. But in a final twist, on 6 April 1999, the constitutional chamber of the **Cour Suprême** heeded requests for annulments posted by the government, and the infuriated leaders of the FRDD-AFDS fell back on their radical claims, demanding that Baré Maïnassara leave the presidency, and calling Nigeriens to exercise "their natural right of resistance" (Ousmane). The country fell into a state of maximum tension, with an illegitimate government clearly unable to operate and a society in which seeds of violence were being sown by the legitimate political leadership. On 9 April 1999, Baré Maïnassara was killed by soldiers at Niamey's military airport, and the Fourth Republic was terminated.

The Fourth Republic was the first Nigerien regime since the **democratization** process started in 1991 to sign agreements with the International Monetary Fund and the World Bank on the **privatization** of Niger's **parastatals** and the trimming of the **civil service**. As a result, the political crisis was compounded with incessant civil service strikes, which considerably obstructed the operation and government.

FOYER DES METIS. Throughout the colonial period, French troops had affairs and sometimes relationships with local **women** but whom they never married. These encounters often resulted in children who were generally ignored by their fathers. As early as the 1910s, the colonial government considered this a problem that should be addressed. It first set up so-called orphanages starting in 1919, in Porto-Novo (Dahomey, now Benin) and in Kayes (French Sudan, now Mali), this latter one being transferred to Bamako in 1924. Niger's mixed-race children were initially sent to Dahomey, with the colony of Niger paying 8,000 francs per year to Dahomey for their **education** and care. Two "mulatto orphanages" (*orphélinats métis*) were established in Niger in 1923, one in **Zinder**, then the colony's capital, and the other in **Niamey**. The rationale for these orphanages was to "gather mulatto children of both genders abandoned by their paternal parents [*sic*], in order to provide, free of charge, for their material living expenses and their general and professional education in ways that will later allow them to earn their living." In 1940, the orphanages were renamed Foyers des Métis (the Mulattos' Home), a phrase that better reflected the fact that the children's maternal families were known and their mothers were alive, although in most cases, ties were severed by the transplantation to the *foyer*, and could be partially reformed only in later life. The colony of Niger hosted three Foyers des Métis in Zinder, Niamey, and **Maradi**. The latter, transferred from the *foyer* of Fada N'Gourma, which reverted to the colony of Haute-Volta (now Burkina Faso) when it was reconstituted, had only female inmates. The *foyers* were suppressed in October 1960, a few months into independence. The children were reunited with their maternal families, but the state continued to pay to each a special allowance for the remainder of their education.

The *foyers* were a typical colonial institution in that they were predicated on the notion that even the mixed and cast-off offspring of the ruling white race should receive special favors from the government. In Niger, where family names are rare and where one's last name is generally one's father's first name, mixed-race children are distinguished for bearing the (female) first name of their mother as their last name. *See also* FRENCH OCCUPATION.

FRANCE. Niger was created and ruled by France as a colony from the early 1900s to 1960, and when France relinquished sovereignty on the country in August 1960, it kept a central place in the **economy** and the **foreign policy** of Niger. Niger's relationship with France has been determined chiefly by the evolution of France's "African policy" and its interest in Nigerien **uranium**. France's African policy was resolutely neocolonialist in the 1960s and was afterward defined by the imperative of protecting French interests and promoting French influence through ensuring political and, to some extent, economic stability in its former African colonies. In the 1990s, France's African policy somewhat unraveled and was reorganized on narrower bases, but the country remained Niger's key partner.

France shaped the transfer of political sovereignty to Nigerien politicians in 1958–1959, excluding the **Sawaba** party through electoral frauds organized by its last colonial administrator, Dom Jean Colombani, and imposing the Francophile administration of the **Parti Progressiste Nigérien** (PPN-RDA) at the head of the new state. In 1959, French president Charles de Gaulle replaced the Ministry of the Colonies by a Ministry of Cooperation which organized France's new relationships with its former colonies—called now *les pays du champ*, literally, "the countries of the field (of action)"—in the domains of technical and military assistance. Cooperation created multifarious links between the French government and Niger's **educational** and public administration, as well as between the French and Nigerien armies. French cooperation agents taught in Nigerien public schools, usually from the high school to the university, they also worked as technical advisors in a variety of Nigerien agencies. Moreover, the French government maintained institutional links with the Nigerien state through bilateral treaties channeling loans, subsidies, and budgetary aid to Niger's government, right up to the late 1980s.

Although this framework provided France with a significant amount of influence on Niger's successive regimes, it was inadequate for Niger's needs, especially in the development of a productive sector, and it did not create reliable dependence on the part of Niger. Thus, while President **Hamani Diori** was very supportive of French policy in the Sahara in the early 1960s—thereby antagonizing the Algerian resistance and subsequent post-1962 independent government—he was much more reluctant to help France support the Biafran rebellion that threatened to destroy the Nigerian federation toward the end of that decade. In the early 1970s, Diori strove to revise the generous conditions of uranium **mining** he had granted to France in view of Niger's dramatic **drought** and hunger crisis, and the French government pointedly failed to protect him when the Nigerien army organized a coup against his regime.

France, very likely, was not behind the coup, however, as the crisis in the early 1970s had only worsened the contradictions in the **First Republic** regime and terminally crippled its ability to rule. Indeed, the new military regime's relationship with France started on a rather chilly note, as **Seyni**

Kountché ordered the French army to pull the troops it had stationed in **Niamey** out of Niger and generally scaled down military cooperation with France. Moreover, the **Office National des Ressources Minières** (ONA-REM) was set up to better look after Nigerien interests in the mining sector and, crucially, in the booming exploitation of uranium, led by France. In the heady days of the *régime d'exception*—1974–1982—the rulers of Niger indeed hoped to end France's governing influence on the country through fast-paced economic development fueled by uranium money and affordable international credit. Niger's ties with France, however, ran deeper than its rulers perhaps cared to consider. Thus, Niger's economy depended on the **health** of its **currency**, the **CFA franc**, which was pegged to the French franc and managed by the French treasury through mechanisms that put severe controls on Niger's access to reserve credit. In this way, Niger in the 1980s imported the inflation that plagued the French economy and also was directly hit by the successive devaluations of the French franc, which reduced the value of the CFA franc relative to the U.S. dollar, the currency in which the country's debt was held. Subsequently, the French franc revalued, pushing the CFA franc up and heating up the exchange rates of that currency with those of neighboring countries.

The deep financial crisis into which Niger fell after 1982 was greatly caused by this state of affairs, and by the late 1980s, France was starting to prod the country into following the leadership of the International Monetary Fund (IMF), thereby scaling down its own level of commitment. In 1987, the French treasury helped the Nigerien government finance its first **civil service** trimming program, the Programme d'Appui à l'Initiative Privée et à la Création d'Emploi, which subsidized civil servants to leave their position and create small businesses. The program was too modest to be successful, however, and subsequent Nigerien resistance to IMF conditionalities led France to significantly reduce its economic assistance to Niger, especially since it now inscribed its aid policy within the multilateral approach recommended by the international financial institutions.

When Niger's finances collapsed in the early 1990s, compelling the government to suspend salary payments through several months, France did not use the mechanisms of the CFA monetary union to bail the country out and instead resorted to a devaluation of the currency (1994) as a blanket solution to the recession which was devastating the entire Franc Zone. Both France's unwillingness or inability to help out in the early 1990s and the 1994 devaluation were interpreted as a betrayal in Niger, considerably damaging the image of France in the country; even though France had never been very popular in Niger, it had thus far been seen as the country's only reliable partner, when push came to shove.

The fact of the matter was that, in the 1990s, France was reshaping its African policy, which was terribly hurt by its misconduct in the Rwandan genocide (1994) and the general perception that while the United States was now promoting freedom and democracy in Africa, it still hung on to stability through dictatorships protective of its strategic interests. Thus, in Niger, President Jacques Chirac provided personal support to coup-maker **Ibrahim Baré Maïnassara** even after it became clear that he was bent on restoring authoritarian rule (1996), going to the lengths of sending to Niamey a renowned French jurist, Jacques Mazeaud, to justify one of Baré Maïnassara shadier constitutional manipulations. However, Chirac's support for Baré Maïnassara also allowed him to broker a compromise between the Nigerien president and his political opposition in 1998, in view of the fateful regional **elections** of 1999. It was certainly not his fault when Baré Maïnassara decided to renege on the conditions of the agreement through yet another manipulation—which ended up costing Baré Maïnassara his life.

France was the first country visited by the new Nigerien prime minister, **Hama Amadou**, in 2000, and the goal of the visit—which was met—was to secure critical French budgetary support after the country's later political vagaries had exhausted the funds of the state. France was all the more intent at contributing to stabilize Niger because it now had a renewed interest in the country's uranium. In the early 2000s, the French uranium sector was consolidated by manager Anne Lauvergeon, who founded **AREVA** by merging COGEMA and Framatome, the two major French nuclear enterprises. The highly ambitious and very wealthy new enterprise targeted Niger as the main source of its uranium ore, and this deeply entangled France into Nigerien internal politics, both in relation to the intermittent **Tuareg** unrest in the areas of uranium exploitation and to Nigerien decision makers whom AREVA officials openly courted. Understanding this trend, Niger's president **Mamadou Tandja** used the threat of "diversifying" Niger's mining partners to compel an explicit French support for his constitutional coup of 2009. On 27 March 2009, prior to signing the agreement which granted to AREVA rights of exploitation on the giant uranium mines of **Imouraren**, French president Nicolas Sarkozy attended a reception at which Mamadou Tandja announced that he would seek an extension of term limit declared unlawful by the country's **Cour Constitutionnelle**.

France's involvement in Niger was complicated by the attacks of the Algerian Islamist terrorist group **Al-Qaeda in the Islamic Maghred (AQIM)** which targeted its nationals living and working in Niger. Several French people were kidnapped in the northern desert, including at **Arlit** (September 2010), while an attack on two Frenchmen in Niamey ended tragically with the death of the victims and their abductors (January 2011). In March 2011,

France attacked the Libyan government to prevent it from suppressing an insurrection in eastern **Libya**, leading to a collapse of authority in Libya and a potential strengthening of AQIM, which then had access to all manner of weapons from the arsenals of Libya. While deploring this development, newly elected Nigerien president **Mahamadou Issoufou** rejected a French proposition to station French soldiers in Niger. However, France has been allowed to discreetly step up its so-called military cooperation with Niger, especially in the areas of uranium production.

France remains Niger's first economic partner, and its cultural influence, through the large Francophone population of the country, is towering. *See also* AGENCE FRANÇAISE DE DÉVELOPPEMENT; COLONIE DU NI-GER; FOREIGN AID; FRENCH OCCUPATION; OPERATION CHEVAL NOIR; TAZARTCHÉ; UNION ECONOMIQUE ET MONETAIRE OUEST AFRICAINE.

FRANCO-ARABE. In 1957, the first autonomous government of Niger (still under French overrule though), led by **Djibo Bakary**, opened a *madrasa* (**Arab**-Islamic school) in the town of **Say**, considered a historical Islamic site in Niger. The *madrasa* was specifically aimed at teaching the texts and **languages** indispensable to the knowledge of the Islamic **religion** and the training of the appropriate teaching personnel. The teaching of the French language was also prescribed, but the *madrasa* of Say was clearly a religious school which the Nigerien government wanted to establish so as to stress the Islamic identity of the emerging Nigerien nation. To wit, it was directly placed under the tutelage of the government council and under immediate control of the vice-president of the government council.

After independence, however, the dominant paradigms of national development and secular development led the Nigerien government (now under **Hamani Diori**) to enact a law that changed the *madrasa* of Say into a secular-oriented school in which a good dose of French and secular courses were introduced alongside Arabic and religious subject matters: 15 hours of Arabic against 10 and a half hours of French (1966). The *madrasa* thus became a Franco-Arabic school, placed under the tutelage of the Ministry of National Education, when it would have been run by the Ministry of the Interior had it been considered a religious school. The form of education thus created was hybrid, half secular and half religious. Moreover, while the religious aspect is predominant in the primary cycle, it starts to dwindle away at the secondary level, and becomes rather insignificant at high school level; Islamic subject matters are not examined at the *baccalauréat* examinations which conclude high school studies.

The Franco-Arabic system grew comparatively rapidly, especially given the fact that the state strongly favored secular schools. The first Franco-

Arabic secondary school (CEG V) was opened in **Niamey** in 1973 with funding from the **Libyan** government, and it catered for the entire territory, which, given the great distances of Niger's vast landmass, was not stimulating for the growth of the sector. In 1979, the government created a direction of the *madrasas* at the Ministry of National Education to better plan out the development of the sector, and three years later, a second Franco-Arabic secondary school was established in **Zinder** (1982). By then, numerous primary schools and private *madrasas* had already appeared, and the system was completed by the first Franco-Arabic high school, created in Niamey in 1984.

In 1986, the old project of setting an Islamic university in Say finally came to fruition, and this provided a new outlet to the Franco-Arabic system's high school graduates, who had hitherto either defaulted to the secular system or sought scholarships to carry on their studies in the Middle East—not necessarily in religious fields but taking advantage of their mastery of Arabic to broaden their higher learning educational opportunities.

In the 1990s, the demand for a religious Islamic **education** boomed in Niger, especially in the **Hausa** regions of the east which were strongly influenced by developments in northern **Nigeria**. Promoters in Zinder and especially **Maradi** imported from there a new form of religious school, modeled in its organization and its methods on the secular schools but teaching exclusively religious subject matters. They are locally known under the name *Islamiya*, but the state initially called them pirate schools, seeing in them a new form of education that challenged its hallowed principle of *laïcité* (public secularism). The rapid multiplication of such schools indicated that they were responding to a massive social demand, characteristic of the deeper Islamization of Nigerien society in the 1990s decade. The great majority of the *Islamiya* schools were founded by enthusiastic businesspeople who were eager to work for the cause of **Islam** but lacked the skills and vision to sustain a school or an educational undertaking more generally. By the late 1990s, they had tended to seek government assistance, and therefore to let their purely religious *Islamiya* schools turn into the semi-religious Franco-Arabic schools, thus ensuring a final victory of that system.

Yet the boom of the *Islamiya* had shown that there was a massive demand for an education that took into account Niger's deeper Islamization. In 1998 the state came up with a response to the new situation, which consisted in launching an ambitious overhauling of the entire Franco-Arabic system. The reform, currently under implementation through several programs funded through loans from the Islamic Development Bank, aims not at changing the workings of the system but at mending and expanding it. In this light, a complete set of Nigerien handbooks in all Arabic language subject matters has finally been printed, putting the Franco-Arabic system on the same footing as the secular system where Nigerien handbooks had long replaced the French handbooks that were used in the 1960s. The expansion of the system into vocational education is experimental, while **Koranic schools** are increasingly viewed as a form of preschooling for the Franco-Arabic system.

FRANCOPHONIE. See ORGANISATION INTERNATIONALE DE LA FRANCOPHONIE.

FRENCH OCCUPATION. The first European travelers to visit what later became Niger were the Germans **Heinrich Barth** and Edward Vogel, who during the period 1853–1855 went from Niger to Chad via **Say**, Sokoto, **Zinder**, **Gouré**, and Kouka (Bornu). In 1870 another German traveler, Gustav Nachtigal, also on his way to Chad, passed along the classic Fezzan–Bornu route touching on **Bilma** and **N'Guigmi** in Niger, and in 1891–1892 the French army officer Vincent Monteil crossed the Niger River at Say going as far as Bilma via Sokoto and N'Guigmi. Following these first exploratory visits, in December 1897 a 37-man mission was sent to the court of **Damagaram** at Zinder and onward to Chad, led by Captain **Marius-Gabriel Cazemajou**, to expand **France**'s colonial control. Initially well received, Cazemajou was later assassinated by a court faction fearing France's real intentions, and the column retreated. Following that debacle, the **Mission Afrique Centrale-Tchad** was dispatched primarily to punish Damagaram and to explore further the Niger–Chad territories. Its swath of destruction even prior to arrival in Damagaram was terminated by the killing of its two leading officers, Voulet and Chanoine. The column—under new command—attacked Zinder, killing Sultan **Amadou Kouran Daga** in Roumji on 13 September 1899. Consequently the French third military territory was set up to encompass the area of Sorbon-Haoussa (on the Niger River north of **Niamey**) up to Zinder.

In 1901 **Agadez** was taken with a force of 70 troops, and other areas began to feel the French presence. In adjudicating various interclan and interethnic disputes that they encountered (especially among the **Tuareg**), the French helped those groups willing to assist them in their push toward Chad and in the impending battle with the Darfourian empire-builder **Rabah**. A decisive battle with the **Kel** Gress ensued in **Damergou**, following which many of the latter clan migrated to Chad. Several of these clans continued east all the way to Sudan before trickling back to Niger fully 30 years later. The French authority among the Tuareg was also disputed in numerous instances and led to several violent revolts, including those of Fihroun and of **Kaocen**. In the south, periodic anticolonial grievances erupted in the form of local **rebellions**, especially in the early 1900s.

By 1920, however, French occupation was consolidated in the territory, and Niger moved from being treated as a military territory to being administered as a colony. *See also* COLONIE DU NIGER; MISSION AFRIQUE CENTRALE-TCHAD.

FRONT DE LA OUMMA ISLAMIQUE (FOI). Moribund Islamist party. Political **Islam** had gained strength in Niger as in some neighboring countries (**Nigeria**, Algeria, and Mali in particular) since the Iranian Revolution, and the successes of the Islamic Salvation Front party in Algeria became an inspiration for Islamists in Niger. In November 1990 several Islamist intellectuals announced they would register the FOI as a political party. Provisions in the new **constitution** that forbade **political parties** based on **religion** quashed this. Islamist activists instead created associations and agitated against the concept of *laïcité* (public secularism) which the constitutional committee had used to prevent the establishment of their party. Though they succeeded in banning the word itself from the definition of the state in the constitution of 1992 (and from all those that followed afterward), its content (separation of state and religion) was affirmed by each of Niger's constitutions, and the word was used in various constitutional clauses.

FRONT DE LIBÉRATION DE L'AIR ET DE L'AZAWAD (FLAA). Originally a broad **Tuareg** irredentist front, from which several splinter groups seceded in June 1993, namely the **Armée Révolutionnaire de Libération du Nord Niger** (ARLN) and the Front de Libération Témoust (FLT). The front claimed to represent both **Aïr** and **Azawagh**. Headed by **Rhissa ag Boula**, who was also the vice-president of the rebel coordinating group, the **Coordination de la Résistance Armée** (CRA), the FLAA had between 400 and 800 men, some heavily armed with matériel from remnants of Hissene Habre's army after the latter was ousted in Chad. The FLAA wanted Nigerien military removed from its platform region and demanded that Niger adopt a federal organization.

FRONT PATRIOTIQUE DE LIBÉRATION DU SAHARA (FPLS). Tuareg irredentist armed group, comprising some 200 combatants and demanding the separation of Niger's Saharan regions from the country. It was created late in the **rebellion** period, in January 1994, and was headed by **Mohamad Anako**. It shared its turf with the **Armée Révolutionnaire de Libération du Nord Niger** (ARLN).

FRONT POPULAIRE POUR LA LIBÉRATION DU NIGER (FPLN). Organization set up with the aim of overthrowing President **Seyni Kountché**. Headed by **Hamani Diori**'s son, **Abdoulaye Hamani Diori**, and Khamed Moussa (former cabinet director of the Ministry of Defense under Diori), the

FPLN recruited mostly disgruntled **Tuareg** and was involved in several raids in Niger in the mid-1980s, and especially on 29 May 1985. Based in Tripoli, **Libya**, it had a coordinating office in Tamanrasset in Algeria. Abdoulaye Diori's actions resulted in the freshly released Diori being imprisoned anew. Several of the key leaders of the FPLN in the 1990s joined in the Tuareg uprising. *See also* TUAREG REBELLION.

FULANI. Large ethnic group known in English and **Hausa** under this name, as *Fulan* in **Zarma**, *Peul* in French (from Wolof), *Fellata* in **Kanuri**, *Fulbe* (their own name, with *Pullo* being the singular), and at times as **Bororo**. The Fulani are a mostly Muslim people estimated at over 27 million, scattered throughout West and Equatorial Africa, but found in larger numbers especially in northern **Nigeria**, Niger, Mali, Guinea, Senegal, and Cameroon. They are everywhere a minority, except for Guinea where they make up a plurality of the population (about 40 percent). In Niger, most Fulani live in the region of **Tillabéri** (25 percent), with strong minorities in the regions of **Zinder**, **Maradi**, and **Dosso**. Their **language** is Fulfulde, which exists in several dialects. As **cattle**-owning, nomadic groups, they are known as Bororo, or Bororoje (which refers to their red, long-horned zebu cattle) in the Chad-Niger-Cameroon area, where they speak the purest Fulfulde and are least affected by **Islam**. This group refers to itself as **Woodabe**.

Coming into Niger from the west with their cattle, the Fulani in this part of West Africa (the Central Sudan) were not united until the rise of **Usman Dan Fodio** in the 19th century. Their distant and even recent past and origins have always been clouded with mystery, but many scholars have assumed an Ethiopian, and a few have posited a possibly Jewish, origin.

Niger's 2001 **census** placed the number of Fulani in Niger at 9 percent of the country's population. Many of these, especially along the **Niger River**, have become totally sedentary and have picked up the local language (especially **Zarma** in the west and Hausa in the center-east). They have also mixed with the **Songhay** to spawn the mixed ethnicity of the **Kurtey**.

G

GABDI. Traditionally an elderly woman in the **Zarma-Songhay** regions, with a position of social authority. In modern times, the term applies to a class of so-called emancipated **women** in their late 20s and early 30s, generally unmarried or divorced, with a reputation of stylishly living off wealthy men. Most dreaded and desired in Niger's heterosexual male fantasies are the *Gabdi Lalo* (literally, "aggravated *gabdi*" or "super *gabdi*"), whose sexual wiles and financial appetite are perceived as infinite. Women in the larger Zarma-Songhay towns (**Niamey** and **Dosso**) who identify as *gabdi* often form convivial clubs that organize festive get-togethers and support many of these towns' music bands by their patronage. They also play a political role in the key support faithfully provided to one of the country's leading politicians, **Hama Amadou**. Although the *gabdi* lifestyle originates in Zarma-Songhay traditions and is dominated by Zarma-Songhay women, it has become a Niameyan phenomenon and thus includes converts from other Nigerien cultures. Indeed, the concept is close in traditional meaning to the **Hausa** *Karuwa*, even though in this context, it did not evolve to mean "prostitute" (*waykuru*, in **Zarma**).

GAMATIÉ, ALI BADJO. An economist and **civil servant**, Gamatié was appointed finance and **economy** minister in 2000, a position in which he stayed until 2003. His tenure was marked by Niger's international debt cancellation in the framework of the Heavily Indebted Poor Countries (HIPC) initiative as well as by major government cutbacks in 2002, pursuant to agreements signed with the International Monetary Fund and the World Bank in 1998. Generally perceived at that point as a close associate of Prime Minister **Hama Amadou**, Gamatié was lambasted by the independent press for his sponsoring of legislation that would raise publishing taxes, thus financially stifling the press, as well as for his alleged complicity in the passing of legally dubious government contracts. He was replaced by **Ali Lamine Zeine** in 2003 and moved to Dakar (Senegal) as vice-governor of the **Banque Centrale des États de l'Afrique de l'Ouest** (BCEAO), the institution that issues Niger's **currency**. In 2008, during the corruption court case against former prime minister Amadou, Gamatié testified (from Dakar) that Amadou made unauthorized use of treasury funds. It shortly appeared that, in the wrangle between Amadou and President **Mamadou Tandja**, Gamatié had moved into Tandja's camp (whose daughter he married). He was thus appointed, in 2008, special advisor to the president for mineral affairs and conducted the negotiations with the French **mining** company **AREVA** for the €1 billion deal on the exploitation of the **Imouraren uranium** mine.

The following year, after Tandja had overthrown the **constitution** of the **Fifth Republic**, Gamatié was appointed prime minister (October), though the position, under the new constitution, carried few real powers. In February 2010, the army ousted Tandja, a day after Gamatié had read on national television a hard-line speech reaffirming the president's rejection of any contestation of his power, including especially by the **Economic Community of West African States** (ECOWAS). ECOWAS had suspended Niger's membership and it was rumored that Tandja intended to withdraw the country's membership altogether. Gamatié, together with former finance minister Zeine and former interior minister **Albadé Abouba**, was detained longer than other cabinet ministers. He was finally released for medical reasons, and shortly thereafter left Niger for **France**.

GANDA, OUMAROU (1935–1981). Born in **Niamey**, Ganda, after having completed his primary **education**, joined in 1951 the French Far East expeditionary corps and was sent to fight as a soldier in Indochina. He returned to Niger in 1955 and moved to Côte d'Ivoire where he worked as a longshoreman on Abidjan's dockyard. He met there the French anthropologist **Jean Rouch** who was applying his new methods of *cinema vérité* to the study of Nigerien communities in Côte d'Ivoire and Ghana. Ganda worked as an assistant for Rouch and also assumed the lead role in his movie *Moi, un Noir* (*I, a Negro*) in 1958. The experience introduced Ganda to filmmaking, and when, a few years later, he returned to Niger, he quickly became involved in the Franco-Nigerien cultural center's culture and **cinema** club, where he acquired further technical and direction training.

Ganda's first film, *Cabascabo*, came out of a screenplay contest organized by the club in 1968. In the 1970s, Ganda made several dramatic films (*Le Wazzou polygame*, 1970; *Saïtane*, 1972; *L'Exilé*, 1980) and documentaries. *Le Wazzou polygame* won the FESPACO (the African cinema festival of Ouagadougou) grand prize in 1972. The diversity, originality, and seriousness of Ganda's work made of him the greatest in a generation of talented Nigerien filmmakers who cropped up in the 1970s and died out in the 1980s. Ganda's premature death of a heart attack in 1981 effectively signaled the end of the golden age of Nigerien cinema. A FESPACO prize and Niamey's city cultural center are named after him.

GAO. Capital of the **Songhay** state since 1010 and the main political center of the empire that grew out of that state in the 15th century. Founded earlier, around 850, and known by Arab travelers as Kaw Kaw, Gao became the capital after the Islamization of the Songhay, replacing the island of **Koukya** in that role. In the 14th century, the scholar and adventurer Ibn Batuta visited Gao and described it as one of the largest and finest Sudanic towns. It was conquered by Moroccan troops in 1595, following which it went into a long decline. In it are found the tombs of the **Askias**, though in reality only one tomb remains visible. On the **Niger River**, it is the terminus of vessels from Mopti, and it is well connected by tracks and unpaved roads to Algeria and a paved road to **Niamey**. At the time of the Songhay and Mali empires, the town was also an important caravan entrepôt at the juncture of several important cross-Saharan routes. Currently the town of 87,000 is within the Republic of Mali. Many of its inhabitants have formed a very large diaspora in Niamey (a capital much closer to the town than Bamako) where the *Gao boro* (people of Gao) are an integral part of the social and economic fabric.

GARBA, BELLO TIOUSSO. Political leader, head of a small, post-1991 **political party**—the Union pour la Démocratie et le Progrès (UDP-Amintchi)—aligned behind the anti-**MNSD Alliance des Forces du Changement** (AFC) coalition. Garba made himself a name as a defender of African traditions against **Islam**. He died in the late 1990s.

GARBA, MAHAMAN (1954–2009). Born in Kornaka, a village in the northern sections of the region of **Maradi**, he was trained as a musicologist at the Institut National des Arts in Dakar (Senegal) in 1976–1980. He subsequently earned a doctorate in ethnomusicology and served as director of the arts and letters service at the Ministry of Youth, Sports, and Culture and as music professor at the Youth, Sports, and Culture National Institute. In 2005, he supervised the Arts Department of the Fifth Game of the **Francophonie**, held in **Niamey** that year.

Garba issued a few records of music, some of which were popular in the late 1980s. But he was most well known in Niger for his efforts at professionalizing musicians and at prodding the state to develop a consistent cultural policy. His premature death in May 2009 was thus felt as a great loss in Niger's music community. *See also* DANCE AND MUSIC.

GARDE NATIONALE DU NIGER (GNN). *See* GARDE REPUBLICAINE.

GARDE REPUBLICAINE. The older name of the Forces Nationales d'Intervention et de Sécurité (FNIS) and of the Garde Nationale du Niger

(GNN). They were formed under President **Hamani Diori** as a personally loyal presidential guard. The Garde Républicaine put up a fight before succumbing to the assault during the **coup of 15 April 1974** that toppled Diori, and was subsequently totally restructured. It was placed under the command of Captain Moussa Hassane and expanded, at one stage, to a force of 2,000. Trained by Moroccan officers, the guard was as close to President **Seyni Kountché** as it had been to Diori. In the late 1990s, it received large influx of former **Tuareg** rebels, as a component of the peace deals of the various Tuareg fronts with the Nigerien government in 1995. Faithful to its tradition as a repressive and loyal presidential instrument, the FNIS served President **Mamadou Tandja** in his attempt to overthrow democratic rule in Niger and unsuccessfully defended him during the **coup d'état of 18 February 2010**. In 2011, it was renamed Garde Nationale du Niger.

GATE-GATE. One of the several names given by the local population to the rampaging Voulet-Chanoine column. The term is **Zarma**; in other areas the local equivalent is Sara-Sara. *See also* MISSION AFRIQUE CENTRALE-TCHAD.

GAYA. Town of 28,385 on the Benin–Niger border, demarcated by the **Niger River**, which is spanned by the Malanville Bridge. Also a *département* of 253,000 people in the region of **Dosso**. It is the main crossing point for much of Niger's imports and exports that use the **Organisation Commune Bénin-Niger** railway and the port of Cotonou in Benin.

GAZIBO, MAMOUDOU. A political scientist, Gazibo studied at the Universities of **Niamey** and Bordeaux and teaches at the University of Montreal in Canada. He has specialized in the study of democracy in developing countries, and became a vocal diaspora voice—becoming notably a regular guest of Radio France International news broadcast—against President **Mamadou Tandja**'s attempt to install a dictatorship in 2009. After Tandja was toppled, Gazibo was appointed president of the committee that prepared the draft **constitution** of the **Seventh Republic**, priding himself on the speed and low cost with which the committee worked. Upon completion of this task, Gazibo returned to his university in Canada.

GAZOBI, ISSAKA (1943–1997). Physician and head of gynecological services at **Niamey** Hospital. Gazobi was educated at the University of Dakar's medical school and taught at the **University of Niamey**. In the 1980s, he became a celebrity physician in Niamey's maternity wards. After his death, the main maternity hospital in Niamey was named after him.

GHADAMSI. Historically powerful merchants from Ghadames—an oasis south of Tripoli, in contemporary **Libya**. Called *Adamusawa* in **Hausa**, Ghadamsi had been established in small numbers in many centers in Niger until the early years of the colonial area. Their economic power was far out of proportion to their actual numbers (for example, in 1899 there were only 10 in **Zinder** and 12 in Djadjihouma); they were among the principal organizers and financial backers of trans-Saharan trade, many forming trading chains from the Mediterranean coast all the way to Kano. Their prime importance was in providing a bridge between the coastal communities, the economic condition of which they were familiar with, and the interior countries. With the decline of the caravan trade, they either returned to Libya or settled permanently in some of the larger urban centers in the interior. In the case of the Niger communities, most relocated farther south in northern **Nigeria**, especially Kano.

GIDA. The basic unit of the extended family, in **Hausa**. The word means house. The supreme authority within it is called the *mai gida* (literally "owner of the house"), a paterfamilias assisted by the main wife or *uwar gida* (literally "mother of the house"). *Mai gida* has become a Nigerien vernacular for translating the French word *patron*, i.e., modern-educated people of middle-class standards of living. *Windi* is the **Zarma-Songhay** equivalent.

GOBIR. The contemporary Gobir tradition says that the Gobirawa (as people of the Gobir are called in **Hausa**) came from Baghdad (Iraq), a mark of the relatively recent Islamization of this branch of the Hausa people, which made Middle Eastern origins prestigious. The historical consensus is that the Gobirawa are the most important of the people who dwelled in the ancient **Aïr** region, from which they moved southward sometime around the ninth century, as a result of desertification and the political troubles created in North Africa by the expansion of **Islam** (especially the turbulent arrival of the **Tuareg**). The fact that the sultan of Aïr (seated in **Agadez**) is still today a Gobir from the village of Dogerawa is certainly testimony to the age-old ties of the Gobirawa with the Aïr region.

The Gobirawa moved south in stages, settling the Tarka and Kaba valleys, and colonizing the arable lands that stretch between the **Arewa** and the **Katsina**, and that took the names *Gobir Tudu* (High Gobir) to the west and *Gobir Fadama* (Large Gobir) to the east. The southeastward expansion of the Gobirawa brought them against another Hausa group, the Katsinawa, who occupied the fertile territory between the **sultanate of Damagaram** (to the northwest) and the kingdom of Zamfara (to the south), centered on the city of Birnin Katsina and the outpost of **Maradi** in the northern part of their kingdom. The Gobir rulers moved their seat closer to Katsina, from their early capital at **Birnin Lalle**, to Birnin Naya, not far from the rich alluvial lands of the Gulbin Maradi (the Maradi River valley). When the Katsinawa destroyed Birnin Naya in the mid-17th century, the Gobirawa founded a new capital nearby, at Gwararame.

The power of the Gobir kingdom was finally established in the early 18th century, partly thanks to the actions and policies of the warlike King Soba (1680–1694). The Gobirawa then proceeded to infiltrate the kingdom of Zamfara (southwest) and took advantage of a political crisis there to attack it. Under the leadership of King **Babari**, they captured Birnin Zamfara (capital of the Zamfara kingdom) and were ceded the northern sections of Zamfara territory, in which they established their new capital at **Alkalawa**. The Gobir kingdom soon reached the apogee of its might under King **Bawa Jan Gwarzo** (1771–1789). It then included territories situated today in **Nigeria** (the northern sections of the states of Sokoto and Zamfara) and in Niger (**Birni-N'Konni**, **Guidan Roumdji**, **Madaoua**, and **Mayahi**). However, the kingdom faced internal and external threats. Within the kingdom, conquered populations (Zamfarawa and Kabawa) were not fully reconciled to Gobir supremacy, and **Usman dan Fodio** was building a radical religious (**Islam**) censure of the government. Outside of the kingdom, neighboring states envious of Gobir success were waiting for their opportunity. As long as Jan Gwarzo maintained the unity of Gobir government, these threats were suppressed, but immediately after his death in 1789, the Gobir kingdom was put to severe tests.

In 1795, a war with the Katsinawa resulted in the death of the Gobir king, Yakuba, whose severed head was ignominiously dispatched to Birnin Katsina. The government weakened and was eventually unable to check the onset of the jihad launched by dan Fodio in 1804. In 1808, jihadi troops killed the Gobir king, **Yunfa**, during a battle at Alkalawa, and the Gobir leadership retreated north, thus fixing the bulk of Gobirawa into regions that were to become Nigerien. Subsequently the leader of the Sokoto jihad, dan Fodio, conquered all the Hausa kingdoms that were afterward incorporated into Nigeria, including the southern and richer part of the Katsina kingdom. The Katsina leadership moved north, settling in Maradi and striking a survivor's alliance with the Gobir leadership, which settled in **Tibiri**, 5 km west of Maradi. United around their former bone of contention, the Gulbin Maradi, the Gobirawa, and Katsinawa resisted the Sokoto jihad until the colonial takeover, which folded them into the French empire, while the Sokoto territory went under British sovereignty.

Today, the Gobirawa and the Katsinawa are the two dominant groups in the Nigerien administrative region of Maradi. The Gobirawa are also a sizeable component of the southern circumscriptions of the region of **Tahoua** (*départements* of Birni-N'Konni and Madaoua).

GOUNGUIA. *See* KOUKYA.

GOURÉ. *Département* of 227,400 people in the region of **Zinder**, with headquarters in the town of Gouré, which has an estimated population of 13,500 and is 170 km east of Zinder, on the section of the **Route de l'Unité** leading to **Diffa**. An important administrative and **agricultural** center, Gouré has lost most of its traditional village appearance.

GOURMANTCHÉ. Ethnic group which is much more numerous in neighboring Burkina Faso (where is located their main town, Fada N'Gourma), they are found in Niger near the Burkina Faso border along the **Niger River**'s W bend. They make up 0.4 percent of the country's population, a small minority bigger only than the **Arabs**. They provide most of the gardening work of the city of **Niamey**. Though such a small minority, some of the great names of Niger's public life hail from their community, including in the early period of independence the politician and writer **Léopold Kaziendé**. Most of the Gourmantché are Roman Catholic.

GOVERNMENT OF NIGER (MAY 2011).

Mahamadou Issoufou	Head of State
Brigi Rafini	Prime Minister
Mohamed Bazoum	Minister of Foreign Affairs
Amadou Boubacar Cissé	Minister of Planning, Territorial Organization, and Community Development
Abdou Labo	Minister of Interior, Decentralization, and Religious Affairs
Karidjo Mahamadou	Minister of Defense
Soumana Sanda	Minister of Public **Health**
Marou Amadou	Minister of Justice, Government Spokesperson
Foumekoye Gado	Minister of Mines and Energy
Kalla Ankouraou	Minister of Equipment
Moussa Bako Abdoul Karim	Minister of Urban Planning
Saley Saidou	Minister of Trade and Private Sector
Salifou Labo Bouche	Minister of Communication and New Technologies
Kadidiatou Dandobi Maikibi	Minister of Population, **Women**'s Promotion, and Child's Protection

Ouhoumoudou Mahamadou   Minister of Finance
Nana Hadiza Noma Kaka N'Gade   Minister of Professional Training and Employment
Mamadou Youba Diallo   Minister of Higher **Education** and Scientific Research
Mariama Elhadj Ibrahim Ali   Minister of National Education
Oua Saidou   Minister of Agriculture
Issoufou Issaka   Minister of Water Resources and the Environment
Mahamane Ousmane   Minister of Stockbreeding
Maimouna Almou Salami   Minister of Transport
Kounou Hassane   Minister of Youth, Sports, and Culture
Haoua Abdou Yahaya Baaré   Minister of Industrial Development, Craft, and **Tourism**
Fatouma Zara Boubacar Sabo   Minister of **Civil Service** and Labor

GOVERNMENT OF NIGER AT INDEPENDENCE (1960).

Hamani Diori   President Council of Ministers
Saidou Djermakoy Issoufou   Minister of Justice
Diamballo Yansambou Maiga   Minister of Interior
Barcougne Courmo   Minister of Finance
Adamou Mayaki   Minister of **Economy**
Ibra Kabo   Minister of the **Civil Service**
Harou Kouka   Minister of Labor
Ikhia Zodi   Minister of Youth and Sports
Leopold Kaziendé   Minister of Public Works
Boubakar Ali Diallo   Minister of Public **Health**
Maidah Mamadou   Minister of **Agriculture** and Forestry
Yacouba Djibo   Minister of Stockbreeding
Mouddour Zakara   Secretary of State for Interior
Samna Maizoumbou   Secretary of State to the Presidency
Nicholas Leca   Director of the Presidential Cabinet

GOVERNORS, COLONIAL, OF NIGER.

Commissioners
1912–1913   Lt. Col. Charles-Camille Thierry de Maugras
1914–1916   Col. Paul-Celestin-Marie-Joseph Venel
1916–1918   Col. Charles-Henri Mourin
1918–1919   Col. Marie-Joseph-Félix Mechet
1919–1920   Col. Claude-Paul-Emile Lefebvre
1920–1921   Maj. Maurice-Gustave-Fernand Renauld
1921–1922   Col. Lucien-Emile Ruef

Lieutenant Governors

1922–1929	**Jules Brévié**
1930	Alphonse-Paul-Albert Choteau
1931	Louis-Placide Blacher
1932–1933	Théophile-Antoine-Pascal Tellier
1933–1934	Maurice-Léon Bourgine
1934–1935	Leon-Charles-Adolphe Petre
1936–1937	Joseph-Urbain Court

Governors

1937–1938	Joseph-Urbain Court
1939–1940	Jean-Alexandre-Leon Rapenne
1941–1942	Maurice-Emile Falvy
1942–1954	Jean-François Toby
1955–1956	Jean-Paul Ramadier
1956–1958	Paul-Camille Bordier
1958	Louis-Félix Rollet
1958	Don-Jean Colombani

High Commissioner

1959–1960	Don-Jean Colombani

GROS, AMADOU MOUSSA (General). **Tourism** minister during the **Second Republic** and secretary-general of the Defense Ministry under the **Mouvement National pour la Société de Développement** (MNSD Nassara) government of **Hama Amadou** in 1995, he moved to being a close collaborator of President **Ibrahim Baré Maïnassara** after the latter installed his **Fourth Republic** regime. An unsinkable military politician, General Gros was appointed after the **coup d'état of 18 February 2010** personal chief of staff of President **Djibo Salou**.

GROUNDNUT. Historically significant cash crop, which has lost much of its value to Niger's **economy** only in the 1980s. Groundnuts were first introduced in Niger in the mid-1920s, throughout the southern band of the country but with a concentration around **Maradi** and **Zinder**. As early as 1935, 3,527 tons of groundnuts were sold in Maradi alone, and 9,340 tons on the various markets around Zinder, leading to an unprecedented commercial boom that attracted several commercial houses, including the Compagnie Française d'Afrique Occidentale (CFAO) and several Nigerian and Lebanese houses. Niger rapidly attained the rank of second-largest producer of groundnuts in the French empire, and buyers in Marseilles and Bordeaux favored the crop from its fields because of its high fat content. In 1945 Niger exported 10,566 tons; by 1952, 39,855 tons; and at independence, 76,720 tons. The highest production occurred in 1966–1967, when 312,000 tons were exported. During this period, groundnuts were the primary export of Niger and the mainstay of state revenue. Though **uranium** was discovered and **mining** began in the late 1960s, it was then a cheap ore, moreover exclusively sold to **France**, so Niger's dependence on its cash crop was extreme.

This changed first with the **Sahel drought** of the early 1970s which saw production and exports plummeting to an insignificant 3,758 tons in 1975—a year in which moreover the production was destroyed by Rosette disease. That year, the Nigerien government reoriented the activities of the groundnut marketing company, the **Société Nigérienne de Commercialisation de l'Arachide** (SONARA), whose twin high rises used to dominate Niamey's skyline. It was granted the monopoly of marketing and exportation of cowpeas, though the venture—which resorted to the mechanisms used for the marketing of groundnuts—was inconclusive. The real threat to groundnut production proved to be a combination of internal and international factors which evolved in the late 1970s and early 1980s. In 1977, the Nigerien government all but abolished its fiscal demands on the peasantry, who, needing less regular cash income, stopped concentrating so much on cash crops. Furthermore, the hunger of the early 1970s had transformed food crops into domestic cash crops, which led to a surge of cereal cultivation. Cowpea also emerged in that period as a better export crop to the nearby market of **Nigeria**, which offered very attractive prices for the commodity. On the international market, the development of the European Agricultural Policy abolished the preferential deals which Niger had with French buyers and subsidized European competition. Lastly, other fat-yielding crops took over the international market. As a result of all these events, groundnuts ceased to be a relevant cash crop in Niger, as in other Sahelian countries, by the mid-1980s, though it is still produced for domestic consumption.

The decline and fall of groundnuts adversely impacted Niger's economy. While the state had attempted substituting uranium for groundnut as its key export, the uranium glut of the mid-1980s (at a time when it had also become clear that groundnut had lost its earlier value) left it with no comparable alternative.

The groundnut sector had been organized by SONARA, which was founded in 1963 in that view. SONARA had three shelling factories in Tchadoua (capacity of 45,000 tons), **Dosso** (30,000 tons), and Malbaza (15,000). It delivered the produce to two **oil** mills, in rates that varied between 20,000 tons in 1964 and 30,000 tons in 1969. In 1970 the **Société Industrielle et Commerciale du Niger** (SICONIGER) produced 20,656 tons, and the Société des Huileries du Niger (SHN) 9,982 tons. Since then three new oil mills have been constructed in Niger, one each by SICONIGER, SHN, and SEPANI. The whole sector was dismantled in the late 1980s, with SONARA itself being scrapped in 1990. Yet groundnut production and cultivation unexpectedly bounced back in the 1990s, becoming profitable again by 2000 and attaining very high production rates by the end of the decade.

Below are the stages of the groundnut industry in Niger:

1912	Construction of the Kano (Nigeria) railway; development of groundnut in the eastern and central regions of Niger.
1924	Exports reached 1,500 tons
1938	Exports increased to 13,700 tons
1942	Establishment of the Société Industrielle et Commerciale du Niger (SICONIGER)
1938–1945	Slowdown due to war
1950	Rapid increase of production to 193,000 tons in 1957
1957	Establishment of the Société des Huileries du Niger (SHN) and of the Société Industrielle et Alimentaire de Magaria (SIAM)
1960	Production levels at 150,000 tons
1962	SIAM is closed down and the Société Nigérienne de Commercialisation de l'Arachide (SONARA) is established
1965–1970	Groundnut products accounted for 65–72 percent of the country's total exports
1966	Record production of 311,900 tons
1967	Record level of land areas sown with cereals being 432,000 ha
1972	Start of Project Revival of Groundnut Cultivation; production level of 260,000 tons
1972–1989	Decline of groundnut production: land areas reduced by 50 percent and production by 80 percent between 1960 and 1984
1975	Destruction of groundnut production by Rosette disease
1987	End of Project Revival of Groundnut Cultivation
1989	SONARA closed down
1990–1996	Renewed increase both in terms of land areas cultivated and of production reaching, in 1996, 416,000 ha and a production of 196,000 tons, 10 times that of 1990
2000	250,000 ha harvested and 110,000 tons produced

GUIDAN ROUMDJI. A small town of 10,800 people, at about 30 km west of **Maradi** on the **Route de l'Unité,** and headquarters of the *département* of the same name, which has a large, mostly **Gobir Hausa** peasant population of 439,431.

GULBI. The **Hausa** term for long, fossilized valleys and alluvial plains of 2 to 5 km in width. They are known in **Fulani** as *Dallol*. The most important is the Gulbin **Maradi**, in the vicinity of Maradi, although there are minor ones through the **Gobir** regions.

GUM ARABIC. Crop of the acacia tree normally harvested by seminomadic groups during their transhumance patterns. Sudan has a quasi monopoly over world markets, exporting up to 80 percent of the tonnage. Since 1964 gum arabic had been a monopoly of **COPRO-NIGER** in Niger, which exported up to 1,000 tons of it per year in the 1970s. It is cultivated especially in the **Gouré** region of Niger, and was frequently smuggled into **Nigeria**, where it fetched a much higher price than that paid by COPRO-NIGER (in the 1970s, 65–75 **CFA francs** per kilogram). With the onset of the **Sahel drought** in the mid-1970s, which drained the region of its nomadic populations, a world shortage of the crop (used especially in paints) developed, boosting domestic prices to 200 CFA francs. Niger never attained the production levels of the 1960s, and indeed quantities harvested are very small.

H

HAJJ. The pilgrimage to Mecca, which is a duty required of all Muslims who have the means or opportunity to make the pilgrimage to the center of **Islam**. In 1970, official Saudi Arabian figures noted that the total number of pilgrims from Africa was 90,109, though the true figure is undoubtedly higher. Of this number, some 5,000 came from Niger. The figures for 1980 were of the same order, and those for 1990 slightly higher. In recent years, the demand for the *Hajj* has grown exponentially in Niger, leading to the establishment of many travel agencies opened specifically for the organizing of the pilgrimage. At the request of the Nigerien government, the Saudi government gradually increased the yearly quota allocated to Niger to 10,000 in 2010. Men who have concluded the *Hajj* are entitled to add the prefix **Alhaji** or El Hadj to their names. **Women** are prefixed Hajia or Hadjia.

HAMA, BOUBOU (1906–1982). Born in Fonéko near **Téra** in Niger's sixth year of existence as a French establishment, Boubou Hama might in some ways be the most significant figure of Niger's brief history to date. Transcending the social prejudices of his native **Songhay** community (where he belonged in the low ranks of slave descendants), Hama rose to become a very active politician, a dedicated cultural worker and scholar, and a prolific writer. His writing output (over 60 published books) easily ranks him as the most prolific African author in the 20th century, though his books are scarcely known outside of Niger and adjacent French-speaking countries—a fact that is unrelated to the literary and intellectual qualities of many among them.

Hama's primary **education** took place in western Niger and in places (Dori and Ouagadougou) now located in Burkina Faso but then temporarily attached to the colony of Niger. He completed his training as a teacher at the famed **École William Ponty** in 1929 in Dakar and was subsequently posted as teacher and school headmaster to **Niamey**, **Tillabéri**, and Dori. From 1950 to 1957, he directed the Institut Français d'Afrique Noire (IFAN) in Dakar.

Hama's political career started with an awareness of the marginalized position of Niger even within the French empire: extremely weak school attendance rates, scanty equipment and industrial activities, tiny salaried employment mostly filled by individuals from other colonies, and a political representation assumed by a deputy from the French Sudan (now Mali), Fily Dabo Sissoko. A few months after the Conference of Brazzaville, in which **France** tried to chart reforms in its African empire, a group of young educated Nigerien men clandestinely met on an island on the **River Niger** to set up a committee called Groupe de la Deuxième Conférence de Brazzaville in order to organize the defense of the public interests of the colony's natives. Hama was elected president of the group, which started then radical agitation against the colonial regime.

On this basis, Hama started a political career as a member of the **Parti Progressiste Nigérien** (PPN-RDA), which he represented at the inter-African **Rassemblement Démocratique Africain** (RDA) constituent congress in Bamako (French Sudan, now Mali), in 1946. In 1956, he became the president of the PPN-RDA, a position he retained until the **coup d'état of 1974**. A French West Africa grand councilor for Niger in 1958, he rose also that year to the top position which he held for the remainder of his official career, that of president of the **Territorial Assembly**, which became the Legislative (1959) and finally the **National Assembly** (1960). This made him nearly as powerful as President **Hamani Diori**, with whom he teamed up to run a fairly authoritarian, single-party regime.

His memberships in various committees (consultative committee for **agricultural** production, consultative committee for higher education, scholarship commission, and investments commission) testify to the variety and specificity of his public commitments, which also included significant cultural activity. Hama was, for instance, instrumental in the framing and implementation of the scheme which brought to life both the **Musée National** in Niamey and the Franco-Nigerien cultural center. He was also energetically involved in the canvassing and writing of the Nigerien humanities handbook which replaced colonial manuals. In April 1974, the regime of which he was such a central figure was overthrown by the military and Hama was first put under house arrest in Niamey, and then transferred to a military cantonment in **Agadez** before being brought back to the Camp Bagagi (another cantonment) in Niamey. He was released in July 1976 and resumed his scholarly activities, participating to a colloquium in 1977 and a seminar in 1981, and continuing to write research essays to the final weeks of his life. He died in Niamey in January 1982.

Hama's more enduring legacy resides in his scholarly and literary work, based on extensive research throughout the **Sahelian** regions of West Africa and an original philosophical view of Africa's history and of its potential contribution to global civilization. The corpus of his work could be divided into five categories: the antiquarian anthropological work devoted to the various communal cultures that make up the Nigerien national tapestry (e.g., *Recherche sur l'histoire des Touareg sahariens et soudanais*, 1967); the fabulist narratives often culled from Songhay mythologies (e.g., *Izé Gani*, posthumous, 1985); the collection of facts and data on Niger's disappearing traditional bodies of knowledge which remain in unpublished notebook form; the personal, philosophical, and lyrical semifiction (e.g., *Kotia Nima*, 1969); and the extensive essays that span philosophical, anthropological, and political interests relative to Africa in the world (e.g., *Essai d'analyse de l'éducation africaine*, 1968).

The Musée National in Niamey has been named after him. In 1989–1999, the Nigerien government also awarded a Prix Boubou Hama to honor writers and scholars. The laureates were Issa Ibrahim (1989), **André Salifou** (1991), **Abdourahamane Mariko Kélétigui** (1992), **Abdoulaye Mamani** (1993), Adamou Idé (1996), **Idé Oumarou** (1997), and Boubé Gado (1999). *See also* CIVIL SERVICE; LITERATURE.

HAMADAS. Rocky desert plateaus, a much more frequent feature of the Sahara desert, especially within Niger, than the image of endless sand dunes (*ergs*) popularized in fiction.

HAMANI, DJIBO (1943–). Hamani graduated from the Universities of Grenoble (1971) and Aix (1975) with degrees in history, the earliest history doctorate holder after **André Salifou**. He has written several books on Niger's history and headed the history section of the **Institut de Recherches en Sciences Humaines** (IRSH) in the early 1990s. In 1991, Hamani was one of the personalities vying for the presidency of the **Conférence Nationale**'s Haut Conseil de la République (HCR). He desisted in favor of his colleague André Salifou, which famously made the latter cry on national television. In recent years, Hamani, disgusted at the corruption of democratic governance in the Nigerien context, became an Islamist intellectual, pushing for a greater and deeper Islamization of Niger's educational system, and imagining Niger as essentially a Muslim nation in his *L'Islam au Soudan Central: Histoire de l'Islam au Niger du VIIe au XIXe siècles* (2007). Yet in 2009, when President **Mamadou Tandja** suppressed the **Fifth Republic** in his bid to stay in power, Hamani became one of the rare university professors to openly and vocally oppose his project. After Tandja was toppled, the transitory executive military outfit **Conseil Suprême pour la Restauration de la Démocratie** (CSRD) appointed him a member of the **Conseil Consultatif National** that served as a transitory parliament. *See also* ISLAM.

HAMIDOU HIMA, DJIBRILLA (Colonel) (1965–). Better known in Niger as "Commandant Pelé" owing to his passion and support for soccer in the country. Born in **Niamey** where he attended primary school, Hamidou Hima started a military career from his secondary **education** years, attending the secondary studies section of the military school at Bingerville (Cote d'Ivoire) in 1977–1989 up to the *baccalauréat* degree. In between, he also received military training in Morocco and **France** and joined the Nigerien **armed forces** in August 1986. He was posted chiefly in the rough northern stations of the army, at **Dirkou**, Madaouela, and **Agadez**, and was therefore directly engaged in combat against **Tuareg** rebel fronts in the 1990s, earning immense popularity among the troops. He was consequently co-opted into the **Conseil de Réconciliation Nationale** (CRN) set up by **Daouda Malam Wanké** after the toppling of President **Ibrahim Baré Maïnassara** (April 1999) and promoted to battalion chief in October of that year. He also took up the presidency of Niamey's soccer league and of the Association Sportive des Forces Armées Nigériennes (ASFAN).

Under the **Fifth Republic**, Hamidou Hima was appointed to the crucial military position of commander of defense zone number one—i.e., Niamey, the capital, **Tillabéri**, and **Dosso**. That military region is the most sensitive in the country, and Hamidou Hima's appointment was a mark of trust from President **Mamadou Tandja**. Tandja also pulled strings to get him elected president of Niger's national soccer federation, the Fenifoot, on 25 July 2009. Hamidou Hima thus appeared nested within Tandja's ploy to destroy the democratic regime in July–August 2009. Yet when Squadron Chief **Djibo Salou** moved to remove Tandja in February 2010, he received the support of Hamidou Hima in keeping Niamey under control. Hamidou Hima subsequently became one of the key officials in the provisional executive organ **Conseil Suprême pour la Restauration de la Démocratie** (CSRD).

HASKÉ. The first independent Nigerien newspaper after the Islamist *Iqra* (founded in **Maradi**), *Haské* (which means "light" in **Hausa**) was founded in 1990 in Niamey by Ibrahim Cheick Diop, a former government journalist who had taken one of the early retirement grants provided by the state in the late 1980s to trim off the **civil service**. Hugely successful in its first year as a symbol of the opening up of Niger's political system, the paper was subjected to government naggings and was briefly issued from Benin. After the boom of the independent press in 1991, its importance declined and toward the end of the decade, it was issued very irregularly. Diop himself had by then started a new career in the United Nations system. *See also* MEDIA.

HASSANE, AMADOU (1931–). Former vice-president of the **National Assembly**. Born on 15 February 1931, in Garendèye (**Dosso** district) and educated in **Niamey**, **Zinder**, and Dosso, Hassane commenced his career as a nurse and founded the radiology station in Niamey's National Hospital, of which he later became head (1954–1957). In 1957 he was elected **Parti Progressiste Nigérien** (PPN-RDA) deputy from Dosso, and in December 1958 he was elected **Afrique Occidentale Française** (AOF) grand councilor from Niger. Reelected to the National Assembly through 1974, he also represented Niger at the Organisation Commune des Régions Sahariennes (1959) and served as the National Assembly's first vice-president after 1965. He also was (until the **coup d'état of 1974**) advisor to the Constitutional Chamber of the **Cour Suprême**, vice-president of the Board of Directors of the **Société des Mines de l'Aïr** (SOMAIR), and secretary-general of the PPN.

HASSANE, SIDO (1932–1980). Former secretary-general of the trade **union** Union Nationale des Travailleurs du Niger (UNTN). Born in Koygourou in 1932, the brother of **Amadou Hassane** who became the vice-president of the **National Assembly**, Hassane attended schools at **Dosso** and Kollo and in 1948 commenced teaching on the primary level. He taught in **Dogondoutchi**, **Abalak**, and Kao (**Tahoua** region), Dosso, and Bonkoukou (**Filingué**), finally in 1958 becoming director of the high school Lycée National Issa Korombé in **Niamey**, remaining in that post until 1974. He was deeply involved in union activities after 1956 and was a member of the Syndicat National des Enseignants du Niger (SNEN), the union of Niger schoolteachers. He was elected its deputy secretary-general in 1961 after a 1960 union seminar in Tunis sponsored by the International Confederation of Free Trade Unions. In 1962 Hassane also became deputy secretary-general of the UNTN and in 1969 the union's secretary-general. In 1972 he became a member of the Conseil Economique et Social and traveled abroad widely. He was imprisoned after the **coup of 1974** and died in prison in **Tillabéri**.

HAUKA. Spirit cult which emerged in the early 1920s, largely but not exclusively as a reaction to the consolidation of colonial overrule. In many of its aspects, it is also a modern expression of the religious culture that had engendered, in a remoter past, the **Holley** and **Bori** rituals. Its advent was signaled by the coming of a hitherto unknown group of foreign, many of them European-like, spirits who first manifested themselves during a public **dance** of young adults in the then-small village of **Filingué**. The spirits introduced themselves as Hauka spirits and claimed to have come from the Red Sea and to be guests of the spirit Dongo (the master of thunder in the Holley pantheon). They said they had followed a **Hausa** pilgrim who had returned to Niger from Mecca. Their leaders were Gomno Malia (governor of the Red Sea), Mayaki (war leader), Kapral gardi (corporal of the guard, from French *caporal de garde*), and Babule (the blacksmith). Their appearance was peculiarly military, with a behavior of salutations and drills similar to those of the French military and the use of burning torches to stroke their unharmed body. The French, heeding the worries of local chiefs, immediately repressed the new cult, temporary arresting 60 Hauka adepts under order from a district commissioner named Major Crochichia. This, however, did not deter the cult's adept, who simply adopted Crochichia among the Hauka spirits as Kumandan muugu (Hausa for "the wicked commander") or Korsasi. Preexisting spirit cults were also initially hostile to the Hauka, which the Hausa called *babule* (spirits of fire) and the **Zarma-Songhay** *zondom* (malicious madmen). Thereafter, the cult developed into an independent movement throughout western Niger, enlisted mainly young adults, and established new settlements that appeared to organize resistance to the colonial administration and local chiefs.

The colonial administration ended up banning the movement and imprisoning or exiling—to Haute-Volta and Côte d'Ivoire—its main leaders. The movement went underground, emerging in the Gold Coast (Ghana) where western Nigerien seasonal migrant workers had started to travel in the 1930s. There, the Hauka pantheon continued to grow, including Kafaran Salma, possessing the name of **Niamey**'s first district commissioner, Lieutenant Salaman; Kafaran kot (corporal of the coast); and Lokotoro (doctor), among many others. The spirits traveled back and forth between Niger and the Gold Coast, along with their adepts, and they were gradually accepted into the **Songhay** Holley pantheon under the sponsorship of Dongo mediums. Despite some last-ditch resistance of the Holley priesthood, Hauka eventually constituted the sixth spirit family of the Songhay pantheon, joining in the struggle of certain spirit groups against witchcraft.

Given the great fluidity of the boundary between the Holley and the Bori cults, as well as the many connections between the Zarma-Songhay and Hausa-speaking people living in the towns of the Gold Coast, as well as in Niger, the Hauka cult soon associated with the Bori cult as well, producing there some equivalents of the spirits of Western Niger: Soja (the soldier), the Mushe (Sir, from French *Monsieur*) spirits, which were French (including Komandan, commander; Kabran sakitar, corporal secretary). Crossing into northern **Nigeria**, the Hauka spirits soon started to have also English-slanted names.

The Hauka spirits, all of them European or closely connected to the Europeans, reflect therefore the colonial experience from a local, Nigerien (and northern Nigerian) point of view. More specifically, they mirror the consolidation phase of colonial overrule of the 1910–1930s, which was dominated by military authority and the oppressive instruments derived from the *Indigénat* system. They also comment on events in which the French and the

British were involved, extending spirit geography to faraway lands—such as the Red Sea, Constantinople, Marseilles, and Germany (an echo of events in World War I, when thousands of young men especially from western Niger were recruited in the French army). As the colonial regime gradually relaxed its grip in the 1940–1950s, the Hauka cults merged with the ancient Holley and Bori cults and started to express more localized concerns and events. They never built on postcolonial regimes in the way in which they built on the early colonial regime, indicating in all likelihood that the trauma of occupation by and hegemony of a foreign culture had faded out by the 1960s. *See also* RELIGION.

HAUSA. The largest ethnic group in West Africa, and a predominantly Muslim people, numbering around 40 million in the early 2000s. The Hausaland straddles **Nigeria** (with over 30 million Hausa in the north-central and northwest sections of the country) and Niger (6.7 million from the **census** in 2001), with other smaller concentrations throughout West and Equatorial Africa. The Hausa **language** belongs to the Chad group of the Hamito-Semitic language group and is infused with Arabic words consequent to heavy **Arab** influence and the Hausa gradual but nearly wholesale conversion to **Islam**. Many terms also come from the **Kanuri** language as a result of their former close contact with, and domination by, the **Bornu Empire**. Their language is the lingua franca of some 50 million people, mostly through trade from Ghana to southern Chad. In Niger the Hausa are found in the center and eastern regions in a broad arc from east of **Dogondoutchi** to east of **Zinder**. At around 52 percent of the population, they are the largest ethnic group of the country.

Hausa history commences as that of a **Sahelian** group taken between the pressures of the **Tuareg** in the north, **Songhay** in the west, and Bornu in the east, and thus forming a compact demographic "wedge" with no unifying political formation of its own. The name *Hausa* seems recent, and the people are known as Afuma in ancient texts, though this designation is now uncommon.

According to tradition, seven states were formed by the Hausa, who never knew political unity. Rather, they created walled and trading city-states with a hinterland whose width depended on success at war. The states had precise internal hierarchical organization and ground their earliest legitimacy in being ruled by sons of the queen of Daura—the mother of the Hausa people—and a legendary eastern hero, generally thought to have come from Yemen. The states were **Gobir**, Daura, Kano, **Katsina**, Zazzau, and Rano (since disappeared). Gobir at the height of its power straddled a large territory on both sides of the current Niger–Nigeria border. The **Fulani** jihad at the beginning of the 19th century conquered most of the Hausa states and drove many groups into areas now in Niger, from which they tried to regain their homelands (from **Maradi** and **Tibiri**, for example). The area north of Katsina (now ruled by a Fulani king) became a major war zone for a whole century, as Fulani and Hausa armed might clashed. Following the Fulani conquests the major autonomous Hausa states, all in Niger, were **Damagaram**, **Tessaoua**, Maradi, Gobir, **Konni**, and **Arewa**. The Fulani states to their south were Sokoto, Gwandu, Katsina, Daura, and Kazaure.

In Niger, the Hausa are subdivided into a number of subgroups, the most important being (going from east to west) (1) the Damagarawa (singular: Badamagare), a recent subgroup formed out of a mix of Daurawa (with their main center in Niger being **Magaria**, while their ancient capital of Daura is in Nigeria) and Kanuri by the **sultanate of Damagaram**, living therefore in the region of Zinder which covers the older Damagaram territory; (2) the Katsinawa (singular: Bakatsine), with their Nigerien center at Maradi and their ancient capital being Katsina in Nigeria; (3) the Gobirawa (singular: Bagobiri), the largest subgroup, occupying the area west of Maradi up to **Birni-N'Konni**, now the largest Gobir town, even though the seat of the main Gobir king is in the small town of Tibiri, 5 km out of Maradi; (4) the **Arawa** of the Arewa (Singular: Ba'are), around Dogondoutchi, a group which, farther west, becomes for all practical purposes **Zarma**, under the name **Maouri**; (5) the **Adarawa** of the **Ader** (singular: Ba'adare), around **Tahoua**; (6) the Kurfayawa (singular: Bakurfaye), around **Filingué**, a group which, farther west, merges with the Songhay, under the name of **Soudié**.

HAUTE COUR DE JUSTICE. Composed of **National Assembly** deputies who elect their president, the Haute Cour de Justice, a section of the **Cour Suprême**, was empowered to impeach and try members of the government, including the president of the republic, for crimes while in office as well as for treason. The court was abolished after the **coup d'état of 1974** and reinstated in 1992 (**Third Republic**), 1999 (**Fifth Republic**), and 2010 (**Seventh Republic**).

HAWAD (1950–). A poet and painter from the **Aïr**, Hawad is based in **France** and defines himself as a **Tuareg** as opposed to a Nigerien. His work—a great deal of which is written in Tuareg **language** and script—is a manner of surrealist reflection on Tuareg identity, culture, and suffering. Hawad scarcely belongs to Nigerien **literature**—only arguably through his area of birth—and is in fact unknown in Niger, his productions being read mostly in the sizable publics of Western Tuaregophiles.

HEADS OF STATE. Since independence in 1960, Niger has had nine heads of state: **Hamani Diori** (1960–1974); General **Seyni Kountché** (1974–

1987); General **Ali Saibou** (1987–1993); **Mahaman Ousmane** (1993–1996); General **Ibrahim Baré Maïnassara** (1996–1999); Major **Daouda Malam Wanké** (1999); **Mamadou Tandja** (1999–2010); General **Djibo Salou** (2010–11); and **Mahamadou Issoufou** (2011–).

HEALTH. Nigerien populations used to master a very rich pharmacopoeia and sets of therapeutic techniques, some of which are still practiced by so-called traditional healers with a renewed vibrancy in the 1990–2000s. It has been often noted that healers are able to cure more completely and at much lower costs a number of minor physical ills, but their practice is unregulated, their training unmonitored, and their knowledge unassessed—with all the attendant risks for their clients. Therefore, they are at the margins of Niger's health system, in which they are represented by those French-educated professionals who strive to build a bridge between local medical knowledge and the European science of healing introduced by the colonial regime.

The modern health system was started by the French who applied here, as in their other colonies in Africa and Asia, the discoveries made in the struggle against "tropical diseases" in the late 19th to early 20th centuries, chiefly to protect the troops and the colonial administration (malaria, yellow fever) but also the colonized population (cholera and food-based diseases especially). Thus, the French deployed in the colony a small corps of physicians, racially divided, with European physicians normally in the service of whites and African physicians (an administrative category, the *mèdecin africain*) working for the natives. They also developed very efficient hygiene services in charge of eradicating sources of harmful germs in and around settled areas and of vaccinating the population. The flagship of the emerging health system was the hospital of **Niamey,** whose first buildings were constructed in 1922, with the addition of a surgical unit as early as 1938 and of a psychiatry service in 1955.

The health system was considered a public service by the colonial administration, and this orientation was strengthened by the newly independent state of Niger which saw in the development of free health care a key way of establishing its legitimacy. In the 1960s, health infrastructures were thus financed by the state to provide heavily subsidized services and drugs, notably through the **Office National des Produits Pharmaceutiques et Chimiques** and a network of health centers in small towns. The **uranium** boom of the mid-1970s led to an attendant boom of public investment in the health system, but this quickly proved to be unsustainable. A schedule of fees was adopted in 1987, starting a gradual phasing out of free health care. The order of physicians was created the following year—graduating into the Ordre des mèdecins, pharmaciens, chirurgiens-dentistes, infirmiers et sage-femmes

(Order of Physicians, Pharmacists, Dentists, Nurses and Midwives) in 2011—as a sign of the gradual liberalization of the sector. By the mid-1990s, the public health system had become fully fee-based, and a liberalized health sector started to develop, especially as the state funded the training of pharmacists abroad (University of Dakar in Senegal and of Abidjan in Côte d'Ivoire especially), as the **University of Niamey** lacked a school of pharmacy. While in the two previous decades there were only a small number of private pharmacies, all in Niamey, by 2011 pharmacies have become a common sight in every neighborhood of the capital as well as in the main towns of the country. The public system closed most state-run pharmacies (*pharmacies populaires*) but maintained an infrastructure of three national hospitals (two in Niamey and one in **Zinder**), six regional hospitals, 42 district hospitals, 578 health centers, and around 1,600 rural health units (*cases de santé*). This was justified by the fact that private practice developed chiefly in Niamey and in the major towns, and the public system remains geared to catering for the poor and needy, in the often flawed organizational conditions of the public service.

Niger's health system does not quite meet the minimal norms of the World Health Organization (WHO) in terms of extension and diversity of services. It has around one physician for 105,000 people (WHO norms being of one for 10,000), one nurse for 7,000 people (closer to WHO norms of one for 5,000), and one midwife for 5,000 people. This last figure does meet WHO norms, although services are concentrated in urban areas while the bulk of the population lives in rural areas, pointing to the general problem of Niger's health system: accessibility. Thus, of the 245 pharmacies and drugstores of the country, 95 are in Niamey (38 percent), leading to an imbalance of one pharmacy for 8,800 people in the capital as against one for 54,000 in the country at large. The accessibility problem is exacerbated by the fact that most health services, public and private alike, have been fee based since the 1990s, and thus have become out of reach for the majority of the population in most cases. As a result, traditional healing has gained a renewed currency, including in urban areas, while the sale of cheap drugs on the street by illiterate traders has grown exponentially in all urban areas. Despite the periodic outcry of the physicians and pharmacists **union** (the Syndicat des Pharmaciens, Mèdecins et Chirurgiens-dentistes) about this, the state quietly tolerates this development, in view of the great poverty in the country. Indeed, Nigeriens struggle to square, in this domain as in many others, indigence with the demands of donors and international financial institutions for the development of profitable markets and economic activity. In this light, maternal health care has been highlighted as a central objective of the United Nations Millennium Development Goals, leading donors and the state to make here an exception in the commoditization process of health care. In 2006, prenatal, childbirth, and mother-and-infant health care were fully subsidized by the state, with the assistance of several donor agencies, including the **Agence Française de Développement**, UNICEF, and the United Nations Population Fund. In four years, infant mortality was reduced by 34 percent by the new policy, which has been each year reinstated by the government. This, however, is only one bright spot in an otherwise rather grimmer landscape. *See also* IKHIRI, KHALID; ZIKA, DAMOURE.

HIMA SOULEY, HAMADOU (1959–). The son of a **Niamey** trader, Hima Souley left his law studies at the **University of Niamey** in 1985 to take over the thriving import-export empire that was built by his father around the monopoly trading of Nestlé products in Niger. The Etablissement Hima Souley et Fils was soon turned into a household name in the country as it expanded into rice and sugar trading, and Hima Souley became one of the key representatives of the so-called informal sector in Niger. In the democratic era, Hima Souley avoided direct involvement into politics, unlike many of his peers, but has been understood to side with and fund chiefly the **Mouvement National pour la Société de Développement** (MNSD Nassara), the dominant **political party** in the region of Niamey.

HOLLEY. The Holley is a class of supernatural beings, or spirits, belonging to the larger **Songhay** pantheon. They are distributed in six families and have many powerful and/or nefarious abilities. They are also closely associated to non-Songhay and non-**Zarma** populations. The most ancient and prestigious family, that of the Torou, was formed by Harakoy Dikko, a female water spirit of enchanting **Fulani**-like beauty, and her large offspring, born from her continuous amorous entanglements with humans and other spiritual beings alike, including especially Dandou Ourfama, a heavenly spirit who fathered many of the Holley. Among her children, the most powerful is Dongo, who, armed with a hatchet and wielding a bell, masters thunder. He is attended by Kiray (the Red One), a red-footed eagle who masters lightning. In her eternal quest for love, Harakoy Dikko ended up bedding a cemetery *djinn* (*zinni*, a different category of spirit in the Songhay pantheon), spawning the terrifying family of the Hargey, cold-like corpses who threaten pregnant **women** with death in labor. It is believed indeed that it is by killing women in labor that the Hargey reproduce themselves. There are then three families of wilderness (*ganji*) spirits: the Ganji Kwarey (white spirits of the wild), clearly associated with light-skinned Muslims (Moors and **Tuareg**); the Ganji Bi (black spirits of the wild), who wash themselves with the earth and eat excrement; and the **Hausa** Ganji (Spirit of the Hausa), who dwell on the left bank of the **Niger River**, the side of the river called "Hausa" by the **Zarma-Songhay** because it is bordered by the Hausaland. These are in the habit of driving people insane before drinking their blood, and they also practice gender cross-dressing. The sixth family of spirits, the **Hauka**, arrived in the early 1920s, traveling from the Red Sea area following an invitation from Dongo.

The Holley are not the only supernatural beings in the complex and evolving Songhay pantheon, but they are the ones whose powers are harnessed by humans in the most common Songhay religious ritual, the Holley hori (the "play" of the Holley), a possession ceremony during which the medium becomes the "horse" of the Holley and delivers remedies that might be related to personal as well as collective problems. In this light, the Torou are the most important Holley for collective life, since they control the natural elements and are consulted every year in a special ceremony, the *yenendi* (literally "refreshing"), to predict and control the rainy season; the Ganji Bi are consulted for all problems related to the earth and **agriculture** (including, for instance, a locust invasion) and are called forth using the *bitti* drum and air possessed by every Zarma-Songhay village. Collective endeavors—a hunt, a war—also require appeal to the appropriate family of Holley, always resorting to some sort of animal sacrifice to thank the spirit who responded.

The Holley have been historically linked to the political evolution of the Songhay, as their characterization evidently point to issues of alterity and enmity. Nefarious and wild, the Holley are indeed also foreign, being born in other ethnicities and races (including French, with the Hauka). Their dwelling place (*ganji*, the wild) is also the opposite of that of the Songhay (*koyra*, town, and note that **koyroboro** or townspeople, is a generic name through which the Songhay designate themselves). Lastly, the Songhay word for madness, *holley*, either derives from their name or was given to them following the seemingly demented form that they bestow on their "horse" during the possession trance.

In the 20th century, the Holley have gradually retreated in the countryside and in urban popular or peripheral neighborhoods, owing to the progress of both **Islam** and Western-style modernity, but neither they nor other spirits have disappeared altogether. In fact, they seem to have adjusted to modern life by, among other things, responding to the myriad private problems of individuals toiling and competing in large towns and cities, instead of only tackling the simpler collective problems of yore. Their history is still in the making. *See also* RELIGION.

I

ID EL-FITR. Muslim celebration of the breaking of the fast at the end of Ramadan, one of Niger's most popular festivals with the Id El-Kebir. Called also in the **languages** of the country the "small festival," it is characterized by special preparations of chicken and guinea hen. *See also* ISLAM.

ID EL-KEBIR. Muslim celebration of the day of the Prophet Ibrahim's sacrifice of a ram, occurring two months after end of Ramadan. It is also known in Niger's **languages** as the "great festival" (a literal translation of the Arabic name) and **Tabaski,** and is characterized by the slaughter of one or several rams. *See also* ISLAM.

IDRISSA, ALI (1971–). A **civil society** and **media** leader, Idrissa currently heads the transparency monitoring association Réseau des Organisations pour la Transparence et l'Analyse Budgétaire (ROTAB), the Nigerien section of the international nongovernmental organization (NGO) Publish What You Pay, and the Radio Télévision Dounia (RTD). He is also the vice-president of the Comité de Réflexion et d'Orientation Indépendant pour la Sauvegarde des Acquis Démocratiques (CROISADE), the militant pro-democracy association of **Marou Amadou**. By training an accountant, Idrissa first worked in the commercial sections of media organs and groups before becoming intensively involved in civil society activities and being loosely associated with the political action of **Hama Amadou** (said to be the real owner of RTD), where Idrissa was recruited in 2007. These varied positions proved crucial when opposition mounted against the attempt at a constitutional coup d'état by then-President **Mamadou Tandja** in 2009 (**Tazartché**). RTD became the main media platform for the opposition, notably airing the fearless speeches of Marou Amadou and being as a result repeatedly shut down by the regime. When Tandja was removed in February 2010, Idrissa was appointed vice-president of the transition back to democracy consultative assembly, the Conseil Consultatif National, headed by Marou Amadou. After the elections of 2011, he returned to his normal activities in the civil society.

IFEROUANE. Historically major caravan stop 310 km north of **Agadez** in **Aïr**. Reached by a track after a spectacular but rugged 9–10-hour drive, the large oasis is at the foothills of the Tamgak Mountains (2,000 meters) and is surrounded by fine palm and date groves and vegetable gardens. Always competing with the much more prosperous and bigger Agadez for the trans-Saharan **caravan routes** and trade terminus, by the 19th century Iférouane had essentially secured primacy, contributing to the further decline of its rival, so remarked upon by **Heinrich Barth** in 1850. Today still an important entrepôt for trade from the north, Iférouane is an important stop on the northern **tourist** circuit; many side trips from the village lead to stunningly beautiful sites, including to the peak of El Mecki. The oasis has about 5,000 sedentary inhabitants, and its **economy** in recent times has suffered considerably from the **Tuareg rebellions**, at one point in November 2008 turning into a ghost town for several weeks. Iférouane is also the hometown of Prime Minister **Brigi Rafini**.

IKELAN. Name of the caste of black slaves of the **Tuareg** in **Tamasheq**, with singular form *akli*. Half of their agrarian produce went (and still goes, where the institution exists) to their overlords, and they must tend their gardens. Exclusively cultivators and herders of the Tuareg livestock, the Ikelan do not nomadize like the Berber Tuareg. The name is roughly equivalent to **Bella** in **Songhay** and **Buzu** in **Hausa**. Its opposite is Illelan (singular: *elelli*), signifying free men. While there are distinct subcategories in the Tuareg social hierarchy, the most fundamental division is between the Ilellan and the Ikelan. The Ikelan situation has given rise in the 1990s to the movement of the *Touareg noirs* (Black Tuareg), which seeks to emancipate those Ikelan who are still in actual bondage. *See also* TIMIDRIA.

IKHIRI, KHALID (1948–). Born in Digiri, not far from **Filingué**, in the **Tuareg** communities of northwestern Niger, Ikhiri attended primary school at Bonkounkou, in his home district, and later studied **education** at the teachers' schools of **Tahoua** and **Zinder**. In 1970, he earned a special high school *baccalauréat* degree (Bac Merlin) in **France**, and studied chemistry at the University of Paris XI and at the French Centre National de la Recherche Scientifique (CNRS), obtaining a doctorate in 1978.

Ikhiri then returned to Niger to teach chemistry at the **University of Niamey** and was appointed head of the Chemistry Department of the university.

While in France, Ikhiri was active in the African **student** unions, and this experience led to a founding membership in the **Association Nigérienne de Défense des Droits de l'Homme** (ANDDH) in April 1991. He was elected ANDDH president at that point and has kept the position ever since.

Ikhiri has published extensively in scientific journals, while experimenting with herbal medicine, for which he has opened shop in Niamey.

ILLELA. Small town of 16,000 some 90 km north of **Birni-N'Konni** and 59 km south of **Tahoua**, not to be confused with the town of the same name in **Nigeria**, also near Birni-N'Konni. The **Tuareg** of Aggaba established it as the capital of **Ader** after his conquest of the region and relocation from Birni-n-Ader in the early 18th century. In that period, the Hausa-**language** title of *sarkin* Illela was adopted by the Tuareg rulers as opposed to *sarkin* Ader.

Illela is currently a *département* in the region of Tahoua, with headquarters in the town itself. Illela has great **tourist** attractions in its well-preserved traditional **Hausa** architecture. It is the hometown of President **Mahamadou Issoufou**.

IMOURAREN. Site of extremely rich **uranium** ore deposits (the richest by far in Africa). Some 80 km south of **Arlit**, the deposits are estimated at 150,000 tons of exploitable ore. Discovered in 1966 by the French Commissariat à l'Energie Atomique (CEA), the site was originally developed by a consortium involving Niger's **Office National des Ressources Minières** (ONAREM), the French CEA, and CONOCO of the United States. Depressed global prices for uranium in the 1980s delayed implementation of the project, with CONOCO in particular reneging on its original participation agreement. The project was afterward shelved until the steady rise in uranium prices in the 2000s. In view of this new circumstance, the French returned to the site for further exploration, through AREVA NC (a branch of **AREVA** formerly known and operating in Niger under the name COGEMA) in 2006, and successfully applied for an exploitation permit three years later. The process was partly politicized, as President **Mamadou Tandja** used **France**'s need for Imouraren to extract support from the French government to his ploy of destroying Niger's fledgling democracy. Thus it was in the company of French president Nicolas Sarkozy, who flew to **Niamey** explicitly to attend to AREVA's interests, that Tandja formally launched his bid to change or suppress the **constitution** in May 2009.

The final agreement between AREVA and the state of Niger gave 66.65 percent of the Imouraren **mining** company to AREVA and 33.35 percent to the state of Niger. The site powerfully contributes to Niger's position as AREVA's main provider of uranium. *See also* TAZARTCHÉ.

INDIGÉNAT. Legal framework established in Algeria in the 1830s and expanded into other French colonies in 1889. It was formalized by the *Indigénat* code, adopted in 1865, which imparts to the populations in the French colonies an apartheid-like inferior status. Under this code, *indigènes* (natives) were subject to punishment (including jailing and flogging) for "disrespectful actions," "unauthorized meetings," or "offensive words to an agent of the government including when not in service." *Indigènes* also did not enjoy freedom of circulation, being obliged to secure a travel permit to leave the territory of their home district. Sanctions under the code's legal regime also encompassed confiscations, including of land. Moreover, *indigènes* were under obligation to perform *corvée* (forced labor), including for European planters under certain circumstances, to pay a poll tax and, in times of war, a so-called *taxe de sang* (blood tax), i.e., forced military impressment. The severity and restrictions of *Indigénat* were justified as a price paid by colonized populations for the benefit of "civilization," but they also served to protect the European ruling and trading groups, which were always a very small minority having to maintain distance and fear as bulwarks of their status.

Only an assorted group of notables, customary chiefs, and certain categories of *évolués* or *assimilés* escaped the rigors of the regime in the colony of Niger, much less than 1 percent of the total population. Resistance to it chiefly involved mass migrations into neighboring British colonies, especially **Nigeria** and the Gold Coast (now Ghana). It also fueled agitation among the African *évolués*, and struggle against it was at the origin of the early success of the **Parti Progressiste Nigérien**. It was gradually dismantled in 1944–1946, as the colonies were graduating into overseas territories with a modicum of internal autonomy. For many Nigeriens of adult age in that period, the abolition of *indigénat* is as important an event as independence in 1960. *See also* ASSIMILATION POLICY.

INNA. In the **Gobir** chiefdom in particular, but elsewhere as well (in the **Hausa** states), the *inna* is the second most important personality after the king or paramount chief. A woman of royal lineage, a **Bori** initiate, and with ultimate control over all the Bori priestesses and priests, she is chosen by the king to assist him in his duties. The exact title may vary from chiefdom to chiefdom and is synonymous with *iya* in **Katsina**, *magaram* in **Zinder**, and *magajiya* in Daura. So powerful was the *magaram* in Zinder that she was the only person given a state pension in 1906 by the French when they temporarily abolished the sultanate.

INSTITUT DE RECHERCHE EN SCIENCES HUMAINES (IRSH). IRSH is the successor institute to the Niger branch of the Institut Français d'Afrique Noire (IFAN, established here in 1944, later Institut Fondamental d'Afrique Noire) and the Centre National de Recherches en Sciences

Humaines (CNRSH), putting that outfit under the jurisdiction of the newly created **University of Niamey** (1974). Under the leadership of Diouldé Laya, CNRSH and then IRSH conducted basic research in the humanities, social sciences, and hard sciences, and also published the invaluable *Études Nigériennes* series. The **Musée National** was also under its nominal responsibility. After Laya's tenure, IRSH suffered considerably from mismanagement and neglect. It is now mostly a deserted shell, its library rich in rare documents on Niger's past nearly inaccessible and its equipment falling into disuse and disrepair.

INSTITUT NATIONAL DE DOCUMENTATION, DE RECHERCHE ET D'ANIMATION PEDAGOGIQUES (INDRAP). Public institute created on 4 March 1974 to engage in research, experimentation, and development of methods, procedures, and tools that would improve the Nigerien **educational** system. This means essentially an active participation in the creation of school curricula, especially in the constant objective of fine-tuning them to the Nigerien social and cultural context, and also the fact that INDRAP is the main player in the conception publishing, distribution, and updating of school handbooks. As of 2006, INDRAP employs 80 persons, 40 of whom are researchers. It has five departments subdivided in *cellules*. The Department of Letters and Human Sciences includes five cells: French, Arabic, English, History-Geography, and National **Languages** (i.e., **Hausa**, **Zarma**, Fulfulde, **Kanuri**, and **Tamashaq**). The other two departments concern the hard sciences and the arts of training (*animation-formation*).

INSTITUT NATIONAL DE LA RECHERCHE AGRONOMIQUE DU NIGER (INRAN). Agronomy research organ set up in January 1975 through nationalization of the French research institutes that used to operate in the country. It is Niger's main agricultural R&D outfit, with its main purpose being the attainment of food security and rural development. INRAN focuses on crops, animal sciences, forestry, fisheries, and environmental issues. Activities are carried out at four regional agricultural research centers, based in **Niamey**, Kollo, **Maradi**, and **Tahoua**. Each center oversees research stations and units called Point d'Appui au Développement (PAD). INRAN is under tutelage of the Ministry of **Agriculture**.

INSTITUT PRATIQUE DE DÉVELOPPEMENT RURAL (IPDR). Vocational and technical training school in **Niamey**, focused on livestock production, and operating mostly from Kollo, a small town in Niamey's vicinity. *See also* AGRICULTURE; CATTLE.

ISLAM. The 2001 national **census** determined that 98.7 percent of Nigeriens are Muslim, a figure that means that Niger has the most Islamized population in West Africa after Mauritania. Yet as recently as the first half of the 20th century, such was not the case.

Islam appeared in the northern parts of what is now Niger's territory about a century after the establishment of the **religion** in 630. It gained strongholds among certain classes of people (mostly from the political elite and trading families) in the **Aïr** and in **Damagaram** but was in subsequent centuries very marginal to most of Niger's ethnic communities. However, while the various animist cults (**Holley** among the **Zarma-Songhay** and **Bori** among the **Hausa**) remained the preponderant form of religion, they slowly associated with Islam, producing over time hybrid rituals especially in large settlements and trading outposts. Islam being generally more successful where states and commerce shaped political and economic orders, it was especially in the Damagaram, a satellite state to the Islamic empire of Kanem-Borno, that Islam tended to prevail. In the early 16th century, the **Songhay Empire**'s government became very active in promoting Islam throughout its territory (the eastern parts of which overlap with the territory of western Niger) and in the neighboring kingdoms of the Hausa. This affected especially the larger Hausa states, which are today part of the territory of **Nigeria**, and the Hausa of Niger became the keepers of the older traditions of the ethnicity. Such is to date especially characteristic of the **Arna** of **Maradi**'s area and the **Arewa** Hausa around **Dogondoutchi** and **Lougou**.

In the 17th century, the Sufi **Qadiriyya** proselytism of the Kunta family (originating in today's Mauritania) reached the Hausaland and was very successful in establishing Qadiri orders in **Zinder** and **Katsina** (a city in Nigeria which was then ruling Maradi). At the same time, the collapse of the Songhay Empire deprived Muslim communities of a powerful backer and heightened resistance to the faith-propagation missions (*dawa*) that they felt duty bound to undertake. Islam receded. This situation started to change only in the early 19th century, when various **Fulani** clerical warriors launched jihads throughout the **Sahelian** band of West Africa. While those jihads were centered on lands that are now in the territories of Mali and Nigeria, they had significant impacts on Nigerien territory as well. The Fulani warriors generally failed to gain control over the Songhay and **Zarma** of Niger, but they carved out chieftaincies for themselves in their lands, and used these territorial bases to promote Islam. More importantly, the Sokoto Empire, which conquered all the Hausa kingdoms in what is now Nigerian (and not Nigerien) territory, started to play in the area a role similar to that which the Songhay Empire played in the 16th century. This enabled a further development of the Qadiriyya Sufi order (to which **Usman Dan Fodio**, the founder of the Sokoto Empire, belonged) in particular in both western (**Say**) and eastern (Zinder) Niger. Yet Islam still remained marginal in the area, isolating the future territory of Niger almost perfectly from the successful expansions that were occurring in the future territories of Mali and Nigeria.

In an apparent paradox, it is the **French occupation** of Niger which ended up giving a decisive boost to Islam in this part of West Africa. In western Niger, colonial occupation put an end to the belligerent independence of a tapestry of small chieftaincies and established a *pax gallica* based on state hierarchy and commerce, something that these lands had not known since the fall of the Songhay Empire. In eastern Niger, where states and commerce already existed among the Hausa of Maradi and Zinder, French rule instrumentalized the ruling dynasties and their reliance on Islam for norms of government. At the same time, by tearing down (Zarma-Songhay) and disrupting (Hausa, **Tuareg**) existing social and political systems, the French let loose social elements who found an expression for their grievances in the moral and political toolbox of Islam. More generally, the development of trade and urban life triggered by colonial policies favored the development of Islam, which, in the region, had always thrived in urban centers and among merchant communities.

Islam therefore progressed under French rule in Niger not only because it was actually helped by the colonial government (which was often but not always the case), but more importantly because its rival, animism, suffered from the structures and policies of colonial rule and receded into the rural areas. By the 1940s Islam had become the preponderant religious culture in Niger, but outside of a few purist social enclaves (such as the *Ineslimen* caste among the Tuareg) it remained very much mixed with local rituals and could be said to cohabitate with, rather than replace, animism.

In the 1940s, two key events pushed Islam to the fore in Niger: the first was the participation of Nigerien men in World War II, in which they saw combat in North Africa, Syria, and Lebanon, discovering lands in which Islam was a hegemonic culture. The second event was the 1946 abolition of the infamous colonial ***Indigénat*** code, which strictly limited the mobility of **France**'s African subjects. These events opened up Nigeriens to a world in which they could further strengthen the creed which was becoming the defining religion of their society. One of the first actions of the autonomous government set up in Niger in 1957 in the framework of the French Union was the creation of a **Franco-Arabic** *madrasa* in Say, whose mission statement included the teaching of Islamic learning (1958).

When Niger became independent in 1960, it adopted most of the principles of the French Republic, including the rule of separation between religion and government in the public sphere expressed in the concept of *laïcité*. As a result, the progress of Islam did not translate into state power and did not prevent the prevalence of secular values in government.

The **Hamani Diori** government (1960–1974) set up a formal national Islamic association, but it was one which was incorporated in the structure of the single-party **Parti Progressiste Nigérien** (PPN-RDA) and was thus staffed on the basis of party loyalty, with attendant loss of credibility. In 1974, a new, more autonomous state-sponsored association was established by **Seyni Kountché**, the **Association Islamique du Niger** (AIN), with the explicit view of using Islam as a mobilizing ideology and a government tool. In the following years AIN was able to create a national network of Islamic authorities and informal civil servants (Islamic judges intervening in matters of marriage and inheritance) while also producing the authorized brand of Sunni Islam in Niger, screening, for instance, Islamic missions from the Middle East in order to exclude Shi'ism. Kountché also accepted the pan-Islam-based aid of **Libya**, which had already funded, under Diori, the creation of the first Franco-Arabic secondary school in Niamey, and which offered to Niger the Grand Mosque of Niamey. In the 1980s, Kountché generally strengthened Niger's ties with **Arab** and Islamic countries, and his active diplomacy in that regard led to the election of **Hamid Algabid**, his former prime minister, at the helm of the Organization of the Islamic Conference, as well as to the opening of an **Islamic University** in Say in 1986.

Kountché's policy produced a kind of Nigerien Islam, a blend of moderate Sunni theology and local social practices, governing Nigerien lives in carefully circumscribed preserves that left the state free to commit to the secular work of modernization and development.

But it is also the case that in the 1980s, Islam was shaped in Niger as elsewhere by the Iranian Revolution. The concept of an Islamic government and state became then convincing, and the Saudi government spending on Sunni propaganda in West Africa only served to financially bolster voices that demanded the end of secular rule. In Niger, this evolution took an intellectual form, which was more influenced by the Iranian Revolution in the earlier half of the decade, and by the rise of the Islamic Salvation Front in Algeria in the late 1980s; but it also took a popular form, shaped by the emergence, in northern Nigeria, of a strict Sunni orthodox movement, the Izala. Izala theology sought to purify Islam of practices and rituals deemed un-Islamic, and Izala groups soon started to clash with more traditional Nigerien Sunnis, who were generally backed in those instances by state authorities. As Niger's regime liberalized, however, the politically minded Islamic groups came to the fore, and a strategic alliance between intellectual and popular Islamists effectively put in place an Islamist movement in the early 1990s.

By then, it can be assumed that the very high percentage of Muslims that the 2001 census revealed was already reached in Niger, but Islamic culture was not hegemonic, as Nigeriens also practiced animism and were ruled chiefly according to secular norms and *laïcité* (public secularism). A shift occurred in the 1990s whereby Islam started to become a hegemonic culture, weighing down on resilient animist practices, especially in the cities, and organizing itself in a vibrant associative life that clamored for the Islamization of government. The trend deeply affected Nigerien society, especially as it combined with pauperization and structural adjustment in the 1990s. Profane popular forms of entertainment as in traditional **dance and music** dwindled away, and social codes and manners took on a turn that is more characteristic of the Middle East than of older African cultures. This was especially the case in Zinder and Maradi, the two Nigerien Hausa regions closest to northern Nigeria, and this was truer of the urban popular classes than of the French speaking so-called intellectual classes (who account for about 10 percent of Niger's population).

But entertainment fashions recovered in the late 1990s as the country's economic situation improved, and even Islamic preaching tended to become a new form of entertainment. Preaching, through radio and television broadcast, on the occasion of a *dawa* (Islamic training mission) in villages or town quarters or through the large-scale gatherings of the *Wa'azin Kasa* (National Sermon), has become a social function and literary genre in its own right, generally conducted in Hausa and Zarma, with leading preachers becoming national stars. Mosques are often extended into *markaz* (Islamic center) sometimes complete with a *madrasa* or an adult training center in Arabic and religious matters. Important effects of the shift came about at the social level, as the rise of Sunni orthodoxy effectively served as a break in the extension of liberal civil rights to **women**. The counter-emergence of Islamic legality boosted the role of Islamic authorities, transforming in particular the AIN and its regional branches into a court system administering family matters (divorce and inheritance) in civil action for the vast majority of the population. The arrangement, though informal since the state of Niger does not recognize AIN's judicial authority, is tacitly accepted by the justice administration, which traces a limit only at cases pertaining to penal action. Moreover, in response to the progress of Sunni orthodoxy, Sufi orders also started to organize, especially around the **Tijaniyya** Niassite town of **Kiota**.

On another account, while consistently upholding principles of *laïcité* (although the word itself was buried into clauses and paragraphs) through all of the **constitutions** adopted in the democratic era (1991–2010), despite the vocal hostility of Islamist associations, the Nigerien state strove to accommodate the shift by creating, in 2006, a Haut Conseil Islamique (a consultative state-sponsored Islamic organ) and a Ministry of Religious Affairs. These, however, are hesitant moves, and while by the end of the 2000s Islam has become the hegemonic culture of Niger, it has also acquired a complexity and diversity of expression which contribute to guarantee the survival of the creed's normative rivals, secularism and animism. *See also* BORNU EMPIRE; NIASSISM.

ISLAMIC UNIVERSITY OF SAY. University funded by the Organization of the Islamic Conference (OIC) with monies coming chiefly from Saudi Arabia, as part of the scheme of establishing modern higher **education** institutions with a religious slant in the poorer quarters of the Islamic world. The scheme was developed at an OIC summit in 1974 (Lahore, Pakistan) but came to fruition only 10 years later, with the Say university approved at the OIC summit of 1984 (Sanaa, Yemen) and inaugurated two years later. Another one was opened in Uganda in 1988. The Islamic University of Say—whose official name is Oum Al-Qura University of Niger—has two faculties (Shari'a and Islamic Studies, and Arabic **Language** and Literature), one institute of teachers' training, an African Center for the Revalorization of the Islamic Heritage, a technical and vocational training center called IQRA, a section of postgraduate studies, and a **women**'s college for Islamic Studies and the Arabic Language. It publishes the *Annals of the Islamic University of Niger* (Arabic) and caters to the entire West African region, although the majority of students come from Niger.

ISSA BERI. Name of the **Niger River** in **Zarma**. It means "the Great River"; also the name of Niamey's oldest high school, the Lycée Issa Béri.

ISSA, HAOUA (1925–1990). Mostly known as Haoua Zaley. A member of the Koirategui nobility of **Dosso** (she was a relative of one of the kingdom's *zarmakoy*, Alpha Atta), she persisted in embracing the career of a praise singer, normally reserved to the inferior caste of griots in the **Zarma-Songhay** society, triggering the long-standing hostility of her family. She first made her name in the musical genre of the *zaley*, which did not praise the mighty and wealthy in view of rewards but rather the virtues and elegance of beloved young men. Financial rewards she had, however, as her talents found a niche in the tastes of the budding class of the (all male) modern cadres of the colony of Niger in the 1940s and 1950s. She is thought to be the first Nigerien musical artist to have benefited from the introduction of copyright law in the country; she ended her career in the 1960s. *See also* DANCE AND MUSIC.

ISSA, IBRAHIM (1929–1986). Poet and novelist, born at **Gouré**, in a nomadic **Fulani** family. Issa authored the first extensive Nigerien narrative in

French **language**, *Grandes Eaux Noires* (1959), a novelistic, lyrical reflection on the history of Africa and the unity of humankind, which is set in a remote period in the immense, craggy expanses of the Nigerien **Sahel**. Political activism kept Issa away from **literature**, and he suffered in particular from the period he spent in **Seyni Kountché**'s Saharan jail in 1976. Upon his release, he put out a collection of witty and political poems (*La Vie et ses facéties*, 1980) and an autobiography, *Nous de la coloniale* (1982).

ISSOUFOU, MAHAMADOU (1952–). An **Ader Hausa**, the highly educated leader of the intellectuals' party, Issoufou was born in the district of **Illéla**, near **Tahoua**. A **mining** engineer, he served as national director of mines in 1980–1985 and then as secretary-general of the **Société des Mines de l'Aïr** (SOMAÏR), Niger's main mining company. At the onset of the liberalization and **democratization** process, Issoufou set out to create a progressive party together with various left-leaning intellectuals, including philosophy professor **Bazoum Mohammed** and the future founder of the weekly *Le Républicain*, **Maman Abou**. Though they hoped to transcend the country's regional and ethnic divisions, the party that emerged in 1991, the **Parti Nigérien pour la Démocratie et le Socialisme** (PNDS Tarayya) predictably had its popular base in the region of Tahoua, while its very intellectual (university professors and elite people in the liberal professions and the trade **unions**) leadership was broadly national.

At the first multiparty legislative **elections** of 1993, PNDS had a good showing, winning 13 seats, one of which went to Issoufou. Issoufou then negotiated with **Mahaman Ousmane**, **Moumouni Adamou Djermakoye**, and a number of smaller party leaders the creation of a coalition opposing the return of the former single party, the **Mouvement National pour la Société de Développement** (MNSD), to power through the presidential election. When Ousmane came second after the first round of the election, Issoufou, who had come third, supported him for the runoff; upon Ousmane's victory, Issoufou was appointed prime minister in 1993.

Issoufou's government found Niger's coffers empty, while his party's left-leaning intellectual ethos inhibited cooperation with the International Monetary Fund. As a result, the Nigerien state went bankrupt, failing to pay salaries and emoluments for several months, a situation worsened by the devaluation of the **currency** that Niger shares with the Franc Zone African states, the **CFA franc**, in 1994. At the same time, Issoufou had to face constant obstructionist maneuvers organized at the **National Assembly** by MNSD strategist **Hama Amadou**, while soon finding himself in a fight over the control of public markets allocations with President Ousmane.

In September 1994, Ousmane signed a decree weakening the powers of the prime minister, upon which Issoufou immediately resigned and removed his party from the ruling coalition. Issoufou then sided with MNSD in the ensuing elections, supporting Hama Amadou's accession to the premiership in 1995. An enraged Ousmane refused to cooperate with Amadou's government, which led to a political gridlock and a **coup d'état in January 1996**.

When the coup-maker **Ibrahim Baré Maïnassara** showed that he intended to stay in power and tailor Niger's political regime to his position, Issoufou emerged as his most principled opponent and was twice put under house arrest, together with MNSD's **Mamadou Tandja** and deposed President Ousmane. Thanks to his ties with the unions, he was able to coordinate resistance to the Baré Maïnassara regime with trade and labor union leaders, besetting the government with strikes. Baré Maïnassara was toppled and killed in 1999 by the military, and a new **constitution** installed the **Fifth Republic** during a short transition. Issoufou's leadership had matured in that period, keeping its main base in the region of Tahoua but appearing as the other truly national party, apart from the MNSD. As such, he, and not Mahaman Ousmane, was the key opponent of the Tandja-Amadou team at the elections of 1999. The coalition he put together, which included Djermakoye's **Alliance Nigérienne pour la Démocratie et le Progrès** (ANDP Zaman Lahiya) and **Hamid Algabid**'s Rassemblement pour la Démocratie et la République (RDP Jama'a), was narrowly defeated by the MNSD-led coalition.

As an opposition leader, Issoufou attacked the government on its management of public finances and roused public indignation around several high-profile affairs, the most damaging being the so-called Affaire MEBA, when a European Union audit into funds made available to the state of Niger for spending on the development of primary **education** (MEBA stood for *Ministère de l'Education de Base et de l'Alphabétisation*) revealed gaps, holes, and questionable market allocation procedures. Inflating such scandals, Issoufou considerably undermined MNSD's grip on power and succeeded also in attracting Mahaman Ousmane and his **Zinder** stronghold into his camp by funding his party and his campaign. However, on the eve of the election, Amadou plucked Ousmane away from the PNDS coalition, which, together with some other unexpected factors, led to Issoufou's defeat at the 2004 elections.

Leading a broad coalition at the **National Assembly**, Issoufou maintained the strategy of attacking the government on public finance scandals, insisting in particular that Prime Minister Amadou (and not only a few cabinet ministers) should pay for the MEBA failings. In that period, Issoufou was approached by President Mamadou Tandja who set up regular meeting sessions with him, seeming therefore to dissociate himself from his own party leader in order to favor his rival. Issoufou saw in this unexpected support a way to undermine the MNSD and prepare a PNDS victory at the 2009 elections.

Thanks to Tandja's faction at the National Assembly, he was finally able to see through a no-confidence motion which felled the Amadou government in June 2007. He also collaborated with the judicial indictment of Amadou at the National Assembly the following year. But when, upon the jailing of Amadou, Tandja and his supporters started to float ideas of a third, unconstitutional, term of office for Tandja, Issoufou realized that the normal democratic game had crumbled. He started to clamor for the release of Amadou and to issue pronouncements on the defense of democracy and the constitution.

In 2009, after Tandja publicly disclosed his intention of staying in power, Issoufou led other **political parties** at the National Assembly to seek a statement from the **Cour Constitutionnelle** condemning Tandja's project. He then went ahead with organizing the preparation of a high treason motion against the president. But Tandja dissolved the National Assembly before the motion was ready, and Issoufou refocused resistance in the framework of a Front pour la Défense de la Démocratie (FDD). The FDD, which gathered all the major parties, including a split party of the MNSD cunningly set up by Amadou during a short visit to Niger in July 2009, boycotted the **constitutional referendum** organized in August 2009 to establish a **Sixth Republic**, as well as the legislative elections of October 2009. It was later joined by a similar movement organized by former president Mahaman Ousmane, the Mouvement pour la Défense de la Démocratie et de la République (MDDR), and both groupings formed the **Coordination des Forces pour la Démocratie et la République** (CFDR). The CFDR spearheaded many demonstrations, which were ruthlessly repressed by Tandja's right-hand man, **Albadé Abouba**. During that period, Issoufou also called the military to action, invoking the right of people to reject unlawful government. The military responded with an ambiguous statement which did not seem to commit them to anything and disheartened Issoufou's followers.

When eventually the army removed Tandja from power in February 2010, Issoufou was the first political leader to openly salute the action. He was shortly thereafter announced as PNDS candidate for the incoming presidential election. He won the presidency in the March 2011 runoff ballot, thus becoming the first president of Niger's **Seventh Republic**. In July 2011, an assassination plot against him was defused. It was seemingly masterminded by a few crackpot coup-makers in the lower ranks of the **armed forces**, in cahoots with civilians fearful of the new government's anticorruption probes.

The early policy statements of the Issoufou administration indicate that its purpose is to bring the state back into a redefined national development agenda, after two decades of lackluster **economic liberalization**. Thus, a Ministry of the Plan has been reinstated and the concept of **development plans** revived. More generally, key ministries—including the Ministry of the

Plan and the Ministry of Foreign Affairs—are busy setting up in-house think-tanks to define policy on the basis of research and brainstorming, a political method worthy of the "party of the intellectuals."

IXA, RHISSA (1946–). Painter and draughtsman born at Inates, at the border with Mali. Ixa partly grew up among nomadic **Tuareg**, and his art has been in later years almost entirely inspired by Tuareg transhumance and folklore. In the early phase of his career, in the 1970–1980s, Ixa knew a phase of original creativity and experimentation and gained international fame. Given the restrictive economic conditions of art production in Niger, he has since developed a more artisanal vein, churning out in his small home workshop in **Niamey**'s posh suburb of Kwara Kaano countless images of ancient Tuareg lifestyle using a variety of materials and sizes and targeting mainly a clientele of Western **tourists**. He was also employed by the Nigerien government to decorate a number of important public buildings, including the Ministry of Urban Planning and the Palais des Congrès, Niamey's national conference hall.

J

JACKOU, SANOUSSI (1940–). Born into a noble (*biya maradi*) mixed **(Tuareg/Hausa)** family of Kornaka, north of **Maradi**, Jackou followed a rather typical course of study for Nigeriens at the close of the colonial era: primary schooling in his home district, secondary **education** in **Niamey** and then in Abidjan (Côte d'Ivoire), higher education in **France**, first at the University of Dijon where he studied mathematics and physics, then in Tunis (Tunisia) and Paris where he specialized in law and economics. Jackou returned to Niger in 1970 to take up a position at the planning commission as supervisor for waters, energy, and mines planning. In 1972, he was moved to the National Education Ministry to assist the newly created **University of Niamey**'s rector in the establishment of the colleges and institutes of the university. He then taught agronomy at the university while also being appointed director for industrial development of the newly created regional grouping of the Communauté Economique de l'Afrique de l'Ouest (CEAO). Jackou's brilliant career was interrupted in 1976 when he was arrested by the military government and jailed on the charge of conspiracy to overthrow the regime. He was released in November 1987, a few months after the death of President **Seyni Kountché**, and quickly reintegrated the **civil service**, becoming in 1989 the head of the Economics Department at the University of Niamey.

The democratic opening of the early 1990s enabled Jackou to return to politics with less risks and greater opportunities. He was first among the group of Hausa culturalist leaders who founded the **Convention Démocratique et Sociale** (CDS Rahama), of which he was the vice-president, before launching, in 1996, his own party, the Parti Nigérien pour l'Autogestion (PNA Al'ouma). On these bases, he became a famously vocal figure in Nigerien politics, eccentric, often blunt, and always loquacious, embracing at times quite divisive stances—repeatedly attacking, for instance, "**Zarma-Songhay** hegemony" over Nigerien politics—and being generally a conservative force who notably struck an alliance with Islamist groups to defeat laws for the promotion of **women**'s rights in Parliament in 2006.

His political career is indeed chiefly parliamentary and is defined by maneuverings to peg his small party to one or the other of the big players in order to maintain influence and a seat at the **National Assembly**. He was deputy for

CDS Rahama in 1993–1994 and in 1995–1996, and then consistently for his own party from 1996 to 2009. To help his career, he founded the weekly *Roue de l'Histoire* which has, however, grown into a relatively independent paper, sometimes highly critical of policies openly supported by Jackou. This points to the fact that Jackou is far more flexible, and much more of an opportunist, than many of his public pronouncements may imply. During the entire duration of the **Fifth Republic**, his party was officially in the opposition, allied to the **Parti Nigérien pour le Socialisme et la Démocratie** (PNDS Tarayya), but Jackou was also a broker between that party and a faction in the ruling **Mouvement National pour la Société de Développement** (MNSD Nassara) which was loyal to President **Mamadou Tandja** and opposed to Prime Minister **Hama Amadou**. This much became clear when PNDS, PNA, and the Tandja faction engineered the fall of the Amadou government through a successful vote of no confidence at the National Assembly in June 2007. When Tandja attempted to overthrow the Fifth Republic through the **Tazartché** operation two years later, Jackou stuck with the opposition until it appeared to be losing ground and then moved into the camp of the Tazartché and became a prominent member of the parliament established by Tandja during the ephemeral **Sixth Republic**. After the dissolution of the Sixth Republic, Jackou reconnected with all major forces in Nigerien politics and started building a new position for himself.

JAMA'AT IZALAT AL-BID'A WA IQAMAT AL-SUNNA. A Salafist Muslim movement, the **Izala** (as it is known in Niger) spread from **Nigeria** (it emerged in the Nigerian religiously hotbed city of Jos) into Niger. It was initially successful among the younger generation of *Alhazai* in **Maradi** and was assisted by the pauperization that hit Niger's youth in the 1990s. Izala theology puts a premium on Islamic learning rather than age and status, and encourages frugality and hard work. While in the late 1980s the movement was seen as a threat to the country's **Islamic** establishment, it became mainstream in the course of the 1990s. The name *Izala* has thus been generally abandoned (or else identified with Nigeria) and replaced by Nigerien variants, such as *Ahl as Sunna* or (in the **Zarma**-speaking area) *Sunnanke*, denoting a sense of Sunni orthodoxy and legalism.

K

KADADE. *See* ZAMBO, KADADE.

KADAYE. Capital of the Gobirawa after the fall of their kingdom to the **Fulani** under Mohammed Bello and the sacking of their former capital of **Alkalawa**. Kadaye was founded in 1815 and was itself destroyed after a Gobirawa rebellion and abandoned in favor of Dakourawa. *See also* GOBIR.

KADI, OUMANI (1933–). Longtime **National Assembly** deputy and traditional leader. Born in 1933 in **Illela**, where he belongs to the ruling traditional family, Kadi was one of the scions of princely groups who gave the **Mouvement Socialiste African** (MSA), later **Sawaba**, its early electoral edge. He was elected as MSA deputy for **Birni-N'Konni** in March 1957 and, after shifting to the **Parti Progressiste Nigérien** (PPN-RDA), continued being elected until the **coup d'état of 1974**. In the National Assembly he occupied various positions in the committees and was, among other things, secretary of the assembly bureau between 1958 and 1965. In 1990, he became *chef de canton* of Illela.

KADI OUMANI, MOUSTAPHA (1961–). Born in **Illela**, in the region of **Tahoua**, in 1961, Moustapha Kadi Oumani (son of **Kadi Oumani**) is a labor law specialist who became a human rights activist in the late 1990s, along with his friends **Marou Amadou** and **Nouhou Arzika**. The trio emerged as important players in the Nigerien **civil society** when they spearheaded a national mass movement in 2005, the Coalition Equité Qualité contre la Vie Chère au Niger (Fairness and Quality Coalition against High Costs of Living in Niger), organizing resistance against consumer taxes pushed through the Nigerien **National Assembly** by pressures from the International Monetary Fund. After the government tried to co-opt them in a campaign to explain and justify the new fiscal policies, Kadi and Arzika eventually fell out, while Amadou temporarily retired from public life. Kadi then reverted to his interests in labor issues, especially as they relate to the **mining** industry. He founded the Collectif de l'Organisation pour le Droit à l'Energie (CODDAE) and was elected vice-president for the African section of the French-based international nongovernmental organization (NGO) Droit à l'énergie SOS Futur. CODDAE aims to mobilize Nigeriens in defense of their labor and environmental interests especially as regards the exploitation of **uranium** ore in the desert of the northern **Aïr** regions, but its main objective is the development of a national energy policy that would push Nigeriens some steps forward into accessing the good life. This message is publicized by the monthly journal of CODDAE, *Energie pour tous*.

Kadi, who is a member of the mixed **Fulani** aristocracy of the **Ader** (a historical region now included in the administrative region of Tahoua), published in 2007 an impassioned essay against the resilient practice of slavery in **Tuareg** society, *Un Tabou brisé* (A Broken Taboo), an action all the more brave because it puts him at loggerheads with the privileged status groups to which his family belongs. In 2009, he became, together with Marou Amadou, one of the main civil society militants against the **Tazartché** operation mounted by President **Mamadou Tandja** to maintain his grip on power. After the failure of the Tazartché in February 2010, Kadi was decorated officer of Niger's National Order.

KADO. People of mixed **Songhay-Gourmantché** origins who are found in small numbers in the **Téra** area.

KAKA, NOMA (1920–1993). Born in **Dogondoutchi**, Kaka was educated at **Niamey**'s primary school (1933–1936) and at the **École William Ponty** of Sébikhotane, in Senegal (1936–1939) where he was trained for a teaching career. He served in the campaign of **France** at the outbreak of World War II as a member of Abidjan's Special Platoon in a Senegalese Tirailleurs Battalion and, after France's defeat, returned to Niger where he started teaching at two Niamey schools. During that period, he befriended **Hamani Diori**, **Djibo Bakary**, and other modern-educated locals, joining them to found the **Parti Progressiste Nigérien** (PPN-RDA) in 1946. He signed the 1948 petition of PPN's radical wing demanding the departure of Governor Jean Toby and was as a result moved to the colony of the French Sudan (now Mali), serving there in teaching positions until 1953.

Back in Niger, Kaka rekindled his political interests within the PPN, becoming one of the leading members of the party. After PPN emerged triumphant from the process of Nigerien independence, Kaka was appointed to several sensitive positions as president of the **Cour de Sûreté de l'État** (the legal adjudicator of political repression) in 1964 and as minister of defense (1965–1970). His later portfolios in the cabinet were those of minister of rural **economy** (1970–1972) during the height of the **Sahel droughts** and minister of mines and geology (1972–1974) at a time when Niger was trying to devise a new **mining** policy to draw more revenues from its **uranium** ore. Kaka's career ended with the **coup d'état of 1974**, after which he was put under house arrest in Niamey until 1980, and then in Dogondoutchi until the death of **Seyni Kountché** in 1987. He was afterward able to spend his last years a free man.

KAKASI, BOULI (1937–). Born in Gotheye, in the Zarmaland, Kakasi is the most well-known representative of the **Zarma** genre of praise and court-ship songs, the *zaley*. She has become, with **Hama Dabgue**, emblematic of the decline of traditional Nigerien music. Both were artists supported by powerful state actors (such as **Aissa Diori** in the case of Kakasi) or wealthy socialites, and both live now in misery, a sign, to a large extent, of the shift of Nigerien culture to **Islam**-influenced artistic expressions. *See also* DANCE AND MUSIC.

KANDADJI DAM. Important dam under construction on the **Niger River** between **Ayorou** and **Tillabéri**. A much debated project since the 1960s, feasibility studies were first concluded in 1980 for a hydroelectric dam, which was replaced in the 2000s by a new project more in sync with the new international awareness of the protection of the environment and the vulnerability of ecosystems. The estimated cost of the initial project was 185 billion **CFA francs**, a sum exploding to 400 billion in 1988 due to inflation. Though there was some international backing for the dam, the cost (especially for transshipment of equipment and machinery from the coast), and the major variations in water levels of the Niger River (in late 1985 it was nearly dry at **Niamey**) soon became stumbling blocks. Sited 65 km from the Mali border and 180 km from Niamey, the dam would have allowed the irrigation of 140,000 hectares of land and would have produced up to 900 gigawatts of electricity per year. It also would have opened up southwest Niger, assisted internal fisheries projects, and made most of the Nigerien section of the Niger River much more navigable than it now is.

However, work on the dam proceeded very slowly until projects of funding improvements of the valley of the river in Mali and Niger (the most endangered sections of the river) matured in 1997, chiefly under impulsion from the African Development Bank.

After signing several agreements in the 2000s, the government of Niger secured enough funding from a pool of development banks in the **Arab** world (including the Islamic Development Bank, the Saudi Fund for Development, the Kuwaiti Fund, and OPEC) to launch works for the construction of the dam and the improvement of the surrounding lands in 2010. The Russian consortium Zarubezhvodstroy was contracted to build the dam itself, to the tune of 84.7 billion CFA francs. Initially reluctant to invest in the project, Western donors—the World Bank and the **Agence Française de Développement**—later warmed up to it, considering the commitments Niger's government secured from Arab donors. The new dam seeks to achieve most of the objectives of the earlier project, through methods that put a premium on the preservation of ecosystems and funding for the relocation and economic benefit of 38,000 people (notably all the inhabitants of the villages of Kandadji and Ayorou) displaced by the works.

KANEM-BORNU EMPIRE. *See* BORNU EMPIRE.

KANEMBU. Ethnic group located mostly in Kanem (Chad) and in smaller numbers in **Nigeria** and in Niger, where they are found in the vicinity of **Lake Chad** and in **Kaouar**.

KANTOU. *See* ANGO, YAKUBA.

KANURI. Usually called **Beri Beri** (their **Hausa** name) and lumped together with other small eastern groups (such as the Manga), the Kanuri are found in small numbers from **Zinder** to **Diffa** and in the **Kaouar** oases. The dominant ethnic group of the **Kanem-Bornu Empire** and found in large numbers in the Borno province of **Nigeria** and in western Chad, the Kanuri spilled into Niger from their bases farther south during their establishment of control over Kaouar. The 2001 **census** numbered the Kanuri at 513,116, out of a total Nigerien population of over 10 million.

KAOCEN, AG MOHAMMED WA TEGUIDDA (1880–1919). Kaocen was born in the **Ikelan** caste (the servile, dark-skinned bottom layer of **Tuareg** society) in the **Damergou**, among the Igirnazan fraction of the Ikazkazan Tuareg. He left the region when the French conquered it in 1900, moving to Gouro, in the Kanem (Chad) and adhering to the **Sanusiya** militant Sufi order in 1909. The order, which was founded in 1837, had been very successful among the Tuareg in the Hoggar (Algeria), **Aïr**, and Damergou. As a Sanusi adept, Kaocen went to the Fezzan in 1913 and put himself at the disposal of the Sanusi master and ruler Sidi el-Abed. There, he started to organize to take control of the Aïr (which the French were in the process of occupying), corresponding to that effect with the sultan of **Agadez, Abderahman Tegama**, and receiving armament from Sidi el-Abed. After a few years of preparations, Kaocen decided to strike in 1916. **France** was then involved in World War I, and its grip on the northern desert, far from its bases of operation in the southern savannah, was very shaky. Thanks to the efforts of Tegama, the French—who had a fort outside of Agadez—were not sufficiently on their guard when a Sanusi column about 1,500-men strong, marched toward Agadez in December 1916, where it besieged the town. The French sent in reinforcements and eventually forced Kaocen to lift the siege, but he then successfully organized an insurrection throughout the Aïr and into the Damergou, inflicting a serious defeat on the French in the district of **Tanout** in August 1917. The following year, however, Kaocen responded to a call from the Sanusi master Sidi el-Abed, who wanted to rid himself of Alifa, an **Arab** warlord who had taken the fort of Mourzouk (evacuated by the retreating Ottoman) and declared himself lord of the Fezzan. Kaocen attacked Alifa but was defeated and captured on the battlefield. Alifa's troops brought him to Mourzouk where he was hanged on 5 January 1919. *See also* KAOCEN REVOLT.

KAOCEN REVOLT. A religious-political militant movement aimed at ending and reversing French colonial conquests in the central Sahara and **Sahel**, perceived chiefly as a Christian takeover of the area, and developing in regions now included in Niger (**Damergou** and **Aïr**), Chad, and **Libya** (Fezzan and Tibesti). The movement had three leaders: the eponymous **Kaocen**, a low-caste Black **Tuareg** warrior; the **Sanusiya** master of the Fezzan, Sidi el-Abed; and the sultan of Aïr, **Abderahman Tegama**. Important to the movement was also the participation of powerful Ikazkazan (Kaocen's clan) Tuareg warlord, Al-Moctar Kodogo. The movement started out with the siege of **Agadez**, organized in coordination between Kaocen and Sultan Tegama, in December 1916. It was more precisely a siege of a fort that the French had built outside of Agadez. Despite repeated attacks, Kaocen forces were unable to capture the fort, though they occupied the town itself. Eventually, French reinforcements came from **Zinder** in early March 1917, the siege was lifted, and Kaocen, the sultan, and their supporters left Agadez. The irate French, craving revenge, organized the cold-blooded massacre of the men who stayed behind, chiefly elderly clerics and **Arab** merchants. Food, animals, market goods, and books were confiscated and stored at the fort, and *tirailleurs* (African colonial troopers) were let loose in the town to plunder, kill, and rape. The same events later happened at In Gall, which also had supported the Kaocen attack.

Subsequently, the French mounted a hunt to defeat Kaocen but failed to register any decisive success, being even routed by him near Goulouski (**Tanout** district) on 29 August 1917. Kaocen had been reinforced by Kodogo in late June and was poised to whip most of the Aïr into action against the French; the latter adopted the strategy of securing alliances among Tuareg leaders, in a bid to isolate the Senoussiya core of the movement. This was successful inasmuch as most Senoussiya leaders had to retreat into the Tibesti, from where they launched raiding operations into the French-controlled **Kaouar** and Djado. In 1918, however, the Senoussiya's situation further deteriorated when an Arab adventurer, Alifa, filled the void left by the Ottomans (defeated in World War I) at Mourzouk (now in Libya) and declared himself sole ruler of the Fezzan. To oppose him, the Senoussiya master Sidi el-Abed called in Kaocen, effectively ending the threat that he had so grievously represented for the French. Indeed, Kaocen was roundly defeated by Alifa in Zeila in January 1919 and subsequently hanged at Mourzouk. His associate, former sultan Tegama, escaped capture at Zeila and trekked back south, where a French column in the Kaouar caught him. Brought back to Agadez, he was murdered in his cell by a *tirailleur*, under instructions from the *cercle* commander of Agadez, in April 1920. A **Toubou** chief on French payroll had killed Kodogo the previous month.

The results of the Kaocen revolt were quite negative for local populations. The trans-Saharan trade never recovered from the event, which was a final blow precipitating its already well-advanced decline; large numbers of dromedaries, the desert's vessel, had been killed; hunger, war, disease, and destitution decimated the human population; many clans were fleeced by the French and relocated farther south, around Zinder, **Tessaoua**, and Kano. The French, on the other hand, won the possibility of finally occupying undisturbed the northern sections of Nigerien territory. *See also* FRENCH OCCUPATION; REBELLIONS.

KAOUAR. A scenic arid region in the remote northeastern area of Niger, at the border with **Libya** and Chad. It is dominated by a 150 km-long cliff, which reaches its highest point at Peak Zoumri (576 m). Salts and dates are produced in its oases, the most notable being **Bilma** (a *département* in the region of **Agadez**), **Dirkou**, Aney, and Seguedine. Its main inhabitants are **Toubou** but it was historically a bone of contention between several **Tuareg** groups and was for several centuries controlled by the **Bornu Empire**. Kaouar played a central role in the *azalay* caravan trade.

KARMA REVOLT. A social and political revolt of peasants in the **Niger River** valley, lasting from December 1905 to March 1906, and headed by Oumarou Karma. The revolt came on the heels of the **Kobkitanda** rebellion led by the blind cleric **Alfa Saibou** and was similarly a reaction against the transformation, by colonial taxation and social rearrangement, of the old **Songhay** and **Zarma** social organization. In 1905, in preparation for the revolt, Oumarou Karma ordered the destruction of the telegraphic line, set road and water ways under surveillance, assaulted convoys, and planned to recapture western Niger from the French. French military columns converged from Dori, **Gao**, **Tahoua**, and **Zinder** to crush the uprising. The repression lasted for three months (January–March 1906). After a first set battle in which the French destroyed the village of Karma (the event is remembered in the region as Karma Karo, or the Plunder of Karma), Oumarou Karma fled into the **Zarmaganda**, where the French failed at first to seize him. In March 1906, a French column found his whereabouts, with the help of the *zarmak-oys* of Dosso (**Aouta**), of Tondikiwindi (Korridé), and of Damana (Karanta), as well as the **Tuareg** chief Anawar. The forces of Oumarou were defeated and Oumarou himself is supposed to have died at the hand of Anawar. *See also* REBELLIONS.

KARUWAI. Traditional supporters and active members of the **Bori** spirit cult. Plural form is *karuwai*. They are all **women**, leading a nonconventional lifestyle. In modern times, the word has also come to mean "prostitute" in **Hausa**. *Gabdi* is the **Zarma-Songhay** near-equivalent.

KATSINA. See NORTHERN KATSINA.

KAURA. In the pre-**Fulani Katsina** and in the legitimate Katsinawa successor state (as well as in some other states), the commander of the armies and especially of the cavalry. Nominally a slave, the *kaura* traditionally resided outside the capital city.

KAZIENDÉ, LEOPOLD (1912– 1999). Former minister of economic affairs. Born in 1912 in Kaya, Haute-Volta (Burkina Faso) of Mossi origins, Kaziendé (who was a Catholic) was educated at Kaya and Ouagadougou before proceeding to Dakar's **École William Ponty** (1929–1932). The part of Haute-Volta in which he was born having been merged into the Colony of Niger in 1932, Kaziendé became Nigerien and did not return to a Haute-Volta citizenship once that territory was reconstituted. Graduating as a teacher, he spent the next 26 years teaching and as a headmaster in **Birni-N'Konni**, **Filingué**, **Maradi**, **Dosso**, and **Niamey**. In 1953 he obtained a diploma from **France**'s teachers' training school in Saint-Cloud.

An early member of the interterritorial **Rassemblement Démocratique Africain** political party and Niger's branch, the **Parti Progressiste Nigérien** (PPN), Kaziendé was one of **Hamani Diori**'s early friends and associates. With the rise of the Diori regime, Kaziendé was appointed minister of public works (1958) and remained in that position (reappointed several times) until 1965. During this period he also served on several management boards, including as director general of **Air Niger**. One of the most experienced and competent people in Diori's cabinet, Kaziendé's ministry was expanded in

1965 to include mines, **transportation**, and urban affairs. In 1970 his abilities were given extra scope when he was appointed minister of economic affairs, commerce, industry, and mines—a veritable superministry—though the last three were dropped from his portfolio in 1971. Later the same year he was again shifted, this time to the sensitive Ministry of Defense, where he served until the **coup d'état of 1974**. He was imprisoned after the coup, and a commission of inquiry subsequently found him guilty of embezzlement of 38 million **CFA francs** and of fiscal fraud of 6.5 million, which he was ordered to pay back to the treasury. He was released from prison in April 1978. Despite his age, in 1992 he was a cofounder of a resurrected PPN party headed by Oumarou Youssoufou Garba. He died in Niamey in 1999.

KEITA. Town of around 8,600 people in the *département* of the same name (population 320,000), 600 km from **Niamey**, in the **Tahoua** region.

KEITA, RAHMATOU. A journalist, filmmaker, and writer, Rahmatou Keita was born in Niger's **Songhay** country and studied philosophy and linguistics in Paris, **France**. She settled in that city, working for several French television channels, including Antenne 2 (now France 2) for which she prepared the news magazine *L'Assiette anglaise*, winning two Sept d'Or (the key French TV award). Meanwhile, since 1982, she had been steadily making documentary movies on all kinds of subjects, including the series *Femmes d'Afrique* (**Women** of Africa). Her last one, *Al'lèèssi . . . une actrice africaine* (2003), is a film biography of Nigerien actress **Zalika Souley**. She also wrote a book on the theme of an African observing homeless life and white poverty in France, *SDF, sans domicile fixe* (1983). In 2009, she was the honorary president of the African film festival of Ouagadougou. *See also* CINEMA.

KEL. In **Tamasheq** meaning "people of." It is used as a prefix to a specific **Tuareg** clan (or clans) comprising a confederation.

KIOTA. A small town of about 7,000 in the vicinity of **Dosso** and also a rural **commune** gathering about 30 villages with a total population of 21,000. The town is located in the *département* of **Birni N'Gaouré**, of which it is 25 km distant. Kiota is currently the Sufi capital of Niger, having overtaken **Say** which had steadily declined in this respect in the course of the 20th century. It owes this relatively recent position to the actions of **Cheik Aboubacar Hassoumi**, who settled his **Tijaniyya Niassite** congregation there in the late 1940s and baptized the town in 1971 as Kiota Dar al-Ahbab (Arabic for "Kiota, the Home of Friends"). Through this branding, Kiota prides itself on its cosmopolitism as indeed, besides native **Zarma**, large communities of

Tuareg, **Fulani**, and other groups reside in the town. During the Maoulid (the Prophet Muhammad's birthday) celebration, the population of Kiota easily triples as visitors flock from throughout Niger, **Nigeria**, and other West African countries. Many other adoration and propitiation ceremonies are organized through the year. The mosque and mausoleum, though smaller than those found in the Tijaniyya metropolises of Senegal (Kaolack, Tivaouane, and Touba) are in the same elegant and ornamental oriental style.

KOBKITANDA. A **Zarma** village 60 km southeast of **Dosso**, settled in 1902 by people wanting to live in independence of a *zarmakoy* lordship and the encroaching colonial regime. A Kouré-born holy man, **Alfa Saibou**, joined in the venture to preach **Islam** and resistance to Christian overrule, leading the Kobkitanda people to build a wall (*birni*) in order to equip their village for war while also training themselves in war drills. These goings-on, as well as Alfa Saibou's frequent trips to Sokoto (British **Nigeria**), raised the suspicions of faithful French ally *Zarmakoy* **Aouta** of Dosso (who also wanted to take possession of Kobkitanda and its fertile land). The *zarmakoy* alerted the commander of the *secteur* of Dosso, and in early December 1905, two *gardes cercles* (colonial gendarmes) were sent over to the village to collect taxes and assess the situation there. They were murdered, and further emissaries sent to arrest the perpetrators were turned down. On 28 December, a repressive force of 45 *garde cercles,* 120 cavalrymen provided by Dosso, and a contingent offered by the **Fulani** chief Bayero departed for Kobkitanda, arriving there on 4 January 1906 to be immediately taken in a pitched battle. The French lost only 4 men (including the leader of the column, Lieutenant Tailleur) compared to 51 among the Kobkitanda fighters. Many escaped farther south, to Sambera, a similarly independent-minded village, which was attacked by the French with the assistance of the *mayaki* (war chief) of Dosso. After Sambera was vanquished, Saibou crossed into British Nigeria, joining the revolt that was brewing there in the village of Satiru, 25 km north of Sokoto, and helping to organize the insurrection against the British colonial government. In February 1906, he became the main leader of the revolt and was contacted by the sultan of **Damagaram**, **Amadou dan Bassa**, who was trying to create a large alliance against both the French and British overlords. Satiru forces were, however, crushed in a set battle with the British, which led to the capture and execution of Alfa Saibou in March 1906. *See also* REBELLIONS.

KOMA BANGOU. *See* SAMIRA.

KOMADOUGOU YOBÉ. River, flowing into **Lake Chad**, which for 150 km forms Niger's border with **Nigeria**. Along its valley is found a high density of population. The river was virtually dry for nearly a decade, starting to flow only in 1985. *See also* MANGA.

KONNI. Small **Hausa** state centered on **Birni-N'Konni** between **Gobir, Ader,** Sokoto, and **Maouri.** For some time tributary to Gobir, which conquered the region (1750), Konni submitted in the early 19th century to the **Fulani** under **Usman dan Fodio.**

KORANIC SCHOOLS. The schools are called in Niger *écoles coraniques* in French and more popularly *makaranta*. This latter **Hausa** word means reading place, with an Arabic root (*Iqra*: "read," root also for the word *Quran*), and it describes very well the main activity in the Koranic school: reading the Quran. The Koranic schools are the oldest formal **education** institutions in the territory of Niger. They appeared in Islamic communities as primary schools teaching the Quran and the basic tenets of the **religion,** chiefly through the method of rote learning. The schools were concentrated in the regions where **Islam** was particularly developed, such as among the **Tuareg,** in **Say,** or in the **Damagaram.** Under the colonial regime, they expanded dramatically and gradually became common throughout the Nigerien territory. However, since they were defined as religious schools, they fell under the jurisdiction of the Ministry of the Interior, under **France**'s policy of *laïcité* (public secularism). The independent Nigerien state inherited that policy and did not integrate the Koranic schools in its educational system but favored the development of a *madrasa* system. Since virtually every Nigerien child attends the Koranic schools, and given that the population perceives the *madrasa* as part of an Islamic educational system, the Koranic schools have contributed to the rapid expansion of the *madrasa* system, especially in the 1990s.

The fact that Koranic schools are not integrated into the educational system chiefly means that they have remained informal outfits, dependent on the irregular and meager funding of parents and the occasional wealthy patron, but also very easy to set up. They have thus proliferated at every street corner, and especially in the vicinity of neighborhood mosques. The educational reform programs of the 2000s have started to consider them as possible means of boosting Niger's schooling rates, and formal experimental Koranic schools have been initiated in which the traditional reading of the Koran is supplemented with the learning of basic algebra and elements of the French **language.** *See also* FRANCO-ARABE.

KORI. **Hausa** term synonymous to Arabic *wadi*, denoting a temporary watercourse in eastern and northern Niger.

KOROMBÉ, ISSA. A late-19th century **Zarma** warlord from Koygolo, Issa Korombé spent 20 years training and steeling himself in Wanzarbé, the **Songhay** land famed for traditional knowledge of war, witchcraft, and medicine, before attempting, mostly successfully, to undermine the **Tuareg** and **Fulani** grip on the Zarmaland, together with two **Zarma-Songhay** princes, Daouda Bougaran (from the **Dendi**) and Hamma Fandou (from **Kiota**). The main success of the three men was to considerably limit Tuareg initiatives in the area while preventing the forces of the Sokoto Empire to help the Fulani in the Zarmaland to assert themselves and dominate the country. Korombé himself was part of a class of Zarma-Songhay professional warriors (the *wongari*, literally "war stallions") who, once general peace had settled in their country, moved into the Gourounsi (now in Burkina Faso) in search of new fights. Korombé remained in the Zarmaland where he faced the unexpected arrival of two Fulani warlords from western Sudan (now Senegal and Mali), Ahmadou Sekou and Albouri N'Diaye. The two men were fleeing the French colonial progress and clashed with the lords of the Zarma (*zarmakoy*) who enlisted Korombé to defend them. However, he was defeated and killed in 1895 at a battle in Boumba. One of the oldest high schools in **Niamey**, the Lycée Issa Korombé, bears his name.

KOUKA, HAROU (1922–2008). Kouka was born in **Zinder** and went to school in **Gouré**, Zinder, and **Niamey** before heading to Dakar, Senegal, where he studied medicine until 1947. He worked as a *médecin africain* (African physician) mostly in the eastern regions of the colony of Niger, while entering politics as a member of the **Parti Progressiste Nigérien** (PPN-RDA). He was on the same ticket as **Hamani Diori** at the legislative **elections** of 1956 and headed the **health** workers' **union**. When the PPN-RDA emerged as the ruling party of the newly independent country in 1958–1960, Kouka took up a string of ministerial positions: minister of labor (1958–1959), of labor and social affairs (1959–1960), of labor and health (1960–1963), of national **education** (1963–1972), of public works, **transportation**, and urban planning (1972–1974). His most significant position was as minister of education, an office which made him one of the main architects of Niger's educational system. Upon the **coup d'état of 1974**, he was arrested and interned in various military camps, at **Agadez**, and then in Zinder at the Camp Tanimoune where Diori himself was interned at the time. He was released in 1978, but soon afterward came an unjustified prohibition to practice medicine throughout the territory of Niger, followed by putting him under house arrest at Kazoé, a village about 1,400 km east of Niamey where his father was born (1980). Kouka was released from this banishment only after the death of the paranoid General **Seyni Kountché**, in 1987. He resumed some political activity in Niamey, temporarily presiding over the political bureau of a revived PPN-RDA and also accepting a position in the **Fourth Republic**'s Conseil des sages (Council of the Wisemen). But he generally led, until his death in 2008, the private life of a retired physician.

KOUKYA. Also known as **Gounguia**, a word meaning "the islet," it is the ancient, pre-Islamic capital of the **Songhay** on the Niger River and currently in Mali. Its ruins have never been positively identified, though the town, founded in 690 CE, is thought to be 140 km from **Gao** on the Niger River. Koukya was replaced by Gao as the capital of the Songhay state around the year 1010.

KOUNTCHÉ, AMADOU (1924–?). Early opposition leader and elder brother of President **Seyni Kountché**. Born in Fandou Damana on 17 July 1924 and a civil administrator by training, Kountché was a member of the Union Progresiste Nigérienne (UPN), later Bloc Nigérien d'Action (BNA), and was elected on its ticket to the **Territorial Assembly** to represent **Niamey**. He served in that capacity between 1952 and 1957. In March 1957 he was elected on the **Parti Progressiste Nigérien** (PPN-RDA) ticket from **Filingué** but was dropped from the assembly and the party in 1964 in a purge of former opposition members. In 1966, he took up duties as a civil administrator with the municipal administration of Niamey. After his brother's **coup d'état of 1974**, he was appointed to the modest but pleasant position as *sous-préfet* of the *arrondissement* of **Tillabéri**. He retired shortly after the death of his brother but remained the *chef de canton* of Tondikandia with the title of *zarmakoy*.

KOUNTCHÉ, SEYNI (1931–1987). Born in Damana Fandou into a family belonging to the **Zarma** aristocracy of the area (Tondikandia), Kountché began his military career in the French colonial army in the late 1940s. A sergeant of the French army, he transferred to Niger's army in 1961 and was sent to an officer's training school in Paris (1965–1966), after which he was appointed deputy chief of staff of the armed forces. In 1973, he was promoted to armed forces chief of staff. This was a time when the **Hamani Diori** presidency was reaching its nadir; although the internal threat of **Sawaba** uprising had been significantly reduced, the economic situation was catastrophic as the country faced severe **droughts** in 1973–1974, followed by famines and compounded by the effects of the **oil** shocks of the mid-1970s on the urban **economy**. Harassed by **unions** and **students** who demanded an opening of the regime, Diori tried to pressure the French into increasing Niger's **uranium** royalties and was eventually ousted by the **coup d'état of 15 April 1974** mounted by Kountché.

In the first years of his rule, Kountché dismantled the Diori regime, send-ing several of its dignitaries, including the former president, into faraway jails or putting them under strict house arrest, and brutally thwarting plots in the military to remove him; there were two such attempts in 1975 and 1976. Un-popular with the intellectual classes (unions and students) who had agitated against the Diori regime in view of a more democratic outcome, Kountché benefited, however, from the windfall of an increase in uranium revenues allowing him to fund an ambitious "development society" program. This involved creating a series of state-sponsored corporatist bodies intended to organize the "living force" of the country: the **Association des Femmes du Niger** (AFN), the **Association Islamique du Niger** (AIN), and the *samariya* youth organization. He also installed technocratic bodies that were to imple-ment an **agricultural** policy based on the expansion of produce processing and the overhauling of Niger's energy infrastructure.

While in the first few years of his rule the government was staffed by mili-tary personnel, Kountché initiated in the early 1980s a civilianization process, whereby governments came to be dominated by civilians under the leader-ship of a prime minister (necessarily a civilian and implicitly a **Hausa** or a **Tuareg**), although ultimate control rested in the **Conseil Militaire Suprême** (Supreme Military Council) of which he was the head. This process was part and parcel of a broader "normalization" process predicated on the notion that military rule was an *état d'exception* (exceptional circumstance) and Niger must be restored to a *gouvernement républicain* (republican rule). In this view, the regime was considerably reorganized in the 1980s, certain freedoms were cautiously granted (limited freedom of expression, broader freedom of association), and a national charter was written in 1985 and proposed in a **constitutional referendum** in 1986.

Meanwhile, Kountché's grip on power was weakening. In 1982, he had ac-knowledged the failure of his initial development program, which came about as uranium revenues fell while Niger's debt was soaring. This led Kountché to promote austerity measures based on International Monetary Fund ini-tiatives, and discontent focused on the corruption of his entourage and the profiteering ways of some in his family circles (including especially his wife, Mintou Kountché). In 1984, he averted yet another coup d'état attempt, clum-sily engineered by one of his closest friends, a businessman by the name of **Amadou Oumarou** also known as Bonkano. Moreover, he was already suf-fering from the brain cancer which would eventually kill him, though this was kept secret. This did not prevent him from severely repressing a Tuareg attack engineered by **Libya**, which had claims on Niger's northern regions similar to those it was enforcing on Chad's Aouzou strip, and which used **Abdoulaye Hamani Diori**, ousted President Diori's son, to conduct the operation.

Kountché died in a Paris hospital in 1987. His "development society" project was tentatively carried on under his successor, **Ali Saibou**, in the framework of the single party **Mouvement National pour la Société de Développement** (MNSD), but the civilianization and normalization processes he had started pushed Niger further in the direction of **democratization**.

Unpopular with the intellectual classes until his death, Kountché was feared and loved by the popular classes, and his character and sayings have become almost mythical. He is the only Nigerien leader whose taped speeches have become a staple on the market. While many in his entourage had enriched themselves, Kountché died with very few assets to leave to his family. *See also RÉGIME D'EXCEPTION.*

KOY. "Lord" in **Zarma-Songhay**, as in *zarmakoy* (Lord of the Zarma) or in *Irkoy* (God, literally "Our lord").

KOYROBORO. Townspeople, in **Songhay** (with the pronunciation "kwaraboro" in the **Zarma** variant of the **language**). The term is used to designate the Songhay people, especially at **Gao**, opposing them to alien people who are presumably *ganjiboro* (people of the wild). The opposition is not specifically **Zarma-Songhay**. *See also* DOGUWA.

KURFEYAWA. Small, **Hausa**-speaking **ethnic group** that is also known as **Soudié**, in its **Zarma**- or **Songhay**-speaking incarnation. The Kurfeyawa migrated to villages north of **Tahoua**, pushing the resident Kallé farther south. Many of their settlements are at the foot of major geological faults, which serve as protection against attacks by other groups.

KURTEY. Ethnic group usually attached to the **Zarma-Songhay** ensemble. They are the result of intermarriage of **Fulani** with **Songhay** and **Zarma**. As a Fulani subgroup migrating consequent to an internal schism from Macina upstream on the **Niger River**, they came into Niger around 1750 under the leadership of Chief Maliki. Settling first at **Gao**, they later descended down the Niger River to settle on the islands off **Tillabéri** and **Niamey** around 1820. Currently the area is populated by Kurtey and **Wogo**. Excellent pastoralists, they tended the **cattle** of the Songhay, associated with the **Sorko** and **Kado** in the area, and adopted the local **language** and most local customs. However, they also retained some distinctly Fulani traits and customs. Many Kurtey are currently around Niamey, especially from Koutoukalé (a short distance north of Niamey) to **Say** (65 km south of Niamey), where they settled as followers of Alfa **Mamane Diobo**.

In a period prior to the onset of the colonial era, the Kurtey were greatly feared for their nighttime slave-raiding assaults up the Niger River (in pirogues). These at times reached settlements as far away as 500 km and in general ranged from Say to Timbuktu, with those captured slaves not integrated into Kurtey households being sold at Say and Sansanné-Haoussa. Due to this preoccupation with slave raiding, they were often regarded as nothing more than river pirates. Some Kurtey have migrated farther downstream to near Zaria in **Nigeria**. Like the Wogo, they cultivate river rice, **millet**, and tobacco and engage in fishing and cattle herding, a remnant of their Fulani origins. Like the Wogo, considerable numbers go south, to Ghana, to engage in seasonal labor; indeed, at any one time as much as 40 percent of the adult male population of Kurtey villages may be abroad.

L

LAKE CHAD. Large, shallow, freshwater lake on which converge the international boundaries of Chad, Niger, **Nigeria**, and Cameroon. The lake's major source of water is the 1,200-kilometer Chari River, which is augmented in N'Djamena (Chad) by the Logone River, both entirely within Chad. The surface of the lake varies tremendously depending upon climatic conditions. In the past the lake has encompassed as much as 25,000 sq km and as little as 3,500 sq km. During the **Sahel droughts** of 1968–1974, for example, the lake contracted to one third of its normal size, and crossing from Niger to Chad was possible on foot. In 1985 it shrank to barely 3,500 sq km, and none of its surface water even fell within Niger's international boundaries.

In prehistoric times Lake Chad was a vast inland sea stretching into Chad's Tibesti Mountains and was connected with the Nile River system via affluents. At the time the lake's surface covered some 300,000 to 400,000 sq km. Niger's portion of Lake Chad is 3,000 sq km of its northwest segment. The lake's altitude is 280 meters, and the average depth is from 1 to 4 meters, with annual variations of 1 to 3 meters.

LANGUAGES. Niger has a relatively small number of languages, compared to most other sub-Saharan African countries. Ten languages are used in the country, in order of users (French excluded): **Hausa**, **Zarma-Songhay**, **Tamashaq**, Fulfulde, **Kanuri**, **Boudouma**, Gulmancema, **Toubou**, dialectal Arabic, and Tassawaq. Given Niger's rates of school attendance, the prevalence of French in formal schooling and its relative importance in everyday dealings in the major towns, over 5 percent of Nigeriens may be proficient French-speakers (Francophone) and up to 10 percent may have some command of the language—that is, as many as users of Tamashaq and Fulfulde.

Hausa is the native language of 52 percent of Nigeriens, but the language is also widely used in other parts of the country, especially the far east and the north, as well as in **Niamey**, where it is the second language after **Zarma**. In fact, Hausa is so present in the capital that the city may be considered bilingual for all intents and purposes. The importance of Hausa derives both from population and trade. Zarma-Songhay is confined to the western region of the country but is the lingua franca there, used not only by the Zarma (around 20 percent of population) and **Songhay** (4 percent) but also by other ethnicities in western Niger who have their own language (**Fulani**, **Tuareg**, and **Gourmantché**). No other language, beyond Hausa, Zarma-Songhay, and to some extent French, has a similar lingua franca status in the country. Tamashaq is spoken almost exclusively by the Tuareg, Fulfulde by the Fulani, Kanuri by the Kanuri, Boudouma by the Boudouma, Gulmancema by the Gourmantchés, Arabic by the **Arabs**, and Tassawaq by Saharan Songhay tribes whose Songhay dialect creolized with Tamashaq to produce Tassawaq.

As a result, Niger's national culture is dominated by the three principal languages, although only French and Arabic (in the **Franco-Arabe** system) are extensively used in formal **education**. Experimental schools were set up in the 1970s to develop formal schooling in Hausa and Zarma, but that educational sector has not quite taken off. Fulfulde, Hausa, and Tamashaq have historically possessed a writing system, using Arabic characters (*Ajami*) for the two former languages and an original script, called *tifinagh*, in the case of Tamashaq. Both scripts are still in use, though they are taught informally and outside the national education system. The experimental Hausa- and Zarma-language schools use Latin script, customized by the **Institut National de Documentation, de Recherche et d'Animation Pédagogique** (INDRAP). *See also* ETHNIC GROUPS; SONAIKINE.

LAOUALI, OUMAROU (1949–). Better known under his nickname Gago, Laouli is part of the younger crop of **Maradi**'s *Alhazai* (the merchant patriciate of that city). His only formal schooling was Quranic studies in **Zinder** and **Nigeria**, quickly followed up, in traditional Maradian fashion, with an initiation in business. Gago's career is emblematic of the changed conditions in Maradi's and Niger's **economy** in the 1990–2000s. While businessmen in Maradi in the 1970–1980s tended to specialize in import-export trading despite pressures from the state to invest in manufacturing, the crisis of the import-export model which nearly destroyed the economy of Maradi during much of the 1990s led many younger businessmen to move toward manufacturing, and Gago was especially successful in this regard. He purchased most of the disused state manufacturing infrastructure of the region of Maradi and turned them into profitable ventures. Thus, Gago bought the old **groundnut oil** producing plant of former **Société Industrielle et Commerciale du Niger** (SICONIGER), which now produces the OLGA (Oumarou Laouali Gago) oil products. He also turned, in 1996, an old mattress-making state enterprise into the booming Entreprise Nigérienne de Production de Mousses (ENIPROM), which produces mattresses and bedroom and living room furniture sold throughout Niger, where ENIPROM has become a household name. Together with Sani Souley Koukou, another Maradi businessman, he also bought the state brick-making company and turned it into Briquèterie de Maradi (BRIMA), which thrives on Maradi's 2000 building boom. Gago's enterprises and businesses make him the first Nigerien private employer in the region of Maradi and perhaps in Niger as a whole.

LAYA, DIOULDE (1937–). Sociologist and former director of the **Institut National de Recherches en Sciences Humaines**. Born in 1937 at Tamou (**Say**) and educated in Say, Kollo, and Bamako (Mali), Laya continued his higher studies in Senegal, at Dakar (1957–1962 and 1967) in sociology. Between 1962 and 1970 secretary-general of the Nigerien Commission of the United Nations Educational, Scientific and Cultural Organization (in the Ministry of **Education** in **Niamey**), he was appointed director of the Centre National de Recherches en Sciences Humaines in 1970. He has published a number of works on African oral traditions. He now lives in retirement, though remaining a fixture of Niamey's scholarly life.

LETE ISLAND DISPUTE. *See* BENIN–NIGER BOUNDARY DISPUTE.

LIBYA. Niger's relations with Libya have been chiefly shaped by the policies of Libya's longtime head of state, Colonel Muammar Khadafi (in power since his coup of 1969 and until his fall in August 2011). Kadhafi's rather garbled expansionist policy was at first based on an assortment of pan-Islamic and pan-Arab ideology interlaced with a socialist orientation; starting in the late 1990s, it became based on a pan-African ideal that expressed Kadhafi's disappointment with the **Arab**-Islamic world. During the first period, Kadhafi sought at the same time to transform Niger into a client state of Libya and also to annex a good chunk (30,000 sq km) of the country's northeastern region which borders Libya and which was supposedly ceded to Italy (Libya's former colonial overlord) by **France** (Niger's former colonial overlord).

Initial relations of Kadhafian Libya with Niger were good: President **Hamani Diori** accepted Kadhafi's patronage when the latter encouraged the spread of Arab-**Islamic** culture in Niger by funding the establishment of a **Franco-Arabe** secondary school in **Niamey**, paying also for teaching personnel and material, and by opening a cultural center in Niger's capital. Diori also signed a mutual-defense agreement with Libya in 1974. Diori's ouster, President **Seyni Kountché**, accepted Kadhafi's gift of the imposing and elegant North African–style Grand Mosque of Niamey. But relationships started to sour when Kountché rejected Kadhafi's claims on Nigerien territory and generally grew hostile to Libya's influence in the country. Kadhafi immediately attempted to destabilize or remove Kountché, playing on budding **Tuareg** resentments to partly fund one of the first coup attempts of the *régime d'exception*. By the early 1980s, Niger–Libya hostility was full blown and the Kountché government started to define Nigerien nationalism in public speech in opposition to the activities of the "*impérateur* Kadhafi" (*impérateur* being a French-language neologism coined by Nigerien propagandists to mean pretty much the same thing as *impérialiste*, i.e., imperialist, but with even more lugubrious undertones). Meanwhile, Kadhafi started to recruit Nigerien and Malian Tuaregs in his Islamic Legion, a paramilitary force set up in 1972 to serve as a tool in his grandiose plans for a United States of the **Sahel**.

The Islamic Legion had thus far served to assist Arab cultural supremacists in Chad and Sudan but became a training ground for Niger's future Tuareg rebels, whose dreams of a Tuareg state of the Sahara Kadhafi lavishly fanned. In May 1985, an armed Tuareg band led by **Abdoulaye Hamani Diori**, a son of former President Hamani Diori, crossed into Niger and attacked military installations in the craggy and arid area of **Tchintabaraden**, triggering military reprisals against northern Tuareg communities and reinforcing the nascent anti-Tuareg outlook of the Nigerien army. Despite the failure of the attack, Kadhafi continued to develop a patron–client relationship with leaders of Tuareg communities in Niger and was subsequently accused by the government of Niger of funding and arming Saharan rebel fronts in the early 1990s.

However, the death of Kountché and the transformation of Niger's political regime, combined with Kadhafi's growing disappointment with the Arab-Islamic world, gradually changed Niger–Libya relations. Niger's new democratic politicians started to travel to Tripoli (Libya's capital), seeking Kadhafi's largesse and patronage. In 1998, Kadhafi stepped up his policy of political patronage directed at sub-Saharan countries—after six years of a Western-imposed embargo during which he did not receive any of the expected support from Arab countries—and created the Community of Sahel-Saharan Countries (CEN-SAD), of which Niger became a founding member. Niger was at the time ruled by coup-maker **Ibrahim Baré Maïnassara** who was spurned by Western countries for his refusal to restore democratic governance in the country. Together with the president of Chad, he violated the embargo on air travel to Libya to visit Kadhafi in July 1998 and later received a visit from Kadhafi in Niamey. Baré Maïnassara's also opened Niger to Libyan investments, with notably the establishment of a bank formally tied to the CEN-SAD, the Banque Sahélo-Saharienne pour l'Investissement et le Commerce (BSIC).

The assassination of Baré Maïnassara (April 1999) was loudly deplored by Kadhafi, and indeed, the new Nigerien governments reinstated some of the wariness that the state of Niger traditionally showed to Libya since the

Kountché era. Henceforth, Libyan investments and influence in Niger grew weakly, in contrast with what obtained for instance in the two other Lybian sub-Saharan playgrounds, Mali and Burkina Faso. Yet, in most of the 2000 decade, Niger's relations with Libya were quite good, with the state of Niger authorizing the Libyan ruler to regain influence in the country, especially with the Tuareg—now seemingly peaceful—and the Sufi groups, chiefly the **Niassites** at **Kiota**. The latter received much support in the organization of their grand annual festival, the Maoulid (birthday of the Prophet Muhammad) as well as in the development of Franco-Arabe **education** at Kiota, and Kadhafi took the habit of celebrating the Maoulid at **Agadez**. Moreover, Kadhafi managed to get the state of Niger to inscribe the Islamic New Year in the country's calendar of celebrations—another Sufi symbolism. In this way, Kadhafi powerfully helped Niger's "moderate" **Islam**—generally propounded by the Sufi—to withstand the inroads of Sunni fundamentalism, which had thus far been the only Islamic current to benefit from foreign sponsorship (Saudi Arabia). Lastly, through CEN-SAD mechanisms, Libya became one of the beacons of Nigerien economic migrations, practically on par with the older subregional destinations of the Gulf of Guinea.

However, in the late 2000s, the two countries' relations again became complicated and took some rather negative turns. When in January 2007 a new **Tuareg rebellion** broke out in Niger's north, the Nigerien government quickly claimed that Libya was behind it, and with good reasons. In April 2007, at the height of the crisis, Kadhafi was solemnly proclaimed "leader of the Tuareg sultans" and the commandment drum of the Tuareg clans was transferred to Tripoli. A few months later, Niger expelled a Libyan diplomat who was allegedly caught relaying Kadhafi's financial support to the rebels of the **Mouvement des Nigériens pour la Justice** (MNJ). Despite Kadhafi's official protestations, his role in the release of 25 MNJ hostages in March 2008 appeared to prove that he was indeed pulling many of the strings in the rebellion. In 2009, a rapprochement occurred between Niger's president, **Mamadou Tandja**, and Kadhafi, as the Nigerien ruler looked for allies in order to bear the international and regional isolation into which his constitutional coup of the **Tazartché** was landing him. This led Kadhafi to broker a peace agreement between key MNJ leaders and the Nigerien government in 2009.

Tandja was, however, removed in February 2010 by the **armed forces**, which had some scores to settle with former rebel leaders. Thus, the **Conseil Supérieur pour la Restauration de la Démocratie** (CSRD) ordered the arrest of **Rhissa ag Boula**, an exiled rebel leader who had murdered a man in cold blood in 2004 and who had unwisely returned to Niger, expecting to be left free. To force the Nigerien government to release ag Boula, Kadhafi arrested a group of Nigerien immigrants in Libya under trumped-up charges, threatening the CSRD of having them executed. When the CSRD ignored this, Kadhafi effectively had three Nigeriens executed at Tripoli, prompting transitional president **Djibo Salou** to travel to Libya where he negotiated the freeing of the remaining Nigerien hostages of Kadhafi in exchange for the extra-legal release of ag Boula. Ag Boula then fled to Tripoli, leaving the Nigerien public embittered about Libya.

This recent chain of events explains very much why Nigeriens did not show support, either formal or spontaneous, to Kadhafi when France, Great Britain, and the North Atlantic Treaty Organization (NATO) attacked him in 2011. The conflict, however, led to over 200,000 Nigeriens fleeing Libya in very difficult conditions, while many were killed by Libyan insurgents (or otherwise) who accused them of fighting for Kadhafi, but also following a Libyan tradition or practice of anti-black violence. When the anti-Kadhafi, NATO-supported Libyan insurgents finally seized Tripoli in August 2011, the Nigerien government promptly recognized their executive organ, the National Council of Transition (NCT), as Libya's government. When subsequently high-profile members of the Kadhafi regime—including one of the sons of the deposed ruler—crossed into Niger, fleeing the NCT's grasp, the Nigerien government faced a diplomatic conundrum (unlike Algeria, which also received members of Kadhafi's family at the time when its government did not recognize the NCT) but resolved not to extradite the fugitives. *See also* COUP OF 15 MARCH 1976; MUSSOLINI-LAVAL BOUNDARY AGREEMENT.

LITERATURE. Though there existed in the regions that were to become the Republic of Niger a variety of scripts—*ajami*, or Arabic script, used to write in local **languages**, especially **Fulani** and **Hausa**, and the **Tuareg** script *tifinagh*—there was no written literature in Niger before the colonial period. Writing was essentially for the purposes of historical records and **religion** and did not develop an expressive art form with a range of specific genres. On the other hand, the rich oral literature expressed itself in a variety of genres, among which may be mentioned a wealth of tales and legends, proverb making (especially developed among the **Zarma-Songhay** where it is called *ya-say*), poetry (especially developed among the Tuareg and the Fulani), satirical and lyrical songs, theatrical plays (in the Hausa tradition of the Wasan Kara especially), and epic stories. This latter genre is particularly popular among the **Zarma**-Songhay and has produced the most popular Nigerien literary artist in any Nigerien vernacular (in this instance, the Zarma language), **Djado Sékou**. The social structures which used to support the production of oral literature have, however, been considerably corroded by modern lifestyles and **Islam**, and Nigerien oral literature is apparently a declining tradition.

Contemporary Nigerien literary artists now overwhelmingly use the Latin script and French language to produce works that follow the genres of Western literature: novels, poetry, short stories, plays, and essays. Literacy **education** in the Hausa and Zarma languages has led to the emergence of an as-yet very little known but growing body of literature using the Latin script to produce works in those vernaculars. But Niger's dominant literary tradition is today Francophone, even though it developed significantly later than that of other Francophone countries (with perhaps the exception of Burkina Faso and Togo). The first Nigerien literary works were a product of the culture of the celebrated colonial school **École William Ponty**, at which playwriting and acting was a favored form of entertainment as early as the 1930s. In the 1940s and 1950s, many alumni of William Ponty produced in **Niamey**, **Zinder,** and other Nigerien towns plays that generally satirize the lifestyle of the new class of modern-educated Nigeriens or sometimes the abuses of the colonial system: *Les Invités du Bar Welcome* of **Mahamane Dandobi** negatively portrayed the advent of modernity in Niger in the guise of alcoholism and a mindless pursuit of pleasure; Marcel Inné put on the stage the theme (which would later be recurrent in Nigerien literature) of exodus in *Partir et Souvenir*, while Yacouba Djibo, in *Le Marché noir*, described the hardship of life in the new cities. These works were, however, chiefly hobbyist dabbling for people who did not see themselves as writers or even literary artists.

Most literary works produced about Niger through the colonial period were put out by French writers. French Nigerien literature—literary works written by Frenchmen about Niger or using Niger as a setting—curiously appeared very early and the field is surprisingly crowded. There are thus glimpses of future Niger in Jules Verne's *Cinq semaines en ballon* (1863, 2 chapters out of 44) and in Henri de Noville's *Trésor de Ménandre* (1902), and in the course of the first half of the 20th century, the territory and Colony of Niger were the setting of a spate of colonial fiction, many belonging to the boyish genre of the adventure novel. Yet this literature is not strictly colonial as it outlasted the colonial period. It started with *Ma Femme au Niger* (1919), by Edouard de Meringo, a cheerless tale of infidelity and other sexual improprieties in the small colonial society at **Tahoua** and other places. In 1926, the governor of **Afrique Occidentale Française** (AOF), Maurice Délafosse, penned under the pseudonym Louis Faivre a stylishly written romantic story, *Toum* (1926), smartly delving into the complexities of a relationship between a French colonial administrator and a Nigerien girl from **Tessaoua**. Christian Chéry's *La Grande Fauve* (1955) took up a similar theme but made of it a tale of jealousy and blood, as his French hero—a petty civil servant—is driven to murder a businessman for the sake of a Nigerien girl, in a drama that develops between Zinder and **Diffa**. Stéphane Desombre's *L'Atlantide* *du Nord* (1974), set in 1947, is also a story of love and passion involving three protagonists, a Frenchman, a beautiful Fulani Nigerien woman, and a beautiful Swedish woman. The romance ends, however, not in screams and murder but more trivially, in dampening meningitis. More recently, development agronomist Guy Belloncle published *L'Hivernage* (1980), a novel serving chiefly to propound his theses on Sahelian **agriculture**, and Michel Claux tells, in *Ton Blanc arrive avec le courier* (1991), the quasi-autobiographical story of a French cooperation agent and of his thwarted love affair with a Nigerien woman, set in 1967, in an unnamed Nigerien region. The Voulet and Chanoine theme (the **Mission Afrique Centrale-Tchad**) also inspired several French writers, including a short story (*La Marche vers le soleil*) published by Jean d'Esme in a short stories collection, *Sable de feu* (1949), and as early as 1905 (only six years after the events) a play by François de Curel, *Le Coup d'aile*.

The first Francophone Nigerien self-contained literary work, the novel *Grandes eaux noires* by **Ibrahim Issa** (1929–1986), appeared only in 1959, some 23 years after the publication of the first Senegalese or Beninese Francophone novels for instance. This lateness means that the Nigerien novel did not follow the great literary arc of precolonial nostalgia, anticolonial struggle, and the denunciation of postcolonial authoritarianism and despotism which are symptomatic of most modern African literatures. Instead, the Nigerien novel developed its own very peculiar themes, dominated by the idiosyncratic relationships that authors developed with national identity, Nigerien society, and history and even, in the case of the towering **Boubou Hama** (1906–1982), universal philosophy.

Thus, while early Nigerien literature reflected the expected confrontation of Africans with colonial domination, this was generally in ways which put little emphasis on anger and revolt but rather stress common human problems and aspirations. *Grandes eaux noires* (1959, reissued in 2010) is symptomatic of that attitude. The novel does concentrate on the historical relationships between whites (Europeans) and blacks (Africans), but Issa rejects both the idealization of precolonial Africa found in many other near-contemporary African novels, and the then-rampant negative European perceptions of Africans. In fact, *Grandes eaux noires* is ill-described by the term "novel" and is rather a mix of fiction and of a lyrical and philosophic essay whose major theme is the unicity of humankind and the history of Africa. Its first publisher called it a "*chant du passé de l'Afrique*" (a song of Africa's past), an awkward yet telling designation which would also apply well to most of the novelistic writings of Boubou Hama, the writer whose prolific production dominates Nigerien literature in the 1960s. Hama transmuted both his personal experience and the historical evolution of Africa in relation to world history into vast philosophic reflections, in works which mix lyrical narratives to ethnographic descriptions and complex sagas often inspired by the **Songhay** pantheon, of which he was one of the best experts. Hama was also a dignitary of the ruling **Parti Progressiste Nigérien** (PPN-RDA), of which his younger fellow-writer, **Abdoulaye Mamani** (1932–1993) was a junior member, before joining the **Sawaba** opposition party, outlawed by the PPN government in 1959. Mamani left Niger and edited Sawaba's journal in exile, in Ghana, Mali, Algeria, and Egypt. He published his first literary works, *Poémérides* (1972) and *Le Balai* (1973), during his stay at Algiers, where he worked for an Algerien state cultural agency. He returned to Niger after the fall of the **First Republic** (1974) and worked on his masterpiece, the historical novel *Sarraounia*, published in 1980.

Internal political divisions have clearly contributed to preventing Nigerien writers to create literary and intellectual movements, but many among them instead concentrated on the very description of political ills, either in an openly propagandistic way, such as **Ousmane Amadou** (1948–) or with subtler touches such as **Idé Oumarou** (1937–2002). Others chose to be completely apolitical and to follow the Hama lead of composing lyrical-philosophical narratives inspired by old Nigerien lore. **Bania Mahamadou Say** (1935–2004) and **Abdourahamane Mariko Kélétigui** (1921–1997) were the greatest representatives of this trend, and so are minor authors such as Boubé Zoumé (1951–), Issa Albert (1943–), and Oumarou Kadry Koda (1973–), the latter specializing in writing for children.

Whatever the case, all Nigerien literary production seems to be primarily shaped by relationship to the land and the country's history. Amadou's *Quinze ans ça suffit!* denounced the **Hamani Diori** regime and extolled the military saviors, but the novel was also very much about **drought** and hunger in this most **Sahelian** country. In his *Aboki ou l'appel de la côte* (1978), Mahamadou Halilou expressed the ingrained love of migrant Nigeriens for the miserable and parched country that they have left behind. Mamani's *Sarraounia* transformed the Voulet and Chanoine theme into a **Sarraounia** theme, that is, revisited the same historical story which also transfixed Niger's French writers, but this time from a Nigerien rather than a French perspective.

In recent times, three authors distinguish themselves for the originality, quality, and quantity of their production: the historian and novelist **André Salifou** (1942–), the poet and playwright **Alfred Dogbé** (1962–), and the poet **Hawad** (1950–), the latter being, however, based in **France** and barely belonging to Nigerien literature.

Remarkably, Francophone Nigerien literature is entirely devoid of noted female writers.

LOGA. *Département* of 134,000 people in the region of **Dosso**, and a town of 28,400, which is the headquarters of the *département*. In the 1980s, Loga was famous for high drug abuse (in the Nigerien context) and was famously disparaged as "Niger's Jamaica" by President **Seyni Kountché**.

LOI-CADRE DEFERRE. The "Framework Act," thus called because it provided an open framework in which the government was enabled to legislate by decree, it was passed by the French national assembly in June 1956 on the initiative of Gaston Deferre (minister of the colonies and overseas territories) and Ivorian deputy Félix Houphouët-Boigny. The law created in the overseas territories (most colonies, including Niger, having become such in 1946) government councils elected through universal suffrage, thereby formally reinforcing the internal autonomy of **France**'s possessions. Although the electoral system was still unfavorable to native populations, the double electoral college (one for Europeans and the assimilated minority, the other for African masses) was replaced by a single one. A major consequence of the Loi-Cadre was to break the federal coherence of **Afrique Occidentale Française**, thereby paving the road to independence of each colony as a single nation-state instead of a unit in a federal West African state. Moreover, while the president of the council—chief of the internal executive branch—was a local elected official the governor of each territory remained an appointed representative of the French government with extensive control over **currency**, economic and financial policy, schools' curricula, radio broadcast, police, and defense forces. He was also empowered to annul the outcome of deliberations in the Council of Government as he saw fit.

LOUGOU. An **Arna** village in the **Dallol Maouri**, Lougou is generally considered the oldest extant human settlement in the **Arewa**. Lougou traces its origins back to the kingdom of Daura (the original **Hausa** kingdom) when one only daughter of a deceased king, frustrated by the succession by her uncles, fled to the area and established a queenship—a kingdom in which only **women** could rule. The monarch's title is *sarrouania*, the feminine of *sarki* (king in Hausa). The Lougou settlement is the nucleus of the Gubawa (or Goubé as they are called in the **Zarma**-speaking areas west of Lougou), the people found there as native of the place by the subsequent waves of Hausa- and Zarma-speaking populations who came in the region after the 14th century. Power in Lougou is rooted in spiritual forces, notably symbolized by the Tunguma, the rock of justice, and many resilient pre-Islamic practices. The traditions of Lougou state that 14 queens have ruled before the current ruler of the village, *Sarraounia* Aldjima Gado. Of these, the most renowned is **Sarraounia Mangou**, who bravely opposed the infamous Voulet and Chanoine colonial expedition in April–June 1899. *See also* MISSION AFRIQUE CENTRALE-TCHAD.

LOULAMI. Capital of the **Dendi** branch of the **Songhay Empire** following its collapse to Moroccan power in the **battle of Tondibi**. Long since disappeared, Loulami was probably in the vicinity of the contemporary **Say**.

M

MADAOUA. *Département* of 319,374 people, mostly **Gobir Hausa**, with minorities of **Tuareg** and **Fulani**. It is part of the region of **Tahoua** and its headquarters are in a town of the same name. The town itself, 510 km to the east of Niamey, has a population of 30,000, though it forms, with the 79 administrative villages and *tribus* and the 27 hamlets and *campements* taken in its communal territory, a decentralized agglomeration of 102,277 people. It is an important regional center in Niger's **cotton** and **onion** belt, with a big Sunday market famous for offering the best specimen of *kilishi*, the Hausa sheet of dried and baked meat. Madaoua is also a major center of traditional wrestling sports.

MAGAJIYA **(also Magagia).** High priestess of **Bori** and leader of the free **women** (now considered as prostitutes) who run the cult. The *magajiya* (also **inna**, *iya*, or *magaram*, depending on the place) regulates all conflicts that arise between initiates. During Bori ceremonies she is aided in her duties by the *sarkin Bori*, who are usually men and collect taxes from each initiate, organize the ceremonies and Bori life in their communities, and in general serve as the regional administrators of the cult. The *magajiya* is a very powerful figure, chosen for her intelligence, leadership qualities, and strong personality; because of her role in those regions where the ritual is widespread, her political support is usually greatly sought after. In **Niamey** the *magajiya* played a major role during the Second World War and at the time of the 1958 referendum when she opted for the **Parti Progressiste Nigérien** (PPN-RDA) party and delivered it a strong vote. Indeed, since then the chief *magajiya* (of Niamey), who presides over the other *magajiyas* of the various town quarters, has been a member of the PPN politburo. Moreover, it was the *magajiyas* of Niamey who created, in 1956, the Association des Femmes and in 1958 the Association de Jeunes Filles du Niger and the **Union des Femmes du Niger**. *Magajiya* is a **Hausa** term that is also used by the **Songhay**; other titles exist in non-Hausa areas.

MAGARIA. Town of some 19,421 people that is 92 km west of **Zinder**, headquarters of the *département* of the same name, in the region of Zinder. In the immediate pre-independence era a bastion of the **Sawaba** party, Magaria was founded by Massabaki, a prince of Daura Zongo (one of the original **Hausa** states) and eventually fell under the sway of **Damagaram**. The area used to produce between 36 percent (in 1958) and 51 percent (1968) of Niger's **groundnut** crop.

MAIGA. A name found extensively among **Songhay** nobility, denoting descent from the **Askia Mohammed**, similar to *Sharif* (descendants of the Prophet Muhammad's family) for Muslims, for instance. They are also known as *Maamar Hamey* (the offspring of Maamar, Maamar being the vernacular name of Askia Mohammed). *See also* SONYANKÉS.

MAIGA, DIAMBALA YANSAMBOU (1910–1976). Diambala was a post office official and a financial agent who served throughout the colony of Niger in 1929–1957, working successively in **Niamey**, **Bilma**, **Agadez**, **Maradi**, **Zinder**, and back to Niamey. He was a founding member of the **Parti Progressiste Nigérien** (PPN-RDA) and was elected PPN territorial councilor for **Tillabéri** in 1957. In 1958, he was appointed interior minister and held that position through independence and until the PPN-RDA regime was toppled in 1974. He thus appeared as the third man in the triumvirate formed with President **Hamani Diori** and **National Assembly** president **Hama Boubou**. As interior minister, he was in particular in charge of the repressive tasks of the Diori era, which included a fair amount of torture and a number of effective death penalties—something (executions) practiced in Niger only in that period. He died in Niamey in 1976.

MAIGA, DJINGARAYE (1939–). Born in Mali at Ouatagana, a small town at the border with Niger where Maiga grew up and settled. He is the last still-active representative of Niger's great era of **cinema** production of the 1970s. He started off with a documentary short film portraying the passion of a boy for ball playing (*Le Ballon*, 1972), a film very different from the vision of dark social critic that he developed later. All of Maiga's movie titles comprise the adjective *noir* (black, as in bleak and depressing) in them: *Etoile noire* (1975), *Nuages noirs* (1979), *Aube noire* (1983), *Vendredi noir* (2000), and *Quatrième nuit noire* (2008). The most famous of these is *Nuages noirs*, a complex opus which deals with the difficulties of intercultural marriage (the Muslim **Sahelian** man from Niger marrying a coastal Christian girl while a **student** in Dahomey, and returning with her to **Niamey**), political corruption, and social injustice to **women** (the young Nigerien man divorcing his coastal wife under family pressure and marrying a Nigerien girl whom he repudiates the next day because she is not a virgin, leading to the latter's social destruction). In between these, Maiga produced a number of astonishingly cheerful documentaries, closer to his inspiration in *Le Ballon*.

MAIGA, YOUSSOUFA (General) (1943–). Born in 1943 at Laatakabiyé, in the vicinity of **Téra**, Maiga was educated at **Niamey**'s Roman Catholic mission school, at the Roman Catholic Collège de Lassalle of Ouagadougou (Burkina Faso), and at Niamey's Lycée National high school. He then took up military training, first in a French-linked military high school in Germany (Lycée Maréchal Ney of Sarrebruck), then in gendarmerie training centers in Niamey and Maisons-Alfort (**France**), followed up by various training and educational periods, including in military command (Maisons-Alfort) and criminology (University of Paris–Assas). Maiga started his career in the gendarmerie in November 1964 and served as commander of gendarmerie headquarters throughout the territory in the period 1967–1977, briefly holding the office of director of the national police from June 1974 to July 1975. In 1980, he was appointed *préfet* of **Tahoua**, remaining in that post for a year before entering the cabinet as minister of national **education** (1981–1982).

As the ***régime d'exception*** started its civilianization process, Maiga was removed from the cabinet and sent back to his paramilitary fold, at the second-to-highest office of the gendarmerie (chief of the national gendarmerie). In 1984, he started a diplomatic career, first as defense attaché of Niger's embassy in the United States and then as ambassador to Germany, where he was residing when Niger adopted a democratic regime (1991). He returned home the following year to head the highly sensitive general inspectorate of the **armed forces** and was for a while very close to President **Mahaman Ousmane** as his personal chief of defense staff (1994–1995). At that point, Maiga had become one of the bigwigs of Niger's military. Appointed high commander of the national gendarmerie, the highest office of the corps, in March 1995, he remained in that post beyond the **coup d'état of January 1996**, and indeed was chosen by the coup-maker Colonel **Ibrahim Baré Maïnassara** as vice-president of the **Conseil de Salut National** (CSN), the provisional executive military organ that was set up to head the state prior to the institution of the **Fourth Republic**. After the CSN was dissolved, Maiga took up the ambassadorship to Algeria. Retired a few years later, Maiga was appointed in 2011 governor of the region of **Tillabéri**.

MAI-GARI. Hausa for village chief, with *gari* meaning village or town and *mai* being a prefix for owner.

MAINÉ-SOROA. *Département* in the region of **Diffa**, which encompasses a population of 136,000 and includes the *arrondissement* of Goudoumaria. The small town of Mainé-Soroa, which is the headquarters of the *département*, has a population of 10,000.

MALAM YARO (1852 ?–1921). Important long-distance merchant. Born to a family that traced its origins from Egypt but was established in **Damaga-ram** for two generations, Malam Yaro—whose actual name was Moussa ben Abdoulahhi, and whose father was a religious scholar from the **Kanuri** town of Kulumfardo—grew up in **Zinder** and **Agadez** and established a vast commercial network stretching from **Bornu** to Tripoli on the coast. With strong family ties with the **Tuareg** (having married a woman of the Kel Tafidet drum group) that facilitated his trade, Malam Yaro became a prime supplier of goods to the French forces in Niger as well. Malam Yaro seems to have seen himself mostly as an **Arab** man, nurturing blatantly racist opinions on the inhabitants of Damagaram (including the sultans) and basing his commercial empire on slave labor, both in trade and in farming.

Using his family scholarly pedigree (**Islam**) and his great practical intelligence and sense for opportunities, Malam Yaro became an important personality in the Damagaram court, a trusted advisor to the sultan, and was very favorably regarded by the French until 1906. Indeed, they had earlier considered elevating him to the throne, an idea that he firmly turned down. (This was out of gratitude for his assistance to the ill-fated **Mission du Haut-Soudan** of Captain **Marius-Gabriel Cazemajou**.) In 1906 he was discovered to have taken part in Sultan **Amadou dan Bassa**'s conspiracy against the French. Malam Yaro seems to have believed that the swelling tide of Islam-based insurgency that spawned **rebellions** throughout the region against the French and the British in 1905–1906 would drive out the Europeans, and he decided to side with the camp he thought would be winning. He was punished for this miscalculation and exiled to Côte d'Ivoire.

The French, however, found his influence useful and did not consider him really dangerous, so they returned him to Zinder in 1909. At that time, they were trying to salvage Zinder's trade with North Africa, so as to dodge the pull of British **Nigeria**, which was gradually replacing North Africa as southern Niger's commercial magnet. In fact, the world which saw the rise of Malam Yaro's commercial empire was doomed: Not only was the trans-Saharan trade increasingly a thing of the past, but much of Malam Yaro's economic strength was based on the exploitation of slave labor, which French overrule had expunged. Upon his return to Niger after three years' exile, he tried rebuilding his business but it received two fatal blows: the 1912 arrival of the railroad to Kano, which killed off the trans-Saharan trade, and the devastating Kakalaba famine of 1914, during which many of his creditors fled or died. An impoverished Malam Yaro turned to peddling amulets and other such magical trinkets to **women** and children, and died penniless in 1921. Some of his children, however, later rebuilt the family's wealth in Niger and Nigeria.

MALAMA HOUDA. The Egyptian-born wife of a Nigerien cadre of the **Franco-Arabe** educational system, Malama Houda is a powerful religious conservative voice in contemporary Niger, thanks to her televised **Hausa**-language preaching, based on her native command of Arabic and Islamic texts. Her doctrinal tenets are rigidly orthodox and literalist, and they are re-markably supportive of masculine power, as Malama Houda vocally defends early marriage, wife beating, and female genital mutilation. These views are, however, shaped and colored by a deep-seated resentment against the Western agenda for Muslim countries, and make of Malama Houda a typical representative of reactive Islamism in Niger. *See also* ISLAM; WOMEN.

MALAMA ZAHARAOU. Daughter of **Cheik Boubacar Hassoumi** and **Saida Oumoul Khairy Niass** of **Kiota**, educated at the **Islamic University of Say** (theology), the **University of Niamey** (sociology), and the University of Khartoum in Sudan, Malama Zaharaou represents the Sufi **Tijaniyya** voice in feminine preaching in Niger. She advocates **women**'s advancement through the development of self-help groupings based on religious sociability and openness to Western modernity adjusted to local circumstances. As such, Malam Zaharaou was co-opted in 2006 as a member of the state-sponsored Haut Conseil Islamique (HCI), which is supposed to promote a "Nigerien Islam"—that is, one that is immune to perceived **Arab** extremism.

MALBAZA, CIMENTERIE DE. *See* SOCIÉTÉ NIGÉRIENNE DE CI-MENTERIE.

MALI YARO. *See* BOUREIMA, DOULAYE.

MALLAM YOUNOUS (1688?–1746). The founder of the state (later sul-tanate) of **Damagaram** in the early 18th century. Born around the end of the 17th century, Mallam Younous studied under his father, a cleric named Maina Kadey, in the latter's center of Belbelec. He acquired local fame for his piety, miracles, and saintly demeanor and was made chief of the Gueza village in 1736. His lineage expanded the original dominions into the power-ful Damagaram kingdom.

MAMANI, ABDOULAYE (1932–1993). Poet and writer born at Goudou-maria, in far eastern Niger, Mamani is most famous for his historical novel

314 • MAMIDOU, SEYDOU

Sarraounia, which tells the story of the clash, at **Lougou**, between the French colonial forces led by Voulet and Chanoine and **Sarraounia Mangou**. The novel, based on extensive oral and archival research, was adapted into a 1986 film by Mauritanian director Med Hondo (the film was also called *Sarraounia*). Mamani died in a car crash while traveling to **Niamey** to receive the Prix **Boubou Hama**, which was awarded him that year. He was also the author of a number of poetry books (*Poémérides*, *Eboniques*), a stage play (*Le Balai*, 1972), and a collection of short stories (*Paris-Dakar et autres nouvelles*, 1987). Mamani's early work was published in exile in Algeria, where he was living as a **Sawaba** partisan. Upon his return in Niger in 1974 following the fall of the **First Republic**, he was jailed in 1976 by President **Seyni Kountché**, who had grown suspicious of all political activists during the unstable first three years of his rule. It was during his time in jail that he conceived the *Sarraounia* project and also met fellow writer and political activist **Ibrahim Issa**. In the later period of his life, Mamani was busy setting up a museum in **Zinder**, a project that has been stopped by his premature death.

MAMIDOU, SEYDOU (1962–2002). Better known as Dinozor (from *dinosaure*, French for dinosaur) and Dargné, Mamidou's flamboyant and famously extended scores, based on **Zarma-Songhay Holley** (animist) ritual music, dominated the *maquis* (Ivorian-style music bars) scene in **Niamey** in the 1990s. An extravagant lifestyle of sex and booze is most likely the cause of his premature death in 2002, but a legend developed around the event, claiming that Dargné was killed (spiritually eaten) by an elderly **Dosso** woman, Woybor Zeno (Old Woman, in **Zarma**), who prominently figures in his most well-known number as a powerful sorceress. Dargné's band, Toubal, is still intermittently active. *See also* DANCE AND MUSIC.

MANGA. Region in Niger and name of **ethnic group**. The Manga are a small **Kanuri**-speaking group residing east of **Zinder**, north of **Gouré** between the **Komadougou Yobé** River and the Mounio. Their origin is not known. Though regarding themselves as distinct from the Kanuri (whom they view as strangers), the Manga are quite probably of Kanuri extraction, and their territory was all along a province of the **Kanem-Bornu Empire**, and known as Mangari. The Manga never created any states in their territory, and in 1855, exploiting Bornu's decline and the **Fulani** pressures, Sultan **Tanimoun** of **Damagaram** annexed the entire area to his own kingdom. The area is astride the Niger–Chad border and is a series of plateaus without much vegetation. It is also inhabited by the **Daza Toubou** and the Hassaouna **Arabs**.

MAOURI. Ethnic group found in the **Dallol Maouri** valley, also known as **Arawa** in **Hausa**. There are various legends as to their origins. One refers to the derivation of this Hausa-speaking group from a temporary Bornuan dynasty in the valley following which the **Arewa** chiefdom was established as Kaosa (30 km southeast of **Dogondoutchi**) under nominal Gobirawa suzerainty. A highly localized ethnic group (with its core in the Dogondoutchi area), the Maouri can be differentiated into two groups: the Arawa and the Gubawa (Goubé in the **Zarma**-speaking areas). The former have the strongest links with Bornu, arriving late and conquering the Gubawa and dividing power between the political head—the *sarkin* Arewa, of their own group—and the *sarraounia* head, the ritual queen of **Lougou** and of the Gubawa.

The term *Maouri* is mostly used by the Zarma and **Fulani** to refer to the Dogondoutchi region and population. More specifically, the Maouri are those Arawa who settled among the Zarma west of Dogondoutchi, becoming a Zarma-speaking population.

MARADI. Region encompassing 38,500 sq km and a population of 2,236,000 people with an average density of 53.5 per sq km, the highest by far in Niger. This represents 20 percent of the population of Niger, the biggest proportion of all the seven regions of the country. The city of Maradi, which hosts the regional council, is a *communauté urbaine* of about 148,000 people, the third-largest urban settlement in the country. The region includes the *départements* of **Aguié**, **Dakoro**, **Guidan Roumdji**, Madarounfa, **Mayahi**, and **Tessaoua**. These are subdivided into 33 *arrondissements*, and 112 urban and rural **communes**. The region has also two sultanates, the **Katsina** (seated at Maradi) and the **Gobir** (seated at **Tibiri**, 5 km away from Maradi). The population is in majority Katsina and Gobir **Hausa** (nearly two millions), followed by **Fulani** (185,300) and **Tuareg** (70,000) with a smattering of outsiders.

Centrally located, the city of Maradi is 670 km east of **Niamey**, 250 km west of **Zinder**, and 250 km north of Kano in **Nigeria**, with which it is tightly connected for economic reasons. Much of the original town was badly damaged by the major floods that struck this region in 1945 and the current settlement was moved up on a plateau, along the main thoroughfare which is a section of the **Route de l'Unité** running in from Niamey and out to Zinder, and branching off southward to the Nigerian border. The western side of the thoroughfare comprises the early resettlements of Limantchi (the clerical quarter) and Maradawa (the political quarter) where can be found the central mosque and the palace of the sultan of Katsina-Maradi. The eastern side comprises the newer neighborhoods and the local airport.

Before 1998, Maradi was a *département* which had been subject to much administrative reorganization during the colonial and postcolonial period and was finally reconstituted in 1963, after being temporarily disbanded in 1960. Previously suppressed as an individual region in 1926, it was reconstituted with three cantons in July 1944.

Maradi competes with Niamey as the economic capital of the country. It is the terminus of a paved road from Kano, where much of Niger's **groundnut** crop used to be shipped. In the 1970s–1980s, Maradi was also a major import trade center, receiving goods from Lagos and Kano. In more recent years, it has become a dry harbor for northern Nigeria through a partnership between merchants in Maradi and in Katsina and Kano. To avoid the risky and costly transit between southern Nigeria and northern Nigeria, and also to dodge importation monopolies, northern Nigerian merchants use Niger's installations at the ports of Cotonou and Lomé to ferry over all kinds of goods, with Maradi serving as the axis of importation and reexportation. The Nigerien government protects the transit which, besides stimulating Maradi's commercial **economy**, contributes in very large measures to the customs taxes of a region which is the state of Niger's chief contributor in that field.

Little is known of the history of the region prior to the arrival of the Gobirawa and, farther south, the Katsinawa. The name of the region and town is also subject to some controversy, deriving from either a corruption of Maryadi ("the refuge," the name of a goddess to whom the valley belongs) or the title of a Katsinawa official.

A Katsina province that fell to Fulani (Sokoto jihadist) rule (as did Katsina itself), the Maradi area became in the early 19th century the refuge of those Katsinawa expelled from their territory farther south. In 1807 the Fulani under Umaru Dallaji overcame Katsina, defeating the Hausa ruler Magajin Halidou, who escaped to the northeast with some of his followers. After his suicide, **Dan Kassawa** was selected as the *sarkin* Katsina (king of Katsina). The Hausa refugees went to **Damagaram**, where they lived for two years before settling at Gafai on the border of Damagaram and the Maradi province, now under Fulani rule. They remained in Gafai for 10 years, building up their strength and eventually occupying Maradi following a local revolt against the Fulani in the city.

After installing themselves in Maradi, war became the prime rationale of the expatriate state, since all ardently believed—at least at the outset—that their stay would be only temporary until Katsina was regained. The history of Maradi in the 19th century is therefore the story of a never-ending tug-of-war between the Fulani of Katsina and the Katsinawa of Maradi. Maradi's allies in this struggle were the Gobirawa—also expelled by the Fulani—and, tacitly, Damagaram, which had escaped conquest by Sokoto.

For some time the Gobirawa and Katsinawa lived together in Maradi, but eventually a joint effort was made and Tibiri was built for the Gobirawa in 1836 some 8 km northwest of Maradi. Under **Dan Baskore**, a determined military assault of 10,000 warriors and a cavalry from Gobir, Maradi, Damagaram, and their Kel Owey **Tuareg** allies reached to within 8 km of Katsina before being repulsed. By 1845 an uneasy stalemate had developed between Maradi and Katsina, with periodic mutual assaults across their respective frontier zones but without any major victories on the part of either of the two protagonists.

Of the various rulers of Maradi, one of the most important was Dan Baskore, under whose leadership the kingdom prospered and became finally entrenched when a large wall was erected to protect the town.

The *sarauta* (monarchy) of Maradi is administratively composed of three customary departments to which was recently added a "modern" one: the Right Hand, the Middle, and the Left Hand of the *sarauta*, plus its secretariat (modern department). The Right Hand, led by the *galadima* (the most senior civil servant of the monarchy, akin to a prime minister) is composed of three dignitaries who, together with the *galadima*, form the electoral college as well as the interim government when the king is dead or removed: the *Yan Daka*, the *Yari,* and the *Bagalam*. The princes who have rights of succession also belong in the Right Hand. The Left Hand is made up of the war leaders and animist priests (*maîtres féticheurs*) of the monarchy: the **kaura** (commander in chief of the armies, and especially of the cavalry), the *Waziri*, the *Magagin Bakabé*, and others. The 12 **dogari** (guards) who surround the king in state also belong in the Left Hand. The Middle department is a later-day adjunct arising from the Islamization of the monarchy. It comprises the clerical administration of the town—imams of main mosques—led by the *Sarkin Mallameye*, a grand mufti. Since the death of *Sarki* **Bouzou dan Zambadi**, the new king, **Maremawa Ali Zaki**—a modern-educated man—has redefined the *sarauta* of Maradi as a development chieftaincy, implicated in the various improvement projects and programs of the region of Maradi. This, and the judicial tasks of the **sarki**, have given rise to a chief's secretariat, in charge notably of keeping written records and organizing the nontraditional activities of the king.

The king lists of the Katsinawa successor state of Maradi are subject to various controversies as to the precise dates of the reigns of several rulers. The following is one chronology: Dan Kassawa, 1807–1825; Rauda, 1825–1835; Dan Mari, 1835–1848; Binoni, 1848–1853; Dan Mahedi, 1853–1857; Dan Baura, 1857–1858; Dan Baskoré, 1858–1879; Barmou, 1879–1883; Mazawaje, 1883–1885; Mallam, 1885–1886; Mazallatchi, 1886–1890; Dan Kaka, 1890–1891; Dan Daddi, 1891; Mijinyawa, 1891–1893; Kouré, 1898; Mijinyawa, 1898; Kouré, 1898–1904; Mahaman Burje, 1904; Kouré, 1904–1920; Ali Dan Kimalle, 1920–1922; Dan Koulodo, 1922–1944**; Mahaman dan Baskore**, 1944–1947; Mahaman Bouzou dan Zambadi, 1947–2003; Maremawa Ali Zaki, 2005– .

To indicate the provisional nature of the Maradi state, all kings have been titled *Sarkin Katsina* and not *Sarkin Maradi*, even though Katsina was never regained by the old Hausa ruling house. In Niger's **administrative organiza-tion**, the king of Maradi had the title of *Chef de Province du Katséna*, which was changed, in September 2010, into that of *Sultan du Katséna-Maradi*.

MARIA THERESA DOLLAR. One of several **currencies** in Niger in the precolonial era and the first two decades of French rule in the country. Minted in Vienna and imported via the Maghrib, the Maria Theresa dollar (*Thaler* in German) was better accepted in Niger than the French franc right up to the 1920s. Indeed, the French themselves continued to import the coin (still minted though no longer legal tender in Europe) for some time in order to ensure receipt of services from the local population. The name *thaler* was changed into *dala* in local languages, a word which still denotes currency in both **Zarma** and Nigerien **Hausa.** Thus: 10 **CFA francs** would be *dala hinka* in Zarma and *dala biyu* in Nigerien Hausa—the name of the Nigerian cur-rency (naira) having supplanted the memory of the *thaler* in Nigerian Hausa.

MARIKO, FATIMATA GANDIGUI (1964–). Better known as Fati Mariko, she was educated at primary and secondary levels in **Niamey** and Bougouni (Mali) and later on acquired skills in typing before finding her true vocation in music. In 1986, she became an overnight star in Niger thanks to the hit *Djana-Djana* which she produced with the group Marhaba. Mariko is especially fa-mous in Niger for being the only female hit singer to have sustained a working career for nearly three decades, partnering at times with male stars close to her style of music (modernization of **Zarma-Songhay** ritual and folk songs), as well as hip hop bands. *See also* DANCE AND MUSIC.

MARIKO KELETIGUI, ABDOURAHMANE (1921–1997). A veterinar-ian and writer, Mariko Keletigui was a long-serving administrator in Niger, though his family relocated there from the French Sudan (now Mali) dur-ing the colonial era. He served as director of cooperation in the Ministry of Rural **Economy** (1962), head of the development service in the same ministry (1963–1965), and simultaneously general director of the Société du Riz du Niger and administrator of SOTRAMIL. After 1965 he directed the **Union Nigérienne de Crédit et de Coopérative** (UNCC) and the **Caisse Nationale de Crédit Agricole** (CNCA). He was the author of a number of books on development problems (*Le Niger d'abord: Réflexion sur les défis au développement au Niger*, 1993; *La Mort de la brousse: La degradation de l'environnement au Sahel*, 1996), **Sahelian** folktales (*Sur les rives du fleuve Niger: Contes sahéliens recueillis en pays haoussa, zarma, mandé, peul, manding, banmanan, dogon, touareg, bornouan, mossi*, 2000), and various other topics (*Souvenirs de la boucle du Niger*, 1980; *Les Touareg ouellemin-*

den, 1984; *Poèmes sahéliens en liberté*, 1987). In 1992, he received the Prix **Boubou Hama**, an award created three years earlier to honor writers and scholars. *See also* LITERATURE.

MASSALATCHI, ABDOULAYE MOUSSA. A journalist at the government daily *Le Sahel*, Massalatchi left it in 1989 to found a monthly economic journal, *Le Marché*, which failed to thrive. While periodically seeking to revive and continue this project, Massalatchi serves currently as the Niger's correspondent for Reuters news agency. *See also* MEDIA.

MASSAOUDOU, HASSOUMI (1954–). A geologist and founding member of the **Parti Nigérien pour la Démocratie et le Socialisme** (PNDS Tarayya) and close friend of President **Mahamadou Issoufou**, Massaoudou, an eloquent speaker, was the party's first secretary for information and propaganda. After PNDS's electoral victory as a member of the **Alliance des Forces du Changement**'s coalition in 1993, he was appointed minister of **communication**, culture, youth, and sports on 23 April 1993 under Prime Minister Mahamadou Issoufou, serving until the resignation of Issoufou on 5 October 1995. Massaoudou, one of the most vocal opponents of **Ibrahim Baré Maïnassara**'s authoritarian restoration of 1996–1997, was arrested on 13 July 1996 and tortured in detention, with mock executions being used. After Niger's return to democracy, he won a parliamentary seat at the legislative **elections** of November 1999 and headed the PNDS parliamentary group during the ensuing legislative term. In 2004, Massaoudou was elected first deputy secretary-general of the party.

During President **Mamadou Tandja**'s 2009 constitutional coup, Massaoudou delivered many impassioned and principled speeches against the attempt; especially after the suppression of the **Cour Constitutionnelle**, he claimed to no longer be considering Tandja as Niger's president and took to calling him "Monsieur Tandja" ("Mister Tandja," as opposed to "President Tandja"). After Tandja's removal by the military in February 2010, Massaoudou headed Issoufou's campaign for the presidential election, and upon the PNDS's candidate victory in March 2011, he was appointed director of the cabinet of the president with the rank of minister. *See also* TAZARTCHÉ.

MATAMEYE. *Département* of 170,700 people in the region of **Zinder** with headquarters in the town of the same name, which has around 20,000 inhabitants. Within the *département* is found the important village of Kantché.

MATANKARI. Important town in the *arrondissement* of **Dogondoutchi** in the **Dosso** *département* north of Dogondoutchi. Former capital of the

Arawa, Matankari has a population of 15,000 people and is named after the founder of the Maouri kingdom. In 1688 the town reputedly had a population of 20,000. Prior to the **French occupation**, Matankari was the residence of the *sarkin* **Arewa**. When the French set up their regional headquarters at Dogondoutchi, the *sarki* relocated his palace there. The region around Matankari is very scenic.

MAX. *See* ALI DJIBO, AMADOU.

MAYAHI. *Département* of 392,200 people in the region of **Maradi**, with administrative headquarters in the small town of the same name, which has a population of 9,800.

MEDIA. During the colonial period, the administration published a specialized journal, *Cahiers nigériens*, starting in 1933, and later replaced by another paper intended for government workers, *Niger Information* (1955). Meanwhile, the newly empowered Nigerien political and **union** community transiently issued a number of periodical papers: first, in 1952, a union broadsheet titled *Talaka* (*The Commoner*), published as the French Overseas Labor Code was being prepared in Paris. The following year, on 13 April 1953, the first issue of *Le Niger* appeared under the aegis of the **Parti Progressiste Nigérien** (PPN-RDA), a paper that will become a government weekly at independence (1960) and renamed *Sahel-Hebdo* after the **coup d'état in 1974**. On 17 November 1961, the newly independent state issued the first number of the government daily *Le Temps du Niger*, with the claim that "nothing is as dangerous in a country than the press handled by dirty hands." *Le Temps du Niger* compiled dispatches from Agence France Presse while covering also the activities of the government, and all journalists, including those of Radio Niger, were civil servants.

After the coup d'état of 1974, the media were overhauled by the new regime, with *Le Temps du Niger* becoming Le **Sahel**, Radio Niger becoming **Voix du Sahel**, and the government television channel Télé Sahel being created on the ashes of an experiment in school television. Under the incipient political liberalization of the early 1980s, a number of private papers were authorized, although they were restricted to dealing with cultural, economic, and sports topics: *Le Kazel* (published by a wealthy **Kanuri** trader close to the regime, Elhadj Kazelma) starting in October 1984, *L'Opérateur économique*, *Miroir du Football*, *Promo Sport* and *Le Marché*.

After the death of President **Seyni Kountché** in 1987, the pace of political liberalization accelerated under **Ali Saibou,** and several government journalists left the tedious and heavily policed government papers to launch a series of independent newspaper: first ***Haské*** in 1990 (founded by Ibrahim Cheick Diop, a former journalist at *Le Sahel*) and then in 1991 *Le Républicain* and *Le Démocrate*. Despite this evolution, the government had strengthened the public media sector in the years leading to **democratization**; in July 1987, it created the *Agence Nigérienne de Presse* (ANP), which collects news dispatches from international news agencies and used to publish an excellent periodical magazine, *Nigérama*, with extensive social, cultural, and economic reporting on the various regions of the country. With the gradual decrease of state subsidies, ANP has become a shadow of its former self and issues *Nigérama* sporadically and only on request. In 1989, the department of the written press at the Ministry of Information was expanded into a state organization, the Office National d'Edition et de Presse (ONEP). ONEP prints and distributes the government's papers—*Le Sahel* and *Sahel Dimanche*, the new name of *Sahel-Hebdo*—throughout the country.

A few years later, the development of the private media was stimulated by the full adoption of freedom of expression in the **constitution** of 1992. In 1993, three ordinances of the transitional government liberalized the sector and set up a regulatory authority, the Conseil Supérieur de la Communication (CSC). But the free press experienced its first brush with powerful officials when a series of defamation lawsuits targeted the bolder investigative reporting. Moreover through the 1990s, dozens of newspapers were created, most of them issuing only a few numbers before vanishing into thin air, and many ending up losing their independence to prominent politicians, often switching sides depending on money offered. This behavior was promoted by low circulation—on average, 1,500 copies weekly, even though *Haské* was able to sell up to 12,000 weekly when it was the only nongovernmental paper available—and low advertisement revenues, as well as by a general lack of professionalism among the venturesome editors of the day. This very disorder, however, testified to the vibrancy of the new Nigerien media. Several private radio stations were also created in that period, at first broadcasting only in **Niamey** and environs but soon setting up antennas in the rest of the country.

The development of the media was, however, checked under the **Fourth Republic** by the authoritarian tactics of President **Baré Maïnassara** (1996–1999). University scholar Souley Adji was thus famously kidnapped and brutalized after publishing a series of highly critical articles against the would-be dictator, while **Convention Démocratique et Sociale** (CDS) militant Oubandawaki met the same fate following his interventions on the private radio channels. In March 1997, the headquarters of the Radio Anfani (then regarded as the main platform of the opposition and the critics of the regime) were ransacked by armed men. Four months later, in July, the regime adopted a very restrictive ordinance which made it more difficult to create a press organ while increasing penalties for press offenses. The CSC was moreover transformed into a rubber-stamp organ at the beck and call of the ruler.

After the removal of the Fourth Republic in 1999, the clauses that impeded the creation of new press organs were revoked, but the founders of the **Fifth Republic** conveniently kept the repressive clauses that enabled politicians to better intimidate journalists than under the **Third Republic**. Press offenses could incur a month to five years of jail term and fines running from 10,000 to a million **CFA francs**. On the other hand, the new regime fully liberalized the audiovisual sector in April 2000, while the CSC regained its autonomy. Several private television channels were soon established, among which Radio Télévision Ténéré (RTT), Radio Télévision Dounia (RTD), Canal 3 (which belongs to a Beninese businessman), and the Islamist Radio Télévision Bonferey (RTB) have risen to prominence during the 2000s. RTD, though private, is close to **Hama Amadou**, a prominent politician from the **Mouvement National pour la Société de Développement** (MNSD-Nassara) party and prime minister from 2000 to 2007. As such, under the plucky management of **civil society** leader **Ali Idrissa**, it became the main media platform for the opponents of President **Mamadou Tandja**'s constitutional coup of 2009.

In the course of the 2000s, the state made extensive use of its repressive powers against the media, with *causes célèbres* being *Le Républicain*'s editor and owner Omar Lalo Keita and Mamane Abou and Radio France Internationale correspondent Moussa Kaka. The latter in particular was jailed for one year in 2007–2008, a victim of Tandja's hard-line stance against the **Mouvement des Nigériens pour la Justice Tuareg rebellion** of 2007–2009, of which he was accused of being an accomplice. At the same time, the mercenary nature of much of the written press did justify some of the legal problems which it ran into, and several attempts were made to curb both the tendency and its legal consequences. In March 2007, media bosses set up a self-regulatory institution, the Conseil de Presse, tasked with supervising media ethics and issuing press cards. The Conseil de Presse is made up of seven members, four of whom come from the audiovisual media (two private and two public) and three from the written media (one private, one public, and one retired).

Tandja's attempt at installing a dictatorship in 2009 was opposed by nearly all of the written press, despite considerable pressure and attempts at bribing. The dogged resistance was both principled and rooted in the fear that a dictatorial regime would do away with the free press. As a result of their opposition to the **Tazartché**, the media, and especially the written media, were an important component of the transition of 2010. They were able to see through, under very favorable conditions, the process of the estates-general of the Nigerien press, which the overthrown government had reluctantly agreed to organize under pressure from the European Union. A key outcome of the estates-general was the complete removal of jail terms from the sanctions that could be meted out to journalists who are found at fault. The **Seventh Republic** has thus restored the propitious climate of the Third Republic, while it appears that 20 years of experience in practicing the difficult arts of the freedom of the press have significantly improved the accountability of Niger's media. *See also* DEMOCRATIZATION; EDUCATION; OFFICE DE RADIO-DIFFUSION ET TELEVISION DU NIGER.

MILLET. One of Niger's staple crops, a basic subsistence crop together with sorghum. Niger is Africa's second-biggest millet producer (after **Nigeria**), and the crop is believed to have been first cultivated in history in regions spanning Niger and Mali. Over 65 percent of Niger's surface is planted with the crop, the harvest of which grew from 1,362,785 tons in 1980 to 2,358,741 tons in 2001. Some 85 percent of this is consumed locally and the rest is sold in the cities, and part of it is exported, usually to Nigeria. The only processing center for millet is Société de Transformation du Mil (SOTRAMIL), founded as a **parastatal** in 1967 in **Zinder** and privatized in 1994. SOTRAMIL produces farina, cookies, and pasta.

Despite the growing production of millet, Niger chronically fails to produce enough of the crop for the needs of a fast-growing population. While some of the country's production trickles off into Nigeria, Niger imports large amounts of millet every year, and situations of food crisis arise partly when importation is hampered, notably by the policies of neighboring countries. *See also* AGRICULTURE.

MINDAOUDOU, AICHATOU (1959–). Born in a **Zinder** family, Mindaoudou earned a doctorate in law at Paris's Panthéon Sorbonne University, in **France**, and taught law at the **University of Niamey**. As a prominent member of the **Mouvement National pour la Société de Développement** (MNSD Nassara), she was appointed minister for social development, population, and the advancement of **women** under Prime Minister **Hama Amadou**'s government in 1995. Her tenure was ended the following year by the coup of Colonel **Ibrahim Baré Maïnassara**. After another coup d'état that ousted President Baré Maïnassara in 1999, Mindaoudou was appointed foreign affairs minister by the transitional head of state, Major **Daouda Malam Wanké**. She was reappointed to that position in 2001, in a reshuffled government, under Prime Minister Amadou. A good friend of President **Mamadou Tandja**, Mindaoudou kept her position throughout his terms, surviving the fall of Amadou's government in 2007. Two years earlier, Mindaoudou successfully defended Niger's case against Benin on the question of an outstanding border dispute, at the International Court of Justice of The Hague. She was removed from government affairs after the fall of Tandja in February 2010. In May 2011, she was appointed by the United Nations joint special representative for the hybrid operation of the United Nations and the African Union in Darfur, Sudan. *See also* BENIN–NIGER BORDER DISPUTE.

MINING. Modern mining started in Niger during the colonial period, with the explorations of the French public agency, the Bureau Minier de la France d'Outre-Mer (BUMIFOM), in the late 1940s and through the 1950s. The timing implies that proper mining activities took off chiefly after independence in 1960. Until 1967 tin ore was the only mineral produced in Niger, extracted by the Société Minière du Niger, with an output of around 50 tons a year. BUMIFOM had alerted the French Commissariat à l'Energie Atomique (CEA) to several **uranium** finds, but it was only in 1967–1968 that the CEA started to organize the exploitation of the mineral. Since then, uranium production has become Niger's prime export. Iron ore was also discovered in the **Say** region, and there are huge coal reserves in the **Aïr**. The iron deposits are not exploited, however, because of the large financial investments necessary. Gypsum is produced in the important Magia (Ader Doutchi) site, while limestone (with reserves of 30 million tons) is utilized by the **Malbaza** cement works. In 1985 significant gold deposits were discovered a few hundred kilometers north of **Niamey** and have come into exploitation through a Canadian–Nigerien joint venture in the early 2000s. In that period, **oil** was found in the region of **Diffa** and exploitation rights were acquired by China in 2008, complete with a 20,000 barrels per day refinery, built in the vicinity of **Zinder** (see table 6).

The **constitution** of the **Seventh Republic**, adopted in November 2010, includes several provisions bearing on the mining of mineral resources. Article 150 prescribes transparency by ordering the publication in the country's official journal of all exploration and mining contracts as well as of revenues broken down by company. Article 152 distributes mining revenues between the state and the territorial administration of the region in which the resource is exploited, while article 153 reserves investments made possible by such revenues to predefined priority sectors (**agriculture**, **cattle**, **health**, **education**, and a fund for future generations). These provisions address both the lack of transparency in the use of mining and natural resources that prevailed under previous regimes and the claim repeatedly made by **Tuareg** insurgents that the Aïr region should benefit more from uranium and coal revenues.

In 2007, Niger applied to the Extractive Industries Transparency Initiative (EITI), an international monitoring system aimed at shielding mining

Table 6. Productivity Trends of Main Mining Sectors (in Tons)

	1948	1971	1975	1980	1985	1990	1995	2000	2005	2009
Uranium		410	1,306	4,132	3,181	2,832	2,974	2,898	3,093	3,245
Coal					158,718	153,919	170,971	158,200	182,060	225,072
Cassiterite	27	107	135	77						
Gold									10	4

revenues from corruption and misappropriation. Initially, the country was accepted in the scheme but failed to complete the reforms necessary for its membership to become effective, owing to the political crisis in 2009–2010. It was finally admitted on 1 March 2011. *See also* CASSITERITE; SAMIRA.

MINISTERE DES AFFAIRES SAHARIENNES ET NOMADES. Cabinet ministry during the **Hamani Diori** era that was actually operative for only two months a year during the *cure salée* trek of herdsmen northward. The ministry was involved in coordinating technical services and socioeconomic activities in the In Gall–Agadez–Teguidda triangle where the bulk of the **Tuareg** influx occurs, during which the minister (usually an influential Tuareg *amenokal*), units of the gendarmerie, and the camel corps all relocate to **Aïr** in order to preserve peace among the volatile Tuareg clans living next to a then-hostile Algeria. *See also* FOREIGN POLICY.

MIRRIAH. Large market town 20 km east of **Zinder**. In the 1900s the market convened three times a week, greatly overshadowing Zinder's Thursday market. Formerly capital of one of the Sossebaki states of the area, Mirriah's defeat at the hands of **Damagaram** cleared the way for the latter's rise to preeminence in the area in the nineteenth century.

Currently Mirriah is a *département* in the Zinder region and includes the rural **commune** of Damagaram-Takaya. The *département* has a population of 600,000. The town itself has a population of 14,000.

MISSION AFRIQUE CENTRALE-TCHAD. Also known as Mission Voulet et Chanoine from its leaders, Captain Paul Voulet and Captain Julien Chanoine. Both men had distinguished themselves in the conquest of the Mossi Empire (now Burkina Faso) in 1896. In July 1898, they were assigned the task of occupying Central Sudan (Niger) by trekking to the **Lake Chad** where they would meet the Mission Foureau-Lamy (which traveled southward from Algeria) and the Mission Gentil (which traveled northward from Gabon). The mission would, on its way, reassert French power over **Damagaram** by avenging the death of Captain **Marius-Gabriel Cazemajou** of the **Mission du Haut-Soudan**, who had been assassinated in **Zinder**.

Assembling in Sansanné-Haoussa on 3 January 1899, and numbering 1,700 (600 infantry, 800 porters, 200 **women**, and 100 children), the force descended down the **Niger River**. Due to crop failures in the area, the mission was initially unable to buy supplies and resorted to looting areas which it crossed, leaving a swath of destruction still remembered in some villages to this day. This grew gradually into a method that culminated in the destruction of the rich village of **Birni-N'Konni** (about 10,000 people) in May 1899. The two commanding officers ended up acquiring ambitions to set themselves up as independent potentates, building a base in the **Arewa** region. The Arewa queen, **Sarraounia Mangou**, fiercely opposed them at that point, until they managed to storm her capital of **Lougou** in June.

When news of the havoc caused by the mission reached French head-quarters, Colonel Klobb and Lieutenant Meynier were sent after it to take command of the column. Leaving **Say** on 12 June 1899 via **Dosso** and **Matankari**, they intercepted the column at Dankori. The rebels killed Klobb, following which the two officers were in turn killed by their troops at Maijirgi. The column proceeded on its mission under Meynier to defeat the Damagaram forces in the battle of Tirmini and to occupy Zinder, declaring a French protectorate over the sultanate.

The Voulet and Chanoine story may have inspired Joseph Conrad's *Heart of Darkness*. It was the topic of **Abdoulaye Mamani**'s *Sarraounia* (1980) and of the subsequent Med Hondo movie of the same title (1986), centered on the resistance of the queen of Lougou, as well as of the 2004 French television movie *Capitaines des ténèbres*—this title being an open reference to the French title of *Heart of Darkness*, *Au Coeur des ténèbres*.

MISSION DU HAUT-SOUDAN. Led by Captain **Marius Gabriel Cazemajou** and aimed at charting for **France** the territories between the **Niger River** and **Lake Chad**, as well as reaching the Darfourian empire-builder **Rabah** (at the time a major force in the interior, having just defeated the vaunted **Kanem-Bornu Empire**) and inducing him to accept (with his territories) the "protection" of France. The mission arrived in **Zinder**, where Sultan **Amadou Kouran Daga** of **Damagaram** regally entertained it. On its departure, however, a court faction murdered Cazemajou out of fear that his real intentions were to link up with Rabah against Damagaram. Cazemajou's murder brought about the dispatch of the **Mission Afrique Centrale-Tchad** in retaliation, the occupation of Damagaram, and the killing of the sultan. These events were recounted in a 1981 Nigerien movie, *Si les cavaliers*, by **Mahamane Bakabé**, with a scenario written by historian **André Salifou**.

MONT BAGUEZAN. Highest summit in Niger, in the 80,000 sq km **Aïr** massif. It peaks at 2,022 meters. This is also the name of Niger's presidential plane.

MONT GREBOUN. Second-highest summit in Niger, in the 80,000 sq km **Aïr** massif. It peaks at 1,944 meters.

MOUDDOUR, AHMED (1941–1976). Former director of the **Union Ni-gérienne de Crédit et de Coopérative** (UNCC). A **Tuareg** born in Bonkoukou (**Filingué**) on 4 September 1941, and the son of **First Republic** dignitary **Mouddour Zakara**, Mouddour was educated in Kao, Arzerori, **Tahoua**, and **Niamey** (1947–1957) and continued his studies in Nogent-sur-Marne (**France**), where he obtained a diploma as public works engineer, and at the Paris École Pratique des Hautes Études (1961–1962), where he obtained a certificate in economics and social sciences. Mouddour returned to Niger to a posting as head of the agricultural region of **Dosso** (1962–1965). In 1965 he became the head of agricultural services at Dosso, and in 1970 was appointed director of the UNCC. In 1972 he was also included in the Conseil Economique et Social of which he became vice-president. Between 1969 and 1974 he was also deputy secretary-general of the Union Nationale des Travailleurs du Niger. After his purge, consequent to the **coup d'état of 1974**, he assisted the anti-**Seyni Kountché** plotters of 1976 by smuggling arms in trucks of **COPRO-NIGER**, of which he had been a director. For this he was arrested, sentenced to death, and executed on 21 April 1976.

MOUMOUNI, YACOUBA (1966–). Born in **Téra**, Moumouni was being groomed for an ordinary **Songhay** rural life when he fled to **Niamey**, aged only 10, and became a street child for two years, until his musical skills attracted the attention of the renowned Niamey music teacher and cultural monitoress Fanta Danté. Under her auspices, Moumouni joined the Ballet National du Niger as a virtuoso practitioner of traditional flute, before teaming up with guitarist Abdallah Alhassane to form the eight-man band Mamar Kassey in 1995. (Mamar Kassey is the popular Songhay name of 16th-century Songhay emperor **Askia Mohammed**.) He became an overnight star in Niger after the release of his album *Denké-Denké*—a phrase which is now also his stage name. Moumouni's music is a typically Nigerien blend of **Zarma-Songhay** and **Fulani** rhythms and instruments, with the songs themselves being mostly composed in the Songhay and Fulani **languages**. Moumouni is the only Nigerien musician well known outside of Niger and especially in the West, where his albums are released mainly by the record label Harmonia Mundi. These include *Denké-Denké* (1999), *Alatoumi* (2000), *Via Campesina* (2006), and *On va voir ça* (2008). Western charts classify his music as jazz-ethnic, pop-ethnic, or Afropop. *See also* DANCE AND MUSIC.

MOUSSA, BOUBAKAR (1932–). **Hamani Diori**'s half-brother and former director of national security. Born on 28 September 1932, in **Niamey**, Moussa was educated in **Filingué** and obtained a teacher's certificate at **Tahoua**'s teachers' training school (1953). Between 1953 and 1958 he taught in

Niamey, **Magaria**, and Karakara before going to Paris, **France**, to obtain a higher studies diploma (1958–1961). He remained in Paris for a few months working at Niger's embassy as chancellor, and in October 1961 was appointed director of national security, serving in that post for the next 11 years (1961–1972). In August 1972 he was appointed secretary of state for internal affairs, serving until the **coup d'état of 1974**. He was imprisoned after the coup on a host of charges and was released about a decade later.

MOUVEMENT DES NIGÉRIENS POUR LA JUSTICE (MNJ). **Tuareg rebellion** movement which operated in northern Niger in 2007–2009. MNJ initially professed to be a movement of Nigeriens calling for justice against the Nigerien government, instead of being a purely ethnic Tuareg movement. Indeed the movement attracted in particular a number of non-Tuareg former members of Niger's military, disgruntled at their treatment in the army, and especially included officers who took part to the **Diffa** mutiny of 2002.

The MNJ inflicted heavy losses on the **armed forces** in early 2007, and President **Mamadou Tandja** reacted with a hard-line stance, accusing the rebels of being mere armed bandits and vowing military repression to restore security. From a European base, the group also created a blog which lambasted in particular President Tandja, endlessly described as a bloodthirsty tyrant. The blog grew popular in Niger, where it responded to people's frustration with a regime that was unable to solve economic problems and was mired in corruption. However, by the end of 2007, MNJ military fortunes started to suffer, especially after Tandja put the region of **Agadez** under an *état de mise en garde*, a newfangled kind of state of emergency that gave the military free rein to control and quell. Moreover, a blog posting that called for the establishment of a **Tuareg** republic persuaded other Nigeriens that the MNJ was an ethnic, rather than a patriotic, group and support for it dwindled in the southern parts of the country.

However, the group continued its struggle, daringly attacking Nigerien towns in the south at the edge of the desert, planting mines in many northern areas, and also resorting to kidnapping. In 2008, mines were also planted and exploded in **Niamey**, **Tahoua**, and **Maradi**, large southern towns thus far untouched by Tuareg unrest. It is not sure, however, that the MNJ had planted these, and the Nigerien government itself—under Tandja—has come under suspicion in that regard.

In 2009, intent at focusing on his overthrowing of the **Fifth Republic**, Tandja relaxed his position vis-à-vis the movement, and talks were soon opened under the mediation of **Libya**'s president, Colonel Muammar Kadhafi. An agreement was sealed in October 2009 at Sebha, in Libya. Frustrated splinter groups denounced the deal made by Aghali Alambo (MNJ's main leader) but the rebellion, which lost the vital support of Libya, gradually died out by early 2010.

MOUVEMENT NATIONAL POUR LA SOCIÉTÉ DE DÉVELOPPE-MENT (MNSD Nassara). The **Hausa** word appended to the acronym of the party derives from the Arabic *nasr*, and means divine support. The MNSD was founded as a single party (referred to as *parti-État* in Niger's official chronicles) in 1989, by President **Ali Saibou**, to mobilize the masses in support of the **Second Republic**. When Saibou acquiesced to the establishment of multiparty democracy in 1990, the MNSD *parti-État* became the MNSD Nassara. It was at first threatened by a leadership division, as one faction in the party supported **Mamadou Tandja** and the other **Moumouni Adamou Djermakoye**, two leading figures of the military regime that preceded the Second Republic. Tandja emerged victorious with the help of the key manager of the party, **Hama Amadou**, and Djermakoye withdrew from the MNSD to create his own party, the **Alliance Nigérienne pour la Démocratie et le Progrès** (ANDP Zaman Lahiya).

In the presidential and legislative **elections** of 1993, MNSD garnered more votes than any other **political party** but lost both elections to the coalition of the **Alliance des Forces du Changement** (AFC) led by the two second-largest parties in the country, the **Convention Démocratique et Sociale** (CDS Rahama) and the **Parti Nigérien pour la Démocratie et le Socialisme** (PNDS Tarayya). The AFC coalition had been put together only to oppose MNSD, and when it eventually fell apart and President Mahaman Ousmane called for early legislative elections in 1995, MNSD allied with PNDS and won the elections. Ousmane very reluctantly appointed Amadou prime minister but resolved to cooperate as little as possible, or even not at all, with the MNSD-led government he set up. The cohabitation situation (where the president and the prime minister belong to opposing parties) promptly led to political gridlock. After the coup d'état by Colonel **Baré Maïnassara** in January 1996, MNSD closed ranks with CDS and PNDS to oppose the regime of the **Fourth Republic** established by the coup-maker to buttress his power.

In 1999, the Fourth Republic was overthrown, and the first elections of the **Fifth Republic** led to MNSD dominance, in alliance with both CDS and ANDP. MNSD's elder leader, Mamadou Tandja, became president, and its junior leader, Hama Amadou, became prime minister. Amadou was also elected president of the party in 2001, since Tandja's position barred him from being the chairperson of a party. At the 2004 elections, MNSD, preserving the alliance of CDS and ANDP, won again the presidential and legislative elections against PNDS, and both Tandja and Amadou were returned to their offices. But in 2006–2007, the party came under pressure from the struggle between its two leaders, and factions of Tandjistes and Hamistes emerged. Tandja arranged for a faction within MNSD to ally with PNDS in order to vote a no-confidence motion against Amadou's government at the **National Assembly**. Amadou resigned and came under a variety of accusations, which led to his jailing in June 2008. These events ended up splitting the party, with supporters of Tandja floating ideas of changes in the **constitution** to allow their champion to seek a third term—which was ruled out by the constitution—and supporters of Amadou putting up resistance to such ideas. In February 2009, Amadou, still in prison, was replaced as president of MNSD by a Tandja appointee and his successor as prime minister, **Seyni Oumarou**. Released for medical reasons soon thereafter, Amadou left Niger for **France** in exile, but returned in July to attend the funerals of Djermakoye who died that month. On that occasion, and before promptly returning to France to escape arrest, Amadou masterminded the creation of a new party, the Mouvement Démocratique Nigérien/pour une Fédération Africaine (MODEN/FA Lumana Africa), which quickly drained MNSD of much of its mass following from its key strongholds in **Niamey** and **Tillabéri**. This move considerably weakened the MNSD potentials in serving Tandja's establishment of a new regime.

In the Nigerien context, the MNSD was a liberal-conservative party, its liberal side better represented by Amadou, and its conservative side by Tandja. It survived Tandja's downfall of February 2010 and was kept firmly in the hands of Seyni Oumarou after a fight put up in the courts by Amadou to wrest it back to himself. MNSD went to the legislative and presidential elections stripped of half its base, and still came off nicely, with 26 seats in the National Assembly and with its candidate being the challenger to the winner at the presidential election. *See also* THIRD REPUBLIC.

MOUVEMENT SOCIALISTE AFRICAIN (MSA). Interterritorial party in French Africa to which **Djibo Bakary** affiliated his party (under the MSA title) prior to the adoption of the new party name—**Sawaba**. In the 31 March 1957 election, Bakary's MSA took 41 seats to the **Parti Progressiste Nigérien** (PPN)'s 19, but shortly after, in 1958, Sawaba's call for a "no" vote in the referendum regarding Niger's participation to the French Community federation brought about its French-engineered eclipse as the PPN emerged with an electoral victory largely contrived by the colonial administration.

MUSÉE NATIONAL BOUBOU HAMA. Opened in December 1959, the museum is 24 hectares in size and owes its unique conception to its first conservator, Pablo Toucet, who worked on it as part of **Boubou Hama**'s project of a Vallée de la Culture (Culture Valley) in downtown **Niamey**. This project includes the **Centre d'Études Linguistiques et Historiques par la Tradition Orale** and the Franco-Nigerien cultural center, all adjoining the Musée National. Set up in a large park originally facing the **Niger River** (though now the view on the river is blocked by the buildings of a state-owned hotel and Niamey's main conference hall, the Palais des Congrès), it hosts a cultural and scientific section and a zoo. Most of the collection was donated by the Institut Français d'Afrique Noire, Boubou Hama, **Hamani Diori**, and the French Centre National de la Recherche Scientifique.

Ethnological, cultural, and archaeological/paleontological artifacts are distributed in small whitewashed exhibition pavilions decorated with **Hausa** and **Tuareg** ornamental patterns. Alongside the six pavilions, the museum comprises two exhibition halls, an artisanal center and market, a smaller artisanal center for disabled craftsmen, an educational center for the arts and crafts, a display of traditional Hausa, **Zarma**, **Songhay**, and **Fulani** dwellings, and a mausoleum which displays the remains of the **Arbre du Ténéré**. The zoo has famously cramped little cages mostly taken over by lions, hyenas, and monkeys, but displays as its prized possession a large pool in which resides a drowsy hippopotamus. The Musée National also hosts temporary exhibitions, including the one mounted in 1969–1970 on Niger's rock painting, drawing, and engravings by Henri Lhote. Unlike many museums in Africa, the Musée National is integrated in the city's life, hosting social events or occasional festivals and receiving a big daily stream of visits.

On average, the Musée's statistics number 170,000 visitors per year, the majority of whom are children and teenagers. It receives an annual subsidy from the state (between 30 and 40 million **CFA francs**) and average annual visit fees provide an income (entry fees are 1,000 CFA francs for non-nationals, 200 CFA francs for national adults) of around 12 million CFA francs. The museum's directors have included Pablo Toucet, 1959–1974; Albert Ferral, 1974–1990; Mahamadou Kélessi, 1990–1992; Mariama Hima, 1992–1996; Mahamadou Kélessi, 1996–1999; and Chaïbou Néino since May 1999. Its official name used to be Musée National du Niger.

MUSSOLINI-LAVAL BOUNDARY AGREEMENT. The unratified Franco-Italian boundary treaty that extended southern **Libya** (then an Italian possession) some 200 miles farther south into Niger, Chad, and a corner of Sudan. Since independence, Libya has regarded the unsigned agreement as binding, and with the rise to power of Colonel Muammar Kadhafi, this led to souring Nigerien-Libyan relations for much of the government of **Seyni Kountché**.

N

NADADAW, IDI (1925–1982). A famed **Hausa** singer born in Madarounfa near **Maradi**, Nadadaw was both a griot praising the wealthy and the notable, and a social satirist. His most famous song is perhaps the socially conformist but highly burlesque piece he composed on the ills of being a bachelor, *Sarkin Goburawe* (King of the Bachelors). *See also* DANCE AND MUSIC.

NATIONAL ASSEMBLY. Niger has had seven republics but really two national assembly traditions. The first tradition came about in July 1960 with the dissolution of the former, colonial era Legislative Assembly in which, although the authorities manipulated the voting, there was a modicum of actual competition, especially prior to the banning of the **Sawaba** party. The National Assembly of 1960–1974 had 60 deputies (50 after 1965), was entirely composed of men from the single-party **Parti Progressiste Nigérien** (PPN-RDA), and had no real decision-making power. It was mostly a tribune for the PPN president **Boubou Hama** (also president of the National Assembly) and a place in which to reward notable supporters of the party's rule, mostly traditional chiefs. The second tradition started in 1993 and continues to date. It is that of a more competitive and vibrant National Assembly, interrupted only twice, in 1996–1999 under President **Baré Maïnassara**'s attempt at restoring an authoritarian mode of government, and under President **Mamadou Tandja**'s parody of democratic rule in late 2009.

The current Nigerien National Assembly is defined by the multiparty semiparliamentary **constitutions** to which the country has stuck since 1992, with the two above-mentioned exceptions. The government is chosen from the ranks of its majority party or rather, given the proportional ballot that also favors small parties, its majority coalition of **political parties**, and it is accountable to the deputies, who could bring it down through a no-confidence vote (which happened three times to date). Since 1993, Niger has known six legislative **elections** (against five presidential), and the assembly was never a docile body, as it clearly appeared when President Mamadou Tandja failed to compel it to pass laws changing the constitution in 2009. There is a sense in which, as with all genuinely working semiparliamentary systems, the National Assembly of Niger is in fact more important than the presidency.

Legal (as in 1995) and practical (as in 2006–2007) situations of cohabitation are decided at that level, and when the government is not in the camp of the president, the latter is virtually powerless.

The National Assembly had 83 deputies in 1993. The number subsequently grew to 113 deputies under the **Fifth Republic** (1999–2009), as well as under the current **Seventh Republic**.

NATIONAL CONFERENCE. *See* CONFÉRENCE NATIONALE.

N'GUIGMI. *Département* in the region of **Diffa**, on the border of Chad, including part of **Lake Chad**, with a seminomadic population of 55,000. The town of N'Guigmi, which is an important border-control post and garrison base, is very isolated, at the end of a poor track from **Zinder** via Diffa. It has a population of 16,000 and is the capital of the *département* of the same name. Another sand track skirts the northern edge of Lake Chad ending at Rig Rig in Chad and is a favorite route for **cattle** smugglers from that country.

Once a fishing village on Lake Chad with few water problems, the periodic contractions of the lake in the past two decades have made the town virtually a desert oasis. In the late 1970s commercially exploitable **oil** reserves were discovered in the region, and an exploitation contract signed with the China National Petroleum Corporation in 2008 started extraction works there.

NIAMEY. Modern capital of Niger and nerve center of the country, though sharing economic pride of place with **Maradi** and **Zinder**. Niamey became the capital of Niger in 1926 (making it one of the youngest capitals in Africa), having been at the outset an insignificant minor fishing village not once mentioned in any of the accounts of European travelers in the 19th century. It had around 600 people at the turn of the 20th century. Five years after being designated capital, it had a population of 1,731; just prior to independence (1959), it still numbered only 31,000 people. Rapid growth since independence has raised Niamey's population to 90,000 in 1971; 155,000 in 1977; 397,000 in 1988; 700,000 in 2001; and an estimated 780,000 in 2010.

Niamey is located in the transition zone between the **Zarma** and **Songhay** countries, with the **Zarmaganda** lying on its eastern side (also called **Hausa** side owing to the fact that the Hausaland starts right after Zarmaganda) and the **Soney** lying to its northwestern side (also called Gurma side, since the **Gourmantché** are the immediate western neighbors of the Songhay). Like so many Nigerien or sub-Saharan African localities, Niamey was in fact initially a set of separate villages or hamlets (really large clan homes, called *windi* in Zarma), whose origins may be guessed by their name: Kalley, from the Kalle Zarma; Gaweye from Songhay either because they came from **Gao** or because they were hunters (*gaw* in Songhay, hunting being a key traditional Songhay activity); and Mawrey, from the **Maouri**. These villages were all located on the "Hausa side" or left bank of the **Niger River**. When Niamey was chosen as an ideal site to host colonial administration, these villages shifted around to make room for the French settlement on the higher lands of the plateau to the northeast. They then coalesced around the two markets that soon appeared as the village was growing into a busy small town: the Habu Bene (Zarma for "High Market," known also by its French name of Grand Marché) and the Habu Ganda (Low Market, initially known in French as Le Marché de huit heures, the Eight o'clock market, owing to the fact that it was essentially selling garden products in the early morning hours, and now called Petit Marché). By the 1930s, the villages had become the traditional quarters of the "African town" to which was added, in the vicinity of Habu Ganda, the **Zongo**, the quarter of African migrants (mostly from Niger's Hausaland). This African town therefore occupied, in typical colonial fashion, the lowlands in the southern part of the settlement, gradually stretching to absorb adjacent Zarma villages (such as Gamkallé and Talladjé); while the European town (hosting through much of the colony's history African functionaries from older colonies) was built on a "rational" grid plan on the high land of the plateau, flanked by another Zarma village, Yantala. The two towns tended to meet around the public buildings that were slowly erected between 1926 and the early 1960s: the justice hall, the town hall, the colonial companies' stores (including Niamey's oldest supermarket close to Habu Ganda), the Legislative Assembly (later **National Assembly**), and the Grand Hotel (initially state owned). Along the plateau riverfront sector, where the graceful neo-Sudanic palace of the colonial governor (now the presidential palace) stands, government residences, offices, and ministries were gradually built. These installations became the nucleus of modern Niamey, especially when they were extended by the first African modern-style quarter, Terminus, developed on lands that flank the Grand Hotel.

The name of the urban settlement thus formed is of uncertain origin. One tradition refers to it as the name of a tree by which the first settlers once rested (Niamé); another tradition refers to its origins from Oua Niammane (later Namma or Niame) stemming from the first Zarma inhabitants of the area led by the founder of the village, Chief Kouri Mali. Another legend refers to the amalgamation of the different villages (Niami: mix up). Several other legends exist as to the origin of its name and the original village. Despite an attempt by the colonial government to create, as early as 1931, a so-called traditional chieftaincy in Niamey on par with what existed in **Dosso** or in the Hausaland, Niamey does not have any recognized customary chief, beyond the *chefs de quartier*.

In the first period of its history (1926–1970), Niamey grew essentially in-ward, filling in the vacant spaces between the old villages, and thus gradually unifying the urban space. The growth was given great impetus by political independence, especially as the new state created a central bureaucracy and stepped up a modern built environment, both public and private. Two great urban developments mark this stage: the renovation of the Habu Bene, with cement foundations, in 1962, and the building of the Kennedy Bridge in 1970. The latter work, by connecting Niamey to the right bank of the Niger River, allowed the extension of the town in that area, around the university which was opened there in 1971–1973. Most of the settlements that appeared on the Right Bank as a result of the building of the bridge are **Fulani** (Lamordé, Nogaré) and Zarma (Bangabana, Zarmagandeye). Later on, many of the inhabitants of Gaweye moved to the right bank, where the Gaweye neighbor-hood is now located; they made room for further state buildings which oc-cupy the riverfront on the left bank, in particular the Hotel Gaweye (still state owned to date) and the Palais des Congrès (Niamey's main conference hall)

The next period (1970–1990) of Niamey's growth is marked by immigra-tions caused by **droughts** and the **uranium** boom. Thus appeared refugee settlements drawing in hungry villagers from the surrounding Zarma country (Bandabari) and **Tuareg** from as far as Mali (Lazaret). Both Bandabari and Lazaret are now solid neighborhoods of Niamey with no memory of their ori-gins, apart from the names: Bandabari means in Zarma, "turning one's back on," as in not being able to share food with friends and relatives, and Lazaret being an old Catholic relief center, originally created for lepers). At the same time, especially after 1974, immigrants from coastal countries (**Nigeria**, Benin, Togo, Ghana) came in, attracted by uranium development, and they gained a quasi monopoly over several aspects of retail trade and imports into Niger. The Igbo communities from southeastern Nigeria still control to this date the auto spare parts business of Niamey. Less conspicuously (because sharing the same Sahelian-Islamic culture as the natives), there also arrived great inflows of settlers from Senegal, Burkina Faso (then Haute-Volta), and Mali. By any estimate, the Malians represent the biggest foreign community in Niamey, though this is not very visible. In this period, Niamey began to grow to the southeast, the northeast, and the right bank (known as Harobanda, Zarma for "Beyond the Water").

In the current period, the city is growing in all directions. Important new developments include the extension of the plateau into a posh new quarter of a sandy suburban character, Kwara Kano (Zarma for "Delightful City"), the transformation of the small village-like Zarma quarter of Talladjé into a big town-like predominantly Hausa neighborhood, the building of the Village de la **Francophonie**, a residential quarter constructed on the occasion of the

Fifth Games of the Francophonie in 2005, and generally the rapid proliferation of new neighborhoods outpacing the very inadequate resources of the
city's municipal authorities.

Though Niger has important secondary towns, it must be noted that Niamey is four times bigger than the second city of Niger, **Zinder**, and remains
the principal center of internal and foreign immigration in the country.

Until 1988, Niamey was, apart from being Niger's capital, the seat of a
département. At that date, the *département* seat shifted to **Tillabéri** while
Niamey became the Communauté Urbaine de Niamey (CUN), governed by
a prefect-mayor, and considered a *département* in its own right. With the
decentralization of 1998, the CUN was erected into a region. As the other
communautés urbaines (Zinder, Maradi, and **Tahoua**) of the country, Niamey is divided into quarters (headed by a *chef de quartier* and elected boards)
grouped into **communes** (headed each by a mayor and a municipal council).
The CUN has 99 quarters and 5 communes. According to the **census** of 2001,
the population is in its majority **Zarma-Songhay** (330,000), closely followed
by the Hausa (224,200) and the Fulani (196,000), with all other ethnicities
represented and a sizable minority of non-nationals.

Niamey is connected by a scenic road along the Niger River with Mali,
passing by **Ayorou**, and is also connected via Fada N'Gourma with Burkina
Faso. The **Route de l'Unité** national highway runs from Niamey to Maradi
and hence to Zinder and **Diffa**, branching off at **Birni-N'Konni** to Tahoua
and **Agadez** as the **Route de l'Uranium**.

NIANDOU, HAROUNA (1946–). Born in **Niamey**, Niandou was educated
there, earning a university diploma in letters before taking up journalism studies in **France**, successively at the École Supérieure de Journalisme of Lille, at
the Centre de Formation des Journalistes at Paris, and at Bordeaux and Tunis
(Tunisia). In between these various educational and training efforts, Niandou
worked, from 1966 to 1988, in many positions for Niger's public **media**,
and was the first general editor of the national television, where he also presented the news in the early 1980s. He briefly moved out of the **civil service**
in 1993–1996 to work for the American aid organization USAID. When
the latter closed its doors in protest of **Ibrahim Baré Maïnassara**'s **coup
of January 1996**, Niandou was able to return into the civil service at high-
level positions. He was appointed state secretary at the Ministry of Social
Development and afterward state secretary at the Ministry of Public **Health**,
before entering the cabinet as minister of public health and minister of water
resources and environment. After the fall of the **Fourth Republic**, Niandou
started a career at the regional technical grouping, the **Autorité du Bassin du
Niger**, of which he became the administrative and financial director. He has

authored an essay on Nigerien written media, *La Presse écrite au Niger*, and another one on Nigerien cinema, *Le Cinéma nigérien en devenir*. He is the brother of **Bibata Niandou Barry** and **Abdoulaye Niandou Souley**.

NIANDOU BARRY, BIBATA (1955–). An attorney and police superinten-dent, Bibata Niandou, better known as Madame Barry, is a militant feminist who founded in 1991 the **Association des Femmes Juristes du Niger**, one of the most vocal feminine associations of the early 1990s. In 2003, she was appointed prefect-president of the *communauté urbaine* of **Niamey** and was much praised for her work in cleaning up the city and organizing the games of the CEN-SAD, a subregional community of **Sahelian** and Saharan states. In June 2007, she took up the position of minister of **women** and child protec-tion, remaining in the cabinet through 2010. Her civic engagement records were stained by her very active support for President **Mamadou Tandja**'s constitutional coup of late 2009, and her ministerial responsibilities were ended by the **coup of February 2010** which removed Tandja from office. As a testament to the way in which Tandja's project divided the Nigeriens, Ma-dame Barry's camp was fiercely opposed by her brother, the political scientist **Abdoulaye Niandou Souley**.

NIANDOU SOULEY, ABDOULAYE. A political scientist, Niandou Sou-ley specialized in the study of political **Islam** and **democratization** in Niger. He was well known in **Niamey** for the public lectures he used to deliver in the early 1990s, though in more recent years he retired from the public stage and was apparently mired in alcoholism. During President **Mamadou Tandja**'s ill-fated attempt at ending democratic governance in late 2009, Niandou Sou-ley seemed to spring back to life, speaking forcefully against the president in public lectures and on national and international radio. When Tandja was finally toppled in February 2010, he was appointed president of institutional and political affairs at the transitional parliament, the **Conseil Consultatif National**. He died shortly thereafter, in July 2010, partly of exhaustion. *See also* NIANDOU BARRY, BIBATA.

NIASSISM. Islamic Sufi order of the **Tijaniyya** persuasion, found in the **Niger River** valley settlements and originally from Senegal. Cofounded by Abdoulaye Niass and his son, Ibrahima Niass (1900–1975), in Kaolack (Sen-egal), it spread in the Hausaland (both in Niger and in **Nigeria**) and in the Yo-rubaland (Nigeria), an unintended result of French colonial efforts at assisting this accommodating brand of **Islam**. The order's most important leader in Ni-ger was, however, the **Zarma** cleric **Cheik Aboubacar Hassoumi** of **Kiota** (near **Dosso**), who married one of Niass's daughters, **Saida Oumoul Khairy**

Niass. Niass himself visited Niger in 1953, giving the order's offshoot there a welcome boost. In recent years, with the development of **civil society**, Nigerien Niassism has found expression in several formal organizations, including the Association pour le Rayonnement de la Culture Islamique (ARCI) and the newspaper *Al-Maoulid*. Through these channels, Nigerien Niassism stresses its attachment to cultural and social action rather than political militancy, and appears very critical of Islamism and Sunni orthodoxy in particular, through defining Nigerien Islam as rooted in its African context instead of replicating idealized **Arab** manners. Moreover, to the preferred modes of action of its rivals—preaching and the ceremony of the Wa'azin Kasa—Nigerien Niassism opposes adoration chanting and the annual grand-scale celebration of the Maoulid, the Prophet Muhammad's birthday. And lastly, while Sunni Orthodox groups treat **Christianity** (and especially its Protestant varieties) with hostility, Nigerien Niassism maintains warm relations with the Catholic Church in Niger. *See also* ISLAMIC ORDERS; RELIGION.

NIGELEC. *See* SOCIÉTÉ NIGÉRIENNE D'ELECTRICITÉ.

NIGER-POSTE. Niger's postal sector was established at independence, with the initial setting up of the Office des Postes et Télécommunications (OPT) service in 1959. The postal service came of age with its adhesion to the Universal Postal Union in 1961. OPT became a full-fledged **parastatal** in 1970. In 1996–1997, it was partly privatized, with its telecommunication branch merging with the Société des Télécommunications Internationales (STIN) to become **Société Nigérienne des Télécommunications** (SONI-TEL) and its postal branch remaining in the state portfolio as Office National des Postes et de l'Epargne (ONPE). In 2005, ONPE's capital was opened to private investment as the company evolved into a mixed-**economy** corporation under the name Niger-Poste. Only the personnel of ONPE bought shares of Niger-Poste, however, and the company remains largely state owned.

NIGER RIVER. Africa's third-longest river, and the world's ninth longest, the Niger rises 250 km from the sea in the Futa Djallon highlands of Guinea (height: 800 meters) and spirals in a huge 4,184-km arc through Mali (where it forms a large inland delta), Niger, Benin, and **Nigeria** before flowing into the Atlantic Ocean. The river's drainage basin is 2,262,000 sq km and its average flow rate is of 6000 m^3. The river flows for some 550 km through western Niger, and a small portion of it forms the border between Niger and Benin. A string of islands there, the most well-known being Lété, was the source of a border dispute between Niger and Benin which was solved only in 2005. The river offers Niger limited navigation possibilities for only 200 km (essentially between **Gaya**/Malanville and **Niamey**), a stretch navigable by shallow vessels, except in times of **drought**.

It receives, in Niger, no affluents on its left side between Tossayé and Malanville, though there are large vestiges of former hydrographic features—the fossilized valleys of Tilemsi, **Azawagh**, and **Dallol Bosso**. On its right bank it receives the Goroubi, Diamangou, and Tapoa affluents. Above the **Parc National du W** the river is joined, from the Benin side, by the Mekrou, Alibori, and Sota rivers. The series of **Sahel** droughts since the mid-1970s has depressed water levels throughout the river's course. In 1985 the Niger River was nearly dry at Niamey, and at its lowest level since 1922. The projected **Kandadji Dam**—between **Ayorou** and **Tillabéri**—is supposed to make the river (in normal years) fully navigable throughout its entire course.

NIGER TRANSIT (NITRA). State agency created by the Ministry of Economic Affairs in December 1974, with the **Société Nationale des Transports Nigériens** (SNTN) possessing 48 percent of the shares. Capitalized with 5 million **CFA francs** and with administrative headquarters in **Niamey**, NITRA is the state's customs agent that manages Nigerien port facilities at Cotonou (Benin) and Lomé (Togo).

NIGERIA. Nigeria is in more than one way Niger's most important neighbor. The most populated country in Africa, endowed with tremendous **oil** riches and the most vibrant **economy** in West Africa, it also shares Niger's longest border—1,500 km—and is arguably Niger's first economic partner, in competition with **France**. Relationships between postcolonial Niger and Nigeria are uneventful at state level, but the constraints that characterize the level of exchanges between the two countries—which could have easily been much higher than they now are—were created during the colonial period.

The border between Nigeria and Niger cuts through the area inhabited by the **Kanuri** (whose main urban center, Maiduguri, is now in Nigeria) and the densely populated Hausaland. Remarkably however, it also follows, through a historical fluke, the border between the emirates of the Sokoto Empire (all falling under British rule) and the **Hausa** refugee states of **Gobir** and **Northern Katsina**, as well as the unconquered **sultanate of Damagaram** (all taken over by France). The separation created new cultural differences between Frenchified and Anglicized Hausa but did not alter the substantial cultural commonalities and many social ties that unite the Hausa across the political border. Moreover, given the fact that the Hausa never historically created large imperial states and generally lived in small, keenly competitive commercial kingdoms, the separation lacks the political meaning of impairing a settled nationality. No pan-Hausa nationalism runs along the border as might have been expected, despite the fact that many social and cultural movements, some with political undertones, that develop in Nigeria (where lay the biggest and more prosperous side of the Hausaland) cross over into Niger.

Colonial France engineered most of the artificial divisions between Niger and Nigeria that persist to date. In the early 20th century, France sought to maintain the Saharan trade routes that connected the **Damagaram** with North African centers, given the fact that it gradually controlled most of the Sahara, as well as the Algerian and Tunisian terminii of the old routes. This policy was undermined in great deal by the British development of the Gulf of Guinea and building of a railroad connecting the great Hausa commercial center of Kano to ports in southern Nigeria. The establishment of **groundnut** basins around **Zinder** (Damagaram) and **Maradi** (Northern Katsina) depended on connections with Kano, a fact which the French authorities found unpalatable.

During World War II, Niger—like all **Afrique Occidentale Française** colonies—was loyal to the government of occupied France, and its zealous right-wing governor, Jean Toby, shut down the border with Nigeria, considered a British territory and therefore an enemy of Vichy France. The measure was quite unsuccessful, however, prompting the French to mull over plans to effectively divert Nigerien trade away from Nigeria. In the 1950s, this led to the establishment of **Opération Hirondelle**, and later to that of the **Organisation Commune Bénin-Niger** (OCBN), which essentially served to organize Niger's import-export trade in connection with the French-controlled ports of Cotonou (Bénin) and Lomé (Togo). While the organization appears to an extent logical given the fact that it also factored in the city of **Niamey**, which is located too far away from Nigerian centers to be a part of the Nigerian routes, it was chiefly meant to reduce the Nigerien Hausaland's dependence on Nigeria. This French outlook prevailed after independence. Thus, President **Hamani Diori** maintained cooperation with Dahomey (Bénin) despite the tense relationships that obtained between the two states during much of his tenure. In so doing, Diori was trying to preserve Nigerien integrity, which he thought could be threatened by a centripetal pull of Niger's Hausa toward their brethren in Nigeria if trade links created a settled dependence. However, unlike France, Diori was not hostile to Nigerian integrity and refused to follow the lead of France and Côte d'Ivoire in helping the Biafran insurgents during Nigeria's late 1960s civil war. In fact, he worked as an active mediator to end the conflict in a way that ensured the survival of the Nigerian federation.

In 1971, the two states set up the Nigeria-Niger Joint Commission for Cooperation (NNJCC), which organized Nigerian assistance to Niger in the areas of infrastructure building and **education** especially. Nigeria also provides

Niger with cheap electricity, which allowed the country to avoid investing in domestic production of electricity for several decades.

Nigeria and Niger collaborate in a number of regional organizations, including most importantly the **Economic Community of West African States** (ECOWAS), and the two countries maintain an embassy in each other's capitals, while Niger also has a very busy general consulate at Kano, a testimony to the intense economic and social relations existing between the Nigerien and Nigerian Hausalands.

However, the relations between the two countries are unequal, as Niger is much more in need of Nigerian cooperation than the other way around. Nigeria has at times considered Niger a nuisance, interfering with its internal economic policy through its large diaspora within Nigeria and the large-scale smuggling cum unrecorded trade which involves the *Alhazai* **of Maradi**, often aided and abetted by Niger's state organizations. Nigeria sporadically resorted to border closures and eviction of Nigerien nationals, especially in the early 1980s, in violation of agreements included in the ECOWAS treaty. But this never affected the relations between the two states, as it was understood to be short-term reactions rather than set policy on the part of Nigeria. *See also* BENIN-NIGER BOUNDARY DISPUTE.

"NIGÉRIENNE, LA." National anthem of Niger, adopted on 12 July 1961. Three Frenchmen composed it: Maurice Albert Thiriet for the lyrics, and Robert Jacquet and Nicolas Frionnet for the **music**.

NORTHERN KATSINA. Northern Katsina (*Katséna Nord*) is the section of the kingdom of Katsina that has become part of Niger's territory, including the *communauté urbaine* of **Maradi** and the *départements* of Madarounfa, **Aguié**, and **Tessaoua**. Like the Gobirawa, the Katsinawa claim an Iraqi ancestry, but interestingly, one mixed with Jews. Katsina royalty and aristocracy believe to this day that they are the offspring of the marriage of Bayajida, an **Arab** man from Baghdad (Bagdaza in Hausa), and of Daura, daughter of a Jewish man by the name of Lamarudu.

Whatever the case may be, a **Hausa** man, Kumayun, founded the Katsina kingdom in the 13th century. It blended a variety of people around its early capital at Durbi ta Kusheyi, about 32 km southeast of Birnin Katsina (the modern capital, now in **Nigeria**)—an original Katsina group, intermarrying with groups known as Durbawa, Tazarawa (founders of the Tessaoua district), Nafatawa, and Jinjino-Bakawa. Katsina blossomed in the 15th and 17th century as the principal gateway to the Hausaland for northern trade, and the kingdom grew rich and powerful. The northern sections of the kingdom were important as strategic assets regarding the maintenance and security of trade routes to the Sahara, the relations with the **Tuareg** and the Gobirawa, as well as for internal migrations into their less populated lands.

The main threat to Northern Katsina came from the **Gobir** kingdom, which under King Soba besieged **Maradi**. The greatest Gobir monarch, **Bawa Jan Gwarzo**, also temporarily captured the town. It is, however, **Usman dan Fodio**'s jihadist attack on the Hausa kingdoms which did away with Katsina's founding house (the Korau), replacing them in 1808 with a **Fulani** jihadi emir (viceroy), Malam Umaru Dallaji. Abuses from the strict jihadist administration led to an uprising and to the founding of a Korau legitimist kingdom in Maradi, the principal town in Northern Katsina. That region had in particular strong traditions of **Arna** (animist) religion, which favored resistance to jihadist inroads. The official policy of the exiled Korau was to regroup and take back the larger and richer Southern Katsina. Accordingly, the ruler, seated in Maradi, took the title *Sarkin Katsina a Maradi* (King of Katsina at Maradi). Maradi was considered only as a *sansanin yaki* (war base), which moreover permitted alliances with the neighboring Gobir kings and the **sultanate of Damagaram**.

But the policy of reconquest floundered, especially when, in the 1850s, the house of Korau was troubled by the royal succession squabbles peculiar to the Hausa princely system (*sarauta*). At the same time the Sokoto Empire (the imperial state born from the jihad) faced **rebellions** in many of the conquered provinces. It sought peace with defiant kingdoms such as the one in Northern Katsina. In this new context, Northern Katsina was torn apart by succession contests. In 1892, King Mijinyawa was thus ejected from the throne by his contestants and ended up creating a new Katsina kingship in **Tessaoua**. A similar story led to the emergence of a kingship in Gazaoua. In the early 19th century, the French took over all of Northern Katsina, and they endorsed the rule of the house of Korau in Maradi and Tessaoua as intermediary to colonial overrule. In independent Niger, the area has been defined as the province of Gobir-Katséna, folded in the administrative region of Maradi. The king of Maradi still hails from the house of Korau and is one of the most prominent traditional chiefs) in the Republic of Niger. His official title of *Chef de Province du Katséna* was changed and upgraded in September 2010 into that of *Sultan du Katséna-Maradi*. (For the list of kings, see the entry on Maradi.)

NOUHOU, ASKIA. Son of Daoud, and grandson of **Askia Mohamed** I. Founder of the kingdom of **Dendi** and first in the short lineage of the Askias—lasting to the mid-17th century—of the southern branch of the **Songhay Empire** following the fall of **Gao** and the **battle of Tondibi** (1591). Ruling for seven years, during which all his efforts were channeled into the struggle to regain the lost heartland of the empire, he assumed leadership over

Songhay after the Moroccan conquest and the death of his brother, Askia Ishaq II, at Tondibi. Hidden in the Niger bend (the W) until troops sent to capture or kill him retreated, he afterward organized his forces to harass the enemy now entrenched in Gao.

OFFICE DE RADIO-TÉLÉVISION DU NIGER (ORTN). Niger's state broadcasting authority, which carries programs in French, **Hausa**, **Zarma**, **Tamasheq**, **Kanuri**, Fulfulde, **Toubou**, Gourmantchéma, and Arabic. Its television channel, Télé **Sahel**, emerged from a French-sponsored experiment of school television attempted in 1964–1977 in **Niamey** and **Dosso**, and eventually shelved for its costliness. The state of Niger used the infrastructure set up during the experiment to test mass television broadcasting during the Football World Cup of 1978. Given the success of the operation, Télé Sahel started to broadcast the following year, at first only four days a week, and with color transmission limited to Niamey and Dosso (where the stations installed by the French were revised for colorization). Broadcasting stations were rapidly multiplied and by 1982 over 80 percent of the country's vast landmass were covered by Télé Sahel broadcasts. Color television also became general. Télé Sahel moved into daily broadcasts in 1988.

In the first half of the 1980s, Télé Sahel invested in producing original documentary movies and even fiction films, besides its extensive coverage of official activities. But at the turn of the 1990s decade, starved of funding, it tended to focus on pedestrian coverage of meetings and seminars, while relying on partnerships with foreign television (and especially the French network Canal France International) for educational and entertainment programs.

The 1990s liberalization of the audiovisual sector brought about a competitive environment, with the founding of several private television channels. In response, ORTN created a second public television channel that uses the same digital technology as its competitors, Tal TV. Tal TV focuses on entertainment and **education**, leaving all official business to Télé Sahel. Also like most of its competitors, Tal TV broadcast only in and around Niamey at this point.

Télé Sahel's budget is provided by the state (52 percent), its own resources (30 percent), and licence fees (18 percent). *See also* MEDIA; VOIX DU SAHEL.

OFFICE DES EAUX DU SOUS-SOL (OFEDES). *See* SOCIÉTÉ D'EXPLOITATION DES EAUX DU NIGER (SEEN).

OFFICE DES PRODUITS VIVRERS DU NIGER (OPVN). State organ created in August 1970 in a context of cereal deficit and low **agricultural** productivity. OPVN was tasked with the mission of collecting cereal, supply deficit-prone regions, and manage security stocks and food aid. Equipped with the monopoly of agricultural trading via the cooperatives, it handled the marketing and price stabilization of some 85 percent of Niger's agricultural produce, including **millet** and sorghum. After the **droughts** of the mid-1970s, it faced immense difficulties in building up its stock of commodities for stabilization purposes. In the early 1980s, OPVN shrank both in staffing and operation, and its mission was redefined in 1984 with the canceling of its monopoly on millet and sorghum marketing and the reduction of its security stock to 80,000 tons of cereal (down from stocking capacities of over 230,000 tons). Other restructuring, starting in 1988, further reorganized OPVN, which emerged in 1999 as an organization aiming exclusively at managing the state's cereal security reserves, consisting in 40,000 tons of locally produced cereal (the national security stock) and a financial endowment geared to the purchase of 40,000 additional tons of cereal (the food security fund). OPVN also runs the sale of food aid that is distributed through the market at low prices.

OPVN has been headed in turn by Slimane Ganoua, 1970–1974; Boubacar Bolho, 1974; Abdou Inda, 1974–1975; Amadou Anabo, 1975–1980; Adamou Souna, 1980–1984; Mahamane Koulou, 1984–1988; Ila Kané, 1988–1991; Abdoulaye Ouhoumoudou, 1991–1992; Abdoulaye Bonkoula, 1992–1994; Abass Adam Melly, 1994–1996; Madou Mahamadou, 1996–1999; Captain Aboubacar Amadou Sanda, 1999–2000; Issaka Hassane Djégoulé, 2000–2005; and Adamou Chaiffou, 2005– .

OFFICE DU LAIT DU NIGER (OLANI). *See* SOCIÉTÉ DE LAIT DU NIGER (SOLANI).

OFFICE NATIONAL DE L'ENERGIE SOLAIRE (ONERSOL). *See* CENTRE NATIONAL D'ENERGIE SOLAIRE (CNES).

OFFICE NATIONAL DES AMENAGEMENTS HYDRO-AGRICOLES (ONAHA). Parastatal set up in 1978 and charged with the systematic extension of irrigated lands tapping the river waters, with a concentration on rice-producing areas. This followed a 12-year experiment in water management effected chiefly in the region of **Niamey**. Initially, ONAHA was a state agency working with producers' cooperatives to help them develop sustainable farm water management systems in the Ader-Doutchi-Magia (cereal and **cotton** irrigation, gardening), along the **Komadougou Yobé** (region of **Diffa**, four sites) and along the **Niger River** (40 rice-producing sites, most of which are in the region of **Tillabéri**, with some around **Gaya** in the region of **Dosso**). It received considerable assistance from the Japanese government in particular.

Following the famous **Zinder** seminar of 1982, during which Niger essentially gave up the ideal of national development in favor of gradual and later accelerated liberalization, ONAHA's mission shrank to providing advice and information services as well as the promotion of system maintenance. In the late 1980s, ONAHA met the same fate as most Nigerien state agencies, being crippled by financial difficulties. It was restructured in the early 1990s, becoming a state agency operating as a commercial organization, and thus competing with private firms to provide services and solutions to farmers. Its trajectory in this new phase is lackluster, as it became (like so many public agencies) a pawn in the political struggles of the democratic era. In 2010, ONAHA was one of the key agencies targeted by the military transition regime that followed the toppling of President **Mamadou Tandja** for thorough reorganization. An engineer and military officer, Captain Mamoudou Amadou Bondabou, was appointed to carry out that mission during the transition period. *See also* ECONOMIC LIBERALIZATION.

OFFICE NATIONAL DES PRODUITS PHARMACEUTIQUES ET CHIMIQUES (ONPPC). State company set up in 1962 with a broad-based mission that gradually included the production of essential drugs under generic license as well as their sale in a network of low-cost pharmacies, the state-run *pharmacies populaires* (peoples' pharmacies), and the supervision of drug import and distribution in the country.

Various production units (four in total) were put in place between 1972 and 1989 for different categories of medicines. A not-for-profit state organ, ONPPC organized the entire pharmaceutical business, from importation and production to storage and distribution. It had (and still has) 3 regional storehouses (**Niamey, Zinder**, and **Tahoua**) and 13 supply centers and branches. In this way it basically managed a state monopoly over pharmaceuticals, especially since it benefited from various discounts and facilities which obliged the small number of private pharmacies to purchase their stock through its services. In 1997, however, the pharmaceutical sector was liberalized, permitting the establishment of private distributors, while ONPPC itself saw its status changed into that of a state agency with a commercial orientation. Its production units were consolidated into two mixed-economy companies, the

Société Nigérienne des Industries Pharmaceutiques (SONIPHAR) and the Société Industrielle Pharmaceutique (SIP).

Anecdotally, ONPPC was headed, before his accession, by the current *zarmakoy* and sultan of Dosso, Maidanda Saidou Djermakoye. *See also* ECONOMIC LIBERALIZATION.

OFFICE NATIONAL DES RESSOURCES MINIÈRES (ONAREM). Public industrial and commercial company created on 26 August 1976 and charged with promoting the research, development, and exploitation (as well as sale) of all mineral resources in the Republic of Niger, and to participate in all joint companies set up. ONAREM holds 33 percent of the shares of **Société des Mines de l'Aïr** (SOMAIR) and holds similar equity in the other **mining** companies. In the mid-1980s, ONAREM discovered gold in a dozen sites 200 km north of **Niamey**, and it initiated an agreement with a Canadian company for the joint exploitation of the ore on the same terms, following more detailed feasibility studies in the mid-1990s. *See also* SAMIRA.

OIL. Oil prospecting, started in the early 1950s, was interrupted in 1965 and resumed in the early 1970s with the government's encouragement and consequent to various promising signs of possible deposits in **Aïr** as well as in neighboring countries. Among the major concessions granted in that period were 245,000 sq km north of **Lake Chad**, given to Texaco (across the border in Chad, several wells came on line in the early 1970s), which committed itself to spend 910 million **CFA francs** in explorations over five years; Continental Oil Company, which obtained a concession over 290,000 sq km in southern Niger, pledging investments amounting to 1,650 million CFA francs over five years; and Bishop Oil and Refining Company, which held a potentially valuable Djado concession of 110,000 sq km and 85,000 sq km in the **Agadez** area, with the commitment to invest 550 million CFA francs in explorations. By the late 1970s, sufficient actual deposits had been discovered (especially in the distant Tin Touma sands in the **N'Guigmi** area) to ensure Niger self-sufficiency in oil, if and when the resources are exploited, but no steady investment was forthcoming.

Things moved ahead only in the 2000s, as new players from Asia appeared in the country's **mining** scene. Thus, in 2004, the Chinese China National Petroleum Corporation (CNPC) took up a joint venture with TG World (an older player from the early 1990s) to secure permits in the **Ténéré** desert. The following year, the Indonesian Petronas announced important findings in the Agadem block, in the northeastern region of Diffa. In 2008, Petronas and Esso's rights on the Agadem block were transferred to CNPC, and the Nigerien government signed a contract of exploitation with the China National

Oil and Gas Development Corporation. The Agadem block has an estimated 483 million barrels potential, and Chinese investments of upward to $5 billion include extraction and the building of a 450 km pipeline and a refinery, the latter in the northern outskirts of the town of **Zinder**. The refinery is due to produce 20,000 barrels a day. Of these, 7,000 barrels would cater to Nigerien demand, and 13,000 percent would be exported mainly to **Nigeria**. The reserves are estimated to amount to some 300 million barrels. Though this is somewhat paltry compared to Nigeria's reserves of 36 billion barrels, it is expected to stimulate business and investment conditions in the country by significantly lowering the cost of energy, especially given that the oil is being refined in the country. *See also* SOCIÉTÉ DE RAFFINERIE DE ZINDER.

ONION. Onions have emerged as an important export crop in Niger in the 1990s and indeed by the mid-2000s officially as the second Nigerien export product after **uranium**. In 1990, Niger had produced 170,000 tons of the bulb, 356,184 at the end of the decade in 1999, and on average 400,000 tons yearly since the early 2000s. The industry, having developed in the liberalization decade of the 1990s, is entirely controlled by private Nigerien and foreign (mostly West African) interests. Domestic consumption averages 13,000 tons a year, leaving plenty (deducting losses due to storage problems) for export. **Gobir Hausa** peasants produce around 80 percent of the crop in the southern areas of the region of **Tahoua**. Onion is harvested in January–April, selling at very low prices in that period. As the year wears on, however, it becomes dearer, increasing tenfold by December. Southern producers discovered, in the early 2000s, that ecosystems in the **Aïr** permitted year-round production, but their efforts there were quashed by the onset of the 2007–2009 **Tuareg** rebellion.

Niger mostly exports into other West African countries, with prime customers being Côte d'Ivoire and Ghana. Nigerien producers are advantaged by the popular quality of their two main types of the produce, the purple colored *violet de Galmi* and the shiny white *blanc de Soumarana*. Part of the production exported to Côte d'Ivoire finds its way to **France**, prompting Nigerien producers to seek European Union certification in order to sell the crop directly on the French market. But the sector is also hampered by the mode of exploitation practiced by small landholders with little access to credit, and more generally by the lack of a streamlined **agricultural** policy in Niger.

OPÉRATION CHEVAL NOIR. Secret French contingency plan, allegedly devised by President Charles de Gaulle himself, to protect **Hamani Diori**, his family, and key aides with French troops stationed in Niger and to spirit them away to Camp Leclerc in case of a coup d'état in **Niamey**. The plan was not put into motion when the **coup of 15 April 1974** actually occurred, allegedly since there was "no one" in Paris at the time (Easter) to authorize its execution, and the French garrison of Niamey was likewise preoccupied with a hunt over the holiday. More likely, the failure to intervene was a ploy by Jacques Foccart, **France**'s longtime "African policy" operator, to drop Diori who had become bothersome over **uranium** revenues. The French garrison was subsequently removed by the new Nigerien regime.

OPÉRATION HIRONDELLE (Operation Swallow). Arrangement set up by the colonial government in 1953 to evacuate Niger's **groundnut** crop via a railroad in Dahomey to the Atlantic port of Cotonou and thence to Europe. One key objective of Opération Hirondelle was to cut dependence on the British-owned Kano–Lagos route, but it proved to be a very slow, cumbersome, and inefficient arrangement due to the major problems of evacuating the big-volume crop in just a few weeks onto a rail-and-truck network that is both outdated and in a state of disrepair. It was advantageous to Benin, however, for its Cotonou–Parakou railway would otherwise have been grossly underutilized in the southbound direction. The projected expansion of the railway to Niger—ever in discussion—could alleviate some of the problems. The arrangement was organized by an intergovernmental organization, the Organisation Commune Dahomey-Niger (OCDN), later **Organisation Commune Bénin-Niger** (OCBN), which had to be heavily subsidized.

In time, Opération Hirondelle was abandoned, but its infrastructure gave rise to the current "special transit" when the Niger–Benin route proved valuable to northern Nigerian importers in view of **Nigeria**'s internal organizational problems. The connection Cotonou–**Maradi** has thus become the most important axis of the new arrangement, further increasing the dependence of Cotonou's port on the Nigerien trade.

The name "Opération Hirondelle" was likely inspired by the code name of the 1953 French airborne raid on the Viet Minh supply depots in Lang Son, during the Indochina War.

ORGANISATION COMMUNE BÉNIN-NIGER DES CHEMINS DE FER ET DES TRANSPORTS (OCBN). Joint Benin-Niger organization (known as OCDN when Benin was known as Dahomey), founded in 1959 with a Beninese majority control (63 percent) of the shares. The OCBN's main activities were running the railroad from Cotonou to Parakou (entirely in Benin), the Parakou–**Niamey** transshipment by trucks of goods destined for Niger, the joint management of the Cotonou wharf, and coordination of **Opération Hirondelle**. The Cotonou–Parakou line is 438 km long, and the remaining 880-km section to the border and **Dosso** has been projected for decades. The high building costs and low traffic (except when Niger's crops have to be evacuated) have stalled execution of the project, despite the fact that feasibility and fund-raising efforts have been mounted periodically.

ORGANISATION DE LA RESISTANCE ARMÉE (ORA). Successor, in 1995, to the **Coordination de la Résistance Armée**, which signed the April 1995 peace agreement with the government, formally ending the first **Tuareg rebellion**. The organization was somewhat looser than the CRA, and was headed by **Rhissa Ag Boula**, who was also head of the CRA.

ORGANISATION INTERNATIONALE DE LA FRANCOPHONIE (OIF). Successor organization to the Agence de Coopération Culturelle et Technique (ACCT). ACCT was founded on 20 March 1970 by a convention signed in **Niamey**, and under, inter alia, the active diplomacy of Niger's president, **Hamani Diori**. Its objectives, with funding mostly from **France**, Canada, and Belgium, are to intensify cultural and technical cooperation among member-states in matters of **education**, training, science and technology (but not research), **agriculture**, culture and communication (but not television), law, environment, and energy. In 1970, ACCT had 21 members. This membership had doubled by 1995, when it became the Organisation Internationale de la Francophonie. By 2010, OIF had 75 member-states, categorized into 56 full members and 19 observer states.

OIF countries make up 800 million of the world's population, and the organization has extended cooperation into the domains not covered by ACCT through four so-called direct operators, the Agence Universitaire de la Francophonie (AUF) for academic research, TV5 for television, the Université Senghor d'Alexandrie in Egypt, and the Association Internationale des Maires Francophones. Its first secretary-general (elected in 1997, the year in which the position was created) was former United Nations secretary-general Boutros Boutros-Ghali. He was succeeded in 2003 by former Senegalese president Abdou Diouf. OIF organizes the annual Jeux de la Francophonie, the fifth edition of which were held in Niamey in December 2005.

OUALLAM. Town of 7,800 people in the *département* of the same name (population 281,000) in the **Tillabéri** region; also the main urban settlement in the historical region of **Zarmaganda**.

OUBANDAWAKI, ISSOUFOU OUSMANE (1948–). Born in **Birni-N'Konni** where he went to primary school, he further studied at the Lycée National in **Niamey**, gaining his scientific *baccalauréat* in 1969, before moving to **France** where he completed a course of studies in aviation at the École

Nationale d'Aviation Civile, at Sceaux. Upon graduating from the school at Sceaux, Oubandawaki went to the University of Montreal, with a scholarship from the United Nations Development Programme (UNDP), to undertake a course of studies for a master's in the **economy** of airborne transportation. After returning to Niger, he was appointed to the country representation for the Agence pour la Sécurité de la Navigation Aérienne en Afrique et à Madagascar (ASECNA), climbing to the position of general manager of the service in Niger in 1985. He was afterward promoted to various high-profile positions within ASECNA's general headquarters in Dakar (Senegal) until 1996, when, upon becoming president of Niger, his friend **Ibrahim Baré Maïnassara** appointed him defense minister and then transport minister. As defense minister, he had a bill adopted that considerably increased the pension to the widows and orphans of troops deceased in combat (this was an aftermath of the 1990s **Tuareg rebellions**). At the Ministry of Transport, he presided over the liberalization of the sector, leading to the emergence of Niger's vaunted passenger **transportation** business.

In 1998, Niger supported his candidacy to the position of general manager of ASECNA, which he won at a meeting in Bata (Equatorial Guinea). His tenure lasted until 2004, when Oubandawaki started to position himself as a presidential hopeful in Niger, creating a nongovernmental organization (Amélioration Gestion Intégrée des Ressources, AGIR) to offer wells and microcredit to rural populations and thus popularize his name. He then proceeded to create the party Alliance pour le Renouveau Démocratique (ARD Adaltchi Mutunchi) and ran for the presidency in 2011. He came seventh of 10 candidates with 1.93 percent of the vote.

OUMAROU, ABOUBACAR SANDA (1931–). Born into **Zinder**'s royal family in the **Birni** (Zinder's traditional heart), Sanda did some primary and secondary **education** in Zinder and was enthroned sultan of Damagaram in 1978. The **sultanate of Damagaram** was recognized as the highest title in Niger's traditional peerage, but Sanda is famous especially for an extended judicial battle that started when he was deposed from the throne in 2001.

In July 2001, Sanda was accused of fraud and swindling, embezzlement, drug trafficking, and other crimes, with evidence provided by his own siblings and an allegedly defrauded trader. The government removed him from the Damagaram throne and put him under house arrest in **Niamey** with heavy fines. The defense rejected the accusations and denounced a conspiracy between the sultan's siblings and powerful politicians in Niamey acting for electoral purposes. The case against the sultan collapsed after the main witness for the prosecution (the defrauded trader) withdrew his claims, but trial was postponed until July 2009 when a court in Niamey eventually found him not guilty, released him from house arrest, and ordered the state to compensate him. In the meantime, however, Sanda had lost the throne to one of his relatives and his first action as a free man was to launch a campaign to be restored into the position. In June 2011, a ruling of the **Cour Suprême** finally reinstated him as sultan.

The events served to highlight the precarious position of Niger's traditional rulers; threats of violence against state officials in Zinder after the Sultan's arrest failed to materialize and while Sanda was exiled and isolated in Niamey, the new state-backed sultan was soon firmly in place. Niger's traditional peerage was thus clearly revealed as a mere state organization, freely manipulated by state officials even in its highest reaches.

OUMAROU, AMADOU (Lieutenant) (1943–). Key conspirator in the somewhat botched 1983 attempted coup against President **Seyni Kountché**. Better known in Niamey as **Bonkano**, a nickname which means "the fortunate" in **Zarma**, Oumarou was President Kountché's personal aide and confidant. Virtually illiterate, he used his control of the portals of the presidential office to dispense patronage, in the process enriching himself tremendously. His interests included construction, commerce, trucking, and **banking**. Of **Fulani** background, he offered a 100 million **CFA franc** mosque to his neighborhood of Karagué, on **Niamey**'s Fulani-settled right bank, and donated various sums for charitable purposes—all, the rumor went in Niamey, in order to atone for his crimes. In 1983 Oumarou utilized his status in the presidential office to lure and arrest a number of key military officers (including **Ali Saibou**, the future president, after Kountché's death) as a prelude to a takeover. When the conspiracy failed, due to the alertness of one of the commanders, Oumarou slipped into exile to **France**. In 1991, during the proceedings of the **Conférence Nationale**, Oumarou was given personal immunity and returned to testify before a committee investigating the fiscal improprieties of the Kountché era, throwing further light on high-level mismanagement and corruption. He unsuccessfully tried to return to politics and his wealth also withered in due course. *See also* COUP OF 5 OCTOBER 1983.

OUMAROU, IDE (1937–2002). Former secretary-general of the Organization of African Unity (OAU) and former foreign minister of Niger. Born in **Niamey**, and a graduate of **École William Ponty** and the Institut des Hautes Études d'Outre-Mer (IHEOM), the former colonial cadre training institute École Coloniale, in Paris, Oumarou was trained as a journalist. He commenced his career as an editor in the Ministry of Information, and in 1961 was appointed editor of *Le Niger*. In 1963 he became director-general of information, serving until October 1972, when he became director of posts and telecommunications.

Shortly after **Seyni Kountché**'s **coup of 1974** he joined his presidential staff as *chef du cabinet*, becoming Kountché's closest aide for the next five years. In 1980 he was promoted by Kountché to head Niger's delegation to the United Nations, and in that capacity he presided over the Security Council between May 1980 and January 1981. On 14 November 1983, Oumarou was recalled to Niamey to become foreign minister, serving until July 1985 when the Organization of African Unity elected him its secretary-general. He ran for another term of office in July 1988 but was defeated by Tanzania's Salim Ahmed Salim, returning to Niamey to serve as General **Ali Saibou**'s minister of state and special advisor.

Oumarou was an author as well. His novel *Gros Plan* won the coveted Grand Prix Littéraire d'Afrique Noire in 1978. This was followed by *Le Représentant* in 1984. He also published, in 1996, a memoir of his work under President Kountché, *Temps forts avec Seini Kountché*. *See also* LITERATURE.

OUMAROU, MAMANE (1946–). Diplomat and former prime minister. A **Kanuri** from eastern Niger, Oumarou served as ambassador to Canada, mayor of **Maradi**, and minister of youth, sports, and culture under President **Seyni Kountché**. Briefly prime minister of Niger, in November 1983 (the first to hold the office), Oumarou was afterward appointed head of the **Conseil National de Développement**, serving until 1988 in what was at the time envisaged as the second most important post in Niger. After Kountché's death, his successor, General **Ali Saibou**, reappointed Oumarou prime minister of Niger in May 1989. The position was eliminated in December 1989. He was later appointed Niger's envoy to Saudi Arabia until his retirement. In 2008, President **Mamadou Tandja** appointed him mediator of the republic, an office which, in view of the **Tazartché** constitutional crisis which Tandja then proceeded to trigger, proved to be a lifeless sinecure bestowed on Oumarou as a favor.

OUMAROU, SANDA (1904–1978). Former sultan of **Zinder**. Born in 1904 and the son of **Amadou dan Bassa** and grandson of **Tanimoun**, Oumarou came to the throne in 1950. His full name was Sanda Oumarou dan Amadou. He was the father of deposed sultan **Aboubacar Sanda Oumarou**.

OUMAROU, SEYNI (1950–). A **Songhay** man from **Tillabéri**, Oumarou combined a short formal **education** with business savviness and experience in administrative affairs, leading him to the position of general manager of the

Nigerien paper-processing enterprise (Entreprise Nigérienne de Transformation du Papier, ENITRAP) in 1987–1988. The position gave him a springboard for wealth building as he subsequently became Niger's major marketer of stationary materials. A close friend of **Mouvement National pour la Société de Développement** (MNSD)'s secretary-general **Hama Amadou**, he was appointed special advisor to the prime minister when Amadou was briefly at the helm of government in 1995.

In 1999, the transitional government of **Daouda Malam Wanké**, the ouster of President **Baré Maïnassara**, chose him for the Ministry of Trade and Industry, a position he retained under the government set up by Hama Amadou upon MNSD's victory at the polls that year. In the following years, Oumarou moved between several cabinet portfolios until the fall of the Amadou government at the National Assembly in June 2007. By then, he had become closer to President Mamadou Tandja who chose him to succeed Amadou as prime minister. The appointment allowed Tandja to maintain MNSD's unity, since Oumarou, like Amadou, had his support base in the region of Tillabéri, a major MNSD stronghold. Furthermore, Tandja maneuvered to have Amadou ousted from the MNSD presidency, and this resulted in Oumarou becoming MNSD's president in January 2009, at an extraordinary party congress in **Zinder**. This did not go without conflicts, consummated by a weakening of the MNSD after Amadou managed to mastermind the creation of a split party in July 2009.

Supporting Tandja's bid to overstay his last term and change Niger's political regime, Oumarou organized a **constitutional referendum** in August 2009, and though the results were massively fraudulent, he assisted Tandja in establishing the **Sixth Republic**. He then stepped down from the premiership in order to stand as a parliamentary candidate for the legislative **elections** of October 2009. Following the elections, which were boycotted by Niger's major parties, the **Economic Community of West African States** (ECOWAS) suspended Niger's membership, and Oumarou headed a Nigerien delegation that traveled to Abuja (**Nigeria**) in November to begin talks on the country's political crisis (although the Tandja regime's official viewpoint was that there was no political crisis in Niger). Later in the month, he was unanimously elected speaker of the **National Assembly**, but this position, like the Sixth Republic itself, was short lived, as the army toppled Tandja in February 2010.

In the period after the coup, Oumarou faced several charges of conspiracy to stir unrest (as president of the MNSD he had called for the immediate release of former President Tandja) and embezzlement (he was arrested, charged, and released on bail). In August 2010, the MNSD had announced that Oumarou was its presidential candidate, and at the first round of voting on 31 January 2011, he came in second with 23.24 percent of the vote against 36.06 percent for **Mahamadou Issoufou** of the **Parti Nigérien pour la Démocratie et le Socialisme** (PNDS Tarayya), and 19.82 percent to Hama Amadou. Amadou having called his voters to support Issoufou into runoff, Issoufou easily beat Oumarou in the second round of voting held in March 2011. Oumarou gracefully acknowledged defeat and started leading the opposition.

OUSMANE, MAHAMAN (1950–). Born in the **Birni** (old town) of **Zinder**, Ousmane was a statistician and economist recruited in one of the military regime's teams of technocrats in the 1980s and was otherwise of little note. However, as Niger was veering toward liberalization and **democratization** in the late 1980s, the prestige of his high **education** combined with his *Birni* upbringing and his high state apparatus job gave him compelling influence in the politics of his home region. He emerged as the obvious leader of an ethno-regional movement founded by intellectuals from Zinder and **Maradi**, in defense of Zinder and **Hausa** interests against the perceived political hegemony of the **Zarma-Songhay**, the Association Mutuelle pour la Culture et les Arts (AMACA). Largely in response to AMACA, a Zarma-Songhay–based association, Energie de l'Ouest, was established, so much so that when Niger finally adopted democratic institutions and a multiparty regime in the early 1990s, associations and parties based on region and ethnicity were outlawed in the name of national unity. AMACA then became a **political party**, the **Convention Démocratique et Sociale** (CDS Rahama), presided over by Ousmane.

CDS remained wedded to Zinder-based interests, but while this prevented it from expecting large voting shares in Zarma-Songhay regions or even in Hausa regions outside of Zinder, it did command nearly exclusively the votes of Zinder, which is the third-most-populated district in Niger. At the time, none of the new parties, as opposed to the single-party state holdout, **Mouvement National pour la Société de Développement** (MNSD Nassara), had a monopoly over such a large share of the electorate. This gave Ousmane a strong position in the negotiations among the new parties to form a coalition that would defeat the MNSD at the presidential election of 1993. He emerged thus as the figurehead of the **Alliance des Forces du Changement** (AFC), the anti-MNSD coalition, scooping the votes of just about all former presidential candidates in the runoff round of the election (he was second to the MNSD's candidate, **Mamadou Tandja**, in the first round), and becoming the first democratically elected president of Niger.

While Ousmane benefited from this atypical situation in the late 1980s and could thus start a promising political career, he was neither charismatic, flexible, nor particularly astute and went on to rapidly squander his opportunities. The coalition cobbled together in the narrow view of defeating the MNSD could survive that outcome only through skillful leadership, which Ousmane failed to provide. Tiffs with his allies, and particularly his prime minister **Mahamadou Issoufou**, leader of the **Parti Nigérien pour la Démocratie et le Socialisme** (PNDS Tarayya), led to an about face when the PNDS left the coalition and sided with the MNSD. Faced with a hostile majority, Ousmane dissolved the Parliament, hoping that new **elections** would give him the opportunity of renegotiating a favorable coalition. This failed to happen, thanks to the greater skills of the MNSD's leadership, and Ousmane had to reluctantly appoint in 1995 the MNSD leader, **Hama Amadou**, prime minister, after having vainly attempted to form a minority government (quickly overthrown by a no-confidence vote). Placed in a situation of cohabitation (where the president and the prime minister belong to opposing parties), Ousmane decided to block the operation of government by refusing to attend cabinet meetings, thereby withholding his presidential signature on bills and appointments. He would thus effectively stall the government of Niger until constitutional timing would allow him again to dissolve Parliament and to organize new elections. The **coup d'état of 27 January 1996** ousted him on the eve of the date at which he was constitutionally allowed to dissolve the **National Assembly**.

This episode seems to have permanently damaged the career of Ousmane as a presidential hopeful. In the following years, he lost his monopoly over Zinder as MNSD and offshoots of CDS made large inroads into his stronghold. At the same time, he did not manage to broaden the basis of his party, even though it was becoming clear that regional fiefs could not win the presidency. However, he was able to redefine his position as that of a kingmaker when his support at the 1999 and 2004 elections proved essential to the success of MNSD over PNDS. Although generally despised in Niger for his perceived greed, avarice, and poor leadership, Ousmane remains very popular in Zinder, and the MNSD rewarded his support with the position of speaker of the National Assembly, which he filled throughout the 2000 decade. In 2003, he was also elected President of the Interparliamentary Committee of the **Union Economique et Monétaire Ouest-Africaine** (UEMOA), and in 2006, Speaker of the **Economic Community of the West African States** (ECOWAS) Parliament.

At this point, Ousmane had grown into being a fixture of the Nigerien political stage, and had become a normal politician, instead of the inflexible firebrand that he was in the 1990s. His public image thus changed into that of a supple practitioner of compromise and moderation, more at home with the ethos of representative democracy. When President Mamadou Tandja started to dismantle the institutions of democracy in 2009, Ousmane did not at first associate himself with the combative stance adopted in response by Mahamadou Issoufou and Hama Amadou, the two other major Nigerien politicians. Instead he tried working behind the curtains to dissuade Tandja until July 2009, when it became clear that such efforts were futile. Ousmane then joined the other parties in the struggle against Tandja, boycotting the **constitutional referendum** organized in August 2009 to usher in a new regime, as well as the legislative **elections** of October 2009. These moves were made from a distance, as Ousmane prudently settled in Abuja (**Nigeria**), where the ECOWAS Parliament is seated. In retaliation, Tandja jailed several of his friends and advisors and an arrest warrant was issued against him. Ousmane returned to Niger when Tandja was ousted by the military in February 2010 and posted his candidacy to the presidential election of 2011. He came in fourth with 8.42 percent, a position that means that he had lost his kingmaker status.

P

PARASTATAL SECTOR. The Nigerien parastatal sector followed the usual trajectory of this sector in many developing countries: a boom in the 1960s, growth issues in the 1970s, crisis in the 1980s, shrinking in the 1990s, and the subsequent boom of a substitute private sector in the 2000s. True to this scenario, most of Niger's major public companies were put in place in the first decade of independence, as part of the national development project that was then de rigueur in Africa and other newly independent Third World regions. In Niger, these public companies were tied to the **agricultural** sector, either as processing units or marketing outfits. Most of these units suffered from the **Sahel droughts** of the early 1970s, with the state struggling to keep them alive and adjust their activities to more difficult conditions, both internally and internationally. The **uranium** boom of the late 1970s allowed the Nigerien state to stay the course of state-led national development and further parastatals were established. In fact, their number, which had reached 54 in 1981, went up to 66 in 1984.

But this growth was problematic, since it was happening against the backdrop of rapidly falling uranium prices and adverse economic changes at the international level. In particular the rise of the U.S. dollar and the successive devaluations of the French franc—to which Niger's **currency** was pegged at a fixed rate—created a climate of high prices and soaring debt. The public sectors piled up losses and sharply contracted government revenues, leading to a series of closures and **privatizations**. Moreover, the very idea of state-led national development abruptly fell into disrepute at the turn of the 1980s, and critically so among the Western donor states which controlled the international financial institutions. As a cash-strapped Niger became dependent on these institutions—the World Bank, the International Monetary Fund (IMF)—it was gradually forced to relinquish that option, which entailed slashing through parastatals.

In 1986 as many as 20 of Niger's parastatal companies were thus slated to be closed in the first round of a rationization program that was supposed eventually to contract the public sector to only 25 enterprises. At accession (1988), President **Ali Saibou**, finding, as he publicly announced, "the coffers of the state empty," signed a series of agreements with the IMF (after the first one in 1983 and three others in 1986) and subsequently cut borrowing, restricted credit, froze wages, and pledged to downsize the **civil service**. A Structural Adjustment Program (SAP) called for major employment cuts in a parastatal sector then employing more people than the civil service itself (29,000 vs 24,000), in a country with only 14,000 workers employed in the private sector.

The SAP was not immediately implemented, however. Despite the fact that the state desperately needed the loans that would then have ensued, the program would have also led to a social and political crisis which the Nigerien leadership did not wish to face. It was indeed deterred by vociferous early resistance from unionists (who had paralyzed the **economy** by general strikes, including a five-day one in 1990 on this very issue), and **students** (directly affected by freezes in hiring by the civil service and the state sector). The layoffs in turn led to a waning of the modern consumers' class, a group of people made up essentially of those on the state's payroll, and foreign commercial companies (CFAO, OPTORG, Unilever, etc.) disinvested from the country or considerably reduced their operations, which made things even harder for the state. Moreover several of the former state enterprises required infusions of new capital and renovations (to make them at least minimally attractive to private investors) that the government could not afford.

By the mid-1980s, eight state enterprises had been privatized, eight (through a reduction in the government's equity) were under private management, five had been liquidated, and three had had their activities merged within a ministry. Among the first affected were the agricultural bodies, the **Union Nigérienne de Crédit et de Coopérative** (UNCC) and the **Office des Produits Vivriers du Niger** (OPVN), which were drastically restructured and partially privatized. This signaled that Niger was giving up the mainstay of its national development project, agricultural policy. In the late 1980s, public sector **banks** and financial institutions collapsed, and a few more parastatals were restructured, but during the turbulent transitional years (1990–1993) there was little further development in that respect.

In October 1994 the new democratically elected government again opened the issue, and, in a clear indication that Niger was switching to **economic liberalization** as the new road to prosperity, stated that an additional 15 of the country's state enterprises would soon be privatized. This was to start with such iconic assets as the electricity company **Société Nigérienne d'Electricité** (NIGELEC), the transport company **Société Nationale des Transports Nigériens** (SNTN), and the cement works company **Société Nigérienne de Cimenterie** (SNC). While the two latter companies were effectively privatized by the 2000s, NIGELEC remains a state company to date. Similarly, the Grand Hotel was sold off to private Nigerien capital and renovated, but the Hotel Gaweye remained in the state portfolio, and was renovated with public money. Among the erstwhile strategic sectors, the telecommunications branch of the postal company was privatized as **Société Nigérienne de Télécommunications** (SONITEL) and urban water distribution was consolidated in a private company, the **Société d'Exploitation des Eaux du Niger** (SEEN), which was farmed out to **France**'s Veolia (then Vivendi Waters).

By the late 1990s, privatization of parastatals was capped by economic liberalization which picked up pace under President **Baré Maïnassara** (1996–1999) and led to the development of a sizable private sector. State intervention took the form of a watchman institution, the **Autorité de Régulation Multisectorielle** (ARM), created in 1999 to oversee private sector activities and respect for the rules and legislation pertaining to privatization contracts.

PARC NATIONAL DU W. Wildlife refuge and nature preserve shared by Niger (300,000 hectares), Burkina Faso (330,000), and Benin (500 hectares) in the double bend of the **Niger River** area as it flows through the last outcroppings of the **Atakora** mountains. The park gets its name from the W shape of the double bend of the Niger. The Niger portion of the park, the most accessible and developed, is 165 km south of Niamey. The best time for visits is between November and February. It is reached via a road from Niamey that passes through Diapaga; by boat from Niamey to Boumba, and to the next 15 km by road to Tapoa; or by DC3 air service during the tourist season. The park has some lovely, though modest, gorges, swamps, and rocky outcroppings, and varied wildlife that includes elephants, lions, buffalo, gazelle, and monkeys.

PARTI NIGÉRIEN POUR LA DÉMOCRATIE ET LE SOCIALISME (PNDS Tarayya). The Hausa word *tarayya* which is appended to the party's acronym, means "coming together." The PNDS was founded in 1990 by a group of **union** leaders and officials of the administration and **parastatal sector** cadres.

This **political party** has been from its creation headed by **Mahamadou Issoufou**, but key leaders include **Mohammed Bazoum** and **Hassoumi Massaoudou**. Though the party's main stronghold is the region of **Tahoua**, where Issoufou is from, PNDS has developed a national reach, and has increased its electoral appeal over the years. It is also known as the "*parti des intellectuels*," and spearheaded the democratic movement that led to the **Conférence Nationale** in 1991.

In 1993, PNDS allied itself with the **Convention Démocratique et Sociale** (CDS Rahama) and a number of less important parties in the **Alliance**

des Forces du Changement (AFC), a coalition set up to prevent the return to power of the **Mouvement National pour la Société de Développement** (MNSD), which represented the regime that was overthrown by the National Conference. After the coalition won the presidential and legislative **elections**, Issoufou became prime minister. But PNDS soon fell out with CDS, and Issoufou resigned in December 1994. PNDS then struck a deal with MNSD against CDS, and the new coalition won the legislative elections that President **Mahaman Ousmane** had convened after Issoufou's government walked out. PNDS provided ministers for the new MNSD-led government, but the cohabitation between Prime Minister **Hama Amadou** and President Ousmane was fraught with disagreements and conflicts, leading to an institutional gridlock and a **coup d'état in 1996**.

Under the **Fourth Republic**, PNDS joined its rivals MNSD and CDS in a common front opposing President **Baré Maïnassara**'s authoritarian rule. PNDS' connections with the unions were important in spurring the incessant strikes which undermined Maïnassara's regime. After the **coup d'état of 1999**, which put an end to the Fourth Republic, PNDS sought an alliance with CDS against MNSD, but CDS eventually preferred MNSD, thus ensuring that PNDS lost both the presidential and the legislative elections that were organized that year. However, it was the largest opposition party in the **National Assembly** and was able to attract a number of smaller parties to its side. Starting right after the second elections of the **Fifth Republic**, in 2004, President **Mamadou Tandja** initiated a rapprochement with PNDS leader Issoufou, establishing regular meetings with him at the presidential palace, allegedly to keep away from the fractious behavior in the 1990s that prevented entente between the parties on stable government. The meetings also signaled a rift within the MNSD between the followers of President Tandja and those of Prime Minister Amadou, which the PNDS hoped to exploit. To this end, the PNDS lent a hand to President Tandja's engineering of the fall of Amadou's government in June 2007, and submitted the motion of no-confidence that led to the event. Soon thereafter, the PNDS's leadership realized, however, that President Tandja intended to subvert the **constitution** of the Fifth Republic and they started a rapprochement with ousted Prime Minister Amadou.

In July 2009, PNDS, a number of minor parties, **civil society** groupings, and the union's umbrella organization Confédération Démocratique des Travailleurs du Niger (CDTN) united to form the **Coordination des Forces pour la Démocratie et la République** (CFDR) in order to oppose President Tandja's dismantling of the Fifth Republic and imposition of an authoritarian **Sixth Republic**. The CFDR became the main political opponent to Tandja's ambitions, especially after Amadou created a new party out of the MNSD and joined the organization. In February 2010, Tandja was deposed by the **armed forces**, an action which the PNDS welcomed.

PNDS is a member of the Socialist International and is, in the context of Niger, a left-wing party. It emerged the all-out victor of the elections of 2011, with 39 seats in the National Assembly and the presidency of the republic. It has, however, secured this result thanks to an alliance with Hama Amadou's party, the Mouvement Démocratique Nigérien pour une Fédération Africaine (MODEN/FA Loumana Africa). *See also* THIRD REPUBLIC.

PARTI PROGRESSISTE NIGÉRIEN (PPN). The **political party** was founded on 12 May 1946, mainly due to grievances from Niger's local educated elite (chiefly graduates from **Niamey**'s primary school and Senegal's **École William Ponty**), who felt that the colony of Niger was the underdog of **France**'s West African empire. Living conditions in Niger were so forbidding at the time—especially from a European point of view—that Niger was considered a "penitentiary assignment" for colonial officials. Moreover, given that the French government invested very little in the colony's educational system, it relied mostly on trained natives of more favored colonies—mostly Dahomey, the French Sudan (now Mali), and Senegal—to run Niger's embryonic **civil service**. Native Nigeriens tended to feel shunned by the colonial regime and humiliated by the condescension of foreign Africans.

But beyond these proto-nationalist concerns, the party's founders were also attuned to a more radical criticism of the colonial regime, which came from pan-African nationalists and French leftists. The former movement was in particular embodied by the **Rassemblement Démocratique Africain** (RDA), an inter-African political party clamoring for further autonomy and even independence, and founded in Bamako (French Sudan) in October 1946, a few months after the PPN's establishment. In September 1947, the PPN joined the RDA, becoming its Nigerien branch. But given the fact that the RDA was linked, in France, to the French Communist Party, the PPN was initially highly suspicious in the eye of Niger's right-wing colonial governor, Jean Toby. In June 1948, Toby, in cahoots with customary chiefs (including the prominent *zarmakoy* of **Dosso**), **Francis Borrey** (a French civil servant), and a number of low-status *évolués*, set up the Union Nigérienne des Indépendants et Sympathisants (UNIS) party. This, combined with a policy of repression against the PPN, changed the political landscape of the country and effectively created the two main political tendencies that would come to dominate Niger's political history: the conservative traditionalist tendency, always pro-government and generally organized around the control that traditional rulers and (at a later point) Islamic clerics have on the populace, and the intellectual modernist tendency, generally suspicious of government and organized around trade unions and (after 1991) **civil society** and the independent **media**. In the earlier stages in the 1950s, the tendencies were also roughly ethnicized, with the traditionalist camp being more identified with the **Hausa** regions, and the modernist camp being tied to the **Zarma-Songhay** regions. The fate of the PPN after the creation of the UNIS indicate, however, that the traditionalist tendency was also very successful in the Zarma-Songhay regions as, with some support from the colonial admin-istration, the UNIS came to dominate Niger's political life throughout the colony's regions, especially after 1952.

At that juncture, the PPN had suffered further weakening after RDA disso-ciated itself from the French Communist Party (1951). One radical member, **Djibo Bakary**, left the party in 1953 to create a trade **union** federation, the Union des Syndicats Confédérés du Niger (USCN), before joining a rival party, the Union Démocratique Nigérienne (UDN). After the departure of the right-wing Governor Toby in 1955 and his replacement by left-wing Jean-Paul Ramadier, the PPN experienced a recovery. The PPN essentially benefited from the fact that administrative support to the UNIS ceased. The UNIS was plunged in a crisis that led to the creation of a split party, the Bloc Nigérien d'Action (BNA), in 1956. Meanwhile, the PPN sought to strengthen its own ideological basis of pan-African nationalism and in September 1957, proposed a merger of all French Equatorial and West African political parties into a single African party. This failed, even as Bakary's **Sawaba** managed a reduced and radical version of this strategy by forming with the Senegalese Parti de la Convention Africaine the Parti du Regroupement Africain (PRA). These various shifts had an unexpected result: given that the PRA policy line was to oppose France's attempt at retaining the colonial system through federalist arrangements, and the UNIS had been terminally weakened by its mid-1950s crises, the erstwhile radical PPN appeared as the only party of note through which France could play its hand in Niger.

The PPN responded positively to French prodding and decided to be its flag bearer in the referendum on the Communauté Française (French Community, a federal unit) that was organized in 1958. Bakary's Sawaba, on the other hand, called on the population to reject France's proposal. Though Sawaba was by then more popular than the PPN, straddling effectively the east–west ethnic divide of Nigerien politics (Bakary, himself a **Zarma**, had his major stronghold in the densely populated Hausa region of **Zinder**), the PPN was fully backed by the administration of new governor Dom Jean Colombani, specially com-missioned by Paris to rig the ballot and ensure a PPN victory. The PPN, leading a coalition of smaller parties in the aptly named Union pour la Communauté Franco-Africaine (UCFA), won all the **elections** organized between 1958 and 1960 and emerged as Niger's ruling party at independence (3 August 1960). Ominously, during the period leading to independence, the PPN was able to force the smaller members of the coalition to merge with it, passed a series of decrees that considerably restricted political expression through rival parties, and outlawed Sawaba. Thus, while the **constitution** of 1960 did not formally expunge multipartyism, it rendered its exercise impossible in practice, pushing moreover the only rival force (Sawaba) into insurrectional opposition.

Unlike Sawaba, the PPN did not have an ethnically broad-based leadership and was perceived as a Zarma-Songhay, or western Nigerien, party. The general perception that PPN thus ushered in an era of Zarma-Songhay hegemony in Niger—a perception especially painful for the Hausa majority—would remain a sore point in Nigerien politics until the onset of **democratization** in 1991. However, the PPN's undeniable hold on Niger also rested on the fact that it successfully mixed traditionalist and modernist tendencies. Thus, while its educated leadership (chiefly Zarma-Songhay) invested heavily in modernist causes—**education**, industrialization, scientific research, setting up quite rapidly (given the pitiable colonial legacy) a working educational system culminating in the **University of Niamey** (1973)—the party intensely courted traditional chiefs and clerics, packing its **National Assembly** with chiefs and their relatives, mostly from the Hausaland (given especially the lack of a developed chiefly system in the Zarma-Songhay regions).

PPN rule was initially marked by a policy of national development that was accommodating to French interests. The newly independent country became heavily dependent on French assistance, repaying its international patron through various forms of exclusivity, including in the exploitation of **uranium** ore, discovered by a French public corporation in the late 1950s. President **Hamani Diori** promoted the creation of the **Francophonie** organization, a watered-down version of the Communauté Française, and its organs were set up in Niamey in 1970. He was also a strong supporter of councils and regional organizations that gathered France's former colonies (**Conseil de l'Entente, Organisation Commune Bénin-Niger**, Communauté Economique de l'Afrique de l'Ouest), in the belief that they were instrumental in preserving Niger's national unity, always threatened by Hausa inclinations for Anglophone **Nigeria**, where the bulk of the Hausa reside. For all these reasons, Sawaba's virulent opposition to the PPN regime was couched in a credible anticolonialist language, while internal agitation from trade and **student** unions (quick to form after the creation of the university) consistently described Diori as a "stooge of imperialism."

Yet when the PPN regime faced its gravest crises with the **droughts** and **oil** shocks of the early 1970s, which sent Niger and its state apparatus reeling, France declined to succor its ally. Battered by internal turmoil, the PPN regime sought assistance from **Libya**, and President Diori pressured the French for a renegotiation of the terms of the uranium contract. He was toppled in the **coup of April 1974**, a few days before a meeting with French negotiators, and the PPN was written out of existence.

To legitimize their own regime, the military of the **Conseil Militaire Suprême** developed a campaign against the PPN through institutional mechanisms as well as cultural tactics (**Ousmane Amadou**'s novel *Quinze ans ça suffit!* and the subsequent Ivorian movie *Pétanqui* by Yéo Kozola), describing its rule of Niger as essentially marked by disorder, corruption, and mismanagement.

The old party name (rather than the party itself) was resurrected with the onset of civilian rule in the 1990s, and a new PPN party emerged, headed by older PPN bosses, Oumarou Youssoufou Garba and **Leopold Kaziendé**. It competed in the 1993 legislative elections, and supported Garba's presidential bid the same year. The party won only two of the National Assembly's 83 seats; seeking a greater political impact in January 1995, it merged with another small party to form the Front Démocratique Nigérien (FDN), headed by Oumarou Youssoufou Garba and Mohamad Moudour. It was part of the **Alliance des Forces du Changement** coalition. Its prize candidate, **Abdoulaye Hamani Diori**, failed, however, to secure his election to the legislature. It was more successful in the legislative elections of 1999, after which the new PPN became one of Niger's more enduring minor parties. *See also* COLONIE DU NIGER; POLICE ECONOMIQUE.

PEUL. *See* FULANI.

POLICE ECONOMIQUE. Post-1976 police force charged with investigating economic and customs crimes and offenses (including hoarding and smuggling) as well as fiscal irregularities. It was under the control of General **Seyni Kountché** and was active during the **Sahel droughts** and their aftermath. The force was dismantled in 1978.

POLITICAL PARTIES. Niger has known three periods of political party activity: the first one occurred during the final stage of French colonial overrule, in 1946–1960; the second evolved under Niger's **First Republic**, in 1960–1974; and the third and current one started in 1988. There was a hiatus under the military regime of 1974–1988. The three periods of party activity, while being each very distinctive, also show some permanencies in the way in which Niger's political life began to be organized at an early stage.

1946–1960. The first stage started when the French Fourth Republic, acknowledging that postwar conditions called for political opening in the colonies, arranged for a modicum of local political representation in the African imperial ensembles (1946). The colonies, now transformed into overseas territories, could send deputies to the French legislature, though the number of seats accorded to these ensured that they would remain a minority section of the National Assembly in Paris. A group of educated Nigeriens immediately seized on the opportunity to create the **Parti Progressiste Nigérien** (PPN-RDA), on the basis of local grievances and pan-African nationalism. PPN in effect soon linked up with the inter-African **Rassemblement Démocratique Africain** (RDA), which was itself tied to the Parti Communiste Français (PCF) in **France**. This particular circumstance is at the origins of the dominant trends of all subsequent Nigerien party systems: the ideological division between traditionalists and modernists and the ethno-regional divide between the west (**Zarma-Songhay**) and the center–east (**Hausa**). Greater acceptance in the Zarma-Songhay regions of French **education** ensured that the leadership of PPN was a nucleus of educated Zarma-Songhay men. Thus, the PPN was both Zarma-Songhay and modernist (progressive) in orientation. To oppose its demands, the right-wing governor of Niger, Jean Toby, helped bring into being the Union Nigérienne des Indépendants et Sympathisants (UNIS), with the backing of customary chiefs, and around the leadership of a French civil servant (**Francis Borrey**) and a mixed-race educated man from **Zinder** (**Georges Condat**). Given especially the greater influence of customary chieftaincy in the Hausa regions compared to the Zarma-Songhay regions (where the only chieftaincy of some note was that of **Dosso**), UNIS appeared at once as Hausa and traditionalist (conservative) in orientation. In fact, however, the identification of the parties by these broad divisions are less clear-cut than would at first appear. PPN was nudged into its role by Toby's strategizing and would have otherwise sought the support of customary chiefs, while UNIS was very influential in the Zarma-Songhay regions themselves, where conservative sentiments were no less important than in the Hausaland. The main point is that these broad divisions were established, and while no party would ever fully embody any of them, they have consistently shaped the character of Nigerien party systems, generating trends between parties and within parties as well.

This much was confirmed when PPN split in 1951 over the issue of RDA's dissociation with the PCF; then a radical leftist offshoot was created around the leadership of **Djibo Bakary**, the Union Démocratique Nigérienne (UDN), while the root PPN, led by **Hamani Diori** and **Boubou Hama**, identified the party primarily with pan-African nationalism rather than progressive revolution. Both PPN and UDN were perceived as antigovernment by the colonial authorities and were locked out of power in favor of UNIS. The departure of Governor Toby and his replacement with socialist Jean-Paul Ramadier (governor in 1956–1957) pushed Bakary's leadership to the fore, as his party was reshaped into a radical affiliate of the **Mouvement Socialiste Africain** (MSA) and the French Socialist Party (SFIO), and helped into victory—

especially given the post-Toby crisis and eventual decomposition of UNIS. A critical period was soon ushered in by the French project of salvaging imperial control through a federal ensemble, the Communauté Française (French Community). At that juncture, RDA, which was led by the Ivorian politician Félix Houphouët-Boigny, was ready to accommodate the French, while the Parti du Regroupement Africain (PRA), which was led by the Senegalese politician Léopold Sédar Senghor and to which Bakary's **Sawaba** was now affiliated, was hostile to the project; indeed, Bakary's party took the name *sawaba* (a Hausa word for freedom) in defiance of France's neocolonial efforts.

The new governor of Niger, Paul Camille Bordier, tried delinking Bakary from Senghor's hard-line stance without success, and the French retaliated by sending in Dom Jean Colombani as their new governor, with the mission of defeating Bakary in the referendum on the Communauté Française scheduled for 1958. Colombani struck an alliance with the only rival force of note, PPN. PPN campaigned for the Communauté Française, predictably won, and gathering all the smaller parties of Niger in a Union pour la Communauté Franco-Africaine (UCFA), prevailed in all the **elections** that followed. In the period leading up to independence, the PPN leadership passed a number of decrees that made it impossible for a rival party to operate, so much so that while the **constitution** of Niger's First Republic did not formally establish one-party rule, that was what occurred in reality. More importantly, Sawaba was specifically outlawed and its members persecuted.

1946–1959. Niger's most important parties during the multiparty era follow.

Parti Progressiste Nigérien-Rassemblement Démocratique Africain (PPN-RDA). Founded in 1946 and ruled independent Niger from 1960 to 1974 (for specific details, see entry for these parties).

Union Progressiste Nigérienne (UPN). Splinter group formed around Georges Condat that left the PPN to form the Union Nigérienne des Indépendants et Sympathisants (UNIS) party and then, in March 1953, left that party in an effort to realign with the PPN. This effort aborted, the UPN rejoined the UNIS party, which by this time had changed its name to Bloc Nigérien d'Action.

Union Nigérienne des Indépendants et Sympathisants (UNIS). Founded in 1948 by former members of the PPN and other previously unaffiliated elements. Its leadership included the *zarmakoy* of Dosso (initially a PPN leader). The origin of the UNIS party is traceable to the schism earlier, in 1946, over the PPN's continued affiliation with the interterritorial RDA party. Its main chiefly leaders included Georges Condat and **Ikhia Zodi**. It suffered major secessions in 1953–1955 when the former opted out of UNIS over its demand that links be reestablished with the PPN in an effort to unite the Niger nationalist movement. Establishing the UPN party, Condat's efforts were rebuffed by the PPN and he returned to the UNIS fold. By that time the party had practically collapsed over the question of affiliation with the new interterritorial movement, the Convention Africaine (a successor to the French National Assembly caucusing group, Indépendants d'Outre-Mer, in which the future president of Senegal, Leopold Sédar Senghor, was most active). The bulk of UNIS—including Condat's defunct UPN—formed the Bloc Nigérien d'Action leaving a few leaders totally isolated within the shell of UNIS. These leaders, including Francis Borrey and Zodi Ikhia, trailed very badly in the 1957 elections, and the party disappeared shortly thereafter, being transformed into the Convention Africaine–affiliated Forces Démocratiques Nigériennes.

Bloc Nigérien d'Action (BNA). Successor to the UNIS party after the major schism that split it apart over affiliation with the interterritorial Convention Africaine. The BNA was constituted of the rump of the UNIS party that opposed affiliation with the latter, leaving their former leaders Zodi Ikhia and Francis Borrey with the empty shell of UNIS. The BNA was also rejoined by a faction that had left UNIS previously, the UPN. In the 1955 elections, the party's Condat-**Seydou** (the latter being the *zarmakoy* of Dosso) ticket obtained 127,000 votes to the PPN's 83,000. In November the BNA merged with Djibo Bakary's Union Démocratique Nigérienne to form a Mouvement Socialiste Africain affiliate, later renamed Sawaba ("freedom" in Hausa). The main leaders of the BNA were *Zarmakoy* Issoufou Seydou and Amadou Mayaki.

Forces Démocratiques Nigériennes (FDN). Successor party of UNIS after the split that brought about the formation of the BNA. The FDN was affiliated with the interterritorial Convention Africaine and was very short-lived since it had hardly any followers.

Parti Indépendant du Niger-Est (PINE) or Union des Nigériens de l'Est (UNE). Largely stillborn party formed of a faction that opted out of the PPN in 1946 over the latter's affiliation with the interterritorial RDA. The faction merged with UNIS in 1948. It claimed to defend the interests of the Hausa against what was already perceived to be a Zarma-Songhay hegemony in Nigerien politics.

Mouvement Socialiste Africain (MSA). Name of an interterritorial movement with which Djibo Bakary's UDN became affiliated. Though Bakary's party also campaigned under the MSA label, his party is discussed under Sawaba.

Sawaba. The rallying call (*sawaba* means "freedom" in Hausa) of the MSA branch in Niger, with a stronghold in Zinder. Sawaba originated from the previous Union Démocratique Nigérienne.

Union Démocratique Nigérienne (UDN). Sawaba's predecessor. Formed in 1954 by PPN dissidents objecting to the parent interterritorial (RDA) party's disaffiliation from the French Communist Party, the UDN was led by former coleader of the PPN, Djibo Bakary, and was quite popular and powerful in the Hausa east, though it counted very few Hausa among its leaders. Aided by traditional chiefs, especially Hausa and **Fulani**, the UDN absorbed the BNA party in 1956 and joined the radical interterritorial party MSA, campaigning under this name until the new party name of Sawaba was adopted. Sawaba briefly controlled Niger's political life, being in a majority in the **Territorial Assembly** and with Bakary as head of the local executive. The party suddenly lost control in 1958 with its dual French-engineered defeat in that year's **constitutional referendum** and territorial elections.

Union pour la Communauté Franco-Africaine (UCFA). It was a temporary loose electoral alliance led by the PPN party in its ultimate electoral fight with Sawaba in 1958, which was to result in the latter's collapse and the rise of the PPN to the status of governing party. Assisted by the retreating colonial administration (which was hostile to Sawaba), UCFA obtained 54 of the 60 seats in the legislature, and Sawaba only four. Following the elections a new political party was supposed to be established, but the PPN leadership coaxed and cowed its allies in the UCFA into merging with the PPN and keeping its name.

Interterritorial Parties. There were several interterritorial movements with which Niger's parties affiliated themselves. These have all been noted previously, including their alliances. In summary they were (1) Rassemblement Démocratique Africain (the Niger affiliate from its inception was the Parti Progressiste Nigérien). (2) Indépendants d'Outre-Mer (more of a caucusing group of Francophone African deputies in the French National Assembly; its prime supporters in Niger were Zodi Ikhia and Francis Borrey of UNIS; the IOM was later to create the Convention Africaine [CA]). (3) Convention Africaine (in many ways successor to the IOM, its Niger affiliate was the practically stillborn Forces Démocratiques Nigériennes after the bulk of UNIS deserted Zodi Ikhia and Francis Borrey over the issue of affiliating the party with the CA). (4) Mouvement Socialiste Africain (the Niger affiliate had for some time the same name; later it became the Sawaba party). (5) Parti du Regroupement Africain (in many ways the outgrowth of the Mouvement Socialiste Africain interterritorial party, the Niger affiliate was the Sawaba party).

1960–1974. De facto single-party system under PPN-RDA. PPN-RDA swallowed all minor parties of the previous era in 1958, through the temporary coalition Union pour la Communauté Franco-Africaine (UCFA), and used its hold on the legislature to outlaw its only substantial rival, the Sawaba party. As sole governing party, PPN-RDA strove to build a party structure that covered the entire social surface of Niger. The party used the state administration to gain control over salaried workers and created a number of corporate organizations to link **women**, traditional chiefs, and Islamic clerics to the party organization. Peasants and youth were also organized in local committees, giving the party the ability to reach directly into community life without depending on local authorities. Despite there being only one party in activity, the state maintained elections rituals, which were used very much as a control instrument over the country's elite (those of the *chefferie traditionnelle* and high state officials) as well as a legitimation pantomime. PPN-RDA was, however, never able to completely eliminate Sawaba rivalry. The banned party had kept a loyal following which PPN-RDA's repression drove underground but which enabled exiled Sawaba leaders to organize several attempts at violently subverting PPN-RDA rule. Thus, in September–October 1964, Sawaba commandos infiltrated Nigerien territory and sparked a number of insurgencies in the countryside. The following year, on 13 April, a Sawaba militant tried killing President Hamani Diori with a grenade at a prayer ceremony. PPN-RDA never succeeded in completely stamping out Sawaba, but by the early 1970s, it had become sufficiently entrenched to contain the threat. However, it proved no match to a military takeover, especially after three years of **drought** and economic decline had reduced the regime's legitimacy to a shambles. After the **coup d'état of April 1974**, PPN-RDA was suspended, together with all party activity.

1974–1988. The military *régime d'exception* under General **Seyni Kountché** operated without political parties but gradually set up an organized movement embodying the ideals of a "development society." The **Mouvement National pour la Société de Développement** (MNSD) was a broad-based mobilization tool with a bureaucracy based on notions of technocratic expertise rather than on the concept of party loyalty.

1988–Current. The **Second Republic** put in place after the death of President Seyni Kountché (1987) institutionalized the MNSD into a *party-État* (a state-party) just as PPN-RDA during the First Republic. Elections were held in 1989, which served to co-opt aspirants to power and influence. Although the military was still present at the top of the party hierarchy, MNSD also promoted the technocratic cadre of the "development society" into a manner of political career.

Though the Second Republic was not a multiparty system, multipartyism was in fact included in the draft constitution of the new regime and was weeded out only at the final stages of adoption. The regime, at any rate, organized a greater political openness, which led to the formation of several political associations, the nuclei of future parties. These quickly agitated for further opening and a full multiparty regime. As a result of the political crisis that developed following the deaths of **students** confronted by security forces in a **Niamey** demonstration in February 1990, the regime further opened up and revised the constitution to adopt multipartyism. Despite these moves, the Second Republic was ended by a kind of civilian coup d'état during the **Conférence Nationale** of 1991, and a large number of political parties were created under the very favorable legislation that came out of the transition to the **Third Republic**.

Aside from these political associations, there were a number of ambiguous organizations that could not last as participants in the democratic game: thus especially the **Front Populaire de Libération du Niger** (FPLN), an organ used by **Abdoulaye Hamani Diori**, under **Libyan** sponsorship, to seize power in a way that had shown its potentials in many Chadian coup d'états. The group, headquartered in Tripoli, had in it several members who had plotted against Kountché, such as **Khamed Moussa** and **Liman Chaafi** (a Libyan national), its president. Abdoulaye Hamani Diori ended up dissolving it to join a revived, but diminutive, PPN-RDA. Some groupings were crackpot clubs that quickly faded out of the emerging Nigerien public stage, showing it to be inhospitable to radical projects; such was the case of the Mouvement Révolutionnaire pour la Libération Nationale (MRLN), the Parti Islamique Intégriste (PII, disallowed by secularist laws), the Front Démocratique Uni (FDU), the Parti Socialiste Révolutionnaire (PSR), and the Mouvement Nigérien des Comités Révolutionnaires (MOUNCORE). In general, most of the new parties were unrepresentative nonentities that struggled to survive, adopting sometimes successfully the strategy of piggybacking onto more successful outfits. The following were the parties that were able to pattern themselves along the major features of Nigerien politics that were mentioned earlier in this entry: the **Parti Nigérien pour la Démocratie et le Socialisme** (PNDS Tarayya), often referred to as the party of the intellectuals, embodies the modernist and progressive tendency, with little ethnic connotation; the **Convention Démocratique et Sociale** (CDS Rahama) is a more traditionalist party, with solid identification to the Hausa and especially to the region of Zinder; the **Alliance Nigérienne pour la Démocratie et le Socialisme** (ANDP Zaman Lahiya) is likewise traditionalist and ethnic, rooted in the Zarma city of Dosso; and the **Mouvement National pour la Société de Développement** (MNSD Nassara) recaptures the strategy of uniting modernist and traditionalist modes and straddles the ethnic divide with its strongholds in the regions of **Maradi** (Hausa) and **Tillabéri** (**Songhay** and Zarma). These four parties have remained throughout this period the main political parties of Niger, with MNSD and PNDS leading the way and a number of smaller parties managing to survive in their shadows by entering into various circumstantial coalitions.

While most Nigeriens quickly took to the party system and saw in it the normal way to seek power and influence, many **Tuareg** and **Toubou** groups chose to express their political ambitions in irredentist movements, resorting to violence to attempt detaching various areas of the desert north from Nigerien sovereignty. This resulted in the formation of a number of fluid fronts or movements of liberation, which are also noted below.

The following presents the four main parties which have dominated Niger's political life since 1991.

Alliance Nigérienne pour la Démocratie et le Progrès (ANDP–Zaman Lahiya). It started out as a Club des Amis de Moumouni Adamou Djermakoye (CAMAD, Club of Moumouni Adamou Djermakoye's Friends) set up by **Moumouni Adamou Djermakoye**, disgruntled over rival **Mamadou Tandja** winning MNSD leadership. Djermakoye, a prominent member of MNSD, wanted its presidency; he was sidelined, however, in favor of Mamadou Tandja, thanks to the strategizing of the party's secretary-general, **Hama Amadou**. Rather than accepting an inferior role within MNSD, Djermajokoye left the party and created ANDP, which immediately captured the vote of Dosso and its surrounding region, where Djermakoye's family had held customary sovereignty since 1902. ANDP first sided against MNSD in the elections of 1993, joining CDS, PNDS, and six other parties in the **Alliance des Forces du Changement** (AFC), a coalition created to oppose MNSD's return to power. ANDP started at that point to develop a pattern of siding rather with PNDS than with MNSD. In 1995, when PNDS left AFC to strike an alliance with MNSD, ANDP followed it in this move. In the aftermath of the coup d'état which ended the stalemated Third Republic in 1996, ANDP first supported the coup-maker's, Colonel **Ibrahim Baré Maïnassara**, bid to the presidency before finally joining forces with the other major parties which had united against his authoritarian projects. In 1999, after the ending of Baré Maïnassara's regime and the restoration of democratic governance, ANDP allied itself to PNDS against MNSD and found itself therefore in the losing coalition, as the MNSD-led bloc of parties emerged victorious at the legislative and presidential elections that year. Since that event, ANDP has regularly shifted sides between the MNSD (which it supported at the elections of 2004) and PNDS (which it supported at those of 2011). Despite the death of its founder, Djermakoye, in July 2009, ANDP remains a force to be reckoned with in contemporary Nigerien politics. At the last legislative elections, in January 2011, it has indeed emerged as Niger's fourth-strongest party, thus overtaking CDS (eight seats versus two for CDS).

Convention Démocratique et Sociale (CDS-Rahama). This is the party of President **Mahaman Ousmane** (in office: 1993–1996), which secured 22 seats in the 1993 legislative elections, making it the second largest in Niger, after the MNSD (which got 29). The CDS also delivered to Ousmane the second-largest number of votes in the first ballot of his 1993 presidential bid, and following the coalescence behind him of virtually all the other non-MNSD parties, he beat Tandja, the MNSD candidate. The CDS is largely a Hausa party, and more specifically a party of **Damagaram** or Zinder, heavily supported by the rich traders of that region, and sustained by the general dissatisfaction of the Hausa at their being shunted from the center of power since independence despite being the largest ethnic group in the country. The CDS was the senior partner in the AFC government until the parliamentary crisis of 1994 that led to new elections in January 1995. At these the former opposition (MNSD), the PNDS (which had precipitated the crisis) and another small party gained 43 of the **National Assembly**'s 83 seats, forming the government, with the CDS transformed into part of the opposition. In 1996, the CDS was removed from power by the coup d'état of Colonel Ibrahim Baré Maïnassara, and it formed an alliance with its former adversaries, MNSD and PNDS, in the interest of the democratic form of governance which had come under threat. After Baré Maïnassara was eventually murdered and a **Fifth Republic** established, CDS secured a position of kingmaker between MNSD and PNDS, and its support for the former twice allowed it to win the presidency in 1999 and in 2004. In 2009, CDS belatedly joined the opposition movements that had formed to oppose President Mamadou Tandja's attempt at ending democratic governance. Tandja had sought much of his popular support in the regions of Zinder and **Diffa**, which had been fiefs of CDS, and in the process, he successfully weakened the grip of that party on its strongholds. At the legislative elections of January 2011, CDS was reduced to only three seats by the invalidation of its lists in the region of Zinder, thus shrinking below newer and minor parties and being vastly outpaced by its former peers, PNDS and MNSD. From being the consistent third party of Niger, it is now its seventh party. This, however, does not reflect its true weight.

Parti Nigérien pour la Démocratie et le Socialisme (PNDS-Tarayya). The party of President **Mahamadou Issoufou**, with coleaders **Mohamed Bazoum** and **Hassoumi Massaoudou**. Allied to CDS against MNSD in the first party coalition of the democratic era, the PNDS shifted to MNSD owing to tiffs between Issoufou (then prime minister) and President Mahaman Ousman. This eventually led to a cohabitation situation—after Ousmane had called legislative elections in the vain hope of regaining control of Parliament—and a political gridlock in 1995. After the Third Republic was ended by the coup d'état of Colonel Ibrahim Baré Maïnassara, PNDS spearheaded the opposition's resistance to his regime and grew into the second-strongest party of the country when democratic governance was restored in 1999. It twice challenged MNSD dominance in 1999 and 2004, as the only other party of national—instead of regional—scope, and emerged as the favorite at both the legislative and the presidential elections of 2011. It won 39 seats out of 113, the largest share of the new National Assembly, and it has thus overtaken MNSD as Niger's greatest party.

Mouvement National pour la Société de Développement (MNSD-Nassara). The party benefited from the network of patronage and influence created under the *régime d'exception* and the Second Republic when it was created as a single party. MNSD remained throughout the **democratization** period the largest party of Niger, with a national constituency resting chiefly on the clout of the merchant class and, to a lesser extent, of traditional chiefs. It took a coalition of all the newly created parties of the early democratization period to bar a return of MNSD to power at the legislative and presidential elections of 1993. In 1995, MNSD led a winning coalition after President Mahaman Ousmane (CDS) dissolved Parliament and unwittingly ushered in an MNSD-PNDS government through the legislative elections organized that year. In the period 1996–1999, during which coup-maker Ibrahim Baré Maïnassara tried to establish a regime at his beck and call, MNSD sided with PNDS and CDS to oppose him. The ensuing political crisis was ended by another coup in 1999, and new democratic elections, which resulted in a victory of an MNSD-led coalition at both legislative and presidential polls. MNSD again won the 2004 elections but unraveled in 2009, as the conflict between its two leaders, President Mamadou Tandja and former Prime Minister Hama Amadou, resulted in the latter creating a new party, the Mouvement Démocratique Nigérien pour une Fédération Africaine (MODEN/FA-Lumana Africa). At the legislative elections of 2011, this split proved to have considerably weakened MNSD: it won 26 seats, while the MODEN/FA acquired 23. These scores ranked the two parties at second and third place behind PNDS, which gained 39 seats. The evolution was confirmed by the results of the first round of the presidential election, which saw PNDS's Mahamadou Issoufou come in first, with MNSD's Seyni Oumarou in the second place, and MODEN/FA's Hama Amadou in the third place.

Many smaller parties emerged and disappeared in the 1990s, a few among them enduring to the present day. Elections are the occasions of either their mortality or their survival. In the recent elections of 2011, a crop of new emerging small parties has considerably displaced the previous contingent. The new cohort includes:

Mouvement Démocratique Nigérien pour une Fédération Africaine (MODEN/FA-Lumana Africa). Founded in July 2009 by the self-exiled former Prime Minister Hama Amadou, MODEN/FA is a split party of MNSD which took away nearly half of the constituency of that party. A telling indication of the potency of MNSD, its new offshoot was immediately positioned by electoral results as Niger's third party. In the first round of the 2011 presidential election, Amadou came third and pledged support for Issoufou (PNDS) in the runoff.

Rassemblement pour la Démocratie et le Progrès (RDP-Jama'a). When Colonel Ibrahim Baré Maïnassara overthrew the Third Republic in January 1996, he first pledged to restore civilian rule without himself running for the presidency. That pledge floundered as he created a Comité de Soutien à Ibrahim Maïnassara Baré (COSIMBA), a support club of a motley group of politicians and opportunists that evolved into a movement, the Union National des Indépendants pour le Renouveau Démocratique (UNIRD), and finally the RDP party. **Hamid Algabid**, a former prime minister of the regime of exception under President **Seyni Kountché**, was elected to the head of the party in August 1997. RDP won all elections under Baré Maïnassara's **Fourth Republic**, through massive and open fraud, but its rule was ended by the **coup d'état of April 1999**, at which Baré Maïnassara was murdered. RDP survived the event and geared up for the elections that were organized a few months thereafter. It split over who—Chairman Algabid or vice-chairman **Amadou Boubacar Cissé**—should be the party's candidate. Algabid won the contest through a judicial ruling and Cissé left to found his own party, UDR. RDP came in fifth in the presidential election of 1999, with 10.8 percent of the vote. It backed PNDS in the runoff, thus finding itself in the losing coalition. By 2004, RDP had lost ground, obtaining only 4 percent of the vote, but this time it supported the MNSD-led coalition, and emerged as a member of the winning camp. In the 2011 rounds of elections, RDP won seven seats and became the fifth-strongest party in the National Assembly, but it had no candidate for the presidency, thereby fully an example of the support party in Niger's party system.

Union pour la Démocratie et la République (UDR-Tabbat). It was founded in 1999 by Amadou Boubacar Cissé (popularly known as ABC), a former prime minister of President Baré Maïnassara. Cissé was the vice-chairman of the ruling party under Baré Maïnassara, the RDP-Jama'a and left it to found UDR after a ruling from the Cour d'État confirmed Hamid Algabid, RDP's chairman, as the leader of that party, against Cissé's claims. UDR had a very poor showing in the 1999 elections, failing to secure any seats in the National Assembly. It was more successful in 2004 and entered Parliament as a member of the opposition coalition led by PNDS, after winning two seats in a split ticket with the Union Nationale des Indépendants (UNI) of **Amadou Ali Djibo**. UDR boosted its image when Cissé emerged as one of the most vocal opponents to President Mamadou Tandja's late 2009 efforts to install an authoritarian regime. It obtained six seats in the legislative elections of 2011. It had a poorer showing in the presidential election, where its candidate (Cissé) won only 1.61 percent of the vote.

Union Nationale des Indépendants. This is the latest avatar of a party founded by Amadou Ali Djibo, who had launched a number of small parties after leaving the MNSD in the early 1990s. UNI was founded in August 1999, in view of the October presidential race that year, and placed seventh and last (with 1.7 percent of the vote) in the first round. It then moved to back PNDS in the runoff and remained in the PNDS coalition in the 2004 elections as well. At that point, UNI managed to secure for the first time a seat in the National Assembly. In the 2011 election, UNI won that same single seat and is thus the smallest of the eight parties of the current National Assembly.

The Irredentist Movements. A dozen irredentist liberation movements emerged in Niger in the early democratizing years. Four of these were, until 1995, coordinated in Paris by the **Coordination de la Résistance Armée** (CRA) and four formed the Mouvement des Fronts Unifiés de l'Azawad (MFUA). They were divided along clan lines and had different aims and visions for the Tuareg north (autonomy, federalism, independence) and various religious goals.

The Mouvement des Fronts Unifiés de l'Azawad (MFUA) was set up in 1991 after a splintering into its constituent parts of the previous Mouvement Populaire pour la Libération de l'Azawad (MPLA), headed by Iyad ag Ghali and headquartered in Mali. (The latter mobilized a segment of the Tuareg there.) After the MPLA initialed peace accords with the Mali government, the following groups opted out and later set up the MFUA: Mouvement Populaire de l'Azawad (MPA), Front Populaire de Libération de l'Azawad (FPLA), **Armée Révolutionnaire de Libération de l'Azawad** (ARLA), and Front Islamique Arabe de l'Azawad (FIAA).

The Coordination de la Résistance Armée (CRA) was formed in 1993 and was headed by **Mano Dayak** and **Rhissa Ag Boula** to group the following liberation fronts. The Front de Libération de l'Aïr et de l'Azawad (FLAA) was the first to organize in Niger and is the only one to claim a sphere of operations in both Aïr and Azawak; Front de Libération Temust (FLT); **Armée Révolutionnaire de Libération du Nord Niger** (ARLN); and Front Patriotique de Libération du Sahara (FPLS). The CRA gave way in 1995 to the **Organisation de la Résistance Armée** (ORA), a somewhat looser organization that initiated the final peace accord in mid-April 1995 formally ending the **Tuareg rebellion** of the 1990s decade.

One other liberation movement from the mid-1990s period can be noted. The Front pour le Renouveau Démocratique (FRD), formed in 1993 but primarily active since 1995 and distinct from all the others in that it operated in the southeast (near **Lake Chad**) rather than in the north, was a Toubou–**Kanuri**–Shoa **Arab** movement.

In late 2007, a new liberation group was formed, the **Mouvement des Nigériens pour la Justice** (MNJ), focusing especially on the exploitation of **uranium**, whose revenues they deem should accrue more to the northern region's benefit. To the traditional ambush and raiding mode of operation of Tuareg rebel fronts, MNJ and its split organizations have added hostage taking.

POUSSI NATAMA, MOUSSA (1965–2008). Poussi's music, based on **Zarma-Songhay** lore and animist **religion**, dominated the stage in **Niamey** in the early 1990s, together with the work of **Saadou Bori**. Poussi himself ascribed his long decline in the 2000s, terminated by premature death, to the tormenting influence of the **Holley** (powerful preternatural beings in the Zarma-Songhay pantheon) who inspired his art. He died the same year as the artist who was considered his Hausa counterpart, Saadou Bori. *See also* DANCE AND MUSIC; RELIGION.

PRIVATIZATION. *See* ECONOMIC LIBERALIZATION.

QADIRIYYA. Historically the most important Muslim religious order in much of Niger, especially in **Damagaram**, and including **Fulani**, **Hausa**, and **Tuareg** adherents. The order was founded by Abdel Kadir al-Jilani (1077–1166) in Baghdad and spread to Morocco around 1450. The oldest branch established in sub-Saharan Africa was set up in Kano, **Nigeria**, in the 17th century, probably after lodges were founded in **Aïr** down from present-day Mauritania. The order was strong in **Zinder**, **Tahoua**, and **Agadez** but rapidly lost ground in the 1920s to the **Tijaniyya** order. Its current strongholds are Zinder and Agadez, and it is especially prevalent among the Tuareg (who also flocked to the Khalwatiya) and the **Arab** Kunta clans. *See also* ISLAM.

R

RABAH ZUBEIR (1845?–1900). Sudanese slave raider and builder of a vast personal empire stretching from Sudan through parts of Chad into northern Cameroon. Rabah commenced his swath of military conquest, destruction, and slave raids from the east, from Darfur (now in Sudan), and by 1893 his troops had defeated the once mighty **Bornu Empire** and pillaged its capital, Kukawa. Though he never entered areas currently within Niger, both his presence at the periphery of **Damagaram** and his ambitions for a farther westward expansion influenced **Zinder**'s court, especially at the time of the arrival of the French mission of Captain **Marius-Gabriel Cazemajou**. Cazemajou's murder in Zinder was in part out of fear in one segment of the court that his true mission was to link up French ambitions with Rabah's aspirations in the area. Niger was the staging ground for one of the three military columns mounted by the French aimed at his destruction. It was within Niger that one of the columns recruited porters, auxiliaries, and camels for its drive toward Chad and the 1900 battle of Kousseri, which brought about the destruction of Rabahist power and the death of Rabah himself.

RADIO NIGER. See VOIX DU SAHEL.

RAFFINI, BRIGI (1953–). Born in **Iférouane** in the **Aïr**, on 7 April 1953, Raffini is an administrator, trained at Niger's École Nationale d'Administration (now **École Nationale d'Administration et de Magistrature**) and at **France**'s Institut Internationale d'Administration Publique and École Nationale d'Administration. He served for several years in the territorial administration as *sous-préfet* before entering the cabinet in 1987, under President **Seyni Kountché**, as state secretary of the Ministry of the Interior, and then (under President **Ali Saibou**) as minister of **agriculture** and the environment. In 1989–1991, he occupied one of the highest offices of the **Second Republic**, that of the president of the consultative assembly, the **Conseil National de Développement**. With the onset of democratic governance, Raffini was part of the faction of the **Mouvement National pour la Société de Développement** (MNSD) which followed **Moumouni Adamou Djermakoye** in the setting up of the **Alliance Nationale pour la Démocratie**

et le Progrès (ANDP Zaman Lahiya). He seems to have been briefly tempted to collude with the irredentist **Tuareg** armed movements which engaged in Niger's first **Tuareg rebellions** of the early 1990s, but eventually stuck to national party politics.

In 2004, he was elected mayor of Iférouane for the Rassemblement pour la Démocratie et le Progrès (RDP Jama'a), the party created by the late President **Ibrahim Baré Maïnassara**. RDP, which was traditionally aligned behind MNSD, supported the **Parti Nigérien pour la Démocratie et le Socialisme** (PNDS Tarayya) in the 2011 **elections**, and Raffini eventually left it altogether to adhere to PNDS. He was subsequently appointed prime minister by President **Mahamadou Issoufou** in April 2011. His appointment to that position is interpreted also as a gesture toward the Tuareg community, which always complains of being marginalized in Niger, although it should be noted that Raffini occupied a similar position under the Second Republic and had distanced himself, in 2009, from the second Tuareg rebellion (2007–2009) by describing it as promoting anarchy and cleavage. Other interpretations have it that President Issoufou had thus installed at the prime-ministership a man coming from outside the PNDS and who would thus owe his elevation entirely to his patron.

RASSEMBLEMENT DÉMOCRATIQUE AFRICAIN (RDA). Francophone Africa's first and most influential political movement, with branches in most of **France**'s African territories. Founded in 1946 at a congress in Bamako (Mali) which various Francophone leaders attended (including an important delegation from Niger) and headed by Côte d'Ivoire's Houphouët-Boigny, the RDA was initially very militant and allied, at the French National Assembly in Paris, with the French Communist Party. The RDA's territorial affiliate in Niger was the **Parti Progressiste Nigérien** (PPN). *See also* POLITICAL PARTIES.

RASSEMBLEMENT DÉMOCRATIQUE DE FEMMES DU NIGER (RDFN). Civic organization for **women** founded in **Niamey** in March 1992. It had been long headed by **Mariama Gamatié Bayard** and included in its ranks several high-profile feminine personalities, such as Mariama Ali, minister of social development, population, and women in 1993–1994. In alliance with the **Association des Femmes du Niger** (AFN) and the **Association des Femmes Juristes du Niger** (AFJN), RDFN has militated throughout the 1990s for the adoption of a Family Code alleviating some of the legal disabilities hampering women in Nigerien society. In the 2000s, it has adopted the networking strategy now favored by **civil society** organizations, to promote development projects targeting women. RDFN, like many of Niger's civil society groups, depends heavily, however, on foreign donor funding and agenda, and has little active connections with its constituency.

REBELLIONS. In the early years of the **French occupation** of the territory that was to become the colony of Niger, there were many movements of unrest and conspiracy against the new power, and at least two major rebellions in the western and northern parts of the country.

*The 1905–1906 Insurgencies in the **Zarma** and **Songhay** Areas.* Their immediate causes were the tax regime and the extractive policies imposed on these regions by the French in the early 1900s. Considering the regions that would later become western Niger as only a passageway to the **Aïr** regions, Hausaland, and the **Lake Chad** area, the French dealt with them quite ruthlessly on several scores: They tampered with the existing political systems, replacing uncooperative rulers with friendly ones; they established an insensitive poll tax system which disorganized the labor and market practices of the area by replacing voluntary contributions with rigid fiscal obligations; and they exacted forced levies of men, animals, and food on the populations to support their eastward progression. These policies were key in worsening large-scale famines in the region (1902), as well as flight to neighboring British territories (**Nigeria**, Gold Coast) and the creation of refuge settlements faraway from French lines of communication, to escape as best as possible the grasp of the colonial power. They also resulted in the two insurgencies of 1905–1906.

The first revolt started in one of the refuge settlements, **Kobkitanda**, which had organized as a village around the leadership of a charismatic blind cleric, **Alfa Saibou**. Saibou virulently preached against taxation and the French-supported chiefs, called to arms against the white Christians, and predicted the arrival of a large Muslim army which would help boot them out by the following **Id el-Kebir** (a Muslim festival which was then due to happen in February 1906). Not content with talking, Alfa Saibou also secretly toured the region in a radius of about 400 km around Kobkitanda, sending letters to notable persons in places which he did not visit (including Karma). The revolt broke out after men in Kobkitanda murdered two *gardes-cercles* (African colonial gendarmes) who had been sent out to collect taxes. The French mustered forces and struck back in January 1906, destroying Kobkitanda forces in a set battle and then razing several of the villages in the **Dallol** region in retaliation for the help they provided the uprising. Alfa Saibou himself managed to escape into the British colony of Nigeria, joining the large uprising of the Satiru revolt there, under the name Shaibu dan Makafo (**Hausa** for Shaibu the Blind). He was captured by the British and beheaded on Sokoto's marketplace in March 1906. Meanwhile, in Karma, a few kilometers north of **Niamey**, a nobleman of a mixed Zarma and Songhay ethnicity, Oumarou, organized a new insurgency against the French. Oumarou (later known as Oumarou Karma) had suffered slights from the French manipulations of customary authority in the area, and he headed a movement of discontent that spanned the Songhay and Zarma northwestern parts of Niger. Though a personal friend of Alfa Saibou, Oumarou Karma rooted his own insurrection in local traditional **religion**, rather than in **Islam**. He attempted to disorganize French coordination by cutting telegraph lines (the material making up the lines was reused to manufacture arrows) and disrupting their river and ground convoys. The French mustered even greater forces than in the case of the Kobkitanda revolt, bringing in troops from Dori (Haute-Volta), **Gao**, Kati (French Sudan), **Zinder**, and **Dosso** as well as cavalrymen furnished by allied chieftains in the area. After three months of operations on the right and left bank of the **Niger River**, the French eventually secured the death of Oumarou Karma at a clash in the **Zarmaganda**, thus ending the **Karma revolt** (March 1906).

The Several Revolts in the **Tuareg** *North.* A holy war had been declared by the **Sanusiya** order, which had been expanding from Kufra into Kanem in Chad, clashing with the northward expansion of the French. This resulted in numerous skirmishes between French troops and Sanusiya believers. The Niger area upheaval was picked up, in particular, by **Kaocen Ag Mohammed** and, earlier, by Fihroun. Other factors adding fuel to the revolts were the general anarchic spirit of the Tuareg (who never lived for long under an organized state formation), loss of Tuareg camel wealth in the various French levies—or unpaid "purchases"—for the earlier conquest of Chad, the French abolition of slavery and the slave trade on which the high-caste Tuareg lifestyle depended, and the severe 1911–1914 **droughts** that hit **Damergou** and **Aïr** especially hard. The most serious of the Tuareg revolts was the second one—of Kaocen—who arrived secretly at **Agadez** in December 1914 with a large force of troops armed with modern rifles and a cannon. Kaocen besieged the fort which the French built near Agadez and controlled the entire region for three months, until reinforcements were sent up from **Zinder**. The rebels eventually joined Sanusiya fights farther north into present-day **Libya**, where Kaocen was captured by an **Arab** warlord and hanged at Mourzouk in 1919. *See also* KAOCEN REVOLT; SARGAJI REVOLT.

RÉFORME ADMINISTRATIVE, 1964. Administrative reform of 17 July 1964, effective 1 October 1965, which divided Niger into seven *départements*, 32 **arrondissements**, and approximately 150 **communes**. The administrative reform was directed toward both rationally setting up the country's administrative framework and decentralizing as much as possible decision making to allow better development prospects and greater mass participation. Toward this end, a Conseil d'Arrondissement was set up in each of these local units. They were, until 1972, consultative, and since then executive. *See also* ADMINISTRATIVE ORGANIZATION.

RÉGIME D'EXCEPTION. The regime of exception is the name given in Niger to the military government of the late 1970s–early 1980s, in reference to the fact that a "normal" regime would be a republic, that is, a form of liberal democracy. It was installed on 15 April 1974, when Lieutenant-Colonel **Seyni Kountché** and his friends in the **armed forces** overthrew President **Hamani Diori**, terminated the **First Republic**, and created the **Conseil Militaire Suprême** (CMS) as the country's leading organ. Later in the month, the coup-makers bestowed on the CMS all legislative and executive powers "until such time when circumstances would allow a return to the normal play of institutions." Kountché was the "President of the Supreme Military Council, head of the state" (he avoided being styled "president of the republic," owing to the nature of the *régime d'exception*). The regime presented itself as a military technocratic effort, immune from politics, and working to mobilize the population for the tasks of development. The initial years were marred by infighting, as Kountché had to dispose of some of the officers of the CMS, notably Commandant **Sani Souna Siddo**, accused in August 1975 of plotting a coup in cahoots with erstwhile **Sawaba** leader **Djibo Bakary**, and then, in March 1976, Commandant **Moussa Bayéré** and Captain **Mohamed Sidi**, who attempted a coup d'état with the participation of **Ahmed Mouddour**, secretary-general of the **union** umbrella organization Union Nationale des Travailleurs du Niger (UNTN).

However, the CMS did put in place early on several corporatist bodies aimed at mobilizing the population: the *samariya* youth organizations and the **Association Islamique du Niger** (AIN) in September 1974, and then the **Association des Femmes du Niger** (AFN) in September 1975. Moreover, it launched two annual sports and culture events, the national wrestling championship (1975) and the national youth festival (1976), which were held in turn in the country's *département* capitals, and which came to give to Nigeriens the sense of a national culture. These varied structures were to work within the frame of a "development society," formally established as a national commission in July 1981.

At that point, the *régime d'exception* started to transition into a normal regime by downgrading the military presence in government and by instituting, in 1983, a civilian prime ministership first held by **Mamane Oumarou**. Oumarou was also soon (August 1983) appointed president of the **Conseil National de Développement**, the technocratic consultative assembly in charge of implementing the development society project whose mission had been charted by the national commission. In 1984, despite escaping another coup attempt, Kountché pushed the "normalization" process further by installing a commission tasked with the preparation of a national charter that would serve as the constitutional basis for the development society. The charter granted also freedom of association and more limited freedom of expression. It was presented to the Nigerien public throughout the year 1985 and adopted by referendum in 1986. The referendum voting was tightly controlled, but the extended campaign that preceded it allowed unions and **students** to clamor for freedom of expression and a multiparty democracy. Moreover, the state of Niger lacked the financial muscle to fund the ambitions expressed in the national charter. While in the first years of the regime of exception, the state thrived on a short-lived **uranium** boom, by the mid-1980s falling uranium revenues, mounting debt, and the hidden inflation imported from a devalued French franc (to which Niger's **currency**, the **CFA franc**, was pegged on a fixed parity) all contributed to emptying state coffers. The regime was therefore increasingly open to the instructions of the International Monetary Fund, which made of the high government spending of the development society a pipe dream. Seyni Kountché died in 1987 of a brain tumor, and his successor, **Ali Saibou**, moved out of the *régime d'exception* into the **Second Republic**.

Nigerien commentators use the phrase "*régime d'exception*" also for the rule of **Ibrahim Baré Maïnassara** under the **Fourth Republic**, denying it the true essence of republican governance.

RELIGION. The bulk of Niger's population is Muslim (98 percent), with a small minority of **Christians** (less than 2 percent). A sizable fraction of both Muslims and Christians are also animist, and a tiny minority is exclusively animist. Most of the animists are **Maouri** or **Arawa** and **Arna**, with some **Manga**, **Boudouma**, and **Songhay**. In recent times, animistic rituals have regressed outside of these enclaves but have not disappeared, even in urban settlements where **Islam** is hegemonic. Furthermore, the two great animist pantheons of the Songhay (**Holley**) and the **Hausa** (**Bori**) suffuse Nigerien popular culture, especially in **dance and music**, where they translate into entertainment lore.

The majority denomination among the Christians is, historically, Roman Catholicism and came in following workers from the coastal French colony of Dahomey (now Benin). Niger's Catholic Church is today part of the Conference of Bishops of Burkina Faso and Niger, and has an archbishopric in **Niamey** (founded as a bishopric in 1961 and currently headed by **Michel Cartatéguy**) and a bishopric in **Maradi** (established in 2001 and currently headed by Ambroise Ouédraogo). The church counts about 16,000 faithful,

RELIGIOUS ORDERS • 387

most of whom reside in Niamey, with a plurality of expatriates from Benin, Togo, and Burkina Faso. The Catholic mission in Niger was originally set up by Bishop François Steinmetz of Dahomey in January 1931. In the 1940s other missionaries (not affiliated with the latter's Missions Africaines de Lyon) started their work in the **Zinder** area. Protestant missionaries arrived in the Zinder area as early as 1924, moving on to **Tibiri** (near Maradi) a few years later. Several of these missions came to Niger via northern **Nigeria**, as, for example, two American societies—Sudan Interior Mission and the Africa Christian Mission—established in Zinder, **Dogondoutchi**, **Madaoua**, and **Galmi**, where the Sudan Interior Mission has established a large field hospital.

Among the Muslim majority, the **Tijaniyya** order is the dominant one after wresting primacy from the **Qadiriyya** during the first decades of the 20th century. Other orders, badly trailing these two, are Hamallism and **Sanusiya**, though **Niassism** (a Senegalese-originated branch of Tijaniyya) has in recent decades made some steady inroads from its stronghold at **Kiota**, and various shades of Wahhabi creed have come to the fore during the 1990s.

The Songhay and **Zarma** areas of western Niger have been mostly affected by the Islam of the western **Sahel** and its clerical orders. In eastern Niger, Islam came mostly via **Bornu** (which dominated the area until roughly the mid-18th century), and the faith shows there some of its original eastern flavor and peculiarities. In the north, the Sanusiya influence has been felt strongly, especially by the **Tuareg** and the **Toubou** of **Aïr** and **Kaouar**. *See also* RELIGIOUS ORDERS.

RELIGIOUS ORDERS (Muslim). There are numerous Muslim Sufi religious orders in Niger, though the dominant one by far is the **Tijaniyya**, which attained primacy over the **Qadiriyya** in the first decades of the 20th century. Established by Sidi Abu Abbas Ahmad al-Tijani in Fez (Morocco) in 1800, under patronage from the Moroccan sultan Moulay Sulayman, it propagated in West Africa chiefly through the jihad of the **Fulani** Toucouleur clerical warrior, Alhaj Umar Tall (mid-19th century). It became hegemonic first in regions that are now in Senegal and western Mali, and the French later encouraged it as a force of accommodation of colonial overrule. In this way, it further spread into the interior of West Africa, especially in the Hausaland. It first reached Zarmaland through a more circuitous route, when **Cheik Hanafi Moustapha** brought it back from the eastern Sudan in the early 20th century, and it blossomed there in its **Niassite** guise under the leadership of **Cheik Boubacar Hassoumi**.

The Qadiriyya has been established in Niger since the 18th century, when it was the local majority order. Founded in Baghdad early in the 12th century, it arrived in Niger in the 17th century, chiefly through the connections of migrating Fulani clerical families with the propagators of the order in West Africa, the Moorish family of the Kunta (Mauritania). The Qadiriyya provided the doctrine and organization at the basis of **Usman Dan Fodio**'s jihad and was thus especially strong in both Hausaland and Zarmaland (in this latter area, through **Say**) throughout the 19th and early 20th century. Colonial authorities feared, however, that it was at the basis of the many **Islam**-slanted revolts and conspiracies of the early 20th century, both in Niger and in **Nigeria**. It was therefore spurned in favor of Tijaniyya.

Hamallism struck roots mostly among the oppressed slave or former slave (especially Fulani)—*ramaibe*—during World War II. Khalwatiya became one of two dominant orders among the **Tuareg** (the other being **Sanusiya**) arriving in Niger from Egypt in the mid-16th century but not spreading much beyond the Tuareg of **Aïr**. The Sanusiya established itself in Aïr around 1870 and spread via the **caravan route** to **Kaouar**, In Gall, and **Iférouane**; one of its important centers became Djididouna, though contemporarily Kaouar, and **Bilma**, specifically, are probably its main centers. It adopted a virulent anti-infidel (and thus anti-French) line in the first decade of the 20th century and declared, from Kufra, **Libya**, a jihad against the French that was headed by the Tuareg and **Toubou** in Niger, and by other groups in **France**'s other Saharan colonies. As a result, the French endeavored to stamp out the order wherever they could.

Other minor orders to be found in Niger include Chadeliya and Taibiya. A 1920 **census** of the Islamic clerics in Niger found that there were 771 belonging to the Qadiriyya, 332 to the Tijaniyya, 21 to the Sanusiya, 3 to the Chadeliya, and 1 to the Taibiya. The **Zinder** *cercle* at the time counted 169 Tijaniyya, 91 Qadiriyya, 4 Sanusiya, 3 Chadeliya, and 1 Taibiya clerics. In the **Tahoua** *cercle*, the figures were 420 Qadiriyya and 8 Tijaniyya. Since this census, the Qadiriyya membership has drastically shrunk and the Tijaniyya expanded. No reliable figures such as these of 1920 are currently available, however, mostly because the postcolonial state does not have the anxious French urge to control them. All that can be noted on this score is that while some of the orders have grown irrelevant, others have boomed—chiefly the Tijaniyya. *See also* RELIGION.

REPATRIATIONS. Large numbers of Nigeriens resident in other African states (but mostly in West Africa) have been forcibly repatriated over the years for a variety of reasons. The two best-known instances were the 200,000 Nigeriens expelled from Ghana in 1970 for reasons of economic nationalism in Ghana. Their reintegration into the Niger **economy** caused the government a great deal of fiscal stress. Earlier, in 1964, an undetermined though smaller number of Nigeriens were expelled from Dahomey as retaliation against Niger's earlier expulsion of its large Dahomean expatriate community. And in 1982 the massive expulsions of foreigners from **Nigeria** caused major dislocations and fiscal hardships to Niger, which was faced with an influx of over 100,000 of its nationals.

RIZ DU NIGER (RINI). A state company set up in 1968 with 250 million **CFA francs** in capital to process rice planted by farm cooperatives. It commenced with the capacity of producing 10,000 tons of rice annually, a sum since doubled, though rice production plummeted in the 1980s. The company has three plants, in **Tillabéri**, Kirkissoye, and Kollo. Consistently operating below capacity (and never producing over 17,250 tons), the company has long been scheduled for restructuring or **privatization**. It is now only 30 percent state owned. *See also* PARASTATAL SECTOR.

ROUCH, JEAN (1917–2004). French anthropologist, filmmaker, and one of the foremost scholars of Niger. Trained originally as a civil engineer, Rouch worked in the colony of Niger on road construction sites (1941–1942) before joining the Free French Forces (1942–1945) resisting **France**'s German occupation during World War II. After a postwar stint as a journalist at Agence France Presse, Rouch returned to Niger where he gradually developed new interests as an ethnologist (focused on the **Songhay**) and a filmmaker. Rouch's film work is in particular at the origin of the *cinema vérité* genre in France, a medley of surrealist inspiration, direct **cinema** aesthetics, and shared anthropology methods applied, in the case of Rouch, to western Nigerien seasonal migrants to the southern coast of West Africa (Accra and Abidjan in particular).

Rouch is also the father of Nigerien cinema, as he stayed in the country after independence and trained most of the 1960s Nigerien movie directors, including especially **Oumarou Ganda**. The training was often in the form of close collaboration with the many films that Rouch made between 1949 and 1979. Indeed, if the early films portrayed the lives, rituals, and hunting feats of the Songhay and the **Sorkos**, Rouch moved at midcareer into longer narrative movies, starting with *Jaguar* (1955), thus employing many young Nigeriens as assistants and actors. After settling in France in the early 1970s, Rouch taught at the Musée de l'Homme in Paris. He would make frequent trips back to Niger until the last one in 2004, when he died in an automobile accident near **Birni-N'Konni** (February 2004). His remains are buried at the old Christian cemetery of **Niamey**.

ROUTE DE L'UNITE. Name of the paved highway that links up far western Niger (starting in **Tillabéri**) to far eastern Niger (ending in **N'Guigmi**), over a distance of about 1,300 km. The road crosses all of Niger's regional capitals, with the exception of **Tahoua** and **Agadez**. It was partly funded by Canada (the segment between **Diffa** and N'Guigmi), and its complete name is Route de l'Unité et de l'Amitié Nigéro-Canadienne. The administration knows it also as the *Nationale 1*, that is, "National Highway 1." It was baptized in the name of national unity, usually conceived in Niger as the union of the **Zarma-Songhay** (west) and the **Hausa** (east). Most of the section between **Zinder** and N'Guigmi through Diffa had long been in a state of advanced degradation, until President **Mamadou Tandja**, a native of the region of Diffa, used his presidential powers to organize its repair in the late 2000s.

ROUTE DE L'URANIUM. Name of the 650-km highway through which Niger's **uranium** exports travel. The road commences at **Arlit**—with feeder roads from the other mines in the vicinity—and runs through **Agadez** to **Tahoua**, before connecting with the **Route de l'Unité** in **Birni-N'Konni**. It then merges with that highway until **Dosso**, where it diverges southward to the Benin border, uranium being evacuated through the Beninese port of Cotonou. The 650-km road was paved between 1976 and 1980. It is regularly maintained through contracts with the **mining** companies.

S

SAADOU BORI. *See* ABODAN, SAADOU.

SABIRI. The most ancient population of **Dosso**. Under their *sandi* (chief), the Sabiri had a privileged status in Dosso until **Aouta** became *zarmakoy* (lord) of Dosso. The *sandi* is the official who enthrones the *zarmakoy*.

SAHEL. Arid transitional zone between the desert north and the subtropical south. Running across much of Central and West Africa, the zone encompasses most of central and northern Niger. Though the Sahel usually has regular rainfall, any disruption of the climate (as during the recent series of prolonged **droughts**) can transform the affected areas into desert. The term *Sahel* is Arabic for "fringe" or "border." It is conceived as the shores of the great sand sea of the Sahara desert.

SAHEL, LE. Niger's governmental daily, formerly named *Le Temps du Niger*. Edited and distributed by the Ministry of Information, its circulation has inched up over the years to 4,000. The ministry also publishes a weekly—*Sahel Hebdo*, now called *Sahel Dimanche*—with a similar circulation. It was until 1989 the only newspaper in the country. *See also* MEDIA.

SAIBOU, ALI (1940–2011). President of Niger between 1987 and 1993, and former chief of staff of Niger's **armed forces**. Born in Dingazibanda near **Ouallam** in the **Zarmaganda**, Saibou decided at an early age on a military career and enrolled in the Saint-Louis (Senegal) preparatory school in 1954. He then joined the First Senegalese Tirailleurs Regiment. He saw military action in 1960 in Cameroon (where he was wounded) while with the Fifth Regiment Interarmes d'Outre-Mer (RIOM) of **France**. He was transferred to the Nigerien army in August 1961, with the rank of sergeant. After attending officer's school, he was placed in command of units at **N'Guigmi** (1969) and **Agadez** (1973), attaining the rank of captain. He was in that town when **Seyni Kountché** overthrew President **Hamani Diori** and his prompt overnight drive with troops to **Niamey** in support of Kountché brought about his promotion to major and elevation to the cabinet as minister of rural **economy**

and the environment. On 20 November 1974, he was also named chief of staff of the armed forces. He retained that position until Kountché's death in 1987. He then arranged to succeed Kountché with the support of a strong military clique and an appeal to the military rule of "command to the oldest in the highest rank."

At the end of Kountché's rule, Niger was veering toward civilian rule with the adoption of a charter in 1986. Because he was both far less politically minded than Kountché and genuinely indifferent to political power, Saibou precipitated the movement at his accession. Under the motto *"décrispation"* (relaxation), he made effective most of the formal liberties granted by the charter in the framework of a **constitution**, which he pushed through in 1988. This, combined with the deteriorating economy, created a new zeitgeist that clearly pointed toward the end of authoritarian single-party rule.

In 1989–1990, **Tuareg rebellion** in the **Ader** region and **union** and **student** rioting resistance to International Monetary Fund and World Bank policy packages pushed the regime toward a tilting point. The death of three (or perhaps more) students on 9 February 1990 during a demonstration started its effective undoing. Faced with clamors for change and justice, Saibou and the officials of the single-party **Mouvement National pour la Société de Développement** (MNSD) granted all democratic freedoms and drafted a multiparty regime constitution. This was perceived by opposing groups (quickly establishing parties and associations) as a ploy to retain power through **democratization**, and the intellectual classes which staffed them demanded a national conference, similar to the one that was being held in neighboring Benin but serving also as a people's court for trying the alleged crimes of the military regime and possibly extending into the **First Republic**. Saibou did not put up much resistance and was retained as titular head of state during the proceedings of the **Conférence Nationale** and until the 1993 **elections**. The conference eventually adopted a constitution that was a replica of the one drafted by MNSD officials, but it enabled the emerging leaders to build their public persona while also giving the new **political parties** the time to gain some texture.

Saibou afterward retired to his large house in Niamey and his farms in Dingazinbanda, accepting to appear in **Baré Maïnassara**'s Conseil des Sages (Council of the Wisemen), set up after the **coup d'état of January 1996**, and also being the first dignitary visited by **Djibo Salou** after he overthrew **Mamadou Tandja** in February 2010.

Ali Saibou was also the last ruler in the 30 years of **Zarma-Songhay** monopoly over Niger's presidency. He died in Niamey in October 2011.

SAIDA OUMOUL KHAIRY NIASS (1941–). Daughter of Cheikh Ibrahima Niass (the founder of the **Tijaniyya** Niassite order in Senegal) and widow of **Cheik Aboubacar Hassoumi** (the founder of the **Kiota** branch of **Niassism** in the region of **Dosso**), she is popularly known as Maman Senegal. Founder of two **Franco-Arabe** schools in Kiota, she has been most successful in organizing Tijaniyya **women** in her association, Jamiyat Nassirat-Dine, which runs credit facilities and organizes many economic activities and feminine self-help community work throughout western Niger. Her daughter, **Malama Zaharaou**, is a renowned preacher and a member, for Kiota, of the consultative state-sponsored Islamic organ Haut Conseil Islamique.

SALA, MOUSSA (Lieutenant Colonel). Former commander of Niger's armored unit and minister of public **health**. Since 1966 head of Niger's small armored unit, Moussa joined the military cabinet after the **1974 coup d'état** as minister of public health and social affairs. In mid-1975 he was shifted to head the Ministry of Transport and Public Works but was returned to his old ministry (stripped of social affairs) in 1976, when he was also promoted to major. Appointed minister of **education** in September 1978, Sala was held personally responsible for the eruption of **student** unrest in the country in 1980 and was dropped from the cabinet in February 1981. Sala was rehabilitated after General **Ali Saibou**'s rise to power, and in 1989 was named **Mouvement National pour la Société de Développement** (MNSD) deputy from **Dosso** to the **National Assembly**. He served in that capacity until the assembly was dissolved in 1991. He died in the mid-1990s.

SALIFOU, ANDRE (1942–). Historian, author, politician, and diplomat. Born in 1942 in **Zinder** and educated locally, in **France** (at the University of Toulouse), and at the Abidjan (Côte d'Ivoire) École Nationale d'Art Dramatique, Salifou is Niger's first doctorate holder in the discipline of history (1970). He has written several plays, one of which—*Tanimoune*—was first performed in Algiers in 1969 and gained him much acclaim. He also founded and directed many amateur theatrical groups. Between 1967 and 1973 teaching at the École Normale teachers' school of Zinder, he was its director between 1969 and 1970. In 1973 he went to Dakar to serve with United Nations Educational Scientific and Cultural Organization (UNESCO) office there until 1978, and then became director of social and cultural affairs of the Francophone African countries' Organisation Commune Africaine et Malgache (OCAM). He returned to **Niamey** a year later to become the director of the school of **education** of the **University of Niamey**, in due course emerging as its dean. In the late 1980s, he participated in focusing pressure on the **Second Republic**'s authorities for political liberalization; when the **Conférence Nationale** was convened in 1991, he was elected president of the Haut Conseil de la République (HCR), the interim (until **elections** produced a regular) legislature of Niger.

Barred, together with other former heads of state and government leaders, from running in the forthcoming presidential elections, Salifou joined forces with Illa Kané to form a **political party**, the Union des Patriotes Démocrates et Progressistes (UPDP-Shamuwa). The party won only one seat in the **National Assembly**, filled by Salifou for his Zinder constituency. He then joined the **Mouvement National pour la Société de Développement** (MNSD Nassara) in opposition protest against the ruling coalition's monopoly of positions and offices, once being arrested together with 90 other personalities in April 1994. Dissatisfied with the minor role he was playing under the **Third Republic**, Salifou was among those who fully supported the coup-maker of January 1996, Colonel **Baré Maïnassara**, in his attempt at installing a new system. He was appointed minister of state in charge of higher education and research, and then minister of state in charge of foreign relations (1996–1997). After the toppling of Baré Maïnassara in 1999, Salifou attempted a UPDP comeback as presidential candidate but garnered only 2.08 percent of the vote. He subsequently started a diplomatic career, at the **Organisation Internationale de la Francophonie** (special envoy to the Comoros in 2001), the African Union (special envoy to Madagascar in 2002, to Côte d'Ivoire in 2003).

Despite this hectic career, Salifou is a prolific writer, second only to **Boubou Hama** in Niger—and perhaps in French-speaking sub-Saharan Africa as a whole—in output. His endeavors include several historical works, including the book form of his doctoral dissertation, *Le Damagaram ou sultanat de Zinder au XIXe siècle* (1971); a number of historical plays, including *Tanimoune* (1973), *Si les Cavaliers avaient été là* (1985), *Le Fils de Sogolon* (1985), and *Ousman Dan Fodio, serviteur d'Allah* (1988); and a few novels such as *Tels pères, tels fils* (1994) and historical essays, among which is *La Question touarègue au Niger* (1993). More recently he has published an essay on democracy, *Entretien avec mes enfants sur la démocratie en Afrique* (2004), a historical essay on the slave trade and the first biography of a former Niger president, *Biographie politique de Diori Hamani* (2010). *See also* FOURTH REPUBLIC.

SALOU, DJIBO (1963–). Born in the village of Namaro, about 40 km west of **Niamey**, Salou studied up to the high school *baccalauréat* degree before joining the army in 1987. After attending the military officers' school of Bouaké (Côte d'Ivoire), he underwent special training in artillery in China (1998 and 2001). This was rounded off by instruction in military leadership (*État-major*) received at Morocco's Collège Royal d'Études Militaies Supérieures. He served as instructor of the **Forces Armées Nigériennes** (FAN) in **Agadez** and as United Nations field commander in Côte d'Ivoire (2004) and United Nations military supervisor in the Democratic Republic of Congo (2006). In the Nigerien military, Salou's unit is the 121st commandment, support and service squad, better known through the shorthand Compagnie d'appui (support squad), of which he is the commander. The Compagnie d'appui is known for the key role it played in all the military coups organized in Niger, which is attributable to the fact that while it has no special department or task within the army, its support and service mission puts it in touch with all the military departments and squads of the FAN.

On 18 February 2010, Salou masterminded a coup d'état which cut through the knot of the political crisis created by President **Mamadou Tandja**'s unconstitutional bid to stay in power beyond his term of office. The coup was supported by the rest of the army, the bulk of Niger's political class, and more importantly, the population itself—as a crowd of more than 10,000 took to the streets in Niamey to dance at the ousting of Tandja the following day. In a matter of two weeks, the army came up with a procedure to restore civilian rule under the supervision of a military staffed **Conseil Supême pour la Restauration de la Démocratie** (CSRD). In the weeks before the establishment of the CSRD, military leaders discussed the direction that should be given to the takeover of state power, many among them being of the opinion that the army should remain in charge for a few years in order to root out corruption and restore state organizations to better working conditions. But under pressure from civilian politicians and the international community, Salou favored a yearlong transition consisting essentially of the writing of a new **constitution** and the organizing of a **constitutional referendum** and of local, legislative, and presidential **elections**. Alongside a civilian-dominated caretaker government, a set of civilian institutions were established to run the process: a constitutional court, a transitional parliament called the **Conseil Consultatif National**, and a constitution drafting committee which completed its mission in May 2010. The period was also marked by the setting up of state financial inspections to retrieve from various bigwigs of the **Fifth** and **Sixth Republics** and their assorted clients the money that they had embezzled, totaling several billions of **CFA francs**. Salou promised to commit the funds thus secured to the building of a second national hospital in Niamey, but this decision might not be fulfilled by his successors.

In January–March 2011, Salou organized the rounds of elections that restored Niger to democracy and left the presidency. *See also* DEMOCRATIZATION.

SAMARIYA (also *Samaria*). Traditional organizations resurrected by **Seyni Kountché**'s military regime and given a modern developmental function. Meaning "youth" in **Hausa** (the singular being *samari*), the *samariya* were groups of youth (organized by age) coordinated at the village level under a *sarkin samari* to perform whatever tasks they were delegated by the village chief or the *sarkin samari*. Largely stagnating in the 1960s, the groups were resurrected after the **coup d'état of 1974** by Kountché, who called upon them to assume a major effort in several developmental tasks, such as brick-making and the construction of schools and classrooms. In 1981–1982, the *samariya*—by now officially set up in every one of Niger's 9,000 villages—were given a key role in the newly enunciated development society, though their economic role has always been modest and as a tool for popular mobilization even less. They were chiefly important in the organization of the annual youth festivals that celebrated Niger's cultures through the *régime d'exception* and dwindled out of existence in the 1990s.

SAMIRA. Site of the latest and most productive of the gold mines discovered in the *département* of **Téra** (region of **Tillabéri**). An older gold deposit was discovered at Koma Bangou by the **Office National des Ressources Minières** (ONAREM), in 1985. The discoveries there, yielding between 15 and 200 grams of gold per ton of rock, triggered an influx of artisanal miners. In May 1994, the Nigerien government signed an agreement with a Canadian company, Etruscan, for feasibility studies. The study determined that the exploitation would not be commercially viable and Etruscan closed operations. The site was subsequently taken over by artisanal miners, despite Etruscan's still valid concession; Koma Bangou turned into a gold rush town of around 50,000 people, mostly Nigeriens but with substantial proportions of people from other West African countries. A richer deposit was discovered at Samira Hill, not very far from Koma Bangou. In 2004, Etruscan returned, with another Canadian company, Semafo, to set up a joint venture with the state of Niger (which holds 20 percent stake in its operation), in a Moroccan-headquartered company, the Société des Mines du Liptako (SML). The reserves at Samira were estimated at 19 tons to be exploited over six years, but the deposits are believed to be only one site in a constellation of gold deposits stretching between Gotheye and **Ouallam**, and constituting the "Samira Horizon." Semafo is busy exploring that part of the region of Tillabéri.

SANDI. Head of the non-**Zarma** indigenous population, which in the **Dosso** chiefdom is roughly equal to the *zarmakoy* whom he actually formally enthrones after selection from the **Aouta** family. The *sandi* is always consulted by the *zarmakoy* on important matters. *See also* SABIRI.

SANUSIYA. A Sufi (mystic) order stressing return to the basic precepts of **Islam**, avoidance of contaminating influences from the infidel world, and direct interpretation of Islam. The order struck roots in **Libya** in the 19th century and had a deep impact farther south toward the latter part of that century. Founded by the Algerian scholar al-Sayyid Muhamad bin Ali al-Sanusi al-Khattabi (called in Libya the Grand Sanusi, al-Sanusi al-Kabir), Sanusiya was established in Libya after his return from Mecca where he had organized his first lodge. Moving his headquarters to the interior Jaghbub (190 km from the coast) where an Islamic university was also founded (the second after Cairo's Al-Azhar), al-Sanusi won the allegiance of various tribes in the interior of Libya, and others involved in long-distance trading. In light of this success, the order developed a more African-oriented proselytizing ambition, and the center of the order was shifted to Kufra in 1895, from which its influence radiated into **Aïr** and **Kaouar** (in Niger) and Kanem and Ouadai (in Chad). Much of the conversion of these areas to the Sanusiya occurred after al-Sanusi's death and was carried out by his two lieutenants, Sidi Muhammad al-Barrani and Muhammad al-Suni.

The Sanusiya's expansion southward coincided with **France**'s northward progress, and the two forces clashed bitterly from the turn of the century into the 1920s. In Niger the Sanusiya established itself first in Aïr in 1870 (especially in **Agadez**, In Gall, **Iférouane**, and a few other minor centers). Emissaries were sent as far afield as **Zinder**, both to gain converts and open lodges and to mobilize the population against the French. The order did not strike deep roots among the **Tuareg** and the **Toubou**. The Sanusiya currently has a number of lodges, especially in Kaouar. *See also* RELIGION; RELIGIOUS ORDERS.

SARA-SARA. One of the several local names for the rampaging Voulet-Chanoine column in Niger. In **Zarma** the equivalent is **Gate-Gate**. *See* MISSION AFRIQUE CENTRALE-TCHAD.

SARGAJI REVOLT (1899–1900). Localized anti-French revolt lasting from August 1899 to December 1900 and affecting the region north of **Dosso** (and flaring up again in 1905), ethnically a mixed area of Gubey, **Tuareg**, **Maouri**, and **Zarma**. Among the complex reasons for the revolt was the attachment of the traditionally independent villages of Sargaji and **Loga** to the authority of the *zarmakoy* of Dosso, a prime ally of **France**. The refusal of the two villages to submit to Dosso's authority led to hostilities that spread throughout the area. Two campaigns (in August 1899 and February 1900) led to French defeats; only in November 1900 did a strong French column armed with rapid-firing weapons succeed in razing the villages and setting the prime conspirators to flight. *See also* REBELLIONS.

SARKI. King in **Hausa**. The term is used for the king of a large region (such as the **Gobir**), the chief of a village, or the official head of any organization, ritual, or ceremony, for instance, *sarkin Bori*. It is the root for *Sarauta* (royalty), the traditional system of kingly rule in Hausaland. Feminine is *Saraunia*, generally spelled *sarraounia* in Niger.

SARRAOUNIA MANGOU. Late 19th-century queen of **Lougou**, in the **Arewa** (*sarraounia* is feminine for *sarki*, the Hausa word for "king"). Little is known about her life. Sovereign of a people whose identity was deeply shaped by a local pantheon and its rites and beliefs, the **Arna**, Sarraounia Mangou successfully opposed the encroachments of the Islamic empire of Sokoto and bravely confronted the new power of the French, when it arrived in the Arewa in the form of the blood-soaked **Mission Afrique Centrale-Tchad**. Sarraounia Mangou held the column for much of the early months of 1899, but her capital of Lougou was finally stormed in April that year, and the queen disappeared. The exact moment and circumstances of her death are unknown. Her life was the object of a novel—*Sarraounia*, by **Abdoulaye Mamani**—and a movie drawn from the novel by Mauritanian director Med Hondo. The village of Lougou remains to date a queenship.

SASSALE. Kurtey slaves, originating in the Sassalé village near Dessa, who developed a reputation as griots specializing in obscene songs and dances.

SAWABA. In **Hausa**, "independence" or "freedom"—the rallying call of **Djibo Bakary**'s **Mouvement Socialiste Africain** and later the official name of that party, founded in 1957. The party lost the 1958 referendum (in which it called for a "no" vote) by 358,000 (for the **Parti Progressiste Nigérien**, PPN) and 98,000 for Sawaba, and shortly thereafter lost the territorial **elections**, thus losing political primacy in Niger. These losses were largely engineered by the retreating colonial government, which resented Bakary's antagonism to **France**'s agenda, and wanted to leave the country to a friendly regime at independence. With the rise of the PPN the Sawaba party was banned (in 1959) and several years later attempted a comeback through violent means, among which were the October 1964 attacks on several border and customs posts and the April 1965 grenade attack on President **Hamani Diori**, the reaction to which was so harsh that Sawaba for all practical purposes stopped its quest for power. In 1964, moreover, it was estimated that it had only about 300 to 400 militants and fewer guerrillas trained (in particular) in Kwame Nkrumah's Ghana. The party had at various times been labeled communist, which is erroneous, though certainly it was radical. After the

coup d'état of 1974, Sawaba leaders, including Djibo Bakary, were invited to return to Niger on the condition that they refrain from politics. The party name, as a suffix, was resurrected by Djibo Bakary with the onset of competitive elections in the early 1990s, but not only has it not garnered more than a small number of votes, it has also split into two, with Bakary heading one of its components. *See also* POLITICAL PARTIES.

SAY. Historically important **Fulani** and Muslim stronghold. The city was founded in 1825 by Alfa **Mamane Diobo**, a **Qadiriyya** Sufi master who came to the area from Djenné (Mali) in 1810 via **Gao**, and was in full control of the area around Say by the time of his death, in 1834. Though Diobo was no conqueror, his control over Say was ensured by both his clerical renown and the diplomatic protection of the Sokoto Empire, also founded by a Fulani Qadiriyya Sufi master, **Usman Dan Fodio**.

The town was occupied by **France** on 9 May 1897 and administered from Dahomey until 1907. In 1928, it became part of the *cercle* of **Niamey**. Located about 57 km from Niamey, not far from the **Parc National du W**, the town (now a *commune urbaine*) has today 12,000 people but bears little resemblance to the ancient center of Islamic learning and piety. In recognition of its former role, however, Niger's first *madrasa* was set up here in 1957, and in 1974 the Organization of the Islamic Conference designated Say as the site for an Islamic university for West Africa. The new university, the **Islamic University of Say**, opened its doors in October 1986, with Dr. Abdullah Ben-Abdul-Muhsin El-Turki as its rector.

Say is connected to the capital by an all-weather road and has a colorful Friday market to which many tourists flock. Nearby are found iron deposits with 50 percent iron content.

In its heyday the town of Say was widely known from Gao to **Gaya** as a center for Islamic learning and piety. It is reputed to have had at one time 30,000 inhabitants and to have launched its own trans-Saharan caravans. It has retained from those days a traditional government held by the descendants of Diobo in the office of *alfaize* (literally, son of the cleric, in **Zarma**). Succeeding to Alfa Mamane Diobo (1825–1834), the *alfaize* have been: 1834–1860, Boubacar Modibo; 1860–1872, Abdourahmane; 1872–1874, Moulaye; 1874–1878, Abdoulwahidou; 1878–1885, Saliha Alpha Baba; 1885–1893, Amadou Satourou Modibo; 1893–1894, Halirou Abdoulwahabi; 1894–1910, Halirou Abdoulwahidou; 1910–1913, Diabiri Modibo; 1913–1956, Alhassane Hama Gao Modibo; 1956–2002, Abdoussalami Alhassane; 2002– , **Amadou Issa Cissé**. The first five (through 1893) were sons of Alfa Mamane Diobo, and thereafter came his grandchildren and their children.

Currently Say is a *département* of 283,000 in the region of **Tillabéri**. Its main populations are Zarma and Fulani with a strong **Gourmantché** minority and a smattering of **Songhay** and **Kurtey**. *See also* FRANCO-ARABE.

SAY, BANIA MAHAMADOU (1935–2004). Administrator, youth leader, and prolific writer and poet. Born in 1935 in Tillakaina, outside of **Tillabéri**, and educated as an administrative accountant, Say served as a teacher before being selected to become director of the national budget office. He was much involved in the cultural activities of the *samariya*, on which he wrote an essay, *La Samaria* (1981). In 1980 a book of his poems was published in Niger. His works include the poetry collection *Algaita*; several novellas, including *Le Voyage d'Hamado* (1986) and *Akosombo, le festin des sorciers* (1991); and satirical writings. *See also* LITERATURE.

SAY–BARROUA LINE. A straight line between **Say** and Barroua (on **Lake Chad**) that delineated, in the **Anglo-French Treaty** of 1890, the French (northern) and British (southern) spheres of influence in the area. **France**'s haste in ratifying the border was indicative of a gross overestimation of the extent of British control and influence south of the line, costing France the highly populated areas of northern **Nigeria**. The Say–Barroua Line was later somewhat revised in favor of France.

SECOND REPUBLIC. The Second Republic came into being after a **constitutional referendum** organized by President **Ali Saibou** on 24 September 1989. It was the culmination of the normalization process organized by the previous president, **Seyni Kountché**, to end the so-called *régime d'exception* installed at the **coup d'état of April 1974**. Though it seems that Kountché had intended the normalization to result in the adoption of a national charter which organized a tightly state-controlled "society for development" (1986), Saibou pushed this farther into a constitutional government, still authoritarian as it was based on single-party rule of the **Mouvement National pour la Société de Développement** (MNSD) but fairly liberal in terms of freedoms of expression and association. The Second Republic's **constitution** gave extensive powers to the president, presumably allowing him to carry out policies as he saw fit. However, the regime had come into being under inauspicious circumstances; the worsening of the financial crisis and of the economic recession which started out in the country early in the 1980s decade meant that by the late 1980s the Nigerien state was absolutely broke.

The government was forced to sign agreements with the International Monetary Fund, the World Bank, and other donors, which antagonized its premier constituency (civil servants and other state workers) and eventually led to a swelling protest movement at the **University of Niamey**. The latter was especially triggered by the tentative implementation of a World Bank–sponsored educational reform project which was scheduled to shift resources from higher **education** to primary education, drastically trimming scholarships, and reducing university staff and services. The policy led to unrest among the **students**. During a student demonstration on 9 February 1990, some policemen used real bullets and three (and perhaps more) students were killed. The event angered the public and chastened the authorities of the Second Republic who proposed a constitutional reform to introduce full multiparty democracy in the system, drafting a new constitution to that effect. The opposition—students, workers **unions**, civil and political associations, the latter quickly morphing into **political parties**—refused this solution, preferring the organization of a national conference that would, among other things, try the crimes and errors of both the *régime d'exception* and the Second Republic. On 29 July 1991, the **Conférence Nationale** convened and proclaimed itself sovereign, thereby terminating the Second Republic in what was effectively a bloodless but verbose civilian coup d'état.

SEKOU, DJADO (1930–1988). Easily the greatest known **Zarma**-language literary artist, Sekou was born in Gomno, near Hamadallahi in the **Zarmaganda**, and flourished in the 1970–1980s, apparently after traveling extensively in Mali to acquire the learning required for his storytelling art. Sekou specialized in epic storytelling, simply called *faakaray* (entertainment) or *deede* (narrative) in Zarma. These were adapted from epic legends and cycles developed out of the 19th-century wars of conquest and resistance between **Fulani** jihadists (such as Alhaj Umar Tall, called Umaru Futiyu in Sekou's stories) and Bambara lords and kings in contemporary Mali. Other Nigerien Zarma-language storytellers have exploited the same material, but none has achieved the universal appeal of Sekou, whose performance provided to today's Zarma-speakers a host of proverbs and sayings. Sekou's narratives, widely published in the forms of audiotapes, have undergone rather infelicitous attempts at French renderings and remain today throughout the Zarma and **Songhay** country of Niger the only work of secular literary art to successfully compete with Islamic preaching. *See also* ISLAM; LITERATURE.

SEVENTH REPUBLIC. Niger's most recent political regime, adopted through a **constitutional referendum** on 2 November 2010. The new regime essentially restores the **Fifth Republic**, which had been dismantled by **Mamadou Tandja** in August 2009 to be replaced by a short-lived **Sixth Republic**.

SIDHAMED, SEIDNALY (1957–). Better known under his nom de guerre of **Alphadi**, Sidhamed is a fashion designer born in Timbuktu (Mali) from Nigerien parents in a large transnational Saharan family of chiefly **Arab** background. Alphadi studied **tourism** in Paris in the 1970s and first worked as a civil servant in Niger's tourism ministry. He had also taken classes of design and dressmaking at Paris's Atelier Chardon Savard (**France**). In 1983, while still working at the tourism ministry, he created his first collection, which was two years later shown at Paris's Salon International du Tourisme. His career took off, as he received many international awards and built a prestigious network of friends and business partners in the Paris fashion world. In 1998, he organized the first edition of the Festival International de la Mode Africaine (FIMA) in the dunes of Tiguidit, in Niger's desert north, bringing in high-couture stars such as Yves Saint-Laurent, Kenzo, and Thierry Mugler, together with a host of young African designers. Alphadi's intention was to make of the festival a biennial event, and FIMA's second edition was organized in **Niamey** in 2000. It provoked the anger of Islamic associations, whose mass protests degenerated into scenes of violence in Niamey and **Maradi**. Many Islamic associations were subsequently banned, and the FIMA, which had the full support of the government, went on unhindered. Since then, Alphadi has been able to organize it regularly. Subsequent editions were held in 2003, 2007, 2009, and 2011, making of the festival a routine event generally taking place on scenic sites along the **Niger River**, always in the vicinity of Niamey.

SIDI, MOHAMED (Captain). Ringleader of the March 1976 uprising against the **Seyni Kountché** regime, who was wounded in the fighting. He was condemned to death in his subsequent trial and was executed on 21 April 1976. Prior to the **coup d'état of 1974** that led to the rise of Seyni Kountché, he had been chef de cabinet of the minister of defense. *See also* COUP OF 15 MARCH 1976.

SIDIBÉ, ISSOUFOU. Sidibé heads the Confédération Démocratique des Travailleurs du Niger (CDTN), a more radical alternative to the mainstream **union**, the **Union des Syndicats des Travailleurs du Niger** (USTN). Sidibé thus took a stance against President **Mamadou Tandja**'s candidacy in the 2004 **election**, claiming that he treated workers' demands with contempt. In 2005, Sidibé's CDTN was central to the organization of the ghost town campaigns which shut down the main Nigerien towns and cities for several days in protest against a new value added tax on goods and services adopted by the government under instructions from the International Monetary Fund. During the 2009 political crisis, Sidibé became one of the main anti-Tandja orators, and the CDTN joined the **political parties** in the **Coordination des Forces pour la Démocratie et la République** (CFDR) coalition. After Tandja dissolved the constitutional court in July 2009, Sidibé called for a "ghost country" strike on the model of the 2005 event, but the call was unheeded and the CDTN resorted to organizing more traditional general strikes in August. CDTN was thus instrumental in fueling the crisis atmosphere which undermined Tandja's attempt to establish a dictatorship, and which eventually led to his removal through a **coup d'état in February 2010**.

SIDIKOU, ABDOU (1927–1973). Former secretary of state for foreign affairs. Born in 1927 in Kouré (near Niamey) where he was *chef de canton*, and educated locally as well as at the **École William Ponty** (Dakar, Senegal), Abdou Sidikou continued his **education** at the Dakar faculty of medicine and that of Paris (**France**), graduating from the latter in 1956. He served his internship at the Hôpitaux de la Seine (1956–1957) and continued specialization in serology, biology, and bacteriology, returning to Niger to become chief pharmacist at **Niamey**'s National Hospital (1957–1959). In 1959 he was brought into the government as cabinet director of the minister of **health**, and in 1962 moved into the diplomatic world when he was appointed ambassador to the United States, the United Nations, and Canada. In September 1964 he was shifted to head his country's embassy to West Germany, Benelux, Austria, Scandinavia, and the European Economic Community, and in November 1965 returned to Niamey to become secretary-general for foreign affairs. On 14 April 1967, he was promoted to secretary of state for foreign affairs. In January 1970 he was shifted, for health reasons, and appointed secretary of state attached to the presidency. He was throughout also Niger's inspector of pharmacies. Abdou Sidikou died on 26 July 1973.

SIDO, SANI SOUNA (Major) (1933–1977). Former minister in the early years of **Seyni Kountché**'s rule. The *chef de cabinet* of **Hamani Diori**'s military cabinet prior to the **coup d'état of 1974**, Sido was not brought into the conspiracy because of his proximity to Diori. After the coup, however, in part because of his popularity among the troops, he was brought into the **Conseil Militaire Suprême** and appointed its vice-president and also minister of interior, mines, and geology. He rapidly developed into a strong competitor to Kountché, and friction multiplied between the two officers though they appeared on the surface to be on good terms. By the end of 1974, Sido was stripped of his other military duties and demoted from the Ministry of Interior to directorship of the newly created **Conseil National de Développement**. He was accused on 2 August 1975 of plotting to do away with Kountché and was imprisoned. He died in **Agadez** in June 1977 allegedly of epilepsy, but in reality was executed under instruction from the *préfet* of Agadez, Lieutenant Colonel **Bagnou Beidou**. During the 1991 **Conférence Nationale**, the event became a cause célèbre of sorts and a number of officers, including Beidou, were imprisoned for his murder. However, Beidou had acted upon orders from on high and was released shortly after the conference ended. *See also* ARMED FORCES.

SIXTH REPUBLIC. A seven-month authoritarian regime installed by **Mamadou Tandja** through a **constitutional referendum** on 4 August 2009. The referendum was heavily manipulated and was boycotted by the opposition. Nigeriens voted against it mostly through record low participation rates—below 5 percent—in most of the country, though the regime drew significant support in the regions of **Maradi, Zinder**, and **Diffa** (the two latter are Tandja's home regions). The regime installed a presidentialist system and was to be ushered in by a transitional period of three years during which Tandja intended to eradicate opposition and bring Nigeriens to heel. Legislative **elections** organized in October 2009 resulted in a rubber-stamp Parliament dominated by the Tandjiste faction of the **Mouvement National pour la Société de Développement** (MNSD Nassara) and a smattering of small opportunistic parties and individuals (so-called independent candidates). It was terminated when Squadron Chief **Djibo Salou** toppled Tandja on 18 February 2010. The episode is known in Niger under the name of **Tazartché**, and the supporters of Tandja's projects are called Tazartchistes.

SOCIÉTÉ D'EXPLOITATION DES EAUX DU NIGER (SEEN). Niger's water company for urban areas. In Niger, water provision is divided between urban and rural distribution, with differing modes of exploitation and operation. Urban distribution of potable running water was originally ensured by the electricity company **Société Nigérienne d'Electricité** (NIGELEC; dating back to 1961 as SAFELEC), while exploitation of rural water in wells and boreholes was developed by the Office des Eaux du Sous-sol (OFEDES), created in 1963. In 1980, both NIGELEC and OFEDES came under the supervision of a Water Ministry created that year. The ministry first attempted to develop water distribution in rural areas by levying a tax on NIGELEC's water bills, which were then collected in a special fund, the Fond National de l'Eau, set up in 1983. The fund lasted until 1990, but meanwhile the water sector was restructured with the support of the World Bank, and a public water company, the *Société Nationale des Eaux* (SNE), was created (1987). The SNE took over the activities of both NIGELEC (which was restricted to electricity provision) and OFEDES (which disappeared).

While SNE benefited from the removal of the FNE in 1990, it did not thrive, owing to a variety of factors, including especially the devaluation of the **CFA franc** in 1994 and the continuous political instability in the country, which hindered rational management and the implementation of policy agreements with donors. Despite these difficulties, SNE was comparatively efficient, ensuring in particular a rate of 80 percent in the correct functioning of its networks. However, donors pressured for **privatization** in view of the liability that the state represented during much of the period. In 1996, the government of Niger signed with the International Monetary Fund a structural adjustment program which included a large-scale privatization and liberalization scheme. In the new framework that then emerged, SNE was privatized in stages, through the creation of a Société du Patrimoine des Eaux du Niger (SPEN), a donor-backed state organ, which in turn reached an agreement with the giant French firm Vivendi Waters (now Veolia) to provide water services in 52 urban settlements through the Société d'Exploitation des Eaux du Niger (SEEN). Veolia owns 51 percent of SEEN, with 34 percent going to private Nigerien businesses, 10 percent to SEEN's employees, and 5 percent to the state. The target population was thus of 2,600,000 in 2009, of which 1,819,000 had access to SEEN's services (this was up from a serviced population of 1,215,000 in 2001). In this way, urban distribution of water had been again separated from rural distribution, which became the preserve of small local undertakings financed by decentralized communities and nongovernmental organizations. Rural areas' water needs currently have 60 percent rate of coverage on average, with the sparsely populated region of **Agadez** leading the way with a rate of coverage in modern wells and boreholes of 92 percent and the region of **Tahoua** closing the ranks with a rate of coverage of 50 percent. In contrast, SEEN's rate of coverage is currently at 80 percent on average. *See also* PARASTATAL SECTOR.

SOCIÉTÉ DE LAIT DU NIGER (SOLANI). Private successor of the Office du Lait du Niger (OLANI). OLANI was created in 1971 as a state organ with backing from the United Nations in view of helping Niger to provide cheap fresh and powdered milk and dairy products to the population, especially children. It built on Niger's large livestock sector, which already fed an artisanal milk and dairy business. Though the state of Niger wanted to hang on to OLANI, the company was hard hit by the crisis of the early 1990s and especially the **currency** devaluation of 1994. **Economic liberalization** moreover brought about a more competitive environment in which the private company Niger-Lait became a major rival. In 1998, OLANI was one of only three of the 13 companies slated for **privatization** to be effectively sold off to private Nigerien capital. Though SOLANI's production is variable, depending as it does on the seasons since much of the raw product is drawn from traditional herding, the company produces on average 4 million liters of milk yearly.

In general the milk and dairy products sector boomed in Niger in the 2000s, with Niger-Lait usually outperforming SOLANI and both having to compete with Laban-Niger. While all three companies were initially centered on **Niamey**, they have expanded in recent years into almost all the other regions. They often face there the successful competition of homegrown companies such as Coopérative Laitière de Niamey (around Niamey), Tarmamoua Ader (in **Tahoua**), and Grande Laiterie de Zinder (in **Zinder**). Moreover, semi-industrial units (such as Kany-Lait in Niamey) propose interesting taste variations that allow them to hold out in specific niches. SOLANI, however, keeps an edge through its efforts at preserving the standard of quality and traditions of OLANI. *See also* CATTLE; PARASTATAL SECTOR.

SOCIÉTÉ DE RAFFINERIE DE ZINDER (SORAZ). A joint venture between the Chinese **parastatal** China National Petroleum Corporation (CNPC), which owns 60 percent of the plant, and the government of Niger (40 percent), the refinery was built on a $980 million investment to receive crude **oil** from the Agadem area through a 450-km pipeline. Established in the barren **Damergou** region to the north of **Zinder**, it has a 20,000 barrel-per-day capacity. The very high costs involved in building it in a notoriously waterless area are likely to have a negative impact on costs of operation and production, and ultimately on the pricing of finished products. The refinery was initially projected to be located somewhere on the banks of the **Niger River**, but former president **Mamadou Tandja** decided on Zinder, in the run-up to his plans to ending democratic rule with support base in that region. *See also* TAZARTCHÉ.

SOCIÉTÉ DES BRASSERIES ET DES BOISSONS GAZEUSES DU NIGER (BRANIGER). Created in 1967 by Brasseries et Glacières Internationales, BRANIGER manufactures soft drinks, sodas, juices, and mineral waters among other drinks. In a more lucrative venture, it also brews beer. It is paradoxically (for a predominantly Muslim country) one of the most prosperous businesses in the country, thanks to the addiction of Niger's **civil service** class and modernized youth to the bar and *maquis* (an Ivorian-style rambunctious music bar) lifestyle. It produces a characteristic beer stamped with a giraffe logo and nicknamed *conjoncture* in the 1980s by civil servants suffering from the austerity measures then taken by the government given the "*conjoncture économique*" (economic conditions). The name has stayed, with the variant *conjonka*. Although evidently not suffering from the depressed economic conditions, BRANIGER had, however, to face the competition of other companies under the liberalized conditions of the 1990s. The Castel Group bought it in 1993, but new investments were not forthcoming until August 2009, when the Nigerien government signed a decree giving to BRANIGER a preferential regime reinstating a degree of monopoly. As a result, BRANIGER doubled its capital the following year, from 1.5 billion **CFA francs** to nearly 3 billion. *See also* ECONOMIC LIBERALIZATION; PARASTATAL SECTOR.

SOCIÉTÉ DES PRODUITS CHIMIQUES DU NIGER (SPCN). Mixed-economy company set up in **Niamey** in 1980, though in existence since 1965 under a different share distribution. Capitalized at 225 million **CFA francs** with the original participation of the Blohorn Group, the company produces an array of soaps, cosmetics, powders, and detergents. Its productive capacity is over 4,500 tons of soap a year. A generally successful company, SPCN has concentrated on the making of soaps after the 1994 devaluation increased costs for the importation of the ingredients needed for cosmetics making. The main competition comes from **Nigeria**. *See also* ECONOMIC LIBERALIZATION; PARASTATAL SECTOR.

SOCIÉTÉ MINIÈRE DE L'AÏR (SOMAIR). **Uranium**-processing company, the first to be established in Niger. Established on 7 July 1967 after an accord granting it a concession over 360 sq km in the **Arlit** area, SOMAIR was capitalized with 60 million French francs, with 45 percent of the shares originally held by the French **parastatal** Commissariat à l'Energie Atomique (CEA), 40 percent by two private French companies (Compagnie de Mokta–El Hadid and Compagnie Française des Minerais d'Uranium), and 15 percent by the Niger government, which retained the right to increase its share to 20 percent. Niger's share—through the **Office National des Ressources Minières**, which holds the equity—has since increased to 36.6 percent. The structure of the capital changed considerably in later years, as the French state interests were consolidated into an **AREVA** ownership of 63.4 percent.

The company is at the origin of the creation of the town of Arlit. It currently employs 600 persons, mostly Nigerien nationals. There are now only six expatriate French people working at SOMAIR. *See also* ECONOMIC LIBERALIZATION.

SOCIÉTÉ NATIONALE DE COMMERCE ET DE PRODUCTION DU NIGER (COPRO-NIGER). Better known as COPRO-NIGER, the company was originally capitalized with 150 million **CFA francs**, but after major deficits this was raised to 600 million CFA francs. The shares were owned by the state (33 percent), the **Banque de Développement de la République du Niger** (18.2 percent), the **Union Nigérienne de Crédit et de Coopérative** (15 percent), and 28 individual shareholders. Created as a state trading organization in April 1962, COPRO-NIGER had, throughout the country, 28 agencies and 60 sales outlets employing more than 200 workers. It held a monopoly over certain imports, the full list of which varied, and was assigned a monopoly over the purchase of certain locally produced crops. Thus, in 1969 COPRO-NIGER was given the monopoly over the import of concentrated milk, green tea, sugar, salt, cigarettes, textiles, and sacks. Earlier, in 1964, it lost its monopoly of the purchase of Niger's **groundnut** crop, and in 1968 of meat and several other commodities.

COPRO-NIGER had been plagued by a host of deficit-producing problems stemming in part from Niger's poor **transportation** system, the immense distances involved, and a poor commercial network in the country outside the urban centers. Its primary purpose—for which the monopolies were granted—was to ensure stability of food prices and to ensure a system of retail and wholesale outlets throughout the country, especially in the remote areas of the country shunned by private businessmen. Moreover, it was used as a political instrument to spur commercial activities in regions such as northern Niger that suffered from marginalization in the postcolonial era. However, its monopolies were also damaging to private business, and a few of them were lifted in 1985 to create a degree of competition beneficial to consumers. Eventually COPRO-NIGER became a casualty of Niger's early spell of **economic liberalization**, during the first half of the 1990s. Under pressure of the World Bank, it was scrapped by the state in 1995. Some of its agencies—notably the key one in **Maradi**—were bought by private Nigerien local, while others disappeared. *See also* ECONOMIC LIBERALIZATION; PARASTATAL SECTOR.

SOCIÉTÉ NATIONALE DES TRANSPORTS NIGÉRIENS (SNTN). Before independence, trucking and **transportation** developed in Niger chiefly in relation to the marketing of **groundnut**. Trucking companies were branches of French companies with a monopoly on colonial markets, in particular the Compagnie Transafricaine (a holding company with branches in Côte d'Ivoire, Haute-Volta, Mali, Niger, and Dahomey). There were few local trucking businesses and only those traders with connections with the French commercial houses could afford to purchase a truck. At independence, the Nigerien government stimulated national trucking mostly through credit access and contracts with public companies. In 1963, the state created, with SAGA (the majority company in the Compagnie Transafricaine) the Société Nationale des Transports Nigériens (52 percent owned by SAGA and 48 percent by the state of Niger). SNTN had both commercial and public activities. On the commercial side, it carried imported goods from ports in neighboring countries and **uranium** from the desert north. It also maintained passenger transportation lines between **Niamey** and the main towns of the country. On the public side, it commuted civil servants to their workplace, in theory in exchange for compensations from the state, but in reality without any compensation.

To compensate for this, the state of Niger regulated a monopoly situation in favor of SNTN and scuttled competition, with other companies thriving only on lines not served by the company. However, its interventions in the company's operations prevented the accumulation of productivity gains, and by the early 1990s, SNTN was in dire financial straits. In 1994, the state of Niger agreed to a restructuring plan proposed by the International Monetary Fund, and the passenger transportation operations of SNTN were privatized into the Société Nigérienne de Transport des Voyageurs (SNTV). The new company operates in a liberalized, highly competitive context and has become just one among many other transportation companies, specializing in interurban passenger transportation. The other operations of SNTN are in decline and for much of the 2000s, the society has been entangled in a legal battle with the **bank** BIA Niger, to which it owed 555 million **CFA francs** in 2002, now increased (after judicial penalties) to over 2 billion CFA francs in 2010. *See also* ECONOMIC LIBERALIZATION; PARASTATAL SECTOR.

SOCIÉTÉ NIGÉRIENNE DE BANQUE (SONIBANK). Private bank set up in **Niamey** on 29 August 1990 to take over the deposits of the BDRN, which was in liquidation and possessed 70 billion **CFA francs** in unrecovered debts. It was capitalized at 2 billion CFA francs. The Tunisian **banking** company STB contributed 25 percent, the **Banque Centrale des États d'Afrique de l'Ouest** (BCEAO) contributed 10 percent, the West African Development Bank also contributed 10 percent, and various public Nigerien interests (the finance and **economy** ministry, the national social security fund, and the Société Nigérienne des Produits Pétroliers) contributed the rest. *See also* ECONOMIC LIBERALIZATION; PARASTATAL SECTOR.

SOCIÉTÉ NIGÉRIENNE DE CIMENTERIE (SNC). Popularly known as **Cimenterie de Malbaza**. It was established in 1963 with a capital of 900 million **CFA francs** in Malbaza, 36 km east of **Birni-N'Konni**, to replace costly imports of cement from abroad. The Malbaza area is very rich in raw material used for cement production. Its production price in 1969 was 13,000 CFA francs a ton, or twice the world market price of cement (though just about equal to the price of imported cement, given the high cost of transport from the coast). In the early years, the factory worked at two-thirds capacity and produced an average of 40,000 tons of cement a year. In the 1990s, this decreased to 30,000 tons a year, while Niger's annual cement demand was 150,000 tons. Cement was thus imported from Benin, Burkina Faso, and **Nigeria,** even though the SNC production was of a higher quality owing to the raw material available in Niger (limestone and gypsum). In time, SNC's cement factory price has also increased to 85,000 CFA francs a ton, retailed at 105,000 CFA francs a ton, while the price of imported cement ranges between 105,000 and 110,000 CFA francs a ton. SNC was privatized in 1998, and its production rates have slightly increased, returning to the levels achieved in the 1960s (40,000 tons a year). *See also* ECONOMIC LIBERALIZATION; PARASTATAL SECTOR.

SOCIÉTÉ NIGÉRIENNE DE COMMERCIALISATION DE L'ARACHIDE (SONARA). Mixed-economy company established in May 1962 as the sole exporter of **groundnuts** from Niger, entrusted also with centralization of all groundnut purchases in the country in order to reduce costs and speed the process of Nigerienization in this field. The state controlled 60 percent of the share capital. All intermediate purchasers of groundnut were required by law to sell their stocks to SONARA. In 1970 SONARA was one of Niger's largest enterprises, being capitalized at 1.4 billion **CFA francs**. It had groundnut-cracking plants at Dosso and Tchadoua (a third one in Malbaza had to be closed down), with a capacity of 70,000 tons. After the sector's crisis in the 1970s and its rapid decline in the 1980s, SONARA, which had unsuccessfully tried to reconvert into the trading of cowpeas, was scrapped in 1989. *See also* AGRICULTURE; ECONOMIC LIBERALIZATION; PARASTATAL SECTOR.

SOCIÉTÉ NIGÉRIENNE D'ELECTRICITÉ (NIGELEC). NIGELEC is the country's electricity company. Large-scale electricity supply emerged in Francophone West Africa only after 1946 and was at first organized by a mixed-economy company set up in 1950, the Energie Electrique de l'Afrique Occidentale Française (EEAOF), controlled by Electricité de France (EDF, **France**'s national electricity company). In 1959, EEAOF was turned into the intergovernmental Société Africaine d'Electricité (SAFELEC), and its Nigerien section operated until 1968, when it was replaced by NIGELEC. The company was founded with state capital (from the state itself and also from the development bank **Banque de Dèveloppement de la République du Niger** (BDRN), the groundnut company **Société Nigérienne de commercialization de l'Arachide** (SONARA), as well as the municipalities serviced) to which was added French public participation (Caisse Centrale de

Coopération Economique) and loans from the French Banque Internationale pour l'Afrique Occidentale (BIAO). NIGELEC was initially tasked with the provision of electricity and clean water, and its ownership by the state was necessitated by the lack of attraction of the landlocked country for major international private companies. It now provides only electricity service.

NIGELEC organizes the supply of electricity in the heavily populated southern band of the country through minor local production in thermal plants and through interconnection with **Nigeria**'s electricity supply (up to 80 percent of NIGELEC's supply). The sparsely inhabited northern area is supplied through the coal company SONICHAR, which caters chiefly to the **mining** industries of the **Aïr** and the city of **Agadez**. There were pressures from the International Monetary Fund to privatize NIGELEC in the 1990s, but when the company failed to attract buyers in the initial run-up to **privatization**, the state of Niger changed its mind and decided to hold on to NIGELEC as a strategic asset. This was partly motivated by the need former president **Mamadou Tandja** had for NIGELEC as a backroom financier for his political projects; during his term in office, the company was run by his close friend Ibrahim Foukori. In the period 2000–2009, NIGELEC allocated over 9 billion **CFA francs** to Tandja's propaganda pet project, the President of the Republic's special program, generally against the wishes of the board of administration. Other cases of politically motivated gross mismanagement have been found and triggered the temporary arrest of Foukori in 2010.

NIGELEC is currently owned by Nigerien interests. Its capital of 3.3 billion CFA francs (up from only 65 million at creation) is distributed among the state (94.65 percent) and the company's personnel (4.10 percent), with trifles going to the BIA (a **bank**) and the cities of **Niamey**, **Zinder**, **Maradi**, and **Tahoua**. NIGELEC's monthly bill to the Nigerian Power Holding Company of Nigeria is on average of $1.5 million at a purchase rate of 20 CFA francs per KWH, with sales rate at 80 CFA francs per KWH. The rate of electrification of the country is very low, standing at 10 percent in urban areas and much less in rural areas. Significant contrasts exist also between the capital Niamey, which has a 100 percent rate of electrification and about 60 percent of its population subscribe to NIGELEC services, and other towns; thus, the next town in line, Maradi, has only 6 percent of its population subscribing to the company's services. However, the situation is in rapid evolution. While, for instance, in 1996 Niamey alone had 31,085 subscribers against 26,467 in the rest of the country, in 2005 only 54 percent of subscribers were Niamey residents, pointing to a trend that reduces the imbalance. Projections indicate that the demand for electricity will double by 2020, stressing a challenge for which NIGELEC and the state of Niger will have to respond in measures worrisome in view of their present inadequacy. The building of the dam at

Kandadji now underway and the West African regional interconnection plans that are being prepared notably in the framework of the **Economic Community of West African States** (ECOWAS) might solve some of the issues. *See also* ECONOMIC LIBERALIZATION; PARASTATAL SECTOR.

SOCIÉTÉ NIGÉRIENNE DE PRODUITS PETROLIERS (SONIDEP). State agency capitalized at 500 million **CFA francs**, created on 20 January 1977, to ensure the regularity of import and distribution of Niger's petroleum supply. It remains state owned, having failed to attract buyers under a World Bank–sponsored **privatization** scheme. *See also* PARASTATAL SECTOR.

SOCIÉTÉ NIGÉRIENNE DES TELECOMMUNICATIONS (SONI-TEL). The telecom sector of Niger was created in 1959, with the establishment of the **parastatal** Office des Postes et Télécommunications (OPT). It was further expanded by the establishment of the Société des Télécommunications Internationales du Niger (STIN), which was tasked to take charge of international telecommunications. The sector was first restructured in 1986 and then largely privatized in 1996–1997. A state-manned postal service was created as Office Nationale des Postes et de l'Epargne (ONPE), while telecommunications were consolidated by the merger of OPT's telecom branch with the STIN to create the SONITEL. The new company, capitalized at 22.7 billion **CFA francs**, was partly sold in 2001 to a Chinese-Libyan consortium, DATAPORT (uniting the Libyan Laaico to the Chinese ZTE), which owned 51 percent of the equity. The state of Niger kept 34.11 percent of the company with the rest going to Nigerien private capital and the company's personnel. The deal proved disappointing and was the object of relentless condemnation in Niger's **media** throughout the 2000s.

The crisis had become acute especially after the 2004 mobile phone market opened, which saw SONITEL's mobile phone branch SAHELCOM outperformed by foreign newcomers such as CELTEL. SONITEL also recorded a debt of over 40 billion CFA francs despite a 140 percent increase in service fees and had to face protests and strikes from workers over pay and working conditions. In 2009, the Nigerien government canceled the **privatization**, took over the company at 100 percent, and prospected for other buyers. In January 2011, SONITEL and its mobile phone branch SAHELCOM were sold off to the Libyan company Green Network, under conditions widely believed to violate the rules of the private sector regulatory authority, the **Autorité de Régulation Multisectorielle** (ARM). Green Network was a branch of a Libyan sovereign fund which developed a strategy of expansion in Africa predicated on low cost telecommunication and an agenda that appeared to be more political than economic. However, the deal collapsed two months later, when **Libya** came under attack by Western powers supportive of Libyan insurgents.

Niger's telecommunications sector is marked by competition in the mobile phones subsector, where foreign private companies (AIRTEL, Orange, and MOOV) beat SAHELCOM. Though SONITEL holds a near-monopoly on Internet communication, it also faces in that subsector the competition of Orange, which secured in 2007 the first combined landline, mobile phone, and Internet communication license for a foreign company in the country. *See also* NIGER-POSTE.

SOCIÉTÉ NIGÉRIENNE DU CHARBON D'ANOU ARAREN (SONICHAR). Mixed-economy enterprise set up on 5 May 1975 with a capital of 760 million **CFA francs**—now 19.7 billion CFA francs—to exploit the 6 million tons of coal deposits discovered in Anou Araren, some 1,000 km northeast of **Niamey** and 40 km northwest of **Arlit**. Production commenced at the open-cut mine in 1981 of Tefereyre (75 km northwest of **Agadez**), and output is around 180,000 tons a year on average. SONICHAR was created largely to tackle Niger's energy crisis, especially in the northern region of Agadez, while also catering for the **uranium** mines that developed in the late 1970s. It ran into difficulties in the early 1980s, with the rise of the dollar against a devalued French franc (to which Niger's **currency** was pegged at a fixed parity rate) and falling uranium prices but overcame its problems by 1986, although with adjustments to a new economic environment. The coal extracted is used to produce electricity on site for the various uranium mines in the immediate vicinity and for the towns of Arlit, **Akokan**, and Agadez.

After the restructurations of the 1990s, the company is now chiefly Nigerien owned with the state's share up at 69.3 percent and minority shareholders, including a number of local companies as well as the Islamic Development Bank, which has 10.14 percent of the equity. One of the largest coal-producing companies in Africa, SONICHAR employs 296 workers (down from 442 in 1982). Running costs have been higher than anticipated, and the electricity produced is also very expensive, considerably deflecting earlier expectations that SONICHAR could help spur the transformation of Niger's north. The quadrupling of Niger's demand for electricity between 1970 and 1985, and more since, however, has brought about expansion in SONICHAR's operations. The company started off in 1981 with a capacity of 16 MW of electricity and increased it in 1982 to 37.7 MW. Only 40 percent of the electricity consumed by Niger is produced in the country, and 34 percent of this comes from SONICHAR, making the northern region the only one to be catered for from the country. *See also* ECONOMIC LIBERALIZATION; PARASTATAL SECTOR.

SOLY, ABDOURAHAMANE (1930s–). Born in the late 1930s, Soly followed the typical (for the small number of children who then had access to formal schooling) Nigerien course of study at the close of the colonial era: primary **education** in his home district (**Tahoua**) and then secondary education in **Niamey** and in Porto Novo (Dahomey, now Benin). After earning his high school *baccalauréat* degree, Soly went into military service at a post in Ouidah (Dahomey) and as Niger was becoming independent, he was sent to the newly created University of Dakar for higher education (1958). He received a master's degree in private law in 1962 and subsequently undertook professional training at the Bordeaux Centre National d'Études Judiciaires (1962–1966). This led to a distinguished **civil service** career in Niger's civil service and justice administration, culminating in his appointment as justice minister in 1987. By then Soly had become severely vision-impaired and was famous for combining intensive intellectual activities (many lectures and writings) with blindness. He ended his professional career in 1998 after serving nine years as attorney-general at the **Cour Suprême**.

He remained, however, an active public intellectual, in particular coming out over the summer of 2009 in public conferences and press interviews against President **Mamadou Tandja**'s attempt at overthrowing the **Fifth Republic**. After the failure of the attempt in February 2010, Tandja's military ousters appointed Soly vice-president of the constitutional council in charge of providing a legal framework to the transitional institutions set up at that juncture.

Along with his many articles in the press, Soly has published an essay on Niger's **democratization** process (*Conférence nationale du Niger*, 1994), an essay in Islamic spiritual meditation (*Le Chemin du pèlerin*, 1994), and a collection of folk tales (*Contes et nouvelles, recueil pour une veillée*).

SONAIKINE. The **Songhay** name for the Songhay **language**, also called *koyrakine* ("language of the country"). The language has three principal, mutually intelligible, dialects. It is generally considered a Nilo-Saharan language, unrelated therefore to any in the West African region, but akin to languages in Sudan and Uganda. Lexically, it has taken in some influx from Arabic and liberally imbibed from its neighbors, such as the **Tuareg** in the northern sections and the **Hausa** in the southern sections of its area of extension. Songhay is also used as a ritual language by communities in the western Nigerien Sahara and in northwestern **Nigeria**, a vestige from the era of the **Songhay Empire**.

SONEY. An area in the northwestern corner of Niger, including the regions of Anzourou and Wanzarbé and the towns of **Téra** and **Tillabéri**. This is considered the heartland of the **Songhay** (the word "Soney" is "Songhay" as pronounced by the Songhay), the sanctuary of their ancient pantheon and priestly class, and the place in which the lineage of the original Sonni dynasty retreated after the coup d'état of 1493, creating a secret society of magicians, the **Sonyankés**.

SONGHAY (or Songhai, Sonrai, pronounced more like "Soney"). Broad constellation of ethnic communities, including the Koyroboro of **Gao**, the Songhay proper around **Tillabéri**, the **Sorkos** (islanders of the **Niger River**), and the **Dendi** south of **Dosso** and into Benin, to whom one might add with some reason the **Zarma**, who claim difference but share the same **language** and manners. The Songhay essentially live along the Niger River valley, from Niafounké (Mali) to the region of Parakou (northern Benin) throughout the western regions of Niger. The Dendi are principally found on the Niger–Benin border (and in a few areas of northern Benin) and are essentially those Songhay elements which resisted the Moroccan conquest of the heartland of Songhay and of Gao. Other groups frequently lumped together with the Songhay are the **Kurtey**, who are former **Fulani**, strongly intermarried with Sorko, and found on the islands of the Niger between **Niamey** and Tillabéri and between Niamey and **Say**, as well as in **Nigeria** near Zaria; the **Wogo**, who are found intermingled with the Kurtey; and the **Tyenga** of Dendi. There are strong Songhay communities in the Bambara cities of Djenné, Mopti, and Bamako and a large diaspora in Ghana (Accra and Kumasi especially). There are also remnants of Gao Songhay (Koyroboro) in **Agadez** and surrounding regions, presumably having settled there during the conquest of **Aïr** by Gao in the 16th century.

The Songhay are mostly agriculturalists, hunters, and fishers, growing rice and **millet** and letting the Fulani tend their livestock. Their population in Niger is today estimated at about 1 million (the bulk of the Songhay live in Mali), and together with the Zarma (with which they are generally associated in Niger as the **Zarma-Songhay** ethnicity) they form about 21 percent of the country's population, the second-largest ethnic group after the **Hausa**.

There is no clear origin of the Songhay, nor should we expect one. The group is most certainly the coalescence, along the Niger River and its island-ers (the **Sorkos**), of a variety of riverine settlers whose identity was shaped initially by the development of the trans-Saharan trade through Timbuktu (a predominantly Songhay town) and Gao. An ambitious dynasty in the town of **Koukya** (most likely initially an island, from the Songhay word *goungia*, islet), the *Za* or *Dya*, slowly developed its power from the eighth century onward, becoming partly Islamized after 15 rulers and later moving to Gao. There, they soon became powerful enough to rebel against the tutelage of the

Bambara Empire of Mali. The Za dynasty was followed by a related lineage, the *si* or *sonni*, from which came the founder of the **Songhay Empire**, **Sonni Ali Ber**, who took power in 1464. The gradual expansion of the power of Gao is the real matrix of a Songhay identity, as the empire tended to homogenize language and manners along the river, through all Songhay lands, on the basis of the culture of the **Soney**. This was reinforced by the fact that the successor dynasty, the **Askia**, though of Sarakhollé origins, promoted a further element of coherence in the empire's culture, **Islam**. The breakup of the Songhay Empire in the early 17th century loosened the bonds between the various regions inhabited by the Songhay, and the language itself subsequently differentiated into several dialects, some of which are barely intercomprehensible. The Niger River valley remains, however, a unifying link. *See also* BATTLE OF TONDIBI.

SONGHAY EMPIRE. The Songhay Empire was the greatest of the states created in West Africa—larger in extension than any of the modern countries in the region, stretching from the Senegal River valley to the **Aïr** and into Hausaland, though it essentially developed along the **Niger River** valley, its backbone. It took shape in the late 15th century, under the reign of **Sonni Ali Ber**, who became king of **Gao** in 1464 and started a career of conquests and administrative reforms that birthed the empire in the matter of some two decades. In particular, **Sonni** Ali conquered the rich commercial town of Djenné as well as Timbuktu, a trading hub with a brilliant Islamic scholarly tradition. He also established a central government system and developed several new offices of control and administration, the most important of which was arguably that of the *hikoy* (master of the boats, running the river fleet which carried the Songhay troops). Sonni Ali was briefly succeeded by his son, Sonni Barou (1492–1493), but the latter was removed through a coup d'état by **Askia Mohammed**, a high-ranking officer in the Songhay army.

Askia Mohammed continued Sonni Ali's policy of conquests and regular administration, but also profoundly reshaped the empire's government through the application of stringent Islamic rules and legislation. He thus received the title of "Lieutenant of the Caliph for the Land of the Blacks" from the caliph of Mecca during a pilgrimage; by the end of his reign, the Songhay Empire had many of the traits that were found in the large Islamic states of Asia (the Ottoman, Safavid, and Moghul empires). But this was intermingled with the African traditions of the Songhay, the Bambaras, and the Sarakhollés, the dominant peoples in the empire. It was also under Askia Mohammed's reign that the empire reached its limits, absorbing the Aïr (1500) and the Teghazza in the north and subduing much of Hausaland in the south, but meeting with failure in its attempts to conquer the empire of the Mossi.

In much of the 16th century, the Songhay Empire successfully confronted the threat that came from the sultanate of Morocco, until the latter launched a major expedition in 1591. The invading Moroccan troops were armed with firearms, a technology then barely known in rudimentary forms in West Africa, and it defeated the Songhay at the **battle of Tondibi**.

The empire did not collapse entirely, putting up lasting resistance in its southern provinces, which eventually became a small kingdom ruled by the last Askias (**Dendi**). The kingdom eventually disintegrated into factions by the mid-17th century. Meanwhile, the Moroccan occupiers were unable to maintain the territorial cohesion of the empire, which floundered in about a decade, becoming part of the small Bambara kingdoms that would dominate the area in the 18th century. The Songhay retained political dominance chiefly in the parts of their empire that are now included in Nigerien territory. Rulers of the Songhay Empire: ?–1464, Sulayman Dandi; 1464–1492, Sonni Ali; 1492–1493, Sonni Barou; 1493–1528, Muhammad Ture; 1528–1531, Farimundyo Musa; 1531–1537, Muhammad Bunkan; 1537–1539, Ismail; 1539–1549, Ishaq I; 1549–1582, Daoud; 1582–1586, Muhammad II; 1586–1588, Muhammad Bani; 1588–1591, Ishaq II.

SONNI. Title of the rulers of the Kingdom of **Gao** and of the **Songhay Empire**, assumed by the son of the 20th *dya* (or *za*) of the Songhay. There were 19 *sonni* kings between 1335 and 1493, when the **Askia** dynasty replaced it.

SONNI ALI BER (?–1492). Sonni Ali the Great was the 18th sonni of the **Songhay** at **Gao**, and the true founder of the **Songhay Empire**. Assuming power in 1464, he greatly expanded Songhay's territory, including into large areas currently in Niger. It was under Sonni Ali that Timbuktu was captured in 1468, followed by Djenné (1473) and Mopti (1477). Sonni Ali died in battle in 1492. His son and successor, Sonni Barou, was toppled in 1493 by one of Ali's lieutenants, Mohammed Touré (**Askia Mohammed**), who set up the Askia dynasty.

Sonni Ali's power was believed to be rooted into Songhay mystic **religion**; the highest caste of Songhay animist mediums or priests, the **Sonyankés**, claim him as the originator of their preternatural abilities.

SONYANKÉS. A hereditary and closed high caste of **Songhay** priests settled in the **Soney**. They claim to draw their original magical powers from **Sonni Ali Ber**.

SORKO. One of the major **Songhay** subgroups, found along the **Niger River** from Timbuktu down to **Niamey**. Divided into two branches—the Faran and the Fono—the Sorkos are master fishers and dominate all riverine commercial activity between Djenné and **Gao** (both in Mali). They were prominent in the foundation of the **Songhay Empire**. Thanks to their knowledge of the river, they played a major role in **Sonni Ali**'s conquests and expansion of the Songhay Empire. The Sorkos of Niger inspired much of the early cinematographic work of **Jean Rouch**. *See also* ETHNIC GROUPS.

SOSSEBAKI. A Bornuan lineage that ruled a series of small states in the area between **Zinder** and Kano. Sossebaki was the surname given to Mohammed Ouba n'Saraki, one of the successors of Mohammed Nafarko, meaning "mouth-sucker." The latter, a son of the sultan of **Bornu**, had been sent to pursue escaping slaves in the 10th or the 12th century and was made chief of the population among which he found himself. The small chiefdoms that were eventually established were initially tributaries of Kano and then of Bornu. One of the better-known mini-states was centered around **Mirriah**. Most of them were eventually conquered by Zinder in the establishment of the **Damagaram** kingdom in the 18th century.

SOUDIE. Also known as **Kurfey**, the Soudié are an **ethnic group** of mixed **Hausa** animist ancestry, originally residing in **Gobir** and forming a small confederation of clans. Chased from **Tahoua** by the **Tuareg** Ouilliminden in the period 1820–1850 and settling in the **Zarmaganda**, the Soudié adopted the **Zarma** customs and **language**, except for those Kurfey who remained Hausa speaking and are still referred to as Kurfey rather than Soudié.

SOULEY, ZALIKA (1947–). Born in **Niamey**, Zalika Souley started at age 19 a career as the first professional sub-Saharan actress in history, with a role in **Moustapha Alhassane**'s *Le Retour d'un aventurier* (1966) in which, in the lead female role (Reine Christine, from the famed Swedish queen) she gallivanted on horseback, wearing blue jeans and a cowboy hat. She afterward worked mostly for **Oumarou Ganda**, starring in his movies *Cabascabo* (which was on the selection of the Cannes film festival of 1969), *Le Wazou polygame* (which won the top award of the African film festival of Ouagadougou in 1972), and *Saïtane* and *L'Exilé*, the last opus of the great moviemaker. She also featured in Moustapha Alhassane's 1972 film, *FVVA (Femme, Voiture, Villa, Argent)*. In 1981, she appeared in *Pétanqui*, a movie by the Ivorian director Yéo Kozola (inspired by **Ousmane Amadou**'s propaganda novel against the **First Republic**, *Quinze ans ça suffit!*) and the next year in **Djingaraye Maïga**'s *Aube Noire*.

By then, the Nigerien movie industry was entering its declining phase, and Souley did not earn (or save) much from her career. She was briefly

(1978–1985) employed by the national television corporation, the **Office de Radio-Télévision du Niger** (ORTN), and upon losing that job found herself working as a telephonist at a Niamey hotel and then in 1987 as a cultural supervisor at the popular *Centre Culturel Djado Sékou* of Niamey. She attempted a **cinema** comeback in **Moustapha Diop**'s *Mami Watta*, which was, however, a flop. In the 1990s, her life and career were much honored, as she received several decorations from Niger and foreign states, and a documentary movie, *Zalika*, was made on her life by the Nigerien documentary filmmaker Jean-Pierre Kaba. But her financial prospects remained dim, as she struggled to support her six children. Under the government of President **Baré Maïnassara**, she received some stipends and support from the state, which were curtailed after the fall of Baré Maïnassara's regime in 1999. She migrated to the United States in 2000, doing odd jobs to survive and earn spare money, quite forgotten until 2003,when another Nigerien documentary filmmaker, **Rahmatou Keïta**, made of her life a beautiful and poignant movie, *Al'lèèssi . . . une actrice africaine*. She returned to Niger in 2009.

SOUMAILA, ALMOUSTAPHA. Niger's long-serving minister of planning, and one-time minister of finance and planning. Soumaila first joined the cabinet when appointed in September 1984 to General **Seyni Kountché**'s government, and was retained in that capacity by General **Ali Saibou** (1987–1991) right until the transition government took over in September 1991. Soumaila had earlier served under General Kountché as secretary of state for commerce and **transportation** between January 1983 and September 1984. After the **Mouvement National pour la Société de Développement** (MNSD)—the party created under Ali Saibou's rule—came back to power in February 1995, Soumaila was reappointed minister of finance and planning until the **coup d'état of January 1996**. MNSD again returned to power in 1999, leading to several appointments for Soumaila, including one as general manager for the organization of the Fifth **Francophonie** Games which, amid rumors of conspiracy and embezzlement, cost him his reputation and freedom from 2005 until February 2007, when he was granted release.

STUDENTS. Students have been a thorn in the flesh of all governments of Niger, but especially with the wave of fiscal austerity that afflicted the country in the late 1980s. The **Hamani Diori** government had for a long time been opposed by the country's modern-educated youth, and government–youth confrontations were numerous, especially in the 1970s. Of the various eruptions that occurred, one in particular was the 1969 disorder in **Zinder** and **Niamey**, which was repeated on 19 January 1970 when students in the three secondary schools of Zinder went on strike. When the minister of

education declared the strike illegal—it was over higher stipends, shorter terms, and diplomatic recognition of the Union of Soviet Socialist Republics and China—and closed the schools in town, Niamey's students went on a sympathy strike. The situation was further inflamed by an open letter to the strikers by the unpopular **Boubou Hama**, who addressed the students paternally as "my children" and reminded them of the privileged status they occupied in the country. The strike eventually collapsed after three weeks.

In November 1970, Nigerien students joined in a strike at the University of Abidjan where they were pursuing higher studies. The Côte d'Ivoire government promptly expelled them (as well as nationals from other countries). Even as Niger initiated its own national university, its expelled students were transported directly to military camps where many were roughed up, sparking secondary school strikes in sympathy. The **armed forces** were called out a month later to restore order. Student unrest continued into 1971 and erupted again in 1972 over the visit to Niger of French president Georges Pompidou, who received a tomato on the head on that occasion. On 12 February 1972, the Niger embassy in Paris was taken over by Nigerien students in **France** opposing the Diori government, though their invasion was brief. Since in this instance, as in others, French technical assistants and teachers in Niger had given the students moral support (and according to Diori and Hama, active support), relations with France deteriorated during the year. Schools were closed for some time due to the strike in Niamey in sympathy with the Paris demonstrators, but they were reopened on 21 February; in May 1972 a commission was set up to initiate educational reforms. The gesture did not succeed in soothing student grievances, and again the Paris embassy was seized on 9 November 1973, in sympathy with continued student unrest in Niger (which had been going on for some six months) and a strike that had paralyzed Niger's schools since October of the previous year. The Niamey strike was a long one, lasting from 22 October 1972 until February 1973. Student ringleaders were arrested, and in a closed trial in **Tillabéri** many—together with a handful of teachers who had allegedly incited the students—were given stiff prison sentences.

It was not surprising, therefore, that when the **coup d'état of 1974** occurred, the country's students were solidly behind it. Yet, within six months disenchantment set in with the nonideological tenor of the new military regime. In both 1975 and 1976, strikes and calls for major reforms (many of these of an academic nature) were directed at President **Seyni Kountché**, thought to be hostile to the restive youth. Intermittent confrontations continued until the 1980s. Strikes occurred in 1979, 1982, and again in the mid-1980s, necessitating the closure of the educational establishment for varying periods of time.

By the late 1980s, however, the frequency of confrontations began to escalate, caused primarily by the harsh austerity regime that began to affect all aspects of the Nigerien social fabric. The **parastatal sector** was in shambles and piling up deficits, the **civil service** had become a major expenditure, all at a time when **uranium** revenues—which once had fueled the transformation of the country from a **groundnut**-producing Sahelian backwater—were declining. Decisions to trim the civil service and stem the automatic recruitment of college graduates into it, as well as projected closures of a large number of parastatals demanded by international donor agencies as a precondition for bailing out the parlous **economy** were violently resisted by students, often joined by the **union** umbrella **Union des Syndicats des Travailleurs du Niger** (USTN) in sympathy strikes.

On 9 February 1990, a huge boycott of classes commenced, developing into a demonstration in downtown Niamey (over various academic cuts and a government decision to restrict civil service employment as a result of the World Bank–sponsored Project Education III), which was prevented by military troops from crossing a bridge. When the procession would not stop, the troops fired at the students, officially killing three (but likely more). Though the **Ali Saibou** government tried to contain the damage by selective reshuffling of the cabinet and military high command, outrage at the incident merged with the budding democratic movement to call for the adoption of multiparty democracy. Constant union-led unrest and pressure from an increasingly independent intellectual class finally resulted in the convening of the **Conférence Nationale** of 1991, which led to **democratization**. The initial spark had been given by the students' unrest.

Neither the transition government (1991–1993) nor democratization since 1993 has brought a respite from ongoing student unrest and government–student confrontations. Indeed, on 18 May 1993, students expressed their disgust with the new government (triggered by shortages of school supplies) by going on a rampage that saw the setting on fire of the headquarters of four **political parties**, including the **Parti Nigérien pour la Démocratie et le Socialisme** and the **Convention Démocratique et Sociale**. The financial straits of Niger still required fiscal austerity. At the same time, the recession and the departure of a large number of expatriates and foreign companies and the jobs they created have made even more acute the desperate search for a salaried position in a country where all along the public payroll had been the major employer. Periodic strikes and demonstrations have erupted every year since over late payment of student grants, just as the civil service (and the armed forces) have rebelled over similar delays in back pay. In that period, the students transformed the 9 February anniversary into a tradition for organizing massive protest demonstrations.

In February 2001, student unrest reached higher level as violent protests in Niamey led to the cold-blooded killing of a gendarme and severe retaliation from the government of Prime Minister **Hama Amadou**, which gathered sufficient evidence to jail 16 students. In the ensuing showdown with the **Union des Scolaires Nigériens** (USN), the government clearly sacrificed its popularity to secure a final solution to the student unrest issue. The core of USN militants organized an 11-day hunger strike, followed up by marches and demonstrations, while Amadou appointed **Bouli Ali Diallo** rector of the **University of Niamey** to implement measures that included the stationing of gendarmerie forces on campus—breaking the hitherto respected *franchises universitaires* (university freedoms).

Since that episode, student unrest in Niger has somewhat abated, de-escalating from confrontations with the government to internal confrontations with university administration. Most of the reforms, which considerably increased registration fees and stiffened conditions of access to social benefits, were passed with surprisingly little resistance from students; the 2000s witnessed a long string of normal academic years, disturbed chiefly by teachers' strikes rather than student unrest. These circumstances might well endure as Niger has opened three new universities in **Tahoua**, **Maradi**, and Zinder, thus alleviating a major source of student dissatisfaction: the social costs of settling in Niamey for students from faraway parts of the immense territory. Meanwhile, 9 February as Nigerien Student Day has gradually become a tradition of boisterous juvenile occupation of public space rather than the occasion for riotous protest marches.

T

TABASKI. Muslim festival, also called Fête du Mouton (Ram Day). The word derives from *Peské* (Jewish for Easter, close to *Pâques* in French, for instance) and curiously gained currency chiefly in Francophone West Africa. The variant *Tafaska* is used in Berber North Africa. *See also* ID EL-KEBIR.

TADELIZA. Capital of the nascent **Agadez** sultanate prior to the designation of Agadez as its permanent capital in 1434. Despite the shift of the center of political authority to Agadez, Tadeliza remained the principal center of **Aïr** for a century. It was conquered around 1500 by the **Songhay Empire** and later razed. The city's precise location was subject to much speculation. There is a small village and a *wadi* (fossil river) with the same name, but that was not the location of the ancient center, which was finally traced in 1973 by Lhote to the area on the right bank of the Irazer-n-Agadez, near the small village of Irezen Melouldnin, 20 km from Agadez, the inhabitants of which had not forgotten the nature of the ruins nearby.

TAHOUA. A region and *département* roughly corresponding to the historic **Ader** region. It is approximately equidistant (at 440 km) from **Niamey** and **Agadez**. The town is Niger's fourth or fifth largest (in competition with Agadez), with 72,450 people. The region encompasses 1,908,100 people over 150,260 sq km. The population of the *département* is a mixture of Ader **Hausa**, **Fulani**, **Tuareg**, and, especially to the south, **Gobir** Hausa and **Arawa**. The town of Tahoua was originally formed of three **Arna** villages that were eventually absorbed into the municipality. The region includes the *départements* of Tahoua, **Birni-N'Konni**, Bouza, **Illela**, **Keita**, **Madaoua**, and **Tchintabaraden**, **Abalak**, and the *arrondissements* of Tillia, Dogu-eraoua, and Bagaroua. Though a typical Hausa town and an important communications and trade artery, Tahoua has little tourist interest. The regions between Tahoua and Birni-N'Konni, however, have villages with handsome architectural traditions that signal the transition from the western **Sahel** (Mali) to the central Sahel of the Hausaland.

TAL NATIONAL. A music band operating under the motto "*la culture est notre pétrole*" (culture is our **oil** [rent]), Tal National was formed in 2006 by a group of musical artists (singers and players) led by a former lawyer and current lead singer, Issoufou Halmadal, better known as Almeida. Tal National, which performs in Niger's major **languages** (**Hausa** and **Zarma**, sometimes mixed with French) has become the most popular music performer in the country, as measured notably by its contributions to the Bureau National des Droits d'Auteur, the highest nationally. At times tied to major individual singers such as **Mali Yaro** and Seini Maiga, Tal has created a truly Nigerien musical style through blending the musical traditions chiefly of the Hausa, the **Zarma-Songhay**, the **Tuareg**, and the **Fulani**. It caters not only to the *maquis* bar scene but also to **Niamey**'s popular concerts patronized by clubs of **women** living the *gabdi* lifestyle (a sociological equivalent of the French *demi-mondaine*). *See also* DANCE AND MUSIC.

TALIBI, MOUSSA HAMIDOU (1965–). A philosophy professor with a doctorate from the University of Dakar, Talibi's busy career has been marked by the occupation of key levers in his professional field: elected president of the association of Nigerien philosophy teachers in 2000 (still current), he was also the head of the Philosophy Department at the **University of Niamey** from 2005 to 2008 before moving to the position of secretary-general of the higher **education** teachers' **union**. During former president **Mamadou Tandja**'s ill-fated attempt to establish a dictatorship in 2009, the union was the only organization of its level to have openly supported the project, breaking with a long-standing commitment of university teachers to Niger's **democratization**—though many individual university teachers disagreed with the union's stance. Under Talibi, the union appears to put its corporate interests first and foremost and to have renounced its erstwhile political role.

TAMASHEQ. Tuareg name for the Berber language spoken by the **Tuareg**. It has many variants, two of which are prevalent in Niger, the *tamasheq tahoua* (*tawallammat*) and the *tamasheq tayart*. The language has its own alphabet, the *tifinagh*. In Niger, it was given a Latin alphabet only in 1999; it has had one in Mali since 1967. The Tuareg like to call themselves *Kel Tamashaq* (the people of the Tamasheq), the word "Tuareg" itself being an Arabic one.

TAMBARI. Royal drums, part of the symbols of chiefdom in **Tuareg** clans. They are of pre-Islamic Tuareg origin, though they are also found among several non-Tuareg **ethnic groups**.

TAMESNA. The **Tuareg** Ouilliminden name for Talak, the steppelike desert between **Aïr** and Adrar des Ifora.

TANDJA, MAMADOU (1938–). Born in **Maïné-Soroa**, a small town in the far eastern region of Niger, Tandja is of **Kanuri** and **Hausa** cultures and **languages** although his family came from the Sarakhollé communities of Mauritania and Mali, where he still maintain kinship ties. His formal **education** was short, mostly acquired in Niger's École Nomade (nomadic school, tailored to the needs of desert communities), and he soon joined the army and the circle of **Seyni Kountché**'s friends. A key member of the **Conseil Militaire Suprême**, the ruling organ set up by Kountché after he seized power in the **coup d'état in 1974**, Tandja was also appointed *préfet* of **Maradi** in 1976, then minister of the interior in 1979. Kountché having taken up that position for himself in 1981, Tandja was moved to the prefecture of **Tahoua** that year. He remained in that position until 1988 when he was appointed ambassador to **Nigeria**. Two years later he returned to Niger as minister of the interior.

In 1991, the single party established by President **Ali Saibou** in 1988, the **Mouvement National pour la Société de Développement** (MNSD), became a normal **political party**, and Tandja won its leadership against rival **Adamou Moumouni Djermakoye**, thanks to the support of the party's key manager, **Hama Amadou**. But MNSD's bid for the presidency in 1993 was opposed by the **Alliance des Forces du Changement** (AFC), a general coalition of nearly all the new political parties of the country, which wanted an alternative above all. Tandja lost to AFC's leader **Mahaman Ousmane**, but his party won a sizeable share of the **National Assembly**'s seats. Tandja, however, kept a low profile, leaving the task of undermining AFC to Amadou. In a secret pact with Tandja, Amadou's mission was to engineer the accession of Tandja to the presidency, and in return, Tandja was to choose him as his successor. Amadou managed to wrest governmental power from Ousmane at the legislative **elections** of 1995, but the latter blocked government operation by refusing to cooperate with the prime minister (Amadou), plunging the country into a political crisis terminated by a **coup d'état in 1996**.

MNSD and Tandja initially approved the coup, but when it became clear that the coup-maker, **Ibrahim Baré Maïnassara**, intended to stay in power, they came out against him, leading to a brief putting of Tandja under house arrest along with other political leaders (July 1996). Together with Mahaman Ousmane and the leader of the **Parti Nigérien pour la Démocratie et le Socialisme** (PNDS Tarayya), **Mahamadou Issoufou**, he was again briefly arrested at the end of 1996 following a pro-democracy rally. However, Baré Maïnassara was overthrown and killed in 1999, and the new coup-makers quickly restored civilian rule, organizing elections in which an MNSD-led coalition emerged victorious. Tandja was thus elected president. His first term was marked by policies of government spending reduction following agreements with donors, some of which caused unrest among **students** and within the military. But Tandja did not appear involved, as his prime minister,

Hama Amadou, managed the policies and the crises while his finance minister, **Lamine Zeine**, a close friend, managed relations with donors. Tandja's first strong stance as president was to oppose **media** description of Niger's 2004–2005 food crisis as a famine and to launch a vaunted Special Program of the President of the Republic, aimed at building thousands of schools and infirmaries in the country's vast rural areas. Although the funds came from donors, the channel of a president-backed program was supposed to improve ownership and delivery.

With a broadened coalition, Tandja won the election of 2004 but started to distance himself from Prime Minister Amadou while instituting regular meetings with the opposition leader, Mahamadou Issoufou. The rapprochement was a ploy intended to cajole Issoufou into a maneuver to remove Amadou through a parliamentary no-confidence vote. Tandja secretly wished to stay in power beyond his second and last term, and considered the prime minister the key threat to that project. During that period, the antagonism between Tandja and Amadou became manifest as the latter publicly disagreed with the president's hard-line stance on the matter of the **Tuareg** insurgency that started in 2007.

In June 2007, Tandja's friends in the MNSD, united in a Tandjiste faction, voted against their government and with the opposition in a no-confidence motion, forcing Amadou to resign. Tandja then attempted several moves to jail Amadou, while stepping up the propaganda about his special program's achievements on public radio and television and floating ideas of seeking a third term to "complete the work underway." This project was soon dubbed **Tazartché**, from a Hausa word meaning "to carry on," while Tandja and his supporters from the MNSD, along with **Nouhou Arzika**, a prominent member of the **civil society**, a small number of breakaway **Convention Démocratique et Sociale** (CDS) politicians, and the leaders of a number of minor parties called it the *Refondation de la République* (Refounding of the Republic).

In 2008, Tandja worked to secure a broad-based support for the project with mixed results. The major leaders showed either open hostility (Issoufou, Djermakoye) or reluctance (Ousmane), while the civil society leaders, with the single exception of Arzika, were unanimously opposed to what they called the "dismantling of democracy." So did much of the written press, the popular private radio and television network Dounia, and the leading trade **unions**, including the judges' and attorneys' unions, but with the marked exception of the university professors' union (also bribed by the promise of benefits such as homes and salary increases). On the other hand, Tandja coaxed the support of traditional chiefs, which, despite their showing of popular legitimacy, are on the payroll of the state, and he concentrated resources extracted from French, Chinese, and other companies interested in **mining** Niger's deserts on buying off the higher military echelons.

Thanks to the support of traditional chiefs, Tandja could pitch the project as based on the people's wishes, against the whims of intellectuals in **Niamey**. But the deeper division was ethno-regional, since Tandja's project drew genuine support from the regions of **Diffa** (in which his hometown of Maïné-Soroa is located), **Zinder**, and Maradi, while the regions of Tahoua, **Dosso**, and **Tillabéri** (the latter surrounding the capital city of Niamey, also hostile to Tandja) were massively opposed to the Tazartché. It was not, as might have been the case, a Hausa versus **Zarma-Songhay** contest, since Tahoua is a Hausa region and erstwhile Hausa supremacist Ousmane sided with Zarma-Songhay leaders; as ever, Niger's ethnic divisions were trumped by the ambitions and maneuvering of the major political leaders, who thrived on the democratic game and dreaded to be put out of job by a dictator. Besides, to retain control over MNSD, Tandja had to appoint as prime minister an influential politician from the **Songhay** region of Tillabéri, **Seyni Oumarou**.

With Amadou in jail, the MNSD under some level of control, the military leaders bought off, and the traditional chiefs enlisted as clapping hands, Tandja felt safe enough to announce, during a visit of **France**'s president Nicolas Sarkozy, that he would push for constitutional reform to suppress the two-term limit. Immediately, a political crisis burst out full blown: The political parties formed a coalition, the Front pour la Défense de la Démocratie (FDD, Front for the Defense of Democracy) under PNDS leadership; civil society groups created umbrella organizations to start denunciation campaigns, using the Radio Television Dounia's network (which was repeatedly shut down in the following months); and trade unions organized strikes. The parties' initial strategy was procedural: They sought a **Cour Constitutionnelle** statement that pronounced Tandja's project illegal and unconstitutional, and they then started to formulate a parliamentary motion to indict the president for high treason at the **Haute Cour de Justice**. Tandja however dissolved the National Assembly in June, before the motion was passed, and the following month, he shut down the Cour Constitutionnelle, exceeding his constitutional powers.

Endowing himself with discretionary powers, he prepared a referendum asking the people to grant him three years of dictatorial power, followed by elections organized in the framework of a presidentialist **constitution** with no term limit. The FDD boycotted the **constitutional referendum** which was held on 4 August 2009 with record low participation rates in the country's western regions and in Tahoua and high participation rates in Zinder and Maradi. Tandja went on however to proclaim the **Sixth Republic** and to organize legislative elections in October. These were also boycotted by the FDD, joined by another opposition coalition established by CDS. After the October elections, the opposition coalitions stepped up confrontation on the streets while seeking support at the level of the European Union (which condemned

Tandja's actions and suspended aid) and of the **Economic Community of West African States** (ECOWAS, which suspended Niger's membership of the community and organized several mediation missions). In response, Tandja tried to intimidate the opposing leaders by issuing arrest warrants against Ousmane (then settled in Nigeria), Amadou (in France), and Issoufou (who stayed in Niger but was not arrested). These efforts relied especially on the silence of the **armed forces**, the assistance of the paramilitary Force Nationale d'Intervention et de Sécurité (FNIS, the former republican guard), and the ruthlessness of the minister of the interior, **Albadé Abouba**. But they were undermined by the resistance of the judicial system, whose powerful unions were opposed to the Tazartché.

In January 2010, it appeared that the instability was not financially sustainable, and Tandja resolved to take drastic measures, including, rumors had it, a military purge and a formal pulling out of ECOWAS, which had become a major base of the political and civil society oppositions. But on 18 February 2010, he was toppled by an army squad led by squadron chief **Djibo Salou**. After a short stay in a military barracks, he was moved to the Villa Verte, a plush residence for state guests, where he was put under house arrest. In September 2010, his family lodged a complaint at the ECOWAS Justice Court for arbitrary custody, which resulted in the court ordering the state of Niger to release him. In response, Nigerien authorities announced that Tandja may be formally tried for embezzlement. In January 2011, he was moved to the prison of Kollo, outside Niamey. Charges against him were dropped only after the establishment of Niger's new government in May 2011. *See also* COUP OF 18 FEBRUARY 2010.

TANIMOUN DAN SULEYMAN (1811–1884). Sultan of **Damagaram**, 1841–1843 and 1851–1884, and one of that kingdom's most illustrious kings. Known also as Baki Jataw or Tanimoun Dari, Tanimoun was a son of Suleyman, and his rule over Damagaram alternated with that of his brother Ibrahim. He was appointed sultan by the sultan of **Bornu**, at the time Damagaram's nominal suzerain, but was expelled from the throne by his brother Ibrahim. He regained the throne in 1851 after returning to the good graces of the court of Bornu, where he resided for part of the intervening years. A strong sovereign and leader, Tanimoun centralized Damagaram's government and administration, encouraged **Tuareg** settlement in the outskirts of **Zinder** (thus gaining their military allegiance in his expansionist policies), and greatly built up Damagaram's army, of which he is regarded as the true founder. In 1871 the kingdom possessed 6,000 rifles and 40 cannons, and could draw many thousands of foot soldiers. Despite seven rejections by Bornu of Zinder's request to fortify the city, Tanimoun ordered the walls built, and the remnants remain to this day. At their construction they were reputed to be 9–10 meters high and 12–14 meters thick at the base, with seven city gates and a total circumference of four and a half kilometers. Tanimoun's tomb is found on the old sultanate's palace grounds in Zinder.

TANKOANO, AMADOU (1953–). Academic, born on 7 February 1953 and educated at the University of Nice in public law and international economic law. Upon his return to **Niamey**, Tankoano rapidly rose through the ranks at the local university, being appointed the first dean of the school of economics and law, which he had helped found, in 1985. He has also been counselor to the **Cour Suprême** since 1987. He specialized in commercial and international patent law, on which he published widely, and was one of Niger's legal agents at the 2005 hearings of the International Court of Justice which adjudicated the **Benin–Niger border dispute**.

TANOUT. *Département* in the region of **Zinder**, with a population of 332,000 and headquarters in its namesake, a small town of 14,200, 160 km north of Zinder.

TAOUA. Daughter of the leader of the second wave of Gobirawa to move into **Aïr** in the 12th century. Remnants of her tomb at Kouchewa are still visible and are venerated by the animist population of the area.

TAPOA. Niger River affluent in the immediate vicinity of the **Parc National de W**. With a basin of 5,500 sq km and a length of 260 km, the Tapoa forms a 20-meter waterfall near the park, joining the Niger via a narrow and sinuous gorge obstructed by large boulders. The region has phosphate deposits. In 1981 an agreement was reached with **Nigeria** for their joint exploitation, but little has come of it.

TARGUI. The singular for a **Tuareg** male.

TASAR. Ruler of the **Tessaoua** dependency of **Maradi** until its break from Maradi. The name comes from the founder of the dynasty, Tasar Ibrahim, who was succeeded by 24 chiefs, until the onset of the colonial era.

TASSILI. Tuareg name for the *hamadas*—the rocky desert plateaus of Niger.

TAYA, ELHADJI MAHAMANE (1951–1988). Born in **N'Guigmi**, a far eastern town of predominantly **Kanuri** culture, Taya first studied economics at the **University of Niamey** before embracing a successful musical career, which made of his work the dominant sound in Nigerien pop music in the late 1980s. The Centre de Formation et de Promotion Musicales (CFPM) of Niamey, the country's only training and musical promotion institute, is named after him. *See also* DANCE AND MUSIC.

TAZARTCHÉ. This **Hausa** phrase, which means "it must go on," has taken the quite common political usage (through Nigerian Hausa, which spells it "Tazarce") of "overstaying in office." In Niger, it became popular as the name given throughout the country to the constitutional crisis of 2009, triggered by former president **Mamadou Tandja**'s bid to remain in power after his last term of office. Tazartché divided Nigeriens in Tazartchistes (pro-Tazartché) and Anti-Tazartchistes. The division went through families, regions, and **ethnic groups**, with individuals from any of these backgrounds falling into both camps. However, as developments at the end of the crisis revealed, many Tazartchistes were opportunistic followers and cheerleaders of Tandja's project, and its main principled supporters are generally (though not always) individuals from the regions of **Diffa**, **Zinder**, and **Maradi**, which had always constituted Tandja's electoral power base. Anti-Tazartchisme was more firmly principled and developed as a defense of democratic governance as well as of rule of law grounded in French-inherited ideals of citizenship and the republic.

Tandja sought to carry out the Tazartché ploy through financial largesse, perks, and patronage to the elite (both civilian and military), and a series of populist, ethno-regional, and patriotic appeals. In the first vein, he claimed to be indispensable for Niger's economic prosperity, referring to the achievements—some real, most sham—of his Programme Special du Président de la République (the President of the Republic's Special Program) development spending in public **health** and local schooling, as well as to a number of public works (the **Kandadji Dam**, a second bridge in **Niamey**) which he wished to "complete." In the second vein, he cultivated Hausa sentiment, still bruised from the historical 1960–1991 **Zarma-Songhay** dominance of Niger's political life, finding echoes for this chiefly in Zinder and Maradi, but not in the other Hausa regions of **Arewa** and **Ader**, fiefs of opposition leader **Mahamadou Issoufou**; and in the third vein, he took, for a while, a tougher stance on French domination of Niger's **uranium**, putting forward a policy of diversification favored by China's interests in Niger's minerals and natural resources, and also making of the suppression of the **Tuareg rebellion** of 2007–2009 a matter of national pride. These diverse grounds for Tazartché appealed differently to different groups of people, with the most successful across the board being the development spending tactic, and the least successful the hard-line approach to the Tuareg insurgency. What follows is a timeline of the Tazartché project from origins to failure.

22 December 2005: Tandja is sworn in for a second term; he pledges to "respect and enforce respect for the **constitution**" and takes an oath for this on the Quran.

26 October 2008: Tandja states he "will step down at the end of his term" in an interview with the French daily *Le Monde*.

21 December 2008: Rally at the **National Assembly** of supporters of the extension of the presidential term limit. Rallies will increase in occurrence in early 2009, being organized throughout the country.

27 March 2009: During a visit of French president Nicolas Sarkozy, Tandja announces that he will seek a constitutional revision through a **constitutional referendum** to extend the presidential term limit.

8 May 2009: Consulted by opposition parties on this project, the **Cour Constitutionnelle** declares that such a referendum would be unlawful.

26 May 2009: Tandja dissolves the National Assembly. As per the constitution, he now has 90 days to organize legislative **elections**.

29 May 2009: In a rambling televised speech, Tandja announces that he will organize the referendum, as that is the wish of the Nigerien people.

2 June 2009: Tandja signs a decree installing a handpicked technical committee to draft a new constitution.

5 June 2009: The Council of Ministers sets referendum vote for 4 August 2009.

12 June 2009: The Cour Constitutionnelle issues a binding decision against the referendum.

14 June 2009: Thousands demonstrate against the referendum in Niamey and other towns.

17 June 2009: The national bar association calls for respect of the 12 June Cour Constitutionnelle ruling.

18 June 2009: A strike ordered by the seven main trade **unions** of the country is cancelled by court ruling.

25 June 2009: Rescheduled national 24-hour strike.

26 June 2009: The Cour Constitutionnelle reaffirms its 12 June ruling. Tandja invokes article 53 of the constitution and assumes emergency powers.

29 June 2009: Tandja disbands the Cour Constitutionnelle, overstepping his legal powers.

1 July 2009: A national work stoppage is ordered by unions.

4 August 2009: The constitution adopted at referendum removes the presidential term limit and extends Tandja's power for three years as a "transition period."

20 October 2009: The 2009 legislative elections are organized and boycotted by the opposition. Niger is suspended from the **Economic Community of West African States** (ECOWAS).

22 December 2009: Scheduled end of Tandja's last term as per **Fifth Republic** constitution.

14 February 2010: The reconciliation dialogue is suspended. Thousands attend antigovernment demonstration in Niamey.

16 February 2010: A closed-door ECOWAS meeting at Abuja (**Nigeria**) ends in a call for Niger's quick return to constitutionality.

17 February 2010: A defiant televised speech of Prime Minister **Ali Gamatié** rejects ECOWAS' call.

18 February 2010: The presidential palace is attacked by army men; Tandja is captured.

19 February 2010: The United Nations and the African Union (which suspends Niger) condemn the coup. Opposition parties, **civil society** organizations, and the unions release statement of support for the junta that had emerged from the coup and call for rapid elections.

20 February 2010: Massive demonstrations are in Niamey in support of the coup leaders and new elections.

21 February 2010: The coup leaders assure ECOWAS mediators of a short transition to civilian rule, the timing to be defined by political dialogue. Tazartché is buried.

TCHANGA. *See* BOUREIMA, MOUMOUNI.

TCHANGARI, MOUSSA (1969–). Born in **N'Guigmi**, in the far eastern regions of Niger, Tchangari initially studied in the country's **Franco-Arabe** semireligious (**Islam**) schooling system: *madrasa* in N'Guigmi, followed by a Franco-Arabic secondary school in **Zinder**, a Franco-Arabic high school in **Niamey**, and the expected entry at the **Islamic University of Say** after the *baccalauréat* degree in 1988. But then Tchangari abruptly changed course, leaving **Say** and theology to enter the **University of Niamey**'s department of philosophy, where he earned a bachelor's degree in 1995. The period was very militant, with two academic years lost to **student** strikes and the upheaval of the **democratization** process of 1991 in which Tchangari, as the secretary-general (1989–1990) and then the president (1990–1991) of the **Union des Scolaires Nigériens** (USN), played a key role. He was the leading representative of the students at the **Conférence Nationale** but left his position the following year in order to learn English at the **Usman Dan Fodio** University of Sokoto, in **Nigeria**. He was also, in April 1991, a founding member of the **Association Nigérienne de Défense des Droits de l'Homme** (ANDDH).

Upon his return from Nigeria, Tchangari started a career as a journalist and a leftist activist. He contributed first to the satirical weekly *Le Moustique* and then to the left-leaning (at the time) weekly *Tribune du Peuple*, before founding his own **media** group, *Alternative*, on the basis of a radical democratic ideology. During that period, Tchangari was very active as an organizer of the private press; a founding member of the Nigerien association of the private press journalists in 1995, he was also, from 1992 to 2002, the secretary-general of the Association Nigérienne de la Presse Indépendante (ANPI). In 2001, he turned his energies toward more militant activities, with the founding of the radical association Alternative Espaces Citoyens, of which he was elected secretary-general. The association wanted Niger to adopt participatory and decentralized democracy, and in this view, it started to organize the Nigerien Social Forum in 2003 with such success that the government took restrictive measures against later editions of the event and Tchangari was chosen as the coordinator of the African Social Forum in 2008.

During the 2005 civil disobedience campaigns organized against a new value added tax on goods and services which scared the government, Tchangari and Alternative Espaces Citoyens pushed for a mass uprising and a political revolution, but they were sidelined by the forces of accommodation and moderation led by the Coalition Equité Qualité (which also involved **Marou Amadou**, **Nouhou Arzika**, and **Moustapha Kadi**). In 2008, Alternatives Espaces Citoyens organized the African Social Forum in Niamey, subjecting the government of Niger to a barrage of criticisms, and announcing its intention to organize an awareness caravan that would tour the country and whip up citizen's conscience. The government forbade it.

In 2009, when President Mamadou Tandja overthrew the **Fifth Republic**, Tchangari adopted an ambiguous position: Alternative Espaces Citoyens kept aloof from the events, claiming that all Nigerien politicians were equally bad and that Tandja only revealed the contradictions in the system. The association came under suspicions of harboring sympathies for Tandja's project, especially after another of its most prominent members, Souley Adji, appeared to offer advice to the president on how best to dodge his critics in a journal article. It must be noted that Tchangari as well as Adji are from the same eastern districts as Tandja, a circumstance which heightened those suspicions.

After Tandja was toppled in February, Tchangari vainly clamored for a participatory constituent assembly for the drafting of the post-Tandja **constitution**: he was overruled by the consensus of the political class and the international community.

Aside from these militant activities, Tchangari and his friends in Alternative Espaces Citoyens have produced many valuable, radical-slanted studies of Niger multifarious social ills.

TCHINTABARADEN. *Département* in the region of **Tahoua** that was the prime area of nomadization of the Ouilliminden Kel Dinnik **Tuareg** group. Formerly known as Tahoua-Nomade, it encompasses the *arrondissements* of Abalak and Tillia and has a population of 85,000, downward from 104,000 in 1977—the only Nigerien circumscription to register a negative population growth. The northern part of the region of Tahoua in which this *département* is entirely located is the hardest hit by desertification. The *département* is headquartered in Tchintabaraden, an oasis 75 km north of Tahoua, with a large village of 8,142, upward from 5,000 in 1988. It hosts a camp of Niger's **armed forces** which had often been a target of Tuareg armed attacks, including one in the early 1980s organized by **Abdoulaye Hamani Diori**. More recently Tchintabaraden was attacked in 1990, in the aftermath of which the Niger armed forces undertook mass reprisals on the Tuareg tribes of the area, accusing them of aiding assailants. The number of civilian casualties is unknown, figures ranging from 63 (according to the government) through 600 to 700 (estimated by humanitarian organizations), to 1,500 (according to Tuareg groups). In 1991, the **Conférence Nationale** indicted both Niger's minister delegate for defense, **Bagnou Beidou**, and the then-*préfet* of Agadez, Kimba Kollo, for their role in the repression, though the **Cour Suprême** later exculpated them. The events at Tchintabaraden were evoked in the mid-1990s by Tuareg irredentist forces as a cause for their rebellion against the state of Niger. *See also* TUAREG REBELLIONS.

TEDA. A branch of the **Toubou** found mostly in northern Chad, and in much smaller numbers in eastern Niger. They call themselves Tedagada (those who speak Tedaga). Both Toubou branches speak similar dialects, which are related to the **Kanuri** language. In Niger the Teda are to be found in **Kaouar** and especially in the Djado area the between Agadem and Soutellan, and are often called Braouia by other **ethnic groups**. The Teda are Muslim, with most of the clans in Niger belonging to the **Sanusiya** order. Both in Niger and in neighboring Chad the Teda spearheaded the anti-French, anti-infidel drives from the onset of the colonial era into the 1920s. In Chad, the Teda have been in rebellion against the regimes of Ndjamena since 1966. Certain clans have been pushed into Niger by this rebellion, and the Niger government has been extremely apprehensive about the possibility of the **rebellions** spreading into its territory. This did not occur, despite several incidents in the late 1960s, but after Hissene Habre's ouster in Chad in 1990 elements of his army fled to Niger, sold their arms to the rebelling Tuareg, and in 1993 joined in a rebellion in Niger's desolate southeastern region. *See also* TUAREG REBELLIONS.

TEGAMA AGH BAKHARI, ABDERAHMAN (1880?–1920). Sultan of **Agadez** at the time of the **Kaocen revolt**. Born in Doguerawa around 1880, Tegama was an energetic leader in very trying times for his people. He sided with the budding rebellion in **Aïr** aimed at freeing it from colonial and infidel rule. After the rebellion collapsed and the siege of Agadez's French fort was lifted, Tegama escaped to **Kaouar (Bilma)** but was betrayed to the French by the local **Toubou** in May 1919. He was brought to **Zinder** and imprisoned. The French were reluctant to put him on trial because of the disturbances that this might stir up, and Tegama was murdered in his cell on 29 April 1920. His death was for years passed off as suicide.

TEMPS DU NIGER, LE. Daily mimeographed newspaper published since 1960 by the Niger Information Service in Niamey, with a circulation of 1,300. Following the **coup of 1974**, the paper's name was changed to *Le Sahel* on 29 April that year.

TENDE. Spirit cult practiced by some **Tuareg** in **Aïr**, similar to the **Bori** and **Holley** cults farther south. *See also* RELIGION.

TÉNÉRÉ. Area of shifting dunes stretching over some 400,000 sq km between **Aïr** and **Kaouar**. In prehistoric, wetter days fully vegetated and settled (by inhabitants who left numerous cave engravings), the Ténéré is now totally uninhabited. In the western part, some stunning sand-dune formations dominate the landscape, while in the north the desert is essentially a monotonous sand plain. The term Ténéré is actually the **tamasheq** word for "desert"; the equivalent **Arab** word is Sahara. *See also* ARBRE DU TÉNÉRÉ.

TÉRA. Town of 18,900 some 180 km northwest of **Niamey**. Also a *département* encompassing 296,000 people in the region of **Tillabéri**. In the 17th century, Téra was a small **Songhay** state centered on the large village of that name. It is today the largest purely Songhay urban settlement in Niger. *See also* DENDI.

TERRITORIAL ASSEMBLY. The Territorial Assembly succeeded the **Conseil Général** in February 1952. In line with changes throughout overseas French colonies, the Assemblée Territoriale possessed wider powers. Still elected by a double electoral college, of its 50 deputies 15 were elected by the first (European) and 35 by the second (African) college. In the March 1952

elections the Union Nationale des Indépendants et Sympathisants (UNIS) party captured 34 of the 35 African seats and one of the European seats.

In December 1958—following the electoral defeat of the **Sawaba** party—the organ transformed itself into the **Assemblée Constituante** in order to ratify the **constitution** of 25 February 1959, and on March 12, 1959, it became a legislative assembly. Among the presidents of the assembly, successors to Moumouni Aouta, *zarmakoy* of **Dosso**, were **Georges Mahaman Condat** and Malick N'Diaye. The assembly elected two councilors to the French Republic and three to the French Union as well as five councilors to the **Afrique Occidentale Française** (AOF) Grand Council in Dakar, Senegal.

TESSAOUA. Important historic town of 31,300 people, 137 km east of **Maradi** and 117 km west of **Zinder**. Also, a *département* of 335,900 people in the region of Maradi. Historically a vassal of **Katsina** (before the Sokoto **Fulani** conquest), Tessaoua continued its allegiance to Maradi after the Katsinawa relocated to that town. Far to the east of the continuing **Hausa**-Fulani tug-of-war, Tessaoua (which in 1851 had a population of 15,000) was ruled by the **tasar** and was quite independent in most matters. This de facto independence eventually led to a split from the nominal suzerainty of Maradi.

THIRD REPUBLIC. The **constitution** of the Third Republic was adopted through a **constitutional referendum** on 26 December 1992. Although coming out of the labors of the **Conférence Nationale**'s committee of fundamental texts (which also drafted an electoral code and several other legal framework documents), it was not very different from the draft constitution proposed by the declining **Second Republic**. It was a semiparliamentary (or semipresidential) constitution copied from the French Fifth Republic constitution. The Third Republic was the first Nigerien political regime in which the rules of liberal representative democracy were applied. In what will become a pattern in the country's political life, the more technocratic institutions of democracy (the **Commission Electorale Nationale Indépendante** and the **Cour Suprême**) worked perfectly, ensuring that the rules of the game were enforced in an exemplary way. But the more political institutions (the **National Assembly** and the presidency) soon became battlefields between inflexible political leaders, feuding for the protection of clique interests, personal prestige, and regional and **ethnic** preference.

The first government of the Third Republic was formed by a coalition of new **political parties** united only by their intent to prevent a return to power through **elections** of the erstwhile single party, the **Mouvement National pour la Société de Développement** (MNSD). That coalition, **the Alliance des Forces du Changement** (AFC), soon collapsed under the pressure of the rivalry between President **Mahaman Ousmane** of the **Convention Démocratique et Sociale** (CDS Rahama) and Prime Minister **Mahamadou Issoufou** of the **Parti Nigérien pour la Démocratie et le Socialisme** (PNDS Tarayya). In 1995, the legislative elections returned MNSD to power at the National Assembly, forcing President Ousmane to appoint MNSD's **Hama Amadou** prime minister. The cohabitation situation did not work well, as Ousmane refused to attend cabinet meetings, hindering considerably the operation of government. Key to these feuds was the control of the public markets commission, which constitutional rules gave to the prime minister's office but which the presidency wanted. There was also a fight over appointments. These instruments, along with cabinet positions, were essential to rewarding followers, and Ousmane had lost them through his defeat in the legislative elections. In January 1996, the delay that Ousmane was constitutionally forced to observe before dissolving the National Assembly would expire, and he was clearly determined to then act on his powers in a move that was expected to escalate the crisis and worsen the gridlock. On the eve of the expiration of the delay, on 27 January 1996, Ousmane was overthrown by his chief of defense staff, Colonel **Ibrahim Baré Maïnassara**, who proceeded to suspend and eventually to terminate the constitution of the Third Republic.

Despite its rocky history, the Third Republic installed the forces and logics that still dominate Nigerien politics to date: the main parties and leaders, and the remarkable feature of efficiency in supervisory institutions which puts the country on par with the most advanced liberal democracies in the world. *See also* COUP D'ÉTAT OF 27 JANUARY 1996.

TIBIRI. Ultimate independent capital of the Gobirawa following their long series of clashes with, and rebellions against, the **Fulani** Sokoto Empire. Currently Tibiri is the political center of Niger's eastern Gobirawa, with a population of 10,000 and a very important weekly market. The main mosque and the royal palace are prominent sites in the town, and the *inna* (animist priestess) of **Gobir** also lives there. Located just 5 km outside of **Maradi**, Tibiri was built in 1836 by a joint Katsinawa-Gobirawa effort after the two groups lived peacefully together in Maradi for several years. The two groups also cooperated in the struggle to regain their territories to the south from which they had been expelled by the Fulani. In 1860 a dissident Gobirawa group seceded from Tibiri and set up its own center of antiestablishment dissidence (with Fulani help) at Sabon Birni, which was some time later conquered by the legitimate forces of Gobirawa.

TIJANIYYA. Dominant **religious order** in Niger that since the 1920s nearly completely replaced the **Qadiriyya**, previously dominant in the area. The order is popular in particular among the **Kanuri**, the **Zarma**, and the **Songhay**. Its most important strongholds are **Kiota**, **Niamey**, **Gouré**, and **N'Guigmi**.

Founded by Sid Ahmed al-Tijani (a Moor from Trarza) in the late 18th century, the order spread widely in subsequent centuries. The Tijaniyya in Niger at first opposed the French intrusion, but an understanding was reached and the order became the one favored by the French administration. Later, Hamallism arose as a reaction to this alliance.

TILLABÉRI. A mixed **Songhay** and **Zarma** small town with a population of 16,200 (of 30,000 for the urban **commune** which includes neighboring villages), and a region encompassing a population of 1,859,000. Midway on the scenic road connecting Niamey (140 km south) with **Ayorou**, Tillabéri is the center of a grain-growing region and currently also produces rice and sugar cane. Its market days attract sellers and buyers from as far north as **Gao** (Mali). The district of Tillabéri (a *département*) includes the towns of Ayorou and Sansanné-Haousa.

TIMIDRIA. A civic association-cum-nongovernmental organization formed in 1991 under the leadership of Ilguilas Weila and a group of dark-skinned or Black **Tuareg** of slave background. The word means solidarity or brotherhood in **Tamashaq**, and the association militates for the emancipation of the tens of thousands of dark-skinned slaves who form the underbelly of Tuareg society. In the early 2000s, Timidria provoked an international outcry and the irritation of the Nigerien government by claiming that the country numbered about 800,000 slaves. Though the numbers were clearly inflated and also included people who had slave background as opposed to being actual slaves, the claims succeeded in putting the issue of slavery on the public stage in Niger. In recent times, Timidria has moved more into NGO roles, setting up community projects in the semiarid areas, delivering farm equipments, fertilizers, and such; this can be viewed as an assistance to the economic transformation through which Black Tuareg, by combining **agriculture** and **cattle** rearing, are slowly freeing themselves from their overlords.

TONDIBI, BATTLE OF. Tondibi was the site of the major clash between Moroccan (and some Spanish mercenary) troops and the armies of the **Songhay Empire** on 12 April 1591. The Moroccan trans-Saharan assault was mounted in November 1590 and succeeded by virtue of surprise and the muskets carried by a sizable contingent of the 4,000-man force. By contrast the 40,000 troops sent to oppose them did not have a single musket among them and had not been exposed to rifle power in the past. The battle changed the course of history in the region, leading to the collapse of the Songhay Empire.

Narratives of the battle often include the fact that a strategy used by the Songhay army was to use thousands of bulls at the vanguard of the army to attack Moroccan horses and thus break a force that was chiefly of cavalrymen. The ploy backfired badly when the Moroccans shot their guns and scared the bulls, which then turned against the Songhay army at the back.

In the Songhay language, Tondibi fittingly means black stone.

TONDIBIA. Important military camp 12 km from **Niamey**, specialized also in the training of new recruits and the on-the-field instruction of young military officers. It hosts a garrison and the Groupement d'Instruction des Forces Armées Nigériennes (GI/FAN), which also provides customized military training for gendarmes at the end of their own instruction.

Tondibia served as an initial custody facility for several higher officials of the First Republic after the **coup in April 1974** and for toppled President **Mamadou Tandja** in February 2010.

Tondibia should not be confused with Tondibi, the site—now located in Mali—at which a Moroccan invading army defeated the **Songhay Empire** in the **battle of Tondibi**). Tondibi means black stone and Tondibia *the* black stone.

TOUBOU. Collective name for several branches of an **ethnic group** found in the southern Sahara, and specifically in northern Chad and Niger and in southern **Libya**. Their name comes from the **Kanuri** for "inhabitants of Tu," the local name for the Tibesti Mountains to the east of **Kaouar**. The two major Toubou branches are the **Teda**—found in large numbers in Chad and in smaller concentrations in Djado, **Bilma**, **Agadez**, and in general in Kaouar in Niger—and the **Daza**, who are found in much larger numbers in Chad and Libya but in very small numbers around **Lake Chad** in Niger and in general in the **N'Guigmi area**. Estimates of the total population of the Toubou vary greatly, but it is thought that their maximum numbers do not exceed 350,000, most found in Chad (some 50 percent) and Libya (30 percent).

The ethnic origin of the Toubou is still clouded in mystery, especially since their dark complexion and their language are quite different from the Berbers from whom it is assumed they originated and with whom they share unique and strikingly similar ABO blood-group patterns. According to one reconstruction of their origin, the Toubou are descendants of white nomads from the Nile Valley who arrived between the seventh and ninth centuries in the region of Tibesti–Kaouar, an area where they helped found the Kanem kingdom, and then in the early 13th century were pushed out of the region northward. In subsequent centuries, by now ethnically intermixed with other groups, they arrived in the areas they formerly occupied in search of new pastures. Early in the 19th century, this new migration gained momentum under Ottoman pressure from Libya.

At the onset of the colonial era the Toubou, fierce Senoussi adherents and highly independent, resisted for nearly two decades the entry of the French into their regions. Muslim, nomadic, and aggressive, the Toubou have traditionally exacted a levy (10 percent) on all caravans (that they did not plunder) passing through their strongholds, or from sedentary settlements (for instance, Kaouar), exacting a tribute from the populations there.

Niger's Toubou, mostly in the vicinity of N'Guigmi and Kaouar, control the salt pans of the area and have a political entity called the sultanate of Kaouar. Their supremacy of the region was shattered, however, by the **Tuareg** in the 19th century, though they were allowed to retain their intermediary role between the Kanuri population of the oases and the Tuareg overlords. They arrived in Niger from Kufra (Libya) via Tibesti (Chad) and first settled in the **Komadougu Yobé** River area before being pushed farther north by the existing, and more powerful, Mobeur. Among the most important Toubou clans, which are all quasi autonomous, are the Kecherda, Azza, Dogordo, Gadana, and Ouandalla. Since the onset of the **Tuareg rebellion** in Niger in 1990, the Toubou have been restless. Augmented by those remnants of Hissene Habre's armies which fled N'Djamena after losing out to a rival, in 1993 the Toubou set up a new "liberation front" for their region in southeastern Niger. This turned into a tug-of-war around scarce resources with **Arab** and **Fulani** groups and dwindled into irrelevance by the mid-1990s.

TOURAWA. Title of the war chief of the sultan of **Agadez**. The second most important personality after the sultan, the *tourawa* has traditional command over all the **Arabs** residing in **Aïr** (*tourawa* is **Hausa** for "the whites") and also leads the annual or biannual **Bilma** caravan. *See also* AGADEZ, SULTANATE OF.

TOURISM. Despite some impressive tourist attractions (along the **Niger River**, the **Parc National du W**, the **Tuareg** encampments, and of course the stunningly beautiful **Aïr** massif), tourism has been slow to develop in Niger. This has been in part a result of the relatively undeveloped tourist infrastructure and in part because exploration of Aïr has been largely for the venturesome and hardy. Only 18,000 tourists visited Niger in 1977, of whom 55 percent came from Europe, just over a third from **France**. In that year the entire country had only 16 hotels (seven in Niamey, the others rather tiny), with fewer than 700 beds in all. Since the advent of the military regime, a serious program of developing the country's tourism was embarked upon.

Also, the paving of the **Route de l'Uranium** made distant **Agadez** and Aïr a long day's drive from **Niamey** rather than a rugged expedition in its own right. Hotel construction and renovation increased room and bed capacity. A new hotel—the Gaweye—on the Kennedy Bridge in Niamey by itself (with its 250 rooms) increased capacity by 30 percent. A decade later, in 1987, over 43,000 tourists visited Niger (a 25 percent increase), giving the country's hotels a 2 billion **CFA franc** turnover.

In 1990, the **Tuareg rebellion** in Aïr put an end to rosy hopes of the tourist industry's further coming of age. At the same time, the government's acute budgetary straits forced it to pass the running of most of the larger state-run hotels to private management teams. In that year Niger had nearly a thousand rooms, Agadez's airport was upgraded to an international airport to accept charter flights from Europe, and the tourist possibilities in the **Tahoua** and **Zinder** regions were being developed. All these options have been put on hold as tourist figures plummeted.

TRANSPORTATION. Niger is landlocked, undeveloped, far from the coast, and has wide population dispersal; thus, inadequate internal communications and external import-export linkages have always been a major constraint to development in Niger. At independence, Niger had no tarred roads, inheriting only a rudimentary network of laterite and sand tracks from the French administration. Until 1963, the only blacktopped stretch of road outside a town connected the **Niamey** airport to the presidential palace over a few kilometers. In the 1960s, Niger had to devote upward to 9 percent of public expenditures to roads and communication, much more than any other West African country—on account both of what little it had, and the huge distances it was dealing with. Canadian financing provided a relief in the building of the nearly 1,000 km-long **Route de l'Unité** and by 1978, the country had a 7,657-km network of national roads, which included 1,892 km of paved roads. Several principal railroads, none of which is fully satisfactory, were used, are used, or could be used for Niger's foreign trade. They all exist in neighboring countries only and include:

The Nigerian railroad system, which terminates at two localities 125 and 262 km from major Niger towns. The routes tend to be heavily used by importers and exporters, for they are the least costly. Thus on the heyday of that trade, 80 percent of Niger's **groundnuts** were dispatched from **Zinder** to Kano, and on to Apapa on the coast, the remainder going via Benin. The route was, however, not fully satisfactory, for Niger's groundnut season coincided with **Nigeria**'s and the latter's crop received priority on the railroad. Moreover, the massive delays at Nigeria's ports have made the import of goods from overseas via Nigeria extremely hazardous.

The Régie Abidjan–Niger that links Côte d'Ivoire's Abidjan port with Ouagadougou in Burkina Faso, which is 590 km from Niamey. The route had become quite useful since the European Union funded repairs of the road in the 1990s, but the crisis in Côte d'Ivoire shifted much of the connection to the Ghanaian port of Tema.

The Algerian railroad system that now terminates near Colomb-Béchar (at Adabla). There have been some exploratory talks regarding its extension to **Gao** (Mali) and thence to Niamey, though the project appears even less economical. In the fall of 1977 a trucking link was established between the Algerian Colomb–Béchar terminus and Kano, Nigeria, with the massive port congestion in Nigeria (and the added costs on goods this created), making shipping of goods from Europe over the trans-Saharan route economical again, but this lasted only temporarily.

The Dakar–Niger railroad, linking Senegal with Mali and ending at Koulikoro (Mali), just beyond Bamako. Its extension has been discussed on several occasions, though the entire project is likewise tentative. And in any case, the port of Dakar is much too far from Niamey, compared to generally better (deep sea waters and other conditions) options nearby.

*The **Organisation Commune Bénin-Niger (OCBN)** and **Opération Hirondelle***, which OCBN route links Niamey via **Dosso** and **Gaya** to Parakou in Benin by regular truck schedules, and from Parakou by railroad to the port of Cotonou. The route is extensively used by Niger, especially for its imports, as well as for the evacuation of some of its mineral output (**uranium**, for instance). The Benin railroad, however, was in a state of acute disrepair in the 1970s and 1980s, requiring expensive renovations and the purchase of new rolling stock, something Benin was reluctant to undertake due to its own acute fiscal straits. The rail bed was improved, however, and some new (mostly passenger) rolling stock was purchased in the mid-1980s when Niger threatened to divert its transit trade to other routes, but the route is still not fully satisfactory. The extension of the OCBN railroad north into Niger has been envisaged for over five decades, and discussions have been revived recently to include other neighboring countries.

Niger has two highways, the Route de l'Unité, linking the Mali-Burkina-Benin borders with the Chad border, and the **Route de l'Uranium** built to ferry the mineral from Arlit to Benin, linking up with the Unity Road in **Birni-N'Konni**. The road from **Arlit** to Dosso to Niamey and Gaya has been mended, but the Unity Road from Birni-N'Konni to Zinder and beyond is in a state of disrepair. The entire road network is as follows:

Paved roads	3,760 km (27.1 percent)
Laterite roads	2,860 km (20.7 percent)

Serviced tracks	2,880 km (0.6 percent)
Rudimentary tracks	4,225 km (30.6 percent)

An important development in the 1990s is the growth of passenger transportation, following the liberalization of the transport business and the end of the monopoly of the **Société Nationale des Transports Nigériens** (SNTN). Dozens of private bus companies emerged, mostly run by **Zarma-Songhay** (Garba Maissadjé, Africa Assalam, Sounna Transport, etc.) and especially **Tuareg** (Rimbo Transport, Aïr Transport, Azawad Transport, etc.) businessmen. These have revolutionized to some extent Niger's transportation industry, as Niger's bus companies have become easily the most present in the West African region, linking Niamey to Ouagadougou (Burkina Faso), Cotonou (Benin), Lomé (Togo), Accra (Ghana), Abidjan (Côte d'Ivoire), Bamako (Mali), and Dakar (Senegal), and sometimes partnering with companies in Burkina Faso and Mali, the only other countries in that part of Africa with a comparatively extensive regional network of passenger transportation.

TUAREG. Largely nomadic **ethnic group** found in a large area centered on the Ahaggar Mountains (Algeria) and including concentrations in Niger, Algeria, Mali, and **Libya**. In Niger their number is 1,017,000 according to the most recent **census** (2001), or 9 percent of the population. They are thus the third-largest group in the country, after the **Hausa** and the **Zarma-Songhay**, although smaller than these by a very large margin and almost equivalent in size to the **Fulani**. Estimates of their total number in Africa vary widely, although those who claim Berber ancestry and constitute the upper-tier class of Tuareg society in most regions (though not in the **Aïr**) are probably everywhere a sizable minority ruling over a majority of Tuareg with a southern black ancestry and slave background.

Berber Tuareg are educated in the clan and tribe system characteristic of desert Berbers and nurture a very elevated sense of their lifestyle and ethnic worth. Black Tuareg are often autonomous communities (despite their nominal slave status) with a culture that intermediates between that of their black neighbors and that of the Berber Tuareg; they are called **Bella** by the Zarma-Songhay and Bugaje (singular, **Buzu**) by the Hausa. Black Tuareg are also household slaves living with Berber Tuareg communities, the only actual slaves still existing in Niger and Mali, though this is illegal, and these are the **Ikelan** proper.

Tuareg arrived in the current territory of Niger around the 11th century, settling in the Aïr region where they displaced Hausa agriculturalists, together with desertification. The original seven clans to arrive in Aïr were united in a federation as the Itesen. The Tuareg do not usually call themselves Tuareg—this being an **Arab** appellation—but rather refer to themselves by their clan's or their tribal confederation's name and more generally as Kel **Tamashaq**, i.e., "those who speak Tamashaq." Each clan (*taousit*) is composed of various families under the leadership of one of several chiefs, the *amrar*. Several large clans, or tribes, form a Tuareg *kel*, or "People of . . . " Several *kels* may combine to appoint a joint supreme chief, or *amenokal*, though this term may also signify any chief on the clan level.

Tuareg hierarchy recognizes several distinct castes. The most elevated are the Imajeren, which means "the noble," followed by the Imrad, also freemen but subordinate to the former. The Ineslemen are a religious, nonfighting, sacerdotal caste whose very orthodox practice of Sunni **Islam** put them at variance with over groups attached to the ancient customs and manners of the community. At the bottom of the caste system come the Ikelan (in Tuareg) or Bella (in Songhay) or Buzu (Hausa) slaves. Originally the Ikelans' role was to tend palm groves or vegetable gardens while their overlords trekked the desert. There are also several specialized occupational castes, including the Inadin artisan and silversmith caste, which is considered separate and outside regular Tuareg society, being freemen, but spurned for their commercial way of life. They tended to form an important class, however, whenever the Tuareg managed to establish a state formation, as their diplomatic services and relative wealth proved key to running a political regime.

The Tuareg language is Tamasheq, which comes in closely related dialects; its written script, *tifinagh*, is related to the ancient Libyan language.

Following the arrival in Aïr of the first Itesen wave, other clans drifted in over the centuries. Certain of these clans eventually became sedentary; many remained nomadic or seminomadic, and their patterns of transhumance have at times covered large areas.

Politically the Tuareg have never constituted one entity. They formed a number of sultanates, however, such as that in **Agadez** in the 15th century. Elsewhere, smaller entities were established after the conquest of territory and sedentary populations, as in the **Ader** and **Tahoua**. Converted to Islam, and later to the **Sanusiya** religious order, though retaining many pre-Islamic customs, the Tuareg resisted the imposition of French rule over their areas; they saw them both as infidels and rivals for the exploitation of settled black populations.

During the **First Republic** (1960–1974), the Tuareg were treated with special consideration, and one of their *amenokals* served in the cabinet (as often as not resident in Agadez) as minister of Saharan affairs. Free salt, tea, and sugar were distributed to the migrating clans during the *cure salée* at In Gall, and Aïr was administered with a gentle hand—part of a keen awareness of the great volatility of a population occupying a region close to then-inimical Algeria.

The *régime d'exception* (1974–1988) upended this policy. In the 1980s **Libya** tried to foment the growth of subnationalism among Niger's Tuareg following the break in diplomatic relations with **Niamey**. A number of Tuareg civil servants were enticed by Libyan blandishments and left for Tripoli, and on at least three occasions former president **Hamani Diori**'s self-exiled son, **Abdoulaye Hamani Diori**, with Libyan support led groups of Tuareg in assaults against Nigerien military installations in Aïr and Ader (including **Tchintabaraden**) in an effort to attain a comeback for his father. After one armed incident in 1985, Kountché expelled thousands of "non-Nigerien" Tuareg from Niger.

Tuareg grievances took on a new nature following the effects of the **uranium** boom of the late 1970s–early 1980s. Prominent among those effects are the considerable immigration of workers from other parts of Niger, and the fact that top positions in the **mining** industry were generally held by educated black southerners. For Berber Tuareg, this resulted in a world turned upside down, given their traditional social prejudices against dark-skinned people. Playing into the destabilizing policies of Libya, they reacted against this evolution by assaulting Nigerien military installations, leading to a cycle of repressions, which culminated in the violent Tchintabaraden events of 1987. The latter were a consequence of an enduring trait of the relations between Niger's army and Berber Tuareg communities: the difficulty of distinguishing friends and foes in an atypical environment (the desert) and the fact that unlike other nomadic populations, the Berber Tuareg had, by the late 20th century, built a consistent tradition of hostility toward the state, either colonial French or postcolonial Nigerien. The hostility moreover took on the form of the dream of a Tuareg republic in the Sahara, which became the basis of irredentism in the 1990s.

Though this was the more spectacular face of Tuareg developments in recent times, it is perhaps only a symptom of the deeper evolution which is seeing the transformation of that society by forces unleashed by **democratization**—namely, the emancipation of large groups of Black Tuareg and the emergence of a Tuareg elite in Nigerien southern towns and cities as the north becomes increasingly inhospitable, in economic and political terms.

The main Tuareg confederations of clans in Niger are:

The Kel Aïr: They nomadize in the Aïr as their name indicates.

The Kel Dinnik: "Those of the East." Since the 18th century, they form, with the Kel Ataram ("Those of the West") the two branches of the large Ouillimiden confederation. They nomandize through Niger and Mali and speak, besides a variant of Tamasheq called Tawallammat, dialects of Arabic and **Songhay**. In Niger, principally the Ouilliminden Kel Dinnik are found, resident in the **Azawagh**.

The Kel Gress: One of the largest Tuareg confederations, with clans found as far south as within the northern parts of **Nigeria**.

The Kel Owey: The name means "Those of the beef," which refers to their **cattle**-herding vocation and the head of cattle that they give as symbolic tribute to their suzerain, the sultan of Agadez. They are headed by an *anastafidet* and used to control the Kaouar *azalay* trade. That monopoly was challenged by the Imouzourag in the 18th century but was guaranteed to the Kel Owey by the French, when the Kel Owey were able to supply them with camels for their expeditions in Chad. The Ikazakazan, from whom came **Kaocen**, the Sanusi warrior, are a subgroup of this confederation. *See also* AGADEZ, SULTANATE OF; TUAREG REBELLIONS.

TUAREG REBELLIONS (1991–1995, 2007–2009). The **Tuareg** rebellions of Niger (and Mali) play out a conflicted pattern of reaction to state power, which has also become increasingly rooted in the structures of Tuareg society, marked by a stark master–slave divide.

There is a Tuareg pattern of resistance to state power which, though related to the fact that the Tuareg never built large states or strong state formations (as did the **Songhay** and the **Hausa**), has been, in the 20th century, mostly the consequence of a tradition of resistance born under French rule. Colonization unsettled Tuareg society in more serious ways than it did sedentary societies by cutting the economic lifelines through the Sahara desert, drawing internal and external boundaries that constrained their nomadic traditions, and setting up a stable administrative state which armed and educated southern blacks whose previous state of peaceful anarchy had left them vulnerable to attack.

The fledgling Nigerien state of the 1960s secured Tuareg peace by leaving the northern region largely out of state policy, especially since it appeared to be poor, immense, and arid, with a very low population density. But renewed state interest in the late 1970s, following the **uranium** boom, awoke the dormant tradition of resistance, which flared up when Colonel Muammar Kadhafi of **Libya** enlisted Nigerien Tuareg in his Islamic Legion and fueled an irredentist dream for a Tuareg Saharan republic in the 1980s. The attacks on Nigerien military installations as well as coup attempts combined with these attacks incurred reprisals from **Seyni Kountché**'s government, and solidified Tuareg grievances with blood (repression) and exile (thousands of Tuareg were driven into Algeria by Niger's **armed forces**).

In the early 1990s, with the onset of **democratization**, Tuareg groups were able to publicize these grievances, especially the legitimate claim to reinstallation and compensation for Kountché's expulsions. To these grievances, however, was added the angst of the upheaval introduced in Tuareg society by both the uranium boom and democratization. The uranium boom had opened up the northern region to southern Nigeriens, who first went there as mine workers and then gradually discovered the untapped **agricultural** and commercial potentials of the region. They tended to enter into working agreements with the lower-caste members of Tuareg society, more open to labor and trade, and together, they created an around-the-year **onion** production sector under the favorable climate of the southern parts of the region of **Agadez**. More importantly, they also started turning swaths of nomadic zones into agricultural lands. In this way the democratization era immediately triggered an attack, from within Tuareg society, on the master–slave structure of that society, which is the hidden base of the vaunted (Berber) Tuareg culture of tea drinking, music, and camel parading—chiefly leisure activities.

Thus, on the one hand the various rebel fronts of the mid-1990s officially grounded their insurgency in the Nigerien state's alleged refusal to provide satisfactions for the repressions of the *régime d'exception*, as well as in the aspiration for a separate or several separate states; but on the other hand, the fact that these rebellions were led by Berber Tuareg against a so-called cultural genocide revealed the deep-seated and quite reactionary nature of the movements.

The rebel movements never represented a serious threat to the state of Niger. Those in 1991–1995 took advantage of the fact that Niger had started a democratization process and did not have for much of that period (1991–1993) a fully operational government, while also being unable to control and use its unpaid military. It is therefore a testimony of the weakness of the insurgencies that they were not able to seriously threaten such a debilitated state. In fact, they floundered into infighting and division, and only ended up creating an untenable state of insecurity in the north, ruining **tourism**, halting southern colonization, and constraining **mining** activities. The economic impact of insecurity forced the government to consider the demands of the Tuareg fronts, which were: (1) the evacuation of all Nigerien armed forces from **Aïr**; (2) a federal system, with the north (Aïr and **Azawagh**) being one component with complete administrative and military autonomy; (3) an infusion of funds for the benefit of the north; and (4) the integration of Tuareg youth into the army. The contradictoriness of the demands reflects the divisions between the Tuareg fronts, and while some of them appeared unacceptable to the Nigerien government, the main difficulty was to establish dialogue with a unified rebellion, rather than with dozens of shifting and splitting groupings. The condition for peace talks was reached when most Tuareg rebel fronts united in a loose federation, the **Organisation de la Résistance**

Armée (ORA), for the purpose of discussions with the government. At an Algeria-brokered peace meeting, the two last demands were considered consistent with Nigerien sovereignty, and a program of enlisting Tuareg youth in Niger's various military and paramilitary corps was designed and gradually implemented—a process which did incur the resentment of southerners. Niger's concessions to the Tuareg at the Ouagadougou agreements (1995) were much narrower than those of Mali (where the Tuareg had a similar tradition of resistance to state power), chiefly because of the state of Niger's interest in retaining control over the mineral riches of the north.

As peace was restored in the north, tourism was revived and southern immigration into the region of Agadez resumed on a large scale. By 2005, the region had become the second magnet of Niger's internal migration, after **Niamey**. This led to a new Berber Tuareg malaise: the influx of black southerners meant now a rise of intermarriages, and especially of prosperous or hard-working black men marrying Berber Tuareg **women**, prized for their fair beauty. More generally, it meant cultural contacts, which revived Berber Tuareg fears of losing their culture to a general Nigerien hodgepodge dominated by the Hausa and, to a lesser extent, the **Zarma-Songhay**. Moreover, while Libya had scaled down its support to Tuareg irredentism, a new strategic greed (rather than grievance) motivation arose with the development in the Sahara of large scale traffics—especially of narcotics and cigarettes toward Europe. Lastly, the main component of the peace agreement of 1995, the recruitment of front men into Niger's armed forces, was to be implemented in cooperation with former front leaders, and the latter tended to organize recruitment with a view to building patronage in their communities rather than rewarding former fighters.

All these motivations crystallized to cause the second rebellion in 2007. The Nigerien government, under President **Mamadou Tandja**, reacted with a hard-line position, especially after rebels inflicted severe initial defeats to the Nigerien army. The region of Agadez was put under a state of emergency, and the army was given free rein to restrict freedoms and organize repression. Northern **economy** was rapidly ruined, with many businesses relocating to the south and southern migrants leaving it in droves. Meanwhile, the main rebel group, the **Mouvement des Nigériens pour la Justice** (MNJ), attracted sympathies in the south through a blog that subjected the Nigerien government to relentless criticism on the basis of patriotism and social justice issues. Sympathies abated, however, in early 2008 when a posting showed a flag of a Tuareg republic, and internal criticism of the government's open war option declined in the south. Internationally, criticism came only from nongovernmental organizations and humanitarian organizations, and by mid-2008, reverses were more numerous in the rebel's camps than in the government's—a turn of events which ensured unhindered access to the uranium and coal mines.

The insurgency suddenly attracted wide international attention after a Canadian diplomat, working for the United Nations and desirous to seeing firsthand the sufferings of Tuareg communities in the northern parts of the region of **Tillabéri**, was abducted by armed Tuareg or **Arab** men working for **Al-Qaeda in the Islamic Maghreb**. As a result, international pressure on both Niger and Tuareg fronts (via Libya) increased and, by late 2009, peace was brokered at Tripoli. The main condition, to which the state of Niger agreed, was again recruitment of fighters in the various armed forces of the country. Indeed, while the rebellion, or more precisely the support it had within Tuareg society, had complex causes, its ultimate fuel is unemployment and poverty in a changing society, coupled with a tradition of confronting the state with violence.

The Tuareg rebellions of Niger and Mali have drawn the sustained attention of the Western **media**, which tend to see them as the romantic battle of a brave and free people against a despotic African state, with racial undertones. Facts and events, however, indicate that they are more sadly the expression of the greater vulnerability of the Tuareg to the forces of modernity and of the poverty of both Niger and Mali, materially unable to cushion that community from the inevitable effects of those forces. It is worth noting moreover that they have so far always involved a very low-intensity warfare (casualties numbering well below 1,000 both in the mid-1990s and in the 2007–2009 rebellions), which therefore has not caused national trauma or inflicted lasting damage to relations between the Tuareg and other populations in these countries.

TYENGA. A small ethnicity believed to be the oldest inhabitants of the lower **Niger River** valley, and especially of **Dendi**. The Tyenga language—which is nearly extinct—is also spoken by a few clans in **Nigeria**, though most members adopted **Songhay** and later also **Hausa** in the Nigeria side of the border. The Tyenga were pushed into the Dendi from Sokoto, which they had been chased out of by the Hausa. There are only a few thousands of them in Niger, though many more live in northern Nigeria. In Niger, they have tended to become assimilated in the **Zarma-Songhay** group, owing to their location in the south of the region of **Dosso**. See also ETHNIC GROUPS.

U

UNION DES FEMMES DU NIGER (UFN). Defunct **women**'s organization, created on 6 October 1958 under the leadership of **Hamani Diori**'s wife,
Aissa Diori, and scrapped by the military regime that toppled Diori in 1974.
In the following year, UFN was revived as the **Association des Femmes du
Niger** (AFN), but its ethos was quite different. Initially based on traditions of
women's self-help grouping in Niger, it emphasized participation of women
in improvement efforts in their communities but capped this with demands
specific to women, such as **education**, women-specific job creation, and
legislation to protect women as wives and mothers. UFN founded the local
women's network associations out of which AFN would subsequently build
its own constituency. Though it did not succeed in shaping Niger's legislation
to the advantage of women, it is at the origin of the remarkable presence of
women in the public sphere in Niger, which culminated in the struggles and
a number of victories in recent years.

UNION DES SCOLAIRES NIGÉRIENS (USN). Organization of **students**
which claims authority over all Nigeriens in school, from primary to higher
education, though it is viewed chiefly as a university students association
by the state. USN is one of Niger's earliest corporate interest associations,
having been founded in July 1960, and despite the very small number of
Nigeriens then in the formal education system. Its affiliated associations
now include the Union des Etudiants Nigériens de l'Université de Niamey
(UENUN) and several other Nigerien student associations abroad. Extremely
combative and a hotbed of radical leftist ideals in the 1970s–1980s, its officers were harassed during the *régime d'exception* (1974–1987), which it saw,
just as the previous **Hamani Diori** regime, as a stooge of imperialism; it was
recognized by government only in 1990.

   As the Nigerien government increasingly adopted austerity measures that
threatened scholarships and future careers, USN's planks started to focus less
on the transformation of society and politics and more on the corporate interests of students, and especially of university students. It was to protest against
World Bank–sponsored higher education budget cuts that UENUN organized

the fateful march of 9 February 1990 which led to the collapse of the **Second Republic**. USN was subsequently formally recognized by the state (28 December) and took part the following year in the **Conférence Nationale**, where its representatives were at the forefront of accusatory motions against the army and officials from the previous regimes.

The violent contestations between USN and successive Nigerien governments in the 1990s were all based on financial grievances and neglect for higher education infrastructures, which put the union in sync with army troops and trade **unions**. The evolution was also marked by strong underground ethnicization in the early 2000s, with hostility brewing between **Hausa** and **Zarma-Songhay** students in particular. The USN of the late 2000s has thus little left of what it was at its origins, and it was not unexpected that it vocally supported President **Mamadou Tandja**'s project at ending democratic governance in the summer of 2009. Tandja had bought out the union's leadership, while a majority of university students came from the regions of **Zinder** and **Maradi**, which provided the president's main support basis in the country.

UNION DES SYNDICATS DES TRAVAILLEURS DU NIGER (USTN). Successor, after the **coup d'état of 1974**, of the Union Nationale des Travailleurs du Nigers (UNTN). USTN used to encompass 31 individual **unions**. Uneasily tied to the military regime in the 1980s, it became in the 1990s a major force—via strikes or threats of strikes—in the drive toward political liberalization and **democratization** in Niger. USTN was thus instrumental in the coalition of associations and unions which forced President **Ali Saibou** to agree to democratization through the **Conférence Nationale** in 1991, a circumstance which led to an overrepresentation of the unions (considering that fully 80 percent of Nigeriens are active in the informal **economy** and the **agricultural** sector) in the gathering. This allowed them to sink the early measures taken by Ali Saibou's government to implement the International Monetary Fund's structural adjustment package while also resisting the imposition of a national solidarity tax aimed at bolstering the finances of the **armed forces** fighting **Tuareg** and **Toubou** insurgencies. USTN's resistance to structural adjustment was not ended even by the crisis of 1994, when the **CFA franc** was devalued and state workers were left unpaid for several months. It took the authoritarian clout of **Baré Maïnassara**'s regime to implement the drastic IMF and World Bank–sponsored austerity measures that included freezing recruitments, executing **civil service** cuts, and launching a **privatization** program (1996–1998). An aggrieved USTN responded by extensive strikes that paralyzed the administration and stalled the government, leading an exasperated Baré Maïnassara to state, "Everything's fine—we save money on their salary" (strikers were not paid for the days of strike).

In the late 1990s, several breakaway trade and labor unions emerged, of which the most important is the Confédération Démocratique des Travailleurs du Niger (CDTN), founded in 2001. Moreover, the liberalization of union law has extended unionization to a variety of petty urban professions, such as cab drivers, butchers, truck drivers, and even the beggars (who, in Niger's Islamic context, are considered a profession), and this was important in organizing the national resistance against a 19 percent increase of the value added tax on goods and services in 2005, during which a coalition of unions and civic associations against high costs of living in Niger virtually sent the entire country on strike for several days.

During the 2009 political crisis, USTN joined the five other trade confederations of the country under the leadership of CDTN to organize the first all union general strike of the country since the establishment of the **Fifth Republic** in 1999. Even more than the general strikes under the Baré Maïnassara regime, this one was politically motivated in opposition to President **Mamadou Tandja**'s project at ending democratic governance.

USTN's membership stands at 60,000, its secretary-general is Abdou Maigandi, and it is affiliated with the International Trade Union Confederation and the Organization of African Trade Union Unity. *See also* SIDIBE, ISSOUFOU; TAZARTCHÉ.

UNION ECONOMIQUE ET MONETAIRE OUEST-AFRICAINE (UEMOA). Regional economic integration organization that includes all the West African users of the **CFA franc currency**: Benin, Burkina Faso, Côte d'Ivoire, Guinea Bissau, Mali, Niger, Senegal, and Togo. UEMOA succeeded the Union Monétaire Ouest Africaine (UMOA) on 10 January 1994, two days before the devaluation of the union's single currency. In the late 1980s, the UMOA region was devastated by a recession which had been deemed by economists comparable only to the one which brought the former Soviet Union to its knees. The recession was caused by two major shocks: the general collapse of the price of mineral and **agricultural** raw materials (including **groundnut** and **uranium** in the case of Niger) and the real-term appreciation of the CFA franc, following the rise in value of its anchor currency, the French franc. This significantly lowered exchange rates with countries outside the Franc Zone (including, importantly, **Nigeria** in the case of Niger) at the worst possible time for the region. All macroeconomic indicators in the zone simultaneously deteriorated, leading to a devaluation of the currency and the adoption of macroeconomic reforms that necessitated the development of economic integration alongside currency integration. UEMOA therefore replaced UMOA—and also the old and dormant Communauté Economique d'Afrique de l'Ouest (CEAO)—and instituted mechanisms of macroeconomic surveillance to monitor the implementation of stringent convergence criteria.

Also, a number of community institutions were gradually set up: a Conference of Heads of State; a Council of Ministers organized by the community's central **bank**, the **Banque Centrale des États d'Afrique de l'Ouest** (BCEAO); a Commission of the UEMOA; a Court of Justice; a General Accounting Office (Cour des Comptes); an Interparliamentary Committee; a Regional Consular Chamber; and two banks, the BCEAO, which also created the Banque Régionale de Solidarité (BRS), and the Banque Ouest-Africaine de Développement (BOAD).

Technically efficient, UEMOA lacks an overarching political vision, and its main development initiatives, the common market (1998) and the common agricultural policy (Politique Agricole de l'Union, 2001) bestow on the region the colonial identity of a provider of agricultural raw materials (organization of commercial crops essentially in view of export toward the European Union) and a consumer of finished goods (very low common external tariffs inconsistent with the local development of industrial productive activities). This organization points to the fact that UEMOA is very much guided by French policy and continues, in a changed international context, the economic traditions of the **Afrique Occidentale Française** (AOF); indeed, all member-states of UEMOA, minus Guinea Conakry plus Guinea Bissau, were also member colonies of AOF. Moreover, UEMOA's agenda is on several levels in contradiction with that of the bigger West African regional organization, the **Economic Community of West African States** (ECOWAS), which was chosen by the African Union as its "pillar of integration" for the West African region in 2002. *See also* ECONOMY.

UNION NIGÉRIENNE DE CREDIT ET DE COOPERATIVE (UNCC).

Modern farmer's cooperatives were introduced in Niger by the colonial government in the form of contingency funds closely supervised by the administration, the Sociétés Indigènes de Prévoyance, de Secours et de Prêts mutuels (SIP), in 1934. Initially created in Algeria in 1893 to cope with natural calamities and the endemic plundering raids of Berber nomads, they became, in sub-Saharan territories such as Niger, important sources of funding for the *mise en valeur* (development cum exploitation) of the colonies, since membership was mandatory and was in fact a form of hidden taxation. SIPs could also serve, however, to subsidize rent **agriculture**, when they were forced to purchase unsold production through direct government interference. SIPs were replaced by more democratic Sociétés Mutuelles de Développement Rural in 1956, with a management board largely elected—two thirds—from among local people. Moreover, a law of 1955 allowed the creation of autonomous farmers' cooperatives, leading to the establishment of the two first grassroots farmers' cooperatives in Niger, those of the rice growers at Kollo (1955) and the market gardeners at **Mirriah** (1957).

At independence, the government opted for the development of a cooperative movement funded by cheap access to public credit from production to marketing. UNCC was set up in 1962 with the mission of organizing that development, in particular through the establishment of a network of affiliated local and departmental **unions**. The UNCC scheme operated relatively well until the mid-1970s, organizing the rent crop (**groundnut** and **cotton**) market and ensuring steady incomes to farmer producers. The *régime d'exception* reoriented UNCC toward more political roles, in its "developmental society" vision which required a corporate integration of the peasantry in the state. This evolution did away with the relative autonomy of farmers' cooperatives, an essential element of UNCC's success. Moreover, greatly owing to the decline of its key rent crops, UNCC market organization mission had lost much of its economic significance by the early 1980s, and its scrapping was demanded as early as 1982 by state agricultural experts (seminar of **Zinder**). In 1984, it was effectively removed and replaced with the Union Nationale des Coopératives (UNC), which closely tied the cooperatives to the state in a centralized pyramidal ordering consonant with the **Conseil National de Développement**'s general organization. After the financial crisis of the state came to a head in the late 1980s, UNC was among the first state organizations to be reformed. While the pyramidal control organization of the union was retained, the cooperatives were given greater autonomy—meaning in practice that they received less help from the state.

In the early **democratization** period (1991–1996), UNC was left dormant by the state, leaving farmers' cooperatives entirely to their own devices, a circumstance which stimulated the emergence of a variety of self-help farmers' organizations. In 1996, a law on rural cooperatives liberalized the creation of farmers' cooperatives and organizations and the following year, UNC was killed off. Since farmers had already started to organize before legislative permission, it came as no surprise that by 1999, the state has registered 1,114 farmers' organizations, which later consolidated in the course of the 2000s, creating the umbrella organization Plateforme Paysanne du Niger (PFPN), established in 1998.

UNIONS. Most of Nigeriens work in subsistence **agriculture** and the informal **economy**, so the number of workers' unions is very low, with two of them attracting most of workers in the formal sector: the historic **Union des Syndicats des Travailleurs du Niger** (USTN), a federation with a membership of around 60,000 and the breakaway Confédération Démocratique des Travailleurs du Niger (CDTN).

Aside from the large federations, and often affiliated to them, there exists in Nigerien towns a large array of occupational unions, and some of these—such as the cab drivers' union—have impressive clout and discipline. Unionization has grown apace with **democratization**, and many trade unions are also politically committed to the defense of democracy. That is in particular the case of the Syndicat Autonome des Magistrats du Niger (SAMAN), the judge's union, whose members have drafted all Niger's **constitutions** since 1991 and staunchly opposed President **Mamadou Tandja**'s project of scrapping democracy in 2009. USTN's 1990–1991 strikes were as political as they were corporate, mixing resistance to austerity and structural adjustment programs with vocal contestation of the authoritarianism of the **Second Republic**. Similarly, in 1996–1999, USTN organized strikes to oppose **Ibrahim Baré Maïnassara**'s restoration of authoritarian rule as well as **privatization** plans and attendant **civil service** cuts. In 2009, it was the breakaway CDTN that was at the vanguard of a kindred struggle against Tandja's own authoritarian project.

Owners' unions include the Syndicats des Commerçants, Importateurs et Exporteurs du Niger (SCIMPEXNI), Syndicat Patronal des Entreprises et Industries du Niger (SPEIN), and Syndicat des Transporteurs (ST), while certain professional unions are exclusively focused on the defense of occupational interests and standards, such as the Syndicat des Pharmaciens, Médecins et Chirurgiens Dentistes (SYMPHAMED).

UNIVERSITE ABDOU MOUMOUNI DE NIAMEY (UAM). Officially established in 1973 as the University of Niamey, it grew out of the Centre d'Enseignement Supérieur created in September 1971 to consolidate a number of postsecondary institutions that were founded after Niger's independence in 1960. It took its current name in 1992, after the distinguished physicist **Abdou Moumouni Dioffo** who had died the previous year. Dioffo was rector of the university in 1979–1983.

The only public university of the country until 2011, UAM has five faculties, three research institutes, one teachers' school, and a university hospital. Three affiliated technology institutes were set up in **Maradi**, **Tahoua**, and **Zinder**, and these are now the bases for the establishment of three new public universities in these towns.

UAM is built on an extended campus on the right bank of the **Niger River** (known as Harobanda, i.e., **Zarma** for "beyond the water"). As a result, the university is separated from the centers of power in downtown Niamey, which have developed on the left bank. **Student** demonstrators always need to cross the bridge for their marches to have an impact, and this led, on 9 February 1990, to a deadly clash between students and security forces who were trying to prevent them from crossing the bridge. Niger's democratic transition can be traced back to that event, which radically undermined the **Second Republic**'s legitimacy. Since the deadly clashes of February 2001, at which the students killed a gendarme, the state has moved ahead of the bridge and stationed permanently a gendarme post right by the campus.

The university currently has around 9,000 students.

UNIVERSITE ISLAMIQUE DU NIGER. See ISLAMIC UNIVERSITY OF SAY.

UNIVERSITY OF NIAMEY. *See* UNIVERSITE ABDOU MOUMOUNI DE NIAMEY.

URANIUM. Niger is currently the world's third-largest uranium producer, though with 8 percent of the global output, it is far behind Canada and Australia. Not all potential uranium reserves have been tapped, however, especially as the commodity suffered a global glut in the 1980s–1990s and further prospecting was abandoned for two decades. Uranium currently represents between 30 and 35 percent of Niger's exports (as opposed to an average of 80 percent in the late 1970s) and 5 percent of its gross national product. It has spawned a large array of subsidiary industries both in Niger and in **France**, including the maintenance of the **Route de l'Uranium**, usually contracted out to French enterprises.

Uranium was discovered in various parts of Niger's northern desert in the late 1950s and early 1960s by a French public agency, the Commissariat à l'Energie Atomique (CEA), and an agreement was signed with the Nigerien government to reserve exclusivity of access to France, which was then opting for nuclear energy as its main source of electrical power, and also as the basis for its so-called energetic independence. Commercial exploitation commenced in 1971, under the dual leadership of French-controlled COGEMA and the **Société des Mines de l'Aïr** (SOMAÏR). SOMAÏR has a Nigerien participation of only 36.6 percent via the **Office National des Ressources Minières** (ONAREM). Uranium boomed in the mid-1970s, and by the end of the decade, a community of 250 mostly French expatriates had settled in **Arlit** and **Akokan**, towns born of uranium exploitation and complete with all kinds of modern amenities, including stores directly supplied from France. Nigeriens also migrated there en masse from all parts of the country, and in the early 1980s, Arlit peaked at 60,000 people, becoming one of the largest urban centers in the country.

ONAREM was formed in December 1974 by the military regime to centralize and administer the government's uranium holdings and to watch over the government's interests. Moreover, owing to friction with France—which controls much of their market—the Francophone uranium-producing countries set up a joint-marketing organization whose task was to ensure high prices for the mineral.

Uranium exports from Niger increased rapidly after the first shipment of 400 tons in 1971. Niger's uranium mines started to be operated only five to six years after the discovery and assessment of deposits, as opposed to an average of 20 years for mines elsewhere. By 1974, SOMAÏR (then the sole fully operative **mining** company) was exporting 1,400 tons of processed/enriched mineral ore valued at 15 billion **CFA francs**. The **Compagnie Minière d'Akouta** (COMINAK) was created in June 1974 (with capital from CO-GEMA, ONAREM, and smaller shares for Japanese and Spanish investors) to exploit the underground mines at Akokan. With the entry of new uranium companies, tonnage increased to over 4,500, and (highly optimistic) estimations projected a possible annual production of 10,000 tons by the year 1990.

The uranium boom collapsed in 1980. Lower global demand, coupled with excess production by other countries, first seriously depressed prices and later severely eroded global demand. Niger's uranium production began to decline in the 1980s, since excess ore could not be sold economically at the depressed prices—30,000 CFA francs a kilogram in 1980; 17,000 in 1992. Production declined from a peak of 4,400 tons in 1980, first to around 3,500 tons, and then more sharply to 2,000 tons.

Uranium prices reached an all-time low in 2001, with international market prices falling to $7 (3,500 CFA francs) per pound. Then the volatile commodity price rose again to a peak of $137 (68,000 CFA francs) per pound in a bubble period in 2007—its highest value in 25 years. There was consequently a scramble back to deserted mines, including those in Niger, where France's **AREVA** started to invest heavily.

Uranium has played an important role in Niger's politics. The boom in the late 1970s contributes to explain some of the issues which led to the **Tuareg** unrest and open **rebellion**, but more importantly, uranium profoundly shaped Niger's relations with France. In the 1970s, France built for itself a situation of exclusivity in the exploitation of Niger's uranium, thereby generating prices unrelated to the world market and primarily shaped by demand in France and reexportation on the world market. Niger's government received royalties with little control over and no real understanding of the pricing of the commodity. In an attempt to remedy the large-scale economic crisis that was engulfing his regime, President **Hamani Diori** pressured the French to modify the terms of the exclusivity agreement and was toppled on the eve of a tense cycle of negotiation, with no intervention from the French squad stationed in Niamey, largely for the protection of his power. More generous terms were given to the new military regime of **Seyni Kountché**, especially since this reflected the condition of the market after the **oil** shock of 1973.

During the global glut of the 1990s, France consolidated its nuclear sector, and GOGEMA merged into AREVA, the biggest uranium company in the world today; AREVA, SOMAÏR, and COMINAK own respectively 66 percent, 63 percent, and 34 percent of shares in the **Imouraren** mines. Uranium had become competitive again in the late 2000s, and Nigerien uranium became the mainstay of AREVA's expansion strategy: It provides energy for over half France's nuclear electricity plants and is refined and reexported on the world market, together with AREVA's state-of-the-art nuclear technologies. To protect this central asset from growing Chinese competition, AREVA intensely lobbied Niger's government and politicians. This was done to the extent that, when President **Mamadou Tandja** decided to publicize his intention to unconstitutionally overstay his final term, he was able to do so in the approving presence of France's president, Nicolas Sarkozy, brought to **Niamey** as an AREVA high-level advocate.

Though the mines at Imouraren (the second largest in the world) are not yet in operation, AREVA already makes annual profits of upward to €430 million from its other Nigerien mines. It has adopted a policy of recruiting local staff and boosting its corporate responsibility profile with charity work throughout the country. Yet, as acute poverty and food crises show all too well, Niger profits very little, if at all, from the mineral riches dug from its soil. *See also* ECONOMY.

URANIUM ROAD. *See* ROUTE DE L'URANIUM.

URBAN CENTERS. In 2001, Niger's latest **census** numbered the country's urban population at 1,745,000 people, making up 16.2 percent of the country's population. The following is a ranking of Niger's 10 greatest urban centers. These figures are those of population within urban settlements, as opposed to within the larger administrative units of municipalities; for instance, the town (urban settlement) of **Tillabéri** has 16,000 people while the **commune** of Tillabéri, which includes a number of satellite villages, has 30,000 people. Thus, Tillabéri does not make it into this list. The figures reported here may therefore be smaller than those reported in individual entries, which at times record population within the municipalities:

1.	Niamey	676,000
2.	Zinder	171,000
3.	Maradi	147,000
4.	Agadez	78,000

5.	Tahoua	73,000
6.	Arlit	68,000
7.	Dosso	43,000
8.	Birni-N'Konni	43,000
9.	Tessaoua	32,000
10.	Dogondoutchi	29,000

VOIX DU SAHEL. Established as Radio Niger in 1958 and operating on 91.3 MHz FM and 9705 kHz shortwave, it gained its current name in 1974. Funded by the state, it has long been the only national radio station in the country, offering programs in French and seven Nigerien **languages**. Since the liberalization of the mid-1990s, Voix du Sahel has to compete with several national private radio stations, including Radio Anfani, Radio Television Dounia, and the Islamist Radio Television Bonferey. *See also* MEDIA.

W

WANKE, DAOUDA MALAM (?–2004). Of mixed **Hausa** and **Songhay** ethnicity, Wanké was born in the town of Yellou, south of **Dosso**, and was a major in Niger's military when he became the main hand in organizing a coup d'état against President **Ibrahim Baré Maïnassara** in 2009. The affair could be more accurately described as a successful assassination plot, and the Baré Maïnassara government remained in place after the killing of the president. It ran routine business while an institution set up by Wanké, the **Conseil de Réconciliation Nationale**, busied itself over the drafting of a new **constitution**, eventually adopted as the **Fifth Republic**'s constitution at the end of the year. The constitution enshrined a general amnesty to all those involved in the death of Baré Maïnassara, ensuring that Wanké would not be tried for the murder of Baré Maïnassara.

Wanké's nine-month rule also allegedly allowed him to raid the treasury and to subsequently set up a business after he left the presidency. But he soon afterward developed several different health problems, traveling to Morocco, **France**, and Switzerland to seek medical cure, and finally dying in **Niamey** in 2004. Rumors ascribed his sudden, incurable, and fatal illnesses to the dark magics of the celebrated animist shamans of the **Arewa**, the region of origin of Baré Maïnassara.

WEST AFRICAN ECONOMIC AND MONETARY UNION (WAEMU). *See* UNION ECONOMIQUE ET MONETAIRE OUEST-AFRICAINE.

WINDI. Zarma or **Songhay** for "compound," the basic social unit among settled West African populations. A *windi* is the dwelling of an extended family, made up of the smaller homes—sometimes as many as 20 or 30—of related nuclear families and their dependents. In the traditional **Zarma-Songhay** social hierarchy and snobbery, there are *windi beri* (great compounds, often translated into French as "*grande famille*") with an aura of nobility and wealth and *windi kaina* (little compounds, left untranslated) denoting lack of resources and character. *See also* GIDA.

WODAABE. Nomadic **Fulani** herders. The name means "the people of the taboo," that is, those who respect the ancient tenets, or taboos, of the Fulani culture, in contrast with urban-dwelling, **Islam**-practicing, little-Fula-speaking Fulani. Other Fulani call them **Bororo**, that is, "**cattle** camps dwellers," a word that is more common among outsiders. Woodabe herd the long-horned zebu cattle, following the Sahelian and Sudanic dry and wet seasons, traveling south–north as the rainy season sets in in the **Sahel**, in groups of several dozen relatives, typically several brothers with their wives, children, and elders. Their territory of transhumance extends from northern **Nigeria** and northern Cameroon into Niger and Chad, though the majority of Woodabe are Nigeriens. Although they have converted into Islam over the centuries, the Woodabe live chiefly by the old Fulani code of conduct, which has its most colorful manifestation among them in the *gerewol* festival, in the course of which young men showcase their beauty (especially in terms of white eyes and white teeth as well as height) and skills and are judged by young **women**, with the event often ending in a number of marriages. *See also* ETHNIC GROUPS.

WOGO. Small **ethnic group** found in Mali, **Nigeria**, and Niger. In Niger they are often found intermingled with the **Kurtey** on the **Niger River** islands off **Tillabéri** and **Niamey**. Arriving from the vicinity of Lake Debo to Bourra (Ansongo) in Mali and of Sarakhollé-**Sorko** ethnic mixture, a Wogo branch came down the Niger River, reaching its present locations in Niger and Nigeria starting round 1810. Islamized, the Wogo fought numerous battles with the Kurtey, whom they found settled on the islands before them. Courageous and very industrious, the contemporary Wogo are excellent agriculturalists, and many become seasonal farmworkers in Ghana. They are ethnically homogenous, and the three Wogo segments (in Mali, Niger, and Nigeria—the latter migrating from Bourra to Zaria around 1890) are strongly linked. Their numbers in Niger are hard to determine but estimates revolve around 30,000. They speak the **Songhay language**.

WOMEN. In Niger, as in any society, the situation of women is not homogeneous, but it has tended to become more homogeneous as the country itself has developed a national culture and in accordance with the evolution of its social and economic fortunes. What follows sketches the historical statuses of women in Niger's past, the rupture introduced by colonial modernity (1900–1960), evolution during the developmental state period (1960–1987), and current developments shaped by the conflicting rises of liberal **democratization** and Islamic Sunni orthodoxy since the early 1990s.

Before Colonization. In historical times, the life and conduct of women were governed by norms developed in ethnic cultures, which varied extensively and often displayed patterns of matriarchy alongside more conventional patriarchal elements. Thus, among the **Hausa** and the **Zarma-Songhay**, the traditional animist religions were managed principally by women priestesses, the most powerful deities (such as Harakoy Dikko among the Songhay or the **Doguwa** spirits among the **Arewa** Hausa) were female, and in some cases sovereign power belonged to women, as in the Arewa priestly kingdom (or more appropriately, "queendom") of **Lougou**. Among the Saharan communities of the **Tuareg** and the **Toubou**, women were in some measure the real heads of the household, as the tent and garden—the basic elements of Saharan material life—often belonged to them. Furthermore, older ethnic norms—still active among the Tuareg in particular—allow women to initiate divorce and inherit in the same way and amounts as men. Ancient Nigerien lives were spent on farmlands organized by large patriarchal households living on farms apportioned from communal domains. In these contexts, the division of labor favored monogamy or bigamy, the stability of marriages, and the entrenchment of reciprocal rights and obligations between husband and wife. Women could also accumulate personal wealth independent from the household, a right especially strengthened by Islamic rules.

While in modern days Nigeriens generally expect women to be wives and mothers but not leaders, recorded history among Niger's ethnic communities indicate that female leadership was not a rare thing in past centuries. The Songhay princess Kasai (16th century) and the Arewa queen **Sarraounia Mangou** (19th century) are still remembered in collective memory and celebrated as icons of Nigerien feminine power. Much of the art created and developed within ancient Nigerien societies was to a large extent the fruit of women's skills and labor: mural decorations, ornamental pottery and basketry, household weaving, singing and proverb making (hence the Hausa *zabia*, or diva, and the Zarma-Songhay *yasay*, or proverb making, done while pounding cereal), and so forth. On the whole, it appears that the roles and powers assumed by women in the past were superior to what occurs today.

Colonial Modernity. The colonial regime profoundly reshaped Nigerien societies to adjust them to the demands of the colonial **economy** through taxation, monetarization, and the installation of pyramidal hierarchies both at the local political level and within households. Additionally, the colonial administration promoted **Islam** as the culture that mediated its authority in Niger because it has written legal codifications administered by a recognizable (from the modern French perspective) judicial system. A side effect of these transformations was the destruction of the ancient status of women in

Niger, in social, legal, and economic terms. Socially, the rapid progress of Islam under colonization did away with the central place women occupied in communal religions and, more importantly, bestowed on men the control of the family and of patrimonial property (land especially) which had thus far been more equally shared. This change was in turn strengthened not only by the colonial administration's reliance on Islamic law but also by **France**'s own Napoleonic Code (Code Napoléon) in which women were considered legally minor and husbands held the *puissance paternelle* (paternal power) over the family—a legal concept only recently replaced with the concept of *autorité parentale* (parental authority) in France itself, but not in Niger.

The fact that so much power was socially and legally granted to men also had a substantial economic impact on women's lives. Although Islam in fact encourages women to accumulate their own wealth and to engage in trade, other circumstances, such as smaller inheritance share (half that of male siblings under Islamic law) and little access to land, limit their capital and general investment muscle in the Nigerien context. Moreover, in Hausaland, where Islamization brought also a fair degree of Arabization, the practice of confining women in the house developed especially among the class of notables, where the availability of pecuniary wealth could have otherwise spurred feminine business-mindedness. More generally, Islamic conceptions of feminine decency restricted the movement of women beyond the market-place, even though the Islamic rule of male guardianship of women in the public space never became a Nigerien custom.

Developmental State. Niger's two first political regimes—the **First Republic** of 1960–1974 and the *régime d'exception* of 1974–1987—were both authoritarian systems which bought into the idea of a corporatist organization of society in the service of national development. Ideas of specific rights and subgroup emancipation were largely foreign to them, especially during the first two decades of independence. In the period after colonial liberalization (1946), women had started to organize chiefly as self-help groups interested in fostering the well-being of the communities to which they belonged. Many such groupings cropped up, especially around old matriarchal traditions deriving from the ancient spirit cults of the Hausa and the Zarma-Songhay. It is on the basis of this associative movement that the government of **Hamani Diori** created, in 1958, the **Union des Femmes du Niger** (UFN). UFN's agenda was women emancipation through jobs and friendly legislation, but the ruling party, the **Parti Progressiste Nigérien** (PPN-RDA), also used it as a women's mobilization tool. In practice, in the developmental atmosphere of the era, UFN focused on the material burdens of women and the alleviation of domestic chores without addressing underlying impediments, leaving in particular Niger's laws and customs untouched in that regard. It is to be noted that these impediments were somewhat lighter in the first decades of Niger's existence as a nation-state than they have become in more recent times.

The military regime that succeeded the First Republic in 1974 reformed all of its corporatist bodies and generally granted them a greater autonomy, paradoxically. This was partly due to the fact that the new regime had no single-party organization into which to tie these bodies: They received their own budgets, granted by the state, but managed by themselves, and they could thus develop separate agendas. Thus UFN was replaced with an association, the **Association des Femmes du Niger** (AFN), which was created in 1975 in the excitement aroused by the United Nations World Conference on Women held that year at Beijing, China. The women who staffed the new association were much more educated than UFN's leadership, and they defined their mission in terms of rights specific to women, in social, legal, and economic terms. In 1976, they pressured President **Seyni Kountché** for the adoption of a comprehensive Family Code, which would end women's minor status, modify inheritance rules, and do away with the *puissance paternelle*. Kountché, however, had also created an **Association Islamique du Niger** (AIN), which viewed the code proposal as an attack on the Sunni Maliki legal tradition upheld by most of Niger's Muslim clerical classes.

Throughout the 1980s, the government engaged in a difficult balancing act between AFN and AIN, reaching, by the death of Kountché (1987), a consensus text which organized a series of concessions and opting out or opting in clauses for marriage contracts, though the thorny issue of inheritance was not entirely solved. However, the draft code was not adopted, as the new president, **Ali Saibou**, had to busy himself in reframing the regime of exception and installing the **Second Republic**. The short-lived and troubled existence of that regime put women's issues on the sideline, until the establishment in 1991 of two independent associations set up by highly educated women in the **civil service** and the judicial system: the **Rassemblement Démocratique des Femmes du Niger** (RDFN) and the **Association des Femmes Juristes du Niger** (AFJN). Dynamically headed by **Mariama Gamatié Bayard**, RDFN shaped the initial terms on which women's issues should be dealt with by any democratic Nigerien government.

Liberal Democracy and Islamic Orthodoxy. In the early 1990s, the adoption of liberal democracy—which was at the time a large wave overthrowing or temporarily upsetting Africa's authoritarian regimes—brought also the propagation of human and subgroup rights, often aided by generous funding from Western governments and nongovernmental organizations as well as the United Nations system. But in countries such as Niger, with a society increasingly subject to the cultural hegemony of orthodox forms of Sunni Islam, democratization also implied the propagation of Islamic law by associations created for that purpose. These were in particular, in the early 1990s, the **Association pour la Diffusion de l'Islam au Niger** (ADINI-Islam) that was very active in **Maradi** and the **Association Nigérienne pour l'Appel et le Salut Islamique** (ANASI). The outwardly secular state never formalized Islamic law in Niger's codes and administration, but it was very cautious not to antagonize Islamic associations on matters, such as the Family Code, on which they could easily mobilize the masses.

The 1990s decade was thus a combative period for both feminists and Islamists, during which each camp registered defeats and victories. The first victory was won by the feminist camp on 13 May 1991, when thousands of women marched on the building into which the **Conférence Nationale**'s preparation committee had convened. The women stormed into the building and demanded representation at the all-male conference, upon which five seats were granted to women. The day of 13 May subsequently became the Nigerien Woman's Day and a national holiday, but the more immediate reward was the establishment by the National Conference of a committee in charge of preparing and adopting a Family Code. Victory was closely followed by defeat, however, as the transition government failed to adopt the Family Code and electoral politics later kept ambitious politicians away from the hot-potato issue. Most Nigerien politicians did not consider women a constituency in their own right, and in fact, the key weakness of the feminist position in the country does come from the fact that the rights-advancing movement is entirely organized by a small nucleus of educated women, often well-to-do, and more connected to international networks than to the masses of downtrodden women in rural Niger.

However, the increasing number of feminine associations and pressure from the United Nations had enough traction over the years to slowly open up the political system to women's issues. In 1999, President **Daouda Malam Wanké**, a military officer with no political ambitions presiding over a transition government, rammed through the ratification of the United Nations Convention for the Elimination of all Discrimination against Women (CEDAW). In 2000, however, it was Prime Minister **Hama Amadou** himself who pushed through reforms on political and administrative quotas, guaranteeing 25 percent of all elective and cabinet positions to women, and setting up an Observatoire National de la Promotion de la Femme (ONPF) headed by cabinet minister Aïchatou Foumekoye. Amadou, the leading politician of the Zarma-Songhay region of Niger, is the only Nigerien politician to consider women as a constituency, clearly owing to the fact that Zarma-Songhay women have more successfully preserved their autonomy than women in other parts of the country, even among the popular classes. (Indeed, Amadou's main support organization was a women's political club, the Groupe de Réflexion sur le

Genre au Niger au Vingt-et-unième siècle, GRGN 21). These are, however, symbolic victories; in 2004, **elections** sent only 14 women to a National Assembly of 113 deputies—a 12.3 percent rate, below the legally determined quarter rate. The government appointed after 2004 moved closer to respecting the prescribed rate, with six women in a cabinet of 27 members (23 percent).

Subsequent Nigerien governments strove to respect the quotas, but though these are important developments, they are of interest chiefly to the small minority of educated middle class women who are in the position of vying for office. For the most part, women's lives in Niger are governed by Islamic rules and the laws of marriage, with (from the women's perspective) a number of more positive effects and an arguably greater deal of negative effects. Thus, in Nigerien practice, the household is entirely supported by the husband, with no participation from the wife, who is free to commit her income or wealth to purely personal pursuits, either in trade or in leisure. Moreover, the husband must clothe, feed, and pay for the **health** care of his wife or wives. In practice, Nigerien husbands strive to abide by these rules, but when they do not, serious social problems ensue, since there is no legal sanction for failing to fulfill a husband's obligations. In most cases, women burdened by domestic chores, especially in rural areas, have no time to actually engage in trade or leisure and may find themselves compelled to support the household in the case of the husband's failure to do so. Given the social restrictions imposed upon them, the unwarranted obligation may be quite daunting and goes a long way toward explaining the great poverty of a significant portion of Nigerien households.

The Islamic legal restrictions on inheritance—the main channel of resource transfer in Nigerien society—are even more serious: Girls inherit half the inheritance of boys, a provision technically justified by the fact that, in the view of Maliki law, the boys' inheritance is usufruct and should enable them to provide for their sisters if the latter are repudiated by their husbands or are widowed. Wives inherit even less: one eighth of the husband's patrimony, to be further subdivided if they are co-wives in a polygamous household. These restrictions are drastically implemented when it comes to inheriting land and real estate, all important sources of stable income and financial security. Lastly, wives cannot initiate divorce under Islamic Maliki law, even though they can dispute the terms of the divorce, usually at the civil case courts maintained by AIN. These courts are an unofficial but state-sanctioned outgrowth on Niger's judicial system, which adjudicate only civil cases on the basis of arbitration rather than litigation. Women in urban areas may also bring their case to the secular courts, where they can initiate a divorce on the basis of the civil code inherited from France, and through litigation. In practice, this rarely happens, especially outside of Niamey.

In the mid-1990s, Niger's feminist organizations adopted a strategy of national consolidation to coordinate their efforts and created the **Coordination des ONG et Association Féminines du Niger** (CONGAFEN), which established linkages with the **Association Nigérienne de Défense des Droits de l'Homme** (ANDDH) and other rights-defending groups in the country. CONGAFEN focuses on the promotion and implementation of international conventions on women's rights, which feminine organizations consider as temporary compensations for the lack of a Family Code. The organization was instrumental in pushing the Nigerien government to sign the African Union Maputo Protocol on Women's Rights in 2004, but the National Assembly repeatedly refused to ratify the document, which vocal conservative deputies described as a Western ploy to destroy the Nigerien family. A more promising front is educational policy, where two decades of girls' **education** promotion extensively funded by Western donors has started to bear fruit in the main urban centers; in Niamey, certain schools have now more female students than male students and initial equality of schooling is becoming the norm—though the rate of girls dropping out, often for reasons of marriage, is still much higher than the rate of boys doing the same.

The organizations represented within CONGAFEN are all secular, with the exception of the Roman Catholic Union des Femmes Catholiques du Niger. A year prior to its establishment, a group of Islamic associations had founded the Association des Femmes Musulmanes du Niger (AFMN), in 1994. AFMN strategically demands the adoption of a Family Code, just as all other feminine associations, under the condition, however, that the code be entirely based on Islamic law. AFMN does not represent the position of all Islam-slanted feminism in Niger, however. A deep doctrinal rift exists between an Orthodox Sunni current, currently best represented by one of AFMN's key leaders, **Malama Houda**, and feminist preachers such as the late Malama Zeinab, famed for her virulent and sarcastic attacks on masculine power, and **Malama Zaharaou**, representative of the Sufi **Tijaniyya** position which underplays Islamic law in favor of social and educational work.

In 2003, Niger adopted a penal code that includes a number of provisions protective of women, providing for jail terms in cases of domestic battery and female genital mutilation. The latter, which had always been very marginal in Niger, was reduced by half by 2006 (from 5 to 2.2 percent), thanks to a proactive policy of implementation. The former measure will have greater effects only as Niger's formal judicial system extends its as yet paltry reach in the country. Indeed, this detail points to the fact that women's plight in Niger is to a great extent an outcome of the weakness of state organizations, normally in charge of extending and implementing individual and group rights but severely curtailed by the 1990s structural adjustment policies and the virtual scrapping of the national development project.

YACOUBA, HENRI DUPUIS (General) (1924–2008). Former inspector general of the Niger **armed forces**, and at the time the most senior officer in the armed forces. Yacouba was born on 10 March 1924 in Timbuktu (French Sudan, now Mali) and was trained from an early age for a military career by his father, a soldier in the French colonial armies. Just prior to independence he was promoted to officer rank and moved to **Niamey** as one of the few indigenous officers of the newly created Niger army. Yacouba then served as head of personnel services in the Niger Ministry of Defense (December 1961–August 1966) while simultaneously being *chef de cabinet* of the minister of defense (December 1962–August 1966). He was then appointed director of national defense in the ministry of the same name and in July 1973 also assumed the post of inspector general of the armed forces. After the **coup d'état of 1974**, in which Yacouba was involved in a nonactive way, he was promoted; by August 1976 he had attained the highest rank in the armed forces, as a general, the first in Niger. Immediately after the coup he was brought into the military cabinet as minister of **education**, youth, and sports. In a 1975 shuffle, he dropped the portfolios of youth and sports, and in another shuffle the same year he was named minister of posts and telecommunications. The following year Yacouba was implicated in the **coup attempted on 15 March 1976**, having recently been dismissed from the cabinet. At the time his "driving ambition" was cited as the reason both for his purge from the cabinet and for his involvement in the conspiracy. He was reintegrated into the government in a minor, mostly honorific, post consequent to a reassessment of his minor role in the 1976 plot, and he served in that capacity between 1976 and 1985, when he was retired from the armed forces. After **Seyni Kountché**'s death in 1987, Yacouba—though in retirement since 1985—was reappointed by General **Ali Saibou** to his honorific post, as token compensation for his being shunted aside by Kountché.

YAKUDIMA. In the precolonial **Damagaram** hierarchy, a son or brother of the sultan, and heir apparent, who resided as governor of the village of Damagaram ta-Kaya.

YENENDI. Important **Holley** rite, usually performed in May or June (at the end of the dry season) and aimed at invoking the rains. It is especially celebrated in the **Tillabéri** region.

YUNFA (r. 1801–1808). The last king of the **Gobir** before the kingdom was downsized by the **Fulani** jihad of **Usman dan Fodio**. Yunfa, a nephew of **Bawa Jan Gwarzo**, pursued the policy of opposition to Islamic insurgency that started in the kingdom during the reign of that monarch a few decades earlier. By his accession, however, the Muslim insurgents had become a conquering force who was able to besiege several times **Alkalawa**, the capital of Gobir, the most powerful **Hausa** polity until the late 18th century. Jihadists eventually stormed Alkalawa in 1808, killing Yunfa in the battle for the city.

Z

ZAKARA, MOUDDOUR (1916–1976). Former *amenokal* of the Ouil-liminden **Tuareg**, former minister of finance and of Saharan and nomadic affairs, and after 1959 in effect minister resident in **Agadez**. Born in 1916 in Diguina (**Filingué**) and eventually (after 1952) *chef de canton* of Imanan (composed of largely sedentary Tuareg) and *amenokal* of the Ouilliminden Kel Dinnik (one of the largest Tuareg confederations), Zakara was educated in **Niamey** and worked as a simple clerk in the colonial treasury (1932–1938). He was transferred to **Tahoua** in 1938, and between 1940 and 1947 he served as **Tamasheq** interpreter in the Nomad Affairs Division of the colonial government's Tahoua headquarters. Between 1947 and 1957 special agent and representative of the government (after his appointment as *chef de canton*), Zakara was elected to the **Territorial Assembly** in 1957 as **Mouvement Socialiste Africain** deputy and in 1959 as Union pour la Communauté Franco-Africaine deputy, serving in that body as its vice-president. In 1958 he was brought into the cabinet of **Hamani Diori** as secretary of state for internal affairs, a key post, and served in this capacity until 1962. Zakara's responsibilities were enlarged in 1965 to include posts and telecommunications. In 1970 his duties were again redefined as minister of finance, Saharan, and nomadic affairs, and he held these portfolios until the **coup d'état of 1974**. The treasurer of the association of customary chiefs in Niger, he participated in various traditional ceremonies, leading the traditional *cure salée* departure of the Ouilliminden livestock in August. After the 1974 coup d'état, Zakara was imprisoned for embezzlement of 55 million **CFA francs** and fiscal fraud of 19 million CFA francs—the second-worst offender of the Diori associates. He was serving a jail sentence for those offenses when he fell ill and died in the hospital in May 1976.

ZAKI, MAREMAWA ALHADJI ALI (1939–). Born into the royal family of the **Katsina** in **Maradi**, Ali Zaki studied public administration at Niamey's Centre de Formation Administrative (precursor of the **École Nationale d'Administration et de Magistrature**) and worked as cabinet director to the national **education** minister, **Dan Dicko Dan Koulodo**, in 1972–1974. After the **coup d'état in 1974**, he followed Dan Dicko Dan Koulodo to the

Agence de Coopération Culturelle et Technique (ACCT) of the Francophone countries in Paris. Upon returning to Niger, Zaki resided in Maradi where he dabbled in some trading involving rice and petroleum products with **Nigeria**. In 2003, the ruling king of the Katsina in Maradi, **Bouzou dan Zambadi**, gave him the title of *Maremawa*, traditionally bestowed on "wise princes" in the Katsina court.

In October 2005, some time after the death of Bouzou, he was elected king of the Katsina in Maradi by the royal electoral college, and he was formally appointed by the state in November of the same year. In September 2010, the state elevated the kingship of Maradi to the rank of sultanate in Niger's traditional peerage, and the official title of the customary ruler of Maradi is henceforth, in French style, *Sultan du Katsina-Maradi*.

***ZALEY.* Zarma-Songhay** musical genre famous in the 1940–1950s, and dominated by **women** singers who often celebrate the virtues of the men whom they appreciated or liked. As a result, the word *zaley*, or *zalay*, came to mean "amorous seeking," indiscriminately of men toward women or vice-versa. The *zaley* is arguably the first cool and fashionable musical genre to have captured a young audience in Niger, before the international trends of the *yéyé* (from **France**), reggae, disco, and others. The genre was in particular represented by **Haoua Issa**, nicknamed Haoua Zaley. *See also* DANCE AND MUSIC.

ZAMBO, KADADE (1947–). A wrestling champion from **Tahoua**, Zambo was one of the stars of Niger's national wrestling championships in the late 1970s and early 1980s. He was especially famous for being unlucky, as he never won the top champion saber despite usually reaching the finals, a circumstance that made him the favorite of the public until his retirement in 1983, with gifts and a large cash award from President **Seyni Kountché**.

ZARMA (also Djerma, Zerma, Dyerma). The Zarmas' homelands (the **Zarmaganda**, northeast of **Niamey**, and encompassing Zarmataray to the southeast and around Niamey) are all located within the territory of Niger, unlike with any other ethnicity of the country, but they have large diasporas chiefly in Ghana and Côte d'Ivoire (where they are known as Zaberma) as well as smaller diasporas in **Nigeria** (Kebbi) and as far afield as the Republic of Sudan where a Zarma-speaking community traces its origins to stranded Zarma Mecca pilgrims. Moreover, in their language and manners, the Zarma are barely distinguishable from the neighboring **Songhay**; although both groups claim difference, they are usually lumped together as the **Zarma-Songhay** or the Songhay-Zarma in Niger's public discourse.

Like the Songhay, the Zarma have a system of vocational caste. Each caste derives or is linked to a preternatural force governing its main occupation; so wood artisans and lumberjacks are linked to the spirits of trees, potters to the spirits of earth and fire, hunters to the doubles of animals and their protecting spirits, and so forth. The priestly caste of the *zima* reproduces itself through initiation rather than inheritance, and is thus not really a caste. *Zima* are in relation with the dead, and they can serve as mediums for **Holley** spirits. Though in recent times they appear to have been somewhat displaced by the Islamic clerics, it is also the case that they have transmitted some of their roles and practices to this newer category of priests. All of these traits apply to the Songhay as well.

A wide array of oral traditions offers disparate accounts of the origin of the Zarma, the most common referring to their Malinke and Sarakhollé origins from Mali, whence they migrated southeastward. Their main towns are Niamey, **Dosso**, and **Ouallam**. They were patchily Islamized until the 16th-century efforts of the Songhay emperor **Askia Mohammed** and of some of his successors to establish **Islam** as the dominant religion and culture in their realms. Though Islam receded after the collapse of the **Songhay Empire**, it remained a faint element in Zarma culture, revived in the 19th century's contacts with the **Fulani**. These consisted of wars of plunder and conversion from Fulani jihadists as well as in the more benign influence of the Fulani Sufi master **Mamane Diobo** who founded a **Qadiriyya** congregation in the town of **Say**, between Niamey and Dosso. Diobo in particular channeled the influence of the Fulani Islamic government of the Sokoto Empire in the area.

In the 17th century, the Zarma peacefully settled the **Dallol Bosso** valley, which they called **Boboye**, and they proceeded from there to the area of Dosso, allying themselves with its original inhabitants to fight the **Maouri** of the Dallol Raffi. Under pressure from the **Tuareg** to the north, the Zarma also soon faced the jihads of Fulani armies, including those of the Sokoto Empire, which made inroads into Zarma lands and was not pushed back until around 1870.

The French arrived in the Zarma regions in the late 1890s, at a time when the *zarmakoy* of Dosso was striving for prominence over other Zarma chiefs and warlords. The French struck an alliance with Dosso to control the area, but the task proved daunting as they soon faced widespread unrest, spurred by their efforts to impose hierarchy and taxation on the looser political system of the Zarma. This led to a series of revolts in 1905–1906, with a first insurgency organized by **Alfa Saibou**, the blind cleric of **Kobkitanda**, and involving also the Satiru insurgency against the British in the neighboring Sokoto area, followed by a second insurgency under leadership from the Songhay of Karma, but with a strong participation from the Zarma. The brutal quelling of these revolts by the French led to the consolidation of the *zarmakoy* of Dosso as leader of the Zarma (although that leadership remained generally circumscribed in reality to Dosso and its vicinity) and, more importantly, to an opening of Zarma society to French influence. Never organized in an extensive state or kingdom, the Zarma presented the French with a fierce but anarchic resistance (1905–1906), which afterward gave way more easily to accommodation of and participation in French rule.

Yet during the colonial period, the Zarma developed a seasonal migration pattern to the southern coastal areas of West Africa (to the Gold Coast, now Ghana), in part to flee French taxation and also owing to their poor lands, both of which causes were at the origin of the many famines that dotted the 20th century in the Zarma lands. Over time, this has created large Zarma diasporas in Benin, Togo, Ghana, and Côte d'Ivoire, with considerable impact on the economic well-being and outlook of the Zarma homelands in Niger. In most countries where they have settled, the Zarma have acquired a reputation for hard work and honesty.

The Zarma **language** is spoken in Niger by some 2 million people and is part of the Nilo-Saharan family of languages. Together with the Songhay, the Zarma make up 22 percent of the population of Niger, a bloc of about 3 million people, second only to the Hausa in that constellation. Given this minority position (albeit a large one), the Zarma-Songhay saw their political dominance (as defined by the occupancy of the presidency) come to an end with the onset of multiparty **elections** in 1993. Since then, the Zarma have tended to vote for **Moumouni Adamou Djermakoye**'s **Alliance Nigérienne pour la Démocratie et le Progrès** (ANDP Zaman Lahiya), and for that reason, the **Hausa** language name of the party (*zaman lahiya*, peacefulness) was jocularly turned into *zarmay laya* (Zarma for "the line of the Zarma"). That is true especially for Zarma in the Dosso area, while those in other areas have tended to follow the leadership of the **Mouvement National pour la Société de Développement** (MNSD Nassara)'s Songhay bosses. *See also* ETHNIC GROUPS.

ZARMA-SONGHAY. Sometimes also referred to as Songhay-Zarma. Though the **Zarma** and the **Songhay** claim to be different ethnicities in Niger, they speak the same **language** (with minor dialectal differences in pronunciation) and share the same customs and social organization. In fact, the Zarma are believed to be a Songhay subgroup, either originally or through assimilation. In Niger, they are lumped together for practical purposes, and they thus form a large ethnicity occupying the western regions of the country, and assimilating there a variety of minority groups with clear linguistic and cultural differences, such as sedentary **Fulani**, the **Gourmantché**, the

Tyenga, the **Maouri**, the **Soudié**, and the Goubé; the latter four groups are considered **Hausa**, under different names (respectively, Tyengawa, **Arawa**, Kurfeyawa, and Goubawa), when the Zarma-Songhay regions transition into the Hausaland to the east. *See also* ETHNIC GROUPS.

ZARMAGANDA. The lands northeast of **Niamey**, around **Ouallam**, constituting most of the *département* of Ouallam. The name means Zarmaland and the area has served as the base from which the **Zarma** are believed to have moved and colonized much of the regions southeast of Niamey (**Boboye**) starting in the 17th century. The tomb of Mali Bero, the mythical Zarma hero who is said to have carried the Zarma here from the shores of the Lake Debo (Mali) on a flying mat, is in the Zarmaganda, where it is still today a revered shrine. Both Zarmaganda and the regions later colonized by the Zarma are called Zarmataray—an untranslatable word designating the prevalence of Zarma manners and **language**.

ZARMAKOY. Executive office in Zarma villages. It has never quite evolved into a kingship outside of **Dosso** but has often tended to be monopolized by a small number of aristocratic families in any location.

ZEINE, ALI MAHAMANE LAMINE (1965–). Born in **Zinder**, Zeine is an economist who started a career in Niger's finance ministry in 1991, prior to finishing up his studies with a doctoral degree earned at the University of Marseilles (**France**) in 1998. In 2001, he became President **Mamadou Tandja**'s cabinet director and was subsequently appointed finance and **economy** minister in 2003. A close associate of Tandja, Zeine remained in post throughout the two terms of his patron, surviving the fall of Prime Minister **Hama Amadou**'s government in 2007. As finance minister, Zeine was very much appreciated by the World Bank and the International Monetary Fund for the manner in which he implemented their stringent conditionalities through the country's economic policies. He was also a loyal handyman for Tandja in his mobilization of financial resources during the preparation of his constitutional putsch against the **Fifth Republic** in 2009. As such, Zeine was the only cabinet minister, together with Prime Minister **Ali Gamatié** and interior minister **Albadé Abouba**, to be put under house arrest for some time after the **coup of 18 February 2010**, while his files were being investigated. Unlike Abouba, but like Gamatié, he was quickly released.

ZIBO, ALI (1949–2007). Decorated for his music and singing at the first National Youth Festival held in **Zinder** in 1976, Zibo went on to study telecommunications in Dakar in the early 1980s but did not forget his earlier inclinations. Upon his return to Niger, he embraced a career in music and artistic activism. He is especially well known on the latter score for his involvement with the copyright protection agency Bureau Nigérien du Droit d'Auteur (BNDA), of which he was the president, and for his activities in several international music competitions. While he lacked the glamour and celebrity of contemporary pop artists such as **Alhadji Taya**, **Moussa Poussi Natama**, and **Saadou Bori**, his work was arguably more important as he directed all the trend-setting bands of Nigerien beat from the 1970s to his premature death in 2007: Amicale de Niamey (1972–1974), Les Ambassadeurs du Sahel (1974–1976), Caravane (1976–1985), and Sahel Jazz du CFPM Taya (2003–2005). He was also the leader of the celebrated Groupe Musical Sogha. *See also* DANCE AND MUSIC.

ZIKA, DAMOURE (1923–2009). A traditional healer and film actor, Zika hailed from a long line of **Sorko** (**Songhay** fishers and masters of the river) healers. Still a child, he became a friend of **Jean Rouch**, when the latter was studying and filming the art of his grandmother, a renowned healer and spirit medium. Zika subsequently appeared in most movies made by Rouch, including the early *Bataille sur le Grand Fleuve* (1950–1952), in which his preteen self is spotted splashing about in the **Niger River**. In the 1960–1970s, Zika featured in nearly all the movies shot in Niger, working for **Oumarou Ganda**, **Moustapha Alassane**, and **Djingaraye Maïga**, as the male equivalent of sorts of **Zalika Souley**. Unlike Souley, however, Zika was able to cash in on his fame to develop his knowledge of traditional medicine, establish a traditional healing clinic in Niamey, and host a show on the topic on national radio **Voix du Sahel**. He was injured in the 2004 car crash in which Jean Rouch died, and died in Niamey in April 2009, following a long illness. *See also* CINEMA.

ZILLY. *See* BOUKARY, SANI MALAM CHAIBOU.

ZIMA. Priestly caste of the traditional **Songhay** spirit rites. One is not born into the caste, however, but initiated into it. A *zima* is a medium who is capable of receiving the **Holley** spirits in himself and of serving as a bridge between the human and spirit worlds. Forbidden to intercede with the major spirits, the *zima* are the priests most in contact with the average person. A superior high caste, hereditary, closed, and very secretive *zima* group, the **Sonyanké** are the nobility of the *zima* and deal directly with the major deities of the Songhay spirit world.

ZINDER. Niger's second-largest city and historic capital of the **sultanate of Damagaram**. The town has a population of 171,000. The Communauté

Urbaine de Zinder is also the headquarters of the region of Zinder, which has a population of about 2 million and a territory of 152,863 sq km. The main **ethnic groups** are the **Hausa**, the **Fulani**, and the **Kanuri** with minorities of **Tuareg** and **Toubou**. The region includes the *départements* of **Gouré**, **Magaria**, **Matameye**, **Mirria**, and **Tanout**. As Niger's only major city in the immediate precolonial era, the town served for a while as the capital of the colony (1911–1926).

Despite the relocation of the capital to **Niamey**, Zinder remains an important center in its own right, squarely in the three M triangle—the **Mirriah**, **Matameye**, **Magaria** area of **groundnuts**, cereals, and sugar cane production—with a large **cattle** market directed at Nigerian trade. During the precolonial era an important terminus of the trans-Saharan caravan trade, Zinder rose to prominence slowly as a result of the expansion of the sultanate of Damagaram in the 19th century. It greatly benefited during that period from the shift in caravan trade away from **Katsina** to Kano consequent to the Fulani conquests of **Usman Dan Fodio**. It also possessed a "double" slave market to which many suppliers flocked (the kingdom's two biggest slave markets were both in Zinder—at **Zongo** and **Birni**), shipping northward once a year (to Fezzan via **Aïr**) slaves and kola nuts, and receiving guns and cowrie shells (for use as a **currency**) from the coast. The French dominance in the early 20th century did away with the trading in slaves and reoriented commercial activities toward the southern coast. As an administrative capital and, by the 1930s, a center of groundnut production, Zinder was not quite as adversely affected by the changes as might have otherwise been the case.

Zinder is located 908 km east of Niamey, 488 km south of **Agadez**, and 604 km west of **N'Guigmi**. The oldest part of the town is the *birni*, the old walled city, which is still surrounded by remnants of Sultan **Tanimoun**'s massive 5-km-long ramparts (mid-19th century). One kilometer from it (the separating area is filled in by the modern urban sprawl of residential areas and a military camp) is Zongo, which was once a Saharan **caravan** stop and residence. Today it is Zinder's liveliest commercial center. Dominating the town is the Camp Tanimoun, renamed from Fort Cazemajou after independence. Zinder is famous for the neem trees that line up the road to its entrance over several kilometers as well as the landscape of large boulders found in its downtown areas.

The town numbered only 9,200 people in 1951, but the population climbed to over 33,000 by 1971, overtook Maradi as the second-largest city in Niger around 1980, and currently stands at around 171,000. For a long time Zinder—and not Niamey—was the principal headquarters of the various European trading houses purchasing Niger's commercial crops (**cotton**, groundnuts), though today most have relocated their headquarters to Niamey while retaining branches in Zinder and Maradi. The latter, building stronger connections with the Nigerian cities of Katsina and Kano, has indeed grown much more commercially livelier than Zinder.

Within the *birni* the tombs of three former sultans can be found—Tanimoun, Hanatari, and Moustapha. The city has a big Thursday market and is a major artisan center.

ZODI, IKHIA (1919–1996). Educator, early political leader, and former cabinet minister. Of **Tuareg** origins and one-time director of the Institut Fondamental d'Afrique Noire (**Niamey** branch), Zodi was an early party militant in the **Parti Progressiste Nigérien** (PPN-RDA). In 1946–1947 he joined in the groundswell of opposition in the party that gave rise to the Union des Nigériens Indépendants et Sympathisants (UNIS) faction and later political party. One of its prime leaders despite his youth, his attempt in 1955 to force the party to affiliate internationally with the Indépendants d'Outre-Mer parliamentary group split the party apart and resulted in the desertion of most of its leaders and membership. Some time later, the party changed its name and affiliated with IOM's successor, the Convention Africaine. Earlier, Zodi had secured his **election** to the French national assembly (beating **Hamani Diori** in 1951) and in 1952 was elected **Territorial Assembly** deputy from **Filingué**, and between 1952 and 1957 he sat on the grand council of the **Afrique Occidentale Française** (AOF). In December 1958, he made his peace with PPN and was integrated into Diori's cabinet as minister of **education**, youth, and sports. In December 1960 he was appointed minister of African affairs. It was in that role that he was implicated in the 1963–1964 anti-Diori attempted coup, purged, sentenced to death, and with the sentence commuted, imprisoned in a military camp. He was not released from prison until February 1971. For all practical purposes, Zodi's driving ambition brought his early promising career to a standstill. He has played no significant role in Niger since. *See also* DIALLO, HASSAN A.; POLITICAL PARTIES.

ZONGO. Throughout most of West Africa and parts of Equatorial Africa, the "temporary" residence of strangers. The *zongo* is often outside the village or town proper. (Often with rapid urbanization, the *zongo* finds itself swallowed up, becoming the center of the town.) In general, however, it is a separate and distinct quarter altogether, which in larger *zongos* are divided internally along ethnic lines. The term means "thorn enclosure," implying temporary living quarters, as opposed to habitation within the *birni*, or fortified city. Of Niger's various *zongos*, that of **Zinder** is by far the most important. In Niamey a *zongo* quarter has existed since 1936 (though a *sarkin zongo* has existed since 1906). It sprang up next to the town's then only market (today's *Petit Marché*).

Bibliography

INTRODUCTION

The people of what is now Niger are first described in a book by the chatty Arab traveler Abu Abdullah Ibn Battuta in the late 1350s, where they appear as the scary forerunners of the integrally black lands farther south, in which no light-skinned person could hope to dwell with safety. This is perhaps fitting, given the name of the country—although the fear may have been unwarranted. Ibn Battuta went in the Sahel to visit the Muslim monarch of the Mali Empire, and over two centuries later, Muslim Songhay chroniclers such as Mahmoud Kati, Abderrahman Sadi, and others talked far more extensively about the region and its populations (*Tarikh el-Fettach, Tarikh es-Soudan*, and other writings) than he could do.

The scholarly traditions supported by the large empire of the Songhay disappeared, however, some decades after the fall of the polity, and writing—especially on the lands now included in the Republic of Niger—became rare and confidential. Still, the darker period that set in seems to have produced many written documents—in both Arabic and local languages using Arabic script—aside from the lists of monarchs (*Chronicle of Agadez*) that are already publicly available, but they are privately kept by clerical families in the country, under lock and key. The *Manuscrits Arabes et Ajami* (MARA) section of Niamey's *Institut de la Recherche en Sciences Humaines* (IRSH) has been conducting for the past few years an inventory of these writings, which may fill in gaps—despite the expected narrowness of their focus—on our knowledge of Niger's past after the fall of Songhay.

Of course, the bulk of what came in modern times—starting in the mid-19th century with Heinrich Barth's witty and enlightened remarks on a section of central Niger running north–south from Aïr to Gobir—is in European languages, mostly French, however with English providing a mounting body of works. Indeed, the growth of literature on Niger—contrasting with a meager scholarly output in the first half of the past century—has been such that what follows should be taken much more as a bibliographic guide of sorts rather than as a comprehensive or exhaustive bibliography of Niger. So the notes start with some general studies covering grounds on African—especially West African—history, a number of themes important to contemporary Niger (democracy, the Sahel), and the colonial policy of France in the region. The latter include some gems, such as Robert Delavignette's *Afrique Occidentale Française*, a spectacularly well-written and well-informed personal reflection on enduring West African realities that clearly transcends its period of composition.

Because of the peculiar history of the southern Saharan areas roughly corresponding to Niger's Ténéré desert—a story of lush and wet plains supporting hulking saurians, which turn into a hospitable savannah for early humans before gradually drying into the barren wilderness that they now are—archaeology has had a field day in Niger. The greatest deal of the work here was done during the late colonial and early independence period by French expeditions—with the output of Henri Lhote towering—though new finds are still being made in recent years, as is shown by the Gado, Maga, and Oumarou 2001 walkthrough.

Nigerien historians call Niger before French colonization *l'espace nigérien* ("the Nigerien area") to specify that for centuries past, there was no sovereign territory that bore the name. Therefore, the early accounts and monographs of European travelers (or explorers as they have been historically called) and literati generally encompassed sections of West and Central Africa larger than the "Nigerien area." After French administration settled, colonial officials published articles on the specific section of

Niger that they were administering, and the first studies of the entire colony were also motivated by practical policy: thus Abadie's *Colonie du Niger* of 1927 or Marty's study on Islam in Niger in 1931 (to be found in the "Islam" subsection of "People, Society, Religion" here). In relation to the latter point, let us note that unlike in the previous editions of this dictionary, authors and texts generally have single entries, even though many works could have figured equally fittingly in various subdivisions of the bibliography. The bibliography is thus shortened and focused, with the downside being that the reader should have in mind several levels of relevance when looking for a particular work or author.

Moreover, the bibliography now includes many works by Nigerien scholars who have become increasingly more productive in the 1990–2000s, and this is one of the reasons behind the transformation of the former "Anthropology and Ethnology" section into a "People, Society, Religion" section. The anthropological and ethnological studies which were the prevailing approach of Nigerien populations by colonial-era scholars are still represented here, and they are in general well worth consulting. But new perspectives in the West and the growing output of Nigerien scholars in all fields previously covered by colonial anthropo-ethnology have evidently profoundly reshaped the literature in this domain, making it less fascinated by exoticism and more attracted to issues, manners, and thought. Good examples of this evolution in the same geographic sector of Niger are Susan Rasmussen's intellectually sophisticated work on the Tuareg and Aboubacar Adamou's discriminating explorations of their lands. The four-volume anthology of Songhay-Zarma oral literature of Fatimata Mounkaila is an imposing result of the local development of Nigerien scholarship, defining very characteristically the country's quiet intellectual independence. Such independence does not mean that Nigerien scholarship is disconnected from Western higher education institutions, and a particular effort has been made here and in all of the sections pertaining to the social sciences and humanities to report dissertations from French and American universities—including, for the former, dissertations defended by Nigerien scholars. Reference sources, such as Kimba Idrissa's *Historiographie nigérienne*, also include master's theses in history, mostly presented at the University of Niamey.

Indeed, social sciences and the humanities dwarf in this bibliography entries on hard sciences, which in part reflects the reality of research in Niger—but only in part. Certainly a more developed scientific bibliography will be needed in future editions of this tome, but it has been here somewhat sacrificed to the requirements of balance and size. This is also—to an extent—true of literature, which is here included in a section with cinema and the arts. There is, however, a substantial compensation in this case, given that the dictionary has an extensive entry on literature and many authors have their individual entries as well, and the option has been to focus on works on Nigerien literature rather than on productions of Nigerien literature.

Niger has some of the most beautiful and stunning landscapes in Africa, but security issues have made it in recent years a risky place to visit for Westerners. Still, there are many good travel guides in French (not listed here), and the U.K.-based Bradt travel books publisher has issued its first Niger guide in 2006. Many *beaux livres*, as the French phase goes (for glossy picture books), could provide the consolations of armchair traveling for the wary. Thus, for instance, the photographer Maurice Ascani, who has been working in Niger for the past five decades, has started to publish in book form his treasure trove of pictures on the country, starting in 2010 with *Niamey à 360°*, which offers aerial views of the capital from the 1960s to today; his is travel in both space and time.

The Internet also provides abundant sources of information on the country—ones with the benefit of regular updating. A list of URLs—selected partly on the basis of apparent durability—has been added to the reference section. It must be pointed out that Nigerien government institutions strive to maintain websites, though in many cases quite desultorily. Newspapers and magazines very rarely maintain websites but accept the regular posting of their issues—in most cases, the entire paper in PDF format—on media compilation websites tamtaminfo.com and nigerdiaspora.net, created and maintained by Nigerien IT specialists as a hobby.

Apart from the Internet and a small number of libraries with good Africanist collections in the United States, not much can be gleaned on Niger outside the country itself, France (at the overseas archives of Aix-en-Provence and the University of Bordeaux in particular), and Senegal, which holds at Dakar a good deal of the former *Afrique Occidentale Française*'s archives. But many of the reference resources listed at the end of the bibliography provide good perspectives on the country's past and present; as far as history of the present is concerned, some international newspapers—*Jeune Afrique* and *Le Monde diplomatique*—keep the articles they publish on the country through the years in online archives. The publisher L'Harmattan also has a large and growing Nigerien department, in which most of the works are available as eBooks, instantly downloadable from the Internet.

GENERAL WORKS

Annan-Yao, Elizabeth. *Démocratie et développement en Afrique de l'Ouest. Mythe et réalité*. Dakar: CODESRIA, 2005.

Bernard, Yves. *Mil, merveille du Sahel*. Paris: L'Harmattan, 2008.

Bernus, Edmond, and Sidikou A. Hamidou. *Atlas du Niger*. Paris: Japress, 2005.

Bernussou, Jérôme. *Histoire et mémoire du Niger de l'indépendance à nos jours*. Toulouse: Méridiennes, 2009.

Brunschwig, Henri. *Le Partage de l'Afrique Noire*. Paris: Flammarion, 1971.

Cassou, Marcel. *Sur les routes de la faim. Comment survivre au Sahel?* Paris: L'Harmattan, 1997.

Chafer, Tony. *The End of Empire in French West Africa: France's Successful Decolonization?* Oxford, New York: Berg, 2002.

Chailley, Marcel. *Histoire de l'Afrique Occidentale Française*. Paris: Berger-Levrault, 1968.

———. *Les Grandes Missions Françaises en Afrique Occidentale*. Dakar: IFAN, 1953.

Chipman, John. *French Power in Africa*. Oxford: Blackwell, 1989.

Cornevin, Robert. *Histoire des Peuples de l'Afrique Noire*. Paris: Berger-Levrault, 1960.

———. *Histoire de l'Afrique*. 2 vols. Paris: Payot, 1967.

Cuoq, Joseph. *Histoire de l'Islamisation de l'Afrique de l'Ouest.* Paris: Paul Geuthner, 1984.

Delavignette, Robert. *Afrique Occidentale Française.* Paris: Editions Géographiques, Maritimes et Coloniales, 1931.

Deloncle, Pierre. *L'Afrique Occidentale Française: Découverte, Pacification, Mise en Valeur.* Paris: Editions Ernest Leroux, 1934.

Dubresson, Alain, Jean-Yves Marchal, and Jean-Pierre Raison (eds.). *Les Afriques au sud du Sahara.* Paris: Belin-Reclus, 1994.

Echenberg, Myron. *Colonial Conscripts: The Tirailleurs Senegalais in French West Africa, 1857–1960.* Portsmouth: Heinemann, 1990.

Englebert, Pierre, and Katharine Murison. "Niger: Recent History." In *Africa South of the Sahara.* London: Routledge, 2007.

Finley, Diana. *The Niger.* London: Macdonald Education, 1975.

Gautier, E. F. *L'Afrique Noire Occidentale.* Paris: Larose, 1935.

———. *Le Sahara.* Paris: Payot, 1948.

Gazibo, Mamoudou. *Introduction à la politique africaine.* Montreal: Presses de l'Université de Montréal, 2006.

———. *Les Paradoxes de la démocratisation en Afrique: Analyse institutionnelle et stratégique.* Montreal: Presses de l'Université de Montréal, 2004.

Giri, Jacques. *Le Sahel au XXIe siècle: Une essai de réflexion prospective sur les sociétés sahéliennes.* Paris: Karthala, 1989.

Kio Koudizé, Aboubacar. *Chronologie politique du Niger de 1900 à nos jours.* Niamey, 1991.

Ki-Zerbo, Joseph. *Histoire de l'Afrique noire.* Paris: Hatier, 1972.

———. *Le Monde africain noir.* Paris: Hatier, 1964.

Klein, Martin A. *Slavery and Colonial Rule in French West Africa.* Cambridge: Cambridge University Press, 1998.

Les Dynamiques transfrontalières en Afrique de l'Ouest. Collective, ENDA DIAPOL. Ottawa: CRDI, ENDA DIAPOL, Karthala, 2007.

Martin, Gaston. *Histoire de l'Esclavage dans les colonies françaises.* Paris: Presses Universitaires de France, 1948.

Morgenthau, Ruth Schachter. *Political Parties in French-Speaking West Africa.* Oxford: Oxford University Press, 1964.

République du Niger. *Paris: La Découverte "l'état du monde."* 2010.

Richard-Molard, J. *Afrique Occidentale Française.* Paris: Berger-Levrault, 1949.

Salifou, André. *Le Niger.* Paris: Karthala, 2002.

Sarraut, A. *La Mise en valeur des colonies françaises.* Paris: Payot, 1953.

Seffal, Rabah. Niger. *Cultures of the World.* New York: Benchmark Books, 2010

Spitz, G. *L'Ouest Africain Français.* Paris: Editions Géographiques, Maritimes et Coloniales, 1947.

Stride, G. T., and Caroline Ifeka. *Peoples and Empires of West Africa.* New York: Africana, 1971.

Suret-Canale, Jean. *Afrique noire: l'Ere coloniale.* Paris: Editions Sociales, 1971.

———. *Afrique noire: De la décolonisation aux indépendances.* Paris: Editions Sociales, 1972.

———. *Afrique noire: Géographie, Civilisation, Histoire.* Paris: Editions Sociales, 1973.

Suret-Canale, Jean, and Richard Adloff. *French West Africa.* Stanford, Calif.: Stanford University Press, 1957.

ARCHAEOLOGY AND PREHISTORY

Alionen, H. *Préhistoire de l'Afrique.* Paris: N. Boubée, 1955.

Ba, Amadou Hampaté, and G. Dièterlen. "Les fresques d'époque bovidienne du Tassili, N'Agger et les traditions des Peul; hypothèses d'interprétation." *Journal de la Société des Africanistes* 36, no. 1 (1966): 141–57.

Beltrami, Vanni. "Repertorio dei monumenti cosiddetti 'pre-Islamici' presenti nel territorio dell'Aïr ed aree limitrofe." *Africa* (Rome) 34, no. 4 (1979): 417–23.

———. "Repertori delle stazioni paleolitiche e neolitiche dell'Aïr e dell regioni circostanti." *Africa* (Rome) 35, no. 3/4 (1980): 489–504.

———. *Repertorio preistorico-archeologico del territorio dell'Aïr ed aree limitrofe.* Rome: Istituto Italo-Africano, 1987.

Bernus, S., and P. L. Gouletquer. "Approche archéologique de la Région d'Azalik et de Tegidda n Tesemt." Paris: CNRS, 1974.

Binet, C. "Notes sur les ruines de Garoumélé (Niger)." *Notes Africaines,* no. 53 (January 1952): 1–2.

Bouesnard, L., and R. Mauny. "Gravures rupestres et sites néolithiques des abords est de l'Aïr." *Bulletin de l'IFAN* (ser. B) 24, no. 1/2 (January–April 1962): 1–11.

Brouin, G. "Du nouveau au sujet de Takedda." *Notes Africaines,* no. 47 (1950): 90–91.

———. "Un îlot de vieille civilisation africaine: le pays de Ouacha (Niger Française)." *Bulletin du Comité d'Etudes Historiques et Scientifiques de l'AOF* 21, no. 4 (October–December 1938): 469–79.

Camps, Gabriel. "Le chars sahariens: Images d'une société aristocratique." *Antiquités Africaines* (Paris) 25 (1989): 11–40.

———. "Ten Years of Archaeological Research in the Sahara, 1965–1975." *West African Journal of Archaeology* 7 (1977): 1–15.

Castro, R. "Examen de creusets de Marandet (Niger)." *Bulletin de l'IFAN* (ser. B) 36, no. 4 (October 1974): 667–75.

Chamla, M. C. *Les Populations anciennes du Sahara et des régions limitrophes. Etudes des restes osseux humaine néolithiques et protohistoriques.* Paris: Arts et Métiers Graphiques, 1968.

Chantret, F., R. de Bayle des Hermens, and H. Merle. "Deux nouveaux gisements néolithiques de la région d'Agadès: Ibadanan et Ntarhalgé." *Notes Africaines,* no. 132 (October 1971): 85–93.

———. "Le Gisement préhistorique de Madaouéla, République du Niger." *Bulletin de la Société Préhistorique Française* 65 (1968): 623–28.

Chudeau, René. "Les monuments lithiques du Sahara." *Anthropologie* 30 (1920): 111–14.

Clark. J. Desmond. "An Archeological Survey of Northern Aïr and Ténéré." *Geographical Journal* 137, no. 4 (1971): 455–57.

———. "Human Populations and Cultural Adaptation in the Sahara and Nile during Prehistoric Times." In *The Sahara and the Nile Quaternary Environments and Prehistoric Occupation in Northern Africa*, edited by Martin A. J. Williams, 527–82. Rotterdam: Balkema, 1980.

Courtin, J. "Le Ténéréen du Borkou, Nord Tchad." In *La Préhistoire, problèmes et tendances*, 133–38. Paris: CNRS, 1968.

De Beauchêne, Guy. "Niger 1963: Recherches archéologiques." *Objets et Mondes* 6, no. 1 (1966): 69–80.

———. "Nomades d'il y a 5000 ans." *Niger* (Niamey), no. 1 (October 1967): 47–50.

———. "Recherches archéologiques au Niger en 1966." *Actes du Premier Colloque Internationale d'Archéologie Africaine (Fort-Lamy)* (1969): 50–61.

Desplagnes, L. "Une mission archéologique dans la vallée du Niger." *Géographie* 13 (1906): 81–90.

De Zeltner, Franz. "Des Dessins sur les rochers à Aïr qui appartient au territoire des Touareg." *Anthropologie* 23 (1912): 101–4; 24 (1913): 171–84.

———. "Les gravures rupestres de l'Aïr." *Anthropologie* (1916): 171–84.

———. "Objets en pierre polie de l'Aïr." *Bulletin et Mémoire de la Société d'Anthropologie de Paris* (1912): 394–97.

Echellier, J. G., and S. P. Roset. "La céramique des gisements de Taqalaqal et de l'Adrar Bousio." *Cahiers des Sciences Humaines* 22, no. 2 (1986): 151–58.

Fagan, B. M. "Radiocarbon Dates from Sub-Saharan Africa." *Journal of African History* 8 (1967).

Faure, Hugues. "Disque néolithique trouvé dans la région du Nord-Est de l'Adrar Bous (Niger)." *Notes Africaines* (October 1960): 110–11.

———. "Sur quelques dépôts du Quaternaire du Ténéré." *Compte Rendu de l'Académie des Sciences* 249, no. 25 (1959): 2807–9.

Feger. "Note sur les pyramides de pierre de la région de Konni (Niger)." *Notes Africaines no. 29* (January 1946): 5.

Franz, H. "On the Stratigraphy and Evolution of Climate in the Chad Basin during the Quaternary." In *Background to Evolution in Africa*, 273–83. Chicago: University of Chicago Press, 1967.

Gado, Boubé, Abdoulaye Maga, and Amadou Idé Oumarou. *Eléments d'archéologie ouest-africaine, IV, Niger.* Nouakchott: CRIAA, Paris: Sépia, 2001.

Gallay, Alain. "Peintures rupestres récentes du bassin du Niger." *Journal de la Société des Africanistes* 34, no. 1 (1964): 123–39.

Gardi, René, and Jolantha Neukom-Tscudi. *Peintures rupestres du Sahara.* Lausanne: Payot, 1962.

Gironcourt, Georges de. "Les inscriptions lithiques du Niger et de l'Adrar." In *Bulletin de la Section Géographique du Ministère d'Information Publique.* Paris, 1914.

Grebenart, D. "Néolithique final et âge des métaux au Niger, près d'A-gadez." *Anthropologie* 89, no. 3 (1985): 337–50.

———. *La région d'In Gall-Tegidda n'Tesemt. Niger: Programme archéologique d'urgence. 1977- 1981.* Niamey: IRSH, 1985.

Greiget, J. "Description des formations retracées et tertiaires du bassin des Iulle-meden." Paris: BRGM, 1966.

Huard, Paul. "Contribution à l'étude des spirales au Sahara central et nigéro-tchadien." *Bulletin de la Société Préhistorique Française* 63, no. 2 (1966): 433–64.

———. "Gravures rupestres des confins nigéro-tchadiens." *Bulletin de l'IFAN* 15, no. 4 (1953): 1569–81.

———. *Mission Berliet Ténéré-Tchad.* Paris: Arts et Métiers Graphiques, 1962.

———. "Les missions Berliet au Sahara." *Libyca* 8 (1960): 323–35.

———. "Une nouvelle date pour le néolithique saharien: Celle du Ténéréen." *Libyca* 8 (1960): 259–60.

———. "Nouvelles gravures rupestres du Djado, de l'Afafi et du Tibesti." *Bulletin de l'IFAN* (ser. B) 19, no. 1/2 (1957): 184–223.

———. "Premier aperçu sur la préhistoire du Ténéré du Tafassasset." *Documents Scientifiques du Mission Berliet*, 149–78. Paris: Arts et Métiers Graphiques, 1962.

———. *Le Sahara avant le désert.* Toulouse: Editions des Hesperides, 1974.

Huard, Paul, G. Breaud, and J. M. Massip. "Répertoire des sites paléolithiques du Sahara central, tchadien et oriental." *Bulletin de l'IFAN* (ser. B) 31, no. 3 (1969): 853–74.

Huard, Paul, and J. M. Massip. "Monuments du Sahara nigéro-tchadien." *Bulletin de l'IFAN* (ser. B) 29, no. 1/2 (1967): 1–27.

Huard, Paul, and R. Mauny. "Prises de dates résultant des travaux de la mission Berliet-Ténéré." *Bulletin de la Société Préhistorique Française* 65, no. 5/6 (1960): 270–72.

Joleaud, L. "Vertèbres subfossils de l'Azaoua." *Comptes Rendu de l'Académie des Sciences* (1934): 599–601.

Joubert, C., and R. Vaufrey. "Le néolithique du Ténéré." *Anthropologie* 50 (1941–46): 325–30.

Kelessi, Mahamadou. *Etat actuel des recherches sur le néolithique dans l'Aïr et ses régions adjacentes.* Niamey: Université de Niamey, 1987.

Kelley, Harper. "Harpons, objets en os, travailles et silex taillés de Taferjit et Tamaya Mellet (Sahara nigérien)." *Journal de la Société des Africanistes* (1934): 135–43.

Killick, D., et al. "Reassessment of the Evidence for Early Metallurgy in Niger, West Africa." *Journal of Archeological Science* 15, no. 4 (1988): 367–94.

La Région d'In Gall Tegidda n Tesemt: Programme archéologique d'urgence, 1977–1981. Niamey: IRSH, 1985.

Laforgue, P. "Quelques objets néolithiques du Niger." *Bulletin du Comité d'Etudes Historiques et Scientifiques de l'AOE* 21 (1938): 147–48.

Lapparent, A. F. de. "Les dinosaures du Sahara central." *Travaux de l'Institut de Recherches Sahariennes* 19, no. 1/2 (1960): 7–24.

———. "Reconnaissance des gisements à dinosauriens du Tamesna." *Travaux de L'Institut de Recherches Sahariennes* 10 (1953).

Law, R. C. C. "Garamantes and Trans-Saharan Enterprise in Classical Times." *Journal of African History* 8, no. 2 (1967): 181–200.

Lebeuf, Jean Paul. *Carte Archéologique des abords du lac Tchad.* Paris: CNRS, 1969.

Le Coeur, Charles. "Une chambre des hôtes de la ville morte de Djado." *Notes Afric-aines,* no. 43 (October 1943): 9–10.

Lhote, Henri. "Découverte de chars de guerre en Aïr." *Notes Africaines,* no. 127 (July 1970): 83–85.

———. "Découverte des ruines de Tadeliza, ancienne résidence des sultans de l'Aïr." *Notes Africaines,* no. 137 (January 1973): 9–15.

———. *L'Epopée du Ténéré.* Paris: Gallimard, 1961.

———. *Les Gravures de Nord-Ouest de l'Air.* Paris: Arts et Métiers Graphiques, 1972.

———. "Recherches sur Takedda, ville décrite par le voyageur Ibn Battouta et situé en Aïr." *Bulletin de l'IFAN* (ser. B) 34, no. 3 (1972): 430–70.

———. "Saharan Rock Art." *Natural History* 69, no. 6 (June–July 1960): 28–43.

———. *Les Chars rupestres sahariens: Des Syrtes au Niger par le pays des Garaman-tes et des Atlantes.* Paris: Errance, 1982.

———. "Les salines du Sahara: La saline de Taguidda-n-tisemt." *Terre et la Vie* 3, no. 12 (December 1933).

Maley, J., et al. "Nouveaux gisements préhistoriques au Niger oriental." *Bulletin ASEOUA,* no. 31/32 (1971): 9–18.

Mascarelli, M., and R. Mauny. "Découverte d'un biface de longeur exceptionelle au Kaouar." *Notes Africaines,* no. 70 (April 1956): 38–39.

Mauny, R. "Contribution à la préhistoire de l'Aïr. In *Contribution à l'étude de l'Aïr,* 537–40. Paris: Larose, 1950.

———. "Découverte d'un atelier de fonte du cuire à Marandet (Niger)." *Notes Afric-aines,* no. 58 (April 1953): 33–35.

———. "Etat actuel de nos connaissances sur la préhistoire de la colonie du Niger." *Bulletin de l'IFAN* 11, no. 1/2 (January–March 1949): 141–58.

———. "Objets subactuels en fer trouvés en pays Teda et à l'est de l'Aïr." *Notes Af-ricaines,* no. 97 (January 1963): 24–25.

Milburn, Mark. "Aïr Occidental: Essai de chronologie relative de quelques monu-ments lithiques." *Almogaren* (Hallein) 7 (1976): 147–54.

———. "On Pre- and Protohistory of Ténéré Tafassasset." *Leba* (Lisbon) 6 (1987): 37–60.

Monod, Théodore. *Contributions à l'étude du Sahara occidental. Gravures, peintures et inscriptions rupestres.* Paris: Larose, 1938.

Morris, R. W. B., and Mark Milburn. "Some Cup-and-Ring Marks of Western Aïr." *Almogaren* (Hallein) 7 (1976): 143–45.

Mourgues, Gaston. "Gravures rupestres chez les Touaregs nigériens." *Afrique Fran-çaise* 44, no. 8 (August 1934): 145–48.

Nicolas, Francis. "Inscriptions et gravures rupestres." In *Contribution « l'étude de l'Aïr,* 541–51. Paris: Larose, 1950.

Niger '86: Viaggio nella preistorica. Milan: Centro Studi Archéologie; Africana, 1987.

Pedrals, Denis Pierre de. *Archéologie de l'Afrique Noire: Nubie, Ethiopie, Niger sahélien, L'Aïr tchadien. Niger inférieur . . .* Paris: Payot, 1950.

Poncet, Yveline. *La Région d'In Gall. Tegidda n Tesemt.* Niamey: IRSH. 1983.

Posnansky, Marrick, and Roderick McIntosh. "New Radiocarbon Dates for Northern and Western Africa." *Journal of African History* 17, no. 2 (1976): 161–96.

Prévost, Marius, and Lucien Mayet. "L'Oasis du Kaouar et la préhistoire du Sahara oriental." *Nature,* no. 2658 (March 15, 1925): 161–68.

Quéchon, G. "Groupements de lances néolithiques de la région de Termit." *Cahiers des Sciences Humaines* 22, no. 2 (1986): 203–16.

Quéchon, G., and J. P. Roset. "Prospection archéologique du massif de Termit (Niger)." *Cahiers d'ORSTOM 11,* no. 1 (1974): 85–104.

Regelsperger, G. "Du Niger au Tchad. La Mission Tilho." *Mois Colonial et Maritime* 1 (1909): 97–109.

Reygasse, M. "Le Tenéréen: Observations sur un faciès nouveau du Néolithique des confins algéro-soudanais." In *Congrès Préhistorique de France. XIe session, Periqueia 1934,* 577–84. Paris: SPF, 1935.

Rodd, F. R. "Some Rock Drawings from Aïr in the Southern Sahara." *Journal of the Royal Anthropological Institute* 68 (1938): 99–111.

Roset, Jean-Pierre. "Art rupestre en Aïr." *Archaélogia* (Paris), no. 39 (March–April 1971): 24–31.

———. "Deux modes d'inhumation néolithique au Niger." *Cahiers d'ORSTOM* 14, no. 3 (1977): 325–30.

Rouch, Jean. "Gravures rupestres de Kourki (Niger)." *Bulletin de l'IFAN* (1949): 34–53.

Roy, A. "Vestiges de Takedda, ancienne capitale des Igdalens, centre minier et caravanier d l'Aïr au XIVe siècle." *Notes Africaines,* no. 29 (January 1946): 5–6.

Ruhlmann, Armand. "Le Ténéréen." *Bulletin de la Société de Préhistoire du Maroc* (1936): 3–15.

Schobel, Jürgen. *Ammoniten der Famille Vascoceratidae aus dem Unteren des Damergou-Gebietes. République du Niger.* Uppsala: Palaeontological Institution of the University of Uppsala, 1975.

Sereno, P., H. C. E. Larsson, C. A. Sidor, and B. Gado. "The Giant Crocodyliform *Sarcosuchus* from the Cretaceous of Africa." *Science* 294 (2001): 1516–19.

Smith, Andrew Brown. "Adrar Bous and Karkarichinkat: Examples of Post-Paleolithic Human Adaptation in the Saharan and Sahel Zones of West Africa." PhD diss., University of Califomia–Berkeley, 1974.

———. "The Neolithic Tradition in the Sahara." In *The Sahara and the Nile: Quaternary Environment and Prehistoric Occupation in Northern Africa,* edited by Martin A. J. Williams and Hugues Faure, 451–65. Rotterdam: Balkema, 1980.

Tillet, Thierry. *Le Paléolithique du bassin tchadien septentrional.* Paris: CNRS, 1983.

Toucet, P. "La Préhistoire au Niger." *Communauté France-Eurafrique,* no. 126 (November 1961): 31–36.

Vedy, Jean. "Contribution à l'inventaire de la station rupestre de Dao Timni-Woro-Yat (Niger)." *Bulletin de l'IFAN* (ser. B) 24, no. 3/4 (July–October 1962): 325–82.

———. "La station rupestre de Ziri-Betidai (Niger)." *Bulletin de l'IFAN* (ser. B) 23, no. 3/4 (July–October 1961): 456–75.

Vernet, Robert. *Le Sud-ouest du Niger. De la préhistoire au début de l'histoire.* Paris: Sépia, 1996.

EARLY ACCOUNTS AND MONOGRAPHS

Abadie, Maurice. *Afrique Centrale: La colonie du Niger.* Paris: Société d'Editions Géographiques, Maritimes et Coloniales, 1927.

———. "La colonie du Niger." *Géographie* 47, no. 3/4 (March–April 1927): 169–90.

Alexander, Boyd. "From the Niger by Lake Chad to the Nile." *Annual Report of the Smithsonian Institution* (1909): 335–400.

———. "From the Niger by Lake Chad to the Nile." *Geographical Journal* 30 (1907): 119–52.

Alexander, J. *Whom the Gods Love: Boyd Alexander's Expédition from the Niger to the Nile, 1904–7, and His Last Journey, 1908–10.* London: Heinemann, 1977.

Alibert, Louis. *Méhariste 1917–1918.* Paris: Delmas, 1936.

Arnaud, E., and M. Collier. *Nos Confins sahariens.* Etude d'Organisation militaire. Paris: Larose, 1908.

Auguste, T. "Le Pays de Zaberma." *Afrique Française* (1901): 25–32.

Auzou, Emile. "La Boucle du Niger." *Revue des Deux Mondes* 147 (1898): 163–88.

Ayasse. "Première reconnaissance: N'guimi, Agadem, Bilma." *Revue des Troupes Coloniales* 1 (1907): 552–82.

Baillaud, E. "Les territoires français du Niger: Leur valeur économique." *Géographie* (1900): 9–24.

Barbier, J. V. *A travers le Sahara. Les Missions du Colonel Flatters.* Paris: Librairie de la Société Bibliographique, 1884.

Barth, Heinrich. *Travels and Discoveries in North and Central Africa.* 3 vols. Reprint. London: Frank Cass, 1965.

Baudry L. "Le Niger économique." *Géographie Commerciale* (1897): 337–46.

Bernus, S. *Henri Barth chez les Touaregs de l'Aïr.* Niamey: Etudes Nigériennes, 1972.

Bindloss, Harold. *In the Niger Country.* 1898. Reprint. London: Frank Cass, 1968.

Binger, Louis-Gustave. *Du Niger au Golfe de Guinée par le pays de Kong et le Mossi.* Paris: Musée de l'Homme, 1982.

Bouchez. *Guide de l'Officier méhariste au territoire militaire du Niger.* Paris: Larose, 1910.

Bovill, E. W. (ed.). *Mission to the Niger.* 4 vols. Reprint. Cambridge: Cambridge University Press, 1966.

Brosselard, G. *Voyage de la mission Flatters au Pays des Touareg Azd-jers.* Paris: Jouvet, 1911.

Buchanan, Angus. *Exploration of Air: Out of the World North of Nigeria.* New York: Dutton, 1922.

———. *Sahara.* London: John Murray, 1926.

Buret, A. *Le Territoire Français Niger-Tchad.* Brussels: Imprimerie Nouvelle, 1905.

Burthe d'Annelet. *A Travers l'Afrique Française. Du Cameroun à Alger par le Zinder, l'Aïr, le Niger, le Ahagar.* 2 vols. Paris: Roger, 1932.

———. *A Travers l'Afrique Française. Du Sénégal au Cameroun.* 2 vols. Paris: Didot, 1939.

Chudeau, René. "L'Aïr et la région de Zinder." *Géographie* 15, no. 6 (May 15, 1907): 321–36.

———. "D'Alger à Tombouctou par l'Ahaggar, l'Aïr et le Tchad." *Géographie* 15, no. 5 (1907): 261–70.

———. "Le cercle de Bilma." *Géographie* 21, no. 4 (April 1910): 264–66.

———. "Notes sur l'ethnographie de la région du Moyen-Niger." *Anthropologie* (1910): 661–66.

———. "Le pays des Touaregs Ioulliminden." *Géographie* 21 (1910): 221–36.

———. *Sahara Soudanais, Mission au Sahara.* 2 vols. Paris, 1909.

Cortier, Maurice. *Mission Cortier 1908, 1909,1910.* Paris: Larose, 1914.

———. "De Zinder au Tchad." *Comptes Rendus de l'Académie de Sciences* 143 (1906): 193–95.

———. "Teguidda-n-tesemt." *Géographie* (September 5, 1905): 159–64.

De Bary, Erwin. *Le Dernier Rapport d'un Européen sur Ghat et les Touareg de l'Aïr.* Paris: Librairie Fischbacher, 1898.

Delevoye, M. *En Afrique Centrale, Niger-Bénoué-Tichad.* Paris: Le Soudier, 1906.

Denham, Dixon, and H. Clapperton. *Narrative of Travels and Discoveries in Northern and Central Africa in the Years 1822, 1823, and 1824.* London: John Murray, 1826.

Desplagnes, Louis. "Notes sur l'origine des populations nigériennes." *Anthropologie* 17 (1906): 525–46.

———. *Le Plateau central nigérien.* Paris: Larose, 1907.

Foureau, F. *D'Alger au Congo par le Tchad.* Paris: Masson, 1902.

———. "De l'Algérie au Congo Français par l'Aïr et le Tchad." *Géographie* 2 (1900): 936–61.

———. *Documents scientifiques de la Mission Saharienne (Mission Foureau-Lamy)* 1898–1900. 3 vols. Paris: Masson, 1905.

François, G. "La Mission Desplagnes dans le plateau central nigérien." *Bulletin du Comité d'Afrique Française* (April 1907): 159–63.

———. "La Mission Tilho. La frontière entre le Niger et le Tchad." *Afrique Française,* no. 2 (1909): 56–62.

Gadel, A. "Notes sur l'Aïr." *Bulletin de la Société de Géographie de l'AOF,* no. 1 (March 31, 1907): 28–52.

———. "Notes sur Bilma et les oasis environnants." *Revue Coloniale* 7, no. 51 (1907): 361–86.

———. "Les oasis de la région de Bilma." *Bulletin de la Société de Géographie de l'AOF* 2, no. 30 (1907): 85–114.

Gaden, Henri. "Notice sur la résidence de Zinder." *Revue des Troupes Coloniales* 2 (1903): 608–56, 740–94.

Gallieni, Joseph Simon. *Explorations du Haut-Niger.* Paris, 1883.

Gautier, E. F., and R. Chudeau. *Missions au Sahara.* Paris: Armand Colin, 1909.

Goldstein, Ferdinand. "Die Saharastädte Ghat und Agades." *Globus* 92 (1907): 171–75, 186–88.

Hall, D. N., et al. "The British Expedition to the Aïr Mountains." *Geographical Journal* 137, no. 4 (December 1971): 445–67.

Hallett, Robin (ed.). *The Niger Journal of Richard and John Lander.* New York: Praeger, 1965.

Hourst, Emile Auguste Léon. *French Enterprise in Africa: The Personal Narrative of Lieutenant Hourst of His Exploration of the Niger.* London: Chapman and Hall, 1898.

Ibn Battuta, Abu Abdullah Muhammad. *Travels in Asia and Africa, 1325–1354.* Columbia: South Asia Books, 1986.

Jacobs, A. *Les voyages d'exploration en Afrique du Docteur Barth en 1849. Le désert, le Tchad, le Niger.* Paris, 1860.

Kerillis, Henri de. *De l'Algérie au Dahomey en Automobile.* Paris: Plon, 1925.

King, W. J. Harding. *A Search for the Masked Twareks.* London: Smith, Elder, 1903.

Laird, M. G., and R. K. Oldfield. *Narrative of an Expedition into the Interior of Africa by the River Niger.* London: Bentley, 1920.

Lander, R., and J. Lander. *Journey of an Expedition to Explore the Course and Termination of the Niger.* London: Murray, 1833.

———. *The Niger Journal of the Landers.* Reprint. London: Routledge and Kegan Paul, 1965.

Lanoye, F. de. *Le Niger et les explorations de l'Afrique centrale depuis Mungo-Park jusqu'au Docteur Barth.* Paris: Hachette, 1860.

Lenfant, Eugène Armand. "De l'Atlantique au Tchad par la voie Niger-Bénoué-Toubouri-Logone." *Afrique Française,* no. 6 (1904): 186–99.

———. "Exploration hydrographique du Niger." *Comité des Travaux Historiques et Scientifiques. Bulletin de Géographie Historique et Descriptive* (1903): 25–133.

———. *Le Niger, voie ouverte à notre empire africain.* Paris: Hachette, 1903.

Leo Africanus. *The History and Description of Africa.* 3 vols. Cambridge: Cambridge University Press, 2010.

Mattei, A. *Bas Niger, Bénoué, Dahomey.* Grenoble: Vallier, 1890.

Meniaud, Jacques. *Les Pionniers du Soudan avant, avec et après Archinard, 1879–94.* 2 vols. Paris: Société des Publications Modernes, 1931.

Mohamed ben Otsmane el-Hachaichi. *Voyage au Pays des Senoussia à travers la Tripolitaine et les pays Toureg.* Paris: Challamel, 1903.

Monteil, Charles. *De Saint-Louis à Tripoli par le Lac Tchad.* Paris: Alcan, 1894.

Moullet. "Le Ténéré, Kaouar, Tibesti. Du Tibesti au Hoggar." *Revue des Troupes Coloniales* 28 (1934): 105–25, 269–90.

Muteau. *Le Niger et la Guinée.* Dijon, 1882.

Nachtigal, Gustav. *Sahara and Sudan.* Trans. by A. G. B. Fisher and H. J. Fisher. 4 vols. London: Hurst, 1971.

Paulhiac, H. "Maures et Touareg." *Revue de Géographie* 55 (1905): 74–79, 99–103.

———. "Le pays de Zaberma." *Bulletin du Comité de l'Afrique Française* 11 (1901): 25–32.

Péroz, Etienne. *Au Niger: Récits de campagnes 1881–1892.* Boston: Adamant Media Corporation, 2010.

Pietri, Camille. *Les Français au Niger: voyages et combats.* Charleston, S.C.: Nabu Press, 2010 (reissue from 1923).

Regelsperger, G. "Du Niger au Tchad. La Mission Tilho." *Mois Colonial et Maritime* 1 (1909): 97–109.

Richardson, James. *Narrative of a Mission to Central Africa Performed in the Years 1850–51.* 2 vols. London: Chapman and Hall, 1853.

Richardson, Robert. *A Story of the Niger.* London: Nelson and Sons, 1888.

Rodd, Francis J. Rennell. "A Journey in Aïr." *Geographical Journal* 62 (1923): 81–102.

———. "Une mission anglaise en Aïr." *Bulletin du Comité d'Etudes Historiques et Scientifiques de l'AOF* 11, no. 4 (1928): 695–707.

———. "A Second Journey among the Southern Tuareg." *Geographical Journal* 73 (1929): 1–19, 147–58.

Salaman. "Notice sur le Moyen Niger." *Revue Economique Française* 27 (1905): 471–90.

Toutée, Georges Joseph. *Dahomé, Niger, Touareg.* Paris: Armand Colin, 1905.

———. *Du Dahomé au Sahara.* Paris: Armand Colin, 1907.

Von Bary, Erma. *Le Dernier Rapport de Von Bary sur les Touaregs de l'Aïr, Journal de Voyage 1876–77.* Paris: Fischbacher, 1898.

PEOPLE, SOCIETY, RELIGION

General Studies

Bellot, Jean Marc. "Les femmes dans les sociétés pastorales du Gorouol." *Cahiers d'Outre-Mer* 33, no. 130 (April–June 1980): 145–65.

Bovin, Mette. "Ethnic Performances in Rural Niger: An Aspect of Ethnic Boundary Maintenance." *Folk* (Copenhagen) 16/17 (1974): 459–74.

Bullington, James R. *Adventures in Service with Peace Corps in Niger.* Charleston, N.C.: BookSurge, 2007.

Calame-Griaule, G. "Notes sur l'habitation du plateau central nigérien." *Bulletin de l'IFAN* 17 (1995): 477–98.

Capot-Rey, R. *Nomades Noirs du Sahara.* Paris: Plon, 1958.

Chilson, Peter. *Riding the Demon: on the Road in West Africa.* Athens: University of Georgia Press.

Chudeau, R. "Peuples du Sahara central et occidental." *Anthropologie* 24 (1913): 185–96.

Cohen, Ronald. "The Structure of Kanuri Society." PhD diss., University of Wisconsin, 1960.

"Coutumiers Azna." In *Coutumiers juridiques de l'AOF.* Vol. 3, 303–16. Paris: Larose, 1939.

Donaint, P. "Les Cadres géographiques à travers les langues du Niger, contribution à la pédagogie de l'étude du milieu." *Etudes Nigériennes*, no. 37 (1975).

Echard, Nicole. "Histoire et phénomènes religieux chez les Asna de l'Ader." In *Systèmes de Pensée en Afrique Noire*, 53–77. Paris, 1975.

Fuchs, Peter. *Das Brot der Wüste: Sozio-Ökonomie der Sahara Kanuri von Fachi.* Wiesbaden: Steiner, 1983.

Gallais, Jean. *Hommes du Sahel.* Paris: Flammarion, 1984.

Griaule, Marcel. "L'Arche du Monde chez les populations nigériennes." *Journal de la Société des Africanistes* 18, no. 1 (1948): 117–26.

Guermond, Yves. "Paysans du Niger sahélien." *Cahiers de Sociologie Economique* (Le Havre) (May 1966): 1889–2170.

Horowitz, Michael M. "Ecology and Ethnicity in Niger." *Africa* 44, no. 4 (1974): 371–82.

———. *The Manga of Niger*. New Haven, Conn.: Human Relations Area Files, 1972.

Horowitz, Michael M., et al. *Niger: A Social and Institutional Profile*. Binghamton, N.Y.: Institute for Development Anthropology, 1985.

Jaffré, Joël, and J. Dorou. *La Caravane du Sel*. Paris: Denoel, 1978.

Karl, Emmanuel. *Traditions Orales au Dahomey-Niger.* Niamey: Centre Régional de Documentation pour la Tradition Orale, 1974.

Kimba, Idrissa. *Guerres et Sociétés. Les Populations du "Niger" occidental et leurs réactions face à la colonization (1896–1906).* Niamey: IRSH, 1981.

Le Coeur, Charles. "Initiation à hygiène et à la morale de l'alimentation chez les Djerma et les Peuls de Niamey." *Bulletin de l'IFAN* no. 8 (1946): 164–80.

———. "Méthodes et conclusions d'une enquête humaine au Sahara nigéro-tchadien." In *1ère Conférence Internationale des Africanistes de l'Ouest, Comptes Rendus*. Vol. 2, 374–81. Paris: Maisonneuve, 1951.

Le Coeur, Charles, and M. Le Coeur. "Tombes antéislamiques du Djado." *Notes Africaines*, no. 21 (1944): 1–2.

Lhote, Henri. *Aux Prises avec le Sahara*. Paris: Les Oeuvres Françaises, 1936.

Ligers, Z. *Atlas d'Ethnographie Nigérienne*. 2 vols. Paris: 1974.

Lobsiger-Dellenbach, Marguerite. "Contribution à l'étude anthropologique de l'Afrique Occidentale Française (Colonie du Niger); Haoussas, Bellahs, Djermas, Peuls, Touaregs, Maures." *Extraits des Archives Suisses d'Anthropologie Générale* (Geneva) 16, no. 1 (1951).

Malfettes, Raymond. "Le canton de Dessa." *Archives des Etudes Nigériennes*, no. 1 (1964).

———, (ed.). *Pastoralism in Tropical Africa*. London: Cass, 1975.

Morel, Alain. "Villages et oasis des Monts Bazzans (Massif de l'Aïr-Niger)." *Revue de Géographie Alpine* 1 (1973): 247–66.

Muller, Jean-Claude. *Du bon usage du sexe et du mariage. Structures matrimoniales du haut plateau nigérien*. Paris: Harmattan, 1992.

Nicholas, Guy. "Aspects de la vie économique dans un canton du Niger: Kantché." *Cahiers de l'SEA*, no. 5 (1962).

———. "L'Evolution du Canton de Kantché. Etude ethnologique d'une société de l'Est du Niger." Master's thesis, Bordeaux University, 1957.

Oxby, Clare. *Les Pasteurs nomades face au développement*. London: International African Institute, 1975.

Perron, M. "Le Pays Dendi." *Bulletin du Comité Historique et Scientifique de l'AOF* (1924): 51–83.

Piault, Marc H. *Populations de l'Arewa. Introduction à une étude régionale*. Paris: Études Nigériennes, no. 13, 1964.

Poncet, Yveline. *Cartes ethno-démographiques du Niger*. Études Nigériennes, no. 32, 1973.

Raulin, Henri. "Cadastre et terroirs au Niger." *Études Rurales*, no. 9 (April–June 1963): 58–77.

———. "Société sans classes d'âge au Niger." In *Classes et associations d'âge en Afrique de l'Ouest*, edited by D. Paulme, 320–29. Paris: Plon, 1971.

Riou, A. "Le Niger géographique et ethnologique." *AOF Magazine* (Dakar), no. 6 (May 1954).

Robin, Jean. "Description de la province de Dosso." *Bulletin de l'IFAN* 9, nos. 1–4 (1947): 56–98.

———. "Note sur les premières populations de la région de Dosso (Niger)." *Bulletin de l'IFAN* 1, no. 2/3 (April–July 1939): 401–4.

Robinson, Pearl T. "African Traditional Rulers and the Modern State: The Linkage Role of Chiefs in the Republic of Niger." Master's thesis, Columbia University, 1975.

Rochette, R., A. Guillon, and J. Hernandez. "Dogondoutchi, petit centre urbain du Niger." *Revue de Géographie Africaine* 56 (1968): 349–58.

Rosman, Abraham. "Social Structure and Acculturation among the Kanuri of Northern Nigeria." PhD diss., Yale University, 1962.

Rouch, Jean. "Les pêcheurs du Niger: Techniques de pêche, organisation économique." *Comptes Rendus de l'Institut Français d'Anthropologie* 5 (January–December 1951): 17–20.

———. *Petit Atlas ethno-démographique du Soudan entre Sénégal et Tchad.* Paris: Larose, 1942.

———. "Toponymie légendaire du 'W du Niger." *Notes Africaines*, no. 46 (April 1950): 50–52.

Van Hoey, Léo Frans. "Emergent Urbanization: Implications of the Theory of Social Scale Verified in Niger, West Africa." PhD diss., Northwestern University, 1966.

Vital, Laurent. *Rituels de possession dans le Sahel.* Paris: Harmattan, 1992.

Education

Alou, Mahaman Tidjani. "Les Politiques de formation en Afrique francophone: École, état et sociétés au Niger." PhD diss., University of Bordeaux, 1992.

Barbey, Guy. "L'Aventure de la télévision scolaire du Niger." *Coopération et Développement*, no. 39 (January–February 1972): 22–29; no. 40 (March–April 1972): 7–15.

Bergmann, H., and Iro Yahouza. *Niger: Étude sectorielle sur l'éducation de base.* Eschborn: GTZ, 1992.

Clair, Andrée. *Les Découvertes d'Alkassoum.* Paris: Editions Farandole, 1962. [School text.]

———. *Dijé.* Paris: Editions Farandole, 1962 [School text.]

———. *Issilim.* Paris: Editions Farandole, 1972. [School text.]

———. *Le Voyage d'Oumarou.* Paris: Editions Bourrelier, 1962 [School text.]

Clair, Andrée, and Boubou Hama. *Le Boabab Merveilleux.* Paris: Editions Farandole, 1971. [School text.]

Diawara, I. "Cultures nigériennes et éducation: Domaine Zarma-Songhay et Hausa." *Présence Africaine,* no. 148 (1988): 9–19.

Hama, Boubou. *Education Africaine: Sentences, maximes, proverbes et locutions Zarmas, Songhays, Haoussas, Peuls et Bambaras.* Niamey, 1972.

———. *Essai d'analyse de l'éducation africaine.* Paris: Présence Africaine, 1968.

———. *Pour une dialogue avec nos jeunes: Démarches pédagogiques.* Niamey, 1972.

Hama, Boubou, and Marcel Guilhem. *Niger, récits historiques.* Paris: Ligel, 1967.

Hima, Mariama. "L'Education à travers les contes dans la société songhay-zarma." Master's thesis, École des Hautes Etudes en Sciences Sociales, Paris, 1978.

Hukill, Mark Alan. "Télévision Broadcasting for Rural Development in Niger." MA thesis, University of Hawaii, 1984.

Hutchison, John P. "Language Policy for Education in Niger." In *Languages in International Perspective*, edited by Nancy Schweda-Nicholson et al., 279–94. Norwood, N.J.: Ablex, 1986.

Koley, Glenda Dickison. "Mission Primary School Dilemma: Day or Boarding School for Nationals of the Republic of Niger?" MA thesis, Columbia Bible Collège, 1984.

Madougou, Amadou. *Kokari ou la lutte silencieuse de l'enseignant.* Paris: L'Harmattan, 2003.

Mai Moussa, Gapto. *Les Déterminants de la scolarisation des enfants au Niger.* Sarrebruck: Editions Universitaires Européennes, 2011.

Meunier, Olivier. *Bilan d'un siècle de politiques éducatives au Niger.* Paris: L'Harmattan, 2000.

———. *Dynamique de l'enseignement islamique au Niger. Le cas de la ville de Maradi.* Paris: L'Harmattan, 1997.

———. (ed.). *Variations et diversités éducatives au Niger.* Paris: L'Harmattan, 2009.

Olkes, Cheryl. "Information-Seeking with Mass-Media in the Republic of Niger: An Exploratory Study of Town and Country." PhD diss., University of Texas–Austin, 1978.

Tchangari, Moussa (ed.). *Le Droit à l'éducation au Niger. Rapport d'analyse des politiques et du financement de l'éducation de 2000 à 2007.* Niamey: Alternative Espaces Citoyens, 2008.

Triaud, Jean-Louis. "Note sur l'enseignement Franco-Arabe en Niger." *Islam et Sociétés au Sud du Sahara,* no. 2 (1988): 155–56.

Wilson, Wendy. "Cooperatives as a Vehicle of Adult Education in Africa." *Journal of Negro Education* 56, no. 3 (1987): 407–18.

Wynd, Shona. "Education, Schooling and Fertility in Niger." In *Gender, Education and Development: Beyond Access to Empowerment*, edited by Christine Heward and Sheila Bunwaree. Trowbridge: Redwood Books, 1999.

Yenikoye, Ismael Aboubacar. *Faut-il enseigner dans les langues nationales? L'exemple du Niger.* Paris: L'Harmattan Niger, 2007.

———. *L'Université Abdou Moumouni de Niamey: organisation et aspects qualitatifs de l'enseignement au Niger.* Paris: L'Harmattan Niger, 2007.

Islam

Alidou, Ousseina. *Engaging Modernity: Muslim Women and the Politics of Agency in Postcolonial Niger.* Madison: University of Wisconsin Press, 2011.

Alio, Mahaman. "L'Islam et la femme dans l'espace public au Niger." In *Afrique et développement*, 3–4, 2009.

Etat et Islam au Niger. *Actes du colloque de Niamey, Novembre 2007.* Université de Niamey: FSEJ.

Garçon, Loïc. *Etude de l'évolution des pratiques de l'Islam au Niger.* Niamey: Bureau de l'Ambassade du Canada au Niger, 1998.

Glew, Robert. "The Construction of Muslim Identities and Social Change in Zinder, Republic of Niger." PhD diss., Michigan State University, 1997.

Grégoire, Emmanuel. "Islam and the Identity of Merchants in Maradi." In *Muslim Identity and Social Change in Suhsaharan Africa*, edited by Louis Brenner, 106–15. Bloomington: Indiana University Press, 1993.

Hamani, Djibo. *L'Islam au Soudan central: Histoire de l'Islam au Niger du VIIe au XIXe siècle.* Paris: L'Harmattan, 2007.

Kang, Alice. "Bargaining with Islam: of Rule, Religion and Women in Niger." PhD diss., University of Wisconsin, 2010.

Laizé, M. "Islam dans le Territoire Militaire du Niger." *Bulletin du Comité d'Etudes Historiques et Scientifiques de l'AOF,* no. 2 (April–June 1919): 177–83.

Marty, Paul. *Etudes sur l'Islam et les tribus du Sudan.* 4 vols. Paris: Larose, 1920.

———. "L'Islam et les tribus dans la colonie du Niger (ex-Zinder)." *Revue des Etudes Islamiques* 4 (1930): 333–432; also Paris: Paul Geuthner, 1931.

Masquelier, Adeline. *Prayer Has Spoiled Everything: Possession, Power and Identity in an Islamic Town in Niger (Body, Commodity, Text).* Durham, N.C.: Duke University Press, 2001.

Meunier, Olivier. *Les voies de l'islam au Niger dans le Katsina indépendant du XIXe au XXe siècle.* Paris: Publications scientifiques du Muséum, 1998.

Miles, William S. "Shari'a as De-Africanization: Evidence from the Hausaland." *Africa Today* 50, no 1 (2003): 51–75.

Niandou Souley, Abdoulaye. "Les 'licenciés du Caire' et l'Etat du Niger." In *Le Radicalisme islamique au Sud du Sahara. Da'wa, arabisation et critique de l'Occident*, edited by René Otayek, 217–37. Paris: Karthala-MSHA, 1993.

Norris, H. T. *Sufi Mystics of the Niger Desert.* Oxford: Clarendon Press, 1990.

Robinson, Pearl T. "Islam and Female Empowerment among the Tijaniyya in Niger." Research Note, September 2005. http://www.scribd.com/doc/35822151/Islam-and-female-empowerment-among-Tijaniyya-in-Niger (accessed 26 November 2010).

Triaud, J. L. "L'Islam et l'Etat en République du Niger." In *Islam et Etat dans le monde aujourd'hui*, edited by Olivier Carré. Paris: Presses Universitaires de France, 1982.

Villalón, Leonardo A. "The Moral and the Political in African Democratization: The 'Code de la Famille' in Niger's Troubled Transition." *Democratization* 3, no. 2 (1996): 41–68.

Zakari, Maikoréma. "La naissance et le développement du mouvement Izala au Niger." In *Islam, société et politique en Afrique sub-saharienne. Les exemples du*

Sénégal, du Niger et du Nigeria, edited by Jean-Louis Triaud. Paris: Les Indes Savantes/Rivages des Xanthons, 2007.

———. *L'Islam dans l'espace nigérien de 1960 aux années 2000*, 2 vols. Paris: L'Harmattan, 2009.

Local Religions

Besmer, Fremont E. *Horses, Musicians and Gods: The Hausa Cult of Possession.* South Hadley, Mass.: Bergin and Garvey, 1983.

Broustra-Monfouga, Jacques. "Approche ethnopsychiatrique du phénomène de possession. Le Bori de Konni (Niger), étude comparative." *Journal de la Société des Africanistes* 43, no. 2 (1973): 197–220.

Faulkingham, Ralph H. "The Spirits and Their Cousins: Some Aspects of Beliefs, Rituals, and Social Organization in a Rural Hausa Village in Niger." University of Massachusetts, Department of Anthropology, Research Report no. 15, Amherst, 1975.

Gruner, Dorothée. "Der Traditionelle Moscheebau ara Mittleren Niger." *Paideuma* (Frankfurt), no. 23 (1977): 101–40.

Hama, Boubou. "Le culte des ancêtres, quelques tableaux de la vie d'un prêtre de la terre." *Notes Africaines,* no. 31 (July 1946): 22.

———. "L'Esprit de la culture sonraie." *Présence Africaine,* no. 14/15 (June–September 1957): 149–54.

———. "Note sur les Holé." *Education Africain* (1941–1943).

Henley, Paul. "Spirit Possession, Power, and the Absent Presence of Islam: Reviewing *Les maîtres fous.*" *Journal of the Royal Anthropological Institute* 12, no. 4 (2006): 731–61.

Idrissa, Kimba. "Une révolte paysanne et anticoloniale: la prêtresse Chibo et le mouvement baboulé/hawka au Niger (1925–1927)." In *Sociétés Africaines*, no. 3 (1996).

Lallemand, Suzanne. *La mangeuse d'âmes: Sorcellerie et famille en Afrique noire.* Paris: Harmattan, 1988.

Masquelier, Adeline. "Narratives of Power, Images of Wealth: The Ritual Economy of Bori in the Market." In *Modernity and Its Discontents*, edited by Jean Comaroff and John Comaroff, 3–31. Chicago: University of Chicago Press, 1993.

———. "Ritual Economies, Historical Meditations: The Poetics and Power of Bori among the Mawri of Niger." PhD diss., University of Chicago, 1993.

Nicolaisen, Johannes. "Essai sur la religion et la magie touarègues." *Folk* (Copenhagen), no. 3 (1961): 113–62.

———. "Les 'Juments des Dieux': Rites de possession et condition féminine en pays hausa (Vallée de Maradi, Niger)." *Etudes Nigériennes*, no. 21 (1967).

Nicolas-Monfouga, Jacqueline. *Ambivalence et culte de possession. Contribution à l'étude du Bori hausa.* Paris: Anthropos, 1972.

Paslan, Michela. *Anthropologie du rituel de possession Bori en milieu hawsa au Niger. Quand les génies cohabitent avec Allah.* Paris: L'Harmattan, 2010.

Rasmussen, Susan Jane. *La religion et la magie songhay.* Brussels: Editions de l'Université de Bruxelles, 1989.

Schmoll, Pamela G. "Black Stomachs, Beautiful Stones: Soul-Eating among Hausa in Niger." In *Modernity and Its Discontents*, edited by Jean Comaroff and John Comaroff, 193–220. Chicago: University of Chicago Press, 1993.

Vidal, Laurent. *Rituels de possession dans le Sahel: exemples peul et zarma du Niger.* Paris: L'Harmattan, 2000.

Bozo/Sorko

Baa, M. *La geste de Fanta Maa, archétype du chasseur dans la culture des Bozo.* Niamey: CELTHO, 1987.

Dieterlen, Germaine. "Note sur le génie des eaux chez les Bozo." *Journal de la Société des Africanistes* 12 (1942): 149–55.

Francis-Boeuf, Jean. "Etude sur les Bozos du Niger occidental." *Outre-Mer* 3 (1931): 391–405.

Griaule, Marcel, and Germaine Dieterlen. "L'Agriculture rituelle des Bozo." *Journal de la Société des Africanistes* 19, no. 2 (1949): 209–22.

Ligers, Z. *Les Sorko (Bozo), maîtres du Niger: Etude ethnographique.* 3 vols. Paris: Cinq Continents, 1964–1967.

Rouch, Jean. "Banghawi–Chasse à l'hippopotame au harpon par les pêcheurs sorko du Moyen-Niger." *Bulletin de l'IFAN* (1948): 361–77.

———. "Les Sorkawa, pêcheurs itinérants du Moyan-Niger." *Afrika* 20, no. 1 (January 1950): 5–25. Translated to English in *Farm and Forest* 10 (1950): 36–53.

Ydewalle, Serge d'. "Avec les pêcheurs Sorko du Niger." *Jeune Afrique,* no. 897 (March 1978): 71–73.

Fulani

Ba, Amadou Hampaté, and Germaine Dièterlen. *Koumen: Texte initiatique des pasteurs Peul.* Paris: Ecole Pratique des Hautes Etudes, 1974.

Baba, Diallo. *La Tradition historique peule.* Niamey: Centre d'Etudes Linguistique et Historique par Tradition Orale, 1977.

Beauvilain, Alain. *Les Peuls du Dallol Bosso.* Niamey: Institut de Recherches en Sciences Humaines, 1977.

Beckwith, Carol. "Niger's Wodaabe: People of the Taboo." *National Géographic* (October 1983): 482–509.

———. *Nomads of Niger.* New York: H. N. Abrams, 1993.

Bonfiglioli, Angelo Maliki. *Dud'al Histoire de famille et histoire de troupeau chez un groupe de Wodaabe du Niger.* Cambridge: Cambridge University Press, 1988.

———. "Evolution de la propriété animale chez le WoDaaBe du Niger." *Journal des Africanistes* 55, no. 1/2 (1985): 29–37.

Botting, Douglas. *The Knights of Bornu.* London: Hodder and Stoughton, 1961.

Bovin, Mette. "Nomads of the Drought: Fulbe and Wodaabe Nomads between Power and Marginalization in the Sahel of Burkina Faso and the Niger Republic." In *Ad-*

aptative *Stratégies in African Arid Lands*, edited by Mette Bovin and Leif Manger, 29–57. Uppsala: Scandinavian Institute of African Studies, 1990.

Brakenberry, E. A. "Notes on Bororo Fulbe or Nomad Cattle Fulani." *Journal of the African Society* 23, no. 91/92 (1924).

Brandt, H. *Nomades du Soleil*. Lausanne: Clairefontaine, 1956.

Dièterlen, Gennaine. "Initiation among the Pastoral Peul Tribes." In *African Systems of Thought*, edited by M. Fortes and G. Dièterlen. London: Oxford University Press, 1965.

Dupire, Marguerite. "Contribution à l'étude des marques de propriété du bétail chez les pasteurs Peuls." *Journal de la Société des Africanistes* 24, no. 2 (1955): 123–44.

———. "Les facteurs humains de l'économie pastorale." *Etudes Nigériennes* no. 6 (1972).

———. *Organisation sociale des Peul. Etude d'Ethnographie comparée*. Paris: Plon, 1970.

———. *Peuls Nomades. Etude descriptive des Wodaabe du Sahel Nigérien*. Paris: Institut d'Ethnologie, 1962.

———. "La Place du commerce et des marchés dans l'économie des Bororo (Fulbe) nomades du Niger." *Etudes Nigériennes*, no. 3, 1961.

———. "The Position of Women in a Pastoral Society: The Fulani WoDaaBi." In *Women in Tropical Africa*, edited by Denise Paulme. Berkeley: University of California Press, 1963.

———. "Trade and Markets in the Economy of the Nomadic Fulani of Niger." In *Markets in Africa*, edited by Paul Bohanan and George Dalton, 335–64. Evanston, Ill.: Northwestern University Press, 1962.

Dupire, Marguerite, and Michel De Lavergne de Tressan. "Devinettes peuples et Bororo." *Africa* 25, no. 4 (October 1955): 355–92.

Gallois, Jean. "Les Peuls en question." *Revue de Psychologie des Peuples* (Le Havre), no. 3 (1969): 231–51.

Hama Beidi, Boubakar. *Les Peuls du Dallol Bosso: Coutumes et mode de vie*. Saint-Maur, France: Sépia, 1993.

Hopen, C. E. *The Pastoral Fulbe Family in Owandu*. London: Oxford University Press, 1958.

Johnston, H. A. S. *The Fulani Empire of Sokoto*. London: Oxford University Press, 1967.

Kaartinen, Timo. "The Wodaabe Flight: Inversion of Hierarchy in a West African Pastoral Community." *Soumen Anthropologi* 14, no. 4 (1989): 3–10.

Kintz, D. "Les Peuls de Maradi." PhD diss., University of Bordeaux, 1977.

Layya, Juuldé. *La Tradition Peule des Animaux d'Attache*. Paris: Anthropos, 1973.

———. *La Voie Peule*. Paris Nubia, 1984.

Legal, V. "Acculturation spontanée et acculturation forcée chez les Wodaabe nomades du Niger." MA thesis, University of Paris, 1971.

Loftsdottir, Kristin. *The Bush Is Sweet: Globalization, Identity and Power among WoDaaBe Fulani in Niger*. Uppsala: Nordic Africa Institute, 2008.

Luhi, Charles. "Les Bororo et leurs légendes." *France Eurafrique*, no. 218 (July 1970): 28–31.

Mohamadou, Eldridge. "Les peuls du Niger oriental: Groupes ethniques et dialectes." *Camelang* (Yaoundé), no. 2 (1969): 57–93.

Riesman, Paul. *Freedom in Fulani Social Life.* Chicago: University of Chicago Press, 1979.

Seydou, Christiane. *Bibliographie Générale du Monde Peul.* Niamey: IRSH, 1977.

Soehring, A. "Nomadenland im Aufbruch. Bericht über die Cure Salée 1965 in der Republik Niger." *International Afrika Forum* 2, no. 2 (April 1966): 178–81.

Stenning, Derrick J. "Cattle Values and Islamic Values in a Pastoral Republic." In *Islam in Tropical Africa,* edited by I. M. Lewis. London: Oxford University Press, 1966.

———. *Savannah Nomads: A Study of the Wodaabe Pastoral Fulani.* London: Oxford University Press, 1959.

Tauxier, L. *Moeurs et Histoire des Peuls.* Paris: Payot, 1937.

Tremearne, A. J. *The Niger and the Western Sudan.* London: Hodder and Stoughton, 1910.

Van Offelen, Marion, and Carol Beek. *Nomades du Niger.* Paris: Editions Chêne, 1983.

———. *Nomads of Niger.* New York: Abrams, 1983; London: Collins, 1984.

Wilson-Fall, Wendy. "Resource Management in a Stratified Fulani Community." PhD diss., Howard University, 1984.

Zaborowski. S. "Les Habés et les Peuhls du Niger oriental." *Revue Anthropologique* 22 (1912): 242–47.

Hausa

Bartel, Noirot. "Une province hausa du Niger: Le Tessaoua—essai sur les coutumes." *Renseignements Coloniaux* (February 1937): 20–24; (May 1937): 41–45.

Bonté, Pierre, and N. Echard. "Histoire et histoires. Conception du passé chez les Hausa et les Twareg Kel Gress de l'Ader." *Cahiers d'Etudes Africanes* 61/62 (1976): 237–96.

Charlick. R. B. "Power and Participation in the Modernization of Rural Hausa Communities (Niger)." PhD diss., University of California–Los Angeles, 1974.

"Coutumes haoussa et peul." In *Coutumiers juridiques de l'Afrique Occidentale française.* 3 vols. Vol. 2, 261–301. Paris: Larose, 1933.

Echard, Nicole. *Bori, aspects d'un culte de possession hausa dans l'Ader et le Kurfey.* Paris: EHESS, 1989.

———. "L'Habitat traditionnel dans l'Ader (pays hausa. République du Niger)." *Homme* 7, no. 3 (July–September 1967): 48–77.

———. "Note sur les forgerons de l'Ader (pays haoussa, République du Niger)." *Journal de la Société des Africanistes* 35, no. 2 (1965): 353–72.

———. "La pratique religieuse des femmes dans une société d'hommes. Les Hausa du Niger." *Revue Française de Sociologie* 19, no. 4 (October–December 1978): 551–62.

Erlmann, Veit, and Habou Magagi. *Girkaa: Une cérémonie d'initiation au culte de possession boori des Hausa de la region de Maradi (Niger).* Berlin: D. Reimer Verlag, 1989.

"La famille haoussa." *Niger* (Niamey), no. 8 (November 1969): 18–27.

Faulkingham, Ralph H. "Political Support in a Hausa Village." PhD diss., Indiana University, 1970.

Glew, Robert, and Chaibou Babalé. *Hausa Folktales from Niger*. Athens: Ohio University Center for International Studies, 1993.

Hamani, Djibo. *L'Adar précolonial (République du Niger)*. Contribution à l'étude de l'histoire des états Hausa. Paris: L'Harmattan, 2006.

Keith, Nancy Jean. "Feeding, Weaning and Illness in Young Hausa Children." PhD diss., Michigan State University, 1991.

Levy-Luxereau, A. *Etude Ethno-zoologique du pays hausa en République du Niger*. Paris: Musée d'Histoire Naturelle, 1972.

Nicolas, Guy. "Les Catégories d'ethnie et de fraction au sein du système social Hausa." *Cahier d'Etudes Africaines,* no. 59 (1975): 359–441.

———. *Cosmologie Hausa*. Paris: CNRS, 1965.

———. "Développement rural et comportement économique traditionnel au sein d'une société africaine." *Genève Afrique,* no. 2 (1969): 359–441.

———. *Dynamisme sociale et appréhension du monde au sein d'une société Hausa*. Paris: Musée de l'Homme, 1969.

———. "Essai sur les structures fondamentales de l'espace dans la cosmologie Hausa." *Journal des Africanistes,* 36, no. 1 (1966): 65–107.

———. "Fondements magico-religieux du pouvoir politique au sein de la principauté Hausa du Gobir." *Journal de la Société des Africanistes* 39, no. 2 (1969): 199–231.

———. "The 'Other' Hausas." *West Africa,* no. 3130 (July 4, 1977): 1348–49.

———. "Particularismes régionaux au sein de la culture Haoussa: Aspects Nigériens." *Bulletin des Etudes Africaines* 1, no. 1 (1981): 111–31.

———. "La pratique traditionnelle du crédit au sein d'une société subsaharienne, vallée de Maradi, Niger." *Cultures et Développement* 6, no. 4 (1974): 737–73.

———. "Processus de résistance au 'développement' au sein d'une société africaine." *Civilisations* 21, no. 1 (1971): 45–66.

———. "Les relations sociales dans la société haoussa." *Synthèses Nigériennes*, no. 1 (February 1968): 17–27.

Persyn, René. *Les Talakas*. Paris: La Pensée Universelle, 1978.

Pilaszewicz, S. "The Craft of the Hausa Oral Praise-Poets." In *Folklore in Africa*, edited by S. Biernaczky, 269–76. Budapest: Lorand Eotros University, African Research Project, 1984.

Pucheu, Jacques (ed.). *Contes haoussa du Niger*. Paris: Karthala, 1982.

Rousselot, R. "Notes sur la faune ornithologique des cercles Maradi et de Tanout." *Bulletin de l'IFAN* (1947): 99–137.

Salamone, F. A. *The Hausa People*. 2 vols. New Haven, Conn.: HRAF, 1983.

Saunders, Margaret Overholt. "Marriage and Divorce in a Muslim Hausa Town: Mirria, Niger." PhD diss., Indiana University, 1978.

Smith, Mary F. *Baba of Karo: A Woman of the Muslim Hausa*. New Haven, Conn.: Yale University, 1981.

Smith, Michael. "The Hausa Markets in Peasant Economy." In *Markets in Africa*, edited by Paul Bohanan and George Dalton. Evanston, Ill.: Northwestern University Press, 1962.

Spiltler, G. "Herrschaft über Bauern: Staatliche Herrschaft und islamischurbane Kultur in Gobir." Paper, Frankfurt University, 1978.

Thom, Derrick. "The City of Maradi: French Influence upon a Hausa Urban Center." *Journal of Geography* 70 (1971): 472–82.

———. "The Niger–Nigeria Borderlands: A Politico-Geographical Analysis of Boundary Influence upon the Hausa." PhD diss., Michigan State University, 1970.

Maouri

Karimou, Mahamane. *Les Mawri Zarmaphone.* Niamey: IRSH, 1977.

Latour Dejean, Eiaine de. "Shadows Nourished by the Sun: Rural Social Differentiation among the Mawri of Niger." In *Peasants in Africa*, 104–41. Beverly Hills, Calif.: Sage, 1980.

Leroy, P. "Une population nigérienne. Les Maouri." *CHEAM*, no. 1486 (1949).

Monteil, Vincent. "Note sur la toponomie. L'Astronomie et l'orientation chez les Maures." *Hesperis* 26 (1949): 189–220.

Piault, Colette. "Contribution à l'étude de la vie quotidienne de la femme Mawri." *Etudes Nigériennes*, no. 10 (1965).

Piault, Marc Henri. *Histoire Mauri: Introduction à l'étude des processus constitutifs d'un état.* Paris: CNRS, 1970.

———. "Les Mawri de la République du Niger." *Bulletin du cercle des Jeunes Anthroplogues* (1966).

———. "Les Mawri de la République du Niger." *Cahiers d'Etudes Africanes* 7, no. 28 (1967): 673–78.

———. "La personne du pouvoir ou la souveraineté du souverain en pays mawri (Hausa du Niger)." In *La Notion de personne en Afrique Noire*, 459–65. Paris: CNRS, 1973.

Rochette, R. "Au Niger Tibiri, village Maouri." *Revue Géographie Alpine,* no. 1 (1965): 101–30.

Rochette, R., J. D. Gronoff, F. Masseport, and A. Valancot. "Doumega, Dioundiou, Kawara, Debe. Villages des Dallols Maouri et Fogha." *Etudes Nigériennes*, no. 19 (1967).

Soudié/Kurtey/Wogo

Da Silva, M. "Enquête sur les moeurs et coutumes soudiées avant l'occupation française." *Bulletin d'Enseignement AOF,* 23 (January–March 1934).

Echard, Nicole. "Histoire du Peuplement: Les traditions orales d'un village sudyé, Shat (Filingué, République du Niger)." *Journal de la Société des Africanistes* 39, no. 1 (1969): 57–78.

Kaziendé, Leopold. "Origine des Sudiés." *Education Africaine* 29, no. 104 (1940): 32–44.

Olivier de Sardan, Jean-Pierre. "Marriage among the Wogo." In *Relations of Production: Marxist Approaches to Economie Anthropology*, edited by D. Seddon, 357–87. London: Frank Cass, 1978.

——. *Systèmes des relations économiques et sociales chez, les Wogo (Niger)*. Paris: Institut d'Ethnologie, Musée de l'Homme, 1969.

Rousselot, R. *Les Wogo du Niger. Etudes Nigériennes*, no. 20 (1965).

——. "Les voleurs d'hommes. Notes sur l'histoire des Kurtey." *Etudes Nigériennes*, no. 25 (1969).

Toubou

Baroin, Catherine. *Anarchie et Cohésion sociale chez les Toubou: Les Daza Késerda (Niger)*. Paris: Editions de la Maison des Sciences de l'Homme, 1985.

——. "Dominant-dominé: Complémentarité des rôles et des attitudes entre les pasteurs deda-daza du Niger et leurs forgerons." In *Forge et Forgerons*, edited by Yves Monino, 329–81. Paris: ORSTOM, 1991.

——. "Effets de la colonisation sur la société traditionnelle Daza." *Journal des Africanistes* 47, no. 2 (1977): 123–31.

——. "Esclaves chez les Daza du Niger." In *Itinéraires en pays peul et ailleurs*, 321–41. Paris: Société des Africanistes, 1981.

——. "Les marques de bétail chez les Daza et les Azza du Niger." *Etudes Nigériennes*, no. 29 (1972).

——. "The Position of Tubu Women in Pastoral Production: Daza Kesherda, Niger." *Ethnos* 52, no. 1/2 (1987): 137–55.

——. "Techniques d'adoption en milieu animal. Les Daza du Niger." In *L'homme et l'Animal*. Paris: Institut Inter-Ethnoscience, 1975.

Chapelle, J. "Etude sur les Toubous, nègres sahariens." *CHEAM*, no. 804 (1946).

——. "Les Toubous." *CHEAM*, no. 1039 (1947).

Cline, Walter. *The Teda of Tibesti, Borku and Kawar in the Eastern Sahara*. Menasha, Wis.: George Banta, 1950.

Gamory-Dubourdeat, P. M. "Notes sur les coutumes des Toubous du Nord." *Bulletin du Comité d'Etudes Historiques et Scientifiques de l'AOF* (1926):131–52.

Heseltine, Nigel. "The Toubbou and Gorane." *South African Archaeological Bulletin* 14, no. 1 (1953): 21–27.

Le Rouvreur, Albert. "Agadem et Djado: Deux aspects du Teda." *CHEAM*, no. 1142 (1948).

Tubiana, Jérôme. *Contes toubou du Sahara. Contes recueillis au Niger et au Tchad*. Paris: L'Harmattan, 2007.

Tuareg

Aghali Zakara, Mohamed. *Psycholingustique touarègue*. Paris: INALCO. 1992.

Aghali Zakara, Mohamed, and Jeannine Drouin. *Traditions touarègues nigériennes*. Paris: Harmattan, 1979.

Altanine ag Arias. *Iwillimiden*. Niamey: CNRSH, 1970.

Aymand, A. *Les Touaregs*. Paris: Hachette, 1911.

Barth, Heinrich. "Die Imoscharch oder Tuareg, Volk und Land." *Petermanns Mittelungen* 3 (1857): 239–60.

Bernus, Edmond. "L'évolution de la condition servile chez les Touaregs sahéliens." In *L'Esclavage en Afrique Précoloniale*, edited by C. Meillassoux, 27–47. Paris: Maspero, 1975.

———. "Quelques aspects de l'évolution des Touareg de l'Ouest de la République du Niger." *Etudes Nigériennes*, no. 9 (1963).

———. *Touaregs, chronique de l'Azawak*. Paris: Plume, 1991.

———. *Touaregs Nigériens, Unité Culturelle et diversité régionale d'un peuple pasteur*. Paris: ORSTOM, 1981.

Bernus, Edmond, and A. A. Arias. "Récits historiques de l'Azawagh. Traditions des Iullemmeden Kel Dinnik." *Bulletin de l'IFAN* 32, no. 2 (April 1970): 434–85.

Bernus, Edmond, and Suzanne Bemus. "Du sel et des dates. Introduction à l'étude de la communauté d'In Gall et de Tegidda-n-Tesent." *Etudes Nigériennes*, no. 31 (1972).

Bleeker, Sonia. *The Tuareg, Nomads and Warriors ofthe Sahara*. New York: Morrow, 1964.

Bonté, Pierre. "Le Lion et la gazelle: Etats et Touaregs." *Politique Africaine*, no. 34 (1989): 19–29.

———. "Production et échanges chez les Touareg Kel Gress du Niger." Master's thesis, University of Paris, 1970.

Brock, Lina Lee. "The Tamejirt: Kinship and Social History in a Tuareg Community." PhD diss., Columbia University, 1984.

Cabannes, R., et al. "Etude hémotypologique des populations du massifs du Hoggar et du plateau de l'Aïr." *Bulletin et Mémoire de la Société d'Anthropologie de Paris* 4 (1969): 143–46.

Campbell, Dugald. "Islam et noblesse chez les Touaregs." *Homme*, no. 115 (1990): 7–30.

———. *La tente dans la solitude: La société et les morts chez les Touaregs Kel Ferwan*. London: Cambridge University Press, 1987.

———. *On the Trail of the Veiled Tuareg*. London: Seeley, Service, 1928.

———. "Why Do the Tuareg Veil Their Faces?" In *Contexts and Levels: Anthropological Essays on Hierarchy*, edited by R. H. Barnes et al. Oxford: JASO, 1985.

Chaker, Salem (ed.). *Etudes Touarègues: Bilan des recherches en sciences sociales: Institutions—chercheurs—bibliographie*. Aix-en-Provence: Edisud, 1988.

Claudot-Hawad, Hélène. "Des Etats-nations contre un peuple: Le cas des Touaregs." *Revue de l'Occident Musulman et de la Méditerranée* (Aix-en-Provence) 44 (1987): 48–63.

———. "Femmes touarègues et pouvoir politique." *Peuples Méditerranéens* (Paris) 48/49 (1989): 69–79.

———. "Les Touaregs ou la résistance d'une culture nomade." *Revue de l'Occident Musulman et de la Méditerranée* 51 (1989): 63–73.

———. *Les Touaregs: Portrait en fragments*. Aix-en-Provence: Edisud, 1993.

Clauzel, J. "Les hiérarchies sociales en pays tuareg." *Travaux de l'Institut de Recherches Sahariennes* 21, no. 1 (1962): 120–75.

Coulomb, J. *Zone de Modernisation Pastorale du Niger*. Paris: IEMVT-SEDES, 1971.

"Dix Etudes sur l'Organisation sociale des Touaregs." *Revue de l'Occident Musulman et de la Méditerrannée*, no. 21 (1976), special issue.

Garba, Amadou. "Chez les Touareg on prend le voile quand on est devenu un homme." *France-Eurafrique,* no. 196 (June 1968): 39–40.

Grégoire, Emmanuel. *Touaregs du Niger: Le destin d'un mythe.* Paris: Karthala, 1999.

Hama, Boubou. *Recherche sur l'histoire des Touaregs Sahariens et Soudanais.* Paris: Présence Africaine, 1967.

Hamani, Djibo. *Au carrefour du Soudan et de la Berbérie: Le sultanat Touareg de l'Ayar.* Paris: L'Harmattan, 2006.

Ichefegh, Attoujani. "Problèmes économiques, sociaux et politiques du développement chez les Touaregs Iwellemmendan de la République du Niger." Ottawa: Ottawa University Institute of International Coopération, [1974?]

Jean, Camille-Charles. *Les Touareg du sud-est; Leur rôle dans la politique saharienne.* Paris: Larose, 1909.

Lefevre, Witier, and J. Ruffie. "Note sur l'hétérogénéité biologique des Touaregs." *Revue de l'Occident Musulman,* no. 11 (1972): 99–105.

Leupen, A. H. A. *Bibliographie des populations Touarègues.* Leiden, Netherlands: Afrika-Studiecentrum, 1978.

Mariko, Keletigui. "Political Systems of Pastoral Tuareg in Aïr and Ahaggar." *Folk* (Copenhagen) 1 (1959): 67–131.

———. *Les Touaregs Ouelleminden.* Paris: Karthala, 1984.

Nicolas, Guy. "Un village bouzou du Niger: Etude d'un terroir." *Cahiers d'Outre-Mer* 15, no. 58 (April–June 1962): 138–65.

Norris, H. T. *The Tuaregs: Their Islamic Legacy and Its Diffusion in the Sahel.* London: Aris and Phillips, 1975.

Palmer, H. R. "The Tuareg Veil." *Geographical Journal* 68 (November 1926): 412–18.

Prasse, K. *Dictionnaire touareg-français.* 2 vols. Copenhagen: Museum Tusculanum Press, 2003.

Ramir, Sylvie. *Les pistes de l'oubli: Touaregs au Niger.* Paris: Editions du Félin, 1991.

Rasmussen, Susan J. "Accounting for Belief: Causation, Misfortune, and Evil in Tuareg Systems of Thought." *Man* 24, no. 1 (1989): 124–44.

———. "Gender and Curing in Ritual and Symbol: Women, Spirit Possession and Aging among the Kel Ewey Tuareg." PhD diss., Indiana University, 1986.

———. *Poetics and Politics of Tuareg Aging: Life Course and Personal Destiny in Niger.* DeKalb: Northern Illinois University Press, 2009.

———. *Spirit Possession and Personhood among the Kel Ewey Tuareg.* Cambridge: Cambridge University Press, 1995.

Reeb. "Les Iklan ou les Touaregs Noirs." *CHEAM,* no. 1226 (1947).

———. "Les Noirs au sein de la société touarègue." *CHEAM,* no. 1291 (1948).

Renaud, J. "Etude sur l'évolution des Kel Gress vers la sédentarisation." *Bulletin du Comité des Etudes Historiques et Scientifiques de l'AOF* 2 (1922): 252–62.

Richer, A. *Les Touareg du Niger: Les Ouilliminden.* Paris: Larose, 1924.

Rodd, Francis Rennel. "The Origin of the Tuareg." *Geographical Journal* 67 (1926): 27–52.

———. *People of the Veil.* London: Macmillan, 1926.
———. "A Second Journey among the Southern Tuareg." *Geographical Journal* 73 (1929): 1–19, 147–58.
Saenz, Candelaris. "They Have Eaten Our Grandfather: The Special Status of Aïr Twareg Smiths (Niger)." PhD diss., Columbia University, 1991.
Si Gunga Mayga. "Les Touaregs en pays Songhay." *Niger et Pays Voisin* séries, Cahier 18, texte 1, Fonds Vieillard. Dakar: IFAN Library.
Soehring, Anneliese. "Nomadenland im Aufbruch: Berichte über die 'cure salée' 1965 in der Republik Niger." *Internationales Afrika-forum* (April 1966).
Spittler, Gerd. *Les Touaregs face aux sécheresses et aux famines: Les Kel Ewey de l'Aïr (Niger) 1900–1985.* Paris: Karthala, 1993.
Vautier, Maguy. *Vents de sable.* Paris: L'Harmattan, 2006.
Worley, Barbara. "Property and Gender Relations among Twareg Nomads." *Nomadic Peoples* 23 (1987): 31–35.
———. "Women's War Drum, Women's Wealth: The Social Contribution of Female Autonomy and Social Prestige among Kel Faday Twareg Pastoral Nomads (Niger)." PhD diss., Columbia University, 1991.

Zarma/Songhay

Ardant du Picq, Charles Pierre. *Une population Africaine: Les Dyerma.* Paris: Larose, 1933.
———. "Une population Africaine: Les Dyerma." *Bulletin du Comité d'Etudes Historiques et Scientifiques de l'AOF* 14, no. 4 (October–December 1931).
Baba Kake, Ibrahima. *Djouder, la fin de l'Empire Songhay.* Dakar: Nouvelles Editions Africaines, 1975.
Baba Kake, Ibrahima, and Gilbert Comte. *Askia Mohamed, l'apogée de l'Empire Songhay.* Paris: Editions ABC.
Bernard, Yves, and Mary White-Kaba. *Dictionnaire zarma-français (République du Niger).* Niamey: ACCT, 1994.
Bisilliat, J. "Maladies de village et maladies de brousse en pays songhay." *Cahiers d'ORSTOM* 18, no. 4 (1981/1982): 475–86.
Bisilliat, J., and D. Laya. "Représentations et connaissances du corps chez les Songhay-Zarma: Analyse d'une suite d'entretiens avec un guérisseur." In *La Notion de personne en Afrique*, 331–58. Paris: CNRS, 1973.
Bisilliat, J., E. Pierre, and C. Pidoux. "La notion de Lakkal dans la culture Djerma Songhai." *Psychopathologie Africaine* 3, no. 2 (1967): 207–63.
Bornand, Sandra. *Le Discours du griot généalogiste chez les Zarma du Niger.* Paris: Karthala, 2005.
———. *Parlons zarma: Une langue du Niger.* Paris: L'Harmattan, 2006.
Bouchet, Alain Paul. "Perspectives thérapeutiques et sociales des phénomènes de transe de pays songhay." PhD diss., University of Paris, 1988.
Boulnois, Jean, and Boubou Hama. *L'Empire de Gao: Histoire, coutumes et magie des Sonrai.* Paris: Maisonneuve, 1954.
Clauzel, J. "Des noms songhay dans l'Ahaggar." *Journal of African Languages* 1, no. 1 (1962): 43–44.

Cushman, Amanda. *Zarma Folktales of Niger.* Niantic: Quale Press, 2010.

Davis, Richard Eugène. "Response Innovation in a Zarma Village: Contemporary Tradition in Niger, West Africa." PhD diss., University of Connecticut, 1991.

Diarra, A. "La notion de personne chez les Zarma." In *La Notion de personne en Afrique Noire*, 359–72. Paris: CNRS, 1973.

Diarra, Fatoumata-Agnes. *Femmes Africaines en devenir: Les femmes Zarma du Niger.* Paris: Editions Anthropos, 1971.

———. "Les relations entre les hommes et les femmes et les migrations des Zarma." In *Modem Migrations in Western Africa*, edited by Samir Amin, 226–38. London: Oxford University Press, 1974.

"Documents jerma: Les coutumes." *Niger et Pays Voisin* series, Cahier 53, Fonds Vieillard. Dakar: IFAN Library.

Ducroz, Jean-Marie, and Marie-Claire Charles. *L'Homme Songhay tel qu'il se dit chez les Kaado du Niger.* Paris: Harmattan, 1982.

Dupuis-Yakouba, A. *Les Gow, ou chasseurs du Niger. Légendes songai de la région de Tombouctou.* Paris: Leroux, 1911.

Gado, Boubé. *Le Zarmatarey. Contribution à l'histoire des populations entre Niger et Dallol Mawri.* Niamey: IRSH, 1980. Also PhD diss., University of Paris, 1979.

Hale, Thomas A. "Kings, Scribes and Bards: A Look at Signs of Survival for Keepers of Oral Tradition among the Songhay-Speaking Peoples of Niger." In *Folklore in Africa Today*, edited by S. Biernaczky. Budapest: Lorand Eotros University, 1984. Also in *Artes Populares* 1 (1983): 207–20.

———. *Scribe, Griot and Novelist. Narrative Interpreters of the Songhay Empire.* Gainesville: University of Florida Press, 1990.

Hale, Thomas A., et al. *The Epic of Askia Mohammed.* Bloomington: Indiana University Press, 1996.

Kaba, Lansiné. "The Pen, the Sword and the Crown: Islam and Revolution in Songhay Reconsidered." *Journal of African History* 25, no. 3 (1984): 241–56.

———. "Le pouvoir politique, l'essor économique et l'inégalité sociale au Songhay 1464–1591." *Bulletin de l'IFAN* 45, no. 1/2 (1983).

Karimou, M. "Rôle du 'griot' dans la société sonrai-djerma (Niger)." *Annales de l'Université d'Abidjan* 1, no. 1 (1972): 97–102.

Lateef, N. V. "A Techno-Environmental Analysis of Zarma Cultural Organization." *Bulletin de l'IFAN* 37, no. 2 (April 1975): 388–411.

Lateef, N. V., and N. L. Lateef. "Zarma Ideology." *Bulletin de l'IFAN* 38, no. 2 (April 1976): 377–89.

Mounkaila, Fatimata. *Le mythe et l'histoire dans la geste de Zabarkane.* Niamey: CELTHO, 1989.

Olivier de Sardan, Jean-Pierre. "Un barde, des scribes, et la geste du Songhay." *Cahiers d'Etudes Africanes* 30, no. 2 (1990): 205–10.

———. *Concepts et conceptions songhay-zarma.* Paris: Nubia, 1982.

———. "Contradictions sociales et impact colonial." PhD diss., University of Paris, 1982.

———. "Esclavage d'échange et captivité familiale chez les Songhay-Zerma." *Journal de la Société des Africanistes* 43, no. 1 (1973): 151–67.

———. "Personnalité et structures sociales (à propos des Songhay)." In *La Notion de personne en Afrique*, 421–45. Paris: CNRS, 1973.

———. *Les sociétés songhay-zerma (Niger-Mali). Chefs, guerriers, esclaves, paysans.* Paris: Karthala, 1984.

———. "Unité et diversité de l'ensemble songhay-zarma-dendi." In *Peuplements et migrations. Actes du premier colloque international.* Niamey: CELTHO, 2000.

Rouch, Jean. "Le calendrier mythique chez les Songhay-Zarma (Niger)." *Systèmes de Pensée en Afrique Noire* (1975): 52–62.

———. "Contribution à l'histoire des Songhay." *Mémoires d'IFAN*, no. 29 (1953).

———. "Rites de pluie chez les Songhay." *Bulletin de l'IFAN* 15, no. 4 (October 1953): 1655–89.

———. "Sacrifice et transfert des âmes chez les Songhay du Niger." *Systèmes de Pensée en Afrique Noire* (1976): 55–66.

———. *Les Songhay.* Paris: Presses Universitaires de France, 1954.

Sarr, M. "Les Songhay." *Etudes Maliennes* (Bamako), no. 4 (January 1973), special issue.

Soumaila Hammadou, Moussa Hamidou, and Diouldé Laya. *Traditions des Songhay de Téra (Niger).* Niamey: ARSAN, CELTHO, Karthala, 1991.

Stoller, Paul. *The Cinematic Griot: The Ethnography of Jean Rouch.* Chicago: University of Chicago Press, 1992.

———. "The Dynamics of Bankwano: Communication and Political Legitimacy among the Songhai." PhD diss., University of Texas–Austin, 1978.

———. *Fusion of the Worlds: The Ethnography of Possession among the Songhay of Niger.* Chicago: University of Chicago Press, 1989.

———. "The Negotiation of Songhay Space: Phenomenology in the Heart of Darkness." *American Ethnologist* 7, no. 3 (1980): 419–31.

———. "Ritual and Personal Insults in Sonrai Sonni." *Anthropology* 2, no. 1 (1977): 31–37.

———. "Social Interaction and the Management of Songhay Socio-Political Change." *Africa* (London) 51, no. 3 (1981): 765–80.

———. "Son of Rouch: Portrait of a Young Ethnographer by the Songhay." *Anthropological Quarterly* 60, no. 3 (1987): 114–23.

Stoller, Paul, and Cheryl Olkes. *In Sorcery's Shadow. A Memoir of Apprenticeship among the Songhay of Niger.* Chicago: University of Chicago Press, 1989.

Streicher, Allan Joseph. "On Being Zarma: Scarcity and Stress in the Nigérien Sahel." PhD diss., Northwestern University, 1980.

Surugué, B. "Contribution à l'étude de la musique sacrée Zarma-Songhay." *Etudes Nigériennes*, no. 30 (1972).

HISTORY

Abdelkader, A. "Histoire de l'Aïr du Moyen Age à nos jours." *Niger* (Niamey), no. 19 (March 1973): 10–13.

Aboubacar, Adamou. "Agadez et sa région. Contribution à l'étude du Sahel et du Sahara nigérien." Master's thesis, University of Niamey, 1968. Also Niamey: *Etudes Nigériennes*, no. 44 (1979).

Adamu, Mahdi. *The Hausa Factor in West African History*. London: Oxford University Press, 1978.

Afrique Occidentale Française, Gouvernement Général. *Le Niger*. Paris: Société d'Editions Géographiques, Maritimes et Coloniales, 1931.

Alkali, M. Nur. "The Political System and Administrative Structure of Kanem Bornu under the Saifawa." In *Evolution of Political Culture in Nigeria*, edited by J. F. Ade Ajayi and Bashir Ikara, 33–49. Ibadan: Ibadan University Press, 1985.

Amed Toihir, Saïd, and J. Mahi Matiké. "Famine de 1931 au Niger." In *Wood, Energy and Households*, edited by C. Barnes et al., 51–58. Uppsala: Scandinavian Institute of African Studies, 1984.

Arnett, E. J. *The Rise of the Sokoto Fulani*. Kano, Nigeria, 1929.

Ba, A. K. *Sonni Ali Ber*. Niamey: INRSH, 1977.

Baier, Stephen. "Afirican Merchants in the Colonial Penod: A History of Commerce in Damagaram (Central Niger) 1880–1960." PhD diss., University of Wisconsin, 1974.

———. *An Economic History of Central Niger*. London: Oxford University Press, 1981.

———. "The Transsaharan Trade and the Sahel: Damergou, 1870–1930." *Journal of African History* 18, no. 1 (1977): 37–60.

Baier, Stephen, and D. J. King. "Drought and the Development of Sahelian Economies: A Case Study of Hausa-Tuareg Interdependence." *LTC Newsletter*, no. 45 (1974): 11–22.

Beraud-Villars, J. *L'Empire de Gao*. Paris: Plon, 1942.

Bernus, Edmond. "Récits Historiques de l'Azawagh." *Bulletin de l'IFAN* 32, no. 2 (1970): 431–85.

———. *Touaregs: Chroniques de l'Azawak*. Paris: Plume, 1991.

———, et al. *Nomades et commandants: L'administration et sociétés nomades dans l'ancienne AOF*. Paris: Karthala, 1993.

Bernus, Suzanne (ed.). "Henri Barth chez les Touaregs de l'Aïr." *Etudes Nigériennes*, no. 28 (1972).

Berthelot, André. *L'Afrique saharienne et soudanaise. Ce qu'en ont connu les anciens*. Paris: Les Arts et les Livres, 1927.

———. *Hippolyte Berlier (1919–1992), rédemptoriste: Premier évêque du Niger en terre d'Islam*. Paris: L'Harmattan.

Bisilliat, Jeanne, and Dioulde Laya. "The Caravan Trade in the Nineteenth Century." *Journal of African History* 3, no. 2 (1962): 349–59.

———. *Les Zamou*. Niamey: CNRS, 1972.

Bonardi, Pierre. *La République du Niger*. Paris: APD, 1960.

Buret, Joseph. *Le Territoire Français Niger-Tchad*. Brussels: Société d'Etudes Coloniales de Belgique, 1905.

Carlier, Marc. *Méharistes du Niger: Contribution à l'histoire des unités montées à chameau du territoire nigérien: 1900 à 1962*. Paris: L'Harmattan, 2000.

Chailley, Marcel. "La Mission du Haut-Soudan et le drame de Zinder." *Bulletin de l'IFAN* 16, no. 3/4 (July–October 1954): 243–54; 17, no. 1/2 (Jan.-Apr. 1954): 1–58.

Chanoine, Charles P. J. "Mission Voulet-Chanoine." *Bulletin de la Société de Géographie* 20, no. 7 (1899): 220–35.

Chapelle, Jean. *Souvenirs du Sahel: Zinder, lac Tchad, Komadougou.* Paris: Harmattan, 1987.

Clair, Andrée. *Le Niger, pays à découvrir.* Paris: Hachette, 1965.

Clarke, Thurston. *The Last Caravan.* New York: Putnam, 1978.

Clauzel, J. "L'administration française et les sociétés nomades dans l'ancienne Afrique Occidentale Française." *Politique Africaine,* no. 46 (1992): 99–116.

Coilion, Marie-Hélène Joséphine. "Colonial Rule and Changing Peasant Economy in Damagherim, Niger Republic." PhD diss., Cornell University, 1982.

"La convention franco-anglaise du Niger: Le 14 juin 1898." *Afrique Française,* no. 7 (1898): 209–18.

Cros, Pierre. *Niger, la paix nazaréenne.* Paris: Thélès, 2009.

Dankoussou, Issaka. *Histoire du Dawra.* Niamey: Centre Régional de Recherche de la Documentation pour la Tradition Orale, 1979.

———. *Katsina: Traditions historiques des Katsinaawaa après le Jihad.* 1974. Reprint, Niamey: CNRSH, 1988.

David, Phillippe. "La geste du grand Kaura Assao." *Etudes Nigériennes* no. 17 (1964).

———. "Maradi, "l'ancien état et l'ancienne ville." *Etudes Nigériennes,* no. 18 (1964).

———. "Maradi précoloniale: L'état et la ville." *Bulletin de l'IFAN,* no. 3 (July 1969): 638–88.

———. *Niger en transition, 1960–1964: Souvenirs et rencontres.* Paris: L'Harmattan, 2007.

Delafosse, Maurice. *Haut-Sénégal-Niger.* 3 vols. Paris: Larose, 1912.

Delavignette, Robert. "Souvenirs du Niger." *Revue Française d'Histoire d'Outre-Mer* 54, no. 1947 (1967): 13–21.

Dionmansu, Sy. *La Pénétration Européenne au Niger.* Niamey: Imprimerie de Souza, 1972.

Djibo, Hamani. "Contribution à l'étude de l'histoire des états hausa: L'Ader précolonial." *Etudes Nigériennes,* no. 38 (1975).

Djibo, Mamoudou. *Les Transformations politiques du Niger à la veille de l'indépendance.* Paris: L'Harmattan, 2001.

Donaint, Pierre, and François Langrenon. *Le Niger.* Paris: Presses Universitaires de France. 1972.

Doombos, Martin R. "The Shehu and the Mullah: The Jehads of Usuman Dan Fodio." *Genève Afrique* 14, no. 2 (1975): 7–31.

Dubois, Félix. *Notre Beau Niger: Quinze Années de Colonisation Française.* Paris: E. Flammarion, 1911.

Dufour. J. L. *La révolte de l'Aïr (1916–1917).* Paris: Centre d'Etudes sur l'Histoire du Sahara, 1987.

Duhard, Jean-Pierre. "La résistance des Tuaregs de l'Aïr." *Saharien,* no. 109 (1989): 8–13.

Dunbar, Roberta Ann. "Damagaram (Zinder, Niger) 1812–1906: The History of a Central Sudanic Kingdom." PhD diss., University of California, 1971.

———. "Recherches historiques au Damagaram." *Mu Kaara Sani* (Niamey), no. 2:15–19.

Ekechi, F. "Relations between the Royal Niger Company and the French Missions on the Niger. 1885–1900." *Umoja* (New York) 2, no. 2 (July 1975): 13–28.

Elliot, G. S. McD. "The Anglo-French Niger-Chad Boundary Commission." *Geographical Journal* 24 (1904): 505–24.

Fluchard, Claude. *Le PPN-RDA et la décolonisation du Niger, 1946–1960.* Paris: L'Harmattan, 1995.

Foulkes. "The New Anglo-French Frontier between the Niger and Lake Chad." *Scottish Geographical Magazine* 22 (1906): 565–75.

Fugelstad, Finn. "Archival Research in Niger: Some Practical Hints."*African Research and Documentation,* no. 16/17 (1978): 26–27.

———. "The Expédition That Lost Its Head." Paper, University of Birmingham, 1975.

———. "Les Hauka: Une interprétation historique." *Cahiers d'Etudes Africaines,* no. 58 (1976): 217–38.

———. *A History of the Niger, 1850–1960.* Cambridge: Cambridge University Press, 1983.

———. "Niger in the Colonial Period." PhD diss., University of Birmingham, 1976.

———. "A propos de travaux récents sur la mission Voulet-Chanoine." *Revue Française d'Histoire d'Outre-Mer* 67, no. 246/47 (1980): 73–87.

———. "Reconsideration of Hausa History before the Jihad." *Journal of African History* 19, no. 3 (1978): 319–39.

———. "Révolte dans le désert. Les mouvements de révolte chez les nomades du Sahara Nigérien (1915–31)." PhD diss., University of Aix-en-Provence, 1971.

———. "Les révoltes des Touareg du Niger (1916–17)." *Cahiers d'Etudes Africaines* 13, no. 1 (1973): 82–120.

Gandah Nabi, Hassane. "La Compagnie Française de l'Afrique Occidentale au Niger (1926–1998)." *Outre-mers* 91, no. 342–43 (2004): 295–319.

Grégoire, Emmanuel. *The Alhazai of Maradi: Traditional Hausa Merchants in a Changing Sahelian City.* Boulder, Colo.: Lynne Rienner, 1992.

Guilleux, C. *Journal de route d'un caporal de tirailleurs de la mission saharienne (Mission Foureau-Lamy), 1898–1900: Sahara, Aïr, Soudan, Lac Tchad, Chari, Congo.* Belfort: Schmit, 1904.

Guitard, Françoise. "Les conditions de l'évolution du commerce: Agadez." PhD diss., University of Paris, 1988.

Hama, Boubou. *Contribution à la connaissance de l'Histoire des Peuls.* Paris: Présence Africaine, 1968.

———. *L'Empire Songhay: Ses ethnies ses légendes et ses personnages historiques.* Paris: P. J. Oswald, 1974.

———. *Histoire des Songhay.* Paris: Présence Africaine, 1968.

———. *Histoire du Gobir et de Sokoto.* Paris: Présence Africaine, 1967.

———. *L'Histoire d'un peuple: Les Zarma.* 3 vols. Niamey: mimeo, 1964.

————. *Histoire Traditionnelle d'un peuple: Les Zarma-Songhay.* Paris: Présence Africaine, 1967.

————. *Histoire Traditionnelle d'un village Songhay Foneko.* Paris: Présence Africaine, 1970.

————. *Le Niger. Unité et Patrie. Ses Bases historiques à travers l'unité de l'histoire humaine de notre pays.* 2 vols. Paris: mimeo, 1962.

————. *Recherche sur l'histoire des Touaregs sahariens et soudanais.* Paris: Présence Africaine, 1967.

Hama, Boubou, and A. Boulnois. *L'Empire du Gao, Histoire, coutumes, et agie des Songhay.* Paris: Maisonneuve, 1954.

Hunwick, J. O. "Religion and State in the Songay Empire." In *Islam in Tropical Africa*, edited by I. M. Lewis. London: Oxford University Press. 1966.

————. "Songhay Bornu and Hausaland in the Sixteenth Century." In *History of West Africa*, edited by J. F. A. Ajayi and M. Crowder. Vol. 1. New York: Columbia University Press, 1971.

Idrissa, Kimba. "La formation de la colonie du Niger: Des mythes à la politique du mal nécessaire (1880–1922)." PhD diss., University of Paris, 1988.

Janvier, J. "Autour des missions Voulet-Chanoine en Afrique Occidentale." *Présence Africaine* 22 (October–November 1958): 86–100.

Joalland, P. *Le Drame de Dankori, Mission Voulet-Chanoine, Mission Joalland-Meynier.* Paris: Argo, 1930.

————. "Du Niger au Tchad." *Bulletin de la Société Normande de Géographie* 24 (1902): 65–84.

————. "De Zinder au Tchad et la conquête du Kanem." *Géographie* 3 (1901): 369–80.

Karimou, M. *Tradition Orale et Histoire: Les Mawri zarmaphones des origines à 1898.* Niamey: IRSH, 1976.

Kati, Mahmoud, et al. *Tarikh el-Fettach*, translated (French) and edited by Octave Houdas and Maurice Delafosse. Paris: Maisonneuve, 1981 (reprint).

Klobb. *A la Recherche de Voulet.* Paris: Argo, 1931.

Konaré, Adama Ba. *Sonni Ali Ber.* Niamey: IRSH, 1976.

Lambert, R. "Les Salines de Teguidda-n-Tesoum." *Bulletin du Comité d'Etudes Historiques et Scientifiques de l'AOF* 18, no. 2/3 (1934): 366–71.

Laya, Diouldé. "La brousse est morte." In *Pastoralists of the African Savanna*, edited by Mahdi Adamu and A. H. M. Kirk-Greene. Manchester: Manchester University Press, 1986.

Le Coeur, Marguerite. *Les oasis du Kawar.* Niamey: IRSH, 1985.

Le Niger au quotidien: Recueil d'histoires vécues au temps de la présence coloniale. Maisons-Laffite: Imprimerie Finet, 1992.

Lovejoy, Paul E. *Salt of the Desert Sun: A History of Salt Production and Trade in Central Sudan.* Cambridge: Cambridge University Press, 1986.

McDougell, Ann E. "Camel Caravans of the Saharan Sait Trade." In *The Workers of African Trade*, edited by C. Coquery-Vidrovitch and Paul Lovejoy, 99–122. Beverly Hills, Calif.: Sage, 1985.

———. "Salts of the Western Sahara: Myths, Mysteries and Historical Significances." *International Journal of African Historical Studies* 23, no. 2 (1990): 231–58.

Mahaman, Alio. "The Place of Islam in shaping French and British Frontier Policy in Hausaland: 1890–1960." PhD diss., Ahmed Bello University of Zaria, 1997.

Mahamane, Addo. "Institutions et imaginaire politiques hausa: le cas de Katsina sous la dynastie de Korau (XVème-XIXème siècles)." PhD diss., University of Aix-en-Provence, 1998.

Mangeot, P. "Le siège d'Agadès raconte par un prisonnier de Kaossen." *Renseignements Coloniaux*, no. 8 (1930): 479–84.

Marty, A. "Histoire de l'Azawagh nigérien." Thesis, University of Paris, 1975.

Mathieu, M. "La Mission Afrique Centrale." Thesis, University of Toulouse, 1975.

Meynier, O. "La guerre sainte des Senoussya dans l'Afrique Française (1915–18)." *Revue Africaine* 83, no. 2 (1939): 227–75.

———. *Mission Joalland-Meynier.* Paris: Editions de l'Empire Française, 1947.

Miles, William F. S. *Hausaland Divided: Colonialism and Independence in Nigeria and Niger.* Ithaca, N.Y.: Cornell University Press, 1994.

———. "Partitioned Royality: The Evolution of Hausa Chiefs in Nigeria and Niger." *Journal of Modern African Studies* 25, no. 2 (1987): 233–58.

Ministère de la France d'Outre-Mer (France). "Le Niger." Paris, 1950.

Ministère des Affaires Etrangères (France). *Niger et Tchad.* Paris: Cussac, 1918.

Monteil, Charles. *Les empires du Mali.* Paris: Maisonneuve et Larose, 1968.

Morou, Alassane. "Etude de l'équilibre vivrier et de sa problématique au Niger." MSc thesis, Laval University, 1981.

Moumouni, Seyni. *Vie et oeuvre du Cheik Uthmân Dan Fodio (1754–1817): De l'Islam au soufisme.* Paris: L'Harmattan, 2008.

Museur, Michel. "Un exemple spécifique d'économie caravanière: l'échange sel-mil." *Journal des Africanistes* 47, no. 2 (1977): 49–80.

Obichere, Boniface. *West African States and European Expansion: The Dahomey-Niger Hinterland, 1885–1898.* New Haven, Conn.: Yale University Press, 1971.

Olivier de Sardan, Jean-Pierre. "Le cheval et l'arc." In *Guerres de lignages et guerres d'états en Afrique*, edited by Jean Bazin and Emmanuel Terray, 191–231. Paris: Editions des Archives Contemporaines, 1982.

———. *Quand nos pères était captifs . . . récits paysans du Niger.* Paris: Nubia, 1976.

O'Mara, Kathleen Khadija. "A Political Economy of Ahir (Niger)." PhD diss., Columbia University, 1986.

Owen, Richard. *Saga of the Niger.* London: Robert Haie, 1961.

Palmer, Herbert Richmond. *Bornu, Sahara and Sudan.* London: Murray, 1936.

———. "The Central Sahara and the Sudan in the Twelfth Century A.D." *Journal of the African Society* 28, no. 112 (July 1929): 268–378.

Perie, Jean. "Notes historiques sur la région de Maradi." *Bulletin de l'IFAN* 1, no. 2/3 (April–June 1939): 377–400.

Perie, Jean, and Michel Sellier. "Histoire des populations du cercle de Dosso (Niger)." *Bulletin de l'IFAN* 12, no. 4 (October 1950): 1015–74.

Perron, Michel. "Le pays Dendi." *Bulletin du Comité d'Etudes Historiques et Scientifique de l'AOF* (1924): 51–83.

Porch, Douglas. *The Conquest of the Sahara.* Oxford: Oxford University Press, 1986.

Pourage, Gérard, and Jean Vanaye. *Le passé du Niger de l'antiquité à la pénétration coloniale.* 2 vols. Paris: mimeographed, 1973.

Rash, Yehoshua. *Des Colonisateurs sans enthousiasme.* Paris: Paul Geuthner, 1973.

———. "Des colonisateurs sans enthousiasme: Les premières années françaises au Damergou." *Revue Française d'Histoire d'Outre-Mer* 59, no. 214 (1972): 5–69; no. 215 (1972): 240–308.

———. "Un établissement colonial sans histoire. Les premières années française au Niger 1897–1906." PhD diss., Univeristy of Paris, 1972.

Riou, Yves. *La Révolte de Kaocen et le siège d'Agadès 1916–17.* Niamey, 1968.

Rivet. *Notice sur le Territoire Militaire du Niger et le Bataillon de Tirailleurs de Zinder.* Paris: Lavauzelle, 1912.

Rothiot, Jean-Paul. *L'ascension d'un chef africain au début de la colonisation: Aouta le conquérant (Dosso-Niger).* Paris: Harmattan, 1988.

———. *Le Niger: Textes et documents d'histoire du 16e siècle au 20e siècle.* Niamey: INDRAP, 1979.

Rottier, A. "Le Sahara oriental. Kaouar, Djado, Tibesti." *Renseignements Coloniaux,* no. 1 (1924): 1–24; no. 2 (1924): 78–88; no. 3 (1924): 101–8.

Sadi, Abderrahman. *Tarikh es-Soudan.* Translated (French) and edited by Octave Houdas and Edmond Benoist. Paris: Maisonneuve, 1981 (reprint).

Salifou, André. "Colonisation et sociétés indigènes au Niger de la fin du XIX siècle au début de la deuxième guerre mondiale." PhD diss., University of Toulouse. 1977.

———. "La Conjuration manquée du sultan de Zinder, 1906." *Afrika Zamani,* no. 3 (1974): 69–103.

———. *Crise Alimentaire au Niger: Les Leçons du Passé.* Dakar: Institut Africain de Développement Economique et de Planification, 1974.

———. "Le Damagaram ou sultanat de Zinder au XIXème siècle." PhD diss., University of Aix-en-Provence, 1970.

———. "The Famine of 1931 in Niger." *African Environment* 1, no. 2 (1975): 22–48.

———. "Les Français, Fihroun et les Kounta 1902–1916." *Journal de la Société des Africanistes* 43, no. 2 (1973): 175–95.

———. *Histoire du Niger.* Paris: Nathan, 1989.

———. "Kaocen et le siège d'Agadez 1916–17." *Journal de la Société des Africanistes* 42, no. 2 (1972): 193–95.

———. "Kaoussan ou la révolte senoussite." *Etudes Nigériennes,* no. 28 (1973).

———. "Malan Yaroh, un grand négociant du Soudan central à la fin du XIXe siècle." *Journal de la Société des Africanistes* 42, no. 1 (1972): 7–27.

———. "Quand l'histoire se répète: La famine de 1931 au Niger." *Environnement Africain* 1, no. 2 (1975): 25–52.

Séré de Rivières, Edmond. *Histoire du Niger.* Paris: Berger-Levrault, 1966.

———. *Le Niger.* Paris: Editions Maritimes et Coloniales, 1952.

Smith, Michael G. "A Hausa Kingdom: Maradi under Dan Baskore, 1854–1875." In *West African Kingdoms in the Nineteenth Century,* edited by D. Forde, 93–122. London: Oxford University Press, 1967.

———. *Herrschaft über Bauern, die Ausbreitung staatlicher Herrschaft und einer islamisch-urbanen Kultur in Gobir.* Bonn: Campus Verlag, 1978.

———. "The Jihad of Shehu Dan Fodio." In *Islam in Tropical Africa*, edited by L. M. Lewis. London: Oxford University Press, 1966.

———. "Traders in Rural Hausaland." *Bulletin de l'IFAN* 35, no. 2 (1977): 362–85.

Staudinger, Paul. *In the Heart of the Hausa States.* 2 vols. Athens: Ohio University Center for International Studies, 1990.

Stewart, Bonnie Ann. "An Operational Assessment of the National Organization of Commerce and Production in Niger." *Agricultural Administration* (May 1981): 209–19.

———. "Peanut Marketing in Niger." *Journal of African Studies* 7, no. 2 (Summer 1980): 123–28.

Stoller, Paul Allen. *Embodying Colonial Memories: Spirit Possession, Power and the Hauka in West Africa.* New York: Routledge, 1995.

———. "Horrific Comedy: Cultural Résistance among the Hauka Movement in Niger." *Ethos* 12, no. 2 (1984): 165–86.

Terrier, Auguste. "La délimitation de Zinder." *Questions Diplomatiques et Coloniales* 14 (1902): 481–91.

Tymowski, Michal. "Le Niger: Voie de communication de grands états du Soudan occidental." *Africana Bulletin* (Warsaw) 6 (1967): 73–95.

Urvoy, Yves. "Chroniques d'Agadez." *Journal de la Société des Africanistes* 4, no. 2 (1934): 145–77.

———. *Histoire des Populations du Soudan Central.* Paris: Larose, 1938.

Zakari, Maikoréma. *Contribution à l'histoire des populations du sud-est nigérien (Le cas de Mangari, XVIe-XIXe siècles).* Niamey: IRSH, 1985.

———. *Tradition orales du Mangari.* 2 vols. Niamey: CNRS, 1986.

POLITICS AND ECONOMICS

Political Issues

Abba, Seidik. *La Presse au Niger. Etat des lieux et perspectives.* Paris: L'Harmattan, 2009.

Abba, Souleymane. "La chefferie traditionelle en question." *Politique Africaine,* no. 38 (1990): 51–60.

Adji, Boukary. *Dans les méandres d'une transition politique.* Paris: Karthala, 1998.

Agoro, I. O. "The Establishment of the Chad Basin Commission." *International and Comparative Law Quarterly* 15, no. 2 (April 1966): 542–50.

Ahmad, Syed Salahuddin. "Niger-Nigeria Relations, 1960–75." *Kano Studies* 2, no. 1 (1980): 59–72.

Allakaye, Joseph Seydou. "La Société de Développement." *Europe Outremer,* no. 624 (January 1982): 11–14.

Alou, Mahaman Tidjani. "Courtiers malgré eux: Trajectoires de reconversion au sein de l'association Timidria au Niger." In *Les courtiers en développement*, edited by T. Bierschenk, J. P. Chauveau, and J. P. Olivier de Sardan. Paris: Karthala, 2000.

———. "Niger: Civil Society Activists Reinject Politics into Public Life." In *The State of Resistance*, edited by F. Polet, 118–22. New York: Zed Book, 2007.

Amuwo, K. "Military-Inspired Anti-Bureaucratie Corruption Campaigns: An Appraisal of Niger's Experience." *Journal of Modern African Studies* 24, no. 2 (1986): 285–301.

Artuso, Mario. *Décentralisation au Niger: résultats et questions ouvertes.* Paris: L'Harmattan, 2009.

Asiwaju, A. J., and B. M. Barkindo (eds.). *The Nigérian-Niger Transborder Cooperation.* Lagos: Malthouse Press, 1993.

Bakary, Djibo. *Silence! On decolonise. Itinéraire politique et syndical d'un militant africain.* Paris: L'Harmattan, 1992.

Baulin, Jacques. *Conseiller du président Diori.* Paris: Eurafor-Press, 1986.

Beïdi, Boubacar Hama. *La Chefferie traditionnelle au Niger.* Niamey: MEN, 2008.

Bellot, Jean-Marc. "La Politique Africaine de la Libye: Le Cas du Niger." *Revue Française d'Etudes Politiques Africaines* (August–September 1980): 20–36.

Berthier, Thierry. "Le Régime politique de la République du Niger." 2 vols. Thesis, University of Roanne [1973?].

Biarnes, P. "Niger: Les raisons de la Chute." *Revue Française d'Etudes Politiques Africaines,* no. 101 (May 1974): 25–28.

Bois de Goudusson, Jean du. "La réorganisation de la chefferie traditionnelle au Niger." In *Année Africaine 1983,* 108–11. Paris: Pedone, 1985.

Bourgeot, André. "Mouvement de libération nationale et réalité du Sahara." *Pensée,* no. 229 (1982): 91–97.

———. "Révoltes et rébellions en pays touareg." *Afrique Contemporaine,* no. 170 (1990): 3–18.

Casajus, Dominique. "Les amis français de la 'cause touarege.'"*Cahiers d'Etudes Africaines* 35, no. 137 (1995): 237–50.

Chaffard, Georges. *Les Carnets secrets de la décolonisation.* Paris: Calmann-Levy, 1967.

———. "Les carnets secrets de la décolonisation: La subversion au Niger en 1965." *France Eurafrique,* no. 190 (Dec. 1967): 35–37.

Charlick, Robert B. *Niger: Personal Ride and Survival in the Sahel.* Boulder, Colo.: Westview Press, 1991.

———. "Power and Participation in the Modernization of Rural Hausa Communities." PhD diss., University of Califomia–Los Angeles, 1974.

Clair, André. *Le Niger Indépendant.* Paris: ATEOS, 1966.

Comité d'Etudes Historiques et Scientifiques de l'Afrique Occidentale Française. *Coutumiers Juridiques de l'Afrique Occidentale Française,* vol 3. *Mauritanie, Niger, Côte d'Ivoire, Dahomey, Guinée Française.* Paris: Larose, 1939.

Comte, Gilbert. "Le Dahomey au sein de l'Entente. La réconciliation avec le Niger." *Europe France Outre-Mer* 42, no. 426/427 (July–August 1965): 22–24.

———. "Niger: De l'uranium et des jardins." *France Eurafrique,* no. 193 (March 1968): 19–22.

Crombe, Xavier, and Jean-Jacques Jezequel (eds.). *A Not-So Natural Disaster: Niger 2005.* New York: Columbia University Press, 2009.

Dahomey. Service d'Information. *The Truth about the Dispute between Dahomey and Niger.* Porto Novo, 1963.

Dayak, Mano. *Touareg, la tragédie.* Paris: Jean-Claude Lattes, 1992.

Decalo, Samuel. "Modernizing Tradional Society under the Ascetic General." In *Coups and Army Rule*, edited by Samuel Decalo, 241–84. New Haven: Yale University Press, 1990.

———. "Niger: Démocratisation réussie, avenir en suspension." In *L'Afrique politique 1994*, 134–58. Paris: Karthala, 1994. 1974 edition: 6–9.

Deschamps, Alain. *Niger 1995: Révolte touarègue. Du cessez-le-feu provisoire à la "paix définitive."* Paris: L'Harmattan, 2000.

Diori, Hamani. *Parole à la nation.* Niamey, 1963.

Discours et messages: Ali Saibou. Niamey: Agence Nigérienne de Presse, 1988.

Djermakoye, Moumouni Adamou. *15 Avril 1975.* Niamey: Nathan-Adamou, 2005.

"Djibo Bakary parle." *Politique Africaine,* no. 38 (1990): 97–110.

Djibo, Hadiza. *La Participation des femmes africaines à la vie politique, les exemples du Sénégal et du Niger.* Paris: L'Harmattan, 2001.

Djirmey, Aboubacar, et al. "Lutte d'identité culturelle au Niger." *Politique Africaine* (March 1992): 142–48.

Faujas, Alain. "La Politique étrangère du Niger." *Revue Française d'Etudes Politiques Africaines,* no. 72 (December 1971): 41–57.

Frère, Marie-Soleil. *Presse et démocratie en Afrique francophone. Les mots et les maux de la transition au Bénin et au Niger.* Paris: Karthala, 2000.

Fugelstad, Finn. "Djibo Bakary, the French and the Référendum of 1958 in Niger." *Journal of African History* 14, no. 2 (1973): 313–30.

———. "UNIS and BNA: The Rôle of 'Traditionalist' Parties in Niger, 1948–60." *Journal of African History* 16, no. 1 (1975): 113–35.

Gabas, Jean-Jacques. *Aides extérieures dans les pays membres du CILSS: Investissement en panne.* Paris: OCDE, 1987.

Gazibo, Mamoudou. "Foreign Aid and Democratization: Benin and Niger Compared." *African Studies Review* 43, no. 3 (2005).

———. "Niger: l'usure progressive d'un régime militaire." *Afrique Contemporaine* 191 (1999).

———. "Les premières elections locales nigériennes: la décentralisation sur fond de crise." In *L'Afrique politique 1999, entre transitions et conflits.* Paris: Karthala, 1999.

———. "La vertu des procédures démocratiques: élection et mutation des comportements politiques au Niger." *Politique Africaine* 92 (2003).

Gobi, Salou. *Le Destin nigérien. Le douloureux enfantement de la Vème République.* Niamey: NIN, 2002.

Golan, Tamar. "The Conseil de l'Entente." PhD diss., Columbia University, 1980.

Gonidec, P. F. *Constitutions des Etats de la Communauté.* Paris: Sirey, 1959.

Grove, A.T. *Niger and Its Neighbors.* London: Taylor and Francis, 1985.

Guillemin, Jacques. "Chefferie Traditionnelle et administration publique au Niger." *Revue Française d'Etudes Politiques Africaines,* no. 213/2 14 (October–November 1983): 115–24.

———. "Note sur l'évolution de l'organisation administrative territoriale de la République du Niger." *Revue Française d'Etudes Politiques Africaines,* no. 201/202 (October–November 1982): 97–103.

Hama Beïdi, Boubacar. *La Chefferie traditionnelle au Niger.* Niamey: Ministère de l'Education Nationale, 2008.

Hama, Boubou. *L'Itinéraire de l'homme et du militant.* Montreal: Hurtubise, 1993.

Hamani, Abdou. *Les Femmes et la politique au Niger.* Niamey: NIN, 2000.

Hetzel, W. "Problems of the Inland Situation of the Republic of Niger." *Erdkunde* (March 1970): 1–14.

Higgot, Richard A. "Colonial Origins and Environmental Influences on the Foreign Relations of a West African Land-locked State: The Case of Niger." PhD diss., University of Birmingham, 1979.

——. "Niger." In *The Political Economy of African Foreign Policy*, edited by T. Shaw and O. Aluko, 165–89. London: Gower, 1984.

——. "Politics in Niger, 1945–71." MA thesis, Birmingham University, 1974.

——. "Structural Dependence and Decolonization in a West African Land-locked State: The Case of Niger." *Review of African Political Economy,* no. 17 (July–August 1980): 43–58.

Higgot, Richard A., and Finn Fugelstad. "The 1974 Coup d'Etat in Niger: Towards an Explanation." *Journal of Modern African Studies* 13, no. 3 (September 1975): 383–98.

Idrissa, Abdourahmane. "The Invention of Order: Republican Codes and Islam Law in Niger." PhD diss., University of Florida, 2009.

——. "Modèle islamique et modèle occidental: le conflit des élites au Niger." *L'Islam politique au Sud du Sahara: Identities, discours et enjeux,* edited by Muriel Gomez-Perez. Paris: Karthala, 2005.

Idrissa, Kimba (ed). *Armée et politique au Niger.* Dakar: CODESRIA, 2008.

—— (ed.). *Le Niger: Etat et démocratie.* Paris: Karthala, 2000.

Issoufou Tiado, Mahamadou. *Le Niger, une société en voie de démolition.* Paris: L'Harmattan, 2010.

Jouvé, Edmond. "Du Niger de Diori Hamani au gouvernement des militaires." *Revue Française d'Etudes Politiques Africaines,* no. 149 (May 1978): 19–44.

Kotoudi, Idimama. *Transition à la Nigérienne.* Niamey: Nouvelle Imprimerie du Niger, 1993.

Kountché, Seyni. *Discours et Messages, 1974–5.* Niamey: Secrétariat d'Etat à la Présidence Chargé d'Information et Tourisme, 1975.

——. *Discours et Messages, 1975–6.* Niamey: Secrétariat d'Etat à la Présidence Chargé de l'Information, 1976.

Laine, Bernard. "Régime Militaire et Société de développement au Niger 1974–83." *Afrique Contemporaine* (January–March 1983): 38–44.

Les "Dossiers noirs" de la politique africaine de la France n° 8: Tchad, Niger. Escroqueries à la démocratie. Collection. Paris: L'Harmattan, 1998.

Lund, Christian. *Land, Power and Politics in Niger. Land Struggles and the Rural Code.* New Brunswick: Transactions, 1998.

Maidoka, Aboubacar. "La constitution nigérienne du 24 Septembre 1989." *Revue Juridique et Politique,* no. 2 (May–September 1991): 112–32.

Maignan, Jean-Claude, Ginette Fabre, and Jean-François Lionnet. *La Difficile démocratisation du Niger.* Paris: CHEAM, 2000.

Mamoudou, Abdoulaye. *A la conquête de la souveraineté populaire: Les élections au Niger, 1992–1999.* Niamey: Démocratie 2000, 2000.

Martens, George R. *Trade Unionism and Politics in Niger.* Lomé, Togo: Regional Economy and Research Center. 1986.

Martin, François. *Le Niger du Président Diori 1960–1974.* Paris: Harmattan, 1991.

Mayaki, Youssouf. *Gouvernance et développement au Niger. Réflexions iconoclastes pour un sursaut citoyen.* Niamey: ECOFI, 2003.

McEwen, A. C. "The Establishment of the Niger/Nigeria Boundary, 1889–1989." *Geography Journal* 157, no. 1 (March 1991): 62–70.

Meyer, Reinhold. "Legitimität und Souveränität des nigerischen Staates." *Afrika-Spectrum* 22, no. 2 (1989): 193–207.

Milcent, Ernest. "L'Evolution de M. Djibo Bakary." *Chronique Sociale de France,* no. 4 (July 1956): 366–67.

Miles, William F. S. "Self-Identity, Ethnic Affinity and National Consciousness: An Example from Rural Hausaland." *Ethnic and Rural Studies* 9, no. 4 (1986): 427–44.

Mouralis, Jean-Louis. "La Cour d'Etat, juridiction suprême de la République du Niger." In *Les Cours Suprêmes en Afrique,* edited by Gérard Conac, 290–306. Paris: Economica, 1988.

———. "Le Niger après Seyni Kountché." In *Année Africaine 1989,* 243–79. Paris: Pedone, 1990.

"Niger after Kountché." *Africa Confidential* (February 18, 1987).

"Niger Builds." *Africa Report* (December 1970): 11–12.

"Niger Chroniques d'un Etat." *Politique Africaine,* spécial issue, no. 38 (1988).

"Niger: The French Disconnection." *Africa Confidential* (September 8, 1972): 3–5.

"Niger Government." *Africa Confidential* (May 17, 1974).

"Niger: Saibou's Hand." *Africa Confidential* (March 3, 1989): 3–4

"Niger: Soutien populaire au Coup d'état militaire." *Revue Française d'Etudes Politiques Africaines,* no. 101 (May 1974): 20–24.

Nubukpo, Kako. "Les conseils nationaux de chargeurs des pays en voie de développement: L'exemple du Niger." *Revue Juridique et Politique* 41, no. 3 (1987): 168–84.

Ofoegbu, Mazi Ray. "Nigeria and Its Neighbors." *Journal of West African Studies* 12 (1975): 3–24.

Olivier de Sardan, Jean-Pierre, and Mahaman Tidjani Alou (eds.). *Les Pouvoirs locaux au Niger, I: A la veille de la décentralisation.* Paris: Karthala, 2009.

Oumarou, Amadou. "Interférences de la loi, la coutume et la 'charia' islamique devant les juridictions nigériens." *Penant* (April–June 1979): 129–33.

———. "La Loi sur la liberté de la presse au Niger." *Penant,* no. 769 (July–September 1980): 254–61.

Oumarou, Hamani. *L'administration des carrières des magistrats au Niger. Une ethnographie du Conseil de la Magistrature.* Niamey: LASDEL Etudes et Travaux, 2008.

Pons, R. "Le problème touareg: Hier, aujourd'hui et demain." *Marchés Tropicaux et Méditerranéens* (May 7, 1993): 1185–91.

Raynal, Jean-Jacques. "De la démocratisation à la démocratie? La constitution ni-gérienne du 24 septembre 1989." *Afrique Contemporaine,* no. 155 (1990): 68–79.

———. *Les institutions politiques du Niger.* Saint-Maur: Sepia, 1993.

Raynal, Maryse. "La diversité dans l'unité: Le système juridictionnel Nigérien." *Penant,* no. 805 (January–May 1991): 61–110.

Raynaut, Claude, and Souleymane Abba. "Trente ans d'indépendance: Repères et tendances." *Politique Africaine,* no. 38 (1990): 3–29.

Armies of Occupation, 181–203. Waterloo, Belgium: Wilfrid Laurien University Press, 1984.

Robinson, Pearl Theodora. "Traditional Clientage and Political Change in a Hausa Community." In *Transformation and Resiliency in Africa,* edited by Pearl T. Robinson and E. Skinner (eds.), 105–28. Washington, D.C.: Howard University Press, 1983.

Salifou, André. *La question touarègue au Niger.* Paris: Karthala, 1993.

———. *Biographie politique de Diori Hamani, premier président de la République du Niger.* Paris: Karthala, 2010.

Thollard, G. "Le problème de l'enclavement du Niger." Mémoire, University of Bordeaux, 1983.

———. *West Africa's Council of the Entente.* Ithaca, N.Y.: Cornell University Press, 1972.

Van Walraven, Klaas. "Decolonization by Referendum: The Anomaly of Niger and the Fall of Sawaba, 1958–1959." *Journal of African History* 50, no. 2 (2009): 269–92.

———. "From Tamanrasset: The Struggle of Sawaba and the Algerian Connection, 1957–1966." *Journal of North African Studies* 10, no. 3/4 (2005): 507–27.

Vieillard, Gilbert. "Coutumiers du cercle de Zinder, 1932." In *Coutumier Juridique de l'Afrique Occidentale Française.* Vol. 3. Paris: Larose, 1939.

Villalón, Leonardo A., and Abdourahmane Idrissa. "Repetitive Breakdowns and a Decade of Experimentation: Institutional Choices and Unstable Democracy in Niger." In *The Fate of Africa's Democratic Experiments. Elites and Institutions,* edited by Leonardo A. Villalón and Peter VonDoepp. Bloomington: Indiana University Press, 2005.

Wall, Roger. "Niger: Politics and Poverty in the Sahel." *Africa Report* (May–June 1983): 59–65.

Waziri Mato, Maman (ed.). *Les Etats-nations face à l'intégration régionale en Afrique de l'Ouest. Le cas du Niger.* Paris: Karthala: 2007.

Yenikoye, Ismael Aboubacar. *Chroniques de la démocratisation au Niger.* 2 vols. Paris: L'Harmattan Niger, 2007.

———. *Ethique et gouvernance: le cas du Niger.* Paris: L'Harmattan Niger, 2007.

———. *Gouvernance sous la Ve République au Niger.* Paris: L'Harmattan Niger, 2007.

———. *Démocratisation et fonction parlementaire au Niger.* Paris: L'Harmattan Niger, 2007.

Economic and Social Development

Abba, Seidik. *Le Niger face au Sida: Atouts et faiblesses de la stratégie nationale contre la pandémie.* Paris: L'Harmattan, 2008.

Adamou, Aboubakar. "Les ressources minières dans l'économie du Niger." *Etudes Scientifiques* (December 1981): 35–40.

Adesina, Akinwumi Ayodeji. "Farmer Behavior and New Agricultural Technologies in the Rain-Fed Agriculture of Southern Niger." PhD diss., Purdue University, 1988.

Afrique Contemporaine 1, no. 225 (September 2008). Special issue on "La Crise alimentaire au Niger."

Alou, Mahaman Tidjani. "Le Partenariat public-privé dans le secteur de l'eau au Niger: Autopsie d'une réforme." *Annuaire suisse des politiques de développement* 24, no. 2 (2005): 161–77.

Arnould, Eric J. "Merchant Capital, Simple Social Reproduction, and Underdevelopment: Peasant Traders in Zinder, Niger Republic." *Canadian Journal of African Studies* 20, no. 3 (1986): 323–56.

———. "Petty Craft Production and the Underdevelopment Process in Zinder, Niger." *Dialectical Anthropology* 6 (1981): 61–70.

———. "Process and Social Formation: Petty Commodity Producers in Zinder, Niger." *Canadian Journal of African Studies* 18, no. 3 (1984): 501–22.

———. "Regional Market System Development and Changes in Relations of Production in Three Communities in Zinder Province, Niger." PhD diss., University of Arizona, 1982.

———. "Social Reproduction in Zinder Province, Niger Republic." In *Households: Comparative and Historical Studies of the Domestic Group*, edited by Robert McNettling, R. R. Wilk, and Eric J. Arnould. Los Angeles: University of California Press, 1984.

Audette, Raymond. "Stockage traditionnel de céréales vivrières en milieu paysan au Niger." MSc thesis, Laval University, 1983.

Azam, Jean-Paul. *Le Niger: La pauvreté en période d'adjustement.* Paris: Harmattan, 1993.

Ba, B. "The Problem of Transferring Technology to the Least Industrialized Countries (the Case of Niger)." *Labour and Society* (Geneva) 1, no. 3/4 (July–October 1976): 121–26.

Baier, Stephen. "The Development of Agricultural Credit in French-Speaking Africa, with Special Reference to Niger." MA thesis, University of Wisconsin, 1969.

———. *An Economic History of Central Niger.* Oxford: Clarendon Press, 1980.

———. "Long Term Structural Change in the Economy of Central Niger." In *West African Cultural Dynamics*, edited by B. K. Swartz and R. E. Dumett, 587–602. The Hague: Mouton, 1980.

Baillaud, Emile. "La mise en valeur des territoires du Niger français." *Annales des Sciences Politiques* 14 (1899): 744–65.

———. "Les territoires français du Niger: Leur valeur économique." *Terre-Air-Mer* 2 (1900): 9–24.

Beaussou, Jean-Jacques. "Genèse d'une classe marchande au Niger." In *Entreprises et Entrepreneurs en Afrique*, 205–20. Paris: L'Harmattan, 1988.

———. "Le Niger Central." Thesis, University of Paris, 1980.

Beck, Alois J. *Theorie und Praxis der "Animation Rurale" im Frankophonen Afrika: Landliche Entwicklung im Departement Zinder. Republik Niger.* Bochum, Germany: Studienverlag Brockmeyer, 1981.

Belloncle, Guy. *Coopératives et développement en Afrique noire sahélienne.* Sherbrooke, Quebec: Centre d'Etudes en Economie Coopérative, 1978.

———. "Une expérience d'animation coopérative au Niger." *Archives Internationales de Sociologie de la Coopération et du Développement*, no. 21 (January–June 1967): 47–73.

———. "Une expérience d'animation coopérative au Niger." In *Villages en Développement*, edited by H. Desroche and P. Rambaud, 201–27. Paris: Mouton, 1971.

———. "Formation des hommes et développement au Niger. Introduction à la problématique nigérienne." *Développement et Civilisations*, no. 49/50 (September–December 1972): 27–37.

Bellot, Jean-Marc. *Commerce, Commerçants de bétail et migration régionale; L'exemple de l'Ouest du Niger.* Bordeaux: Institut d'Etudes Politiques, 1982.

———. "Exportations du bétail et politique nationale: L'exemple des exportations de l'Ouest du Niger." *Revue Française d'Etudes Politiques Africaines*, no. 207/208 (April–May 1978): 77–105.

Brosch, J. "Canada et Niger: De la francophonie à la coopération." *France Eurafrique*, no. 210 (October 1969): 28–30.

Carle, P. "Une expérience d'assistance technique: La création de la Société Nigérienne de Commercialisation de l'Arachide (SONARA)." *Coopération et Développement* (October–December 1964): 14–20.

Chako, Cherif. "Politique agricole et accords internationaux des échanges au Sahel. Cas du Niger. World Bank Document. 2000. http://www-wds.worldbank.org/external/default/WDSContentServer/WDSP/IB/2005/08/26/000160016_2005082 6162606/Rendered/PDF/319260Politiqu1ccordsInternationaux.pdf (accessed 18 September 2010).

Charlick, Robert B. "Induced Participation in Nigerien Modernization: The Case of Matamaye County." *Rural Africana*, no. 18 (Fall 1972): 5–29.

———. "Participatory Development and Rural Modernization in Hausa Niger." *African Review* (Dar es Salaam) 2, no. 4 (1972): 499–524.

Collins, John Davison. "Government and Groundnut Marketing in Rural Hausa Niger: The 1930s to the 1970s in Magaria." PhD diss., Johns Hopkins University, 1974.

Colombe, J. *Textes généraux sur la planification nigérienne.* Niamey: Ecole National d'Administration, [1972?].

Curry, John James. "Local Production, Regional Commerce, and Social Differentiation in a Hausa Village in Niger." PhD diss., University of Massachusetts, 1984.

Dan Moussa, L. "L'Information en tant que stimulant du développement rural au Niger." PhD diss., University of Paris, 1974.

Delpy, Jacques. "Le Développement économique de la République du Niger." Thesis, University of Paris, 1960.

Derriennic, Hervé. *Famines et Dominations en Afrique Noire: Paysans et Eleveurs du Sahel sous le Joug.* Paris: L'Harmattan, 1977.

Dorosh, Paul Anthony, and B. Essema Nssah. *External Shocks, Policy Reform, and Income Distribution in Niger.* Ithaca, N.Y.: Cornell University Food and Nutrition Policy Program, 1993.

Doutresscule, Georges Alexis-Helie. "L'Elevage au Niger." Thesis, Mortain University, 1924.

Dynamique de l'emploi dans un système sahélien, le Niger. Addis Ababa: Bureau International du Travail, 1980.

Eberhart, Frederick B. "Equitable Distribution in Small-Scale Agricultural Projects in the Niger Republic: Trade-Offs in Reaching the Poor." MA thesis, University of Indiana, 1985.

Economic Commission for Africa. *Le développement industriel du Niger.* Mimeo. Addis Ababa, 1965.

Ediafric. *Les Plans de Développement des Pays d'Afrique Noire.* Paris, 1972.

Elbow, Kent M. "Popular Participation in the Management of Natural Resources: Lessons from Baban Rafi, Niger." PhD diss., University of Wisconsin, 1992.

Everts, Arjaan. *Industrialisation des pays d'Afrique s sub-saharienne: Le cas du Niger,* edited by by C. Brochet and J. Pierre. 1986.

Frelastre, Georges. "La Nouvelle stratégie rurale du Niger." *Revue Française d'Etudes Politiques Africaines,* no. 211/212 (August–September 1983): 69–106.

———. "Le séminaire de Zinder et la nouvelle stratégie de la République du Niger." *Revue Française d'Etudes Politiques Africaines,* no. 211/212 (1983): 69–80, 97–106.

Fuchs, P. "Sozio-Ökonomische Aspekte der Dürrekatastrophe für die Sahara-Bevölkerung von Niger." *Afrika Spectrum* 9, no. 3 (1974): 308–16.

Gavin, Sarah. "Land Tenure and Fertility Management in Niger." PhD diss., Stanford University, 1993.

Gérard, M. "Arlit et les retombées économiques de l'uranium sur le Niger." Thesis, University of Aix-Marseilles, 1974.

Gilliard, Patrick. *L'Extrême pauvreté au Niger. Mendier ou mourir?* Paris: Karthala, 2005.

Grégoire, Emmanuel. "L'Etat doit-il abandonner le commerce des vivres aux marchands?" *Politique Africaine* 37 (1990): 63–70.

———. "Le fait économique haoussa." *Politique Africaine* 38 (1990): 61–67.

Guilbert-Nignon, Louise. "Les ouvriers mineurs du Niger." PhD diss., University of Paris, 1989.

Guillaumont, Patrick, and Sylvaine Guillamont. *L'Ajustement structurel, ajustement informel: Le cas du Niger.* Paris: Harmattan, 1989.

Hugon, Pierre. "Les programmes d'ajustement structurel du Niger et l'impact de l'économie nigérienne." *Afrique Contemporaine,* no. 155 (1990).

Jabara, Cathy L. *Structural Adjustment and Stabilization in Niger.* Ithaca, N.Y.: Cornell University Food and Nutrition Policy Program, 1991.

Jacquemin, André. *La Fiscalité des Collectivités Territoriales du Niger.* Niamey: Ecole Nationale d'Administration, 1974.

Judet, P., and R. Tiberghien. *L'Industrialisation de l'économie nigérienne: Diagnostic, éléments pour une problématique, premières pistes pour des stratégies.* Niamey: Ministère du Plan, 1986.

Julienne, Roland. "Les plans de développement des Etats de l'Afrique francophone." *Industries et Travaux d'Outre-Mer,* no. 195 (February 1970): 85–91.

———. "Les plans de développement des états de l'Afrique francophone en 1975." *Industries et Travaux d'Outre-Mer,* no. 266 (January 1976): 11–18.

Justice, C. O., and P. H. Y. Hiernaux. "Monitoring the Grasslands of the Sahel." *International Journal of Remote Sensing* 7, no. 11 (1986): 1475.

Karimou, Goukoye. "L'Animation des collectivités au développement." *Europe France Outre-Mer,* no. 430 (November 1965): 41–43.

Laya, Diouldé. "Interviews with Farmers and Livestock Owners about the Famine." *African Environment* 1, no. 2 (1975): 49–70.

Le Niger: La pauvreté en période d'ajustement. Paris: L'Harmattan, 1993.

Luxereau, Anne. *Changements écologiques et sociaux au Niger.* Paris: L'Harmattan, 2000.

Maiga, Issaka Doulaye. "Difficultés et limites de l'animation rurale: Le cas du Niger, 1964–1974." In *La participation populaire au développement en Afrique Noire,* edited by A. C. Mondjanagni, 155–70. Paris: Karthala, 1984.

Maina, Sanda. "On Food Security in Niger Republic." MS thesis, Michigan State University, 1982.

Meunier, Michel. "Le rôle de l'armature urbaine dans le processus de formation de l'espace: Le cas du Niger." MA thesis, University of Montréal, 1975.

Meyer, R. "Die 'animation rurale' in Niger: Möglichkeiten und Verwirklichungschancen in einer peripheren Gesellschaftsformation." *Afrika Spectrum* 11, no. 2 (1976): 145–55.

Morou, Alassane. "Etude de l'équilibre vivrier et de sa problématique au Niger: Une perspective à long terme." MSc thesis, Laval University, 1981.

Moulton, J. "Development through Training: *Animation Rurale* in Niger and Sénégal." In *Non-formal Education and National Development,* edited by J. C. Bock and G. J. Papgiannis, 25–41. New York: Praeger, 1983.

Nnadozie, E., and M. Dwight. "The Political Economy of Islamic Penetration and Development in Niger." *Scandinavian Journal of Development Alternatives* 9, no. 2/3 (June–September 1990): 205–20.

Nubukpo, Kako. "Le concept de banque et d'établissement financier dans les pays de l'UMOA: Le cas du Niger." *Revue Juridique et Politique* 41, no. 4 (1987): 328–44.

Raulin, Henri. *Le Développement rural: De la région au village: Analyser et comprendre la diversité.* Bordeaux: Groupe de Recherches Interdisciplinaires pour le Développement, 1988.

Roberts, Pepe. "Rural Development and the Rural Economy in Niger." In *Rural Development in Africa,* edited by J. Heyer, P. Roberts, and G. Williams, 193–221. New York: St. Martin's Press, 1981.

Rodary, Pierre. "L'Organisation Commune du Dahomey-Niger (OCDN)." *Bulletin de la Chambre du Commerce du Niger,* no. 144 (Apil 15, 1963): 1–9.

——. "L'Organisation Commune Dahomey-Niger des chemins de fer et des transports." *Industries et Travaux d'Outre-Mer*, no. 116 (July 1963): 634–38.

Rouch, Jean. *Rapport sur les migrations nigériennes vers la Basse Côte d'Ivoire.* Niamey: IFAN, 1957.

Saint André, Christian. "La Compagnie de culture cotonniere du Niger 1919–1927: Intérêts nationaux ou intérêts privés?" PhD diss., University Paul Valéry, 1978.

Schaefer, Kurt Carpenter. "A Portfolio Model of Mixed Farming in Less Developed Countries, with an Application to Project Evaluation in Southeastern Niger." PhD diss., University of Michigan, 1984.

Schneider, James B. "Development as Dialogue: The UNCC Story." *Community Development Journal* 4, no. 3 (July 1969): 151–58.

Sidikou, Hamidou. *Une region sahélienne en crise: le Zarmaganda (République du Niger)*. UNESCO report, 1987.

Somerville, Carolyn M. *Drought and Aid in the Sahel: A Decade of Development Coopération.* Boulder, Colo.: Westview Press, 1986.

Sordet, Monique. "Une Terre ingrate, un exemple d'équilibre ethnique." *Europe France Outre-Mer*, no. 503 (December 1971): 5–7.

——. "Traders in Rural Hausaland." *Bulletin de l'IFAN* 39, no. 2 (1977): 362–85.

Starr, Martha. "Risk, Environmental Variability and Drought-Induced Poverty: The Pastoral Economy of Central Niger." *Africa* (London) 57, no. 1 (1987): 29–56.

Thomas-Peterhans, Randall. "The Stratification of Livestock and the Production and Marketing of Livestock in Southeastern Niger." PhD diss., University of Michigan, 1983.

Tinguiri, Kiari Liman. "Crise économique et ajustement structurel 1982–86." *Politique Africaine* 38 (1990): 78–86.

Toh, K. "Niger's External Debt: Legacy of Uranium-Led Strategy." *Eastern Africa Economie Review* 3, no. 1 (1987): 27–41.

Vourc'h, Anne, and Maina Boukar Moussa. *L'expérience de l'allégement de la dette du Niger.* Paris: OCDE, 1992.

SCIENCES

Linguistics

Abdoulaye, Mahamane Laouali. "Derived Direct Objects in Hausa." *Journal of West African Languages* 21, no. 1 (1991): 75–90.

——. "Les variations en hausa chez les locuteurs natifs. *Cahiers de l'Institut de Linguistique et des Sciences du Langage* 15 (2004): 127–77.

Abraham, Roy C. *Dictionary of the Hausa Language.* London, 1963.

Adam, Yacoudima. *Lexique Kanuri.* Niamey: INDRAP, 1982.

Aghali-Zakara, Mohamed. "Enseignement des langues africaines par la télévision: L'expérience nigérienne." *Bulletin des Etudes Africaines de l'INALCO* (Paris) 3, no. 5 (1983): 3–13.

——. "Essai de psycholinguistique touarègue." *Bulletin des Etudes Africaines de l'INALCO* (Paris) 6, no. 12 (1986): 5–96.

———. "L'interaction des systèmes linguistiques et apprentissage d'une langue: Cas du français et du berbère." *Bulletin des Etudes Africaines de l'INALCO* (Paris) 2, no. 3 (1982): 13–32.

Alawjely, G. ag. *Awgele temajeq-tefrensist.* Copenhagen: Akademisk Forlag, 1980.

Ardant du Picq, Charles Pierre. *La Langue songhay, dialecte dyerma: Grammaire et lexique français-dyerma et dyerma-français.* Paris: Larose, 1933.

Arnott, D. W. "Fula Language Studies: Present Position and Future Prospects." In *Pastoralists of the West African Savanna*, edited by Mahdi Adamu and A. H. M. Kirk-Greene, 87–100. Manchester: Manchester University Press, 1986.

———. "Some Features of the Nominal Class System of Fula in Nigeria, Dahomey and Niger." *Afrika und Übersee* 43, no. 4 (March 1960): 241–78.

Bargery, George P. *A Hausa-English and English-Hausa Vocabulary.* London: Oxford University Press, 1951.

Barth, Heinrich. "Vocabulary of the Language of Agadiz." *Journal of the Royal Geographical Society* 21 (1851): 169–91.

Basset, André. "Parlers touaregs du Soudan et du Niger." *Bulletin du Comité d'Etudes Historiques et Scientifiques de l'AOF* 18, no. 2/3 (1935): 336–52.

Bohm, Gerhard. *Die Sprache der Ful: grammatikgeschichtliche Grundlagen und Entwicklung.* Vienna: AFRO-Pub, 1989.

Caron, Bernard. *Le haoussa de l'Ader.* Berlin: Reimer, 1991.

Casajus, Dominique. "Sur l'argot des forgerons touaregs." *Awal: Cahiers d'Etudes Berbères* 5 (1989): 124–36.

Cew Sonray. Niamey: Centre Régional de Documentation pour la Tradition Orale, 1970.

Cortade, Jean Marie, and Mouloud Mammeri. *Inititation à la langue des Touaregs de l'Air.* Agadez: Fraternité Charles de Foucauld, 1968.

Cowan, J. Ronayne, and Russell G. Schuh. *Spoken Hausa.* Ithaca, N.Y.: Spoken Language Service, 1976.

Cyffer, Norbert, and John Hutchinson. *A Dictionary of the Kanuri Language.* Dordrecht: Foris Publications, 1990.

Dauzats, André. *Lexique français-peul et peul-français.* Albi: Imprimerie Albigeoise, 1952.

Dupuis, Yakouba. *Essai de méthode pratique pour l'étude de la langue songoi ou songai.* Paris: Leroux, 1917.

Eguchi, P. K. *An English-Fulfulde Dictionary.* Tokyo: Institute for the Study of Languages and Culture of Asia and Africa, 1986.

Foucauld, Charles Eugène de. *Dictionnaire abrégé touareg-français (dialecte Ahaggar).* 2 vols. Algiers: Jourdan, 1918.

———. *Dictionnaire touareg-Français.* 4 vols. Paris: Imprimerie Nationale, 1951–52.

Furniss, Graham, and Philip J. Jaggar (eds.). "Problèmes de toponymie haoussa: Les noms de villages de la région de Maradi." *Revue Internationale Onomastique* (Paris) 19, no. 2 (June 1967): 95–127.

———. *Studies in Hausa Language and Linguistics.* London: Kegan Paul, 1988.

Greenberg, Joseph H. "Arabie Loanwords in Hausa." *Word* (New York) 3, no. 1/2 (1947): 86–97.

Hacquard, A., and Auguste-Victor Dupuis. *Manuel de la langue Songhay parlée de Tombouctou à Say.* Paris: Maisonneuve, 1897.

Jarrett, Kevin A. "Dialectes et alphabétisation dans les écoles Kanuri du Niger." *Journal of West African Languages* 18, no. 2 (November 1988): 105–24.

Jolivet, Rémi, and Fabrice Rouiller (eds.). *Pratiques et représentations linguistiques au Niger. Résultats d'une enquête nationale.* Lausanne: Cahiers de l'ILSL no. 15, 2004.

Lacroix, P. F. "Les langues du Niger." *Synthèses Nigériennes,* no. 1 (February 1968): 5–16.

Manessy, G. "Le Français d'Afrique Noire." *Langue Française,* no. 37 (February 1978): 91–105.

Monteil, Charles. "Les apparentements génétiques du Songhay." In *Proceedings of the Fourth Nilo-Saharan Conférence, 1989,* edited by M. Lionel Bender. Hamburg: Buske, 1991.

———. *Les Dialectes du Songhay.* Paris: SELAF, 1981.

Tersis, Nicole. *Le Dendi: Phonologie, lexique dendi-français.* Paris: Bulletin de SELAF, 1972.

———. *Grammaire Zarma.* Paris: SELAF, 1973.

———. *Le Parler Dendi.* Paris: SELAF, 1968.

———. *Phonologie Zarma.* Paris: SELAF, 1973.

———. *Le Zarma. Etude du parler Djerma de Dosso.* Paris: SELAF, 1972.

Tran, Hong Cam. "Approche socio-linguistique de l'emprunt français en hausa." *Etudes Linguistiques* 2, no. 1 (1980): 13–51.

———. "Contribution à l'étude phonétique des nigérismes." *Bulletin de l'AELTA* 2 (March 1981): 40–49.

Waali, Naybi, and Muhammadi Habali. *Kaara Karaatuu.* Niamey: Centre Régional de Documentation pour la Tradition Orale, 1971.

Westermann, Diedrich H. "Ein Beitrag zur Kenntnis des Zarma-Songai am Niger." *Zeitschrift Eingeborenen Sprachen* 11, no. 3 (1921): 188–220.

———. "Nationalsprachenpolitik im Niger." *Zeitschrift für Phonetik* 43, no. 4 (1990): 484–91.

Yanco, Jennifer J. "Language Attitudes and Bilingualism in Niamey, Niger." *Africana Journal* 14, no. 1 (1983): 1–9.

Nature and Environment

Adjanohoun, Edouard J. *Médicine Traditionnelle et Pharmacopée: Contribution aux Etudes Ethnobotaniques et Floristiques au Niger.* Paris: Agence de Coopération Culturelle et Technique, 1980.

Adjanohoun, Edouard J et al. *Contribution aux études ethnobotaniques et floristiques au Niger.* Paris: Agence de Coopération Culturelle et Technique, 1980.

Allan, J. A. (ed.). *The Sahara: Ecological Change and Early History.* London: MENAS Press, 1981.

Bembelo, Arouna. "La Chèvre rousse et son exploitation au Niger." Thesis, University of Toulouse, 1961.

Bergassoli, Michel. "Scope and Conditions for Improved Use of Food and for Development: The Case of Niger." In *Food Aid for Development*, edited by Haitmut Schneider, 69–82. Paris: OECD, 1978.

Brochaye, J. "Le Goruol, République du Niger." Thesis, University of Rouen, 1973.

Buerkert, Andreas, and B. E. Allison (eds). *Wind Erosion in Niger: Implications and Control Measures in a Millet-Based Farming System.* New York: Springer, 1996.

Bui, Elizabeth Nathalie. "Relationships between Pedology, Geomorphology and Stratigraphy in the Dallol Bosso of Niger, West Africa." PhD diss., Texas A&M University, 1986.

Charre, J. "Le Climat du Niger." Thesis, Université du Grenoble, 1974.

Hooker, Jackson William (ed.). *Niger Flora: Or, an Enumeration of the Plants of Western Tropical Africa.* Cambridge: Cambridge University Press, 2011 (reissue).

Jomini, Patrick André. "The Economic Viability of Phosphorus Fertilization in Southwestern Niger: A Dynamic Approach Incorporating Agronomic Principles." PhD diss., Purdue University, 1990.

Koster, Stanley Henry. "A Survey of the Vegetation and Ungulate Populations in Park W, Niger." MS thesis, Michigan State University, 1982.

Mainguet, M. "Carte des degrés de réactivation des manteaux sableux." *Conférence des Nations Unies sur la Désertification* (September 1977).

Mascianis, Marcel-Paul. "Le précambrien de la partie orientale de la boucle du Niger." Thesis, University of Clermont-Ferrand, 1955.

Ministère de la Coopération (France). *Cartographie des pays du Sahel.* Paris, 1976.

Ouattara, Mamadou. "A Study of Two Toposequences of the Dry Valley of Western Niger." PhD diss., Texas A&M University, 1990.

Scott-Wendt, John William. "An Evaluation of the Causes of Soil Infertility in Niger." PhD diss., Purdue University, 1989.

Thom, D. J. "The City of Maradi: French Influence upon a Hausa Urban Center." *Journal of Geography* 70 (1971): 472–82.

Social Sciences and Humanities

Alou, Antoinette Tidjani. "Ancestors from the East, Spirits from the West. Surviving and Reconfiguring the Exogenous Violence of Global Encounters in the Sahel." *Journal des africanistes* 80, no. 1/2 (2010): 75–92.

———. "Niger and Sarraounia: One Hundred Years of Forgetting Female Leadership." *Research in African Literatures* 40, no. 1 (2009): 42–56.

Arnaud, M., and B. Spire. *Urbanisme et habitat: République du Niger.* Paris, 1960.

Arnould, Eric J., and Helen K. Henderson. "Women in Niger." In *Women in Development.* Tucson: University of Arizona, International Agricultural Programs Working Paper no. 1, 1982.

Bandiaré, Ali. "L'Enfant dans la société nigérienne." *Revue Juridique et Politique,* no. 2 (April–June 1977): 371–79.

Barkow, Jérôme H. "Strategies for Self-Esteem and Prestige in Maradi." In *Psychological Anthropology*, edited by T. R. Williams, 373–88. Paris: Mouton, 1975.

Barou, Jacques. "L'Emigration dans un village du Niger." *Cahiers d'Etudes Africaines* 6, no. 63/64 (1976): 627–32.

Bataillou, C. "Modernisation du nomadisme pastoral." In *Nomadisme et Nomades au Sahara*, 165–77. Paris: UNESCO, 1963.

Belloncle, Guy. *Femmes et Développement en Afrique Sahelienne.* Paris: Nouvelles Editions Africaines, 1980.

Bernus, Suzanne. "Niamey, Population et habitat." *Etudes Nigériennes*, no. 11 (1962).

———. *Particularismes ethniques en milieu urbain; L'exemple de Niamey.* Paris: Institut d'Ethnologie, Musée de l'Homme, 1969.

Biston, Pascal. "L'immigration à Niamey. Causes, consequences et perspectives, representation et politique migratoire." Master's thesis, Université Joseph Fourier of Grenoble, 1992.

Bonnecase, Vincent. "Faim et mobilisations sociales au Niger dans les années 1979 et 1980: Une éthique de la subsistance?" *Genèses* 4, no. 81 (2010): 5–24.

Ciucci, L., and D. Maffioli. "L'impact de l'urbanisation sur les modèles de consommation alimentaire de base au Niger." *Africa* (Rome) 43, no. 2 (1988): 292–97.

Clerson, Gérard. "Habitat à Niamey." MA thesis, Université de Sherbrooke, 1972.

Cooper, Barbara. *Evangelical Christians in the Muslim Sahel.* Bloomington: Indiana University Press, 2006.

———. *Marriage in Maradi. Gender and Culture in a Hausa Society in Niger.* Portsmouth, N.H.: Heinemann: James Currey, 1997.

Dandobi, Mahamane. "Les institutions matrimoniales basées sur la tradition et la coutume ne sont pas restée immuables." *Niger* (Niamey), no. 12 (March 6, 1967): 3; no. 13 (March 13, 1967): 5, 8.

———. "Le mariage au Niger." *Revue Juridique et Politique,* no. 1 (January–March 1967): 105–17.

Davis, Richard Eugène. "Responses to Innovation in a Zarma Village: Contemporary Tradition in Niger." PhD diss., University of Connecticut, 1991.

Diarra, Fatoumata Agnès. *Femmes africaines en dévenir, les femmes zarma du Niger.* Paris: Anthropos, 1971.

Diop, M. "Etude sur le salariat: Haute-Sénégal, Niger, Soudan, Mali, 1884–1963." *Etudes Maliennes* (Bamako), no. 14 (1975).

Dudot, Bernard. "Traditions sur les origines de la ville de Niamey." *Notes Africaines,* no. 117 (January 1968): 19–20.

Gado, Bouréïma Alpha. *Une histoire des famines au Sahel. Etude des grandes crises alimentaires (XIXème et XXème siècles).* Paris: L'Harmattan, 1993.

Galy, Kadir Abdelkader. *L'Esclavage au Niger. Aspects historiques et juridiques.* Paris: Karthala, 2009.

Gervais, Raymond. "Les conséquences démographiques de la sécheresse au Sahel: Le cas du Niger, 1969–1974." MSc thesis, Université de Sherbrooke, 1982.

Hama, Boubou. *Le Double d'hier rencontre demain.* Paris: UGE, 1973.

———. *L'Exode rural: Un problème de fond.* Niamey: Editions de la Croix Rouge Nigérienne, 1968.

———. "Textes et Documents sur la ville de Niamey." Niamey: IFAN, 1955.

Harragin, Simon. *The Cost of Being Poor: Markets, Mistrust and Malnutrition in Southern Niger.* London: Report for Save the Children UK, 2006.

Kelley, Thomas A. "Exporting Western Law to the Developing World: The Troubling Case of Niger." Working Paper. Berkeley, Calif.: Berkeley Electronic Press, 2006.

King, M. H. W. "Rural-Urban Migration in Niger." Thesis, University of Michigan, 1977.

Le Niger: La pauvreté en période d'ajustement. Collection. Paris: L'Harmattan, 2000.

Le Thin, Kim Dung. "Etude de la fécondité au Niger à partir d'une sondage, 1970–1971." MSc thesis, University of Niamey, 1976.

Maccatory, Bénédicte, Makama Bawa Oumarou, and Marc Poncelet. "West African Social Movements 'against the High Cost of Living': From the Economic to the Political, from the Global to the National." *Review of African Political Economy* 37, no. 125 (2010): 345–59.

Ministère de l'Economie et de Finances (Niger). Recensement général de la population 1988. Niamey, 1992.

Ministère du Plan (Niger). Direction de la Statistique et de l'Information. Estimations de quelques paramètres démographiques de la population du Niger de 1977 à l'an 2000. Niamey, 1985.

———. Recensement général de la population 1977. Niamey, 1987.

Monnier, A. "Les organisations villageoises de jeunes: Samari." Niamey: CNRSH, 1967.

"Niamey: Capital of the French Niger Colony." *Geographical Journal* 76 (T930): 364.

"Niamey, perle du Niger." *Europe France Outre-Mer*, no. 503 (December 1971): 8–10.

Painter, Thomas Michael. "Making Migrants: Zarma Peasants in Niger, 1900–1920." In *African Population and Capitalism: Historical Perspectives*, edited by Dennis D. Cordell and Joël W. Gregory, 122–33. Boulder, Colo.: Westview Press, 1987.

———. "Peasant Migration and Rural Transformation in Niger." PhD diss., State University of New York–Binghamton, 1986.

Raynaut, Claude. "Circulation monétaire et évolution des structures socio-économiques chez les Haoussas du Niger." *Africa* 47 (1977).

Saunders, M. O. "Marriage and Divorce in a Muslim Hausa Town: Mirria, Niger." PhD diss., University of Indiana, 1978.

Sauvy, Jean. "Un marché africain urbain: Niamey." *Notes Africaines,* no. 38 (April 1948): 1–5.

Séré de Rivières, Edmond. "La Chefferie au Niger." *Penant* 77, no. 718 (October–December 1967): 463–88.

Service de la Statistique (Niger). "La population dans la République du Niger," by H. Wiesler. 2 vols. Niamey, 1973.

Talfi, Bachir. "Quel droit de la famille applicable au Niger? Le pluralisme juridique en question." Research Paper, April 2008. http://www.humanrights.dk/files/doc/forskning/Research%20partnership%20programme%20publications/B.T._Idrissa.pdf (accessed 26 November 2010).

Thom, Derrick J. "The City of Maradi: French Influence upon a Hausa Urban Center." *Journal of Geography* (November 1971): 472–82.

——. The Morphology of Maradi, Niger." *African Urban Notes,* no. 7 (Winter 1972).

Villalón, Leonardo A. "The Moral and the Political in African Democratization: The 'Code de la Famille' in Niger's Troubled Transition." *Democratization* 3, no. 2 (1996): 41–68.

LITERATURE, CINEMA, AND THE ARTS

Aghali, Zakari, and Jeannine Drouin. *Traditions Touarègues nigériennes. Ameroloqis, héros civilisateur pre-islamique, et Aligurran, archétype social.* Paris: L'Hartmattan, 1979.

Bebnoné, Palou. "Kaltouma." *L'Avant Scène,* no. 327 (1965): 33–39.

Beik, Janet. "Hausa Théâtre in Niger." PhD diss., University of Wisconsin. 1984. Reprint. New York: Garland. 1985.

——. "Plays without Playwrights: Community Creation of Contemporary Hausa Theatre in Niger." In *African Literature in Its Social and Political Dimensions,* edited by Eileen Julien et al., 23–31. Washington, D.C.: Three Continents, 1986.

Bernard, Manama, and Yves Bernard. "Le cinéma au Niger." *7e Art,* no. 49 (1984): 5–7.

Bisilliat, Jeanne, and Diouldé Laya. *Les zamu ou poèmes sur les noms.* Niamey: CNRS, 1972.

Card, Caroline Elizabeth. "Tuareg Music and Social Identity." PhD diss., Indiana University, 1982.

Casajus, Dominique. "Le frère, le djinn et le temps qui passe." *Cahiers de Littérature Orale* 12 (1982): 15–38. Also in English in *Research in African Literatures* 15, no. 2 (Summer 1984): 218–37.

——. *Peau d'âne et autres contes touaregs.* Paris: Harmattan, 1985.

——. "Un salon littéraire chez les Touaregs." *Cahiers de Littérature Orale* (1982): 177–78.

Chaïbou, Dan-Inna. "La théâtralité en Pays Hawsa." MA thesis, University of Abidjan, 1979.

Chaïbou, Dan-Inna, and J. D. Pennel. *Bibliographie de la littérature nigérienne.* Niamey: Centre Culturel Franco-Nigérien, 1988.

Choupaut, Yves-Marie. "Boubou Hama, dans son roman 'Kotia Nima' réconcilie les hommes de tous les pays avec leur enfance." *France Eurafrique,* no. 222 (December 1970): 36–38.

Clair, Andrée, and Boubou Hama. *Founya le vaurien.* Paris: Editions G. P., 1975.

——. *Kangué Izé.* Paris: La Farandole, 1974.

——. *La Savane Enchantée.* Paris: La Farandole, 1972.

Coppe, Claudie, and Adamou Garba. *Contes du Niger.* Paris: Nathan Afrique, 1984.

Dandobi, Mahamane. "L'Aventure d'une chèvre; pièce satirique en 4 tableaux." *Traits d'Union* (Dakar), no. 9 (July–September 1955): 76–83.

——. *Kabrin Kabra.* Paris, 1958.

Delisse, Louis François. *Enquête sur l'architecture et la décoration murale à Zinder.* Niamey: OAU-CELTHO, 1986.

Desenclos, A., A. Clair, and H. Coltrane. *Contes du Niger.* Niger (Niamey), no. 10 (May 1970): 20–62.

De Zeltner, Franz. *Contes du Sénégal et du Niger.* Paris: Leroux, 1913.

Diado, Amadou. *Maimou, ou le drame de l'amour.* Niamey: Editions du Niger, 1972.

Diawara, Issoufou. "Moustapha derrière la caméra." *Niger* (Niamey), no. 2 (January 1968): 70–75.

Douze nouvelles du Niger. Niamey: Centre Culturel Franco-Nigérienne, 1988.

Ducroz, J. M., and M. C. Charles. "Recherche sur la prosodie soney." *Etudes Linguistiques* (Niamey) 1, no. 1 (1979): 50–77.

Etienne-Nugué, Jocelyne, and Mahamane Saley. *Artisanats traditionnels en Afrique Noire: Niger.* Paris: Harmattan, 1987.

Ferrand, Gérard. *Anthologie de la poésie nigérienne.* Paris: Centre International de la Pensée et des Arts Français, 1970.

Foucauld, Charles Eugène. *Poésies touaregues.* Paris: Leroux, 1930.

Foucauld, Charles Eugène, and A. de C. Motylinski. *Textes touareg en prose.* Algiers: J. Carbonel, 1922.

Glew, Robert S., and Chaibou Babalé (eds.). *Hausa Folk Tales from Niger.* Athens: Ohio University Press, 1993.

Grandadam, Sabine, et al. *Neuf nouvelles du Niger.* Niamey: Centre Culturel Franco-Nigérienne, 1983.

Haffner, Pierre. "Edgar Ray Sugar Robinson, alias Oumarou Ganda dit: Le conteur." *7e Art,* no. 42 (1982): 16–19; no. 43 (1981): 16–19.

———. "Eine nationale Schule: Niger." *Revue pour le Cinéma Français* 27/28 (November 1989): 35–46.

Hama, Boubou. *L'Aventure extraordinaire de Bi Kado, fils de noir.* Paris: Présence Africaine, 1971.

———. *Bagouma et Tiegouma.* Paris: Présence Africaine, 1975.

———. *Cet "autre" de l'homme.* Paris: Présence Africaine, 1972.

———. *Contes et légendes du Niger.* 6 vols. Paris: Présence Africaine, 1972–76.

———. *L'essence du verbe.* Niamey: CELTHO, 1988 (posthumous).

———. *Izegani: L'enfant vert.* Niamey: Centre Culturel Franco-Nigérien, 1990 (posthumous).

———. *Moisson de ma jeunesse.* Niamey: Imprimerie National du Niger, 1981.

Hama, Boubou, and Andrée Clair. *Le Baobab merveilleux.* Paris: La Farandole, 1971.

Hassane, Diallo Amadou. *A l'ombre des anciens.* Niamey: Imprimerie Nationale du Niger, 1980.

Heathcote, David. *The Arts of the Hausa.* Chicago: University of Chicago Press, 1977.

Hiskett, Mervyn. *A History of Hausa Islamic Verse.* London: School of Oriental and African Studies, 1975.

Ilbo, Ousmane. *Le cinéma au Niger.* Brussels: OCIC, 1993.

Issa, Ibrahim. *Grandes eaux noires.* Paris: Les Editions du Scoipion, 1959.

———. *La vie et ses facéties: Poèmes.* Niamey: Imprimerie Nationale du Niger, 1974.

Issa Daouda, Abdoul-Aziz. *La Double tentation du roman nigérien.* Paris: L'Harmattan, 2006.

Laya, Diouldé, J. D. Pénel, and Boubé Namaïwa (eds.). *Boubou Hama. Un homme de culture nigérien.* Paris: L'Harmattan, 2007.

"Littérature Nigérienne." *Notre Librairie* (Paris) (1991): special issue.

Maiga, Boubou Idrissa. *Poésies nigériennes, enfant du Grand et Beau Niger.* Paris: ABC.

Malanda, Ange-Séverin. "L'exil et le lointain: Hommage à Oumarou Ganda." *Présence Africaine,* no. 119 (1981): 170–75.

Malleval, Félix, et al. *Dix nouvelles du Niger.* Niamey: Centre Culturel Franco-Nigérien, 1980.

Mamani, Abdoulaye. *Poèmérides.* Paris: Oswald, 1972.

———. *Sarraounia.* Paris: Harmattan, 1980.

Mariko, Kélétigui. *Sur les rives du fleuve Niger: Contes sahéliens.* Paris: Karthala, 1984.

Mateso, E. Locha. "Niger." *Anthologie de la poésie d'Afrique noire d'expression française,* 138–46. Paris: Hatier, 1987.

Mercier, Paul, and Jean Rouch. *Chants du Dahomey et du Niger.* Paris: GLM, 1950.

Mester de Parajd, Corinne, and Laszio Mester de Parajd. *Regards sur l'habitat traditionnel au Niger,* 10–14. Nonette, France: Centre de Réalisations d'Etudes et d'Editions Régionales, 1988.

Mohamadou, Halilou Sabbo. *Aboki, ou l'appel de la côte.* Dakar: Nouvelles Editions Africaines, 1978.

Mounkaila, Fatimata. *Le mythe et l'histoire dans la geste de Zabarkane.* Niamey: CELHTO, 1989.

Muzi, Jean. *Anthologie de la littérature orale songhay-zarma.* 4 vols. Paris: L'Harmattan, 2008.

———. *Contes des rives du Niger.* Paris: Flammarion, 1986.

Oumarou, Ide. *Gros Plan.* Paris: Nouvelles Editions Africaines, 1978.

———. *Le Représentant.* Abidjan: Nouvelles Editions Africaines, 1984.

Ousmane, Amadou. *15 Ans, ça suffit.* Niamey: Imprimerie Nationale du Niger, 1979.

———. *Chroniques judiciaires.* Niamey: Imprimerie Nationale du Niger, 1987.

Outman, Mahamat. *Les Sahels.* Paris: Oswald, 1972.

Paraiso, Moustapha Richard. *Une femme qui rêve.* Paris: La Pensée Universelle, 1991.

Pénel, Jean-Dominique. *Littérature Nigérienne. Rencontre: Keletigui Mariko, Mamani Abdoualye, Ide Oumarou, Yazi Dogo, Hawad.* Niamey: Centre Culturel Franco-Nigérien, 1990.

———. *Littérature Nigérienne. Rencontre,* 2. Niamey: Editions du Ténéré and Paris: L'Harmattan, 2010.

———. *Littérature Nigérienne. Rencontre,* 3. Niamey: Editions du Ténéré and Paris: L'Harmattan, 2010.

Prost, A. "Légendes songhay." *Bulletin de l'IFAN* 18, no. 1/2 (January–April 1956): 188–201.

Rauss, Raymond. "L'Art et le récit: Un pont entre deux cultures: à propos du film de Moustapha Diop." *Peuples Noirs: Peuples Africains,* no. 52 (1986): 116–26.

Rouch, Alain, and Gérard Clavreuil (eds.). "Niger." *Littératures nationales d'écritures françaises*. Paris: Bandas, 1986.

Salifou, André. *L'Empereur des menteurs et autres contes haoussa*. Niamey: NIN, 2002.

———. *Tanimoune*. Paris: Présence Africaine, 1973.

———. *Tels pères, tels fils. Une saga sahélienne*. Paris: Karthala, 1994.

Sauty, Louis. *Le Ténéré*. Paris: René Juliard, 1945.

Sauvy, Jean. *Jean Rouch tel que je l'ai connu*. Paris: L'Harmattan, 2006.

Say, Bania Mahmadou. *Algaita, trente et un poèmes du Niger*. Niamey: Imprimerie Nationale du Niger, 1980.

———. *Le Voyage d'Hamado*. Abidjan: Nouvelles Editions Africaines, 1981.

Scheinfeigel, Maxime. "*Cabascabo*: Un film de Oumarou Ganda." *Avant-Scène-Cinéma*, no. 265 (1981): 39–50.

Seydou, Christiane. "Aspects de la littérature Peul." In *Pastoralists of the African Savanna*, edited by Mahdi Adamu and A. H. Kirk-Greene, 101–12. Manchester: Manchester University Press, 1986.

———. *Contes et Fables des Veillées*. Paris: Nubia, 1976.

———. "Panorama de la littérature peule." *Bulletin de l'IFAN* 35, no. 1 (January 1973): 176–218.

———. *Silamaka et Poulori, récit épique peul*. Paris: Armand Colin, 1972.

Souleymane, Yazidou, and Bernard Caron (eds.). *Contes haoussa*. Paris: CILF, 1985.

Standifer, James A. "The Tuareg: Their Music and Dances." *Black Perspectives in Music* (Cambria Heights) 16, no. 1 (Spring 1988): 45–62.

Stephens, Connie Lee. "Relationship of Social Symbols and Narrative Metaphor." PhD diss., University of Wisconsin, 1981.

Tchoumba-Ngouankeu, I. *Autour du Lac Tchad*. Yaoundé: Editions CLE, 1969.

Tersis, Nicole. *En Suivant le calebassier*. Paris: CILF, 1979.

———. *La Mare de la Vérité, contes et musique zerma*. Yaoundé: Editions CLE, 1977.

Tilho, J., and M. A. Landeroin. *Grammaire et contes Haoussa*. Paris: Imprimerie Nationale, 1909.

Traoré, Bini. "L'Exilé d'Oumarou Ganda."*Peuples Noirs: Peuples Africains*, no. 23 (1981): 54–93.

Urvoy, Yves François. *L'Art dans le territoire du Niger*. Niamey: IFAN, 1955.

Vieyra, Paulin Soumarou. "Hommage à Oumarou Ganda: cinéaste nigérien." *Présence Africaine*, no. 119 (1981): 165–69.

Watta, Oumarou. "The Human Thesis: A Quest for Meaning in African Epic." PhD diss., State University of New York–Buffalo, 1985.

Zoumé, Boubé. *Les souffles du coeur*. Yaoundé: Editions CLE, 1977.

TOURISM AND TRAVEL

Adamou, Aboubacar, and Alain Morel. *Niger, Agadez et les montagnes de l'Aïr: Aux portes du Sahara*. Grenoble: Editions de la Boussole, 2005.

Ascani, Maurice, and Hamidou Arouna Sidikou. *Niamey à 360°*. Dakar: Editions Laure Kane, 2010.

Behnke, Alison. *Niger in Pictures*. Brookfield: Twenty-First Century Books, 2008.

Boubacar, Seyni Gagara. *Ecotourisme et Patrimoine: Comment sauvegarder le Parc "W" du Niger?* Sarrebruck: Editions Universitaires Européennes, 2010.

Durou, Jean-Marc, and Pierre-Maris Decoudras. *Bonjour le Sahara du Niger: Aïr, Ténéré, Kawar, Djado*. Richelieu: Editions du Pélican, 2001.

Geels, Jolijn. *Niger: The Bradt Travel Guide*. Chalfont St Peter: Bradt Travel Guides, 2006.

Heinrichs, Ann. Niger. *Enchantments of the World*. Danbury: Scholastic Library, 2001.

Morgan, Ted. *The Strong Brown God: The Story of the Niger River*. Boston: Houghton Mifflin, 1976.

Rabeil, Thomas. *Distribution potentielle des grands mammifères dans le Parc du W du Niger*. Sarrebruck: Editions Universitaires Européennes, 2010.

Ruszniewski, Jean-Yves. *KoKowa: la lutte traditionnelle au Niger*. Paris: Sépia, 2005.

Sellato, Eric. *Niger, la magie d'un fleuve.* Paris: Vilo, 2004.

Silhol, Sandrine. *La Girafe blanche du Niger*. Saint-Sébastien-sur-Loire: Editions d'Orbestier, 2006.

SOURCES, REFERENCE WORKS, AND BIBLIOGRAPHIES

Papers

Africa Contemporary Record: Annual Survey and Documents. London: Africa Research, 1969–.

Africa Research Bulletin, Economic, Financial and Technical Series (online at http://onlinelibrary.wiley.com/journal/10.1111/(ISSN)1467–6346) and Political, Social and Cultural Series (online at http://onlinelibrary.wiley.com/journal/10.1111/(ISSN)1467–825X/issues). Monthly, Wiley-Blackwell, United Kingdom, 1964–.

Africa South of the Sahara. London: Europa Publications, 1971–.

Africa South of the Sahara: Index to Periodical Literature. Washington, D.C.: Library of Congress, Africa and Middle East Division, 1985.

Africa Yearbook. Politics, Economics and Society South of the Sahara. Leiden, Brill. 2005–.

Afrique. Paris: Jeune Afrique, 1968–.

Année Africaine. Paris: Pedone, 1963–.

Année Politique Africaine. Dakar: Société Africaine d'Edition, 1966–.

Asamani, J. O. *Index Africanus: Catalogue of Articles in Western Languages Published from 1885 to 1965*. Stanford, Calif.: Hoover Institution, 1975.

Baier, S. "Archives in Niger." *History in Africa,* no. 1 (1975): 155–58.

Berger, Pierre (ed.). *Exporter au Burkina Faso et au Niger*. Paris: Ubifrance, 2007.

Beudot, Françoise. *Eléments de Bibliographie sur les pays du Sahel*. Paris: OCDE, 1990.

Bibliographie de documents du CILSS et le Club du Sahel. Paris: OCDE, 1989.

Bibliographie de documents et rapports sur les pays du Sahel (1977–1985). Paris: OCDE, 1989.

Bibliographie des Travaux en Langue Française sur l'Afrique au Sud du Sahara. Paris: Centre d'Etudes Africaines, 1982.

Bibliographie ethnographique de l'Afrique sud-saharienne. Tervueren: Musée Royal de l'Afrique Centrale, 1966–.

"Bibliographie sommaire de la République du Niger." *Etudes et Documents,* no. 18 (April 1969).

"Bibliographie Toaurègue: Langue, culture et société, 1977–1987." In *Etudes Touarègues,* edited by A. Chaker, 92–102. Aix-en-Provence: CNRS, 1990.

Blackhurst, Hector (ed.). *Africa Bibliography.* Manchester: Manchester University Press, 1985–1989; Edinburgh: Edinburgh University Press, 1990–.

Blake, David, and Carole Travis. *Periodicals from Africa: A Bibliography and Union List of Periodicals Publishers in Africa.* Boston: G. K. Hall, 1984.

Carson, P. *Materials for West African History in French Archives.* London: Athlone Press, 1968.

Catalogue Systématique de la Section Afrique, Bibliothèque du Musée de l'Homme. 2 vols. Paris, 1970.

Centre de Développement de l'OCDE. *Sécheresse au Sahel. Sélection d'articles de périodiques à partir de Décembre 1972.* Paris, 1974.

Chaïbou, Maman. *Répertoire biographique des personnalités de la classe politique et leaders d'opinion du Niger. 1945 à nos jours.* 2 vols. Niamey: Démocratie 2000, 1999, and 2003.

Chronologie Politique Africaine. Paris: Fondation Nationale des Sciences Politiques, 1960–1970.

Commissariat Général au Développement (Niger). Centre de Documentation. *Bibliographie Sommaire de la République du Niger.* Niamey, 1972.

Conover, H. F. *Official Publications of French West Africa, 1946–1958.* Washington, D.C.: Library of Congress, 1960.

Coulibaly, Siaka. *Eléments de bibliographie sur les pays du Sahel.* Paris: OCDE, 1991.

Deutsche Afrika-Gesellschaft. *Afrikanische Köpfe.* Hamburg, 1971.

Documentation Française (France), La. *Bibliographie Sommaire de la République du Niger.* Paris, 1969.

Donaint, Pierre. "Bibliographie sommaire de la République du Niger d'après le fichier de G. de Beauchêne." *Etudes et Documents* (Niamey), no. 18 (April 1969).

Fugelstad, Finn. "Archival Research in Niger: Some Practical Hints." *African Research and Documentation* 16/17 (1978): 26–27.

Gaignebet, Wanda. *Inventaire des thèses africanistes de langue française.* Paris: CARDAN, 1975, and subséquent intermittent éditions.

Hull, Doris (éd.). *A Current Bibliography on African Affairs.* Monthly, Farmingdale, N.Y.: Baywood, 1968 –.

Idrissa, Kimba. "Historiographie nigérienne. Bilan critique et perspectives." http://www.histoire-afrique.org/article12.html (accessed 23 November 2010).

Institut Fondamental d'Afrique Noire. *Catalogue des Manuscrits de l'IF AN.* Dakar: IFAN, 1966.

International Africa Institute. *Africa.* 1929–. International Africa Institute.

Joucla, Edmond A. *Bibliographie de l'Afrique occidentale française.* Paris: Société d'Editions Géographiques, Maritimes et Coloniales, 1937.

Journal Officiel de la République du Niger. Niamey, 1958–.

Journal Officiel du Territoire du Niger. Niamey, 1933–1958.

Le Rouvreur, Albert. *Eléments pour un dictionnaire biographique de Tchad et du Niger.* Paris: CNRS, 1978.

"Les travaux scientifiques du Président Boubou Hama." *Mu Kaara Sani* (Niamey), no. 1 (n.d.): 40–41.

Lipschutz, Mark, and R. Kent Rasmussen. *Dictionary of African Historical Biography.* Berkeley: University of California Press, 1986.

Marchés Tropicaux et Méditerranéens. Weekly. Paris, 1950–.

Massoni, G., et al. *Liste Bibliographique des Travaux effectués dans le bassin du fleuve Niger par les chercheurs de l'ORSTOM de 1943 à 1968.* Paris: ORSTOM, 1971.

Mauny, Raymond. "Bibliographie de la préhistoire et de la protohistoire de l'Ouest Africain." *Bulletin de l'IFAN* 29, no. 3/4 (July–October 1967): 879–917.

Meillassoux, Claude. *Cartes Historiques d'Afrique Occidentale (Sénégal et Haut-Sénégal et Niger, 1802–1899).* Paris: Musée de l'Homme, 1970.

Ministère du Plan (Niger). *Annuaire statistique.* Niamey, 1985–.

Revue Française d'Etudes Politiques Africaines. Monthly/quarterly. Paris, 1968–1990.

Le Sahel (Niamey). Daily. 1961–.

Sahel: A Guide to the Microfiche Collection of Documents and Dissertations. Ann Arbor, Mich.: University Microfilms International, 1981.

Saix, E. *Cuvette du Lac Tchad: Elément d'une bibliographie.* Paris: Prohuza, 1962.

SCOLMA. *United Kingdom Publications and Theses on Africa.* Cambridge: Heffer, 1963–.

Seydou, Christiane. *Bibliographie Générale du Monde Peul.* Niamey: INSH, 1977.

The 2009 Niger Economic and Product Market Databook. Icon Group International, 2009.

Urvoy, Yves. "Essai de bibliographie des populations du Soudan central (Colonie du Niger)." *Bulletin du Comité d'Etudes Historiques et Scientifiques de l'AOF* 19, no. 2/3 (1936): 243–333.

West Africa. Weekly. London. 1919–.

Witherell, Julian W. *French-Speaking West Africa: A Guide to Official Publications.* Washington, D.C.: Library of Congress, 1976.

Zamponi, Lynda F. *Niger.* Oxford: Clio Press, 1994.

Online

http://web.worldbank.org/WBSITE/EXTERNAL/COUNTRIES/AFRICAEXT/NIGEREXTN/0,,menuPK:382456~pagePK:141159~piPK:141110~theSitePK:382450,00.html (Niger page on the World Bank website).

http://www.africa.upenn.edu/Country_Specific/Niger.htm (Niger page at the University of Pennsylvania African Studies Center. Various resources, data and news).

http://www.afristat.org (Statistical records).

http://www.afrobarometer.org (Statistical records on democracy and governance in Africa).

http://www.afromix.org (Music).

http://www.aiddata.org (Multisource information on global aid flows).

http://www.annuaireniger.com (Phonebook and addresses).

http://www.focusonniger.com (Compilation of news and news sources on Niger, regularly updated).

http://www.friendsofniger.org (Compilation of information on Niger, regularly updated, with an online periodical, *Camel Express*).

http://www.histoire-afrique.org (Growing bibliography and other information on West African history, set up by West African historians. In French.).

http://www.ids.ac.uk/blds/blds.html (Bibliography on development information in print, CD-ROM and online sources, with some full-text articles available).

http://www.imdb.com/country/ne (Niger page of the Internet Movie Database).

http://www.imf.org/external/country/NER/index.htm (Niger page on the International Monetary Fund's website).

http://www.intnet.ne/pnud_fr.html (United Nations Development Programme in Niger. Various resources and data. In French.).

http://www.ird.fr/bani/present.htm (Physical anthropology database on Niger. In French.).

http://www.ird.fr/fr/inst/infotheque/horizon (General resources of the Institut de la Recherche pour le Développement, including some full-text articles. In French.).

http://www.ird.ne (Research papers and information of the Institut de la Recherche pour le Développement in Niger. In French.).

http://www.jeuneafrique.com/pays/niger/niger.asp (*Jeune Afrique*'s Niger articles archive. In French.).

http://www.lasdel.net (Freely accessible recent monographs on Niger's regions, with regular additions. In French.).

http://www.monde-diplomatique.fr/index/pays/niger.html (*Le Monde diplomatique*'s Niger articles archive. In French.).

http://www.nigerdiaspora.net (Compilation of Nigerien newspapers and paper articles, regularly updated. In French.).

http://www.oecd.org/pages/0,3417,en_38233741_38242551_1_1_1_1_1,00.html (Sahel and West Africa Club website. Has regular publications on the West African region's countries as well as data and maps.).

http://www.stat-niger.org/statistique (Statistical information from Niger's national statistical office. Regularly updated. In French.).

http://www.tamtaminfo.com (Compilation of Nigerien newspapers and paper articles, regularly updated, with video postings. In French.).

http://www.uemoa.int (Regularly updated economic data. In French.).

https://www.uni-hohenheim.de/~atlas308/ (Spatial data on sustainable land use planning in Niger and Benin.).

About the Authors

Abdourahmane Idrissa is a Nigerien political scientist. Born and brought up in Niger, he studied philosophy (master's degree) and political science (*Diplôme d'études approfondies*) at the University of Dakar, in Senegal, before moving to the United States with a Fulbright scholarship to carry on his political science studies. He obtained a doctorate from the University of Florida in 2009. Postdoctoral work at the Universities of Oxford and Princeton, as a Global Leader Fellow (2nd Cohort) led him to develop an expertise in the political economy of West Africa, in addition to his earlier focus on African democratization, political Islam, and political theory. Idrissa has published several papers in both English and French as book chapters and peer-reviewed journal articles, chiefly on Niger and the Sahelian region. He currently works on West African regionalism and Francophone (African) political philosophy. Now based in Niamey, Idrissa has founded there a training program in political economy and governance in the Sahel and West Africa and teaches political science courses at the University of Niamey.

Samuel Decalo (MA, PhD in political science, University of Pennsylvania) has taught both at home (University of Rhode Island; Graduate Faculty, New School for Social Research) and abroad (University of Botswana, University of the West Indies). He has published numerous books and articles on Africa and the Middle East, including three other dictionaries in this series (Benin, Togo, Niger) and *Coups and Army Rule in Africa* (Yale University Press). He is professor of political science at the University of Natal, Durban.

CPSIA information can be obtained at www.ICGtesting.com
Printed in the USA
BVOW041629210512

290514BV00002B/1/P